The Cambridge Guide to English Usage

The Cambridge Guide to English Usage is an A–Z reference book, giving an up-to-date account of the debatable issues of English usage and written style. Its advice draws a wealth of recent research and data from very large corpora of American and British English – illuminating their many divergences and also points of convergence on which international English can be based. The book comprises more than 4000 points of word meaning, spelling, grammar, punctuation and larger issues of inclusive language, and effective writing and argument. It also provides guidance on grammatical terminology, and covers topics in electronic communication and the internet. The discussion notes the major dictionaries, grammars and usage books in the US, UK, Canada and Australia, allowing readers to calibrate their own practices as required. *CGEU* is descriptive rather than prescriptive, but offers a principled basis for implementing progressive or more conservative decisions on usage.

Consultants

JOHN ALGEO   University of Georgia

JOHN AYTO   University of Surrey

DAVID CRYSTAL   University of Wales, Bangor

SIDNEY LANDAU   Fellow of the Dictionary Society of North America

KATIE WALES   University of Leeds

The Cambridge Guide to
English Usage

PAM PETERS
Macquarie University

CAMBRIDGE
UNIVERSITY PRESS

PUBLISHED BY THE PRESS SYNDICATE OF THE UNIVERSITY OF CAMBRIDGE
The Pitt Building, Trumpington Street, Cambridge, United Kingdom

CAMBRIDGE UNIVERSITY PRESS
The Edinburgh Building, Cambridge, CB2 2RU, UK
40 West 20th Street, New York, NY 10011–4211, USA
477 Williamstown Road, Port Melbourne, VIC 3207, Australia
Ruiz de Alarcón 13, 28014 Madrid, Spain
Dock House, The Waterfront, Cape Town 8001, South Africa

http://www.cambridge.org

First published 2004

Printed in China by Imago

Typeface Nimrod (The Monotype Corporation) 7.25/9 pt.   *System* LATEX 2_ε [TB]

A catalogue record for this book is available from the British Library

ISBN 0 521 62181 X hardback

Contents

Preface   *vii*

Overview of Contents and How to Access Them   *x*

A to Z Entries   *1–592*

Appendix I   International Phonetic Alphabet Symbols for
                  English Sounds   *593*

Appendix II   Geological Eras   *594*

Appendix III   Perpetual Calendar 1901–2008   *595*

Appendix IV   International System of Units (SI Units)   *596*

Appendix V   Interconversion Tables for Metric and
                  Imperial Measures   *597*

Appendix VI   Selected Proofreading Marks   *598*

Appendix VII   Formats and Styles for Letters, Memos and
                  E-mail   *600*

Appendix VIII   Layout for Envelopes   *602*

Appendix IX   Currencies of the World   *603*

Bibliography   *604*

Preface

The *Cambridge Guide to English Usage* is written for English-users in the twenty-first century. It takes a fresh look at thousands of questions of style and usage, embracing issues that are time-honored yet still current, as well as those newly arising as the language continues to evolve. Some of these come with electronic communication and online documentation, but there are numerous others among the more than 4000 headwords in the book.

At the threshold of the third millennium, English is more diverse than ever in all hemispheres. Research into "new Englishes" has flourished, supported by journals such as *English World-Wide, World Englishes* and *English Today*. At the same time, the quest for a single, international form for written communication becomes more pressing, among those aiming at a global readership. This book is designed to support both global and local communicators. It identifies regionalized elements of usage, grammar and style, with systematic attention to American and British English, and reference to Canadian, Australian and New Zealand English as well. It allows writers to choose styles and usage appropriate to their readership, according to how local or large it is. The local options help to establish and affirm regional identity within, say, North America or Great Britian. But communicating beyond those regions calls for reappraisal of the options, putting a premium on those with the widest distribution worldwide, ideally region-free. *The Cambridge Guide to English Usage* identifies "international English selections" wherever they can be distilled out of the alternatives available, and implements them on its own pages. It empowers readers (as writers, editors, teachers, students) to choose and develop their own style, for their particular purposes.

Many kinds of resource have been brought to bear on the style and usage questions raised. *The Cambridge Guide to English Usage* is the first of its kind to make regular use of large databases (corpora) of computerized texts as primary sources of current English. Numerous examples of British usage have come from the 100 million word British National Corpus (see **BNC**); and of American usage from a subset of 140 million words of American English from the Cambridge International Corpus (see **CCAE**). The corpora embody various kinds of written discourse as well as transcriptions of spoken discourse – enough to show patterns of divergence between the two. Negative attitudes to particular idioms or usage often turn on the fact that they are more familiar to the ear than the eye, and the constructions of formal writing are privileged thereby. Corpus data allow us to look more neutrally at the distributions of words and constructions, to view the range of styles across which they operate. On this basis we can see what is really "standard," i.e. usable in many kinds of discourse, as opposed to the formal or informal. References to "formal" and "informal" within the book presuppose that they lie above and below the broad band of everyday written communication, and together form a three-point stylistic scale.

The relative acceptability of a given usage can also be gauged by means of population surveys. This involves the use of questionnaires on doubtful or disputed usage in spelling, punctuation, the use of capital letters and certain points of grammar. A series of six questionnaires called the "Langscape survey" was published in *English Today* (1998–2001), with the support of the editor, Dr. Tom McArthur. Hundreds of questionnaires from around the world were returned by mail and fax, and through the Style Council website at Macquarie University, where they were analyzed in terms of regional and sociolinguistic trends. Results from Langscape are quoted in some of the book's entries for their insights into people's willingness to embrace particular spellings or usages. They are a litmus test of future directions.

Attitudes to usage often reflect what's said in the relevant language authorities, most notably the *Oxford English Dictionary* (2nd edition, 1989) for British English, and *Webster's Third New International Dictionary* (3rd edition, 1961, reprinted 1986) for American English. These unabridged dictionaries remain monuments to English language scholarship, to which we are all indebted. Though their latest editions are not so recent, their positions tend to be maintained in younger, abridged dictionaries, except where there are good reasons to diverge, e.g. on neologisms or previously unrecorded usage. The *New Oxford Dictionary of English* (1998) and *Merriam-Webster's Collegiate* (2000) have been used to update the verdicts of the unabridged dictionaries, where relevant; and the *Canadian Oxford Dictionary* (1998) and the *Macquarie Dictionary* (3rd edition 1997) are invoked for regional comparisons. Comparative reference is also made to regional usage books, including Fowler's *Modern English Usage* (1926; and later editions by Gowers, 1965, and Burchfield, 1996); to the excellent *Webster's Dictionary of English Usage* (1989), Garner's *Modern American Usage* (1999), and Fee and McAlpine's *Canadian English Usage* (1997). These secondary sources contribute to the diversity of views on changing usage, and articulate local reactions to worldwide innovations.

Issues of editorial style are also treated comparatively, to allow readers to position themselves relative to American or British style, as articulated in the *Chicago Manual of Style* (15th edition 2003) and the *Oxford Guide to Style* (2002). Reference is also made to *Editing Canadian English* (2nd edition 2000) by the Editors' Association of Canada, to the Australian government *Style Manual* (6th edition 2002), and to the New Zealand style manual *Write, Edit, Print* (1997). Those resident in non-English-speaking countries can forge a synthesis of regional styles appropriate to their readerships.

Grammatical cruxes of usage are discussed with reference to modern grammars such as the *Comprehensive Grammar of the English Language* (1985), the *Introduction to Functional Grammar* (1985; 1994) and especially the *Longman Grammar of Spoken and Written English* (1999). The latter is explicitly corpus-based, using data from the Longman corpus of over 40 million words in six registers, to complement or extend the data derived from the BNC and CCAE, mentioned above. *The Cambridge Guide to English Usage* aims to bridge the gap between traditional and modern grammar, and uses terminology from both (e.g. *mood* and *modality*) as entry points to discussing grammatical questions. Elements of discourse analysis are also discussed, for example *information focus* and sentence *topic*, as aids to writing and editing.

Apart from its large range of primary and secondary sources, *The Cambridge Guide to English Usage* draws on the findings of numerous linguistic researchers, named within the text and in the bibliography. Their contributions to our understanding of the intricacies of the English language are legion. Many are corpus linguists associated with the ICAME group (International Computer Archive of Modern English), who have progressively developed the uses of corpora for linguistic description with each new generation of corpus. Other European and American linguists who have contributed greatly to this book are the distinguished consultants named on p. ii, whose careful reading of the MS has enhanced its relevance to different parts of the English-speaking world.

The Cambridge Guide to English Usage also owes much to undated and undatable discussions with colleagues and friends at Macquarie University, in the Linguistics department and associated with the *Macquarie Dictionary*. To Professor Arthur Delbridge, the foundation Professor of Linguistics and Editor-in-chief of the Dictionary who connected me with both, I owe a particular debt of gratitude. Others who provided invaluable support for the publication of the prototype *Cambridge Australian English Style Guide* (1995) were Dr. Robin Derricourt (formerly of Cambridge University Press, Australia), and Hon. Justice Michael Kirby (of the High Court of Australia). In the preparatory stages of *The Cambridge Guide to English Usage*, I was fortunate to be a visiting professor at the Englisches Seminar of the University of Zürich, which gave me access to their excellent BNC search tools and experience of teaching at a European university. Many thanks are due to those at Cambridge University Press (UK) who saw the project through from first to last: Adrian du Plessis, Kevin Taylor and Dr Kate Brett, and my copy-editor Leigh Mueller. Back home in Australia my warmest thanks go to my family, to Fliss, Greg, and especially to John, for his unfailing love and support.

Pam Peters

Overview of Contents and How to Access Them

The alphabetical list in this book contains two kinds of entries: those which deal with general topics of language, editing and writing, and those dealing with particular words, word sets or parts of words. An overview of many general entries is provided on the opposite page. The particular entries, focusing on issues of usage, spelling and word form, are too numerous to be shown there, and simply take their places in the alphabetical list. But for many questions, either general or particular entries would lead you to the answer you're seeking, and the book offers multiple access paths via crossreferences.

Let's say you are interested in where to put the full stop in relation to a final bracket or parenthesis. Any of those terms (full stop, bracket, parenthesis) would take you to the relevant discussion under **brackets**. In addition the general entry on **punctuation** presents a list of all the entries dealing with individual punctuation marks, for both words and sentences.

Questions of grammar are accessible through traditional terms such as **noun** and **verb**, **clause** and **phrase**, and traditional labels such as **dangling participle** or **split infinitive** ... though the entries may lead you on to newer linguistic topics such as **information focus** and **modality**. Aspects of writing and argument (when is it OK to use **I**? what does it mean to **beg the question**?) are discussed under their particular headings, but can also be tracked down through more general ones such as **impersonal writing** and **argument**.

If your question is about current use of a word such as **hopefully**, or a pair such as **alternate** and **alternative**, or **gourmet** and **gourmand**, the discussion is to be found under those headwords. When it's a question of spelling, e.g. **convener** or **convenor**, the individual entry may answer it, and/or direct you on to another (**-er/-or**) where a whole set with the same variable part is dealt with. In the same way, the entry **-ize/-ise** discusses the alternative spellings of countless verbs like recognise/recognize, although there are too many to enter alphabetically. The key spelling entries are listed under **spelling** sections 2 and 3, in case you're unsure what heading to look under. Alternative plural forms can be located via the entry on **plurals**.

As in the text above, the use of boldface means that the word is entered as a headword, and it identifies all crossreferences at the end of entries. Within any entry, further instances of the headword(s) are often boldfaced to draw attention to strategic points about them. Words related to the headword(s) or derived from them are set in italics, as are all examples.

◊ Abbreviations used in the body of the text are explained at their alphabetical place.

STYLE AND STRUCTURE OF WRITING

ARGUMENT & STRUCTURE OF DISCOURSE

Argument
Beg the question
Coherence or cohesion
Deduction
Fallacies
Information focus
Introductions
Paragraphs
Topic sentences

RHETORICAL DEVICES

Analogy
Aphorism
Figures of speech
Irony
Metaphors
Oxymoron
Personification
Symbols
Understatements

SPECIAL STYLES

Commercialese
Digital style
Impersonal style
Jargon
Journalese
Plain English
Technologese

VARIETIES OF ENGLISH

American English
Australian English
British English
Canadian English
International English
New Zealand English
South African English
Standard English

WRITING FORMS

E-mail
Inverted pyramid
Letter writing
Narrative
Reports
Summary

WORDS

FORMS OF WORDS

Acronyms and initialisms
Affixes, prefixes, suffixes
Compounds
Past tense
Plurals
Proper names
Zero forms

SPECIAL EXPRESSIONS

Clichés
Emoticons
Foreign phrases
Four-letter words
Geographical names
Intensifiers

WORD MEANINGS & SENSE RELATIONS

Antonyms
Euphemisms
Folk etymology
Hyponyms
Synonyms

SPELLING

Alternative spellings: ae/e i/y -ize/-ise l/ll oe
-or/-our -re/-er yze/yse
Spelling rules: -c/-ck- ce/-ge -e -f >-v- -o
-y > -i-, doubling of final consonant, i before e

USAGE DISTINCTIONS

Collocations
Near-but-not-identical words
Reciprocal words

EDITORIAL STYLE

EDITORIAL TECHNIQUE

Abbreviations
Audiovisual media
Bibliographies
Dating systems
Indexing
Lists
Prelims
Proofreading
Referencing
Titles

INCLUSIVE LANGUAGE

Ageist language
Disabled
Miscegenation
Nonsexist language
Racist language

PUNCTUATION

Apostrophes
Brackets
Bullets
Colon
Comma
Dashes
Full stop/period
Hyphens
Question marks
Quotation marks
Semicolon

TYPOGRAPHY

Accents
Capital letters
Dates
Headings
Indention
Italics
Numbers and
   number style

GRAMMAR

GRAMMATICAL ISSUES

Agreement
Dangling participles
Double negatives
First person
Modality
Nonfinite clause
Restrictive clause
Split infinitive
Whom

WORD CLASSES

Adjectives
Adverbs
Conjunctions
Determiners
Interjections
Nouns
Prepositions
Pronouns
Verbs

@

This is a symbol in search of a name. English-speakers call @ the "*at* sign," which will do while it serves as the universal symbol of an e-mail address. Its shape is also used along with other *emoticons* to represent expressions of the human face (see **emoticons**). But its resemblance to animals emerges through ad hoc names in other languages. In Danish, it's seen as the "elephant's trunk," and in Chinese as "little mouse." Russian has it as "little dog," Swedish as "cat's foot," and Dutch as "monkey's tail." The best consensus is for "snail," which provides a name for @ in French, Italian, Hebrew and Korean.

◊ On quoting e-mail addresses, see under **URL**.

a or an

Which should it be?

a hotel	or	an hotel
a heroic effort	or	an heroic effort
a RAF training course	or	an RAF training course
a $8 ticket	or	an $8 ticket

A single rule resolves all such queries: **a** is used before words beginning with a consonant, and **an** before those beginning with a vowel. This is straightforwardly applied in *a doctor, a receptionist* and *an astronaut, an engineer*. But note that the rule depends on the sound not the spelling. We write *a union, a unique gift* and *a once-in-a-lifetime experience* because the words following the article actually begin with a consonant sound (the "y" sound in the first two cases, and the "w" sound in the third). The same principle makes it *an hour, an honor,* and *an honest man.* The word following the indefinite article begins with a vowel sound.

When writing abbreviations, the choice between **a** or **an** again depends on the pronunciation of the first letter. So *a US Marine* and *a Unesco project* are quite regular, as are *an MP* and *an HB pencil.* Any abbreviation beginning with F, L, H, M, N, R, S or X takes **an**, because of the way those letters are pronounced. The effect is exploited in advertising for a brand of beer, where the use of A (rather than AN) shows how to pronounce the ambiguous brandname:

> **I CAN FEEL A XXXX COMING ON**
> **AUSTRALIANS WOULDN'T GIVE A XXXX**
> **FOR ANYTHING ELSE**

Preceded by **A**, the brandname must be read as "four ex" not as "exexexex." It nudges readers away from the unprintable or socially unacceptable interpretation of the word, while no doubt capitalizing on it.

Similar principles hold for writing sums of money. Pronounce them and they select **a** for *a £12 shirt* and **an** for *an $80m. loan,* taking the cue from the number (which is said first) rather than the currency symbol (which is written first).

Despite all that, certain words beginning with *h* are made exceptions by some writers and speakers. They would preface *hotel* and *heroic* with **an** rather than **a**, despite pronouncing the *h* at the start of those words. Other polysyllabic words beginning with *h* will be given the same treatment, especially if their first syllable is unstressed. In both American and British English the words *historic, historical* and *historian* are the most frequent of these exceptional cases, but the tendency goes further in Britain, by the evidence of matching databases (LOB and Brown corpora). They show that British writers use **an** to preface adjectives such as *habitual, hereditary, heroic, horrific, hypothetical, hysterical* (and their adverbs) as well as the noun *hotel.* There are far fewer examples in the American data, and the only distinctive case is *herb,* which is commonly pronounced without *h* in the US (though not in the UK or elsewhere). The King James bible (1611) records the use of **an** with other monosyllabic words, as in *an host* and *an house,* though they are supposed to go with *h*-less pronunciations, formerly much more common.

Over the centuries *h* has been an uncertain quantity at the beginnings of words in many European languages. Most words beginning with *h* lost it as they passed from Latin into French and Italian. The Latin word *hora* meaning "hour" became French *heure* (pronounced "err," with no *h* sound) and also the Italian *ora,* without an *h* even in the spelling. English retains an *h* in the spelling of *hour* but not in the pronunciation. The process also shows up in the contrasting pronunciations of *heir* (an early English loan from French) and *hereditary* (a Renaissance borrowing direct from Latin), which embody the same Latin stem. Spelling pronunciation has revived the *h* in some French loanwords like *heritage* and *historian* (those well used in English writing); while others such as *hour, heir, hono(u)r* are *h*-less, in keeping with French pronunciation. Classical loanwords (apart from *honorary, honorarium, honorific*) have settled on pronunciations with the *h* sounded; and they complement the many basic Anglo-Saxon words such as *here, how, him* and *hair, home, honey* in which *h* is pronounced. (See further under **h.**)

Nowadays the silent *h* persists in only a handful of French loanwords (*heir, honest, hono(u)r, hour* and their derivatives), and these need to be preceded by **an**. The *h* of other loans like *heroic, historical* and *hypothesis* may have been silent or varied in earlier times, leaving uncertainty as to whether **an** was required or not. But their pronunciation is no longer variable and provides no phonetic justification for **an**. Its use with them is a stylistic nicety, lending historical nuances to discourse in which tradition dies hard.

◊ For the grammar of **a** and **an**, see **articles**.

◊ For the presence/absence of **a/an** in (1) journalistic introductions, see **journalism and journalese**; and in (2) titles of books, periodicals, plays etc., see under **the.**

a-

The a- prefixed to ordinary English adjectives and
adverbs comes from two different sources. In a few
cases such as *afresh, akin* and *anew*, it represents the
Old English preposition *of*, and so *anew* was once "of
new." In many more cases it was the Old English
preposition *on*, as in:

aback	ablaze	abroad	afloat	afoot
aglow	ahead	ajar	alive	around
ashore	aside	asleep	astray	

Thus *ashore* was literally "on shore."

In each set the two elements of the prepositional
phrase have long since merged into one. But the past
still shows through in the fact that as adjectives they
are used only after the noun they qualify, either
postpositively as in *the way ahead* or predicatively, i.e.
as the complement of a verb, as in *Route 66 is ahead.*
(See further under **adjectives**, section 1.) The
adverbial functions of these words are also evident in
collocations such as *taken aback, go astray* and *get
ahold of* (see further at **ahold**). Others such as **around**
are now both adverbs and prepositions.

Note the apparently similar *apart,* which consists of
French elements (*à part*) rather than English ones. Its
parity with *aside* is examined at **aside (from).**

a-/an-

These are two forms of a negative prefix derived from
Greek. In English its meaning is usually privative, i.e.
"without" or "lacking." It appears as the first
component in some academic and technical words,
such as:

achromatic	analgesic
apathy, apathetic	anarchy, anarchic
aphasia, aphasic	anhydrous
atheism, atheist	anorexia

As the two lists show, the form **an-** occurs before
vowels and *h*, and **a-** before all other consonants. In
most cases the prefix combines with Greek stems
which do not exist independently in English. In just a
few, such as *amoral, asexual, atypical*, the a- combines
with a Latin stem that is also an ordinary English
word. In the case of *amoral*, the prefix makes the vital
difference between *amoral* ("lacking in moral values")
and *immoral* ("contrary to moral values," where *im-* is
a negative).

◊ For more about negative prefixes, see **de-, in-/im-,
non-** and **un-**. See also **dis-**, and other privative affixes
such as **-free** and **-less**.

-a

This suffix is really several suffixes. They come into
English with loanwords from other languages,
including Italian, Spanish, Latin and Greek, and may
represent either singular or plural. In *gondola*
(Italian), *siesta* (Spanish), *formula* (Latin) and *dogma*
(Greek), the **-a** is a singular ending, whereas in
bacteria (Latin) and *criteria* (Greek), it represents the
plural.

Loanwords ending in singular -a are not to be taken
for granted because their plurals may or may not go
according to a foreign pattern, as discussed in the first
section below. Loanwords which come with a plural -a
ending pose other grammatical questions, to be dealt
with in the second section.

1 **Words with the singular -a** mostly make their
plurals in the usual English way, by adding an *s*. This
is true for all the Italian and Spanish words, and many

of the Latin ones. So *gondola* becomes *gondolas, siesta*
becomes *siestas,* and *aroma* becomes *aromas.* The
numerous Latin names for plants, for example
mimosa, ponderosa, protea, sequoia, all take English
plurals. However, Latin loanwords which are strongly
associated with an academic field usually have Latin
plurals as well, thus *formulae* along with *formulas,
retinae* and *retinas* etc. So plurals with *-ae* prevail in
writing intended for scientists and scholars
everywhere, though the forms ending in *-as* are also
available and used in nonspecialized writing and
conversation.

The major dictionaries differ over which words can
take English plurals. *Webster's Third* (1986) indicates
an English plural for all the words listed below –
either explicitly, as first or second alternative, or by
the lack of reference to the plural (this being the
dictionary convention for regular inflections). The
Oxford Dictionary (1989) allows either Latin or
English plurals for those set in italics below, but Latin
only plurals for those set in roman. Note also that
while the *Oxford* presents the Latin plurals as
ligatures, *Webster's* sets them as digraphs (see further
under **ae/e**).

abscissa	am(o)eba	antenna	aorta
aura	caesura	cicada	cornea
echidna	fibula	formula	hydra
lacuna	lamina	larva	mora
nebula	nova	patella	penumbra
persona	piscina	placenta	pupa
retina	stoa	tibia	trachea
ulna	urethra	vagina	vertebra

An English plural is natural enough for those
latinisms which are both common words and
technical terms (e.g. *aura, cicada, cornea, retina*). For
some (e.g. *aorta, urethra*), the occasions on which a
plural might be needed are not very many, and, when
it is, an ad hoc English plural is all the more likely.
Note that for **antenna, patella** and **persona**, the two
plurals are used in different fields (see under those
headings). For the plural of *alumna*, see **alumni**.

Greek loanwords with singular -a can also have two
plural forms. They bring with them their Greek plural
suffix *-ta*, though they soon acquire English plurals
with *s* as well. The Greek *-ta* plurals survive in
scholarly, religious or scientific writing, while in
other contexts the English *s* plurals are dominant.
Compare the *traumas of everyday life* with the
traumata which are the concerns of medicine and
psychology. Other loanwords which use both English
and Greek plurals are:

    dogma lemma magma schema stigma

For both *dogma* and *stigma*, the Greek plural is
strongly associated with Catholic orthodoxy (see
stigma). The Greek plural of *miasma* (*miasmata*)
seems to have lapsed in C21 English (see **miasma**).

2 **Words with plural -a from Latin** are often collective
in meaning, for example *bacteria, data* and *media*.
There's no need to pluralize them, nor do we often
need their singular forms, though they do exist:
bacterium, datum etc. (For more information, see
-um.) The grammatical status of words like *media*
(whether to construe them as singular or plural) is
still unsettled. Those who know Latin are inclined to
insist on plural agreement, on the grounds that *data*
and *media* (not to mention *candelabra*) "are plural."
Yet the argument depends on Latin rather than
English grammar; and is undermined by other cases

such as *agenda* and *stamina,* which are also Latin plurals but now always used with singular verbs in English. The issues of singular/plural agreement are further discussed under **collective nouns** and **agreement** section 1; and at individual entries for **candelabra, data** and **media.**

◊ For Greek loanwords with a plural -a, such as *automata, criteria, ganglia, phenomena,* see **-on.**

a fortiori

This elliptical phrase, borrowed from Latin, means roughly "by way of something stronger." Far from being an oblique reference to fetching the whisky, it's used in formal discussion to mean "with yet stronger reason" and to introduce a second point which the speaker or writer feels will clinch the argument. Compare **a priori.**

à la

In contemporary English this versatile French tag is deployed on many of the frontiers of taste, apart from *haute cuisine.* It is still exploited on *à la carte* menus that offer you taste-tempting dishes *à la duchesse* or *à l'indienne;* and in countercuisine, it can be found in *fast foods à la McDonalds.* But beyond the restaurant business, *à la* can refer to a distinctive style in almost any domain, and the reference point is usually ad hoc, as in *makeup [used] to amuse, à la Mick Jagger,* or *an oversight committee à la New York in the 1970s.* As in those examples, the construction often turns on the proper names of persons or places, titles and institutions. It creates reference points in film – *à la "Casablanca"* – and fiction – *à la "Portnoy's Complaint"* – not to mention health management: *whether to quarantine people with AIDS à la TB.* Increasingly **à la** is found with common nouns as well, as in *law à la modem,* and *seats covered with vinyl à la taxicab,* among the examples from CCAE.

A la is a clipped form of the French *à la mode (de),* which explains the feminine form of the article (*la*). In English it works as a fixed phrase, rather like a compound preposition, and there's no suggestion of adapting its grammatical gender from **à la** to *au* when the following name is masculine (see the Mick Jagger example above).

The grave accent is still often printed on **à la** in English, especially British English, though it is by no means a recent borrowing (first recorded in 1589). No doubt its use is often prompted by a taste for the exotic; and the accent – and the fact that the phrase still tends to be italicized – help to emphasize its foreignness. The *Oxford Dictionary* (1989) updates the entry on **à la** without registering the accentless form, whereas it appears as an alternative in *Webster's Third* (1986).

à la carte

This is one of the many French expressions borrowed into English to cover gastronomic needs. Literally it means "according to the card." At restaurants it gives you the freedom to choose from individually priced dishes – and the obligation to pay whatever the bill amounts to. The **à la carte** system contrasts with what has traditionally been known as *table d'hôte,* literally "the host's table." This implies partaking of whatever menu the restaurant has decided on, for a set price. The phrase goes back to earlier centuries, when the only public dining place for travelers was at the host's/landlord's table. But *table d'hôte* is what

most of us partake of when traveling as tourist-class passengers on aircraft. In restaurants more transparent phrases are used to show when the menu and its price are predetermined: *fixed price menu* (in the UK and US), or *prix fixe* (in France and francophone Canada). In Italy it's *menu turistico.*

Though dictionaries such as *New Oxford* (1998) and *Merriam-Webster* (2000) continue to list **à la carte** and *table d'hôte* with their French accents, they are commonly seen without them in the English-speaking world.

a posteriori

Borrowed from Latin, this phrase means "by a later effect or instance." It refers to arguments which reason from the effect to the cause, or those which work from a specific instance back to a generalization. *A posteriori arguments* are concerned with using empirical observations and induction as the basis of reasoning. They contrast with *a priori arguments,* on which see next entry.

a priori

This phrase, borrowed from Latin, means "from the prior [assumption]." It identifies an argument which reasons from cause to a presumed effect, or which works deductively from a general principle to the specific case. Because such reasoning relies on theory or presumption rather than empirical observation, an *a priori argument* is often judged negatively. It seems to make assertions before analyzing the evidence. Compare **a posteriori.**

abacus

What if there's more than one of them? Technical uses of this word in classical architecture have no doubt helped to preserve its Latin plural *abaci.* This is the only plural recognized in the *Oxford Dictionary* (1989), and the one given priority in *Webster's Third* (1986). But *Webster's* also recognizes the English plural *abacuses,* which comes naturally when **abacus** the word refers to the low-tech, finger-powered calculator. See further under **-us.**

abbreviations

These are the standardized short forms of names or titles, and of certain common words and phrases. The term covers (i) *abbreviated words* such as *cont.* and *no.,* i.e. ones which are cut short or contracted in the middle; and (ii) *abbreviated phrases* such as *AIDS, RSI,* formed out of the first letters of words in a phrase. Both groups can be further divided (see under *contractions* section 1 for **abbreviations** v. *contractions;* and under *acronyms* for the distinction between *acronyms* and *initialisms*). The punctuation given to each group varies according to American and British style, and within them, as discussed below in section 2. However, there's a consensus that most types of symbol should be left unpunctuated (see section 1 below).

Abbreviations of all kinds are now accepted in many kinds of functional and informative writing, as neat and clear representations of the full name or title. Certain **abbreviations** such as *EFT* or *ftp* are in fact better known than their full forms (*electronic funds transfer, file transfer protocol*). The idea that they are unacceptable in formal writing seems to derive from writing in the humanities, where they are less often needed. **Abbreviations** may indeed look strange in the text of a novel or short story. Yet who can imagine a letter which does not carry **abbreviations** somewhere in referring to people and places? Business and technical reports could hardly do without them.

Provided they are not obscure to the reader, **abbreviations** communicate more with fewer letters. Writers have only to ensure that the abbreviations they use are too well known to need any introduction, or that they are introduced and explained on their first appearance. Once the reader knows that in a particular document *CBC* equals the *Children's Book Council* or the *Canadian Broadcasting Corporation* or the *Carpet Bowls Club*, as the case may be, the short form can be used from then on.

1 Abbreviations which are never punctuated. Certain special categories of symbol never appear with a stop/period, anywhere in the world. They include:
- symbols for SI units: *kg, ml* etc. (See **SI units**.)
- compass points: *N, NE, SW* etc.
- chemical symbols: *Mn, Ni* etc.
- symbols for currencies: GB£, A$ etc. (See **Appendix ix.**)

One other group of **abbreviations** which never take stops are *acronyms* like *laser, scuba* (i.e. those which are pronounced like words and written in lower case: see **acronyms**).

2 Abbreviations which may or may not be punctuated, according to regional editorial practice (all other groups of **abbreviations**, of titles, institutions, placename elements and ordinary words and phrases). The various practices and their applications are illustrated below, followed by a discussion of each:
a) using stops with any kind of **abbreviation**
(= traditional American style)

G.A.T.T.   U.K.   Mr.   Rev.   mgr.   incl.   a.s.a.p.

b) using stops with **abbreviations** but not *contractions* (= traditional British style)

G.A.T.T.   U.K.   Mr   Rev.   mgr   incl.   a.s.a.p.

c) using stops for short forms with any lower case letters in them
   i)   *GATT   UK   Mr.   Rev.   mgr.   incl.   a.s.a.p.*
      (all **abbreviations**)
   ii) *GATT   UK   Mr   Rev   mgr   incl.   a.s.a.p.*
      (excluding *contractions*)
d) using stops for short forms consisting entirely of lower case letters:

GATT   UK   Mr   Rev   mgr.   incl.   a.s.a.p.

*Option (a) is the easiest to implement, and has been the traditional practice in the US, though the *Chicago Manual* (1993) noted its erosion amid the worldwide trend to use less punctuation. Familiar **abbreviations** can be left unstopped because the reader needs no reminder that they are shortened words or phrases.
*Option (b) turns on the distinction between **abbreviations** and *contractions,* and gives punctuation to the first group but not the second. In theory a contraction like *mgr* ("manager") is not a "true" abbreviation, but a telescoped word with its first and last letters intact. Compare *incl.* which is clearly a clipped form of "including," and in which the stop marks where it has been abbreviated. This distinction developed in C20 British style (see **contractions**, section 1) but has never been fully standardized (Ritter 2002), and is varied in particular fields (e.g. law) and by publishing houses. It never was part of American style. Canadian editors note the

distinction, though they call *contractions* "suspensions," in keeping with French editorial practice. However, the consistency of the traditional American style is appreciated when the two types of **abbreviation** are juxtaposed (*Editing Canadian English*, 2000). In New Zealand and Australia, the government *Style Manuals* (1997, 2002) have maintained the distinction, though the majority of Australian editors, writers and English teachers surveyed through Style Council in the 1990s (Peters, 1993c) begged to differ.

A particular conundrum for those who observe the distinction is what to do with pluralized abbreviations. Should the plural of *vol.* be *vols, vols.* or *vol.s?* Because the plural abbreviation preserves the final letter, there's an argument for treating it as a contraction and abandoning the stop, although it seems odd to have different punctuation for the singular and plural: *vol.* and *vols* respectively. The stopped alternatives are themselves anomalous. In *vol.s* the plural inflection is separated by a stop from the word it should be bound to; and in *vols.* the stop no longer marks the point at which the word has been clipped. *Vols.* is in fact the British choice (Butcher's *Copy-editing,* 1992, and Ritter, 2002) as well as the American, generally speaking. However, the *Chicago Manual* (1993) embeds the curiosity that Protestant scholars use *Pss.* for *Psalms,* where it's *Pss* for their Catholic counterparts in the *New American Bible.*
*Option (c) According to this option, stops are dispensed with for abbreviations which consist of full capitals, but retained for those with just an initial capital, or consisting entirely of lower case. This is in line with style trends in many parts of the English-speaking world. Capitalized acronyms and initialisms like *OPEC, UNICEF, BBC* are normally left unstopped, as indeed they appear in the *Oxford Dictionary for Writers and Editors* (1981), and are now explicitly endorsed in the *Chicago Manual* (2003). This was the preferred practice of freelance editors in Canada (*Editing Canadian English,* 1987), and those surveyed in Australia via Style Council in 1992. Stopless acronyms/initialisms are normal in the world of computing, witness *ASCII, CD-ROM* etc. Standardized abbreviations for nation-states such as *NZ, SA, USA* usually appear without stops these days. They do contrast, however, with other national abbreviations such as *Can., Germ.* and *Mex.,* which are still to be punctuated, according to both British and American references. Within the US, the two-letter abbreviations used in revised zip codes are standardized without periods, whether they consist of one or two words. Compare *NY* and *WY (New York / Wyoming); RI* and *WI (Rhode Island / Wisconsin).* Despite this growing consensus on leaving stops out of capitalized acronyms and abbreviations, the distinction between abbreviations and contractions still divides British and American style on lower-cased short forms. Hence suboption (ii) involving contractions, which is British-preferred; and (i) the more fully regularized suboption, which accords with American traditional practice.
*Option (d) builds on the trend described in (c). It takes its cue from the presence/absence of an initial capital letter, and applies stops only to those that begin with a lower case letter. The option brings abbreviations such as *Can* into line with *USA,* and

makes no attempt to distinguish between contractions and abbreviations in lower case. This gives it more appeal in America than Britain, because it would require stops to be put back in contractions such as *mgr,* which the British are accustomed to seeing in stopless form. For Americans it goes furthest in the direction of reducing the "fussiness" of word punctuation mentioned by the *Chicago Manual* (1993) – and is easily applied by printers and publishing technicians.

A fifth option, to use no stops in any kind of **abbreviation**, is not commonly seen on the printed page, but appears increasingly in digital style on the internet. It is easiest of all to implement, and would resolve the anomalies created by distinguishing contractions from **abbreviations** (options b, c (ii)). It would also break down the invisible barrier between **abbreviations** and symbols (section 1 above). Leaving all **abbreviations** unstopped is sometimes said to be a recipe for confusion between lower case abbreviations and ordinary words. Yet there are very few which could be mistaken. Those which are identical, such as *am, fig* and *no* are normally accompanied by numbers: *10 am, fig 13, no 2,* and there's no doubt as to what they are. The idea of leaving abbreviations totally without stops may seem too radical for the moment, but it would streamline the anomalies and divergences outlined in this entry.

> **International English selection:** The third option (c (i)) for punctuating **abbreviations** – using periods/full stops for **abbreviations** containing one or more lower case letters – recommends itself as a reasonable compromise between American and British style. It is in keeping with the worldwide trend to reduce punctuation, without any commitment to different punctuation for *contractions* and **abbreviations,** and the anomalies that it creates. (That distinction is embedded in option c(ii), for those who wish to maintain it.)

3 Stopped abbreviations at the end of a sentence.
When an **abbreviation** with a stop/period is the last word in a sentence, no further stop needs to be added:
> *Remember to acknowledge all contributors – the producer, director, screenplay writer, cameramen etc.*

In such cases, the "stronger" punctuation mark (the period / full stop that marks the end-of-sentence) covers for the lesser stop marking the **abbreviation**. This is in keeping with the normal convention (see **multiple punctuation**). By the same token, it masks the editorial decision as to whether the abbreviation should be stopped or not – which readers sometimes need to know. When necessary, it's best to remake the sentence so as to bring the abbreviation in from the end. This was done in discussing examples such as *vol* and *vols* in section (b) above.
◊ For the use of stops with the initials of a person's name, see under **names**.
◊ For the use of the stop/period in **Latin abbreviations**, see under that heading.

abide and abode
At the turn of the millennium, neither of these is much used. The verb **abide** appeared quite often in the King James bible, translating an array of Hebrew and Greek verbs meaning "dwell," "stay," "continue," "remain" and "endure" – senses which linger in the Victorian hymn "Abide with me," often sung at funeral services. Otherwise it survives mostly in the phrase *abide by (a decision),* and in the slightly colloquial idiom *can't/cannot abide* or *couldn't abide* [something or someone]. The participle *abiding* serves as adjective in combination with certain abstract ideals, for example *an abiding concern, his abiding faith in humanity;* and in the compound *law-abiding.* Yet shrinking usage overall leaves people unsure about the past tense. Is it the regular *abided* or **abode**, which was used consistently in the King James bible? The evidence of British and American dictionaries and corpora is that *abided* is preferred. As a noun, **abode** is mostly restricted to legal phrases such as *no fixed abode* and *right of abode.* Other uses, including the cliché *my humble abode,* and freely formed expressions such as *the abode of my forebears,* have an archaic ring to them.

-ability
This ending marks the conversion of adjectives with *-able* into abstract nouns, as when *respectable* becomes *respectability.* Adjectives with *-ible* are converted by the same process, so *flexible* becomes *flexibility.* The ending is not a simple suffix but a composite of:
• the conversion of *-ble* to a stressed syllable *-bil* and
• the addition of the suffix *-ity.* (See further under **-ity**.)

ablative
This grammatical case operates in Latin and some other languages, but not English. It marks a noun as having the meaning "by, with, or from" attached to it. For some Latin nouns, the **ablative** ending is *-o,* and so *ipso facto* means "by that fact." (See further under **cases.**)

The *ablative absolute* is a grammatical construction found in Latin which allows a phrase (all inflected in the ablative) to stand apart from the syntax of the clause or sentence in which it appears. The Latin tag *deo volente* ("God willing") is used in the same way in contemporary English.

able and able to
The use of *(be) able to* as a semi-auxiliary verb dates from C15, though it is not equally used in the US and the UK. The British make more of it, in the ratio of 3:2 according to the evidence of comparable C20 databases (**LOB** and **Brown**). It reflects the greater British use of modals and modalized verb phrases generally (see **modality**, and **auxiliary verbs**).

In both varieties of English, **able to** takes animate subjects much more often than inanimate ones, as in:
> *Thompson was able to smell a bargain a continent away.*

As in that example, **able to** normally combines with an active verb (see further under **voice**). This was the pattern in hundreds of corpus examples, the only counter example with a passive verb being *the chapel was still able to be used* (from LOB). **Able to** seems to insist on being construed with animate, active participants, as if it still draws on the energy of the adjective **able**, expressed in *an able politician* and *able-bodied citizens.* **Able** appears much less often as an adjective than as an auxiliary verb in both British and American data: in the ratio of 1:11 in LOB and 1:12 in the Brown corpus. It occurs mostly in nonfiction genres of writing, perhaps because the approval expressed in it seems detached rather than engaged with the subject.

-able/-ible

Which of these endings to use is a challenge even for the successful speller. They sound the same, and the choice between them seems arbitrary. In fact the choice is usually fixed by the word's origins. Unabridged British and American dictionaries – *Oxford* (1989) and *Webster's Third* (1986) – do allow that certain words may be spelled either way in contemporary English, although they diverge on which have the option, and only a handful of words are given alternative spellings in both:

> *collapsable/collapsible*   *collectable/collectible*
> *condensable/condensible*   *ignitable/ignitible*
> *preventable/preventible*

Those apart, the following are independently credited with alternative spellings by *Oxford* and *Webster's*, marked *O* and *W* accordingly:

> *avertable/avertible (O)*
> *confusable/confusible (O)*
> *connectable/connectible (O)*
> *contractable/contractible (O)*
> *deductable/deductible (O)*
> *detectable/detectible (O)*
> *diffusable/diffusible (O)*
> *discernable/discernible (W)*
> *expressable/expressible (W)*
> *extendable/extendible (W)*
> *extractable/extractible (W)*
> *impressable/impressible (W)*
> *perfectable/perfectible (W)*
> *suggestable/suggestible (O)*
> *transfusable/transfusible (W)*

Others such as *digestable/digestible* and *resistable/resistible* could probably be added to that list, but for the fact that *Oxford* presently marks their -able spellings as cutting out in C19.

The -able suffix is the more widely used of the two in English at large, partly because it combines with any Anglo-Saxon or French verb (*believable, enjoyable*), as well as neo-Latin ones, as in *retractable* or *contactable*. Fresh formations based on neo-Latin can provide alternatives to the well-established loan from Latin, as with *contractable/contractible*, where the first (in the sense "able to be contracted") is a modern word, whereas the second "able to contract" goes back to C16. Yet the opposite tendency is also to be found: *Oxford Dictionary* citations show that some start life with -able, as did *deductable* and *detectable*, and later acquired neo-Latin spellings with -ible. The forces of analogy compete with regular wordforming principles among these words, and because they are readily coined on the spur of the moment, the dictionary records are necessarily incomplete. Any word of this type not yet listed in the dictionary can legitimately be spelled -able, if it's based on a current English verb stem, simple or compound, e.g. *gazumpable, upgradable*. In fact the stem is often a useful clue for spelling the established words. Compare *dispensable* (whose stem is the same as the verb *dispense*) with *comprehensible,* for which there is no English verb "comprehens-." Most words with -ible embody Latin stems with no independent verb role in

English. (This is also true of a very few -able words such as *educable* and *navigable,* derived from the Latin first conjugation, but with enough relatives in English such as *education, navigation,* to secure their spelling.) The -ible words often lack close relatives, and the rationale for the spelling is not obvious unless you know Latin conjugations. The table below lists the most important -ible words, though where there are both positive and negative forms (e.g *credible* as well as *incredible*), it gives just one of them.

accessible	*adducible*	*admissible*
audible	*combustible*	*compatible*
contemptible	*credible*	*deducible*
divisible	*edible*	*eligible*
feasible	*flexible*	*incomprehensible*
incontrovertible	*incorrigible*	*incorruptible*
indefensible	*indelible*	*indestructible*
infallible	*intelligible*	*invincible*
irascible	*irrepressible*	*irresistible*
legible	*negligible*	*ostensible*
perceptible	*permissible*	*persuasible*
plausible	*possible*	*reducible*
reprehensible	*responsible*	*submersible*
susceptible	*tangible*	*terrible*
transmissible	*visible*	

The stems of -ible words come straight from Latin paradigms and are not normally usable as English verbs (*access* and *flex* are exceptions in so far as they now serve as verbs). Most -ible words express rather abstract senses, unlike those ending in -able, which typically build in the active sense of the verb: compare *defensible* and *defendable*. Note also that words ending in -ible take the negative prefix *in-* (as in *indefensible*), whereas those with -able and based on English verbs are usually negated with *un-* (e.g. *undefendable*). See further under in-/un-.

◊ For the choice between *drivable* and *driveable, likable* and *likeable* etc., see **-eable or -able**.

abled

See under **disabled and disability**.

abolition or abolishment

Though both terms are current, the Latin-derived **abolition** holds sway in British as well as American English. In the UK **abolition** is effectively the only term, in data from the BNC, whereas **abolishment** plays a minor part in the US, appearing in the ratio of about 1:17, in data from CCAE. We might expect more of **abolishment**, which is just as old (dating from C16) and has more direct connections with the verb *abolish*. Yet legal and institutional uses of **abolition** give it strong social and political connotations, in the discontinuance of slavery and the death penalty. The productivity of the word is also reflected in derivatives such as *abolitionist*.

Aboriginal and Aborigine

Since around 1800 the term **aboriginal** has been used as a generic reference to native peoples encountered by colonialists in (for them) remoter parts of the world. The capitalized form **Aboriginal** still serves as a collective reference to indigenous groups within the population, especially in Australia, but also in Canada, where it complements the use of *First People / First Nation*. In the US the general term is *Native American* or *American Indian*, and *Indian* is used by the peoples themselves. Use of the term

Amerindian for the North American Indian is mostly confined to linguistics and anthropology. In South Africa the indigenous people are referred to as *black South Africans*. No collective name is needed in New Zealand for the *Maori,* because they are ethnically homogeneous.

In current English, the noun **aborigine** is particularly associated with Australia, but always capitalized as **Aborigine/Aborigines**. Its status vis-à-vis using **Aboriginal** as a noun has been much debated on diplomatic and linguistic grounds. **Aborigine** was believed by some to be more pejorative than **Aboriginal** (though this view is not shared by the people themselves). Others argued that **Aborigine** was an illegitimate *backformation* from **Aborigines**, though few would now call it a linguistic crime (see **backformation**). Neither argument carries weight in terms of common usage. Australian sources on the internet return almost three times as many instances of **Aborigines** as of **Aboriginals** (Google 2002). Successive Australian government *Style Manuals* have swung from one paradigm to another (Peters 1995), and the sixth edition (2002) proposes **Aboriginal(s)** for the noun (singular and plural) as well as the adjective. So **Aborigine(s)** is currently ruled out of official documents, though other publications such as newspapers, magazines and monographs make free use of it.

For indigenous people themselves, generic terms are unsatisfactory whenever a more specific name can be found. Those preferred for particular regions of Australia are listed in the government *Style Manual* (2002), and for the First Nations of Canada in *Editing Canadian English* (2000). The names of federally recognized Native American tribes are listed on the internet at www.healing-arts.org/tribes.htm.
◊ For the use of **Black**, see under that heading.

about, about to, and not about to

The fluidity of its meaning makes **about** a word to watch. But as adverb/preposition, and as a semi-auxiliary in *be about to,* its uses are more generally accepted and more international than is sometimes thought.

About *as preposition and/or adverb* has several meanings which are widely used and current in both the US and the UK:
1) "close to"/"approximately" in time, as in *"come (at) about ten o'clock."* The approximation is handy whether the writer is unsure of the time, or prefers not to put too fine a point on it (see **vague words**). Though often presented as the British counterpart to American use of *around*, the construction is just as familiar in the US, according to *Webster's English Usage* (1989). See further at **around**.
2) "close by," "in the vicinity" (but not visible): *"George is about. Could you hold on?"* The adverbial use is conversational in tone, though it also appears in everyday writing, as in *seeing who is about*. This is sometimes said to be strictly for the British, because Americans prefer *around*. But the US preference is not so strong as to exclude **about**, by the evidence of the Brown corpus.
3) "concerning" or "concerned with," as in *the letter is about reconciliation* (preposition); *that's what it's about* (adverb). The preposition has always been standard usage, and the adverb is freely used in a variety of everyday prose in British and American

databases. The emphatic form *that's what X is all about* is also alive and well, despite the view of *Webster's English Usage* (1989) that it was on the decline. There are hundreds of examples in data from CCAE and the BNC. Most involve impersonal subjects, as in *that's what art / life / free enterprise is all about*. But in American data there are a few examples with a personal subject, as in *that's what this candidate is all about* and *we know what we are all about*.

The most important use of **about** is in the collocation **be about to**, used as a semi-auxiliary verb to express future events or intentions (see **auxiliary verbs** section 3). Its shades of meaning vary with the grammar of the subject (first, second or third person): compare *I'm about to go home* (said with intent) and *The judge was about to pronounce the sentence* (future event). But the negative counterpart **not about to** seems to have developed its own strong sense of determination, irrespective of person. Intention and resolve are both expressed in *I'm not about to stop you* and *Fox was not about to risk waiting for her inside her room* (these examples from the BNC, showing its use in British English). The idiom **not about to** seems to have originated in the American South and South Midland, and it was being used in nationwide publications by the 1960s, and even by two American presidents (Truman and Johnson). Its potential ambiguity attracted the attention of usage commentators including Bernstein, writing in *The New York Times* (1968/9), but there's no hard evidence of confusion with ordinary uses of the semi-auxiliary. **Not about to** probably has some rhetorical value in its negative understatement. See under **figures of speech**.

about face or about turn
See under **U-turn**.

abridgement or abridgment

The *Oxford Dictionary* (1989) prefers the regular **abridgement**, and in British English it's way out in front of **abridgment**, by 34:1 in data from the BNC. In American English the difference is less marked. *Webster's Third* (1986) gives priority to **abridgment**, yet it's only slightly ahead of **abridgement** in data from CCAE. See further under **-ment**.

> **International English selection:** The spelling **abridgement** recommends itself for the purposes of international English, given its regularity and substantial use in American English as well as British.

abscissa

The *Oxford Dictionary* (1989) gives only *abscissae* as the plural of this word, in keeping with its use in formal mathematical contexts. Compare *Webster's Third* (1986), where the absence of plural specifications implies that the regular English plural is to be expected. See further under **-a** section 1.

absent

A new prepositional role for this word has emerged from American legal usage since the 1940s. In examples like *"Absent any other facts, there arises an implied contract"* (from *Webster's English Usage*, 1989), it works like a Latin ablative absolute construction *absente (quo)* "in the absence of (which)." (See further under **ablative**.) It provides a convenient hedge for a conclusion, and, not so surprisingly, has begun to appear in US academic and argumentative writing outside the law itself. There's scant evidence of it in British English.

absolute

This uncompromising word has been put to various grammatical purposes, in reference to (1) adjectives, (2) pronouns, (3) verbs, (4) clauses. In essence it means that the word concerned stands alone in the sentence, without the usual grammatical connections to the phrase, clause or sentence being expressed. Some of the applications outlined below belong to traditional grammar, but collectively they show how freely the term has been applied. Overuse of the term **absolute** would explain why there are alternatives, also noted below.

1 **Absolute adjectives.** The term **absolute** is usually applied to parts of adjectives which by their grammar or meaning are not involved in comparison. Many grammarians use it to refer to the uninflected form of any adjective, e.g. *bright*, as opposed to *brighter, brightest*. (See further under **adjectives**, section 2.) An alternative older name for this part of the adjective paradigm is the "positive" form.

The phrase *absolute adjective* is applied by usage commentators, e.g. *Webster's English Usage* (1989), to adjectives whose meaning doesn't permit comparison. They are also called "uncomparable adjectives," by Garner (1998) and others. Either way the quality they refer to either is or is not, and there are no grades in between. They resist being modified by words such as *rather* and *very,* for the same reason. But the phrase *absolute adjective,* as applied to *unique* and others, suggests that they have only one meaning (see **unique** for its several meanings). The fact that a word may have both comparable and noncomparable senses seems to be overlooked. The lists of supposed *absolute adjectives* varies considerably from one authority to the next – itself a sign of the fuzziness of the category. Most include *complete* and *unique*, but there the similarities end. Among those sometimes included are:

countless	eternal	fatal	first
impossible	infinite	last	paramount
perfect	permanent	previous	simultaneous
supreme	total	ultimate	universal

Many of these are commonly modified by words such as *almost* or *nearly*, which Fowler (1926) allowed even for *unique*. You can posit approximations to an **absolute** state, if not gradations of it. That apart, comprehensive dictionaries show that such adjectives have both nongradable and gradable senses. The gradable sense is clearly being used in "a more complete account of events than ever before." So the notion of *absoluteness* needs to be attached to the sense, not the whole word. If the term *absolute adjective* has any value, it would be to refer to *defining* adjectives (see under **adjectives**):

auxiliary	classic	horizontal	ivory
second-hand	steel		

With their categorial meanings, they cannot be compared. Fowler also used **absolute** to refer to adjectives that serve as the head of a noun phrase: as in *the underprivileged, the young*. In these generic phrases the adjective behaves like a noun, in that it can be pre- or post-modified: *the very young, the young at heart* (*Comprehensive Grammar*, 1985). They are otherwise relatively fixed, always prefaced by *the,* and construed in the plural.

Absolute comparatives are expressions in which a comparative form of an adjective appears, but no real comparison is made. In fact comparisons are often implicit: they were explicit in only 25% of the examples in the Survey of English Usage, according to the *Comprehensive Grammar* (1985). But there could be no comparison at all in conventional or institutionalized expressions such as: *my better half, the finer things of life, Greater London, higher education, the younger generation*. We never imagine a starting point for them in "my good half," "high education" etc., so they are *absolute comparatives*. This is not of course the case with the familiar advertising line: BRAND XXX WASHES WHITER – which invites consumers to conjure up the comparatively murky linen produced by an unnamed competitor, while avoiding any claims for libel.

Absolute superlatives embody the superlative form of an adjective without any specific comparison. Like *absolute comparatives* they are often conventional expressions, and often involve *best* as in: *best practice, best seller, all the best, put your best foot forward*. Others are *worst-case scenario, worst enemy; do one's darndest; on/from the highest authority*. Freely formed examples like *the kindest person, the loveliest day* involve a kind of **hyperbole** (see under that heading).

2 **Absolute pronouns.** This is the term used by some grammarians (Huddleston, 1984) for possessive pronouns which stand as independent nouns, such as: *hers, ours, yours, theirs*. The *Comprehensive Grammar* (1985) calls them *independent* pronouns. See further under **possessive pronouns**.

3 **Absolute verbs** are those not complemented by the usual object or adjunct, as in *They ate*. (See further under **verb phrase** section 3.) This use of **absolute** is also at least as old as Fowler (1926), and appears in some older dictionaries.

4 **Absolute constructions or clauses** are grammatically independent phrases or nonfinite clauses, not integrated with the sentence in which they appear. Some are so conventional as to pass unnoticed, e.g. *that being so, all things considered*. Others created ad hoc by the writer may be censured as *dangling participles* or *unattached phrases:* see further under **dangling participles**.

abstract nouns

These words carry broad, generalized meanings that are not tied to the specific instance or a tangible, concrete item. The essential *abstract noun* is the name for an intangible such as *honesty, justice* or *knowledge*, though modern grammarians recognize many other kinds of words which refer to abstractions or to imputed entities such as *energy, luck* and *research*. Many **abstract nouns** are constructs of the language itself, built up out of other, more specific words. Thus abstractions such as *formality, graciousness, prevention* and *severance* are generated out of descriptive adjectives such as *formal, gracious,* and action verbs such as *prevent, sever*. Even ordinary and familiar words can take on abstract meanings in analytical writing. Think of *field* and *grain*. We usually imagine them in concrete terms, but in expressions like *field of study* and *grain of truth,* they become detached and abstract. Broad cover terms such as *article, creature* and *vehicle* are also abstract until applied to a particular object. A *vehicle* may thus take shape as a car, tram, bus, truck, bicycle or perhaps even a skateboard or wheelbarrow. (For more on the distinction between *abstract* and *concrete nouns,* see **nouns**.)

Abstract nouns are a useful means of building ideas. They help writers to extend their arguments and develop theories. They can encapsulate remarkable insights, and summarize diffuse material under manageable headings. The downside is their too frequent appearance in academic and bureaucratic clichés. In his classic *Complete Plain Words* (1962), Gowers talks of the "lure of the abstract [word]" for British civil servants, and of the need to "choos[e] the precise word." Most American students are familiar with the injunction of their "freshman composition" textbooks to "prefer the concrete to the abstract," although the prevalence of the opposite in professional writing has been noted by researchers such as Lanham (1974) and Couture (1986). Computer software is able to identify some of the abstract language in a text, i.e. words ending in *-tion, -ness, -ity, -ance, -ancy, -ence* and *-ency* and other characteristic suffixes. It cannot identify ordinary words used in abstract senses, let alone decide whether they are appropriate for the subject. *Abstract words* are not necessarily reprehensible, but their cumulative effect on the weary reader needs to be factored in.
◊ For further discussion of related issues, see **gobbledygook** and **nominal**.

abstracts

An **abstract** is a distinctively structured summary, used especially in academic contexts. See under **summary**.

academia, academe and academy

The first of these words is both the most ancient in form and the most popular now, at the start of C21. **Academia** (*Akademeia*) was the name of the Athenian garden associated with the legendary Greek hero Akademos (in medieval times called **Academe**). Plato's school of philosophy took its name from the garden, hence later references to "Plato's Academy."

The use of **academe** to mean "place of learning" is first recorded in Shakespeare's *Love's Labour's Lost,* where it appears in the singular as well as plural (alongside "books") as the source of "the true Promethean fire." Fowler (1926) took Shakespeare to task for using **academe** in reference to an institution rather than a person, and would have liked even less its extended use to refer to the whole academic community and environment. *Merriam-Webster* (2000) embraces all these senses, whereas only the institutional ones appear in *New Oxford* (1998), *Canadian Oxford* (1998) and the Australian *Macquarie* (1997). In American and British usage, **academe** most commonly appears in sets like *arts, academe and the professions.* Otherwise it provides the context for many a work of fiction – apart from Mary McCarthy's novel *The Groves of Academe* (1952), and Mark Stein's play (c. 1980) of the same name. The phrase *groves of academe* now has more than a whiff of cliché about it, but at least it can be varied. Large databases such as the BNC and CCAE show a range of alternatives: *halls of academe* (hybridized with "halls of [higher]

learning"), *realms of academe, world of academe, ivory towers in academe,* and even *the ghetto of academe.*

Fowler's criticism of using **academe** in the sense "academic world" could perhaps have prompted the rise of **academia** as an alternative term since World War II. In fact **academia** outnumbers **academe** by 4:1 in both the BNC and CCAE, and it collocates in much the same way with "halls," "ivory towers," "cloisters," and "groves" itself. Like **academe,** it appears in sets like "labor, business and academia" to designate a sphere of activity and influence. No doubt its more transparent form (ending in the abstract suffix *-ia*) gives it an advantage over its competitor, which lacks formal analogues in English. (See further under **-ia.**)

The phrase *the academy* is very occasionally found as a synonym for **academia** and **academe,** but its usage is mostly worlds apart and has been much broader than either, especially in C19 and earlier C20. In the UK, **academy** served as the common term for an alternative type of school to the classically oriented grammar school; and in North America it was used in reference to private schools. It's now more familiar as the key word in the names of various specialized institutes of the performing arts – *the Royal Academy of Dramatic Art, Franz Liszt Academy of Music* – as well as visual arts and sciences. In the US, the word **academy** is built into the names of defense force training centres such as the *West Point Academy,* not to mention the metropolitan *Police Academy,* immortalized through movies. The American *Academy of Motion Picture Arts and Sciences* lends its name to the *Academy Awards,* and winners there enjoy professional esteem comparable to that of the *Academy exhibitor* among the British art establishment. These various institutions give a specialized meaning to **academy** that distinguishes it from **academe** and **academia,** yet it now lacks generic usages enough to guarantee it a long future.
◊ For the *Académie Française* and other *language academies,* see **language academy.**

accents and diacritics

In speech, an **accent** is a general style of pronunciation which strikes the listener as different, as in *a foreign accent, an Irish accent.* It may involve the stress patterns of words as well as the way sounds are pronounced. The **accents** of written language mostly relate to individual sounds. When superimposed on a particular letter of the alphabet, **accents** show that the pronunciation differs in some way from the unmarked letters. The English spelling system does without **accents,** except for the occasional foreign word (see below). Many other languages make systematic use of **accents** to indicate aspects of sound, stress and pitch. The technical term for *accent marks* is *diacritics.*

The most familar **accents** are those of European languages, such as the French *acute* and the German *umlaut* which mark particular vowels, and the Spanish *tilde* and the Slavonic *háček,* used with particular consonants. Less well-known ones are the small circle used over *u* in Czech, and over *a* in Danish, Norwegian and Swedish, and the slash used with *l* in Polish and with *o* in Danish and Norwegian. (See further at individual entries on **acute, cedilla, circumflex, dieresis, grave, háček, tilde, umlaut.**) **Accents** are also used to mark the strongly stressed syllables of some words of Italian, Spanish and Irish.

Some Asian languages written in the Roman alphabet, such as Vietnamese, have **accents** to show the different tones or pitch that go with a particular word: rising, falling, level etc. The use of **accents** shows the limitations of the alphabet for writing the sounds of diverse modern languages. (See further under **alphabets**.)

Foreign accents/diacritics in English Accents may be included in the English spelling of loanwords, depending on whether the word is a common noun or proper name, and the context of communication.

a) Loanwords which become English common nouns tend to lose their **accents** in the course of time, witness French loans such as *crepe, debut, elite, facade,* and *role*. Their disappearance is helped by the fact that English typewriters and wordprocessors rarely have accents in their repertoire, neither does the internet. In fact there's no reason for **accents** to be retained in words such as *role* or *elite,* where the vowel letters themselves match the pronunciation. The **accents** would mostly be missed by francophones and those for whom it adds cachet or a hint of sophistication. In *Webster's Third* (1986) the unaccented form of all those words is given priority, whereas the opposite holds true for the *Oxford Dictionary* (1989). This difference probably correlates with divergent regional trends, as well as the fact that the original *Oxford* (1884–1928) was much more inclined to mark loanwords as "not naturalized," with **accents** shown to correlate with their perceived foreignness. Though the "foreign" symbol has been removed from many of these loanwords in the second edition (1989), the **accents** remain and accentless alternatives are not yet recognized. *Copy-editing* (1992) suggests that if **accents** are to be marked, all those belonging to the word should be there, e.g. *protégé, résumé*. The more functional approach is to use whatever **accents** are essential to distinguish loanwords from their English homographs. Hence *resumé* with one **accent** to contrast with *resume*. (See further under **resumé**.) Even so, the context may provide all that's needed to identify them as noun and verb respectively, just as it does for *exposé* and *expose*. Only the first could appear in *an exposé of corruption* and the second in *the will to expose corruption*. The difference between *pique* and *piqué* is embedded in their particular collocations: *a fit of pique* v. *a pique table cloth*. When both are adjectives, readers may depend more on the accent to distinguish their attributive use, as in a *flamboyant lamé suit* and *a lame duck*. The accent is more crucial when the homographs work in the same grammatical slot.

b) Well-known foreign names with **accents/** diacritics generally lose them when reproduced in English. Thus *Dvorak* is usually written without the **háček,** *Zurich* without the **umlaut,** and *Montreal* without its **acute**. In some contexts of communication, however, retaining such **accents** assumes some strategic and diplomatic importance. This would be so for British or American authors writing for EU readerships; or for anglophone Canadians when writing French-Canadian names and titles into public documents, such as *Sept-Îles* and *Musée de Nouveau Brunswick*. Note also that **accents** are used on capital letters in Canadian French, though not regularly in Metropolitan French. For further details, see *Editing Canadian English* (2000).

acceptance or acceptation

At the start of C21, these two are scarcely interchangeable as the noun counterpart to the verb *accept*. The latinate **acceptation** could once be used to mean "a state of being accepted or acceptable," but the last trace of it was around 1800, by which time the French-style **acceptance** had replaced it for all practical purposes. Just one application remains for **acceptation**: to refer to the interpretation or understanding of a word which is the focus of academic or legal discussion. American data from CCAE provides a single example in which a court found that "by common acceptation, the description [*white pine*] has acquired a secondary meaning as firmly anchored as the first." On that one showing, and the two British instances in BNC, **acceptation** is close to extinction.

accessory or accessary

Accessory is now the all-purpose spelling for most contexts. **Accessary** used to be reserved for legal discourse, when talking about a person as the *accessary to a crime* or *an accessary after the fact*. But **accessory** is now used in those expressions too, as evidenced by data from very large corpora (BNC, CCAE). They contained no examples of **accessary** apart from a very dubious British example, in which the word was flanked by three misspelled words. Dictionaries which continue to present **accessary** as an alternative spelling are presumably justifying it from specialized legal documents, which perpetuate archaic writing conventions. Meanwhile the spelling **accessory** has always been preferred for the extra item(s) that go with any complex outfit, whether it is a set of clothes, a car or a computer.

accidentally or accidently

The second and shorter spelling is not as obsolete as the *Oxford Dictionary* (1989) claims. Databases show its currency, with a score of British examples in the BNC and almost 100 American ones in CCAE. These numbers suggest that **accidently** is somewhat commoner in American English, and its relative frequency vis-à-vis **accidentally** confirms it: about 1:15 in American data, whereas it's 1:28 in the British data. **Accidently** is sometimes regarded as a spelling mistake or malformation, but its pedigree is obscured by the fact that *accident* was once an adjective, from which it could be derived quite regularly. Common pronunciation of the word (with stress on the first syllable) also supports the shorter form. This is not to say we should prefer it to **accidentally**: rather that it cannot be dismissed as a solecism.

acclaim

Note that the associated noun is *acclamation*. See **-aim**.

accommodation, accomodation and accommodations

Accommodation, and the related verb *accommodate*, may well qualify as the most widely misspelled words in otherwise standard writing of the late C20. Yet "accomodate" was not uncommon in earlier centuries, as the *Oxford Dictionary* (1989) shows. Celebrated authors such as Defoe, Cowper and Jane Austen used it. The insistence on two *m*s thus seems to have firmed up during the last 100 years. It is unquestionably in line with the etymology of the word (its root is the same as for *commodity* and *commodious*). But unless you know Latin, the reason for the two *m*s isn't obvious. One pair of doubled consonants (the *c*s) seems enough for some writers as if a kind of *dissimilation* sets in. (See **dissimilate or dissimulate**.)

Accomodation is still relatively rare in edited prose, however commonly seen in signs and advertisements. British data from the BNC has **accommodation** outnumbering **accomodation** by almost 100:1, and in American data from CCAE the ratio is still close to 70:1. Neither *Webster's Third* (1986) nor the *Oxford Dictionary* presents the single-*m* spellings as alternatives, though they allow consonant-reduced spellings of other words such as *guer(r)illa* and *millen(n)ium,* despite their etymology. The management of double and single consonants is a vexed issue for various groups of English words (see **single for double**).

Until recently, American English was distinctive in using the plural **accommodations** in reference to temporary lodgings or arrangements for lodgings, whereas British English preferred the singular. But the BNC provides evidence of **accommodations** being used now in the UK as well – in advertisements for *oceanfront accommodations,* as well as more abstract discussions describing how *each party is prepared to make substantial accommodations to the other.* Overall there are 45 instances in the BNC, as opposed to thousands in CCAE, but enough to show that the plural form is being recommissioned in Britain. The *Oxford Dictionary* shows earlier British citations up to about 1800.

accompanist or accompanyist
Accompanyist seems to have dropped out of favor, though still heard from time to time. Both spellings were evidenced in C19, and the *Oxford Dictionary* (1989), while preferring **accompanist**, actually had more citations (3:1) for **accompanyist**. *Webster's Third* (1986) also presents the two spellings, putting **accompanist** first. But there's no recent evidence for **accompanyist** in either BNC or CCAE – or anything to suggest that **accompanyist** is a US alternative, as suggested by some dictionaries.

accusative
This is a grammatical name for the case of the direct object of a verb. In "The judge addressed the jury," *jury* is the direct object, and could therefore be said to be **accusative**. The term is regularly used in analyzing languages like German and Latin, because they have different forms for the direct and the indirect object (the latter is called the **dative**).

In English both direct and indirect objects have the same form, whether they are nouns or pronouns. Compare:
> The judge addressed the jury / them (direct object)
> The judge gave the jury / them his advice (indirect object)

Because the words *jury/them* are the same for both roles, the term **objective case** is often used in English to cover both **accusative** and **dative**.
◊ For more about grammatical case, see **cases** and **object**.
◊ For the so-called "unaccusative," see **ergative** and **middle voice**.

ACE
This is an acronym for the Australian Corpus of English, a database of late C20 written Australian English, from which evidence has been drawn for entries in this book. For the composition of the corpus, see under **English language databases**.

-acious/-aceous
These endings have a spurious likeness, although they need never be confused. The words ending in **-aceous** are not everyday words except for the gardener or botanist. How recently did you see *herbaceous* or *rosaceous,* for example? *Farinaceous* comes closer to home in discussions of food or diet, yet all such words originate as scientific creations, referring to particular classes of plants.

By contrast, the words ending in **-acious** are unspecialized and used in many contexts. For example:
> audacious capacious loquacious pugnacious
> vivacious voracious

Note that the *-ac-* in these words is actually part of the stem or root of the word (e.g. *audac-*), to which *-ious* has been added. For more about words formed in this way, see **-ious**.

acknowledgement or acknowledgment
Acknowledgment is given priority in both *Webster's Third* (1986) and the *Oxford Dictionary* (1989), perhaps because of its use by publishers in the front matter of books. Yet **acknowledgement** gets plenty of use in both the US and the UK. In American data from CCAE, the two are almost equally matched, while British evidence from the BNC has **acknowledgement** strongly preferred, by more than 5:1. The spelling which retains the *e* in the middle is more regular in terms of the larger conventions of English spelling (see **-e**). For other words ending in *-dg(e)ment*, see under **-ment**.

> **International English selection:** Since **acknowledgement** is well established in both American and British English, and the more regular spelling, it's the one to prefer in international communication.

◊ For the location of *acknowledgements* at the front of a book, see **preface**.

acro-
This Greek element, meaning either "top" or "end," brings both kinds of meaning into English in loanwords. In words like *acrophobia* and *acropolis* (including the *Acropolis* in Athens) it means a "high position." In others, like *acronym* and *acrostic,* it means the "tip" or "extremity" of the words involved. The *acrobat* is literally "one who walks on tiptoe."

acronyms
An *acronym* is the word formed out of the initial letter or letters of a particular set of words. Thus an *acronym*, like an abbreviation, carries the meaning of a complex title or phrase:
> ASCII (American Standard Code for Information Interchange)
> NATO (North Atlantic Treaty Organization)

UNICEF (United Nations International Children's Emergency Fund)

WHO (World Health Organization)

Acronyms like these are written without stops, and may metamorphose further into words by shedding their capital letters, except for the first one. Thus *NATO* can also be written as *Nato*, and *UNICEF* as *Unicef*. When **acronyms** become common nouns, they are written entirely in lower case. For example:

laser (light amplification by stimulated emission of radiation)

radar (radio detection and ranging)

scuba (self-contained underwater breathing apparatus)

snag (sensitive new-age guy)

Not all **acronyms** are nouns. The adjective *posh* is believed to have begun as an **acronym**, standing for "port outward, starboard home"– unquestionably the choicer side of the ship, if you were a colonial journeying between Britain and India, and wanted to avoid the tropical sun. Another is the adverb *AWOL* (still usually capitalized) which in military parlance is "absent without official leave," but used much more widely in the phrase *gone AWOL,* to cover an unexplained absence.

The desire to create **acronyms** which are both pronounceable and meaningful has exercised many an action group, such as:

ASH (Action on Smoking and Health)

CARS (Committee on Alcohol and Road Safety)

LIFE (Lay Institute for Evangelism)

MADD (Mothers against Drunk Driving)

SWAP (Students Work Abroad Program)

Strategically chosen **acronyms** can also provide a useful mnemonic, as in the *SWOT* analysis of business operations, under the headings of "strengths, weaknesses, opportunities, threats."

Acronyms and initialisms. All the **acronyms** discussed so far comprise strings of letters which combine to form syllables, and can be pronounced as ordinary words. This is not, however, possible with abbreviations like *BBC* or *GNP,* which have to be pronounced letter by letter. Technically they are *initialisms* rather than **acronyms**, although the term is not widely known. (The term *alphabetism* is still less common.) Yet *initialism* began as a nonce word just before 1900, according to the original *Oxford Dictionary* (1884–1928). Though absent from the 1976 Supplement *H–N,* it eventually made a full entry in the second edition (1989). Still it remains a technical term for professional editors and lexicographers, and hardly leaves any trace in large general databases. There are no occurrences of it in CCAE, and only one (in the plural) in the BNC. Data from both corpora show that *initialisms* such as *CBT* (computer-based training) and *FMFFV* (full motion / full frame video) are simply called **acronyms**. The distinction is in any case flawed, because (1) an abbreviation can embody both types, as does *MSDOS;* and (2) the same abbreviation can be pronounced in two ways. Think for example of *AKA* ("also known as") and *UFO* ("unidentified flying object"), which are two-syllabled **acronyms** for some speakers, and three-syllabled *initialisms* for others. *Initialisms* generally keep their capital letters, even when they correspond to strings of lower case words.

active verbs

The term *active* is applied by grammarians to a verb whose action is performed by its own grammatical subject. A classical illustration is the statement: *I came, I saw, I conquered.*

Active verbs contrast with **passive verbs**, where the subject is acted upon by the verb's action. There are three passive verbs in the historical punishment for high treason – *He was hanged, drawn and quartered* – although only the first one is fully expressed with a subject and a part of the verb *be* (see **passive verbs**).

In written documents, **active verbs** are vital because they express action directly as an event, rather than making it a passive process. They are the natural way to keep a narrative moving vigorously along, and many books on good style recommend their use to ensure vigorous prose. Other things to avoid are discussed under **gobbledygook**, and **impersonal style**.

acuity or acuteness

The adjective *acute* has for centuries had two abstract nouns: the latinate **acuity** being first recorded in 1543, and the home-grown English **acuteness** in 1646. **Acuity** is much more frequent than **acuteness** – by a factor of 4:1 in American English (CCAE) and 5:1 in British data from the BNC. Despite unequal shares of usage, they coexist through some specialization in their uses. The corpus data has **acuity** typically referring to sharpness of vision, while **acuteness** is associated with poignancy of feeling, suffering and the symptoms of disease. Yet the BNC also shows some overlap, in that either may refer to sharpness of intellect and observation, where the mind's eye and the seeing eye coincide.

acute accents

The meaning of this mark depends on the language being written. In some European languages it marks a special vowel quality, as in French where it's used for a tense *e* (one pronounced with the tongue higher than for other kinds of *e*). In Czech and Hungarian the **acute accent** can be associated with any of the five vowels. Compare Polish, where it goes with the vowel *o,* and several consonants: *c, n, s* and *z.*

Other languages deploy the **acute accent** to mark prosodic aspects of words. In Greek and Spanish writing, **acute accents** are placed over vowels to show that the syllables they occur in are stressed. Spanish homophones are sometimes distinguished this way: thus *si* ("if") and *sí* ("yes"). In Vietnamese writing, the **acute accent** represents a rising pitch for the syllable concerned.

Double **acute accents** are used in Hungarian on *o* and *u,* making different sounds from the same letters marked with umlauts. See further under **umlaut**.

ad or advert

In the snappy world of advertising, abbreviated forms of the key word are indispensable, though they made their first showing in print some decades before the industry took off. The *Oxford Dictionary*'s record begins in Victorian England, with two citations from mid-C19, and one from 1902 whose author finds it "a loathly little word," yet such was its popularity in the 1920s that *admen* themselves campaigned against it, fearing that it robbed their enterprise of dignity (Mencken's Supplement to *The American Language,* 1945). With only two letters, **ad** is an abnormally brief word for embodying content (see further under **words**), and British dictionaries including the *Oxford* label it "colloquial." American dictionaries such as *Webster's Third* (1986) leave it unlabeled, and American corpus evidence confirms that it's stylistically versatile, appearing in eight different categories of fiction and nonfiction in the Brown corpus, and in newspapers as well as monographs in the more recent CCAE. Reviewing its status, *Webster's English Usage* (1989) concludes that it is acceptable to a large majority of Americans. It also occurs freely in contemporary British English, with over 750 instances (singular and plural) in the BNC, found in many kinds of publication, and connected with various British institutions including Sainsbury's and Yorkshire TV.

Other signs that **ad** is established are the increasing range of compounds based on it. *Adman* originated in the first decade of C20, but CCAE contains many others, usually spaced, such as *ad agency, ad campaign, ad revenues* and *want-ads.* Note that in all but the last example, **ad** means "advertising" rather than "advertisement," though not all dictionaries recognize this.

Advert also originated in C19 (first recorded in 1860), but did not gain popularity until the 1950s. Large databases confirm that it's little used outside Britain. Though the BNC contains more than 800 examples (singular and plural) in BNC data, the tally from CCAE could be counted on the fingers of one hand. Its appearances in BNC texts – mostly the more interactive kinds of discourse – show that it's still "colloquial," as noted in the *Oxford Dictionary.* **Advert** as an abbreviation of "advertisement" keeps its distance from the identical latinate verb **advert** meaning "draw attention," which appears less than 10 times in the BNC, and only in rather formal style.

Both **ad** and **advert** are occasionally punctuated like abbreviations – ad., advert. – and there are examples among the *Oxford Dictionary* citations, though they are not proposed as secondary forms. For most writers **ad** and **advert** are established short forms, like *exam* or *gym,* and there's no need to mark them as abbreviations of "advertisement" or "advertising." See further under **clipping.**
◊ For the choice between **advertisement** and **advertizement**, see further under that heading.

AD or A.D.
This abbreviation stands for the Latin *anno domini,* meaning "in the year of the Lord." It represents a date calculated within the calendar devised centuries ago by the Christian church, which is still the standard for the western world. In the Christian calendar, all years are dated as being either before the presumed year of Christ's birth (BC), or after it (**AD**).

According to a long-established principle of style, noted in Burchfield (1996) and the *Chicago Manual* (2003), **AD** should be written before the number in a date, as in *AD 405,* and *BC* after the number: *55 BC.* Yet there's increasing evidence that "it ain't necessarily so." *Webster's English Usage* (1989) presents counter examples alongside conventional ones; and *Webster's Style Manual* (1985) had earlier observed that, despite the convention, "many writers and editors place *AD* after the date" (as in *405 AD*). It observed that this

makes **AD** dates consistent with *BC* dates – and both then have the same order as when spoken. Database evidence from CCAE as well as the BNC confirms the trend in both the US and the UK, though it's closer to being an equal alternative in the American data. The *Cambridge International Dictionary* (1995) allows both placements.

The developing practice of placing **AD** after the year reference is supported by the now regular habit of having it follow the word *century,* as in *the fifth century AD.* This was the only location for it in many examples from the BNC and CCAE, and it's accepted even by usage authorities who object to placing **AD** after the year. Once again it reflects the order in which the phrase is said, but it was once objected to on the grounds that the word *anno* ("year") came awkwardly after "century." Those who read **AD** in its original Latin terms are however increasingly rare. For most it simply means "in the Christian era," and has a "purely conventional significance," as the *Chicago Manual* (1993) put it. Most scholars and scholarly editors, it says, have "long since withdrawn their objections."

The punctuation and typesetting of **AD** raise a few further questions. The font is usually roman rather than italic, in keeping with the bold feature style of this entry, rather than the italics used in examples. With full typesetting resources it can appear in *small capitals* (see **small caps**), but in wordprocessed text and on the internet it typically appears in full caps. The use/non-use of stops in **AD** is a matter of regional and/or individual policy for capitalized abbreviations (see **abbreviations**). American authorities cited in this entry tend to use periods/stops (**A.D.**) and the British ones not. They are united in leaving no space between the letters of the abbreviation, but setting space between it and the year.
◊ For more about the writing of dates, see **BC or BCE** and **dating systems**.

ad hoc, ad-hoc and adhoc
In Latin this phrase meant "to this" and by extension "for this matter." We use it in expressions like *ad hoc committee,* i.e. one set up for a specific and limited purpose, alongside the regular committee. In this precise context **ad(-)hoc** is neutral in meaning. In wider use it has come to mean "impromptu," and, more negatively, "lacking in forethought or circumspection." Decisions *made ad hoc* often seem arbitrary. These shifts in meaning, and the range of English derivatives (see below), show how thoroughly **ad(-)hoc** has been assimilated.

Ad hoc is still usually set with space, whether used as an attributive adjective, as in *ad hoc measures,* or predicatively (or adverbially) as in *Everything is very ad hoc* (see **adjectives** section 1). In American data from CCAE, the spaced form (**ad hoc**) outnumbers **ad-hoc** by more than 7:1, in keeping with the general American practice of avoiding *hyphens* (see under that heading). The difference is even greater in BNC data (closer to 15:1), though this may have more to do with British preference for preserving the identity of the Latin phrase. The BNC also provides a score of examples of **adhoc** (set solid). This form has yet to be recognized in either *New Oxford* (1998) or *Merriam-Webster* (2000), but it's the natural trend when the word is almost always an adjective rather than adverb, as the databases show. The fact that it has several derivatives is further evidence of its ongoing assimilation.

The nouns derived from **ad(-)hoc** pose issues of spelling, illustrated in the alternative forms *adhoc(k)ing, adhocism / ad hocism, adhoc(k)ery* and even *ad-hoc-ness*, all registered in the *Oxford Dictionary* (1989). The *Addenda* of *Webster's Third* (1986) adds *adhocracy,* a word which could be applied in many domains where *adhoc(k)ery* seems to rule. It conforms neatly to English spelling, and doesn't require any extra letter or hyphen to make it look like a real word. The *Oxford* variants *ad hocism* and *ad hoc-ery* show the persistent use of space to identify the Latin elements, though they highlight etymology at the expense of current meaning, and ignore the problems of suffixation (see further under **-c/-ck-** and **-e**). At any rate, consensus has yet to be achieved on how to spell these words, leaving writers free to select or construct the form which communicates best.

ad hominem

This phrase, borrowed from Latin, is part of the longer expression *argumentum ad hominem* "argument directed at the individual." It refers to diversionary tactics used in legal pleading and political rhetoric, either an appeal to the self-interest of the listener(s), or a personal attack on the opposition (the "mudslinging" of low-level parliamentary debate). Either way it diverts attention from the real issues, and jeopardizes proper debate and discussion. It suggests that the speaker is unable or unwilling to answer the points raised by the other side. (See further under **argument**.)
◊ See also **ad personam**.

ad infinitum

In Latin this phrase meant "to infinity" and was used literally in medieval scholasticism in theological and mathematical argument. But in modern usage **ad infinitum** is always a rhetorical exaggeration – applied to a process which seems to go drearily on and on.

ad lib, ad-lib or adlib

In shortened form, this is the late Latin phrase *ad libitum,* meaning "at one's pleasure," or "as you please." Musicians have known it for centuries as a directive to do as they like with the musical score: modify the tempo, add a few grace notes, omit a few bars of repetition. Only in C20 was the word extended to other kinds of performance (particularly acting and public speaking), in which the speaker may extemporize beyond the script. Often it implies a complete absence of scripting. These more general uses of the phrase have turned it into a colloquial verb, as in *having to ad-lib his way through a weather forecast.*

Both the *New Oxford Dictionary* (1998) and *Merriam-Webster* (2000) have the verb written as **ad-lib**, the last consonant of which is doubled when suffixes are added, as in *ad-libbed, ad-libbing* and *ad-libber*. The dictionaries propose the hyphenated form **ad-lib** for the noun (*an original ad-lib*) and adjective (*his ad-lib masterpiece*) as well, though *New Oxford* uses **ad lib** when illustrating the rather rare adverb. Yet data from the BNC show a mix of **ad-lib** and **ad lib** for verb, noun and adjective in edited texts,

and **ad lib** interchanging with **adlib** in broadcasting autocues (e.g. *Harriet adlib*), where its grammar is indeterminate. Data from CCAE have **ad lib** as often as **ad-lib** for noun, verb and adjective, in line with the greater reluctance of Americans to use a hyphen when spaced forms will do (see under **hyphens**). But **ad(-)lib** evidently varies in both the US and UK – which goes with the free-wheeling nature of the process it refers to.

ad personam

This Latin phrase (literally "to the person") has had two kinds of use in late C20 English:
* to describe appointments which are made to suit the individual candidate, rather than by general criteria
* as a nonsexist variant of *ad hominem*, on the mistaken assumptions that (a) the latter means "at the man" (male) rather than "at the human individual"; and (b) Latin *persona* can be used like "person" in English (see under **-person** and **persona**). Just what equal opportunity it provides for is unclear.
Neither usage is widespread. The second, noted by Bliss (1966), seems to predate affirmative action of the 1980s, while the first makes its appearance in *New Oxford* (1998). There's no sign of either in *Merriam-Webster* (2000).

ad rem

This Latin phrase means literally "to the matter." It is used to identify arguments which stick to the point at issue, and do not resort to diversionary tactics or argumentative tricks. (See further under **argument** and **fallacies**.)

adage

See under **aphorism**.

adaptation or adaption

These are both abstract nouns based on the verb *adapt*. **Adaptation** is older by far with an antecedent in late Latin, whereas **adaption** appears first in C18, apparently formed on the analogy of *adoption*. **Adaption** has never been as popular as **adaptation**, to judge by the way it's cross-referenced to the longer word in both *Webster's Third* (1986) and the *Oxford Dictionary* (1989). In contemporary databases of British and American English, **adaption** is much less common than **adaptation**, in the ratio of about 1:20 in BNC and 1:40 in CCAE. What use it has in American English is typically in references to a literary work being adapted for another medium such as television or film. But occasionally it refers to the adapting of computer software for different platforms, of industries to changing market forces, and of humans to extreme stress. The last is the sole example in CCAE to support the indication of the *Random House Dictionary* (1987) that **adaption** belongs to sociology. Clearly the word is in wider use than its editors – or Fowler (1926) – were aware. **Adaption** is thus a viable alternative to **adaptation**, and goes almost anywhere the verb *adapt* itself can go.

adapter or adaptor

Some *-er/-or* pairs complement each other, one being used for the person and the other for the instrument

(as with *conveyer/conveyor*). But this is not so for **adapter/adaptor**, which are interchangeable in database evidence from both the US and the UK. The chief difference is that **adapter** is much more frequent than **adaptor** in American English, occurring more than four times as often in CCAE; whereas in British English the situtation is reversed with **adaptor** occurring nearly four times as often as **adapter** in the BNC. In both databases, the words were used much more often in relation to mechanical, electrical or electronic devices than to people who adapt something such as a literary work. But the human sense was spelled as both **adapter** and **adaptor**, and there were instances of both *co-adapter* and *co-adaptor* in CCAE.
◊ For other kinds of complementation between **-er/-or** words, see under that heading.

addendum

For the plural of this word, see under **-um**.

addition or additive

Additives are of course **additions**, but **additions** are not necessarily **additives**. **Additive** has the much more restricted meaning of something added in a chemical process, as in photography, or in the processing of foods. But if you're extending your house or family, it will be an **addition**, not an **additive**.

addresses

In the last fifty years, the wording of **addresses** in letters and on envelopes has become increasingly streamlined. Current practice is to use minimal punctuation, and abbreviations for titles, generic elements of street names, and state or province codes. Zip codes / post codes are used in most English-speaking countries, placed after the name of the state in the US and Australia, after the city in the UK, and after the province in Canada. In European **addresses** the post code precedes the name of the city. Examples of each are set out in Appendixes VII and VIII.
◊ For the conventions of e-mail and internet **addresses**, see **URL**.

adherence or adhesion

These abstract words are both related to the verb *adhere*, meaning "stick to." They differ in that **adhesion** usually refers to the physical gluing or bonding of one substance to another, while **adherence** means a less tangible connection, such as the commitment to a religion, philosophy, code of behavior or international agreement. Yet there's some crossover between them, which is acknowledged in American and British dictionaries, and evidenced in the corpora.

The physical bonding expressed in **adhesion** can be chemical (as of household paint sticking to a surface), biochemical (as when bacteria attach themselves to cells) or mechanical (as of the grip of a tyre on the road or a shoe on the ground). In American English there is a further specialized legal use of the term in *contract of adhesion* (one which is attached to a job and cannot be negotiated by the employee). Among the crossover examples from CCAE, **adhesion** was also used in a few references to Christian affiliation (both conformist and nonconformist) and to political policy, in *adhesion to free trade*. These latter areas are the broad domain of **adherence**, which expresses

many kinds of religious affiliation (Christian and non-Christian), as well as political and social commitments (to Keynesian economics, the Berne copyright convention and the new corporate mentality). Some applications were closer to home, as in **adherence** to a low-fat diet, or to a dress code of suits, ties and jackets for legislators. Again there were a few crossover examples in both CCAE and BNC where **adherence** (rather than **adhesion**) was used to express chemical and biochemical bonding. The interplay between the two words shows that they are not quite as specialized in their applications as is sometimes said, although **adhesion** remains the one to which more technical senses are attached. **Adherence** still can be applied more freely, in many human and social situations. This helps to explain why it is much more common than **adhesion**, although the margin is greater in the US than the UK, judging by their relative frequency in data from CCAE and the BNC.

adieu

In several European languages, speakers seem to invoke the divinity when taking leave of each other. **Adieu** (French) and *adios* (Spanish) both mean literally "to God"; and the English *goodbye*, originally "God be with you," spells it out a little more. *Goodbye* is now totally secularized, an all-purpose farewell, whereas **adieu** retains a certain divine melancholy, a sense of the significance of the parting that it marks. Contemporary English uses of **adieu** illustrated in the BNC are mostly to be found in literary fiction, in direct address ("Gentlemen, adieu"), and in narrative comment, usually collocated with the verb *bid* in the sense "declare" (see further at **bid**). When used in nonfictional contexts, *bidding adieu* attaches historic moment to historical departures, as when "bidding adieu to Soviet troops" is coupled with "working out new treaties of good neighbourliness with the Soviet Union."

Adieu appears only very rarely in the plural, leaving some doubt as to whether it should then be the English *adieus* or French *adieux*. The major dictionaries endorse the first rather than the second: *Webster's Third* (1986) does so explicitly, and the *Oxford Dictionary* (1989) implicitly, by the absence of plural specification. However the *-x* plural is still available for those who wish to emphasize the foreign origins of **adieu**, and it's needed of course in titles such as *Les Adieux,* given to one of Beethoven's sonatas.

adjacent, adjoining and adjunct

The first two words imply closeness in space, and both may indicate objects or areas juxtaposed to each other:
> *The company suffered a serious setback when fire gutted much of the adjacent warehouse.*
> *The area ranges from full sun beyond the herb bed to deep shade adjoining the house.*

Adjoining normally implies contiguity, though the common boundary often has to be deduced from context, and may be no more than a right-angle connection, as in *an alley adjoining the main road,* and *houses in adjoining streets*. The sense of contiguity in **adjoining** probably stems from its visible connections with the word *join;* whereas the etymology of **adjacent** ("lying near") is obscure to most. **Adjacent** doesn't require things to be hard up against each other, though they may be, as in *adjacent angles* or the *adjacent organs* of anatomical descriptions. More often, **adjacent** seems to be used when the relative closeness of two objects is not so important, or not known. Consider its use in BNC examples such as *research with grant-maintained and other adjacent schools,* which leaves it open as to how many schools in a given district are covered by the study.

Adjacent is also used to refer to the position of an item immediately preceding or following in a sequence (*Webster's Third,* 1986), and the relationship begins to be a matter of time rather than space. Add this to its already wider range of applications, and it's no surprise to find that **adjacent** occurs more than twice as often as **adjoining** in both American and British English, from the evidence of CCAE and the BNC.

Adjunct is a good deal more abstract than either **adjacent** or **adjoining**, and quite rare as an adjective. Its uses are official, as in *adjunct professor,* meaning one appointed by special (non-tenured) attachment to an institution.

◊ For grammatical uses of the noun **adjunct**, see **adjuncts**.

adjectives

Often thought of as "descriptive words," **adjectives** just as often serve to define or to evaluate something:

a big room   a windowless room   an awful room

The same **adjective** may describe *and* evaluate something, as in *a poky room.* Writers can of course use more than one **adjective** in the same string, to create a multifaceted image. Wine labels and wine commentaries are a rich source of them:

> *intense cool-climate fruit and smoky oak aromas very lively, fine, dry palate with a flinty edge and a long finish*
>
> *a medium-bodied cabernet-style wine, matured in small French casks*

Both simple and compound **adjectives** can go before the key noun, but the more elaborately phrased descriptors ("matured in..." etc.) need to go after it (in *postposition*). Theoretically there's no limit to the number of **adjectives** you can pile up in front of a noun – only the risk of losing the reader with too many. As those wine descriptions show, a set of three or four is plenty, especially if some of them are *compound adjectives* (on which see section 3 below).

Adjectives appear in a conventional order, the evaluative ones coming first, before the descriptive ones, which always precede the definitive ones. This explains the sequences in *smoky oak aromas* and *small French casks.* Note also that the **adjective** modified by *very* comes first in the string, as in *very lively, fine, dry palate.* The same holds for any gradable or comparable adjectives (see section 2 below). Last and next to the noun are the definitive or categorial adjectives, such as *French,* which are nongradable. A further point to note is that definitive adjectives are often nouns conscripted for *adjectival* service, like *oak* in *smoky oak aromas.* (On punctuating sets of adjectives, see **comma**, section 3.)

1 Attributive and predicative adjectives. When **adjectives** precede the nouns they qualify, as in the examples above, they are said to be *attributive.* But many also occur independently after a verb, particularly if they are evaluative or descriptive. Compare for example *small casks* with *The casks were small.* In cases like the latter, adjectives are said to be *predicative,* because they form part of the predicate of the clause, complementing the verb and its subject (see further under **predicate**). Attributive and predicative uses yield different meanings in some cases: compare *an ill omen* with *She was ill.*

Some **adjectives** resist being used in predicative roles. Those such as *utter, mere* (and others when used as *emphasizers* e.g. *a firm friend, the real hero, sheer arrogance*) can only occur as *attributive adjectives.* The same is true of many which serve to define or categorize a noun (like *meeting* in the example *meeting room*), which could not be used predicatively in the same sense, if at all. Other **adjectives** are restricted to the predicative role, including those on the adjective/adverb boundary, such as:

aboard   abroad   aground   ajar   awry

We never say "the ajar door," only *The door was ajar.* Whether *ajar* counts as an **adjective** or an adverb in that exemplary sentence is a conundrum, to be tested by syntactic criteria like those of the *Comprehensive Grammar* (1985). (See further under **a-** and **copular verbs**.)

2 Comparison of adjectives. The *adjective* system allows us to compare one thing with another, and to grade them on the same *adjectival* quality. There are however two systems of comparison, involving (a) suffixes or (b) *more* and *most.* Their application depends largely on how many syllables the **adjective** consists of.

*Adjectives of one syllable are usually compared by means of the suffixes *-er* and *-est,* as in:

fine wine	(absolute)
finer wine	(comparative)
the finest wine	(superlative)

The different forms of the **adjective** – *absolute* (or *positive*), the *comparative* and the *superlative* – make the regular *degrees of comparison* for most everyday English **adjectives**. *Good* and *bad* are the major exceptions with their irregular paradigms *good, better, best* and *bad, worse, worst.* Other exceptions are **adjectives** like *crushed* and *worn,* which have verb (past participle) suffixes embedded in them, and whose degrees of comparison are formed *periphrastically,* i.e. with the help of *more/most.* Idiom occasionally dictates an irregular form for a one-syllabled **adjective**, as in the phrase "a more just society."

*Adjectives consisting of three or more syllables almost always form their degrees of comparison *periphrastically,* i.e. by means of *adjectival phrases* formed with *more* and *most*:

> *an expensive wine*
> *a more expensive wine*
> *the most expensive wine*

Exceptions among three-syllabled **adjectives** are those formed with *un-,* such as *unhappy* and *unhealthy,* whose comparatives and superlatives are as they would be without the prefix: *unhappier, unhealthiest.*

*Adjectives with two syllables are less predictable in their forms of comparison than those shorter or longer. Many can be compared either way, such as:

gentle	*lovely*
gentler / more gentle	*lovelier / more lovely*
gentlest / most gentle	*loveliest / most lovely*

The inflected forms are neat for attributive use, whereas phrasal comparisons are of course bulkier and lend themselves to predicative use, especially for emphasis. Other factors such as the need to use matching forms of comparison for paired **adjectives**, as in *the most simple and straightforward solution,* have been found to explain some of the variation (Leech and Culpeper, 1997).

One large group of **adjectives** – those formed with *-y* – is more regular than the rest, using suffixes for the comparative/superlative suffixes almost always. The following are a token of the many:

angry	easy	empty	funny	happy
healthy	heavy	lofty	merry	noisy
pretty	speedy	tidy	wealthy	weighty

Ad hoc **adjectives** formed with *-y* are compared the same regular way:

craggy	craggier	craggiest
dishy	dishier	dishiest
foxy	foxier	foxiest

Compare **adjectives** ending in *-ly,* which are quite variable. Researchers have found that *early* always used suffixes for comparison, whereas *likely* was almost always compared with *more/most*. Others in the *-ly* group such as *costly, deadly, friendly, lively, lonely, lovely* can go either way. Some **adjectives** such as *costly, deadly, friendly* prefer the inflected form for the superlative, but use periphrasis for the comparative: *more costly, costliest* (Peters, 2000). Both patterns of comparison have been found with adjectives ending in *-le* (*feeble, humble, noble, simple* etc.), though they are more often inflected; and the same is true of those ending in *-ow* (*mellow, narrow, shallow*). Those ending in *-er* (*bitter, eager, proper, sober* etc.) tend the other way, making their comparisons with *more/most*. **Adjectives** with a derivational suffix, such as *-ful* (*hopeful*), *-less* (*graceless*), *-ive* (*active*), *-ous* (*famous*) are always compared phrasally, as are those formed with *-ed* (*excited*) or *-ing* (*boring*). But two-syllabled **adjectives** formed with the negative prefix *un-* (*unfair, unfit, unwise*) are compared by means of inflections, just like their positive counterparts. Beyond all those groups, there are individual **adjectives** which go their own sweet way: *quiet* is almost always inflected; *common, cruel, handsome, minute, polite, remote* appear in both inflected and phrasal comparisons.

Regional studies of the two types of comparison show that American English is slightly more inclined than British to use phrasal comparison with *-ly* **adjectives** (Lindquist, 1998). Some have thought that writers would be more inclined to use phrasal comparison than speakers, though research associated with the *Longman Grammar* (1999) showed the opposite: that the frequency of inflected **adjectives** was higher in all forms of writing (fiction, journalism, academic) than in conversation. Despite these tendencies, writers have some freedom of choice when comparing many everyday two-syllabled **adjectives**, to be exercised in the service of style, rhythm and rhetoric. The only caveat is to avoid using inflections as well as periphrasis in quick succession, as in "the most unkindest cut of all" (*Julius Caesar*, iii:2). Double superlatives like this were acceptable in Tudor English, but not nowadays.

*Uncomparable **adjectives**. Many kinds of **adjective** don't support any *degrees of comparison* – the quality they refer to cannot be graded. A definitive adjective like *French* (in *French cask*) either is or is not true. (*More French than the French* turns it ad hoc into a *gradable adjective*.) Other **adjectives** which cannot be compared are those which refer to an absolute state, such as *first, double, last* and *dead*. Uncomparable **adjectives** like those are sometimes referred to as *absolute adjectives* (see **absolute** section 1).

3 **Compound adjectives** consist of two or more parts, and may or may not include an **adjective**. They are the staple of journalese, as in *the war-torn Middle East* or *power-hungry executives,* but are also used creatively by advertisers, and by authors and poets for artistic purposes. For more about the structure of *compound adjectives,* see **compounds**, and **hyphens** section 2c.
◊ For the grammar of *adjectival phrases* and clauses, see **phrases** and **clauses** section 4.

adjoining or adjacent
See **adjacent**.

adjuncts
Grammarians use this term in two different ways:
* for a particular set of adverbs: see **adverbs**, section 1
* for the *adverbial* component(s) of a clause: see **predicate**, section 1

administer or administrate
These come from French and Latin respectively, and as often the first has many more roles than the second. Dictionaries tend to cross-reference **administrate** to **administer** as if it could be freely substituted for it, yet **administrate** can scarcely take as its object things such as *justice, punishment, medicine, poison, a blow, an oath* or *the sacrament,* all of which collocate with **administer**. **Administer** has a distinctive intransitive use with *to* (once disputed, now dictionary-endorsed) which is found in examples such as *administering to the sick*, and this **administrate** cannot cover. The chief uses of **administrate** are close to the nouns *administration* and *administrator*, in the intransitive sense of "act as administrator" or transitively "manage the administration of" (usually a corporate structure or institution). Neither is common in British English, judging by the dearth of examples in the BNC, but there's a sprinkling of them in American data from CCAE. Intransitive and transitive uses are almost equally represented (the latter involving objects such as "department," "estate," "the act," "private lands"). **Administrate** clearly has a role to play, one that is distinct from **administer**.

admission or admittance
Though similar in age, these two abstract nouns for the verb *admit* have very unequal shares of the linguistic market. The latinate **admission** dominates the scene by about 40:1, according to BNC data. **Admission** scoops up the verb senses of confessing something or letting it slip, as in *an admission of guilt* or *by his own admission,* and **admittance** is only rarely found in such senses. Either word can be used when it's a matter of entering or being allowed to enter (a controlled public place such as a stadium or exhibition), although **admission** is much more common, and the one built into compounds such as *admission price*. Hospitals institutionalize it in their nomenclature, ADMISSIONS being the section where patients are admitted for care. While **admission** invites entry, **admittance** is associated with denying

it, in the conventional sign NO ADMITTANCE. The sign addresses those not authorized to enter a given area because of potential dangers or privacy – not those who work there, who would not be denied access by it. In a more upfront way **admission** can also be associated with exclusive kinds of entry, for example membership of professional groups, as in *admission to the board of solicitors*, or *admission to the Bar*. These official uses of **admission** may nevertheless suggest that the word is to be avoided when the access route is less formal, hence BNC examples such as *admittance to Paradise* and *admittance to the afterlife* (no "admissions board" to control access there!). Unexpected uses of **admittance** may amount to no more than the fact that it seems closer to the verb *admit* than **admission** does, and comes naturally when thinking of the verbal process. The most distinctive application of **admittance** is as a technical term in electronics, where it complements *conductance, impedance* and *resistance* in the structure of electrical systems.

adopted or adoptive

Usage books often present these as reciprocal adjectives, the first representing the perspective of the *adopter*, the second that of the *adoptee*. So **adopted** is the word to expect from parents referring to the child they have taken in, and **adoptive** is the child's word to describe the parents he or she has acquired in this way. This distinction is perhaps a reflex of the *Oxford Dictionary's* (1989) note that **adopted** is used "especially of the child." Yet its definition of **adoptive** allows either perspective: "an adoptive son, father etc." and does not make the two words complementary. Whatever its basis, the "traditional distinction appears to be crumbling" says Burchfield (1996); and the BNC presents both regular and divergent examples, the latter including "adopted parent," and "adopted family," as well as "adoptive children" and even an "adoptive pup" in a veterinary report. In fact the selection of **adopted** or **adoptive** is immaterial because the following noun ("child" or "parent") indicates the perspective.

advance, advanced and advancement

Subtle changes have taken place in the grammar and spelling of **advance** since it first appeared in C13 English. Its original form *avaunce* reflects its French origins, but in Tudor times it was remodeled as **advance**, in accordance with Latin spelling conventions, although it has no exact Latin ancestor. Originally a verb, by 1680 it was also used as a noun, as in *the enemy's advance*, and attributively, as in *advance guard*.

The uses of **advance** as adjective and noun contrast with their grammatical counterparts **advanced** and **advancement**. **Advance** as adjective indicates priority in time and/or space, as in *advance notice;* whereas **advanced** implies being well down the track in terms of achievement or sophistication, as in *an advanced student* or *advanced thinking*. The two cannot substitute for each other. Compare the noun **advance** with **advancement**, where dictionaries suggest there's some common ground in referring to progress in a particular field of endeavor. Yet **advance** can hardly replace the other word in the *American Association for the Advancement of Science*, not because it is an established title but because

advancement is an abstract concept, whereas any **advance** is specific and down-to-earth. *The advancement of civilization* would connote the heightening of cultural mores, whereas *the advance of civilization* could be a comment on the use of mobile phones in the Himalayas. The more abstract properties of **advancement** make it a useful euphemism for getting ahead in one's career or profession, where **advance** is no substitute. Yet there are many more applications of **advance** for which **advancement** is unsuitable, and the first outnumbers the second by more than 9:1 in British English and 4:1 in American English, in comparable databases (LOB and Brown corpora).

adventurous or adventuresome
See **venturous**.

adverbs

Adverbs are the most varied class of English words, with a variety of syntactic roles. Some modify verbs, as the name **adverb** suggests. But many have other roles in sentences which are beginning to be recognized by individual names. The terms used to identify them below are those of the *Comprehensive Grammar* (1985).

1 Types of adverb. Adverbs which detail the circumstances of the verb are these days often called *adjuncts*, to indicate that they connect with the core of the clause without being part of it. Other types of adverb are *subjuncts*, which typically modify other adverbs or adjectives; *disjuncts*, which modify whole clauses or sentences; and *conjuncts*, which forge a semantic link between a sentence and the one before it.

*adjuncts** add detail to whatever action the verb itself describes. They may specify the time or place of the action, the manner in which it took place, or its extent.

(time)	tonight	tomorrow	soon
	then		
(place)	abroad	downtown	indoors
	upstairs		
(manner)	well	quickly	energetically
	thoughtfully		
(extent)	largely	partly	thoroughly
	totally		

*subjuncts** moderate the force of various kinds of word. Many such as *really, relatively, too, very,* modify adjectives and other **adverbs**, as in *very strong/strongly*. Some such as *almost, quite, rather* can modify verbs as well. *Subjuncts* of both kinds have the effect of either softening or intensifying the words they modify, hence the two major groups:

(downtoners)	*fairly*	*rather*	*somewhat*
(intensifiers)	*extremely*	*most*	*so*

Expletives like *bloody* are powerful intensifiers of other adjectives, as in: *a bloody good book* (see further under **intensifiers**). A special subgroup of *restrictive subjuncts* serve to spotlight others and to narrow the focus of the sentence. They include **adverbs** such as *especially, even, only*.

*disjuncts** affect the interpretation of the whole clause or sentence, either as judgements of the likelihood of something happening (*maybe, possibly, probably, surely*); or as expressions of attitude towards the event (*fortunately, mercifully, regrettably, worryingly*). They stand outside the core grammar of the sentence, and can be moved around within it:

> *Fortunately the letter got there in time.*
> *The letter fortunately got there in time.*
> *The letter got there in time fortunately.*

Disjuncts, like *subjuncts,* can be used for emphasis, and have a significant interpersonal role to play in a writing style: see under **interpersonal**.

conjuncts are **adverbs* which play a cohesive role between separate sentences, or clauses. They include words like *also, however, therefore,* and thus express logical relationships such as addition, contrast and causation. (See further under **conjunctions**.)

The same **adverb** can of course be used in more than way. Thus *mostly* can be an *adjunct* or a *subjunct,* depending on whether it quantifies the extent of something, or simply serves to emphasize it. *Too* is an attitudinal *subjunct* in *too hot* and a *conjunct* in *I'm coming too. Yet* can be an *adjunct* of time as in *not yet here,* and a *contrastive conjunct,* as in *small yet tasty apricots.* More controversially, *hopefully* is these days a *disjunct* as well as an *adjunct* (see **hopefully**).

Note also that *not,* the *negative adverb,* is treated separately from other **adverbs** in modern English grammars. This is because of its affinity with negative words of other kinds, such as determiners and pronouns (*neither, no, none*). *Not* has wide-ranging powers within sentences, to modify a word (verb, adjective or another **adverb**), a phrase, or a whole clause. (See further under **not** and **negatives**.)

2 Adverbial structure and form. From all the examples above, it's clear that **adverbs** do not necessarily end in *-ly.* (See further under **-ly** and **zero adverbs**.) Many like *soon* and *well* consist of a single morpheme. There are also *compound adverbs,* for example *downtown* and *indoors.* (See further under **compounds**, and **hyphens** section 2b.) Many **adverbs** are phrases:

> straight away   to the bottom
> in no way   a little bit
> without a care in the world

Adverbial ideas can be expressed through several kinds of clause. See **clauses** section 4c.

3 Comparison of adverbs. Like many adjectives, **adverbs** allow degrees of comparison. Those consisting of one syllable, e.g. *fast, hard, soon,* make their comparative and superlative forms with inflections in the same way as adjectives: *sooner, soonest etc.* **Adverbs** formed with *-ly* enlist the help of *more* and *most,* as in *more energetically, most energetically*.

4 Position of adverbs in sentences. Many **adverbs** can appear at various points in a sentence, as noted above (section 1) for *disjuncts. Adjuncts* can also appear early, late or in the middle of a sentence:

> *Yesterday trading hit an all-time low.*
> *Trading yesterday hit an all-time low.*
> *Trading hit an all-time low yesterday.*

Conjuncts are relatively mobile also. (Compare that last sentence with the one above the set of examples, and see further under **also**.) There are few restrictions on *conjuncts* such as *however,* despite notions to the contrary (see **however**). The position of **adverbs** can be used to alter the emphasis of a statement, and to control the focus. (See further under **information focus**.)

A very small group of **adverbs** (*hardly, never, scarcely*) require inversion of the normal word order when used at the beginning of a sentence. See under **inversion**.

adverse or averse

These words express different kinds of negative orientation: **adverse** relates to external circumstances, while **averse** gets inside the individual:

> *With such adverse judgements on his case, he was still averse to reconsidering the action.*

Adverse is commonly applied to legal or official conditions that are hostile, or to threatening natural forces, as in *adverse weather conditions* or *an adverse reaction to a drug.* **Averse** expresses strong disinclination, though the idiom *not averse to* is used lightly or ironically, as in *not averse to a little whisky.* While **adverse** is mostly used attributively, **averse** is almost always predicative (see **adjectives** section 1). Grammar thus tends to keep them apart – but not entirely. In both the UK and the US, there's evidence of **adverse** being used predicatively, and when the subject is personal there may be some doubt about the writer's intention. See for example:

> *Courts have not been adverse to developing the common law.*
> *Purity campaigners were not adverse to drawing on science to validate morality.*

The use of *not* seems to neutralize the difference between the two words, although the first example is probably still within the legal pale. The second clearly shows the use of **adverse** where you might expect **averse** – except that it lacks the element of understatement which goes with *not averse to* (see under **figures of speech**). The ratio of *not adverse to* to *not averse to* is about 1:3 in American data from CCAE. This confirms the rapprochement of the two idioms noted by *Webster's Dictionary of Usage* (1989), though it has yet to be registered by *Merriam-Webster* (2000). *New Oxford* (1998) notes this use of *not adverse to* as an error, and usage data from the BNC makes it less common in British English as a substitute for *not averse to,* appearing in the ratio of about 1:11.

Despite some convergence between **adverse** and **averse** in common usage, they contrast sharply in botanical descriptions. Leaves *adverse to* the stem turn towards it, while those *averse to* it turn away. These are the literal senses of the two words in Latin, but lost to contemporary English.

advertisement or advertizement

The first spelling **advertisement** is given preference in dictionaries everywhere, including North America. This is as it should be, because there's no evidence of **advertizement** in data from either CCAE or the BNC. Perhaps its currency depends on signs and unedited texts which are not included in those databases. The fact that **advertizement** gets dictionary recognition everywhere is curious, based perhaps on the preferred American pronunciation which according to *Webster's Third* (1986) stresses the third (rather than the second) syllable. It may also represent the assumption that the *-ise* spelling would naturally give way to *-ize* in the US (see further under **-ize/-ise**). But the two instances of the verb **advertize** in CCAE are totally eclipsed by over 1100 instances of **advertise**.

> **International English selection:** The dearth of evidence for the spelling **advertizement** (or even **advertize**) makes the *-ise* forms preferable anywhere in the world.

adviser or advisor

Both these spellings are in current use, though **adviser** is the dominant spelling in both the US and the UK. The ratio in American data from CCAE is 20:1 and in British data from the BNC it's 6:1. Curiously, **advisor** is sometimes said to be "the American spelling." The *Oxford Dictionary* (1989) notes the frequency of the -or spelling in the titles of persons who give advice "especially in the US," and this quasi-official usage has no doubt helped to make people aware of it. Yet the *Oxford* lists **advisor** only as a variant of **adviser**, with no independent headword even for cross-referencing. The spelling **adviser** is consistent with the majority of agent words formed in English (see -er/-or), and it goes back to C17, according to *Oxford* citations, whereas **advisor** is first recorded just before 1900. Whether it is simply a respelling of **adviser** or a backformation from **advisory** is a matter of debate. But whatever its past, **advisor** is registered alongside **adviser** in major British, American, Canadian and Australian dictionaries.

ae/e

In words like *anaemic* and *orthopaedic* the **ae** spellings present the classical Latin digraph **ae**, which became a ligature (**æ**) or just **e** in medieval times. The ligature is still used in the *Oxford Dictionary* (1989), but the digraph appears in abridged and smaller versions, notably the 1993 edition of the *Shorter Oxford* and *New Oxford* (1998). Other British dictionaries such as those of Chambers, Collins and Longman, have always used the **ae** digraph, either because of Fowler's (1926) support for it, or the lack of typographic options. But American dictionaries like *Webster's Third* (1986) make use of simple **e** spellings in most such words, e.g. *anemic, hemorrhage, orthopedic,* instead of the ligature or digraph. The **e** spellings are standard in American English, except for *(a)esthetic* and *arch(a)eology,* where they are in the minority (in data from CCAE the digraphic spellings prevailed by more than 5:1). Canadians too use **e** rather than **ae** spellings, according to the *Canadian Oxford* (1998).

In British English, there's increasing variability in spelling the largish set of classical loanwords including **ae/e**:

(a)eon	*(a)esthetic*	*(a)etiology*
an(a)emia	*an(a)esthetic*	*arch(a)eology*
arch(a)eopterix	*c(a)esura*	*di(a)eresis*
encyclop(a)edia	*f(a)eces*	*gyn(a)ecology*
h(a)ematite	*h(a)emoglobin*	*h(a)emophilia*
h(a)emorrhage	*h(a)emorrhoids*	*leuk(a)emia*
medi(a)eval	*orthop(a)edic*	*p(a)ediatric*
p(a)edophile	*pal(a)eography*	*pal(a)eolithic*
prim(a)eval	*septic(a)emia*	*tox(a)emia*

Some of the most familiar **ae** words appear quite commonly now with just **e** – even in the UK. Data from the BNC confirms it for words such as *medi(a)eval* and *encyclop(a)edia,* and to a lesser extent for *pal(a)eolithic, leuk(a)emia* and *orthop(a)edic.* They constitute a scale, from words where **e** spellings are in the majority or close to it, to those linked up with medical or other kinds of technical usage, where specialists tend to preserve the **ae** (Peters, 2001a). The 1998–2001 Langscape survey showed that at least 25% of British respondents would use **e** spellings in *archeology, leukemia, paleolithic, septicemia.* These words and others such as *orthopedic, pedophile* were

endorsed by 29–50% of respondents from Australia, where **ae** spellings have prevailed in the past. More remarkable still was the higher endorsement by second-language users of English, in Europe as well as Asia. Their support for **e** spellings was almost without exception higher than the British; and a majority of Continental respondents (often 70% +) voted for **e** spellings, except for *aesthetic* and *anaesthetic* – where they stood at 48% and 50% respectively.

Apart from usage data, there are linguistic arguments in favor of the **e** forms. The **ae** digraph is awkward as a vowel sequence with no roots in common English spelling. It makes the ligature bulk too large, and sits strangely alongside other vowels in words like *diaeresis, palaeolithic* and others with the *pal(a)eo-* prefix. In words like *septic(a)emia,* the use of **ae** runs counter to the more general spelling principle that *c* followed by an "a," "o" or "u" carries a "k" sound. (See further under -ce/-ge.)

The use of **ae** is sometimes defended on grounds of etymology: that it helps readers to recognize the meanings of the classical loanwords. But **ae** is not so etymological, when it's a Latin transcription of the Greek diphthong *ai.* The Greek root *paid-* meaning "child" is the one at stake in *encyclop(a)edia* and *orthop(a)edic,* as well as *p(a)ediatrics* and *p(a)edophilia.* Millions of readers without Greek recognize these words as wholes, not through the syllable in which *paid-* is embedded. We no longer look for the **ae** in *pedagogue, pedagogy* and *pederast;* and *p(a)edophile* and *p(a)edophilia* may be expected to go the same way. In nonspecialist usage, *p(a)ediatrician* could also join the group, though it's protected by doctors in some parts of the world (see **pediatrician or paediatrician**). The specialists' tendency to preserve **ae** in those words goes hand in hand with their greater use of **ae** plurals (rather than *-as* ones) for Latin words ending in -a (see -a section 1). They therefore deal more frequently with words embodying the digraph, and its distribution is more significant for them. Yet specialists looking to a wider readership outside the UK, e.g. on the internet, might take note of the various terms in this entry where the *a* of the **ae** digraph is bracketed, as a reminder that in linguistic terms it is unnecessary. Much of the world works without the **ae** digraph.

International English selection: Spellings with **e** rather than the **ae** digraph are to be preferred on linguistic grounds as well as their wider distribution, throughout North America and increasingly in Continental Europe, Australia and elsewhere. In the UK it would streamline the currently uneven situation, whereby some words are already being spelled with **e**, and others vacillating over going that way.

Final notes on ae/e

1 For use of the **ae** in Latin plurals, see -a section 1.
2 The **ae** digraph still substitutes for the ligature in classical proper names such as *Aeneas, Caesar,* as well as Anglo-Saxon ones such as *Aelfric* and *Caedmon.*
3 The **ae** at the beginning of words like *aerial* and *aerobic* is never reduced to **e**. In words like those it is part of the combining element *aer(o)-* ("air"), where *a* and *e* are separate syllables. See **aer(o)-**.

aeon or eon
See ae/e.

aerie or eyrie
See eyrie.

aer(o)-
This is the Latin spelling of a Greek element meaning "air," which is built into words like *aerate, aerobic, aeronautical* and *aerosol*. The overall number of **aero-** words is not large, and everyday words in the group are gradually being replaced by others:

aerate(d)	by	*carbonate(d)*
aerial	by	*antenna*
aeroplane	by	*aircraft, airliner*
aerosol (can)	by	*spray* (can)

Some **aero-** words have already gone. We no longer use *aerogramme* for *air letter* or *aerodrome* as the ordinary term for an airport. The adjectival use of *aerial* in the Australian airline QANTAS (a historical acronym for Queensland and Northern Territory Aerial Services) sounds quite old-fashioned. Still **aer(o)-** survives and remains productive with technical and scientific words, especially in relation to aviation and aerospace itself:

aerobraking	*aerodynamic*	*aerofoil*
aeromagnetic	*aeromechanic*	*aeroneurosis*
aeropause	*aerostatic*	

As the examples show, it combines with both classical and English stems.

aesthetic or esthetic
See ae/e.

aetiology or etiology
See ae/e.

affect or effect
For general purposes, the choice between these words is a matter of grammar: **affect** is a verb, and **effect** a noun. Compare:
> *The strike affected our beer supply.*

with
> *We felt the effect of the strike on our beer supply.*

These are by far the most common uses of those words. But because of their similarity, and the fact that **effect** appears about three times as often as **affect**, the spelling "effect" tends to be inadvertently given to the verb. What complicates the picture is that in rather formal usage **effect** can itself be a verb meaning "bring about," as in:
> *To effect a change of policy, we must appoint a new director.*

And in psychology **affect** can be a noun meaning "the emotion a person attaches to a particular idea or set of them." Yet these latter uses are relatively rare. The psychological use of **affect** makes no showing in parallel British and American corpora (LOB and Brown), and there is one instance of **effect** as a verb to every 10 to 15 as a noun. In the great majority of contexts, it's **effect** as a noun and **affect** as a verb which writers need.

affixes
An **affix** is a meaningful element attached to either the beginning of a word (a *prefix*) or the end (a *suffix*). (See under **prefixes** and **suffixes**.)

afforestation
See **reafforestation**.

African English
This phrase is a paraphrase for "English in Africa" and therefore a collective term for the infinitely varied forms of the language used in the west, south and east of the continent. Within each region the varieties spoken are quite diverse because of their individual colonial histories, and contact with different local languages. English is an official language in west African states such as Nigeria, Sierra Leone and the Cameroon, but it's most widely used there in well-established forms of pidgin (see **pidgins and creoles**). In east Africa (in Kenya, Uganda and Tanzania), English is also an official language, but less creolized because of the official use of Swahili as a lingua franca for the speakers of African languages. In southern Africa, English also takes its official place alongside local languages. See further under **South African English**.

Afro-American or African American
The term **Afro-American** goes back to C19, and has been in widespread use in the 1960s and 70s. During the last quarter of C20, **African American** has also been widely used, but instances of **Afro-American** are still rather more numerous in data from CCAE. For other terms used in the US and elsewhere for persons of African origin, see **black or Black**.

afterward or afterwards
See -**ward**.

-age
Borrowed from French, this suffix came into English with words such as *courage* and *advantage*, and is now used to create many kinds of abstract nouns in English. Some examples are:

anchorage	*bondage*	*breakage*	*cartage*
dosage	*drainage*	*frontage*	*leverage*
parentage	*percentage*	*postage*	*sewerage*
shrinkage	*storage*	*tonnage*	*wastage*
wreckage			

Some words ending in -**age** develop more specific meanings out of the abstractions they originally represented. They may refer to a specific amount of something, as do *dosage, percentage* and *tonnage*, or the payment associated with something: *cartage, corkage, postage*. Others express the result of a process, as do *breakage, shrinkage* and *wreckage*.

Words formed with -**age** normally lose the final -*e* of their stems, as with *dosage, storage, wastage* (see further under -**e**). The most important exception is *acreage* where the *e* in the middle marks the fact that there are three syllables to the word. Other words to note are *lin(e)age* and *mil(e)age*, which may be spelled either with or without the middle *e*. See further **linage** and **mileage**.

aged or age
Should it be *aged 30* or *age 30,* when you want to indicate someone's age? British English uses the first, American English the second. See further under **inflectional extras**.

ageing or aging
See **aging**.

ageism or agism

The first spelling **ageism** is recommended in both *Webster's Third* (1986) and the *Oxford Dictionary* (1989), and is the one found in almost all instances of the word in reference databases of American and British English. The very few examples of **agism** are all to be found in the BNC database – surprisingly when it's American English (not British) that endorses **aging** so strongly (see under that heading). But at least one of the British citations is equivocal:

> *An inaugural meeting of the Alliance Against Ageism in Employment launched a "ban agism in recruiting campaign."*

The newness of **ageism** (first recorded 1969) and the shortness of its stem no doubt combine to make writers spell it out in full. In the longer run, we may expect it to conform to the general rule for words formed with stems ending in *-e* (see **-e**).

ageist language

Stereotypes about age are embedded in language, as for any human characteristic. Some of those relating to the elderly are benign, e.g. *old folks,* but others such as *old fogey* and *old pensioner* carry negative connotations about the person's capacity and their dependence on the state. Language that expresses popular prejudices about old age is to be avoided – unflattering terms such as *old bag/codger/duck/ geezer, geriatric* (or *gerry*), *granny, oldster* – although being colloquial, they're not so likely to appear in official prose. Journalists and broadcasters are nevertheless very aware of negative stereotyping of the elderly in the media, and the need to curb **ageist language** – gratuitous references to a person's age, and the implication that anyone over 65 is over the hill. Stereotyping of any kind makes communication less inclusive (see further under **inclusive language**).

When age is a relevant issue, neutral terms such as *senior, senior citizen* and (collectively) *the elderly* are widely used (see under **seniors** and **elder/eldest**). The phrases *aged care* and *the aged* smack of bureaucracy – the terms of official documents about managing the elderly. Elderly people themselves can make affirmative use of the word "old," but it's pejorative for others to apply it to them.

agenda

This loanword is a Latin plural, meaning "things to be done." But its singular *agendum* is hardly ever seen, and **agenda** itself is always construed as singular in a sentence, with a singular verb:

> *The agenda for the meeting is three pages long.*

This singular use of **agenda** meaning "list of things to be discussed" is only about a century old, according to the *Oxford Dictionary* (1989). Yet the singular use of **agenda** was so quickly established that by 1907 an English plural *agendas* was on record. These days you may even hear it turned into a verb:

> *I'll agenda that item for our next meeting.*

However, that extension of the word is not yet registered in dictionaries. See further under **transfers**.

agent nouns

These are nouns like *teacher* and *calculator* which are very visibly based on verbs (*teach, calculate*), and represent someone or something as doing the verb's action. Other names for them are *agential noun* and *agentive (noun)*. Over the centuries **agent nouns** have been formed in English with *-er* (*dancer*), *-or* (*investor*), *-ant* (*commandant*) and *-ent* (*superintendent*). Only the first type is fully productive in modern English.

aggravate, aggravation and aggro

For too long the word **aggravate** has been shackled by the idea that it should not be used to mean "vex or annoy." The pedantic tradition says it only means "make worse," that being the literal meaning of its Latin components. But the argument is about as sound as suggesting that the word *rivals* should only be used of people who share the same river, since that's how the word originated.

The *Oxford Dictionary* (1989) has citations for **aggravate** meaning "vex or annoy" from 1611 on. They are typically associated with everyday prose rather than lofty writing; and in later C19 writing John Stuart Mill found the usage in "almost all newspapers, and ... many books." Dickens and Thackeray are notable users of it in their novels. But the *Oxford* labels it "fam." (i.e. "familiar"), and others including Mill and Fowler actively censured the usage, one calling it a "vulgarism of the nursery," and the other "a feminine or childish colloquialism." Their condemnation seems to have led other usage commentators to the same judgement, though there are ample examples of its use in general C20 writing. Burchfield (1996) presents British examples of this "later" sense for **aggravate** alongside the "older" one, and allows that they coexist. In American English the two also coexist, though *Webster's English Usage* (1989) reports that the sense "annoy" is somewhat less common than "make worse" in its files. But the *Webster's* data also notes that for *aggravating* and **aggravation** the meanings "annoying"/"annoyance" are more common than those corresponding to "make worse." This suggests the narrow focus of objections to **aggravate**, which have made a fetish of it.

The "later" meaning of **aggravate** is now centuries old and has its place in speech and writing that invoke human feelings. It can scarcely be rejected on grounds of possible misunderstanding, because only a human subject or object of the verb can be annoyed, while other subjects or objects are made worse.

A new frontier for **aggravation** is its application to aggressive confrontation on urban streets, among football crowds and elsewhere:

> *Faced with the alternatives of the dole, or the angry aggravation of the streets, motherhood brings a sense of belonging.*
> *You're not married? Whaddya do for aggravation?*
> *– I live near here. Four muggings away.*

The two examples, from the BNC and CCAE respectively, confirm this aggressive use of **aggravation** in the US as well as the UK. The new sense is quite removed from the abstract or internal senses which have hitherto been debated. It does not seem to have raised objections – perhaps the potential forces have been exhausted on the old bone of contention. In the UK attention has turned to **aggro**, an abbreviation formed with the *-o* suffix, first recorded in 1969. The casualness of its clipped form (see further under **-o**) confirms its origins in informal style, and *Oxford* labels it "slang." Yet most of the 81 examples in the BNC come from academic and journalistic prose, not transcribed speech, and it works in a variety of collocations and compounds, notably *full of aggro, aggro leader* and the putative *Aggro Cup*. These examples show it moving into attributive roles, and the basis on which it's likely to become a fully fledged adjective. In British English it has quickly become the most effective term for an ugly social phenomenon, more direct than **aggravation** in the newest sense. It has still to catch on in American English, to judge by the paucity of natural examples in CCAE, and *Webster's Third* (1986) labels it "British," without any stylistic restriction.

aggressor or aggresser
The second spelling **aggresser** is technically possible, given the existence of a verb *aggress*, which was recorded in C18 and C19 with the potential to form an English-style agent word with *-er* from it. But there are no C20 examples of the verb or its agentive in either the BNC or CCAE. Usage is 100% behind the latinate **aggressor**.

aging or ageing
British and American English diverge in the choice between these two spellings. In the US **aging** serves as the standard spelling for the verb participle, according to *Webster's Third* (1986), and is endorsed by usage for the noun and adjective as well. In data from CCAE, **aging** is overwhelmingly preferred to **ageing**. Both spellings are current in the UK, but there **ageing** is a good deal more common than **aging**, outnumbering it by more than 12:1 in data from the BNC. However the two spellings are used equally for noun and adjective in very similar or identical phrases, such as *ag(e)ing of the population* and *premature ag(e)ing*. Examples of verbal use are elusive, though the regular **aging** might be expected from the fact that the *Oxford Dictionary* (1989) gives no special form for use in the verb phrase. For the noun (*verbal substantive*) and (*participial*) adjective, the *Oxford* gives equal status to the two spellings with only a comma between them, but **ageing** has priority in the sequence.

The linguistic arguments for **aging** are clear. It conforms to the basic English spelling rule of dropping a final *e* from the stem before adding a suffix beginning with a vowel (see **-e** section 1). **Aging** is consistent with *raging, staging* and *waging (war)*, among others. Those who prefer **ageing** would say that *age* needs to keep its *e* because two letters are insufficient to maintain its identity. The argument is somewhat undermined by the existence of words like *axing* and *icing*. **Aging** itself is not new, but has been in print for well over a century, according to the *Oxford Dictionary*. It seems high time to affirm the regular spelling for all applications of the word.

> **International English selection: Aging** is the spelling for communicating with a worldwide audience, because it is standard in the US, familiar enough in the UK, and underpinned by one of the fundamental rules of English spelling.

◊ On the choice between **ageism** and **agism**, see under that heading.

agree
It may surprise Americans as well as the British, that the verb **agree** can be used transitively, as in *the parties had agreed the price* or *all procedures are*

agreed, among various examples in BNC data. Passive constructions like the last have perhaps fostered the more challenging active ones noted by C20 usage writers, though the *Oxford Dictionary* has active examples from C16 and C17. In American idiom, **agree** is almost always followed by a particle, either *on, to* or *with*, according to *Webster's English Usage* (1989), and these constructions are also very familiar in the UK. But *Webster's Third* (1986) notes that the transitive use of **agree** with a following noun complement (as opposed to a clause complement) is "chiefly British."

agreement
In grammar this is a technical term for the way words or word classes are matched in terms of *number* (*singular* or *plural*), *gender* (*masculine, feminine* and [sometimes] *neuter*) and *person* (*first, second* or *third*). An alternative name for the concept is *concord*. The principles of **agreement** can be seen in the selection of congruent word forms in sentences such as:
> *That flower has had its day.*
> *Those flowers have had their day.*

This conventional matching of nouns, demonstratives, personal pronouns / determiners and verbs, to mark them (wherever possible) as either singular or plural, as inanimate (= neuter) rather than animate, and as third person reference, is known as *formal agreement*. It contrasts with *notional* or *semantic agreement*, to be seen in:
> *The general public are still making up their minds.*

In sentences like these, the *formal agreement* of subject and verb would put the verb and following pronoun in the singular because "public" is formally a singular noun, but it's overruled in that example by the plural notion that "public" entails, hence the selection of the plural verb and determiner. Many controversies over **agreement** turn on the interplay between *formal* and *notional agreement*. British English is often said to be more accommodating of *notional agreement* than American English. While this seems to hold for the treatment of collective nouns (see below), there's much more convergence on other frontiers of **agreement**.

Most issues of **agreement** can be addressed within the context of the sentence, looking at the subject and whatever *agrees* with it. The following discussion is therefore structured in terms of several kinds of subject:
1 collective nouns (e.g. *government, mob*)
2 nouns whose reference form ends in *s* (e.g. *economics, Woolworths*)
3 indefinite pronouns (e.g. *anyone, each*)
4 compound subjects (e.g. *John and I, neither John nor I, eggs and bacon*)
5 complex subjects, including quantifiers (e.g. *a book of answers, a total of 20 students*)
All these will be discussed in terms of *formal* and *notional agreement*, as well as *proximity agreement*, where applicable. *Proximity agreement* is **agreement** with the number of the nearest noun, and underscores either *formal* or *notional agreement*, as the case may be. It particularly affects the constructions presented in sections 3, 4 and 5.

1 Collective nouns referring to groups or bodies of people or animals, such as *government* and *mob*, can combine with either singular or plural verbs in spite of their singular form. A very few, such as *cattle,* *people, police* require the plural; and *staff* takes a plural verb most of the time, according to *Longman Grammar* (1999) research. But the *Grammar* reports considerable variability on others:

> *The family has decided to celebrate on Sunday.*
> *The family have decided to celebrate on Sunday.*

The choice of verb makes it either *formal* or *notional agreement*, and carries slightly different implications. The singular verb implies an official consensus of the group, whereas the plural makes the reader/listener more aware that individual members assented to the suggestion. The same subtlety can be expressed with any one of a number of nouns referring to organized or casual groups of people:

audience	assembly	board	choir
class	clergy	club	committee
company	congregation	council	couple
crew	crowd	delegation	department
executive	faculty	family	government
group	jury	mob	office
orchestra	pair	panel	parliament
public	quartet	team	trio
union			

Respondents to the Langscape survey (1998–2001) affirmed the viability of both singular and plural verbs for examples such as *clergy, orchestra, panel,* though American respondents were always more committed to the singular than the British. A study of many such words in newspaper data (Levin, 1998b) likewise found that American journalists made less use of plural verbs than their British counterparts. Yet both groups were strongly disposed to use plural pronouns in **agreement** with collective nouns.

Collective nouns for animals, such as *flock, herd, pack, school, shoal, swarm, troupe* enjoy some freedom in terms of *notional agreement*, like that accorded to the human groups. This applies also to biological terms such as **bacteria**, **algae**, **flora** (see under individual headings) and fauna.

Notional agreement in the plural is possible for a variety of proper nouns which are formally singular. They include:
*Commercial businesses, government institutions and special interest groups, where the plural verb implies corporate activity:

> *Foxtel have sold off some of their assets.*
> *The Red Cross have expanded the Geneva office.*
> *The Ministry of Defence are on our side.*

This happens in British as well as American English, according to *Webster's English Usage* (1989), and the combination of singular verbs followed by plural pronouns is also in evidence.
*Sports teams identified by the proper names of cities and countries are not uncommonly found with plural verbs (and pronouns) in British reportage (but not American):

> *England are all out for 152.*
> *Argentina were beaten 4:2 in their match against Sweden.*

*Metonymic references to governments, such as *Beijing, Baghdad, Washington, Westminster,* may likewise generate *notional agreement* in news reporting and headlines. (See further under **metonymy**.)

◊ For the choice between singular and plural **agreement** with **data** and **media**, see those entries.
◊ For **agreement** with adjectives used to head noun phrases (e.g. *the poor*), see under **absolute** section 1.

2 Agreement for nouns ending in s. Certain kinds of noun end in *s* even though they refer to a single object, raising doubts as to whether a singular or plural verb is required with them. The following clusters of words show clear tendencies for (a) plural **agreement** and (b) singular **agreement**.

a) Plural agreement is normal for many ordinary objects, for example:

> *The jeans look too large on me.*
> *Those scissors were not sharp enough.*

Other examples of the two major groups are:
clothes

bathers	bermudas	bloomers	braces
briefs	corduroys	daks	dungarees
fatigues	flannels	jodhpurs	knickers
leathers	longjohns	overalls	pants
plus fours	pyjamas	shorts	slacks
suspenders	tights	trousers	undies

tools and instruments

bellows	bifocals	binoculars	forceps
glasses	goggles	nutcrackers	pincers
pliers	scales	secateurs	shears
spectacles	tongs	tweezers	

Plural agreement is also usual with various abstract nouns or composites ending in *s,* such as:

amends	arrears	congratulations
contents	credentials	dregs
dues	funds	goods
grounds	headquarters	lodgings
looks	means	odds
outskirts	pains	premises
proceeds	regards	remains
savings	surroundings	thanks
valuables		

Yet some uses of these are exceptional, as when *grounds* or *means* refers to a single, specific item and a singular pronoun is quite possible: *on that grounds, by this means* (see further under **ground** and **means**). A singular verb is sometimes found with *headquarters* and other words which refer to a collective establishment or operation (*barracks, cleaners, gasworks*). For example:

> *The printers is near the traffic lights on Bridge Street.*

b) Singular agreement is usual for various kinds of nouns which serve as standard nomenclature for:
* academic subjects, as in:
> *Economics/linguistics/physics/statistics was not my forte.*
* games and sports, as in
> *Athletics/dominoes/gymnastics/quoits makes a great spectator sport.*
* diseases, as in
> *Measles/mumps is raging through the neighborhood.*

However when words in any of these groups are used to refer to particular objects or instances (and are no longer names) they take plural verbs:

> *His economics sound like those of a shopkeeper.*
> *The dominoes were all in the box.*
> *Measles are breaking out all over her face.*

The names of businesses such as *Lloyds, McDonalds, Oddbins, Woolworths* may take either singular or plural agreement.

> *Woolworths is showing a strong profit margin this year.*
> *Woolworths are offering a discount on rubber bands.*

The use of the singular verb carries a stronger sense of the corporate entity. Although nouns ending in *s* are usually assumed to be plural, the *-s* inflection has other roles in modern English. (See further under **-s**.)

3 Indefinite pronouns. Some of these take a singular verb on all occasions, while others are variable. Those ending in *-body, -one,* and *-thing* have singular verbs on all occasions:

> Any-/every-/no-/somebody has a stake in it.
> Any-/every-/no-/someone like that is entitled to it.
> Any-/every-/no-/something that looks odd should be discounted.

The third sentence shows how the singular requirement carries over into any relative clause depending on the pronoun. Note also that in spite of the *formal agreement* with a singular verb, the pronoun/determiner following an *indefinite pronoun* may have *notional agreement* in the plural, as in:

> Everybody has to pay their taxes.

The *Longman Grammar* (1999) notes that the use of plural determiners and pronouns after *indefinites* such as *everybody/nobody* is common in both speech and writing. It satisfies the need for gender-free expression (see further under **they**). The use of purely *formal agreement*, as in *Everybody has to pay his taxes,* is nowadays felt to be sexist and unfortunate (as if men are the only tax-payers). The exclusivity is avoided in *Everybody has to pay his or her taxes,* yet the phrasing seems cumbersome.

Indefinite pronouns such as *any, either, neither* are more susceptible to a plural verb when they appear as the head of the phrase, as in:

> Any of the books he wrote is/are worth reading.
> Neither of their suggestions appeal(s) to us.

In such cases the plural verb could be prompted by *proximity agreement* – i.e. the adjacent plural noun – or by *notional agreement,* because the phrase implies a set of items. The use of a singular verb in such examples (i.e. *formal agreement*) singles out one item from the set. That apart, the singular construction sounds more precise and stylistically more formal; but examples of the plural verb could be found in written data analyzed for the *Longman Grammar.* Note that there is no requirement for singular agreement after *none* (see further under **nobody**).

4 Compound subjects. In the simplest cases, a coordinated subject such as *John and I* or *brother and sister* takes a plural verb, which makes them joint operators of the action:

> John and I have managed the refurbishment.

But when the coordinates are uneven in length, or when the second coordinate is a singular noun, a singular verb may seem appropriate. See for example:

> JK's article and the negative reaction to it was on her mind.
> Bird songs and the sound of the waterfall makes it a magical place.

In the second example, the effect of *proximity agreement* with the nearer coordinate is to disengage it from the coordination. Singular **agreement** with one rather than both coordinates can be triggered by the use of the more elaborate coordinators, e.g. *as well as, along with, together with.* It can also be found with items coordinated by some common convention, as in:

> His bread and butter was telemarketing.
> Bacon and eggs is on the menu.

In such cases the coordinated items form a notional singular. Singular agreement with *bed and breakfast*

was endorsed by a majority of respondents to the Langscape survey (1998–2001), in both the US and the UK.

Coordinates which are alternatives often have a singular verb in **agreement**, as in *A cup of coffee or a brisk walk is called for.* The singular *is* confirms that that this is *disjunctive coordination,* in which the selection of one coordinate excludes the other. The same relationship is to be found in subjects coordinated with *neither/nor* as in:

> Neither brother nor sister was present.

But the less formal *Neither brother or sister were there* is equally possible, and justifiable as *notional agreement* with both coordinates. Two-thirds of American respondents to the Langscape survey endorsed it, and about half of the British.

Further options arise when the coordinates present a mixture of grammatical persons, especially the first person singular:

> Neither she nor I is?/am?/are? inclined to go.

The use of *is* (third person) sounds awkward after *I* (first person), and *am* too is less than ideal: though it accords perfectly with *I* and provides *proximity agreement,* it makes a disjunction with *she. Notional agreement* would suggest *are,* to bundle *she* and *I* up together as plural, first/third person, but it's still less than an elegant solution. Such sentences probably need redesigning, for example: *I am not inclined to go and neither is she.*

5 Complex subjects. Many a noun phrase has a hierarchy of two (or more) nouns within it, as in *a lot of questions* or *a book of answers.* The following verb will *agree* with whichever noun is the *head* (see further under **noun phrases**). In *a lot of questions, questions* is the head, with *a lot of* its determiner, and so plural **agreement** is called for: *A lot of questions need to be asked.* In *a book of answers, book* is the head, postmodified by *of answers,* and so singular **agreement** is required: *A book of answers comes with the task material.* Those two patterns of **agreement** (both involving *formal agreement*) are the common ones for complex noun phrases, except that lengthy postmodification with plural nouns can trigger *proximity agreement,* in spite of a singular head. See for example:

> Amid the crisis, the status of foreign nationals and aid-workers are uncertain.

This kind of *notional agreement* is normally edited out of the written medium, but not uncommon in speech.

Noun phrases that act as quantifiers can take either singular or plural **agreement**. Compare:

> A total of 192 cars was banked up behind the accident.
> A total of 192 cars were banked up behind the accident.

As elsewhere when there are **agreement** options, the singular verb seems to invoke the set, whereas the plural verb makes us aware of the individual items in it. Both plural and singular agreement were found with quantifiers such as *a group/set of* and *a range/series of,* in the *Longman Grammar* (1999) corpus. Plural **agreement** is more likely for more informal quantifiers like:

a batch of	a bunch of	a handful of
a heap of	a mass of	a pile of
a rash of	a score of	a spate of

More than 70% of respondents to the Langscape survey (1998–2001) endorsed the plural with *a spate of.*

American usage and usage commentators mostly run with the plural for such expressions, according to *Webster's English Usage* (1989), and it's accepted for the verb and following pronoun in British English (Burchfield, 1996).

For **half of** and **none of**, the choice between singular and plural depends on whether the following noun is *countable* (see under **half of the** and **nobody**). **Agreement** issues affecting the phrases **majority of**, **one in/out of** and **number of** are discussed under their respective headings.

Note finally that noun phrases embodying a specific amount which is judged as sufficient, appropriate, right – or the reverse – typically take a singular verb. For example:

> *Twenty dollars takes you to the city and back.*
> *Six weeks in the African desert isn't my idea of fun.*

These again show *notional agreement,* projecting the amount expressed in terms of cost, time, space, volume etc. as a singular item.

Summary: Grammatical **agreement** overall is more regular than the numerous variations of this large entry might suggest. *Formal* and *notional agreement* coincide more often than not. But when they diverge, the choice of singular or plural has a subtle effect on meaning (see Reid, 1991); and it allows writers to narrow or expand their focus. When *notional agreement* and *proximity* both combine against *formal agreement*, they prevail in many kinds of writing. On its own, *proximity agreement* is usually played down.

agriculturist or agriculturalist

Americans strongly prefer the shorter form. In data from CCAE **agriculturist** outnumbers **agriculturalist** by almost 4:1, and *Webster's Third* (1986) presents it as the key term. In British English things are almost the opposite. **Agriculturalist** occurs more than twice as often as **agriculturist** in BNC data, and it's given priority by the *Oxford Dictionary* (1989).

◊ For other pairs of this kind, see **-ist**.

ahold or a hold

This composite word originates in spoken language, but is now quite well established in print, at least in American English. More than 100 examples in CCAE have it occurring freely in quoted speech, and in narrative and commentary on events, with a number of distinct applications. Its most physical meaning is found in police reports on the apprehending of suspected criminals: *before the FBI got ahold of him,* and more metaphysically in reference to contacting anyone, as in *trying to get ahold of him for a month.* It can mean personal or political control, as in:

> *You gotta get ahold of yourself.*
> *If the ultra-conservative right wingers get ahold of the legislature as they did the Republican platform . . .*

It can mean "mental grasp," as in:

> *Our style of music is not very elitist. Everyone can get ahold of it.*
> *The new people haven't gotten ahold of what we're trying to do.*

As in all those examples, **ahold** most often collocates with parts of the verb *get,* but CCAE also has a sprinkling of collocations with *grab* (especially for physical encounters) and *take* (for the less physical

sense of thriving) as in *Maybe this absentee thing will take ahold and get more people to vote.*

Ahold makes no showing at all in British data from the BNC, and is labeled "dialectal" by the *Oxford Dictionary* (1989). Yet the BNC has almost 40 instances of *get/got a hold,* and their uses overlap with those found in American English, as in *get a hold of himself* (= personal control) and *once they get a hold . . .* (of plants thriving). The British **a hold** makes it a regular noun phrase whereas the American **ahold** allows it to be an adverb collocating with verbs in rather the same way as *around* and *aside.* (See further under **a-**.) The two different settings correlate with the fact that *ahold of* is a relatively fixed idiom in American English, whereas in British **a hold** collocates variously with *of, on* and *over,* and is less clearly established in contemporary prose.

-aholic

Though *alcoholic* has been part of the English language for over 100 years, its role in creating names for those with addictions of other kinds is very much of the late C20. Apart from *workaholic,* most of them are playful: *chocoholic/chocaholic, chargeaholic* ("one who overuses credit cards"), *shopaholic.* Many are ad hoc, and few have made into the common language and found places in dictionary headword lists. But the productivity of the ending is remarkable, and it takes its place alongside **-head** and **-phil(e)** as a way of identifying people with particularly strong tastes or appetites for something.

aide or aid

The spelling **aide** comes from the French phrase *aide-de-camp,* meaning "assistant on the field [of battle]." It became part of English military usage, and was subsequently extended to the assistants of diplomatic representatives, and heads of government, as in *the governor's aide.* In the UK those are still its dominant uses, judging by data from the BNC, with few examples of its extension to more ad hoc roles as in "election job for Maxwell aide" or that of the "personal aide and driver." In the US the word is applied to assistants of all kinds in both powerful and lowly roles, associated with the political party machines (*a Republican aide*), the Church (*RC priest made an aide to Auxiliary Bishop*), academia (*anthropologist's aide*) or the local health service (*a home-health aide*). It can refer to a hired bodyguard (*a short-term security aide*) or domestic worker (*a temporary round-the-clock aide . . . to help at home with such basic chores as eating and cleaning*). The term occurs thousands of times in CCAE, and is no doubt particularly useful in news reporting because of its flexibility in referring to spokespersons who wish to be anonymous, or whose exact role and title are not known.

While the noun **aide** is extending itself as a reference to many kinds of assistant, the much older word **aid** maintains its ground as a noun meaning "assistance" and as the verb "to assist." As an abstract noun, **aid** is often qualified in specific phrases like *first aid, foreign aid, hearing aid, legal aid.* There are examples of **aide** replacing **aid** in such collocations (*development aide, federal aide*) in both CCAE and the BNC, but not enough to count as anything other than typos. For the moment, **aide** remains a human rather than abstract noun.

-aim

Verbs ending in **-aim**, such as *exclaim*, all have related nouns ending in *-amation*. Compare:

acclaim	acclamation
declaim	declamation
exclaim	exclamation
proclaim	proclamation
reclaim	reclamation

Both nouns and verbs originated in Latin with the *-am* spelling, but the verbs were respelled **-aim** on the analogy of *claim* in the late C16. Their pronunciation underscores the spelling difference: the **-aim** of the verb goes with its strong stress, whereas the *-am* of the noun is unstressed.

-ain

English verbs ending in **-ain** connect with a rather inconsistent set of abstract nouns. See for example:

abstain	abstinence
detain	detention
explain	explanation
maintain	maintenance
ordain	ordinance
pertain	pertinence
retain	retention
sustain	sustenance

The verbs go back to different conjugations in Latin (where the stems were spelled with *a, e* or *i*), though they all became *ain* in early modern English. The nouns meanwhile are a mix, some borrowed from French (those ending in *-nce*), and some direct from Latin (those ending in *-tion*). The different vowels in the second syllables of some of the *-nce* words (e.g. *abstinence/sustenance*) are the impact of French on the original Latin verb. English thus inherits some of the vagaries of French spelling.

ain't

Few usage issues hit the headlines as **ain't** did in the US in the 1960s, with discomforting consequences. In informal conversation it draws little attention to itself, and the *Oxford Dictionary* (1989) traces its use back to a citation of 1778. But it has long been the bugbear of American school teachers (*Webster's English Usage*, 1989); and its listing in *Webster's Third* (1961) created a furore, despite the explanatory note that **ain't** was "used orally in most parts of the US by many cultivated speakers, especially in the phrase *ain't I.*" The *Chicago Tribune* beat it up into a sensational headline:

> *SAYING AIN'T AIN'T WRONG!*

Others hostile to the new *Webster's* tried to use the entry on **ain't** to discredit the dictionary, ignoring the distinction between spoken and written usage – as often in fundamentalist discussions of language. This very public controversy over **ain't** probably increased the stigma attached to it in the US, and the Harper-Heritage usage panel (1969–75) registered its strongest veto against it. Yet **ain't** is still a signal of "congruent" informality between American speakers, according to *Webster's English Usage*. Data from CCAE confirm this, with **ain't** appearing freely in utterances quoted in newspapers, and in proverbial sayings such as:

> *Things ain't what they used to be.*
> *You ain't seen nothing yet.*
> *If it ain't broke, don't fix it.*
> *This town ain't big enough for both of us.*

It also gets into print in reference to songs such as "Ain't misbehavin'," "Ain't she sweet?" and "It ain't necessarily so," among others. Writers who play on those sayings or song titles can do so with little risk of censure. Through all this, **ain't** seems to be more significantly embedded in American English than in British. In the UK **ain't** is also associated with casual and dialectal speech (*New Oxford*, 1998). The BNC's numerous examples of **ain't** (more than 3500) come from spoken as well as written texts. But its appearances in print are almost always embedded in quoted speech – or quasi-proverbial sayings such as:

> *London may be the centre of England, but it ain't for me.*

The grammar underlying **ain't** is remarkably complex, when you consider that it serves as a contraction for any of the following:

> *am not   is not   are not   has not   have not*

All except *has not* are illustrated in the examples quoted above. Standard English has contractions for most of them, i.e.:

> *isn't   aren't   hasn't   haven't*

But there's no similar contraction for *am not. Amn't* is regarded as childish or dialectal; and *I'm not* (reducing the verb rather than the negative) works only for declarative sentences. For questions, the contraction commonly used in the UK is *Aren't I?* It looks odd written down, because it's the form of the verb used with plural pronouns (*we, you, they*). Fowler (1926) argued that for the first person singular, *ain't* ought to be an acceptable substitute, though it seems to have gone unheeded. *Aren't I* is now the standard form for the question in British English, according to the *New Oxford*. However for some of the American Harper-Heritage usage panel, it was "a genteelism much worse than *ain't I.*"

Historically speaking, both **ain't** and *aren't* are probably descended from *an't*, recorded during the late C17 as the regular contraction. Sound changes of the C18 affected the pronunciation of the vowel "a" before nasal consonants, raising it in some dialects, and lowering and retracting it in others. While **ain't** is a product of the first process, *aren't* represents the second in terms of British (*r*-less) pronunciation – though not general American. If only *an't* was still available, it would avoid the grammatical discomfort and provide a nonstigmatized alternative to **ain't**.

airplane, aeroplane, airliner and aircraft

American English uses **airplane** where British has traditionally used **aeroplane**, or **airliner** for the large passenger carrier. But **aircraft** is now the dominant term everywhere for referring to an individual winged vehicle, not to mention collectives of them:

> *This aircraft is now ready for boarding.*
> *Aircraft are more polluting than is realized.*

British data from the BNC yields thousands of examples of **aircraft** to a few hundred of the other terms put together. Data from the CCAE shows relatively more use of **airplane** in the US, but **aircraft** still outnumbers it by a factor of 3:1, and **airliner** by 10:1. The ratios are little changed when you discount attributive uses such as *aircraft carrier/hangar/ parts.*

◊ For other *aero-* words now being replaced, see **aer(o)-**.

aitch or haitch

See **haitch**.

aka and alias

See under **alias**.

-al

This suffix has two major roles:
* to make nouns out of certain verbs
* to make adjectives out of nouns

1 Nouns with **-al** are regularly based on verbs of two syllables with stress on the second. See for example:

acquittal	appraisal	approval	arrival
betrayal	betrothal	committal	denial
dismissal	disposal	perusal	proposal
rebuttal	recital	refusal	removal
reprisal	retrieval	reversal	revival
survival	upheaval	withdrawal	

Some of the earliest examples are from medieval legal English, and several of those just mentioned have strong legal connections. The type has spread into the language at large, though few new ones have been formed on the same pattern in recent times. *Deferral* and *referral* are the only C20 examples.

2 Adjectives are made by adding **-al** to an ordinary noun, and new ones are continually being formed. A handful of examples are:

bridal	critical	cultural	herbal
magical	musical	national	parental
seasonal	sensational	transitional	

However a good many common adjectives ending in **-al** were borrowed ready-made from medieval Latin, and they may function in English either as adjectives or nouns or both. See for example:

animal	annual	capital	casual	final
funeral	liberal	official	oval	principal
rival	spiral	total	verbal	

Some of these, e.g. *rival*, *total*, are also used as verbs. The question then arises as to whether or not we should double the final *l* before adding verb endings to them: *rival(l)ed, total(l)ing* etc. The issues are discussed at **-l-/-ll-**.

alarm, alarum and alarmed

In C21 English, **alarum** is an archaism which survives only in the accounts of antique clock mechanisms, and in the combination "alarums and excursions" written as stage directions from C17 drama. It has no role as an alternative to **alarm** in its various other uses as noun and verb. **Alarm** meanwhile is extending its reach, visible in the use of **alarmed** to mean "fitted with a security alarm" which has been on record since 1969. It looks exactly like the past participle of **alarm** meaning "arouse fear in," hence the strangely ambiguous notice that says:

THIS DOOR IS ALARMED

Can the "intelligent building" also have feelings?! In this context both **alarm** and the *-ed* suffix contribute to the ambiguity. See further under **-ed**.

albino

The plural of this is **albinos** (not *albinoes*), by specific mention in the *Oxford Dictionary* (1989) and the absence of mention in *Webster's Third* (1986): it details only irregular plurals. See further under **-o**.

alfresco or al fresco

This Italian phrase meaning "in the fresh air" or "out of doors" was first recorded in English in 1753. The *Oxford Dictionary* (1884–1928) marked it as a foreignism, but set it solid as both adverb and adjective, anticipating its full assimilation. *Webster's Third* (1986) also has it set solid, and, in American data from CCAE, **alfresco** leads the way over **al fresco** by 3:2. British usage goes the other way, with **al fresco** outnumbering **alfresco** by 3:1 in BNC data. Neither database gives evidence of a clear distinction between adverb and adjective: compare *eating alfresco / dine al fresco* and *an alfresco supper / the al fresco buffet*. We may conclude that the Italian setting now has more value for British writers, whereas in American usage **alfresco** is becoming fully integrated. A citation from CCAE featuring the *alfresco black-tie Medici awards dinner* says it all.

algae

The Latin word for "seaweed" has become the generic name for a much larger group of both salt- and freshwater plants. Although it carries a Latin plural inflection, its sense in C21 English is often collective, hence its ability to take either singular or plural agreement. (See **agreement**, section 1.) Both constructions are well represented in British and American databases, as in:

The algae offers good cover for minnows.
Algae are never absent from the tissues of the hydras.

American data from CCAE shows **algae** in agreement with singular verbs or pronouns (*it, this*) more often than plural, in the ratio of about 3:2. Singular constructions are also well represented in BNC data, on a par with the plural.

Technically **algae** has its singular in *alga* (see further under -a section 1). But *alga* is largely confined to scientific prose: it makes very little showing in the BNC and even less in CCAE.

alias and aka

Both these originate in the context of law and policing, as ways of linking the alternative names or identities by which suspects are known, e.g. *Gillelmus alias Gilmoure* and *Joe Smith aka "Baby Face" Smith*. **Alias** (in Latin "otherwise") was used this way in C16, whereas **aka** (an acronym for "also known as") appears first in the US after World War II. **Aka** has more quickly broken free from its legal background. It has been used to flag variant names for people and things in American English since the 1970s, and in British English from around 1990. There are BNC citations from a variety of publications in fields such as computing and music technology.

Both **aka** and **alias** have an expanding range of uses in reference to persons and objects at large. They streamline the reviewer's task of identifying actors, their roles and disguises, as in:

Dr Evil aka Lawrence Fullers
Fawlty Towers waiter Manuel alias actor Andrew Sachs

In examples like these, the convention of giving the personal name first is reversed – a freedom which is sometimes exercised within the same document. In CCAE data, an article on *Don Novello aka Father Guido Sarducci* captions the photo as *Father Guido Sarducci aka Don Novello*. The reversability of **aka** and **alias** allows writers and editors to foreground whichever of the two names is more salient in the immediate context.

Both **aka** and **alias** provide alternative names for movies and other entertainment products: *Dawn of the Dead (aka Zombies), W & W Ventures Inc., alias Tooth Fairy Documentation Center. Both are used to juxtapose the common and foreign names of objects, as in Basque pelota (aka jai alai) and the columbine (alias aquilegia). Occasionally the second slot is used for satirical or humorous comment, witness Lord Rees Mogg aka the Pornfinder General and Miki's mum – alias the hand in the '70s Denim aftershave advert. The examples show how far **aka** and **alias** have come from their origins.

Apart from its role as a link word, **alias** has other uses as a noun. Its use to mean "assumed name" dates from C17, but in late C20 computerspeak, **alias** is an alternative address to which the software can transfer electronic data. In this technical sense it also serves as a verb.

Note that **aka** is normally written in lower case without stops, as is typical of *acronyms,* though it's often pronounced as an *initialism* (see under **acronyms**). The variant forms **a.k.a.** and **AKA** with full capitals made very little showing in either BNC or CCAE. Although they would prevent confusion with words borrowed into English such as *aka* (Japanese for "red") and *aka* (a Maori word for a type of vine), the problem seems pretty remote. Such words only come together in very large English dictionaries.

alibi

Like *alias,* the word **alibi** continues to distance itself from its Latin origins. Originally a Latin adverb meaning "in another place," it was similarly used in Tudor court records: *He was alibi.* By mid-C18 its role as a noun was established, and this now dominates, by the evidence of both American and British databases. Just occasionally it serves as a verb, transitive or intransitive:

> ... had reluctantly agreed to alibi her
> Both refused to alibi for their performance.

The second example shows how **alibi** as noun or verb is now also used to mean "(an) excuse," a usage which still carries the label "informal" in *New Oxford* (1998), though it has been around for more than 80 years. *Webster's English Usage* (1989) notes that British censure of using **alibi** to mean "excuse" intensified following Partridge (1942), whereas the early objections of American commentators seem to have dwindled. *Webster's Third* (1986) registers the meaning as standard, without stylistic warnings. In data from CCAE it's used freely in news reporting on sports or political events, as in *preparing your alibi in case you lose* – as well as reviews of movies, where, for example, a mother and daughter *joust, argue and alibi about their relationship with X.* It would not be the first Latin loanword to acquire a new meaning in English.

all and all of

The uses of **all** as pronoun and determiner are common and uncontroversial. Its ability to be either shows up in alternatives such as:

> All of the responses from Canada are positive
> (pronoun)
> All the responses from Canada are positive
> (determiner)

In the second example, **all** is in fact a *predeterminer* (see under **determiners**). Data from the BNC show that *all the* is far more common than *all of the,* and

lends itself to lengthy postmodification, as in: *all the people involved in Stone's $40 million movie ...* Compare *He can't please all of the people all the time,* where the **all of** phrase is not elaborated.

All serves as an adverbial intensifier in idioms such as *all the better* (with a following comparative), and *not all that good* (always following a negative). The second type of construction is on the margins of written usage, but its acceptability in spoken usage was confirmed by Mittins *et al.* (1970) in the UK, and the Harper-Heritage usage panel (1969–1975) in the US.

all right or alright
See **alright**.

all-around or all-round

These two are interchangeable in American English, according to *Webster's English Usage* (1989), though **all-around** is much more popular with writers represented in CCAE, by a factor of 14:1. In British English the opposite is true, and **all-round** dominates the data from the BNC. The very few instances of **all-around** were confined to advertising, as in an *all-around shoe grip.* See further at **around and round**.

allegory

An **allegory** is a narrative which uses fictional characters and events to portray salient aspects of real life, as does Orwell's *Animal Farm* (1945) or Tolkien's *The Lord of the Rings* (1954–5). Dramas and movies can achieve the same:

> A simple tale of a teenager who hijacks a school
> bus to take him to his girl in another town, it is
> also a complex allegory of Love versus the Law ...

Taken separately, the people and events become symbols of things larger than themselves, and collectively they create *allegorical meaning.* **Allegory** was much favored in earlier historical times, partly because it offered artists an oblique way of presenting contentious political and social matters, without running the risk of imprisonment or worse. *Allegories* often carry a strong moral or message, whether it is homiletic (as in Bunyan's *Pilgrim's Progress* 1678) or satirical (as in the work of Byron).

alleluia or hallelujah
See **hallelujah**.

alliteration

This is the literary device of juxtaposing words containing the same initial sound, so as to weld them together as a group. It was much used in English medieval drama, and, among modern poets, by Gerard Manley Hopkins:

> Kingdom of daylight's dauphin,
> dapple-dawn-drawn falcon

Alfred Tennyson used it to achieve sound symbolism or onomatopoeia as well, in:

> The moan of doves in immemorial elms
> And murmuring of innumerable bees

Not only the first sound in the word, but also successive syllables are used for onomatopoeic effect in that example.

The same device can be used in prose, and by those with more commercial aims in mind. In advertisements, alliteration helps to highlight features of the product and package them together:

> *Machines That Make Money* (a computer)
> *Your nose need never know* (a deodorant)
> *A Philips Microwave will give late guests the*
> *Warm Welcome they don't deserve!*

allomorph
See under **morphology**.

allusion or illusion
See **delusion**.

allusive or elusive
See **elusive**.

-ally
This is the usual adverbial ending for adjectives ending in *-ic* (see under **-ic/-ical**). Note however *accidentally* and *incidentally*, where **-ally** replaces an earlier *-ly:* see **accidentally**, and **incidentally**.

alma mater
See under **alumni**.

almost
The adverbial uses of this word, as in *almost died* and *almost undone,* need no comment. More intriguing are its uses in noun phrases, some of which are standard and others on the fringe. Its use as a qualifier in *almost everything, almost nothing* is recognized in grammars and dictionaries, but they diverge on how to explain its grammatical role in expressions such as *an almost saint* and *a victory almost,* examples from the *Oxford Dictionary* (1989). In expressions like these it comes close to being an adjective, and the *Dictionary* explains this special role as "qualifying a substantive (noun) with an implied attribute." *Webster's Third* (1986) simply classes it as "adjective." The *Comprehensive Grammar* (1985) meanwhile interprets this use as "metalinguistic," and comparable to that of other "comment adverbs" (i.e. *disjuncts*: see **adverbs** section 1). However we choose to legitimize the coupling of **almost** with nouns, its use in both the US and the UK is shrinking. The latest American example in *Webster's English Usage* (1989) is from 1972. A lone example in the LOB corpus – *the almost certainty that they will lose money* – suggests its obsolescence in British English.

along
In both British and American English, this word has multiple roles as adverb and preposition, expressing both spatial relations (*along the path, plodding along*) and more abstract connections (*experiments along those lines, expected to go along with the policy*). But Americans make much more use of **along** to express accompaniment, as in:

> ... *the Indians whom the Spaniards had brought*
> *along with them.*

This use of *along with* is not unknown in British English (on a par with the other uses mentioned, in data from the LOB corpus). In the American Brown corpus, uses of **along** for "accompaniment" outnumbered all others by more than 2:1 (Peters, 1998b).

alongside and alongside of
Alongside (of) is still evolving both grammatically and semantically from its nautical origins as an adverb. Dictionaries register **alongside** as both adverb and preposition, and the prepositional role (*alongside the path*) is much more frequent than the first (*Rogers was alongside*), judging by database evidence. *Webster's English Usage* (1989) notes that the transitional form **alongside of** seems to be tailing off, and it makes only small showing in the databases, with about a score of examples in CCAE and the BNC. For example:

> *The automobile is ranged alongside of the oxcart.*
> *We steamed alongside of the pier.*

Both **along** and **alongside of** are mostly used of physical proximity, but occasionally in more abstract ways:

> *Alongside this ideal – perhaps provoked by it –*
> *ran strong counter-currents.*
> ... *a continuity of leadership alongside of infusion*
> *of new leaders.*

alot
This amalgam of *a* and *lot* is still regarded as nonstandard, though it appears in unedited writing and occasionally gets into print. There are some 50 instances in British data from the BNC, almost entirely from three sources: e-mail, TV autocue data, and TV newscasts. Citations obtained by *Webster's English Usage* (1989) are mostly from memos, private correspondence and draft prose. The occasional instance of **alot** might be just a typo, a failure to press the space bar on the keyboard. But its recurrence in typescript or in handwritten manuscripts makes it more significant, as the shadow of things to come. **Alot** lacks real analogues: the nearest is *awhile,* also compounded with the indefinite article, but sanctioned by centuries of use. Other adverbs beginning with *a* involve a reduced form of "on" or "of." See **a-**.

alphabetic or alphabetical
The longer form is strongly preferred in British as well as American English. **Alphabetical** outnumbers **alphabetic** by almost 6:1 in BNC data and 8:1 in CCAE. ◊ For other pairs of this kind, see **-ic/-ical**.

alphabetical order
Alphabetical systems are not all alike. Differences emerge if you look closely at the order of items in a library catalogue, a computer-ordered list and several dictionaries. The two major alternatives within alphabetical systems are letter-by-letter order, and word-by-word order. The differences show up in the sample lists below.

Letter by letter	Word by word
bitter	*bitter*
bitterbark	*bitter end*
bittercress	*bitter pill*
bitter end	*bitterbark*
bitter-pea	*bittercress*
bitter pill	*bitter-pea*
bitters	*bitters*

In the letter-by-letter order, all word spaces and hyphens are disregarded. The order often has unrelated words juxtaposed in the list. Its advantage is that you can easily find compounds with variable spacing, because their location depends purely on the letters. With the word-by-word system, you work only as far as the first word space, and this brings spaced compounds in immediately after their base word, and compounds which are hyphenated or set solid follow after. It pulls related words together in the list, whatever their settings, and works well with words or names whose settings are invariable.

Dictionaries use modifications of the two systems, depending on how far they "unpack" compounds and derivatives associated with the base words into separate entries. *Webster's Third* (1986) goes furthest in the letter-by-letter direction, and unpacks not only compounds but also derivatives such as *bitterly* and *bitterness* to take their alphabetical place. *Merriam-Webster* (2000) and *New Oxford* (1998) unpack the compounds but keep *bitterly/bitterness* as run-ons/run-ins within the main entry for *bitter* (see **run in or run on**). The *Oxford Dictionary* (1989) goes further in the word-by-word system, grouping many sets of compounds together with the base word. The alphabetical system in indexes may be either letter-by-letter or word-by-word, the first being easier for the indexer and the second for the reader. In smaller sized indexes, it makes little difference to the ordering. For the alphabetization of names beginning with **da, de, di, Mac, St, van** and **von**, see individual headings.

alphabetism

This is another name for the *initialism*. See under **acronyms**.

alphabet

The **alphabet** used for writing English and many other languages is derived from one developed by the Greeks more than 2000 years ago. The word itself confirms this, being made up of the ancient Greek names for the first two letters: *alpha* + *beta*. Modern **alphabets** fall into three groups: (1) modern Greek; (2) Cyrillic (or Russian); (3) Roman. Note that other writing scripts such as those used in the Middle East and India are sometimes called "alphabets," though they developed independently of this group with their own sets of symbols.

1 The modern Greek alphabet with its 24 letters is most like the modern Greek original, and it preserves letters such as *lambda, pi* and *rho* which are extensively modified in the *Roman alphabet*. In Greece and elsewhere, it's used for general communication in Greek, as well as within the Greek Orthodox Church.

2 The Cyrillic alphabet, associated with St Cyril and the Russian Orthodox Church, is used for the Russian language and several Slavic languages. It was also applied to certain non-Indo-European languages within the jurisdiction of the former Soviet Union, such as (Outer) Mongolian. Some of its letters are deceptively like those of the *Roman alphabet*, but with quite different sound values. For example, *P* in Cyrillic represents *R*, and *C* is *S*. Ships bearing the initials *CCCP* were registered in the former USSR, which (in romanized transliteration of the Russian) is Soyuz Sovetskikh Sotsialisticheskikh Respublik.

3 The Roman alphabet is the written medium for all the languages of western Europe, and some in eastern Europe. It is also the standard medium for writing languages of all kinds in North and South America, in

southern Africa, as well as some in Southeast Asia, in Australia and the Pacific. The original *Roman alphabet* was expanded in early modern times with the addition of the letters *j, v* and *w* (the first derived from *i,* and the second and third from *u,* which had been both consonant and vowel). Its range is also extended by the accents or diacritics added to particular letters in various languages. See further under **accents**.

alright or all right

The spelling **alright** is controversial for emotional rather than linguistic or logical reasons. It was condemned by Fowler in a 1924 tract for the Society for Pure English, despite its recognition in the *Oxford Dictionary* (1884–1928) as increasingly current. But the fury rather than the facts of usage seem to have prevailed with most usage commentators since. The *Oxford Dictionary* (1989) maintains its detachment with the note that it is a frequent spelling, and its stance is underwritten by more than 8000 citations in the BNC, many from written and edited sources as well as transcriptions of speech. CCAE also has ample examples in everyday reporting, narrative and quoted speech, illustrating its use in familiar idioms such as *doing alright, feeling alright* and *work out alright*.

Dictionaries which simply crossreference **alright** to **all right** (as the "proper" form) typically underrepresent its various shades of meaning as a discourse signal. It may be concessive, as in *Alright, I'll come with you* – or diffident, as in *How're things? Oh alright* – or impatient as in *Alright, alright!* None of those senses is helpfully written as **all right**, which injects the distracting sense of "all correct." Those who would do away with **alright** prefer to ignore its various analogues, such as *almost, already, also, although, altogether, always,* which have all over the centuries merged into single words. Objections to **alright** are rarely justified, as *Webster's English Usage* (1989) notes, and Burchfield (1996) only makes a shibboleth of it. The strength and diversity of its use in Britain correlates with the comment of *Webster's Third* (1986) for America, that it is "in reputable use." At the turn of the millennium, **alright** is there to be used without any second thoughts.

also

This adverb performs several grammatical roles which are uncontroversial. **Also** typically appears in mid-sentence, putting the spotlight on a neighboring word while making longer-range connections:

> *With their usual skepticism they also questioned the figures.*
> *John and Jeanette also will be there.*
> *I will also argue that editors need better recognition.*

Grammatically speaking, **also** is an *adjunct* in the first sentence, a *subjunct* in the second, and a *conjunct* in the third (see **adverbs** section 1). But when **also** appears as a conjunct at the start of a sentence, it raises questions:

> *Also not clear is whether any of the mothers received steroids...*
> *Also, some groups may have so many interconnections that such an approach is impossible.*

This prominent use of **also** has been subject to censure, though more in the UK than the US.

According to Fowler (1926), it gave a "slovenly" feel to the sentence, as of careless afterthought not properly integrated by the writer. It could be said of the second example above, but not the first, where it's a calculated inversion of normal word order. In both, **also** helps to signal an additional point, as often in academic argument. Examples from the Survey of English Usage corpus were mostly in "private speech" by London academics (Taglicht, 1984). Yet Burchfield (1996) – echoing Fowler – associates it with "uneducated speech." The fact is that there are over 6000 instances of sentence-initial **also** in written sources in the BNC, in both monographs and serials (about 5% of all instances of the word). The *Longman Grammar* (1999) shows that the overall frequency of **also** is much lower in ordinary conversation than in news or academic writing. So the stylistic complaints about **also** seem to be misguided, along with the underlying grammatical assumptions. As a conjunct it can legitimately be used at the start of a sentence; and on the evidence there's little reason to question its purposefulness.

alternative or alternate

These words are a shifty pair. Both involve the idea of "the other" from the Latin stem *alter* embedded in them, and in older usage both meant "the other one of a pair." The *alternative plan* would imply there were only two to choose between, just as *alternate years* means "in every second year." But the strict sense of *alternation* is now much less central to **alternative**, and mostly confined to scientific and numerical uses of **alternate** and its derivatives, as in *alternating current*. In current usage both **alternate** and **alternative** are extending themselves as adjectives along similar lines. As nouns they are increasingly different.

Alternative now often refers to a set of more than two options, as recent dictionaries acknowledge. The *alternative fuel vehicle* is one that runs on anything other than petrol/gasoline. The possibility of several options is strongly associated with the noun **alternative** as well, as in *one of several alternatives* and *a number of alternatives*, recurrent phrases in the BNC. De Bono allows for "195 alternatives" in his *Atlas of Management Thinking* (1990).

The adjective **alternate** is also registered with the meaning "offering choice" in *Webster's Third* (1986), without comment. Its use in official English in postwar Britain is registered in a complaint of Gowers (1954), though the *Oxford Dictionary* (1989) labels it "US." British resistance to it continues – as far as *New Oxford* (1998) is concerned. Its usage note reports that although the reading program found **alternate** used to mean "offering choice" in 25% of all instances of the word, this was "still regarded as incorrect by many." British use of **alternate** is nevertheless exemplified in its use in a variety of phrases in the BNC, such as *alternate source of income, alternate harvesting systems, alternate means of transport*. Using **alternate** for this sense of **alternative** is recognized in Australia, as in *alternate routes to Adelaide* from the *Macquarie Dictionary* (1991), and it's current in Canada also (*Canadian English Usage*, 1997). Clearly the trend is worldwide.

The most recent development for **alternative** and **alternate** is their use as adjectives to refer to a social or cultural practice which is different from that of the conventional mainstream culture. This use of **alternative** is registered in both the *Oxford Dictionary* (1989) and *Webster's* (1986); and it's illustrated in BNC examples such as:

> *Alternative methods of pain relief such as acupuncture and hypnosis are not generally available on the NHS.*

It appears in *alternative bookshop/medicine/technology,* not to mention *the alternative look* [of a hairstyle] *with dashes of golden copper lights ... added to the longer areas at the top and sides.* **Alternate** too is now being used in this sense, as in *alternate lifestyle magazine*. According to *Webster's English Usage* (1989), the sense has been around since the 1960s, and it's acknowledged through crossreference in *Merriam-Webster* (2000). *New Oxford* (1998) knows about it but keeps it at arm's length: "chiefly North American." The constraining influence of etymology (which has delayed recognition of the new meanings for **alternative**) seems now to be operating on **alternate**. Yet **alternate** and **alternative** do seem to share the same adjectival roles, and, not surprisingly, the shorter synonym recommends itself to many.

The noun **alternate** stands apart from all this, used to mean "someone who substitutes for another in the performance of duties." From its origins in theatre to refer to the understudy for a stage actor, it serves around the world in a variety of bureaucratic and legal contexts as well as the sporting arena.

although or though

See under **though**.

aluminum or aluminium

Both these were coined around 1810, along with *alumium,* and *alumina,* for the ore and the metal extracted from it. **Aluminum** was Sir Humphrey Davy's name for the metal, and it has remained the standard spelling in the US (see *Webster's Third,* 1986); and also in Canada, according to the *Canadian Oxford* (1998). But in the UK it quickly changed to **aluminium**, which was felt to have a more "classical" sound than **aluminum**, according to the *Oxford Dictionary* citation from 1812. No-one could deny its consistency with the names of other elements such as *potassium, chromium* and *zirconium*. **Aluminium** is the standard spelling for *New Oxford* (1998), and it overwhelms **aluminum** by more than 100:1 in data from the BNC. The British spelling is also preferred by Australians, as indicated by the *Macquarie Dictionary* (1997).

alumni, alumnae and alma mater

Both **alumni** and **alumnae** connect graduates with the institution which gave them their degree, male graduates being designated by the first, and female by the second. Yet the male term is often used to include the other, as in the *Melbourne University Alumni Association*. The words are Latin plurals, with **alumnus** as the singular form for **alumni**, and **alumna** for **alumnae**. (See further under -**us**, and -**a** section 1.)

Alumnus and *alumna* are literally the "foster child" of the **alma mater** "fostering mother," as universities and colleges have been called since C17 – making them the ultimate extended family. Such families are extended even further in American usage, where **alumni** can be associated with all kinds of training institutions, from the US Naval Academy to the Henry Park Primary School.

a.m., am, A.M., AM or AM

This is the standard abbreviation for times that occur from midnight to midday. It stands for the Latin phrase *ante meridiem,* literally "before noon." Like other lower case abbreviations, **a.m.** is often punctuated with stops, in line with regular practice in both the US and the UK (see **abbreviations**, sections 2 [a], [b] and [c].) Without stops, **am** could just be mistaken for the first person verb *(I) am.* But it's rather unlikely, given that the the time reference is almost always accompanied by numbers, as in *10 am.* In British data from the BNC, times expressed with **am** (unstopped) are always in the majority over those with **a.m.**, though both forms are current. The American convention of printing the abbreviation in small caps, as *10 AM*, also makes the stops unnecessary. When small caps are unavailable, full caps may be used. The *Chicago Manual* (1993) recognized the stopless practice alongside its own preferred policy of using stops (*10 A.M.*) in all kinds of abbreviations. Both stopped and stopless forms are used in Canada (*Editing Canadian English,* 2000) – as in Australia, though the government *Style Manual* (2002) recommends the stopless lower case forms.

What time is *12 a.m.?* The Latin makes it "12 before noon," and therefore "midnight," whereas people used to translating **a.m.** as "in the morning," would think of it as "12 noon." Using *12 noon* or *12 midnight* prevents any ambiguity. The *Chicago Manual* (2003) notes the use of *12 M* for "12 noon," where *M* is again Latin *meridies* ("midday") – while indicating that it's rarely used. It would certainly help with "noon," but there's no parallel abbreviation for "midnight." The ultimate remedy is to use the "twenty-four hour clock" which makes 12 midnight into 24:00, though it's still mostly reserved for itineraries and institutional schedules.

To separate the hours from the minutes in a time reference, a colon is used in North American style, as in *12:05 am* (i.e. just after midnight). British and Australian style use a stop, as in *12.05 am.*

◊ For the use of AM for "amplitude modulation," see under **FM**.

◊ Compare **p.m. or pm**.

ambi-/amphi-

This prefix, meaning "on both sides," appears as **ambi-** in a few Latin loanwords, such as *ambidextrous, ambiguous* and *ambivalent.* As those examples show, it carries the sense of unsettled values, likely to switch from one alternative to the other.

The prefix **amphi-** is the equivalent in Greek loanwords, such as *amphibian, amphora* and *amphitheatre.* In these words the prefix simply implies "both sides." The *amphibian* lives on both sides of the high-water mark; an *amphora* has handles on both sides; and the *amphitheatre* has its audience both in front and behind, in fact, all around.

ambience or ambiance

In English these both represent the French *ambiance* meaning "surroundings." The anglicized spelling **ambience** connects it with the adjective *ambient,* and it's become the general-purpose word for any kind of physical or atmospheric context: *staffroom ambience, European ambience, druggy ambience, motherly/sisterly ambience.* The French spelling **ambiance** once enjoyed a more esoteric existence in the realms of artistic criticism, as a word for the setting or context of a piece of art or music. But it too is used like **ambience** in current American and British English. Database examples have it applied to decor as in *warehouse ambiance* and *hot tropical ambiance,* and sometimes more abstractly as in *competitive ambiance* and *an ambiance of war and hatred.* Both spellings are well used in the US, though data from CCAE puts **ambiance** ahead of **ambience** in the ratio of about 5:2. The opposite holds in the UK, judging by BNC data in which **ambience** is far more common than **ambiance**. The two spellings are nevertheless recognized by *New Oxford* (1998), as by *Merriam-Webster* (2000) – leaving writers an uncommon freedom to use either.

ambiguity

This word is often used in the general sense of "uncertainty of meaning" or "fogginess of expression." More literally it means "capacity for dual interpretation" – an expression which leaves the reader swinging between two possible meanings. **Ambiguity** in the second sense can occur in a single phrase, as for example in *progressive anarchy.* (Does it mean "anarchy which leads to progress" or "anarchy which gets worse and worse?") Classified advertisements can generate **ambiguity** in what they juxtapose, as in:

Free to good home: 4-year-old rottweiler, good guard dog, eats anything, loves children

Potential owners might be warned, though the advertiser was no doubt unaware of the **ambiguity**. The same goes for the pharmacist whose slogan was: *WE DISPENSE WITH CARE.* Less amusing are the cases of bad writing, as in the review of a movie whose makers were concerned with men trying to understand women. "They have no idea what they are all about" says the reviewer. We're confused too! The cure for such **ambiguities** lies in rewording the sentence or rearranging its components.

Yet **ambiguity** is also used creatively and deliberately. A classic study of it in English literature is Empson's *Seven Types of Ambiguity* (1930); and modern advertisers and copywriters use it to stimulate and hold their readers. The tension between two competing meanings engages the mind, especially when both are applicable in the context. For example, in the headline:

Why public servants are revolting

And in the slogan of a used-car salesman:

We give you a Good Deal

Ambiguity of this kind works rather like *double entendre,* except that neither of the meanings generated is risqué. (See **double entendre**.)

ameba or amoeba, and amebic or amoebic

See under **amoeba**.

amend or emend

See **emend**.

America and Americans

The *Americas* take their name from Amerigo Vespucci, an Italian astronomer and navigator who sailed under the Spanish flag, and in 1497 explored the Atlantic coast of what we now know as South America (Brazil, Uruguay and Argentina). Ten years later, a German map-maker attached the name **America** to the coastline Vespucci had charted. Vespucci was the first to discover continental **America**, so it was christened in his honor, even though Columbus reached the Caribbean islands in 1492.

For many people, **America** means "the United States of America," not the whole of North America, let alone Central and South America. (See also **Latin America**.) The citizens of the United States usually refer to themselves as **Americans**, and *America the beautiful* does not seem to include Canada. Canadians, in fact, prefer not to be thought of as **Americans**, so the feeling is mutual. This book indicates wherever possible whether the usage described is specifically associated with the United States, or common throughout English-speaking North America (= *North American*).

◊ For use of *US* and *the USA*, see **USA**.

American English

This variety of English now has the largest body of first-language speakers in the world. It originated with pockets of English settlers on the Atlantic seaboard of North America: a small group from the West country who took land in Virginia in 1607, and the better known "Pilgrim Fathers," many of them from East Anglia, who settled in New England in 1620. Those English communities evolved into the "Thirteen Colonies," though it was a narrow coastal settlement by comparison with the vast areas to the north, west and south which were then under French and Spanish control. But within 200 years, the English-speaking immigrants had acquired a mandate for the whole continent, and English was the common language.

The American Declaration of Independence from Britain in 1776 meant much more than political separation. Linguistic independence was also a felt need, and its outstanding spokesman, Noah Webster, issued a series of publications proposing language reforms from 1783 on. The movement also found expression in the phrase "the American language," first recorded in the US Congress in 1802. In his *Compendious Dictionary of the English Language* (1806), Webster urged Americans to detach themselves from English literary models. The dictionary enshrined spellings that now serve to distinguish American from British English, such as *color, fiber* and *defense*. (See further under **-or, -re** and **-ce/-se**.) Webster's later and much larger *American Dictionary of the English Language* (1828) included many Americanisms, words borrowed from Indian languages, e.g. *caribou, moccasin, tomahawk, wigwam,* and ones created in North America out of standard English elements, e.g. *land office, log house, congressional, scalp* (verb).

American English is distinctive also in its loans from other European languages represented on the continent. From Dutch come *boss, cookie* and *waffle*, from French *chowder* and *gopher*, and from Spanish *plaza* and *tornado*. These various kinds of Americanisms are the unique contribution of the New

World to English at large, documented in the *Dictionary of American English* (1938–44) and especially the *Dictionary of Americanisms* (1951). Other major dictionaries of C20 were the *American Heritage* (1969), *Random House* (1966) and *Webster's Second* and *Third International* dictionaries (1934, 1961), each of which published later editions.

The distinctiveness of **American English** can also be seen in countless expressions for material and technological innovations of C19 and early C20. American use of *gas, kerosene, phonograph* and *tire* contrasts with the British *petrol, paraffin, gramophone* and *tyre*. **American English** remained untouched by spelling modifications which were fostered in British English during C19, hence its preference for *check, curb, disk* and *racket*, where British English has *cheque, kerb, disc* and *racquet* for certain applications of those words. Other examples where **American English** preserves an older spelling are *aluminum, defense, distill* and *jewelry* (rather than *aluminium, defence, distil* and *jewellery*).

Across the American continent, dialect variations are to be found, particularly in pronunciation and the vernacular vocabulary such as *teeter-totter* v. *see-saw,* and *fairing off* v. *clearing up*. Words like these link people's speech with particular regions – broadly speaking the South, the mid-West, and the North / Northern Inland. The mapping of geographical variants began in 1928 with the *Linguistic Atlas* projects in various regions. It continued with nationwide surveys for the *Dictionary of American Regional English* (*DARE*) in the 1960s, and sociolinguistic research of the 1970s, emphasizing social and ethnic dialects in American cities. In the 1990s, the need to synthesize regional and social data on variation was matched by more sophisticated computer resources, illuminating the demography of American dialects as never before. The social significance of dialect has also been highlighted in nationwide debates on the kinds of English to be used and taught in the classroom, centring on Michigan in the 1970s and California in the 1990s. (See further under **Black English**.)

A notional *standard American English* underlies the written form across the continent, and is relatively uniform, except when the writer wishes to conjure up a local or colloquial voice. This is not to say that Americans do not differ on points of written usage, as they have always done. The liberal views of Webster on things such as the use of *whom* and *shall* v. *will* contrast with the strictures of school grammarians of C19, the archetypal Miss Fidditch and Miss Thistlebottom. Usage books of C20 present the same wide range of opinion, some allowing American usage to distance itself from accepted British usage (e.g. on whether *bad* can be an adverb), and others seeking to bring it back into line with British English. The seminal *American English Grammar* published (1940) by Charles Fries, uses descriptive and inductive techniques to account for **American English** as it actually is.

American English is often more regular than British, as in the use of stops in most abbreviations, and the rules for deploying final punctuation in relation to quotation marks. (See **abbreviations** section 2a and **quotation marks** section 3c.) Other areas of difference beween American and British are indicated under **punctuation**.

amid, amidst, among or amongst

These four prepositions share much the same grammatical functions these days, but differ somewhat in their regional distribution and their applications. Overall the shorter forms (**amid** and especially **among**) are much more frequent than the longer ones, as the relative percentages show in both British and American databases:

	BNC	CCAE
amid	3.8%	6.2%
amidst	1.7%	0.4%
among	78.8%	93.1%
amongst	15.7%	0.3%

The rarity of **amid** and **amidst** in British English helps to make them the literary and formal options for **among/amongst**. In American English **amongst** is also very uncommon, and the only one in general use is **among**.

The choice between **among** and **amongst**, according to Fowler (1926), turned on whether the following word began with a vowel. He was extrapolating from a small set of C19 citations from the *Oxford Dictionary* (1989) where **amongst** was preferred. The idea is not supported by much larger amounts of contemporary data from the BNC, where **among** and **amongst** had very similar ratios of vowels to consonants following (both about 1:7). Contrasting examples such as *among other things / amongst others* are indifferent to the sound following, so the explanation clearly cannot be phonetic. The following example would suggest that writers may use both for "elegant" variation:

> *The Group of 15...held a summit meeting in Caracas, Venezuela on Nov. 27–29, attended by, **amongst** others, the heads of government of India, Indonesia, Malaysia and Senegal. . . .:third world debt and protectionism **among** industrialised countries featured prominently in the discussion.*

The tenacity of **amid(st)**, in spite of its minority status in both American and British English, can be explained in terms of its semantics and grammar. In fact it seems to be more versatile than **among(st)**, expressing relationships in space and the social environment, as well as abstract contexts for which **among(st)** is unsuitable.

	amid(st)	among(st)
old pine trees	x	x
the landscape	x	
press releases	x	x
bizarre publicity	x	(x)
speculation	x	
the silence	x	
army officers	x	x
the militia	x	x

The table shows that **among(st)** is grammatically restricted. Effectively it can be used with plural nouns, and collective singular ones like *militia* which comprise a number of similar, countable entities. *Publicity* is ambiguous, and lends itself to **among(st)** only if the context makes it a series of press releases, rather than an abstraction. Abstract concepts like *speculation*, *silence* and *landscape* are *mass nouns* rather than collective ones, and do not lend themselves to **among(st)** at all. It seems that **amid(st)**

works with both mass and countable nouns, whereas **among(st)** goes only with the latter. (See further under **count nouns**.)
◊ Compare **while or whilst**.

amoeba or ameba, and amoebic or amebic

Respondents to the Langscape survey (1998–2001) mostly preferred **amoeba** over **ameba**, even in the US. In fact both *New Oxford* (1998) and *Merriam-Webster* (2000) foreground **amoeba/amoebic**, which makes the convergence less surprising. It is of course a technical term, at home in scientific writing, not the daily news. For other words where American English uses e rather than *oe*, see **oe**. The plural of **amoeba** is discussed under **-a** section 1.

amok or amuck

Contemporary American and British dictionaries all prefer the first spelling, though the second was foregrounded in the *Oxford Dictionary* (1884–1928), being used in most of its citations from earlier centuries. Database evidence now runs very strongly in favor of **amok**. It outnumbers **amuck** by about 12:1 in the BNC, and by 25:1 in American data from CCAE.

The spelling **amok** is closer to the original Malay word *amoq* meaning "frenzied," while **amuck** reflects the way it was and is commonly pronounced, at least outside the UK. Dictionaries such as *Merriam-Webster* (2000), the *Canadian Oxford* (1998) and the Australian *Macquarie* (1997) still give priority to the pronunciation with "muck" as the second syllable, whereas *New Oxford* (1998) gives the pronunciation with "mock" – more consistent with the now dominant spelling. **Amuck** is probably *folk etymology*, though the connection with "muck" sheds little light on the word. See **folk etymology**.

among

See **amid, amidst, among or amongst**, and **between or among**.

ampersand

This word covers a variety of symbols used to represent the word "and." In official names and company titles, it has a shape like the figure 8, as in *Marks & Spencer's*. Its alternative older shape looks like the Greek epsilon: &, as in Beaumont & Fletcher. Both these forms have been available in printing, though only the first is common on typewriters and wordprocessors. In handwriting many people use a form like a cursive plus-sign: +, as in *bread + butter*.

The **ampersand** is not now used for general purposes in printed text, but replaced by "and" itself. It occurs only in references to:

1. corporations, e.g. *P & O*, and publishing companies, e.g. *Harper & Row*
2. statutes and parliamentary acts, as in *Acts of Settlement 12 & 13*
3. the joint authors of a work, as in *Gilbert & Sullivan, Rodgers & Hammerstein*.

The third point is the only case where you might actually introduce an **ampersand** into a text: to clarify pairs of authors when there's a string of names mentioned in quick succession. There is otherwise no need to use **ampersand** when citing joint authors in text or parentheses – though British editors have made a practice of inserting **ampersands** into parenthetic references (*Copy-editing*, 1993). Current editorial practice in both the UK and the US is to restrain the use of **ampersands**, and to "silently" replace them with "and" (Ritter, 2002). The *Chicago Manual* (2003) recommends removing **ampersands** from the titles of published works. Style manuals agree on the need to retain **ampersand** in corporate names, although the *Chicago Manual* relaxes this for the names of publishing companies listed in bibliographies (e.g. *Harper and Row*), so long as consistency is maintained for all company names. **Ampersand** is to be avoided when citing the names of persons involved jointly in a legal case (Butcher, 1993), lest the litigants seem to be a company.

The word **ampersand** is hybrid Latin, a telescoping of "and per se and" which can only be translated as "& by itself makes 'and'." It records the fact that for centuries **ampersand** stood at the end of the list of alphabetic symbols A–Z in school primers – as the final symbol which in itself represented a whole word. No doubt the list was chanted in many a C19 classroom, and the word "ampersand" stands as a monument to rote learning.

amuck or amok
See **amok**.

an
For the choice between **an** and **a**, see **a or an**.

-an
This common suffix generates adjectives from proper names, both personal and geographical. See for example:

Elizabethan	*Gregorian*	*Hungarian*
Lutheran	*Mexican*	*Mohammedan*
Republican	*Roman*	*San Franciscan*
Tibetan		

As these examples show, the suffix may be simply added to the end, or may replace a final *-e* or *-o* in such words. If the final letter is *-y* it changes to *i* before the suffix. (See further under **-e** and **-y>-i-**.) In many cases, the suffix coincides with the final *-a* of a name, as in:

Alaskan	*Asian*	*Australian*	*Estonian*
Indian	*Jamaican*	*Persian*	*Romanian*
Russian	*Spartan*	*Syrian*	*Victorian*

Because the resulting ending is quite often *-ian* (as in *Asian*), the **-an** suffix has given birth to *-ian* as a suffix in its own right. It is common with proper names, as in:

Bostonian	*Brazilian*	*Canadian*	*Christian*
Darwinian	*Freudian*	*Miltonian*	*Natalian*
Wagnerian			

The *-ian* suffix also appears in some ordinary adjectives, such as *mammalian* and *reptilian*, and a good many nouns referring to roles and professions:

grammarian	*guardian*	*musician*	*optician*
physician	*politician*	

Note that a number of similar-looking words like *comedian, historian, librarian* are really examples where a final *y* has become *i* before the suffix **-an**.

One other variant of this suffix is *-ean*, which belonged originally to a number of classical words:

Antipodean	*Chaldean*	*Epicurean*
European	*Herculean*	*Mediterranean*
Procrustean	*Promethean*	

For these, and for *Jacobean* and *Singaporean, -ean* is the only possible spelling. Note however that several others may be spelled either *-ean* or *-ian:*

> *Argentinean/Argentinian,*
> *Aristotelean/Aristotelian, Boolean/Boolian,*
> *Caesarean/Caesarian, Hermitean/Hermitian,*
> *Shakespearean/Shakespearian.*

For most of them *-ian* is now the most common ending, but see under individual headings.

-ana
See under **-iana**.

anacoluthon
This learned word refers to a very common feature of spoken language – its grammatical discontinuity. When speaking off the cuff or on the run, we frequently start a sentence, stop, and continue on another tack. For example:

> *"That computer problem of yours – Why didn"t*
> *I – All we need to do is to call up FILE . . . "*

Once past the **anacoluthon** of the first two sentences, the speaker manages to complete one. But the listener has already got enough to follow his drift because of the predictable phrases that make up everyday talk. So the **anacoluthon** doesn't impair spoken communication too badly. It does need to be edited out of writing.

◊ For the plural of **anacoluthon**, see under **-on**.

anaemic or anemic
See under **ae/e**.

anaesthetic or anesthetic
See under **ae/e**.

anagrams
An **anagram** is a word puzzle in which the letters of one word can be rearranged to form another. For example:

instead	*sainted*
mastering	*emigrants*
parental	*paternal*

The letters may be arranged in any order, as the examples show. Compare *palindrome*, in which the same letters must be read in reverse order. Samuel Butler's *Erewhon* is therefore strictly an **anagram**, not a **palindrome**. (See further under that heading.)

analogue or analog
The British choice here is **analogue**, whether it's a matter of electronics as in *analogue v. digital technology;* chemistry (finding **analogues** of other compounds); or nontechnical uses as when referring to something *analogous* in function to something else. Thus the American Congress is the **analogue** of the British parliament. Elsewhere in the world, in the US, Canada and Australia, **analog** is usual in electronic applications of the word, such as *analog computer, analog gauges,* and often found in chemical applications as in *the highly processed seafood analog used primarily for imitation crab,* from CCAE. For nontechnical uses, Americans (though not Canadians or Australians) use both **analog** and **analogue**. Compare examples such as *speed listening as an analog to speed reading* with *a musical analogue to Esperanto*. With these various uses **analog** appears twice as often as **analogue** in CCAE data, which

Merriam-Webster (2000) endorses for the adjective, but still puts second to **analogue** for the noun.
◊ On the history of the two spellings, see **-gue/-g**.

analogy

This is a matter of the perceived likeness between things. **Analogies** work rather like metaphors in poetry, but are used in speaking and writing either to explain something, or to bring the audience to a particular point of view. An imaginative geography teacher might explain how a cyclone moves *by analogy with* the way spaghetti behaves when you twirl it up a fork. The parliamentarian who is keen to lower the speed limit for jumbo-sized trucks or semitrailers might refer to them as "juggernauts of the highway." As the second example shows, an **analogy** may embody a judgement (positive or negative), which gives it persuasive force. The word *juggernaut* projects the vehicle as something enormous, primitive and harsh, which mows down everything in its path.

A *false analogy* is one which suggests conclusions which are misleading or inappropriate to the topic. Take for example the suggestion that crosscultural communication is like a game between people who are playing badminton on one side of the net and tennis on the other. This **analogy** works only in a light-hearted context. Where there are serious concerns about crosscultural misunderstanding, it distorts and trivializes the issues, implying that they can be reduced to a set of sporting rules, and one side just has to agree to work by the rules of the other.

analytic or analytical

In both American and British English, **analytical** has the numbers over **analytic**: a factor of more than 3:1 in CCAE as well as the BNC. But the databases show both used with the same noun: *analytic/analytical mind, analytic/analytical technique, analytic/analytical philosophy*. The choice is free, as with some but not all **-ic/-ical** pairs. See further under that heading.

analyze or analyse

American and British English divide on these spellings. *Webster's Third* (1986) foregrounds **analyze**, which was preferred by Dr. Johnson in his dictionary (1755). The *Oxford Dictionary* (1989) makes **analyse** its primary spelling, while noting that neither has the etymological edge over the other. Database evidence confirms the regional split. In CCAE **analyze** overwhelms **analyse** by a factor of 100:1, whereas in BNC data **analyse** is strongly preferred, by about 10:1. See further under **-yze/-yse**.

anaphora and anaphoric

In rhetoric and grammar, these words are put to different uses.
*For the rhetorician, **anaphora** in the strictest sense involves repeating a word or several at the start of successive sentences, as in Churchill's declaration:
> *We shall not flag or fail. We shall go on to the end. We shall fight in France...*

Rhetorical **anaphora** is also found in any phrasal pattern repeated with strategic variation, as in Lincoln's hope:
> *...that government of the people, for the people, by the people, shall not perish from this earth.*

*For grammarians **anaphora** is a semantic relationship between two successive noun phrases which refer to the same thing. Thus a pronoun is **anaphoric** to its antecedent:
> *He popped the question and she made the most of it.*

There the pronoun *it* harks back to "the question," and *he* and *she* to persons mentioned in earlier sentences. **Anaphora** normally refers back to something previously mentioned, although the opposite, i.e. *forward-looking anaphora* (called *cataphora*) can be set up – at least within the same sentence:
> *On its arrival in Bangkok, the aircraft was cordoned off.*

In that example *its* anticipates "aircraft" and is *cataphoric* to it.

The concept of **anaphora** is sometimes used of the relationship between the tenses of successive verbs, or verbs and adverbial expressions of time, where one creates the context or a reference point for the second:
> *The boss had fired the secretary and installed a personal assistant.*
> *After the weekend I shall be in Frankfurt.*

Anaphora is a vital element in the cohesion of discourse, and in maintaining the consistency of meanings in it. See further under **coherence or cohesion**.

-ance/-ence

Because these suffixes sound exactly alike, and both make abstract nouns, it seems perverse that they are not interchangeable in most English words. Usually there's no option, and only one spelling will do. But the previous letters or sounds often serve as a clue, to save you reaching for the dictionary. With any of the following, the spelling is **-ence**:

-*cence* (with the first *c* pronounced "s") *innocence magnificence reticence*
-*gence* (with the *g* pronounced "j") *convergence diligence indulgence*
-*quence consequence eloquence sequence*
-*scence convalescence effervescence fluorescence*

When other letters come before the ending, the spelling (**-ance** or **-ence**) can sometimes be settled through related words where the doubtful syllable is stressed. So to get *preference* correct, think *preferential*. The same technique works for:

confidence	deference	difference	essence
influence	penitence	providence	prudence
reference	reverence	sentence	

For **-ance** words, a related word ending in *-ate* or *-ation* can help you to get some of them right. So *dominance* can be reliably spelled by thinking of *dominate* or *domination*. The same technique works for:

luxuriance	radiance	significance	tolerance

and many others.

Two small groups require special attention, because of their sheer perversity:

assistance resistance

versus

existence insistence persistence subsistence

By rights they should all have **-ence** because they go back to the same Latin stem. But the French were inclined to spell them all with **-ance**, and their legacy remains in the first pair. Would that the classical respellers of the English Renaissance had done a more thorough job on this set (see **spelling** section 1), or that dictionaries permitted us to spell them either way.

A very few words may be spelled with either **-ence** or **-ance**. They include *dependence/dependance* and *independence/independance*. The spelling with **-ance** is in each case more common in the US (see further under **dependent**). The same is true for **ambience/ambiance** (see under that heading).
◊ For variation between **-ance** and **-ancy**, or **-ence** and **-ency**, see **-nce/-ncy**.
◊ For the choice between **-ence** and **-ense**, see **-ce/-se**.

-ancy/-ency

These suffixes, like *-ance* and *-ence*, create many a spelling problem. But there are ways of predicting which spelling to use, just as with *-ance* and *-ence*. See **-ance/-ence** for details.

and

And is the most common conjunction in English, and ranks among the top three words in terms of overall frequency. It serves to join together words and phrases as well as clauses, though the balance of the two depends on the type of discourse. Academic writers make much use of **and** to connect words and phrases, according to the *Longman Grammar* (1999); whereas in everyday writing and speech, **and** is more often used to coordinate clauses. Because it simply adds something to whatever went before, speakers can easily build ideas with it on the run. A vital element in the breathless narratives of children, it also helps impromptu speech-makers:
> *"Now let me tell you a little about the background to this proposal and the petition. And before I address the question of how best to ... "*

As the example shows, **and** can just as readily appear at the start of a sentence as in the middle, although this has raised the eyebrows of prescriptivists and teachers for decades. *"It's wrong to use **and** at the start of a sentence,"* they say. Their judgement is based on a very literal interpretation of the role of a conjunction – that it must conjoin things within a sentence, and cannot, should not, must not link things across sentence boundaries. Grammarians now recognize that **and** can be used as a *conjunct,* to provide a semantic link with the previous sentence. (See **conjunctions and conjuncts**, and **coherence or cohesion**.)

To use **and** repeatedly at the start of a sentence would be stylistically unfortunate. Like *but, it* or any other word, it quickly becomes monotonous and predictable. Yet there can be stylistic or rhetorical reasons for repeating **and**:
> *He commanded the multitude to sit down and took the five loaves and the two fishes, and looking up to heaven, he blessed, and brake, and gave the loaves to his disciples, and the disciples to the multitude. And they did all eat, and were filled, and they took up the fragments that remained twelve baskets full. And they that had eaten were about five thousand men, beside women and children.* (Matt. 14:19–21 AV)

Of course this translates the wording of the Greek New Testament, but it shows how the repetition of **and**, especially at the start of the second and third verses, helps to stress the enormous scope of the miracle.

and/or

At its best, **and/or** is a succinct way of giving three alternatives for the price of two. Thus:
> *The child's father and/or mother should attend the meeting.*

is equivalent to:
> *The child's father, or mother, or both of them should attend the meeting.*

As long as there are just two coordinates, the meaning of **and/or** is clear, though the reader may have to pause over it to tease out the alternatives. When there are more than two items, the number of possible alternatives goes up and becomes unmanageable. Try:
> *The child's mother, father and/or guardian should attend the meeting.*

With three coordinates, the meaning is inscrutable, and expressions of this kind are no doubt the ones which give **and/or** its bad reputation for ambiguity. It is sometimes said to belong in the contexts of legal and business writing, yet the citations in *Webster's English Usage* (1989) show that it's widely used in informative writing for the general reader.

anemic or anaemic

See under **ae/e**.

anent

This Anglo-Saxon fossil is rare outside the domain of law. The only British example in the BNC is from Scottish industrial law:
> *... a deputation of female compositors had insisted on an agreement anent the same.*

In American data from CCAE the few examples come from newspaper columns – writers with sententious content who are apparently seeking an elevated style:
> *Anent your editorial: what exquisite irony lies in the Reagans' agonizing...*

Anent is of course shorter than "concerning," and less bureaucratic than "with respect to." But that's about all there is going for it.

anesthetic or anaesthetic

While Americans and Canadians prefer the first, the British and Australians are more inclined to the second. See further under **ae/e**.

aneurysm or aneurism

The first spelling is now dominant in both British and American English. In database evidence **aneurysm** outnumbers **aneurism** by a ratio of 29:1 in the BNC and 13:1 in CCAE. It was not always so. The *Oxford Dictionary* (1884–1928) found that **aneurism** was more common in its C19 citations, even though **aneurysm** rendered the word's etymology more exactly. (The stem consists of *an(a)-* "up" plus *eurus* "wide"). The familiarity of the *-ism* ending, and the interchangeability of *y* and *i* in English spelling no doubt helped to create and support **aneurism** for quite some time (see **i/y**). This would explain the slightly higher frequency of **aneurism** in American English, though *Webster's Third* (1986) weighs in behind **aneurysm**. **Aneurism** has almost had its day.

angle brackets

See **brackets** section 1e.

Anglo- or Anglo

With or without a hyphen, the meaning of **Anglo(-)** varies with context. In compound adjectives it trades meaning with its other half – witness *Anglo-Saxon*, where it connects with a historical culture vested in the south and midland parts of England, and *Anglo-American* where its meaning is usually political, involving joint action by the UK and US governments.

As a noun in the form **Anglo** (and *Anglos*), it refers to a person's language, but always in contrast with whatever other language(s) are used in that quarter of the world. In Quebec where the term originated in 1800, it identifies English-speakers as opposed to the French, whereas in the southwestern US, including California, the contrast is first and foremost with Spanish speakers. In Scotland, **Anglo** means anyone from south of the border, even if they play football for Scottish teams. Although it need not be derogatory, it creates a "them and us" division with social implications. See further under **racist language**.

annex or annexe
British English is inclined to make a verb of the first and a noun of the second (especially in the sense of an extension to a building, as in the *boarding annexe* to a school). Examples of **annexe** in the BNC were almost entirely of this kind. But the database also shows **annex** working as a noun, in fact more often as noun than verb. Its frequency is helped by its being the regular spelling for an appendix to a legal or bureaucratic document, and it's also found meaning "building extension," as in *a new annex to Chelmsford College of Further Education, the Bar Council's Warwick Court annex,* and even *the use of annex setts* (by badgers)! Americans make little use of the word, by the dearth of evidence from CCAE, but according to *Webster's Third* (1986) use **annex** for all applications of the word.

Annex(e) has effectively been twice-borrowed from French into English. The original loanword was put to legal purposes, trimmed down to **annex** for both noun and verb before 1700. It was reborrowed as **annexe** in C19 for architectural uses. Who knows if the French spelling helps to grace the drawings of a not-altogether-graceful extension?

annul
This legal verb is a backformation from the French loan *annullement,* and appears in early modern English as *annulle* and **annul**. The trimmed form has been the standard spelling in both British and American English since C19.

anoint or annoint
The first is the accepted spelling everywhere. The second was used in C15 and C16, but is now extinct according to the *Oxford Dictionary* (1989). American usage books of C20 still find reason to comment on it, and there are plenty of examples on the internet. The ratio of **annoint** to **anoint** on the internet (just on 1:15, by a Google search in 2002) – means the spelling isn't to be taken for granted. The spelling **annoint** no doubt results from misanalysis of the word into *an-* + *noint*, by analogy with *announce*.

anorexic or anorectic
The first form is much more common in both American and British English. **Anorexic** outnumbers **anorectic** by almost 10:1 in data from CCAE, and by almost 100:1 in the BNC. For other pairs of the same kind, see **-ctic/-xic**.

-ant/-ent
These suffixes are alike in sound and meaning, and both are found in common adjectives and nouns. Yet for most words, convention has made one or other the only one acceptable. For some, the standard spelling can be predicted from the letters or sounds immediately before the ending.

The following groups are always spelled with **-ent**:
  -cent (when *c* is pronounced "s") *magnificent*
  -gent (when *g* is pronounced "j") *diligent intelligent*
  -quent   eloquent
  -scent   evanescent   obsolescent

Note that the words fitting these patterns always have at least two syllables before the ending. These apart, a word's spelling may be predicted from related words whose pronunciation makes the elusive vowel unmistakable. The sound of *accidental* would put you right on *accident*, and *consonantal* helps with *consonant*.

A very small number of these words can appear with either **-ant** or **-ent**. They are typically ones which work as both adjectives and nouns, like **dependent/dependant** (see further under that heading). In such cases writers may, as the *Oxford Dictionary* (1989) suggests, reserve the **-ent** for the adjective, and use **-ant** for the noun. But this distinction does not sit comfortably with the fact that **-ant** is the ending of many adjectives, or that adjectives and nouns shift into each other's roles. Less frequent examples, such as **propellant/propellent** and **repellent/repellant**, seem to be settling arbitrarily on the first one in each case (see under those headings).

For **ascendant**, **defendant** and **descendant**, the **-ant** spelling alone is current and used for both noun and adjective: see individual headings.

Though both spellings survive for **confidant/confident**, they present different meanings. See **confident or confidant(e)**.

antagonist and protagonist
See **protagonist**.

Antarctic(a)
Being a geographical term, this word typically appears with a capital letter (see **capital letters**). Either *the Antarctic* or **Antarctica** are used to refer to the region around the South Pole. But when used as an adjective, the word may be spelled either with or without a capital, depending on whether it refers directly to the South Pole, or is being used figuratively. This makes the difference in:
  Mawson succumbed to the Antarctic climate
and
  My azaleas are slow to flower with this antarctic weather.
◊ Compare **Arctic**.

ante-/anti-
These prefixes mean very different things.
1 The Greek anti- (meaning "against, opposed to") is well established in words like:
  anticlimax   anticyclone   anti-intellectual antisocial
not to mention
  antidisestablishmentarianism

Anti- is regularly used to form new words, such as *anti-abortion, anti-business, anti-government, anti-Semitism*. Newer words with **anti-** often carry a hyphen in British English, according to *New Oxford* (1998), whether or not the base word begins with a capital letter (see **hyphens**). But *Merriam-Webster* (2000) shows how American English gives a solid setting from the start to most words formed with **anti-**, whether a vowel or consonant follows: *antiabortion, antibusiness, antigovernment*. Hyphens are used only before a capital letter, as in *anti-Semitism*.

2 Ante- from Latin means "before," as in:
> antecedent   antedate   antediluvian
> antepenultimate   anteroom

It is never hyphenated. These days it's hardly ever used to form new words, but has yielded its place to *pre-* (see **pre-**).

One curious exception to all the above is the word *antipasto*, borrowed from Italian. Though it means the things you eat before the main meal, the Italians have fixed the spelling with **anti-** not **ante-**.

antenna

This Latin loanword has two plurals, the anglicized **antennas** and the latinate **antennae**, which have rather different applications. In both British and American English, **antennas** is put to specialized use in referring to the devices that receive radio, TV and satellite signals. **Antennae** covers the biological uses of the word in reference to the feelers of insects, snails and prawns etc. The plural **antennae** is also used in figurative references to that human facility to sense social and political currents in the environment, as in the following examples from the BNC and CCAE respectively:

> *However decent the man, his political antennae were too insensitive.*
> *Children have faultless antennae for detecting when adults are serious.*

Those are the broad distinctions. However both databases harbor examples in which **antennae** is used for the electromagnetic device, and in CCAE about 1 example in 5 was spelled that way. The American data also provided some rare examples in which **antennas** was used for biological and human applications, notably Nancy Reagan saying she used "all my little antennas to ferret out White House personnel problems." But the First Lady's commitment to the regular English plural was heavily outweighed by the general preference (more than 90%) for **antennae** in this application. See further under **-a** section 1.

anthrax

For the plural of this word, see **-x** section 3.

anthropomorphism

See under **personification**.

anti-

See **ante-/anti-**.

anticlimax

See under **climax**.

antipodes or Antipodes

This remarkable word was coined by Plato, to mean "those with their feet placed opposite." It reminds us that the Greeks of the fourth century BC understood not only that the world was round, but also that through gravity all the world's inhabitants trod the earth in the same way, whether in the northern or southern hemisphere. Those on one side of the world therefore had their feet opposite to those on the other. Or, as Shakespeare expressed it, they were "counterfooted."

The word has been used of both people and places on opposite sides of the globe, and so Mongolia and Argentina are **antipodes** relative to each other, not just for Britain vis-à-vis Australia and New Zealand. Strictly speaking, the word could be also used by Australians and New Zealanders in reference to Britain, although the course of history has meant it being most often used by the British in reference to Australia. Both the *Oxford Dictionary* (1989) and *Webster's Third* (1986) give preference to the lower case form, although instances of **Antipodes** outnumbered **antipodes** in this application by more than 3:1 in the BNC. The capital letter serves to differentiate this specific geographical sense of the word from the generic sense of "opposite," as in *Violence and voting are antipodes*. But not all writers use it.

antivenin, antivenene, antivenine or antivenom

The spelling **antivenin** is given preference in the major American and British dictionaries, with **antivenene** offered as the lesser alternative. **Antivenine** is noted only in the *Oxford Dictionary* (1989). Spelling variation between *-in* and *-ine,* and between *-ine* and *-ene* affects other chemical compounds (see **-ine**), but has little public impact. These three however interconnect with first aid and public safety, and health authorities in many places now endorse **antivenom** instead, following a recommendation of the *Lancet* magazine in 1979. It appears in the World Health Organization's Committee on Venoms and Antivenoms. **Antivenom** is clearly more transparent, and makes for more reliable communication when life is threatened.

The reference databases provide little evidence on any of the terms. Only **antivenin** could be corroborated in American data from CCAE, and none of them appears in the BNC. (Life-threatening events involving snakes are of course relatively uncommon in the British Isles – thanks to St Patrick!) An internet search (Google, 2002) confirmed that all four words are still current, though the use of **antivenene** is very low, and **antivenine** rates only a few hundred examples worldwide. By contrast **antivenom** and **antivenin** both notched up several thousand, with **antivenom** ahead by a factor of 7:5. Thus **antivenom** seems to be establishing itself – the specialists' sensible choice has gained popular support.
◊ Compare **flammable/inflammable**.

antonyms

These are pairs of words with opposite meanings, like *wet* and *dry*, or *dead* and *alive*. Many **antonyms** like *wet/dry* are words from opposite ends of a scale, and one can imagine intermediate stages on the scale between them, like those expressed in "rather wet" and "almost dry." In linguistic terms they are *gradable antonyms,* which permit degrees of comparison (see **adjectives** section 2).

Antonyms like *dead/alive* are also opposites, but without a continuous scale between them. If you say that an animal is "half-dead," you are really saying that it's still alive. In fact the use of one word entails negating its opposite: *alive* means "not dead," just as *dead* means "not alive." The two words complement each other in meaning and are therefore called *complementary antonyms*.

A third group of **antonyms**, such as *buy/sell, parent/child* and *before/after*, form pairs that are not so much opposite as reciprocal in meaning. As those examples show, the words may refer to reciprocal actions or relationships, or corresponding relationships in time or space. The term for such **antonyms** is *relational opposites*, or *converses*. Comparative expressions, such as *higher/lower* also fall into this class.

Note that all pairs of **antonyms** have a common denominator between them:

> *wet/dry*　　(level of moisture or saturation)
> *buy/sell*　　(exchange of goods for money)

So any pair of **antonyms** is in fact concerned with the same thing: they just take contrasting perspectives on it.

any and any-

These raise grammatical questions as well as issues of style. As an indefinite pronoun, **any** can stand for either singular or plural, and the verb agreement varies accordingly:

> *Is any of their advice to be taken seriously?*
> *None of those apples. We don't want any that are wrinkled.*

The personal pronoun agreeing with **any** is very often *they, them, their:*

> *If any of the staff come, make them welcome.*

This use of *them* (*they/their*) with **any** is now the most neutral form of agreement, whatever objection may be made in terms of formal agreement (see further under **they**). The use of *him* or *her* in that sentence would turn it into an expectation about the sex of the staff attending. The agreement with *anyone* and *anybody* likewise frequently involves *they, them, their*, again maintaining the indefiniteness, and in spite of a singular verb. (See further under **agreement** section 3.)

Other **any**-compounds are adverbs, some of which (*anyhow, anymore, anyway, anywhere*) are regularly set solid. The solid setting of *anymore* meaning "any longer" is widely used in the US and elsewhere outside the UK (Burchfield, 1996); and it contrasts usefully with the juxtaposed determiners *any* and *more* in *Any more news?* But *anymore* (as adverb) tends to be replaced by the spaced *any more* in formal British style. The BNC's examples of *anymore* meaning "any longer" (almost 300) come from interactive or colloquial writing:

> *The joke isn't funny anymore.*
> *They don't make films like his anymore.*
> *"Anytime, anywhere," the note had said.*
> *They'll explain it to anyone, anytime . . .*

The last two examples show how the setting of established **any**-compounds provides a pattern for the newer ones. *Anytime* appears more than 100 times in BNC data, again in informal discourse. Writers of more formal prose may wish to space out *any more* and *any time,* but it makes no difference to the adverbial meaning.

Some **any**-compounds are strongly associated with American rather than British English. This is so for *anymore* used in positive rather than negative constructions. Compare the examples given above with *Listening is a rare art anymore,* where it means "nowadays." *Anyplace* and *anywheres* are also most at home in American English, the former gaining ground as the latter seems to be losing it, according to *Webster's Dictionary of Usage* (1989). The use of *anybody* and *anyone* is a further point of regional divergence: see under **-one or -body**.

aorta

For the plural of this word, see under **-a** section 1.

Aotearoa

See **New Zealand**.

apart or aside

See **aside (from)** and **apart (from)**.

apeing or aping

See **aping**.

apexes or apices

Dictionaries allow both **apexes** and **apices** for the plural of *apex*, though they differ over the order. The *Oxford Dictionary* (1989) puts the Latin **apices** first, while *Webster's Third* (1986) makes it **apexes**. Data from the BNC suggests that while academic writers may use **apices**, **apexes** is likely in other kinds of nonfiction. **Apexes** also appears as part of a newish verb, used in sportscar racing, and elsewhere: [*Music that*] *apexes at the solo.* Verbal use of *apex* is noted in *New Oxford* (1998) and *Merriam-Webster* (2000).
◊ For other Latin loanwords of this type, see **-x** section 2.

aphorism, adage, axiom, maxim, proverb

All these words refer to statements of received wisdom, and brevity is the soul of all of them. Dictionaries often use the words as synonyms for each other, yet there are aspects of each to differentiate.

An **aphorism** is above all pithy and terse, as in *Least said, soonest mended,* whereas the wording of an **adage** has a centuries-old flavor to it: *He who pays the piper calls the tune.* A **proverb** expresses its practical wisdom in homely terms: *A stitch in time saves nine.* The **maxim** is also drawn from practical experience, but turned into a general principle and rule of conduct: *People who live in glass houses shouldn't throw stones.* The **axiom** is the most abstract of the set, a statement embodying a recognized truth which is felt to need no proof: *Crime does not pay.* The wording of **axioms** is a little more flexible than that of the other four: it can for example be turned into the past tense.

All five types of saying express common wisdom, and they seem to evoke a widely held set of values which can be used to bring people on side. With their more or less fixed wording, many can be invoked without even being quoted in full. You only have to say "People who live in glass houses" to remind an audience of that maxim, and of how vulnerable they are. Many an argument has deflected a challenge or gathered strength in this way.

aping or apeing

Both these spellings seem to have their adherents. A majority (58%) of the 1100 respondents to the Langscape survey (1998–2001) preferred **apeing** to **aping**. Yet in both British and American databases, all examples of the word were spelled **aping**. The shorter spelling is of course the more regular one: see further under -e section 1.

apoplectic or apoplexic

See under -ctic/-xic.

apostrophe

This has two distinct meanings:
1. a punctuation mark, for which see **apostrophes** (next entry);
2. the rhetorical practice of "turning aside" (translating the Greek word as literally as one can).

The term **apostrophe** was first used of dramatic speeches in which an actor, turning aside from fellow actors on stage, directs his remarks towards the audience. It may be an appeal to someone present, or an invocation to an absent party. An example of the latter is found on the lips of Shakespeare's Antony in *Julius Caesar*:

> "O Cicero, thou shouldst have been present at this hour"

In other literary works, poetry or prose, an **apostrophe** is any section in which the author diverts attention away from the main narrative with an invocation. In his novel *Lolita*, Nabokov does it with *"Gentlemen of the jury,"* and *"Gentlewomen of the jury."*

apostrophes

As punctuation marks, **apostrophes** are used primarily for indicating:
1. the omission of a letter or letters from a word
2. possession or attribution

In spite of its Greek name, the *apostrophe* began to be used as a punctuation mark only in C17. It was first and foremost a mark of omission, as in *think'st* and *mislik'd*, where the vowel was dropped from the verb's suffix to maintain the rhythm of verse. **Apostrophes** have also been put to use with certain kinds of abbreviations in writing, e.g. *C'tee* for *committee* (see **contractions** section 1).

The use of **apostrophes** to mark possession grew out of their use to mark omission. In earlier centuries the genitive suffix for many nouns had been *-es*; and though it had long been contracted to plain *-s* without any obvious problems of communication, C17 scholars wanted to indicate the lost letter. Some even assumed that a genitive expression like *the kings castle* was really a contraction of *the king his castle,* and so the **apostrophe** in *the king's castle* marked the remnant of the hypothetical lost word. The oddity of this explanation for examples such as *the queen's ship* – where the pronoun would have been *her* – seemed to escape attention.

Apostrophes became the regular mark of possession on singular nouns during C18, and were extended to plural nouns in C19. Their sense of possession was at one time so strong that it was thought improper to say *the table's legs,* because this seemed to attribute possessive powers to something inanimate. Scruples of this kind have long since gone by the board, and daily papers are full of phrases like *today's announcement* and *Japan's ambassador,* where the **apostrophe** marks association or affiliation rather than possession.

The role of **apostrophes** has thus expanded in several ways over four centuries. Though no longer used for the lost verb inflection, they now serve to mark omissions and contractions of other kinds within the verb phrase, as in *it's, I'll, we'd* and *John's not here,* as well as *hasn't* and *don't.* (See further under **contractions** section 2.)

1 Standard uses of apostrophes with nouns are as follows:
* *apostrophe s* for singular nouns, marking possession or attribution, as in *a spectator's car, the class's response.* It makes no difference for common nouns if they end in an *s* or not, whereas proper nouns ending in *s* may be given special treatment (see section 3 below).
* *apostrophe s* for plural nouns not ending in *-s,* such as *women's work, the mice's squeaking.*
* an **apostrophe** alone for the possessive of plural nouns ending in *-s,* as in *the spectators' cheers.*

Note that the *apostrophe s* is normally added to the final word of a compound possessive expression, as in *mother-in-law's tongue* or *Laurel and Hardy's humor.* But when a compound phrase identifies two independent possessors, the *apostrophe s* may be added to both, as in *her father's and mother's names.*
◊ For the choice between *apostrophe s* and **apostrophe** alone in *each others* and other ambiguous cases, see under **number**.

2 The disappearing apostrophe. Apostrophes are not now obligatory in a number of kinds of expressions. They include:
* plural nouns in phrases which express affiliation, for example, *teachers college* and *senior citizens centre.* This C20 trend is widespread in the English-speaking world. Burchfield (1996) notes it in corporate names and titles such as *Diners Club* and *Farmers Weekly,* while *The Right Word at the Right Time* (1985) had already found it in British institutions such as *Sports Council, Parks Department* and some generic items such as *trades union.* In the US it's recognized by the American Associated Press stylebook, and for corporate and institutional names (e.g. *Department of Veterans Affairs*) by the *Chicago Manual of Style* (2003). The *Guide to Canadian Usage* (1997) finds both older and newer practices in *Teachers' Federation* and *Music Educators Association.* The Australian government *Style Manual* (2002) recommends elimination of **apostrophes** on plural nouns used attributively (see **adjectives** section 1). This makes for consistency in items such as *drivers licence, girls school, proofreaders marks,* where the **apostrophe** doesn't mark possession – and the time spent worrying about whether it should really be *driver's licence* or *drivers' licence* would be better used elsewhere. But there are special cases which seem anomalous without the *apostrophe s,* such as *Children's Book Week* (because "childrens" is not a regular form of the word), and *A Visitor's Guide to Darwin,* where the plural form would seem discrepant with the preceding *A* (cf. *Visitors Guide to Darwin*). Thus context is the final arbiter as to whether **apostrophes** are needed, as always.

* plural expressions of time and space, such as *five weeks leave* (compare *a week's leave*), and *three kilometres distance* (cf. *a kilometre's distance*). **Apostrophes** are not critical in quantitative expressions like these, because they work attributively, like the examples discussed in the previous paragraph. The **apostrophe** is routinely omitted from plural quantitative nouns in US newspapers, and it's a recognized practice for time expressions in Canada (*Editing Canadian English,* 2000), in the UK (Butcher, 1992), and in Australia, according to the government *Style Manual* (2002).
* numbers and dates, such as *in his 60s, fly 767s, during the 1980s.* All the regional style manuals including the *Chicago Manual* (2003) agree on this. **Apostrophes** are usually there in the plural of single numbers, as in *All the 2's and 3's were missing*.
* sets of letters, such as *MPs, PhDs, IOUs.* One advantage of not using the **apostrophe** in these plural initialisms is that it's then available for the possessive, as in *MP's action under scrutiny*. Single letters in lower case still usually mark the plural with **apostrophes**, as in *Dot the i's and cross the t's.* (See further under **letters as words**.)
* placenames involving possessive forms. **Apostrophes** are not required at all in placenames in the US and Australia, thanks to intervention by the Board on Geographic Names and the Geographical Names Board respectively. This action obviates the problem of unpredictable use of **apostrophes** in British placenames, where *Kings Cross* and *St Albans* contrast with *King's Lynn* and *St Martin's,* and the **apostrophe** stands between *St Helens* in Lancashire and *St Helen's* on the Isle of Wight. Individual names may be checked against the British *Post Office Guide,* and the *Oxford Atlas* gazetteer. In Canada, where practice is also variable, the authority is the Canadian Permanent Committee on Geographical Names.
* company names such as *Harrods, McDonalds, Woolworths.* The absence (or presence) of the **apostrophe** is of course fixed by trademark. In Canada the 1977 Charter of the the the French Language requires anglophone companies to drop the English possessive from their names when operating in Quebec.

3 Apostrophes with personal names ending in *-s.* What to do for the possessive form of proper names ending in *-s* has led to a variety of opinions and still-evolving practices. The earlier convention was to exempt all of them from the regular *apostrophe s,* and mark them with just an **apostrophe**, as in *Jones', Jesus', Keats', Robbins'* etc. This general rule has since been reduced to a few special cases:

a) literary, classical and religious persons whose names end in *s* should have just the **apostrophe**. All others have the full *apostrophe s:*
   Jones's   Menzies's   Keats'   Jesus'
   Xerxes'   Euripides'
b) literary, classical and religious persons whose names consist of two or more syllables and end in *s,* should have the plain **apostrophe**. All others have the regular *apostrophe s:*
   Jones's   Menzies's   Keats's   Jesus'
   Xerxes'   Euripides'
c) any name whose last syllable is pronounced with a long "eez" sound should have just the **apostrophe**,

whereas others have *apostrophe s:*
   Jones's   Menzies'   Keats's   Jesus's
   Xerxes'   Euripides'
d) any name whose possessive form is pronounced with the same number of syllables as the plain form should have the plain **apostrophe**. The application of this rule depends of course on the vagaries of pronunciation. Do most people pronounce the possessive of *Jones* with one or two syllables? (Perhaps it depends on who you are keeping up with!) Apart from this, rules such as (a) to (c) overlap in their application, and the outcome depends on which one prevails. British authorities such as Butcher (1992) and *Hart's Rules* (1983), which admit rules based on pronunciation, effectively leave it up to the individual, which is fine if both writer and editor agree on this.

Much greater consistency is achieved by doing away with special cases, and treating names ending in *-s* to the full *apostrophe -s,* just like any other noun. This is recommended by the *Chicago Manual* (2003) and the Australian government *Style Manual* (2002). The practice is easy to apply, and deals effectively with English and foreign names, French names ending in a silent "s," such as *Camus's* and *Dumas's,* not to mention *Arkansas's.* The *Chicago Manual* still allows for a little of conventions (a) and (c) above, and acknowledges the lingering use of the **apostrophe** alone after names ending in "s," in some quarters. *Canadian English Usage* (1997) also recognizes the classical tradition (a), while noting that it is "always acceptable to add *-s* to a name that ends in *s.*"

◊ For the choice between *it's* and *its,* see **its**.
◊ The choice between using *apostrophe s* and nothing at all in statements like *They wouldn't hear of Henry('s) coming* is a matter of grammar. See further under **-ing**.

4 The superfluous apostrophe. The use of **apostrophes** in ordinary plural words, sometimes known as the "greengrocer's apostrophe," is familiar in hand-written shop signs everywhere in the English-speaking world: *banana's for sale; fresh prawn's; latest video's.* In the US, the "Great Apostrophe Plague" is noted in John Simon's aptly named *Paradigms Lost* (1980). In Australia, the so-called "Apostrophe Man" keeps tabs on "apostroflation," with a constant supply of examples to report to the *Sydney Morning Herald,* both downmarket (*auto's*) and upmarket (*gateaux's*). Superfluous **apostrophes** are a symptom of unedited prose and of the inexperienced writer, who is inclined to add a "flying comma" to any final *s* for good measure. As applications of the **apostrophe** begin to shrink, expert writers and editors are also less certain about its use, hence the many details of this entry. Burchfield, quoted in a 1985 news article (see *Webster's English Usage,* 1989), commented that the **apostrophe** had probably reached the limits of its usefulness, and might only be retained for contractions. A return to C17 simplicities with the **apostrophe** might not be a backward step.

◊ For the use/nonuse of **apostrophes** in locative expressions such as *at the printers,* see **local genitive**.

appall or appal
See under **single for double**.

apparatus
For the plural of this word, see under **-us** section 2.

appareled or apparelled
See under **-l-/-ll-**.

appendixes and appendices
Like many loanwords from Latin, **appendix** has two plurals: the Latin **appendices** and the regular English **appendixes** (see further **-x** section 2). Some reserve **appendixes** for medical references to the colonic appendage, and make **appendices** the plural for the sections of additional material at the back of a book. Americans use both plurals for the latter, but are somewhat more inclined to use **appendixes**, by the evidence of CCAE where it outnumbers **appendices** by about 3:2 in referring to the back end of a book or report. The instances of **appendices**, as in *found only in the appendices of history,* suggest its conservation by writers with a literary bent. The American data generally lines up with *Webster's Third* (1986), which puts **appendixes** ahead of the classical plural. British preferences are quite the opposite. The *Oxford Dictionary* (1989) prioritizes **appendices**, and its prevalence is underscored by data from the BNC, where **appendices** outnumbers **appendixes** by a factor of more than 30:1. Yet the handful of instances of **appendixes** referred to sections added at the back of a book or report, as they might in American English. The supposed line of demarcation between **appendixes** and **appendices** breaks down in both the US and the UK.

The medical operation of excising the **appendix** is called an *appendectomy* in the US and Canada. In the UK *appendicectomy* remains just as common, judging by their relative showing (11:6) in the BNC. But in English worldwide, the shorter form clearly dominates. An internet search (Google, 2002) returned 13 instances of *appendectomy* for every 1 of *appendicectomy*.

appointer or appointor
See under **-er/-or**.

apposition
Just what counts as **apposition**, and how to punctuate the phrases *in apposition* are the major issues. Grammarians differ over the criteria for **apposition**, such as whether the *appositives* have to be grammatically identical in form, juxtaposed, and phrased so that either could be omitted without impairing the syntax: see the *Comprehensive Grammar of English* (1985). In fact the three sentences below all present **apposition** in its strictest form.
> *Swami Svaratnaram, their yoga teacher,*
> *prescribed the routines.*
> *She was born in Pymble, a suburb of Edinburgh.*
> *He ordered a martini, the drink that went with the*
> *company he kept.*
Appositives like those, being syntactically equal in rank, are effectively *nonrestrictive* (see **relative clauses** section 4). They are therefore punctuated with commas, as shown.

Yet various familiar kinds of **apposition** are *restrictive,* in that one *appositive* serves to define the other, and their syntactic relationship is one of dependency. Like *restrictive relative clauses,* they are not separated by commas, witness:
> *the soprano Kiri Ti Kanawa*
> *the year 2000*
> *your brother James*
> *the River Ganges*
> *the term "responsible government"*
In the regular forms of proper names, the title or descriptor may be seen as having a *restrictive appositive* function: *Lord Mountbatten, President Eisenhower; Mount Egmont; Lake Titicaca.* But when such names are glossed, as in *Eisenhower, president of the US from 1953–1961,* the comma marks a *nonrestrictive apposition.* The titles in such *appositions* do not need to have capital letters: see **capital letters** section 1d.

A *parenthesis* differs from an *appositive* in not being grammatically matched with another constituent of the sentence (the subject, object etc.). It is therefore usually set off with brackets: see further under **parenthesis**.

appraise, apprise and apprize
These spellings intersect with two distinct words. **Appraise** meaning "estimate the value of" always contrasts with **apprise** meaning "notify." **Apprize** served as a variant for **appraise** in older American English, and in Scottish law, but is now the American alternate for **apprise**, according to *Merriam-Webster* (2000). The chances of the two uses being confused are reduced by the fact that they are differently construed:
> *The sheriff apprized the ship's cargo.*
> (= **appraise**)
> *The sheriff apprized them of its value.* (= **apprise**)
The *of* construction is characteristic of **apprise**, whether the verb is active or passive:
> *The company was apprised of the cargo's value.*
Compare *The ship's cargo was appraised for its value.*

Apprise is increasingly a rather formal word, and much less common than **appraise** in data from CCAE and the BNC. There's no sign of **apprize** in either the American or the British database. Institutional uses of **appraise** in assessing work performance have no doubt boosted its frequency, as well as that of the related abstract noun *appraisal.* It outnumbers *apprisal* by more than 1000:1 in the reference databases – and there are none of *apprizal.*

appropriacy and appropriateness
Dictionaries are unanimous that **appropriateness** is the abstract noun for *appropriate.* Yet **appropriacy** is very occasionally heard, and breaks the ice in the BNC with a handful of examples from rather academic writing. There are analogues for it, in the relationship between *literate* and *literacy* or *adequate* and *adequacy* – if it needs any explanation.

apropos
This telescopes the French phrase *à propos* meaning "to the purpose." As a simple adverb or adjective, **apropos** means "right or opportune" in relation to whatever is going on: *The remark was apropos.* But when followed by *of* and another word or phrase, e.g. *apropos of the election,* it sets up a prepositional phrase. At the start of an utterance *apropos of* is used to highlight a new topic of conversation, and therefore serves as a **discourse marker** (see further under that heading). It often signals a change of subject.

Sometimes speakers change the topic of conversation more or less abruptly, with the phrase *apropos of nothing*. Whether the new topic is really unrelated to what went before, and entirely unmotivated, is for the listener to judge. The phrase still implies that the speaker is very conscious of altering the topic of conversation.

Apropos is usually written as a single word, according to dictionaries everywhere in the English-speaking world. However the *Oxford Dictionary* (1989) notes the French form *à propos* with accent as an alternative. British and American databases provide a handful of examples in which it appears spaced as *a propos,* without the accent.
◊ See also **malapropisms**.

apt to or likely to
See **liable**.

aquarium
The Victorian *aquavivarium* quickly translated itself into **aquarium**, and into a public and domestic institution. The English plural **aquariums** is strongly preferred by Americans, by its dominance of the data from CCAE. But their British counterparts use both **aquariums** and the Latin plural **aquaria**. The two plurals appear in roughly equal numbers of BNC texts – even in the same text – suggesting that the choice is quite open. See further under **-um**.

-ar
This ending appears on a few nouns and many adjectives in English. The nouns are a mixed bag, representing:
* people:
  beggar burglar bursar friar pedlar
  scholar vicar
* objects and animals:

agar	altar	briar	budgerigar
calendar	caterpillar	cellar	cigar
collar	cougar	dinar	dollar
exemplar	fulmar	grammar	hangar
molar	nectar	pillar	poplar
seminar	vinegar		

In some cases, the **-ar** is a direct legacy of medieval Latin. *Bursar* is from *bursarius,* and *calendar* reflects *calendarium* (see further under **calendar or calender**). Others, e.g. *collar* and *pillar,* were written with *-er* in earlier English and later respelled with **-ar**, perhaps to show that they were not agent words and that the ending was not really a suffix (see further under **-er**).

The desire to differentiate homonyms probably helps to account for others like *altar* (as opposed to *alter*) and *hangar* (as opposed to *hanger*). The spelling of *liar* i.e. "one who tells lies," differentiates it from the possible agent word *lier* ("one who lies around"). But the **-ar** spelling seems awkward for words like *beggar* and *pedlar,* which also look like agent words and might be expected to have *-er* spellings. In American English *pedlar* has been replaced by *peddler,* whether it refers to someone *peddling* cocaine in New York, or pots and pans in the Alleghenies. In fact, neither *beggar* nor *pedlar* is an agent word. Their origins are rather obscure, but they appeared fully fledged in Middle English, and the verbs *beg* and *peddle* are backformations from them (see **backformation**). Here again the -ar spellings

show that, historically speaking, they are not agent words.

Apart from that mixed bag of nouns, -ar is regularly found on adjectives borrowed from classical or medieval Latin. See for example:

angular	cellular	circular
crepuscular	familiar	globular
insular	jocular	linear
lunar	muscular	particular
perpendicular	planar	polar
rectangular	regular	singular
solar	stellar	titular
triangular	vehicular	vulgar

◊ For the choice between *peninsular* and *peninsula,* see **peninsula**.

Arabian, Arabic or Arab
All three words serve as adjectives relating to the *Arabian Peninsula,* where the first Muslim state was established around AD 600, known now as *Saudi Arabia.* **Arabian** is used in general references to the culture and geography of the region, as in *Arabian Nights* and *Arabian deserts.* **Arabic** mostly refers to the language, scripts and symbols associated with *Arab peoples,* and is applied to the languages of countries such as Syria, Jordan, Irak, Egypt, Tunisia, Algeria. Curiously, what we know as *Arabic numerals* originated in India, and are known by the **Arabs** themselves as "Indian numerals." But **Arab** is now the most frequent and widely used adjective, no doubt because of the power and influence of **Arabs** outside *Arabia* itself: hence the *Arab countries/leaders/nations* of the *Arab League.*

Arabic loanwords
Words borrowed into English from Arabic languages often vary in their spelling because of their variability in the source language. Arabic words are constructed out of triliteral roots (i.e. roots consisting of three consonants), which are combined with particular vowels to form sets in the same semantic field. Thus the root *k t b* appears in the word for "book" as well as "write." In fact the vowels vary somewhat from dialect to dialect, and the same word borrowed at different times and places could be differently transliterated in English. This helps to account for variants such as *kabob/kebab* etc., and also the active respelling of older Arabic loans such as *sheik.* See further under **kebab, kilim, sheikh, sheriff.**

arbor or arbour
See under **-or/-our.**

arced or arcked, and arcing or arcking
See under **-c/-ck-.**

arch-/archa-/archae-/arche-/archi-
These five forms represent just two prefixes, both inherited from Greek:
1 **arch-/archi-** meaning "principal, chief" and
2 **arch(a)(e)-/archi-** meaning "beginning"
Words embodying the first prefix are:

archangel	archbishop	archduke
archenemy	archiepiscopal	archipelago
architect		

Words embodying the second prefix are:

archaic	archaism	arch(a)eology
arch(a)eometry	archetype	archiplasm
architrave		

45

The different forms and pronunciations of the prefixes are the result of the way they were treated in Latin, Italian, French and English – not strictly in line with the Greek. The choice between *archaeometry* and *archeometry* etc. is essentially a matter of American or British spelling: see further under **ae/e**.

In fact, the two prefixes seem to have developed from the same source. The Greek word *arche* meant both "beginning" and "principality," just as the verb *archein* meant both "be first" and "govern or rule." The two come together in *archives,* documents which record the origins of things, and which were kept at the Greek *archeion* or headquarters of the local government.

-arch/-archy

The Greek suffix **-arch** means "chief" or "ruler," much like the prefix *arch-/archi-* (see previous entry). It forms nouns like *matriarch, monarch* and *patriarch.* Complementing it is the suffix *-archy* meaning "rule or system of government," which forms the corresponding abstract nouns:

>   *matriarchy   monarchy   patriarchy*

as well as

>   *anarchy   hierarchy   oligarchy.*

archaeology or archeology

The choice between these is not just a matter of American or British spelling, though **archaeology** is given priority in the *Oxford Dictionary* (1989), and **archeology** in *Webster's Third* (1986). The response patterns to the Langscape survey (1998–2001) were more complex, with 25% of British respondents endorsing **archeology**, and more than 70% of those from Continental Europe. Around 70% of US respondents endorsed **archeology**, but this means a substantial minority preferred **archaeology**; and in American data from CCAE, **archaeology** outnumbered **archeology** in the ratio of 5:2. For *archaeologists* the world over, including the US, the first spelling projects the flavor of antiquity. Here as often, specialists differ from the general public in the spellings they prefer. See further under **ae/e**.

archaisms

These are words and expressions that belong to times past. Feudal relations of past centuries are embedded in *liege lord* and *yeoman* from medieval times, and distinctive socio-political roles in the *emancipists* and *suffragettes* of more recent history. References to the *warming pan, chamber pot, penny farthing* and *horse-drawn carriage* help to conjure up material aspects of earlier historical periods. Measuring distances in *leagues* and quoting prices in *guineas* have the same *archaizing* effect.

Archaisms of another kind are the ordinary function words and expressions which have somehow gone out of fashion. Examples are: *forsooth, methinks, howsoever* and *verily.* They have less power to set a particular historical period, and are more likely to draw attention back to the writer and the writer's style. They suggest a certain self-conscious use of language, which can either be effectively ironic, or annoyingly precious. The boundary between *archaic* and old-fashioned language is somewhat fluid and subjectively determined. Whether you class words like *albeit, goodly, perchance* and *rejoice* as **archaisms** or just old-fashioned words depends on individual education and experience of language. Those who read older literature are more likely to feel that such words are part of the continuum of the English language, and only a little old-fashioned. Those whose reading comes from the last decades of C20 (plus C21) will probably feel the words are *archaic.*

archeo- or archaeo-

See under **arch-**.

archipelago

For the plural of this word, see under **-o**.

archives or archive

The plural **archives**, used to refer to an organized or institutional collection of historical documents, is increasingly challenged by the singular **archive** in American and British English. Alongside the older usage found in *National Archives, York Minster archives* etc., stand newer institutions such as the *National Sound Archive* and the *Urban Archive Center* etc. **Archives** is still in the majority in both names and ordinary phrases, in data from CCAE and the BNC. Yet computer *archiving* systems show **archive** taking on the role of verb/participle, and its use as attributive adjective can be seen in *archive disks/footage/sources/tapes,* among numerous examples in the databases. With all these grammatical roles, the form **archive** looks set to command the future, though the **archives** established so far will not lose their importance.

Arctic or arctic

The capitalized form is standard in geographical references to such things as the *Arctic Circle, Arctic Ocean* and *Arctic Zone.* The latter is also commonly referred to simply as the **Arctic**. Other strictly adjectival uses of the word are lower-cased, whether in the names of identified fauna and flora – *arctic fox, arctic tern, arctic willow* – or more generally in reference to *arctic temperatures* and *arctic clothing.* The plural form **arctics** is used in American and Canadian English to refer to the warm, waterproof overshoes needed in the extreme cold.
◊ Compare **Antarctic(a)**.

aren't I

See under **ain't**.

Argentina, Argentine, Argentinean or Argentinian

These all connect with the large South American state variously known as **Argentina**, the **Argentine**, and the *Argentine Republic.* Data from both American and British sources confirm that **Argentina** is now many times more popular than the **Argentine**. The databases also show that **Argentine** is the most common form of the adjective, strongly preferred over **Argentinian/Argentinean** in both the US and the UK.

When referring to the inhabitants of **Argentina**, there's again more than one possibility: *Argentines* (in three syllables), and *Argentineans* or *Argentinians* (in five). Americans prefer *Argentines,* by the evidence of CCAE; whereas *Argentinians* is the preference of British writers registered in the BNC. Neither database has much evidence of *Argentinean(s),* though

Webster's Third (1986) gave them priority over
Argentinian(s). The *Oxford Dictionary* (1989) has
Argentinian alone.
◊ For other examples of *-ean/-ian,* see under **-an.**

argot

This C19 French loanword refers to the jargon of a
sharply defined class of people, what C21 linguists
might call a "sociolect." As originally applied, **argot**
meant the language of the underworld, e.g. thieves or
convicts. These days it can be associated with any
community or activity, as in the following examples
from British and American databases: *academic argot,
teenage argot, street argot, Unix argot;* or *the argot of
CB radio / horse racing / defense contracting* – not to
mention that of stockbrokers, involved in *trading
(arbitrage, in the argot).*

arguably

There's a latent ambiguity in **arguably** as to whether
one is arguing for or against a proposition. The
affirmative use is often spelled out by an
accompanying superlative or evaluative expression,
as in *arguably the most powerful package, arguably a
hazardous occupation, arguably the buy of the season,*
among more than 600 examples in the BNC. The word
allows writers to have it both ways, to say that "a case
can be made out" without actually committing
themselves to it. The equivocation takes over in some
instances, as in *what is merely arguably right,* and the
word comes closer to its negative use "capable of
being disputed." But whether distanced from or closer
to a given point of view, **arguably** leaves the advocacy
to someone else.
◊ For the choice between *inarguably* and *unarguably,*
see **inarguable.**

argument

Many things pass for **argument** which do not merit
the name. Those who would persuade all too often
shortcircuit the argumentative process, by attacking
or appealing directly to the interests of the listener
(*argumentum ad hominem*), or to the listener's
hip-pocket nerve (in neo-Latin *ad crumenam*). The
argument may be just a *non sequitur, ad hoc,* or *ex
silentio;* and worse perhaps, goes on *ad infinitum.*

A proper **argument** addresses the issues
(*argumentum ad rem*), and develops either inductively
(*a posteriori*) or deductively (*a priori*). We owe these
Latin phrases to scholars in rhetoric and philosophy
between C16 and C18 (see individual heading for more
about each). A few other argumentative tactics and
tricks go by English names, for example: *begging the
question,* and posing a *leading question.* (See also
under **analogy,** and **fallacies.**)

The spelling of **argument** (minus the *-e* of *argue*)
looks like an exception to the rule for words formed
with *-ment* (see under **-e**). In fact the word was
borrowed ready-made from French, with its spelling
harnessed to the Latin *argumentum.*
◊ For what grammarians call the *arguments of the
verb,* see under **cases.**

-arian

A latter-day suffix, **-arian** has developed from several
sources. Some of the words embodying it, like
librarian and *veterinarian* derive from medieval Latin
words ending in *-arius;* while others like *egalitarian*

are modeled on French antecedents. Many have
simply been formed by analogy in English. Whether
adjective or noun, they refer to attitudes of mind, and
moral, religious or political beliefs. For example:

antiquarian	*authoritarian*	*disciplinarian*
humanitarian	*libertarian*	*millenarian*
parliamentarian	*proletarian*	*sabbatarian*
sectarian	*totalitarian*	*utilitarian*
vegetarian		

Note that in *grammarian, Hungarian* and others, the
-ar belongs to the word's stem: see further under **-an.**

arise or rise

See **rise.**

Aristotelian or Aristotelean

All modern dictionaries give preference to
Aristotelian and for some it's the only spelling
recognized. Though the original *Oxford Dictionary*
(1884–1928) preferred the classically backed
Aristotelean, it recognized that **Aristotelian** was
more common even then.
◊ For other words which vary between *-ian* and *-ean,*
see under **-an.**

armfuls or armsful

See under **-ful.**

armor or armour

See under **-or/-our.**

aroma

In spite of its classical appearance, **aroma** is now
always pluralized in the English way. It originated as
the Greek word for "spice," and kept its Greek plural
aromata when borrowed into Latin. This form of the
plural was once used a little in English, according to
the *Oxford Dictionary* (1989). It also explains why the
French for "aroma" (in our sense) is *aromate.* But
contemporary English uses **aroma** for a distinctive,
usually attractive smell, and the plural **aromas.**

-aroo

This jokey suffix probably owes something to
trans-Pacific contact in both C19 and C20. In US
English **-aroo** was highly productive in the 1940s,
generating many casual and short-lived coinages
such as

congaroo	*jivaroo*	*jugaroo*	*kissamaroo*
vibaroo	*whackaroo*		

as well as

babyroo pepperoo snoozamoroo switcheroo

with alternative spelling of the penultimate syllable.
The journal *American Speech* (Bolinger, 1941) found
the source for **-aroo** in Spanish, as naturalized in the
American word *buckaroo* and its Spanish counterpart
vaquero "cowboy." Bolinger noted "coincidental
support" from the Australian word *kangaroo,*
providing the word with its bouncy overtones. Yet it
seems significant that **-aroo** became highly
productive during World War II, at just the time when
American servicemen enjoyed *R and R* ("rest and
recreation") in Australia.

For Australians, **-aroo** is a neutral element of
Aboriginal origin, found in the names of fauna and
flora, including *kangaroo, wallaroo, calgaroo,
willaroo,* and in placenames in several eastern states:
Coorparoo (QLD), *Gundaroo* (NSW), *Liparoo* (VIC). It

is also the formative element in *jackaroo,* the C19 Australian word for a "farmhand," as well as *jillaroo,* his C20 female counterpart. The coincidental uses of *jackaroo* and *buckaroo* suggest early trans-Pacific communication, though scanty evidence makes it hard to say in which direction the influence operated. Later Australian and New Zealand (NZ) formations of the 1940s, such as *jambaroo, jigamaroo, shivaroo* belong to the wartime vogue for **-aroo**, and mimic the American coinages. Both in the US and Australia, some were spelled with **-eroo** (see under that heading). Most were too transient to become standardized one way or the other.

around and round
Large differences in the regional frequencies of these two set the scene. As adverb or preposition, **around** is much commoner than **round** in American English, by more than 40:1 in the Brown corpus. In British English they come much closer but the majority goes the other way, with **round** outnumbering **around** by just 7:6 in the LOB corpus. **Round** has uses as an adjective (*a round face*), a noun (*theatre in the round*) and verb (*she rounded on him*), none of which are fulfilled by **around.** But **around** is the American preference for several adverb and prepositional uses which might be performed by **round** or other words in British English. Compare:

> *He looked around the room / round the room.*
> *They hadn't seen anyone around/about.*
> *A shield of prayer was thrown around him / round him.*

In fact **around** is now common enough in such applications among British writers, as Burchfield (1997) demonstrates. Even the use of **around** to mean "approximately" is far from being distinctly American usage. There was no statistically significant difference in data from the Brown and LOB corpora on this point (see Peters, 1998a). Examples from LOB such as *a crowd of around 30,000* and *the price rose to around $253* show that this use of **around** to mean "approximately" is at home in Britain.

arouse or rouse
See **rouse.**

arrant or errant
Collocations such as *arrant knave* and *knight errant* give an antique flavor to both of these adjectives, yet both have some current uses. The sense of "wandering/straying" was once common to both, and remains in both physical and figurative uses of **errant.** British data from the BNC presents examples such as *errant feelings/temper* as well as an *errant foot* and the *errant strand of hair.* But by far the commonest use is in reference to persons who are in some way out of line, and there is mild censure in *errant husband, errant secretary, errant citizen* etc. Other **errant** persons in American data from CCAE included the *errant sailor/builder/doctor/lawyer* and *arbitrageur.* Both databases have **errant** used in reference to stray bullets, but Americans apply it more freely to a vehicle which has gone off track, whether *bus, light-plane* or *satellite,* and to devices which play up, such as computers, radio transmitters and even domestic alarms. American English also makes much more use of **errant** in reporting on misdirected shots by golfers and other sportsmen.

In **arrant** the sense of waywardness is now overlaid with heavy censure. Its only surviving roles are as an intensifier of usually negatively toned nouns, particularly *arrant nonsense,* though in BNC data it also goes with *sexism, rudeness, hypocrisy* and *mischief-making. Arrant coward* and *arrant coxcomb* show more direct censure of the person, as does *arrant anti-Semite* from CCAE. Yet **arrant** makes little showing in either database. The few British examples seem hoary with age, and the mere handful of American ones put it close to extinction. Further evidence of its decline can be seen in mistaken uses of **errant** for **arrant** in each database: *errant nonsense, an errant traitor.* Here and elsewhere, **errant** is gaining ground.

ars gratia artis
This sententious phrase borrowed from Latin means "art for the sake of art" or "art for art's sake." In its French form "l'art pour l'art," it was much touted by C19 French Romantics and used in support of the notion that art could be indifferent to moral and social values. The phrase is wonderfully enigmatic, and can be quoted either to invoke a lofty aestheticism, or to justify irresponsible artistic activity. It serves as the motto of MGM films, displayed at the start of each movie along with the roaring lion. Whether you read the motto as an artistic affirmation or an ironic comment will depend on whether it prefaces *Out of Africa* or *Tarzan the Apeman.*

artefact or artifact
See **artifact.**

articles
This is a grammatical term for two kinds of words: the *definite article the* and the *indefinite article a/an.* **Articles** are the commonest words on the page: almost every English sentence has one. Yet their role and meaning is subtle, and often a problem for people learning English as a second language.

The prime function of **articles** is to signal that a noun is to follow, sooner or later. See for example:

> *the brown fox*
> *the proverbially quick brown fox*
> *a sports car*
> *an expensive state-of-the-art sports car*

Articles normally come first in the noun phrase. However both *a* and *the* can be preceded by predeterminers (see under **determiners**); and *the* by bulkier quantifiers such as *one of, some of, none of.*

The chief difference between *definite* and *indefinite articles* is in the specifications they put on the following noun. The *indefinite article* indicates that the noun is being mentioned for the first time in the discourse in which it occurs. See for example:

> *On my way through Hong Kong, I bought a camera.*

Compare the effect of the *definite article:*

> *When I showed the camera to customs, they charged me 33% duty.*

Using the word *the* implies that you have already referred to the object or concept in question. In this case, "the camera" must be the one bought in Hong Kong. It isn't any camera, but one for which some specific information has already been supplied.

Note however that writers can supply that specific information immediately after the noun in question, as in:

> The camera which I bought in Hong Kong cost me 33% duty.

Still the use of *the* implies that the noun will be detailed in the immediate context. The chief exceptions are universal and generic uses of the *definite article,* such as *the air* and *the tiger is an endangered species* (see **the** section 2). Those apart, the *definite article* is one of various devices which make for cohesion in English. (See further under **the** and **coherence or cohesion**.)

The use and choice of **articles** differs slightly in some regions of the English-speaking world. Where Americans speak of being *at the university* or *in the hospital,* the British would say *at university* or *in hospital.* Use of the *definite article* varies within the UK – being less used in northern dialects than in the south. The selection of *a* or *an* for the *indefinite article* is less predictable in the US than in the UK. In American speech *a* may be used instead of *an* before words beginning with a vowel sound: *a area, a oven.* See further under **a or an**.

artifact or artefact

All major dictionaries recognize both spellings, but while **artifact** is cited first by American and Canadian dictionaries, the British and Australian prefer **artefact**. The *Oxford Dictionary* (1884–1928) gave preference to **artifact**, but changed to **artefact** in the second edition (1989). Data from the BNC confirms that **artefact** is now more common and more widely used in British English, by a factor of 6:1; whereas CCAE data shows that in American English **artifact** is used almost exclusively.

The word has few close relatives in English, the nearest being *artifice* and *artificial.* The analogy with those no doubt helps to maintain **artifact**, whereas **artefact** has little to support it but closeness to the original Latin *arte facto* ("made by art").

-ary/-ery/-ory

In British pronunciation, these three suffixes all sound alike. Whether the vowel is *a, e* or *o,* it is pronounced as an indeterminate vowel (*schwa*) or eliminated entirely, and offers no clue to the spelling. American pronunciation meanwhile puts more stress on the first vowel of the suffix, and the sound is quite clearly one vowel or the other. Compare American and British ways of saying *dormitory* and *secretary.* Without the American pronunciation to help, grammar and meaning are the best way to sort them out.

Check first whether the word is an adjective or a noun.

*If it is an adjective, the ending is either **-ary** or **-ory**. Overall there are fewer ending in **-ory**. To discover which ones should be spelled **-ory**, have a look at the letters preceding the suffix. If they are *-at, -ct* or *-s,* you are most likely to be dealing with cases of **-ory**. See for example:

compulsory	cursory	derogatory
illusory	introductory	mandatory
obligatory	perfunctory	satisfactory
valedictory		

The very many words with **-ary** have other combinations of letters before the suffix:

complimentary	dietary	disciplinary
elementary	hereditary	plenary
revolutionary	rotary	rudimentary
solitary		

*If the word is a noun, the ending could be **-ary**, **-ery** or **-ory**. Overall there are more ending in **-ery** than either of the other two, but you can be more certain of the spelling by being aware of how these words fall into certain semantic groups. For example:

-ary These are typically either nouns referring to a person's role:

actuary	dignitary	legionary
mercenary	secretary	

Or else to something in which a collection of objects is to be found:

aviary	breviary	dictionary	dispensary
granary	library	rosary	summary

-ery These nouns may refer to general states or styles of behavior:

buffoonery	drudgery	flattery	mystery
savagery	slavery	snobbery	trickery

Or else to occupations, trades and the tools or goods associated with them:

archery	bakery	brewery
butchery	confectionery	drapery
grocery	hosiery	joinery
machinery	millinery	printery
saddlery	surgery	tannery
winery		

-ory Nouns ending this way typically refer to a place in terms of the characteristic activity that takes place there:

conservatory	depository	dormitory
laboratory	observatory	repository

◊ For the difference between **accessory/accessary**, **mandatory/mandatary** and **stationery/ stationary**, see individual entries.

as

This little conjunction provides many kinds of links in written English, including comparative, temporal and causative. It also serves as a relative pronoun, preposition and adverb. There are style and usage issues affecting all of these roles.

1 Comparative as. On its own, conjunctive **as** prefaces adverbial clauses:

> You can set up house there as you wish.
> They never join in as they used to.

The use of **as** rather than *like* in the second kind of sentence has long been prescribed in British English, though without recognition of the finer points. (See further at **like**.) Doubled up, **as** forms a correlative with itself, as in:

> as loud as they could
> not as difficult as she expected

When the comparison is negative, as in the last case, the word *so* can replace the first **as**: *not so difficult as she expected.* This alternation is established in some conventional positive expressions of this kind:

> as far as / so far as I'm concerned
> as long as / so long as they play ball.

2 Temporal and causative as. These are not problematic in themselves, but sometimes hard to distinguish:

> As he walked through the church, the organ began playing.
> He began to whistle the tune as no-one else was there.

Does **as** express cause or time in these cases? Time is more likely in the first and cause in the second, but either is possible. Such ambiguity does no harm in conversation; and poets or dramatists may indeed exploit it to allow more than one interpretation of the discourse. But in expository and argumentative prose, an ambiguous **as** may blur the structure of thinking. Research associated with the *Longman Grammar* (1999) showed that *causative* use of **as** was actually much rarer than *temporal* use across all spoken and written styles. American speakers and writers proved less inclined to make *causative* use of **as** than their British counterparts.

3 Relative as. This use of **as** ranges from the standard to the colloquial. In the following sentence it takes the place of the pronoun *who:*

> *Childcare facilities are available to all such staff as have been employed for more than two years.*

Burchfield (1997) confirms that the construction of *as* with *such* or *the same* remains standard in British English, and *Webster's English Usage* (1989) offers examples from contemporary American sources. Now mostly confined to American English is the contraction of **as** in *all's,* as in

> *All's you have to do is press a couple of buttons.*

The contraction is rather informal and rarely seen in print (only two examples in CCAE).

4 Prepositional as. The comparative use of **as** (*lonely as a cloud*), and projective use into a role or character (*as parents they were learning all the time*) is uncontroversial – except when followed by personal pronouns that distinguish subject and object (*I/me, he/him* etc.). In practice these constructions are rare in serious nonfiction, according to the *Longman Grammar;* and in fictional writing where they do freely appear, the subject and object pronouns are about equally used. In conversation the object pronouns hold sway.

5 Adverbial as. The uses of **as** as adverb are rather abstract, indicating restrictions on the time or scope of an action, for example *as now, as yet.* They are stylistically neutral, at home in various kinds of discourse. Compare:

> *as of June 19 / as from June 19*
> *as per your instructions*

These uses of **as** are commonly associated with contracts and business writing.

ascendant or ascendent

Most dictionaries have **ascendant** as the first spelling, whether the word is a noun or an adjective. In C19 the two spellings were given equal billing by the *Oxford Dictionary,* though even then citations ran heavily in favor of the *-ant* spelling. The phrase *in the ascendant,* borrowed from astrology, may have helped to popularize it.

Likewise *ascendancy* and *ascendance* seem to have prevailed over *ascendency* and *ascendence,* according to dictionaries and language databases. See further under **-ant/-ent.**

Asian or Asiatic

These words are almost equally old, but they are not now equally usable. In the US as well as the UK, **Asiatic** is felt to be disparaging, probably because of its use as a racial designator, as in the San Francisco *Asiatic Exclusion League* of 1907 (previously the *Japanese and Korean Exclusion League*), and the

anti-Asiatic riots in Vancouver (1906-7), against Hindus and Sikhs. American wartime nomenclature such as the *Asiatic campaign* and the *Asiatic-Pacific theater of operations* also carry hostile implications. Since the 1940s **Asian** has increasingly replaced **Asiatic** for all ordinary purposes: what were previously *Asiatic countries/people/art/languages* are now *Asian countries/people/art/languages.* In BNC data, **Asian** outnumbers **Asiatic** by almost 20:1 and in CCAE by more than 600:1.

The continuing uses of **Asiatic** in both databases are academic, in analyses of ancient Greek and near-Eastern cultures, and of Marxist theory on the *Asiatic mode of production.* Clearly the geographical reference points differ in ancient history and in political philosophy. Other rather generalized uses of the word are to be found in zoological and botanical names such as the *Asiatic clam / black bear / lily / bittersweet.*

The geographical reference points for **Asian** are just as diverse, and may involve any part or parts of that large continent. In British English **Asian** often connects with the Indian subcontinent in discussions on immigrants and immigration. In other contexts **Asian** can refer to Central Asia (*the central Asian khanates, including Khiva, Bukhara and Kokand*); or to Southeast Asia including the offshore islands (*S.E. Asian languages, including Korean, Japanese and Javanese*). In the US and Australia, this is probably the most common application of the word. Australians sometimes debate whether they too are "part of Asia," but the phrase raises questions of political and cultural identity rather than geography.

aside (from) or apart (from)

Americans use both these adverbs/prepositions, but are more inclined to **aside**, in the ratio of 5:4 in data from CCAE. British inclination runs the other way, so that **apart** outnumbers **aside** in the BNC by about 5:2. So despite regional preferences, both words are current in the UK as well as the US. The differing frequencies do however help to explain why **aside from**, meaning "not taken into account," is much less used in British English (the ratio is about 1:6 in BNC data); whereas **aside from** and **apart from** appear almost equally in American data from CCAE. Idioms such as *these things aside* and *aside from everything else* are also much less common in British English, where they are formulated with **apart** (Peters, 1998b).

aspect

This is part of the grammatical meaning of some verbs, interacting with the tense yet independent of it. It gives a perspective on the verb, indicating whether its action is complete or still going on. The difference is clear in:

> *The official party had arrived.*
> *The official party was arriving.*

Both verb phrases are in the past tense, but while the first is *perfect* in its **aspect** (i.e. the action is complete), the second is *imperfect* (also called *progressive, continuous* or *durative)* in its **aspect** (i.e. the action is still going on). In some languages this difference is shown entirely by the endings of the main verb, but English does it with a combination of the particular auxiliary verb and participle. The auxiliary *have* plus the past participle forms the *perfect aspect;* and a part of the verb *be* plus the present participle forms the *imperfect.* (See further under **auxiliary verbs** and **participles.**)

1 Use of the imperfect (-ing) aspect with stative verbs.
Standard English resists using the *imperfect aspect* with *stative verbs,* or rather, verbs used to represent timeless states or open facts. Instead they are expressed with the simple present:

Two and two make four.
Finland has many lakes.
Steve is overweight.
Everyone enjoys a party.
They spend little time watching television.

Verbs expressing mental and emotional states also resist the *imperfect.* For most contexts, it could not be used to paraphrase:

I love detective stories.
She believes everything he says.
They spend little time on the garden.
We all hope for a better future.

When *imperfect* forms are used with such verbs, they seem to point at the recency or temporariness of the state:

They are (now) spending little time on the garden.
We are all hoping for a better future (in these difficult times).

In some regional varieties of English, notably Indian English, the *imperfect* is nevertheless used generally with stative contructions, e.g. *I am loving detective stories,* without implying any restrictions on the state of mind. Compare: *I'm loving detective stories since you introduced me to Marele Day,* which could just be said by English-speakers anywhere. It is however unlikely to be seen in standard prose.

2 Regional variation in use of the imperfect and perfect aspects. American speakers use the *imperfect* (-ing) *aspect* more often than their British counterparts: the ratio is 4:3 in conversational data from the *Longman Grammar* corpus. By contrast, British writers are more given to using the *perfect* (-ed) *aspect* than American writers, again by a factor of 4:3 in the *Longman Grammar* research. The differential is at its most marked in news reporting, but it impacts on other registers as well. One consequence is that adverbs such as *already* and *just,* which are sometimes said to require the present perfect, can combine with the simple past in American English. Compare:

We already gave him a response (American)
We have already given him a response (British)

The British tendency to make more use of the English present perfect is analogous to that of the French with the *passé composé* (Engel and Ritz, 2000), which has largely displaced the simple past for everyday purposes.

assibilation
See under -er/-a.

assist
This verb can be complemented in a variety of ways. It can take a simple object, as in *assist the war effort.* But **assist** is more often construed with a particle of some kind:

* with *in:*
to assist the user in meditation
assist in the development of American football
can assist in removing the confusions
assist Namco in creating the next generation of arcade games

* with *with:*
to assist an elderly person with the completion of their tax return
can assist with obtaining an overview

Both constructions can take abstract nouns and/or -ing forms as complements, but the -ing type are far more frequent after *in,* in data from the BNC. This correlates with the fact that the *assist in* construction is much more common than the *assist with* construction, in both British and American databases.

An alternative construction with **assist** is *to* + infinitive, as in:

assist you to negotiate a contract
assist families to overcome problems

The construction with *to* plus infinitive requires an object, whereas the other two do not. The three types of complementation are largely interchangeable in terms of semantics, though the first is rather more formal in style.

assonance
A half-rhyme in a string of words is known as **assonance.** It can involve either words with the same vowel sound but different consonants following:

Feed the man meat.

or else different vowels between the same consonants

Butter is better.

The latter is sometimes distinguished as *consonance.* Whether in art or advertising slogans like those above, **assonance** helps to bind the key words together. The echoic link reinforces the underlying grammatical structure.

assume or presume
A good deal of ink has been spilled over the difference between these words, about their relative strength in expressing the idea of "take for granted," and whether facts or beliefs are involved. One of the most important differences is the simple fact that **assume** is much more common than **presume,** in both British and American English. In both Brown and LOB databases, instances of **assume** (including *assumed/assumes/assuming*) outnumber those of **presume** by more than 12:1. **Assume** slips easily into everyday discussion, drawing less attention to itself and more to the particular point which the speaker wants to foreground. **Presume** seems to draw attention to itself and to the presumptive act on the part of the speaker.

◊ On *assuming that,* see **dangling participles.**

assurance or insurance
When is **insurance** not **insurance?** The answer used to be "When it's *life assurance.*" The *Oxford Dictionary* (1884–1928) noted this, but also that the distinction was not made originally (there were cases of *marine assurance*), and that it did not prevail everywhere (*life insurance* was also to be found). *Life insurance* is now much more frequent than *life assurance,* at least by the evidence of the internet. The ratio between them was about 5:2 in a Google search (2002). However among the most prominent businesses registered under each name, *life assurance* tended to come from non-English countries (Germany, Egypt, Thailand, Philippines) and from Canada, whereas *life insurance* companies were often sited in the US or England.

assurer or assuror
See under -er/-or.

asterisk

The **asterisk** sign * has no standard role in punctuation, but is put to a variety of purposes by writers, text editors and printers; and by specialists in particular fields.

*General uses of the asterisk
1 as a mark of omission or ellipsis
2 as a typographical dividing line, to make a break in a narrative (a set of asterisks spaced across the whole page)
3 to refer readers to footnotes
4 to enumerate the items in a list (see **lists** section 2)

The first of these uses is vigorously discouraged by both the *Chicago Manual* (1993) and *Hart's Rules* (1983), and clearly it's unnecessary when we have the apostrophe to mark an omitted letter, and three dots for the ellipsis of whole words. The question remains of what to do when quoting four-letter words without wanting (or being permitted) to spell them out. To use **asterisks** for the missing letters, as in "F*** you," seems to draw attention to the word, which may of course be what the writer intends. The set of **asterisks** embellishes the places of the missing letters so as to positively invite the reader to fill them in. A complete row of **asterisks** across the page marks a more substantial break than extra line space, and often signals a discontinuity in the focus of the text.

The third use, as a footnoting device, is the most commonly encountered of all uses of the **asterisk**. One or more **asterisks** helps to lead readers to the occasional footnote at the bottom of a page, especially in texts which also make use of numbered endnotes. They thus provide an auxiliary referencing system for the author, or for editors who wish to add special-purpose footnotes. In tables of numbers the **asterisk** can draw the reader's attention to footnotes, and substitute for superscript numbers which might be confused with the numbers of the table itself. However square-bracketed numbers, not **asterisks**, are often used these days within tables of numbers.

*Specialized uses of the asterisk
–in statistics, **asterisks** mark the three levels of probability conventionally used in analyzing numerical findings. Three **asterisks** correspond to a probability of less than .001 that the phenomenon occurred by chance; two **asterisks** to a probability of less than .01; and a single **asterisk** to less than .05.
–in computing, the **asterisk** indicates an unknown character or characters, used as a wildcard for more comprehensive effect (a search for *affect** would find instances of *affected/affecting/affects* as well as *affect*)
–in historical linguistics, **asterisks** mark conjectural, reconstructed forms of words:
Indo-European *treies becomes "three" in English.
Linguistic theorists also use the **asterisk** for constructions that are grammatically unacceptable, such as **The sky is shattering.*

astro-

This Greek element meaning "star" is built into a number of words relating to the sciences of star-watching, both ancient and modern. Some of these words, like *astronomy* and *astrology,* come direct from Greek. Others like *astrobiology, astronaut, astrophysics, astrosphere* are recent formations. The *astrolabe* was a medieval navigating instrument. Its C20 counterpart is the *astrocompass.* All these words have retained their scientific roles apart from *astronomic(al),* which doubles as a colloquial word for "skyhigh." Like other paired adjectives of this kind, *astronomic* and *astronomical* differ little in meaning (see **-ic/-ical**).

Also related to **astro-** are *asterisk* and *aster* (the flower), where the emphasis is on the visual shape of stars rather than their uses. Both were borrowed into English via Latin.

asyndeton

This Greek loanword refers to the lack of a coordinating word between items in a series. In a series of three or more, **asyndeton** is the norm for all but the last pair. See for example:
> *on Monday, Tuesday and Wednesday*
> *... wouldn't eat bread, pasta, porridge or potatoes*

For writers, the **asyndeton** has the rhetorical effect of piling one example on top of another (see further under **rhythm** section 2). This rhetorical effect can be extended by not using a coordinator such as *and* and *or* between the last pair of words:
> *... put a stop to all such jokes, jibes, snide remarks*

Pure **asyndeton** like this is less common than *polysyndeton* (i.e. mixed forms of linkage, explicit and nonexplicit), shown in the first pair of examples. *Polysyndeton* helps the reader to anticipate the end of a series, especially when there is no change of typeface to mark it. But when a different typeface is used for the series of examples, the coordinator is superfluous and may seem fussy, insisting on talking the reader through what is obvious from other cues. This is why pure **asyndeton** is often used in the sets of examples presented in this book.
◊ For the use of commas between items in a series, see **comma** section 3b.

at

Contemporary idiom packs meaning into this small word at the end of a sentence:
> *This is where their thinking is at.* (= the present frontiers)
> *Yeah. That's where it's at.* (= things are happening)

At the end of the sentence, the final stress falls on **at**, and earns it predictable censure from those who see it as blatant use of a preposition-at-the-end-of-the-sentence. But in this role, **at** is clearly not a preposition but an adverb, complementing the subject of the clause. (See further under **predicate** section 1.) No doubt the contemporary flavor of the idiom also draws comment, and the fact that it smacks of spoken rather than written English.

The collocation *at about* raises eyebrows in some quarters as an *oxymoron.* (How can something be both there, and somewhere there?) The objection is rather perverse, since *about* normally modifies the following phrase as in *at about 12 noon,* and makes sense in that context.

at sign @
See entry at the start of the letter *A.*

ate

See under **eat**.

-ate

A slightly loaded question: how would you pronounce the following?

> *animate   articulate   designate   duplicate*
> *graduate   moderate   separate   syndicate*

All these words, and some others ending in **-ate**, are pronounced in two ways. The pronunciation depends on the words' grammatical role – whether they serve as adjectives, verbs or nouns.

1 Adjectives ending in -ate are pronounced with just one main stress which is early in the word, either on the first syllable (as in *animate*), or the second (as in *articulate*). They often have a past passive meaning: *designate* (as in *governor designate*) means "having been appointed," and *separate* "having been divided off." (In Latin they were all past participles of first conjugation verbs.) These adjectives often provided the stem for the development of verbs in English, and from those verbs we have a fresh crop of participial adjectives alongside the older ones. See for example:

> *animate/animated   designate/designated*
> *separate/separated*

The meaning of the later ones is of course more closely related to the verb. A few **-ate** adjectives have no verb counterparts however:

> *affectionate   considerate   dispassionate*
> *proportionate*

2 Verbs ending in -ate are the most common words of this kind. They are pronounced with two stresses, one early and one on the final syllable, so that it rhymes with "mate." Many such verbs date from C15, as do all of the following:

> *abbreviate   consecrate   contaminate   dedicate*
> *equate   frustrate   incorporate   inoculate*
> *mitigate   recreate   terminate   translate*

Alongside verbs like those with Latin stems, **-ate** has long been the formative in words with French or English stems:

> *assassinate   hyphenate   marinate   orchestrate*

All those originated in C16. Since then **-ate** has remained a highly productive verb suffix, attaching itself to stems from any language. Occasionally there are duplicate verb forms in **-ate** such as *commentate* (alongside *comment*) and *orientate* (alongside *orient*). To some, such **-ate** forms seem redundant, though they may develop their own specialized meanings. (See further under **comment** and **orient**.)

3 Nouns ending in -ate are few in number, and have a single early stress like the adjectives. There are two distinct kinds, one official and the other scientific. The older ones are official words referring either to an office or institution:

> *consulate   directorate   electorate   syndicate*

or to the incumbent of a particular office or status:

> *curate   graduate   magistrate*

Many were borrowed from Latin, though some have been formed in English on non-Latin bases, e.g. *caliphate, shogunate.* The scientific words ending in **-ate** refer to chemical compounds which are salts of acids ending in -*ic,* including:

> *acetate   lactate   nitrate   permanganate*
> *phosphate   sulfate*

Compare the scientist's use of the suffix **-ite**.

-athon

This freshly evolved suffix refers to an endurance test of some kind, taking its cue from the word *marathon,* the Olympic contest in long-distance running. That word was actually a placename, the site of the Greek victory over the Persian army in 490 BC. Yet its latter syllables have helped to generate many a suburban contest based on sticking at one particular activity: the *dance-a-thon* and the *bowlathon,* as well as the *rockathon* (for continuous rocking in the rocking chair) registered in the *Guinness Book of Records.* Many **-athons** are designed to raise money for a good cause, e.g. the *bike-athon for cerebral palsy,* though this becomes rather blatant in the *begathon* held by an American radio station to raise money. Most **-athon** words are created for the event and disappear with it. *Walkathon* and *talkathon* however are both established – listed in *Webster's Third* (1986) and the *Oxford Dictionary* (1989) and on record since the 1930s. *Talkathon* in the US is still associated with political endeavors, as a synonym for "filibuster" as well as the term for the extended talkback radio/TV done by a campaigning politician. But in Britain it's the length rather than any cause which makes it a *talkathon.* The *Oxford* citations show it being used of a very lengthy BBC discussion, and a protracted conversation between intimates.

Not surprisingly, English creations ending in **-athon** are pluralized with -*s,* rather than Greek plurals. See further under **-on**.

◊ For the usually mistaken use of *Jonathon* for *Jonathan,* see **Jonathan**.

-ation

Many an abstract noun in English ends this way. Some have been borrowed from Latin; many more have been formed in modern English from verbs ending in -*ate.* Almost all the verbs in the entry on **-ate** above have nouns ending in **-ation.** The close relationship between *animation* and *animate, articulation* and *articulate* etc. makes it very easy for writers to vary and modify their style without having to hunt for synonyms. For example:

> *There was animation in their faces at the prospect of refreshments.*
> *The prospect of refreshments animated their faces.*

Verbs in **-ate** provide a ready cure for writing which is heavy with **-ation** words. They require some rewording of the sentence, but that's part of the cure.

A small group of nouns ending in **-ation** are related to verbs ending in -*ify,* not -*ate.* For example:

> *beautification (beautify)   gratification (gratify)*
> *identification (identify)   justification (justify)*
> *simplification (simplify)*

In these cases the verb has been borrowed through French, whereas the noun goes back to Late Latin.

-ative

This is the ending of a body of adjectives which form a tight network with nouns ending in -*ation,* and to a lesser extent the verbs ending in -*ate.* The following are some of many **-ative** adjectives with counterpart nouns as well as verbs:

> *cooperative   creative   generative*
> *illustrative   participative*

Other such adjectives connect with nouns in *-ation,* but no verb in *-ate:*

> *affirmative   conservative   consultative*
> *declarative   evocative   representative*

Some adjectives in **-ative** are of course used unchanged as nouns, e.g. *affirmative, alternative, cooperative.* See further under **transfers.**

-ator

This is a very productive agentive suffix, associated with verbs ending in *-ate.* As the following examples show, it refers either to instruments or to people who are agents of the verb's action:

> *calculator   demonstrator   investigator*
> *perpetrator   radiator*

These **-ator** words form a large and open-ended group of agentive words which are spelled with *-or* rather than *-er.* The reason is that many **-ator** words come direct from Latin, where agentives of this kind were always *-or.* The Latin spelling has provided a firm model for many similar formations in modern English.

atrium

For the plural of this word, see under **-um.**

attend or tend

These verbs live separate lives most of the time, and coincide in just one area of meaning: "take care (of someone or something)."

> *He was attending to the fire.*
> *He was tending (to) the fire.*
> *A nurse attended to the injured at the scene of the accident.*
> *A nurse tended (to) the injured at the scene of the accident.*

Attend in this sense is always accompanied by *to,* whereas **tend** can do without it. However this use of **tend** is declining, and is now mostly restricted to dealing with fires and first aid. **Tend** could not replace **attend** *(to)* in other contexts, for example, in phrases like *attending to the customers,* or *attending to his business.*

　Tend to meaning "be inclined to" is very much current usage, as in *the press tends to overreact.* There, **tend** works as a kind of auxiliary verb or **catenative** (see further under that heading). **Tend** ("be inclined") and **tend** ("take care of") are in fact independent words. The origins of the first are to be found in the French verb *tendre* ("stretch"), while the second is actually a reduced form of **attend.**

attester or attestor

See under **-er/-or.**

attorney-general

The plural of this word is discussed under the heading **governor-general.**

attributive adjectives

See **adjectives** section 1.

au naturel

This French phrase meaning "in the natural (state/way)" was first used in gastronomy, to make a virtue of leaving food items uncooked, or else cooked plain without spices and garnishes. By the beginning of C20 **au naturel** began to be used in its second sense

"undressed," or as the coy phrase has it "as nature intended." In 1905 it was just a matter of *ankles au naturel,* according to an *Oxford Dictionary* (1989) citation, but it now implies a state of undress which would appeal to a *naturist* (see **naturalist or naturist**).

au pair, à deux and a quattr'occhi

The French phrase **au pair** means not so much "in a pair" as "on an equal footing." It is thus rather a euphemism for the financial arrangement whereby someone lives with a well-to-do family, acting as an all-purpose assistant in exchange for board and lodging, but with no standard wage. **Au pair** is significantly different from **à deux,** another French phrase which does mean "in a twosome," but implies a private meeting or meal from which others are excluded. An Italian phrase which picks up the same idea of privacy and exclusiveness is **a quattr'occhi,** meaning "between four eyes."

audi(o)-

This Latin element meaning "hear(ing)" occurs in its full form in *audiology* and *audiovisual,* and is blended into *audible, audience, audition, auditorium.* The same element is found in *audit* and *auditor,* reminding us of the historical practice of checking accounts in a public hearing: they were actually read aloud. Because this is now a private business, the sense of "hearing" is lost from both *audit* and *auditor* – except when they refer to a student who participates in a course by attending lectures but without being assessed in it.

audiovisual media

The need to refer to material other than print has raised new questions for bibliographers. *Audiovisual materials* require their own bibliographical practices, depending on whether they are films, videos, sound recordings of music, speeches or interviews, computer programs, maps, works of art, or museum objects.

　Many such items are available only in limited editions, and in the case of works of art they are unique, so that the place where they are kept (i.e. the repository) is very important. An additional issue with sound recordings is the need to recognize the role of both the originator/composer of the work and the performer; or for interviews, both the subject (interviewee) and interviewer (the person with substantial responsibility). In citing all such kinds of material, the medium needs to be identified, in square brackets immediately after the title.

1 Films, movies, videotapes, television programs. Most films, movies, video recordings and TV productions are the product of collaboration, and so the title rather than any individual author is featured first:

> *Crocodile Dundee* [motion picture] Directed by Peter Faiman. California. Rimfire Films. 1986. Distributed by CBS FOX.
> *The Story of English* [video recording] Directed by Robert McCrum, William Cran and Robert MacNeill. London. BBC Enterprises. 1986.

After identifying the title and medium, the reference may mention the person with either artistic or administrative responsibility (the director and/or producer). If the item is not in the hands of a commercial distributor, the repository in which it's held is indicated.

2 Recordings of music and the spoken word, including interviews. Recordings of music usually feature the work of a composer or author, as well as that of a performer. But for citation purposes, the first gets priority:

> Beethoven, L. van *Beethoven or bust* [sound recording] Realised by Don Dorsy on digital synthesizer in Anaheim, California. (1988) Compact Disc by Telarc International.
> Mansfield, K. *The garden party* [sound recording] Read by Dame Peggy Ashcroft in Marlborough, Wiltshire. (1983) Cover to Cover Cassettes.

In citations of interviews, the name of the interviewee takes precedence, though that of the interviewer should also be given:

> Suzuki, David. *Margaret Throsby in conversation with David Suzuki and Edward Goldsmith* [sound recording] Perth WA (1989) ABC Radio Tapes.

For sound recordings made from a general broadcast, titles may have to be supplied, as in that last example. Note also that it helps to indicate to the reader what kind of format the sound is recorded on: audiocassette, compact disc etc.

3 Electronic media: computer programs, CD-ROMs, on-line documents. The first two media are analogous to published books in terms of the bibliographic information needed. The third has more in common with unique objects stored at a particular location (see below, section 5).

a) **Computer programs.** These are usually referenced first by title, although if there is a known author, his/her name is given first. A typical example is as follows:

> *Grammatik* [computer software] San Francisco, California. Reference Software International. (1991)

b) **CD-ROMs.** Reference to any particular unit on the CD-ROM requires the reader to work through a main menu to the relevant submenu. The access path is indicated with one or more dashes.

> *The ICAME Collection of English Language Corpora* [CD-ROM] Bergen, Norway; Norwegian Computing Centre for the Humanities, 1993. Helsinki Corpus – Early Modern English texts.

c) **On-line documents: internet and WorldWideWeb materials.** Because the message is separable from the medium, both need to be included in the reference. The identifying details of the document are given first, including the primary author, title of composition and title of host document, if different. Because electronic documents can be regularly updated, both the date of publication and the date of citation need to be supplied. The second is usually given in terms of the month and day (arguably, the particular hour of the day might be important, but it's not regularly shown). The mode of access is shown through the URL address, which also indicates the forms in which it can be downloaded and printed.

> EAGLES Guidelines [On-line] Italy, Expert Advisory Group on Engineering Standards, 1996 Available from the Internet:
> URL: www.ilc.pi.cnr.it/EAGLES96/browse.html#topics
> [cited 10 September 1998]

Chevrons may be used to enclose the internet address, especially if it runs on to the next line (see **URL**). The ultimate reference on citing on-line material is International standard ISO/FDIS 690-2.

4 Maps. References to individual sheet maps usually begin with a regional title, and include any series identifier, as well as the scale:

> North Island New Zealand [map] New Zealand Department of Lands and Survey (1966) 1:1,637,000.

5 Works of art, archival and museum objects. Because these items are unique, the repository in which they are kept is a vital element. For works of art, the reference highlights the creator and its title:

> Senbergs, Jan *The Constitution and the States* [wall panels] (1980) High Court of Australia, Canberra.

For archival objects and museum realia, a descriptive title must be found as the focus of the reference:

> Black-glazed bowl [realia] fourth century BC. Item MU 328 Ancient History Teaching Collection, Macquarie University.

As in this example, a catalogue number leads the reader to the particular object, if there's more than one of the kind in the repository.

augur or auger

Neither of these is a common word, which leaves some writers in doubt as to which is which. **Augur** is a verb that mostly makes its appearance in the idiom *it augurs well...* The words *augury, inaugural* and *inaugurate* are derivatives of it. The second word **auger** is a tool or machine for boring holes. With its *-er* ending it resembles other workshop instruments, e.g. *screwdriver, spanner,* yet **auger** is not itself an agentive word. It goes back to Old English *nauger* (a blend of *nafu,* "nave/hub of a wheel" + *gar,* "spear"), which was misanalyzed in C15 as (*an*) *auger.*

auntie or aunty

Both spellings are current for the cognate female relative, though **auntie** is the primary one in *Webster's Third* (1986) and the *Oxford Dictionary* (1989). The recommendation is taken more seriously in the US, judging from CCAE data where it outstrips **aunty** by almost 10:1. Popular characters such as *Auntie Mame* and *Auntie Em* in *Wizard of Oz* have perhaps underscored it. In the UK, the ratio between **auntie** and **aunty** is rather closer: 5:2 in data from the BNC.

The *-ie* spelling puts **auntie** among the colloquialisms for familiar persons and phenomena such as *cabbie, chappie* and *sweetie* (see further under **-ie/-y**). The *-y* spelling also serves in a variety of colloquialisms: *hippy, baddy, druggy,* as well as informal kinship terms such as *daddy, granny* and *mummy/mommy.* We may assume that **aunty** associates the word with the latter group.

The use of **Auntie** in reference to the BBC dates from 1962, the implications being rather equivocal and not-so-affectionate. In Australia the analogous ABC was likewise dubbed **Aunty**, in a context of strong competition from its commercial rivals. It did generate affirmative action both in-house and in the community, with one Melbourne support group styling themselves *Aunty's nephews and nieces.*

aura

For the plural of this word, see **-a**.

Australia and Australians, Aussies and Oz

During C17 and C18, **Australia** was known as "New Holland," a reminder of the fact that the Dutch were the first Europeans to locate and visit the land. The name **Australia**, derived from the Latin *terra Australis* ("Southern Land"), was used by Cook, but owes its establishment to Governor Macquarie in early C19. **Australian** was first applied to Aboriginal people in 1814 by Matthew Flinders, but within ten years it also referred to others living on the continent. The word is used in the original sense by linguists speaking of the *Australian languages*.

The clipped form **Aussie** originated in World War I as a term for "Australia," "an Australian," and as the general-purpose adjective. The spellings *Ossie* and *Ozzie* showed up very infrequently in the same period, according to the *Australian National Dictionary* (1990). But the use of **Oz** took off in the 1970s, helped no doubt by publicity surrounding the radical *Oz Magazine* (1967–73).

Australian English

With the arrival of the First Fleet, **Australian English** began among settlers and convicts drawn mostly from southern and eastern England. Within a generation, the differentness of Australian speech was being commented on, for better or for worse. Yet only in C20 (and after two world wars) did **Australian English** attain its majority, and secure recognition of its place in the English-speaking world.

Distinctively Australian vocabulary developed in response to the new social and physical environment. The conditions of transportation, the development of new pastoral lands and the gold rushes all demanded their own terminology. Some of it came from standard English (e.g. *block, bush, squatter, emancipist*), and some (e.g. *barrack, billy, fossick*) from English dialects. Convict slang drawn from the British underworld provided other words such as *swag*.

New vocabulary was required for Australian flora and fauna, and the naming process went on throughout C19. The names for Australian fauna were sometimes borrowed from Aboriginal languages, and sometimes compounded out of English elements, and the same animal or bird might be referred to either way. So the *dingo* was also the *native dog*, the *kookaburra* was the *laughing jackass* or *settler's clock*, and the *koala* the *native bear*. By the end of C19, this variation had mostly been ironed out, leaving fewer rather than more Aboriginal names. Few people remember that *bettong* was the name for a small kangaroo, *tuan* for a flying squirrel, and *wobbegong* for the carpet shark. The names for Australian flora and fauna were the staple of a dictionary titled *Austral English*, published in 1898 by E. E. Morris. Items from Morris's list of Australianisms were incorporated into the *Oxford* and *Webster's* dictionaries in the first half of C20.

A wide-ranging account of the informal and colloquial aspects of **Australian English** was first made by S. J. Baker in a volume first published in 1945, titled *The Australian Language*, echoing H. L. Mencken's *The American Language* (1919). Baker recorded the slang of many Australian subcultures: the racetrack, the pub, the two-up game, and above all that of Australia's military forces in two world wars. Not all the words that he discussed were strictly speaking Australianisms, but they were and are part of the resources of **Australian English**. Like Mencken, he presented his findings in a series of essays with word lists embedded in them, not as a dictionary.

The first comprehensive dictionary of **Australian English**, the *Macquarie Dictionary,* appeared in 1981 with 80,000 headwords. It included all standard Australian words and meanings, as well as *Australianisms* (expressions which originated in Australia and are often still unique to that country): words for new cultural and social phenomena, for the local flora and fauna as well as slang and colloquialisms. The *Australian National Dictionary,* published in 1990, concentrates on Australianisms alone, a total of 10,000 headwords, with substantial historical information on each via citations.

Australian English does not seem to have diverged in its grammar from that of standard English elsewhere. In casual conversation some Australian-speakers (like English-speakers elsewhere) make nonstandard selections of tense, such as *come* for *came, done* for *did,* and *kep* for *kept;* and *but* can occur as a sentence-final item (see **but**). However, none of this appears in print, except when an author quotes or aims to represent nonstandard speech. The morphology of Australian English words is based on the same resources as English everywhere, although Australians make fuller use than others of informal shortenings of words with *–o* (as in *milko* for "milkman"), and with *-ie* (as in *barbie* for "barbecue"). The latter suffix is sometimes said to be childish, but in Australia its use is widespread among adults, and words formed with it are part of the informal style of popular daily newspapers.

The only distinctively Australian detail of morphology one might point to is in the handful of reduplicative words (e.g. *mia-mia, willy-willy*), which embody the exact reduplication used in various Aboriginal languages. In English generally the echoic type of reduplication (*ping-pong, walkie-talkie*) is much more common, and words with exact reduplication remain informal (see further under **reduplicatives**).

The details of Australian written style (i.e. editorial style) are not strongly standardized, in that most publishing houses and newspapers print their own style guides for their writers and editors. The Australian government *Style Manual,* now in its sixth edition (2002), sets the standard for federal government publications, and is referred to by other Australian institutions and corporations.

Beyond the genres of official publishing, different editorial practices may seem appropriate, and with both British and American publishing houses at work in Australia, the range of styles is probably increasing rather than decreasing. The institution of regular "Style Council" conferences since 1986 has helped to inform editors about variable and changing trends in style. (Contact the Linguistics Department, Macquarie University, for information about them.) There is no language academy to refer to in Australia (any more than in Britain or the US), but the Style Council conferences provide a consultative forum for discussing and assessing the options in written **Australian English**.

◊ See further under **language academy**.

Australianisms
See **Australian English**.

author and authoress

Sensitivity to unnecessary gender specification has curbed the use of **authoress**, and its numbers in British and American databases are minuscule. In data from the BNC the frequency of **authoress** is about 1% of that of **author** – and less than that in CCAE. Female writers are regularly referred to as **author**, and it is only the odd occasion which generates such citations as *authoress and artist Miss Fleur Cowles and her husband* ... (in which case the commentator is clearly going out of ?his? way to mark the writer's gender).

The verb **author** has recently returned to common usage after centuries of disuse. Before becoming "obsolete" in C17, it evidently supported both the meanings current now: (i) be the author of, and (ii) create or originate (something). The first meaning is the commoner for *authored* in BNC citations, while *authoring* is mostly associated with computer *authoring tools*, a new application of the second meaning. In CCAE *authoring* supports both meanings. Writers' reputations are evidently based on such things as "authoring a poetry book" or "authoring five cookbooks," while another's distinction was to be "winner of the 1987 Nobel Peace prize for authoring the peace plan." Other American examples apply the word to someone who is the architect and prime mover of legislation, but there are no parallels in data from the BNC. Both American and British English make use of the verb *co-author* ("be joint author of ").

authoritarian or authoritative

These words take rather different attitudes towards authority. In **authoritarian** there is resentment of high-handed leadership, whereas in **authoritative** the leadership provided is welcome and respected. **Authoritative** is much the older of the two, dating from C17, whereas **authoritarian** dates only from C19. The social and political practices of the Victorian era seem to be embedded in the latter.

auto- and auto

Borrowed from Greek, the prefix **auto** meaning "self" or "on its own" is familiar enough in words like:

autobiography	autocracy	autocrat
autograph	autoimmune	automatic
automaton	automobile	autonomous
autonomic	autonomy	

A less obvious example is *autopsy,* which is literally "inspection with one's own eyes." Its reference nowadays is so restricted to postmortems that one would hardly venture a joke about an "autopsy" of the food served in the company canteen, though in past centuries (up to C18), the word was not so specialized in its meaning.

From its use in *automobile,* the prefix **auto-** can also mean "associated with motor cars," as in *auto-electrician, auto-mechanic.* In American English these would appear spaced rather than hyphened, in keeping with the fact that **auto** has a life of its own as an abbreviation of *automobile.*

In the phrase *auto-da-fe,* borrowed from Portuguese, *auto* means "act" (of faith). It was a euphemism for the execution of those tried by the Inquisition, and usually applied to the burning of "heretics."

auxiliary verbs

These verbs combine with others to make up a verb phrase, and help to indicate **tense**, **aspect**, **voice**, **mood** and **modality**. (See under those headings for more about each.) *Auxiliaries* complement the *main verb* (also known as the *full verb* or *lexical verb*), bringing grammatical meaning to bear on its lexical meaning. The verb phrase may contain as many as three *auxiliaries* (or even four), as the following set shows:

> *was added*
> *was being added*
> *had been added*
> *might have been added*
> *might have been being added* (at that time)

A verb which has no accompanying *auxiliary* is known as a *simple* verb (compare **compound verbs**). The *auxiliaries* are often classed into two subgroups: *primary auxiliaries* and *modal auxiliaries,* which form closed sets. There is also an expanding set of semi-auxiliaries/semi-modals.

1 The primary auxiliaries are *have, be* and *do. Have* and *be* have the special characteristic of combining with participles, present and past, in order to express **aspect**, and the **passive** voice (see further under those headings). *Have* and *be* never combine with the "bare" infinitive, as do the *modal auxiliaries* and the verb *do* itself. In the continuous flow of discourse, the *auxiliaries have* and *be* sometimes appear unaccompanied by participles, but this is when the relevant participle can be inferred from a previous sentence. So for example it is natural enough to say (or write):

> *I haven't met the new assistant yet. Have you?*

The main verb participle *met* (and its object) are understood through the use of *have* in the question. *Primary auxiliaries* can also stand alone as main/full/lexical verbs, as in:

> *He has a large office.*
> *They are in the bottom drawer.*

In those cases, each verb carries its own lexical meaning: *have* a possessive meaning, and *be* an existential meaning.

The auxiliary *do* has special roles in helping to formulate the interrogative (*Do I like spaghetti?*) and negative statements (*I don't like spaghetti*). All interrogative and negative statements are phrased with *do,* unless they already contain one of the other *auxiliaries* (*primary* or *modal*). *Do* has other roles as a substitute verb:

> *I enjoy spaghetti much more than they do.*

Here *do* stands for the main (lexical) verb *enjoy* and its object in the second clause. Once again, *do* performs this function unless there is another *auxiliary* present. Compare the following with the previous example:

> *They wouldn't enjoy the spaghetti as I would.*
> *They can't enjoy the spaghetti as I can.*

When *do* works as a main verb in its own right, it means "work on (something)," as in *doing one's accounts* or *doing the milk run.*

2 The modal auxiliaries express shades of possibility, certainty and obligation, with a "bare" infinitive following. Two of them, *will* and *shall,* can also express future time, although there may be an overtone of certainty or obligation there as well:

> *You will be in my power!*
> *The vote shall be taken as soon as the motion is put.*

The key *modal auxiliaries* are:

> can   could   may   might
> must   shall   should will
> would

These are the grammarians' "central modals," contrasting with those in the next section. (See further under **modality and modal verbs**.)

◊ For the use of paired modals (e.g., *might could*), see **double modal**.

3 Semi-auxiliaries, semi-modals, periphrastic modals. English makes use of a number of *quasimodal* verbs, whose meaning resembles that of one or other of the verbs in section 2, and seems to paraphrase it:

i)

> *dare (to)*   (compare *could*)
> *need (to)*   (compare *must*)
> *ought to*   (compare *should*)
> *used to*   (compare *would*)

ii)

> *be able to*   (compare *can*)
> *be about to*   (compare *will*)
> *be going to*   (compare *will*)
> *be likely to*   (compare *will*)
> *be obliged to*   (compare *must*)
> *be supposed to*   (compare *should*)
> *be willing to*   (compare *would*)
> *have to*   (compare *must*)

Quasimodals behave somewhat like modals, in not requiring *do*-support in negative constructions. But those in the second set are always followed by the *to*-infinitive, and it's usually so for those in the first (see further under **dare (to), need, used to, ought**). The *Comprehensive Grammar* (1985) calls the first set "marginal modals" and the second "semi-auxiliaries" (since all involve the use of *primary auxiliaries*). Alternative names used in the *Longman Grammar* (1999) are "marginal auxiliaries" for the first set, and "semi-modals" for the second, though *semi-modal* is also used to cover both groups (excluding *dare*). To avoid the dual use of *semi-modal* and prevent misunderstanding, the cover term *quasimodal* is used in this book for both types of periphrastic modal.

◊ Compare **catenatives**.

avail

As a noun, **avail** is now mostly fixed into the negative idiom *to no avail*, and its occasional variants *to little avail, to any avail* and the rhetorical question *To what avail?*

The verb **avail** still has plenty of vitality as a reflexive form, as in *anxious to avail themselves of the instruction afforded to their children*. This is standard in both American and British English, but a sprinkling of other constructions, both transitive and intransitive, appear in the databases, some of which suggest a nostalgia for older usage. Transitive uses such as *it will not avail him as a defence* (BNC), *one whose mercies might avail him better* (CCAE), and intransitive ones like *God does avail much* sound just idiomatic, and American writers seem able to vary the intransitive construction:

> *Driving under military escort will not avail.*
> *No kind of summitry will avail unless the Soviet Union continues …*

As in these examples, negative predications can be formulated with **avail**. Those embodying a positive statement seem more marginal: *enables budget travelers to avail of low-cost flights* (CCAE); *[computer] design to avail of advanced telecommunication infrastructures* (BNC). Here **avail** means "take advantage"; elsewhere it means "provide": *the bill would avail health insurance to the uninsured in Iowa; the forum would avail him the opportunity to get just that* (both CCAE). These perhaps experimental constructions seem to connect with the ubiquitous adjective *available*, though the derivational process is ad hoc. They are mutants in the evolution of language, but for the moment rather marginal.

avenge or revenge

See **revenge**.

averse or adverse

See **adverse**.

avocados or avocadoes

A majority of respondents (73%) to the Langscape survey (1998–2001) preferred **avocados** for the plural of avocado. In fact it's the only plural indicated in the *New Oxford* (1998) and *Merriam-Webster* (2000). The currency of **avocadoes** must be explained by reference to other vegetables (*tomatoes, potatoes* etc.) and/or greengrocer's spelling. See further under **-o** section 1.

await or wait

See **wait**.

awake or awaken

See under **wake**.

aware

This has long been a predicative adjective, like others formed from Anglo-Saxon with the prefix a- (see under that heading). Changes in its grammatical role are signaled by the presence of modifiers, e.g. *fully aware, hardly less politically aware,* showing its closeness to becoming a "central" adjective, by the criteria of the *Comprehensive Grammar* (1985). A further sign of this development is its attributive use in the US, in examples such as *an aware parent, an aware and educated population* from CCAE. Burchfield (1997) confirms the trend in the UK also.

aweing or awing

See under **-e** section 1.

awesome

The older and more literal meaning still stands in many combinations, such as *an awesome sight* and *awesome responsibility,* along with definitely secular applications such as *awesome military power* and *the most awesome hydroelectric plant.* But in colloquial usage and mass-market writing, the reverential sense of **awesome** is diffused into an all-purpose epithet of approval. It is particularly prevalent in sports writing, in both the US and the UK. The following are tokens of the many examples in both the BNC and CCAE:

> *She has also gained an awesome reputation in racing.*
> *It is not an awesome lineup. But it is local.*

In both databases **awesome** also injects hyperbole into advertorials on consumer products: *an awesome driver's car; the speed [of the computer's operation] is awesome*. Though the usage began with adolescents, and approval of the *awesome jeans jacket with rhine stones,* it now evidently serves a variety of adult purposes.

awhile

This word is found with solid setting in both British and American English, though more of its uses are sanctioned in the US. *Webster's Third* (1986) allows that **awhile** may be adverbial as in *settled awhile,* as well as the object of the preposition *for.* Thus *for awhile* is accepted, and there are hundreds of examples in CCAE. The *Oxford Dictionary* (1989) stands by the etymology of the phrase and finds only *for a while* acceptable. Its position is not entirely borne out by data from the BNC, in which *for awhile* makes up about 15% of the 89 instances of **awhile.** The *Oxford* does however hint at the "unification of sense" which may be there in **awhile**, and in idioms and collocations such as *not yet awhile, stay awhile, stood awhile in thought,* any strict notion of time seems to be being played down. Separating **awhile** into *a while* may seem to make too much of what is – after all – a vague time period.

axe or ax

The spelling **ax** is earlier, and the major spelling in American English, outnumbering **axe** by more than 4:1 in CCAE. According to the *Oxford Dictionary* (1884–1928), **ax** was "better on every ground," including etymology, phonology and analogy. Yet its citations show that the spelling **axe** gained support in Britain during C19, and the second edition of the *Dictionary* (1989) confirms that **ax** is no longer in use, as does the BNC.

The best argument for the spelling **axe** is that it contrives to make the word consist of three letters. It thus conforms to the principle that while function words may have less than three letters, content words usually have a minimum of three (see further under **words**). The extra *e* is of course dropped when it becomes a verb *axing* and *axed,* at which point its redundancy is obvious. (See further under **-e** section 1.)

axiom

See under **aphorism**.

axis

For the plural of this word, see **-is**.

aye or ay

These two spellings represent two pronunciations and two different meanings. **Ay**, pronounced to rhyme with "day" (or sometimes "die"), is an old-fashioned adverb meaning "ever." **Aye**, always pronounced to rhyme with "die," is the formal expression of affirmation used in public meetings, institutionalized in the Navy response *Aye Aye sir*. In the British parliament **aye** becomes a noun meaning "one who votes in the affirmative," as in: *The ayes have it.* In the US Congress the affirmative votes are the "yeas."

The shorter spelling **ay** is occasionally used for the parliamentary vote. But it then overlaps with the adverb, apart from challenging the principle that English content words generally have a minimum of three letters (see under **words**). All this makes **aye** much the better spelling for the affirmative word.

B

-b/-bb-

Words ending in the letter **-b** often become **-bb-** before adding a suffix beginning with a vowel sound. The doubling happens whenever the suffix begins with *e, i* or *y;* and with *-le* and *-ly,* which both involve the indeterminate vowel (see **schwa**). For example:

ad-libbed	*bobble*	*clubbed*	*cobwebby*
crabby	*dubbing*	*glibbest*	*hobnobbed*
knobbly	*robber*	*rubbed*	*snobbish*
snubbed	*stabbing*		

These spellings show the consonant-doubling used in English words of one syllable – or two, the second of which has an independent life as a monosyllable. (See further under **doubling of final consonant**.) Note that the vowel in all of them is short. When it's long or a diphthong, the *b* stays single, as in *booby* and *bribed.*

The doubling principle applies also in abbreviated words with short vowels such as *confabbed* and *women's libber.* For them, the double *b* is a sign of being anglicized (from latinate originals: *confabulation* and *liberation* respectively).

baby and babe

Both American and British English use **baby** as the ordinary, unmarked term for an infant, and to describe the offspring or offshoots of other animals and plants, as in *baby rabbits, baby carrots.* Brand and product names use **baby** to indicate the small of the species, e.g. *babybel* (for the smallest wax-packaged cheeses), and *baby grand* (for the miniature grand piano). With all these applications, **baby** is much more common than **babe**, the difference being about 15:1 in the US and 45:1 in the UK, by database evidence.

In standard English, a **babe** is not usually an ordinary **baby**. Its use in the King James bible connects it with the Nativity, as in the *babe wrapped in swaddling clothes.* Idioms like *newborn babe, babe-in-arms* and *sleeping like a babe* are more often figurative than references to infants. Otherwise, **babe** in this sense survives mostly as an intimate word for the family or the neighborhood, as when the local newspaper hopes that *both mum and babe will be problem-free.* Meanwhile in British advertising, the **babe** is beginning to grow up, to become the *Bovril Babe.* An advertorial on the latest swimming fashions foreshadows *what the nifty water babe will be wearing next year* – playing on the title of Kingsley's *Water Babies.* Other BNC citations suggest the "American" use of **babe** as a casual term of endearment is catching on, at least in British novels: *Do you want a hand, babe?*

In American English, **babe** has long been both a term of endearment and a way of referring to female companions and sex symbols. In some examples from CCAE, **babe** has divine allure, as in *babe of paradise;* in others it has commodity value: *a bankable star and a bit more of a babe.* Yet the idiom *political babe in the woods* makes **babe** naive and gender-neutral. On the baseball scene, **babe** can be used man to man:

> *"You're out of here, babe," Perlozzo told his first baseman.*

Such usage is probably helped by the memory of *Babe Ruth*, whose legendary status allows his name to be used in surprising places, as in *the Babe Ruth of conflict resolution.* Baseball apart, **babe** can now be heard in casual reference to an attractive adult – and as a term of endearment – anywhere in the English-speaking world.

bacillus

For the plural of this word, see under **-us** section 1.

back-

This is a formative element in quite a few English compound words:

backbench	*background*	*backhand*	*backlash*
backlog	*backslider*	*backstroke*	*backwash*
backwater			

Back- serves to indicate location or direction, and like other adverbs and particles it is normally set solid with the word it's prefixed to. (See **hyphens** section 2b.)

As the examples above show, it normally combines with ordinary English stems, whereas *retro-*, its classical equivalent, combines with scholarly words from Latin and Greek. See further under **retro-**.

back channels

See under **interjections**.

back matter

See **endmatter**.

back of, in back of and in back

American English does without *the* in all these constructions, and so they may sound elliptical and alien to British ears. Yet **back of** is more than four centuries old, according to the *Oxford Dictionary* (1989), and known everywhere in the English-speaking world in the phrase *back of beyond.* Productive use of **back of** can be found in British fiction (Burchfield, 1996). In the US, Canada and Australia, it gets a lowish level of use in expressions like *back of the range* and *back of the supermarket,* drawing attention to what is in the hinterland or behind/beyond the immediately visible. It makes a useful paraphrase as in the following example from CCAE:

> *Behind it is ... Cannery Row Memorial Park ..., and back of that, the site of the "Palace Flophouse."*

Back of can also be used figuratively, as in:

> *The party made gains but stayed well back of the Democrats in House seats.*

This parallels its quite frequent use in sports reporting: on the golfer, *one stroke back of the leader,* or the horse closing strongly, *a half-length back of Mykawa*.

In back of is sometimes used in sports reports too, as of the athlete surprised at being *2.14 seconds in back of the winner*. It can be used more abstractly, as in:

> One could even respond to a ... *voice in back of the speaker's question* ...

Most often **in back of** explains physical locations, as in:

> *Buildings in back of the charred commercial structure were also damaged.*
> *Subway tracks ran in back of all the houses on her side of the street.*

As these examples from CCAE show, **in back of** usually means "beyond the back of" (and outside it), so that it contrasts with *in the back of,* which locates something inside. In fact American use of **in back of** complements the common English use of *in front of*. It is relatively recent, however, according to *Webster's English Usage* (1989), and potentially ambiguous outside the US. Curiously the use of **in back of** may be a response to ill-founded criticism of **back of** – not on grounds of ambiguity, but because it was thought colloquial. *Webster's English Usage* affirms the place of both expressions in standard American English.

The phrase **in back** is also an Americanism, often used of getting into or being in the rear seat of a vehicle. So the US headline:

> *THIEF TAKES VAN WITH CHILD ASLEEP IN BACK*

corresponds exactly to the British:

> *THIEVES DRIVE OFF MOTHER'S CAR WITH BABY IN BACK SEAT*

In British English, this headline would be paraphrased as "in the back seat" in the article itself, but not in American. Other CCAE citations from newsreports show that **in back** is the common phrase: as when the driver *assumed that the passenger in back was Patrick*; or when *Wilson stays at the wheel; Elzie sits in back assembling the packages* – the traveling cottage industry. **In back** is used to indicate other spatial relations, as in: *women swinging their way down darkened streets with footsteps in back following them*; and the hall *open to concertgoers sitting on the lawn in back*. In British English the phrase would be "behind" or "at the back" respectively.

The three phrases of this entry all point to the fact that **back** retains more of its adverbial character in American idiom than in British.

back slash

See under **slash**.

backchannels

See **interjections**.

backformation

New words are most often developed from smaller, simple words, as *rattler* is from *rattle* and *assassination* from *assassin*. Just occasionally words (especially verbs) are formed in the opposite way, distilled out of pre-existing words which are construed as complex ones (see further under **complex words**). So *burgle* is from *burglar, accrete* from *accretion,* and *electrocute* from *electrocution.* Some other verbs derived in this way are:

donate	edit	enthuse	extradite	laze
liaise	reminisce	resurrect	scavenge	sidle
swindle	televize			

Compound words also lend themselves to **backformation**, witness the following verbs:

baby-sit	day-dream	dry-clean
lip-read	self-destruct	spring-clean
window-shop		

Most of the **backformations** just mentioned have become standard English, but many others are transient. More than half of those appearing in American and British glossaries of new words are not taken up in dictionaries, according to Ayto's (1998) research.

To some writers **backformations** of any kind are unacceptable, as if their unusual origin makes them illegitimate words. Some *backformations* seem rather superfluous, because they duplicate an existing verb. Thus *orientate,* backformed from *orientation,* means much the same as *orient,* and is cross-referenced to it in many dictionaries – though there are regional differences in their distribution (see further under **orient and orientate**). Other **backformations** like *commentate* (from *commentator*) are certainly earning their keep alongside the existing verb (*comment*), and cover different areas of meaning (see further under **comment**). It seems pedantic to deny their legitimacy on account of their origins. Their newness often attracts attention though even that is relative to people's exposure to them. Some examples like *remediate* (1969) and *surveil* (1960) are older than they feel; *revulse* (as in *I was revulsed by it*) has been registered in American dictionaries since the 1930s, though not yet in Britain (in this passive sense). The motive for backforming *revulse* from *revulsion* is clear enough: the formally related verbs such as *revolt* and *repel* seem too remote.

Note that the singular *Aborigine* was at one stage censured as a backformation from the plural *aborigines,* which was the only form used in Latin (see further under **Aboriginal**). For examples of other words derived in a similar way, see **false plurals**.

backshifting

See **sequence of tenses**.

backslash

See under **slash**.

back-to-back

Since World War II, **back-to-back** has been taken up increasingly as an adjective meaning "consecutive." Busy people now have *back-to-back meetings,* sportsmen *back-to-back games,* and politicians *back-to-back news conferences.* Continuous time may be expressed as *back-to-back weeks* or *back-to-back years.* The intricacies of business deals are caught up in *back-to-back purchases.* These usages originated in the US according to the *Oxford Dictionary* (1989), but they also register in British English in examples such as *back-to-back semi-finals,* [*phone*] *calls back-to-back,* and *back-to-back trading system,* among examples from the BNC. In fact, the adjective **back-to-back** has long been used in the UK (since 1845) to refer to a kind of high-density suburban architecture: *back-to-back houses* (or just *back-to-backs*), associated with old industrial towns. This particular spatial sense appears not to have crossed the Atlantic, though

Americans certainly use **back-to-back** in reference to simple physical arrangements such as *back-to-back seats* in a railway car. Spatial uses of **back-to-back** are more or less transparent, but its temporal uses are also well established worldwide, recognized in Canadian and Australian dictionaries (*Canadian Oxford,* 1998, and the *Macquarie Dictionary,* 1997), as well as British and American.

backward or backwards
See under **-ward.**

bacteria and bacterium
To classicists and scientists, **bacteria** is unequivocally plural, and so *These bacteria are dangerous* is the only way to construe the word. The answer is less clear cut for others, especially in the US. Extensive data from nontechnical sources in CCAE show that the word is quite often construed as a collective or singular noun, as indicated by singular verb agreement:

> *Make sure that all the bacteria was taken care of*
> *A bacteria called Listeria monocytogenes was found in icecream*

Singular examples like these and plural ones occur in the ratio of about 2:5 in the database. Singular agreement often shows up when a particular strain of **bacteria** is being identified for the public, as in the second example. British sources contained in the BNC also provide evidence of **bacteria** in singular constructions:

> *Normal skin bacteria breaks down into irritating free-fatty acids.*
> *When a bacteria or a virus gets into us ...*

Such examples are from nonscientific communication, but they confirm the use of **bacteria** as a collective or singular noun, which needs to be recognized in dictionaries.

Bacteria is of course a Latin plural (see **-a**), whose singular is the rather rare **bacterium.** The ratio between them is 10:1 in British data from the BNC, and about 12:1 in American English from CCAE. The rarity of **bacterium** helps to explain why **bacteria** itself is increasingly used as a singular, at least in nonscientific writing.

bad or badly
No-one could dispute the fact that **bad** is first and foremost an adjective (*a bad shot*), and **badly** an adverb (*He played badly*). This division of labor was stressed by C18 and C19 grammarians, and as long as **badly** is a regular adverb of manner (as in *behaving badly*), it holds. But **bad** has adverbial roles of its own, sanctioned by idiom, which effectively make it a **zero adverb** (see further under that heading).

What is the role of **bad** when combined with verbs like *look, smell, sound, taste?* Being *copular verbs,* they can combine with adjectives or adverbs, and **bad** could be either in the idioms *it looks/sounds bad if ...,* or *the meat smells/tastes bad.* (See further under **copular verbs.**) But when *the meat has gone bad,* **bad** is clearly more an adverb: compare *the meeting went well.* Further down the track is *We didn't do too bad, did we?* which is idiomatic in North America and Australia, but not generally accepted in Britain. American English allows **bad** with all the verbs mentioned so far, and others, according to *Webster's English Usage* (1989). *Needs it bad* and *wants it bad* are standard idioms in which **bad** serves as an intensifier. American usage commentary has however become

polarized: in the earlier C20 it went with this use of **bad,** but turned to censure in the second half. Purist reactions from Bernstein (1958) and the Harper-Heritage usage panels (1969, 1975) promoted the idea that *wants it badly* is "correct" style. Evans and Evans (1957) nevertheless thought that the construction with **bad** would become standard. This view gains supports from CCAE data, where instances of *want/wants/wanted it bad* outnumber those with **badly** by 5:2. Although the majority of constructions with **bad** are from quoted speech rather than newspaper commentary/editorial, they appear – varying with **badly** – in both types of discourse:

> *"Now everybody wants it bad."*
> *It can be done if we want it bad enough.*

The forcefulness of the construction with **bad** no doubt recommends itself to columnists, and the boundary between spoken and written styles is not hard and fast. More debatable now in the US are intensive uses of **bad** with less common verbs such as *hate, hurt, screw up* (as in *it hurts bad*), though there are handfuls of each in CCAE. The database confirms that *(be) bad off* (i.e. "lacking money or resources") is current American idiom, outnumbering *(be) badly off* by more than 3:1.

For the British, even *wants it bad* is too informal to appear in standard prose, according to Burchfield (1996) – let alone *it hurts bad* or *bad off.* The limits of acceptability for **bad** are set with copular verbs involving states of being or becoming. *Feel bad* appears in both written and spoken texts in the BNC – and is in fact much more common than *feel badly,* by a factor of 5:1. But there's no place for *hates it bad.*

The frontiers for **bad** as adverb are thus different in the US and the UK, and still being negotiated. Highly charged attitudes to its use are not so surprising, given the emotive and evaluative word that it is.

baggage or luggage
The first *Oxford Dictionary* (1884–1928) noted the American preference for **baggage** and British for **luggage,** remnants of which can still be found in the US terms *baggage car* and *unclaimed baggage* as opposed to *luggage van* and *left luggage* in the UK. But **baggage** and **luggage** are now used interchangeably in American and British English for the miscellany of bags, suitcases and odd-shaped objects which go with the traveler. Data from CCAE and the BNC show that **luggage** is the more common of the two – at least for American and British writers – although in airport signs, **baggage** is the word that strikes the eye, and it's built into terms such as *baggage systems, baggage handlers* and *excess baggage.*

Other, unrelated uses of **baggage** would help to explain why writers in both the US and the UK are increasingly inclined to use **luggage.** Since C17 **baggage** has been used to refer negatively to someone's political, philosophical or psychological commitments, as in:

> *dump their ideological baggage*

or

> *the cold-war baggage of his predecessors*

In British English it's possible to use **luggage** this way (as in *their psychological luggage*), according to *New Oxford* (1998). But there's scant evidence of it in BNC, and all such predispositions are construed with **baggage.** This negative use of **baggage** is taken further in the phrase *carry(ing) too much baggage,* which makes any aspect of a political candidate's past an impediment to his chances of success.

For centuries **baggage** has also been used in allusive references to women. In C17 sources it was applied with relish, as in *a saucy baggage*, though this usage now seems dated or sexist. It may owe something to the notion of *army baggage*, helped by earlier French *bagasse* ("camp follower"), as suggested by *Webster's Third* (1986). In current use **baggage** is most often an off-handed or derogatory term for the woman who wasn't born yesterday:

> *No-one could say the old baggage lacked for courage.*
> *She's a talentless baggage who should keep her mouth shut.*

Baggage in this sense elaborates on the use of *bag* for "an unlikable woman." Negative uses of **baggage** would help to explain why more writers are inclined to use **luggage** when referring to the traveler's bags.

bail or bale

These two spellings have been interchanged in several contexts, leaving some doubt as to which now goes where, especially in figurative extensions of the essential words.

The origin of **bale** as in *bale of hay* is the Old French word *balle* meaning "package"; while for **bail(s)** as in cricket, it's the older English *baile* meaning "stick." A more literal use of **bail** is found in agricultural contexts, for the wooden partitions or frames by which farmers separate or restrain large animals. In Australia and New Zealand this was figuratively extended in the verb *bail up*, used originally of the bushranger waylaying travelers for their valuables, and now of anyone who buttonholes another against his/her will.

The legal uses of **bail** derive from another Old French word, the verb *bailler* meaning "keep in custody." The expression *bail* (someone) *out* ("help [someone] out of difficulties") originates in this legal context, hence its spelling in:

> *... bail out the Northern line from a vast increase in traffic.*

In fact this spelling is little used in the UK for the extended verb, according to BNC evidence, but much used in the US, as well as Australia and New Zealand. In the UK **bail** is usually a noun, caught up in phrases such as *on bail* and *grant/refuse bail*.

Nautical use of *bail out* was traditionally spelled the same way, but by coincidence, since the phrase embodies the Old French word for a bucket: *baille.* In the US it is still spelled *bail out,* but *bale out* was gaining ground in the UK during C19, according to the first *Oxford Dictionary* (1884–1928), and has become the preferred spelling of the second edition (1989). When it comes to airmen making a parachute jump from their aircraft, this too is *bail out* in American English. It is *bale out* in the *Oxford Dictionary* (1989), yet not because it's regarded as an extension of the nautical usage (an emergency measure in / exit from a vehicle). Instead, the dictionary relates it to the noun **bale**, and sees the manoeuvre as one where the parachutist exits from the aircraft like a *bale (of hay etc.)* through a trapdoor.

In all this we see two solutions to a dilemma. The American solution is to use **bail** for every meaning except the nonlegal noun (*bale of hay, straw, wool*). The British solution is to reserve **bail** for legal uses

(and cricket), and assign **bale** to other uses, especially the verbs associated with taking emergency measures and/or helping someone out of difficulty. The following examples from the BNC and CCAE respectively show the contrast for both transitive and intransitive uses:

> *He could perhaps bale uncle out of the difficulties.* (tr.)
> *Kennedy would bail out the intelligence agency if need be.* (tr.)
> *He ordered the crew to bale out.* (intr.)
> *The crew of a 12-foot skiff bail out after their boat capsized.* (intr.)

The same spellings are applied in the related noun/modifier, as in British *a bale-out scheme* and American *a government bailout*. Etymologists may shake their heads, but at least there's consistency.

Quite independent of all that is the **bale** in *baleful*. Its spelling never varies, because it reflects the Old Norse word *bal*, meaning "fate."

balk or baulk

The first spelling **balk** has much to recommend it. Apart from the analogy with common words like *talk* and *walk,* **balk** is the earlier spelling. In the US **balk** is standard for verb and noun uses, and the only spelling to be found in CCAE. **Baulk** is much more in evidence in the UK. Its use increased in the later C19, according to the *Oxford Dictionary* (1884–1928), and *New Oxford* (1998) makes it the primary spelling. Data from the BNC confirm the dominance of **baulk** for the noun referring to a large wooden beam, as in *holed amidships by a baulk of timber*. But **baulk** and **balk** are used equally for the verb, meaning "resist," "stop short." The divergent senses of verb and noun might explain the different spelling conventions in British English, although they are not differentiated elsewhere. Canadians – like Americans – prefer **balk** for both noun and verb, according to *Canadian Oxford* (1998), and Australians **baulk**, according to the *Macquarie Dictionary* (1997).

> **International English selection:** The spelling **balk** is to be preferred for both noun and verb, given its wide distribution and etymological consistency.

◊ Compare **caulk, calk** or **calque**, where several meanings are involved.

ballot

Should the *t* be doubled when this word has verb suffixes added to it? No is the answer, in terms of both practice and principle. *Balloted/balloting* are used in more than 95% of instances in both British and American databases (BNC and CCAE). The spellings conform to the common principles for doubling: see further under **-t**.

balmy or barmy

The colloquial adjective for someone who's losing their mind is spelled **balmy** in the US, and **barmy** in the UK. The first evidence of this sense (from the 1850s) is attached to **balmy** by the *Oxford Dictionary* (1989), as an extension of its rather vague use in expressions like *balmy weather*. This explains the continuing use of **balmy** in American English, whereas **barmy** is a British respelling of **balmy** dating from the 1890s, now used regularly for the sense "crazy" as in *gone barmy*. So in the UK **balmy** is reserved for the climatic sense of "warm, benign," and only rarely used to mean "crazy" (in less than 5% of all instances in BNC data). **Barmy** could hardly be substituted in the US, because the standard dialect is rhotic, i.e. pronounces the "r" after a vowel.

Some dictionaries including *New Oxford* (1998) present **barmy** as derived independently from *barm,* a technical word for the froth on fermenting beer. Admittedly the *Oxford Dictionary* (1989) records figurative uses of **barmy** on isolated occasions from C17 on, but they refer to the creative brain in a ferment rather than suspected insanity. The two states of mind are of course proverbially close – though perhaps the *barmy army* of drunken hooligans at European football matches has provided a more direct link with *barm.*

bandeau

For the plural of this word, see under **-eau.**

banjos or banjoes

The word **banjo** has been in English long enough (since C18) to have acquired a plural with *-es* as well as just *-s.* But **banjos** is now the preferred spelling, endorsed by over 75% of those responding to the worldwide Langscape survey (1998–2001). Both *Merriam-Webster* (2000) and *New Oxford* (1998) put **banjos** ahead of **banjoes** for the plural. See further under **-o** section 1.

banquet

On whether to double the *t* before verb suffixes are added, see under **-t.**

Bantu

Within southern Africa, the connotations of this word have been more pejorative than elsewhere, due to its oppressive use as a racial designator in the *Bantu Education Act* of 1953. In the post-apartheid era, it has been somewhat rehabilitated, with nine **Bantu** languages recognized among the official languages of South Africa (see under **South African English**). For anthropologists and linguists, **Bantu** has always referred to a distinctive culture or language group, eminently worthy of attention.

bar

For the use of this word as a preposition, as in *bar none,* see under **barring.**

barbaric, barbarous or barbarian

These have all been used since C16 to express the civilized person's distaste for savagery, and condemnation of it. There's little to differentiate them, except that **barbaric** is the most frequent of the three as adjective, in data from the BNC, and **barbarian** has a parallel life as a noun for someone with savage or uncivilized ways. Note also that whereas **barbarous** always expresses condemnation, the judgement in **barbaric** varies with the phrase it appears in. In *barbaric cruelty* it's clearly negative, while in *barbaric splendor* it connotes something which though primitive is impressive in its own way.

In origin all three words represent a much less harsh judgement about those who stand outside our society and culture. The root *barbar-* embedded in

them was used by the Greeks to describe the speech of the neighboring nations, which they found unintelligible. Thus **barbarians** were originally people who spoke a different language; and the name given to the *Berbers* may have originated in this way also. In modern English the tables are turned in the idiom "It was all Greek to me."

barbarism

This word was once much less harsh as a comment on words and idioms (see previous entry). In C16 **barbarism** simply referred to a foreign word borrowed into English, though from C18 on, it served to stigmatize what were deemed mistakes in English words. *Barbarisms* were words malformed in terms of conventional usage or the usual patterns of word-formation, e.g. *normalcy.* They contrasted with *solecisms,* which were other kinds of error in syntax (see **solecism**). This technical application of **barbarism** makes it less heavy-handed, as Fowler (1926) noted. But commentators less scrupulous than Fowler have been known to deploy **barbarism** with all its primitive force to put down a particular usage. **Barbarism** then becomes a verbal weapon, often deployed in the face of popular support for the expression the writer/speaker wishes to expunge. It invokes social sanctions against it: no civilized person would utter it! See further under **shibboleth.**

barbecue or barbeque

The first spelling is much more common. In American data from CCAE, **barbecue** outnumbers **barbeque** by 19:1, and in the BNC it's just on 30:1. **Barbecue** has exclusive backing from the *Oxford Dictionary* (1989), being much closer to the original word in Haitian Creole: *barbacoa* ("a framework of sticks on which meat is smoked"). It first appears in C17 English as *barbacue,* sometimes referring to a makeshift bed, and by 1733 had acquired its sense of a form of entertainment involving alfresco cooking and dining. Its popularity in the southern hemisphere is reflected in the shortened form *barbie,* used in Australia and New Zealand.

The second spelling **barbeque** seems at first sight to frenchify the word, although the French would pronounce such a word with just two syllables, to rhyme with "dalek." In fact the *-que* probably represents the third syllable of various abbreviations for the word, as *bar-b-que, Bar-B-Q* and *BBQ.*

barrel

In British English, the final *l* of **barrel** is doubled before adding verb suffixes, in American English it stays single. Compare *double-barrelled surname* with *double-barreled shot gun.* For further discussion, see **-l-/-ll-.**

barring and bar

As prepositions identifying exceptions, these are both relatively uncommon and may raise questions of usage. **Barring** usually associates with negative events, as in *barring accidents / a disaster / injuries / any last minute hitches.* It commonly appears at the start of a sentence, raising suspicions that it may be a "dangling participle," although its connections with the verb *bar* are now scarcely there (see **dangling participles**). For example:

Barring coups, the four Southern Cone presidents will all still be in office in 1994.

In fuller context, the phrase with **barring** has a good chance of being read absolutely, as intended: "Provided there are no coups d'état ... " (See **absolute** section 4.) Whether foregrounded in a sentence or set off in parentheses, it highlights a proviso to the statement being made.

The preposition **bar** is a similarly efficient way of mentioning an exception to an implied set:

closed to all bar buses and taxis
everything bar the kitchen sink

As in those cases, **bar** attaches itself to the pronoun that encompasses the whole set. The idiom *bar none* is attached to a superlative phrase, as in:

the best young backs in the country bar none
the sexiest actress in the world bar none

The examples all show how **bar** is tied into formulas, whereas **barring** enjoys more flexible and productive use. When the two coincide, as in the following, **barring** seems to win out:

Nothing barring a major disaster can prevent her from becoming a main attraction. (Why not *Nothing bar a major disaster ... ?*)

Examples like this from the BNC suggest that **barring** is gaining ground while **bar** is losing it. The same trend emerges in data from CCAE, where examples of **barring** run in to hundreds, and those that there are of **bar** are confined to the idiom *bar none*.

based on

This argumentative phrase is sometimes felt to introduce a "dangling participle." See further under **dangling participles**.

bases

What are the bases of power in this country? The reader may well puzzle over whether this is the plural of *base* or *basis*. It could be either, and though pronunciation would make it one or the other, the difference is masked in the spelling. Often the context helps to settle the issue, as in *American bases overseas* – but not always. As the first example showed, clarification may be needed. For more about the plurals of words like *basis*, see **-is**.

basic or basal

Both these were derived from the word *base* in the earlier C19, **basal** in 1828 and **basic** in 1848, according to the *Oxford Dictionary* (1989). In spite of its slightly later start, **basic** makes a much greater impact on contemporary English, being frequent in both writing and speech, and outnumbering its rival by more than 20:1 in the BNC. The applications of **basal** are specialized and technical, confined to the fields of medicine, biology and geology except for the *basal readers* used in primary education.

Basic English

To facilitate communication across language barriers, a reduced version of English, called **Basic English** was compiled by C. K. Ogden in 1930. Its inventory of 850 key words provides the wherewithal for discussing everyday things: 100 operations (mostly *function words*), 400 general and 200 picturable things (mostly nouns, a few verbs), 100 qualities and 50 opposites (= adjectives). Although some of the selections inevitably seem dated and culture-specific (e.g.

servant), it would support general conversation anywhere. The larger objectives of **Basic (English)** are reflected in its being an acronym for *British American Scientific International Commercial,* though it would need to be supplemented with scientific terms – not to mention the names of countries and currencies – to go any way towards international communication. **Basic English** was endorsed by both Churchill and Roosevelt in the 1940s, but did not achieve any formal status as an auxiliary language. The essential notion of a reduced but fully functional English vocabulary has nevertheless been taken up in the "defining vocabularies" of certain dictionaries, whose publishers aim to ensure that the dictionary definitions are intelligible to learners with limited English.

basically or basicly

Basically is the standard way of spelling this adverb, on record since 1903. The eminently sensible **basicly** is not yet recognized in the major dictionaries, nor the BNC, and it makes only a single appearance in CCAE. As yet the word seems to be bound by the *- ally* convention for adjectives ending in *-ic,* though it would not be the first to break out. See further under **-ic/-ical**.

bassinet or bassinette

See under **-ette**.

bathe or bath

Ablutionary practices are culture-specific. But in the English-speaking world there's added complexity from the fact that the verbs **bath** and **bathe** can connote different uses of water. The British use the verb **bath** to mean "take a bath" or "give a bath" (to a baby), while **bathe** normally refers to washing a wound. In addition **bathe** can mean "take a swim" in the sea, hence the *bathing costume* and the *bathing boxes* for changing one's clothes at the edge of the beach. In American usage, **bathe** refers not only to swimming but also to washing the baby, or oneself, by means of a bath or shower, and the verb **bath** is reserved for technical applications. Canadians can use either **bathe** or **bath** for personal ablutions, according to the *Canadian Oxford* (1998). Australians distinguish between them much like the British (*Macquarie Dictionary,* 1997), but tend to use the verb *shower* for the cleansing activities in the bathroom.

Note that when written down, *bathing* and *bathed* are ambiguous for readers familiar with both **bath** and **bathe**. Which verb do they relate to? Paraphrases such as *having a bath/bathe* and *had a bath/bathe* may be needed – unless the context (indoor/outdoor) settles it as one or other kind of encounter with water. Metaphorical expressions such as *bathed in sunlight* are also susceptible to misreading.

bathos

This Greek word for "depth" is used in literary criticism to refer to an anticlimax, an abrupt shift from the elevated or sublime to the trivial or ridiculous. When **bathos** is deliberate, the effect may be funny, ironic or satirical. Unintentional **bathos** reflects negatively on the writer, as triteness or banality of style. Either way the effect is not one of **pathos** (see further under that heading).

baulk or balk
See **balk**.

bayonet
Dictionaries in the UK, US, Canada and Australia all foreground *bayoneted* and *bayoneting* for the inflected verb forms. *Merriam-Webster* (2000) notes the spellings with two *t*s (*bayonetted, bayonetting*) as alternatives, which can be justified if the main stress falls on the third syllable (see **doubling of final consonant**). But with main stress on the first syllable, the spellings with one *t* are appropriate. It may as well be used if – as often – the pronunciation is unknowable or unimportant.

BC or BCE
The letters **BC** ("before Christ") remind us that our dating system has a religious foundation. Yet the fact that **BC** is an English phrase confirms its modern origins: it was coined in C18. Compare the Latin abbreviation *AD* (short for *anno domini*), which has been used in Christian annals and records since C6.

The inescapably Christian connotations of **BC** have led some to prefer **BCE**, intended to represent "before the common era." **BCE** seems to have originated in the US in the 1960s, as a way of embracing Jewish and Christian interests in the western historical calendar. However **BCE** can still be read as "before the Christian era," so the problem remains – as well as the fact that the "common" calendar has no connection with the dating systems used in Islam or other Asian traditions. These problems also affect *CE*, the corresponding term intended to replace *AD*.

BC and **BCE** are both placed after the date itself: *50 BC, 50 BCE*. Compare the position of *AD*, discussed under **AD or A.D.** All these abbreviations can be written without stops. The fact that they consist of capitals is one reason for this (see further under **abbreviations** options 2 [c] and [d]). Another is the fact that they are usually accompanied by numbers, which make plain their dating function.

◊ For alternative ways of indicating dates, see **dating systems**.

be
The verb **be** in its numerous forms is the most common in English. It has more distinct forms than any other verb, with three for the present: *am, are, is;* two for the past: *was, were;* and two participles: *being, been* as well as the infinitive **be**. In some regional dialects of English, **be** serves instead of *am, are, is* for all persons of the present tense. In Black English, **be** indicates repeated or habitual action: *People be leapin' outta their seats.*

The most essential role of **be** is as one of the primary auxiliary verbs of English, used to express continuous action (to grammarians, the imperfect aspect), and the passive voice, as in the following:
> *you are asking* (continuous action / imperfect)
> *you are asked* (passive)

Compare *you ask* with no auxiliary, expressing simple action in the active voice. (See further under **auxiliary verbs**, **aspect** and **voice**.)

The verb **be** can also be used as a main verb on its own, in an existential sense:
> *I think therefore I am.*

Or it can be used as a copular verb, linking the subject of the clause with its complement:
> *Their plan is a great leap forward.*

(See further under **copular verbs**.)

The present forms of **be** are often contracted with their subject pronoun in the flow of conversation, as *I'm, you're, she's, we're, they're*. The third person singular *is* forms contractions with many kinds of nouns, both proper and common:
> *Jane's being taught the piano.*
> *Stalin's dead.*
> *Dinner's in the oven.*

For the use of these forms in writing, see **contractions** section 2.

Note finally that **be** (and *were*) have residual roles as subjunctives in modern English. See further under **subjunctive**.

be-
This prefix dates back to Old English, and is an inseparable element of verbs like *become, begin, behave, believe*. In modern English it serves mostly as a grammatical agent, turning intransitive verbs into transitive ones, as in *belie, bemoan, bewail;* or creating verbs from nouns and adjectives: *becalm, befriend, bejewel, belittle, bewitch*. Ad hoc words generated with **be-** are transparent enough to be understood on first encounter:
> *They stood ready for the rodeo, leather-jacketed and bespurred.*

Words formed with **be-** (or any affix) are less likely to find a permanent place in dictionaries than other kinds of neologism, according to Ayto's (1998) research.

beat or beaten
While **beat** is standard for both present and past tense of this verb, it's sometimes used instead of **beaten** for the past participle as well. In C18 this was ordinary written usage, and *Merriam-Webster* (2000) notes it as a current alternative for American English. However the use of **beat** as past participle is mostly found in particular idioms where the participle is passive, for example *get/got beat* and *(can't) be beat*. Database evidence of this (from CCAE and the BNC) comes particularly from sports reporting in the US, and casual conversation in the UK:
> *We got beat by a very good football team.*
> *If we get beat, it's my fault.*

Can't be beat (used of notional competition, as in *a location that can't be beat*) is standard American idiom, according to *Webster's English Usage* (1989). Almost all instances of it in CCAE had **beat** rather than **beaten** as the past participle, whereas they were very rare in the BNC. Written data from CCAE also show the use of **beat** (as past participle) in the phrasal verb *beat up*, referring to acts of violence:
> *...took him out of the Bronx where he had been beat up*

In the same construction, writers represented in the BNC use **beaten**:
> *He was beaten up by a gang of white boys...*

Yet the participial adjective *beat-up* is found in English everywhere, referring especially to battered vehicles, as well as furniture, clothes and other things rather the worse for wear, from the *beat-up hotel* to *beat-up sneakers*.

Although **beat** is built into various idioms as past participle, its appearance otherwise in that role connotes spoken rather than written style. **Beaten** is far more common as the past participle in active or passive verb phrases, and not seriously challenged by **beat** across the range of prose styles in the UK or the US (Peters, 1993b). The distinct past participle remains part of the writer's repertoire.

beau ideal

This phrase is often interpreted in reverse. In French *le beau idéal* means "ideal (form of) beauty" or "the abstract idea of beauty." Those who understand the French (where *idéal* is an adjective following the noun) use it this way in aesthetic discussions in English. But without an accent, **ideal** looks like an English word, and so the phrase is often taken to mean "beautiful ideal," and applied in many contexts to the perfect model of something: *the beau ideal of the family.*

beaus or beaux

After centuries of use as an English noun meaning "boyfriend," **beau** still poses the question as to whether its plural form should be French or English. In British English, **beaux** has the upper hand, being the preferred form of the *Oxford Dictionary* (1989), and dominant in the BNC, by about 4:1. American dictionaries allow either **beaus** or **beaux**, and the examples in CCAE are about equally divided. Both forms could be found in versions of the same story in the *Atlanta Journal,* and businesses may cash in on either: the *Beaux Tie Grill* was matched by *Belles and Beaus Bridal and Formal Wear.* Americans are perhaps more inclined to **beaus** because of the need to distinguish it from a very different use of **beaux** in architectural comments such as [*that*] *giant beaux arts bath house* (= Union Station), where *Beaux Arts* is decapitalized as often in American style.

bedevil

Normal British practice is to double the final *l* before adding verb suffixes to words like this (see **-l-/-ll-**). However about 1 in 8 examples of *bedevil(l)ed* in the BNC keeps the *l* single, as in American English.

beet and beetroot

The same vegetable goes by different names in North American and British English, according to its uses. In the US and Canada, **beet** is the culinary term for the garnet-colored vegetable used in mixed salads and Russian-style borscht. Its color becomes a simile for embarrassment in *blushing like a beet.* When used in agriculture as a source of sugar, it's referred to as *sugar beet.* The British use *sugar beet* or just **beet** for the agricultural crop, as in *productive acres of beet and potatoes.* In the UK **beetroot** serves as the standard term for the vegetable on the table, as it does in Australia – but not in North America.

beg the question

This phrase refers to a frustrating argumentative tactic, though it may be understood in one of three ways. Its curious wording reflects the fact that it translates the Latin phrase *petitio principii* ("begging the principle"), meaning that the speaker/writer assumes the fundamental premise or issue that ought to be discussed. Typically the issue is woven into another assertion or premise which effectively submerges it. The actual terms used in a discussion can **beg the question**, as recognized in the following:

> *Some definitions of mental illness beg the question of what constitutes normal behavior.*

The problem with *begged questions* is that they compromise the scope of the discussion, preempting what the participants would need to focus on in order to gain a fresh perspective.

The argumentative sabotage in *begging the question* is recognized by those who use it to mean "evade the issue." This alternative use is acknowledged in *Webster's Third* (1986), the *Canadian Oxford* (1998) and the Australian *Macquarie Dictionary* (1997). While this understanding of **beg the question** strains the meaning of *beg,* it's pragmatically closer to the original sense of the phrase than when it simply means "raise the question," as in:

> *Doesn't three guitarists in three albums beg the question that Chadwick might be just a little hard on his sidemen?*

This third use of **beg the question** is now the commonest of the three, according to *New Oxford* (1998).

begin (to)

English allows two kinds of construction with **begin**:

> *They began to feel relaxed after the meal.*
> *They began feeling relaxed after the meal.*

The *-ing* construction gained ground in American English since the 1960s, probably through news reporting, and is now a well-established alternative to the *to* construction. Meanwhile in British English the *to* construction is still strongly preferred, according to Mair's (1998) research.

behalf of

On behalf of is the standard collocation in English everywhere, though alternatives are around in both the US and the UK. In British data from the BNC, about two thirds of all instances were *on behalf of X* (or *on X's behalf*). But the rest was a mix of *in behalf of, of behalf of* and just plain *behalf of,* as in *the claims of NUS to speak behalf of individual students.* Dictionaries note that Americans use *in behalf of* as well as *on behalf of,* but in data from CCAE the latter is much more common, by about 20:1. There's no evidence that *in behalf of* is restricted to a single sense, as commentators have sometimes suggested. The two senses associated with *on behalf of* ("in defense of" / "to the benefit of") and "as agent/representative for") are both to be found in the American corpus for *in behalf of*:

> *efforts in behalf of corporate clients*

versus

> *sent telegrams in behalf of their 10,000 members*

However as the examples show, the two senses are not clearly separable.

An extension of the second sense into "on the part of" is occasionally heard and seen: *That was a great shot on behalf of the young winger.* It smacks of running commentary and the desire to embellish the facts. In edited text, this use of *on behalf of* would probably amount to overwriting the simple fact that "the young winger produced a good shot." Examples of this newest use of *on behalf of* are nevertheless making their way into print, according to Burchfield (1996), but it has yet to be registered in dictionaries.

◇ Compare *on the part of,* discussed at **part of**.

behavior or behaviour
See under **-or/-our**.

behove or behoove
This verb is almost a fossil in British English, used only in impersonal constructions with *it* to express a duty, as in "it would behove xx to . . ." Instances of its use in the BNC can be counted on the fingers of one hand, and all are from formal writing. Its spelling in UK is **behove**, whereas in the US it's always **behoove**. In American English it enjoys a slightly more varied existence, appearing in more and less formal contexts, and in more interactive prose – witness the following from CCAE:

> *It would behoove the Senate to act promptly.*
> *Would it behoove you to look at your duty roster?*
> *It didn't behoove me financially to go overseas.*

In other examples, the verbs accompanying **behoove** were *will, may* and *might,* giving it a wider range of modality and shades of obligation, from a broad imperative to the individual's sense of what is fitting. See further under **modality**.

Beijing
See under **China**.

belie
This word implies that things are not as they seem:

> *These days her voice and lifestyle belie her upbringing.*

With **belie**, appearances mask something very different underneath, hence the fact that **belie** is sometimes confused with *underlie*. But while *underlie* refers to the actual structure of things physical or psychological, **belie** always implies a misrepresentation of them.

Because **belie** is derived from the verb *lie* "tell lies," its past tense is *belied* (not *belay*). For the past tense of *underlie*, see **underlay**.

benefit
Should you double the *t* before adding verbal suffixes? The answer from the great majority of writers, both American and British, is no. In American data from CCAE, *benefited/benefiting* outnumber *benefitted/benefitting* by about 8:1, and in BNC data the ratio is more than 10:1. Thus common usage supports the regular spelling, according to the principles discussed under **-t**.

Benelux
See under **Netherlands**.

benzine or benzene
These two spellings are used to distinguish different chemical substances. **Benzine** is a mixture of hydrocarbons obtained in the distillation of petroleum. For Americans it is also a synonym for "gas." **Benzene** is a single species of hydrocarbon molecule, with various industrial applications. Confusion of the two spellings by nonchemists is hardly surprising, given that *-ine* and *-ene* are interchangeable in the names of other household

chemicals (see further under **-ine**). In fact **benzene** was originally **benzine**.

beseeched or besought
Either of these can be used as the past form of *beseech*. The *Oxford Dictionary* (1989) retains a note from its first edition to say that **beseeched** is "regarded as incorrect," but in BNC data it's the preferred form, outnumbering **besought** by more than 10 times. American dictionaries register **besought** and **beseeched** (in that order) as equal alternatives, but again usage gives stronger backing to the second. **Beseeched** is more frequent than **besought** in CCAE, though by a lesser margin (2:1) than in the British data.

beside or besides
Do these mean the same thing? The answer is yes and no. As a preposition **beside** has the more immediate and physical meanings "next to" and "in comparison with," while **besides** covers the more detached and figurative ones "in addition to" and "apart from." Compare:

> *The ticket machine was beside the driver.*
> *There was no-one besides the driver in the bus.*

But **beside** is very occasionally used in a figurative sense like the one shown in that second sentence, according to the *Oxford Dictionary* (1989) and *Webster's English Usage* (1989).

As adverbs, **beside** and **besides** share the figurative role:

> *He enjoyed a big salary, a company car, and everything else beside(s).*

Yet only **beside** can appear when the sense is that of physical proximity:

> *The president was on the platform and his wife stood beside.*

Overall then, **beside** seems to be gaining on **besides**, at least in the roles of preposition and adverb. The preference for adverbs without *s* can be seen elsewhere: see **-ward**.

Yet **besides** is unchallenged as the conjunct meaning "moreover":

> *Besides, he felt they owed it to him.*

In that role it cannot be replaced by **beside**.

besought or beseeched
See **beseeched**.

bet or betted
The past form of the verb **bet** can be either **bet** or **betted**, according to all major dictionaries. **Bet** is more than likely for the past participle:

> *Being a mathematician, he bet(ted) for years by a random number table.*
> *She had bet her savings on that horse.*

See further under **zero past tense**.

bête noire
Borrowed from French, this phrase allows us to refer discreetly to something or someone we can't stand. In reverse order **bête noire** means "black beast," or less literally "bugbear" – though with a touch of the sinister that puts it higher up the stylistic scale. The *e* of **noire** is there to agree with **bête**, which happens to be a feminine noun in French. So the *e* should remain, even if your difficult person is masculine: **bête noire** applies to either gender. Yet the phrase is sometimes

seen in English as *bête noir*, a spelling which is registered in *Webster's Third* (1986) as an alternative. American examples from CCAE showed it to be indifferent to gender, applied to men, political opponents and even one's mother-in-law. Examples of *bête noir* are also to be found in the BNC, though the form is not recognized in British dictionaries.

Dictionaries in the UK, US, Canada and Australia all crown **bête noire** with its French circumflex, though it's not crucial to the identity of the phrase (see **accents**). The plural is shown as *bêtes noires*, with plural marking on both words (noun and adjective), as in French. See further under **plurals** section 2.

better or bettor

The spelling **bettor** for a person who lays bets undoubtedly helps to distinguish it from the adjective/adverb **better**. It would be indispensable if you had to write:

He was a better bettor than his partner.

Yet the juxtaposition of the two seems far-fetched. **Bettor** is less likely than *punter* in most contexts – you could bet on it.

In fact the spelling **better** is used generally in the UK for the person who lays bets, and it had the backing of Fowler (1926). It is more natural than **bettor** as the agent noun from an English verb (see further under **-er/-or**). In the US however, **bettor** is the preferred form, as shown in *Webster's Third* (1986).

better or more well-

Compound adjectives with a built-in comparative can be constructed in two ways. Should it be *a better known author* or *a more well-known author*? See under **well and well-**.

between or among

These words share more common ground than they used to. **Between** was formerly reserved for situations where just two things or people were being related – *shared between husband and wife* – and **among** complemented it when there were three or more: *shared among the relatives*. The restriction on the use of **between** has certainly gone by the board, and Gowers declared it to be "superstition" in *Complete Plain Words* (1954). It is not uncommon for **between** to be used in expressions referring to more than two groups or reference points, as in *a balance between deference, quotation and his own critical comment.* But **among** is still reserved for situations where there are at least three parties involved. One could not say "among husband and wife." See further under **amid(st) or among(st)**.

between you and me (or I)

Those who always use **between you and me** have it easy, because it's in line with what the traditional grammarians regard as correct use of pronouns. Yet **between you and I** is certainly used too, and for some people it is the usual formula to highlight a confidential point of conversation. The real issue is whether it should appear in writing.

The phrase **between you and I** has a long history of both use and censure. Literary authors from Shakespeare on confirm its currency, yet it fell foul of C18 grammarians, and their zeal to preserve the remaining case distinctions (nominative/accusative) among the English pronouns. They argued that in

between you and ???, both pronouns are objects of the preposition, and must therefore be accusative. This makes no difference for *you* but it demands *me* rather than *I* as the second pronoun. Of course, if it were *between me and my dog*, no-one would say or write otherwise. The use of *me* comes naturally then, because it is directly governed by *between*. The *I* probably gets into **between you and I** because it's further away from the governing word.

Other factors may help to foster the use of *I*, such as the fact that the phrase quite often comes immediately before the subject/nominative of a clause, as in:

Between you and I, they won't be here much longer.

Using *I* may be a kind of hypercorrection, according to the *Comprehensive Grammar* (1985), based on oversensitivity about using *me* (see further under **me**). The vacillation over *me/I* is symptomatic of shifting case relations among pronouns generally (Wales, 1996). But because **between you and I** seems to have become a **shibboleth** (see under that heading), it's to be avoided in writing. In fact a confidential **between you and I/me** is unlikely to occur to anyone writing a formal document, because of the impersonal character of the style that goes with it.

beveled or bevelled

For the choice between these spellings, see **-l-/-ll-**.

bi-

This prefix comes from Latin with the meaning "two," though in a handful of English words it means "twice." Examples of the first meaning ("two") are easily found in everyday and general words such as:

bicentenary	*bicycle*	*biennial*	*bifocals*
bigamy	*binary*	*binoculars*	*bipartisan*

as well as scientific words such as:

bicarbonate	*biceps*	*bicuspid*	*biped*
bisexual	*bivalve*		

The second meaning ("twice") is found only in *biannual* and sometimes in *bimonthly* and *biweekly*. It arose only in C20, and unfortunately makes for chronic difficulty in interpreting those words. None of the other number prefixes 1 to 10 has this duality of meaning (see **number prefixes**). The distinction between *biennial* and *biannual* is easiest to remember if you're a gardener working with *biennial asters* which last for two years, or someone who attends *biennial exhibitions* which take place every two years. Without the support of such contexts, a reader may well be in doubt. Does a *biannual meeting* take place twice a year or every two years? Dictionaries which distinguish *biennial* ("every two years") from *biannual* ("twice a year"), also note that *biannual* is sometimes used with the meaning of *biennial*. For a writer, there is always the risk of not being interpreted as you intend and it's safer to use a paraphrase. One can replace *biannual* with "twice a year," and *biennial* with "every two years."

Alternatively you could use the prefix *semi-* and *semiannual* instead of *biannual*, as *Webster's English Usage* (1989) suggests. This works well enough for *semimonthly* and *semiweekly* also, because *semi-* combines with both classical and English words (see **semi-**). *Fortnightly* is also useful as a paraphrase for "every two weeks / twice a month," in something intended for British readers. But *fortnight* and *fortnightly* are unfamiliar to Americans.

◇ Compare the prefix **di-**.

biannual or biennial

See under **bi-**.

bias

When **bias** becomes a verb, should its inflected forms be *biased* and *biasing*, or *biassed* and *biassing?* The spellings with one *s* were overwhelmingly preferred by 94% of respondents to the worldwide Langscape survey (1998–2001). They are the primary spellings in all the major dictionaries: *New Oxford* (1998), *Webster's Third* (1986), *Canadian Oxford* (1998), the Australian *Macquarie* (1997). The forms with double *s* were evidently quite common in C19, but with both Fowler (1926) and the *Oxford Dictionary* (1884–1928) arguing against them, their currency has been greatly reduced. The single *s* spelling represents the more regular principle for verbs ending in a single consonant, though British and American English don't always agree on this (see **doubling of final consonant**).

The plural of the noun **bias** is not commented on in the dictionaries, which implies that it is the regular *biases*. It helps to reinforce the single *s* forms for the verb.

Bible or bible

Does this word need to be capitalized when it refers to the volume of holy scriptures which is the cornerstone of Christianity? Half of all respondents to the Langscape survey (1998–2001) said yes "always," but for a third it was "sometimes" and for the rest "never." The survey produced markedly different results from the UK and the US: while 62% of British respondents said "always," only 35% of Americans did. This divergence no doubt reflects their different orientation to the use of capitals generally (see **capital letters**), rather than any religious difference. In this book, **bible** is usually lower-cased because it appears in paraphrases of the formal title, e.g. *the King James bible*. Figurative uses of the word, such as the "cyclist's bible" or "military planners' bible," naturally have the word without a capital.

bibliographies

Bibliography is the general name for the consolidated list of works referred to by the author. Note that in some academic disciplines, it includes any item read or consulted in writing the book. Others prefer to restrict the list to items which are actually cited in the text, which makes it a "List of references" rather than "Works consulted."

The form of the **bibliography** varies with the chosen referencing system in matters such as the order of items, alphabetization, and the forms of names. There are also many small points of style in punctuation and abbreviations which vary with the publishing house, the journal and its editor, and a writer should always check for their particular preferences. Generic disciplinary guides are to be found for:

* *humanities* in the *Chicago Manual of Style* (2003) and the *MLA (Modern Languages Association) Style Manual* (2nd. ed. 1999)
* *social sciences* in the *APA (American Psychological Association) Style Manual* (5th. ed. 2001)
* *natural sciences* in the *CBE (Council of Biology Editors) Manual* (6th. ed. 1994 = *Scientific Style and Format*).

What follows are token **bibliographies** to illustrate the different formats used to complement each of the main referencing systems:

A. short-title references, in the text and footnotes/endnotes
B. author–date references (also called the "Harvard" or name–year system)
C. number system (with "Vancouver" style)

For the forms of the references themselves, see **referencing**.

A. Bibliography to go with short-title references

Algeo, John "Desuetude among new English words." *International Journal of Lexicography* 6:ii; 1993.

Preston, Dennis R. "Where the worst English is spoken." In *Focus on the USA*, edited by Edgar W. Schneider. Amsterdam, John Benjamins: 1996.

Trudgill, Peter and Hannah, Jean. *International English: a guide to the varieties of standard English.* London, Edward Arnold: 1982.

B. Bibliography to go with author–date references

Algeo, J. 1993 Desuetude among new English words. *International Journal of Lexicography*, 6: ii.

Preston, D. R. 1996 Where the worst English is spoken. In *Focus on the USA*, edited by E. W. Schneider. Amsterdam, John Benjamins.

Trudgill, P. and Hannah, J. 1982 *International English: a guide to the varieties of standard English.* London, Edward Arnold.

C. Bibliography to go with number system, using Vancouver style

1 Trudgill P, Hannah J. *International English: a guide to the varieties of standard English.* London, Edward Arnold: 1982.

2 Preston DR. Where the worst English is spoken. In Schneider EW ed., *Focus on the USA.* Amsterdam, J Benjamins: 1996.

3 Algeo J. Desuetude among new English words. Int. J of Lexicography 1993; 6:2.

Points to note
**Order of entries:
– The order of entries is alphabetical in A and B. In C the order is dictated by the numbers, which run in accordance with the appearance of each item within the text.
**Authors' names and initials
– In all three systems the names of all authors are inverted (Ritter, 2002). The practice of inverting the first author's name but not the second or others is in abeyance.
– Initials are occasionally used in A for the full first names of authors, usually in B, and always in C. In C the initials are written without stops, and the word and is omitted between the names of joint authors.
**Date of publication
– The date is placed immediately after the name(s) of the author(s) in B, but not A or C.
**Titles of articles, chapters, books and journals
– The use of capitals in titles and subtitles varies, though the minimal capitalization of librarians has much to recommend it. (See further under **titles.**)
– The titles of articles or chapters of books have in the past been set in quotation marks. This practice is now rare in the natural sciences (see *CBE Manual*, 1994), and declining in the social sciences and humanities (*Webster's Style Manual*, 1985). The *Chicago Manual* (2003) notes that quote marks are not

used for the titles of articles and chapters in author–date style (B). Speaking for British practice, Butcher (1992) notes that they are not essential in **bibliographies**.

– Italics are normally used in A and B to set off the title of the book or the name of the journal.

– In Vancouver style (C) the generic parts of the names of journals are abbreviated. The recognized abbreviations for medicine and biomedical research are detailed each year in the January issue of the *Index Medicus*. Abbreviations for other fields of research may be found in *Chemical Abstracts, World List of Scientific Periodicals,* in British Standard BS 4148 and in American National Standard Z39.5 1985.

– In references to chapters or parts of a book, the book's title should appear before that of the editors, according to the *Chicago Manual*. However the Vancouver system gives the name(s) of the editor(s) first.

**Publishing details

– In the publication details, the place of publication often precedes the name of the publisher. This was not always so, but it's the practice of both Butcher's *Copy-editing* and the *Chicago Manual;* and it makes good sense these days in the era of multinational publishing. If the place is subsumed in the actual name of the publisher, as for *Melbourne University Press,* there's no need to repeat it.

– In Vancouver Style (C), the publisher's name may be abbreviated, for example with *Univ Pr* for "University Press." See *CBE Manual* (1994) for further details. Ampersands should be used, as in *Harper & Row,* in both B and C styles.

**Punctuation

– The overall trend in punctuating *bibliographical* entries is to greater simplicity. Periods / full stops are preferred as the device between separate items, instead of the array of commas and parentheses used in the past. Within each component, commas and colons may be used, as shown above.

bicaps

See **capital letters** section 4.

bicentennial or bicentenary

The celebration of a national 200th birthday calls for extensive public use of either or both of these words, as nouns and adjectives. Americans celebrating their two centuries of independence called it the **bicentennial.** This usage came naturally, and it has the backing of the *Oxford Dictionary* (1989), because it builds in the Latin root for "years" (*enn-*). Yet Fowler (1926) argued that **bicentenary** was to be preferred for the noun, on grounds of analogy (see under **centennial**); and that **bicentennial** should be used only as adjective. British usage as represented in the BNC still goes along with this. Most instances of **bicentenary** were unequivocally nouns (i.e. non-attributive use), whereas most of those for **bicentennial** were adjectival – or at least attributive – as in *bicentennial celebrations* (see further under **adjectives** section 1).

Australians celebrating their 200th birthday in 1988 faced the dilemma of knowing both American and British usage. The *Australian Bicentennial Authority* decided to call the event *the Bicentenary,* and thus seemed to put Fowler's distinction in place. Yet the event was commonly referred to as *the Bicentennial.* Three factors help to explain this:

* the much reported American and French *bicentennials* of the same decade
* the fact that **bicentennial** in its attributive use (as in *Bicentennial Authority*) is easily understood as a noun, since nouns often take on that role in English, witness *birthday celebration.*
* the fact that many classical adjectives have evolved into independent nouns in English: see further under **-al** and **-ary**.

The Australian *Macquarie Dictionary* (1997) and the *Canadian Oxford* (1998) both allow that **bicentennial** can be a noun as well as adjective – like **bicentenary**.

> **International English selection:** Since **bicentennial** serves as an independent noun in American, Canadian and Australian English, there is no reason to replace it with **bicentenary** in that role.

biceps and forceps

The plural of **biceps** could be *biceps, bicepses* or even *bicipites* if you know your Latin. Most people choose between the first two, effectively using either the zero plural or the regular English *-es* plural. The use of just *biceps* as the plural is probably swelled by those who are unsure whether one or more rippling **biceps** is being referred to. With its final *s* **biceps** looks already like a plural, and it probably diverts the uncertain user from adding a further plural ending to it. In any case, it's a perfectly acceptable form. Other muscles such as the *triceps* and *quadriceps* have the same alternative plurals.

Forceps is both similar and a little different. The plural could be *forceps, forcepses* or *forcipes*. (The Latin plural of **forceps** differs because it derives from the verb *capere* [*cip-*] "take" rather than the noun *caput* [*capit-*] "head.") With **forceps** there is a stronger incentive to settle on the zero plural, because of the analogy with *pliers, scissors* and other familiar tools with double blades or arms. On whether **forceps** takes a singular or plural verb, see **agreement** section 2.

bid, bade or bidden

Two Old English verbs have coalesced into one in **bid**, one meaning "ask, demand" and the second "declare, command." By C15 their meanings and past forms had become intertwined, and the tangled legacy is still with us in uncertainties as to which past forms to attach to which meaning. At auctions and in card games, both the past tense and the past participle are **bid**:

> They said he bid millions for the house.
> I've never bid three no trumps so often in one evening.

But when the verb comes up in reference to commands and greetings, the usual past tense is *bade*, and the past participle *bidden*, as in *She had bidden him a quick goodnight*. These inflected forms now have a slightly old-fashioned flavor to them, and are sometimes replaced by *bid*. As a noun, the word shows up regularly in newspapers (see **headline words**).

biennial or biannual

See under **bi-**.

biker, bikie, cyclist or cycler

Three different lifestyles and subcultures go with
these words, though all denote persons devoted to
two-wheeled vehicles, whether motorized or
pedal-powered. The word **biker** is applied in both the
US and the UK to recreational and mountain *bike*
riders as well as members of motorcycle gangs, with
their often violent and lawless activities. *Biker gear*
(i.e. leather jackets) and *biker movies* are associated
with the latter, although the scene is complicated in
the US by the so-called "Rubbies" (Rich Urban Bikers)
who scarcely fraternize with the conventional
groupies. Australians meanwhile use **bikie** to
designate the motorcycle gang members and
distinguish them from recreational riders (= **biker**).

Cyclist serves in both the UK and the US to refer to
the independent recreational **biker** as well as the
professional cycling champion. Again the collocations
help to show which subculture is intended: *mountain
cyclists* on the *hiker–biker* trail or the *Olympic cyclist*.
Some dictionaries note **cycler** as a synonym for
cyclist, but there is scant evidence of its use in British
or American corpora.

Though **biker** and **cyclist** overlap in their coverage
of the cycling scene, the context normally clarifies
which of the three subcultures is intended. **Biker** is
less frequent than **cyclist** in either American or
British databases, though the difference is more
marked in British English. In CCAE they appear in
the ratio of 2:3, whereas in the BNC it's about 1:3.
Constraints on **biker** are suggested by the label
"informal" or "colloquial" found in British
dictionaries. Yet the stylistic difference has nothing to
do with their relative age, since both are on record
from the 1880s. Rather it may correlate with word
forms. **Cyclist** keeps the classical look of the word
(based on Latin *cyclus*), whereas **biker** abbreviates
and anglicizes it. Linguistic scruples like these are
probably reinforced by the negative associations of
biker with motorcycle gangs.

-bility

See **-ability**.

billet

On whether to double the final *-t* when this word
becomes a verb, see **-t**.

billion

The value of **billion** is now 10^9 everywhere in the
English-speaking world, even in the UK. British usage
has changed during the last twenty years, bringing it
into line with American on this crucial issue, and so a
billion means "a thousand million" (Ritter, 2002),
rather than "a million million." The changeover was
led by British financial institutions such as the
Treasury, and has been reflected in reporting by the
London *Financial Times* and *The Economist* for some
time. It puts Britain out of step with the EU, where
both France and Germany use the term
milliard/Milliarde for "a thousand million," and
billion means "a million million." But it is in step
with the US, Canada (*Canadian English Usage*, 1997),
and the Australian government *Style Manual* (2002).

There is nevertheless some continuing danger
within the UK of **billion** being understood in terms of
the old value. British style guides such as Butcher's

(1992) urge writers to spell out numerical values
involving *billions* whenever they are critical. So
however convenient it is to put £4 *billion* or £4 *b*. in
the headline, or anywhere else, it's more ambiguous
than £4,000,000,000, or £4000 million.

The meaning of **billion** affects the value of *trillion,
quadrillion, quintillion* etc. Thus in the
English-speaking world, the *trillion* is now 10^{12},
whereas for France and Germany it's 10^{18}. And so on.

The variable values for **billion** etc. have not been a
problem for mathematicians and scientists, who
routinely deal with very large numbers in terms of
powers of ten. Astronomers measure the vast
distances of the universe by means of *light-years* or
parsecs (the distance equal to a heliocentric *parallax*
of one *second* of arc). Geologists bypass **billion** by
estimating past time in terms of the *mega-annum
(Ma)* or *millions of years* (variously abbreviated as *my,
m.y., m.yr*). In the North American system the most
remote time is expressed with the one unit, e.g. *3400
Ma*, whereas the European geologic system uses both
mega-annum and *giga-annum* (*CBE Manual*, 1994). So
3400 Ma equals *3.4 Ga*.
◊ For more on the standard numerical prefixes, see
Appendix IV; and on geological eras, Appendix II.

bimonthly

See under **bi-**.

binary multiples

See **bytes**.

bingeing or binging

See under **-e** section 1d.

bite or byte

See under **bytes**.

bivouac

English borrowed this from French which
transliterated it from Swiss German *beiwacht*. In C18
its spelling varied from **bivouac** to *bivouaq* to
bivouack, but the verb forms, more often than not,
were *bivouacked* and *bivouacking*. Most respondents
(69%) in the Langscape survey (1998–2001) preferred
the *-ck-* spelling over just *-c-*, in line with English
spelling conventions for verbs ending in *-c*. See
-c/-ck-.

biweekly

See under **bi-**.

black or Black

This word has been used since C17 to translate the
Spanish *negro*, and to refer to the dark-skinned people
encountered by colonial settlers in Africa, Australia
and elsewhere. In the US it chiefly referred to Africans
transported as slaves and was a common designation
until after the Civil War, when replaced by the older
"colored" and then "Negro" (see further under
colo(u)red). **Black** was revived by the Civil Rights
Movement around 1970 as an affirmation of ethnic
identity, and actively promoted in the slogan *Black is
beautiful*. In expressions like *Black Power* and *Black
English* it always carries a capital letter, but not in
generic references. Data from both CCAE and BNC

show that **black** resists capitalization, even when paired with other ethnic descriptors, as in *blacks and Mexicans*. Newspaper coverage of events in South Africa also uses lower case:

> ... *acute shortage of housing for blacks in South Africa's urban areas*

But Australian Aborigines use **Black** (with capital letter) in self-reference, paralleling the American *Black Power* movement, and affirming the general principle of capitalizing ethnic names (see **capital letters** section 1b). Compounds such as *blackfella* are not however capitalized. In the UK, **black** may refer to either Jamaican or Asian immigrants, and is not a solidarity name for the people concerned.

Like any racial designator, the word **black** can be prejudicial to the peoples referred to, especially when used indiscriminately by whites. The fact that **black/Black** is used in self-reference by the people concerned does not license others to do the same. The dilemma prompted the late C20 search for alternatives which could be used in public communication, with some success in establishing geographic/national names, such as *African American, African Canadian* etc. They have the advantage of being in line with those for other immigrants, e.g. *German-American,* and of allowing for finer discriminations as in *Nigerian Canadian (Jamaican, Trinidadian* etc). See further under **racist language**.

Black English

Recognition of ethnic varieties such as **Black English** is relatively recent, and represents acknowledgement of its status as one of the "English languages" (McArthur, 1998). American **Black English** probably developed out of the plantation creole used by African slaves and became then *decreolized* in contact with standard American English, although its relationship with white Southern dialects is still debated. In three decades it has been the most intensely researched form of American English (Schneider, 1996), its name revised several times, from **Black English** to *Black English Vernacular (BEV)* to *African American English Vernacular (AAVE)*. In 1996 its status as a separate dialect or language, called *Ebonics*, was highlighted in the debate over the attempts of one California school district to obtain funding for disadvantaged students under a bilingualism support program. Most of the characteristics of *AAVE* are paralleled in regional dialects of English, although several features of its noun and verb morphology are unique (Wolfram and Schilling-Estes, 1998). They include the omission of *-s* from plural and possessive nouns; of *-s* from the third person singular present tense of verbs; and special uses of *been* and *be,* to indicate action done a long time ago, and habitual use (see under **be**).

In other parts of the world, the term **Black English** continues to be used to designate the variety used by ethnic Africans. In Britain, the variety of English used by Caribbean immigrants in London is also referred to as **Black English**. In western and southern Africa, **Black English** as used by indigenous people distinguishes it from English used by European settlers and their descendants. (See further under **South African English**.) In Australia the variable forms of Aboriginal English are known to their users as *blackfella talk*.

blamable or blameable

American English prefers **blamable**, as indicated by *Webster's Third* (1986), whereas the British preference is **blameable**, according to the *Oxford Dictionary* (1989). The first spelling embodies the regular convention of dropping a final *-e* from the verb before adding a suffix that begins with a vowel (see **-e**).

blanch or blench

Both these verbs connect with the French adjective *blanc* ("white"): **blanch** means "make something white," and **blench** "become white or pale." **Blanch** is often found in recipes for preparing food, as in:

> *First blanch the almonds in boiling water.*

In constructions like these, **blanch** is always transitive. Contrast **blench**, which refers to a human reaction to stress and strain, and is intransitive:

> *My handbag would make a strong man blench.*

Yet in both British and American English, **blanch** is now used intransitively in the same way as **blench**:

> *Tough guys don't blanch.*

Data from the BNC show **blanch** used in this sense is gaining ground over **blench**, outnumbering it by 2:1. In the US, **blench** is already obsolescent, by its absence from CCAE data. The *Oxford Dictionary* (1989) records the extinction of several senses of **blench** ("become pale"), under the impact of an identical Old English verb meaning "recoil or shy away." In fearful situations a human being may (1) turn pale and/or (2) shy away, and **blench** could mean either or both. It can be important to know whether the protagonists stood their ground or not, and the ambiguity of **blench** lets a narrative down at the critical moment. With **blanch** it's more straightforward: just a matter of turning white.

◊ Compare the use of *blink* to mean "flinch": see under **blink**.

blanket

When used as a verb (in *blanketed*), this word conforms to regular spelling rules. See **-t**.

blends

See **portmanteau words**.

blink

New applications of this verb intersect with old, and with several different constructions. Its essential physical meaning, i.e. "close and open the eye," is extended now to a range of devices that flash regularly, from distress signals to the cursor on your computer. See for example:

> *Traffic signals blink yellow.*
> *The red light on his car phone began to blink.*

The emotional significance of *blinking* in showing surprise remains a not uncommon use, often in negative constructions as in:

> ... *doesn't blink at the mess*
> *No-one should blink when* (an Olympic site is converted to a prison)
> *The reference librarian didn't even blink. He gets requests like that everyday* (for a book on the methodology of murder)

Transitive constructions, such as *didn't blink an eye* (or *an eyelash*) also embody this sense of (not) showing surprise.

The physical and emotional aspects of *blinking* are of course a liability amid the continuous tension of competitive sport, whether it's baseball or boxing. Hence the importance of not being the side to *blink first*. Spectators too must be provided with *no-blink* coverage of the game by the TV station (no responsibility if they doze off themselves). This metaphorical use of **blink** to mean "lose concentration" and so "give way" has leaped out of the sporting arena, at least in North American English, and can be applied to a backdown in politics. Among the various examples in CCAE, it becomes a question of *which side will blink first* (in talks with Israel). This usage is recognized in both *Merriam-Webster* (2000) and the *Canadian Oxford* (1998), but not yet in *New Oxford* (1998) or the Australian *Macquarie Dictionary* (1997).

Blinking is everywhere used as a metaphor for having the eyes closed when one might be expected to notice something untoward. This too can be transitive or intransitive, as in the local problem of *blink-your-eye deals,* or the international one when nations *blink at [another's] political and human rights outrages*. Both *at* and *away* appear in such constructions, witness *blink the problem away for a year.* Control of one's own *blinking* is definitely imputed here, whereas in most other uses it is deemed involuntary, or at least subject to external forces.

Modern **blink** seems to be the intersection of two different verbs. Its owes its spelling to the Scottish form of Old English *blench* "recoil"/"flinch" (see under **blanch or blench**) – which underpins its use with that sense in North America. Its association with the eyes is thought to come from the Middle Dutch verb *blinken* ("shine"; cf. German *blinken*, "sparkle").

bloc or block

Borrowed from French *bloc* in C14, **block** is anglicized in spelling and supports an array of meanings both physical and figurative. In C20 it was for several decades used to refer to political groupings, for example when referring to the *block vote* of Welsh miners.

The spelling **bloc** is a C20 reborrowing of the same French word, used only in the political sense. In English its earliest application (1903) was to political alignments in western Europe, but after World War II the most common collocations were *communist bloc / Eastern bloc / Soviet bloc*. It is now used freely of political groupings of any persuasion, anywhere in the world, whether supranational – e.g. *imperial bloc, Islamic bloc, trading bloc* – or intranational. In American data from CCAE, the *malleable suburban voting bloc*, or the *bloc of white voters* may be the key to the next election. Clearly **bloc** is taking over where **block** might previously have served, whenever it correlates with a *power bloc*. Hence the significance of a *bloc of seats* in the Serbian parliament, as opposed to the contiguous *block of seats*. It explains also the choice of spelling in a *geographical bloc, off limits to Palestinian police,* referring to a settlement in Gaza.

blond or blonde

As often when there's a choice of spellings, people assign different roles to them. The common practice with these is to use **blond** in reference to males, and **blonde** for females. This is rather like what French does with grammatical as well as natural gender (see **gender**), and the tendency can be seen in both American and British English. Most citations in both CCAE and the BNC have **blond** and **blonde** applied on the basis of natural gender, whether speaking of a person, or the color of her/his hair: *a stunning blonde, a blonde woman, blonde hair.* Although references to a man as *a blond* were rare in both databases, *blond hair* was frequently associated with a male head: *an idealised portrait of Jesus with blond hair and blue eyes.* In both corpora, **blond** was associated with nonhuman color references, as in *built of blond stone* or the *blond-dune area in Namibia.*

Yet for some writers, there's a grammatical distinction to be made with **blond** and **blonde**, whereby **blonde** is reserved for the noun (the stereotyped female), and **blond** used as the general adjective in *blond-haired, blond wood* etc. This is illustrated in the juxtaposition of *British Blondes* with *thanks to [whom] blond hair became a mark of feminine beauty*, in a citation from the *New York Times Book Review* (1983) quoted in *Webster's English Usage* (1989). The sense of a grammatical divide probably derives from the fact that **blond** is not often used as a noun in either British or American English: its frequency in that role is low in both the reference databases. By the same token, the two words appear freely as adjectives – the main difference being that **blonde** is more common as adjective in BNC data (in the ratio of about 3:2), whereas in CCAE, **blond** has a slight lead over **blonde** (a ratio of about 6:5). However the adjectival data from both databases confirm the strong tendency to use **blonde** in female references and **blond** in those to males, i.e. the natural gender principle.

The clichéd application of **blond(e)** to female and male hair color has meant a loss of specificity, hence the need to qualify it as *ash/gray/silvery blond(e)* among CCAE examples, and *dark/strawberry/platinum blonde* from the BNC. Both databases provide evidence of *peroxide blond(e)*. The ages of the persons referred to extends now from juveniles – *a blue-eyed blond tot* – to the cricketing idol – *blond, handsome, with great charisma* – to the follicularly challenged: *his hair – blond, thinning on top*. The sexist implications of **blond(e)** may be dwindling.
◊ Compare **brunette or brunet**.

bloody

Used as an intensifier, **bloody** was once a word to blush over. However the *Oxford Dictionary* (1989) records this use since 1785, and it has long been a feature of talk among men, though avoided (like other swear words) in mixed company. The former taboo and its association with casual and coarse communication still combine to limit its appearances in print. Among the examples in CCAE, some seem to exploit the literal connection with *blood* as well, and the ambiguity could no doubt be used in defence if necessary:

> *bloody brutes like Rambo*
> teach them a bloody lesson in betrayal and revenge
> SHEER BLOODY MURDER (reported from a
> Johannesburg newspaper)

Other examples are unmistakably expletive, though put on the lips of sports trainers:

> *"Unless you bust a bloody gut . . . you'll never win*
> *a bloody race."*

Or reviewers of movies, influenced as it were by the dialogue itself:

> *. . . a bloody awful denouement.*

Or John Lennon: *"They still use the bloody comparisons."*

How common is it overall? In nonfiction, including journalism, quite rare. Less than 3% of all instances of **bloody** in CCAE were intensifiers (even if we include ambiguous examples like those above). In the BNC things appear on first sight to be the reverse: little use of **bloody** in its literal sense of "associated with blood," and much of the intensifier (*bloody idiot; waste of bloody time* etc.). Yet almost all instances of intensifier use come from (i) transcribed speech, and (ii) fictional dialogue designed to communicate the intensity and rhythm of everyday speech. Writers who are not exercising novelist's license are still pretty circumspect about using it in print.

blow, blew, blowed and blown

The verb **blow** uses **blew** for its past tense and **blown** for the past participle as long as it refers to a moving stream of air. In earlier centuries the regular **blowed** was also used occasionally for both, but it survives with the general meaning only in dialect. No doubt this has something to do with the use of **blowed** (and *blow*) in imprecations such as *Well I'll be blowed* or *I'm blowed if I'm going to,* on record since 1781 according to the *Oxford Dictionary* (1989). For most speakers, **blowed** is imbued with that colloquial color.

blue

For the spelling of *blu(e)ish* and *blu(e)ing,* see under **-e** section 1h.

blurb

This word has made it into standard English, despite its glutinous feel and jokey origins. Coined by American humorist Gelett Burgess in 1907, **blurb** remains the only simple way to refer to the remarks printed on the dust jacket of a book to promote sales. Since then it has consolidated its identity as a genre of advertising, with predictably glowing words (*brilliant, extraordinary, masterly, outstanding*) and often extravagant claims about the book's contents. **Blurb** is now also applied to discursive promotional material used for various kinds of entertainment or infotainment, on movie flyers, concert programs, tourist pamphlets and software packaging. The *blurb's* hyperbole no doubt raises skepticism in most readers, but the word itself has established its place in the English language. In North American English it can be used as a verb as well as a noun, according to *Merriam-Webster* (2000) and the *Canadian Oxford* (1998). **Blurb** appears in the BNC in a variety of text-types, and is given unqualified acceptance as a noun in *New Oxford* (1998), though it regards the verb as "informal."

BNC

See **British National Corpus**.

-body or -one

For the choice between *anybody* and *anyone* etc., see **-one**.

bogey, bogie or bogy

These spellings represent three different words, referring to:

1 a score in golf (originally par; now one over par)
2 the wheel assembly under a railway/railroad wagon
3 a bugbear; something you dread

A primary spelling for each has been evolving, though with considerable interplay between them as the secondary spellings show. The table below sets the order of spellings from the *Oxford Dictionary* (1989) and *Webster's Third* (1986).

	bogey	*bogie*	*bogy*
1 golf	*Ox1, W1*	*Ox3, W3*	*Ox2, W2*
2 wheel assembly	*Ox3, W2*	*Ox1, W1*	*Ox2, W3*
3 bugbear	*Ox2, W1*	*Ox3, W3*	*Ox1, W2*

The dictionaries agree on the preferred spelling for the golfing term (**bogey**), and that **bogie** should be used for "wheel assembly," but diverge over the primary spelling for "bugbear." Data from both CCAE and the BNC show that **bogy** is now very rare in the US as well as the UK, and that **bogey** is often used for this sense. The use of *[old] Bogey* in preemptive references to the Devil may have helped it along. *Bogeyman* now far outnumbers *bogyman* for the compound, by more than 3:1 in CCAE, and 50:1 in the BNC.

Though **bogey** now spells the golfing term as well as "bugbear," their contexts of use help keep the two senses apart – except perhaps for superstitious golfers. And though the plural *bogies* once served both **bogy** ("bugbear") and **bogie** ("wheel assembly"), it's now firmly attached to the latter. As a proper name, **Bogie** refers to the American movie star Humphrey Bogart (1899–1957), at least in the US; and **Bogey** to the British Colonel Bogey, who gave his name to the standard (par) score in golf (*Brewer's Dictionary*, 1986), and a military march associated with two world wars. ◊ For other words which vary between **-ie** and **-y** or **-ey** and **-y** in spelling, see **-ie/-y** and **-ey**.

boggle

This curious verb seems to derive from the same Celtic word for "ghost" as *bog(e)y* ("bugbear") and *bug* ("gremlin") (see further under **bogey** and **bug**). The earliest use of **boggle** (C16) is of a horse starting in fright as if from "seeing a ghost." A similar sense is embodied in *the mind boggles,* and this intransitive construction is the normal pattern for **boggle** in British English. In American English it's turned around. *It boggles the mind* is much more common than *the mind boggles,* and transitive uses of **boggle** outnumber the intransitive by about 8:1, in data from CCAE. American usage allows some variation of the idiom, so that the object of *boggling* may be *the imagination / my creativity* or *the most analytical mind* – not to mention *the White House* as in *Computer sabotage boggles the White House.* Extended uses of the intransitive construction can be seen in BNC data, as in:

> *the mind boggles at the potential*
> *the mind boggles at what might happen*

Apart from using *at,* the data show the occasional use of *with* instead of *at* when the complement is a noun phrase, and *that* when it's a clause.

bogy, bogey or bogie

See **bogey**.

bon mot or mot juste

These phrases, borrowed from French, are both idiomatic in English. **Bon mot** (literally "a good word") refers to a memorable witticism or clever remark. The plural is *bons mots* if one aims to maintain the authentic French effect (but see **plurals** section 2). The **mot juste** (literally "the right word") is "the well-chosen word," one which suits the context perfectly.

bon vivant or bon viveur

The French phrase **bon vivant** has the longer history in English (from the end of C17), whereas **bon viveur** is a latter-day pseudo-French formation of C19. **Bon vivant** is still much more widely used to refer to one who enjoys the pleasures of good living, but the presence of the other has prompted some demarcation disputes over meaning.

For some, the two phrases are synonymous. For others, the focus of **bon vivant** is especially on the epicurean delights of the table, whereas **bon viveur** implies the indulgences of the trendy man-about-town (and the "Don Juan"). The connotations of the phrases vary with people's attitudes to such codes of behavior, some finding them redolent with sophistication, others with reprehensible self-indulgence.
◊ See also **gourmet or gourmand**.

bona fides and bona fide

These are two forms of the same Latin phrase with different applications. **Bona fides** is used in English to mean "good faith or honest intention," and agrees with a singular verb as in:
The litigant's bona fides was queried by the judge.
A shortage of Latin outside the court of law has it often understood as a plural (see **false plurals** for other examples). Verb agreements in both American and British databases confirmed this, and there were no instances with a singular verb. This shift in agreement is probably fostered by extended applications, so that it can now mean "proof(s) of being genuine" or "credentials," as in:
... unidentified sources whose bona fides have not been established
These extensions of **bona fides** showed up first in the context of intelligence operations, according to *Webster's English Usage* (1989); then diplomatic contexts, as in the following from the BNC and CCAE:
Mr de Klerk's bona fides remain unproven.
South Africa's bona fides are now accepted.
In American English **bona fides** may be acknowledged in almost any field of endeavor, political, professional or personal: *egalitarian bona fides; literary bona fides; the home-ec. teacher's bona fides; bona fides as a spokesman for black rage.*

Bona fide is the ablative of *bona fides*, meaning "in good faith" (see further under **ablative**). It serves as an adverb-cum-adjective in expressions like *bona fide offer* and *bona fide traveler,* where the nouns themselves have strong verb connections.

bonus

For the plural of this word, see **-us** section 1.

bony or boney

See under **-y/-ey**.

book titles

For details about how to set out the titles of books, in bibliographies and elsewhere, see **titles**.

bored with or bored of

In both American and British English, **bored with** is the standard collocation, at least for writers. In data from CCAE and the BNC, most instances of **bored of** were confined to quoted or transcribed speech. Perhaps **bored of** owes something to the "Our Gang" film *Bored of Education,* whose maker Hal Roach won an Academy Award for it in 1936 and again in 1984. The title has been a springboard for others, as in *chairman of the bored of International Dull Folks Unlimited.*

born or borne

Though identical in pronunciation, the spelling of these words marks their different domains of meaning. **Born** is only used in expressions which refer to coming into the world, whether it is an actual birth (*born on Christmas Day*) or a figurative use (*not born yesterday*). **Borne** serves as the all-purpose past participle of the verb *bear*, as in:
The oil slick was borne away by the tide.
Both **born** and **borne** are related to the verb *bear,* and there was no systematic difference in their spelling until the last quarter of C18. Earlier editions of Samuel Johnson's dictionary (up to 1773) gave the past participle of *bear* as either "bore or born." But **borne** had been widely used in C16 and C17, and it gradually replaced the other two as the general past participle, leaving **born** with its restricted role.

Bosnia Herzegovina

See under **Yugoslavia**.

bosom or bosoms

The singular form **bosom** ("human breast") has a long history, reflected in idioms such as *bosom pals, welcomed to the bosom of the family* and religious phrases such as *the bosom of Abraham, in the bosom of the Father.* It occurs much more often than **bosoms**, in both BNC and CCAE, in the ratio of more than 6:1 and about 4:1. In references to female anatomy **bosom** is not intrinsically erotic, though on the pages of a romantic novel it may become so. It may be explicitly anerotic, an element of pity, as in *all her poor sad bosom,* or satire: *heaving bosom appropriately cantilevered for the occasion.*

The plural **bosoms** is a recent development, as of 1959, according to the *Oxford Dictionary* (1989). It draws attention to the twinness of the female **bosom**, and appears naturally enough in titillating contexts (or commentaries on them), as in the movie moment at which *bosoms heaved and manhood stirred.* Its association with seduction sometimes makes for unintended comedy, as in the attempt to avoid a scandal in *the bosoms of the Church*; or the unskilled historical novelist whose knights *smote their armored bosoms in a gesture of fealty*.

bossa nova

Not Italian for "new manageress" but the name of a lively dance rather like a tango, with a jerky rhythm. The phrase is actually Brazilian slang for a new style or approach, and is not to be interpreted literally in terms of its Portuguese components, which mean "new bump."

botanic or botanical

Both words are adjectives associated with *botany,* though **botanic** has had little general use since C18. It mostly survives in long-established titles/names such as the *Royal Botanic Society,* the *Botanic Lexicon* and *Botanic Garden(s)* from Cambridge to Edinburgh and Brooklyn to Santa Barbara. More recent foundations are *Botanical Gardens,* and **botanical** is the usual form for other adjectival uses, as in *botanical specimens/illustrations/guidebooks.* The two spellings contrast in:

> Dr Short . . . *is the Australian botanical liaison officer for the Royal Botanic Gardens at Kew.*

Botanical is thus much the more productive form of the word, outnumbering **botanic** by almost 2:1 in BNC data and 6:1 in CCAE.
◊ For other pairs of words like this, see under **-ic/-ical**.

both or both of

See under **of**.

bourgeois

The implications of **bourgeois** ("citizen") are rarely neutral, though the precise nature of the judgement it passes, whether political, social or aesthetic, is relative to context. When first used in C17 English, it brought its French reference to those who earned their living in the city (e.g. by mercantile means) and incurred some contempt by so doing from landed gentry. Following the industrial revolution, and in Marxist thinking, **bourgeois** correlated with the privileged managerial class and exploiters of the proletariat. Contemporary expressions of the model are to be found in statements like the following from the BNC:

> *The notion of thrift carried little meaning; it was essentially part of a bourgeois economic outlook largely incompatible with proletarian living conditions.*

From both political angles, **bourgeois** has the negative vibes associated with "middle class."

In C20 English **bourgeois** acquired a further critical meaning as in *bourgeois taste,* implying aesthetic or social values which are conventional, mediocre and even philistine. This seems to be a democratized extension of the original political sense, as in:

> *Free verse has been exposed as decadent, and modern art as the shopworn property of the bourgeois masses.*

Sometimes the word seems to serve simply as a putdown, as in *That's a terribly bourgeois view.* In such cases, the person challenged might well riposte by asking whether the speaker's use of **bourgeois** was revisionist or not!

bow or bows

Whether in the **bow** or the **bows**, the action is at the front of the ship. For sailors, the plural **bows** is the usual expression because there is both a port and a starboard **bow** which meet at the stem in front. But landlubbers see only "the pointed end" of the ship, and are more inclined to use **bow**.

BP

These letters, when preceded by an approximate date *5000 BP,* stand for "before the present" (i.e. before AD 1950, the reference date). The abbreviation refers to a chronological system based on radiocarbon dating, used increasingly by archeologists, historians and scientists. The **BP** system relies on measuring the radio-isotopes of remains from a particular culture or era, and deducing their age from the relative decay of carbon atoms in them. The dates derived this way are not particularly exact, and a plus or minus factor has to be proposed. Scientists note the laboratory used as their reference point for **BP**, according to the *CBE Manual* (1994), using *P* for Philadelphia, *Q* for Cambridge, UK, and so on. For example:

> *950 ± 100 BP (P1234)*

Like other dating abbreviations, **BP** is left unstopped, and can be set either in full or small caps. See under **AD or A.D.**; and further under **dating systems**.

bracket

When **bracket** is used as a verb, there's no reason to double the *t* before suffixes (*-ed* and *-ing*): see **-t**.

brackets

The role of **brackets** is to separate a string of words or characters from those on either side. They come in five different shapes each with its own functions which are detailed below. The punctuation problems which arise with parentheses in particular are also discussed below, sections 2 and 3.

1 Types of brackets
a) Parentheses ( ), sometimes called "round brackets," often enclose a parenthetical comment or parenthesis within a carrier sentence:

> *Angkor (the ancient capital of the Khmer empire) is situated hundreds of miles upstream from Phnom Penh.*

In such a sentence the parenthetical words could also be set off with either commas, *em rules / dashes* or spaced *en rules / dashes* (see **dashes** section 1). The three types of punctuation are also used by some to represent different degrees of separation. Commas are felt to make the least separation between the parenthesis and the rest of the sentence, then *parentheses,* and then dashes. Yet whether all three levels can be usefully exploited in the same sentence is doubtful.

Practice and principle vary even for indicating two levels of parenthesis. Some authorities allow a combination of dashes with *parentheses* – with dashes on the outside, according to the *Chicago Manual* (2003), or on the inside, following *The Right Word at the Right Time* (1985). When nested **brackets** are needed, American style combines *square brackets* with *parentheses* (the **brackets** on the inside). British style as expressed in the *Oxford Guide to Style* (2002) warns against doing this, because of the convention of using *square brackets* for editorial interpolations (see section 1b below). Instead it recommends using *parentheses* within *parentheses,* taking care to close each set in turn.

Other uses of *parentheses* are to:
* enclose optional additions to a word, when the author wants to allow for alternative interpretations or applications of a statement. For example:
  Students will take their additional subject(s) in their own time.
* enclose numbers or enumerative letters in a list. If they are in continuous text it's usual to put

brackets on either side: (i), (ii) etc., but when they stand at the margin in a list (as in this entry), the second bracket alone is enough.

* enclose a whole sentence which forms a parenthesis within a paragraph.
* provide a locus for author–date references (see **referencing**).

b) **Square brackets** [ ] are conventionally used in prose to indicate editorial additions to the text, whether they explain, correct, or just comment on it in the form of *[sic]*. Other examples are:

> *... went home [to New Zealand] and died shortly after.*
> *... [cont. p. 166]*

In mathematics, *square brackets* are used in a hierarchy with *parentheses* and *braces*, but there the convention runs counter to that mentioned in (1a), and *parentheses* are to be dealt with before *square brackets*, according to both *Chicago* and the *CBE Manual* (1994).

In linguistics, *square brackets* are used to enclose phonetic (as opposed to phonemic) symbols. Cf. (1d) below.

c) **Braces** { }, sometimes called "curly brackets," are used as distinguishing **brackets** in mathematics, after *parentheses* and *square brackets*. The conventional order for enclosures is thus {[( )]}, working from the inside out.

In linguistics *braces* identify the morphemes of a language. (See under **morphology**.)

d) **Slash brackets** / /, also called *diagonal brackets* or "slashes," serve to separate the numbers in a date, as in 11/11/88. In Britain they were used in sums of money to separate pounds from the smaller denominations (see further under **solidus**).

In linguistics, *slash brackets* mark phonetic symbols which have phonemic status for the language concerned. The phonemes of English are listed in Appendix I, using the symbols of the International Phonetic Alphabet.

e) **Angle brackets** ⟨ ⟩ are used in mathematics as the outermost set in the hierarchy ⟨{[( )]}⟩. In linguistics they show the graphemes of a particular writing system, for instance the ⟨gh⟩ in *ghost*. As printed they are sometimes identical with paired *chevrons* (see further under that heading).

2 Use of stops with brackets/parentheses.
Punctuation outside any pair of *parentheses,* and especially after the parenthesis, is determined by the structure of the host sentence. Compare the following sentences:

> *Their last act was passable (no unexpected mishaps), and so the show earned a modicum of applause.*
> *The last act of the show was passable (no unexpected mishaps) and amusing.*

Without its parenthesis, the second sentence would certainly not have had a comma, so there's no reason to add one with the parenthesis.

Within the **brackets** themselves there is minimal punctuation: only exclamation or question marks if required, unless the parenthesis stands as an independent sentence. Compare:

> *He said (no-one would have predicted it) that he would run for president.*
> *He said he would run for president. (No-one would have predicted it.)*

Note in the first of these sentences, the absence of initial capital and full stop in the parenthesis, because

it is embraced within another sentence. Only when the parenthesis contains a title, or some stock saying, would capitals be introduced:

> *Tomorrow's lecture (Language and Social Life) has been cancelled.*
> *Their grandmother's imperative (Waste not want not) had them saving every plastic bag that came into the house.*

3 The final stop/period: inside or outside a parenthetical bracket? When a sentence ends with a parenthesis, the point to check is whether the parenthesis forms part or all of the sentence. If it is the whole sentence, the stop goes inside; if the parenthesis is only the last part of the sentence, the stop goes outside. Compare:

> *He said she was guilty. (No-one believed him.)*
> *He said that she was guilty (in spite of appearances).*

Note that this rule for the placement of the final period is the same throughout the English-speaking world, whereas the ones relating to stops and quotation marks are variable. See **quotation marks** section 3c.

Brahmin, Brahman and Brahm(a)

Several applications need to be distinguished in deciding between these spellings. Either **Brahmin** or **Brahman** may be used for:

1 a member of the highest or priestly caste among the Hindus
2 a breed of Indian cattle used in crossbreeding animals for warmer latitudes.

The *Oxford Dictionary* (1989) gives priority to **Brahmin** while *Webster's Third* (1986) makes it **Brahman.** However data from British and American corpora show that **Brahmin** is actually the commoner spelling for sense 1 and **Brahman** for sense 2. **Brahmin** is essentially the older spelling, according to the *Oxford*, which helps to explain why it's also the spelling used for the *Boston Brahmins* (members of the old established families of New England, highly cultivated and aloof), and elsewhere in American English for individuals of the same type. The concept is applied in Australia in references to the *Adelaide brahmin* (lower case). The few examples of *brahmin* (lower case) in the BNC were used in reference to the Hindu caste, but otherwise upper case prevailed in the British and the American evidence.

One further use of **Brahman** emerged from the databases. Both CCAE and the BNC yielded several instances in which **Brahman** referred to the pervasive world spirit or oneness of all things in Buddhist philosophy. This seems to be C20 innovation. The *Oxford Dictionary* gives **Brahm** and **Brahma** as the distinctive spellings for this, but there are no citations for it after mid-C19.

breach, breech or broach

Breach is the hinge in the interplay between these, since it sounds exactly like **breech**, and comes close to **broach** in meaning. **Breech** is the least common of them, once a general word for "trousers" (cf *breeches*), but now mostly found referring to the rear end of something, and used in association with childbirth (*breech birth*) and a style of guns (*breech loaders*).

Breach comes from the same root as the word *break*, though its applications are much more limited. It can refer to a physical break, as in a *breach in the* *dike* (or in the defences of the football team), but more often it connotes a figurative rupture, in law or in personal relations: *a breach of the peace, a breach of promise.* As a verb **breach** also appears in both figurative and physical senses. Its figurative use in *breach the agreement* is uncomplicated, whereas the physical sense in *breach the dike* is at some risk of overlapping with **broach.** The effect of *breaching a dike* is not unlike that of *broaching a keg:* in either case liquid pours through the hole. Still there's a difference, in that *breaching* is normally the work of nature and *broaching* a human act. **Broach** is a term from joinery and carpentry for a tapered spike used to enlarge a hole. The more figurative use of **broach** in *broaching a subject* is again a matter of opening something up, this time a reservoir of discussion.

Note also *brooch* ("a piece of jewellery"), pronounced exactly like **broach.** The two words come from the same French source and were spelled alike until about 1600.

Breathalyzer or breathalyser

The trademark **Breathalyzer** dates from the 1960s, and in North American usage the word is still capitalized more often than not. In data from CCAE the upper-case form (as in *Breathalyzer test*) outnumbers the lower-case one by more than 2:1, though the verb *breathalyze* is accepted without a capital letter. Elsewhere both noun and verb appear freely in lower case. In the UK the spelling **breathalyser** is used from the first *Oxford Dictionary* (1989) citation, and this dominates in BNC data, along with *breathalyse* for the verb. The lower-case spellings with *-yse* also prevail in Australia, according to the *Macquarie Dictionary* (1997). For those conscious that *analyse* is blended into the latter part of the word, *-yse(r)* seems preferable, but there are counter arguments. See **analyze or analyse.**

breech, breach or broach

See **breach**.

brethren or brothers

Brethren was the ordinary plural of *brother* until the late C16, when it gave place to **brothers**. The King James bible nevertheless keeps **brethren** all through, and it survives in more conservative religious discourse. Protestant evangelical groups such as the *Plymouth Brethren* preserve the older plural, where Catholic orders use the modern one, as in *Christian Brothers*. See further under **plurals** section 1c.

briar or brier

Two different shrubs may be indicated by these two spellings, but they have never been distinguished by them. Both **briar** and **brier** have been used for:
(1)   the wild rose and the thorny bush that bears it
(2)   white heath
Brier is the older spelling for the wild rose, originally Old English but challenged by the variant **briar** from C16 on. The *Oxford Dictionary* (1989) puts **brier** first, while noting **briar** as "now more common." The two spellings appear in the same order for the white heath from southern France, first mentioned in the later C19. *Webster's Third* (1986) also makes **brier** the primary spelling for both plants. Yet **briar** is strongly preferred in both British and American databases, outnumbering **brier** by more than 3:1 in the BNC and

6:1 in CCAE. **Briar** is used whether it's a simple reference to the plant, or caught up in compounds such as *briar patch* (full of thorn bushes), or *briar pipe* (made from the root of the white heath). Placenames real and fictional (the *Briar Patch* of Joel Harris's "Uncle Remus" stories) have probably reinforced the use of **briar**.

brilliance or brillancy

See under **-nce/-ncy**.

briquet or briquette

See under **-ette**.

Britain, British, Briton, Britisher and Brit

The term **Britain** is familiar shorthand for *Great Britain*, the island which geographically contains England, Wales and Scotland; or else the *United Kingdom*, a political entity comprising Great Britain and Northern Ireland (see **UK**); or else the *British Isles*, including *Great Britain*, the whole of Ireland, and all the offshore islands.

The adjective **British** is used in reference to many aspects of the culture of Great Britain, yet there's no straightforward general term for its inhabitants. **Britisher** is an Americanism which the British do not warm to, and Americans themselves make relatively litte use of it, by the evidence of CCAE. The abbreviation **Brit** has gained popularity since World War II, though it seems to be more freely used in the US than the UK. In BNC data it mostly appears in newspaper headlines, and in breezy reporting on sport and popular music. But American writers use it in a wider variety of contexts, and in more discursive writing – witness examples from CCAE such as *a founding sister of Brit feminism* and *a Brit's eye view of American youth*. Such uses on both sides of the Atlantic show that it has shed the disparaging overtones once attributed to it.

Briton has advantages over both **Britisher** and **Brit**. In spite of historical overtones, it seems to be regaining ground as a general appellation, and is almost twice as frequent as **Brit** in both CCAE and BNC. It doesn't smack of headlinese, and is not restricted to sports / pop music reporting. Yet the identification of an individual **Briton** is still very much associated with journalism in the BNC, as in *A Briton will command and direct NATO troops* or *the first Briton to climb Everest without oxygen*. The plural **Britons** does however appear in a wider range of nonfiction writing.

None of the **British** labels (**Britisher, Brit, Briton**) are relished by the non-English inhabitants of UK, who naturally prefer to be identified as *Welsh, Scottish, Irish* (see further under **Ireland and Irish**). In using those more specific names, as well as *English*, there are gains in precision for all.

British English

The expression **British English** is generally used to distinguish the standard form of English used in Great Britain and Northern Ireland from the varieties used in other parts of the world. British pronunciations as shown in most dictionaries are in fact those associated with southern and eastern dialects (and with speakers from the middle and upper classes). The grammar and core vocabulary of "standard English" are also from southeastern

England, yet they are the staple of written English from anywhere in the UK – if it aims to reach readers beyond its place of origin. The term **British English** as used in this book refers to the common written language, which through various media and styles communicates to a wide reading public.

Contemporary **British English** is not of course the same as the pre-standardized variety of English that crossed to America from 1600 on, or the mix of dialects that was transported to colonies in other parts of the world in C18 and C19. (See under **American English**, **Australian English**, **Canadian English**, **New Zealand English**, for the particular dialects concerned.) **British English** has itself evolved during the last four centuries. The pre-Renaissance vernacular was expanded with thousands of classical loanwords, often in alternative forms (e.g. *barbarian/barbaric/ barbarous*; *tragic/tragical*). Cultural connections with France, Italy, Spain and the Netherlands fostered the adoption of words from modern European languages, from *ballet* to *bullet, scherzo* to *stiletto*. The huge volume of borrowings also supplied the formative elements for neo-classical terms – combining forms such as *electro-/geo-/hydro-* and *-graphy/-logy/-lysis*. It prompted some fine-tuning of the appearance of English words (see for example the entries on **check** and **quay**, and **spelling** section 1). The interplay between classical and French models for spelling is still with us in alternatives such as *-or/-our* and *-ize/-ise*.

The characteristic written features of **British English** owe much to C18 and C19 linguistic movements, which were not felt so strongly elsewhere. A plethora of grammars and dictionaries appeared to fill the void left by unsuccessful attempts to establish an English language academy in C17 and C18 (see **language academy**). Some of these publications held more authority than others, most notably Samuel Johnson's *A Dictionary of the English Language* (1755), reprinted with very few changes for 75 years, and Lindley Murray's *A Grammar adapted to different Classes of Learners* (1795). They symbolize the collective desire to codify the language and put bounds on unruly variation.

The industrial revolution stimulated scientific inquiry on all fronts, including the English language, and the *Oxford English Dictionary* (published 1884–1928) is a monument to it. Its Scottish-born editor, James Murray, inspired the collection of 1.8 million citations of English usage, to provide a history of the English lexicon century by century from the Norman Conquest on. In keeping with its historical stance, the dictionary is strictly descriptive and avoids judgements about style or usage which would be at risk of anachronism (see further under **descriptive or prescriptive**). Work on the dictionary began more than two decades before the publication of the first volume. In its shadow, controversy raged over what was or was not good English. The Dean of Canterbury (Henry Alford) published his "Plea for the Queen's English" in 1863, which drew a fierce critique titled "The Dean's English" (1864) from Washington Moon, a Fellow of the Royal Society of Literature. The two jousted publicly over many points of usage, and Moon's work, with excerpts from Alford, ran to several editions. The prescriptive tradition was thus maintained by individual authors through C19, and launched into C20 by *The King's English* (1906)

compiled by the brothers Fowler. The *Dictionary of Modern English Usage* (1926) by H. W. Fowler is likewise famous for its stoutly worded prescriptions, though they are mitigated by extensive use of citations. This gives "Fowler" more weight than his imitators, and successive reprintings of his work into C21 have kept his judgements in circulation. His influence is stronger in the UK than elsewhere (Peters and Delbridge, 1997) in terms of detail. But his use of the word *usage* has been claimed in the titles of works on American, Canadian and Australian English.

The grammar of **British English** owes much to the work of European scholars, most notably Otto Jespersen, whose *A Modern English Grammar on Historical Principles* (7 vols. 1909–49) is in the descriptive tradition of the *Oxford Dictionary*. The *Comprehensive Grammar of the English Language* (1985) distinguishes British from American grammatical usage from time to time, using data from the Survey of English Usage begun in 1959 at University College London. The *Longman Grammar of Spoken and Written English* (1999) makes systematic use of database evidence to describe common usage, to show how it varies in different genres of writing, and to contrast British and American patterns of speech.

Against this backdrop of description and prescription, written **British English** remains in some ways more pluralistic than other varieties, for example in allowing *-t* as well as *-ed* for the past tense of verbs such as *leap*. It tolerates both *-ize* and *-ise*, *-able* and *-eable,* where North American English prefers the first in each case. It embraces more exceptions to the general spelling rules, as in the exemption of *l* from the spelling conventions associated with final consonants (see **doubling of final consonant**). In punctuation the British conventions often create subcategories of style which are not observed elsewhere, e.g. in punctuating abbreviations (see **contractions** section 1); and the positioning of stops relative to quote marks (see **quotation marks** section 3). Yet typically one or other British convention overlaps with the American, providing common ground for "international English."

British National Corpus (BNC)

A most important source on contemporary British usage is the **British National Corpus (BNC)**. Compiled in the early 1990s, the database consists of over 100 million words from 4124 texts in computerized form. It includes 10 million words of (transcribed) spoken British English and 90 million words of printed or written material, of which 75% is nonfiction and 25% imaginative or creative prose. The written material was published from 1975 on, apart from a small number of slightly earlier fictional texts, which were included on grounds of their continuing popularity. The range of genres and audiences included is large and diverse, from mass-circulating newspapers and magazines to monographs by major publishers to the products of small local presses, as well as e-mail and scripts and autocues for television. The spoken data was collected from the contexts of business, education, religion and politics, as well as radio phone-ins and the everyday conversation of citizens from 4 socio-economic groups in 38 different locations throughout Britain.

With this wide range of computerized source material, the **BNC** provides empirical and quantifiable evidence on current usage. It shows what is common English idiom, used in many genres of communication, as well as which forms of expression are relatively uncommon – either older ones becoming obsolescent or totally new arrivals. Usage can be correlated with particular corpus genres, such as journalism or academic prose, and with broader communicative styles, such as the formal or the interactive. The **BNC** represents the current state of the language comprehensively. It avoids the problems of bias and selective taste that are inherent in the comments of individuals and committees on usage.

The **BNC** was compiled by a consortium involving major publishers: Oxford University Press, Longman (now Pearson Education) and Chambers (now Chambers Harrap), as well as Oxford University Computing Services, the Lancaster University Centre for Computational Research on the English Language, and the British Library Research and Innovation Centre. Collateral funding was provided through the Department of Trade and Industry, under the Joint Framework for Information Technology, the Science and Engineering Council and the British Academy. Further details on use of the corpus can be obtained via the internet address: http://info.ox.ac.uk/bnc.

broach, breach or breech
See **breach**.

broadcast or broadcasted
The past form of the verb **broadcast** is usually identical with the present:

> *Iliescu broadcast a further plea for ethnic tolerance.*
> *Weather forecasts are broadcast incessantly.*

British writers hardly use **broadcasted** at all, by its very slight showing in BNC data. Among American writers it's relatively more common, and used for the past form as well as the participial adjective, in data from CCAE:

> *... radio station that broadcasted anti-Tutsi propaganda*
> *"Today" has broadcasted live from the Vatican.*
> *... a man who matched the broadcasted description.*

These *-ed* forms are in line with the more general American preference for regular verb inflections (see further under **-ed**).

broke
As an adjective for a person or company without monetary resources, **broke** is more than 300 years old. In C17 it was an alternative past participle of the verb *break*, alongside *broken*. By 1716 it was a synonym for "bankrupt," and losing respectability as a past participle for the other senses of *break*. Samuel Johnson threw his weight behind *broken* with the comment that "a distinct past participle is more proper and elegant." Johnson's censure seems to have cast a long shadow over **broke** even in this specialized sense as a paraphrase for "bankrupt"; and British usage commentators are still inclined to dub it "informal" or "slang." While **broke** ("bankrupt") hardly appears in the BNC, it makes a modest showing in CCAE and seems to belong to standard American usage, as noted by *Webster's English Usage* (1989).
◊ Compare *gone bust*, under **bust**.

brooch or broach
See under **breach**.

brother-in-law
See **in-laws**.

brothers or brethren
See **brethren**.

Brown corpus
See under **English language databases**.

brunette or brunet
The first is the older and much more common word internationally. **Brunette** dates from 1713, while **brunet** (from 1887) is rare, at least in British English (it registers not at all in the BNC). In American English **brunet** is seen a little more often, though still **brunette** outnumbers it in CCAE by about 20:1. Surprisingly perhaps, the instances of **brunet** were almost all references to women, in examples like *catty brunet, the now-brunet Madonna*, and there was scant evidence of its being the "male" counterpart to **brunette**. For some American writers, it seems that **brunet** is simply a shorter equivalent to **brunette**, to be used just as one might prefer *omelet* to *omelette* (see further under **-ette**).

In both CCAE and BNC, **brunette** is almost always a noun. When modified, the accompanying adjectives are mostly approving, though often sexist, ranging from *pretty, shapely, stunning, vivacious* in BNC to *slinky* and *drop-dead-gorgeous* in CCAE. Compare **blond or blonde**.

bucketfuls or bucketsful
See under **-ful**.

budget
On how to spell this word when verb suffixes are added to it, see under **-t**.

buffalo, buffalos or buffaloes
The *Oxford Dictionary* (1989) and *Webster's Third* (1986) give **buffaloes** as the plural of **buffalo** – except when it stays as **buffalo**, in the discourse of hunters and environmentalists (see **zero plurals**). But **buffalos** was endorsed by the majority of respondents to the Langscape survey (1998–2001). For British respondents it was a small majority (53%), whereas for the Americans it was 76%. Continental respondents (69%) were also much more inclined towards the regular spelling **buffalos**. See further under **-o**.

buffet
This string of letters represents two different words, both of which raise spelling queries when used as verbs. The older **buffet** has been a verb meaning "strike with repeated blows" since C13. It keeps a single *t* when suffixes are added: *buffeted, buffeting*.

The other **buffet**, associated with a flat-topped piece of furniture on which food can be displayed (as for a *buffet lunch*), is a C18 borrowing from French. In English it's still pronounced in the French fashion, so that it half rhymes with "café." Very occasionally it works as a verb (in the same way as *banquet*). It then takes the standard suffixes and is written in exactly the same way as the older word (*buffeted, buffeting*),

81

even though still pronounced as if the *t* were not there. See further under **-t**.

bug

For Americans **bug** is a household word, with several applications developed over the last 150 years. Few would question their stylistic status, according to *Webster's English Usage* (1989). The British also make good use of **bug**, with hundreds of examples in the BNC. It lends itself to casual discussion of things that upset the equilibrium of body, mind or machine – which works against it on the scale of stylistic precision. The *Oxford Dictionary* (1989) and *New Oxford* (1998) query some uses of **bug** with the labels "slang" and "informal," though all can be found across a range of spoken and everyday written texts in the BNC. In formal discourse the word might still seem out of place, but it's otherwise well assimilated.

In current usage, **bug** can refer to:
1. an insect
2. a surveillance device
3. a germ or infection
4. an enthusiasm
5. a computer problem

Attached to the first three senses are verbs, whose stylistic status in British English is much like that of the noun, as discussed below.

1 bug "insect." This is the oldest sense, recorded since C17, and standard in the US for any kind of six-legged creature, and so it naturally appears in compounds such as *bug repellent,* and also in more specific names such as *bedbug, ladybug, June bug.* The generic use of the word is labeled "dialect or US" in the *Oxford Dictionary* (1989), but becomes the primary sense in *New Oxford* (1998), with no restrictive labels. Its increasingly standard use in the UK is confirmed in BNC citations such as *bug spray* and *water placed around the room to attract the bugs.* The use of the adjective *bug-eyed* "(with bulging eyes [like an insect])" – listed without comment in *New Oxford* – also suggests that the British are not unfamiliar with the generic use of **bug**. However there's little sign in the UK of the American verb *bug out,* used of eyes that "stand out on stalks," as in:

> *He clasped his head and his eyes bugged out.*

2 bug "a microphone concealed for surveillance." As a noun this was first recorded after World War II (1947). It must have been around earlier, by the fact that it was already on record as a verb (meaning "plant a surveillance device") at the end of World War I. *Webster's English Usage* affirms that these uses of **bug** are standard American idiom, and they are listed without restrictive labels by *New Oxford,* where the *Oxford Dictionary* labeled them "slang." Both noun and verb are well represented in the British and American databases. *Bugging* can be carried out within buildings, on vehicles or a telephone line:

> *... harassed by the KGB. My telephone and apartment are bugged.*

In keeping with the secretive process, *bugging* is usually expressed in the passive. The further reaches of the word are the *political campaign bugged* and *parties bugged for blackmail.*

3 bug "germ/infection." **Bug** has been used to refer to an infection-causing micro-organism since 1919, according to the *Oxford Dictionary. New Oxford* labels it "informal," and examples such as *flu/stomach bug* turn up more often in spoken than written data in the

BNC. The related verb **bug** "annoy" as in *it really bugged me* is also associated with speech rather than writing. *Webster's English Usage* notes that the noun has escaped censure in the US; and there's no doubt that the verb is used more freely in print. It carries more shades of meaning, especially the sense "pester," as in:

> *... the sort of side dish your mother always bugged you to finish*

In CCAE data, the scope for word play with **bug** ("insect") is also enjoyed:

> *Iowans bugged by pesky fruit flies*
> *... bugged by X's gnat-picking*

4 bug "enthusiasm." Both Americans and the British use the noun **bug** to refer offhandedly or self-deprecatingly to an enthusiasm: *the acting/spring-cleaning bug* or *the motorcycle/triathlon bug.* This again is "informal" according to *New Oxford,* but unobjectionable as far as *Webster's English Usage* is concerned. In CCAE data it appears in the same kinds of prose as the other uses of **bug**.

5 bug "computer problem." This most recent use of **bug** – to refer to a "gremlin" in the computer (an unexplained problem with software or hardware) – is accepted worldwide. It owes something to C19 use of **bug** to refer to a mechanical defect, but also seems to hark back to the ultimate origins of **bug** in a Celtic word for "ghost" or "devil." (Compare **boggle** and **bogey**.) A connection with **bug** as "insect" can also be found, with the help of Ambrose Bierce's (1906) definition of the fly as "a monster of the air owing allegiance to Beelzebub." Though the *Oxford Dictionary* decided to keep **bug** meaning "ghost" separate from the other senses, they seem to have plenty in common.

◊ For the verbs *bug off* and *bug out* meaning "leave," see under **bugger**.

bugger

Like most words with taboo connections, **bugger** has a substantial history, going back to 1598, according to the *Oxford Dictionary* (1989), and no doubt earlier. Its colloquial meanings are also well established. **Bugger** as a rough equivalent to "chap" dates from early C18, and this is still its most frequent use in contemporary written English, by the evidence of BNC and CCAE. It mostly appears in quoted speech, and always it's rich in attitude. Its tone is offhanded, which often seems to intensify the reference, whether to persons:

> *Some bugger is wearing it!*
> *Then you're a sillier bugger than I thought.*
> *I can't keep up with the old bugger.*

Or to objects:

> *a multipurpose little bugger* (said of a word)
> *... lift the little gold bugger* (of winning the World Cup)
> *... gnawing little bugger at the back of my mind*

Bugger has a role in imprecations, paraphrasing *damn.* The verbal formula *bugger it/him/her/them* is on record from late C18, though the first recorded case of *a bugger* (as in *no-one gives a bugger*) is from C20. Other phrasal verbs including *bugger off* ("go away") and *bugger up* ("make a mess of") are also C20 additions to the repertoire. Most recent are the curtailed forms *bug off* and *bug out* ("leave quickly"), which mask the key word lest it offend. Unabbreviated verb uses nevertheless appear quite freely in the spoken material from the BNC, and constitute about

40% of all instances of the word. In CCAE by contrast, there's only small evidence of **bugger** as a noun, and hardly any as a verb, only *Bugger it all*. The evidence suggests that **bugger** is more freely used in the UK than the US, a conclusion also reached by *Webster's English Usage* (1989), and by Burchfield (1996) on the basis of dictionary evidence.

The word **bugger** is very occasionally an agent noun associated with the verb **bug**, meaning "one who plants/operates surveillance devices," or the device itself. See **bug** section 2.

bullets

These are the newest addition to the punctuation repertoire, though different in that they precede the strings of words that they mark off, rather than following them. **Bullets** differ also in taking on a variety of graphic shapes. They can be rendered as dashes or asterisks within the standard set of punctuation marks; or as small black circles, hollow circles, lozenges, arrows, stylized hands etc., as the software provides.

The chief function of **bullets** is to itemize the components of a vertical list, when there's no need for more specific enumeration with numbers or letters (see **lists** section 2). Because they highlight sets of information that can be scanned by the eye, they facilitate reading on screen, and are therefore recommended in the structure and styling of digital documents. See **digital style**.

bunch of

For some, the feel of this phrase depends on its complement. In a *bunch of grapes/flowers* or a *bunch of keys,* it's quite neutral and stylistically unremarkable anywhere in the English-speaking world. In the US, **bunch of** is also a general collective, as in *a bunch of colleges* or (more figuratively) *a bunch of ideas;* and it's freely applied to people. These seem to have developed during C20 and established themselves, according to *Webster's English Usage* (1989). Canadians also use them, but might find the application of **bunch of** to people somewhat "informal," and/or derogatory, given the gloss "a group, a gang" in the *Canadian Oxford* (1998). *New Oxford* (1998) uses the same label ("informal") for British English, yet it's the disparaging aspect of **bunch of** which stands out of its appearances in the BNC. Whether "they" are a *bunch of amateurs/second-raters* or *cocooned scientists, extremist Freemasons* or *individualistic head-in-the-sand poseurs* – the writer has no time for them. Constructions like these are hardly colloquial or casual, and suggest that **bunch of** is less neutral in the UK than the US when applied to a group of people.

bungee, bungy or bungie

For the ultimate adrenalin rush, *bungee jumping* rather than *bungy jumping* is preferred overwhelmingly as the spelling in American data from CCAE. **Bungee** also has a clear majority of 2:1 in the BNC. But the word predates the sport: as **bungy** it's recorded in the 1930s as the term for the elasticized cord used in launching a glider, and for tying up bundles, the bulging suitcase etc. It shares its pronunciation and probably its past with **bungie**, a word for india rubber, which could well be Hindi. The Indian connection might explain why **bungee** is now the most popular spelling: compare *suttee,* and see **-ee.**

bureau

For the plural of this word, see **-eau**.

burgle or burglarize

These two verbs appeared on opposite sides of the Atlantic within a year of each other, **burglarize** in 1871 and **burgle** in 1872. Still **burglarize** is very much the American choice, outnumbering **burgle** by almost 20:1 in CCAE. But **burglarize** has no support in the UK, and is absent from the BNC. Instead **burgle** serves the purpose, and examples appear in a variety of British sources. For both speakers and writers, **burgle** projects the meaning of "break and enter" more efficiently than the legal phrase, and it's indispensable when (as usually) a passive construction is needed:

In 1990 nearly a million homes were burgled.

Burgle seems to have surmounted the hurdle of being a **backformation** (see further under that heading).

burka, burkha or burqa

This Arabic word refers to the all-covering dress worn by certain Muslim women that masks their faces apart from a slot for the eyes. The *Oxford Dictionary* (1989) has it on record since the 1830s, with a variety of spellings. It makes **burka** the primary spelling, as does *Webster's Third* (1986), with **burqa** and **burkha** as alternatives. An internet search (Google, 2003) confirms that **burka** is the commonest spelling worldwide, outnumbering **burqa** by 5:3, and **burkha** by 7:1. Yet together, **burqa** and **burkha** come close to matching the numbers for **burka.** Their considerable presence shows the active respelling of Arabic loanwords at the turn of the millennium, affirming their foreign origins. See further under **q/k**.

Burma or Myanmar

Within the United Nations, the *Burmese* nation is represented as **Myanmar**, the name decreed in 1989 by the Law and Order Restoration Council of the military government. It was intended to replace **Burma**, the English colonial name, as a symbol of the nation's new identity. However within **Burma** the use of **Myanmar** has been shelved because the National League for Democracy, who won the 1990 election by a huge majority, has not yet been allowed by the military to assume its place in government.

burned or burnt

These alternative past forms of *burn* raise questions. Are they interchangeable, or is there some crucial distinction? American English uses **burned** regularly within the verb phrase, and overall in more than 85% of examples in CCAE. **Burnt** is reserved for special attributive uses as in *burnt cork, burnt almond*, and *burnt-out,* used of vehicles and buildings as well as persons.

In British English, the two are about equally used. **Burned** has a very slight edge over **burnt** (53% to 46%), which goes with the fact that **burnt** can appear in ordinary verb constructions such as *Their fire burnt low* and *The house was burnt down.* The use of **burnt** is sustained partly by its being often pronounced with "t," according to the *Comprehensive Grammar* (1985), though this is unprovable. Others explain the choice of **burned** or **burnt** as depending on the grammar of the verb:

* **burned** = continuous action (i.e. *imperfect*); **burnt** = completed (*perfect*)
    The fire burned low v. *The fire had burnt through acres of forest*
* **burned** = intransitive; **burnt** = transitive
    The fire burned low v. *She burnt her hand on the stove*
* **burned** = active; **burnt** = passive
    The fire had burned through v. *Her hand had been burnt*

Because these principles overlap, they produce conflicting outcomes. This problem – and/or the lack of grammar – would explain why **burned** and **burnt** seem to be used interchangeably in BNC data. Compare the intransitive uses in:
    The flame burnt steadily towards the light
    Lights still burned in the bookshop.
That said, the data show British writers to be generally more inclined towards **burned** for the simple past (*the spirit burned her throat*), whereas they use **burned** and **burnt** about equally for the past participle. Like their American counterparts, they do prefer **burnt** for attributive uses as in *burnt toast*.

International English selections: Against divergent practices, it makes sense to standardize on the regular form **burned** for the past tense and participle of the verb, rather than assuming that any systematic or meaningful distinction can be made with the two spellings. For the adjective, **burnt** is clearly supported worldwide.

◊ For other verbs with the same alternative past forms, see **-ed**.

burqa, burkha or burka
See **burka**.

burst
This verb is exactly the same for past and present tense. For other examples, see **zero past tense**.

bus
The standard plural for **bus** is *buses,* as dictionaries indicate; and there's little sign of *busses* as plural in either American or British databases. But what about the inflected forms of **bus** as a verb: should they be *buses* (*bused, busing*), or *busses* (*bussed, bussing*)? Larger dictionaries present them as alternatives, in that order, yet database evidence suggests opposite trends in the US and the UK. The British preference for double *s* spellings is clear in BNC data, with twice as many examples of *bussed* as of *bused*. But in American data from CCAE, instances of *bused* outnumber *bussed* by about 8:1. In Canada, *bused* and *busing* are also the usual spellings, according to *Canadian English Usage* (1997). The forms with double *s* are more regular for a single-syllabled verb of this kind (see further under **doubling of final consonant**). The American preference for single *s* may however reflect the influence of the noun **bus**, and/or the need to distinguish the verb **bus** from the colloquial word *buss* ("kiss"). Thus when a president *bussed his photograph,* there's no doubt about what actually happened!

bust and busted
The verb **bust** has no connection with an identical noun **bust** referring to the upper portion of a person's anatomy. Rather **bust(ed)** has split off from the verb *burst,* and developed its own identity and meanings. It has acquired a regular past tense **busted** alongside the zero past tense **bust**: compare *busted an arm* with *bust their way in.* **Bust** is then a synonym for *break/broke/broken,* and it supports an array of more figurative meanings, as when its object is a union or "infrastructure." In other collocations the object implies being caught red-handed as in *cadets busted for cheating* or *busted for possession of illegal substances.* Other examples in CCAE show **busted** meaning "framed" (i.e. charged with a crime one didn't commit). The hundreds of examples of **busted** in CCAE confirm its widespread use in the US, in line with its rising status (*Webster's English Usage,* 1989). In British English, **busted** is used in much the same ways as in the US, to mean "broken," as in *wheezing like a busted old fan,* and "raided by police," as in *the party was busted by the Vice Squad.* The BNC's examples come from everyday writing or speech, confirming that such usage is still "informal," as noted by *New Oxford* (1998). However Burchfield (1996) found the expression *busted his leg* "entirely neutral." The status of **busted** in British English is clearly changing from "nonstandard," as it was dubbed by the *Comprehensive Grammar* (1985).

The use of **bust** in *gone bust* "gone bankrupt" is quite well represented in BNC data from both reported conversation and financial comments intended for nonspecialists. It appears more frequently in the British database than the American, although CCAE data have it in a wider range of applications, beyond the strictly financial to marriages and ideas.
◊ Compare **broke**.

but
The fact that **but** is a conjunction does not prevent it from being used at the beginning of a sentence. The point is that it then becomes a *conjunct* (see **conjunctions and conjuncts** section 1). Generations of young writers have been taught not to begin sentences with **but**, yet their professional counterparts seem relatively unconcerned. More than 20% of the uses of **but** in the BNC were sentence-initial, not including those from transcripts of speech. In conversation **but** is quite often heard at the beginning of an utterance as the speaker alerts listeners to an imminent change of tack in the topic under discussion. Signaling this to one's audience (or readers) may be vital, if they are to follow new developments in an argument. Still it is counterproductive to use **but** or any other *discourse marker* repeatedly (see further under that heading.) For alternative devices that express contrast, see **conjunctions** section 3.

buzz words
See **vogue words**.

by, by-, bye- and bye
The English particle **by** appears as a prefix meaning "near to" or "beside" in words like:
    bypass   byroad   bystander   byway

It appears with the less physical meaning "associated with" or "derivative from" in others such as:

> byname   byplay   byproduct   byword

The trend is to set these words solid, though dictionaries differ as to which particular words from the second set are still to be hyphenated. All give a hyphen to the most recent word of this type *by(-)line* ("indication of authorship at the head of a newspaper article"), although those in the newspaper business are less inclined to do so. The fact that the word is increasingly used as a verb *bylined* is another factor that fosters the set-solid form.

When it comes to *by(e)law,* you may choose between **by** and **bye**. The spelling with **bye** hints at the word's history in Old Norse *byr* meaning "town"; while **by** looks like a reinterpretation of the first syllable as the English prefix **by-**. North American dictionaries prefer *bylaw* set solid, and this is the dominant form in American English, judging from CCAE data. *New Oxford* (1998) and the Australian *Macquarie Dictionary* (1997) prefer *by-law,* although actual usage is more variable. Data from the BNC yields examples of *bylaw, by-law, byelaw* and *bye-law,* among which the last was the most frequent. The instances of *bye-law* were mostly embedded in juridical statements and legal reports, whereas *byelaw* and *by-law* were more frequent in nonlegal writing. *Bylaw* appeared only a handful of times.

By(e)-election is allowed the same options as *by(e)(-)law* by some, though it really is based on the prefix **by-**, and there's no historical justification for **bye-**. In BNC data, *by-election* is the commonest form by far, with hundreds of examples whereas *byelection* and *bye-election* had less than a score each. *By-election* is the only spelling in American data from CCAE.

By/bye also appears in a few places as an independent noun. In Canada, Australia and the UK, it's used in various sports for the round in a competition when a team is conceded a pass, because of the lack of a competitor. In cricket a **bye** or *leg bye* is a run gained on the side, i.e. not from contact between bat and ball. In *by the bye,* **bye** is again a noun meaning "something aside," though it's often written as *by the by,* as if it had something in common with *by and by* (which is correctly written with two *by*s). Note

also the informal *bye-bye,* a telescoping of "(God) be with you," said twice over.

◇ Contrast the English prefix **by-** with the Latin *bi-*, discussed under **bi-**.

by reference to or with reference to

See **reference to**.

bytes

The computer term *byte* was coined in the 1960s as a companion to *bit* – not any small piece but a blend of "binary digit," i.e. a unit of computerized information, coded as 1 or 0. A *byte* equals 8 bits in most operating systems. With the rapid growth of computer capacity, *kilobytes* have given way to *megabytes, gigabytes* etc., yet being based on a binary system, the computer terms don't match up exactly with those of the SI system, whose decimal prefixes they use (see Appendix IV). To distinguish the two, a fresh set of symbols and names embodying *bi* was established in 1998 by the International Electrotechnical Commission, associated with NIST (National Institute for Science and Technology). These are shown in the table below, and contrasted with the values of the common terms with their metric prefixes.

	bytes		bits
	official name/ symbol		value in bits
1 kibibyte	kibi	Ki	2^{10} bits = 1024 bits *(1 kilobyte = 1000 bits)*
1 mebibyte	mebi	Mi	2^{20} B = 1,048,576 B *(1 megabyte = 1,000,000 B)*
1 gibibyte	gibi	Gi	2^{30} B = 1,073,741,824 B *(1 gigabyte = 1,000,000,000 B)*

The symbol *B* for **bytes** is standard; however, there's a plethora of existing symbols for the *megabyte,* originating from different manufacturers (see **megabyte**).

As visual and sound information converge, the *megabyte* of information is more easily confused with the *soundbite* beloved of radio broadcasters, which gives a punchline. The *bite* of *soundbite* is directly related to the common verb ("sink your teeth into").

c., ca. or ca
See under **circa**.

-c/-ck-
English spelling sometimes demands that we double
the last letter of a word before adding -ed, -ing and
other suffixes (see under **doubling of final
consonant**). Normally this means repeating the letter,
as with *beg* > *begged* etc., but when the last letter is **c**,
it's "doubled" by making it **ck**. See for example:

bivouac	bivouacked	bivouacking	bivouacker
frolic	frolicked	frolicking	frolicker
mimic	mimicked	mimicking	mimicker
panic	panicked	panicking	panicker
picnic	picnicked	picnicking	picnicker
traffic	trafficked	trafficking	trafficker

The same happens when -y is added, witness *panicky*
and *colicky*. This special treatment for a final **c** is
necessary to ensure that it keeps its "k" sound before
the suffix. When followed by *e, i* or *y*, a **c** usually
sounds as "s," as in *racer, racing* and *racy*
(see **-ce/-ge**).

Adding the *k* into *panicked* etc. looks strange partly
because the inflected forms are much less used than
the simple form *panic*. A variable *k* is also somewhat
unusual. Much more often it's fixed into the spelling,
as in thousands of words like *deck, derrick* and
rickshaw, not to mention *kite, knee, leek, plankton*. In
fact *k* has come and gone from some of the words listed
above: spellings such as *logick, musick* and *physick*
were used in early modern English (up to C18), until it
was felt that the *k* in them was superfluous. But the *k*
reappears before the suffix in *panicked* and the rest,
like a ghost from the past.

Some technical words ending in *c* are exceptions,
and do not add in a *k* before suffixes beginning with *e*
or *i*. Engineers and scientists prefer *arced/arcing* to
arcked/arcking. Technical words derived from *zinc*
are written *zincic, zinciferous, zincify* and *zincite*. The
less technical *zincky* follows the general rule.
◊ For the inflected forms of **sync**, **talc** and **tarmac**, see
individual headings.

cabala, cabbala, kabala, kabbala or qabbalah
All these refer to an esoteric Jewish tradition, or,
more broadly, to any mystical doctrine. Choosing
among the spellings is a matter of regional
preferences, and whether you want to stress the
Hebrew origins of the word. *Merriam-Webster* (2000)
gives priority to the forms with one *b*, while *New
Oxford* (1998), *Canadian Oxford* (1998) and the
Australian *Macquarie* (1997) prefer those with two *b*s.
The spellings with one *b* are in line with antecedents
in medieval French and Latin (and other related
words such as *cabal*). Those with two *b*s reflect the
spelling of the Hebrew original, although other
adjustments as in **qabbalah** are needed to hebraicize

it fully. The *k*-spellings enjoyed some currency in C19,
but a hundred years later, those with *c* seem to have
prevailed.
◊ For other examples of similar spelling variation, see
under **k/c** and **single for double**.

cabanossi or kabanossi
See under **k/c**.

cabby or cabbie
See under **-ie/-y**.

cactus
Most respondents to the Langscape survey (1998–2001)
preferred *cacti* for the plural of this word: see **-us**
section 1.

caddy or caddie
Caddy is the only spelling for the container of tea –
which may also be the obvious place to hide the
household keys. The word is derived from Malay *kati*,
where it refers to a particular measure of weight,
approximately 600 grams.

When it comes to golf, the spelling varies a little.
Caddie is more usual and given preference over
caddy in the major British and American
dictionaries – at least for the noun. For the verb the
Oxford Dictionary (1989) has **caddy** as the preferred
spelling, and its use is illustrated in several BNC
examples, such as *arranged for him to caddy at the LC
Club*. *Webster's Third* (1986) keeps **caddie** as the
primary spelling for both verb and noun.

The word is believed to have come from Scottish
English in C19. Originally it was the French *cadet*, but
you may hear the informal Scots *laddie* in it also. That
apart, the -*ie* suffix serves as a familiarity marker on
other English nouns: see **-ie/-y**.

Caesarean, Caesarian, Cesarean or Cesarian
Add in the choice between capitalized and
uncapitalized forms of the word, and you have eight
possible spellings. Yet database evidence from the US
and the UK shows that forms with capitals are a good
deal more common than those without. Historical
uses of the word are almost always capitalized;
whereas references to the obstetrical procedure are
lower-cased occasionally in CCAE, and quite often in
BNC data (**caesarean**/**caesarian** appeared in more
than 50% of instances of the word).

Given the choice between *ae* and just *e* in the first
syllable, historians everywhere use the first. The
adjective **Caesarean**/**Caesarian** is tied to the name
Caesar, and so keeps the classical *ae* spelling even in
the US (see further under **ae/e**). When referring to
obstetrics, British writers maintain the *ae* in both
general and medical publications. Americans writing
for a general audience tend to do the same, though the

medical preference for **cesarean** shows up occasionally in data from CCAE.

The choice between *-ean* and *-ian* is relatively clear cut, and both British and American writers tend to use *-ean* in *Caesarean (cesarean) section.* In CCAE data spellings with *-ean* outnumber those with *-ian* by more than 15:1. The two are more equally represented in the BNC, though **Caesarean** has the edge (4:3) in terms of the number of texts in which it appears. Among historians however the preferred spelling seems to be **Caesarian**.

Despite the careful maintenance of Julius Caesar's name in the spelling of the obstetrical procedure, it seems very unlikely that he himself was born by *C(a)esarean section* – as legend has it. Only in the last hundred years have surgical births become a regular procedure, and safe enough to ensure the survival of both mother and child. In earlier times surgical deliveries like this were indeed performed, but only to release an unborn child from a dying mother. Julius Caesar's mother bore two more children after him, so she can scarcely have had a *C(a)esarean* performed on her. The tradition probably arose from the fact that the name *Caesar* seems to embody the Latin stem *caes-* meaning "cut." The name was however borne by several of Julius Caesar's ancestors. See further under **folk etymology**.

caesura or cesura

The first is the primary spelling in *Merriam-Webster* (2000), and the only one as far as *New Oxford* (1998) is concerned. For the plural, see **-a** section 1.

café, cafe or caffe

In French *café* is both the coffee shop and the beverage. Only the first sense has been fully anglicized, but now so much a suburban institution that it freely appears without the French accent in shop signs and in print – hence the jokey pronunciation with one syllable. Both *New Oxford* (1998) and the Australian *Macquarie Dictionary* (1997) list the accentless form **cafe** as the primary spelling, whereas *Merriam-Webster* (2000) and the *Canadian Oxford* (1998) prioritize **café**. Actual database evidence is hard to obtain because accents tend to be filtered out by the software. Yet there may still be some cachet in the foreign accent, whether or not the place serves *haute cuisine*. The phrases referring to what you drink at a **cafe**, e.g. *café au lait* or *café-filtre*, often carry the acute accent. Where Italian coffee-making practices prevail in the English-speaking world, the beverage becomes **caffe**, but not often with the grave accent it would carry in standard Italian. Its foreignness is still underscored in the italianate phrases *caffe crema* or *caffe latte* in which it typically appears.

caftan or kaftan

See under **k/c**.

cagey or cagy

Less than a century old, this word still varies in spelling, and the more regular **cagy** has yet to prevail. Both *Merriam-Webster* (2000) and *New Oxford* (1998) make **cagey** the primary spelling, and in the Langscape survey (1998–2001) it was preferred by the majority of respondents worldwide. See further under **-y/-ey**.

calculus

In Latin this meant "pebble, stone," and the sense continues in *renal calculi* (kidney stones), *vesical calculi* (in the bladder) and medical terms for other concretions of the older human body. The plural *calculi* is straight Latin (see further under **-us**). But when **calculus** refers to one of a set of subdisciplines of mathematics such as *differential calculus* or *integral calculus,* their plural is the regular English *calculuses.*

caldron or cauldron

See **cauldron**.

calendar or calender

The spelling of the last syllable makes a difference. With **calendar** you have the word for a system by which time is calculated, whereas **calender** refers to machinery used in manufacturing cloth or paper.

Calendar is the commoner of the two words by far. Its *-ar* ending is an integral part of the stem of its Latin forebear *calendarium* ("account book"). The Roman account book took its name from the fact that accounts were tallied on the first day of each month, known in Latin as the *calendae* (or *kalendae*). So time and money were reckoned together.

The other word **calender** refers to the machine whose rollers put a smooth finish on paper or cloth as it passes through. The word originates as a medieval spelling for the word "cylinder" which helps to explain the *-er*.

caliber or calibre

See under **-re/-er**.

calico

For the plural of this word, see under **-o**.

caliper or calliper

Dictionaries everywhere prefer **caliper(s)** for the measuring instrument and other mechanical devices that go by this name. In American data from CCAE **caliper** is the only spelling, whereas in the BNC it shares the field with **calliper.** The spelling **caliper** keeps the word closer to its only English relative *caliber/calibre,* of which it's a C16 variant.

caliph, calif, khalif or kaliph

Modern dictionaries give preference to **caliph** for spelling this word for an Arab ruler. Arabic scholars prefer **khalif**, it being closer to the original form of the word. On the variation between **caliph** and **calif**, see **f/ph**; and for **caliph** v. **kaliph**, see **k/c**.

calisthenics or callisthenics

See **callisthenics**.

calix and calyx

The *i* and *y* make a significant difference with these. **Calix** is the ancient Latin word for the chalice used in the Catholic Church. It maintains its Latin plural **calices**. The second word **calyx** refers to the protective covering of a flower bud (and collectively to the sepals). At bottom it's a neoclassical use of the Greek *calux* ("shell"). Its plural in scientific discourse is always **calyces**, but in general use it would be **calyxes**. See **-x** section 3.

calk or caulk
See **caulk**.

calliper or caliper
See **caliper**.

callisthenics or calisthenics
This C19 word for graceful gymnastic exercises combines the Greek elements *kallos* ("beauty") and *sthenos* ("strength"). In Britain **callisthenics** is the primary spelling according to *New Oxford* (1998), and it prevails among a small set of examples in the BNC. But in North America **calisthenics** is presented as the primary spelling in both *Merriam-Webster* (2000) and *Canadian Oxford* (1998), and it's the only spelling to be found in data from CCAE.

callous or callus and calloused or callused
In theory, these complement each other as adjective and noun referring to a thickened patch of skin, the latter illustrated in *the callus on his index finger*. (For other pairs of this kind, see under **-ous**.) In practice the adjective **callous** gets used figuratively, in the sense of "having a thick skin," i.e. hard-hearted or brutal, witness *callous murder* or *callous dismantling of the welfare state*. Amid scores of examples in the BNC, the figurative sense dominates.

All this explains the need for the adjectival derivative **calloused**, which in BNC data almost always expresses physical hardening of the skin, as in *a big, strong hand, roughly calloused from field work*. It presupposes a verb "to make or become callous" which is registered in both the *Oxford Dictionary* (1989) and *Webster's Third* (1986), though it appears only as past and present participle. The spelling **callused** is much rarer and implies a derivation directly from the noun (see further under **-ed** section 2). It therefore serves as a way of emphasizing the physical meaning, in citations such as *heels can become callused*. Yet the figurative sense seems to haunt it too in *the callused offspring of earth*.

calque
See under **caulk**.

Cambodia
The name **Cambodia** has been reinstated for the Southeast Asian republic. It replaces *Kampuchea*, promoted during the Khmer revolution as the proper noncolonial name, and proclaimed in the official name *People's Republic of Kampuchea* in 1979. The name has since become notorious, and **Cambodia** continues as the name registered at United Nations.

camomile or chamomile
The spelling **chamomile** reflects the Latin *chamomilla* and its putative origin in the Greek *chamaimelon* ("earth apple"). It dominates in pharmacy and herbal recipes, whereas the French-derived **camomile** prevails in literary and nontechnical contexts. So the *camomile lawn* and *camomile tea* (as a social rather than therapeutic drink) help to make **camomile** the commoner spelling of the two in the UK, by the evidence of the BNC. In the US, **chamomile** is still the preferred spelling, according to *Merriam-Webster* (2000) and in data from CCAE.

can or may
There is no simple division of labor between these, and like any well-worked words they have shades of meaning which are sometimes hard to pin down. In interactive contexts, **can** vacillates between:

> *be able to* (ability)
> *be allowed to* (permission)
> *be possible that* (possibility)

The meaning often depends on context, and the status of the speakers. So **can** could express ability or permission in *I can come with you*, depending on whether the speaker ("I") is allowed to exercise his or her discretion in such matters. In a similar way, circumstances would decide whether in *It can make things hard for you* **can** expresses ability or possibility. In written discourse **can** is less equivocal, and only rarely expresses permission in academic prose, according to the *Longman Grammar* (1999). The *Grammar* shows that academic writers commonly use **can** to express ability as well as logical possibility – just like **may**. **Can** and **may** have similar frequencies overall in academic writing, whereas in other kinds of discourse (written and spoken) **can** is very much more common.

The most common use of **may** nowadays is to express the sense of possibility, as in *It may decide the future*. This is true even in conversation according to the *Longman Grammar*, although **may** can still embody a sense of permission, depending on the circumstances and the status of the interlocutors. The point of *They may leave by the first train* could be either permission (if the speaker enjoys lofty status), or else possibility (with neutral status). When expressing permission, **may** seems more conspicuously polite than **can**. Compare statements such as:

> *You may go if you wish.*
> *You can go if you wish.*

And the requests:

> *May I open the window?*
> *Can I open the window?*

The higher level of politeness and deference in **may** is a commonplace of usage books, often made categorical and without reference to its other grammatical functions. Data from the Longman corpus show that **may** is relatively rare in conversation, where it's outnumbered by **can** more than 20 times over. This, and the fact that **may** is now strongly associated with academic writing, support the feeling that it expresses things more formally.

◊ See further under **could or might**; **may or might**; and under **modality**.

Canadian English
Outside North America, Canadians are sometimes mistaken for Americans, but the Canadian variety of English is its own unique blend of British and American English. The foundations were laid by American Loyalists in C18, who moved into Canada from the eastern seaboard of the US, and were subsequently joined in C19 by new immigrants from Britain, especially Scotland. The **Canadian English** vocabulary includes loanwords from Canadian Indians, such as *caribou, kayak, toboggan* and *totem*, which have become part of English worldwide. The same goes for certain French words such as *anglophone, francophone*, which were first assimilated

into English in Canada through contact with French speakers in Quebec. From east to west in Canada, there are considerable differences in vocabulary; and regional dictionaries of provincial vocabulary, such as that of *Newfoundland English* (1984) and of *Prince Edward Island English* (1988) appeared before any comprehensive national dictionary such as the *Canadian Oxford Dictionary* (1998).

When written or printed, **Canadian English** varies in the extent to which it reflects American or British usage. Generally speaking, newspapers and magazines use American spellings such as *color, center* and *anemic,* in line with the Canadian Press Stylebook; whereas Canadian book publishers tend to use the British alternatives (*colour, centre, anaemic* etc.). Research by Ireland (1979) highlighted some regional differences, in that those resident in Ontario were more likely to use *-our* spellings than those in the provinces east or west of them. The punctuation of **Canadian English** again shows both American and British tendencies, but American practices prevail in the preference for double quote marks in many book publishers, as well as newspapers and magazines. Notable exceptions are the University of Toronto Press and the Canadian branches of Macmillan and Oxford University Press, which all prefer British style. In the absence of a specifically Canadian style guide, Canadian editors work with British or American style according to the task and its intended readers, as is clear from *Editing Canadian English* (2000).

A large endowment to support and promote standard **Canadian English** was vested by J.R. Strathy in the Strathy Language Unit, established in 1981 at Queen's University, Kingston Ontario. The Strathy Corpus of Canadian English was planned and developed there by the Unit's first directors (W.C. Lougheed, followed by M. Fee); and the corpus provided extensive data for the *Canadian Guide to English Usage* (1997).

canceled or cancelled
See under -l-/-ll-.

candelabra
By origin **candelabra** is a Latin plural, like *bacteria* and *data,* and so its Latin singular is **candelabrum.** But **candelabrum** is not much used in contemporary English, judging by its low frequency in British and American databases; and its role as singular is often subsumed by **candelabra,** as in *a massive candelabra* or just *a candelabra.* This singular use of **candelabra** is noted in all regional dictionaries, American, Canadian, British and Australian, without censure except in *New Oxford* (1998). Of course **candelabra** also serves as plural (*a pair of candelabra, matching candelabra*), and in many contexts where its grammar is indeterminate, as in the title *Behind the candelabra: my life with Liberace.* Plural uses of **candelabra** (and instances of **candelabrum**) occur in writing concerned with antiques or ceremonial uses of the branching candlestick. Meanwhile the unmistakably singular use tends to turn up in narrative contexts, where the **candelabra** is a token of showiness or showmanship. In botanical names such as *candelabra primula, candelabra tree* (Euphorbia ingenuus), **candelabra** again seems to be singular.

Current uses of **candelabra** thus tend to mask its plural identity, so it's not unnatural to take it as

singular and then create an English plural for it: **candelabras.** Though **candelabras** is frowned on by some, both *Webster's Third* (1986) and the *Oxford Dictionary* (1989) acknowledge it, as well as **candelabrums.** Contemporary databases provide no support for **candelabrums,** but **candelabras** is clearly in use in both the US and the UK. If it matters that there was more than one branching candlestick to light the room, **candelabras** says it.

candidacy or candidature
Both mean the "status or standing of a candidate," and date from mid-C19. *Webster's Third* (1986) labels **candidature** as "chiefly Brit.," suggesting that Americans are more accustomed to **candidacy,** and evidence from CCAE bears this out, with examples of **candidacy** by the thousand, and only one of **candidature.** In Britain both words are current, but **candidacy** is again more common than **candidature,** outnumbering it by more than 2:1 in data from the BNC. In many contexts the two words seem to be interchangeable, whether they involve candidates for political parties, for local government or for head of state. Perhaps the only context in which **candidature** prevails is that of academic qualifications, where *Ph.D. candidature* etc. seems to be conventional.

cannon or canon
What's in a letter? In these divergent words, guns and missiles contrast with the laws and standards of the Church.

The spelling **cannon** is reserved for a large gun, formerly mounted on a carriage, and for the shot fired by it (the *cannon ball*). It also refers to particular shots made in billiards and croquet.

Canon is the spelling for two kinds of meaning, both originally associated with the Church:
* for a member of a religious group living under *canon law,* or a clergyman attached to a cathedral
* for the body of laws associated with a church, or other formulated practices, as in the *canon of the Mass.* Outside the Church it has come to mean any law or standard, or a reference list of items which are deemed authentic, e.g. the *canon of Shakespeare plays.* The *canon of saints* comprises those officially recognized by the Catholic Church.

Both aspects of **canon** go back to a Latin word meaning "rule or measuring line." Ultimately it was the Greek *kanon,* a derivative of *kan(n)e* meaning "a rod or reed." This, strangely enough, is also the ultimate source of **cannon.** The hollowness of the reed and its usefulness as a firing tube gave rise to **cannon,** whereas the straightness of the rod is the semantic basis of **canon.** Other words derived from the same Greek source are the English *cane* and Italian *cannelloni.*

canoe
Should it be *canoeing* or *canoing?* See under -e section 1g.

cantaloupe, cantaloup, cantalope or cantelope
In references to this freshly luscious melon, the first spelling dominates citations from both British and American databases, and it's rightly given preference in major dictionaries. Yet all highlight the second as an alternative (not in the databases); and the third and

fourth, noted in *Webster's Third* (1986) as well as the *Oxford Dictionary* (1989), connect with a not uncommon pronunciation which rhymes with *antelope*, and creates a spurious etymology for an inscrutable word (see further under **folk etymology**).

Cantaloupe in fact enshrines the name of a quite different animal. The origins of the word are in *Cantalupo* ("song of the wolf,") the name of one of the Pope's former estates near Rome on which the fruit (brought from Armenia) was first developed. This explains why the vowel of the middle syllable should be *a* rather than *e*, but leaves us with the option of French *loup* ("wolf") or the anglicized -*loupe* for the last syllable.

Canton
See under **China**.

canvas or canvass
Dictionaries give the spelling **canvas** to the noun referring to a heavy fabric with a variety of applications from art to camping; and **canvass** to the verb meaning "solicit votes or voting support," and its associated noun. But the spelling distinction is only about a century old, and unabridged dictionaries such as *Webster's Third* (1986) and the *Oxford Dictionary* (1989) show that either spelling has been and is possible. Database evidence suggests that this interchange is uncommon in current British English, given that the BNC's examples (e.g. *paintings on oil and canvass*) are mostly in transcriptions of speech. In American data from CCAE it's a little more common, and the interchange goes both ways: compare *translating vision to canvass* with *a canvas of investment opportunities*. As the second example shows, the noun **canvas(s)** is freely used in the US of investigations or surveys that have nothing to do with the electoral process. A **canvass** may or may not be carried out face to face, witness the *telephone canvass,* and can be associated with neighborhood detective work (the *police canvass*) or implementation of local regulations: *a door-to-door canvass to confiscate home-grown fruit*. In the UK **canvass** (as noun) is mostly associated with securing votes or surveying public attitudes, whereas the verb can also be used to mean "ascertain" (*canvass the views of members*) and "discuss" (*canvassing the future*), as in the US.

The noun **canvas** comes from *cannabis* ("hemp"), and so a single *s* is all that etymology can justify. The verb **canvass** apparently derives from it, though authorities disagree on how. Dr. Johnson believed it originated in the practice of sifting flour through a piece of canvas, which is figuratively extended to the sifting through of ideas, one of the earliest recorded meanings. The *Oxford Dictionary* however relates **canvass** to **canvas** through a jolly practice alluded to by Shakespeare: that of tossing someone in a large canvas sheet, which could be figuratively extended to mean the public thrashing and airing of ideas. Yet neither explanation accounts for the sense of soliciting votes – the key to its most important modern uses.

Spelled as **canvass**, the verb presents no problems when suffixes are added: *canvassed, canvassing*. As **canvas** it would raise the question as to whether to leave the *s* single as in *canvased, canvasing*. (See further under **doubling of final consonant**.) The

plural of the noun **canvas** is simply *canvases*, on the analogy of *atlas(es)*.

capacity to, capacity for and capacity of
These are several ways of coupling **capacity** with a following verb, all current and with scant differences in meaning. **Capacity to** takes an infinitive, as in *capacity to learn, capacity to muddle through*, and it's the most frequent of the three constructions in both the US and the UK, by the evidence of CCAE and the BNC. The alternatives **capacity for** and **capacity of** take a verbal noun (-*ing* form), as in *capacity for getting around* and *capacity of evoking quieter forms of heroism*. The construction with *for* is a good deal commoner than the one with *of,* especially in American data. Both are occasionally also used with abstract nouns as in *capacity for fun, capacity of observation*.

capital or capitol
Both *Capitol Hill*, the seat of federal government in the US, and the building which houses the American Congress are spelled **Capitol** (with an upper case initial). It was the name of the temple of Jupiter in ancient Rome. The same word **capitol** (usually with lower case) is given to the headquarters of any of the US state assemblies, such as the *Texas state capitol*. Various *Capitol theatres* scattered throughout the world also use the name, as does the *Capitol* recording company.

The chief city in any state or country is its **capital**, in lower case. Note that the Australian federal parliament is housed on *Capital Hill*, within the ACT (Australian Capital Territory).

capital letters
These are so named because they "head" the beginning of a sentence, or a word or expression of special significance. (*Capital* embodies the Latin word caput, "head.") **Capital letters** are larger than ordinary letters, and often different in shape – angular rather than rounded, as is evident in the differences between *F* and *f, H* and *h*, and *M* and *m*. Printers refer to them as "upper case" letters because they were stored in the upper section of the tray containing the units of typeface, while the ordinary letters ("lower case" letters) were kept in the lower and larger section of the tray. (For the use of *small capital letters,* see **small caps**.)

Fewer initial *capitals* are now used in writing English than in earlier centuries. In C18 they were used not just for proper names, but also for any words of special note in a sentence, especially the noun or nouns under discussion. This practice survives to some extent in legal documents, which still use more **capital letters** than any other texts, partly perhaps to provide a focus for the reader in long legal sentences. Elsewhere the use of *capitals* has contracted to the items mentioned in the following sections (1a) to (1f). The use of *capitals* in abbreviated references (section 3) is more variable, as in the writing of book titles (see under **titles**; see also **Bible**). The gradual disappearance of **capital letters** from proper names which become generic words is discussed in section 2.

Capital letters are a matter of regional difference. British writers and editors are more inclined to use **capital letters** where Americans would dispense with them. This divergence may well owe something to the fact that the original *Oxford Dictionary* (1884–1928) put a **capital letter** on every headword, whereas *Webster's Third* (1986) has them all in lower case, and adds a note to say whether each is usually or often seen with a *capital*. The traditions thus established no doubt underlie the semantic and aesthetic values writers invest in **capital letters**, though logic doesn't always support their conclusions. "When in doubt use lower case" is the pragmatic advice of the *Oxford Dictionary for Writers and Editors* (1986).

1 Capitals for proper names

a) The distinguishing names and designations given to a person are always given initial capitals. In some cases, e.g. *Patience Strong,* the capitals serve to confirm that the common words do indeed form a personal name, but most personal names (e.g. *James Simpson*) consist of elements that have no place in the common language. Capitals are used with names whether they are true given names, pseudonyms like *Dorothy Dix*, or nicknames such as *the Iron Duke.* The names of fictitious persons like *John Doe* and fictional characters like *Sherlock Holmes* are capitalized. Literary personifications (e.g. *Truth*) are also conventionally marked by their special capital letter: see **personification**. References to the Deity are regularly capitalized, and, in some ecclesiastical traditions, the attendant personal pronouns *Him* etc. as well. See further under **God**.

Extra **capital letters** are often given in English to foreign names involving articles and prepositions, though they would not be capitalized in the language from which they come. So words like *da, de, della, le, la, van* and *von* quickly acquire *capitals*, as a glance at the telephone book would show. A Dutch personal name like *van der Meer* becomes *Van Der Meer,* and eventually *Vandermeer.* Celebrated names of this kind, such as *da Vinci, de Gaulle, della Robbia* and *van Gogh,* do resist this capitalization more strongly. Yet they too acquire a **capital letter** when used at the beginning of a sentence. On the use of one or two **capital letters** in names such as *FitzGerald/ Fitzgerald* and *McLeod/Macleod,* see under **Fitz-** and **Mac**.

b) National and ethnic names are regularly capitalized, whether they refer to nations, races, tribes, or religious or linguistic groups. Hence:

Altaic	Aztec	Caucasian
Christian	Danish	Hausa
Hindu	Japanese	Muslim
Navaho	Semitic	Tartar
Tongan	Tutsi	Ugric

References to the Canadian *First Nations* and to Australian *Aborigines* and *an Aboriginal* people are always capitalized for this reason. See also **black or Black** and **colo(u)red**.

c) The names of organizations and institutions are to be capitalized, whenever they are set out in full. (For abbreviated references, see below, section 3.) Most institutional names consist of a generic element e.g. *department* and another word or words that particularize it e.g. *education; finance and administration.* When cited in full, both generic and particularizing words are capitalized, but not any small function words linking them (prepositions, articles, conjunctions). See for example:

The Church of Jesus Christ of Latter-Day Saints
Department of Immigration and Ethnic Affairs
IBM Global Services

Museum of Contemporary Art
Printing and Allied Trades Union
Returned Services League of Australia
Royal Society for the Prevention of Cruelty to Animals

The names of vehicles of transport are capitalized, whether they are brand names such as *Boeing 747* or *Ford Falcon*, or unique names such as the *Orient Express* or *HMS Dreadnought*. Individual vehicle names are normally italicized as well.

d) Official titles and offices are capitalized whenever they are used to name a particular holder or incumbent, e.g.

Cardinal Newman
Chancellor Kohl
Lieutenant James Varley
Lord Denning
President Ronald Reagan
Secretary of State Henry Kissinger
Senator John Harridene

When the title or office is used in apposition to the individual's name, capitalization practices vary. American English is not inclined to capitalize, whether the title follows the name, or precedes it without being part of it:

Fiorello La Guardia, mayor of New York
the mayor of New York, La Guardia
French president De Gaulle
Charles De Gaulle, president of France

In British English such titles carry **capital letters** when they come before the individual's name, but not if they follow, according to Ritter (2002). So a reference to *French President De Gaulle* would be fully capitalized. Older British style put *capitals* on titles used on their own, as in *the Bishop of London was in attendance* (*Hart's Rules,* 1983). But this is no longer necessary except to prevent ambiguity (Ritter); and Americans just would not, according to the *Chicago Manual* (2003). Neither would put a capital on generic or plural references to an office: *when he became king; the prime ministers of England.* British and American practices also coincide on using upper case / *capitals* in honorific titles and forms of address such as *His Grace, Her Majesty, Your Excellency.*

Senior title- and office-holders in institutions other than church and state are not regularly capitalized. In newspapers and other general publications, references to chief executive officers in business and industry are typically lower-cased, as in:

chairman of Kraft Foods
managing director of Reader's Digest

In-house company publications and prospectuses may nevertheless capitalize all references to their executives.

e) Geographical names and designations are capitalized whenever they appear in full. In some cases this helps to distinguish them from phrases consisting of identical common words e.g. *Snowy Mountains, Northwest Territory,* but in most cases the *capitals* simply help to highlight unique placenames for countries and cities e.g. *India, Delhi,* as well as local and street names e.g. *Park Avenue, Times Square.* They are also used for individual topographical names such as the *Mississippi River* and the *South Downs.* The names of special buildings and public structures are also capitalized whenever they are given in full form, as with the *Eiffel Tower* or the *Statue of Liberty.*

When two or more geographical names are combined in a single expression, the generic part of the names is usually pluralized and kept in lower case if it follows rather than precedes:

> *the Hudson and Mississippi rivers*
> *the Atlantic and Southern oceans*

Cf.

> *Mounts Egmont and Hutt*

This practice is established in many parts of the English-speaking world, and detailed in the *CBE Manual* (1994), the Australian government *Style Manual* (2002), and the *Chicago Manual* (2003). But whether the generic word precedes or follows in the official form of the name can be difficult to ascertain. (See further under **geographical names** section 1.)

Compass directions are capitalized when abbreviated – *S, SW, SSW* – but lower-cased when written out in full: *south, southwest, southsouthwest.*

f) References to unique historical events and periods are capitalized if they are the standard designation:

> *Black Hole of Calcutta*
> *Bronze Age*
> *the Reformation*
> *Roaring Twenties*
> *World War II*

However ones which are paralleled in different places at different times do not need *capitals*: *gold rush, industrial revolution.*

Special feast days, holidays and public events are given initial *capitals*:

> *the Adelaide Festival*
> *Bay to Breakers*
> *Boxing Day*
> *Fourth of July*
> *Good Friday*
> *Yom Kippur*

While the regular names of days and months are capitalized (*Saturday, September*), those for less well-known points in the calendar are left in lower case: *solstice, equinox.*

g) Scientific nomenclature for animals, plants, fungi, bacteria, viruses and diseases have a capital letter for the genus, but not for the species name:

> *Larus pacificus*
> *Begonia semperflorens*

Both parts of the expression are normally italicized. However the common English names for flora and fauna are not capitalized or italicized, when they coincide with the genus name. Hence:

> *acacia   capsicum   citrus   herpes*
> *octopus   pterodactyl*

(See further under **scientific names**.)

Astronomical names for the stars, planets, asteroids etc. are capitalized:

> *the Great Bear*
> *the Milky Way*
> *the Southern Cross*

However when the name consists of both a particular and a generic element e.g. *the Crab nebula,* only the particular part bears a *capital*.

h) Commercial names, including trademarks, brandnames and proprietary references should be capitalized as long as their registration is current. Those which become household words steadily lose the initial *capital* – witness *cellophane, escalator, nylon, thermos* – and many a trademark has lapsed in the course of time. An added problem in international English is that a commodity such as *aspirin* is now

free of trademark restrictions in the UK and the US, Australia and New Zealand, but not Canada. Dictionaries usually indicate when a particular word originated as a trademark, and their use of upper or lower case for the headword is some indication of their judgement on its current status as a proprietorial or generic item. Thus the *Oxford Dictionary* (1989) lists *aqualung, jeep and caterpillar* with lower case, but *Frigidaire, Hoover* and *Levis* with upper case, choices which seem to be largely based on the accompanying citations. This correlates with its disclaimer to the effect that there is no legal significance in the use or nonuse of a **capital letter** on such names. But *Webster's Third* (1986) lists all such words with upper case (a departure from its standard practice for all other headwords), and thus presumably avoids litigation. Even large dictionaries are retrospective in their coverage, and cannot perhaps be expected to be up to date with the changing status of words coined as trademarks. The ultimate reference on their status is the registry of patents in each English-speaking country. (See further under **trademarks**.)

The proprietary names of drugs require a *capital*, whereas generic ones may be lower-cased. Thus *hydrocortisone (Celestone-V)*. For general purposes, i.e. when not concerned with the trialing of a proprietary drug, the writer would naturally use generic names. For up-to-date information on non-proprietary names, consult the twice-yearly *British National Formulary* or the annual *Dictionary of Drug Names* of USAN (United States Adopted Names Council) and USPC (United States Pharmacopeial Convention).

In computer terminology, the names of computer languages and proprietary programs and systems are usually given *full caps:*

> *CD-ROM   FORTRAN   HTML   JAVA*
> *PC   UNIX*

This is in line with common practice for *acronyms* (see **acronyms**), though not all computer terms are strictly that, as the mix of examples shows.

The names of newspapers, magazines and serials always bear initial capital letters:

> *Christian Science Monitor*
> *Daily Telegraph*
> *English Today*
> *New Scientist*

The definite article/determiner (*the*) is not normally capitalized (or italicized) in such references. (See further under **the** section 4.)

2 When capital letters disappear from proper names. Since a **capital letter** marks the fact that a name is unique (or at least relatively so, in the case of "common" personal names such as *Anne, James* etc.), we might expect them to disappear when the name becomes the byword for something. This has certainly happened to words such as *sandwich* and *wellington*, where the meaning of the common noun is far removed from the person concerned. Eponymic words like those are most likely to be lower-cased when they take on a derivational suffix, as for example in *machiavellian, pasteurize, spoonerism*. (See further under **eponyms** and **suffixes** section 2.)

Capital letters disappear more slowly from geographical and national names which have become the byword for something. No doubt this is because the regular geographical/national use of the word (with a *capital*) is current, and some writers flinch at *french polish* (with lower case) because they are so accustomed to *French exports*. Dictionary makers are also reluctant to decapitalize such words because of the inconsistencies they seem to create in a column of compound expressions.

Yet Fowler (1926) and others since have recommended lower-casing expressions like *french windows* and *venetian blinds,* because the geographical/cultural connection is tenuous and scarcely felt. We might all agree to delete the **capital letter** in phrases such as *dutch courage, french leave* and *chinese burn,* which owe more to Anglo-Saxon prejudice than anything else (see further under **throwaway terms**). Many people would remove the *capital* from geographically named fruits and vegetables like *brussels sprout, french bean, swiss chard,* because they are grown all over the world. This was clear in responses to the Langscape survey (1998–2001), and the majority also resisted routine capitalization of *alsatian* and *siamese*. The names of animal breeds like these continue to be capitalized in publications produced by official breeder organizations, yet the trend away from *capitals* is evident in newspapers and books for the general market. Wine regulators encourage the use of *capitals* for grape varieties (but not for wine names), so that it should be *Chardonnay, Riesling* and *Shiraz,* but *champagne, moselle* and *sauterne*. Yet uncertainty in the general public about that distinction, and the unfamiliarity of the places embodied in some of the wine names, means that many people simply lower-case them all. The town names enshrined in the names of cheeses – *cheddar, edam* and *stilton* – are not universally known, and again most respondents to Langscape resisted capitalizing *Stilton*. Overall then **capital letters** tend to disappear from common nouns derived from place names, though the trend is retarded in certain contexts.

3 Capital letters in abbreviated designations and titles. After introducing a name or the title in full, most writers abbreviate it for subsequent appearances – it would be cumbersome otherwise. The word retained is often lower-cased. So the *Amazon River* becomes *the river, Brigadier R. Sande* becomes *the brigadier,* and *the National Gallery* becomes *the gallery*. The practice is set out in the *Oxford Guide to Style* (2002) and extensively illustrated in the *Chicago Manual* ch. 8. It was endorsed worldwide by a majority of respondents to the Langscape survey (1998–2001). The use of lower case helps to show that it is not the official name/title, and avoids drawing unnecessary attention to it once it is a "given" rather than "new" item in the stream of information. (See further under **given and new**.)

Some established abbreviations do nevertheless retain the *capital:*

a) *the Channel* (for the *English Channel*); *the Keys* (for the *Florida Keys*); *the Reef* (for *Great Barrier Reef*)

b) abbreviated names of organizations continue to bear *capitals* when they consist of the particular, rather than the generic part of the name, as in *a new look for Veterans Affairs; the budget for Health*

c) many organizational names are abbreviated as an initialism or acronym in full caps: *AMA, BBC, GATT, HMSO, NAACP*

Other exceptions to the general principle are the tendency mentioned above in section 1d, to capitalize even abbreviated references to the chief executive roles, e.g. *the Prime Minister, the Chancellor,* and the tendency to retain capitals in in-house publications,

when referring to company or organization personnel, e.g. the *Human Resources Manager,* the *Directors*. In British style the word *Government* often carries a **capital letter** even in shorthand references to a particular government (Ritter, 2002). But in American, Canadian and Australian style, *government* is lower-cased except when the word appears within the official title: see the *Chicago Manual* (2003), *Editing Canadian English* (2000) and the Australian government *Style Manual* (2002). The danger of overcapitalizing is noted in *Copy-editing* (1992), once exceptions begin to be admitted.

4 The use of mid-capitals (also called bicaps, incaps and intercaps). Some organizations and businesses go by compound names with a **capital letter** in the middle, e.g. *AusInfo, HarperCollins*. The *mid-capital* is thus part of their trademark or business identity, and it defies the general practice of using a hyphen before a capital letter in mid-word (see **hyphens** section 1c). The practice is established in personal names such as *FitzGerald* and *McIvor:* see under **Fitz-** and **Mac or Mc**.

5 Capital letters in crossreferences to chapters, figures, tables etc. Editorial practices vary over whether words such as *chapter* should carry an initial *capital* in textual references to other chapters, as in:

> See chapter 4 for further discussion.
> The contrasting data are presented in figures 6 and 7.

The *Chicago Manual* uses lower case whether the word is given in full, as in these examples, or abbreviated to *ch., fig*. etc. British authorities diverge: the *Oxford Guide to Style* (2000) has them in *capitals,* whereas *Copy-editing* (1992) explicitly allows either style – so long as it's used consistently. *Copy-editing* notes that *table* is never abbreviated, and recommends against using the other abbreviations except in parentheses and footnotes.

6 The use of capital letters in book titles and other compositions. **Capital letters** may be used minimally, moderately or maximally in the titles of books and articles, as well as other published or broadcast works. See further under **titles**.

◊ For using *capitals* to mark individual letters as words, see **letters as words**.

◊ For making use of *capitals* for typographical effect, see under **headings and subheadings** (*layout and typography*).

capital punishment
See under **corporal**.

capitol or capital
See **capital**.

cappuccino
Dictionaries present **cappuccino** as the standard spelling for Italian-style coffee made with a topping of frothy steamed milk, now fully assimilated in the English-speaking world. The phrase *cappuccino cowboys* makes its point in American cities. **Cappuccino** is the dominant spelling in data from CCAE and the BNC, yet the databases also contain a sprinkling of the variants *capuccino* and *cappucino,* in around 10% of all instances of the word. They can also be seen on menus and restaurant blackboards – evidence of the English tendency to drop a consonant or two from loanwords (see further under **single for**

double). **Cappuccino** is the only legitimate spelling for those who wish to connect it with its origins in the Italian word *cappuccio* meaning "hood." The hood gave a name to the *Capuchin* order of friars, a French form of the name, which again shows the loss of one of the two *ps*.

There is another connection with the Capuchins, because the Capuchin friar (in Italian *cappuccino*) wore a chestnut-colored robe, whose hue was then called *cappuccino*, according to the *Grande Dizionario della Lingua Italiana* (1962). Thus **cappuccino** describes the color of the coffee beneath the foam – neither black nor white but brindle.

In English the plural of *cap(p)uc(c)ino* is normally *cappuccinos*, though in an Italian *ristorante* or *trattoria*, it could well be *cappuccini*. See further under **Italian plurals**.

capsize

This is the one word (of more than one syllable) which must always be spelled *-ize*, even by writers who prefer to use *-ise* in *organise, recognise* etc. (see further under **-ize/-ise**). The second syllable is not something added to the root, but an integral part of its source – in the Spanish verb *cabezar* ("sink by the head").

carat, karat or caret

Both **carat** and **karat** are used in assessing the value of gold, though the first is much more common than the second. In American English the two spellings sometimes correspond with different measures, **carat** being a unit of weight (about 200 milligrams), and **karat** a measure of its purity. (Pure gold is 24 *karats*.) Yet **carat** often serves for both, according to the major American dictionaries, and in Britain this is standard practice. The abbreviation for **carat** is *ct.* or *car.*, and for **karat** it is *kt.*

Both **karat** and **carat** seem to have developed from the same source, though neither comes very close to the Arabic *qirat*. Rather they reflect the mediating languages: Greek *keration* and Italian *carato*. Both meanings (weight, and purity) were current in C16 English, and the fact that the second one is sometimes spelled *caract* suggests that it may have developed under the influence of the Middle English word *caracter*, which was later used to mean both "sign, symbol" and "worth, value."

Different altogether is the word *caret*, a technical word used by editors and printers for the omission mark ∧. Borrowed from Latin in C17, it means literally "(something) is lacking" – whatever is supplied.

carburetor or carburettor

The spelling with one *t* is preferred in the US, whereas in the UK it has two in keeping with regional differences over the treatment of the last consonant before suffixes when the stress comes late in the word. (See further under **doubling of final consonant**.) Representative databases (CCAE, BNC) and dictionaries (*Webster's Third*, 1986 and the *Oxford Dictionary*, 1989) confirm the American/British preferences. The dictionaries register other spellings with *-er* (*carbureter/carburetter*), but neither of these appears in database evidence. They nevertheless show the derivation of the word from a little-known verb/noun *carburet*, coined at a time when chemical compounds were named with the addition of the French suffix *-uret*. The same compounds are nowadays christened with *-ide*.

carcass or carcase

Dr. Johnson's preference for the first spelling seems to be winning out. In the US **carcass** dominates in data from CCAE, and it's the more popular of the two in BNC data, by more than 3:1. The *Oxford Dictionary* (1884-1928) noted that **carcase** was about as common as **carcass** in C19, but since then its use has declined. Canadians, like the Americans, prefer **carcass**, according to the *Canadian Oxford* (1998); whereas Australian usage is more mixed (Peters, 1995), like the British.

Carcass is a C16 respelling of the word modeled on French *carcasse* (in Middle English it had been *carcays* or *carkeis*). Those earlier forms seem to be reflected in the spelling **carcase**, though the spelling of the second syllable could equally be *folk etymology*, an attempt to inject meaning into an opaque word (see further under **folk etymology**).

cardinal or ordinal

See under **ordinary**.

careen or career

The era of sailing ships made **careen** ("tilt a vessel on its side") a familiar nautical term, used to describe the ship's motion under sail as well as when beached for repair and maintenance. New modes of transportation in C20 have seen the verb applied to other vehicles, so that cars, trucks, buses and planes can now *careen*, but the emphasis is on fast and uncontrolled movement:

a hit-and-run driver careened into his car

Careen can also be used figuratively, as in *careened from one crisis to another.* All these uses are at home in the US, by the evidence of CCAE. They are still quite rare in British data from the BNC, where the verb **career** serves much the same purpose:

a fully-laden truck careered through the traffic lights

. . . even as these thoughts careered through B's troubled mind.

British commentators have in the past been inclined to treat extended uses of **careen** as mistaken uses of **career**. But *New Oxford* (1998) recognizes them without censure, as does the *Canadian Oxford* (1998) and Australian *Macquarie Dictionary* (1997).

cargoes or cargos

Dictionaries everywhere put **cargoes** ahead of **cargos** as the plural form, and British and American databases show that writers are much more inclined to use the first. Yet respondents to the Langscape survey (1998–2001) showed less commitment to **cargoes**. British respondents were almost equally divided between the two plurals, while 70% of European respondents and 85% of Americans preferred **cargos**. These results suggest ongoing change, as for other words of this kind: see **-o**.

caroled or carolled

See under **-l-/-ll-**.

case

See **in case, in case of, and in the case of**.

cases

Nouns and pronouns play various roles in clauses, and their particular function in a given sentence is known as their **case**. Grammatical **cases** are in many languages associated with a particular ending or inflection. English nouns show it for the genitive or possessive, with the *apostrophe "s,"* as in: *cat's breakfast, today's program.* English pronouns adjust their forms for the accusative as well as the genitive:

nominative	I	he	she	we	they	who
accusative	me	him	her	us	them	whom
genitive	my	his	her	our	their	whose

Yet the nominative/accusative distinction for English pronouns is increasingly neutralized in certain contexts (see for example **me**, and **whom**) – which suggests evolution towards a "common case" (Wales, 1996). **Case** distinctions are much more visible in languages such as German, with its separate *accusative* and *dative* forms for many nouns. Latin had them for the *ablative* and *vocative cases* as well. (See further under **accusative**, **ablative**, **dative** and **vocative**.) Aboriginal languages in Canada and Australia use other **cases** which are rare in European languages, such as *instrumental, locative* and *privative* (expressing the lack of something).

Because English nouns lack distinctive inflections for subject and object, traditional grammars identify their **case** in terms of their *function* relative to the verb or other constituents of the clause. So the subject noun (or noun phrase) is said to be in the *nominative* (or *subjective*) *case,* and the object noun / noun phrase to be *accusative* (or *objective*) in its **case.** The *dative case* would be found in a name or noun phrase that served as indirect object (see further under **dative** and **object**).

Modern English *case grammar* has stimulated fresh analysis of the system of **cases**, in terms of the so-called *arguments* of the verb and its *valency.* It allows (*Cambridge Grammar of English,* 2002) that verbs may take one or more arguments:

* one argument

> (*monovalent:* subject only; = intransitive) *they agreed*

* two arguments

> (*bivalent:* subject + direct object;
> = monotransitive) *they thanked him*

* three arguments

> (*trivalent:* subject + indirect object
> + direct object : = ditransitive)
> *they sent him a fresh proposal*

(See further under **transitive**.) Though the nomenclature varies, this approach helps to explain the flexible wording of English clauses, and the different roles of the grammatical subject for active and passive verbs: the active subject is typically the verb's *agent* or *senser,* while the passive one is the verb's *goal* (Halliday, 1994).

caster, castor or Castor

These spellings cover a range of meanings between them, and are interchangeable for some but not others. The spelling **castor** is standard when referring to (1) a particular type of fur hat, or (2) an oil used in making perfumes, both being associated with the beaver (in Greek *kastor*). The *-or* spelling also goes with *castor oil* extracted from the *castor-oil plant (Ricinus communis)* or the *castor bean* as it's called in the US and Canada. *Castor-oil politics* are of course analogous to medicinal use of the extract – and unpalatable, whatever their purgative value.

The spelling **caster** derives from the English verb *cast,* and refers naturally enough to one who or that which *casts.* Both human and nonhuman applications are to be found in the context of fishing, since **caster** refers to the flycasting fisherman, as well as his choice of **caster** rather than maggot or **worm as** bait. A different kind of *casting* takes place when making movies or staging plays, but there again the role of **caster** is spelled so as to reflect its origins.

In more remote applications of the word, **caster** varies with **castor** as the spelling for:

1 containers that dispense sugar, pepper or some other condiment
2 swiveling wheels attached underneath movable furniture
3 pivoting device connecting the axle of a vehicle with the front wheels

In American data from CCAE, these senses are usually spelled **caster**, although *Webster's Third* (1986) registers both spellings for them. In British English the spelling is often **castor**, judging by BNC evidence and dictionary variants, and the same is true in Australia and Canada. The connection with the verb *cast* has evidently not been obvious enough to regularize the spelling everywhere – apart from the overlap between *-er* and *-or* generally, which must also be a factor in the confusion. (See further under **-er**.)

In Britain the fine grade of sugar is increasingly spelled **caster**, in keeping with the fact that it's the type for the *sugar caster.* Yet this connection has also been masked by the spelling **castor** in the past, and there are still a few examples of *castor sugar* to be found in the BNC. In American usage it generally goes by the name *superfine sugar,* .and the spelling is unambiguous.

None of the above connects with **Castor** of *Castor and Pollux,* the twin sons of Zeus and Leda, whose stars (the Gemini) have traditionally been coupled together – though radio astronomers now believe they are light years apart.

cata-/cat-/cath-

These all represent a Greek prefix meaning "down or down to the end," and so also "complete." It appears in a number of loanwords, such as:

cataclysm	*catalepsy*	*catalogue*	*catapult*
cataract	*catarrh*	*catastrophe*	*catechism*
catheter	*cathode*	*catholic*	

The examples show how **cath-** appears instead of **cata-** before words that began in Greek with an *h*, and **cat-** before other vowels. In some neoclassical words, the prefix has a negative meaning ("wrongly"), as in *catatonic* and *catachresis.*

catachresis

Usage critics sometimes deliver their judgements with this obscure Greek word, literally "a misuse." It implies that the wrong word has been chosen for the context, as when *credible* is used for *creditable* or *martial* for *marital,* where the amusement value of the mistake is not salient. (Compare **malapropisms**.)

Gowers (1954) makes the nice point that **catachresis** is itself misused from time to time, by writers who apply it to an expression which is stylistically flawed, but hardly "wrong."

catalogue or catalog

The idea that **catalogue** is British and **catalog** American shortcircuits the facts. *Webster's Third* (1986) gives equal status to the two spellings, and in CCAE's written texts they are equally current. **Catalog** is however prominent in libraries, filing systems and mail-order flyers. British usage is much more focused on **catalogue**, and it's the standard spelling as far as *New Oxford* (1998) is concerned. In BNC data, **catalog** appears only in specialized documents for library professionals, who are more familiar than most with the *Library of Congress Catalog*.

The duality of American usage entails two sets of spellings for the verb, and *Merriam-Webster* (2000) notes *catalogued, cataloguing* as well as *cataloged, cataloging*. The latter are rather uncomfortable in terms of common spelling rules (see **-e**, and **-ce/-ge**). Other **-gue/-g** words are discussed under that heading.

> **International English selection:** Catalogue is well established in both American and British English, and linguistically regular as a base for the verb forms *catalogued* and *cataloguing*. On both counts it seems preferable.

catalyze or catalyse

British and American English diverge on these. In the US, **catalyze** is the primary spelling, according to *Merriam-Webster* (2000), and it's the only spelling in data from CCAE. But **catalyse** is strongly preferred in the UK, as indicated in *New Oxford* (1998), although *catalyze* appears in a few, mostly technical examples in the BNC. For other *-yse/-yze* pairs, see **-yze/-yse**.

cataphoric and cataphora

See under **anaphora**, and **coherence or cohesion** (section 2).

catapult

This is the only spelling recognized for this word, and some dictionaries recognize only one pronunciation for it (with the last syllable pronounced like the first one in *ultimate*). A little attention to what people say shows that there are several pronunciations for the last syllable, one of which makes it sound like the first syllable in *poultry*. Since this is a diphthong, it's not surprising that an alternative spelling *catapault* has been sighted several times over in a highly respected newspaper (Weiner, 1984) without being subedited out. It appears on the internet, in just over 1% of the thousands of examples of the word found by a Google search in 2002. The word is one to keep your eye on.

catastrophe

The plural of this word is still usually *catastrophes*, despite the occasional appearance of *catastrophies,* at least in American English. It is not acknowledged in *Webster's Third* (1986) though *Webster's English Usage* (1989) reports that its editors were aware of it, and there are a few instances in CCAE. Such a plural

implies *catastrophy* as singular, an alternative form recorded during C17 but not since, according to the *Oxford Dictionary* (1989). Google searches of the internet carried out in 2002 found thousands of examples of both *catastrophy* and *catastrophies*, though they represent less than 2% of all instances of the word. In standard English, **catastrophe** resists anglicization of that last syllable and retains its classical look. Compare the anglicized *trophy* ("prize won in war or competition") from Greek *trophe*.

catchup, catsup or ketchup

See under **ketchup**.

catenatives

These resemble and yet differ from *auxiliary verbs*. Common examples are:

> *He seems to think the same way.*
> *We began planning the Christmas party.*
> *They remembered leaving the keys under the mat.*
> *You love to surprise your family.*

Like auxiliaries, **catenatives** forge links with other nonfinite verbs, though with *to* infinitives or *-ing* forms, not "bare" infinitives. The **catenatives** also differ from auxiliaries in the meanings they express. Instead of paraphrasing the modals like other semi-auxiliaries (see **auxiliary verbs** section 3), they qualify the action of the following verb (as do *seem, begin*), or else set up a mental perspective on it (as do *remember, love*). Other examples like *seem* are:

> appear cease chance continue fail
> finish get happen help keep
> manage stop tend

Others like *remember* are:

> attempt consider detest endeavor
> expect forget hate hope
> intend like prefer regret
> resent risk strive try
> want

Note that some **catenatives** can take either *to*-infinitives or *-ing* constructions as their complement, others only one of them.

Catenatives are relatively new in the classification of English verbs, and grammarians still debate which belong to the class. The *Comprehensive Grammar* (1985) admits only the first group mentioned above, whereas the *Introduction to the Grammar of English* (1984) allows both. The latter questions whether a third group of verbs could also belong, ones whose complement is a *to*-infinitive but which require a noun phrase in between:

> *He advised her parents to come.*

Other examples of this type are:

> ask entreat invite oblige remind
> request teach tell urge

These verbs typically express some kind of speech act. The *Longman Grammar* (1999) groups the three types together with those which take a content clause as complement (see **content clause**), and uses the term "controlling verbs" for all.

cater for or to

Database evidence confirms that **cater** is usually construed with *for* in British English and *to* in American English. Compare *cater for all tastes, cater for exceptional persons* (from the BNC) with *cater to a specialized clientele, cater to our every whim* (CCAE). There are however counter examples in each corpus, witness *cater to the frat pack* (BNC), and *cater for the black community* (CCAE), suggesting that some American/British writers are already embracing the other construction.

In American English (but not British) **cater** can be used transitively: *cater meals, cater three more wedding receptions, cater various events at the White House;* and absolutely, as in *we will cater.*

cater(-)corner, cater(-)cornered, catty-corner or kitty-corner

All these variants and more are used in North America to refer to the direction diagonally opposite across a space, outdoors or inside:

> ... *an abandoned house catercorner to the church*
> *Two women sat catty-corner from each other, chatting.*
> *The family lived kitty-corner across the fields from my grandfather.*
> *He sat at the end of the defense table, turned catercorner toward the jury.*

The forms shown in these examples: **catercorner**, **catty-corner** and **kitty-corner**, are about equally represented in CCAE data, but **cater(-)cornered** makes little showing. American English generally makes less use of *-ed* in compound words (see **inflectional extras**). *Merriam-Webster* (2000) settles on the widely used **catercorner** for its headword, though *DARE* also notes the prevalence of **kitty-corner** in northern areas of the US, as in Canada (*Canadian English Usage,* 1997). As often, unsettled spellings reflect the opaqueness of the word – for all but gamblers, who might know *cater* as the term for "four" on the dice (from the French *quatre*). Across the face of the dice the dots are **catercorner** to each other.

cathode or kathode

See under **k/c**.

Catholic or catholic

What's in a capital letter? Written without it, **catholic** implies "universal, all-embracing" and is uncontroversial and unfettered in meaning:

> *Since her taste was catholic she enjoyed almost any of the videos people brought her.*

With a capital, **Catholic** becomes the focus of theological argument. Technically it might then refer to the whole Christian Church, the Church universal, irrespective of orthodoxies and denominations. In practice **Catholic** frequently refers to the Catholic Church based in Rome, where the point is simply to distinguish it from the Protestant and Orthodox churches (Greek and Russian). Examples such as *a Catholic country, Spain's Catholic kings* and *Catholic primary schools* all illustrate this use of **Catholic** to mean *Roman Catholic,* as do references to the *Catholic-Nationalists* of Northern Ireland. But in England one needs to distinguish between *Roman Catholic* and *Anglo-Catholic* (the "high" movement within the Church of England), and thus the term **Catholic** is often qualified one way or the other. Some Protestants and Anglo-Catholics use *Roman Catholic* (as adjective/noun) to insist that the referents cannot lay claim to the Church universal. Yet theological contentions are not necessarily uppermost in the minds of ordinary members of the Roman Church who

prefer to be called just **Catholics**. The term **Catholic** is usefully inclusive in North America, where Spanish, Italian and Irish church traditions are all well established; and in Australia, with both Irish and Italian traditions.

◊ Compare **Protestant.**

caucus

This term for the group who develop political strategies for a particular party probably comes from the Algonquian word for "elder, adviser." It owes nothing to Latin, and so the plural is *caucuses.* **Caucus** can be used of a meeting of that political executive group, and it also serves as a verb: *Party members caucused last week over the issue.*

cauldron or caldron

Whatever the brew, **cauldron** is the standard spelling in the UK. The *Oxford Dictionary* (1989) gives it priority, and it dominates in data from the BNC. In the US the field is more evenly divided: both spellings are well represented in CCAE, but instances of **cauldron** still outnumber those of **caldron** in the ratio of 7:3. **Caldron** nevertheless takes precedence in *Webster's Third* (1986), hence the fact that it's often thought of as the American spelling. **Cauldron** is given as the primary spelling in *Canadian Oxford* (1998) and the Australian *Macquarie Dictionary* (1997).

Cauldron and **caldron** are both respellings of the original loanword *caudron* from medieval French, designed to show its connection with the Latin *caldarium* ("hot bath"). The spelling **caldron** is the earlier of the two, dating from the Middle Ages, whereas **cauldron** is a Renaissance respelling. Dr. Johnson's dictionary put its weight behind **caldron**.

International English selection: Though it's a compromise spelling, **cauldron** currently has the broader base of usage, in North America as well as Australia and Britain.

---

caulk, calk or calque

These three spellings represent several developments from the Latin verb *calcare* ("tread").

1 To **caulk** (a boat or anything else) is to press a filler substance into the spaces between the pieces of wood, tile etc. of which it's made, in order to make it water- or air-tight. The spelling **caulk** is given preference for this over **calk** in British, Canadian and Australian dictionaries, whereas in American dictionaries it is the other way round.

2 **Calk** is the primary spelling for (i) the small projection on a horseshoe designed to prevent slipping, and (ii) the spiked plate on the soles of shoes worn by loggers. The same spelling also applies to the industrial process in which a design is transferred by pressure from one sheet to another. This usage is occasionally spelled in the French way as **calque**.

3 **Calque** is the regular spelling for a "loan translation," the linguistic analogue of the industrial process of *calking,* but pronounced in the French way so as to rhyme with "talc" rather than "talk." A **calque** is an expression created in one language to parallel a particular word or phrase in another. It matches the original expression in structure, but slots into it words from the borrowing language. For an

97

English example of a **calque**, think of *commonwealth* coined in C16 to represent the Latin "res publica." They are equivalent apart from the different sequences of adjective and noun in the two expressions. See further under **commonwealth**.

caveat emptor

This Latin phrase, borrowed into English in C16, means "let the buyer beware." In law it expresses the principle that the seller of goods is not responsible for the quality of the goods, unless the goods are under warranty. In more general usage it urges buyers to subject purchases to close scrutiny.

caviar or caviare

The first is the authentic French spelling, the second an anglicized form from C18. Dictionaries make them equal alternatives, though the *Oxford Dictionary* (1989) gives priority to **caviare** and *Webster's Third* (1986) to **caviar**. In fact **caviar** prevails in both British and American databases. Citations in the BNC run 2:1 in favor of **caviar**; and amid hundreds of American examples of the word in CCAE, **caviare** is not to be found. So **caviar** dominates in edited English texts, whatever else happens on menus and product labels.
◊ Other French loanwords to acquire an extra *e* are discussed under **-e** section 3.

c.c. or cc, CC or C.C.

This abbreviation found at the foot of business and institutional letters stands for "carbon copy." The *Oxford Dictionary for Writers and Editors* (1981) allowed only **c.c.** (with stops), to differentiate it from the abbreviation **cc** for "cubic centimetre." But the use of **cc** for "carbon copy" is acknowledged in most dictionaries, British and American. British correspondents definitely prefer to put the abbreviation in lower case, where their American counterparts may use upper-case forms. *Webster's Third* (1986) presents it without stops as **CC**, whereas the *Random House Dictionary* (1987) has it as **C.C.**

The function of **c.c./cc** is to tell the letter's addressee that an exact copy has been sent to those people named/listed alongside, a convention which serves two rather different purposes. It undoubtedly saves the addressee the effort of sending further copies to the other people named. Effectively it also warns the addressee that others have been informed about the contents of the letter. For more about commercial letter writing conventions, see under **commercialese**.
◊ Note that the abbreviation **c.c./cc** ("cubic centimetre(s)"), once used in measurements of liquid volume and engine capacity, has been superseded among SI units by *cm³* and L. See Appendix IV.

CCAE

The Cambridge International Corpus of American English, abbreviated as **CCAE**, has supplied the data on American usage for many entries in this book. The database consists of approximately 140 million words, of which approximately 120 million come from written sources such as newspapers and monographs, fiction and nonfiction published between 1986 and 2000. It also contains about 22 million words transcribed from spoken sources.

CD-ROM

This is code for "compact disk read-only memory," where *CD* distinguishes it from other computer memory systems such as hard or floppy disk, and *ROM* from the computer's *RAM ("random access memory")*, which can be both read and written to. With these two significant parts **CD-ROM** is always hyphened and normally capitalized, like other computer abbreviations (see **capital letters**, section 1h).

While **CD-ROM** is now the common name for the electronic commercial product, computer specialists work with *CD-Rs,* which can be written on once, and *CD-RWs,* which can be written to, erased and rewritten.

CE

This abbreviation coming after a date means "Common Era." See further under **BC**.

-ce/-cy

For alternative spellings like *permanence/permanency,* see **-nce/-ncy**.

-ce/-ge

Words ending in **-ce** or **-ge** need special attention when suffixes are added to them. Most words ending in **-e** drop it before adding any suffix beginning with a vowel. (Think of *move, moving* and *movable*; and see further under **-e**.) But words with **-ce** and **-ge** vary according to the first vowel of the suffix.

If it begins with *a* (as in *-able, -age, -al, -an*) or *o* (as in *-ose, -ous, -osity*), the word remains unchanged and keeps its *e*. See for instance:

   replaceable   manageable   outrageous
In words like these, the *e* serves a vital purpose in preserving the *c* or *g* as a "soft" sound: compare *replaceable* with *implacable,* and *outrageous* with *analogous.*

But if the suffix begins with *e* (as in *-ed* or *-er*), *i* (as in *-ing, -ism, -ist*) or *y*, words ending in **-ce** or **-ge** can drop their *e*. Think of the following words based on *race*:

   raced   racer   racing   racism   racist   racy
The "s" sound is maintained in each of them through the vowel of the suffix.

Alternative means of preserving the "soft" "*c*"/"*g*" sounds can be seen in the spellings of *forcible* and *unenforceable,* of *tangible* and *changeable.* The words ending in *-ible* came direct from Latin, while those with *-eable* have been formed in English. See further under **-able/-ible**, and also **-eable**.

-ce/-se

In pairs such as *advice/advise* and *device/devise,* the **-ce** and **-se** have complementary roles, with **-ce** marking the noun and **-se** the verb. The **-ce** is of course pronounced "s," and the **-se** "z." In Britain and Australia this spelling convention also affects *licence* and *practice,* so that *license* and *practise* must be verbs, while *licence* and *practice* are nouns. This makes no difference to their pronunciation, but demands a modicum of grammar to get each spelling in its rightful place. In American English one spelling serves for each word, whatever its grammatical role (see further under **license** and **practice**).

Regional differences also emerge in the American spelling of *defense, offense* and *pretense,* as opposed to

British *defence, offence* and *pretence*. The -ce spellings commit British (and Australian) writers to inconsistencies such as *defence/defensive, offence/offensive* and *pretence/pretension,* which Americans are spared. Canadians labor with both systems, according to the *Canadian Oxford* (1998), using the -ce spelling for *defence/offence* and -se for *pretense.*

The spellings *defense, offense* and *pretense* are not only more straightforward, but just as old as the spellings with -ce. Anglo-Norman scribes introduced *c* into the spellings of both native and borrowed words of English, some of which have become the standard form, e.g. *once* (earlier "ones") and *grocery* (earlier "grossier").

International English selection: The -se spellings for *defense, offense* and *pretense* have the great advantage of consistency with their derivative forms *defensive, offensive, pretension.*

-cede/-ceed
Why should words like *exceed, proceed* and *succeed* be spelled one way, and *concede, intercede, precede, recede* and *secede* in another? All these words go back to the Latin verb *cedere* ("yield or move"), but the second group are much more recent arrivals in English, mostly post-Renaissance, whereas the first set were actively used in C14 and C15. Middle English scribes turned the Latin *ced-* into -ceed to bring those words into line with native English ones such as *feed* and *need,* which were pronounced the same way. The words ending in -cede came into English from written sources during the Renaissance, hence both their bookish flavor and their classical spelling.

The divergent spellings of *proceed* and *precede,* and of *proceeding(s)* and *procedure,* can be explained in the same way. The classical spelling of *procedure* confirms that it was borrowed later into English (in C17). Its *-ced-* spelling goes with the foreign suffix *-ure,* whereas the -ceed goes with the English *-ing* ending.
◊ For the spelling of **supersede,** see **supersede or supercede.**

cedilla
This is one of the less familiar foreign accents to come into English, and the only one to be written beneath the letter it affects. It comes with a handful of loanwords from French such as *façade* and *garçon,* and with the Portuguese *curaçao.* In both languages the **cedilla** keeps a *c* sounding like "s" before *a, o* and *u.* Before *e* and *i,* it's not needed because those vowels keep the *c* soft anyway. The **cedilla** comes and goes in the spelling of French verbs, depending on the following vowel:

nous annonçons	"we announce"
vous annoncez	"you announce"
vous recevez	"you receive"
ils reçoivent	"they receive"

In English the **cedilla** on loanwords is often left out because of its absence from many keyboards and wordprocessors.

The name **cedilla** comes from the Spanish *zedilla.* It means "little *z,*" a rough way of describing its shape. But it was first used in writing French words in C16, as an alternative for *cz* in *façade* or for *ce* in *receoivent.*

celebrant and celebrator
The first of these is associated primarily with religious services, in phrases such as *chief celebrant and preacher* or *principal celebrant at the funeral mass.* In American English, **celebrant** also has its secular and democratic uses, as an artful way of referring to participants and revelers at public festivities: *a celebrant holds his beer mug at the German-American festival,* and *no anti-celebrant is safe on the streets [of New York] from breakfast [on St Patrick's Day].* In British English, **celebrant** is occasionally used of the protagonist for a particular cause or point of view, seen in BNC examples such as *celebrant of the English country station* and *celebrant of the mystique of the public school.* American examples of these more abstract uses can be found in CCAE examples such as *celebrant of the life of Whitman* and *a John Ford-like celebrant of the American West.*

The alternative **celebrator** is little used, despite being closer in form to the essential verb *celebrate,* and recommended by American usage writers of the 1950s to avoid secularization of **celebrant.** In fact **celebrator** appears only a handful of times in CCAE: in references to the reveler, as in *New Year's celebrator,* and to the protagonist, as in *celebrator of diversity.* The BNC contains a solitary example of its use in *narrator and celebrator of these blisses,* suggesting ad hoc formation from the verb rather than the establishment of the noun in British English.

Celsius or centigrade
Celsius is the official name for the **centigrade** scale of temperature used within the metric system. The scale was devised by the Swedish astronomer Anders Celsius (1701–44), using the freezing and boiling points of pure water as its reference points. They establish a scale from 0 degrees to 100 degrees. The **Celsius** scale dovetails with the *Kelvin* scale of temperature, which offers an "absolute zero" temperature of 273 degrees, the theoretical temperature at which gas molecules have zero kinetic energy. **Celsius** temperatures have been gradually adopted in Britain (and more quickly in Australia) to replace the Fahrenheit system. Older kitchen stoves, and cookery books, are of course calibrated in degrees *Fahrenheit.* In the US, temperature is still generally measured on the Fahrenheit scale. (See further under **Fahrenheit** and **metrication.**)

The name **Celsius** is preferred to the metric name **centigrade** as a way of highlighting the names of famous scientists – part of the naming policy of the Bureau International de Poids et Mesures. Like other scientific eponyms **celsius** can appear without an initial capital letter (see under **eponyms**), though in BNC data it's still capitalized more often than not. For **centigrade,** the ratio of capitalized to non-capitalized forms is about 50/50.

Celtic or Keltic
The name **Celtic** (pronounced "keltic") is used to refer collectively to the peoples of Wales, Scotland and Ireland, who emigrated across Europe more than 2000 years ago. Thus the term *Anglo-Celtic* used in Canada and Australia refers collectively to immigrants from all parts of the British Isles, as opposed to those who emigrated from Continental Europe and elsewhere.

The original *Celts* left traces of their civilization in various places across Continental Europe, in Switzerland, Spain and in France. The people of present-day Brittany still speak a *Celtic* language, Breton, which is closely related to Welsh. Together, Breton- and Welsh-speakers make up a larger Celtic-speaking population (over 1 million) than the speakers of Scottish and Irish Gaelic (between 100,000 and 200,000, according to estimates in the *Cambridge Encyclopedia of Language,* 1987). **Celtic** (pronounced "seltic") is nevertheless the rallying cry for the Scottish football team based in Glasgow (as well as that of the Boston-based basketball team).

Keltic reflects the original Greek name for the Celts: *Keltoi*. It has been more used by scholars than writers at large, and serves to distinguish the ancient nomadic people from their modern descendants.

cement or concrete

In their physical applications, these words are sometimes interchanged, as when a *concrete mixer* is referred to as a *cement mixer.* **Cement** is of course the bonding agent in **concrete**, although concrete's strength comes from the other ingredients, i.e. the steel reinforcing or crushed stones. The substitution of **cement** for **concrete** is therefore an everyday instance of *meronymy* (see under **synechdoche**). Figurative uses of **cement** pick up the sense of bonding as in *social cement,* and the sense is extended in BNC examples of its use as a verb, as in *cement a relationship, cement his authority, cement that deep family loyalty to the institution.* The figurative uses of **concrete** are typically adjectival, as the opposite of *abstract* in *concrete terms, concrete social consequences* and the *concrete world of experience.*

censor or censure

As verbs these seem to overlap because both involve strong negative judgements. They differ in that **censor** implies official control of information which is deemed dangerous for the public, and results in the proscription or banning of such things as books, movies or news items. It is a preventive measure, whereas **censure** voices public criticism of things already done, as when members of government are *censured* in a formal parliamentary motion.

As nouns the two words go their separate ways, **censor** as an agent word "one who censors," and **censure** as the abstract noun for "strongly voiced criticism."

centennial or centenary

These are registered as both adjective and noun in most dictionaries, and there's no controversy over their being "adjectives." However it becomes debatable when they act as qualifiers, as in *Elgar's birthday centenary celebrations,* where they might equally be regarded as nouns in attributive roles. Both **centennial** and **centenary** look like Latin adjectives, so there is more room for doubt about their role as nouns, especially if they are relatively rare. Database evidence shows that **centenary** is a rarity for Americans, whereas **centennial** is little used by the British.

British use of **centennial** (as adjective or noun) has probably been constrained by Fowler's express preference for **centenary**, because it matched up better with *bicentenary, tercentenary* etc. and

sesquicentenary (150 years). In BNC data **centenary** outnumbers **centennial** by about 25:1, and it's freely applied to the hundredth anniversary of persons (Prokofiev, Mondrian, James Joyce) as well as institutions large and small (Science Museum, Birmingham's Book Room).

Comparable American data from CCAE shows extensive use of **centennial** (adjective or noun) for the 100-year celebrations of anything from the transcontinental railroad to the Statue of Liberty, and it appears – more permanently – in the names of high schools, tennis competitions, city parks and a range of mountains, among other things. Thus **centennial** is the dominant term, outnumbering **centenary** in CCAE by about 10:1. Canadians and New Zealanders share the American preference, while Australians are ambivalent. See further under **bicentennial**.

centi-

This prefix means "one hundredth," as in *centimetre, centisecond* and other words of measurement used within the metric system (see further under **metrication** and **number prefixes**). Yet **centi-** is derived from the Latin word *centum* meaning "one hundred," and this is its meaning in words like *centenary* and *century,* borrowed direct from Latin.

Note by way of curiosity that most *centipedes* do not actually have 100 feet or legs (50 pairs), but anywhere between 15 and 170 pairs. (Compare *millipede:* see under **milli-**.)

centigrade or Celsius

See under **Celsius**.

centre/center on or around

Just which particle should be used with the verb *centre/center* is sometimes debated, though the major dictionaries are accommodating. *Webster's Third* (1986) makes it clear that any of a number of particles is possible (*in, at, on, upon, about, (a)round);* and the *Oxford Dictionary* (1989) shows both shift from *in* to *on,* and the acceptability of *(a)round.* So why the fuss about using **centre/center around**? *Webster's English Usage* (1989) traces it to American college composition books of the 1920s, whose authors found it "illogical," apparently because they were thinking in strictly geometrical terms. In fact mathematicians tend to use *centre/center at.*

American and British databases show that **center/centre on** constructions are a good deal more frequent than **center/centre around**, by about 5:1, but both serve to identify a focus or topic of interest:

> ... *an economy centered on agriculture*
> *The debate should not centre on cost.*
> *Antiwhaling could centre around alternatives to whale products.*
> *Speculation centered around such companies as T-C Inc.*

As in these examples, there's some tendency to use *around* with a plural topic, though both CCAE and BNC could provide counter examples. The writer may be pinpointing a focus of attention, or the "circle" of interest around it, but either way it works without any strict spatial analogy. *New Oxford* (1998) accepts this use of **centre/center around**, as being well established and idiomatic. Its meaning may be less focused than the one assumed by its critics, but it clearly indicates the starting point for discussion.

◊ For the choice between **centre** and **center**, see **-re/-er**.

centuries

In the Anglo-Saxon historical tradition, we number **centuries** by thinking ahead to the boundary with the next one. So the *nineteenth century* includes any dates from 1801 to 1900; and the *twentieth century*, all those from 1901 to 2000. The tradition is based on the fact that the first **century** of the Christian era dates from AD 1 to AD 100, and could not be otherwise since there was no AD 0.

Whatever the justification, this system of reckoning seems rather perverse. For one thing, it runs counter to the ordinary numerical system, in which we think of decimal sets running from 0 to 9 in each "ten," or 00 to 99 in each "hundred." We might reasonably expect the last century to include dates from 1900 to 1999: at least they would all have the number 19.. in common. But no, it's 1901 to 2000, with the present **century** starting on 1 January 2001.

That was also the first day of the *twenty-first century*, again somewhat perversely, since all but the last year in it will begin with 20 ... (2010, 2020 etc.). Yet the convention of referring to the years of one **century** by the next one on is thoroughly established in English, and in other (north) European languages including French, Dutch and German. In both Italian and Spanish however, a reference to a **century** such as the *Quattrocento* or *el Siglo XIV* means "the 1400s" (the famous century of Renaissance painters). In formal English *quattrocento* would be translated as "the fifteenth century," though expressions such as *the 1400s* recommend themselves as clearer and more direct.

Abbreviations for indicating particular **centuries** are not standardized and include the following:

15th century	*XV century*	*XVth century*
15th cent.	*15th c.*	*15C C15*

The first set provide little compacting, and reflect the general reluctance to use abbreviations in the humanities. The *Chicago Manual* (1993) proposes rather that any references to **centuries** should be spelled out in full, as *fifteenth century* etc. Others endorse the use of roman numerals in them as a gesture towards abbreviation, though it may be counterproductive in terms of ease of reading. Those more accustomed to abbreviation accept that the word **century** can be reduced without impairing communication. Among those in the second set above, the pair with lower case are British style (Ritter, 2002), whereas those with upper case are American. Their compactness is an asset in texts where they occur often (such as this book). *C15* has some advantage over *15C* in that it could never be mistaken for a reference to temperature reading in degrees Celsius (*15°C*).
◊ For indicating dates that span the turn of the **century**, see under **dates**.

ceramic or keramic

See under **k/c**.

ceremonial or ceremonious

Both words relate to the noun *ceremony,* and **ceremonial** even substitutes for it occasionally, as in *court ceremonial* and *ceremonials committee*. But as an adjective **ceremonial** simply means "used in, or as of a ceremony," for example *ceremonial sword,*

ceremonial dress. **Ceremonious** is both a synonym for **ceremonial** and a value-laden word which suggests an emphasis on ceremony for its own sake, or as a mask in strained interaction: *he took a relieved and ceremonious farewell*. The latter is its only distinctive sense, but it's in the eye of the beholder and not always clearly separable from the other. **Ceremonious** is actually quite rare in both British and American databases (BNC and CCAE), and **ceremonial** evidently satisfies writers' needs most of the time.

certified or certificated

Certified, borrowed from French in C14 is older by far, and has many applications in terms of guaranteeing public safety (*certified building/food/seed/wines*) and professional standards (*certified accountant / timber infestation surveyor*). The procedures of *certifying* persons as dead or insane are other major uses of the word, as in the following examples from the BNC:

> *A police surgeon later certified Mr Heddle dead. He fantasized about having her certified and getting a lot of sympathy.*

The rarer and more cumbersome **certificated** is a C19 backformation from *certificate,* implying that the object or person has qualified according to a set of standards. In both British and American English it's used in relation to aircraft and ships, and to particular professions, such as teachers, nurses, librarians, notaries. But in Britain its use is boosted in eduspeak, where particular skills and training programs are **certificated**, as in *certificated foundation course in art and design; all core skills will be certificated on the Record of Education and Training*.

cesarean or caesarian

See **Caesarean**.

c'est à dire

Borrowed from French, it means "that is to say." The Latin abbreviation *i.e.* says the same in fewer letters, and its efficiency is important in documentary writing. In more discursive writing the bulkier French phrase may serve to underscore a reformulation of ideas which the author is about to offer.

ceteris paribus

Borrowed from Latin, this phrase means "all other things being equal." It is used in argument to limit a conclusion or generalization on which writers feel they may be challenged. It provides academic protection for their claim, since it is usually impossible to show whether all other things are equal or not.

cf.

In English scholarly writing this stands for the Latin *confer* meaning "compare." In Latin it would be a bald imperative, but in English it invites the reader to look elsewhere for a revealing comparison.

chacun à son goût

Drinking habits and gout are not really uppermost in this phrase borrowed from French, which means "each one to his own taste." In French the word *chacun* is masculine, though the phrase is intended as a general observation: everyone has their own tastes. It often serves to preempt debate based on differences in taste, and therefore functions in the same way as the older Latin maxim: *de gustibus non est disputandum* ("concerning matters of taste there can be no argument"). Both the French and Latin sayings can also be used more offhandedly, to say "There's no accounting for taste."

chairman

Some women who chair meetings are quite content to be called **chairman**. They see it simply as a functional title, like that of *secretary* and *treasurer*, which indicate a person's official role in an organization. Others relish the challenge that the word has sustained from the feminist movement, amid pressures to promote nonsexist language. Yet the problem with **chairman** is seen differently by different people, and so the solutions vary.

Critics of the word **chairman** are sometimes concerned that it seems to make women in that role invisible. The alternatives they suggest are *chairwoman* or *lady chairman,* which draw attention to the sex of the person concerned, as do terms of address such as *Madam Chairman* and *Madam Chair*. More often the concern is that **chairman** seems to foster the expectation that only a man could fulfil the role. They propose nonexclusive, gender-free alternatives, such as *chairperson* or *chair*. Neither of these solutions seems wholly satisfactory, because:
* *chair* combines awkwardly with any verb implying human action – even though it has done this since C17, according to the *Oxford Dictionary* (1989), as in a Royal Society minute on a matter *referred to me by this Honourable Chair.*
* *chairperson* suffers from the fact that it more often substitutes for *chairwoman* than for **chairman**, and thus tends to have female connotations. This could change, given a steady increase in the proportion of male *chairpersons* mentioned in current data from the BNC and CCAE. But until then the best solution is to seek an independent, gender-free term, such as *convener, coordinator, moderator* or *president.*
◊ For further discussion of these issues, see **nonsexist language**.
◊ For other compounds like **chairman**, see under **man, man-** and **-man**.

chaise longue or chaise lounge

This French expression meaning "long chair" is applied in English to that eminently relaxing piece of furniture which supports the legs in a resting position, and keeps the upper body at a sufficient angle to allow us to keep up a conversation.

Because of the comfort it offers, the **chaise longue** is sometimes referred to as a **chaise lounge** – with just a slight rearrangement of the letters of the second word. It is after all a chair in which you lounge about, and it shows folk etymology in action, trying to make sense of an obscure foreignism (see **folk etymology**). **Chaise lounge** was first recorded well over a century ago in Ogilvie's *Imperial Dictionary* (1855), and its use is widely recognized outside Britain (in American, Canadian and Australian dictionaries), though the *New Oxford* (1998) simply labels it "US." *Webster's English Usage* (1989) noted its frequent use in the furniture trade and advertising, and that it also appears occasionally in general and literary writing. **Chaise lounge** and **chaise longue** are about equally

common in CCAE; and the corpus shows that **chaise lounge** is usually a piece of outdoor patio furniture – except when it's a *Scottish oak chaise lounge*. The outdoor/indoor distinction created some angst for journalists reporting on a murder in which the body was found *under a chaise lounge/longue inside the enclosed porch [of the house]*. The **chaise longue** meanwhile is often mentioned among collections of antiques (*the Empire-style chaise longue*), or as an objet d'art, like the *chaise longue of hammered scrap metal too hard to lie on*. If it is a **chaise lounge**, the French order of words still helps to distinguish it from the *lounge chair,* the general term for an "easy chair" – not obviously designed for lounging in but rather for the *lounge (room)*, which in both Britain and Australia is the sitting room of a private house.

For the plural of **chaise longue**, *Merriam-Webster* (2000) indicates **chaise longues** and **chaises longues**, in that order. The first treats it like an ordinary English compound (see under **plurals**), while the second is fully French. With the anglicized **chaise lounge**, we may expect **chaise lounges.**

chalky or chalkie

The endings serve to distinguish the adjective **chalky** ("covered with or consisting of chalk") from the noun **chalkie**, used informally in Australia and New Zealand to refer to a teacher or, before computerization, a stock exchange assistant.

challenged

In the contexts of equal opportunity or political correctness, depending on your point of view, this word has taken off as a formative of compounds. American examples from the domain of education are *developmentally challenged* and *physically challenged,* where teachers grapple with the unequal genetic endowments of their students. Unfortunately the cumbersome phrases are themselves a challenge, and now often parodied in ad hoc formations such as:
> *vertically challenged* ("short" or sometimes "very tall")
> *follicularly challenged* ("bald")
> *sartorially challenged* ("showing bad taste in dress")
> *circumferentially challenged* ("overweight")

Alternative ways of referring to those with disabilities are discussed under **disabled**.

chamois, chammy or shammy

Chamois is the French name for the European antelope from whose skin a soft leather was originally prepared. Similar leathers prepared from the skins of goats or sheep are also called **chamois**, and even **chammy** or **shammy,** reflecting the sound of the word in English. However both *New Oxford* (1998) and *Merriam-Webster* (2000) associate the spelling **shammy** with the soft polishing cloth made of imitation leather – *sham chamois,* as you might say.

chamomile or camomile

See **camomile**.

chancy or chancey

See **-y/-ey**.

channeled or channelled

The choice between these spellings is discussed at -l-/-ll-.

Chanukah or Hanukkah

See **Hanukkah**.

chaperon or chaperone

These two spellings are very evenly matched in their appearances in American and British databases, for both noun and verb. **Chaperon** is the standard French form, given priority in *Merriam-Webster* (2000), whereas *New Oxford* (1998) puts **chaperone** first, in keeping with the fact that English-speakers typically pronounce it to rhyme with "tone." Historically the **chaperon(e)** was female, and the gratuitous *-e* may reflect this perception – though sex is no impediment to being a **chaperon(e)** nowadays. The data from the BNC and CCAE have it applied to men who act as team managers for junior sportspersons, and male teachers who supervise students on excursions.
◊ For other examples of French words given a feminine -e, see under **-e** section 3.

charted or chartered

These past forms of the verbs *chart* and *charter* can be mistaken for each in spoken English, and hence are sometimes interchanged in print. They sound alike in dialects of English which are non-rhotic, i.e. ones in which *r* is silent after a vowel. So as pronounced by many Britons from southern and eastern areas, and by Antipodeans, the two words are indistinguishable, whereas for most American and Canadian speakers, the *r* of the second syllable of **chartered** sets them apart. Note also that most British speakers use different vowels in the second syllables of **charted** and **chartered**, which further help to distinguish them.

The verb *chart* is a matter of cartography or mapping, either literally or figuratively. During C18, the coasts of New Zealand and eastern Australia were finally **charted**; but in C21, it's outer space that remains *to be charted,* and areas of social and political behavior that are *uncharted territory.*

As a verb *charter* means "set up by charter," and so institutions may be **chartered** to fulfill public functions; and individuals such as *chartered accountants* or *chartered engineers* have obtained the right to engage in professional practice. The idea of being hired under a specialized contract underlies the *chartering* of a vehicle (a bus, ship, helicopter etc.), but the fact that it means contracting to cover a particular geographical distance brings it close to **chart**.

chassis

In the plural this French loanword is usually left unchanged:
> *A pile of rusty automobile chassis lay at the foot of the cliff.*
However an English plural *chassises* is recognized in *Webster's Third* (1986).

chastise or chastize

Despite appearances, this word was not formed with the *-ise/-ize* suffix. It originates as a mutant form of the verb *chasten*, which was *chastien* in Middle English. Against this background there's no case for spelling it **chastize**, as if it went back to Greek – and no problem

if your policy is to use *-ise* spellings wherever the *-ise/-ize* options appear: see further under **-ize/-ise**. But if your policy is to use *-ize* spellings, **chastise** and a number of others should still be spelled with *-ise* on grounds of etymology, according to Fowler (1926) and American commentators such as Copperud (1980). A sprinkling of examples spelled **chastize** (about 3% of all instances of the word) was nevertheless found in a Google search of the internet in 2002.

chateaus or chateaux

For the choice of plurals, see **-eau**. In French the word has a circumflex, but it is now rarely reproduced in English.

chauvinism

This word has always represented extreme attitudes: bigoted devotion to one's own nation, race or sex, and a corresponding contempt for those who do not belong to it. The word enshrines the name of *Nicolas Chauvin*, an old soldier of Napoleon I whose blind devotion to his leader was dramatized in popular plays of the 1820s and 30s. The *chauvinists* of C21 are those who assume the superiority of their own country or race, and close their minds to the value of others. (See further under **racist language**.)

The phrase *male chauvinism*, popularized in the 1970s, is the attitude which assumes the superiority of men over women. See further under **female**.

cheap and cheaply

At one level of analysis, these are simply adjective and adverb respectively, as in:
> *He bought a cheap jacket at the market.*
> *Their support was bought quite cheaply.*
But as the second example shows, the regular adverb **cheaply** tends to carry the abstract sense of "at low cost," rather than "at a low price." The latter meaning is often expressed simply by **cheap**, as in:
> *The jacket was going cheap at the market.*
In copular constructions like that, it's debatable whether **cheap** is really an adverb or an adjective (see further under **copular verbs**). Whatever the grammar, it is perfectly idiomatic, and does not need to be corrected to **cheaply**.
◊ For other adverbs of this type, see **zero adverbs**.

check or cheque, and checker or chequer

The English-speaking world at large uses the first spelling for many applications of the verb **check** meaning "stop, restrain, verify, tick," and the corresponding nouns. And at supermarkets, workshops, cloakrooms and luggage offices, the person who *checks out* the goods is called in nonsexist terms a **checker**. Only when it comes to money is there a great divide, with Americans continuing to use **check** for a personal bank note, while **cheque** is preferred by Canadians, Australians and the British.

Cheque is very much a latter-day spelling, first appearing at the beginning of C18. It was used by the Bank of England to refer to the counterfoil issued for a money order – literally a way of checking each one and preventing forgery. **Cheque** soon became the name for the money order itself in Britain. The system was adopted somewhat later in the US, though the spelling has remained **check**.

In the same way C18 British English adopted the spelling **chequer** for a pattern of squares, as in the game *chequers* and the *chequerboard,* as well as the figurative *chequered career*. It replaced the longer-established **checker** which continues in American and Canadian English. North American motoring writers are therefore spared the anomaly that confronts their British and Australian counterparts, of referring to a *chequered flag* which has black and white *checks* on it.

chef d'oeuvre

Borrowed from C17 French, this phrase means "masterpiece." More literally, it means "the culmination of the work." It can be used of an outstanding work in any artistic field: literature, music, opera, painting, sculpture and even gastronomy. But when your hired caterer produces *hors d'oeuvres* which are a **chef d'oeuvre**, that is a lucky coincidence.
◊ Compare **hors d'oeuvre**, and **magnum opus**.

chemist, pharmacist or druggist

See under **pharmacist**.

cheque and chequer

See under **check**.

cherubs or cherubim

See under -**im**.

chevrons

The *chevron* is a V-shaped bar. One or more **chevrons**, set on the sleeves of military and police uniforms, show the rank of the wearer.

In mathematics and statistics, a *chevron-shaped* mark turned horizontally has a specific meaning depending on its direction: < before a number means "is less than," and > means "is greater than." Computer programmers attach other functions to the same signs:
> means "direct output to"
< means "take input from"
In computer programming, **chevrons** are also used in pairs like *angle brackets* to frame special codes and commands (see **brackets** section 1). Note however the angle brackets used in mathematics have a broader span, ⟨⟩, as opposed to < >, where full type resources are available.
◊ For the use of **chevrons** in citing internet addresses, see **URL**.

chiasmus

This word, borrowed from classical Greek, refers to an elegant figure of speech. It expresses a contrast or paradox in two parallel statements, the second of which reverses the order of items in the first:
Martyrs create faith, faith does not create martyrs.
Glory to God in the highest, and on earth peace towards men.
As the examples show, the second statement may play on the words and/or the structure of the first. Both are played on in the following newspaper headline, highlighting the opening up of the Berlin Wall in 1989:
TUMBLING WALL SENDS WALL STREET SOARING
The **chiasmus** has a pleasing symmetry in which the contrasting statements are balanced. It draws attention to word order, which we tend to take for granted in English prose because it is largely

regularized. It provides elegant variation on the standard patterns of clause and phrase.

chicano, Chicano and Chicana

As a noun this word is always capitalized, though *Webster's Third* (1986) notes the lower-case **chicano** as an alternative for the adjective. Both forms are registered in the *Oxford Dictionary* (1989), but in the *New Oxford* (1998) only **Chicano**. The editorial convention of capitalizing ethnic and national designations would require **Chicano**, whatever its grammar (see under **capital letters** section 1). **Chicana** is the strictly feminine form for a female Mexican American, used only as a noun.

The word is a clipping of the Mexican Spanish adjective *mejicano/mejicana,* i.e. "Mexican." Its earliest American use in the 1940s was to refer to militant groups of Mexican immigrants. This gave it strong political overtones that linger, even though the word is now applied more generally to US citizens of Mexican origin. The word *Hispanic* provides a less emotively charged way of referring to the Mexican-American, though it is also less specific because it includes other Spanish-speaking immigrants, e.g. those from the Caribbean. As often, the straight geographical name *Mexican-American* is both specific and neutral. See further under **racist language**.
◊ Compare **Hispanic** and **Latino**.

chilli, chili, chile or chilly

The first three are alternative spellings for a pepper or a peppery vegetable discovered in the New World. In Britain and Australia the primary spelling is **chilli**, which is believed to render the original Mexican Indian word most exactly. But in American and Canadian English, the spelling **chili** is given preference and often featured in the spicy Mexican dish *chili con carne*. The actual Spanish form of the word is **chile**, hence its use in *chile con carne,* in parts of the US where Spanish is better known.

The fourth spelling above is a separate word meaning "rather cold" in all varieties of English. But in British English it's yet another possible spelling for the pepper, according to the *Oxford Dictionary* (1989).

China

The division of **China** into two political entities in 1949 makes it important to distinguish them:
Chinese People's Republic = *Mainland China* (capital: Beijing)
Chinese Nationalist Republic = *Taiwan* (capital: Taipei)
The estimated population of *Mainland China* in 1990 was over 1 billion, that of *Taiwan* about 20 million.

In *Mainland China* the communist revolution led to far-reaching linguistic reforms, including the development of a standard form of Chinese, *Putonghua,* which involved the modifying and streamlining of more than 2000 traditional characters of the Chinese system. Like "Mandarin" it's based on the Beijing dialect, but serves as the native language of more than half the people. Other major dialects are clustered in the south of the country:
∗ Wu in Shanghai and on the Yangzi valley
∗ Yue in Guangzhou and Guandong
∗ Min in Taiwan and adjoining provinces on the mainland

∗ Hakka used by small groups within the other
southern dialect areas

A phonetic alphabet *Pinyin* has been used to develop
romanized scripts for minority language groups, and
for children beginning their education. It also has
public uses on street signs and the railway system.
Pinyin was officially adopted in 1938, though it was far
from the first attempt to romanize Chinese characters.
Earlier systems include the Wade-Giles, developed by
British scholars in C19; Gwoyeu Romatzyh, designed
by Chinese scholars in the 1920s; and Latinxua
devised by Russians in the 1930s. *Pinyin*'s roots are in
the third, but it differs in the spelling of certain
consonants. Some which strike westerners as unusual
are the use of:

> *q* for pre-palatal "ch"
> *x* for pre-palatal "sh"
> *zh* for retroflex "j"
> *c* for alveolar "ts"

Amid this linguistic evolution, many Chinese
placenames have changed, at least in the forms now
reaching the western world. Some of the most
dramatic are the substitution of *Beijing* for "Peking,"
Guangzhou for "Canton," and *Tianjin* for "Tientsin."
Others less revolutionary are *Xian* for "Sian,"
Shandong for "Shantung," *Chong Qing* for
"Chungking" and *Nanjing* for "Nanking." The
changes of consonants in these examples show which
letters are typically affected, but it's a good idea to
check Chinese names in a large up-to-date atlas.

Chinaman or Chinese

The word **Chinaman** is generally felt to have
derogatory overtones, probably going back to popular
prejudice against Chinese immigrants amid the
American goldrush, where the word originated. In
American English it's not helped by *John Chinaman,*
the derisively named stereotype who didn't stand a
Chinaman's chance of making it. Such connotations
make **Chinaman** dangerous, and public apology was
needed in 1990 for a joking reference to a (black)
footballer surnamed *Rice* – as "a Chinaman whose feet
never touch the ground." Even in an ethnically
neutral situation, **Chinaman** is unsafe for ethnic
reference.

In Britain **Chinaman** was apparently a neutral
term for Fowler in the 1920s, when he presented it as
the ordinary term for an individual from China, and
perhaps for two or three of them (*Chinamen*). But
Gowers revising Fowler in post-imperial Britain
(1965) found **Chinaman** derogatory, and this opinion
is echoed in later dictionaries such as *Collins* (1991)
and the *New Oxford* (1998), though it can scarcely be
as derogatory as *Chink* (see further under **racist
language**). British dictionaries also comment that
Chinaman now sounds oldfashioned – smacking too
much of imperialism in a post-imperial era, perhaps.
Its historical quality is certainly borne out in a
number of retrospective citations among the BNC
data. A neutral substitute for **Chinaman** can be found
in using **Chinese** as a noun, although some people
find it unsatisfactory for the singular, as in *a Chinese.*
If so, *Chinese person* or *Chinese citizen* would serve as a
paraphrase.

Cricketers use **chinaman** (definitely lower case) to
refer to a tricky kind of delivery by a left-handed spin
bowler to a right-handed batsman. It may have
originated as an oblique reference to a Chinese player

on the West Indies side between the wars. At any rate
it's first attributed to a Yorkshire cricketer in 1937. It
is known also in Australian cricket, but applied to a
ball which breaks in the opposite direction – a matter
of semantics rather than physics.

chiseled or chiselled

For the choice between these, see under **-l-/-ll-**.

chlorophyll or chlorophyl

Dictionaries everywhere give preference to
chlorophyll, and it recommends itself on grounds of
etymology. The word is a modern compound of the
Greek *chloro-* ("green") and *phyllon* ("leaf"). The
alternative spelling **chlorophyl** is recognized in
North American dictionaries, though it makes no
showing in CCAE (against some 50 instances of
chlorophyll). For etymologists, the spelling
chlorophyl has the disadvantage of connecting it
with a different Greek word, *phyle* meaning "tribe";
but for whatever reason users everywhere seem to
have settled on **chlorophyll**, the longer and
etymologically preferable form. The final double *l*s
seem to have stabilized better than in some other
English words (see **single for double**).

choosy or choosey

See under **-y/-ey**.

chord or cord

Is it *vocal chords* or *vocal cords?* In contemporary
American English *vocal cords* is more common than
vocal chords, by a factor of 2:1 in CCAE – and *Webster's
Third* (1986) put its weight behind it. The *Oxford
Dictionary* (1989) uses *chords* as the reference point for
the word (at **chord** and under "vocal"). The two
spellings are about equally represented in the BNC,
but *cords* is preferred in technical contexts of writing,
and *chords* in a variety of others. No doubt the
popularity of *chords* connects with the fact that the
vocal cords are so often mentioned in connection with
sounds and singing.

Both **chord** and **cord** derive from a Greek and then
Latin word spelled *chorda,* which meant both "gut"
and "string of a musical instrument." In the Middle
Ages it was just **cord**, and this is still the spelling for
plain ordinary string etc., and for anatomical uses of
the word, as in *spinal cord* and *umbilical.* The *vocal
cords* are however not cord-like in shape, and are more
accurately described as "vocal folds."

The spelling **chord** in mathematics results from the
"touching up" of **cord** during the English
Renaissance, when many words with classical
ancestors were respelled according to their ancient
form. The musical **chord** was also respelled, as if it
came from the same source. In fact it is a clipped form
of *accord* ("a set of sounds which agree together"). Of
all the cases of **cord** mentioned so far, it least deserves
to have an *h* in its spelling.

Christian name

See **first name**.

chrom(o)- and chron(o)-

Chromo- is a Greek root meaning "color." In English
it occurs as the first part of modern compounds such
as *chromosome*, and as the second part in others such

as *monochrome*. It also occurs by itself as *chrome,* the nontechnical equivalent of the element *chromium.*

Chrono-, also a Greek root, means "time." It is embodied in words such as *chronology* and *chronometer* as well as *diachronic* and *isochronous.* In almost all cases, the prefixes and suffixes help to make the distinction between the two roots. Only in *chromic* and *chronic* does the difference depend entirely on their respective roots.

chute, shute or shoot

These are alternative spellings for the channel used to convey wet or dry substances to a lower level, as in *down the chute.* By origin **chute** is the French word for a fall of water, whereas **shoot** shows folk etymology at work, emphasizing the rapid flow within it (see further under **folk etymology**). **Chute** is the primary spelling in both *Merriam-Webster* (2000) and *New Oxford* (1998), and it dominates in data from CCAE and the BNC. There are very few examples of **shoot,** and **shute** is extremely rare.

cicada

For the plural of this word, see under **-a** section 1.

cider or cyder, and cipher or cypher

See under **i/y**.

circa

This prefix meaning "around" comes direct from Latin. Historians use it with dates that cannot be given exactly and should be interpreted with some latitude. For example

Chaucer was born circa 1340.

When spelled out in full as in that example, **circa** is often italicized. When abbreviated as *c.* or *ca.* it is now usually set in roman (see further under **Latin abbreviations**). On whether or not to put a stop on *ca.,* see **abbreviations** section 2.

In the antiques business, the abbreviation helps to protect the vendor against too literal interpretation of the dating of items in the catalogue:

Chippendale chair c.1760

circum-

This prefix meaning "around" appears in a number of Latin loanwords in English:

circumambulate circumcision circumference circumnavigate circumscribe circumspect circumstantial

It has generated few new words in modern English, perhaps because of its ponderousness, which the examples demonstrate.

circumflex

This is an accent which has come into English with quite a few French loanwords, such as *château, entrecôte* and *fête,* as well as in phrases borrowed from French:

chacun à son gôut raison d'être tête à tête

The absence of the **circumflex** from most English typewriters and wordprocessors means that it is quickly lost and forgotten once the loanword becomes assimilated. Those unacquainted with French are unlikely to know that there might ever have been a **circumflex** on words like:

baton chassis crepe depot hotel role

In French the **circumflex** often marks the disappearance of a letter (such as *s*) from the spelling of the word, as is clear when we compare château with *castle,* fête with *feast,* and hôtel with *hostel.* **Circumflexes** have also marked the loss of vowels from particular words, or the fact that the vowel was once long. But from its first appearance in C16 French, the applications of the **circumflex** have been various and inconsistent. Unlike the acute and grave accents, it does not correspond to a particular pronunciation of the vowel it surmounts. The etymological information it provides is less important to English than French users of the word (though even in France there have been concerted efforts recently to do away with the **circumflex,** on the grounds of its redundancy). This further reduces the incentive to keep the **circumflexes** on French loanwords in English.

cissy or sissy

See **sissy**.

citation-sequence referencing

This is an alternative name for the referencing system that identifies sources by a continuous set of numbers. See **Vancouver style**.

citrus or citrous

Though dictionaries keep **citrous** "on the books" as the adjectival form of **citrus,** it never appears in data from either CCAE or the BNC. Instead **citrus** is used freely as the attributive in *citrus aromas, citrus fruits* etc. (see **adjectives** section 1).

The word **citrus** is a C19 addition to English, and it takes an English plural: **citruses.** Dictionaries recommend *citrusy* for the informal adjective.

civil or civic

Both these adjectives relate ultimately to the city and its citizens, but they differ in their range of meaning. **Civic** enters into expressions which are strongly associated with a city, such as *civic centre* and *civic pride;* whereas **civil** often relates to the citizens of the country at large, as in *civil service* and *civil war.*

Civil is the older of the two, appearing first C14, and developing a wide range of meanings in the following centuries. The different kinds of antonyms it has developed are revealing:

civil as opposed to	*uncouth, rude*	
civil " "	*military*	
civil " "	*ecclesiastical*	

Civic meanwhile dates from C16, is still narrow in its range, and occurs much less often, according to the evidence of language databases.

-ck/-cq

These provide alternative spellings in pairs such as **racket/racquet, lackey/lacquey** and **lacquer/lacker.** See further under those headings.

clad or clothed

These are now mostly complementary in their roles rather than interchangeable. Only **clothed** works nowadays as the past tense of the verb *clothe:*

She clothed the children in home-made and hand-me-down items.

Clothed also serves as the active past participle (*she had clothed the children. . .*). In either of these verbal roles **clad** would sound old-fashioned or literary. Yet

clad is definitely the strong contender in current British and American English for the passive past participle and the adjective:

> *He was clad only in a short towelling robe...*
> *Clad in waterproofs and wellies, we walked along the river.*

It readily forms compound adjectives, such as *khaki-clad men; a blue-clad figure; Gucci-clad Latinos; a youthful, jeans-and-leather-clad operative.* Figurative extensions also abound, as in *tree-clad slope, a granite-clad sixties block,* not to mention the *iron-clad guarantee, excuse* or *alibi.* **Clothed** is no substitute in these more figurative and technical usages. The technical verb **clad** meaning "be/provide cladding for" (usually a building structure) has developed alongside, with applications in architecture as well as nuclear technology.

clamor or clamour

See under **-or/-our**.

classic or classical

The relationship between these words is changing. Both imply that something is in a special class, and in their three centuries of use there has been a great deal of overlap between them, as with other **-ic/-ical** pairs (see further that heading). Both words relate things to the classics of high culture, and especially to the civilizations of ancient Greece and Rome – hence the phrase *to study the classics.*

But since the late C19, **classic** has been widening its frontiers and associating itself with all sorts of everyday things, not just matters of culture. The noun **classic** was applied to important horse races last century, and to motor races this century. With a capital letter, **Classic** now typically refers to a golf or tennis tournament. Elsewhere the word **classic** may be applied to anything from a familiar political ploy to the less outrageous types of fashion. The criteria for using the word may or may not be obvious to others, only that it's intended to express approval and to commend. The original *Oxford Dictionary* observed it, commenting that such usage was "burlesque, humorous." A century later it seems perfectly standard and straightforward.

While **classic** has become a more popular and subjective word, **classical** maintains the higher ground. It is suffused with a sense of history and great artistic traditions: *classical music* is associated with a period of outstanding music in western Europe in C18 and C19; and *classical ballet* embodies what for many is still the acme of balletic technique, developed last century.

Occasionally **classical** is used in the freer ways now enjoyed by **classic**. There is however another rival for that informal terrain: *classy.* Its links with the word *class* ("high class") are still quite strong, but it is acquiring overtones of "stylish," "superior," which bring it close to the attitudinal uses of **classic**. *Classy* is more direct and down-to-earth however, so it can probably coexist with **classic** for some time to come.

clauses

The **clause** is the basic grammatical unit in any sentence. Whether they know it or not, people produce many more **clauses** than sentences whenever they communicate. At its bare minimum, a **clause** consists of two elements:

* a subject (S) (whatever is being identified for comment), and
* a predicate (P) (whatever is stated about the subject)

For example:

> *The dollar is rising.*
>   S   P
> *A dreamy expression came over her face.*
>   S   P

The predicate always contains a finite verb, e.g. *is rising, came* in these examples. But often there are other elements such as objects, complements, adverbs or adverbial adjuncts (such as *over her face*). See further under **predicate**.

With their subject/predicate structure, **clauses** are clearly different from phrases (which revolve around a single *head:* see **phrases**). Note however that modern grammarians also recognize *nonfinite clauses* (usually without a subject or finite verb) in subordinate constructions. (see below, section 3, for *subordination*, and also **nonfinite clause**.) The number of **clauses** in a sentence, and the relationship between them, is the basis of distinguishing several different types of sentence: *simple, compound* and *complex.*

1 **Simple sentences** consist of a single **clause**, like the two examples above. They may however embody extra adverbials and dependent phrases:

> *After months of decline, the dollar is rising.*
> (adv. phr.)   S P
> *The dollar finally began to rise, despite economic anxiety.*
>   S   (adv.)   P (v. phr.)   (adv. phr.)

Thus *simple* sentences may have several phrases in them.

2 **In compound sentences,** two or more **clauses** are *coordinated*, i.e. linked in such a way as to have equal status as statements. (Hence *coordination* as the name for this relationship, or alternatively *parataxis*.) The *coordinates* are usually joined by conjunctions such as *and, but, or* or *nor,* though a semicolon or occasionally a comma can also serve to coordinate. For example:

> a) *They came and they brought their dog.*
> b) *They came; their dog came with them.*
> c) *I came, I saw, I conquered.*
> d) *She didn't answer or show any emotion.*

Compound sentences that are coordinated with punctuation rather than conjunctions (as in [c]) are said to have *asyndetic coordination.* (See **asyndeton** and **comma splice**.) When the same subject appears in two **clauses** coordinated by a conjunction, it's often omitted from the second **clause**, as in (d). In sentence (a) however, the subject is repeated in the second **clause** to draw extra attention to it. (See further under **ellipsis** section 1.)

3 **In complex sentences** the **clauses** are linked so as to give one of them superior status. The superior one is known as the *main clause* (or *principal clause*), while the other is subordinated to it and so is called the *subordinate* (or *dependent*) *clause.* The relationship is thus one of *subordination* or *hypotaxis.* The differentiation of roles is marked by the use of particular conjunctions, sometimes called *subordinating conjunctions* (see further under **conjunctions**). The following are complex sentences:

He pleaded insanity so that the charge would be dropped.
    main clause   subordinate clause
Because he pleaded insanity, the charge was dropped.
    subordinate clause   main clause

Notice the different effect of the *subordinate clause* in these sentences. In the first it simply acts as a coda to the *main clause*; in the second it draws attention to both the *main clause* and itself, because of its prime position. (See further under **information focus**.)

4 Types of subordinate clause. In traditional grammar the three types distinguished are:
    relative (or adjectival)   noun (or content)
    adverbial (or adjunct)

As their names suggest, they function as adjectives, nouns and adverbs respectively, in relation to the *main clause*.

a) Relative clauses attach further information to nouns or pronouns in the main clause:
    The book which I had in my hand had once been banned.
    The book was written by someone who mocked conventional values.

The examples show how *relative clauses* serve to define or further describe the noun or pronoun which they modify. (See further under **relative clauses** section 4.)

b) Noun clauses take the place of a noun or noun phrase in the *main clause:*
    They explained what was going on.
    What was going on took some explaining.

The *noun clause* works as either subject, object or complement of the *main clause*. In the first example it is the object: in the second, the subject. (See further under **noun clause**.)

c) Adverbial clauses attach further information to the verb of the *main clause*, detailing how, when, where or why the action or event took place:
    Her eyes lit up as if the sun had risen. (HOW)
    His eyes lit up when he heard the news. (WHEN)
    She would venture where others had failed. (WHERE)
    He would venture because the time was ripe. (WHY)
    She would succeed although they weren't yet out of the woods. (CONCESSION)
    He would succeed if only he could raise the capital. (CONDITION)
    They worked on it as no-one ever had before. (COMPARISON)
    The project would work so that no-one would doubt its value. (RESULT)

Modern grammars such as the *Comprehensive Grammar* (1985) distinguish *adverbial clauses* of similarity/comparison like the one above from *comparative clauses* proper. The latter have a comparative or equative element in the *main clause* (eg. *more, -er*), which connects with *than* or *as* in the *subordinate clause:*
    He liked a bigger house than I did.
Comparative clauses are thus regarded as an additional type of subordinate **clause**.

clear and clearly

These two appear as you might expect in *a clear voice* and *speak clearly*, as adjective and adverb respectively. **Clearly** also has adverbial roles as an intensifier, as in: *He clearly wanted a decision*, and *Clearly not!*

But **clear** also serves as adverb:
    Stand clear of the doors
    They kept clear of townships by day.
In expressions like these, **clear** is idiomatic and could not be replaced by the regular *-ly* form. Other examples of uninflected adverbs are discussed under **zero adverbs**.

cleave

This word is really two words, both verbs, meaning:
1 "be attached (to)," "stick (to)," as in *the 24-hour sleep–wake cycle to which humans cleave*
2 "split," "cut through," as in *gritty pioneers driving oxen to cleave the soil...*

Neither is common in English nowadays, though the second is better represented than the first in both American and British databases. While **cleave** (1) often expresses an attachment to things past (*he cleave[s] to the antique idea of the library*), **cleave** (2) has found a new technical use with microbiologists who *cleave enzymes* etc. in genetic engineering. But **cleave** (2) has provided us with *cleavage,* the butcher's *cleaver,* and a number of expressions such as *cloven-footed, cloven hoof, cleft palate* and *cleft stick.* These fossils show the earlier confusion between the two verbs as to their past forms. The form *cloven* belongs only to **cleave** (2), while *cleft* was originally part of **cleave** (1), but eventually annexed by **cleave** (2).

cleft sentences

A **cleft sentence** is one in which the normal sequence of subject/verb/object is interrupted and even rearranged, so as to spotlight one of them in particular. Compare:
    Jane noticed the unusual signature.
with its cleft counterparts:
    It was Jane who noticed the unusual signature.
    It was the unusual signature that Jane noticed.
The *it was* (or *it is*) of **cleft** sentences draws special attention to whatever follows, underscoring it as the topic of the sentence (see further under **topic**). A similar rearranging of the basic sentence elements (known as the *pseudo-cleft sentence*) helps to foreground the action of the verb, as in:
    What Jane noticed was the signature.
Both *cleft* and *pseudo-cleft sentences* help to sharpen the information focus in a sentence, and to signal a change of focus when necessary. (See further under **information focus**.)

    Cleft sentences raise several questions of grammatical agreement:
* Can the verb in the clause after *it is / it was* be plural? Yes, and in fact it should be, if its subject is plural:
    It is her relatives who have insisted on it.
* What happens with the pronouns? In formal style one uses the subject (nominative) form of pronouns: *I, he, she, we, you, they*. The verb agrees with that pronoun:
    It is I who am unsure.
    It is s/he who is unsure.
    It is we/you/they who are unsure.
However informal usage allows the object pronouns: *me, him, her, us, them.* The third person singular verb is then used for either first or second person singular (as well as third):
    It's me who is unsure.
    It's you who is in need of help.

* What other conjunctions apart from *who* can be used? The relative *that* is often used in **cleft sentences**, in references to people as well as objects. *That* is also preferred to *when* and *where* by some, who would correct *It was on Sunday when I saw him* to *It was on Sunday that I saw him.* The basis of their objection is not explained, and *when/where* are certainly used as relative pronouns in cleft constructions. In speech, intonation makes their relative role clear, whereas in writing it may be ambiguous until you reach the end of the sentence. As often, our control of written language has to be tighter for reliable communication.

clench or clinch

These words both suggest an intense grip. Fists may be *clenched,* and a bargain may be *clinched.* **Clinch** really derives from **clench**, with the vowel changing under the influence of the following *n.* In earlier centuries they shared some meanings, especially in carpentry (*clenching* or *clinching* nails) and in nautical usage. **Clench** now has limited uses, collocating mostly with an individual's hands, teeth, jaw and stomach, while **clinch** has new physical meanings in the hold used by boxers or wrestlers on each other, and the *passionate clinch* of people in noncombative encounters. In commonplace sports reporting, **clinch** collocates with the title, or victory, or just a place in the semi-finals. The competitive connotations of **clinch** lend themselves to business, as in *clinch part of the Malaysian order for frigates;* or politics, as in *clinch up to 500 of the 577 National Assembly seats.* These various uses of **clinch** make it now much more frequent than **clench** in both British and American English databases.

cleptomania(c) or kleptomania(c)

See under **k/c**.

clerk

The occupational status of this word has declined over the centuries. In Chaucer's *Canterbury Tales* (c. 1387) the *Clerk of Oxenford* was an academic, and highly literate, fit to be a *cleric* or member of the *clergy* (all three words are closely related). By C16 the word **clerk** had become secularized, and could refer to the person responsible for the records of an institution, as in *clerk of the court.* In current British and Australian English it now refers to the rather lowly office role of keeping accounts, filing documents, photocopying etc. The connection with paper documentation is less central in North America, where the **clerk** may be employed in retailing as a *sales clerk,* or in hotel reception as a *desk clerk.* In American English, *clerk* also serves as a verb, referring to more and less clerical roles. Compare:

> . . . *clerking for a federal circuit court judge.*
> *He clerked in his father's Atlanta store.*

◊ For other occupational terms whose application varies around the world, see *chemist* (under **pharmacist**), **engineer**, **lawyer**, **optician**.

clew or clue

The detective's **clue** and the carpenter's **clew** (originally "a ball of string") come from one and the same root, and were spelled either way in early modern English. During C17 the two spellings were increasingly attached to the meanings they hold today,

though traces of variability (in the use of **clew** for **clue**) could still be found in American English in the 1940s and 50s, according to *Webster's English Usage* (1989). CCAE yields no evidence of it in the 1990s, however.

clichés

These are tired, overworked turns of phrase like the one in the sign on a certain news editor's desk which read:

> *All clichés should be avoided like the plague.*
The advice of Spike Milligan on the same subject did succeed in avoiding **cliché** itself:

> *Clichés are the handrails of an infirm mind.*
Clichés are a particularly tempting resource if you have to write a lot in a short time. For journalists it's a way of life, and a crop of **clichés** can be harvested from the pages of most daily papers, predictable phrases which readers can skim over: "Urgent – – held behind closed – – ." Fill in the blanks! The word *cliché* is French for "stereotype(d)," and once referred to the stereotype block cast from an engraving, from which multiple copies could be printed. Linguistic **clichés** recast unique events in hackneyed terms. Resisting **clichés** takes mental energy, and for mass media communicators there is the depressing prospect that today's striking thought is tomorrow's platitude, and next week's **cliché**, as Bernard Levin (1986) put it.

Writers sometimes use **clichés** deliberately as a way of parodying a style, and the parody itself controls and limits their use. There's more danger of **clichés** getting out of hand when writers use them to make things effortless for the reader, a danger of losing the reader altogether. Information theory reminds us that readers need at least a modicum of stimulation from the unexpected, to keep them reading. When the content of a text is itself predictable, the language has to provide the stimulation.

Writing the word cliché. **Cliché** comes to us from French with an acute accent, showing that the final *e* is a separate syllable. Like many other accents, it's often left off in English, though without it *cliche* just could be a one-syllabled word like *creche, cache* etc. Those who know the word would never pronounce it with one syllable – hence the Tory jibe about the British prime minister whose speeches consisted of "clitch after clitch after clitch."

When *cliche* becomes a verb in English, its past participle or adjective can be written in several ways:

> *clichéd   cliché'd   clichéed   cliche'd   cliched*
The first three depend on having the acute accent in your typing or printing facilities. If it's not available, the fourth style helps the reader more than the fifth. For more about adding *-ed* to words ending in a syllabic vowel, see **-ed** section 3.

climax

In Greek this meant "ladder," and in rhetoric it implied an ascending series of steps, each one more impressive than the one before. Nowadays we apply the word only to the last step in the series, the point which is the culmination of all that has gone before.

Developing a **climax** is the core of narrative art, whether the composition is as long as a novel or as brief as a fable. A build-up is achieved by many writers through the space they devote to setting the scene and developing characters. All such detail helps to involve the reader, to raise the level of tension gradually, and to build the **climax**.

In argumentative writing also, one needs to plan to develop the discussion step by step towards a **climax**, in order to convince the reader. Many writers make their strongest argument the last one in the series, to ensure the impact and prevent *anticlimax* – that sense of let-down – creeping in at the end.

Even when drafting sentences, it pays to work up to the weightiest item when you have a series to present. Compare

> *Next across the line were an Olympic athlete, a wheelchair victim pushed by his red-hot companion, an army recruit in full battle gear, and a footballer*

with

> *Next across the line were a footballer, an Olympic athlete, an army recruit in full battle gear, and a wheelchair victim pushed by his red-hot companion.*

Assuming that the order in which the competitors finished is unimportant, the second version is more effective because it exploits the escalating amount of detail in each item to engage the reader. The first version simply has one thing after another, like a jumbled catalogue. In the second version the items have all been harnessed to create a mini-climax.
◊ See also **rhythm** section 2, and **bathos**.

clinch or clench
See **clench**.

cling, clung and clang
The English verb **cling** ("hold tightly on to") originally had *clang* as its past tense, but by C15 it had been superseded by **clung**, at least in standard southern English. (See further under **irregular verbs** section 3.) It left room for the Latin verb **clang** ("sound noisily"), first recorded in C16.

clipping
New words are sometimes formed from older ones by a process of cutting back or clipping. The *clipped form* may consist of the end, the beginning, or the middle of the full word, as with the following:

> *bus* (from omnibus)
> *exam* (from examination)
> *flu* (from influenza)

Of the three types, the ones which are clipped back to the first syllable(s), like *exam*, are the most common. Some other common examples are:

> *ad   bra   deb   deli gym lab   memo*
> *mike   photo pram pro   taxi telly zoo*

Many such *clippings* are now the standard word, displacing the original word/phrase entirely – as with *brassiere, perambulator, taximeter cab* – or else nudging it into the more formal styles of writing – as with *advertisement, gymnasium, memorandum*. Those involving spelling adjustments, such as *mike* and *telly*, tend to retain their informality.

As if brief was not really beautiful, English-speakers sometimes extend their clippings with the addition of informal suffixes such as *-ie/-y*. This is of course the source of colloquialisms such as:

> *bookie cabby chappie druggy footie*
> *hanky junkie*

Formations like these are particularly frequent in Australian English, less so in American and Canadian English. Australians also make use of **clippings** formed with the suffix *-o*, such as *arvo* (afternoon), *compo* (compensation), *rego* (registration). See further under **-ie/-y** and **-o**.

cliquey or cliquy
See under **-y/-ey**.

closures to letters
For the use of *yours sincerely* etc., see **Yours faithfully**. The position of the *complimentary close* is shown in examples in Appendix VII.

clothed or clad
See **clad**.

cloven
See **cleave**.

clue or clew
See under **clew**.

co-
The prefix **co-** implies joint activity in a particular role:

> *co-author   co-editor   co-pilot   co-sponsor*
> *co-star*

This meaning is relatively new, extrapolated from the meaning "together" which it has in older formations such as:

> *coaxial   coeducation   coequal   coexist*
> *cohabit   coincide   co(-)operate co(-)ordinate*

These older words show how **co-** was originally used with words beginning with a vowel or *h*, and as a variant of the Latin prefix *con-* or *com-*. **Co-** is the only one of them which is productive in modern English, and since C17 it has increasingly been used with words beginning with any letter of the alphabet. A number of mathematical words show this development:

> *coplanar   coset   cosine   cotangent   covalence*

Co- has in fact replaced the earlier *con-* in *coterminous*, and C17 English raised *cotemporary* as a variant for *contemporary*. It seems to stress the historical sense of that word (living in the same period; see further under **contemporary**).

A perennial question with **co-** is whether or not to use the hyphen with it. As the examples show, the ad hoc words in which it means "joint" are often given hyphens, but the hyphen is left out of the established ones, except those which are liable to be misread and perhaps misunderstood, e.g. *co-worker*. The debate usually centres on those in which **co-** precedes an *o*, such as *co(-)operate* and *co(-)ordinate*. In the US they are set solid like the rest, though usage in the UK is still somewhat divided. BNC data show substantial support for both forms, weighted towards the hyphened forms, but *New Oxford* (1998) prioritizes the solid setting, which must be the way of the future. In Canada, Australia and New Zealand, the major dictionaries and editorial references all support the solid setting. If you follow suit, there can be no misunderstanding because no other words look remotely like them, and the problem of misreading becomes trivial.

Co- words which remain bones of contention are clippings or backformations such as *co-ed, co-op* and *co-opt.* On these, British writers are totally in favor of the hyphen, and their American counterparts more divided. *Coed* outnumbers *co-ed* by more than 2:1 in CCAE data, but *co-op* and *co-opt* prevail over *coop* and *coopt.* The solid settings are thus beyond the frontier for most. Again we might ask how essential the hyphen is. Could the words be misread and misunderstood without it? (What could they be mistaken for?) Without a capital letter *a coed school* can scarcely be misread in terms of *Coed,* the Welsh placename element. Does *the University Coop* really suggest chickens coming home to roost? Homographic words are usually disambiguated by their context (see **homonyms**), and the hyphen becomes redundant. But there's no harm in a little redundancy!

cocotte or coquette

Both these French loanwords are about women and sexuality, but if the **coquette** makes men her victims, men have the advantage over the **cocotte.** Cocotte is colloquial French for prostitute, while *grande cocotte* is the expression for the upmarket type kept in luxury by her lover. Alternatively, she is a *poule de luxe* (roughly "a luxury bird"). The **coquette** differs in the flirtatious independence she maintains while exploiting the affections of her admirers. Both words are ultimately derived from *coc,* the Old French word for "rooster."

codex

For the plural of this word, see -x section 3.

coed or co-ed

See under **co-**.

cogito ergo sum

This Latin phrase meaning "I think therefore I am" is surprisingly well known in the English-speaking world. The seminal utterance was that of French philosopher Descartes in 1637, which has been mediated through British philosophers of C19 and C20. The words seem to express the essence of existentialism, and the ultimate syllogism (see **deduction**). Descartes himself insisted that the statement was simply a way of asserting the involvement of self in any act of thinking. He was concerned about the basis of knowledge, and how far intuition plays a part in it.

coherence or cohesion, coherent or cohesive

There are broad differences between **coherence/cohesion** and **coherent/cohesive,** even though all four are related to the verb *cohere* ("stick together"). None of them retain the literal meaning of the verb itself, but the second word in each pair still carries a sense of bonding together, as in the *cohesion within the party* or a *cohesive defense force.* The first word in each pair has moved further away, and implies a consecutive and logical linkage from one thing to the next, as in the *coherence of his argument* or a *coherent plan.* This extended meaning is underscored in the negatives *incoherence* and *incoherent.* **Cohesion**

and **cohesive** lack established negatives – a sign that they are more recent arrivals (from late C17 and C18), whereas **coherence/coherent** are from C16.

1 Coherence in writing. Communication of any kind needs to be both **coherent** and **cohesive:** to be integrated and logical in its development, as well as effectively bonded in its expression. The **coherence** comes from thinking about the sequence and integration of ideas, whether you are writing or speaking. Even a fiction world has to be imaginatively consistent and provide plausible dramatic development. In nonfiction it's vital that the statements made are somehow related, as being matched or deliberately contrasted, or linked as general/particular, problem/solution or cause/effect. Some underlying logic of development, e.g. deduction or induction, is needed, though it may not be spelled out as such. (See further under **deduction, induction** and **argument.**)

2 Cohesion in writing is the network of verbal connections on the surface of the text, which link one reference with another and mark the continuity of ideas. In fiction, the pronouns *he* and *she* help to keep tabs on the protagonists, as in the following extract from Cliff Hardy's *Heroin Annie*:

> When she came out at twenty to six she was recognisable from her walk; she still moved well, but there was something not proud about the way she carried her head. Her hair had darkened to a honey colour and she wore it short. In a lumpy cardigan and old jeans she headed across the pavement to a battered Datsun standing at the kerb; no-one stood aside for her.

This "portrait of a lady" keeps its focus on Annie with the unobtrusive aid of *she* and *her* in successive sentences. **Cohesion** is also provided by the sequence of references to her appearance, and then the street phenomena, pavements, car, the crowd, as reminders of the dramatic context.

In nonfiction, the pronouns (especially *it, this* and *that*) and *the* as well, are again important in ensuring continuity of reference. Other **cohesive** aids in informative and argumentative writing are the conjunctions, which forge links between one statement and another, and make explicit the underlying relationship (of similarity, contrast, cause and effect, etc.; see further under **conjunctions**). The links between clauses or phrases can also be made by **ellipsis** (see under that heading). Yet much of the **cohesion** still comes through the words that express the subject matter, and through synonyms and antonyms which maintain the same meaning. (See further under **synonyms, antonyms, hyponyms** and **synedoche.**)

Note that most **cohesive** links work *anaphorically,* i.e. by reference back to an antecedent. Yet it is possible to forge a forward-looking **cohesive** link, as in narratives which begin:

> It was the most delightful of occasions – an alfresco lunch in relaxed company.

This *cataphoric* form of **cohesion** is however much less common than the *anaphoric.* See further under **anaphora.**

Most writers succeed in maintaining enough **cohesive** links in the texts they compose. But the conjunctions deserve extra thought, to ensure that those chosen underscore the logical links between statements (see **conjunctions** section 3); and it pays to check any sequences of pronouns, in case ambiguity has crept in. See for example:

> *He waited until the boss had finished reading his letter.* (Whose letter was it?)

Such problems are always more obvious when you come back to edit at a later stage.

3 Noncohesive texts. In fact, it takes effort to write something which is totally lacking in **coherence** and **cohesion**. One author who tried was hailed as a great poet, in a notorious Australian literary hoax. This was "Ern Malley," the pseudonym adopted by James McAuley and Harold Stewart when they offered for publication a set of verses concocted out of bits and pieces from the books that happened to be on their desks at the time. "We opened books at random, choosing a word or phrase haphazardly. We made lists of these and wove them into nonsensical sentences." A sample of the result, from the poem "Egyptian register," begins:

> *The hand that burns resinous in the sky*
> *Which is a lake of roses, perfumes, idylls*
> *Breathed from the wastes of the Tartarean heart*
> *The skull gathers darkness like an inept mountain*
> *That broods on its aeons of self-injury ...*

Knowing the intention behind it, you are unlikely to look for **coherence** or meaningful connections in it. But Max Harris who published the poems in 1944 certainly did. It shows how ready we are to assume that printed text is **coherent** and **cohesive**, though it's as well to maintain a little skepticism.
◊ Compare **gobbledygook**.

cohort

How many people does it take to make a **cohort**? One or many? Originally the **cohort** was a unit of the Roman army (about 600 men), and this meaning, as well as the more loosely defined "retinue," are still around at the turn of the second millennium:

> *He moved out of the studio, followed by his cohort of technicians and production assistants, who thumped him on the back ...*

But the commonest meaning in current British English is its application to a notional experimental, educational or sociological group, as in *a birth cohort, dropouts from a primary school cohort 1980–5,* or *an ageing cohort of teachers.* This technical application has quickly become commonplace, as in the following from BNC and CCAE

> *the cohort for the minibus gathered*
> *a new cohort of frank but liberal commentators on race*

Since World War II, usage originating in North America has **cohort** as a synonym for a single "colleague," "partner," "accomplice" or "companion," and this is its meaning in about half of its appearances in CCAE. Examples include: *a distinguished cohort, his cohort in the Cimarosa concerto [for Two Flutes], a cohort in crime, his cohort in drug dealing.* In American English **cohort** can also be used figuratively, as for the tennis player who looked *as if frustration were her cohort.* The **cohort** as human companion was first recognized and challenged by American usage writers in the 1950s, but is now accepted by *Webster's Third* (1986) and *Merriam-Webster* (2000). In Britain the usage is also quite widespread, despite the *Oxford Dictionary*'s (1989) label "chiefly US." A usage note in *New Oxford* (1998) comments that **cohort** was used to mean

"colleague" in the majority of citations from the current Oxford Reading Programme; and a handful of instances are to be found in the BNC, typically in media and business reporting:

> *But what of Chloe's Playaway cohort, Brian Cant? He left Allied Dunbar last October, at the same time as chief executive Mike Wilson, a 20-year cohort who was viewed as his successor, and sales director Keith Carby.*

Citations like these do not support the *New Oxford*'s label "derogatory," however unpopular the word is with some in Britain, as a newish Americanism.

cole(-)slaw or cold(-)slaw

Both names say something about this salad of raw cabbage, though **coleslaw** is closer to its origins in Dutch *koolsla*. The first part is cognate with the English word *kale,* and the second, a Dutch colloquial abbreviation of *salade*. **Cold slaw** is folk etymology making sense of the unfamiliar first element – and perhaps registering English protest at uncooked cabbage. Its record from 1794 is half a century earlier than the first instance of **coleslaw**, and four out of the five *Oxford Dictionary* (1989) citations for C19 are for **cold slaw**. This early start helps to explain why **coldslaw** is still known in American usage, and registered in *Webster's Third* (1986). However it makes little showing in CCAE, where **cole(-)slaw** is the dominant form. In terms of setting, **coleslaw** outnumbers **cole slaw** by about 5:2, and **cole-slaw** is very rare. Data from the BNC shows that **coleslaw** is also the most popular form in the UK, and there's no sign of any of the others.

Coliseum or Colosseum

Any place of entertainment which calls itself a **coliseum** or **colosseum** invokes the famous *Colosseum* of Rome, the huge amphitheatre built by Vespasian in the first century AD. Its name expresses all that we know in the word *colossal,* and it was evidently the ultimate entertainment centre. Smaller amphitheatres and stadiums, built on the same model elsewhere in the Roman Empire, turned it into a generic word, and it comes to us through medieval Latin (and Italian) as **coliseum**. This form of the word is used by Byron in reference to Vespasian's original, when he declares (through Childe Harold):

> *While stands the Coliseum, Rome shall stand ...*

The neo-Latin form *Coliseum* is the one taken up by C20 entertainment centres in London and its suburbs; and especially for large, covered or partly covered sporting venues across the American continent from New York to Los Angeles. In generic and familiar references to such structures, it appears as **coliseum**, without a capital letter. The name *Colosseum* is now mostly reserved for Rome's magnificent ruin, apart from the *Colosseum Theatre* in Johannesburg, and the Tokyo *Ariake Colosseum,* a sports stadium. Others who have capitalized on the classical form of the name are the jazz-rock bands *Colosseum I* and *Colosseum II.* The word is still portentous, despite changes in public sports and entertainments.

collapsible or collapsable

The first spelling is given priority in both *Webster's Third* (1986) and the *Oxford Dictionary* (1989), though they make the second an acceptable alternative. The spelling **collapsible** would connect it with its Latin antecedents, while **collapsable** represents the fact that it originated in C19 English, and is based on the English verb *collapse*. **Collapsible** is the only one to appear in data from CCAE and the BNC. See further under **-able/-ible**.

colleague and collegial
See **collegial**.

collectable or collectible
These spellings present a regional divide, though they are equally acceptable. **Collectable** is the simple English formation based on the verb *collect*, and preferred by the British according to the *Oxford Dictionary* (1989); whereas *Webster's Third* (1986) gives priority to the latinate form **collectible**. Data from BNC shows that **collectable** is much preferred in Britain for all adjectival uses, ranging from the most literal (*a collectable tax, a car collectable on your arrival*) to the now common sense of "being a collector's item," as in *Chinese art is still collectable*. The few BNC citations for **collectible** all converge on the latter meaning. By contrast CCAE confirms the strong American preference for **collectible** for all meanings of the word, from the *collectible amount for lawsuits* to *rare and collectible comic artworks*. The use of **collectible** as a noun (*a collectible*) is more evident in the American data. The very few American examples of **collectable** are all adjectives, but with hundreds spelled **collectible**, it doesn't add up to grammatical division of labor (**collectable** for the adjective and **collectible** for the noun). Americans prefer the neoclassical here, but not always. See further under **-able/-ible**.

collective nouns
A **collective noun** is a singular term which designates a group of people, animals or objects. Those referring to people usually connote some kind of organization or structure:

audience	class	committee	congregation
council	crew	crowd	family
government	mob	orchestra	parliament
squad	staff	team	tribe

Such words raise questions of grammatical agreement, since they can be used to represent either the collective body or its individual members (see **agreement** section 1).

Collective nouns for animals often appear as the head of a noun phrase, e.g. *herd of elephants, flock of sheep, swarm of bees*. Many are not species-specific (cf. *herd of cows, flock of crows,*) and so the exact type of animals must be specified, at least on first reference. As complex phrases they usually take singular agreement; but when reduced to *herd* they can be construed in the plural, like human **collective nouns**, at least in British and Australian English. *Collective terms* for objects behave rather like the animal terms, in taking singular agreement when they indicate the configuration of a set of items, e.g. *a bunch of keys, a crop of plums, a pile of logs*. However when these terms are used as general quantifiers, as in *a bunch of losers, a crop of winners,* they often take plural agreement (see **agreement** section 5).

The term **collective noun** is also associated with some very traditional *collective* words applied to one species only, such as *covey of partridges, gaggle of geese, pride of lions*. They are models for facetious references to particular human groups, such as the *haggle of vendors* and the *decorum of deans* (or the *decanter of deans*). Among the many others created for amusement are:

> *a column of accountants*
> *a consternation of mothers*
> *a goggle of tourists*
> *a guess of diagnosticians*
> *a quaver of coloraturas*
> *a recession of economists*
> *a slumber of old guard*

The danger of libel looms larger, the further you go with such phrases – which probably explains why their use is limited.

collegial
This is still the only the spelling registered in dictionaries for the adjective referring to the attributes of a *colleague*. But the alternative pronunciation with a hard "g" sound, registered in *Webster's Third* (1986) and *Merriam-Webster's* (2000), shows the mental link with *colleague* – and scope for spellings such as "collegual," "collegal," "colleagual," "colleagal." All four (in descending order of frequency) could be found by a Google search of the internet in 2002. Though collectively they make up only 1 in 1000 instances of the word, they highlight the problem of deriving an adjective from *colleague,* which is an English respelling of the French *collègue*. "Collegual" reconnects with this – and avoids the distracting connections with *college* which go with **collegial**, in its spelling and standard pronunciation.

collocations
Collocation is the tendency of words to go with particular others in a sequence. There may be only one word which can go with a particular verb, as in *the mind boggles* or *with lips pursed*. Why this is so is not obvious, any more than the reason why we speak of *melted butter* and *molten lead*. They are just some of the conventional **collocations** of English.

Collocations of another kind are to be found in phrasal verbs: *bear up, browned off, butt in, carry out* etc., where distinctive meanings are latent in the combinations of verb and particle. Compare *carry out a plan* with *carry out the rubbish*. Knowing which particle to use in the non-literal **collocation** is a challenge for the second-language learner. Even native speakers may puzzle over the slightly different **collocations** used in speech and writing. In written documents, *wait for* (someone) is the standard **collocation**, whereas in conversation it's often expressed as *wait on*. Thus some **collocations** vary according to context, and/or the structure of the sentence. The choice of particle after *different* has a lot to do with both: see **different from, different to, and different than**.

Collocations differ from *idioms* in that their meaning is never so far removed from the literal value of their components, or anything like a figure of speech. Compare expressions such as *a red herring* and *shoot (oneself) in the foot* (= true idioms) with any of the examples in the previous paragraph; and see further under **idiom**.

Collocations differ from *clichés* in that they have an accepted place in the language, and are not thought of as hackneyed expressions in need of replacement. See further under **clichés**.

colloquialisms

These are expressions used in casual conversation. They smack of easy-going exchanges between people, where there's no need to dot the *i*s and cross the *t*s:

> *Hang on a tick, we'll get the cabbie to put the bike on top, and be there in time to have a bite.*

The **colloquialisms** of spoken discourse are often short or shortened words like *tick, bike* and *cabbie,* familiar abbreviations which reduce demands on the listener, and telescope the less essential syllables. Contractions such as *we'll* work in the same way to communicate more (or at least as much) with less. *Colloquial idioms* like *hang on* and *have a bite* also contribute to an allusive style which relies on the context and other knowledge shared by the speaker, e.g. what the time frame is. When conversing we take a lot for granted to ensure the ready exchange of words. **Colloquialisms** express basic rather than precise meanings, and the speaker's desire to minimize verbal barriers. The communicative value of **colloquialisms** is thus almost the antithesis of formal writing. Where verbal precision is paramount, they would be counterproductive. Yet in more interactive styles of writing, a sprinkling of **colloquialisms** helps to lighten the discourse. The main issue then is to ensure that their currency is as wide as the likely readership. See further under **dialect**.

colloquium

For the plural of this word, see under **-um**.

Colombia or Columbia

See **Columbia**.

colon

The **colon** is a handy punctuation mark for showing that examples or specific details are about to come. The examples may continue the line of the sentence, as in the following:

> *Most of their publications are technical: textbooks for students of economics and law; manuals for computer users and specialist dictionaries.*

Alternatively, the examples after the colon may be set out on the line(s) below, as in countless entries in this book.

The **colon** reassures readers that what follows will give them the specifics, and that they are not simply being offered an empty generalization. It allows the writer to detail something or give a set of examples without overloading the introductory part of the sentence. Note that what comes after the **colon** is not usually a sentence itself – a point on which *colons* differ from semicolons (see under **semicolon**). Style manuals agree (*Chicago Manual,* 2003; *Oxford Guide to Style,* 2002) that the word following the **colon** stays in lower case, unless it's a formal quotation, slogan or motto. For example:

> *On the laboratory door was a new sign:*
> *Trespassers prosecuted.*

The word following a **colon** in the subtitle of a book or article may be capitalized (see further under **titles**).

A **colon** is quite often used these days before presenting an extended quotation from a printed source (whereas the combination of *colon plus dash* [:–] for this is obsolescent). Direct quotations from someone's speech are now also prefaced by a **colon**, especially in newspapers and magazines, where once

a comma was the standard punctuation. The use of commas with quotations is increasingly confined to literary fiction. (See **quotation marks** section 3.)

Other uses of colons:

* to separate the headings in memos from the specific details:

> *MEMO TO: Leslie Smith, Manager*
> *FROM: Robin Jones*
> *SUBJECT: Uniforms for staff*

In the US, business letters also have a **colon** following the salutation, as in:

> *Dear Mr Smith:*
> *Your letter (3/9/03) arrived too late for the order to be modified ...*

* to separate the main title from the subtitle of a book (see under **titles**)
* to separate elements in literary and biblical citations

> *Romeo and Juliet Act V:ii*
> *Revelation 12:20*

* to separate elements in bibliographical references, such as the publisher from the place of publication, or the date of publication from the page numbers (see **referencing** sections 2 and 3)
* to indicate ratios in mathematics, as in *3:1*

A further use of the **colon** in the US and Canada is to space the hours from the minutes in expressions of time, e.g. *5:30 pm.* In Britain and Australia, a stop is used, as in *5.30 pm.*

color or colour

See under **-or/-our**.

colo(u)red

The meaning of **colo(u)red** in racial identification depends on the country in which it's used. In South Africa it refers to persons of mixed descent, and was used (with or without capital letter) in apartheid laws to define such a group. (See further under **miscegenation**.) In the US, **colored** has a long history dating back to C18, and remains an alternative term for people of African-American background. Its essence has recently been reaffirmed through the phrase *people of color* (sometimes construed to include Latinos as well, but not Asians). In British usage, **coloured** is a dated term, applied to non-whites of any race. Like many which express racial discrimination, it may give offense.

Colosseum or Coliseum

See **Coliseum**.

Columbia or Colombia

Both names honor *Christopher Columbus,* as does *Colón.* The different forms of his name result from its being differently written in Italian, Spanish and Latin. *Columbus* was of course an Italian by birth, and his name stands in its Italian form (*Colombo*) for the chief city of Sri Lanka. In South America it's written into the mountainous state **Colombia** and the *Colombian Basin* to the north of it. When Columbus settled in Spain, he adopted the name *Cristobal Colón,* and *Colón* lives on as the name of cities in Argentina, Panama and Cuba.

Columbus, the form most familiar to English-speakers, is the Latin version of the explorer's name. In North America it becomes **Columbia** in the several towns that bear the name, as well as the *District of*

Columbia (which spells out the abbreviation *DC*), *Columbia University* and the Canadian state of *British Columbia*.

combated or combatted, combating or combatting

Contemporary dictionaries suggest that the spellings with one *t* are now preferred in the US, Britain and Australia, and evidence from CCAE and the BNC puts **combated/combating** ahead. But Canadians prefer to spell them with two *t*s, according to the *Canadian Oxford* (1998).The *Oxford Dictionary* (1989) shows that the spellings **combatted/combatting** were once more common, no doubt when the word's second syllable was stressed. (See further under **doubling of final consonant**.) The older spelling survives in the heraldic word *combattant*, whereas its modern military counterpart is *combatant*.

come and

See **try and**.

comic or comical

The first of these adjectives is more closely linked with comedy, as in *comic opera* and *a comic character*. **Comical** is more loosely used of anything that generates laughter, as in *a comical expression*. But the boundaries between them are not too sharply drawn, as with other pairs of this kind. See further under **-ic/-ical**.

comma

Commas are an underused punctuation mark, the chief casualty of the trend towards open punctuation (see **punctuation** section 1). They have a vital role to play in longer sentences, separating information into readable units, and guiding the reader as to the relationship between phrases and items in a series.
1 A single comma ensures correct reading of sentences which start with a longish introductory element:
a) *Before the close of the season, you should see this stimulating new play.*
b) *Before the season closes, you should see this stimulating new play.*
Whether the sentence begins with a phrase as in (a), or a clause as in (b), it benefits by having a **comma** to show where the introductory element ends and the main statement begins. The **comma** allows the reader to pause between the two parts, and to absorb each one properly. Introductory strings of words often express the ongoing theme of a paragraph, or serve to highlight a change or adjustment to the theme (see further under **information focus**).
When the introductory string is short (just two or three words), the separating **comma** may not be necessary – except to prevent misreading. In a case like the following, the **comma** is essential:
Down below the bridge deck was half submerged in the river.
A **comma** following "down below" will prevent the reader having to go over the sentence twice to get its structure. **Commas** can also make a difference to the reading of a sentence with a relative clause (see **relative clauses** section 4), and those with negatives in them (see **negatives** section 2).

2 Pairs of commas in mid-sentence help to set off any string of words which is either a parenthesis or in apposition to whatever went before.
The ancient trees, oaks and elms, were sprouting new leaves. (apposition)
Dead canyons, all nature in them reduced to desiccation, came alive with the sound of rain. (parenthesis)
Note that a pair of dashes could have been used instead of **commas** with the parenthesis, in both formal and informal writing.
3 Sets of commas separate serial items, such as:
a) **strings of predicative adjectives,** as in: *It looks big, bold, enticing.* Note that strings of attributive adjectives do not necessarily need to be separated: *She was driving a flashy red sports car.* The adjectives in sequences like those are of several different types (evaluative, descriptive, definitive), and are in no danger of misreading. Where they belong to the same type, as in *a long, turgid, boring lecture,* **commas** are useful separators. (See further under **adjectives**.)
b) **a series of nouns or noun phrases,** as in: *Drinking at the waterhole were cockatoos, emus, budgerigars and kangaroos of several kinds.* Whether there should or should not be a **comma** between the two last items (the so-called *serial comma* or *series comma*) is sometimes hotly debated. American editorial practice, as described in the *Chicago Manual* (2003) insists on a **comma** before the *and*, although *Webster's Standard American Style Manual* (1985) admits that the *serial comma* is as often absent as present in its citation files. In British practice there's an Oxford/Cambridge divide. The *serial comma* has always been part of "Oxford" style, according to Ritter (2002), whereas Butcher (*Copy-editing*, 1992) notes both practices and the need to observe either consistently. In Canada and Australia the *serial comma* is recommended only to prevent ambiguity or misreading, according to *Editing Canadian English* (2000) and the Australian government *Style Manual* (2002). In a sentence like the one shown above, a *serial comma* is not needed to disambiguate the items. However it's a different matter with the following:
Drinking at the waterhole were cockatoos, emus, flocks of budgerigars and kangaroos.
Since the word *flock* does not collocate with *kangaroos*, a **comma** before *and*, to separate *flocks of budgerigars* from *kangaroos* is desirable. Note that once there are **commas** within individual items in a series, semicolons must be used to separate each item from the next:
Drinking at the waterhole were white cockatoos, jostling each other for position; a mob of kangaroos, large and small; and a surprisingly tentative group of emus.
4 The disappearing comma
* with numbers (see **numbers** section 1)
* with dates. Depending on the order (day, month and year, or month, day and year), the **comma** may or may not be necessary. See under **dates**.
* with addresses on envelopes. To ensure accurate reading by the electronic scanners, postal authorities now recommend the omission of commas (and all punctuation) from addresses on envelopes. (See further in Appendix VIII.)
◊ For the *decimal comma,* see **numbers** section 1.
◊ For *inverted commas,* see **quotation marks**.

comma splice

In novice writing, the use of **comma splice**, as in the following, is usually treated as a grammatical fault:

> *These are all new kinds of international problem not envisaged by the founders of United Nations, its terms of reference are not well suited for intervening in civil wars.*

That "sentence" is in fact two sentences, joined only by a comma, and the relationship between them is unclear. Ideally there would be either (a) heavier punctuation (a semicolon or full stop / period) at the junction; or (b) an appropriate conjunction, such as *since* or (in this case) the relative pronoun *whose* instead of *its*. The two statements would come across better with any of those adjustments.

The degree of fault in **comma splices** is nevertheless relative to the length of the components and how well integrated they are. Patterned examples such as *I came, I saw, I conquered* and *Man proposes, God disposes* are clear, rhetorically effective, and stand uncensured. In fact they provide examples of *asyndetic coordination*. See further under **clauses** and **asyndeton**.

commands

In English, **commands** are most directly expressed through what grammarians call *imperatives*. They are the short, sharp forms of verbs which are used on the parade ground, or in written instructions:

> *Squad, march!*
>
> *Switch on the automatic control to the oven. Set the clock to the desired starting and finishing times. Select the temperature . . .*

In instructions and recipes imperatives are regularly found at the start of sentences.

Other, less direct ways of expressing **commands** are also available in English, particularly if you want to soften the abruptness of the imperative, and to adopt the role of counselor rather than commander in the document you're writing. The following sentences illustrate the range from direct **command** to oblique instruction:

> *Switch on the oven.*
>
> *You must first switch on the oven.*
>
> *Make sure you switch on the oven.*
>
> *The oven should be switched on.*

In face-to-face situations, the **command** can be rephrased as a question: *Could you switch on the oven?* This seems to allow more discretion to the other party, turning the instruction into a kind of collaboration. See further under **imperative**.

comme il faut

Borrowed from French, this phrase means "as it should be." It was adopted into English in the courtly C18, to refer to matters of etiquette and correct social behavior. It commends as proper conduct whatever it is attached to. The phrase allows more freedom of choice than certain other French phrases which refer to etiquette. *De règle* means "required by rule or convention"; and *de rigueur* (roughly "in strictness") suggests that the whole weight of social opinion is behind it, to make it an absolute necessity.

comment or commentate

Those who **commentate** usually do so to earn a living, providing continuous commentary on events as official media representatives. Anyone can **comment**, i.e. make ad hoc remarks about something. Yet **commentate** is sometimes disparaged, as a clumsy and unnecessary extension of **comment** (which it isn't); or else as a backformation from *commentator* (which hasn't stood in the way of other useful words). See further under **backformation**.

commercialese

Letter writing has its conventions, and letters written in the name of business can be the most stylized of all. The routine nature of many business letters fostered the growth of jargon and formulaic language, in phrases such as:

> *further to your letter of the 12 inst.*
>
> *re your order of the 27 ult.*
>
> *your communication to hand*
>
> *please find enclosed*
>
> *for your perusal*
>
> *at your earliest convenience*

Clichés such as these sound increasingly stilted, and business firms these days generally encourage their letter writers to avoid them. Better to use direct, fresh language, and to communicate in friendly terms if possible. (See **letter writing**.)
◊ For the conventional layout of letters, see Appendix VII.

commitment or committal

Both words are of course from the verb *commit* and provide an abstract noun for it. Some dictionaries seem to say that they are interchangeable, yet they differ in their breadth and frequency of use. **Commitment** is much more common and widely used for committing oneself to anything, be it a religion, amateur sport, or reducing the consumption of paper. The statement "I have another commitment" can mean almost any activity. **Committal** by contrast has been particularly associated with legal processes, the *committal hearing* and *committal proceedings*, which involve the examination of evidence before a full trial. The formal burial of a body is also referred to as a **committal.** So there are ritual and legal overtones to **committal** which **commitment** is free of.

common or mutual

Common has numerous meanings, but it contrasts with **mutual** in emphasizing sharing rather than reciprocation in a relationship, as in *common origin* or *common interest*.

Mutual involves reciprocity. *Mutual satisfaction* implies the satisfaction which two people give to each other, and *mutual agreement* emphasizes the fact that something is agreed to by both parties (assuming there is no tautology). Reciprocity is carried to excess in a *mutual admiration society*. **Mutual** has also long been used to refer to a reciprocal relationship which is enjoyed by more than one other person, as in the title of Charles Dickens's *Our Mutual Friend,* published in 1865. Yet for some reason this usage was censured in later C19, as the *Oxford Dictionary* (1989) notes. The dictionary also noted that **mutual** was the only possible word in expressions like Dickens's title. (When class distinctions were so important, who would take the risk of referring to "our common friend"!) The linguistic propriety of using **mutual** has never bothered insurance companies, which offer thousands of "mutual insurance" policies, and many build the word **Mutual** into their company titles, as in *Colonial Mutual*.

common gender
See under **gender**.

common nouns
These contrast with *proper nouns*: see under **nouns**.

commonwealth and Commonwealth
The word **commonwealth** has always been a political football. It was first used by social reformers of early C16, who wanted to express in English the notion of the ideal republic, existing for the common good, and not advantaging the rich and powerful. (*Weal[th]* then meant "welfare" rather than "affluence," and *common* was to match *public*.) Several of the original American states, including Massachusetts, Pennsylvania and Virginia, are *commonwealths* by charter, and the word expressed republican and antimonarchic ideals which were popular in C19 America. The notion is institutionalized in titles such as *Virginia Commonwealth University, Commonwealth Transportation Board* and *Commonwealth (or Commonwealth's) Attorney.* The ideals embedded in **commonwealth** appealed to Australian federationists for similar reasons, and it was set into the nation's official title (the *Commonwealth of Australia*) at the Federal Convention held in Sydney in 1891. Other former British colonies such as Canada and New Zealand adopted the title *Dominion*.

The republican associations of **commonwealth** were presumably not strongly felt by the British government when it renamed what had been the British Empire as the *British Commonwealth*, with the king or queen as its head. At the same time the *Imperial Institute* became the *Commonwealth Institute*, and the *Imperial Games* the *Commonwealth Games*. The adoption of the word for this post-imperial purpose led successive Australian prime ministers in the 1960s to declare publicly their preference for "Australian Government" rather than *Commonwealth of Australia*. At the turn of the millennium the term "Commonwealth style" is still used by some for editorial practices associated with federal government documents, but longer-term uses of **Commonwealth** are caught up in the debate over Australia becoming a republic.

The *Commonwealth of Independent States (CIS)*, consisting of 12 former Soviet nations, is the newest political grouping to embrace the word. See further under **Russia**.

comparatives
◊ For *comparative forms* of adjectives, see under **adjectives**.
◊ For *comparative clauses*, see under **clauses** section 4c. See also **than**.

compared with or compared to
Do the following mean the same?
> a net loss of 8 *compared with* the 1990 result...
> a net loss of 8 *compared to* the 1990 result...
What difference there may seem to be is probably affected by one's regional background (American or British) – despite the fact that the major English dictionaries give separate definitions to the two structures. *Webster's Third* (1986) and the *Oxford*

Dictionary (1989) both suggest that **compared with** is used when the comparison is part of a broad analysis, and **compared to** when it's a matter of specifically *likening* one thing to another. But the distinction is probably more honored in the breach than the observance. *Webster's English Usage* (1989) found little correlation between the two particles and the two meanings, and that the two meanings were not necessarily separable anyway. It concluded that any tendency to choose **compared to** for the meaning "liken" could only be demonstrated for the active verb, not when it was passive or just a past participle. The very similar frequencies of **compared to** and **compared with** in data from CCAE also suggest that the two constructions are used indifferently in American English.

In British English **compared with** is a good deal more frequent than **compared to**: the ratio is about 2:1 in BNC data. Also noteworthy is the fact that **compared to** appears more often than **compared with** among spoken data and scripted dialogue. This suggests that it's the more informal of the two constructions, the one you use when speaking off the cuff, rather than when crafting your prose.

The preference for **compared with** was once underpinned by the latinist's insistence that *with* was the only possible particle, because the prefix in *compare* is the Latin *cum* "with." Like other Latin-derived principles of usage, its influence has been more pervasive in Britain, and helped to underscore the use of **compared with**. Yet even there, **compared** is increasingly construed with **to**, on the analogy of similar words and structures such as *likened to* and *similar to*.

The regional preferences for construing **compared** apply also to the adjective *comparable*. In British usage *comparable to* and *comparable with* are both freely used, appearing in the ratio 4:3 in BNC data. American usage meanwhile is strongly inclined to *comparable to*, by the evidence of CCAE.
◊ Compare *averse to*, discussed under **adverse or averse**.

comparison of adjectives and adverbs
For their *degrees of comparison* (*comparative, superlative*), see **adjectives** section 2 and **adverbs** section 3.

compendium
For the plural of this word, see under **-um**.

compensable or compensatable
Unabridged dictionaries such as *Webster's Third* (1986) and the *Oxford Dictionary* (1989) recognize both these as adjectives to the verb *compensate*. Smaller dictionaries have only **compensable**, and it's the only one to register its presence in data from the BNC and CCAE.

competence or competency
Dictionaries often give these as alternatives, and in some contexts they are synonymous in their now dominant sense of "sufficient capability or skills." But English databases show that **competence** occurs much more often than **competency** in general applications, by a factor of more than 10:1. Apart from that, both words have their special domains. Newly developed meanings in linguistics, biology and

geology are attached to **competence**; while
competency prevails in education and vocational
training, where *competency-based training* insists that
students take away identifiable skills.

The two words have shared a number of meanings.
When first recorded in English **competence/
competency** connected with the verb *compete*
("contest"), expressing meanings which are now
attached to *competition*. But in Latin and in
Renaissance English, *compete* also meant "come
together" and figuratively "be convenient or fitting."
The present-day meanings of **competence/
competency** ("fitness or adequacy") are fossils of this
now extinct sense of *compete*, preserved in legal usage
and largely confined there until C18.

In C20 English, **competency** has acquired a plural
form, often found in the phrase *core/key competencies*.
This makes it a countable noun, while **competence**
remains a mass noun only. Such grammatical
differentiation is not uncommon among **-nce/-ncy**
pairs. See further under that heading, and under
nouns.

complacent or complaisant

Complacent has been making inroads into the
domain of **complaisant** during the last two centuries.
Both words ultimately derive from the Latin verb
complacere ("please"), though the meaning is more
evident in **complaisant**, the form borrowed from
French. In English **complaisant** has meant "eager to
please" or "obliging" in a positive sense, while
complacent, the regular Latin form, usually means
"pleased with oneself and with the status quo." Its
overtones now are somewhat negative, suggesting
uncritical self-satisfaction and a reluctance to
improve things.

Complaisant is now a rare word, greatly
outnumbered by **complacent** in both American and
British databases, and suffering from convergence
with it. Examples such as *a complaisant House of
Commons* and *his apparently complaisant wife* show
complaisant meaning not just "eager to please" but
"overready to condone," i.e. much the same as
complacent. It looks like the final stage in this verbal
encounter, with no distinct or neutral identity for
complaisant. Writers wishing to use it in the sense of
"willing to please" should be advised that the
paraphrase is a more reliable means of making their
point.

For **complacent** there have been two abstract
nouns: *complacence* and *complacency*. The first (and
older) form with *-ce* is now giving way to the second
with *-cy*. For other examples of this, see **-nce/-ncy**.

complement or compliment, and complementary or complimentary

These identical-sounding words represent earlier and
later developments of the same Latin word
complementum ("something which completes"). The
spelling **complement** still corresponds to that kind of
meaning, as in:

> His creativity and her business sense are the
> perfect complement for running the gallery.

A similar meaning is the one used by grammarians
when they speak of the *complement to the
verb/noun/adjective/preposition*. See further under
complementation.

The spelling **compliment** which we use to mean "a
commendatory remark" comes through Italian and
French. This extension of meaning can be explained
in terms of etiquette, where a **compliment** is that
which completes or rounds off an act of courtesy. Until
C17, the spelling **complement** represented this sense
also, but it has since been taken over by **compliment**.
In everyday writing, **compliment** is more often
needed than **complement**, and sometimes mistakenly
used for it, in both British and American databases.

The adjective **complementary** correlates with
complement, meaning "that which goes with
something else to make a whole." It typically occurs in
analytical writing, as in *complementary colors,* or *two
vitally important and complementary goals.* By
contrast **complimentary** is an everyday word,
correlating with **compliment** as in *the directors were
complimentary to us.* **Complimentary** is also the
spelling for referring to something given free of
charge, such as *complimentary tickets* to an exhibition,
performance or sporting event, or the *complimentary
bottle of wine* from the restaurant which wants you to
think well of it, despite a small problem with the main
course. The *complimentary close* at the end of a letter
is likewise used to oil the social wheels when
corresponding (see Appendix VII). Again
complimentary is sometimes used mistakenly for
complementary. There's a particular challenge for
American sports reporters in dealing with
complementary players as well as *complimentary
passes* (for the game). But the two spellings cause
visible problems for other writers represented in
CCAE and the BNC, as in *complimentary colours* and
the *complimentary hot sauce* designed to go with
avocados. The databases also show **complementary**
being used for **complimentary**, as in *complementary
glass of champagne,* or the *complementary camera*
with every travel booking of $1000 or more. This is the
more common direction of the mistake, according to
New Oxford (1998), which would reflect the fact that
complementary is more than twice as common as
complimentary, in data from the BNC. But the
opposite holds in American English, with
complimentary about twice as common as
complementary in data from CCAE.

complementation

In the context of modern English grammar, the notion
of **complementation** begins with whatever serves to
complement the verb and complete the verb phrase.
This will depend on the verb itself, whether it is
copular, intransitive or *transitive* (*monotransitive* or
ditransitive): see further under those headings. (For
complement clauses, see **content clause**.)

Not all items found *complementing* the verb are its
complement, strictly speaking. Some grammarians
reserve the term *complement* as far as possible for
those items which are *required* to complete the verb
phrase, including:

* *subject complement,* as in *She is **the apple of his eye***
* *object complement,* as in *She thinks him **a genius***
* certain obligatory adverbs, as in *It costs **five
pounds**; They walked **five miles***

This use of *complement,* to mean something *obligatory*
in a given grammatical construction, makes it
contrast with the optional *adjunct*. See further under
adverbs, section 1, and under **predicate**.

On the analogy of its use in the verb phrase, the term **complementation** is now also applied to *complementary structures* within the noun phrase, adjective phrase and prepositional phrase. Here again the term *complement* is reserved for obligatory elements, as in

1 *(noun complement): their reliance **on the family***
2 *(adjectival complement): fond **of country walks***
3 *(prepositional complement): without **the rhetoric***

For more detail on the structure of the noun phrase and its postmodification, see under **noun phrase**.

complex sentences
See **clauses** section 3.

complex words
A *complex word* embodies more than one distinct component but only one which can stand alone. See for example:

> *child*ren *denigrat*ed *evolution*ary re*model* *water*ing

The independent (or free-standing element) has been italicized in each case. In cases such as *hungri*est, *rac*ism and *traffic*king, the italicized part should still be regarded as the free-standing element, since there's no doubt that *hungry, race* and *traffic* can stand alone. The alternative forms they take in **complex words** are simply dictated by the following suffix and certain basic rules of English spelling. (See under **-y > -i-, -e**, and **-c/-ck-** for the three involved in those cases.)

Complex words have either prefixes, suffixes or both attached to their free-standing element, signaling aspects of grammar and meaning. See further under **prefixes** and **suffixes**, and individual examples such as **ante-/ anti-, -al, -ate, be-** etc.

◊ Compare **complex words** with **compounds**.

compliment or complement
See **complement**.

complimentary or complementary
See under **complement or compliment**.

complimentary close/closing
See under **letter writing** and **Yours faithfully**, and Appendix VII.

compline or complin
The name for the last church service of the day has been growing with the centuries. Its regular French antecedent had neither *n* nor *e*, being *compli* ("completed"). However on English soil it began to be called *compelin,* and it was **complin** in C16 when Cranmer removed it as a separate service from the *English Prayer Book*. In scattered references over the next three centuries it appears as **compline**, and when the service was reinstated by the Anglican Church in 1928, the spelling with *e* was used. In the current *English Prayer Book*, and in Catholic liturgical books, the spelling is **compline**.

The second edition of the *Oxford Dictionary* (1989), unlike the first, gave priority to **compline**, and it's preferred in all modern dictionaries including the *New Westminster Dictionary of Liturgy and Worship* (1986). However the standard pronunciation still seems to go with the older spelling **complin**. The addition of the unhistorical *-e* may be an instance of

frenchification, though the motive is less clear than in other cases. See **frenchification**.

compos mentis
See **non compos mentis**.

composed of or comprised (of)
See **comprise**.

compound sentences
See **clauses** section 2.

compound verbs
Grammarians have applied this phrase to several kinds of verbs which consist of more than one word:

* Those which embrace one or more auxiliary verbs, such as:
  > *was going   am being taken   would have liked*
  (See further under **auxiliary verbs**.)
* Those which combine with particular particles to express a meaning, such as:
  > *compare with   differ from   give up   protest against*
  (See further under **phrasal and prepositional verbs**.)
* Those which are compound formations, such as *downgrade* and *shortlist*. See under **compounds**.

compounds
These are expressions which consist of two (or more) separable parts, each of which can stand as a word in its own right. English has very many of them, of which the following are only tokens:

> *nouns* *audiotape   car park   daylight-saving takeover*
> *adjectives* *airborne   home-made   icy-cold keen-eyed*
> *verbs* *baby-sit   blackball   blue-pencil overturn*
> *adverbs* *downtown   overseas   upmarket worldwide*

Although four examples have been given in each group, there are infinitely more *noun compounds* overall. Note the variation in each group (except the adverbs) over the use of hyphens, and spaced or solid setting. **Compounds** are sometimes said to progress from being spaced as separate words, to being hyphened, and then set solid, but the pattern is far from universal. In American English they may skip the hyphened stage (see **hyphens** section 1d); and some, especially longer ones like *daylight-saving,* may never progress beyond the hyphenated stage (in British English, or spaced, in American) however well established they are. *Compound adjectives* and *verbs* often go straight to the hyphened or set-solid stage, which ensures that they are read as a single grammatical unit. *Noun compounds* actually need it less because their structure is underpinned by that of the noun phrase itself. (See further under **noun phrases** and **hyphens**.)

Whatever the setting, the two parts of a *compound* come together in terms of meaning, and this special integration of meaning makes it more than the sum of its parts. A *car park* is unlike a *national park* in almost every way, in spite of the common element *park*, because both are **compounds**. For the plurals of *compound nouns,* see **plurals** section 2.

Compounds differ from *complex words* in that the latter have only one part which can stand alone. Compare *football* with *footing, machine gun* with *machinery, worldwide* with *worldly* and so on. (See further under **complex words**.)

◊ For *blends* such as *brunch, electrocute* and *telecast*, see **portmanteau words**.

comprehensible or comprehensive

These words are both related to the verb *comprehend*, which in Latin (and earlier English) meant "take a grip on"; and the sense of holding or including (many things) is still the most common one for **comprehensive** nowadays. A *comprehensive approach* (to a problem) takes in almost every aspect of it, just as a *comprehensive school* is intended to teach subjects right across the educational curriculum, not just the academic or technical strand. But the verb *comprehend* has for centuries also meant "have a mental grasp of or understand." The *Oxford Dictionary* (1989) shows that this is actually the first recorded meaning in C14 English, though the more classical meaning was in use then too. The notion of understanding is the primary meaning for **comprehensible** ("able to be understood"). Just occasionally **comprehensive** also shows this development of meaning as well, when used in the sense of "having understanding":

> *They were not fully comprehensive of the corruption within their ranks.*

Though recorded from time to time over the last three centuries, this usage is not common nowadays – mostly confined to formal style and deliberately lofty writing.

comprise, composed of or comprised of

Comprise is a verb over which many people pause, and three constructions are now acceptable with it. Traditionally it meant "include," "contain," as in:

> *The show comprises lesser known Spanish artists.*

This construction, still current, provides an alternative to the passive of *compose*, as in: *The show is composed of lesser known Spanish artists.* Between them they offer a stylistic choice between more compact expression (with **comprise**) or something less dense (with **composed of**). But the two seem to be blended in other uses of **comprise**.

* **comprised of** meaning "made up of," as in:
> *The show is comprised of lesser known Spanish artists*

This construction occurs more freely in American than British English in database evidence. The ratio of **comprised of** to **composed of** is about 1:5 in CCAE and 1:11 in the BNC.

* **comprise** meaning "combine to make up," "constitute":
> *Lesser known Spanish artists comprise the show*

This third construction is the mirror-image of the traditional use of **comprise**. It begins with the parts that make up the whole, rather than the whole which consists of certain parts. Approximately 25% of BNC examples, and more than 75% of CCAE examples use **comprise** this way, especially for numerical statements, as in:

> *Blacks comprise 60% of the department's employees.*

The verb **comprise** is clearly polysemous. Its particular meaning depends on whatever the writer puts as subject of the verb (the whole, or its parts).

Readers take their cue from that. The second edition of the *Oxford Dictionary* (1989) recognizes all three uses of **comprise**, as does *Webster's Third* (1986). None of them can now be considered incorrect.

American dictionaries allow *comprize* as an alternative spelling to **comprise**, but there's scant evidence of its use in CCAE. See further under **-ize/-ise**.

concensus or consensus

See **consensus**.

concerto

For the plural of this word, see under **Italian plurals**.

concessional clause

This type of adverbial clause is disussed under **clauses** section 4c.

conciseness or concision

These both serve as the abstract noun for the adjective *concise*, and are about equally current in American English, by the evidence of CCAE. But British English seems to prefer **conciseness**, which is much the more common of the two in data from the BNC. **Concision** actually appears much earlier, as a C14 loanword according to the *Oxford Dictionary* (1989). But it was never so widely used as to inhibit the formation of the English word **conciseness** in C17. The parity of *concise* with *precise* probably adds an element of uncertainty to the choice between **conciseness** and **concision**.

◊ Compare **precision or preciseness**, and see further under **-ness**.

concomitance or concomitancy

See under **-nce/-ncy**.

concord

See under **agreement**.

concrete or cement

See **cement**.

concrete nouns

These contrast with *abstract nouns*. They refer to visible, tangible things such as *apple, bridge, ceiling, house, student, water*, as well as observable aspects of behavior such as *laughing, running, shouting, typing*, and natural phenomena which have some measurable correlate, such as *electricity, heat, humidity* and *wind*. They may be either *mass nouns* like *flesh* and *water*, or *count nouns* like *apple* and *student*. See further under **count and mass nouns**.

concurrence or concurrency

See **-nce/-ncy**.

conditional

In languages such as French and Italian, the **conditional** is a special form of the verb which shows that an event or action may take place, not that it will. The **conditional** suffixes resemble those of the future tense, though they are distinctive:

          *French   je viendrais (*conditional*)
                     je viendrai (*future*)
          *Italian   (io) verrei (*conditional*)
                     (io) verrò (*future*)

English verbs have no **conditional** forms, and instead the modal verb *would* is commonly used to translate *conditionals* from French and Italian.

The **conditional** expresses the writer's judgement that the fulfillment of the verb's action depends on something else. For example:

Je viendrais mais je n'ai pas d'auto.
(I would come but I don't have a car.)
Si j'avais un auto, je viendrais.
(If I had a car, I would come.)

As the last example shows, **conditional** statements in English are often attached to a *conditional clause,* prefaced by *if, unless* or *provided that,* which are a type of adverbial clause. (See further under **clauses** section 4c.) *Conditional clauses* are sometimes divided into (a) *open* and (b) *impossible* ("*unreal,*" *hypothetical*) conditions. The first is illustrated in the last example above, the second in sentences such as *If I were a driver, I would take you with me.* See further under **subjunctive** section 2.

condominium and condo

The origins of **condominium** in C18 international law are now totally eclipsed by its domestic use, yet both involve joint management (of another country, or of the premises in which an apartment or unit may be individually owned, bought and sold). The domestic use of **condominium** began in C20 American English, and is now well established in Canada and increasingly familiar in Australia. It just registers its presence in the UK, in BNC references to a *holiday condominium on the Riviera* and the *superbly presented condominium...above Flatts inlet.* The plural of **condominium** is *condominiums* (see under **-um**).

The abbreviation **condo** appeared first in the 1960s, according to an *Oxford Dictionary* (1989) quotation, and it's current in Canada and Australia, according to the *Canadian Oxford* (1998) and the *Macquarie Dictionary* (1997). For Australians, **condo** is a natural member of the set of informal words ending in -o: see under **-o** section 1.

confederation and confederacy

In British English, official uses of **confederation** give it a high profile. It is of course extensively used in reference to trade union organizations (e.g. *Confederation of Shipbuilding and Engineering Unions*) and also employer groups such as the *Building Employers Confederation.* Trade union and employer groups in other countries are also designated this way, witness *Confederation of Czechoslovak Trade Unions* and *Swedish Employers' Confederation.* References to political alliances, real or hypothetical, are also expressed via **confederation**. All these applications make **confederation** much more familiar and contemporary in Britain than **confederacy**, whose uses are mostly historical, as in *a confederacy of peoples...in the region of the lower Rhine;* or *the confederacy associated with the Roman Empire.*

In American English, **confederacy** or rather **Confederacy** has the high profile in its very specific geo-historical meaning from the Civil War, when the *Southern States of the Confederacy* (south of the Mason–Dixon line and east of the Mississippi) took on the Union in the north. Those 11 southern states (*the Confederacy*) still form an identifiable subset of the US in terms of cultural politics, and community groups such as the *United Daughters of the Confederacy* help to keep it in the public consciousness. The word can also be used generically, as in *A confederacy of dunces,* the Pulitzer-prize-winning novel by John Kennedy Toole, but the novel's southern setting makes the connection with *the Confederacy* more than coincidental. Apart from its inescapable connection with the South, **confederacy** has a few other historical uses, in references to C18 alliances with American Indians (e.g. the *Iroquois confederacy*) and early baseball organizations (the *Iowa Baseball confederacy*). **Confederation** meanwhile shoulders a burden of generic references to trade, industry and professional groups, as in *the national confederation of publishers, a loose confederation of ranchers, miners, loggers,* and *that electronic confederation called the Internet.* In CCAE data, it occasionally appears as part of an institutional title, but much less often than in the BNC. Overall **confederation** seems to enjoy more general usage in American English than in British.

In Canadian English, **confederation** is frequently used as a generic term in place of *federation.* For Canadians, **Confederation** has historical significance in refering to the original (1867) federation of the four eastern provinces (Ontario, Quebec, Nova Scotia, New Brunswick). *The Confederation* now connotes all ten provinces.

confident or confidant(e)

These both relate to *confidence:* **confident** (adjective) means "having confidence in oneself," whereas a **confidant** or **confidante** (noun) is one who receives the confidences of others. Originally (up to C18) **confident** was the spelling for both noun and adjective.

Although **confidante** looks like a French loanword, the French themselves use *confidente.* Their word referred to a conventional stage character who was privy to the secrets of the chief characters. The English spelling of **confidant(e)** with *a* is conceivably a way of representing French pronunciation of the last syllable (with stress and a nasal vowel); at any rate it distinguishes it visibly from **confident**.

The presence or absence of *e* on **confidant(e)** might be expected to correlate with the sex of the person in whom one confided (with **confidante** for a woman, and **confidant** for the man). In practice **confidant** is used for both men and women, as dictionaries and databases confirm. And though **confidante** is more often used of women in the BNC and CCAE, there's no lack of counter examples among the British/American data: *he was a confidante of Mr Honecker; writer Gus B., the confidante of the New York social set.* Some usage writers, e.g. Burchfield (1996), *Canadian English Usage* (1997), Garner (1998), emphasize the need to use **confidante** for women only. We scarcely need it at all, given that **confidant** covers both men and women.

conform to or conform with

Of these two possibilities, Fowler (1926) commented that "idiom demands *conform to,*" and in both American and British English it's much the more common of the two. In data from CCAE as well as the BNC, **conform to** outnumbers **conform with** by about 5:1. This may seem to vindicate Fowler's judgement at the turn of the millennium, or rather his influence! But **conform with** continues to be used, perhaps under the influence of the phrase *in* *conformity with* where *with* is the standard collocation. There is nevertheless no requirement that the two constructions should match up, as is sometimes argued with *different/differ*. (See under **different**).

◊ See also **compared with or compared to**.

conjugations

The verbs of a language often fall into distinct classes or **conjugations** according to their patterns of inflection and characteristic vowels.

In Latin there were five major **conjugations**, the most distinctive of which was the first with *a* as its stem vowel. Its descendants in English are the many words ending in *-ate, -ator, -ate, -ation* and *-ative*. Most modern European languages have many more than five different classes of verbs, with numerous subgroups created by changes to word forms over the centuries.

The Old English **conjugations** involved seven types of "strong" verb as well as the so-called "weak" **conjugation**, both of which have fractured into small subgroups. Remnants of the strong **conjugations** still alter their vowels to indicate the past tense and past participle, and often add *(e)n* to the latter. They include:

sing	*sang*	*sung*	cf. *ring, swim*
ride	*rode*	*ridden*	*drive, write*
bear	*bore*	*borne*	*tear, wear*
break	*broke*	*broken*	*speak*
take	*took*	*taken*	*forsake*

Verbs of the weak **conjugation** simply add *-(e)d* or *-t* for both the past forms, though some also show vowel changes and spelling changes developed in Middle/ early modern English:

live	*lived*	*lived*	cf. *love, move*
keep	*kept*	*kept*	*creep, meet, sleep*
sell	*sold*	*sold*	*tell*
say	*said*	*said*	*pay*

Strong and weak elements are now mixed in verbs such as:

do	*did*	*done*
shear	*sheared*	*shorn*
show	*showed*	*shown*

See further under **irregular verbs**.

conjunctions and conjuncts

Though both **conjuncts** and **conjunctions** serve to join words together, only the second term is well known. The common **conjunctions** link words belonging to the same phrase or clause:

bread and butter   white or black coffee
The passengers were tired but happy.

Conjunctions also link whole clauses together, as in:

The baker had bread rolls but there were no bagels left.

When linking clauses, **conjunctions** serve either to *coordinate* them as equals, as in the examples above, or to *subordinate* one to the other. There are different sets of conjunctions for each type.

1 The major coordinating conjunctions are:

and but or nor yet

In grammatical terms they link together main clauses (see further under **clauses**). They appear at the head of a clause, and allow the subject following them to be deleted if it's the same as the one just mentioned. See for example:

Marion came and (she) demolished the cheesecake.
Others saw her at it yet (they) didn't comment.

Conjunctions like these can appear at the start of a sentence:

Others saw her at it. Yet they didn't comment.

The "conjunction" thus becomes a *conjunct*, forging a cohesive link with the previous sentence while being grammatically unconnected. (**Conjuncts** are further discussed under **adverbs** section 1; and exemplified in section 3 below.) Grammarians and some teachers have in the past objected to the use of *but* or *and* at the start of a sentence, presumably because they recognized them only as **conjunctions**, not as **conjuncts** (see further under **and** and **but**).

2 Subordinating conjunctions serve to link a subordinate clause with the main clause on which it depends (see **clauses** sections 3 and 4). They include:

how	*when*	*where*	*whether*	*why*
while	*since*	*as*	*before*	*after*
once	*till*	*until*	*(al)though*	*if*
because	*for*	*whereas*	*than*	

Complex subordinating conjunctions include:

as if	*as though*	*as soon as*	*as far as*
in case	*in order that*	*provided that*	*so that*

Many *subordinating conjunctions* also introduce nonfinite clauses e.g. *while dancing, once announced, if chosen.* New *subordinating conjunctions* can evolve out of adverbs, and are indeed in use. (For the status of *directly, however, likewise, plus, so, therefore, thus* as **conjunctions**, see under individual headings.)

3 The logic of conjunctions and conjuncts. Apart from their role in sentence grammar, **conjunctions/ conjuncts** relate ideas to each other, helping to show the logic behind the information offered. In fact they express a number of logical relationships – addition, contrast, causation or circumstance (especially time). These logical meanings are embodied in both *coordinating* and *subordinating conjunctions,* and in **conjuncts** and their paraphrases, as shown in the following table. **Conjunctions** whose status is marginal are shown in parentheses.

*Addition

conjunctions:	*and*	*(likewise)*
	nor	*or*
	(plus)	
conjuncts:	*additionally*	*also*
	alternatively	*besides*
	furthermore	*likewise*
	moreover	*plus*
	similarly	*too*
phrases:	*as well*	*in addition*
	in the same way	

*Contrast

conjunctions:	*although*	*but*
	(however)	*though*
	whereas	*yet*
conjuncts:	*however*	*instead*
	nevertheless	*otherwise*
	rather	
phrases:	*against this*	*by contrast*
	on the contrary	

*Causation

conjunctions:	*as*	*because*
	for	*since*
	(so)	*(therefore)*
	(thus)	

conjuncts:	consequently	hence
	so	then
	therefore	thus
phrases:	as a result	because of this
	for this reason	on account of this
	to this end	

*Circumstance

conjunctions:	although	as
	(directly)	since
	though	when
conjuncts:	granted	meanwhile
	next	now
	soon	still
	then	
phrases:	at this point	despite this
	even so	in that case
	in the meantime	that being so
	under the	up till now
	circumstances	

The table shows that the same word may signal more than one kind of logical meaning. Either temporal or causal relations can be expressed by *as, since, then,* depending on the statements they are coupled with. Because they are ambiguous in some contexts, writers need a repertoire of **conjunctions** and **conjuncts** from which to choose ones which clarify and underscore logical relations within the argument. Variety itself is important. If *thus* appears three times on the same page, its use begins to seem decorative rather than logical.

conjuncts

See under **adverbs** section 1, and **conjunctions**.

conjurer or conjuror

Both spellings are acceptable, and *Webster's Third* (1986) and the *Oxford Dictionary* (1989) both give preference to **conjurer**. Certainly **conjurer** was recorded earlier, in C14 English, while **conjuror** first appeared a century later. In Britain it gained ground over **conjurer** in C19, and now outnumbers it in the BNC by more than 2:1. In American English **conjurer** still prevails, by the evidence of CCAE data. The spelling with -*or* suggests some confusion with *juror,* and analogy with other "role words" derived direct from French. **Conjurer** makes it a simple English formation based on the verb *conjure.* See further under -**er/-or**.

conk or konk

See under **k/c**.

connectible or connectable

Both spellings are acceptable, and **connectable** can be justified on the grounds that the word is a C18 English formation, based on the verb *connect.* Yet the pressure to spell it **connectible** on the analogy of other Latin-derived adjectives such as *perfectible* is quite strong, and the *Oxford Dictionary* (1989) makes **connectible** its first spelling. The complete absence of the word from *Webster's Third* (1989) would nevertheless lead readers to expect it to be spelled in the regular English way (**connectable**), as with any undocumented word. See further under -**able/-ible**.

connection or connexion

See under -**ction/-xion**.

connector or connecter

These spellings with the Latin and the English suffix are juxtaposed as equals in many dictionaries including *Webster's Third* (1986) and the *Oxford Dictionary* (1989). **Connector** is always put first, which is fully vindicated by data from BNC and CCAE. In fact **connecter** makes no showing at all in either corpus, suggesting that it may be time for dictionaries to demote it from the headword. Yet **connecter** is still the natural English formation from *connect,* as it was for Faraday, pioneering electrical systems in early C19. Modern technical usage nevertheless has **connector,** perhaps on the analogy of *conductor, resistor* and other electrical terms. (See further under -**er/-or**.)

connotation

The **connotations** of words are the associations which they raise in the minds of people using them. These associations would be the same for most users: think of *holiday* or *holidays* which generally *connote* pleasure and relaxation – a day out of the regular week, or time out of the regular year for students and many working people. Yet the same word may hold special **connotations** for individuals and subgroups in the population. For working mothers, the school *holidays* or *vacation* raise mixed feelings because the words *connote* a time when life is actually more complicated. One needs to arrange care and entertainment for the children (and relax with them as far as possible), as well as continue one's normal working routine. The **connotation** of words may thus be rather different for speaker and listener, or writer and reader.

The **connotations** of words may also change over the course of time, as with *enthusiasm,* which is positively valued nowadays, though in C17 and C18 it was a derogatory word – associated with extreme religious emotion. The fact that **connotations** vary and change shows how unstable they are.

By contrast, the *denotations* of words (whatever they refer to or identify) are relatively stable. So *holidays* or *vacation* denote a period of days which makes a break in the normal schedules of work or study. Both students and working mothers would agree on that as the core meaning. Yet some words and especially slang have relatively little *denotation,* and their chief force is in their **connotation**. The slang uses of *screw* as a noun denoting "prison warder" or a verb meaning "have sexual intercourse" are heavy with contempt. The **connotations** serve your purpose if your aim is to insult, but make them unusable for neutral communication.

Apart from their positive or negative values, words often have stylistic **connotations**. Compare *read* with *peruse. Read* is the ordinary word for the skill which literate people take for granted; while *peruse* is the rather rare and formal word used mostly when asking your superior to read or scrutinize a document. *Peruse* turns reading into a superior activity, commensurate with the boss's status. A stylistic value is thus also a part of the **connotation** of a word, and something which can change or become neutralized. Rather formal words (like *vacation*) and colloquial ones (like *flu*) now merge with other elements of the standard language.

consensus or concensus

Dictionaries all agree that the word should be spelled **consensus**, because like *consent* it goes back to the Latin verb *consentire* ("agree"). Yet the spelling **concensus** persists. The *Oxford Dictionary* (1989) registers it as an obsolete variant of **consensus**, though without citations to demonstrate its use. Current use of **concensus** in both the UK and the US is confirmed by a number of examples in both BNC and CCAE, though they pale into insignificance beside the thousands of instances of **consensus**. A Google search of the internet in 2002 nevertheless found **concensus** in about 1.5% of all instances of the word. The numbers are thus small but pervasive, and the reason for their occurrence is not far to seek – in confusion with *census*, which is about public information if not public attitudes. The spurious link makes the spelling **concensus** a **folk etymology** (see further under that heading). Like other latinisms which are obscure to many in C21, **consensus** may eventually be (re)credited with an alternative spelling. ◊ Compare **idiosyncrasy or idiosyncracy**, and **supersede or supercede**.

consequent or consequential

These adjectives share some common ground in referring to that which follows as a result of something else, as in

> ... *a statement explaining the overbooking policy and the consequent risk to "reservations."*
> *The consequential shock almost paralysed him.*

Consequential in this sense is often a legal term, in BNC examples such as *indirect or consequential damages,* and the *consequential costs* or *losses* mentioned in accounting. But it also means "important," "weighty," in *a consequential congressional leader* or *a country more consequential than Granada,* among various examples from CCAE. With its extra syllable, **consequential** thus seems to have official or portentous overtones. The briefer **consequent** has a wider variety of uses in economic, scientific and social analysis.

consist of or consist in

In current English, **consist of** enjoys much more widespread use than **consist in**, outnumbering it by 20:1 in BNC data, and 75:1 in data from CCAE. Still some writers make a point of using **consist in** when identifying an abstract principle, and **consist of** when specifying the several (usually physical) components of something. The distinction is exemplified in the following:

> *True education does not consist in being taught just anything.*
> *The kit consists of scissors, thread and sewing cards.*

In fact this distinction emerged only in C20, and is more often observed in formal style than in impromptu speech. The verb *consist* actually has a trail of obsolete collocations behind it. Once upon a time it was *consist on* and *consist by*.

consistence or consistency

See under -nce/-ncy.

consonance or consonancy

See under -nce/-ncy.

consonants

See under **vowels**.

consortium

For the plural of this word, see under **-um**.

constitutionist or constitutionalist

See under **-ist**.

contact clause

This is a grammatical term for the relative clause without relative pronoun, such as *The video **you get with the appliance** explains how to use it.* In speech it is often the way *relative clauses* are expressed, where intonation makes very clear which noun they are attached to. The term was coined by Jespersen (1909–49), but is not used by the authors of the *Comprehensive Grammar* (1985) or the *Longman Grammar* (1999). See further under **relative clauses** section 1.

contagious or infectious

These both imply that something spreads from person to person, and provided it is not an identifiable disease, you could use either. Both have been used figuratively since C18. At first they mostly coupled with words implying negative social phenomena, such as folly and panic, but C19 saw **contagious** associated with vigor, and **infectious** with good humor, as well as other positive collocations of this kind.

In medical usage, it is important to distinguish them. **Contagious** there has the quite specific meaning of being spread from person to person by physical contact, while **infectious** simply means "communicable or capable of being spread by any means," making it the broader term. An *Infectious Diseases* hospital is concerned with those which are spread by water, moist air, insects etc., not just human contact.

contemporary or contemporaneous

As adjectives, both can mean "occurring at the same point or period in time," and both collocate with *with*:

> *Shakespeare was contemporary with Queen Elizabeth I.*
> *The use of cast iron in China was almost contemporaneous with that of forged iron in Europe.*

Some have suggested that **contemporaneous** usually couples with inanimates and **contemporary** with human beings, as these examples happen to show. But if there is any such tendency, it probably results as much from the fact that **contemporary** is an everyday word, while **contemporaneous** appears most often in academic and abstract discourse.

Only in C20 has **contemporary** (as adjective) developed the meaning "modern" or "of our times," which it does not share with **contemporaneous**. It appears in expressions such as *contemporary theatre,* as a substitute for the word *modern,* which by now sounds a bit old hat. This newer meaning of **contemporary** occasionally lends ambiguity to statements in which the older meaning could also apply:

> *Dickens shares with contemporary novelists a concern with social issues.*

Without further information the reader cannot tell whether C19 or C20/21 novelists are being invoked for comparison. Are they Dickens's *contemporaries*, or those of the writer/reader? Note that the noun **contemporary** is free of this ambiguity, and that, unlike the adjective, it is followed by *of*:

Dickens was a contemporary of Thackeray.

Other points to note:

* **Contemporary** has no adverb, but relies on **contemporaneous** for it: (*contemporaneously*)
* The variants *co-temporary* and *cotemporary* enjoyed considerable use in C17 and C18, but are now rare. They make no showing in CCAE, and there's only one example in the BNC. See further under **co-**.

contemptible or contemptuous

These adjectives are complementary in meaning. **Contemptuous** is the attitude of those who hold something (or someone) in *contempt*. Whatever they hold in *contempt* is **contemptible** – for them at least. Behind both words is the lost verb *contemn*, which was used by Shakespeare and in the King James bible. By C19 it survived only in literary usage: when uttered it could scarcely be distinguished from *condemn*. The judgement in both verbs is extremely negative, and still reinforced in the case of *condemn* by its use in law and religion.

content clause

Several kinds of subordinate clause which complement the main clause are grouped together as **content clauses**. Most common and familiar among the **content clauses** are the *noun clause,* as in:

They think *he likes it*
They asked *if I liked it.*
They realized *what was needed. . .*

Less common are the **content clauses** which conceptualize an abstract noun or pronoun, as in:

That he should retire had not occurred to him.
The suggestion *that he should retire* came as a surprise.

Recent grammars such as the *Cambridge Grammar* (2002) include also clauses with a mandative subjunctive (see under **subjunctive** section 1):

They suggested *that he retire immediately.*

The *Longman Grammar* (1999) uses the term *complement clause* to cover all these finite constructions, as well as nonfinite constructions with *-ing* or the *to*-infinitive which perform the same function. Compare:

We hope to come again.
We hope that they'll come again.

The finite *that*-clause allows a different subject, whereas the infinitive does not. A different subject is however possible with *-ing* complements:

I remember that he signed the cheque.
I remember him signing the cheque.
I must remember to sign the next cheque.

As the examples show, the *to*-infinitive expresses potential action rather than enactment of it.

continental, Continental and the Continent

In geography and geology, **continental** can refer to any of the five continents on earth. The noncapitalized form appears in more and less familiar concepts such as *continental shelf, continental drift, continental plate, continental lithosphere.*

But for the British, the capitalized form **Continental** (and **the Continent**) always means *Continental Europe.* This usage predates Britain's membership of the European Union, yet there are hundreds of examples in the BNC to suggest continuing ambivalence about belonging to the European continent. The English Channel is still the watery frontier for *touring the Continent* and partaking of *Continental dishes.* The *continental breakfast* is so well established in English idiom that hotels worldwide use it to identify the quick/inexpensive fast-breaker *minus* eggs, bacon and all the trimmings of the "full English breakfast." As that example shows, some lower-case uses of **continental** also mean "mainland European."
◊ Compare **subcontinental**.

continual or continuous, and continually or continuously

The line of demarcation between **continual** and **continuous** is no longer so sharp. Dictionary definitions in North America, Britain and Australia show that both are now used in the sense of "nonstop," the meaning which used to belong to **continuous**. Their interchangeability on this is evident in BNC examples such as *continual stream of persons* beside *continuous torrential rain.* The once distinctive use of **continual** ("occurring repeatedly, regularly or persistently") is also increasingly shared by **continuous**. Even if we put down to hyperbole examples such as *continuous criticism from the left of politics,* there's the unmistakable fact that *continuous assessment* is now standard educational jargon. (In practice, it is *continual assessment* – luckily for the students concerned. To be assessed repeatedly is bad enough, but to be assessed nonstop would be intolerable.) This and other institutional uses of **continuous** (*continuous monitoring, continuous period of employment, continuous compounding*) help to account for the fact that it is much more frequent than **continual** in BNC data (by more than 4:1). Note also that **continuous** (but not **continual**) can refer to the spatial dimension, as in *continuous tapering of the blade.*

As adverbs, **continually** and **continuously** also have much in common, though their relative frequencies in the BNC are reversed. Again there are examples of **continually** meaning "nonstop," as well as "happening regularly." Compare:

Payments through the year are not continually accrued

with

. . .fingers running continually through tousled blonde hair. . .

And there's **continuously** meaning "happening regularly" as well as "nonstop." Compare:

New species arrive continuously

with

I've lived in London continuously since 1975.

Spatial uses are again exclusive to **continuously**, as in: *The zone extends more or less continuously around the margins of the Pacific Ocean.* But the meaning of both **continuous(ly)** and **continual(ly)** now depends to a large extent on the phenomena to which they are applied.

◊ For the grammatical use of **continuous** in relation to verb forms, see under **aspect**.

continuance, continuation or continuity

Dictionaries in the US, UK and Australia indicate that **continuance** and **continuation** may be substitutes for each other, though each has its own centre of gravity. **Continuance** maintains stronger links with the verb *continue,* implying an unbroken operation or provision (e.g. *continuance of the publishing agreement*), or an uninterrupted stay in the same place or position (*continuance in office*). **Continuation** often implies resumption after a break, whether in the dimensions of space or time:

> *. . . the team's pathetic continuation of form from the previous season. . .*
> *Go up Church Road, then Hollyhome Lane, the continuation of it. . .*

The second example shows how **continuation** comes to mean the physical extension of something. Its capacity to take on more concrete meanings helps to make it much more frequent than **continuance** in present-day English (by more than 4:1 in the BNC).

Continuity emphasizes the lack of breaks or disjunctions in something, as for example in *continuity of service.* The word has assumed particular importance in the audiovisual mass media, where continuity of communication is a point of professional pride. Job titles such as *continuity girl* and *continuity man* identify the person who checks that there are no abrupt changes, inconsistencies, or unexplained pauses in the output. The **continuity** itself is the comprehensive script (for a broadcast) or scenario (for a movie) which details the words, music, sound effects (and camera work) which are going on simultaneously.

continuum

For the plural of this word, see **-um**.

contra-

This prefix originated in Latin as an adverb meaning "against or opposed to." It appears in Latin loanwords such as *contradiction* and *contravene,* and in a few modern English creations, such as:

> *contraception*　　*contradistinction*
> *contraindication*

The prefix is the same in modern Italian and Spanish, and from there we derive *contraband, contralto* and *contrapuntal.*

The so-called *Contras* in Nicaragua were right-wing guerrillas who enjoyed some support from the US government in their struggle against the left-wing regime of President Ortega. In this case *contra* is a clipped form of the Spanish *contrarevolucionario* ("counterrevolutionary"). As that example shows, English often prefers to use the prefix *counter-* instead of **contra-**. See further under **counter-**.

contractable or contractible

Both may turn up in discussions of medicine and health, but they have different applications. **Contractable** refers to something you may *contract,* such as a disease:

> *HIV-AIDS is contractable via shared needles.*

Contractible refers to the capacity of a muscle or other organ to *contract,* as in:

> *The eyelid works by a contractible muscle.*

See further under **-able/-ible**.

contractions

In writing and editing, this term is applied to two kinds of abbreviation, detailed below. Punctuation for the first type is much less uniform than for the second.

1. Contractions as shortened forms of single words from which the middle is omitted – e.g. *Mr, Dr* – as opposed to those in which the end is omitted e.g. *Prof., Rev.* This difference entails special punctuation practices for some writers and editors, who use a full stop/period with the second type but not the first (as just shown). They also treat foreign abbreviations such as *no* ("numero"), *viz* ("videlicet"), *vs* ("versus") this way (see **No(.)/no(.), versus** and **vide**). An older practice for marking **contractions** was to use an internal apostrophe to show where the word was condensed, as in *C'tee* for "Committee," and especially when it helped to show that the duplicated letter was intended, as in *A'asia* for "Australasia" (*Style Manual,* 2002).

The distinction between **contractions** and *abbreviations* was articulated for English by Fowler (1926), though he did not use the word **contraction**, and it seems to have developed as part of the British editorial tradition after World War II. The *Authors' and Printers' Dictionary* (1938) does not mention it; yet it is acknowledged as common practice in *Copy-editing* (1975), and shown in copious examples in the *Oxford Dictionary for Writers and Editors* (1981). Ritter (2002) notes the tradition as well as various inconsistencies that undermine it. Successive editions of the Australian government *Style Manual* (1966–2002) have maintained it, despite research showing the opposite trend (*Style on the Move,* 1993). In North America such **contractions** are known as *suspensions,* but the practice of punctuating them differently is not widespread. *Chicago Manual* (2003) mentions it only in passing, and associates it with the British and the French. In Canada the practice is mostly observed in government documents, according to *Canadian English Usage* (1997). Its anomalous consequences as well as its importance in French editorial practice are noted in *Editing Canadian English* (2000). So the English-speaking world is far from united over whether to distinguish **contractions** from other abbreviations by omitting the stop. Second-language users of English canvassed in the Langscape survey (1998–2001) were clearly more inclined than the British to use stops in **contractions** as well as abbreviations.

◊ For a full discussion of the options, see **abbreviations** section 2.

2. Contractions as telescoped phrases such as *don't, I'll, there's, we've.* In all such cases the apostrophe marks the place where a letter or letters have been omitted. Note that with *shan't* and *won't,* a single apostrophe is all that is used, even though they have shed letters in more than one place. (In C19 English they appeared with two, as *sha'n't, wo'n't.*)

Contractions like these affect one of two elements in the verb phrase:

* the word *not,* when it follows any of the auxiliaries:
> *isn't*　　*wasn't*　*can't*　　*couldn't*
> *doesn't*　*don't*　　*didn't*　*hasn't*
> *haven't*　*hadn't*　*mustn't*　etc.

* the *auxiliary* itself, especially following a personal pronoun:
> *I'm*　*you're*　*s/he's*　*we're*　*they're*　(*be,* present only)
> *I've*　*you've*　*s/he's*　*we've*　*they've*　(*have,* present only)
> *I'd*　*you'd*　*s/he'd*　*we'd*　*they'd*　(*have,* past)

I'd   you'd   s/he'd   we'd   they'd   (would)
I'll   you'll s/he'll we'll they'll (will)

The last set are sometimes said to be contractions of *shall,* but this is very unlikely. (See under **shall** section 2.)

As the list shows, the **contractions** from different auxiliaries are sometimes identical, e.g. *I'd, s/he's.* But the following verb helps to show whether *I'd* stands for *I had* or *I would.* When that verb is an infinitive, as in *I'd keep, I'd* must be "I would"; whereas with a past participle as in *I'd kept,* it is "I had." (See further under **auxiliary verb**).

In conversation and informal writing, auxiliary verbs can be telescoped with almost any kind of word or phrase which serves as the subject: a personal pronoun, a demonstrative or interrogative, a noun or noun phrase, and so on:

That's going too far.
There's a lot more rain coming.
Who'd want a thing like that?
The word's getting around.
The king of Spain's on his way here.

In just one instance the pronoun itself is contracted: *let's.* There were of course others like that in older English, e.g. *'tis, 'twas, 'twere,* which now survive as dialectal expression, as in the title of McCourt's novel *'Tis* (1999).

Contractions like those mentioned above are very common in speech, and appear increasingly in writing, in newspaper columns and magazines across the range from popular to quality press. Contracted forms such as *don't, won't, it's* and *that's* appeared quite often in Westergren-Axelsson's (1998) study of British publications of the 1990s. In the past they were felt to be too colloquial for the written medium, and editors of academic journals are still inclined to edit them out. The writers of formal documents may feel that they undermine the authority and dignity of their words. But the interactive quality that **contractions** lend to a style is these days often sought, in business and elsewhere. They facilitate reading by reducing the space taken up by predictable elements of the verb phrase, and help to establish the underlying rhythms of prose. For all these reasons, **contractions** are used from time to time in this book.

contralto

For the plural of this word, see **Italian plurals**.

convener or convenor

The spelling **convener** is older and better supported in the *Oxford Dictionary*'s (1989) citations, and the first preference in *New Oxford* (1998), *Merriam-Webster* (2000) and the Australian *Macquarie Dictionary* (1997) – all except the *Canadian Oxford* (1998), which prioritizes **convenor**. Data from CCAE puts **convener** ahead of **convenor** in American English by a factor of 2:1. But in Britain, **convenor** enjoys considerable support and is almost equally well represented in the BNC, as if the latinate *-or* suffix gives it a formal status that the common *-er* of English cannot. See further under **-er/-or**.

convergence or convergency

See under **-nce/-ncy**.

conversationalist or conversationist

British preference for the longer form is well known. **Conversationalist** is given priority in the *Oxford Dictionary* (1989), and it outnumbers **conversationist** by 17:1 in BNC data. Current American usage goes the same way: **conversationalist** is the only form to be found in CCAE, though *Webster's Third* (1986) registers **conversationist** as equal alternative.
◊ For other similar pairs, see under **-ist**.

conversion

This term (or *zero derivation*) is used by grammarians to refer to the word-forming process described under **transfers**.

conveyer or conveyor

Conveyer is the older form, and the one for ad hoc agentive uses such as *a conveyer of good news* (see further under **-er/-or**). But **conveyor** has established itself in the fields of law and engineering, and is the spelling normally used for any mechanical carrying device.

convince or persuade

The infinitive construction *convince X to...* provides an alternative to the clausal *convince X that...* See further under **persuade**.

cookie or cooky

Both spellings have been used for the gastronomic meanings of this word, though the Scottish bun was originally **cooky**, and the crisp American sweetmeat is almost always **cookie**. The American use is also familiar to the British, judging by its frequency in the BNC, though in the form of *chocolate chip cookies* rather than the *frozen yogurt cookie sandwich.* (The gastronomic potential of the **cookie** defies imagination!) Canadians and Australians tend to distinguish the **cookie** from other kinds of sweet biscuit by their shape, which is irregular on top from the fruit, nuts or chocolate chips added to the mixture.

Colloquial usage has added human dimensions to **cookie** itself, as:

1   a familiar or endearing term for a woman or girl
2   a man or person of a specified character, such as *smart cookie, tough cookie*
3   a cook or the cook's assistant at a camp. This is also spelled **cooky** or *cookee.*

Both human and gastronomic senses are at play in the slogan *Smart cookies don't burn,* used by pharmacists in Northern Ireland to publicize a campaign against sunburn.

In American English, **cookie** is a productive element in a variety of compounds, such as *cookie-pusher* (a term for someone in an unproductive service job, whether as a counter attendant or the diplomat who seems to devote disproportionate attention to social events) or the adjective *cookie-cutter* as in *cookie-cutter houses* or *a cookie-cutter movie* (i.e. something which seems stereotypical when it ought to be individual and original).

The most recent addition to **cookie**'s range of meanings is as an element of computer jargon. Computer programmers developing interactive software for the internet create a **cookie** to collect information about the users, which can be stored and read back for further applications.

co-op or coop

See under **co-**.

cooperate or co-operate

See under **co-**.

coopt or co-opt

See under **co-**.

co(-)ordinate, co(-)ordinator and co(-)ordination

On whether to use the hyphen with these, see under **co-**. For the grammarians' use of the term **co(-)ordination**, see further under **clauses** section 2.

copular verbs

Some languages do without them, but English always links the subject and *subject complement* of a clause with a **copular verb** (see under **complementation**). The verb *be* is the all-purpose *copula* which simply forges an existential link, whereas others indicate that the complement is a current or resulting state of affairs:

* current

appear	feel	keep	look	remain
seem	smell	sound	taste	

* resulting

become	come	fall	get	go
grow	prove	run	turn	

Modern grammars recognize that the *subject complements* of **copular verbs** can be either adjectives / adjectival phrases, noun phrases, or adverbs / adjuncts / adverbial phrases. Compare the following:

The reception was (very) successful.
The reception was a successful event.
The reception went well.

Obligatory adverbs of time and place (*the reception is here / at 6 pm*) often go with **copular verbs** (*Longman Grammar,* 1999). Alternative names for **copular verbs** are *copulative* or *linking* verbs.

coquette or cocotte

See **cocotte**.

cord or chord

See **chord**.

cornea

For the plural of this word, see under **-a**.

cornerways or cornerwise

For the choice between these, see **-wise**.

coronary, coronal and coronial

Though all three adjectives are ultimately connected with the Latin *corona* ("crown"), their applications in English make them quite distinct. The first two are both used in the description of anatomy: **coronary** to the crown-like structures of blood vessels, nerves or ligatures around a body organ or part; **coronal** to the upper section or "crown" of a body structure, such as the head. When used as nouns, **coronary** stands for *coronary thrombosis,* and **coronal** for *coronal suture,* the serrated line half-way up the sides of the skull.

The third adjective is a legal development of the Latin root, originating in Australia. **Coronial** connects with the *Coroner,* whose name makes him an agent of the Crown. His duties include holding a *coronial court* or conducting a *coronial inquiry* into the causes of death – in which **coronal** or **coronary** may also come up.

corporeal or corporal

As adjectives, both relate to the Latin word for "body" (see next entry), but their applications are quite distinct. **Corporeal** has the wider range of uses: in theological dialectic where *man has both a corporeal and a spiritual*; in law (*corporeal moveables, corporeal hereditament*); in philosophical discussions about the human condition. It finds its way into commentaries on higher and lower forms of art, from *Coleridge lamenting that there was a something corporeal in his [Wordsworth's] poetry,* to *Jed's group being on the point of bringing Satan into corporeal existence.*

Corporal leads a much more restricted life, now almost always bound up in the phrase *corporal punishment* (the striking of another person's body, usually with an instrument such as a stick or whip, to induce that person to mend his or her ways). Once common as a form of discipline in schools, its use has declined since the 1980s. But its punitive function lingers in the public mind, and because *corporal punishment* is so similar to *capital punishment* ("legal execution") the two get confused – as presumably in the mind of the caller to community radio, who urged that schools reintroduce *capital punishment* for those who daub graffiti on public walls.

From malapropism to folk etymology: the noun **corporal** ("noncommissioned officer") results from the misspelling of Old French *caporal* from Italian *caporale* (a derivative of *capo* ["head"]), no doubt under the influence of *corps* ("body of troops").

corps, corpse or corpus

These are, respectively, the French, English and Latin word for "body," though none of them nowadays refers to the living human form. The oldest of the three in English is **corpse**, going back to C14. It was earlier spelled *corse* and **corps**, and until about 1700 could refer to bodies either living or dead. Only since C18 has it been confined to the dead body, and only in C19 did the final *e* become a regular part of the spelling. Some explain the *e* as a backformation from *corpses,* the English plural of *corps;* yet many English words were spelled both with and without a final *e* in the early modern era.

Corps came from French in C18 with the silent *ps* of its French pronunciation. It survives in references to organized bodies of people, especially the *corps de ballet,* the *corps diplomatique*, and the military unit which consists of two or more divisions. *Esprit de corps* implies the "common spirit" of a group of people engaged in the same enterprise.

Corpus is the Latin form which appears only as a specialized word, in law, medicine and scholarship. Its legal use in phrases such as *corpus delicti* and *habeas corpus* is discussed under those headings. In medical and anatomical usage it appears in reference to complex structures such as the *corpus callosum* in the human brain. For scholars, a *corpus* may be either a collection of works by selected groups of authors, or a database of language material, sometimes homogeneous, sometimes heterogeneous. (See further under **English language databases**.)

The word **corpus** is usually pluralized in English as **corpora** (its Latin plural form) at least when it appears in scholarly documents. However the native English plural **corpuses** is often said and occasionally written. See **-us** section 3.

corpus delicti

This legal phrase, borrowed straight from Latin, means "the body of the crime." Lawyers use it in an abstract way to refer to the various elements which make up a criminal offence. But it's often (mis)applied by nonlawyers to material objects associated with a crime, and to the victim in a murder case. More lightheartedly, it's occasionally used to refer to a shapely female figure, as if the Latin *delicti* were somehow related to the English words *delicious* and *delight*.

The phrase *(in) flagrante delicto* ("as the crime was being committed") employs the same Latin word *delictum* ("crime"). It too is subject to some ambiguity, partly because of *flagrante*. See further under **flagrant or fragrant**.

corralled or corraled, corralling or corraling

Though redolent of American westerns and C19 frontiers of settlement, **corral(l)ed** and **corral(l)ing** find figurative applications in contemporary politics on both sides of the Atlantic, in securing votes, support and compliance. The stress on the second syllable of *corral* would lead you to expect double *l* in the inflected forms, and all British writers represented in the BNC use **corralled** and **corralling**.The *Oxford Dictionary* (1989) makes no comment on the verb inflections, curiously, since this usually implies that they are simple and regular. Paradoxically *Webster's Third* (1986) gives *-lled* and *-lling* as the only inflected forms, yet both spellings are in current American use. They are amply illustrated in CCAE: among 81 instances, the forms **corraled/corraling** are about 1 in every 3. Their use might be a routine application of the American practice of not doubling final *l* – except that there's no hint that Americans stress the word differently, i.e. on the first syllable. (See further under **-l-/-ll-**.) On this word then, American spelling proves more variable and less regular than the British.

correspond to or correspond with

In earlier usage, a clear distinction was made: **correspond with** meant "exchange letters with," and **correspond to** meant "have a similar function or shape," when two items were being compared. Nowadays **correspond with** is freely used in comparisons of function and shape, though still outnumbered by **correspond to** in data from both BNC and CCAE. The fact that the construction **correspond with** is gaining ground makes interesting comparison with *compare with*, which is losing ground to its rival. See **compared with or compared to**.

correspondent or co(-)respondent

A **correspondent** is a person who regularly writes letters or dispatches. **Co(-)respondent** is the legal term for the third party in a divorce suit. The hyphenated spelling used in Britain, Canada and Australia helps to prevent confusion between the two words. But to prove it's redundant, **corespondent** is

the regular spelling in US dictionaries. For *Webster's Third* (1986) this is in keeping with its normal practice for longer words formed with **co-**.

corrigenda and corrigendum

See under **-um**.

corrupter or corruptor

Unabridged dictionaries (*Oxford,* 1989, and *Webster's Third*, 1986) present **corrupter** and **corruptor** as equal alternatives. Yet database evidence on both sides of the Atlantic runs strongly in favor of the first. **Corrupter** is the only one to appear in the BNC, and it dominates 13:1 in CCAE. It is of course the natural spelling for an English derivative of the verb *corrupt,* though citations in the *Oxford* suggest that it varied with the latinate **corruptor** in previous centuries.

cortex

The plural of this word is discussed under **-x**.

cosh or kosh

See under **k/c**.

cosher or kosher

See **kosher**.

cosseted or cossetted

This curious word has come a long way from its origins down on the farm. It begins as the noun *cosset,* referring to a hand-reared lamb. The later verb adds the senses of petting and pampering, which allow human objects:

* a child (*her mother had cosseted her with supper in bed as a child*)
* a woman (*women of the ruling race were especially cosseted at [Indian] stations*)
* a media personality (*today he would sit in a think-tank, cosseted by secretaries and flattered by calls from talk-show producers*)

Figurative uses have it applied to physical comforts (*occupants are cosseted in a very spacious cabin*), and to economic commodities (*oil has for decades been cosseted with tax breaks*). BNC examples like these show that the word is frequently used in the passive, and almost always spelled **cosseted**, in keeping with the stress being on the first syllable. See further under **-t**.

cost

The past tense of this verb depends on its meaning. In ordinary use, when it means "be priced at," the past is the same as the present:

> *Don't miss a bargain. Yesterday they cost twenty francs. Today they cost fifteen.*

But in business usage, when **cost** means "estimate the monetary costs of doing or producing (something)," its past tense has the regular *-ed* inflection:

> *They costed the publication quite conservatively.*

◊ For other verbs without a distinct past form, see **zero past tense**.

cosy or cozy

This homely adjective for feeling warm and comfortable came into English via northern UK dialects, probably from Scandinavian sources (it seems to be related to the Norwegian verb *kosa,* "be comfortable"). As a noun it's used for the knitted or padded cover used to keep the teapot warm. For both uses the British prefer **cosy**, and there are few examples of **cozy** in the BNC. Australians share their preference, according to the *Macquarie Dictionary* (1997); whereas North Americans prefer **cozy**, and it dominates the data from CCAE. The American spelling accords with their general preference for *z* rather than *s* in such options. See under **-ize/-ise** and **-yze/-yse**.

co(-)temporary
See under **contemporary**.

cotyledon
This Greek word for the embryonic seed leaf takes an English plural **cotyledons**. Other botanical terms based on it do the same, witness *monocotyledons* and *dicotyledons*. See further under **-on**.

could or might
These two modal auxiliaries share some uses, most notably that of expressing possibility. Both can express the writer's opinion about the likelihood of a fact or event – that it was or is possible, or that it may occur in the future:

They could have been there.	*They might have been there.*
It could be a negative indicator.	*It might be a negative indicator.*

In formal writing, **could** and **might** are used this way about equally, according to the *Longman Grammar* (1999). British writers appeared slightly more inclined to use **might**, and Americans to use **could**, in Collins's (1988) research. But in the *Longman Grammar*'s conversational data, **might** is much less used than **could** in the possibility sense everywhere.

   Might once had a role in requesting permission in polite questions, though this now sounds very self-effacing. Compare:
   Might I have the keys please?
with
   Could I have the keys please?
Both **might** and **could** are less direct than *may* or *can* in questions (see further under **can or may**). For the use of *may have* instead of *might have* in subordinate clauses, as in *They said he may have been there,* see **may or might**.

   In conversation **could** is commonly used to express ability, a role that connects with its origins as the past tense of *can:*
   When he was younger, he could sing like Caruso.
This is about twice as frequent as its use to express permission, according to the *Longman Grammar.* However the ability sense sometimes shades into the other, as in:
   Until then, researchers could do surreptitious recording.
With its several uses, **could** is more versatile than **might**, and far more frequent overall. (See further under **modality and modal verbs**.)

   A curious detail of **could** is the *l* in its spelling, which is never pronounced, and only began to be part of its written form from 1525 on. The *l* was added to bring it into line with other modals *should* and *would,* where there are *l*s for good historical reasons. By a further irony, the *l* later disappeared from the pronunciation of *should* and *would,* so that they now rhyme with **could**.

could of
See under **have**.

councilor or councillor, and counselor or counsellor
Americans consistently prefer **councilor** and **counselor**, which have a large majority over the spellings with double *l* in data from CCAE. For **councilor** the ratio is 2:1, and for **counselor** it's more than 60:1. The single *l* spellings accord with the general American practice for final consonants before a suffix (see **-l-/-ll-**). The different ratios no doubt reflect the less consistent indications of *Merriam-Webster* (2000), which gives priority to **councillor** over **councilor**, but puts **counselor** ahead of **counsellor**. For the British, **councillor** and **counsellor** are standard according to *New Oxford* (1998), and they are overwhelmingly preferred in the BNC. Australian English is like British on this, whereas Canadian English positions itself between the British and American. Canadians prefer **councillor**, but use both **counsellor** and **counselor**, according to the *Canadian Oxford* (1998).

   The two words go back to quite separate terms in Latin: *concilium* ("assembly or meeting"), and *consilium* ("consultation, plan or advice"). The older meanings are still more or less there in *council of war,* and *wise counsel*. But the two words were often mistaken for each other in Middle English, especially with the interchanging of *c* and *s* by Anglo-Norman scribes (see under **-ce/-se**). The idea of consultation passed from the second to the first word, so that a *council* became not just a meeting, but a consultative and deliberative body constituted to meet at certain intervals. And *counsel* gained a collective sense, being used for "a group of legal advisers" from C14 on.

   Yet the old distinction between public meeting and private consultation seems to persist in the work of **council(l)or** and **counsel(l)or**, and helps to distinguish them. The **council(l)or** is a member of a publicly constituted body, whereas the **counsel(l)or** is usually consulted privately for his or her advice.

counseled or counselled
For the choice between these, see under **-l-/-ll-**.

count and mass nouns
Many nouns refer to things which can be counted, and so they can be pluralized, witness:

answers	books	doctors
fences	offices	telescopes

They contrast with **mass nouns** (also known as *noncount nouns*). These are almost always used in the singular because they refer to concepts, substances or qualities with no clear-cut boundaries. For example:

butter	education	honesty	information
keenness	mud		

In the singular, **count nouns** can be prefaced by either *a* or *the*, whereas **mass nouns** permit only *the*. Compare *the/an answer* with *the information*. As the examples show, **mass nouns** may be either concrete or abstract (see further under **nouns**).

   Some **mass nouns** can be used as **count nouns** under special circumstances. While *butter* is usually a **mass noun**, both cooks and supermarket assistants may speak of "all the butters in the fridge," meaning the various types of butter – salted, unsalted and cultured. This *countable* use of a noun shows that the *count/mass* distinction is not inherent in the word itself, but in its use. Quite a few nouns are regularly used both ways, sometimes with different meanings. Compare:

> The lambs suffered in the late frosts.
> The butcher has no more lamb.

Knowing which words and meanings are normally construed as **mass nouns** and as **count nouns** in British/American English is one of the more difficult points for non-native speakers. Regional varieties of English in Africa and Southeast Asia often permit *countable* uses of words which would be **mass nouns** in native-speaker varieties, for example:

> Please put your luggages over there. (Malaysian English)
> Thank you for your advices. (Nigerian English)

Linguists (Quirk, 1978; Wong, 1982) have pleaded for greater tolerance by native-speakers on this issue.

counter-

This prefix meaning "against" was borrowed from French. It came into English with loanwords such as *countermand* and *counterpoint*. In modern English words formed with it, it has developed other shades of meaning, suggesting opposition, retaliation or complementary action:

counterattack	counterbalance
counterfactual	counterinsurgency
counterintelligence	counteroffensive
counterproductive	countersign
countersink	counterweight

In the US **counter-** substitutes for *anti-* in *counterclockwise*, but this is the only instance.

Counter- is normally set solid with the word it prefixes, though some British writers would insert a hyphen before a following *r*, as in *counter-revolutionary*. The more important point to note is that *counter* should have space after it in compounds such as *counter lunch* and *counter service*, where it represents the word *counter* ("bench or table at which goods are sold"), not the prefix **counter-**.

coup de

The French word *coup*, literally "stroke," appears in several phrases which have become naturalized in English. To translate it as "act" (rather than "stroke") gets closer to the meaning generally, but it develops a special character in each of the following phrases:

coup d'état	sudden political move, one which overthrows an existing government
coup de foudre	a thunder bolt, or love at first sight
coup de grâce	blow or shot which finishes off someone in the throes of death
coup d'oeil	a quick glance which takes in a whole scene at once
coup de théâtre	dramatic act designed to draw attention to itself

Clearly it's what goes with **coup de** that dictates its meaning. However when *coup* is used on its own in English, it always means *coup d'état*.

coupe or coupé

In French the accent always serves to distinguish these two, but in English it is capricious. **Coupe** without an accent is really the French for "cup," and

it appears most often on menus in the names of desserts – *coupe de fruits* etc. for a sweet, colorful concoction served in a glass dish.

Coupé, literally "cut back," refers to a road vehicle. Originally a type of carriage, it now means a luxury car which seats only two people, with a long, sloping back aerodynamically designed for speed. However the distinguishing accent is not necessarily there when the word is printed in English texts, and this has fostered a pronunciation of the word with one syllable. It makes it identical with the word used on menus.

Even stranger, confusion between the two words means that the **coupe** featured on English menus is sometimes given an accent – just to assure you of *haute cuisine*. To those aware of the difference, a *coupé de fruits* then suggests the ultimate cornucopia: a luxury sports car used to transport a harvest festival supply of glorious fruits to your table!

couple (of)

American and British English differ slightly on the use of *couple* in quantitative expressions. For the British, it's always *a couple of* as in *a couple of beers* or *a couple of weeks later*. Americans use both *a couple of* and just *a couple*, the latter well represented in CCAE data such as: *just a couple years later, a couple dozen boys*, and *a couple hundred fellow deputies*. The *Oxford Dictionary* (1989) records it from the 1920s, and *Webster's English Usage* (1989) concludes that it has a place in ordinary prose, i.e. prose that does not have pretensions. The briefer American form brings the expression into line with other complex determiners such as *a few*, and removes it from the open-ended set such as *a pair of*, in which *pair* becomes the head of the noun phrase. (See further under **noun phrase** and **determiners**.)

court martial or court-martial, and courts(-)martial or court(-)martials

This is one of the few words that Americans are more inclined to hyphenate than the British. The fact that *Webster's Third* (1986) puts a hyphen in both the noun and verb forms may well account for **court-martial** being almost 7 times as frequent as **court martial** in data from CCAE. The *Oxford Dictionary* (1989) meanwhile makes **court martial** the form for the noun and **court-martial** the verb. However British writers do not necessarily toe the Oxford line, and in the BNC, **court-martial** appears in about 1 in every 2 instances of the word used as a noun.

The components of **court(-)martial** are in French word order rather than English, which is the reason for its traditional plural **courts-martial** or **courts martial** (see **plurals** section 2). In BNC data, almost all of the handful of plurals are **courts martial**. There is 1 example of the anglicized plural **court-martials**, which would be "incorrect" according to the *Oxford*. Both plurals are acceptable in American English according to *Webster's*, which registers them as alternatives. **Courts-martial** is still the preferred form in CCAE data, outnumbering **court-martials** by 16:1.

The inflected forms of the verb may be *court-martialled* or *court-martialed*, and *court-martialling* or *court-martialing*, in keeping with the normal British/American divergence on the doubling of final *l*. See further under **-l-/-ll-**.

131

cousins

Are they my *second cousins,* or my *first cousins once removed?* Strictly speaking, they cannot be both. To sort it out, the question to ask is whether they share one set of the grandparents with you. If the answer is yes, then you must be *first cousins.* If the closest common ancestors are your greatgrandparents, then you're *second cousins.*

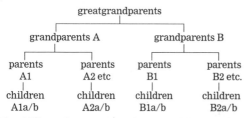

The children of parents A1 and A2 are all *first cousins,* but they are *second cousins* of the children of parents B1 and B2.

The word *removed* means being a generation apart, in either the *first* or *second cousin* line of descendants. So A1a/b and A2a/b are the *first cousins once removed* of B1 and B2 (because B1/B2 have the same grandparents as A1/A2). And if life and time permit, the children of A1a/b and A2a/b would be *first cousins twice removed* from B1 and B2. But when the generations don't line up exactly (as often), the terms *second/third cousin* are sometimes loosely applied to a *first cousin once/twice removed.*

Note also *cousin(s)-german,* an old legal term for *first cousin(s).*

cozy or cosy

See **cosy.**

-cracy

This Greek element meaning "rule (by)" is used in both ancient and modern formations to identify specific kinds of government. We find it in purely Greek words such as *democracy, plutocracy* and *theocracy,* as well as contemporary hybrids such as *bureaucracy, mobocracy* and *squattocracy.*

While **-cracy** forms abstract nouns, its counterpart *-crat* makes the corresponding agent noun "one who participates in rule by," for both older and newer formations. Thus *democrat* stands beside *democracy, bureaucrat* beside *bureaucracy* etc.

Note that *idiosyncrasy* doesn't belong to this set, despite increasing use of the spelling *idiosyncracy.* See further under **idiosyncrasy or idiosyncracy.**

cranium

The plural of this Latin word depends on whether it serves as a technical term in anatomy, or as a jokey reference to the head. Thus a discussion of the *crania of Neanderthal man* would use the Latin plural; and an off-handed comment about getting something into the *thick craniums of politicians* would be the natural context for the English. See further under **-um.**

crayfish or crawfish

Piscatorial specialists know these as different species, but in general usage they are used synonymously to refer to the increasingly rare edible freshwater lobster. In some parts of the world, **crayfish** is also used for the marine spiny lobster. Both spellings are

effectively folk etymology, attempts to render the Middle French loanword *crevis* into meaningful English elements. English transliterations from C15 on make *fish* out of the second syllable, while trying to capture the sound of the first by anything from *crea-* to *crey-* to *kre-* to *cray-.* The variant **crawfish** from C17 finds an English explanation for the first syllable, though *craw* is usually associated with birds.

Both forms of the word survive in the UK, though **crayfish** is much more common in BNC data, outnumbering **crawfish** by about 3:1. In the US, **crawfish** is the more widely known term, and outnumbers **crayfish** by about 3:2 in data from CCAE. **Crawfish** nevertheless has strong associations with Louisiana, so that *crawfish étoufé* ("stuffed crawfish") comes with New Orleans jazz, so to speak. The greater use of **crawfish** in American English has very little to do with its colloquial use there as a verb, meaning "back out (of a political position or action)." For example: *Do we crawfish? Or do we help?* – asked amid discussion of whether to intervene in support of an endangered African leader, fighting for his country's independence. But examples of this in CCAE can be counted on the fingers of one hand.

credible or creditable

These words sometimes overlap in modern usage, because of the newer, colloquial use of **credible.** Essentially **credible** means "believable," as in a *credible account of the accident.* From this it is extended colloquially to mean "convincing," and applied to anything from a politician's words, to the performance by an artist or sports figure:

> *In this last race before the Derby, he's looking very credible.*

The corresponding adverb can also be found with this extended meaning:

> *Hughes played very credibly in B-grade last season.*

If they were rare, these usages might be explained as slips of the tongue for **creditable** ("deserving credit or respect") and its counterpart *creditably.* Yet **creditable** (and *creditably*) are less common and more formal words, ones more often written than said, so they seem unlikely targets in impromptu speaking or commentary.

This colloquial extension of **credible** as "convincing, impressive" brings it remarkably close to meaning the same as *incredible* in its colloquial sense, "amazing, impressive." Not often do a word and its opposite coincide. To borrow the name of a popular TV program: *That's incredible!*

credulity or credibility

These words mostly complement each other, **credulity** meaning "a willingness to believe" and **credibility** meaning "quality of being believable." But the negative tones of the adjective *credulous* ("being too willing to believe") seem to impinge on **credulity,** and make us uncomfortable about saying that something *strains my/your credulity.* Increasingly the phrase we hear uttered is *strains my/your credibility,* and dictionaries now add the meaning "capacity to believe" to **credibility.** Meanwhile *credulousness* is available if we want to stress the fact of being too willing to believe something.

crematorium

For the plural of this word, see -um.

crème de la crème

To be the cream of society is not enough. You have to be **crème de la crème** ("cream of the cream"). The elitist symbolism of cream goes back at least four centuries in English, to when Mulcaster (1581) described "gentlemen" as "creame of the common" (= community). Yet having floated to the top (in those days before milk was homogenized) it could be difficult to maintain your distinctive position except by cultivating things French, and **crème de la crème** makes its appearance in C19, to satisfy that need. To enhance the phrase even further in English, some writers replace the proper grave accents with circumflexes: *crême de la crême!*

The French themselves distinguish carefully between *crème* ("cream") and *chrême* ("oil used for anointing"). Both words actually derive from the same medieval French word *chresme* ("oil for anointing"). But in standard French they have always had different accents, reflecting the belief that they had separate origins.

crenellated, crenelated and crenulated

All these go back to Late Latin *crena* ("a notch"), which is the source of French *crenel* or *crenelle* ("little notch") and of neo-Latin *crenula*. The French words underlie architectural uses of **crenel(l)ated**, while the neo-Latin word becomes **crenulated** or **crenulate** in botany. The shapes referred to also diverge: **crenel(l)ated** normally implies the squarish pattern of projections associated with castle battlements, whereas **crenulate(d)** applies to a pattern with rounded projections and narrow notches (as of certain leaves). The spelling alternatives for **crenel(l)ated** correlate with the usual American/British divide over single and double *l* (see -l-/-ll-). Only **crenellated** appears in the BNC, and in CCAE the data runs strongly in favor of **crenelated**.

creoles

See under **pidgins**.

crescendo

This Italian musical term for a rise in pitch is so well established in standard English as to take an English plural. Both **crescendos** and **crescendoes** are recognized in *Webster's Third* (1986) and the *Oxford Dictionary* (1989), but database evidence from the US and the UK shows that **crescendos** is now much the more common of the two. (See further under -o.) *New Oxford* (1998) also lists **crescendi**, allowing for the musical cognoscenti (see **Italian plurals**).

Becoming standard English has also meant extensions to the meaning of **crescendo**. In the familiar idiom *reach a crescendo* it effectively means "climax," despite musicians and others who would insist that it only means "ascent towards a climax." This meaning is registered as acceptable in both the *New Oxford* and *Merriam-Webster's* (2000), and database evidence has it in various constructions, including *build to a crescendo* and *rise to a crescendo*. As often, technical terms borrowed from specialized areas acquire new meanings in common usage, and these are not under the specialists' control.

crevasse or crevice

These words are in fact from the same source, the medieval French *crevace*, but centuries of separation have helped their spellings and meanings to diverge. **Crevice** meaning "fissure or crack" came into English in C14, as a variant spelling of the original French word. **Crevasse** entered English only in C19, with different meanings on either side of the Atlantic. In the Deep South (probably on loan from Louisiana French), it's recorded from 1814 on to mean a "breach in the bank of a river." A little later than that, British alpine explorers brought back from Switzerland the same word as meaning "deep chasm in a glacier," and this meaning has spread with **crevasse** to other parts of the English-speaking world.

cri de coeur

This French phrase means "a cry from the heart," a plea which is spontaneous, intense and free of affectation. A cry *de profundis* (Latin for "out of the depths") is less personal but more desperate. The words come from the Vulgate version of the beginning of Psalm 130: "Out of the depths have I cried unto thee."

crier or cryer

The spelling **crier** obeys the general rule for verbs ending in *y* (see -y>-i-); and it's overwhelmingly preferred in both American and British databases. It appears in newspaper mastheads, such as the *CROFTON NEWS-CRIER,* and other conventional phrases such as *town crier / market crier*, which help to support more generic uses: *I am not a crier* (="I did not sit and cry"). **Cryer** meanwhile is almost always a proper name, as in *Don Cryer* etc.
◊ Compare **flyer or flier.**

crime passionnel

This French phrase meaning "crime of passion" is not an official legal term, yet it highlights the different treatment given under French and English law to crimes (especially murder) prompted by sexual jealousy. The *Encyclopaedia Britannica* of 1910 explains it thus: "French juries almost invariably find extenuating circumstances" by which to acquit the murderer. This coincides with an English stereotype of the French: as people for whom the affairs of the heart are paramount. The principle for "crimes of passion" seems to be there in the French *Code Pénal*, article 324, which allows husbands finding their wives *in flagrante delicto* to shoot them. Whatever the legal issues, English spelling of the phrase is often erratic. Instead of the French spelling (as above), it may appear as *crime passionel, crime passionelle* and *crime passionnelle*.

criterion and criteria

Dictionaries all present these as the standard singular and plural forms for this Greek loanword (see further under -on). **Criterion** is in fact the less common of the two, outnumbered by **criteria** by more than 1:3 in the BNC and almost 1:4 in CCAE. Thus **criteria** is far more familiar for many, a fact which helps to explain its increasing use as a collective or singular noun. This grammatical development has probably gone further outside Britain than within, but the BNC itself contains examples such as *capability should be the* main criteria and *the Government [should] adopt value for money as its criteria.* In CCAE data, juxtapositions of *the one criteria* and *the only criteria is* clearly show the singular interpretation of the word. In other examples it's quite ambiguous. How many **criteria** are at stake in *That is a substantial increase by any criteria?* For public speakers such ambiguity may well provide rhetorical inflation of what is strictly speaking only one **criterion**.

Criteria not uncommonly serves for the singular in conversation, and in research among young Australian adults by Collins (1979), more than 85% treated it as a singular. *Webster's English Usage* (1986) has citations for it from the 1940s, from a variety of sources including the advertising flyers of certain well-known educational publishers, mass-circulating magazines and academic journals. It notes also the use of the analogical plural **criterias** in speech, though not captured in print. *Webster's Third* (1986) and the *Oxford Dictionary* (1989) also offer **criterions** as an alternative, but it occurs only once in transcribed speech in the BNC, and not at all in data from CCAE.

Though the use of **criteria** as a collective or singular belies its Greek origins, it would not be the first classical loanword to undergo this shift in modern English. Compare *data, media* and other Latin loanwords, whose classical plurals also end in *-a,* and which are also now construed in collective and singular senses. (See further under **-a** section 2.) The key issue for writers and communicators is to decide whether they want their audience to be aware of one or many **criteria** – and to spell it out if it is just one.

The latinized *criterium* is recognized as a common noun by unabridged dictionaries, and appears in the names of racing competitions from France. Being a latter-day formation, its plural is *criteriums* as in *motor cycle criteriums.* See further under **-um.**

Croatia

Once a part of Yugoslavia, **Croatia** declared its independence in 1992 and is recognized by United Nations as a separate state. See **Yugoslavia.**

crochet, crotchet and crotchety

Both these ultimately connect with the French diminutive *crochet* ("little hook"). **Crotchet** was borrowed much earlier, and from C15 had its distinctive English spelling for the musical note which is a quarter semi-breve – though not drawn with a hook like the quaver. In this, the English seem to have misapplied the word *croche* used by the French for the quaver. The term **crotchet** persists in the UK and Australia, but has been replaced by *quarter note* in North America.

By C16 a figurative use of **crotchet**, having *crotchets in the head* (i.e. *bees in one's bonnet*) had added the sense of "whimsical idea" to the word. This sense deteriorated into "perverse, contrary notion," whence the adjective **crotchety** ("irritable, contrary, cranky").

The craft of **crochet** seems to have come into English in the middle C19, and the word appears as both noun and verb. Its French-style pronunciation raises the question of how to spell the inflected verb forms, and whether the *t* should be doubled or not. Dictionaries all propose the regular *crocheted* and *crocheting.* For other French loanwords which raise the same issue, see **-t.**

crocus

The most familiar flower of spring takes an English plural *crocuses* (not the Latin *croci*). Dictionaries agree on this, and database evidence points almost entirely the same way. For the plurals of similar Latin botanical words, see under **-us.**

cross-

This prefix-cum-combining form with its several meanings ("across," "counter," "in the shape of a cross") has generated an extraordinary mass of compounds, some hyphenated, some set solid and some spaced. Compare:

cross-institutional   crossword   cross stitch

Dictionaries often diverge on whether to hyphenate them, and all three settings may be found with a few such as *cross talk.* Where they differ, the *Oxford Dictionary* (1989) is usually inclined to hyphenate *cross-breed, cross-section* etc., where *Webster's Third* (1986) either sets the two elements solid as in *crossbreed,* or spaces them as in *cross section.* See further under **hyphens.**

crossways or crosswise

See under **-wise.**

crudité or crudity

The **crudités** (raw vegetables served with a dip at cocktail parties) are certainly not intended to be seen as evidence of **crudity.** They remind us that *crude* has come a long way in English from meaning "uncooked, raw, unprepared," which its counterpart in French (*cru*) still does. This meaning was overtaken in C18 English by figurative senses such as "lacking in maturity and polish" and "lacking in good character and manners," and these are now dominant in *crude* and **crudity.** The only fossil of the earlier meaning of *crude* is in *crude oil,* but that will scarcely help you to appreciate the delights of the **crudités** put before you.

crueler or crueller, cruelest or cruellest

American writers go for **crueler/cruelest,** which are strongly preferred in data from CCAE, although *Webster's Third* (1986) allows both forms as alternatives. The *Oxford Dictionary* (1989) is silent on the matter, which normally means that the inflected forms are expected to be regular (i.e. **crueler/cruelest**). Spellings with one *l* are the only ones to appear in its citations after 1700 (as the absolute form of the word became *cruel* rather than *cruell*). But British editorial preference for the spellings with double *l* is visible in T. S. Eliot's *Waste Land,* which in the Faber and Faber edition (1944 and later) begins:

April is the cruellest month

The spellings **crueller** and **cruellest** dominate in data from the BNC, in keeping with the British convention of doubling the final *l.* See further under **-l-/-ll-.**

crumby or crummy

Those who wish to draw attention to the crumbs on the tablecloth would naturally use **crumby.** Dictionaries all distinguish it from the disparaging word **crummy** ("of poor quality"), as in *a crummy second-hand car* – though it's a C19 variant of **crumby** (presumably a reference to the crumbs on the floor, brushed off the rich man's table). This disparaging sense and the spelling **crummy** dominate in

American and British databases, and seem to take over even when **crumby** could be appropriate, as when referring to the children's *crummy eating habits* or the *crummy cafeteria lunch*.
◊ Compare **balmy or barmy.**

crystallized, crystalized and crystallised

This derivative of *crystal* is the only one to present spelling options. In American English, it could be **crystallized** or **crystalized**, according to *Merriam-Webster* (2000), but the first spelling outnumbers the second by about 6:1 in data from CCAE. *New Oxford* (1998) puts **crystallized** ahead of **crystallised**, though British writers use them in almost equal numbers, by the evidence of the BNC. Canadians follow the American first preference, according to *Canadian Oxford* (1998), whereas Australians are more likely than any to use **crystallised**, by the *Macquarie Dictionary* (1997). The divergent regional preferences for single or double *l* are discussed at **-l-/-ll-**, and for *-ise/-ize* at **-ize/-ise**.

Other derivatives of *crystal* such as *crystalline, crystallography* are always spelled with double *l*, on both sides of the Atlantic, because of their antecedents in French, Latin or Greek.

-ctic/-xic

These endings create variant forms: *anorectic/anorexic* and *dyslectic/dyslexic* for the adjectives associated with *anorexia* and *dyslexia*. In both cases, the form with **-ctic** is the older one, dating (in the case of *anorectic*) from C19. The spellings with **-xic** have been current since the 1960s, and dominate in contemporary data from both American and British databases. They forge a more visible and audible link with the name of the disorder – though this has not prevented them from being stretched in conversation to cover conditions that are hardly pathological (as when *dyslexic* means "forgetful," and *anorexic,* that someone has lost a little weight).

The C16 adjective *apoplectic* (relating to *apoplexy*, "a stroke") has no alternative in "apoplexic" – as yet. Its current use (since the 1960s) to mean "enraged" may change that.

-ction/-xion

These have been alternative spellings for a small group of nouns:

connection	or	*connexion*
deflection	or	*deflexion*
genuflection	or	*genuflexion*
inflection	or	*inflexion*
reflection	or	*reflexion*

Current usage everywhere nowadays prefers **-ction**, and **-xion** seems increasingly old-fashioned. The forms with **-xion** were borrowed straight from Latin, and reinforced by common knowledge of Latin. With declining knowledge of Latin, the words have been adapted under the influence of the related verb (*connect, deflect* etc.). The only word like these which steadfastly remains as **-xion** is *complexion* – no doubt because of the lack of a related verb.

The choice of **-ction** or **-xion** doesn't affect the meaning of the nouns that still allow it. Note by way of contrast that the adjectives *reflective* and *reflexive* have quite separate realms of meaning, and cannot be interchanged: see **reflective or reflexive.**

cui bono

This rather elusive Latin phrase asks the question "for whom (is/was) the benefit?" or, less literally, "who gains (or gained) by it?" It was originally used by Cicero when defending his clients in court, as a way of querying the motivation for committing a crime. But since its first appearance in English in C17, it has also been taken to mean "to what end?" Several citations in the *Oxford Dictionary* (1989) have it questioning whether something is of practical utility, and being used to express utilitarian values.

cuisine minceur

See under **nouvelle cuisine.**

cul-de-sac

Translated word for word, this unlikely French phrase means "bottom of the bag." In English it has become the byword for a "dead-end" of some kind – structures and situations from which one can only exit the way one came in. In anatomy the **cul-de-sac** is a bodily organ like the appendix which is not a passage through to another, and can become dangerously blocked. In military manoeuvres, a **cul-de-sac** is the difficult position of a force which finds itself checked in front and on both sides, so that the only way out is backwards. In suburban terrain however, the **cul-de-sac** means a quiet street with no through traffic, the kind of street that urban planners try to build into new subdivisions.

In French the plural is *culs-de-sac,* but the hyphens encourage writers to treat it as a compound, and to pluralize it as *cul-de-sacs*. See further under **plurals** section 2.

cum

The Latin preposition for "with" works conjunctively in English, as in *Christmas-cum-birthday present*, to join nouns which identify something or someone with a dual function. It lends itself to ad hoc formations, such as *imitation-cum-spoof, boutique cum museum, economist-cum-strategist, rock star-cum-prodigal son,* among hundreds of examples from both British and American databases. As the examples show, hyphens may or may not be there, and the tendency is to restrict them to either side of **cum** itself, rather than go for a hyphen extravaganza, as in *insurance-magnate-cum-art-collector.*

cum laude

This phrase, borrowed from Latin, means "with praise." It is found in connection with American college degrees, to distinguish four levels of honors:

cum laude	distinction
magna cum laude	with great distinction
summa cum laude	with the greatest distinction
maxima cum laude	″　　″　　″　　″

These phrases all refer to degrees achieved competitively through the examination process. The degree *honoris causa* is acquired without examination, and given as a personal accolade – by universities anywhere in the world.

Other Latin expressions used in connection with exam results are *aeq.,* an abbreviation for *aequalis* ("equal"); and *proxime accessit* (or *prox. acc.*) ("s/he came next"). The latter is some consolation to the person who was the runner-up for a special award or prize.

cumin or cummin

The first spelling is preferred overwhelmingly in contemporary English, by the evidence of British and American databases. **Cumin** with a single *m* also maintains the spelling of its Latin and Greek antecedents.

cumquat or kumquat

See under **k/c**.

cupfuls or cupsful

See under **-ful**.

curb or kerb

In British and Australian English the spelling **curb** serves for the verb "restrain," the noun "restraint," and various restraining devices; while **kerb** is for the concrete or stone step that divides the roadway from the footpath. In American and Canadian English, all are spelled **curb**.

The source of all those meanings is the French word *courbe*, literally "curve." The idea of restraint comes from the **curb**, i.e. curved bit in a horse's harness. The **kerb** on the street evolved from the **curb** which was originally a curved frame or framework around wells and barrels, and then extended to square or rectangular frameworks, including those around trapdoors and along the roof. The spelling for these extensions of the word varied from **curb** to *kirb* and **kerb** – hence the latter for the stone edge that marked the carriageway of improved London streets in C19. But like other late developments in British spelling, it has never caught on in American English.

curly brackets

This is an alternative name for *braces*. See **brackets** section 1c.

currant or current

Getting *-ent* and *-ant* in the right places is a problem with a number of English words (see under **-ant/-ent**); and with **current** and **currant** it has meaningful consequences. Most of the time writers want **current**, which has many more uses in English, as a noun for running water and electricity, as well as an adjective meaning "happening now." All those senses derive from the Old French word for "running" – *corant* – though the word was respelled in English according to its Latin antecedent.

The spelling of **currant**, the small dried fruit which is the staple of Christmas cakes, has a bizarre history. *Currants* were originally named as "raisins of Corinth" (the Greek place with which they were associated), and some medieval recipes give their name in full, as *raisins de corauntz*. Many recipes then reduce the phrase to the last element *corauntz,* which reflected French pronunciation of the placename. The spelling *corauntz* had quite a vogue in C15 England, but English cooks often interpreted it as a plural word, as we see from respellings of it as *corantes, currants* and even *currence.* (See under **false plurals** for other examples.) From these, singular forms were derived in C16 and C17, including *coren, coran, curran, current* and **currant**.

The word **currant** is also applied to quite different plants of the family Ribes, the *redcurrant* and the *blackcurrant*, which are shrubs not vines. Their spelling is also insecure, witness the supermarket product labeled *redcurrent jelly* – an electrifying dish!

currency

See Appendix IX for the names of **currencies** in different countries.

curriculum

The plural of this word is discussed under **-um**.

curriculum vitae

The **curriculum vitae** or *CV* assumes great significance in the UK as the passport to a new job. The portentous Latin suggests a document on "the course of one's life," something you might present on Judgement Day. But strategically what's needed is an outline of your working career so far, not a complete autobiography – a *resumé* as Americans would call it. A **curriculum vitae** begins with a few personal facts, such as age, nationality, marital status, and highest level of education achieved; and then lists the positions you have held, in chronological order but starting with the present. It may help to provide notes on the duties and responsibilities attached to each, if the job titles are less than self-explanatory.

Curriculum vitae is usually abbreviated as *CV* without stops. The lower case form **c.v.** is occasionally used, but always with stops. See further under **abbreviations** section 2.

To conform with its Latin origins, the plural of **curriculum vitae** should be **curricula vitae** (or **curricula vitarum**). But most people when speaking would pluralize it as "curriculum vitaes," as for other foreign compounds in English, and the BNC contains a few examples from edited documents. See **plurals** section 2.

curtsy or curtsey

In most dictionaries **curtsy** and **curtsey** are presented in that order. This accords with current usage in Britain, where **curtsy** appears more often than **curtsey**. The ratio is just on 3:2 in data from the BNC. But in American English **curtsy** almost stands alone, judging by the evidence of CCAE, and has become the standard form.

Through the centuries when *curts(e)ying* was an important social gesture, its spelling was curiously unstable, even for celebrated writers such as Jane Austen. In fact the word has been steadily distancing itself from its origins in *courtesy,* and the interim stages are marked in earlier spellings such as *court'sy, curtesy* and *curt'sy.* However the spelling **curtsey** also reflects the common fluctuation between *-y* and *-ey* at the ends of some traditional words. For other examples, see under **-y/-ey**.

The two spellings support two plurals – **curtsies** and **curtseys** – as well as alternative past forms for the verb: *curtsied* or *curtseyed.*

CV or c.v.

See **curriculum vitae**.

cyber-

This 1990s prefix / combining form for anything associated with computers and digital communication has been extracted from *cybernetics* (the science of automatic control systems, both mechanical and biological). The same root finds expression in "governor." In spite of its technical origins, **cyber-** has proved extremely popular as a means of verbalizing the various responses to the computer age. They range from that of the *cyberphobic* to the *cyberkids, cyberhippies, cyberpunks, cyberchicks/cyberfeminists* among the *Cyberians* who are at home in *cyberspace*. **Cyber**-based institutions such as the *cyber-cafe* are readily identified, and the new frontiers of *cyberart, cyberlaw* and *cybersex* can at least be talked about.

cyclist
See **biker**.

cyclone, hurricane, tornado or typhoon
Though all of these refer to a huge destructive whirlwind, each one has its association with particular parts of the world. **Cyclone** is the term normally used of whirlwinds which affect lands on the rim of the Indian or south Pacific Ocean. It is a meteorologist's word borrowed straight from Greek. In the northwest Pacific and China Sea, **typhoon** is the usual term. Its etymology is much disputed, though it probably owes something to the Chinese *tai fung* ("big wind"), as well as the Greek monster god *Typhon* and the Greek word *typhon* ("whirlwind"). The Greek word is pervasive and seems to have found its way into Portuguese, as well as Arabic, Persian and Hindi; and it is clear that it could easily have been superimposed on the Chinese expression by Europeans who reached the west Pacific.

In and around the Atlantic, Spanish-derived words for whirlwind are the ones used. **Hurricane** is the standard term in the West Indies and the Caribbean coastline, and the Spanish word *huracán* mimics a West Indian one for it. Under American influence, **hurricane** has also spread to the northeastern Pacific and Hawaii. **Tornado** is a purely Spanish concoction out of their words for "thunder" (*tronador*) and "turn" (tornar). It is used by meteorologists of whirlwinds across the Atlantic from Central America to West Africa, but more generally of those that occur within the US, from Tennessee to Ohio. Dictionaries confirm that **tornado** serves both as a synonym for **hurricane**, and as a more specific word for the whirlwind that develops over land and cuts a much narrower path of destruction.

cyder or cider, cypher or cipher
See under **i/y**.

czar, tzar or tsar
Regional tendencies run strongly in favor of either the first or third of these. **Czar** is preferred in the US, according to *Webster's Third* (1986), and it outnumbers **tsar** in CCAE data, by more than 10:1. In the UK, **tsar** became the primary spelling during late C19, according to the *Oxford Dictionary* (1989), and it prevails over **czar** in the BNC by more than 12:1. The word is capitalized in detailed primary references to the **tsars**, as in *Tsar Nicholas I* etc. But it appears without a capital in secondary and generic references.

The compromise spelling **tzar** is very rare in both databases, though listed in some dictionaries. All three spellings attempt to transliterate the word from the Russian to the Roman alphabet, whose symbols do not correspond exactly. (See under **alphabets**.)

Regional preferences apart, the spelling **czar** recommends itself to many because it's closer than **tsar** to the common pronunciation of the word (with a "z" as the first sound). It also seems to reflect the word's ultimate origin in *Caesar*. The argument for **tsar** rests on the fact that it's closer to the Russian spelling of the word; and even in the US, scholars in Slavic studies prefer to use it. Yet American English is also the matrix for new developments of the word **czar**, which are beginning to impact on British English.

From late C19, **czar** became the American byword for a tycoon. Contemporary examples from CCAE include references to *media czar Rupert Murdoch,* the *billionnaire real estate czar,* and the well-placed *daughter of a cosmetics mogul and fashion-industry czar* – not to mention the *tall bald-eagle monetary czar who could move international financial markets with the flick of a cigar!* But the latter day **czar** can also be an executive public servant with a very specific brief. Such is the federal or state *drug czar* (also known as the *antidrug czar*), the *energy czar,* and the *California water czar.* And with ad hoc *czars* also in recreational areas, e.g. the *czar of college basketball* or of *Maryland racing,* the American scene begins to be crowded with them. There must be more than a touch of parody in being called the *czar of prime-time television soap opera.* The *Oxford Dictionary* records generic use of **czar** in Britain since World War II, though its connotations in examples such as *kitchen czar* and the BNC's *decency czar* are definitely negative – more like "petty dictator." None of these semantic developments are associated with **tsar**.

The alternatives **czar/tsar** for referring to the Russian imperial head are paralleled in other derivative words:

> *czardom*   or   *tsardom*
> *czarevna*   or   *tsarevna*
>   (in Russian, the daughter-in-law of the **czar**; in English, the daughter of a **czar**)
> *czarina*   or   *tsarina*
>   (term for the wife of a **czar** used in west European languages)
> *czaritza*   or   *tsaritsa*
>   (Russian term for the wife of a **czar**; the empress).

Czechoslovakia and the Czech Republic
This central European state was formed after World War I, a combination of Bohemia, Moravia and Slovakia. Strictly speaking, only the Bohemians are *Czechs,* but the term *Czech* was often extended to the Moravians and the Slovaks. However the Slovaks maintained their separate identity within **Czechoslovakia**, and negotiated a secession which took effect in January 1993, establishing two new states: the *Slovak Republic* with its capital in Bratislava, and the **Czech Republic**, whose capital is Prague.

da, dal, dalla or Da, Dal, Dalla

These particles are part of various Italian surnames, such as *da Vinci / Da Vinci, dalla Vecchia / Dalla Vecchia* etc. On whether they should be capitalized in English, see **capital letters** section 1a. For indexing purposes they are best alphabetized by the particle itself.
◊ Compare **van and von**.

dais

Thinking of "daisy" helps to secure the spelling of this word, and to underscore the pronunciation preferred by dictionaries everywhere.

The alternative pronunciation which has it rhyming with "bias" is acknowledged in *Webster's Third* (1986), and it correlates with the occasional use of *dias* for the spelling in both American and British databases (CCAE and BNC). Yet another, older pronunciation (making it one syllable rhyming with "pace") is mentioned in *Webster's* and the first edition of the *Oxford Dictionary* (1884–1928), but declared extinct in the second (1989). The presence of two syllables is sometimes marked by the use of a dieresis in the spelling: **daïs**. (See further under **dieresis**.)

The meaning of **dais** has also shifted in the course of time. It is a derivative of the Latin *discus*, which is the rather surprising antecedent for a number of words for furniture: *desco* (in Italian) which becomes *desk* in English, and *Tisch* (the standard German word for "table"). In Middle English and up to 1600, *deis* was the term for a "high table" in a hall, and sometimes by association it referred to the platform the table stood on. The word then disappeared, to be revived by antiquarian writers after 1800, with the meaning "platform" alone.

Dame

For the conventional form of names with this title, see under **Sir**.

dangling participles

Depending on how and where they were educated, people may be highly sensitive or indifferent to **dangling participles** (also known as *unattached* or *misrelated participles*, where *dangling participle* was too much of a stimulus to the imagination). Yet another name for the same peccadillo was *dangling modifier*.

1 The dangling/unattached problem. Whatever term is used, the grammatical problem is how an independent introductory phrase stands in relation to the rest of the sentence. In Latin grammar it's no problem because inflections mark the independence of such phrases (see under **ablative**, and **absolute** section 4). English lacks inflections to do this, and so the introductory phrase will seem to modify the subject that follows it, with strange consequences for the meaning sometimes:

> *Wondering irresolutely what to do, the clock struck twelve.*
> *Having said that, it would be a pity to do it too often.*
> *Now damaged in the stern, the captain ordered the ship back to port.*

Technically there are **dangling participles** in all three sentences – an opening phrase in each is not meant to be attached to the subject of the following clause, though the grammar may seem to push it that way. In the first example the effect is probably distracting, but hardly noticeable in the second (and third). There are semantic and grammatical reasons for this: the contents of the second example are more abstract; and the opening phrase in the third does relate to the object of the sentence.

Castigation of "dangling" constructions almost always focuses on sentences taken out of context. In their proper context of discourse, there may be no problem. The **dangling participle** of the second example (*having said that*) would have a dual function: to draw preceding arguments together, and to alert readers to an imminent change in the argument. It works as an extended conjunctive phrase (see further under **conjunctions**). The third example would sound natural enough in the context of narrative:

> *The bows of the vessel had been scarred by pack ice. Now damaged in the stern, the captain ordered the ship back to port . . .*

The narrative keeps the ship in the spotlight – in the *topic* position in both sentences (see further under **topic**). Even the first example would be less obvious amid a narrative which puts the hero/heroine up front in successive sentences.

In their respective writing contexts the opening phrase in all three of these examples would have a discourse function beyond the sentence itself. If we rewrite the sentences to eliminate the **dangling participles** we lose the topicalizing effect they have. Any sentence in which they create a bizarre distraction should of course be recast. But if the phrase works in the context of discourse and draws no attention to itself, there's no reason to treat it like a cancer in need of excision.

2 Established dangling participles. Note finally that some kinds of *dangling modifiers* are actually the standard phrases of reports and documentary writing. For example:

> *Assuming that . . .*
> *Based on . . .*
> *Concerning the matter of . . .*
> *Considering how . . .*
> *Excepting that . . .*
> *Given that . . .*
> *Judging by . . .*
> *Provided that . . .*
> *Regarding your . . .*
> *Seeing that . . .*

Phrases like these are a commonplace way of indicating the ongoing theme or topic of discussion. (See further under **information focus** and **discourse markers**.) Even the strictest grammarian is unlikely to insist that the substance of those carrier phrases must be attached to the nearest subject noun – any more than with stock phrases such as *barring accidents* or *failing that*.

danse macabre or dance macabre

This phrase, borrowed from French, refers to the traditional "dance of death" which so fascinated the medieval imagination – the dance in which a skeletal figure leads all kinds of people to their doom. Its power in medieval times derived from the ever-present threat of plague, but the motif showed itself as forceful as ever in Australian "Grim Reaper" advertisements concerning the potential spread of AIDS.

Earlier forms of the phrase in English, such as *daunce of Machabree*, show that it was once the dance associated with Maccabeus, the Jewish patriot who led a revolt against Graeco-Roman colonialism in the second century BC. Some suggest that there was a medieval miracle play about the slaughter associated with the revolt. The Dutch *Makkabeusdans* confirms that the tradition was known elsewhere in Europe. But the name *Maccabeus* was no longer recognizable in *Machabree* or *macabré*, and instead became confounded with *macabre*, a word probably of Arabic origin, associated with the gravedigger (*maqabrey*) and graves (*maqabir*). The confusion led to the dropping of the acute accent from the word *macabre*, and to the spelling *macaber* once found in American English (see further under **-re/-er**). The phrase is sometimes anglicized as **dance macabre** (but still with the French word order) according to *Oxford Dictionary* (1989) citations, and a few in American data from CCAE. It often appears in translation, as *dance of death*.

The **danse/dance macabre** expresses the threat of death in the form of frenzied energy, contrasting with the cold symbolism of the skull, the *memento mori* ("reminder of death") which was a subject for Renaissance painters. A third expression of mortality is the Latin phrase *dies irae* ("day of wrath," or Judgement Day), from the opening lines of the Requiem Mass.

DARE

This acronym refers to the *Dictionary of American Regional English*, in five volumes, of which four have appeared (1985–2002). See under **American English**.

dare (to)

This verb is a marginal auxiliary, sometimes construed like an auxiliary with a bare infinitive, or else like a catenative with a *to*-infinitive following (see **catenatives**). Compare:

They dared to speak their minds.
They dared not speak their minds.
They didn't dare to speak their minds.

In current English, **dare** with the *to*-infinitive is used freely in both positive and negative statements. The bare infinitive construction is (a) rare; (b) confined to negative or interrogative utterances: *Don't you dare tell them!, How dare they come here?;* and (c) mostly found in British English, according to the *Longman Grammar* (1999). Elsewhere it survives only in stock idioms such as *I dare say*. The decline of the infinitive construction correlates with increasing use of *do* periphrasis, as in *I don't dare,* especially in American English. Meanwhile British speakers and fiction writers in the Longman corpus can still make negative statements using **dare** without *do* support, as in *I dare not*. The American preference for *do* with **dare** correlates with their greater use of *do* constructions in negatives and questions generally: see further under **do**.

◊ For other marginal auxiliaries, see **auxiliary verbs** section 3.

dashes

The word **dash** is loosely applied to two types of horizontal line characters in printing: the *em dash* and the *en dash*, as they are known in the US and Canada. In the UK and Australia, they are the *em rule* and *en rule*. As the names suggest, the *em dash/rule* is the length of a printed letter *m*, and the shorter *en dash/rule* is the length of an *n*. An *en dash* is slightly longer than a hyphen, and where all three characters are available, each has its own roles:

em dash / em rule   to separate strings of words
en dash / en rule   to link words or numbers in pairs
hyphens   in compounds or complex words

However not all keyboards or wordprocessors have all three; and to compensate, a single hyphen is often used for both *en dash* and hyphen, and three hyphens (or a spaced hyphen) for *em dash*.

1 The em dash / em rule is used either in pairs, or singly. In pairs they mark off a parenthesis in the middle of a sentence:

The most important effect of British colonial development—apart from establishing the tea-drinking habit back home—was the spread of the English language worldwide.

In the *Chicago Manual* (2003), the *Oxford Guide to Style* (2002) and the Australian government *Style Manual* (2002), the *em dashes* that mark a parenthesis are left unspaced. Other British authorities such as Butcher (1992) and *Editing Canadian English* (2000) use a spaced *en dash*. It provides more separation for the parenthetical elements, and has therefore been used in this book. Whichever convention is used, one pair of **dashes** is enough for any sentence. Further parenthetical items within the main parenthesis should be marked off by means of brackets or commas. (See further under **brackets**.)

A single *em dash/rule* may be used like a colon, particularly before a summarizing comment which matches the first part of the sentence:

A loaf of bread, a jug of wine and thou—strictly for intimates!

But the *em dash* is also used to indicate a break (or anacoluthon) in the grammatical structure of a sentence:

A loaf of bread, a jug of wine, and—Why are you smiling?

This use of the dash (*em dash*) in unstructured writing has earned it a reputation as an informal punctuation mark, but the others are quite standard.

The *two-em dash/rule* (two used in quick succession) has several regular uses:

* to show when the text has been discontinued:
  A loaf of bread, a jug of wine——
* to show the deliberate omission of (large) parts of a word, as for instance when representing

"four-letter words" such as *f——*, *c——* (see also under **asterisk**)

* to show where a whole word has been omitted
* to save repeating the name of an author when it occurs first in successive lines of a bibliography or reference list

In British style, the *two-em rule* is spaced in these last two cases, according to *Oxford Style*. The *Chicago Manual* (2003) recommends using a *three-em dash* plus comma or period, according to style.

2 The en dash / en rule (unspaced) is used to connect two words or numbers which set up a span between them:

> the Chinese–American alliance
> Sydney–Hobart yacht race
> pp. 306–9
> 1999–2000

Note that where both the *en dash/rule* and hyphen are available, they can express a difference of meaning:

> Lloyd–Jones (= a partnership between Lloyd and Jones)
> Lloyd-Jones (= an individual with a double-barreled surname)

But in headings and titles consisting of full caps, the *en dash* is used instead of the hyphen in words that are normally hyphenated.

> GOVERNOR GOES PART–TIME

The *en dash* also serves to link a spaced compound with a prefix, as in *quasi–open government policy*; or two hyphenated compounds e.g. *quasi-expert–quasi-disin-terested adviser.*

A *spaced en dash/rule* is used when the words or numbers to be separated have internal spaces. See for example:

> 1 July 1991 – 2 June 1992

In pairs, the *spaced en dash/rule* is also an alternative to the *unspaced em dash/rule* for marking parentheses, as described in section 1 above.

◊ For the uses of **hyphens**, see under that heading.

data

The fact that **data** is a plural in Latin (see under **-a**) has had a powerful influence on its use in English. Writers conscious of its latinity tend to ensure that plural verbs or pronouns are used in agreement with it, as in the following:

> These data were gathered by intensive interviewing. They show . . .

Plural agreement is still insisted on by many in academic circles, where old scholastic traditions die hard. But in general English usage **data** also often combines with singular verbs and pronouns, as if it's conceived of as a collective:

> This data was gathered by intensive interviewing. It shows . . .

This second version actually expresses something slightly different from the first: it projects the data as a mass or block rather than a set of separable items. **Data** thereby becomes a *mass noun,* as noted in the *New Oxford* (1998), and requires singular agreement. The ratio of singular to plural constructions, as shown by verb and/or pronoun(s) is 4:7 in data from the BNC and CCAE. Both *New Oxford* and *Merriam-Webster's* (2000) note that this singular construction is now as much standard English as the plural.

The grammatical number of **data** is often indeterminate because it serves as an attributive or compounding element, in expressions such as *data*

systems, data-processing and *data collection*. Even as a noun, its appearances are not necessarily marked as singular or plural. To show grammatical number it takes a pronoun such as *this/these*, or the present tense of a verb such as *shows/show* or *has/have* (or the past tense *was/were*). Other past tenses and modal verbs provide no indication of number. In fact about 80% of the examples in the American and British databases are indeterminate. Very few are so heavily marked for singular/plural by both pronoun and verb as the examples above, and the verb or pronoun which does the marking can be separated by an intervening phrase, or set in the next clause:

> most polling data over the past year has drawn a picture . . .
> . . . finding the data and downloading it
> . . . demand access to unclassified data, and that it be put . . .
> the data that correspond with paper checks. . .

The separation of **data** from words that agree with it sometimes shows up where editors have intervened in "correcting" singular forms to plural ones (some but not all!) – suggesting to *Webster's English Usage* (1989) that the frequency of plural usage registered in American print owes more to editorial convention than authorial practice. .

In the past, the reluctance to accept singular use of **data** (while admitting its existence) has been expressed in attempts to confine it to particular genres. Commentators have said that it is restricted to spoken English, or to American English, or to technical English. Burchfield (1996) allows it in computing and "allied disciplines" – whatever they are! The further one investigates, the wider the spectrum of writing in which it appears. *Canadian English Usage* (1997) observes **data** with singular agreement in scientific, academic and journalistic writing. Perhaps **data** will become a purely singular/mass noun like *agenda* and *stamina* – Latin loanwords with similar backgrounds. But for the moment it can be construed in either the singular or plural, and writers are taking full advantage of it.

datable or dateable

Both spellings are recognized in *Webster's Third* (1986) and the *Oxford Dictionary* (1989), with priority given to **datable**. It is also the more regular of the two in terms of English wordformation (see **-e** section 1).

dates

Depending on where you are in the English-speaking world, dates may be written in more than one order. The two most familiar are:

*day/month/year
> 11 August 1988   11th August 1988   11th August, 1988
> 11/8/88   11.8.88   11-8-88

*month/day/year
> August 11, 1988   August 11th 1988   August 11th, 1988
> 8/11/88   8.11.88   8-11-88

The trend towards using the cardinal *11* rather than the ordinal *11th* is worldwide, and used in official correspondence everywhere. But the order of items has yet to be standardized. The first order for dates (d/m/y) works from the smaller to larger unit, and it's the one used in Britain and Australia. The *Chicago Manual* (2003) switches its recommendation to the second order (m/d/y) because of its widespread use in the US. But it also notes its ambiguity in the all-number style, and the need for a comma even when the month is named. It still prefers the first order wherever there are multiple dates to be cited. Canadians live with both m/d/y and d/m/y systems, and need to spell out their choice with the first date given in any document.

The potential for confusion among the all-number styles from each set is obvious, and something which those with overseas correspondents need to be careful about. British letters which give a date as *11/8/88* may very well be misinterpreted in North America, and the dates in letters from North America need to be read with caution elsewhere. The problem never arises, of course, if the month is given as a word, or else as a roman numeral (*11.viii.88*), a convention used by some Europeans.

A third possible order for dates is year/month/day: *88/08/11* or *1988/08/11*
This avoids the problems of the other two all-number styles, and it's the order recommended by the International Standards Organization (ISO 8601:1988[E]). It is already widely used in science and computing, and by international companies based in Europe, and increasingly in the US and Canada. As shown in our example, both month and day are indicated by two digits, with zero filling in the space beside the numbers 1–9. In computer usage the year is given its full four digits, and the date may be set without spaces: *19880811*.

In data systems, a different convention has the day and month combined as a single, three-digit number between 001 and 365 (or 366 in a leap year). According to this system, the date *11 August 1988* would appear as *1988224* or *88224*. A space or hyphen can be inserted between the year and the day figure: *1988 224* or *1988-224*. The following table shows the range of numbers for each month:

January 1	*1*
February 1	*32*
March 1	*60* (*61* in leap years)
April 1	*91* (*92*)
May 1	*121* (*122*)
June 1	*152* (*153*)
July 1	*182* (*183*)
August 1	*213* (*214*)
September 1	*244* (*245*)
October 1	*274* (*275*)
November 1	*305* (*306*)
December 1	*335* (*336*)

This method of dating is particularly useful for continuous accounting.
1 Spans of years. When indicating a span of years, a *dash* (en dash / en rule) connects the two numbers. In spite of shared digits, it's often necessary to repeat them in the second number. A period between 47 BC and 42 BC would require both numbers to spelled out in full, as *47–42 BC*, not 47–2 BC, which might seem to be between 47 BC and 2 BC. For four-digit dates AD within the same century, the last two digits are generally repeated in American and Australian style, according to the *Chicago Manual* (2003) and the government *Style Manual* (2002). Thus *1825–29, 1955–58* and so on. However, within the first decade, only one digit is provided: *2003–4*. British style, as articulated by Butcher (1992) and Ritter (2002), recommends not repeating more digits than it takes to show the change, thus *1825–9, 1955–8*. But they make a

special case for numbers between *10* and *19*, as in *1914–18 War*. The argument is that numbers in that decade ("fourteen," "eighteen" etc.) are fused rather than separable compounds (compare "twenty-four"). Style authorities everywhere agree that when dates span the turn of a century, e.g. *1898–1901*, all four digits should be repeated (and that using *1898–901* would be unfortunate).

The *solidus* or *slash* mark is often used for a financial year or other statutory period (such as tenure of office or sporting season) which does not coincide exactly with one calendar year: *1908/9*. It contrasts with *1908–9* where the *dash* indicates a two-year span of time involving both years. This distinction between *dash* and *solidus* then allows us to indicate spans between two financial years, sporting seasons etc.: *1982/3–1983/4*. (See further under **solidus**.)
2 Individual years. Writers referring to individual years normally use all four digits: *By 1986 we had all graduated*. But when speaking, we may allude to a year using just the last two digits – and this form, prefaced by an apostrophe, occasionally finds its way into print, as in *the class of '86*.
◊ For ways of referring to decades and individual centuries, see under **decades** and **centuries**.

dating systems

Several of the world's major religions have provided a calendar for dating historical events. The familiar Christian calendar dates things in relation to the putative year of Christ's birth, AD 1 (see further under **AD** and **BC**). The Islamic calendar is based on the year AD 622, when Muhammad fled from persecution in Mecca to Medina, where he began to develop a following. According to this system, events are dated with the prefix *AH* (= *anno Hegirae*, "in the year of [Muhammad's] hegira or flight"). The Islamic years are however difficult to relate to Christian years because they work on a 355-day lunar cycle. Judaism meanwhile calculates historical time in years from the putative creation of the world. Under this system, the years are also sometimes prefixed *AH* (= *anno Hebraico*, "in the Hebrew year"), which is clearly a trap for the unwary. Alternatively, dates using this reference point are prefixed *AM* (= *anno mundi*, "in the year of the world").

Those seeking a dating system which is neutral as to religion have devised the term *Common Era*, and the abbreviations *CE* and *BCE* ("[before] the Common Era"). But contrary to intention, *CE* is quite often read as "Christian Era," a misunderstanding which is helped by the fact that the first year of the *Common Era is* AD 1. (See further under **BC**.)

Two other secular systems of dating have had their day. The Romans located historical events in relation to the founding of their city in 753 BC. They gave years with the suffix *AUC*, which to them meant *ab urbe condita* ("from the city's founding"), but is usually glossed nowadays as *anno urbis conditae* ("in the year of the city's founding"). In modern times the French Republican calendar was promulgated with the establishment of the Republic in September 1792. It created twelve months, all of thirty days (and five intercalary days), and a new set of names for the months which express the flavor of the season. There's no mistaking the autumn/winter set and the spring/summer set:

Vendemiaire ("the vintage")	*Germinal* ("new shoots")
Brumaire ("mist")	*Floreal* ("flowers")
Frimaire ("frost")	*Prairial* ("grass")
Nivose ("snow")	*Messidor* ("harvest")
Pluviose ("rain")	*Thermidor* ("heat")
Ventose ("wind")	*Fructidor* ("fruit")

The Republican calendar was discontinued with the fall of Napoleon in 1806.

One aspect of the Roman calendar has been extremely long-lived. We owe to Julius Caesar the system of allowing for a normal 365-day year, plus a 366-day year once in every four. This so-called *Julian* (or "Old Style") *Calendar* continued to be used in Europe up to the threshold of the modern era. By then it was evident that the Julian equation for the solar cycle was a slight overestimate and out by 11 minutes 10 seconds a year. The *Gregorian* ("New Style") *Calendar* modified the old formula by reducing the number of leap years. Instead of allowing that every turn of the century (1800, 1900, 2000, 2100, 2200, 2300 etc.) was a leap year, only one in four was (2000, 2400 etc.). The new system took its name from Pope Gregory XIII, and it has been observed in most Catholic countries since 1582. However the state of religious politics being what it was, England remained with the *Julian Calendar* until 1752, by which time the British calendar was twelve days behind the rest of Europe. The *Gregorian Calendar* was not adopted in Russia until 1918.

Finally, there is a **dating system** which uses neither sun, moon or climate as its reference, but the known patterns of radiation in carbon atoms: radiocarbon dating. It relies on the fact that the radiocarbon (= carbon 14) in all living things has a known level of radioactivity, which falls off at a predictable rate after the organism has died. The half-life of carbon 14 is 5700 years, and it continues to be just measurable up to 40,000 years. For obvious reasons the method is more useful to archeologists than geologists generally, and has contributed much to the study of the prehistoric environment and relatively recent climatic changes. An Aboriginal footprint preserved in mud near Ceduna (South Australia) was dated as 5470 BP (± 190 years). (For the suffix **BP**, see further under that heading.)
◊ For **geological eras**, see Appendix II.
◊ For a **perpetual calendar**, see Appendix III.

dative

This is the grammatical name for the case of the indirect object. In some languages such as German and Latin, there are distinct forms and suffixes for nouns, pronouns, adjectives and articles in the **dative** case, to distinguish them from the nominative and accusative. The pronoun *I/me* is as follows in German and Latin:

German	*Latin*	
ich	ego "I" *nominative*	(= subject)
mich	me "me" *accusative*	(= direct object)
mir	mihi "me" *dative*	(= indirect object)

As the translation shows, the **dative** in English is identical with the accusative, and it is only from the syntax of the sentence that its role as an indirect object can be seen. (See further under **accusative**.) Further aspects of case-marking in English and other languages are discussed under **cases**.

daughter-in-law

See **in-laws**.

de, del, della and De, Del, Della

On the question as to whether to capitalize these particles in French, Dutch and Italian surnames (as in *De la Mare, de Haan* and *Del Rosario*), see under **capital letters**. For indexing purposes they are best alphabetized by the particle itself. Compare **van and von**.

de-

The older meanings of this Latin prefix differ from the new. It came into English through everyday Latin loanwords such as *decline, depend* and *descend,* where its meaning is "down or away"; and in ones such as *delude, deplore* and *deride* where it means "put down" in a derogatory sense (*derogatory* itself is another example).

Its usual modern meaning is to reverse an action: either reducing or lowering it, as in *decentralize, de-escalate* and *devalue;* or removing something entirely, as in *defoliate, defrost* and *dethrone.* In *defuse* it may be one or the other, depending on whether the object is a situation or a bomb. This modern usage seems to have developed out of an earlier confusion with *dis-* (see **dis-**). In medieval French, words which had originally had **de-** and those with *dis-* were both written *des-,* because the *s* ceased to be pronounced and people were unsure which words it belonged to.

The earliest English examples of **de-** in its negative and privative sense were strictly technical: *decanonize* and *decardinalize* amid the religious turmoil of C17, and *deacidify* and *de-aerate* out of empirical science in C18. Quite a few modern formations also began as technical jargon: *debrief, decontaminate, demilitarize.* But there are plenty of examples closer to home: *defrost, demist* and *deodorant. Debug* has gone further down the figurative path than *delouse.* As these examples show, new formations are as often based on nouns as verbs.

de facto and de jure

The Latin phrase **de facto** meaning "in fact" or "in reality" comes from the language of law, where it forms a contrast with **de jure** ("according to law" or "lawful"). Even lawyers have had to recognize that things which have no legal standing are a force to reckon with, and **de facto** as an adverb has had vigorous use amid the turmoil of English religious and political history. In current British English it most often works as an adjective to mark ad hoc institutions, such as a *de facto embassy in Hong Kong,* and unofficial or unformulated policies, as in a *de facto form of slavery.* Occasionally **de facto** and **de jure** are juxtaposed, as in the *de facto if not de jure standard* of the computing industry. But **de facto** occurs much more often than **de jure** in reporting and interpreting public affairs, in hundreds of examples in the BNC and CCAE. Americans (more often than the British) use **de facto** to refer to people in ad hoc public roles, as in *de facto president / county executive / press attaché.*

De facto is also used in Australia and New Zealand as a noun and byword for *de facto wife* or *de facto husband* – which is backed by the Australian Family Law Reform Act 1980 and written into tax forms and other documents that take account of domestic relationships. See further under **spouse**.

de gustibus
This abbreviates the Latin saying *de gustibus non est disputandum*. See further under **chacun à son goût**.

de jure
See **de facto and de jure**.

de mortuis
These words invoke the cautionary Latin statement: *de mortuis nil nisi bonum* ("concerning the dead, nothing but good [should be said]," or "speak no ill of the dead"). It represents an ancient taboo as well as a modern social convention, that the shortcomings of those who have died should not be aired: speak kindly or not at all. Though it comes to us in Latin, the saying is attributed to Chilo of Sparta, one of the legendary wise men of Greek tradition, from the sixth century BC. The sentiment is also expressed in brief as **nil nisi bonum**.

de profundis
See under **cri de coeur**.

de règle and de rigueur
See under **comme il faut**.

de trop
This French phrase means literally "too much" or "too many." In English it has long been applied to a person whose presence is superfluous, inappropriate or unwelcome in a given company. It parallels the idiom "playing gooseberry," expressing the idea more directly (if you know French), and more elegantly (if you do not).

Dear
The word **dear** has been used in direct address since C13, and in friendly salutations in personal letters since C15. **Dear** became the formal opener to any kind of letter during C17, which made it semantically opaque. In institutional correspondence the reader may find it dull or inappropriate (if the letter's purpose is to demand that you pay supplementary tax). But for those who still write personal letters, it combines with a first name or nickname to make a warm salutation.

Dear is very strongly associated with paper-based letters, and so seems less natural in e-mail correspondence (see Appendix VII). Those who begin their electronic letters to friends with **Dear** are definitely a minority – less than 20% in Gains's (1998) research. It shares the field with "Hi" (20%), and "Hello" (11%). But almost 40% of personal e-mail and over 90% of administrative e-mail had no salutation at all (as in paper-based office memos). Salutations may seem redundant when the message header identifies the person or group being addressed at the start. A small percentage of personal e-mails (less than 10%) began with the addressee's name alone, as in *Tom: did you get the. . . ?* Most e-mail messages get briskly down to business, and might be at risk of sounding brusque, but for the mitigating effect of conversational and colloquial idiom (Li, 2000) in the body of the message. The message endings used by e-mail correspondents are also far from standardized, and diverge from those used in paper correspondence: see under **Yours faithfully**.
◊ Compare the sample formats for print and e-mail correspondence in Appendix VII.

debarred or disbarred
Dictionaries and usage guides sometimes say these have distinct roles, **disbarred** being reserved for lawyers expelled from the Bar, and **debarred** for any other kind of exclusion from a profession, sporting competition, employment and other more abstract arenas. Only in American English does this come close to the facts. The evidence from CCAE is that **disbarred** is indeed confined to the right to practice law and appear in court; but there are few examples of **debarred**, and *barred* seems to take its place.

In British English, **debarred** is much more common than **disbarred**, by a factor of more than 4:1 in data from the BNC. The uses of **debarred** are many and varied, ranging from the very specific prohibition – *railway companies were debarred from acquiring land* – to other kinds of prevention: *deafness debarred him from lectures*. The relatively few examples of **disbarred** also present a range. Less than half are concerned with exclusion from the Bar, and rather more with being excluded from such things as the armed forces, sports competition and nonlegal professions such as accountancy. An occasional abstract use such as *disbarred from making moral judgement* also appears among the data.

This wider range of uses for **disbarred** has its explanation in the fact that there are actually two verbs written as *disbar*, according to the *Oxford Dictionary* (1989). The older one, labeled "obsolete," is a C16 variant of *debar*, based on its French antecedent *desbarrer*, with the general meaning "exclude." The younger *disbar* ("expel from the Bar") is a C17 creation. The *New Oxford* (1998) takes the radical step of putting the two *disbar* verbs together, allowing that the older usage has indeed continued, and giving *disbar* both legal and nonlegal definitions. But amid this expanding range, the exclusions expressed by **debarred** and **disbarred** don't yet prevent drinkers from consoling themselves at the local bar.

debit
On the spelling of this word when verb inflections are added, see **-t**.

déboutonné
See **en déshabillé**.

debut
Given the importance of *savoir faire* when making a **debut**, it is perverse that the word itself creates uncertainties. In English it no longer needs an acute accent on the first syllable, yet the second syllable has a silent *t* as in French – hence the question of its spelling when it becomes an English verb. The standard practice is to write *debuted* and *debuting* (and continue to pronounce them as if there was no *t*). This is of course what happens with various other French loanwords ending in *-et*, when they are used as verbs in English: see further under **-t**.

deca-/deci-
These prefixes embody the Latin (and Greek) word for "ten." The prefix **deca-** expresses that meaning

straightforwardly in words such as *decade*, *decagon* and *decahedron*. Spelled *deka-*, it has sometimes combined with metric measures such as *dekalitre* and *dekametre,* though neither of those is an SI base unit (see further under **metrication**).

The prefix **deci-** means "one tenth," and it too used to be found with metric measures. But the potential for confusion between **deci-** and **deca-** has long been recognized, hence the attempts to replace **deca-** with *deka-*. In mathematical terms, the prefixes make all the difference between a cup of water (a *decilitre*) and enough for a bath (a *decalitre*). Even so, neither prefix is much used within the SI system, because of the general preference for expressions which involve powers of 1000.

decades

Nowadays the standard style when referring to **decades** is without an apostrophe: for example *1960s* or *in the 60s* (not *1960's*). (See further under **apostrophes** section 2.)

When written purely as words, the *decadic* numbers usually correspond simply with the numbers: *in the sixties and seventies*. Yet verbal references to the first two decades in each century seem to require more than that, hence the "nineteen tens" (*1910s*) and "nineteen hundreds" (*1900s*) – the latter not unambiguously, since it could also refer to the whole century. In the countdown to the new millennium, speculation mounted about how we would refer to the first decade of C21, with the "oh-ohs" and the "noughties"/ "naughties" (see **naught**) as light relief from the plainer "twenty hundreds" or "two thousands." The latter was strongly preferred in an Australian survey (Peters, 1999a), and its potential ambiguity is no problem while the century has yet to unfold. By 2010 all will have settled down with the "two thousand and tens" or the brisker "twenty tens."

◊ For references to other spans of time, see under **dates**.

deceitful or deceptive

Both words involve *deceiving;* but while **deceitful** suggests that it is part of a conscious intention by the perpetrator, **deceptive** just means that one can be misled by appearances. So calling a speech **deceitful** is a judgement about the honesty of the speaker, whereas **deceptive** puts the onus on those listening or reading to watch their own interests.

decessit sine prole

This Latin phrase means "s/he departed [this life] without offspring." Used mostly in law and genealogy, it often appears abbreviated as *d.s.p.* It confirms the fact that the genealogy is complete, rather than a case where genealogists have been unable to trace all the progeny of the person being documented. The same idea is expressed through *obiit sine prole* ("died without offspring": *o.s.p.*) and *sine prole* (*s.p.*).

decided or decisive

These words only come into each other's ambit when **decided** is an adjective, as in a *decided advantage* (or *decisive advantage*?). In such contexts, **decided** means "definite," whereas **decisive** carries the sense of "that which clinches the issue." Thus **decisive** suggests finality, where **decided** is just an interim value.

decimal comma or decimal point

The European convention (also known in Canada) of using a **decimal comma** rather than a **decimal point** is discussed under **numbers** section 1.

decimate

In contemporary English **decimate** has been acquiring new uses, none of which is mathematically precise. Its Latin meaning was exact – "reduce by one tenth" – and in earlier English it was similarly used, as a classical synonym for the Anglo-Saxon word *tithe* ("take one tenth of a person's goods, as a levy or tax"). On rare occasions, the word has also been used to mean "reduce *to* one tenth" (i.e. by nine tenths). The *Oxford Dictionary* (1989) demonstrates this for *decimation*, with a citation from the C19 historian Freeman. He spells out his meaning with the aid of the $\frac{9}{10}$ fraction – evidently anticipating some uncertainty about the word. It tallies with the *Oxford*'s C19 note on the use of **decimate** to mean "devastate or drastically reduce," which it dubbed "rhetorical and loose." We may read between the lines that there was some kind of shibboleth about it, fostered by more widespread knowledge of Latin. But this meaning is nowadays the commonest use of the word in both British and American English, and it's registered without comment in modern dictionaries. With the sense of "reduce drastically," the word appears in many contexts, witness the following from BNC and CCAE:

> ...*communities decimated by AIDS*
> *Torpedo bombers decimated the Italian fleet.*
> ...*housing programs decimated in earlier budgets*
> *Honda decimated the British motorcycle industry.*
> ...*drought that has decimated bird and fish populations*
> *The Communist Party saw its parliamentary representation decimated.*

Among the citations, the mathematical meaning remains only as a distraction – as when we're told that there are now about 18,000 elephants left in Kenya, thanks to poachers *who have decimated the population by 70,000 a year since 1979*. Using exact numbers with **decimate** is ill-advised, whatever its intended sense. They are redundant where it means "reduce by one tenth," and where it doesn't they confound the arithmetic. Precision mathematics is certainly not the point when *decimated* features in sports reporting, as it does on both sides of the Atlantic:

> *Thompson decimated the Christleton bowling.*
> ...*the Huskies have been decimated by injuries*

Yet other developments of **decimate** seem to be American rather than British English. Only in CCAE is the word found to mean "raze to the ground" as in *lava has decimated their homes* or *soldiers decimated entire villages* or the ironic *urban renewal decimated the area*. Also on the frontiers of **decimate** are instances of emotional and personal devastation: a man *decimated by the loss of his wife*, and another *decimated by drug and alcohol abuse*. **Decimate** is thus becoming a general-purpose synonym for "devastate," though not yet acknowledged in *Merriam-Webster's* (2000).

Whatever destruction, damage or disaster it's applied to, **decimate** remains ominous, always expressing a sense of disquiet. Dark connotations have been at the heart of the word since Roman times, when it referred to the punitive measure practiced by the Roman army – the killing of one soldier in ten, as a reprisal against units which mutinied or showed cowardice. The mathematical precision of that meaning has been lost, but the sinister implications are still there.

decisive or decided
See **decided**.

declaim and declamation
The spelling difference is discussed under **-aim**.

declarative
Modern grammarians apply this term to sentences which embody a statement, as opposed to a question or command. In traditional grammar the verb of a **declarative** sentence was said to be *indicative* rather than *interrogative* or *imperative*. See further under **mood**.

declension
Declensions are the different groups or classes to which the nouns of a language belong, according to the way they change for singular and plural, and for the various grammatical cases such as nominative, accusative, genitive (see further under **cases**).

Classical Latin had elaborate noun **declensions**, with individual suffixes for many of the six standard cases, and often a characteristic vowel, such as -a (first **declension**), -*u* (second and fourth **declensions**) and -*e* (third and fifth **declension**). The following are examples of nominative and accusative forms of each:

	nom.	*acc.*
first **declension**:	*domina*	*dominam*
	"woman"	
second **declension**:	*deus* "god"	*deum*
third **declension**:	*miles* "soldier"	*militem*
fourth **declension**:	*manus* "hand"	*manum*
fifth **declension**:	*dies* "day"	*diem*

Older Germanic languages such as Old English and Old Norse had numerous noun **declensions** within the two major groups, known as "strong" and "weak." In modern German there are up to sixteen **declensions**, according to the paradigms in the *Langenscheidt Dictionary* (1997). Most Germanic languages either have or have had **declensions** for their adjectives, also often referred to as "strong" and "weak."

décolleté
See **en déshabillé**.

deductible or deductable
Both spellings are possible for this relatively new word, though **deductible** is the standard form in finance and accounting. This spelling was "rare" in C19 according to the original *Oxford Dictionary* (1884–1928), which gave the regular English form **deductable** as the primary form. But the latinate **deductible** has gained ground since then, according to the *Oxford*'s second edition (1989). It dominates in data from the BNC and CCAE, by more than 60:1. **Deductible** is the only spelling listed in *Merriam-Webster's* (2000), *New Oxford* (1998) and the *Canadian Oxford* (1998), but the Australian *Macquarie Dictionary* (1997) presents **deductible** and **deductable** as equally current. See further under **-able/-ible**.

deduction
This word is often loosely used to refer to any kind of argument. But in logic it denotes a particular kind of reasoning, a process in which a conclusion is drawn after certain premises have been established. Provided that the premises are true, they guarantee the validity of the conclusion. *Deductive* arguments contrast with *inductive* ones, in which the premises can only be said to support the conclusion (see **induction**).

One of the best known forms of **deduction** is the *syllogism*, in which a conclusion is drawn from a pair of premises. For example:

> *All mammals suckle their young.* (major premise)
> *Whales are mammals.* (minor premise)
> *Therefore the whale suckles its young.*
> (conclusion)

The validity of the conclusion depends on (1) the validity of both premises, and (2) the fact that the class of things introduced in the minor premise is included in the class of the major premise. The class which links the major and minor premise is known as the *middle term*.

Similar *deductive* arguments are commonly used in establishing a scientific theory and making predictions from it. They involve setting up and testing a hypothesis which is conditionally asserted within the major premise. The two well-recognized types of argument like this are the *modus ponens* and the *modus tollens*. The following illustrate the two types.

1 Modus ponens
> *If there's an inverse relationship between IQ and the number of siblings in the family, then brighter children will come from smaller families.*
> *Bright children typically come from smaller families.*
> *Therefore there's an inverse relationship between IQ and the number of siblings in a family.*

With the *modus ponens* argument we can assert the antecedent as the conclusion.

2 Modus tollens
> *If there's an inverse relationship between IQ and the number of siblings in a family, then brighter children will come from smaller families.*
> *Bright children don't all come from smaller families.*
> *Therefore there cannot be an inverse relationship between IQ and the number of siblings in a family.*

The *modus tollens* argument is the negative counterpart of *modus ponens,* and works by denying the consequent as the conclusion.

The two patterns of argument may be symbolically represented as follows:

1 *Modus ponens* 2 *Modus tollens*
If p then q   If p then q
    p   not p
therefore q.   therefore not q.

The letters *p* and *q* stand for indicative statements (see further under **indicative**). The *modus tollens* provides the logical framework for testing the *null hypothesis,* used in statistics and much research in the behavioral and social sciences.

Deductive arguments are sometimes referred to as **a priori** arguments. See further under that heading.

defective or deficient
Both these adjectives say that something is unsatisfactory, but they work in different domains.

Defective is used of objects which have detectable flaws, or do not function properly because of missing or damaged parts. **Deficient** expresses a more abstract problem, where there is less than the full complement of a standard quality or attribute. Because of its abstractness, **deficient** is usually qualified in some way, such as "deficient in sensitivity."

With their different applications, the two words rarely cross paths in usage – only where a problem can be identified in either concrete or abstract terms, as in *mentally defective* (= impaired brain function) and *mentally deficient* (= insufficient brain resources). In fact *mentally handicapped* is far more common than either of them, in American and British databases. But where sensitivities are acute, it's sometimes replaced with the broader term **differently abled**: see further under that heading.

defendant or defendent

The standard spelling for the person answering a legal charge is **defendant**, whether the word is technically a noun or adjective. Compare:

> *The defendant showed no remorse.*
> *The judge cautioned the defendant lawyer.*

On its very few appearances in the British and American databases (BNC and CCAE), **defendent** served as a noun (*the defendent appealed...*). Thus it's just a rare spelling variant, not invested with any grammatical meaning of its own. Compare **dependent or dependant**.

defense or defence

While **defense** is standard in the US, and **defence** in the UK, there are linguistic arguments for preferring **defense** (see under **-ce/-se**). **Defence** makes for awkward juxtapositions in international reporting, especially from the British side, as in:

> *This argument does not apply to nuclear defence, such as the Strategic Defense Initiative.*

The spelling difference suggests a writer distancing himself/herself from American style, and unable to see the two spellings as equivalents, as they are in the *Oxford Dictionary* (1989). The British (Canadian, Australian) preference for **defence** seems to have intensified during C20, and it's the dominant spelling in the BNC by more than 500:1. Yet **defense** also appears in the data, not simply in references to the *US Secretary/Department of Defense*. Other organizations round the world with **Defense** in their title act in **defence/defense** of such things as the environment, natural resources, flora and fauna. So when writing about the activities of **Defense** organizations, there's a case for using **defense** for the common noun, for consistency's sake, wherever you are.

deficient or defective

See **defective**.

definite or definitive

The extra syllable in **definitive** makes it more like *definition;* and a **definitive** object has the archetypal qualities of its kind, and serves as a reference point for others. A **definitive** performance of Shakespeare's *Macbeth* is a classic interpretation.

To say something is **definitive** is to make much more ambitious claims for it than with **definite**. **Definite** simply implies that something is exact or has clear, firm limits, as in a *definite proposal*. In some contexts its meaning is further diluted, so that it is little more than an intensifier, as in a *definite step forward* or *They're definitely coming*. See further under **intensifiers**.

definite article

See **articles**.

definitive or definite

See **definite**.

deflection or deflexion

See under **-ction/-xion**.

deforest, disforest or disafforest

All three mean cutting down the trees, but the first is dominant in both American and British English. **Deforest** is the only one to appear in data from CCAE, and it's far more common than the others in the BNC. **Disforest** appears in 1 solitary example, and though there are rather more of **disafforest**, all come from a single historical publication.

defuse or diffuse

See **diffuse**.

degrees

Academic degrees associated with a person's name are normally indicated by two-part abbreviations, representing the level and the field. Both words are capitalized, as in:

> *Jane Brown, B.A.   David Lee, M.Eng.*
> *Jean Lambert, D.Sc.*

But for **degrees** in law e.g. *LL.B, LL.M*, full caps are used for the field (the double *L* signifies the plural of the Latin word for "law"). Other **degrees** based on Latin such as *Ph.D., Litt.D./D.Litt.* have only an initial cap for the field.

The punctuation of *academic degrees* varies with the institution, but American colleges normally put stops on both parts of the abbreviation, in keeping with the general practice of the *Chicago Manual* (1993). Canadians accommodate the stopped style as well as the unstopped (*B.A.* or *BA*). British and Australian style is generally unstopped. This is clear for abbreviations consisting entirely of capital letters (like *BA, MA, MD*), but less so for ones with some lower case letters such as *M(.)Eng(.)* or *Ph(.)D(.)*, which might or might not be punctuated, according to editorial policy: see **abbreviations** option 2 (c) and option 2 (d). In lists of graduates, consistency seems important – with all **degrees** stopped, or all unstopped.

◊ For the use of *(magna) cum laude* etc. with *academic degrees*, see **cum laude**.

◊ For degrees of temperature, see **Fahrenheit** and **Celsius or centigrade**.

degrees of comparison

For the systems of comparison for adjectives and adverbs, see **adjectives** section 2 and **adverbs** section 3.

deixis

Borrowed from philosophy, this term is used in linguistics to refer to the way word meanings can be tied to the situation in which they are uttered.

Without knowing that situation we cannot decode their meaning. Some examples are:

* personal pronouns *I, we* and *you*
* demonstratives such as *this* and *that*
* positional terms like *here* and *there; right* and *left; in front* and *behind*
* points of the compass: *north, east*
* time references such as *tomorrow* and *yesterday; next, last* and *ago; now* and *then*

Words like these are called *deictics,* from the adjective *deictic.* There's no sign yet of a rival "deixic" in dictionaries or grammars – though we might expect it in the longer run. See further under **-ctic/-xic.**

déjà vu

This phrase, borrowed from French, means "already seen." In critiques of artistic or literary works **déjà vu** can be used almost literally to say that the substance is derivative and unstimulating: ... *Paris dealers showing a large number of déjà vu works and recording few sales.* The **déjà vu** in revisionist government policies invites boredom, according to another BNC citation. In sports reporting it simply means the repetition of a win, loss and/or competing with the same opponent(s): *it was déjà vu as he breezed in to outwit O'Hare a second time.*

But when used by psychologists and others, **déjà vu** is a peculiar mental phenomenon whereby people feel they are seeing for the second time something which they can never have seen before. It seems to strike a chord in memory, and yet it can only be a quirk of the mind. The effect is uncanny, though not in the occult realms of "second sight." While the clairvoyant claims to have a view into the future, a **déjà vu** glimpse is always framed in the past.

dekalitre and dekametre

See under **deca-/deci-.**

del/Del and della/Della

On how to treat these elements of surnames, see under **de.**

delirium tremens

Coined in early C19, this medical phrase consists of Latin elements which mean "trembling delirium." The name describes the convulsive state of delirium brought on by prolonged and excessive consumption of alcohol – fits of trembling and sweating associated with terrifying optical illusions. The phrase can be abbreviated to *d.t.* although it's usually written and said in the plural as *d.t.'s,* as if the word *tremens* were a plural noun. The abbreviation often appears in capitals, as *D.T.'s* or *DTs* according to the policy for punctuating abbreviations: see **abbreviations** options 2 (a) or (c).

delusion or illusion

These words both refer to false perceptions, and though they seem interchangeable in some contexts, their implications are slightly different. **Delusion** suggests that the misapprehension is subjective and results from distorted thinking within the individual, or a disordered mind. **Delusions** are chronic or persistent, as for example with *delusions of grandeur.* An **illusion** is a temporary misapprehension produced by external objects or circumstances, as in

an *optical illusion* or *under no illusion.* **Illusions** can be dispelled relatively easily.

In its pronunciation, **illusion** comes close to *allusion,* the abstract noun from the verb *allude.* But while an *allusion* ("passing comment or fleeting reference") can be heard or seen in writing, an **illusion** is all in the mind. There's no English verb associated with **illusion.**
◊ Compare **elusive or allusive.**

demagogue or demagog

See under **-gue/-g.**

demean

This word represents two different words:

* the rather archaic verb **demean** meaning "behave," as in *if I demean myself proudly.* Both it and the noun *demeanor* derive from Old French *demener.*
* the current verb **demean** meaning "lower in dignity or status" is an English formation of C17, based on the adjective *mean.* It may be used either reflexively or nonreflexively. Compare:
    ... would not demean themselves by setting out to acquire popularity
  and
    We will regulate telephone services which demean women and corrupt children.

The second verb provides us with the adjective *demeaning,* as in *a clerical job would be demeaning for her.*

demeanor or demeanour

See under **-or/-our.**

demi-

This French prefix meaning "half" appears in a few borrowed words like *demi-sec* and *demitasse,* and in some hybrid English formations like *demigod* and *demirelief.* It appears as an independent word in the form *demy* (a now obsolete size of paper), with its spelling adjusted in accordance with the English rules for final letters of words. (The reverse process is described at **-y > -i-**).

Demi- is synonymous with *semi* – from Latin and *hemi-* from Greek, and all three are brought into play for subdividing the length of musical notes in British (and Australian) terminology. Thus the *demisemiquaver* is one quarter the length of a *quaver,* and the *hemidemisemiquaver* one eighth of it – a long word for a very brief sound. But North American musical nomenclature does without quavers (and crotchets), and names all notes as fractions of the semibreve. So the *demisemiquaver* is a *thirty-second note,* and the *hemidemisemiquaver* a *sixty-fourth note.*

Demi- lends ambiguity to *demivolt,* unless you happen to have some knowledge of electricity and/or dressage. In fact, it has no place in electrical measurement, but refers to the half turn (with forelegs raised) made by a trained horse.

demise

Death and the law associated with it are the starting points for the word **demise:**
    Many people make wills to anticipate the future and their demise.
It serves to solemnize or euphemize physical death of other kinds, as in: *the demise of his 13-year-old cat* or *her African violet's demise.* Yet in contemporary

English, **demise** often refers to the decline of an institution, custom or fashion. This is the dominant sense in data from both the BNC and CCAE, as in:

> *communism's demise in Eastern Europe*
> *the local barbershop's demise*
> *the void left by the demise of the afternoon edition*
> *the demise of three square meals a day*

Another, more ambiguous extension of the word is to refer to the departure of politicians from office, and the retirement of others from the public arena. It happens when what might be referred to as *political demise* or *professional demise* is just called **demise**. For example:

> *... a rebellion within military ranks triggered Marcos's demise*
> *Alan Bond's demise is a parable of the last 10 years.*

Evidence of **demise** used to mean "loss of position or status" comes from both American and British databases, and it's recognized in *Merriam-Webster* (2000) though not in *New Oxford* (1998). But this use of **demise** (without any indication that it means *political/professional demise*) is safe only in the short term and with readers who know that the person is not yet dead. Otherwise the more deadly possibility will be there to confound their reading of the text. In the longer run, **demise** in the sense of "death" will win out anyway. Writers who want their texts to stand the test of time should still preface the word **demise** with "political," "professional" etc., if that's the intended sense.

demonstratives

Words like *this/these* and *that/those* which draw the reader's or listener's attention to particular objects or persons are **demonstratives**. They function as both adjectives and pronouns:

> *This offer is worth accepting.* (adjective)
> *This is worth accepting.* (pronoun)
> *Those recruits did better than these.*
> (adjective)   (pronoun)

English also has *demonstrative* adverbs (of time, place and manner) including:

> *here/there   hence/thence   now/then   thus*

In modern English the pairs of **demonstratives** (i.e. *this/that, these/those*) express the notion of being either closer to, or further from the writer/speaker. In older English, the words *yon* and *yonder* also worked as **demonstratives**, and expressed a third degree of distance, even more remote from the standpoint of the communicator. In some Aboriginal languages, the *demonstrative* system indicates not only relative distance but direction (i.e. "near to the south," "further away to the west" etc.) See also under **deixis**.

denotation

See under **connotation**.

denounce and denunciation

For the spelling of these words, see under **pronounce**.

dent or dint

See **dint**.

deontic and epistemic

These terms originated in philosophy, but are used by some grammarians to identify the different senses of modal verbs in the following:

> *You may leave now.   You may be right.*
> *He must do it.   He must be on his way now.*

The first in each pair is **deontic**: the utterance involves giving permission or putting an obligation on the subject of the verb. The second is **epistemic:** it expresses a possibility or estimates the likelihood of a fact or event. The two senses are also referred to as *intrinsic* and *extrinsic,* or *root meaning* and *epistemic meaning.* See further under **modality**.

dependence or dependency

Like some other *-nce/-ncy* pairs, the first is typically abstract in its use, so that it's usually modified (before or after) to make it more specific, as in *nicotine dependence* or *dependence on outside finance.* **Dependency** is more specific in itself, referring to a particular dependent unit, and probably best known in its use as a geo-political unit governed by another country: the *Falkland Island Dependencies.* However, **dependency** is also found in phrases such as *drug dependency,* suggesting that for some people it is quite interchangeable with **dependence**. (See further under **-nce/-ncy**.)

Dependence and **dependency** are very much more frequent than *dependance* and *dependancy* in both American and British databases. The *-enc-* spellings are there in their hundreds, whereas instances of *-anc-* spellings can be counted on the fingers of one hand.
◊ Compare *dependent/dependant* in next entry.

dependent or dependant

Uncertainty over spelling this word goes back to C18, when Dr. Johnson offered both spellings for the noun and adjective, with the comment "Some words vary their final syllable." But the *Oxford Dictionary* (1884–1928) stated that *-ant* was more common for the noun in C19, and this has firmed into the preferences of modern British dictionaries: **dependant** for the noun and **dependent** for the adjective.

Data from the BNC shows the grammatical division of labor is not quite as neat as that. While **dependent** is indeed the common form of the adjective, **dependant** serves about equally as noun and adjective. Compare:

> *carers with a dependant in their household*

with

> *more dependant on aid than ever*

and

> *co-operation between mutually dependant classes.*

Still the fact is that adjectival uses of **dependant** are much less frequent than those of **dependent**.

In the US **dependent** is simply used for both adjective *and* noun. Compare:

> *young people dependent on their peers*

with

> *Aid for Families with Dependent Children (AFDC)*

and

> *a disabled or chronically-ill dependent relies on ...*

Dependent appears in thousands of examples in CCAE, compared with about a score of **dependant**, of which more than 90% are adjectival. The data provides ongoing support for the judgement of *Webster's Third* (1986), that **dependent** is the prime spelling in American English, and that **dependant** is a spelling variant without grammatical significance.

If users of English were united on making **dependent** and **dependant** grammatically distinct, it might be worth persisting with. The facts are that it's not perfectly observed in the UK, and disregarded in the US. Those who use **dependant** for the adjective do not cause misunderstanding, since the grammar is always clear from the context, as in the examples above. This being so, one might ask why British dictionaries could not accommodate it – in the name of Johnsonian variation or American liberalism, according to taste. A little flexibility here would be worth a lot, given the arbitrary rule of -*ent* or -*ant* in so many other English words. See further under -**ant/-ent**.

dependent clauses
This is another name for *subordinate clauses*. See further under **clauses** section 3.

deposit
On whether to double the *t* before adding verb suffixes, see -**t**.

deprecate or depreciate
From rather different origins, these similar-looking words have come to overlap in meaning in some contexts, especially when it comes to *self-deprecation* or *self-depreciation*.

In essence **depreciate** means "reduce in price or value." This is the meaning it still expresses in the domain of business and finance, as when *assets are depreciated by 10 percent*. But the word can take on the more figurative meaning of "represent as having little value, belittle," and it then comes close to the extended meaning of **deprecate**. **Deprecate** is essentially "argue against," but by extension means "disparage," as in *The movie star deprecated his acting talent*.

This is why *deprecatory comments* and *depreciatory comments* mean much the same, and compounds such as *self-deprecatory/self-deprecating* and *self-depreciatory* are indistinguishable. With the extra syllable, **depreciate** and its derivatives seem to be the losers in these close encounters. **Depreciate** nevertheless maintains its ground in the world of finance, which it never shares with **deprecate**.

derisive or derisory
The distinction between these words seems to have developed in C20 British English, and since the 1920s, to judge by citations in the second edition of the *Oxford Dictionary* (1989). Both involve laughing something out of court, but their focus is different. **Derisory** attaches itself to the object of *derision*:
> *It was sold at auction for a derisory sum.*

Derisive meanwhile is the attitude of those mocking:
> *The derisive laugh challenged their complacency.*

Thus **derisory** is a synonym for "laughable," and **derisive** for "mocking."

This neat division of labor works – more or less – in British English, where the two words are about equally common. **Derisive** is almost always used to mean "mocking," though **derisory** appears in this sense in more than 10% of the BNC citations, as in *a derisory laugh*, the *derisory song*, and *derisory calls from the crowd*. But American English makes little use of **derisory**: it's outnumbered by 10:1 in data from CCAE, and so both meanings ("mocking" and "laughable") are loaded onto **derisive**:

> *The argument drew derisive laughter.*
> *The distinction between blacks and whites is derisive in this country of mixed races.*

The data also show that the meaning "laughable" is quite rare in the US.

dernier cri
In spite of appearances, this French phrase (literally "the last cry") is closer in meaning to "the last word" than "the last gasp." Though often translated as "the latest fashion," it's certainly not restricted to the world of *haute couture,* and can be applied to "the latest thing" in any field. In some English usage, **dernier cri** seems to carry a certain irony, as if the user was conscious of the literal meaning of the phrase. But in French it is an uncomplicated colloquial idiom which just means "the in-thing."
◊ Compare **bossa nova**.

derogatory or derogative
British and American dictionaries allow both forms for this adjective, though **derogatory** is given priority, and **derogative** often crossreferenced to it. Since first recorded in 1503, **derogatory** has developed several distinct uses; whereas the slightly older **derogative** (dating from 1477) seems to have had little use and no special applications. **Derogative** makes no showing in either BNC or CCAE, yet a Google search of the internet in 2002 found it used in about 2% of all instances of the adjective. It cannot yet be declared "obsolete."

desalination, desalinization or desalinisation
See under **salination**.

descendant or descendent
The first spelling **descendant** has become standard for the "(one) originating from a particular ancestor" – whether it serves as a noun or adjective. The spelling **descendent** is confined to the realms of astronomy and heraldry.
◊ Compare **ascendant**, **defendant** and **dependent**.

descriptive or prescriptive
Language changes all the time in small ways, offering us alternative words, idioms and spellings. Much of the time this passes unnoticed, but when people do notice a new usage around, they may react in one of two ways. They may simply remark on it without passing judgement – the **descriptive** approach. Or they may declare one particular form to be the right one to use – the **prescriptive** approach. *Prescriptivists*, whether they are experts or ordinary citizens, usually plump for the traditional form, whereas *descriptivists* recognize that language changes, and allow that there may be a choice of forms in certain contexts.

In the history of English, language commentators have swung from being typically **descriptive** in C16 and C17, to *prescriptivism* in C18, and later C19 and earlier C20. Under the influence of modern linguistics, more **descriptive** approaches were taken up – especially in the US – during C20. They go hand in hand with better understanding of language change, and better tools for describing it. A third factor is the generally more democratic climate of thinking, which allows that common usage and trends within it are really more powerful in language history than

149

abstract notions of what is correct or "logical" in English. This principle was articulated in Roman times by the poet Horace in the comment "the arbiter, law and standard of speech lies in usage" (*Ars Poetica* lines 71–2). Horace's words were known to and quoted by C18 scholars, yet the idea that common usage should influence judgements about language was little developed in their publications.

Dictionaries and style guides of C20 have varied in their stance, though generally speaking, the smaller the volume the more likely it is to work prescriptively. You need space to offer the full **descriptive** detail on usage. Even larger volumes may resort to *prescriptivism* in the absence of linguistic evidence, a point which is not always obvious to the reader (Peters and Young, 1997). It must be said that some people expect **prescriptive** judgements on what is "correct" and "acceptable," as simple answers to language issues. This C21 book endeavors to provide advice through **descriptive** information on usage, derived from primary and secondary sources. It indicates where particular variants are preferred, and the stylistic contexts with which they are associated – assuming that interested and intelligent watchers of the language would rather have the wherewithal to choose, than have choices made for them.

desert or dessert

The crux presented by these arises out of the several words that can be represented by **desert**.

1 With stress on the first syllable, **desert** is a common noun meaning "sterile dry place," and an adjective meaning "deserted," as in *desert island*. These derive via French from the Latin *desertum* ("deserted" or more literally "unbound"). The verb **desert** as in *deserted his wife* (with stress on second syllable) also comes from the same source.

2 The archaic noun **desert** means "what you deserve," and survives in the phrase *get one's just deserts*. This word is based on the past participle of Old French *deservir*, meaning "deserve."

The noun **dessert** ("sweet course of a meal") sounds exactly like **desert** (2), but the double *s* connects it with the French verb *desservir*, meaning "clear the table" and thus makes it the last course of the banquet. Only rarely do **dessert** and **desert** (2) cross paths and create ambiguity. But it's worth asking what kind of sweet course you expect at the end of a meal, if you *get your just deserts*!

déshabillé

See en déshabillé.

desideratum

For the plural of this word, see under -**um**.

despatch or dispatch

See dispatch.

dessert or desert

See desert.

determinative

This term is generally used by grammarians to refer to the role of *determiners,* possessive nouns and some other items, which precede the adjectives (if any) in a noun phrase and premodify the head noun. However

in Huddleston and Pullum (2002), **determinative** is used for the *determiner* only. See next entry.

determiners

In modern grammars and dictionaries, **determiners** are the words which occupy the first slot in the **noun phrase** (see further under that heading). They include:

* articles: *a   an   the*
* demonstrative adjectives: *this   that   these   those*
* possessive adjectives: *my   your   his   her   its*
  our   their
* quantitative adjectives: *few   both   some   each*
  every   all   no
* cardinal numbers: *one   two   three* etc.

Any of the above could go into the vacant slot in the following:

—— *good book(s)*

Ordinal numbers such as *first, second, third,* and "general ordinals" such as *next* and *last* are also **determiners,** though they typically work in tandem with others, as in *the second/next book from her pen.* Combinations of **determiners** most often involve quantitative words, as in *all the people* and *both my dogs.* The first **determiner** in such structures becomes the *predeterminer.* Other words which can be *predeterminers* are *such* and *what,* which can combine with the indefinite article as in *such an experience, what a business.* Combinations of three **determiners** are also possible, though uncommon. They involve both cardinal and ordinal numbers, as in *the first two students* or *the two first students.* The third **determiner** is then a *postdeterminer.* Modern English also uses *complex determiners,* such as *a few, a lot of, lots of, plenty of,* to express less definite quantities.

detract or distract

See distract.

deus ex machina

This Latin phrase meaning "god from the machine" captures an ancient Greek theatrical practice associated especially with Euripides. It involved hoisting up the divinities who appeared in the play to a position above the stage, from where they could observe and intervene in the affairs of ordinary mortals.

Modern popular culture has a remarkable **deus ex machina** in Superman who descends miraculously to the aid of beleaguered people in innumerable comics, videos and movies. The expression is also applied in contemporary usage to any improbable event or device of plot which provides easy resolution of a difficult situation.

developing countries

This term is now used instead of the less flattering "underdeveloped countries," to describe countries in which the majority of the population are engaged in agriculture rather than secondary industry, and where traditional customs and low rates of literacy prevail. The **developing countries** are typically in Asia, Africa, Latin America and the Pacific region, and they are often former colonies of European powers. Collectively they are sometimes referred to as the "Third World," a term coined when they were seen as independent of both the western and eastern blocs. (See further under **Third World**.) The **developing** countries still tend to have fewer resources and less economic and financial clout than the developed countries of Europe and North America. But they are at least equally represented at the United Nations, and at the Commonwealth Heads of Government meetings.

deviled or devilled
The choice between these is discussed under -l-/-ll-.

devil's advocate
This phrase is a direct translation of the Latin *advocatus diaboli*, the official who was appointed by the Catholic Church to argue against a proposal for canonization, and to draw attention to flaws in the case of the proposed saint. While sympathetic to the cause, he tries to prepare its advocate for any challenges that may be brought against it.

By extension **devil's advocate** has come to mean a person who voices arguments against the position held by most others, and who seems to argue for argument's sake. It is most often used of those who produce negative arguments against what others propose, though it can also apply to those who recommend what most others reject.

devisor or deviser
See under -er/-or.

dexterous or dextrous
Dictionaries recognize both spellings, though **dexterous** is the commoner of the two. In American English **dexterous** outnumbers **dextrous** by 5:1 in data from CCAE, whereas they come closer in British English (**dexterous** prevails by 8:5 in data from the BNC). **Dextrous** is nevertheless the more regular form, according to the *Oxford Dictionary* (1989). It reigns supreme in *ambidextrous,* where there's no alternative.
◊ For other cases in which -*er* becomes -*r*, see -er>-r-.

di or Di
On whether to capitalize this particle in surnames (such as *di Bartolo, Di Maggio*) see under **capital letters.** For the purposes of indexing, the particle is best treated as the first part of the name.
◊ Compare **van and von.**

di-
This prefix meaning "two" appears in borrowed Greek words and neoclassical terms such as:

dicotyledon	*digraph*	*dihedral*
dilemma	*diode*	*diphthong*
diptych	*di(s)syllable*	

Most such words are in specialized areas of learning and scholarship, where **di-** and its Latin counterpart *bi-* share the field to some exent. **Di-** has generated far fewer words in the life sciences; but it's used extensively in chemistry, and has superseded *bi-* in the naming of organic compounds. Only in the well-established names of acid salts, such as *bicarbonate* and *bisulfate,* has *bi-* retained its place. (See further under **bi-.**)

The prefix **di-** can also be a variant form of **dia-,** on which see next entry.

dia-
A legacy from Greek, this prefix meaning "through, across" is a component of borrowed words such as:

diabetes	*diagonal*	*dialect*
diameter	*diagnosis*	*diarrh(o)ea*
diathermy	*diatonic*	

It becomes just **di-** when combined with a word beginning with a vowel, as in *di(a)eresis, diorama* and *diuretic.*

Note that *dialogue* is essentially conversation across a group, because its prefix is **dia-** not *di-* ("two"). Yet *dialogue* is not uncommonly thought to be talk between two parties, probably because it's often contrasted with *monologue*. The term *duologue* exists to specify a conversation between just two people, but is mostly used in dramaturgy.
◊ For the question of whether to write *dialogue* or *dialog,* see **-gue/-g.**

diabolic or diabolical
These two adjectives arrived in English about a century apart (1399 and 1503 respectively) according to the *Oxford Dictionary* (1989), and both have subsequently been used to mean "Devil-like" or "devil-like" as well as "atrociously/inhumanly wicked." British and American databases show that **diabolical** can still be used with either meaning, whereas **diabolic** almost always invokes the Devil or his likeness, as in:
> the diabolic glamour of Nazism
> a grin that alternately looks angelic and diabolic

Diabolic is however rare by comparison with **diabolical,** outnumbered by about 6:1 in the BNC and 14:1 in CCAE. All this suggests that the eclipse of **diabolic** is nigh, while **diabolical** enjoys an ever wider range of applications, from the devilish to the hyperbolic or strictly frivolous. Compare:
> . . . used the cemetery for diabolical activities
> . . . won themselves a draw after a diabolical first half
> "a diabolical dress – a sailor dress with frills" intoned the fashion editor.

The two adjectives have always converged on the same adverb: **diabolically.** See further under **-ic/-ical.**

diacritics
See under **accents.**

diad and diadic
See under **dyad.**

diaeresis or dieresis
See **dieresis.**

dial tone or dialling tone
Around the world, the expression **dial tone** is more widely distributed, being standard in the US, as well as Canada and Australia. **Dialling tone** is used in the UK by the British Telecom network.
◊ For other divergent British/American compounds in which the American is typically uninflected, see **inflectional extras.**

dialect
Dialects are most obvious in the distinctive speech sounds of a particular region, in the "Deep South" vowels of those from somewhere between Texas and Tennessee, and the "burr" of Scottish speakers of English. Within large cities, **dialects** can be the hallmark of particular communities, for example the Cockney of East London, and of Brooklyn or Harlem

in New York. These **dialects** consist not only of different *accents*, but also of words, idioms, and sometimes grammatical patterns that are distinctive to the region or social group.

All aspects of **dialect** may impinge on writing, depending on the subject and nature of the discourse. In *Wuthering Heights*, the Yorkshire **dialect** vested in the puritanical servant Joseph is used to anchor the novel in the bleak northern regions of England:

> *"Sabbath no o'ered, und t'sound o' t'gospel still i' yer lugs, and ye darr be laiking!"* [The Sabbath isn't over, and the sound of the gospel still in your ears, and you dare to play!]

The author of *Huckleberry Finn* uses a range of **dialects** to locate the novel, though *dialectologists* disagree about how many. The most salient are the two used by Huck (South Midland white **dialect**) and Jim the runaway slave (Southern black **dialect**), which serve to remind readers of the socio-ethnic divide among Americans. Regional pronunciations and nonstandard grammar are evident in speech attributed to both, though more consistently in Jim's utterances:

> *"Yo' ole father doan' know, yit, what he's a-gwyne to do. Sometimes he spec he'll go 'way, en den agin he spec he'll stay..."* [Your old father doesn't know yet what he's going to do. Sometimes he expects he'll go away, and then again he expects he'll stay.]

Huck's narrative blends standard with *dialectal* American English:

> *"You don't know about me, without you have read a book by the name of* Tom Sawyer, *but that ain't no matter. That book was made by Mr Mark Twain, and he told the truth, mainly. There was things that he stretched, but mainly he told the truth. That is nothing. I never seen anybody but lied, one time or another..."*

Dialect serves several purposes in the novel, bringing its characters to life, while locating them in the Mississippi region, and connecting them with the larger social parameters of the setting.

Nonfictional writing is much less concerned with individual voices, and offers less scope for **dialect**. Yet the use of regional terms, e.g. *sidewalk* rather than *pavement*, will associate the document and its author with the North American continent rather than Britain. Regional spelling variants such as *plow/plough* can have the same effect – and seem to include or exclude readers, according to where they are coming from. Writers naturally choose the local word or form if their text is to be read within their own region (say the UK or US). The choice is more difficult for those wanting to communicate across regional boundaries, in which case they need to consider the most "international" option available. A familiar colloquial term may prove quite mysterious beyond its own region, however well it speaks to readers within it. The computer manual which refers to a binary switch as a *teeter-totter* will lose readers outside the **dialect** areas of the US and the UK where it's the regular term for "seesaw." Even standard English terms can pose a dilemma for writers looking to international audiences. The Australian playwright David Williamson had to retitle his 1974 drama *The Removalists* as "The Moving Men" for its New York production. In London, it had to be "The Removal Men".

Any questions about the "internationality" of words and phrases can be explored with the help of larger dictionaries, where US/British alternatives are mentioned for particular words. Some learners' dictionaries do it systematically, notably the *Cambridge International Dictionary of English* (1995), from which *dialect-free* options may be extrapolated. But entries in this book explicitly indicate an *international English selection* wherever possible – the option which is regionally neutral and/or accessible to the broadest spread of readers. See further under **international English** and **standard English**.

dialectal or dialectical

These adjectives connect with different nouns. **Dialectal** relates to *dialect* (see previous entry) and to *dialectology*. But **dialectical** relates to *dialectic(s)*, a form of philosophical argument in which the truth is sought through reconciling opposite positions. *Dialectic* originated with Socrates and Plato, but it was given new life by Kant and Hegel in the modern era, and subsequently adapted by Marx in the philosophy of *dialectical materialism*. A more recent extension of the noun *dialectic* makes it simply a way of referring to the tension between two opposing forces, such as church and state, without any philosophical implications. This usage is likely to irritate those with any knowledge of philosophy, and to intimidate those without it.

dialed or dialled

The choice between these is discussed under **-l-/-ll-**.

dialogue or dialog

See under **-gue/-g**.

dialyse or dialyze

See under **-yze/-yse**.

diarchy or dyarchy

See **dyarchy**.

diarrhea or diarrhoea

See under **oe**.

dicey or dicy

Dicey is the less regular of the two spellings, in terms of English word-forming rules (see **-e** section 1). But it reflects the informal flavor of the word, and both *Merriam-Webster* (2000) and *New Oxford* (1998) make it the primary spelling. In database evidence, **dicey** dominates, and it was preferred by the majority of US and UK respondents to the Langscape survey (1998–2001). Yet many respondents from Continental Europe endorsed the more regular spelling **dicy**. Perhaps English spelling would be safer in the hands of non-native speakers!

dicotyledon

For the plural of this word, see under **cotyledon**.

dictum

See under **-um**.

didn't use(d) to and used not to

These constructions are different solutions to the problem of putting the marginal modal *used to* into the negative. All are remnants of an otherwise extinct use of the verb *use* to mean "be accustomed to." See further under **used to**.

dieresis or diaeresis

This is the term for a diacritic used only sporadically in written English. It consists of two dots placed above a vowel, and thus looks rather like the German umlaut. The **di(a)eresis** indicates when the second of two successive vowels is pronounced separately, as in *naïve* and *waiver*. These days it is used primarily in proper names such as *Aïda, Chloë* and *Noël,* and sometimes also *Brontë,* to emphasize the second syllable. In earlier centuries it was also used to show the scansion of common nouns in editions of poetry.

The spelling variants **dieresis/diaeresis** reflect the standard American/British variation in the treatment of Greek diphthong *ai* or *hai* (see further under **ae/e**). In Greek **di(a)eresis** meant "division," "separation," based on the prefix *di-* (i.e. "two") and the verb *hairein* (i.e. "take", "choose"). A much more familiar derivative of the same verb is *heresy* (a separate division of the faith), where the key vowel has long since been spelled with plain *e*. The American **dieresis** is in line with this evolution, whereas the British **diaeresis** preserves the classical root in neoclassical form. With the *ae* ligature untied to make a digraph, it makes an ambiguous and cumbersome sequence of vowels. See further under **ligatures**.

dies irae

See under **danse macabre**.

dietitian or dietician

Contemporary dictionaries in Britain and America give priority to **dietitian** over **dietician**. Yet both spellings are acceptable, and in British English the two are almost equally common, by the evidence of the BNC. In American English however the weight of usage is behind **dietitian**, and it outnumbers **dietician** by more than 7:1 in CCAE. With its two *t*s, **dietitian** has a clearer link with *dietetics,* and this may well have helped to secure its position in C20.

Dietician was endorsed by the original *Oxford Dictionary* (1884–1928) as the "proper" spelling, on the analogy of *physician* and *politician.* Yet uncertainty over the form of the noun was probably fostered by the variety of adjectives related to diet: *dietary, dietic, dietical, dietetic* and *dietetical.* The ones ending in *-ical* have dropped out of use, according to the *Oxford Dictionary,* and *dietic* does not seem to be current. With them much of the support for the letter *c* as part of the stem has disappeared.

different from, different to, and different than

All three constructions have a long history of use, dating back to C16 and C17. Yet much ink has been spilled over their relative correctness, with insufficient attention to their contexts of use. Consider what you would do in the following:

1a   *Bob's approach was different ... Jo's.*
                                (from?/to?/than?)
1b   *Bob's had a different approach ... Jo.*
2a   *Bob's approach was different ... what we expected.*
2b   *Bob had a different approach ... what we expected.*
3a   *Bob's approach was different ... we expected.*

3b   *Bob had a different approach ... we expected.*
Whatever you do in the first two pairs, there's a strong chance you will choose *than* in the third pair. This is because sentences 3a and 3b require a conjunction, and *from* and *to* are essentially prepositions. Those who have learned to shun *than* after **different** will avoid it in 3a/b by rewriting them along the lines of 2a/b, where either *from* or *to* can be used. Yet the use of **different than** in sentences like 3a/b is standard in American English, according to *Webster's English Usage* (1989), and widely accepted in British English, according to the *Comprehensive Grammar of English* (1985), whenever a clause or its elliptical remnant follows (as in sentences 1b or 3a/b above). Data from the BNC shows multiple examples of *than* preceding *what* in type 2 sentences also. These uses of **different than** are frequent in Canada, according to *Canadian English Usage* (1998), and in Australia (Peters, 1995).

When choosing between **different from** and **different to** for constructions like 1a (with a simple noun phrase following), British writers are most likely to write *from* – by about 6:1, according to the evidence of BNC. For American writers the prime choice is between *from* and *than,* which appear in the ratio of 4:1 in CCAE. **Different than** is thus not the most frequent collocation, even in American English, but it's freely used in constructions like 1a, and probably gaining popularity (Hundt, 1998). Americans make little use of **different to**. Overall the corpus data confirms that grammatical issues are more important than regional differences, in deciding what to collocate *different* with. Only in the case of 1a (and the use of *to*) is it strictly a matter of British/American divergence.

The etymological arguments used to support **different from** no longer seem so powerful. The fact that *different* embodies the Latin prefix *dis-* ("away from") does not require the use of *from* after it, any more than with *averse* (see **adverse or averse**). There are natural English parallels for *to* in collocations such as *compared to* and *similar to,* and for *than* in comparatives such as *better than* or *worse than.* The verb *differ* itself combines with other prepositions/particles, for example *differ with* ("disagree"), and so provides only qualified support for using *from*. **Different from** has no exclusive claim on expressions of comparison. Writers and speakers everywhere use **different than** as well, depending somewhat on the grammatical context.

differently abled

This expression has been cultivated in some quarters to refer to persons with a handicap, either physical or mental. It circumvents adjectives such as *disabled, handicapped, crippled,* all of which seem to characterize the person in terms of malfunction or deficiency. **Differently abled** seeks to provide an affirmative alternative, to encourage members of the "abled" population to appreciate the different skills by which those with a disability manage their daily lives.

The intention behind **differently abled** is thus laudable and supportive of those who often suffer from negative stereotyping. But the phrase itself is not widely used – just a handful of examples in CCAE data, and 1 only in the BNC. Its form goes against it, with the polysyllabic adverb positioned up front. The usual position for *differently* is to follow the verb, in database examples such as *angled differently, treated differently, understood differently.*

Affirmative action is necessarily disturbing to the status quo, and linguistic affirmative actions of this kind do encounter resistance and ridicule. Parodies such as *differently advantaged* (living in poverty), *differently pleasured* (sado-masochistic), *differently qualified* (incompetent), satirize the gap between language and reality, and expose the euphemism. This is not an argument for neglecting the sensitivities of people with disabilities, but rather for seeking less cumbersome alternatives. (See further under **disabled**.)

◊ Compare **challenged**.

diffuse or defuse

The first spelling **diffuse** serves for the adjective "scattered or spread thinly":

> *diffuse lighting   diffuse population*

as well as the equivalent verb ("spread out"):

> *Large magnetic clouds would have to diffuse.*
> *. . . an unwelcome truth which the service was easily able to diffuse*

When pronounced, **diffuse** as adjective and as verb are quite distinct: the adjective rhymes with "loose" and the verb with "lose."

Enter **defuse** (meaning "remove the fuse from" or more figuratively "take the heat or tension out of "), often found in the phrase *defuse the situation*. But when it comes to emotions, either **defuse** or **diffuse** can be used, witness *defuse strong feelings* and *to diffuse ill-feeling*, among various examples from the BNC. In other applications, the two also converge:

> *The shock of these artists' social criticism is defused.*
> *Potential wars were diffused with the development projects.*

In such cases, the outcomes of these verbs are much the same, whether the metaphor is that of scattering light or dispersing heat. Readers may feel that one is more appropriate than the other – though light and heat are ultimately the same form of energy.

digestible or digestable

See under **-able/-ible**.

digital style

The computerization of documents allows them to be printed out on paper or delivered via pixels to the computer screen. Both involve digital processes, but it's the delivery of digitized material to screen that raises new questions – about how the text impacts on readers, and whether there are better and worse ways of styling it for readability. Assumptions about typography, such as the use of italics, and of serif versus sanserif fonts, need to be reconsidered (see **italic(s)**; **serif**). The visual structuring of text becomes more important, hence the increased use of headings and vertical lists, to make information more "scannable." With lists come the regular use of bullets (see **bullets**), which need to be recognized as part of our punctuation system, along with the white space that complements each bullet at the end of listed items.

Digital communication via keyboard and screen has generated new media (e-mail, text-messaging) which tend to compact language (see **SMS**), and make use of conventional symbols to convey attitudes (see **emoticons**). There's no suggestion that these abbreviated codes of communication will replace standard English, despite their popularity and effectiveness when the space to communicate in is very small. Still the formats of e-mail differ increasingly from other kinds of correspondence (see **e-mail style**, **Dear** and **yours faithfully**).

The electronic media present their own bibliographic formalities. Conventional ways of referring to internet sources are indicated at **URL**, and under **audiovisual media** section 3c.

digitize, digitise, digitalize or digitalise

The digital age is written into all of them, you might think, although **digitalize/digitalise** originated in C19 medicine, in the use of *digitalis* to treat coronary problems. It too is now applied to the process by which information is made computer-readable, but remains altogether less popular than **digitize/digitise**. In American English the choice is between **digitize** and **digitalize**, and the shorter form prevails, though CCAE confirms that the longer one is also in use. In British English the choice is between **digitize** and **digitise**. They are about equally used in data from the BNC, where there's little sign of the longer forms.

digraph or diphthong

Only the first of these words really relates to writing. A **digraph** is a pair of letters which represents or corresponds to a single sound, such as both the *ch* and the *ie* of *chief*. As these examples show, **digraphs** have their component letters set apart, whereas those of a *ligature* join together to form a single character. In earlier phases of English printing, letter combinations such as *ct* and *ae* were ligatures (ᴄᴛ and æ), but in modern print they are normally set as **digraphs**. (See further under **ae/e** and **oe**, and under **ligatures**.)

Diphthongs are sounds which contrast with pure vowels in that they have the quality of more than one vowel. Pure vowels are pronounced with the tongue held momentarily in one position, whereas **diphthongs** are moving vowels, pronounced by a tongue which is in transit from one position to another. This gives **diphthongs** their dual character, which explains the prefix *di-* ("two") embedded in their name. The Greek word *phthongos* ("sound") is the second element, spelled with three of the **digraphs** of modern English.

Note that "dipthong" is a relatively common pronunciation of **diphthong**, recognized in North American dictionaries (*Webster's Third,* 1986, and the *Canadian Oxford,* 1998), and in the UK by *Collins* (1991) but not *New Oxford* (1998). The spelling *dipthong* has yet to be recognized in any of them, though it appeared in more than 15% of all instances of the word in a Google search of the internet in 2003.

◊ Compare **dip(h)theria**.

◊ For a list of all the sounds of English (consonants and vowels) see Appendix I.

dike or dyke

These spellings represent two different words:

1 a water channel and embankment
2 a lesbian.

British English prefers to use one spelling for the two words, but tradition and usage diverge on which it is. The *Oxford Dictionary* (1989) prioritizes **dike** for both, which is eminently reasonable for the first word, since it's a variant form of *ditch*. The origins of the second word are unclear (or unprintable), and for it too *Oxford* prefers **dike** over **dyke**, and for the associated adjective **dikey** over **dykey**. Its reasons are not explained, though they may be grounded in the fact that many words which vary between *i* and *y* in the end revert to *i* (see **i/y**). A handful of British writers in the BNC use **dike** for either word, but the great majority use **dyke**, and this usage is reflected in the *New Oxford*'s (1998) preference for **dyke** (and **dykey**). Either way, British English supports convergent spelling for the two key words.

American English goes the opposite way, differentiating the two words by means of the two spellings. *Webster's Third* (1986) makes **dike** the primary spelling for "embankment," in keeping with etymology and the original *Oxford*, and it gives **dyke** (and *dykey*) as its preference for "lesbian." These preferences are endorsed by American writers represented in CCAE. They make regular use of **dike** for "embankment," confirming it in numerous placenames, and use **dyke** for "lesbian" on its (rare) appearances.

British writers will thus coincide with American English on one but not the other spelling, depending on which of the two British practices they observe. The alternatives are pretty well known, yet sensitivities may be aroused because of the particular application of **dyke** in the US. This makes it a non-trivial spelling issue for international communicators.

dilettante

This C18 Italian loanword is sufficiently assimilated in English to have an English plural: **dilettantes**. North American dictionaries (*Merriam-Webster,* 2000, and the *Canadian Oxford,* 1998) prefer **dilettantes** over **dilettanti**, and pronunciations with three rather than four syllables. *New Oxford* (1998) and the Australian *Macquarie Dictionary* (1997) do the opposite, preferring the Italian plural and four-syllabled pronunciations. Whether this seems *dilettantish* or evidence of *dilettantism* depends on your point of view. But the existence of those derivatives suggests that it's high time to treat **dilettante** as an ordinary English word.

diminuendo

For this there are three possible plurals. The choice between **diminuendos** and **diminuendoes** is discussed under **-o**; and **diminuendi** under **Italian plurals**.

diminutives

A **diminutive** is an affix which implies smallness of size. Suffixes such as *-ette* or *-let* and prefixes such as *micro-* and *mini-* are all **diminutives**. They are generally neutral in connotation, neither colloquial nor childish.
◊ Compare **hypocorisms**.

dinner

Everywhere in the English-speaking world, this word can raise uncertainties about the sort of meal it refers to. While *lunch* is clearly a midday meal, and *supper* one in the evening, an invitation to *come to dinner* at the weekend can pose a delicate dilemma until an exact time is mentioned.

There are two things at stake. Working people usually have their main meal in the evening, and so from Monday to Friday, and Saturday as well, **dinner** would be eaten with the setting sun, so to speak. On Sunday however, **dinner** used to be the ample midday meal to which many returned from their morning church service. But with changing habits in both eating and church-going, the "Sunday roast" tradition has vanished, and "Sunday dinner" is more and more an evening meal as on other days of the week.

Apart from the question of eating habits, the word **dinner** has had connotations which would be sought by some and avoided by others. It has always been the word for the formal meal arranged for a special occasion, but is also used on a regular basis by many. In the UK, **dinner** is preferred by *U-speakers* (see **U and non-U**), though it may seem pretentious for those lower on the social ladder. Their natural word would be *tea,* which still denotes the main meal of the day – not just a pot of tea and scones – within many British and Australian families. *Supper* is used by Americans and Canadians for the homely evening meal (and also in the UK). But for Australians *supper* is a late evening snack. Where *lunch* is concerned, the English-speaking world is in solid agreement that it refers to a midday meal, which may be light or quite substantial. See **lunch or luncheon**.

dint or dent

Both these go back to an Old English word for a "forceful blow," whence also its use to mean an "impression," typically on metal. Where the **dint/dent** was once a sign of enemy impact on your suit of armor, it now records an unfortunate encounter between your car and another solid object. For this or any other hollow or impression made in a surface, **dent** is the usual spelling in both the US and the UK, by the evidence of CCAE and the BNC. Dictionaries also allow **dint**, but it's rare in the databases, and more often heard than seen. As a verb **dent** is mostly used in the passive, as in *the barge's hull was dented,* and as a participial adjective when referring to *dented cars/cans* or the *kick-dented jukebox*. **Dent** also expresses more figurative kinds of negative impacts, as in *dented market confidence,* or *a dent in their image*.

Dint has a life of its own in the complex preposition *by dint of,* as in *by dint of hard work / persistent lobbying / boundless imagination*. This harks back to its once more general sense of "by force of," though often now diluted to "by means of" or "because of," as in *by dint of experience*.

In the US **dint** is also the conventional way of writing a one-syllabled pronunciation of "didn't" – when rendering dialectal speech.

diphtheria or diptheria

The second spelling represents a common pronunciation of the word, which is now registered in British and American dictionaries (*New Oxford,* 1998; *Merriam-Webster's,* 2000). **Diptheria** has yet to be registered as an alternative spelling, though this is probably only a matter of time. Both British and American databases contain a few citations for **diptheria**, all from printed sources which have undergone some sort of editorial scrutiny.

diphthong or digraph

See **digraph**.

direct or directly

Both these words may be used as adverbs, and in American and Australian English they may be used with any of the meanings attached to the adjective *direct*, in the dimensions of time and space. But British authorities since Fowler have insisted that **direct** as an adverb means "by the quickest route," and cannot / should not (like **directly**) be used to mean "straight away." The two kinds of meaning are not always separable in either word, as in the familiar instruction to Monopoly players:

Go directly to Jail. Do not pass Go . . .

Figurative uses of **direct** also mean "without deviation or delay," in BNC citations such as: *coming into drama training direct from school.* The immediacy of the time frame is surely at least as salient as the notional space and direction in such idioms. The point is that **directly** can be purely temporal:

With public funding it directly becomes a public project.

whereas **direct** always blends time and space.

Apart from its role as an adverb, **directly** also works occasionally as a temporal conjunction:

They came directly they heard the news.

This last usage is recognized in all the major dictionaries, British, American and Australian. The original *Oxford Dictionary* (1884–1928) dubbed it "colloquial," as did Fowler (1926), though he also thought it "defensible." *New Oxford* (1998) registers the use without restrictive label. *Webster's Third* (1986) labeled it "chiefly British," but *Merriam- Webster* (2000) notes it without any regional restriction.

direct object

See under **object**.

direct speech

The most dramatic way of reporting what someone said is **direct speech**, i.e. using not only their words, but their way of projecting them to the listener. Compare:

Hammering his shoe on the American table, Kruschev said: "We will bury you." (direct speech)

with

Hammering his shoe on the American table, Kruschev said that the Russians would bury them. (indirect speech)

The quotation marks in the first version are a sign that the speech is being quoted verbatim. The use of first and second person pronouns (*we* and *you*) shows the direct address of the speaker to his listeners, and re-creates the drama of his words for the reader. In indirect speech the pronouns are commuted into the third person, with the noun *Russians* and the pronoun *them*. The change of modal from *will* (with its high degree of possibility) to the more remote *would*, is another adjustment from *direct* to *indirect speech*. Both kinds of change serve to soften the impact of the statement and push it back into the past. (See further under **modality** and **person**.)

Between *direct* and *indirect speech* there are a number of other ways of quoting or reporting people's words. They include:

Kruschev told them that the Russians would bury them. (narrative reporting of speech)
Kruschev said they would bury them. (free indirect speech)

Kruschev threatened that the Russians would dig their graves. (narrative reporting of act)

These intermediate and oblique forms of reporting offer writers several ways of projecting the substance of actual speech, ways of modifying it and subtly controlling the reader's response.

dis-

This prefix, borrowed ultimately from Latin, often implies reversing the action of a verb. See for example:

disagree	*disarm*	*disclaim*	*disconnect*
discount	*discourage*	*disengage*	*disentangle*
disinherit	*dislike*	*dismount*	*disobey*
disown	*distrust*		

As these words show, it is usually combined with words of French or Latin origin, and with few Old English roots.

When used with nouns and adjectives, it usually implies oppositeness and works as a straight negative:

disadvantaged	*disapproval*	*dishonest*
dishonor	*disorder*	*dispassionate*
displeasure	*disreputable*	*dissimilar*
distaste	*disunity*	

Dis- replaced *des-*, the earlier French form of the prefix, almost entirely in common loanwords of the Middle English period. So for Chaucer *discharge* was *descharge*, and *disturb* was once *destourbe*. The only modern word to have resisted this respelling is *descant*. The respelling of *dispatch* as *despatch* is a different process (see under **dispatch or despatch**).

Dis- overlaps with some other negative prefixes in English, notably (1) *mis-* and (2) *un-*. For the difference between:

1   *distrust* and *mistrust* see **distrust**, and for *disinformation* and *misinformation,* see **mis-**;

2   *disinterested* and *uninterested,* and *dissatisfied* and *unsatisfied,* see under the first of each pair.

Note that **dis-** and *dys-* are separate prefixes, although *disfunctional* is sometimes seen for *dysfunctional*. See further under **dysfunctional**.

disabled and disability

Used in reference to people, these words are now under scrutiny. Signs such as *DISABLED PARKING* have made it the standard way of identifying and providing for individuals with a particular **disability**. But in phrases such as *the disabled* it projects negativity, and may seem to suggest total incapacity on the part of *disabled people*. The simple reversal of that phrase in *people with a disability* is greatly preferred, because it foregrounds people rather than the problem. The alternative *differently abled* is recommended by some, because of its more positive implications and the fact that it does not draw attention to the impaired bodily function, as do *blind, deaf, retarded, spastic* etc. (See further under **differently abled**.)

The lack of specificity in both **disabled** and *differently abled* can be a liability, for those who need to accommodate or provide for people with **disabilities**. Unless it's clear what the **disability** is, there could be problems on both sides. Thus television programs designed to help the deaf need to advertise the fact that they provide for the *hearing impaired* by means of signing. For those unable to walk, the way into public buildings has to be signaled somehow (by means of *Wheelchair access*). This puts the spotlight on the real issue of getting wheels up steps, and takes it off the person who is incapacitated, whether temporarily or permanently.

Not all groups with **disabilities** are inclined to seek more oblique references to their difficulties. The *Deaf Pride* group affirm the use of *Deaf* – and prefer it to be capitalized in any reference to their community, like the names of other national or linguistic groups (see **capital letters** section 1a). The affirmative use of sign languages such as *ASL* (American Sign Language), BSL (British Sign Language), and *Auslan,* their Australian counterpart, helps to accustom the hearing public to these alternative modes of communicating. Their status as community language again justifies the use of capitals.

The concern to avoid negative stereotyping of the **disabled** does not mean that we must expunge words like *blind, deaf, crippled, handicapped* from the language. They have idiomatic and metaphorical uses which do not necessarily prejudice the interests of those with that particular **disability**, as when something *falls on deaf ears*, or a plan is *crippled by the withdrawal of funds.* Arguably such idioms underscore the very problem faced by those with that disability, making it impinge on the wider community. Still such usage needs to be carefully scrutinized in its context and for its implications, as part of the sensitization process. For the fully abled, there's the salutary thought that we all ultimately find ourselves **disabled**, one way or another.
◊ For the basic issues of language engineering, see under **political correctness** and **Whorfian principle**.

disassemble or dissemble
See **dissemble**.

disassociate or dissociate
See **dissociate**.

disbar or debar
See **debarred**.

disc or disk
Both spellings are well used in the UK and the US – despite the notion that **disc** is British and **disk** American. The interplay between them is a continuing saga with new applications affecting their relative frequencies. While **disk** was the normal spelling from C17 on, the *Oxford Dictionary* (1989) records increasing use of **disc** in Britain from late C19 on, to make it "the usual spelling" as far as the Supplement (1972) was concerned. But by the 1990s **disk** is again in the ascendant in British English. So frequent are references to the *computer disk, disk drive, hard disk, disk space* etc. that **disk** is quite a lot more common than **disc** in data from the BNC. **Disc** nevertheless maintains a wider range of uses for *disc-shaped* objects of other kinds: the *licence disc / identity disc, disc brakes*, and especially the *compact disc* and *disc jockey.*

In American English the picture is also divided, but with **disc** appearing much more often than one might expect in CCAE. This is primarily because of its use in *compact disc* or just **disc**, as in *two-disc set* and *disc jockey* again. The convergence of the music and computing industries in the common digital medium means that *CD-ROM* is quite often explained as *compact disc (read-only memory)* as well as *compact*

disk – hardly surprising when the CD and the CD-ROM *diskette* look alike. The *video disc/disk* is another term in which both spellings appear. Yet computer hardware terms are normally spelled **disk**, in *hard disk, disk drive* etc. In other industries such as automobiles, manufacturers and reviewers use both *disc brakes* and *disk brakes,* and sportsmen suffer *herniated discs* and/or *disks.* Astronomers speaking of planetary bodies may use either **disc** or **disk**, but the astronauts journeying into space have prophylactic *dime-shaped discs applied behind the ear* to prevent motion sickness. So although *Webster's Third* (1986) gives **disk** as the primary spelling for most contexts and most compound terms (except in the phonograph record industry), American usage seems to be more fluid and variable, caught between the metaphorical "rock" of *discography* and the *hard drive*, so to speak.

Either spelling could be justified by etymology. The word is a descendant of the Latin *discus* and Greek *diskos,* so it all depends on how far back you wish to go.

discernible or discernable
This word was spelled **discernable** for the first three centuries of its existence, in keeping with its derivation from Late Latin *discernare.* But C19 turned it into the more latinate **discernible**, which has become the standard spelling. Still about 1 in 10 American and British writers use **discernable** (by data in CCAE and the BNC), either in deference to the older tradition, or by using the regular English wordforming principle for English verbs. See further under **-able/-ible**.

discourse markers
In any longish stretch of discourse, whether spoken or written, the reader/receiver welcomes some passing indications as to its structure. Writers and speakers sometimes go so far as to enumerate every structural unit of their discourse: *first(ly), second(ly), third(ly)*; or they may simply mark the boundary between one unit and the next with the help of words such as *another (point), a further (reason)* etc. Such words mark both the beginning of the new unit and the end of the previous one. Contrastive conjunctions and conjuncts such as *but, yet* and *however* may also serve this function when used at the beginning of a sentence. (See further under **conjunctions**.) Like the Monty Python series, they imply "And now for something (completely) different."

More extended types of **discourse markers** are the ones which provide a carrier phrase for identifying the new unit or topic of discussion, such as:

> *apropos of*
> *as far as ... goes*
> *where ... is concerned*

See further under **dangling participles**, and also **topic**.

discreet or discrete
These words both go back to the Latin *discretus* meaning "set apart." This meaning survives much more clearly in the academic word **discrete** (meaning "separate, distinct, unrelated") than the common word **discreet** ("circumspect" or "careful in one's actions and words"). In spite of these considerable differences in meaning, the two spellings were not regularly used to distinguish them until C16.

The nouns *discreteness* and *discreetness* correspond to the two adjectives in their contemporary meanings. *Discretion* is available as a synonym for *discreetness* only.

discrimination, discriminatory and discriminating

Discrimination has two faces, one negative, two positive, which are picked up in the different adjectives related to it. *Discrimination against* a particular social group is a negative phenomenon, implying prejudice as in *racial discrimination, sexual discrimination, discrimination against Catholics, discrimination in the workplace*. These negative values are embodied in **discriminatory** and neutralized in *nondiscriminatory,* a word applied to practices which are designed to avoid prejudicing or disadvantaging any social group. Many institutions, including governments and publishers, have formal codes of *nondiscriminatory language*. (See further under **inclusive language**.) The phrase *positive discrimination* is sometimes used in reference to institutional attempts to *discriminate in favor of* disadvantaged groups.

Other, less political uses of **discrimination** are also positive, though never explicitly called that. These are its psychological and aesthetic uses in referring to the ability to distinguish, and the exercise of good taste and judgement, especially in arts, music, literature and similar cultural domains. The adjective **discriminating** works in exactly this way, as in *the discriminating palate* or *a discriminating section of the concert audience*. Lack of taste and judgement are imputed to the *undiscriminating*, although the scope for **discrimination** is still affirmed. *Indiscriminate* implies the total absence of any principles of selection, and is used of wanton behavior and unmotivated actions, as in *indiscriminate shooting*.

discus

This word takes the regular English plural *discuses,* despite its classical appearance, and the fact that the sport of *discus-throwing* goes back to ancient Greece. Its use on the athletics field has no doubt helped its linguistic assimilation, where other neoclassical words keep their Latin plurals: see under **-us**.

disemboweled or disembowelled

The choice between these is discussed under **-l-/-ll-**.

disfranchise or disenfranchise

Both these words have borne the meaning "deprive of a civil or electoral right" for centuries. **Disfranchise** is the older of the two, dating from C15, while **disenfranchise** made its first appearance in C17. The *Oxford Dictionary* (1989) and *Webster's Third* (1986) give the wider range of meanings to **disfranchise**, but at the turn of the millennium **disenfranchise** is commoner by far, in both British and American English, judging by data from BNC and CCAE. It embodies expanding notions of disempowerment, in *socially and culturally disenfranchised men and women.* New frontiers are its use for a 19-year-old American woman *disenfranchised last year by the hike in the (drinking) age limit,* and the notion of *disenfranchised nerds like Bill Gates* (who felt excluded from the American male machismo). These examples show that **disenfranchise** covers both

having lost a right/privilege, and never having had it at all. References to the loss of a business franchise are also expressed through **disenfranchise**, in the UK as well as the US.

disfunctional or dysfunctional

See **dysfunctional**.

disheveled or dishevelled

For the choice between these, see under **-l-/-ll-**.

disinformation or misinformation

See under **mis-**.

disingenuous

See under **ingenuous or ingenious**.

disinterest, and disinterested or uninterested

The primary and most frequent meaning of **disinterest** is "lack of interest," and in BNC data this is its use about 90% of the time. This helps to explain the uphill battle with **disinterested**, which C20 usage commentators have tried to insist does not mean / cannot be used to mean "bored." They are driven by a desire to neatly distinguish **disinterested** from **uninterested** as follows:

* **disinterested** = "unbiased," "having no vested interest," as in *being asked to step in as the disinterested negotiator*
* **uninterested** = "indifferent," "feeling or showing no mental involvement," "bored," as in *begging an unknown, possibly uninterested deity for help*

Yet the use of **disinterested** to mean "indifferent," "bored" goes back to C17, and though the *Oxford Dictionary* (1884–1928) declared it obsolete, the files were kept open. The second edition of the *Oxford* (1989) updates the record with fresh citations; and databases confirm its currency in both the UK and the US. **Disinterested** means "uninterested," "bored" in more than 25% of all instances of the word in the BNC, and over 40% in American data from CCAE. Both *New Oxford* (1998) and *Merriam-Webster* (2000) register the sense, with usage notes to account for it. A further development, noted in *Merriam-Webster* but not *New Oxford*, is that **disinterested** can mean "having lost interest":

After that we became disinterested in each other.

This makes perfect sense if you construe the word as a combination of privative *dis-* and *interested*. (See further under **dis-**.)

Given that **disinterested** carries several meanings, we effectively rely on the context to show which is intended – as is true of many words. But with all the controversy, it may be better to seek a synonym for it, if you aim to communicate clearly and directly. Possible alternatives have been indicated in the discussion above.

disjuncts

See under **adverbs**.

disk or disc

See **disc**.

disoriented or disorientated

Both forms are used in British English to express the sense of "having lost one's sense of direction," "confused," but the longer form is clearly preferred.

In the BNC **disorientated** outnumbers **disoriented** by more than 2:1. In American English **disoriented** holds sway, with virtually no competition from the other form, on the evidence of CCAE.
◊ Compare **orient or orientate**.

dispassionate
This word sets itself apart from both *impassive* and *impassioned*. See under **impassive**.

dispatch or despatch
Both are acceptable spellings, although **dispatch** gets priority in all major dictionaries in Britain, North America and Australia. In British English the two spellings are about equally popular, judging by their frequencies in BNC. But data from CCAE shows Americans strongly preferring **dispatch**.

Of the two, **dispatch** has the better pedigree. **Despatch** seems in fact to have been a typographic mistake from the headword entered in Dr. Johnson's dictionary. (Johnson elsewhere in the dictionary used **dispatch**.) The mistake survived until corrected in an 1820 reprint of the dictionary, but by then it had established itself in usage. The fluctuation of other words between *dis-* and *des-* (see **dis-**) certainly helped to make it a plausible variant. However the word actually derives from the Italian *dispacciare,* and the frenchified spelling with *des-* is not justified by etymology.

dispensable, indispensable and indispensible
The standard spellings with *-able* reflect their forebears in medieval Latin: *dispensabilis* and *indispensabilis,* and for many dictionaries they are the only spelling. Unabridged dictionaries list the variants *dispensible* and *indispensible* as well, and though the *Oxford Dictionary* (1989) labels them obsolete, there are isolated examples in data from the BNC, despite the prevalence of **dispensable** and **indispensable** overall. The same is broadly true of American English. **Dispensable/indispensable** dominate the data in CCAE, yet there are rather more instances of *indispensible,* occurring in about 1 in 20 cases of the word. *Webster's Third* (1986) allows *indispensible* as an alternative spelling – but not *dispensible,* which is marked as obsolete. In any case, the Latin prefix *in-* probably nudges some writers towards *-ible,* as the more latinate of the two (see further under **in-/un-**).
◊ For the interchange between these suffixes in other English words, see **-able/-ible**.

dispersal or dispersion
The first of these can be used in many contexts, and simply expresses the action of the verb *disperse.* **Dispersal** finds a place in both general nonfiction and fiction, in reference to such things as the *dispersing* of a crowd, or a mass of fog. **Dispersion** has technical overtones because of its uses in describing chemical, physical and statistical phenomena, as in *optical rotatory dispersion* or *dispersion of gross earnings.*

disposal or disposition
Both these relate to the verb *dispose,* but **disposition** preserves the older and more formal of its meanings, in expressing the ideas of "arrangement," "control" and "temper or character." When it comes to *disposing* of something however, **disposal** has taken over, except

in legal contexts. So in dealing with a deceased estate, the will may refer to the **disposition** of property, but in other contexts it is normally **disposal**, as in *waste disposal.* The idiom *at your disposal* ("available for you to use as you see fit") also has **disposal** occupying a slot which was once filled by **disposition**.

dissatisfied or unsatisfied
With their different prefixes, these mean slightly different things. **Dissatisfied** is usually applied to people, and it expresses a specific discontent with emotion attached to it. **Unsatisfied** is used in more detached and analytical ways, to suggest that a certain requirement has not been met. Compare:
> *The candidates were dissatisfied with their campaign manager.*
> *The party's need for leadership was unsatisfied.*
The distinction of meaning ensures the coexistence of these participial adjectives, but only **dissatisfied** is matched by a verb *dissatisfy* and noun *dissatisfaction.*

dissemble or disassemble
These verbs mean very different things. **Dissemble** is a rather uncommon word for masking one's feelings or intentions, as in *no reason to dissemble her curiosity.* It has always been on the outer fringe of English usage, judging by the trail of obsolete meanings for it in the *Oxford Dictionary* (1989). Borrowed from French, the word is not really analyzable in modern English, and has been largely eclipsed by the more transparent *dissimulate* (see next entry). **Disassemble** is a straightforward combination of the prefix *dis-* and *assemble,* the action of taking apart something which was joined together.

dissimilate or dissimulate
What's in a letter? With these two it makes the difference between a latinate synonym for "disguise" (**dissimulate**), and the linguistic term **dissimilate**, meaning "make or become dissimilar." Both are uncommon words: **dissimulate** is hugely outnumbered by *disguise* (as a verb) in BNC data, and **dissimilate** occurs not at all there – which is hardly surprising, given its very specialized role. It describes the process by which one or other of two identical sounds in a word changes to something different. An example is the word *pilgrim,* a direct descendant of the medieval Latin word *peregrinus* (meaning "foreigner," "one who travels around"), where the first *r has/is dissimilated to l.*

dissociate or disassociate
Both these words mean "sever connections," and both have been used since C17. The first is derived from Latin, while the second is a calque of the French *désassocier.* Fowler (1926) gave **disassociate** the thumbs down by saying it was a "needless variant," and both British and American dictionaries give preference to **dissociate**. This accords more with actual usage in the UK than in the US, by the evidence of BNC and CCAE. The British database has **dissociate** outnumbering **disassociate** by more than 3:1, whereas it's the less common of the two in American data, occurring in the ratio 7:9. A regional difference thus seems be developing. With its extra syllable **disassociate** spells out the meaning "put an end to an association," which gives it a *raison d'être* alongside **dissociate**, wherever it's used.

distill or distil

These alternatives are very strongly linked with American and British English respectively, which presents a marked choice for other users of English. The *Oxford Dictionary* (1989) presents them as equally viable, and **distill** is the earlier and more transparent form, showing the word's etymology in Latin root *stillare* ("drip"). (It also underlies the *still* in which *distilling* commonly takes place.) **Distil** was the headword spelling used by Dr. Johnson, though he was distinctly erratic on such words (see **single for double**). It nevertheless set the style used by the great majority of writers in the BNC, whereas almost all citations in CCAE have **distill**. That spelling is of course consistent with all other words derived from the same root (*distillate, distillation, distillery, distiller*), not to mention the inflected forms *distilled, distilling*. All in all there are good reasons for using **distill**.

distinct or distinctive

Both these can be used for emphasis, but their roles are subtly different. **Distinct** is a general-purpose word meaning "clear or definite," while **distinctive** means "having the special character or quality of." Compare:

> There was a distinct smell of marijuana in the corridor.

with

> The distinctive smell of marijuana hung in the corridor.

As the examples show, the word **distinct** simply highlights the following phrase, whereas **distinctive** invokes knowledge shared by both writer and reader on a particular matter.

distract or detract

Both words suggest that the impact of something is undermined, but they identify different communicative problems. With **distract**, the attention of the audience is sidetracked, whereas with **detract** we imply that there's some deficiency in the communication itself, which would devalue it for anyone. Compare:

> The peacock in the dancer's arms distracted us from the dance.
> The jerky movements of the bird detracted from the smooth choreography of the dance.

Detract is normally followed by *from*, whereas **distract** is transitive, with a person or persons following it as the object ("us," in the example above). See further under **transitive**.

distracted, distrait or distraught

These are all variants of the same Latin word *distractus,* a past participle meaning "drawn aside." In English they designate a whole range of mental conditions. **Distrait** is the most recent of them, borrowed from French in C18. It implies being mentally preoccupied and detached from whatever is going on: the person *oddly distrait* hardly communicates with others around. **Distracted** is a C16 English calque of the Latin *distractus,* used of people whose attention is temporarily diverted, or who suffer from too many demands on their attention. **Distraught**, implying severe emotional distress, is an earlier (C14) anglicization of the Latin stem *distract-*.

Its spelling suggests that it was interpreted as a past form like *caught* and *taught*.

distrust or mistrust

Some usage guides suggest that these words differ slightly in meaning (**mistrust** is more tentative), but dictionaries lend no support to it. If anything, the suggested difference probably reflects the fact that **distrust** is the commoner of the two in both the US and the UK (by about 7:4 in CCAE and 3:2 in the BNC). In both American and British data **distrust** is preferred for the verb, appearing twice as often as **mistrust** in that role. **Distrust** is actually the later word, a hybrid formation of Latin and English which had no currency until C16. **Mistrust** is centuries older, and purely English.
◊ Compare **assume or presume**.

ditransitive

See **transitive and intransitive** section 1.

ditto

The **ditto** (") is a pair of marks which signify that the word(s) or number(s) immediately above should be read again in its place. The marks themselves may be vertical like an umlaut (¨), slanting (″), or curved like closing quotation marks ("), depending on the type resources available. The chief use of **ditto** marks is to avoid cumbersome repetition in successive lines of a list or catalogue.

Staff schedule for Christmas period

Saturday	24	December	am	Jones	Lehmann	Taylor
"	"	"	pm	"	"	"
Sunday	25	"	am	"	Wu	Fanuli
"	"	"	pm	"	"	"
Monday	26	"	am	Arnott	Bowie	Yeo
"	"	"	pm	"	"	"

Ditto marks were originally used in C17 calendars to avoid repeating the names of months (*ditto* was once the Italian word for "aforesaid"). In older documents, the letters *do* also served as an abbreviation for it, instead of the pair of marks. For the plural of **ditto**, *Webster's Third* (1986) prefers **dittos** over **dittoes**. This is silently echoed by the *Oxford Dictionary* (1989), where plurals are not indicated if they conform to the regular English pattern. (See further under **-o**.)

Ditto goes further in the US and Canada, as a noun and verb meaning "photocopy." Dictionaries connect these with the proprietary *Ditto* copier, although **ditto** is also used more generally as a verb meaning "repeat."

dived or dove

Outside North America, the past tense of *dive* is always **dived**, which goes back to the verb's origins in Old English. Within North America **dived** and **dove** share the role, and both are acceptable, according to *Webster's English Usage* (1989) and *Canadian English* (1997). **Dove** seems to have originated in Canada and the northern US during C19. Database evidence from CCAE shows that it has spread down the east and west coasts of the US, and serves as an alternative to **dived** in the *Washington Post* and *Atlanta Journal,* as well as the *Los Angeles Times.* In data from New York **dove** is less evident, probably because the *New York Times* (under Theodore Bernstein) campaigned against it. Elsewhere, **dove** and **dived** share the past tense for most uses of the word, whether it's a matter of plunging into water, lunging for the ball, or ducking for cover. **Dove** also takes on the figurative senses, as in:

He dove (dived) into cable TV in the 1960s.
Kim dove (dived) deep into the cookies.

But **dived** is still the only past participle, whatever the sense: *he had dived into the river / cable TV.* Note that compound verbs based on *dive,* such as *nose-dive, belly-dive, crash-dive* and *scuba-dive, sky-dive,* have **dived** for the past tense and past participle.

> **International English selection:** Since **dived** is current within North America and standard elsewhere in the English-speaking world, it's the past tense to use for global communication.

Djakarta or Jakarta and Djogjakarta or Djokjakarta

See **Jakarta.**

do

Like other auxiliary verbs, **do** has several functions. It regularly helps to phrase both negative and interrogative statements, and is occasionally used to express emphasis:

I don't like fresh air.
Do you like fresh air?
They do like fresh air.

These uses are common to both British and American English, yet Americans make rather more use of *do-support* in certain constructions with *have,* where the British find alternative constructions. Compare:

Do you have the time? (American)
Have you the time? (British)

The *Longman Grammar* (1999) found that **do** constructions with the definite article were used three times as often in American conversation and fiction as in British, whereas the British preferred constructions with *have* and *have got.* There was a similar trend (though less marked) with *have to* in negative constructions, where Americans were more likely to say *don't have to* and the British *haven't got to.*

In both American and British English, **do** substitutes for other verbs in connected discourse, in parallel constructions and conversational exchanges:

They asked for a map and I did too.
You wanted to go? I didn't.

British speakers often use **do** as well as other auxiliaries to substitute for another verb, as in *I haven't seen him yet, but I will do tomorrow.* Americans would omit the **do** and reduce it to . . . *but I will tomorrow* (Tottie, 2002).

Aside from those auxiliary roles, **do** functions as a main verb in its own right. Broadly speaking it means "work on (something)," as in *doing the dishes* and *doing the books,* but it takes on different shades of meaning according to whatever it's coupled with, and whatever context it occurs in. So *doing Germany* could mean completing an educational assignment on it, pursuing business connections in all quarters of the country, or touching down in Bonn and Berlin as part of a tourist package.

◊ For the plural of **do** when it serves as a noun, see **hairdo and do.**

docket

Should the *t* be doubled before adding verb suffixes? See under **-t.**

dodo

The proverbially defunct bird still needs a plural for its human analogues. *Dodoes* is given priority over *dodos* in *Webster's Third* (1986), whereas *New Oxford* (1998) reverses the order. As a foreign (Portuguese) word, **dodo** might be expected to take the regular English *s* plural. But it sounds like a nonsense word; and the traditional plural *dodoes* has several centuries of use behind it. See further under **-o.**

doggerel or doggrel

The first spelling is now the usual one for this word for pseudo-poetry or bastardized verse, while the second is one of the various alternatives which show people's uncertainty about where the word comes from. A possible explanation is that it's derived from the Italian *doga* meaning "stick" – it being the kind of verse which hits you over the head with its subtlety. But English-speakers are inclined to find their own word *dog* in it, and a negative meaning like the one embedded in *dog Latin.*

dogma

For the plural of this word, see under **-a** section 1.

doily, doiley, doyly or doyley

Doily is nowadays the most common spelling for the decorative linen or paper napkin used to grace a serving plate. The alternatives exist because the name embodies two variable features of English spelling, *i* varying with *y,* and *ey* with just *y* (see under **i/y** and **-y/-ey**). The word was the surname of a family of successful linen drapers, who, in late C17 England, "raised a fortune by finding out materials for such stuffs as might at once be cheap and genteel," according to the *Spectator* magazine. The aspirations to gentility emerge in yet another spelling of the word as *d'Oyley,* giving it a spurious French connection.

dolce vita

This Italian phrase meaning "(the) sweet life" gives English-speakers a way of alluding to what they would describe as "the good life" – a lifestyle supported by a bottomless bank account, fast cars, country properties, and everything that indulges the senses. Fellini's 1960 movie *La dolce vita* with all those ingredients helped to popularize the idea. A **dolce vita** lifestyle is for those who are free from regular working hours, so that there can be plenty of *dolce far niente* ("sweet doing nothing"), punctuated by moments of intensity.

dollhouse or doll's house

The term **dollhouse** is used in the US and Canada for a child's toy house. In the UK and Australia it's a **doll's house.** For other compounds which are uninflected in American English, see **inflectional extras.**

dolor or dolour

This rare word for "grief" has proved much less popular in English than in French, where it has multiple everyday meanings. It sounds literary rather than contemporary, and suggests a rarefied emotion whether the context is secular or transcendental: *Our Lady of Dolours.* Being largely confined to the written form, its pronunciation has been unstable, varying from "dollar" to "dohlar" to "duller." These coincidences with commoner English words may well have inhibited its use (see further under **homonyms**). Restoration and Victorian poets made **dolour** the familiar spelling, but it presents the usual -or/-our option, should you have to write it into C21 documents.

-dom

This Old English suffix still makes abstract nouns out of more specific ones, although those of C20 have a certain ad hoc quality, and few of them have wide currency. In the US words with **-dom** have been created in media coverage to describe the people involved in particular industries e.g., sports or entertainments:

> moviedom   newspaperdom   oildom
> theaterdom   turfdom

Only *stardom* (actually dating from 1865) seems to be in common use. The American penchant for such words is believed to have been strengthened by the use of *rebeldom* in the American Civil War.

Apart from these mostly temporary formations, English makes use of the suffix in a few words which describe particular states and conditions, such as *boredom, freedom, martyrdom, serfdom*. It also serves to form words which refer to an extent of territory, including *Christendom, earldom, kingdom, princedom* – or *officialdom*, where officials reign supreme.

The word *fiefdom* for "a person's domain of influence" is an early C19 coinage, based on *fief* – which in modern English means the same thing. Those familiar with *fief* regard *fiefdom* as a tautology, but for the rest *fiefdom* is more transparent. *Fiefdom* is far more widely used than *fief* in the US, by the evidence of databases, whereas in the UK the situation is reversed.

dominoes or dominos

Dictionaries all give preference to **dominoes** for the name of the game, as well as the more figurative and political uses of the word in *falling like dominoes*. The game has been known in England since before 1800, hence its traditional English plural -*oes* – rather than the regular -*os* which is now usual for foreign loanwords of this kind. See further under **-o**.

donut or doughnut

See under **doughnut**.

dopey or dopy

The choice between these is discussed under **-y/-ey**.

dot

In e-mail addresses or URLs, the stop used to separate elements of the address is referred to as **dot** everywhere in the world – not as *period* or *full stop*. Already it's built into *dotcom,* the byname for trading companies which conduct most of their business online, with virtual premises on the internet. See further under **URL**.

dot dot dot

This is an informal way of referring to ellipsis marks. See **ellipsis** section 2.

double comparative

One comparative marker is enough in standard English grammar: either *more keen* or *keener,* but not *more keener*. In earlier English there was no particular restraint on this, and Shakespeare's plays provide numerous examples with dramatic effect, as in *more braver* (*The Tempest*), *more hotter* (*All's well that ends well*), *more larger* (*Antony and Cleopatra*), *more mightier* (*Merchant of Venice*). Contemporary speakers may also use a **double comparative** for emphasis, though it's normally edited out of the written medium. A rare example in the BNC is the reference to *more remoter regions of Dartmoor.* See further under **adjectives** section 2.

double entendre

This phrase borrowed from C17 French is most often translated as "double meaning." The alternative meanings are not on the same plane however: one is straightforward and innocent, while the second is risqué. The second meaning is often occasioned by the context or conventional expectations, as in Mae West's legendary greeting to a male visitor:

> Is that a gun you've got in your pocket, or are you just pleased to see me?

In C20 French, the **double entendre** is referred to as *double entente* ("double signification,") and some English speakers use it instead of the older phrase.

double genitive

Despite their apparent redundancy, **double genitive** constructions such as *a friend of ours* or *no fault of Jo's* are established English idiom. Grammarians since C18 have puzzled over the way the construction iterates the *of* genitive with a genitive inflection on the following pronoun or personal noun. But the construction is confined to human referents: compare *a friend of the Gallery / no fault of the Gallery.* The **double genitive** seems to serve two purposes:

* *emphasis.* This is the effect of paraphrasing "not Jo's fault" as *no fault of Jo's,* or turning "our friend" into *a friend of ours.* The **double genitive** unpacks the phrase and foregrounds the noun rather than the person. In conversational examples such as *That book of Bill Bryson's is his best yet,* the construction helps to adjust the topical focus (see **topic** section 4).
* *clarification.* Clearly *a painting of Lady Rich's* and *a painting of Lady Rich* mean different things. The first (a *possessive*) makes the painting part of Lady Rich's collection, while the second (technically an *objective genitive*) says that it is a portrait of the Lady herself. (See further under **genitive**.) The duplication of the genitive marker is thus not redundant but clarifies the fact that the first construction is a possessive genitive.

The **double genitive** construction is not simply a *double possessive,* as it's sometimes called. Rather it is a functional part of English grammar, and has been part of English idiom since C14.

double modal

Constructions involving a sequence of two *modal* verbs do not normally appear in writing, though they are heard in some US dialects, in the Caribbean, and in the UK. Their use in Scots and Irish is reliably attested (Fennell and Butters, 1996), but most widespread in the US, in Midland and Southern (including southeastern) speech communities, black and white. The most commonly reported combination is *might could,* but others sometimes noted are *might can, might should, might would,* and the obsolescent *should ought* and *had ought to.*

The juxtaposition of the two modals in *might could* and *should ought* seems to underscore the points at which they coincide on the scales of modality, for *possibility* and *obligation* respectively. (See further under **modality.**) Modal verbs vary considerably in meaning from context to context, hence perhaps the felt need for a kind of triangulation to underscore either their tentativeness or the intended imperative. Whatever the semantics of the **double modal**, it's associated with spoken rather than written English, except where writers seek to capture the sound of dialect in dialogue or personalized narrative. See further under **dialect.**

double negatives
All the following sentences contain **double negatives**, but is every one of them a no-no?
1. *He didn't say nothing.*
2. *He didn't speak, I don't think.*
3. *He wasn't incapable of speaking.*

Only one of them (the first) is the target of common criticism. The second would pass unnoticed as natural, considered speech; and the third is an accepted way of expressing a subtle observation. The third type of **double negative** often escapes attention because the second negative element is incorporated as a prefix into another word.

Double negatives like those of the first sentence are very conspicuous, and they incur more censure than the others through their social connotations – the fact that they're used in many nonstandard dialects. Sociolinguists find unconvincing the claim that **double negatives** are illogical "because two negatives make a positive." The appeal to mathematics and logic is irrelevant when languages clearly do use **double negatives** (they are standard in languages such as French and Russian). No-one hearing the song line "I can't get no satisfaction" would doubt that it was meant to be an emphatic negative, with the second negative word reinforcing the first. This was exactly how Shakespeare used the **double negative** to underscore a dramatic point: *No woman has: nor never none / shall be mistress of it* (*Twelfth Night*). Rather the introduction of one negative word triggers the use of others, wherever the grammar will bear it. Thus contemporary grammarians speak of "negative concord" or "multiple negation," terms which allow for more than two negatives in quick succession. (See further under **negative concord.**) Still the construction is strongly associated with speech, and writers can find other ways of accentuating the negative.

The **double negatives** of the second and third sentences above have an effect which is far from emphatic. Those in the second sentence make it quite tentative, and give the speaker subtle control over the force of the statement. Subtlety is achieved in the third sentence through the use of a negative word plus a negative prefix (any from the group *in-, un-, non-, dis-, mis-*). The **double negative** again helps to avoid a bald assertion, and paves the way for a new perspective on the topic. Combinations of this kind are quite often used in argumentative writing, as are those which combine a negative with a verb involving a negative process, such as *challenge, deny, disclaim, dispute, doubt, miss, neglect, prevent, refuse, refute.* Other auxiliary negative elements are the adverbs *hardly* and *scarcely,* and the particles *unless* and *without.*

Writers who use two or more of the negative elements just mentioned are unlikely to be charged with producing substandard English. They may well create difficult English however, and sentences which require mental gymnastics of the reader:

> *He would never dispute the claim that there were no persons in the country unable to survive without a government pension.*

It is one of the precepts of the Plain English movement that such multiple negatives are to be avoided, and the reasons are obvious. See further under **Plain English.**

double possessive
See under **double genitive.**

double superlatives
Standard English no longer permits expressions such as *most unkindest,* where the superlative is marked by the preceding *most* as well as the *-est* inflection. In C16 there was no constraint on their use, and Shakespeare uses them in several of his plays to underscore a dramatic judgement. The use of *most highest* in religious discourse is similarly rhetorical, and was exempted by some C18 grammarians (notably Lowth, Bishop of London) from the general censure of **double superlatives.** Grammarians can certainly argue that one or other superlative marker is redundant, and in measured prose one of them would be edited out. Just which depends on the adjective's form. See further under **adjectives** section 2.

doublespeak
This is *double talk,* a combination of euphemism and obfuscation used by institutions and persons to mask unpleasant realities and deceive others as to what is going on. George Orwell's *1984* provides classic examples of **doublespeak,** though he himself did not create the word. It nevertheless spans his *doublethink* and *newspeak,* and lends negative connotations to other formations ending in *-speak.* See further under **-speak.**

doubling of final consonant
To double or not to double, that is the question. It comes up with new verbs made out of nouns and adjectives: what to do with the past forms of verbs derived from *banquet* and *sequin,* for example. It is also the basis of regular differences between British and American spelling. Let's review the general rules before looking at the variations.

In a two-part nutshell, the general rule is that you double the final consonant if:
* the vowel before the consonant is a single one (as in *wetted* or *regretted*), not a digraph (compare *seated* and *repeated*); and
* the syllable before the suffix is stressed (as in *wetted* and *regretted*), not unstressed (compare *budgeted* and *marketed*).

The rule applies to any noun, verb or adjective ending in a single consonant, when suffixes beginning with a vowel or *-y* are to be added. The following examples show how the rule works with various suffixes and after words of one and two syllables:

skims	*skimming*			*bosom*	*bosomy*
win	*winner*	*begin*	*beginner*	*sequin*	*sequined*
step	*stepped*			*gallop*	*galloped*

| stir | stirred | deter | deterred | butter | buttered |
| knit | knitting | admit | admitting | audit | auditing |

(Further examples are discussed under **-p/-pp-, -s/-ss-** and **-t.**) Note that some words, especially those ending in *-r,* vary their spelling because of changes in stress before particular suffixes:

confer	conferred	conference
defer	deferred	deferent
prefer	preferred	preferable
refer	referred	reference

These changes are all in accordance with the rule above. They apply also to derivatives of these words, such as *undeterred, dispreferred* etc.

Exceptions, variations and anomalies Certain kinds of words diverge from the rules just mentioned, in all or some parts of the English-speaking world. They include those ending in:

1 *-x* such as *tax* and *transfix* (never doubled, even when their last syllable is stressed).

2 *-c* such as *panic* (always "doubled" to *-ck*, to preserve their "k" sound: see further under **-c/-ck-**).

3 a syllable which is identical with a monosyllabic word. For example:

backlog	eavesdrop	fellowship	format
handicap	kidnap	leapfrog	overlap
program	sandbag	waterlog	worship
zigzag			

In British English, these words double the final consonant in spite of the lack of stress, to become *backlogged, handicapped, programmed* etc. In American English they may not: alternative spellings such as *kidnaped, programed* and *worshiped* are also in use. See **kidnapped, program** and **worshipped**.

Words ending in *-l* form the largest group of exceptions in British English, and are always doubled, whether or not the last syllable is stressed. In the US the common practice is to apply the general rules given above, and to double only when there is stress on the final syllable. So most Americans write *reveled* with one *l* and *rebelled* with two, whereas the British, and most Australians and Canadians, spell *revelled* in the same way as *rebelled*. These anomalies are discussed further under **-l-/-ll-**.

doubtless or undoubtedly

See **undoubtedly**.

doughnut or donut

In both British and American English, **doughnut** is the dominant spelling. But the spelling **donut** has a high profile, being featured in the names of most major American **doughnut** chains, as well as one-offs such as the *Drive-thru Donut Shoppe!* American writers are therefore not averse to using **donut** when referring to the generic *donut shop* and its staple product. CCAE also contains a scattering of **donut** in more figurative applications of the word, e.g. the *inflated donut* used as a flotation device, or the putative *year of the donut*. These suggest that the spelling is beginning to gain ground beyond its sugary origins, at least in the US.

◊ For the respelling of other words ending in *-ough,* see under **gh**, and **spelling** section 5.

dove or dived

See **dived**.

down-

This familiar particle combines like a prefix with both verbs and nouns, to indicate a descent, or the movement from a higher to lower position. It combines with verbs in *downcast, downfall, downpour, downturn,* and usually bears the stress in those words. When combined with nouns, in *downbeat, downhill, downstairs, downstream,* the stress is more variable, as if it is less fully integrated. Yet in each case, **down-** is set solid with the word to which it is attached.

downtoners

See under **hedge words** and **adverbs** section 1.

downward or downwards

See under **-ward**.

doyly, doyley or doiley

See **doily**.

DR, Dr(.) or dr(.)

In full caps **DR** stands for "dead reckoning," used by ships to estimate their position when neither landmarks nor the sun or stars are visible. As **Dr(.)** before a person's name, it stands for the title "Doctor" (of medicine or any other specialization). Used after the name on invoices it's an abbreviation of "debtor," written **Dr.** according to *New Oxford* (1998), and **dr.** according to *Merriam-Webster* (2000). **Dr(.)** is also the standard abbreviation for *Drive* in street addresses. The use/nonuse of a stop depends on your policy on *contractions*. See **abbreviations** section 2.

draconian, Draconian and draconic

When speaking of harsh laws and severe punishments, which should it be? First choice is **draconian/Draconian** which invokes *Draco,* the punitive Greek legislator of C7 BC, who made death the punishment for almost every public offence. The *Oxford Dictionary* (1989) still has it capitalized, though the lower case form prevails in British and American English. In data from the BNC, **draconian** dominates by more than 4:1, and the proportions are similar in CCAE, except where (in some American newspapers) **Draconian** seems to be cultivated as house style. The word serves to evaluate legislation and official policies on either side of the Atlantic:

> *draconian wage measures*
> *the draconian 42-year sentence had been negated*
> *draconian cuts on Medicare*
> *draconian rules governing drug trafficking*

The adjective **draconic** is quite rare by comparison. It is a neoclassical adjective based on the Latin *draco* ("dragon"), used by scholars and scientists to refer to dragon-like forms in art and nature. But as the *Oxford Dictionary* shows, it has long been confused with the first adjective, and sometimes replaces it. The few occurrences of **draconic** in the BNC and CCAE were almost all of this kind, as in *draconic vagrancy laws* from CCAE. Most dictionaries allow that **draconic** may do service for **draconian**.

draft or draught

The borders between these two spellings are still being adjusted in British English. Both relate to the verb *draw,* whose many descendants range from words for pulling a load, or drawing water, air or money, to sketching, composing a document, dividing up one's livestock or choosing men for military service. The older spelling **draught** has few analogies in English except *laughter,* and the more phonetic **draft** gained ground on it in late C18 and early C19. In American English **draft** is the standard spelling for all uses of the word as noun, adjective and verb (*first draft, draft legislation, draft a new constitution*), and in derivatives such as *drafty* and *draftsman*. In Britain, the scene is much more complicated.

In British English **draft** is now accepted in the contexts of banking, in selecting soldiers and livestock, and especially when referring to the first written version of a document. This last usage accounts for more than 80% of its occurrences in the BNC, as noun, adjective and verb, and they make **draft** overall much more frequent than **draught**. Yet still the business of making technical drawings is distinguished with the spelling **draught**, and in *draughtsman/draughtsperson*. **Draught** persists in references to the taking of fluids, as in *a good draught of ale* and of course *draught beer*. It identifies an *icy draught* under the door, and presents itself also in the adjective *draughty*. The animals used for traction are *draught horses,* and vehicles too may be used for *draught work*. In maritime jargon, **draught** is the measure of how deep the vessel lies in the water (the distance from the waterline to the hull).

English-speakers in other parts of the world take their positions on the borders of this British/American divide. Canadians accept both practices but make more use of the American, according to *Canadian English Usage* (1997). Australians still endorse *draught beer* and *draught horse,* but are uncommitted when it comes to the flow of cool air under the door. They regularly use **draft** for technical drawing as well as for composing documents, and this spelling is confirmed in the official nomenclature *draftsperson* or *drafting officer/assistant,* recommended in the Australian Standard Classification of Occupations (1990). In the context of marine architecture, a survey taken in 1998 showed that the majority of professionals used **draft** rather than **draught** in relation to the *ship's draught*.

Thus boundaries between **draft** and **draught** are still being redrawn – even in British English. The BNC contains 10 examples of *drafty,* suggesting that the spelling comes naturally to some writers, and may not be edited out. *Draughty* appears almost 100 times, however, and is still the one, according to British dictionaries.

dramaturg, dramaturge or dramaturgist

In C19 both **dramaturge** and **dramaturgist** referred to one who wrote dramas for the stage. But **dramaturge** is now applied to the specialist adviser to a theatre company, who devises the repertoire, and investigates and adapts the play scripts for performance. According to *Webster's Third* (1986), the role originated in European theatres. **Dramaturg**, the most recent form of the word, is German in origin, and now the commonest of the three, by the evidence of CCAE. However **dramaturge** is the spelling prioritized by both *Merriam-Webster* (2000) and *New Oxford* (1998).

drank or drunk

See under **drink**.

draughtsman or draftsman

In the UK these spellings distinguish two very different crafts. The **draughtsman** creates technical drawings for architects and engineers: the **draftsman** writes the first version of legislation and official documents. In the US, Canada and Australia, this distinction is not made, and **draftsman** is used for both. See further under **draft or draught**.

dreamed or dreamt

Both spellings are in use for the past forms of *dream,* but **dreamed** is far more common in the US, by a factor of 20:1 in data from CCAE. In the UK **dreamt** is more popular but still in the minority: **dreamed** outnumbers it by 3:1 in data from the BNC. See further under **-ed**.

drier or dryer, and driest or dryest

You can usually count on the fact that **drier** represents the comparative form of the adjective *dry,* while **dryer** is the agent noun referring to an appliance, such as a *clothes dryer*. The *Oxford Dictionary* (1989) and *Webster's Third* (1986) nevertheless make **drier** the preferred spelling for the noun, and it's used by a few British writers represented in the BNC (about 10%), hardly at all by American writers in CCAE. The rare instance of *hair drier* is greatly outnumbered by uses of **dryer** in both domestic and industrial contexts. Newer or less familiar appliances such as the *lettuce dryer* or the *doggie dryer* used in canine *haute couture* are invariably spelled with *y*.

Drier is writers' choice for the comparative adjective in both databases, whether the word refers to climatic conditions, the taste of wine or food, or the analysis of politics, literature and humor, as in *chapters on drier subjects* and the *drier Midwestern drollery*. Whether positive or negatively valued, **drier** is the spelling used. *Webster's* also allows for **dryer**, the regularized spelling, though CCAE contains very few examples of its use.

When it comes to the superlative, American and British usage diverge. **Dryest** is more popular than **driest** with American writers in CCAE, whereas **driest** is the only superlative form to be found in the BNC. The adjective thus seems to be the stronghold of the spelling convention by which final *y* changes to *i* before the vowel of the suffix (see further under **-y>-i-**). In C18 this mutation was also found in *driness* and *drily,* though it is no longer seen in the first of those, and is disappearing from the second (see **drily or dryly**). The resistance of the nouns (*dryness, dryer*) to mutation suggests that the "-*y* becomes -*i*- rule" is increasingly restricted to inflectional suffixes (see **suffixes**). At any rate, the prevailing use of **dryer** for the agent noun ("appliance") makes a useful contrast with **drier** for the adjective – and lends hope that dealing with *some dryer company* doesn't mean an uphill social encounter.

dries or drys

These spellings do double service, as:

* singular form of the verb *dry,* usually **dries** as in *while the glue dries, the soil never dries out*. Very occasionally in American data it is **drys**, as in *depressed real estate market drys up*
* plural form of the noun *dry,* as opposed to "wet." The two terms are used in British English to refer

to distinctive political stances, the **dries** being reluctant to spend public money on social welfare, and proponents of economic rationalism. Their opposition makes a combative headline: *Bone Dries meet the arch-Wet.* In American English the terms refer to those for and against alcoholic prohibition, where the **drys** support it: *wets and drys are separated in the campus pubs.*

drily or dryly

The first of these is much more familiar in British English than any other. In data from the BNC, **drily** outnumbers **dryly** by 5:1, whereas in the American English of CCAE the ratio runs heavily in favor of **dryly**. The American preference for **dryly** correlates with its greater use of *dryer* for both adjective and noun. See further under **drier or dryer**.

drink, drank, drunk and drunken

The parts of this irregular verb have been unstable for centuries, and still seem to be shifting and changing places. The forms **drink**, **drank**, **drunk** are always given as the standard set for present, past tense and past participle, yet larger dictionaries show that things are not so simple. The *Oxford Dictionary* (1989) notes without judgement the "occasional" use of **drunk** for the past tense, while *Webster's Third* (1986) presents it as a colloquial or dialectal form. Both BNC and CCAE contain a sprinkling of it among their spoken samples. The dictionaries also note that **drank** may occasionally be found as past participle. *Oxford* suggests that this is to "avoid the inebriate associations of **drunk**," though there's little evidence of its use – for this or any other reason – even in spoken samples of the BNC. *Webster's* also presents without judgement the use of **drank** for the past participle, and, according to a usage note in the *Random House Dictionary,* this is often done by educated Americans. Still there's little evidence that the variant form appears in written documents, as *Webster's English Usage* (1989) notes.

The form **drunken** (once a past participle) has only a restricted role as attributive adjective: *drunken rage, a drunken sailor.* It thus complements **drunk**, the predicative adjective in expressions such as *They were drunk and disorderly.* See further under **adjectives**.

drink driving, drunk driving or drunken driving

The same legal offence goes by slightly different names in different parts of the world. **Drink driving**, used in the UK and Australia, is based on the euphemistic use of *drink* as a noun meaning "alcoholic liquor," found in idioms such as *took to drink*. In North America **drunk driving** makes it clear that the problem is alcohol, as does **drunken driving**, the occasional alternative. American law dubs it *driving while intoxicated,* or *DWI* for short.

drivable or driveable

See under -eable.

driveling or drivelling

For the choice between these, see -l-/-ll-.

driving licence, driver's license or driver's licence

British drivers carry a **driving licence**, and Americans a **driver's license**. Australians diverge slightly with **driver's licence**; while in Canada both **driver's licence** and **driver's license** have currency.

druggist, pharmacist or chemist

See under **pharmacist**.

drunk or drunken

See under **drink**.

dryer or drier, and dryest or driest

See **drier**.

drys or dries

See **dries**.

d.s.p.

See **decessit sine prole**.

d.t.'s or DTs

See **delirium tremens**.

due to or owing to

Due to has been under a cloud for three centuries, though the basis of objections to it has shifted. Fowler (1926) found the problem in the need to make *due* an adjective or participle properly attached to a relevant noun, not to a notion extracted from a whole clause/sentence. The first sentence below was therefore unacceptable, and should be rewritten as the second or third:

Due to unforeseen circumstances the dinner was postponed.

The postponement of the dinner was due to unforeseen circumstances.

Owing to unforeseen circumstances, the dinner was postponed.

Similar objections had in fact been raised against **owing to** in C18, which quietly faded away as it established itself as a compound preposition. **Due to** began to be used in the same way in late C19 (the first *Oxford Dictionary* citation is from 1897), and objections to it begin to appear early in C20.

Yet Fowler himself noted that this prepositional use of **due to** was "as common as can be", and the *Oxford Dictionary Supplement* (1933) confirmed its frequency in the US. The tide of usage has swept it in, as Gowers admits in his 1965 edition of Fowler, when BBC announcers and even the Queen's own speech-writer have to be counted among its more conspicuous users. There is clearly no reason to perpetuate the shibboleth against **due to**, when the grammatical grounds for objecting to it are so dubious. *Webster's English Usage* (1989) affirms that it is "grammatically impeccable" and used by reputable writers without qualms. See further under **shibboleths**.

dueling or duelling

The choice between these is discussed under -l-/-ll-.

dullness or dulness

Up-to-date dictionaries all give priority to **dullness**, and database evidence confirms that **dulness** is very rare in British English and not used in American. The second spelling exists only as an example of the C18 intervention in the spelling of final *l* in derivative words. See further under **single for double**.

dummy subject

Whatever it might suggest, **dummy subject** is used by grammarians for the role of *it* or *there* in expressions such as:

> *It's raining.*
> *It's tomorrow they were talking about.*
> *There's no clear answer to the question.*

Sentences like these identify their *topic* through the predicate of the clause instead of foregrounding it as the subject – hence the need for the slot-filler, *it* (also known as *prop* it) and *there* (= *existential* there).
◊ See further under **topic** and **cleft sentences.**

duologue or dialogue

See under **dia-**.

Dutch or dutch

See under **Holland**.

dwarfs or dwarves

The first form **dwarfs** is preferred by all dictionaries for the plural of *dwarf*. Database evidence from CCAE and the BNC underscores this, showing that it's the preferred form for both American and British writers, by more than 25:1. The use of **dwarfs** as a verb (as in *this source of income dwarfs social security*) makes up only about 20% of the total, so clearly it's preferred for the plural noun. **Dwarfs** is also sounder in historical terms because the *f* in its spelling is relatively recent, unlike others whose *-ves* plural goes back to Old English. **Dwarves** seems to have arisen on the analogy of *wharf/wharves*, where the plural with *-ves* connects with its antecedents. The number of words with *-ves* plurals is steadily declining, and there's no reason to count *dwarf* among them, on the strength of very sporadic uses of **dwarves**. See **-f>-v-** for other nouns of this type; and **-v-/-f-** for **dwarf** as a verb.

dwelt or dwelled

Dwelt enjoys much more popularity these days in British English, and outnumbers **dwelled** by 10:1 in the BNC. American English shows the same tendency, though less pronounced. The ratio of **dwelt** to **dwelled** is 2:1 in data from CCAE. There was no particular difference according to whether the verb was used in the physical sense "live" (*dwell in*) or the more abstract idiom *dwell on* (= "concentrate attention on"). The greater use of the *-ed* ending by Americans is in keeping with their general preference for more regular endings. See further under **-ed** section 1.

dyad, diad or duad

The spelling **dyad** is preferred in all up-to-date dictionaries, and the only one with multiple examples in CCAE. **Diad** is a current alternative in *Webster's Third* (1986), though according to the *Oxford Dictionary* (1989) it's obsolete. The rare third spelling **duad** also seems to be obsolete by the *Oxford*'s dating, yet is glossed with no indication of obsolescence in *Webster's*. New uses for **dyad** in sociology and theories of communication seem to account for its vitality, as well as the variation in spelling. The tendency to replace *y* with *i* is familiar enough in

other nouns, though **dyad** represents the original Greek root more exactly.

dyarchy or diarchy

Both are recognized spellings, yet dictionaries diverge over which should be given priority. *Webster's Third* (1986) stands alone in preferring **dyarchy**, and this is the only spelling to be found in CCAE. The *Oxford Dictionary* (1989) prefers **diarchy**, based strictly on its view of the etymology (as *di-* + *-archy*), and so it dubs **dyarchy** "erroneous". *Webster's* however suggests that the first element can be traced to Greek *dy-* or *dyo-* (otherwise transliterated as "duo," but with the same meaning as *di-*). Whatever the explanation, **dyarchy** is the more frequent spelling in both BNC and CCAE, and the *Oxford*'s own citations run 5:3 in its favor. Perhaps users of the word feel it looks more consistently Greek as **dyarchy**.

The same divergence in spelling applies to adjectives based on the noun. While *Oxford* gives priority to spellings with *i* in the stem: *diarchic, diarchical* and *diarch(i)al, Webster's* gives them as *dyarchic*, also *dyarchical* or *dyarchal*. Again the *Oxford*'s citations offer rather more support for the spellings with *y*. For the choice between *-ic* and *-ical* endings, see **-ic/-ical**.

dye and dyeing

This word resists the standard spelling rule to drop *-e* before a suffix beginning with a vowel – with good reason – to distinguish itself from *dying*. The distinction is however only about a century old. For centuries, either word could be spelled either way, and those who wished might spell both the same way, relying on the context to communicate the difference. So Addison in C17 spelled both *dye*, while Johnson made both *die*. (See further under **i/y**, **-ie>-y-**, and **-e**.) The convergence of the two words allows a British hairdressing salon to solicit customers under the name *CURL UP AND DYE*.

dyke or dike

See **dike**.

dynamo

The plural of this word is the regular *dynamos*, according to both *Webster's Third* (1986) and the *Oxford Dictionary* (1989). See further under **-o**.

dys-

This Greek prefix means "bad, faulty," and almost all the words it appears in are bad news. It may be that your breathing is labored (*dyspnoea*), you're having trouble swallowing (*dysphagia*), digestion is poor (*dyspepsia*), your bowels are in disarray (*dysentery*), and urinating is a problem (*dysuria*). Apart from its use in designating medical problems, **dys-** also serves to designate intellectual deficiencies (*dyslexia* and *dyscalculia*).

Dys- occasionally forms words which contrast with an opposite number formed with *eu-*, for example *dysphemism* as opposed to *euphemism* (see further under **euphemisms**). The recently coined *dystopia* works on that basis, as an antonym for *Utopia* – misconstrued as "Eutopia." (The name *Utopia* created by Sir Thomas More for his perfect society actually comprises *ou*, "not", and *topos*, "place," i.e. "no place.")

◊ On the interplay between **dys-** and **dis-,** see next entry.

dysfunctional or disfunctional, and dysfunction or disfunction

The largest American and British dictionaries (*Webster's Third,* 1986; *Oxford,* 1989) recognize **disfunctional** as a variant of **dysfunctional**, and *disfunction* for *dysfunction*. The substitution of *i* for *y* in the spelling is not so remarkable (see **i/y**), and both *dys-* and *dis-* have negative meanings. There are just a few examples of **disfunction/disfunctional** in CCAE and the BNC, suggesting that the words are losing their academic flavor, and beginning to be part of more general usage.

e-

In the countdown to the millennium, the letter *e* sprang to life as a prefix. Literally it means "electronic," and more broadly that electronic communication is the key process involved, whether it is *e-business, e-commerce, e-money, e-tailing* (for "retailing"), or *e-books, e-documents, e-mail, e-zines.*

Words formed with **e-** are usually written with hyphens (but see **email**). Without a hyphen the one-letter prefix is somewhat at risk, and indistinguishable from the **e-** which represents the Latin prefix *ex-,* in words such as *education, elation, emergence* (see **ex-**). And if *education* is to be conducted via the internet, it has to be *e-education.*

-e

E is the most hardworked letter of the English alphabet, as every Scrabble player knows. Apart from representing its own sound (as in *let, send*), it often serves as a silent modifier of others (as in *mate, rage*). Sometimes (as in *some, true*) it is a relic of times when far more English words ended in *e* – when "olde shoppe" was indeed common spelling. In the course of history, final *e* has come and gone from many words; and in C21 English it still varies in the spelling of words. Its presence or absence is dictated by a number of rules and conventions:

1 The major rule affecting -e is dropping it before a suffix beginning with a vowel or *y*. This applies to an enormous number of words in English. It happens regularly with the parts of a verb – *hope, hoping, hoped* – and with adjectives: *simple, simpler, simplest.* It also applies whenever words with final *e* are extended into new words:

-able	*note>notable*
-age	*dose>dosage*
-al	*arrive>arrival*
-ation	*conserve>conservation*
-ator	*demonstrate>demonstrator*
-er	*believe>believer*
-ery	*machine>machinery*
-ify	*false>falsify*
-ise	*pressure>pressurise*
-ish	*prude>prudish*
-ism	*elite>elitism*
-ist	*extreme>extremist*
-ity	*saline>salinity*
-ize	*pressure>pressurize*
-ous	*virtue>virtuous*
-ure	*expose>exposure*
-y	*craze>crazy*

The rule does not apply when the suffix begins with a consonant, for example:

-ful	*hope>hopeful*	cf. *hoping*
-ly	*close>closely*	*closing*
-ment	*advertise>advertisement*	*advertising*
-ness	*humble>humbleness*	*humbling*

2 Exceptions and variations to the major rule are as follows:

a) Words suffixed with *-able* such as *lik(e)able, siz(e)able* (i.e. those with stems of one syllable) often retain the **-e** of the stem in British English. (See further under **-eable.**)

b) Words ending *-dge* often lose the *e* before *-ment,* especially in American English. (See **acknowledgement, judgement** and also **fledgling.**)

c) Words ending with *-ce* or *-ge* keep their final *e* before a suffix beginning with *a,* e.g. *embraceable,* and *o,* e.g. *courageous.* (See further under **-ce/-ge.**)

d) Words ending with *-ee* such as *agree* and *decree* drop one *e* before *-ed,* but keep both before *-ing.* So *agreed* but *agreeing.*

e) Words ending in *-inge* such as *singe* may keep the *e* before adding *-ing,* and thus *singeing* is distinct from *singing, springeing* from *springing, swingeing* from *swinging, tingeing* from *tinging.* Some writers keep the **-e** in other rather uncommon verbs of this kind, e.g. *bingeing, hingeing, twingeing, whingeing,* even though there are no parallel words without the **-e** to confuse them with. But no-one keeps the **-e** in the more familiar verbs with *-inge* (e.g. *cringe, fringe, impinge, infringe*), and those with other vowels (e.g. *change, lunge, plunge, sponge*), which always become *cringing, changing* etc., in accordance with the major rule.

f) Words ending in *-ie,* such as *die, lie, tie, vie* change in two ways before *-ing:* they drop their *e* and change the *i* to *y* (see **-ie->-y-**). However *tieing* is recognized in *Webster's Third* (1986) as an alternative to *tying;* and for *stymie* there is both *stymying* and *stymieing* (see **stymie**). The use of *dying* makes a vital contrast with *dyeing* (see **dye and dyeing**).

g) Words ending in *-oe* regularly keep their *e* before *-ing: canoeing, hoeing, shoeing, toeing.* Before *-ist,* it is the same for *canoeist,* but not for *oboist.*

h) Words ending in *-ue* often keep their *e* before a suffix beginning with *i* or *y,* particularly if they have only one syllable. So *clue* and *glue* retain it in *cluey* and *gluey* (to ensure that they are not read as words of one syllable like *buy*). This explains why *blue* appears with *e* in *bluey-green,* but not usually in *bluish.* As a technical term *blueing* is more likely to keep its *e* than in common idiom: *bluing all his pay at the races.* Among standard verbs, the *e* is regularly dropped in inflected forms, as for:

accrue	*argue*	*construe*	*continue*
ensue	*issue*	*pursue*	*queue*
rescue	*subdue*	*value*	

Verbs of one syllable, notably *cue* and *sue,* are less predictable. The much older verb *sue* has had *suing* as its *-ing* form since around 1300, and it's the dominant form by far in hundreds of examples in the British and American databases. But *cue* with its much shorter history (only a little more than a century) has yet to settle into the regular pattern. *Cueing* is sanctioned by the *Oxford Dictionary* (1989) for technical (engineering) uses of the noun, and though nothing is said about the verb, it's the only spelling in the BNC for all forms with *-ing* – whether they involve *cueing the [autocues] to suit the speaker's delivery, unconscious cueing by the human experimenter,* or *cueing individuals into major roles.* In CCAE meanwhile, both *cuing* and *cueing* can be found, and the first is in the majority, even though the second is backed by *Webster's Third* (1986) for all applications of the word. The fact that *cue* is a three-letter word would help to explain its variability: see (i) below.

i) Three-letter words which end in *e* may or may not keep it before suffixes: in *ageism* the *e* is usually there, in *icing* never. Others such as *ag(e)ing, ap(e)ing, aw(e)ing* and *ey(e)ing* may appear either way. The Langscape survey of 1998 showed British respondents preferred to maintain the *e* before the suffix in all of them, whereas for Americans it was only in *eyeing.* Three-letter verbs thus become a new group of exceptions, at least for the British. They apply, to inflected forms, the English spelling principle associated with content words: that they need a minimum of three letters to identify themselves (see further under **words**). Identity problems are of course more likely when such words appear without context in questionnaires and dictionary lists. When the word is established and/or its meaning supported by the context, there's less reason not to spell it according to the major rule. (Compare **aging** and **usable**.)

3 Other spelling conventions with final *e* are:

*A final *e* is sometimes added to a gender-free English word ending in *-ant* or *-ist* to create an explicitly female form of it, for example:

> *artiste   clairvoyante   confidante   typiste*

This is analogous to what happens in French grammar, though in French it is more often used for reasons of grammatical gender than natural gender (see further under **gender**). The use of explicitly female words is often beside the point, and to be discouraged if we care about **nonsexist language** (see further under that heading). In cases like these, the gender-free equivalent is much better established anyway.

*A final *e* is sometimes added to French loanwords used in English, even when they have none in French itself. So there are alternative spellings (with and without the *e*) for words such as *boulevard(e), caviar(e), chaperon(e), complin(e).* The spellings with *e* are really "more French than the French." This is one of several ways in which French loanwords are sometimes touched up in English. (For others, see under **frenchification**.)

*A final *e* often distinguishes proper names from their common noun counterparts, in addition to the initial capital letter. Some examples are *Coote, Hawke, Lowe, Moore.* Not all bearers of such names use these spellings however, and letter writers should always check whether they're corresponding with *Brown* or *Browne, Clark* or *Clarke* etc. (See further under **proper names**.)

*A final *e* is used by chemists to distinguish the names of certain groups of chemical substances – though this technical distinction is not necessarily understood by those who use the spelling *glycerine* rather than *glycerin,* for example. See further under **-ine/-in**.

-eable or -able

The **-eable** ending is a composite of the final *e* of the base word and the **-able** suffix. English spelling requires **-eable** in some words, while it's an option for others. Words such as *changeable* and *traceable* need **-eable** because it serves to preserve the "j" or "s" sound in them (see **-ce/-ge**). Other words such as the following could be spelled either way, depending on your variety of English:

> | | | |
> |---|---|---|
> | *blam(e)able* | *fram(e)able* | *grad(e)able* |
> | *lik(e)able* | *liv(e)able* | *mov(e)able* |
> | *nam(e)able* | *rat(e)able* | *sal(e)able* |
> | *shak(e)able* | *siz(e)able* | *trad(e)able* |
> | *us(e)able* | | |

The choice is broadly regional, but spellings vary more in the UK than the US, as reflected in (or led by) the major dictionaries. *Webster's Third* (1986) gives the **-able** spelling priority over **-eable** for all; whereas the *Oxford Dictionary* (1989) prioritizes **-eable** for most examples such as *likeable, liveable, sizeable* (except that it goes the other way for *usable*). Other dictionaries seem to pick and choose. The *Canadian Oxford* (1998) gives preference to **-eable** in *likeable* and *liveable,* but not in *sizable* or *usable.* In Australia the *Macquarie Dictionary* (1997) prefers *sizeable,* but **-able** for the others. Regional differences were borne out by the 1998 Langscape survey, in which the majority of North Americans (including Canadians) backed the shorter *likable, sizable,* while British respondents and Australians preferred the longer *likeable, sizeable.* Yet older UK respondents were more inclined to use the shorter spellings, perhaps because Fowler (1926) spoke firmly in favor of **-able**. Data from the BNC suggests stronger British commitment to *likeable* (97%) than *sizeable* (85%). Quantitative research on New Zealand English (Sigley, 1999) showed that NZ use of **-eable** is on a par with the British.

Spellings with plain **-able** are in line with the major rule over dropping final *e* (see **-e** section 1). When the stem has two or more syllables, as in *debatable, unshakable, reconcilable, (un)mistakable,* the rule usually prevails everywhere in the world. With stems of only one syllable, e.g. *lik(e)able,* some argue that the *e* is needed before **-able** to prevent misreading. This is an unnecessary extension of the idea that you need a minimum of three letters to represent a stem (see **-e** section 2i). Established and undisputed spellings such as *curable* and *notable* show that the *e* in the middle is inessential. Even new formations such as *drivable* are unlikely to be misread if motor vehicles are already part of the context. The words we read rarely have to stand alone for interpretation, as they do in dictionary lists.

> **International English selection:** The regular rule for words suffixed with **-able** has been used throughout this book, for the reasons just given.

◊ For more on *mov(e)able* and *us(e)able,* see **movable** and **usable**.

each

This word has two faces, expressing the individual yet often by implication concerned with the collective. **Each** therefore presents questions of agreement with verbs and pronouns. As an adjective, **each** usually singles out the individual with singular verb and pronoun:

> *Each spouse is responsible for his/her income tax.*

But the singularity is overruled following a plural subject, as in:

> *Our divisions each take responsibility for their budgets.*

As a pronoun itself, **each** can also take a singular or plural verb, depending on the context and the writer's concerns. See **agreement** section 3, and **they, them, their**.

each other or one another

Prescriptive style commentators have tried to insist that **each other** should be used between two people only, and **one another** when more than two were concerned. Yet Fowler (1926) spoke firmly against this distinction, arguing it had "neither present utility nor a basis in historical usage." His judgement is confirmed in citations recorded in the *Oxford Dictionary* (1989) and *Webster's English Usage* (1989). On the further question of where to place the apostrophe in these expressions, see **other's or others'**.

-ean

See under **-an**.

earned or earnt

In both American and British English, the past form of the verb *earn* is **earned** rather than **earnt**, however it sounds. This accords with the recommendation of *Webster's Third* (1986), while the absence of comment in *Oxford Dictionary* (1989) implies that the verb's inflections are regular. Data from CCAE and the BNC show that **earned** is also the overwhelming choice of British and American writers. This consensus contrasts with British/American divergence over the past form for other verbs such as *burn* and *learn*. See further under **-ed** section 1.

earthen, earthy or earthly

Only the first of these is still completely in touch with the ground. **Earthen** means "consisting or made out of earth or clay," as in *earthen floor*. **Earthy** usually highlights the natural properties of earth which can be recognized elsewhere, as in an *earthy smell,* or its elemental characteristics in an *earthy sense of humor.* Depending on context, **earthy** may carry positive or negative overtones. In the appreciation of wines, it can be ambiguous (Lehrer, 1983), implying a down-to-earth, robust wine to some tasters, and a mouldy bouquet to others.

Earthly takes its core meaning from being the antonym of *heavenly*. When used in expressions such as *earthly pleasures,* it usually implies their limited or short-term nature, in comparison with the infinity of heaven. But it doesn't become a synonym for *heavenly,* when negative elements are attached to it. With the negative prefix *un-,* it denotes eerie elements of the supernatural, as in *unearthly cry*. And in negative idioms such as *no earthly reason* and *not an earthly chance,* **earthly** simply underscores the negative. See further under **intensifiers**.

east, eastern or easterly

When used with lower case, these words all relate straightforwardly to a point, area or direction which is 90 degrees right of the north/south axis for a particular country or city. In the absence of any geographical reference points, it relates to the writer's or speaker's north/south axis.

The main thing to note is that when applied to winds, airstreams or currents, these words denote "from the east," whereas in other applications they mean "to(wards) or in the east." So an *easterly wind* will have its impact on the **eastern** side of a building, and wildflowers in the *eastern region* of a national park will have walkers heading **east** to see them.

When dressed with a capital letter, **East** often carries special historical or political overtones. In *Middle East* or *Far East,* it still represents the European colonial perspective. What was the *Far East* for Britain is the "Near North" for Australia, as its Prime Minister observed in 1939. (Compare the expression *Southeast Asia,* which is free of any "user-perspective.") The difference between European cultures and those of colonial countries was the stimulus for Rudyard Kipling's comment in C19 that "East is East and West is West, and never the twain shall meet." But the need for mutual understanding was better recognized in C20, in institutions such as the East–West Center, established at the University of Hawaii in 1960.

After World War II and during the subsequent Cold War, **eastern** acquired a new political significance in the phrase *eastern bloc,* used in reference to the Soviet Union and its East European satellites. Its communist system and centralized economy contrasted with those of the capitalistic states of western Europe and North America, allied through NATO. But the old east–west division has faded since the breakup of the **eastern** bloc in 1991.

The implications of **Eastern** are different again in references to the *Eastern Orthodox Church,* where the word identifies the group of churches which developed in the **eastern** half of the Roman Empire and were for centuries identified with Byzantium/Constantinople. They include the churches of Greece and Cyprus, Egypt and some cities in the *Middle East,* as well as Russia, Bulgaria, Czechoslovakia, Poland, Romania and Serbia. The group split off from the Catholic Church (based on Rome) in AD 1054.

eastward or eastwards

See under **-ward**.

easy or easily

Despite appearances, **easy** functions as adverb in some common English idioms, such as *rest easy, take it easy* and *go easy on them.* In such expressions it cannot be replaced by **easily** without changing the meaning, or at any rate losing the idiom. As the examples show, they are the stuff of interactive discourse rather than formal style, but that's no reason to "dress" the adverb up, if it is to appear in writing. See further under **zero adverbs**.

eat

The only point at issue with this verb is its past tense: how to say and spell it. In C21 English the spelling has settled down to *ate,* and most Americans, Canadians and Australians pronounce it to rhyme with "late." In the UK *ate* is still often pronunced to rhyme with "let." This accords with the fact that until well on in C19, the spelling **eat** served as both present and past tense, with different pronunciations just like those which distinguish the present and past of the verb *read.* Nowadays *ate* has a lot to recommend it as a distinct spelling for the past tense, and speakers are free to use the spelling pronunciation or not, as they choose.

-eau and -ieu

Words which end in **-eau** or **-ieu** (or *-iau*) are borrowings from French where they are pluralized with *-x*, e.g. *bureau > bureaux.* However once they are at home in English they acquire English plurals as well, e.g. *bureaus.* Those which are totally assimilated may indeed shed their French plural, and in American English *bureaus* is now the only plural form current, judging by the evidence of CCAE – for the commercial *bureau* that specializes in *computer type-setting, design, printing* etc. But in British usage the *Citizens Advice Bureaux* and similar agencies keep the *-x* plural to the fore, and *bureaus* makes little showing in the BNC. Many similar loanwords still have both French and English plurals, including:

bandeau	*bateau*	*beau*	*chapeau*
chateau	*flambeau*	*fricandeau*	*gateau*
manteau	*morceau*	*plateau*	*portmanteau*
reseau	*rouleau*	*tableau*	*tonneau*
trousseau			

In the UK and Canada, the *-x* plural is more likely to be used than in the US or Australia, though it's available anywhere to those seeking to emphasize or exploit the foreign connection. The Australian *patisserie* which advertises its "gateaux's" is trying to make doubly sure!

Likewise *adieu* may be pluralized with either *-s* or *-x*, but the English plural *adieus* is now more frequent and entirely justifiable. The word has been in English for centuries – since Chaucer – and writers of C16 and C17 tended to anglicize the spelling of its root as *adew* and *adue. Purlieu,* another early borrowing, has only the English plural *purlieus.* But *milieu,* borrowed in C19, still more commonly makes its plural as *milieux,* at least in British English. In BNC data, it outnumbered *milieus* by more than 3:1. American preferences illustrated in CCAE again ran the opposite way.

With *fabliau* the plural *fabliaux* is universally preferred. No doubt its users are very much aware of the French origin of the genre.

Ebonics

See under **Black English.**

echo

Borrowed in C14, **echo** has long been pluralized as *echoes*, and this is still the only form for *New Oxford* (1998), *Canadian Oxford* (1998) and the Australian *Macquarie Dictionary* (1997). *Merriam-Webster* (2000) allows both **echoes** and **echos,** and American respondents to the Langscape survey (1998–2001) were almost evenly divided over which to use (54% to 46%). But in data from CCAE there are very few examples of **echos** as a plural noun – and even fewer for its use as a verb (third person singular, present tense). The use of

-es stands firm for this word, despite its erosion in others: see **-o.**

eco-

Words formed with this Greek root show how far it has come from its literal meaning "house"/"home." With *economics* we usually think of state or business finances rather than the household kitty. And with *ecology,* coined only in C19, we focus on the environment and systemic or symbiotic relationships within it. In compounds of C20 and C21, **eco-** takes its cue from *ecology,* hence its latter-day meaning "environment":

ecocide	*eco-defense*	*eco-engineer*
ecofreak	*eco-friendly*	*eco-guerrillas*
ecohazard	*eco-label*	*eco-leftist*
eco-literature	*eco-radical*	*eco-sabotage*
ecospecies	*ecosphere*	*ecosystem*
eco-terrorism	*eco-theology*	*ecothriller*

Eco- has generated a plethora of new words which embody the environmental perspective in politics, economics, social action etc., and sometimes polarized attitudes to it. Many are ad hoc, not listed in dictionaries; and hyphens are a variable element. In examples such as *ecosphere,* **eco-** operates like a prefix or classical combining form, whereas in others (*eco-label*), it comes close to being a compound element. In American data from CCAE, the hyphen is regularly used, although a few **eco-** compounds also appear with space, e.g. *eco group, eco tourism.* Clearly **eco-** is close to being an independent word.

economic or economical

As with many *-ic/-ical* pairs, there is common ground between these, as well as a demarcation difference, though the picture keeps changing. The "economical man" of C19 political philosophy is the "economic man" of C20. Thus **economic** has generally displaced **economical** in references to matters of *economics* and the structure of the *economy* at large; and **economical** now relates to *economy* measures (or *economies*) by which to avoid extravagance and wastage. So while treasurers and governments concern themselves with large-scale **economic** strategies, those responsible for the household finances work on **economical** uses of a small budget. Which is not to say that governments aren't also expected to be **economical.** The two adjectives embody different perspectives on money, one theoretical, the other practical.

Note however that these distinctions are sometimes blurred, at least in colloquial usage, as is acknowledged in dictionaries all over the world. In any case the two different perspectives are not always easy to separate, for example in expressions like *an economic necessity.* There is only one adverb for the two words, *economically,* and we rely on the context to show which sense is intended. Only in the verb *economize/economise* is the meaning unquestionably linked with implementing a practical *economy* measure. See further under **-ic/-ical.**

ecstasy or ecstacy

The spelling **ecstasy** is standard for British and American English, in keeping with the word's origin in Greek *ekstasis,* via Old French *exstasie.* But in English the word has few analogues ending in *-asy,* whereas *-acy* appears in a number of common abstract nouns such as *delicacy, diplomacy, fallacy, privacy.* This accounts for the variant spelling **ecstacy,** marked "obsolete" in the *Oxford Dictionary* (1989) with no citations since C18. The nonstandard spelling with *-acy* is however used by a dozen British writers included in the BNC, all in reference to the common stimulant and hallucinogenic drug, with and without capital letter. **Ecstacy** also appears in data from CCAE, used not only in reference to the drug but in other senses as well: *ecstacy of joy; religious ecstacy; supposed ecstacy of a drug high.* Its use is registered in *Webster's Third* (1986), as a current alternative to **ecstasy** for any sense of the word.

◊ Compare **idiosyncrasy.**

ecu, Ecu or ECU

Whatever its form, this acronym refers to the notional *European Currency Unit.* The lower-cased spelling **ecu** is on a par with upper case **ECU** in terms of relative frequency in the BNC, whereas **Ecu** is used a good deal less. Since 1999, the currency unit which actually changes hands is the *Euro* (see under **Euro- and euro-**).

◊ For other currencies, see Appendix IX.

-ed

Many an English verb takes the **-ed** suffix for its past forms (both past tense and past participle), as for example:

> *bounded claimed departed liked organized wandered*

Verbs like these are the regular verbs of English (see further under **irregular verbs**). In some cases the **-ed** makes a separate syllable (*bounded, departed*), in others it just adds an extra consonant, a "d" sound in *claimed,* and a "t" sound in *liked.* The past forms of some verbs are in fact always spelled with *t,* witness:

> *bent built crept dealt felt kept left*
> *lent meant sent slept spent swept wept*

Among these, the *t* either takes the place of *d* in the stem of the word (as in *bent<bend*), or substitutes for the **-ed** suffix (as in *dealt<deal*). The list was once longer. Spellings such as *past* and *wrapt* are relics of others. Even the "regular" past ending turns out to be not entirely regular.

1 Verbs with both -ed and -t. Several verbs have alternative past forms, including:

> *burned/burnt dreamed/dreamt dwelled/dwelt*
> *kneeled/knelt leaned/leant leaped/leapt*
> *learned/learnt smelled/smelt spelled/spelt*
> *spilled/spilt spoiled/spoilt*

The regular **-ed** forms are dominant in North American English for the past tense/participle of all these verbs except *dwelt* and *knelt,* whereas in British and Australian English both **-ed** and *-t* are used. The use of the *-t* form may have increased in Britain during C20, according to Gowers's 1965 edition of *Fowler's Modern English Usage.* Data from Australia (Peters, 1993b) also shows the persistence of the *-t* spellings for past tense/participle. (See further under **burned, dreamed, dwelt, knelt, leaned, leaped, learned, smell, spelled, spill, spoil.**) When the participle serves as adjective, the *-t* forms are regularly used, as in *spilt milk* and *burnt offering* (or *toast*), even in the US. But the opposite holds for *learn,* for which *learned* is the standard adjectival form, with one syllable in *learned responses,* and two in a *learnéd*

man. The two-syllabled pronunciation (with **-ed** as a separate syllable) is a remnant of medieval English, surviving in few other participial adjectives, apart from *agéd, blesséd, doggéd.* (Those derived from nouns are discussed in section 2 below.)

Some writers attach different grammatical meanings to the **-ed** and *-t* forms: intransitive v. transitive; continuous v. perfect aspect; active v. passive (see under **burned**). But the grammar is vested in the sentence construction, and never depends on the spelling. Other writers – less grammatically inclined – sometimes correlate the use of **-ed** and *-t* with the way they pronounce the word, though this is idiosyncratic and cannot be accessed by the reader. Either way, the spelling doesn't change the meaning of what is written. The variation is redundant and perhaps distracting when the regular **-ed** could be used consistently.

2 Noun-based adjectives with -ed. Not all adjectives ending in **-ed** are based on verbs (i.e. their past participles). Examples such as *pointed, ragged, walled, wooded* show them derived directly from nouns (*point, rag, wall, wood*), rather than an intermediary verb. This is all the more obvious with compound adjectives in **-ed** such as *fair-minded, giant-sized, thin-skinned, three-legged,* which can only be derived from a noun phrase ("fair mind," "three legs"). It also explains why the first component is adjectival rather than adverbial in form: compare *thin-skinned* with *thinly spread.* See also **zero adverbs.**

3 When -ed may be spelled d (i.e. apostrophe d). Though *'d* often stood for **-ed** in C17 English, it now does so only when the verb ends in a vowel: *a, é, i, o,* or *u.* Fowler (1926) recommended it for verbs that are derived directly from nouns (e.g. *cupola'd, mascara'd*); and it has some value for those ending in more than one vowel (e.g. *plateau'd, radio'd, shanghai'd*), as well as those based on foreign adjectives (e.g. *cliché'd, flambé'd*). This use of *apostrophe d* accords with the fact that:

a) apostrophes have long been used to mark omission (see under **apostrophes**); and
b) the **-(e)d** suffix never makes a separate syllable in such words.

Apostrophe d was much more popular with British respondents to the Langscape survey (1998–2001) than with those from other parts of the English-speaking world – who were more inclined to retain the regular **-ed** spellings. Another strategy sometimes used in such cases is to add a hyphen: *mascara-ed, radio-ed.* But it has the disadvantage of seeming to create an extra syllable and had little following, according to a survey reported in *English Today* (1988).

Few words of this kind are entered in dictionaries. When they are, the American dictionaries give them the regular spelling (as in *hennaed, umbrellaed, visaed*); whereas British dictionaries generally give the apostropheed (or rather apostrophe'd) spelling. Though *apostrophe* helps when there are two (or more) different vowels preceding the suffix, it seems unnecessary when the vowels are identical, as in *baaed* and *tattooed.* In any case verbs ending with double e (*agree, filigree, pedigree, referee, tee*) conform to the general rule of dropping their final e before **-ed** (see **-e** section 2d). So the regular **-ed** spelling works well enough in most cases, and offers a clear principle for new or ad hoc verbs.

International English selection: Spellings with the regular -ed are used for verbs in this book wherever they are available, for the reasons discussed in sections 1 and 3 above.

◊ For the choice between *aged 16* and *age 16,* see **inflectional extras.**

edema or oedema

See **oedema.**

edgeways or edgewise

See under **-wise.**

educator, educationist or educationalist

All these words seem to have aspirations beyond the familiar word *teacher,* and represent the desire to express the professionalism involved in pedagogy. Some dictionaries apply **education(al)ist** to those interested in the theory and methods of teaching; and **educator** to those in direct contact with students, whether as lecturer, tutor, classroom teacher or coach. However *Webster's English Usage* (1989) finds little evidence of **educator** for "teacher," rather that it serves as a general term for the educational theorist and administrator; and that **educationist** tends to be used disparagingly in the US (but not the UK). **Educator** is the commonest of the three by far in data from CCAE, and both **educationist** and **educationalist** are rare. British data from the BNC presents roughly equal numbers of **educationalist** and **educationist,** despite Fowler's (1926) preference for the latter. But **educator** is rather more common than either, and again seems to subsume them. The Australian usage commentator Murray-Smith (1989), himself an **educationalist,** recommended **educator** for all applications.

-ee

This ending appears on English words for a number of reasons. Apart from a few simple ones like *knee* and *tree,* such words are often foreign loanwords in which **-ee** is the best way to represent the final syllable in English. So it stands instead of the final *i* in Hindi loanwords such as *dungaree, kedgeree* and *suttee;* and in *chimpanzee,* borrowed from a Bantu language. Yet its most common use in English is as counterpart to the French use of *é* for the past participle, a usage which was established in English law when legal matters were still discussed in hybrid French and English. Many of the words with the **-ee** suffix are ones which designate a legal or quasi-legal role, such as:

appellee	*arrestee*	*assignee*	*consignee*
deportee	*franchisee*	*grantee*	*internee*
lessee	*libelee*	*licensee*	*mortgagee*
parolee	*patentee*	*payee*	*trustee*

Yet as the last example shows, such words can become part of everyday language, as is unquestionably the case with:

absentee	*addressee*	*amputee*	*conferee*
devotee	*divorcee*	*employee*	*escapee*
evacuee	*examinee*	*interviewee*	*nominee*
referee	*returnee*	*trainee*	

The legal or bureaucratic associations of many of these words have nevertheless given **-ee** a formal and organizational flavor; and this is no doubt part of the joke in ad hoc words such as *bumpee, quizzee, holdupee,* formed with everyday verbs. The suffix is productive in many contexts.

The words in the lists above show that **-ee** words do not necessarily form a pair with ones ending in *-er/-or.* The cases which do, like *employee/employer* and *lessee/lessor,* are probably fewer than those like *addressee* or *devotee* which do not. The list also shows that **-ee** words are not necessarily passive, as is sometimes said. Examples such as *conferee, escapee, standee* could only be active in meaning (see **active verbs**); and others such as *absentee* and *retiree* have developed active meanings though they may have originated as passives. Recent examples noted by Bauer (1994) use **-ee** in referring to inanimates in the realms of grammar and linguistics – *cliticee, determinee* – and to corporate entities: *franchisee, takee.* A prototype for the latter could be found in *committee,* and originally it too referred to a single person to whom some duty was assigned. Only from C17 on did it become the word for the group with a collective brief.

Note that **-ee** is sometimes a respelling of the informal suffix *-ie,* especially in some words associated with children, such as *bootees* and *coatee.* Brand names such as *Softees* are also formed with it. See further under **-ie/-y.**

-eer

First and foremost, this suffix serves to identify a person by whatever item they engage with in their work, as with *engineer, mountaineer, puppeteer.* A number of such words have been used in connection with military personnel, including *cannoneer, charioteer, musketeer, rocketeer,* and this seems to have paved the way for its use in civilian forms of contention, as in *auctioneer, electioneer, pamphleteer.* This in turn may have helped to attach a derogatory flavor to words with **-eer,** as with *profiteer, racketeer* and *(black) marketeer.* The negative implications of *(black) marketeer* were exploited in Britain by those reluctant to join the Common Market, as they called the European Economic Community.

Derogatory implications also infect these words when they appear as verbs. There are connotations of excess in *profiteering* and *racketeering,* and relentlessness, as in *commandeer* and *domineer,* though they are loanwords from Dutch. But *pioneer* and *volunteer* are free of any derogatory or contentious associations, whether as nouns or verbs. In each case they were borrowed ready-made into English, and cannot be analyzed in the same way as the English formations.

◊ Compare **-ier.**

eerie or eery

All major dictionaries prefer **eerie** for this Scottish dialect word meaning "weird," though **eery** is more regular as the spelling for an English adjective. (See further under **-y.**) The *Oxford Dictionary*'s (1989) record for *eery* stops in C18, and **eerie** has clearly prevailed.

effect

For the difference between **effect** and *affect,* see under **affect.**

effective, efficient, efficacious or effectual

These words are all about getting things done and having the desired effect, but the first two have many more applications than the third and fourth. **Efficacious** is now used principally to refer to medicines, and remedies secular and spiritual: *efficacious pills, efficacious death, efficacious balm in troubles*. Despite those examples of its attributive use, it most often occurs as a predicative adjective, as in:

> . . . *made no claim that such prayers were efficacious*
> *It was a black lie but efficacious.*

(See **adjectives** section 1.) With these constraints on its use, and its rarity, **efficacious** is now a lofty synonym for **effective**.

Effective has expanded its domain continually since C15, when it was a scholarly word, and even since C17 and C18, when it had particular uses in military and technical contexts. It can now be used in relation to almost anything that achieves the intended result, from *effective advertising* to *effective parenting*. It refers to objects and instruments, as well as methods and strategies, and even to people who harness and mobilize others' efforts towards a particular goal, such as an *effective chairman*. In some contexts **effective** carries the meaning of "being in force," as in *prices effective until December 31*. Very occasionally it means "in fact," as in *took effective control of the city*.

Efficient is most often applied to people who don't waste time or energy and other resources in fulfilling particular tasks, such as an *efficient waiter*. It can also be applied to engines and machinery which give relatively large amounts of power in relation to their consumption: *more fuel-efficient than the previous model*.

A fourth word to consider in this set is **effectual**, which once served as an alternative to **effective** or **efficacious**. In law it's still used to mean "valid" or "binding." But in ordinary usage the sense of "effectiveness" survives only in the negative *ineffectual,* used mostly to describe a person who fails to meet the demands of a task.

-efy or -ify

See **-ify/-efy**.

e.g., eg or eg.

The Latin *exempli gratia* (literally "by way of an example") is the foundation of this common English abbreviation, usually translated as "for example." Like most other Latin abbreviations, it is not nowadays italicized. As a lower case abbreviation, **e.g.** is still typically accorded stops (see **abbreviations**) – at least in American English. In British English it increasingly does without them, and appears as **eg** in more than a third of the examples in the BNC. The third alternative **eg.** was very rare in both British and American corpora.

The punctuation before and after **e.g.** has long been the subject of prescription. A comma used to be considered necessary after it, and is still usual, according to the *Chicago Manual* (2003). But most style guides now dispense with the following comma, and simply emphasize having one before it. Other punctuation marks, such as a dash, colon or opening parenthesis could equally well come before it, depending on the structure of the sentence.

The propriety of using **e.g.** in one's writing has also been subject to taboos and restrictions. Generations of editors have translated it into "for example" whenever it appeared in running text, because it was deemed suitable only for footnotes (according to Fowler, 1926) or tables and parentheses (*Chicago Manual*). The *Manual* still associates the use of **e.g.** in running text strictly with science and technology. The Australian government *Style Manual* is more equivocal, hedging the observation that **e.g.** and other Latin abbreviations are in regular use with the view that they are undesirable in "more formal publications" – except when they contain many shortened forms. Other style and usage guides are more accommodating. *Canadian English Usage* (1997) notes that **e.g.** occurs in writing of "all kinds." As far as Cambridge University Press is concerned, the decision is up to the authors, and **e.g.** is used freely on the expository pages of *Copy-editing* (1992).
◊ Compare **i.e.** and see further under **Latin abbreviations**.

egoist or egotist

These words have identical meaning for many people, both referring to individuals who are seen as preoccupied with themselves and their own interests. Yet for some users they embody slight differences due to their independent origins.

Egoist (and *egoism*) originated in C18 philosophy, amid questions as to whether self-interest was the basis of morality. From this the **egoist** comes to be someone who finds more interest in himself or herself than anyone else. **Egotist** derives from *egotism*, a word used in C18 stylistic discussions to refer to writing which makes excessive use of the first person (*I*). But as *egotism* becomes the outward expression of *egoism*, the two words converge, and dictionaries recognize that they can be synonyms. Both can nowadays refer to self-important behavior of any kind, whether it is boasting about one's achievements, or building public monuments to oneself. In American English, **egotist** seems to be the commoner of the two words, by the evidence of CCAE. But their use in British English is much of a muchness, since they appear in about equal numbers of documents in data from the BNC.
◊ For the choice between *ego(t)istic* and *ego(t)istical,* see **-ic/-ical**.

ei or ie

For the spelling rule which highlights this question, see **i before e**.

either

The question of using singular or plural verbs with **either** is discussed under **agreement** section 3.

elder/eldest or older/oldest

Elder (and **eldest**) date back more than a thousand years as the comparative/superlative forms of *old*. But from C15 on, **older** and **oldest** have steadily gained the upper hand, and the uses of **elder/eldest** are increasingly circumscribed. Only **older** can now be used freely in comparative structures such as *X is older (?elder) than Y*, and applied to objects, abstracts and people in any social group from students to pensioners. **Elder/eldest** is mostly confined to ranking the siblings in the family, and to frames such as *his elder sister, their eldest son,* at least in British

175

English. Americans, Canadians and Australians know these usages also, though they can just as well say *his older sister, their oldest son.* But Americans also make extensive use of **elder** in contrasting the older generation with the younger, as when saying:

> *The elder Whitfields will have their own place.*

(i.e. separate from their daughter and grandson) Or when comparing *the elder Bergman's greatest achievement* with that of his youngest son, also a film director. **Elder** thus commonly appears preceding a proper name. It can even be a company name, as in *the elder PRI power brokers,* stressing generational differences in corporate culture. American English also uses **elder** to mean "older person," as in the expression *elder care,* now contrasted with *child care.* Being *elder-friendly* is also on the socio-cultural agenda in some quarters.

These things apart, **elder** appears worldwide in the expression *elder statesman,* and in Britain in *elder partner* (used for the senior partner in a business). In these, **elder** has shifted its emphasis from age to relative seniority and experience, as also when used as a noun to refer to the senior members of a clan (e.g. *Aboriginal elders*), or the lay officers of certain Protestant churches. This shift is also implicit in the expression *no respect for their elders,* when neither the experience of age, nor age itself, seem to be given their due.

elector or electer

This is always spelled **elector**, by the evidence of British and American corpora – despite the possibility of its being a simple English derivation from the verb *elect.* See -er/-or.

electric, electrical, electronic and electrolytic

The first two invoke the power of electricity, and when its frontiers were being explored in C19, both forms of the word were used in collocations. Expressions such as *electrical battery* and *electrical shock* seem a little surprising nowadays, because we tend to use **electric** when referring to specific things which are either powered by electricity – *electric blanket, electric drill, electric light, electric trains* – or produced by it: *electric current, electric shock.* **Electrical** is used in collocations which are generic, e.g. *electrical appliances/equipment,* or which relate in a more general way to the nature of electricity: *electrical activity, electrical energy, electrical engineer.* Overall **electric** is now the more common of the two, by corpus evidence. (See further under -ic/-ical.)

Electronic embodies the discovery that *electrons* carry the charge in *electric current,* whence the C20 science and technology of **electronics**. They concern themselves with modulating and amplifying the **electric** charge, using semiconductor devices. **Electrolytic** means "working by electrolysis," the process of using an *electric current* to break up a chemical compound.

electrify or electrocute

There is an electric charge in both these verbs, but only with **electrocute** is it fatal. A person may be *electrocuted* by accident, or as a mode of legal execution, as in the US until recently. **Electrify** is primarily used in connection with powering a system with electricity, as in:

> *An American was responsible for electrifying the London Underground.*

But **electrify** is very often used figuratively to mean "excite" or "thrill," as in *an electrifying interpretation of Verdi's* Otello, or when the racehorse turns in *an electrifying performance to win by ten lengths!*

electrolyze or electrolyse

See under -yze/-yse.

electronic documents

See **digital style**.

elegy or eulogy

Either of these may be uttered in memory of someone who has died, but their overtones are different. An **elegy** is an artistic or literary composition which is mournful or contemplative in tone, and may express nostalgia for things past or persons lost. The **eulogy** is a ritual speech or statement which is consciously laudatory and affirmative of what the dead person achieved.

elementary or elemental

These words did service for each other in C19, but they are clearly distinguished nowadays, with **elementary** enjoying much wider use than **elemental**.

Elementary often refers to the elements or basics of any subject you could think of, from physics to piano-playing. *Elementary textbooks* are the ones designed to teach the basics to beginners. Because **elementary** connotes lack of knowledge and experience, it can also be used as a put-down, as in the proverbial "Elementary, my dear Watson" of Sherlock Holmes. However all *elementariness* is relative, and it's a relatively advanced mathematics student who can take *elementary nonhomogeneous linear differential equations* in his or her stride. When physicists speak of *elementary particles*, or chemists of *elementary substances,* the discourse is likely to be technical and demanding.

Elemental relates to older notions about nature. When the physical world was believed to be formed out of the four elements of earth, air, fire and water, **elemental** was the relevant adjective. With the demise of such ideas, **elemental** lives on in figurative expressions such as *elemental fury,* implying the great forces of nature and human nature.

elfish or elvish

See **elvish**.

elision

The disappearance of a vowel, consonant or whole syllable from the pronunciation of a word is known as **elision**. The place of the missing item is marked in writing by an apostrophe, as in *he's, won't* or *shootin', p'lice.* Words and phrases contracted in this way were termed *elisions* by Fowler (1926), among others (see **contractions** section 2).

In certain poetic metres (especially those whose syllables are strictly counted), **elision** is the practice of blending the last syllable of one word into the first syllable of the next, particularly when both are vowels. It was and is a way of keeping the regular rhythm with otherwise awkward combinations of English words.

◊ For the *elision of numbers* in spans, see under **dates**.

ellipsis

Both grammarians and editors make use of this term. In grammar, **ellipsis** means the omission of a word or words which would complete or clarify the sentence. In punctuation practice, **ellipsis** refers to the mark, usually a set of three dots (…), which shows where something has been consciously omitted from a quotation.

1 Ellipsis in the grammar of a sentence. Many ordinary sentences omit a word or words which could be added in to spell out the meaning and clarify the sentence structure. All the sentences below show some sort of **ellipsis**. The ellipted elements are shown in square brackets.

a) *They took glasses from the bar and [they took] plates from the tables.*
b) *They said [that] no-one was there.*
c) *The woman [that/whom] I spoke to yesterday came along.*
d) *Those results are better than [those that] our team could get.*
e) *They are enjoying it more than [they did] last year.*
f) *Herbert loves the dog more than [he does] his wife [does].*
g) *The politics of war are more straightforward than [those of] peace [is].*

Note that the last two sentences have alternative meanings, depending on which of two possible points of ellipsis is addressed. The ambiguity calls our attention to the **ellipsis**, though most of the time it passes unnoticed. Several kinds of **ellipsis**, such as that of the repeated subject in a coordinated sentence (in [a]), or of the conjunction *that* and relative pronouns in subordinate clauses (in [b] and [c]), are well known and recognized by modern grammarians. (See further under **clauses** section 2 and **that**.)

The **ellipsis** of items in comparative statements with *than* (as in sentences [d] to [g]) is also very common, and fuels the grammarian's concern about the role of *than*: is it a preposition or a conjunction? (See further under **than**.) For sentences (d) and (e) it makes no difference, but for (f) and (g), it does affect communication if there's a shortage of context. Writers clearly need to be circumspect.

Yet grammatical **ellipsis** is the hallmark of everyday conversation. In exchanges with others we continually omit elements of the sentence if they simply repeat what has gone before:

Are you coming to lunch? Not until I've collected my mail.
I'll be gone by then. Where to?

As the examples show, the **ellipses** help to connect an answer with the question, and a follow-up with a previous statement. **Ellipsis** is in fact part of the bonding or cohesion of such discourse (see further under **coherence or cohesion**). Apart from contributing to the efficiency of conversation, it is the medium through which we manipulate and expand utterances.

2 Ellipsis in punctuation usually means the set of dots which show where words have been omitted from a text. But because **ellipsis** refers in the first place to the omission itself, the term is sometimes applied to other punctuation marks whose function is the same, including asterisks, and dashes. (See further under **asterisk** and **dashes**.) To avoid ambiguity on this,

some style books refer to *ellipsis points,* and reserve the right to discuss only the dots – as we shall.

Most style manuals recognize the practice of using three dots for an **ellipsis** occurring anywhere within a sentence or between sentences. In Butcher's *Copy-editing* (1992), the *Oxford Guide to Style* (2002) and the Australian government *Style Manual* (2002), the *three-dot ellipsis* is endorsed without question. *Editing Canadian English* (2000) recommends it as "sanity-saving"; and even the *Chicago Manual* (2003) recognizes its use for "most general works and many scholarly ones." Still, the *Chicago* notes the alternative practice of using three dots for an omission within sentences, and four dots (counting in the full stop) for an omission between sentences. In its proper form it makes uneven spacing between the four dots, with the full stop set close to the final word, and the other three dots with equal space on either side of them. The difference is shown below:

He wanted no more of it. … But having said that …

The lack of means to achieve a *four-dot ellipsis* on older typewriters and wordprocessors left many writers and editors with no choice but to use three dots for any **ellipsis**.

All the authorities agree that it's reasonable to begin with a capital letter after an **ellipsis** (whether or not there was a capital at that point in the original), if the resumed quotation constitutes a fresh sentence. The reader is helped thereby. Only in legal and scholarly quotations is this consideration overruled by the need to keep every letter in the same case as the original. One other simplification of older practice with *ellipsis points* is dispensing with them at the start of a quotation. The opening quote marks themselves show that the words cited are an excerpt.

Note finally that a whole line of *ellipsis points* can be used to indicate the omission of a line or lines of verse from a poem, or where whole paragraphs have been omitted from a prose text.

else

This word is usually classified as an adverb (or adjective) in dictionaries, yet its most important roles are as part of a compound pronoun or conjunction, where its legitimacy is only gradually being recognized. Most frequently it's used as part of an indefinite or interrogative pronoun, as in:

anyone else   someone else   what else   who else

So well established are these phrases that **else** can take the possessive form quite easily:

anyone else's car

This usage was once frowned on by those who insisted that **else** was an adverb and so could not be made possessive. The paraphrase they suggested was *whose car else*, which nowadays seems stilted and unacceptable.

Another common role of **else** is to combine with *or* as the complex conjunction *or else*. But in conversation it stands for both of them:

Take the car else you'll be late.

This use of **else** as an independent conjunction occurs particularly in commands and advisory statements, in the context of direct speech. Modern dictionaries do not however recognize it, and though the *Oxford Dictionary* (1989) registered its use as a "quasi conjunction," it had only a few citations from C14 and therefore marked it "obsolete." Yet Burchfield (1996) reports some C20 citations; and the *Right Word at the*

Right Time (1985) found it common enough in informal speech to recommend against its use in writing. Those who write formal documents are unlikely to want to use **else** in this way. But there's no reason to disallow it in other kinds of writing, where direct speech and homely advice have their place.

elusive or allusive

These adjectives can easily be mistaken for each other in speech, being identical in most people's pronunciation, and in some contexts rather alike in meaning: *an elusive charm, an allusive comment.* In both phrases the words imply that something is there and yet not there. But the different spellings confirm that they relate to different verbs (**elusive** to *elude,* and **allusive** to *allude*). Thus an *elusive charm* is one that eludes the beholder and cannot be pinned down, while an *allusive comment* just alludes to something, touching on it in passing, and not dwelling on it. **Allusive** and *allude* are usually linked with things said (or not said), while **elusive** and *elude* relate to things (or people) that disappear or escape.

elvish, elfish or elfin

In more superstitious times, the presence of *elves* and *elf-like* behavior were of common interest, though the spelling has long vacillated between **elvish** and **elfish**. In current American English the two are still about equally used, by the evidence of CCAE, whereas in British data from the BNC, **elvish** has a clear majority. This accords with the stronger British support for *v* plurals in words which maintain them (see under -**f**>-**v**-). It also explains why Tolkien used **Elvish** for the name of the language in *Lord of the Rings.* But these days **elfin** is commoner than either **elvish** or **elfish**, because of its more general use to refer to small, delicate features of face or body: *a thin elfin-faced girl.*

em-/en-

See en-/em-.

em dash or em rule

Both refer to the full dash: **em dash** is its name in North America, and **em rule** in Britain, Australia and New Zealand. See **dashes** section 1.

email, e-mail or E-mail

This abbreviation for *electronic mail* was first seen as **E-mail** in 1982. Since then the first element has swiftly evolved into a productive prefix (see **e-**), and **e(-)mail** is now usually seen with a lower case initial. **E-mail** persists in proprietorial software descriptions in British and American databases, but otherwise it's **e-mail**, with scant evidence of **email** in textual material from CCAE or the BNC. Yet **email** dominates on the internet (Google, 2003), outnumbering **e-mail** by almost 14:1. Google puts its own weight behind **email**, by querying **e-mail** ("Did you mean **email**?") when you search for it.

Dictionaries diverge over which form to use. *Merriam-Webster* (2000) still has **E-mail** for the noun (and **e-mail** for the verb), whereas *Wired Style* (1996) makes it **email**, as does the Australian *Macquarie Dictionary* (1997). The *Oxford Dictionary* (1989) also has **email**, but it's **e-mail** for *New Oxford* (1998) and the *Canadian Oxford* (1998). They too are grappling with the duality of usage, where **e-mail** appears in edited texts but **email** serves for practical purposes on the internet. Editors tend to prefer **e-mail** because of its consistency with other *e*-words, and the new coinings may help it to stage a comeback.

In grammatical terms, **e(-)mail** is also evolving. Being a compound of *mail,* it's a collective noun first and foremost, as in *lots of e-mail.* But many people now use it to refer to a single message, as in *an e-mail from Korea,* which means it also serves as a *count noun* (see **count and mass nouns**). American dictionaries (*Merriam-Webster,* 2000; *Canadian Oxford,* 1998) already recognize this by their definitions, and others will no doubt follow suit. Internet documents searched by Google (2003) were found to contain almost 4 million examples of the plural **e(-)mails**, confirming its widespread use as a count noun.

e-mail style

In their epistolary style, *e-mails* combine elements of the memo with aspects of letter writing. The headers of *e-mails* identifying the sender, receiver and subject are like those of memos (see Appendix VII), as is the fact that *e-mail* messages often do without a salutation or subject line (see under **Dear**). The complimentary close associated with letters is less necessary and much more variable (see under **Yours faithfully**). But the language of *e-mails* is as variable as letters, depending on their purpose (anything from institutional management to personal communication). Thus standard English prevails at one end of the scale, and the abbreviated code of *SMS* or *l33tsp34k* at the other: see **SMS**.

embargo

This C16 Spanish loanword has long been pluralized as **embargoes**, and it's standard in both the US and the UK, according to *Merriam-Webster* (2000) and *New Oxford* (1998). **Embargos** is only rarely found for the plural in either CCAE or the BNC. See further under **-o**.

embryo

The plural of **embryo** is *embryos* for both American and British English, according to *Merriam-Webster* (2000) and *New Oxford* (1998). See further under **-o**.

emend or amend

Neither of these verbs is in common use nowadays: both survive in specialist contexts. To **emend** is the work of scholars, as they edit individual words and expressions in older texts in order to produce a definitive version of the original. The fruits of this work are *emendations.* Those who **amend** documents are concerned with the larger substance – editors seeking to improve the contents of a draft manuscript, or legislators modifying the provisions of legal codes and constitutions. Their work results in *amendments* to the original text.

The plural form **amends** in *to make amends* is a fossil of the once much wider use of **amend**, in references to improving one's conduct and social behavior. Another fossil *They must amend their ways* is now usually expressed as *mend their ways.* As that example shows, *mend* has taken over most of the general functions of **amend** in modern English.

emergence or emergency

There is a clear difference between these now, unlike many -nce/-ncy pairs (see further under that heading). Both are nouns derived from the verb *emerge,* with **emergence** serving as the abstract noun, and **emergency** as the highly specific one, meaning a situation which requires urgent action. The spellings became differentiated only during C19. Predictably, the word with more concrete associations is the one more frequently used. In corpus data **emergency** outnumbers **emergence** by more than 3:1.

emigrant, emigré or expatriate

All these refer to someone who has emigrated away from their native country, but each word has its own implications. **Emigrant** expresses the plain fact that someone has moved permanently away from their country of origin, and is neutral as to the reason for their move as well as their social background. **Emigré** carries more elitist overtones, as well as the implication that the emigration was necessitated by political circumstances. Historically the word **emigré** has been associated with those who fled from the French and Russian revolutions, though it might seem applicable to those who felt obliged to flee communist revolutions in Chile, Afghanistan and Vietnam. The higher social background of **emigré** is clear when the word is contrasted with *refugees,* who may come from any social class.

The term **expatriate** may be applied to those whose emigration was either voluntary or involuntary, though it is often applied to individuals who choose for professional reasons to live in another country, as in:
London has its share of expatriate Australians.
This voluntary exile is sometimes seen as betraying a lack of patriotism, which no doubt explains why **expatriate** is sometimes misconstrued as *expatriot.* There's some evidence of it in the US (in CCAE data), coinciding with the comment of *Webster's English Usage* (1989) that it could become an acceptable variant spelling in the future. (For other examples, see **folk etymology**.) Meanwhile the abbreviated *expat* skirts around the problem, at least in more informal writing.
◊ For the distinctions between **immigrant** and **migrant**, see under **migrant**.

eminent or imminent

While **eminent** is a term of commendation, meaning "outstanding," **imminent** says that something is on the point of happening. Examples such as *an eminent scholar* and *their imminent defeat* show their typical uses, **eminent** referring to people, and **imminent** to events. The two are unlikely to come together in the same utterance – unless of course you're about to be visited by an *eminent person,* in which case it would be possible to speak of an *eminent, imminent visitor!*

Imminent and its adverb *imminently* both focus on events about to happen, whereas *eminently* has little to do with **eminent**. Instead it becomes an intensifier meaning "especially"or "very," as in *eminently likely.* See further under **intensifiers**.

emoticons

This word is a blend of *emotion* and *icon,* coined in computerspeak to refer to "pressbutton" indications of emotion that can be contrived out of the standard keyboard characters. **Emoticons** are used freely in social e-mail and informal *digital style* (see under that heading). The best known *emoticon* is the "smiley" face made up of standard keyboard characters :>)
which may be intensified to the demonic laugh :>D
               moderated to a wink   ;>)
or   reduced to skepticism   :>/
The combinations are not yet standardized, e.g. some use hyphens instead of chevrons for the nose; and some vary in meaning: so :>o can indicate surprise as well as shock. These **emoticons** are thus not yet a universal system of *ideograms* (see further under that heading), apart from the fact that a different set is used in countries such as Hong Kong and Japan (McArthur, 2000). The Asian **emoticons** work in the vertical plane, so that (^ ‿ ^) is the standard smiley, and its opposite number (Y‿Y) symbolizes crying. Both sets of **emoticons** are constrained by the horizontal line of text. We may nevertheless be looking at the prototypes of a new art form – digital mini-portraiture.

emotive or emotional

Though both of these recognize the role of emotion, they identify it in different places. **Emotive** implies that emotion is raised in the audience, and a phrase such as *emotive words* often suggests that the speaker's output is calculated to kindle the emotions of those listening. The word **emotional** simply implies that emotion was expressed by the speaker, or was characteristic of the speech itself. An *emotional speech* can of course have an *emotive effect* on the audience.

empanelled, empaneled or impaneled

While **empanelled** is standard in British English, **empaneled** and **impaneled** are both used in American English. They appear about equally in data from CCAE. See further under **en-/in-** and **-l-/-ll-**.

emphasizer

See **intensifiers**.

employee, employe or employé

Employee is the standard form of this word nowadays, everywhere in the English-speaking world. It seems to have established itself earlier in North America than in Britain, and the original *Oxford Dictionary* (1884–1928) dubbed it "rare except US." The dictionary then gave much fuller coverage to the French form **employé**, and made a point of saying that **employee** was used for female workers. But in its 1933 *Supplement, Oxford* endorsed **employee** as the standard English term, and the idea of a gender distinction disappeared along with the French accent. The *-ee* suffix is of course gender-free in many words (see **-ee**). **Employe** (without accent) is still recognized as an alternative in *Merriam-Webster* (2000). But in CCAE it makes up little more than 1% of all examples of the word, and no showing at all in the BNC.

emporium

For the plural of this word, see **-um**.

en-/em-

These are variant forms of a prefix borrowed from Norman French, meaning "in" or "into," or intensive in function as in *encourage, enrich.* The prefix has been put to fresh use in English, in forming new verbs out of nouns and adjectives:

enable	embed	embellish
embitter	emblazon	empower
encase	encompass	engulf
enlarge	enlist	ennoble
enrapture	enslave	ensnare
enthrall	entomb	entrance
entrench		

As these words show, the **em-** form is used before words beginning with *b* and *p*, and **en-** before all others.

en-/in-

The French prefix **en-** (see previous entry) has long been interchanged with the **in-** prefix from Old English (meaning "in"), and the identical Latin prefix (see further under **in-/im-**). The vacillation between them gave alternative spellings in C18 and C19 to quite a number of verbs (e.g. *endorse/indorse*), and multiple forms to *enmesh*, also found as *emmesh, inmesh, immesh*. Though the *Oxford Dictionary* (1989) and *Webster's Third* (1986) still record the **in-** forms as equal or secondary alternatives, most such words have settled on **en-** during the course of C20 in both British and American English. Only *enclose/inclose* and *enfold/infold* still show a little variability in spelling, by the evidence of British and American databases, though in each case the **en-** form is commoner by far (see **enclose, enfold**). The **en-** form is the only form current in CCAE and the BNC for:

encompass	encrust(ed)	endorse
engender	engraft	enlist
enmesh	enroll	enshrine
enthral(l)	entrench	entwine
entwisted		

A rare exception is *ingrained*, which has prevailed over *engrained* (see **ingrained**). Note also *impassion(ed)*, where **im-** has totally replaced the earlier **em-**. (See also **incumbent**.)

A very few words with **en-/in-** variability have developed distinct meanings for the two spellings, at least in some parts of the English-speaking world. See **inquire/enquire and inquiry/enquiry; insure/ensure; inure/enure**.

-en

These letters represent four different English suffixes:
* a past participle ending, e.g. *taken* (see **irregular verbs** section 7)
* a rare plural ending on nouns, e.g. *children* (see further under **plurals**)
* a means of forming adjectives out of nouns, e.g. *golden*
* a means of forming verbs out of adjectives, e.g. *sharpen*

Only the fourth of these suffixes still generates new words. The first two are fossilized, and the third is not much used except in poetic diction.

Adjectives formed with **-en** are derived from single-syllabled nouns:

ashen	earthen	leaden	oaken	silken
wooden	wool(l)en			

The **-en** ending implies "made out of," and occasionally "looking as if it were made out of," as with *leaden skies* and *silken hair*. The pattern is so simple that we might wonder why its use is so limited nowadays. One reason is that it competes with the *-y*

suffix, which has indeed generated alternative forms for many of the words above: *ashy, silky, wool(l)y*. Another is that when speaking of something actually made out of lead, silk or wool, we can just as well use those words: *lead batteries, silk scarves, wool carpets*. So *ashen, leaden, silken* etc. seem to be retiring to the leisured world of literature.

Verbs formed with **-en** are derived from single-syllabled adjectives (except for *quieten*). The regular pattern is seen in:

blacken	darken	deafen	deepen
lessen	lighten	madden	moisten
redden	ripen	sadden	smarten
stiffen	thicken	whiten	widen

The verbs all imply a change of state, and as things may either be made blacker or become blacker, the verbs can be either transitive or intransitive. Words ending in *m, n, l, r* and any vowel are ineligible for phonetic reasons to become verbs this way, and so *blacken* is not matched by "greenen" or "bluen." Verbs of this kind could once be made out of nouns, as were *frighten, lengthen, strengthen, threaten*, but this is no longer possible.

en dash

This is the North American name for what is known elsewhere (in Britain, Australia and New Zealand) as the **en rule**. See further under **dashes**.

en déshabillé

This French phrase, meaning literally "in (a state of being) undressed," is an elaborate way of noting that someone's dress is informal. The expression also appears in English as *déshabillé* or *deshabille,* or the fully anglicized form *dishabille*. The degree of undress implied by such expressions is very much relative to the situation, sometimes a matter of careless dress, and sometimes its incompleteness. Just how incomplete is suggested by the fact that *dishabille* as a noun once referred to the garment now known as a *negligee* (again borrowed from French).

Other delicate French loanwords used to describe modes of dress which defy convention are *décolleté* ("having a low-cut neckline"), and *déboutonné,* literally "unbuttoned," a sign of social laxness in C19. By extension *déboutonné* came to mean "ready to exchange confidences."

en route and en passant

En route is French for "on the road or way," but has acquired a number of other senses in English. It can mean "along the way," as in *there are caves to be explored en route;* or "in transit," as in *Their neighbors were already en route for Hong Kong*. Some also use it on its own (*En route!*) to mean "let's go." All uses of **en route** have something to do with traveling, whereas **en passant** (literally "in passing") is usually figurative. In examples such as *Their existence is mentioned en passant,* the phrase is a synonym for "incidentally."

en rule

Editors in Britain, Australia and New Zealand use this term for the North American **en dash**, one which is intermediate in size between the hyphen and the full dash. See **dashes** section 2.

enameled or enamelled, and enameling or enamelling

The spellings with one *l* are strongly preferred in the US, and those with two *ll*s in the UK, by the evidence of CCAE and the BNC. See further under **-l-/-ll-**.

enamo(u)red of, with or by

Databases show that **enamo(u)red** most often collocates with **of**, in both American and British English. But unlike the British, Americans also make substantial use of **enamored with**, which is found in about one third of all instances of the word in data from CCAE. **Enamo(u)red by** is rare in both American and British data.
◊ For the choice between **enamored** and **enamoured**, see **-or/-our**.

enclose or inclose, and enclosure or inclosure

The spellings with *en-* are now standard around the world. Spellings with *in-* survive mostly in historical and legal texts in British and American databases, apart from rare examples in transcribed speech.
◊ For other examples of the same type, see **en-/in-**.

encomium

The plural of this word is discussed under **-um**.

encumbent

See under **incumbent**.

encyclopedia or encyclopaedia

American English has **encyclopedia** for its standard spelling, as indicated in *Webster's Third* (1986). British English is more divided, and it may come as a surprise that it's no longer firmly attached to **encyclopaedia**. In fact the *Oxford Dictionary* (1989) presents the two spellings as equal alternatives. Data from the BNC supports the *Oxford* stance, with similar frequencies for the two, in a mix of capitalized and noncapitalized citations, and the same book titles are variously spelled **encyclopedia** or **encyclopaedia**. Though this is poor bibliography, it shows that they are interchangeable as far as common usage goes. See further under **ae/e**.

> **International English selection:** With a usage base in both British and American English, **encyclopedia** is clearly the more useful spelling.

endeavor or endeavour

The choice between these is discussed under **-or/-our**.

endemic, epidemic and pandemic

Since **endemic** is an adjective and **epidemic** most often a noun, we might expect grammar to keep them apart. Yet because they look rather similar, and because both can refer to the presence of disease in a community, they are sometimes substituted for each other:

> Cholera was an endemic/epidemic problem in that overcrowded city.

Their meanings are still rather different however. **Endemic** means "recurring or prevalent in a particular locality," while **epidemic** carries the sense of "(spreading like) a plague," as in *shoplifting has reached epidemic proportions*. Both words may represent aspects of the problem, but the writer needs to distinguish the two for discussion.

The third member of the set **pandemic** was originally (in C17) an adjective meaning "occurring everywhere." It contrasted with **endemic** which connects things with a particular locality. The noun **pandemic**, which owes something to **epidemic**, is used to mean "a plague which affects the whole country."

The tendency of these words to converge need not surprise us, given their common Greek root *-demic*, related to *demos* ("people"). Literally **endemic** is "in the people"; **epidemic** is "upon or among the people" (see further under **epi-**); and **pandemic** ("all the people").

endmatter

For the makers of books, this term covers the various items included at the back of a reference book, including any appendix(es), notes, glossary, bibliography and index(es). The typical order is as just listed. **Endmatter** is often printed in a slightly smaller typeface than the main text. In the US the equivalent term is **backmatter**.

endorse or indorse, and endorsement or indorsement

Spellings with *en-* are standard now around the world, and there are none with *in-* to be found in either CCAE or the BNC. **Indorse(ment)** is still used in American legal texts that refer to the exchange of monetary documents (Garner, 1998), but in everyday usage the check (cheque) is *endorsed*. See further under **en-/in-**.

endpapers

These are the folded leaves glued inside the covers of a hardcover book which join the front cover to the first page and the last page to the back cover.

endways or endwise

See under **-wise**.

-ene or -ine

See **-ine**.

enervate or energize/energise

Despite their similarity, these have opposite meanings. **Enervate** implies a loss of energy, as in *the sun had enervated her to the point of collapse*. **Energize** means being galvanized into action, whether physical or more cerebral: *energized by the new coach*, or *energized by criticism / her enthusiasm*.
◊ For the choice between **energize** and **energise**, see **-ize/-ise**.

enfold or infold

Enfold is the dominant spelling everywhere, but **infold** is recognized in *Merriam-Webster* (2000) as an alternative for general purposes. It appears in about 1 in 5 examples of the word in CCAE. *New Oxford* (1998) registers "technical" uses of *infolded* and *infolding*, and they appear in anatomical and topographic descriptions in the BNC.
◊ For other pairs of this type, see **en-/in-**.

engineer

Since C19 the fields of *engineering* have expanded in many directions: civil, chemical, electrical, electronic, mechanical, metallurgical etc., and a professional **engineer** may be tertiary-trained in theory, design and construction in any of them. The title **engineer** is given to the person in charge of the mechanical functions of a ship or aircraft; and it's also the term for technicians involved in mechanical maintenance, as well as members of army units that carry out *engineering* and construction work. These applications of **engineer** apply everywhere in the English-speaking world. In North America only, those who drive railroad locomotives are *engineers*.

England

See under **Britain**.

English or Englishes

English is the world's most widespread language. Its history is one of almost continuous expansion – from being the language of a few thousand Anglo-Saxon immigrants to Britain in the fifth century AD, to being now the first or second language of at least 750 million people around the world (see Crystal, 1997). On all continents there are nation-states for which it is either *the* national language or one of them.

* *English as national language,* in:

Australia	Bahamas
Barbados	Canada
Falklands	Guyana
Ireland	Jamaica
New Zealand	South Africa
Trinidad and Tobago	United Kingdom
United States of America	

* *English as auxiliary national language,* in:

Brunei	Fiji	Gambia
Ghana	Kenya	Liberia
Nigeria	Papua-New Guinea	Sierra Leone
Singapore	Uganda	Zambia
Zimbabwe		

In several other countries, **English** was until recently an auxiliary national language and remains a *lingua franca* for strategic purposes (e.g. tourism, international affairs):

Bangladesh	*India*	*Malaya*
Pakistan	*Philippines*	*Sri Lanka*
Tanzania		

English is the second language of choice in Russia, China, Japan and parts of the EU.

The volume of international communication in **English** is enormous. Estimates (or guesstimates) have it that 75% of the world's mail, cables and telexes, and 80% of the information on computers is in **English**. It is the language of science and technology and the official medium of communication for ships and aircraft. International organizations mostly use English, whether associated with the United Nations or with sports management. So do the major financial institutions, media networks and travel organizations. Other domains of **English** are international law, tertiary education and in interpreting and translating, as a "relay language" (Graddol, 1997).

Facts like these are sometimes invoked to show that **English** is destined to become the universal medium of communication. But once you begin to look at the details of **English** in any of the countries just named, their divergences are as conspicuous as their convergence. **English** responds to its surroundings wherever it's used. Even in countries where there have always been native speakers (as in the first group

above), **English** still tends to develop new regional characteristics, and to reflect the local culture, society and environment. (See further under **American English**, **Australian English**, **Canadian English**, **New Zealand English**, **South African English**.) In countries like Kenya and Ghana, where English is an auxiliary national language, it rubs shoulders with other languages, borrowing from them and adjusting itself in interaction with them. In early colonial times, this sometimes saw the birth of *pidgin English* (see further under **pidgins**.) More recently it has resulted in "new Englishes" – the nativized or indigenized varieties of post-colonial societies such as India and Sri Lanka (McArthur, 1998), where English has evolved from being the second language of many citizens to being the first.

The development of multiple varieties of **English**, with their own styles of pronunciation, vocabulary and idiom, suggests that the concept of "international English" is not to be taken for granted (see **international English**). The natural tendency towards variation can be constrained in specialized contexts such as communication with ships ("seaspeak") and aircraft ("airspeak"), and tends to happen in the fields of science and technology. But as long as English responds to the infinitely variable needs of everyday communication in innumerable geographical and social contexts, it is bound to diversify. No single set of norms can be applied round the world, to decide what is "correct" or what forms to use. The analogy of Latin – which spread to all parts of the Roman empire and diversified into the various Romance languages – may well hold for English in the third millennium.

English language databases

Databases of language or anything else are only as valid as the raw material they consist of. That material needs to include a stylistic range if we are to evaluate linguistic diversity and change around us. To provide broad objective evidence on current English, a number of computerized databases have been built since 1960. Linguists at Brown University, Rhode Island USA, pioneered with the Brown corpus (i.e. database) of 1 million words of written American English, sampled in clearly defined text categories (newspapers, magazines, books) on a spectrum of subjects with specialized or mass-market readerships. The British counterpart is the LOB corpus (Lancaster–Oslo/Bergen, a collaboration between Lancaster University and two in Norway), which used an equivalent range of samples from 1961. In India (Kohlhapur University), Australia (Macquarie University) and New Zealand (Victoria University), 1 million word databases exactly like Brown and LOB have since been compiled to facilitate intercomparisons of standard English in each region. A similar set of comparative corpora, each 1 million words but half of them spoken English and half written, was compiled as the International Corpus of English (ICE) in the 1990s, by researchers in more than a dozen countries where English is either a first or second official language. The website for ICE is at www.ucl.ac.uk.

The second generation of **English language databases** are much larger, ranging from 25 million to over 200 million words. They have typically been compiled by dictionary publishers, including Collins,

Cambridge (see **CCAE**), Longman and Oxford, the last two being major contributors to the British National Corpus (see further under **BNC**). Their reach into specialized vocabulary and changing idiom is infinitely greater than that of the first generation, and databased evidence is now regarded as fundamental to dictionaries and other language references, as well as teaching materials for ELT and ESL. The corpora ensure that language advice and information in such publications is grounded in actual usage, not dependent on the impressions and preferences of the authors.

engrained or ingrained
See **ingrained**.

enormity or enormousness
Is there any difference between these, apart from their obvious difference in bulk? The short answer now is "Hardly." But according to a usage convention dating back to late C19, there is a line of demarcation: **enormousness** should be used to express the notion of hugeness, vastness or immensity, while **enormity** carries a sense of strong moral outrage, connoting the heinousness of a deed or event. Compare:

> *The enormity and futility of this raid finally swung opinion against city bombing.*
> *... the enormousness of the US budget deficit will mean competition ...*

The distinction is rather difficult to maintain when the adjective *enormous* can now only mean "huge." Writers reaching for its abstract noun not surprisingly tend to harness **enormity** rather than the cumbersome **enormousness**, and in fact the latter makes no showing at all amid 100 million words of the BNC. In the much larger American corpus (CCAE) there are less than 10 examples of **enormousness**. This naturally means that **enormity** (which is well represented in both databases) bears a range of senses in which moral outrage is not demonstrably a component – except as rhetorical overtone (see the first example below). The widened scale of uses for **enormity** ranges from that which is seriously overwhelming, to that which by its sheer size is surprisingly or amusingly beyond the norms.

> *Changes threatening this country ... are of an enormity that still has not sunk in.*
> *Menzies was wilting under the enormity of the work.*
> *... the enormity of the federal deficit*
> *... the enormity of Einstein's intellect*
> *... the enormity of propelling a wheelchair 50 miles a day*
> *... his silver hair outshone only by the enormity of his rucsac*

In a humorous comment like the last, **enormity** has shed all its more alarming connotations. They become diluted in frequent collocations such as *the enormity of the problem/task/challenge*. All such uses occur in edited writing in the corpora, so they cannot be set aside on grounds of informality. The same trends and the actual levels of usage are manifest in both British and American English. This is why dictionaries in the US, UK, Australia and Canada now allow that **enormity** serves as a synonym for **enormousness**: see for example *New Oxford* (1998), *Merriam-Webster's* (2000), *Macquarie* (1997), *Canadian Oxford* (1998).

The *Oxford Dictionary* (1989) shows that **enormity** was around well before **enormousness**, and has been used since C18 to mean "hugeness." This usage was dubbed "obsolete" with the latest citation in 1848, though an intriguing note from late C19 indicates that "More recent examples might perhaps be found, but the use is now regarded as incorrect." Even so the *Oxford* found twice as many citations for **enormity** with that meaning as for **enormousness**. Common usage has never taken account of the shibboleth that somehow attached itself to the use of **enormity** for "vast size." Burchfield (1996) concludes that it may be used in connection with abstracts of overwhelming size, but not physical entities. No such restrictions are mentioned in *Webster's English Usage* (1989). This means that those who need to communicate a sense of outrage should not put too much faith in **enormity**, and would be wise to seek an alternative.

enough
This familiar adjective-cum-adverb is normally complemented by constructions with *to* plus the infinitive. For example:

> *They have enough money to buy their own house.* (adjective)
> *They are rich enough to buy their own house.* (adverb)

An alternative construction for the adverb is also on the increase:

> *They're rich enough that they could buy their own house.*

This use of a comparative clause to complement **enough** is well established in American English, to judge by the hundreds of examples in CCAE.

> *He was an old soldier, ... respected enough that he had some clout.*
> *The weather improved enough that everyone could go out.*
> *The experience was unpleasant enough that no president since has taken such a drastic measure.*
> *... tiny pores, small enough that water droplets can't pass through*
> *... important enough that they not move in haste*

In several of these American examples, *enough that* seems to facilitate expression of the negative. But in British English the last sentence would be expressed as "for them not to move in haste," and constructions with *for* plus subject (case-adjusted) plus infinitive are the usual form. There are few signs of **enough** complemented by a clause in data from the BNC. A rare example is:

> *America will win ... handily enough that it will not want to withdraw from Asia.*

It remains to be seen whether the *enough that* construction will win Britons over.

enquire or inquire, and enquiry or inquiry
See **inquire**.

enroll or enrol, and enrollment or enrolment
The earliest spellings were *inroll* and **enroll**, the double *l* showing the word's origins in French *rolle* ("roll"). However later French *role* seems to have destabilized the English word, fostering "enroule" in C16 and C17, and **enrol** in C18. **Enroll** and **enrol** are presented by *Webster's Third* (1986), as equal

alternatives, and also by the *Oxford Dictionary* (1989), but in the opposite order. The two spellings are however strongly associated with American and British English respectively. This regional divergence stamps itself on the present tense of the verb, where American writers use *I/you/we/they enroll* and *s/he enrolls,* as well as **enrollment** for the noun. British writers have a single *l* in all of them, but still use two *l*s in the past tense (*enrolled*) because of the stress (see **doubling of final consonant**). Canadians and Australians go both ways, some taking advantage of the more consistent American spelling, others following British practice. A Google search in 2002 found **enroll** in more than a third of Australian documents on the internet.

> **International English selection:** The spelling **enroll** is preferable on grounds of etymology, its wide distribution, and its consistency throughout the paradigm.

◊ For the curious history of English spellings with one *l*, see **single for double**.

enshrine or inshrine
See under **en-/in-**.

ensure or insure
See **insure**.

enthrall or enthral
In American English **enthrall** is the standard spelling and the only one to be found in CCAE. British writers prefer **enthral**, by a majority of 2:1 in BNC data, and the *Oxford Dictionary* (1989) underscores the equivalence of the two spellings with its headword as **enthral(l)**. Given that the word consists of *en-* and *thrall,* the spelling with two *l*s has everything to recommend it. The original C16 spelling gave the word two *l*s, but it was subject to the C18 fashion of trimming double final consonants (see **single for double**). The older spelling *inthral(l)* makes no showing in either American or British databases, despite being listed in *Webster's Third* (1986) and the *Oxford* dictionary. See further under **en-/in-**.

entrance or entry
Both these nouns connect with the verb *enter,* and can mean "act of entering," "the place of entering" and "the right to enter." Yet database evidence shows that **entrance** is more often used of the place at which people enter premises, and **entry** of the fact or moment of entering. So on entering the exhibition you could be charged either an *entrance fee* (because it is at the gate) or an *entry fee* (which secures your right to go in). An official *NO ENTRY* sign makes access by that route illegal, whether or not it's physically impossible.

In database evidence, **entrance** is most often a built structure, as in *main entrance* and *entrance foyer;* while **entry** is often more metaphorical, as in *entry into the war* and *student entry to Computing Science.* **Entry** has further developed to mean "something entered," such as a note in a diary or an account book, or an item in a competition.

Both nouns are loanwords from French, **entry** borrowed in C14 and **entrance** in C16. Quite distinct is the verb **entrance** with stress on the second

syllable, formed in English out of *en-* and *trance.* See further under **en-/em-**.

entrench or intrench
See under **en-/in-**.

enure or inure
See **inure**.

envision or envisage
Both verbs have an eye on the future, and are relatively recent words. **Envisage** in the sense "foresee" is first recorded in earlier C19, whereas the record for **envision** starts with Lytton Strachey in 1921. Though both are known, Americans prefer **envision** over **envisage** by about 14:1 in CCAE. In British English **envisage** is overwhelmingly preferred, outnumbering **envision** by almost 100:1 in BNC evidence.

eon or aeon
The choice between these is discussed at **ae/e**.

-eous or -ious
See **-ious**.

epi-
This Greek prefix has several meanings, as seen in the various scholarly loanwords which brought it into English. Its most general meaning "on or upon" is represented in:

> *epicentre   epicycle   epidural   epiglottis
> epithelium   epizooic*

Such words designate things which are physically situated on or above. In others, **epi-** refers to something which is added on or occurs afterwards:

> *epigenesis   epigram   epilogue   episode
> epitaph   epithet   epitome*

When prefixed to a word beginning with a vowel, **epi-** becomes **ep-**, as in *epaxial, epenthetic, epode;* and this also happens before h, as in *ephemeral* ("happening on just one day").

The prefix **epi-** has mostly been productive in the specialized fields of science and scholarship. *Epithet* is among the few to gain a role in popular usage, but not without contention. See **epithet**.

epicene
In the grammar of Greek and Latin, **epicene** was used of nouns which were strictly masculine or feminine by their grammatical class, but could refer to people and animals of either gender. Examples from Latin include *poeta,* a feminine noun which regularly referred to male poets, and *vulpes,* the feminine noun for "fox," which was used of both the vixen and the dog fox. (See further under **declension**.)

In English grammar the term has been transferred from grammatical to natural gender. It is applied to English words which could denote either male or female, such as *artist, cat, clerk, doctor, giraffe, student, teacher, they* i.e. words which are *common* in gender. (See further under **gender**.)

epidemic or endemic
See **endemic**.

epilogue or epilog
See under **-gue/-g**.

epistemic modality
See **deontic and epistemic**.

epithet
The applications of this word are different in scholarly and common usage. Literary scholars apply **epithet** to an adjective, and to a compound adjective if it's a *Homeric epithet* like the "rosy-fingered (dawn)." These uses may perhaps have given rise to the mistaken notion that **epithets** should not be negative (Gowers, 1965), although Johnson's 1755 dictionary had defined **epithet** as a term with either negative or positive qualities, as the *Oxford Dictionary* (1989) still does. This is certainly in line with its application to the nicknames of celebrated or notorious persons, as in *Gregory the Great* or *Ivan the Terrible*. Note that the nickname need not consist simply of an adjective, as in those cases.

But common use of **epithet** and especially **epithets** also makes it a euphemism for the abusive words or names flung in anger or contempt (including swear words). The usage is well established in American English, to judge by numerous examples in CCAE, such as:

> . . . *cars were often spray-painted with racial epithets by white kids.*
> . . . *demonstrators chanted raucous epithets and hurled eggs at the embassy*

Thus **epithets** often connotes public verbal aggression targeting minorities. Only occasionally are **epithets** themselves reported . . .

> . . . *pansy, fairy, nance, fruit, fruitcake and less printable epithets*

This antisocial use of **epithet** is recognized in *Webster's Third* (1986), but not yet in British dictionaries. The very first signs of its use in British English are nevertheless to be found in the BNC:

> *Italians only find skiing interesting when they're shouting epithets or carving each other up.*
> *We were treated to epithets which no Merton man would have allowed to pass his lips in mixed company.*

But as the examples show, this use of **epithets** in British English is (pro tem) a matter of ad hoc abuse and swear words, not the symptom of a broader antisocial agenda.

eponymous or eponymic
Some dictionaries such as *Webster's Third* (1986) present these adjectives as synonyms and variants of each other, whereas others such as the *Oxford Dictionary* (1989) treat them more independently. Either way **eponymous** is given priority, and applied to the person (or proper name) after whom something is named, as in:

> *Andrew Brownswood of the eponymous greetings card maker*
> *The eponymous narrator of Spider (it's a nickname his mother called him)*
> *Hydro Mississauga Ltd of the eponymous Ontario town*
> *Like the eponymous Statue, the word "liberty" comes from French.*

As these examples from BNC and CCAE show, **eponymous** can now be applied to proper names vested in products, compositions, businesses,

institutions, as well as diseases and the placenames and names of nationalities and tribal groups (like *Colombo, American*) to which it was once confined. (See further under **Columbia** and **America**.)

The *Oxford* connects **eponymic** directly with the noun *eponym*, which might give it independent scope but for the fact that only the older senses of that word are registered – those referring to the name-giver (which render the underlying Greek more closely) not the more recent use of *eponym* to refer to the name/word derived (see **eponyms**, final paragraph). The *New Oxford* (1998) which does recognize the latter sense doesn't mention **eponymic**, only **eponymous**. A further complication is that **eponymic** is extremely rare (only one example in CCAE, none at all in the BNC). So for the moment **eponymic** is waiting in the wings, while **eponymous** does double duty for both older and newer meanings of *eponym*. See next entry.

eponyms
Some people gain a curious immortality when their surnames become the byword (and eventually the common word) for a particular product or a practice. The *sandwich* originated this way (named after the portable lunch associated with the Earl of Sandwich, 1718–92); and *braille* is the *eponymous* name for the tactile system which enables the blind to read, invented by Frenchman Louis Braille 1809–52. *Bloomers* take their name from the American feminist Amelia Bloomer 1818–91. **Eponyms** sometimes perpetuate a nickname, as in the case of *grog*. "Old Grog" (referring to his grogram cloak) was the nickname of Admiral Edward Vernon (1684–1757), who reputedly added water to the sailors' rations of rum, and so lent his nickname to diluted alcoholic spirits of any kind. In Australia and New Zealand his nickname has become the byword for cheap forms of liquor.

The items or behavior to which **eponyms** refer are not necessarily a credit to the family name, yet many are no worse than household words:

biro	boycott	brougham	bunsen
cardigan	clerihew	derby	doily
guillotine	leotard	macintosh	morse
pullman	quisling	shrapnel	silhouette
wellingtons			

A more select group of **eponyms** are the ones specifically chosen by the community of scientists to refer to units of measurement, including:

ampere	coulomb	henry	joule
newton	ohm	pascal	watt

The complete list is to be found in Appendix IV.

Note that **eponyms** do not need to be capitalized because they work as common nouns, and are no longer proper names. Their assimilation into the common vocabulary is even more complete in cases where they provide the basis for new complex words, as with:

bowdlerize	chauvinism	galvanize
macadamize	mesmerize	nicotine
pasteurize	sadism	spoonerism

Eponyms abound in the names of flora, celebrating botanists and horticulturalists of many nationalities:

banksia	bauhinia	camellia	clarkia
fuchsia	poinciana	poinsettia	wistaria

These names are written with lower case when they're used as the common name for the plant. However when used as the name of the botanical genus, and accompanied by a species name, they are capitalized. See further under **capital letters** section 1e.

This use of **eponym** to refer to common words derived from proper names (rather than to the name-giver himself or herself) is relatively recent – not recognized in the *Oxford Dictionary* (1989), though *New Oxford* (1998) knows it. *Webster's Third* (1986) and *Merriam-Webster* (2000) anticipate it by reference to a "name derived from / based on [a proper name]." It works of course on the analogy of other linguistic terms such as *synonym, antonym, hyponym*.

equ-/equi-

These are two forms of the Latin root *aequus* meaning "equal," which is found in *equal* itself and in other loanwords such as the following:

equable	*equanimity*	*equation*
equator	*equilibrium*	*equinox*
equivalent	*equivocal*	

In modern English it has helped to create new scholarly words such as:

equiangular	*equidistant*	*equimolecular*
equipoise	*equiprobable*	

The same Latin root is at the heart of *equit-*, a stem which comes to us in French loanwords such as *equity* and *equitable,* words which connote fair and equal treatment for all parties.

Other words beginning with *equ-,* such as *equestrian, equine, equitation,* are extensions of a quite different Latin root: *equus* meaning "horse." Its influence extends to *equip,* though the connection in that case is spurious. The word is of Germanic origin, but appears to have been remodeled in French in the belief that it was related to Latin *equus*.

equable or equitable

What's in a syllable? A sizable difference in meaning – though these words are otherwise similar enough to be mistaken for each other in some contexts. Both embody the Latin root *aequus* ("equal, even"; see **equ-/equi-**), but **equable** preserves the meaning more directly, in its applications to people who have an *equable temperament,* i.e. are even-tempered, and to regions with an *equable climate,* i.e. one which is temperate. **Equitable** comes by a less direct path through French, and is associated with *equity*. It therefore means "even-handed," and implies the fair and just disposition of human affairs, as in an *equitable arrangement*. We trust that judges will deal *equitably* with the matters before them.

The two words are occasionally interchanged by mistake – as in *equitable weather* which then carries the whimsical suggestion that "someone up there" might control the climate, and prevent it from raining indifferently "on the just and the unjust," as the King James bible has it.

equaled or equalled

For the choice between these, see -l-/-ll-.

equilibrium

Should the plural be **equilibriums** or **equilibria**? *Merriam-Webster's* (2000) allows either, whereas *New Oxford* (1998) only mentions the second. The 1998–2001 Langscape survey confirmed the British preference for **equilibria**, and that writers outside Britain (in the US and Australia) for **equilibriums**. The results also showed a broader generational difference: that

equilibria was preferred by those in their later middle years (45 and over), while those under 45 went for **equilibriums.** See further under **-um**.

equivalence or equivalency

These stand on either side of a regional difference. Only **equivalence** seems to be current in British English, by BNC evidence. In American English both are current, but **equivalency** outnumbers **equivalence** by more than 3:1 in data from CCAE.
◊ For other similar pairs, see under **-nce/-ncy**.

-er

When attached to adjectives, this is the regular comparative inflection as in *clearer, simpler, untidier.* (See further under **adjectives** section 2.) Other uses of the suffix are listed at **-er/-or**.

-er/-a

These are alternative spellings for the last syllable of colloquial forms of words such as *chocker/chocka* ("chock full"), *feller/fella* ("fellow"), and especially for proper names such as *Bazza* for *Barry* (as in *Bazza McKenzie*). The additional change from "rr" to "zz" is known as *assibilation*.

-er/-ers

In colloquial English, an **-er** is sometimes substituted for the last syllable (or syllables) of a word, as in *feller* for *fellow, rugger* for *rugby,* and *homer* for the *home run* in baseball. The adaptation is taken further when *champagne* becomes *champers* and *pregnant* becomes *preggers*. Proper names can be made colloquial in the same way in UK and Australia, in ephemeral forms such as *Staggers* for *St Stephens Hall,* and *Makkers* for *Macquarie University*. The added *-s* is a familiarity marker rather than a plural. See further under **-s**.

-er/-or

When you look over the various roles sustained by these two endings, it's remarkable that they overlap so little:

-**er** functions as an agent suffix for verbs, e.g. *hunter*
  as an agent suffix with nouns, e.g.
    farmer
  as a localizing suffix with area and placenames,
    e.g. *New Yorker, Highlander*
  as the comparative suffix for many adjectives,
    e.g. *older* (see under **adjectives**)
  as a colloquial replacement for a final syllable,
    e.g. *feller* (see under **-er/-a** and -**er/-ers**)
  as a variant form of *-re* as in *centre/center*
    (see under **-re/-er**)
-**or** functions as an agent suffix for verbs, e.g. *educator*
    as an ending on borrowed agent words, e.g. *doctor, ambassador*
    as a variant form of *-our,* as in *color/colour* (see **-or/-our**)

The point at which **-er** and **-or** overlap most significantly is in forming agent words out of English verbs, and here even reliable spellers are sometimes in doubt. Should it be:

adapter	or	*adaptor*
adviser	or	*advisor*
*appointer	or	*appointor*
*assurer	or	*assuror*
*attester	or	*attestor*
attracter	or	*attractor*
attributer	or	*attributor*
conjurer	or	*conjuror*
*connecter	or	*connector*
constructer	or	*constructor*
convener	or	*convenor*
conveyer	or	*conveyor*
*deviser	or	*devisor*
disrupter	or	*disruptor*
*exciter	or	*excitor*
*executer	or	*executor*
*granter	or	*grantor*
*licenser	or	*licensor*
mortgager	or	*mortgagor*
*resister	or	*resistor*
*settler	or	*settlor*
*warranter	or	*warrantor*

The pairs in bold are discussed at their own entries in this book. Those asterisked are cases where the **-er** form is the one in general use, and the **-or** one is for specialists, usually in science, technology or law. The remainder are just a token of the ever-increasing group where there are both **-er** and **-or** agent words, and either can be used.

1 Words with -er. Overall there's no doubt that the **-er** group is growing at the expense of the **-or** group. This is because almost all agent words based on English verbs are formed that way. The **-er** suffix can identify people in terms of their work, their recreation or their behavior:

baker	*dancer*	*drinker*	*driver*
hiker	*producer*	*runner*	*smoker*
teacher	*wrecker*		

The suffix is also commonly used to designate machines and instruments by their function:

decanter dispenser divider propeller

The **-er** ending is also the normal one for ad hoc formations, in phrases such as a *prolonger of meetings* or an *inviter of trouble*. Any agent words which are not listed in dictionaries you can safely spell with **-er**.

2 Words with -or. The most significant group of agent words with **-or** are Latin or neo-Latin in origin. Note especially those based on verbs ending in **-ate**, for example:

agitator	*calculator*	*demonstrator*
elevator	*illustrator*	*operator*
precipitator	*radiator*	*spectator*

With other Latin verb groups, the endings are increasingly mixed. Older agentives such as *conductor, contributor, director, instructor, investor* retain the **-or**, while younger ones with latinate stems have **-er**, for example:

computer	*contester*	*digester*	*distracter*
molester	*presenter*	*promoter*	*protester*
respecter			

The older ones with **-or** can sometimes be identified by the fact that their standard meaning has moved some distance away from the formative verb, and seems to designate a role rather than a specific action, e.g. *conductor*. The new formations with **-er** express the ordinary meaning of the verb.

Note that the **-or** ending also goes with certain Latin loanwords such as *doctor, impostor* which clearly cannot have been formed from verbs in modern English. (There is no verb "doct" or "impost.") Other examples are:

divisor	*incisor*	*interlocutor*	*monitor*
precentor	*sponsor*	*transistor*	*victor*

Also spelled with **-or** are a number of medieval loanwords from French, such as:

conqueror	*counsellor*	*governor*	*juror*
purveyor	*surveyor*	*survivor*	

Their **-or** endings are actually a result of their being respelled in early modern English according to the Latin model. In short, you may expect **-or** spellings with older loanwords from either Latin or French, and with younger formations based on verbs ending in *-ate*.

3 A case for spelling reform? Because the **-er** ending is the dominant one for agent words in modern English, it would make excellent sense to allow writers to use it even with those which have traditionally been spelled **-or**, so as to remove the artificial distinction between *computer* and *calculator,* between *demonstrator* and *protester* etc. No vital meaning would be lost in such cases, and it would relieve writers of the unnecessary anxiety about the remaining **-or** spellings. If **-er** were used in all cases where there was a lively English verb, as in *calculater, demonstrater, instructer, invester,* spelling would be more predictable for true agent words. We could still allow for continuing use of **-or** in words which cannot be interpreted as agentives, such as *author, doctor, sponsor, tailor, traitor,* in which the ending seems to be part of the identity of the word. See **spelling, rules and reforms** sections 1 and 4.

-er › -r-

When words are extended with extra suffixes, the less stressed syllables are often reduced in pronunciation, and occasionally this is registered in the spelling as well. It is built into pairs such as:

disaster	*disastrous*	*enter*	*entrance*
hinder	*hindrance*	*monster*	*monstrous*
tiger	*tigress*	*waiter*	*waitress*

For those who use the **-er** spelling in *fiber* etc., it can also be seen in

caliber	*calibrate*	*center*	*central*
fiber	*fibrous*	*luster*	*lustrous*
sepulcher	*sepulchral*	*theater*	*theatrical*

See further under **-re/-er**.

ergative

This term has multiple applications in linguistics, in reference to languages, nouns and verbs. Field linguists use **ergative** to refer to the inflection of nouns as the subject of a transitive verb, when the inflection contrasts with that of the subject of an intransitive verb. An *ergative language* has different inflections for these two kinds of subject, and the inflection for the intransitive subject is the same as that of the object of the transitive verb (see further under **cases,** and **transitive and intransitive**).

English has no **ergative** marking for its nouns, and the term has instead been applied to verbs whose subjects are not agents but "patients" of the action. For example:

The kettle boiled.
This hotel is renovating.
Wax will melt under low heat.
The gap has widened between rich and poor.

Recent research (McMillion, 1998) suggests that **ergative** uses of verbs may be on the increase, and especially in British English. Like the agentless passive, **ergative** constructions allow the writer to report negative facts without pinpointing the agency involved:

> *If the situation worsens, the citizens will need your support.*

The same construction is also known as the "unaccusative." See further under **middle voice**.

-erie or -ery

See **-ery**.

-eroo

This was a popular suffix in America in the 1940s which created ad hoc words such as:

> bummeroo   checkeroo   flopperoo
> jokeroo   kisseroo

The **-eroo** suffix generated a few recorded words in the South Pacific, including the New Zealand term *boozeroo*. But Australian formations such as *jambaroo, jigamaroo, shivaroo* suggest by their spelling that the suffix was identified with *-aroo*, an element derived from *kangaroo*. See further under **-aroo**.

errant or arrant

See **arrant**.

erratum

For the plural of this word, see under **-um**.

-ery

This ending, modeled on the French *-erie,* has been in use in English since C14. It forms both concrete and abstract nouns, of which the following are only a token:

> bakery   imagery   popery   printery
> quackery   rookery   scenery   vinery

Modern French loans with *-erie* such as *coterie, gaucherie, reverie,* resist anglicization, and the ending gives them an edge over English synonyms: compare *patisserie* with *bakery*.
◇ For words with **-ery** derived from Latin, see under **-ary/-ery/-ory**.

escapee or escaper

Escapee is established throughout the English-speaking world as the term for someone who escapes from prison or some other confining institution. It appeared in later C19, one of its earliest applications being to French convicts who escaped from New Caledonia to Australia, 1881.

The word **escaper** is actually older, if we count an isolated example in the King James bible of 1611, or even the first one recorded after that in 1844. With its *-er* suffix, it seems a more regular formation than **escapee** – especially if one assumes that *-ee* is a passive suffix, which was Fowler's reason for preferring **escaper**. But not all *-ee* words are passive in meaning (see **-ee**), and the fact that *-ee* is often found on legal or bureaucratic words makes it apt for one who declines to remain a "guest" of the government. This may explain the popularity of **escapee** in Australia and America (where it outnumbers **escaper** by almost 15:1 in data from CCAE). In Britain the two

are much more evenly matched, though BNC data still puts **escapee** in the majority.

Other agent words based on *escape* belong to different worlds altogether. For an *escapist* it's all in the mind, and for the *escapologist,* it is the dramatic art or sport of extricating yourself Houdini-like from seemingly inescapable cages, chains or ropes.

-ese

This suffix originated as a way of indicating geographical origin, as it still can. The earliest loanwords with it, dating from C15, are *Milanese* and *Genoese,* and by its form the suffix itself must be Italian in origin, not French, as is sometimes said. Later examples of its use in English suggest that it came to be associated with exotic places, and their peoples, cultures and languages:

> Balinese   Burmese   Chinese   Faroese
> Japanese   Javanese   Nepalese   Portuguese
> Sudanese   Vietnamese

The number of Asian places designated with **-ese** is striking.

In C19 the suffix **-ese** acquired another role in designating the distinctive speech style of an individual e.g. *Johnsonese,* or an occupational group e.g. *journalese, legalese, officialese.* Apart from established words such as these, **-ese** appears in ad hoc formations such as *brochurese* and *computerese.* Words formed in this way often have a pejorative flavor.
◇ Compare **-speak**.

Eskimo, Esquimau and Inuit

In Canada the word **Eskimo** (plural **Eskimos**) or the French form *Esquimau* (*Esquimaux*) has been replaced by **Inuit** as a collective way of referring to the Aboriginal people, following the Inuit Circumpolar Conference of 1977 (*Canadian English Usage,* 1997). The principal **Inuit** settlements are in western Arctic, northern Quebec, Baffin Island, and Labrador – although the Innu of Labrador are not **Inuit** but Cree people (*Editing Canadian English,* 2000). In Alaska only one of the four linguistic groups identifies with the name **Inuit**, and the term **Eskimo** continues to be acceptable usage there. No other term can include the whole *Eskimoan people,* according to the *American Heritage Dictionary* (2000).

Inuit is strictly speaking a plural form, with *Inuk* as its singular for the individual. Outside Canada, **Inuit** is nevertheless used for both singular and plural. *Merriam-Webster* (2000) notes **Inuits** as a possible plural in the US.

esophagus or oesophagus

For the choice between these, see **oe/e**.

especially or specially

See **special**.

espresso or expresso

The strong black coffee made by Italians is **espresso**, literally "expressed or drawn out under pressure." The method relies on pressurized steam to extract the flavorsome liquid from ground coffee beans. The spelling **expresso** anglicizes the word and suggests a folk etymology, that it offers you a fast cup of coffee. Although **expresso** can be seen on menus, according to *Webster's English Usage* (1989), it's not so common in edited prose in either American or British English.

In data from both CCAE and the BNC, **espresso** outnumbers **expresso** by more than 10:1.

Like most Italian loanwords **espresso** takes an English plural and a simple *s* at that: **espressos** (see further under **-o**.) However where Italy's haute cuisine is being served, you may hear the plural **espressi**, naturally enough. See further under **Italian plurals**.

esprit de corps
See under **corps**.

Esq.
This abbreviation for *Esquire* once appeared regularly on letterheads and envelopes, as a courtesy title for those who could not claim a title such as *Sir, Dr., Professor* etc., and were not in clerical orders, but were "gentlemen" by virtue of birth, position or education. This represented a large extension of earlier usage, whereby the title *Esquire* was only accorded to the higher gentry, those ranking next to knights. Nowadays the use of Mr. before men's names has effectively taken the place of **Esq**. (See further under **forms of address**.) But in the UK older correspondents still make some use of it, and BNC data registers both historical and current (courtesy) use of it:

> *In the 18th century it was the property of Arthur Eggington Esq JP.*
> *Tuesday evening: W. B. Scott. Esq. in the Chair.*

In current American English, the abbreviation **Esq**. is not common, but sometimes found after the surnames of professional persons, provided no other title (such as *Dr., Mr., Ms., Hon.*) prefaces the name:

> *Mitchell Stephens Esq., a hotshot lawyer from New York*

As in that example, it's often suffixed to the names of people associated with the law, including attorneys, clerks of court, and justices of the peace. In both the US and Canada, it can be used after the surnames of woman lawyers, as well as their male counterparts.

-esque
This ending, found in English *picturesque,* is a clone of French *pittoresque,* and somewhat productive in generating ad hoc adjectives out of proper names, as in *Clintonesque, Chaplinesque, Turneresque* meaning "in the style or manner of (the person named)." As in those examples, **-esque** words are usually coined out of two-syllabled names. The French connection gives the word a *je ne sais quoi* of sophistication, all the more evident when you compare it with *-ish,* which is its Germanic cognate in English. See further under **-ish**.

-ess
This suffix, borrowed from French, is loaded with gender, and its *raison d'être* in the past has been to draw specific attention to the female of the species (with animals, as in *lioness*), and to the female incumbents of particular roles and occupations (as in *air-hostess* and *waitress*). The latter have come under fire as conspicuous examples of sexism in language, and ones which devalue women's participation in the work force. This problem has been felt with all of the following:

actress	authoress	conductress
deaconess	directress	editress
manageress	mayoress	poetess
proprietress	sculptress	stewardess

The feminine ending tends to distract attention from the nature of the occupation itself, making it somehow different from that of the *author, deacon, manager* etc.: it seems to demean the work of the woman who does it. For the *actress* it's a particular dilemma, since gender is essential to the parts they play, and well rewarded in starring roles. But among the rank and file, some women prefer to call themselves *actors*. In other professions, female professionals have solved the problem in the same way, by identifying themselves *authors, editors, managers* etc. Occasionally a synonym or paraphrase can be used, e.g. *flight attendant* for *stewardess*. These and other solutions are discussed in the *Handbook of Nonsexist Writing* (1988), and firmly enjoined by many publishers. For editors and writers, the alternative expression must not be cumbersome, nor leave any doubt that the same occupation is being referred to. (See further under **inclusive language**.)

Other words of this kind do not really undermine women's rights to equal opportunity in the job market. Some are traditional titles: *countess, duchess, princesss;* some designate specific female social roles, such as *heiress, hostess, mistress, patroness* which may need to be identified from time to time. Yet others are just literary fictions, like *enchantress, goddess, shepherdess*. Occasional or literary use of such words hardly poses any threat to the status of women at large; and where they relate to vanishing traditions, they will die a natural death. The **-ess** will simply become an archaic and irrelevant suffix.

◇ For the use of **-ess** in ethnic terms, see **Jewess**, and **negress**.

essays
The classic **essays** of the past were written by philosophers and gentlemen of leisure – from Montaigne and Bacon to Russell and T. S. Eliot – exploring ideas and views on a personally chosen subject. Today's university and college students who write **essays** and papers are their heirs only in the sense that they use them as a vehicle for discussion. Their **essays**/papers are usually written on prescribed topics, and few would risk "flying a kite" in an assessable exercise. Having duly mastered the art of **essay** writing, students graduate to positions in which they never use that form of communication, and letters, reports and memorandums are the order of the day. The only professional equivalent to the traditional **essay** is perhaps the signed editorial column produced by celebrated journalists, who do indeed enjoy the essayist's licence to explore ideas and speak their minds.

essentiality or essentialness
Dictionaries allow that either of these can be the abstract noun for *essential*. But **essentiality** (with six syllables) is more popular than **essentialness** (with four), in small amounts of data from CCAE and the BNC. Writers seeking abstraction seem to go for the whole hog.

esthetic or aesthetic
See under **ae/e**.

estrogen or oestrogen
See under **oe/e**.

189

et al.

See under **etc.**

et seq.

This Latin abbreviation stands for *et sequens* ("and the following [page]"). In the plural it takes the form **et seqq.**, for *et sequentes* ("and the following [pages]"). It was once widely used in scholarly references, as in:

> Newton, *Optics* p. 16 *et seq.*
> Newton, *Optics* p. 16 *et seqq.*

While the first of those refers you to pages 16 and 17, the second is open-ended: the reader decides how far after page 16 to continue in search of relevant material. More specific references are preferred these days for each type, so that the first would be:

> Newton, *Optics* pp. 16–17

and the second, say:

> Newton, *Optics* pp. 16–21

◊ Compare **loc.cit.**, **op.cit.** and **passim**, which are also being replaced by more specific alternatives.

etc.

This abbreviation is usually written with a stop, though this assumes an editorial policy of using stops for lower case abbreviations (see further at **abbreviations** section 2). The stop is used more consistently in American than British English, by database evidence from CCAE and the BNC. But either way, the stop on **etc.** is subsumed by the final full stop when it occurs at the end of a sentence. **Etc.** is regularly printed in roman, not italics (see further under **italics**). Making **etc.** a joint character with ampersand – &c – is not recommended nowadays.

Etc., standing for *et cetera,* is the best known Latin abbreviation in English. The Latin words in it are pronounced in full, unlike *e.g.* and *i.e.* which are simply said as initialisms. Further evidence of its assimilation is the fact that there's no standardized translation for it as there is for *e.g.* and *i.e.* Authors and editors translate **etc.** variously as "and so forth," "and so on," "and such like," "and the like" or "and others," which again shows the gradual extension of its use. It also works as a fully fledged word *etcetera,* and it becomes a colloquial noun *etceteras* with the regular English plural ending.

The original Latin phrase *et cetera* means "and the rest" or "and the others," implying a known set of items which might be used to complete the list preceding it. It relieves the writer of the need to list them, and calls on the reader to supply them. However **etc.** is quite often used more loosely to mean "and others," which presumes nothing of the reader, and just notes that the list is incomplete. Strictly speaking **etc.** refers to things, not people, because the *-a* makes it neuter in gender. For references to people, the Latin abbreviation **et al.** (short for **et alii**, literally "and other persons") is available. (See further under **Latin abbreviations**.)

1 Punctuation with etc. In spite of its thorough assimilation, the use of **etc.** has traditionally been discouraged (along with other abbreviations), and hedged about with rules. The use of commas with it has been the subject of editorial prescription: that there should be a comma before it if the preceding list consisted of at least two items (but not if there was only one); and that there must be a comma after it, except when it was the last word in a sentence. Most style authorities now take a more liberal line. Butcher's *Copy-editing* (1992) asks only for editorial consistency in either using or not using a comma before and/or after **etc.**; and the *Chicago Manual of Style* (2003) relaxes the requirement to use a comma afterwards. In Canada, both older and newer styles coexist, according to *Canadian English Usage* (1997). The Australian government *Style Manual* (1994) adds that the comma before **etc.** is only needed when the sentence might otherwise be misconstrued. When it follows a list, **etc.** is connected by intonation with the previous word, and the comma would be intrusive. Hence its absence in: *in government, defence, production etc.* or *the growing of camellias, rhododendrons, pieris etc.* – among British examples from the BNC. So the "framing" of **etc.** with commas is no longer considered essential, and left to authors' and editors' discretion.

2 The use of etc. in various kinds of writing. Like other abbreviations, **etc.** has been thought unsuitable for many kinds of writing. Strunk and White (1972) called it "a misfit" in formal writing. Butcher (1992) noted the publisher's convention of replacing **etc.** with an English paraphrase, but she advises conferring with the author over it. The *Chicago Manual* (1993) is still unenthusiastic about using **etc.** in "formal prose," and would have it confined to lists, tables and parentheses. What "formal" means in all this is uncertain. *Webster's English Usage* (1989) finds that **etc.** is common in expository writing, and *Canadian English Usage* (1997) that it's more frequent in academic writing than newspapers and magazines. The evidence of databases in the US and the UK is that it occurs in most of the nonfiction genres sampled; and in the Australian ACE database it registered in all types of nonfiction and 5 out of 8 categories of fiction. The traditional restrictions on the appearances of **etc.** are evidently being lifted in many parts of the English-speaking world.

What problem **etc.** could present is rarely discussed, though according to *The Right Word at the Right Time* (1985), it is inelegant and/or discourteous to the reader, and lays the writer open to charges of being lazy or short of information. Yet all such matters are relative to the medium of writing, and to the level of detail required. The writer who supplies a plethora of information is unlikely to be thought careless or ignorant because of an occasional **etc.** Rather it can be seen as signaling the writer's desire to limit the range of examples for discussion, to keep it focused. Stylistically speaking, **etc.** is more efficient than the wordy "translations" used to replace it. But like any stylistic device, it becomes obtrusive with overuse. This means a continuing role for its English paraphrases, as well as complementary devices such as *for example, such as, for instance,* which can be used at the beginning of the list instead of the end. Along with **etc.**, all are elements of a well-stocked writer's repertoire.

ethnic

This word has always been subject to ethnocentricity, i.e. the tendency to take one's own culture as the reference point in judging any others. In early Christian usage it meant "heathen," while C20 and C21 writers often use it to identify any culture other than their own. **Ethnic** thus often means "not of the mainstream," and acquires the connotations of "strange and exotic," as in *ethnic food* or *woollen cardigan with ethnic embroidery.* In these collocations, **ethnic** clearly has a commodity value. The downside of such usage is its apparent lack of discrimination among cultures other than one's own – a tendency to lump them all together. This is not helped by common expressions such as *ethnic minorities, ethnic disturbances, ethnic tensions,* where institutional acknowledgement of racial and cultural difference still seems to project mainstream assumptions, and gloss over whatever problems need to be identified. Of course **ethnic** is the appropriate adjective in abstract discussions of racial and cultural identity, when speaking of an *ethnic group* or the *ethnic mix of the American population.* But in newspaper reports on *ethnic violence,* it's symptomatic of the very social problem it purports to document – a reluctance to identify with disadvantaged and marginal groups. Within the mainstream, *ethnic jokes* perpetuate only racial/cultural stereotypes, and scarcely provide inclusive amusement for all. (See further at **inclusive language**.)

The newish noun **ethnic(s)** is similarly used by members of the social mainstream – in North America and Australia, but not much in Britain – to imply a cultural divide between themselves and immigrants or members of minority groups: *In California we're used to ethnics.* The plural form creates a collective pigeonhole which too easily carries negative messages, as in:

> *His path is peopled by rednecks, ethnics, feminists . . .*
> *. . . interviewed . . . white ethnics, blacks, Latinos and Asians*
> *Only certain ethnics seem to be acceptable.*

What's lacking in such references is proper recognition of the individual cultures and identities involved. (See further under **racist language**.) In more careful writing, **ethnic** combines with specific national names, such as *ethnic Germans* (in Poland or the US), *ethnic Turks* (in Bulgaria), to indicate the particular group whose interests are a matter of concern.

As is evident, **ethnic** is a troubling word which tends to privilege the mainstream culture at the expense of others. Some of the usages outlined above are nonprejudicial and legitimate; but in others the word is simply a front for stereotypical racial/cultural assumptions. It should give pause for thought.

ethos

In common usage this word refers to the characteristic attitudes and values of any group, institution or period of history, as in the *humanist ethos* of C16, or the *get-rich ethos* of the 1980s. In rhetoric and art however it is a technical term for a way of appealing to the audience. See further under **pathos**.

etiology or aetiology

This is a technical term for scientists as well as philosophers. In the sciences **(a)etiology** identifies the causes of disease (or psychosocial disorders), and seeks explanations for geological formations or astronomical events. In philosophy, it focuses on the notion of causation itself. Broadly speaking, the alternative spellings reflect American/British difference where medicine and pathology are

concerned (see further under **ae/e**), though there is a sprinkling of **etiology** among medical references in the BNC. In the other professions it's more an individual matter. For some European philosophers **etiology** is the preferred spelling, as it was for the astronomer Halley. The *Oxford Dictionary* (1989) indicates its acceptance of both spellings.

-ette

This suffix borrowed from French has three main uses in English, to mean:
1 "small" (as in *kitchenette, rosette*)
2 "female" (as in *suffragette, usherette*)
3 "substitute" (as in *leatherette, flannelette*)
The first use of **-ette** has generated a few common terms, such as *couchette, dinette, diskette, flatette, sermonette, statuette,* where the suffix serves as necessary (and sometimes rueful) recognition that the size and scope of the object are diminished in comparison with any archetypes you may think of. The *supermarkette* in an Australian country town makes no false promises. The second meaning has had little use in English generally, although it was productive in America in the earlier half of this century, in formations like *bachelorette, freshette, (drum-)majorette, sailorette* for the members of certain (younger) female groups. Occasionally they were formed from proper names, as in *Latin Quarterettes, the Centaurettes,* and the Topeka *Co-operettes* (the women's auxiliary of the city Co-operative Club). *Undergraduette* had some vogue in Britain between the wars. But the pressure to do away with gender-specific suffixes goes against it now, reinforced by satirical male-chauvinist creations such as *bimbette, editorette, whizzette.* (See **sexism in language**.) In the names of fabrics such as *leatherette,* **-ette** serves to denote a product that is either a substitute for or an imitation of an old-established material. *Flannelette* and the British *winceyette* are further examples.

Loanwords with **-ette**. The use of the **-ette** ending is somewhat variable with *bassinet(te), briquet(te), epaulet(te),* as well as musical terms like *minuet(te), quartet(te), quintet(te), sextet(te).* It appears in full in cultural or consumer contexts where its French connotations are most valued (see further under **frenchification**). More functional loanwords which had earlier had **-ette** were trimmed back to *-et,* as happened with numerous French loanwords like *budget, bullet, facet, pocket, rivet, tablet, turret.* Other significant examples are *toilet* and *omelet:* see individual entries.

etymology

This is the study of the origins and individual history of words: what languages they came from, and how their meaning and form have changed over the course of time. It confronts us with the mutability of language, although *etymological* knowledge has been used to try to prevent language change.

Etymologies are sometimes used to identify an "original" form or meaning for a word, which is then held up as true for all time. This was the basis for a number of the strangest spellings of English, such as *debt, indict, receipt,* whose Latin ancestors (*debitum, indictare, receptum*) are invoked in the letters *b, c* and *p,* added during C15/16. The *etymological* letters were and are superfluous in terms of our pronunciation of those words, which is based on French. Likewise, the fact that *aggravate* contains the Latin root *grav-* meaning "heavy, serious" moves some people to insist that the English word can only mean "make more serious," and ought not to mean "annoy."

Etymological arguments about language are ultimately arbitrary, choosing a fixed point in time (such as classical Latin) as the reference point for language questions. But usage stretches still further back in time. Many Latin words had Greek antecedents, and they can be traced back to Indo-European. See further under **Indo-European**, and **spelling**.

Apart from scholarly uses of **etymology**, there's no doubt that ordinary users of a language like to see a word's meaning reflected in its form or spelling. Words sometimes adjust their spelling in response to an assumed **etymology**. In cases like *bridegroom,* the *etymon* ("original word or form") now enshrined in the spelling is quite wrong. See further under **folk etymology**.

eu-

This Greek prefix brings the notion of "good, fine, attractive or beautiful" to whatever roots it attaches itself to. See for example:

eugenics	eulogy	eupepsia
euphemism	euphony	euphoria

The *euphonium* also owes its name to this prefix (it is simply a variant of *euphony*) though people who live under the same roof as a beginner on the *euphonium* may feel that it is not well named.

The Australian *eucalyptus* tree (literally "fine-capped") is so named after the neat caps which cover the buds.

eulogy or elegy

See **elegy**.

euphemisms

Euphemisms are the fine-sounding words and phrases we use for things which are not so fine or beautiful. The word itself goes back to the Greeks and Greek civilization, suggesting that they had found the need for inoffensive expressions to refer to what was unpalatable, unacceptable and unmentionable in their culture. A little later Cicero wrote about **euphemisms** in letters to his friends (*Epistolae ad Familiares IX*). Contemporary linguistic research suggests that they occur in most languages, and even across languages, for bilingual speakers.

Any culture has its taboo subjects, and will find **euphemisms** for referring to them when reference is unavoidable. The basic bodily functions are a common focus of **euphemisms** in contemporary English, hence the use of *go to the bathroom* for *urinate,* and *have intercourse* for *copulate.* Presumably most people feel some inhibitions or distaste about referring to them. Such **euphemisms** however are a relatively small group by comparison with those created by our social and political institutions, as part of their public rhetoric and as a means to avoid confronting people with uncomfortable and disturbing facts. The funeral industry does it with terms such as *casket* (for coffin), and *professional car* (for hearse). It has created the blended term *cremains,* to reduce people's awareness that they are dealing with cremated remains. The

Australian government does it with the *higher education contribution scheme* or *HECS,* which attempts to put a positive spin on an educational lèvy which generally strikes a negative chord. In various parts of the English-speaking world, the process of *privatisation/privatization* looks increasingly like a name for the withdrawal of government services. Perhaps the *euphemistic* phrase *ethnic cleansing* helped to retard outsiders' responses to the sinister practices that led to Yugoslavia's deconstruction in the 1990s.

Apart from masking the awful truth, **euphemisms** help to "dress things up," when people want to lend status to something – as when barbers call themselves *hair consultants,* and when what used to be called "cooking" is referred to as *home science.* But **euphemisms** with pretensions can easily develop ironic overtones and begin to parody themselves. The burglar alarm expert who calls himself a *security executive* will soon need to find a new job title, if people are to take him seriously. One of the chronic problems with **euphemisms** is their built-in obsolescence. Hardly has a new one become established before its unmentionable past catches up with it. The turnover in terms for the public toilet: *WC, conveniences, rest rooms* etc., is well-known evidence, and we may wonder how long even the male and female icons for them can survive.

The search for replacement **euphemisms** can also be a source of comedy, and some seem deliberately aimed at comic effect. The phrases used to allude to a person's madness are legion, as *round the bend* becomes *round the twist, not the full quid* becomes *a sandwich short of a picnic.* The joke helps to cushion us from the disturbing reality of mental deterioration. **Euphemisms and writing. Euphemisms** are a resource for tactful communication in many situations, and few people want to give unnecessary verbal offense. In written communication, when we cannot be sure how our words will be read, it seems safer to use the occasional **euphemism** in the approach to "touchy" subjects. Many **euphemisms** are drawn from more formal English (e.g. *dismissed* for *sacked*), and more formal vocabulary is part of the verbal repertoire of the professional writer.

This is not to suggest making a habit of lofty expression. Writers who do are indulging not in **euphemism** but *euphuism,* the artificially elevated and embellished prose of John Lyly's *Euphues* (an Elizabethan epistolary novel whose style was satirized by both Shakespeare and Walter Scott). The frontier between **euphemism** and public deception is also one to guard: George Orwell's *1984* reminds us that with the corruption of language we risk the corruption of thought.

Along with a sensitivity to **euphemisms**, writers should perhaps cultivate their sense of the opposite: *dysphemisms* – words and phrases which are likely to prove offensive to the reader. It helps to develop a scale from the most offensive, e.g. referring to someone as a *cunt,* up to the offhanded *bloke* which might only seem offensive in a formal context. Both *dysphemisms* and **euphemisms** are a resource for adjusting one's expression to the needs of the situation. See also **pejorative**.

euphuism

See under **euphemism**.

Euro-, euro-, euro and Euro

As Europe consolidates its political and economic constitution from EEC to EC to EU, new coinings abound with **Euro-**:

> *Euro-ad Eurobeach Eurocrat Euromarket Euro-MP*

As is evident, some relate to EU organizations and the European Parliament; others imply conformity to EU standards and regulations. Most are regularly written with upper case. Among those that relate to EU monetary systems, the lower-case forms with **euro-** are increasingly common. Hence:

> *eurobond eurocheque eurocurrency eurodollar euromarket*

all exemplified in documents contained in the BNC. However neither the *Oxford Dictionary* (1989) nor *New Oxford* (1998) acknowledges the lower-case alternatives as yet.

As the name of the common European monetary unit, **Euro** almost always bears a capital. It can be pluralized as **Euros**, but is just as often left uninflected as in *12 Euro* (see **zero plurals**). In Australia, the **euro** is a type of kangaroo.

◊ See Appendix IX for a list of world currencies.

Europe

For older British citizens, **Europe** is still "the Continent" – that multilingual, multicultural land mass on the opposite side of the English Channel – witness BNC examples such as:

> *She was brought up between India, Europe and England*
> *UK lagers have little in common with genuine bottom-fermented beers from Europe.*

Joining the EEC in 1967 was for many "going into Europe." But having been there for more than thirty years has affected the way the British talk about **Europe**, and the BNC contains many more examples like:

> *The next government will . . . make Britain the brains of Europe.*
> *Birmingham . . . as Europe's leading city of the arts and media*

This perception of Britain as part of **Europe** comes naturally to those outside it. Henry James's novel *The Europeans* is about a British family who come to reside in New England, and for North Americans and Australians, **Europe** has always included both the British Isles and the continental mainland.

evasion or evasiveness

In spite of obvious similarities, these words are different in their makeup and use. **Evasiveness** is the abstract noun derived from the adjective *evasive*, and normally used to describe verbal behavior which avoids confronting the issues that others would like to see addressed. **Evasion** is the verbal noun more closely linked with *evade* and used to refer to specific instances in which a duty or responsibility is shirked, e.g. *tax evasion*. Note that while *tax evasion* is a civil crime, *tax avoidance* (like *tax minimization*) is strictly legal.

even

This word is often used to underscore and draw attention to neighboring words. In speech it can highlight a whole following phrase if the speaker's intonation carries it:

> *He didn't even sign a letter today.*
> (let alone a contract)

But the scope of **even** is more limited in writing because of the lack of intonation. Readers will not necessarily take it as affecting any more than the item immediately following. So the sentence just quoted would need to be slightly rearranged to make its point:

> *He didn't sign even a letter today.*

In that order, **even** draws full attention to "a letter," and thus makes it clear that nothing at all was signed.

◊ Compare **only**, for a similar word whose position in writing is more critical than in speech.

-ever and ever

This is both a suffix and an independent word. As a suffix **-ever** appears in *however* as the set of *wh-* words:

> *however whatever whenever wherever*
> *whichever whoever*

They have two different roles, as *indefinites* and as *intensifiers*.

*As *indefinites,* the **-ever** words usually work as relative pronouns and conjunctions, as in:

> *Whoever thought of it deserves a medal.*
> *The nurse will come whenever you press the bell.*

In casual speech they also function simply as indefinite pronouns or adverbs:

> *Bring your own cup, mug or whatever.*
> *We'll find a spot in the park – wherever.*

*As *intensifiers,* **-ever** words occur only at the beginning of sentences. (Compare the variable positions of the *indefinites*.) They underscore the focus of the question or exclamation that they preface.

> *However can you say that!*
> *Whichever did they mean?*

Fowler (1926) thought that in these cases **ever** should be written as a separate word, as it sometimes is:

> *How ever can you say that!*
> *Which ever did they mean?*

But dictionaries such as *New Oxford* (1998) and *Merriam-Webster* (2000) confirm that **ever** is very often set solid in such cases. Only when it serves to intensify a superlative is it written separately, as in *their best result ever* or *their best ever result*.

every

When **every** is followed by a singular noun (as in *every dog, every week*), there's little doubt that a singular verb goes with it. Singular verbs are also used to agree with *everybody, everyone, everything*. But when it comes to pronoun agreement, there's a strong tendency now to use *they, them, their* with **every** or any of its compounds. (See further under **agreement** section 3.)

◊ For the choice between *everybody* and *everyone*, see **-one**.

every other

In this British idiom, *other* means "second," as in:

> *Time sheets should be submitted every other week.*

For American readers **every other** needs to be paraphrased as *every second (week)*, or *in alternate (weeks)*.

evoke or invoke

There are subtle differences between these. When a memory or reaction is *evoked* in someone, it happens as a byproduct of an activity, not because that was the intended outcome:

His name evoked my student days.
The claim evoked a grunt of approval from the chairman.

What is *evoked* is not directly solicited.

With **invoke**, the subject of the verb is directly soliciting help and support from outside parties, or else appealing to principles for confirmation of an argument:

He invoked the help of the gods.
The company invoked the principle of last in first out.

In just one kind of context, there is potential for overlap – in speaking of contact with departed spirits. Here your choice between **evoke** and **invoke** depends on how much faith you have in the occult. **Invoke** implies some active response from the dead spirits as conjured up in a seance, while **evoke** simply suggests the conjuring up of their memory in the fellowship of their old friends. *Evocation* and *invocation* are distinguished in the same way.

ex-

This Latin prefix embodies two kinds of meaning in English:
* "out of, from"
* "former"

Ex- meaning "out of, from" is blended into hundreds of classical loanwords (nouns, verbs and adjectives), of which the following are only a token:

excavate	exception	excise	exclaim
exclusive	exempt	exorcise	explicit
explosion	export	extend	

The same prefix also appears as *e-* in loanwords such as *edit, elevate, emerge, emigrate.* Whether **ex-** or *e-*, the prefix is always set solid.

Ex- reinvented itself with the meaning "former" in C18 English, forming words which are normally hyphenated:

ex-convict	ex-husband	ex-king	ex-pilot
ex-president	ex-serviceman	ex-wife	

In the same way **ex-** combines freely with compounds, for example:

ex-advertising man	ex-football coach
ex-hairdresser	

-ex

For the plural of words like *apex, index, vortex,* see under **-x**.

ex officio

This Latin phrase means "by right of office." It connotes the duties and/or privileges of a particular office, especially when the incumbent automatically becomes a member of a committee to which others must be elected. The privilege and authority of office are also vested in the Latin phrase *ex cathedra,* meaning "from the seat [of authority]" – either religious or judicial. From that authoritative seat, popes and judges wielded immense verbal power, and their pronouncements and judgements could not be challenged.

Neither **ex officio** nor *ex cathedra* needs a hyphen when it becomes a compound adjective, as in an *ex officio member* or an *ex cathedra statement,* since both are foreign phrases. (See **hyphens** section 2c.)

ex silentio

Those who use an *argumentum e(x) silentio* ("argument from silence") give themselves an enormous licence. They exploit the fact that an author or document is silent on the issue with which they are concerned, and use the absence of comment to bolster their own case. A silence or absence of comment can of course be interpreted in various ways – and in quite opposite ways, as the play *A Man for All Seasons* by Robert Bolt showed so well. The charges against Thomas More turned on arguing that his silence meant a denial of Henry VIII's claims, while the standard aphorism was that silence meant consent: *qui tacet consentire* ("he who is silent [seems] to consent.") Arguments based on silence or the lack of contrary evidence are not really arguments at all, but rhetoric which works on the principle of "heads I win, tails you lose."

exactness or exactitude

Both are registered as abstract nouns for *exact,* in *New Oxford* (1998) and *Merriam-Webster* (2000). The two are equally used by writers in data from CCAE and the BNC.

exalt or exult

With only a letter between them, and some similar connotations, these can be mistaken for each other. Both belong to an elevated style, and elevation is built into the meaning of both. But while **exalt** usually means "raise in status," as in *exalted position,* **exult** ("rejoice, be jubilant") has the spirits running high. The distinction is complicated by the fact that **exalt** is occasionally used to mean "give high praise to," as in *exalted them to the skies.* Yet there's a crucial grammatical difference, in that **exalt** either takes an object or is made a passive verb, whereas **exult** never takes an object and is never passive.

When it comes to *exaltation* and *exultation,* there is little to choose between them. Both express high feelings. If we use *exaltation* for "elation," and *exultation* for "triumphant joy," there's still a lot of common ground between them.

excellence or excellency

In older texts, **excellency** appears where we might expect **excellence**: *admired not only for his gift in preaching but for his excellency and solidity in all kinds of learning.* Nowadays their roles are quite distinct. In both British and American English, **excellency** is normally found capitalized in honorific titles (*your Excellency, his/her Excellency*), while **excellence** continues to serve as the abstract noun. For other pairs of this kind, see **-nce/-ncy**.

except that or excepting that

These limiting phrases are about equally used in British English, in data from the BNC:

He kept quiet, except(ing) that his look changed from friendly to serious.

In American English **except that** is strongly preferred, by the evidence of CCAE. As often, the uninflected form is endorsed in the US: see further under **inflectional extras**.

exception proves the rule

The thrust of this axiom is widely misunderstood, partly because the English version shortcircuits the Latin. In its full form it is a legal maxim: *exceptio probat regulam in casibus non exceptis,* literally "the act of excepting confirms the rule for cases not excepted." By that translation, it describes a reasonable process of argumentation: a principle can be established by selecting those cases to which it applies and setting aside others. (See further under **induction**.)

But by translating *exceptio* into "exception," the statement seems to make the paradoxical claim that an exception confirms the rule. This misunderstanding goes back centuries, according to the *Oxford Dictionary* (1989), since the use of *exception* to mean an exceptional example – rather than the act of excepting – is recorded from mid-C17 on, and is almost as old as the maxim itself.

exceptional or exceptionable

The different values expressed in these words put a gulf between them. **Exceptionable** is always negatively charged, because it describes something people take *exception* to, as in:

Residents whose behavior is exceptionable will be evicted from the hostel.

Exceptional is an objective and definitive word, identifying something as an exception to the general rule, as in *exceptional case*. The *exceptional student* is outside the normal range, and in British (and Australian) English this is applied only at the top end of the scale, to mean "brilliant." In American English it can be used at either end of the scale, and exceptional students may be brilliant or in need of remedial schooling.

With a negative prefix (*unexceptionable, unexceptional*), the two words come closer in meaning. Both can mean "unremarkable" when applied to such things as programs or reports. Those which are *unexceptionable* will not raise objections, but they are as bland as those which are *unexceptional* and contain nothing out of the ordinary. Both words seem to damn with faint praise.

excitor or exciter

See under -er/-or.

exclaim and exclamation

For the spelling of these words, see -**aim**.

exclamation points and exclamation marks

What Americans call the **exclamation point** is known by Canadians, Australians and the British as the **exclamation mark**. Either way, it has its most natural place in printed dialogue and reported speech, to show the dramatic or interactive force of a string of words. It occurs with greetings:

Good evening! Hi! Happy New Year!

with interjections:

Hear, hear! Keep it up!

with peremptory commands:

Don't do it! Get out of here!

and with expressions of surprise, ranging from enthusiastic and sympathetic to the deprecatory:

Absolutely superb! How lucky for you!
What a shambles!

As the examples show, **exclamation points/marks** are often used with fragments of sentences that work as exclamations. They do also occur with fully formed exclamatory sentences:

Don't tell me!
You walked all the way!
Isn't that amazing!

As in the last example, exclamations may be phrased like questions, yet because no answer is being sought, they take an **exclamation point/mark** rather than a question mark. Note also that the **exclamation point/mark** takes the place of a full stop at the end of a sentence.

1 The extended role of exclamation points/marks. Apart from marking utterances which are truly exclamations, **exclamation points/marks** are used by some writers to draw the reader's attention to a particular word, phrase or sentence which they find remarkable or ironic:

The divorce settlement divided the contents of the house equally, so now she can give dinner parties for three!

This use of **exclamation points/marks** has its place in interactive writing, for example in personal letters. But used this way in documentary writing, the effect is more dubious because of the diversity of readers' responses and attitudes. They may not share the writer's sense of irony, and so the reason for using the **exclamation point/mark** may be lost on them. Apart from the danger of inscrutability, **exclamation points/marks** lose their power to draw attention to anything if used too often. Even in informal writing they can be overdone, and those who write documentary prose must be very circumspect with them.

2 Exclamation points/marks and other punctuation.
a) An **exclamation point/mark** which belongs to a quoted statement goes inside the final quotation marks:

Her parting words were "It's on!"

b) The authorial **exclamation point/mark** which comments on a quoted statement goes outside the final quotation marks:

After all that drama he said: "It's not that important"!
After all that drama he asked: "Who'd like a drink?"!

c) An **exclamation point/mark** which belongs to a parenthesis goes inside the closing bracket (see **brackets** section 2).

d) The **exclamation point/mark** precedes points of ellipsis:

It's on!... See you there.

e) The use of double (*!!*) or triple (*!!!*) **exclamation points/marks** generally looks naive or hysterical.

exclamations

The label **exclamation** has always been attached to a very mixed bag of utterances. Anything printed with an *exclamation mark* qualifies, ranging from:

Hell! Damn it! Great!

to more fully fledged utterances such as:

The ideas you have!
What a way to go!
How sensitively he plays!

Grammarians focus first and foremost on **exclamations** which begin with an interrogative word like *how* or *what* and contain the standard clause elements in the standard word order. (See further under **clauses**.) These are the only **exclamations** with a regular form, called *exclamative* in references such as the *Comprehensive Grammar* (1985) – a term which matches up with *declarative, imperative* and *interrogative*. But grammarians also acknowledge that **exclamations** may be formed exactly like statements, commands or questions:

You tried it!   Don't do it!   Isn't she wonderful!
These examples and the ones above show that the full range of **exclamations** cannot be identified by a particular grammatical form. They can be embodied in all types of sentences (declarative/ exclamative/imperative/interrogative), or in fragments of sentences and phrases. (See further under **sentences**.) We know them by their function in discourse – their exclamatory force in dialogue, and the similar force invested in whatever bears *exclamation marks* in writing.

executive summary
See **reports** section 1.

executor or executer
See under -**er/-or**.

exhaustive or exhausting
Though both link up with the verb *exhaust,* these words embody different views of human endeavor. **Exhaustive** has more intellectual connections, and represents the judgement that the endeavor was thorough and complete. An *exhaustive inquiry* is one which works through (*exhausts*) all possibilities. **Exhausting** is more physical, and is concerned with the using up of material resources and human energy. So an *exhausting day* is one which leaves you devoid of energy.

In some contexts either word could occur, and the writer's choice depends on which perspective is sought. An *exhaustive search* for lost hikers implies a full ground and air search with all available resources; whereas *exhausting search* says that it was a grinding day for the rescue party. The first phrase is the detached comment of an administrator of emergency services, the second identifies with those who are actually doing the job.

existence or existance
The first spelling **existence** is unquestionably the standard spelling, grounded in Latin, and the only spelling recognized in dictionaries. But both British and American databases contain a sprinkling of **existance**, and it appears often enough for commentators to issue warnings about it, according to *Webster's English Usage* (1989). The word is one of an anomalous set. See further under -**ance/-ence.**

expatriot or expatriate
See under **emigrant**.

expediency or expedience
As with other -**ence/-ency** pairs, there's room for doubt as to which to use:

on grounds of expedience
on grounds of expediency
In both American and British English, **expediency** is the dominant form, judging by the small showing of **expedience** in CCAE as well as the BNC. In fact **expediency** seems to have dominated since C17, but **expedience** persists and can be used with impunity, since it has no divergent meanings of its own. See further under -**nce/-ncy.**

expiry or expiration
Either of these may be used in reference to the termination of a contract:
with the expiry of the present lease
with the expiration of the present lease
The chief difference between these phrases is one of tone. **Expiry** is a brisker word, suggesting tight planning and tidy systems – though this may have something to do with its brevity, and the fact that it's the word which confronts us every day, in the *expiry date* on credit cards, travel tickets and packaged foods. **Expiration** has the more detached qualities of a formal, latinate word. It seems to speak at a level above the gritty business of arranging contracts and observing their terms, and may indeed serve as something of a euphemism for **expiry** when the latter is an unwelcome fact. Apart from its legal use, **expiration** has some currency among biologists as a synonym for *exhalation*. Altogether, its usage is more academic and abstract than that of **expiry**.

explain and explanation
For the spelling of these words, see -**ain.**

expose or exposé
See under **accents**.

expresso or espresso
See **espresso**.

extendible or extendable
Extendible is given first preference in the *Oxford Dictionary* (1989) and *Webster's Third* (1986), and it's the older spelling, dating from C15. **Extendable** was first recorded in C17, and is the more natural spelling, simply combining the verb *extend* with the English suffix -*able*. In fact, **extendable** seems to be the more popular of the two spellings, in database evidence from both the US and the UK. But the word is one of the few with -*able/-ible* which can be spelled either way. See further under -**able/-ible.**

external, exterior or extraneous
Both **external** and **exterior** refer to what is physically on the outside, though with a slight difference of perspective. **External** is simply what can be seen from outside, as in an *external staircase;* whereas **exterior** suggests a judgement made from inside, as in *no exterior window*. **Extraneous** differs from both in implying that something neither belongs nor is intrinsic to the subject under discussion. *Extraneous suggestions* are not essential or relevant to the main plan, and an *extraneous substance* is foreign matter which has adhered or attached itself to a body, or become blended into a mixture.

extra-/extro-

The Latin prefix **extra-**, meaning literally "outside or beyond," is a formative element in various English words, usually polysyllabic:

extra-atmospheric	*extracurricular*
extramarital	*extramural*
extrasensory	*extraterritorial*

Such words are almost always scholarly ones.

The **extra** of common usage formations, such as *extra time* and *extra dry* is believed to be a clipped form of *extraordinary,* meaning "additional(ly) or special(ly)." (*Extraordinary* could be used as an adverb as well as adjective in earlier English.)

The form **extro-** appears instead of **extra-** in a few modern English words which were coined as opposites to those with *intro-.* Thus *extroduction* matched *introduction,* and *extroversion* matched *introversion.* Very few writers, either British or American. now substitute *extraversion* (or *extravert*), judging by their rarity in both BNC and CCAE – and despite the *Oxford Dictionary* (1989), which has almost as many citations for *extraversion/extravert* as for *extroversion/extrovert.*

◊ Compare **intra-/intro-**.

extraneous or external

See **external**.

extrovert or extravert, and extroversion or extraversion

See under **extra-/extro-**.

exult or exalt

See **exalt**.

-ey

This is both a regular ending and a variable one for English words. In nouns such as *donkey, galley, honey, jockey, journey, monkey, pulley* it's quite regular. The main point to note with such words is that they form their plurals by adding *s* – unlike most nouns ending in *y,* whose plurals are with *-ies* (see **-y>-i-**).

But **-ey** is also a variable spelling for *-y* in a number of English words. In some cases both the older forms with **-ey** (*curtsey, doiley, fogey*) and the younger ones with *-y* (*curtsy, doily, fogy*) have survived, with no differentiation of meaning. In other cases the two spellings have developed different meanings, at least in some varieties of English. See for example the entries for **bog(e)y, stor(e)y** and **whisk(e)y**. The two different spellings mean that there are also two plural forms for each.

Spellings with **-ey** are transitional for a number of colloquial adjectives, such as *chanc(e)y, mous(e)y, phon(e)y, pric(e)y:* see further under **-y/-ey**.

◊ For the choice between *Surrey* and *Surry,* see under that heading.

eyeing or eying

Writers the world over prefer **eyeing**. This was the verdict of most American and British respondents to the Langscape survey 1998–2001. It was also found in more than 95% of examples of the word in CCAE and the BNC. See under **-e** section 1i.

Eyetie or Itie

These are only two of the many spellings for this disparaging reference to an Italian. The archetype, recorded in Boston in 1840, was *Eyetalian,* while variants of it – **Eyetie,** *Eytie, Eytye, Eyety, Eyto* – have been recorded in both American and British English since the 1920s. *Webster's Third* (1986) notes that they may appear from time to time without an initial capital. Alternative spellings of **Itie** (*Iti, Ity*) are also known in British English according to the *Oxford Dictionary* (1989), though they are not registered in *Webster's*.

As spellings, these are less than effective, since the first set with *Eye-* present a distracting folk etymology, and the second set with just *I-* leave the pronunciation in doubt. But we need hardly lament if they miss their target, when their prime purpose is to express ethnic prejudice. The neutral *Italian,* with its straightforward geographical and historical associations, provides better and fairer identification. See further under **racist language**.

eyrie or aerie

Or *eyry* or *aery*? If you have occasion to refer to eagles' nests, the choice of spellings is rich. The original *Oxford Dictionary* (1884–1928) gave preference to **aerie**; but **eyrie** is now the dominant spelling in Britain, according to the second edition (1989), and BNC data confirms this. In American English **aerie** is still preferred, according to *Webster's Third* (1986), which correlates with its large majority in data from CCAE.

The spelling **aerie** connects the word with its French origins, in *aire* ("a threshing floor" or "high level stretch of ground"). However words of that kind were variously spelled *ayre* and *eyre* in early modern English, and use of the second variant was reinforced by the English dialect word *eyre(n)* ("egg(s)"), which suggested a folk etymology for the word, as a place for eggs.

◊ Compare **eerie or eery**.

f/ph

The use of **f** or **ph** is fixed in most English words, reflecting their origins. The **ph** is used in words borrowed from Greek, such as:

phallic   phenomenon   philosophy
phlegm   phosphorus   physics

It also occurs in modern words formed with Greek elements, such as *-phil/-philia, -phobia, phono-/-phony, -graph/-graphy* etc. Words from any other source (Latin, French, Italian or Anglo-Saxon) are spelled with **f**:

fashion   federal   fiasco   flight   foreign
frame   fuse

As the examples show, words with the **ph** spelling are usually scholarly terms, while those with **f** are common usage.

For just a handful of words, the spelling may be either **ph** or **f**. In the case of *sulfur/sulphur*, it depends on whether the use is scientific or not (see **sulfur**). For others such as *calif/caliph* and *serif/seriph*, the **f** is closer to the original word (in Arabic and Dutch respectively), and the **ph** lends them a spurious Greekness. Spellings with **f** prevail for *fantasy/phantasy* and *griffin/gryphon* because they came via Middle French, though they do have Greek antecedents.

F/ph variation also shows up when we refer to the *Filipino* people of the *Philippines*. The islands are named after Philip II of Spain, and the spelling remains in line with the Greek (and English) way of writing his name. The name for the people comes via Spanish, where words with **ph** have all been respelled with **f**. See for example: *física* ("physics"), *filósofo* ("philosopher"), *fotografía* ("photography"). The same replacement of **ph** has occurred in Italian, and in a number of Scandinavian and Slavic languages. But English usually preserves the **ph** in Greek loanwords, and the **ph** grapheme falls in with the set of others compounded with *h: ch, gh, sh, wh.*

-f › -v-

A small group of very old English nouns ending in -**f** make their plurals by replacing it with -**v**-, and adding -*es* for good measure. The group is shrinking, but its active members still include:

calf(calves)   elf(elves)   half(halves)
self(selves)   sheaf(sheaves)   shelf(shelves)
leaf(leaves)   loaf(loaves)
thief(thieves)   wolf(wolves)

Note also that a few words ending in -*fe* (*knife, life, wife*) also substitute -**v**- for -**f**, before adding the plural *s:*

knives   lives   wives

Other words ending in -**f** show change in progress – a trend to replace -*ves* plurals with the regular -*fs* – which is more advanced for some words than others. Database evidence from both the US and the UK shows that the regular plurals prevail now for *dwarf, roof,*

turf; whereas *hoof, scarf, wharf* still tend to have *hooves, scarves, wharves* as their plurals. *Hoofs, scarfs, wharfs* nevertheless make up a substantial minority in the US. The relativities can be seen in the following percentages, based on data from CCAE and the BNC:

	CCAE	BNC
dwarfs (dwarves)	96% (4%)	83% (17%)
hoofs (hooves)	34% (66%)	18% (82%)
roofs (rooves)	100%	99% (1%)
scarfs (scarves)	24% (76%)	3% (97%)
turfs (turves)	100%	55% (45%)
wharfs (wharves)	24% (76%)	17% (83%)

Handkerchief (mostly found in the UK) is usually pluralized as *handkerchiefs* rather than *handkerchieves*.

Many other nouns ending in *f, ff* or *ffe* have always formed their plurals with *s:*

carafes   chefs   chiefs   cliffs   cuffs   giraffes
griefs   gulfs   muffs   proofs   puffs   reefs
ruffs   skiffs   strifes   surfs   waifs

All are relatively recent, i.e. post-medieval additions to English. The plurals of *staff* and *tipstaff* are discussed under **staff, stave and staffer**. The interplay between -**f** and -*ve* in words such as *motif/motive, naif/naive, plaintiff/plaintive* is discussed under individual headings.

◊ For the choice between -**f** and -**v**- in inflected verbs and adjectives, see **-v-/-f.**

faceted

For the spelling of this word when it becomes a verb, see **-t.**

facility or faculty

From a common origin in Latin, these two have developed quite distinct areas of meaning in modern English. **Facility** refers to the ease with which we perform any acquired skill, from opening wine bottles to speaking Spanish. A **faculty** is one of the set of innate powers of perception attributed to people in general. By tradition the *five faculties* are sight, hearing, taste, touch and smell, though the *faculty of reason* adds a sixth. Younger people take all their **faculties** for granted; elderly people cannot, hence the phrase *in full possession of his/her faculties.*

Both **facility** and **faculty** are used of resources beyond those of the individual, but again their applications diverge. **Facilities** has come to mean "physical and organizational resources," whether for arranging conferences or making coffee in your motel room. The term **faculty** is used collectively in Britain, Canada and Australia to mean a department or set of academic disciplines, such as Arts, Science or Law. In American English, **faculty** refers to the whole teaching staff of a university, college or school, distinguishing it thus from administrative and general staff (who are called "staff"). **Faculty** can be construed as a singular or plural entity, witness:

> *Our faculty is one of the best in America.*
> *The faculty is willing to support the idea.*
> *Some faculty were cautious.*
> *Faculty have been getting late salary checks.*

As the examples show, the plural is probably helped by contexts that project *faculty members* as individuals. Overall the singular construction is commoner by far in CCAE, in keeping with the more general American preference for formal agreement (see **agreement** section 1). Yet some database examples with the singular read so awkwardly as to suggest the intervention of editors too committed to maintaining a grammatical tenet: *Over half the faculty is women, The faculty is there as experts to dispense wisdom.* In such cases the plural "are" (i.e. notional/proximity agreement, rather than formal agreement) would have been more congruent with the sense presented by the author. The use of plural agreement has increased in American English since the 1950s, according to *Webster's English Usage* (1989), and is widely accepted among academics. Such usage has long been established in British English.

facsimile and fax

In Latin **fac simile** is a command to "make an exact copy," but its use in English reflects changing technology. In C17 English *fac-simile* was used as a noun for a handwritten copy of a document, especially for legal purposes. Printed **facsimiles** of early manuscripts were first produced in C19, as a resource for scholarship, like the *facsimile edition of Pushkin's notebooks.* **Facsimiles** are of course produced in other mediums in the name of art and architecture, as well as politics, witness the *giant facsimile of a $10,000 contribution check,* used at party rallies to solicit support in an American election. But applications of **facsimile** to something other than words make up only a small proportion of current usage, a minor counterpoint to its everyday use for an electronically produced copy of a document. The technology of the office *facsimile machine* in fact goes back to the less reliable *facsimile telegraphy* and *facsimile radio* of late C19.

In its current applications, **facsimile** is normally replaced by the abbreviation **fax**, especially in combinations like *fax machine* and *send a fax,* but also when it appears as an independent noun and verb: *thank you for your fax; fax me the details.* The presentation of *fax numbers* alongside phone numbers has no doubt helped to spread the word. Its regular use in business communications and in a variety of other contexts means it can scarcely be considered informal, in either British or American English. Rather it has made **facsimile** the formal word. Among data from both BNC and CCAE **fax** outnumbers **facsimile** by more than 7:1. This includes instances of **fax** used as a verb (around 10% of the total), which have helped to establish it.

◊ Compare **memorandum and memo.**

factious, factitious or fractious

None of these is common enough to make its meaning well known. Both **factious** and **fractious** imply uncooperative behavior, and both once meant "tending to split up into petty divisions" (**factious** because it derives from *faction,* and **fractious** from *fraction*).

Nowadays only **factious** carries that meaning, while **fractious** refers to the character of an individual who may be anything from unruly and violent to irritable, but at any rate difficult for others to handle:

> *He was a fractious citizen at council meetings.*
> *The baby was getting tired and fractious with waiting.*

Factitious means "contrived or artificial." It may be applied to human behavior, as in *factitious charm;* or to things without the value they might appear to have, as in *factitious shares.* Distinguish **factitious** from the similar and much more common word **fictitious**: see under **fictional.**

factitive verb

In older grammars of English, this term was used for verbs whose objects could take their own complement, as in:

> *They considered him the least likely candidate.*
> *It drives me mad.*

The constructions created by **factitive verbs** conform to the SVOC pattern (see **predicate** section 3). Their complements may express either a current attribute, as in the first example, or a result, as in the second. For contemporary grammarians they are the less common of the two kinds of *complex transitivity.* See further under **transitive and intransitive** section 1.

factotum

From imperative Latin ("do everything"), this becomes the English word for a "jack of all trades." It was earlier written as two words, or with a hyphen. Its plural is **factotums**, because it's an English compound. See **plurals** and **-um.**

faculty or facility

See **facility.**

faecal or fecal, faeces or feces

The choice in each pair is usually settled by your commitment to British or American spelling norms. See **ae.**

faggot, fagot and fag

In North America **faggot** (or alternatively **fagot**) can be used harmlessly in reference to material objects: a bundle of sticks, or iron rods, or an embroidery pattern. The British share these uses of **faggot**, and they also apply it to a type of meatball made of pork liver. In Britain, **fag** also has harmless uses in referring to a cigarette and a tiresome task, hence the phrases *the fag end (of the day)* and *fagged out* ("tired out"). Being colloquial, they may raise questions of stylistic suitability, but that is all.

When applied to persons, **faggot** and **fag** have always been derogatory and are now a liability. The first has been used for centuries as an unflattering reference to a woman, as in *silly old faggot* – not a model of *inclusive language* (see further under that heading). And the time-honored practice of British boarding schools of making every new boy a **fag** (or slave) to one more senior has had fateful consequences for some:

> *At Eton he had been fag to a charmless older boy who had wasted no time in introducing him to homosexuality.*

That example from the BNC lends force to the largest current problem with these words, given their use in

C20 American English to refer to a male homosexual, as in *fag-bashing* and *Manhattan faggot*. An American politician can pledge such strong curbs on financial institutions as to *make Attila the Hun look like a faggot*. As those examples suggest, the words **faggot** and **fag** carry an emotional charge, which can turn to victimization. The BNC confirms that the homosexual sense of both **fag** and **faggot** is now known in Britain: *people called me a fag for being an actor; I doublebacked through the faggot district*. This usage clearly tangles with existing British uses of these words, apart from adding to the unlovely inventory of sexist language (see further under **sexism in language**). Either way the words pose problems for the writer.

Fahrenheit

Despite official moves to "go metric," the **Fahrenheit** scale (degrees F) of temperature continues to be used in the US. In Canada and the UK, it's being progressively replaced by the centigrade or Celsius scale, as has already happened in Australia and New Zealand. **Fahrenheit** temperatures are calibrated in relation to the lowest temperature that Gabriel Fahrenheit (1686–1736) could achieve by mixing ice, water and certain salts: 0°F. This sets the freezing point of pure water at 32°F, and its boiling point at 212°F. The so-called "comfort zone" for airconditioning is around 70–75°F.

To convert temperatures from **Fahrenheit** to Celsius, simply implement the formula below:

$$(°F - 32) \times \frac{5}{9} = °C$$

(See further under **Celsius**, and **metrication**.)

Whether in *degrees Fahrenheit* or Celsius, we all continue to measure temperatures with the mercury thermometer invented centuries ago by Fahrenheit. It remains more reliable for many purposes than alcohol-based thermometers – except in the microwave oven.

faint or feint

As verbs, these are very different: **faint** is to lose consciousness, while **feint** is to pretend to punch or thrust forward, as a boxer does to draw his opponent's fire at the start of a bout.

Faint is the only spelling possible for the common adjective meaning "weak." Yet either **faint** or **feint** may be used in the technical sense of "lightly printed," used of the least conspicuous grade of lines on ruled paper. Printers prefer the spelling **feint**.

fair or fairly

Both of these have a role as adverbs meaning "honestly" or "without resorting to underhand means," though **fair** is increasingly restricted to a few fixed collocations, such as *play fair* and *fight fair*. Others such as *bid fair, promise fair, speak fair, write fair* (where **fair** means "well") are becoming distinctly old-fashioned. Where it survives in ordinary conversation, **fair** still has a role as an intensifier of other words, as in:

> *It hit me fair and square on the nose.*
> *It fair gets me down.*

(See further under **intensifiers**.)

In more formal discourse the adverb is **fairly**, and it still means "honestly" or "justly." See for example: *campaigned fairly, umpired fairly, divided it fairly*. Yet

by far the commonest use of **fairly**, by more than 10:1 according to the BNC, is as a modifier of other verbs, adverbs or especially adjectives, as in:

> ... *it's fairly knocked about*
> ... *she covered the ground fairly easily*
> ... *a fairly common occurrence*

Most of the time **fairly** serves as a downtoner (see further under **hedge words**). This is standard usage, found in many kinds of writing. More colloquial is its occasional use as an intensifier, as in *It fairly hissed through the broken window*.

fait accompli

This French phrase means "accomplished fact." It is used of preemptive acts which bypass discussion and consultation.

faithfully

Yours faithfully is no longer required as the formal closure to a letter, or thought desirable in many kinds of correspondence. See further under **letter writing**, and **Yours faithfully**.

falafel or felafel

This Lebanese food with various spellings comes from Arabic, where the vowels were not standardized but rendered by ear and/or according to different dialects. The *Oxford Dictionary* (1989) prioritizes **felafel** among the various contenders, and it's the only spelling recorded in the BNC. Meanwhile *Webster's Third* (1986) gave preference to **falafel**, and it outnumbers **felafel** by more than 5:1 in CCAE. **Falafel** is also the first choice for Canadians and Australians, according to *Canadian Oxford* (1998) and the *Macquarie Dictionary* (1997). The Australian writer John Birmingham nevertheless used **felafel** in the title of his humorous novel *He Died with a Felafel in his Hand* (1994), later made into a movie.

fallacies

These are flawed arguments. Speakers and writers get away with them more often than they should, probably because they come in many guises. Some types of **fallacy** have traditional Latin names, others have English ones. The labels do help to distinguish them, so for those who would like to be able to detect **fallacies** in their own argument, or anyone else's, here is an inventory of the major types.

1 **Fallacies in the use of words and their representation of reality**
   a) false analogy (see under **analogy**)
   b) reification: when an abstract word is used as if it referred to a concrete entity. It happens when a theory or principle is expressed as if it were a fact or element of the real world, as when a sociologist says "society forces us to ... "
   c) faulty generalization: when a sweeping generalization is drawn from a small and not necessarily representative set of examples: "The trains are always ten minutes late."
   d) faulty classification: when the terms offered to cover a range of possibilities are insufficient to cover it. Tick-the-box questionnaires often oblige us to use very rough classifications – to show whether we do something *always/often/ sometimes/never*, but there's nowhere to register the fact that we do it rarely but regularly. In its crudest form, the faulty classification may be a

false dichotomy and offer us only two alternatives: *true/false, yes/no, good/bad*. Other familiar forms of false dichotomy are the "black or white argument," and the idea that "whoever is not with us is against us."

2 Logical fallacies

a) faulty deduction: when the argument rests on affirming the consequent, or denying the antecedent. (See under **deduction** for their proper logical counterparts.)

b) using the undistributed middle. This is a flawed syllogism, where the middle term is not made universal through the use of *all*. If it only relates to some of the population in the major premise, no proper conclusion can be drawn. (See further under **deduction**.)

c) circular argument, sometimes called the *vicious circle*, is one which claims as its conclusion the very assumption on which it began. It happens in some essays and theses, when writers divide their material (say newspaper articles) into four categories, discuss each one in turn, and then declare "we may conclude that there are four major types of news report." Similarly flawed arguments are those which beg the question, also known by the Latin phrase *petitio principii*. (See further under **beg the question**.)

d) analytic–synthetic confusion, sometimes known as the "no true Scotsman" **fallacy**. Here an assertion is made which can be tested by empirical evidence, as with "This publication can be obtained at all good bookshops." If the statement is challenged by someone who was unable to get the book at what most people think of as a good bookshop, the defender shifts ground to the terms of the assertion itself, and claims that the bookshop visited could not be a good one. So what appears to be a synthetic statement is defended as an analytic one. (See further under **induction**.)

e) *non sequitur* arguments suffer from a logical gap between the premise and the conclusion. (See under **non sequitur**.)

f) *post hoc propter hoc* arguments make the mistake of assuming that what comes after is a result or effect of whatever went before. (See under **post hoc**.)

f) irrelevant conclusion, also known by the Latin phrase *ignoratio elenchi* ("ignoring of [the required] disproof"). Here the person arguing devotes great effort to proving or disproving something which is beside the point at issue.

3 Diversionary arguments i.e. those which rely on diverting attention from the issues or sidestepping them:

a) forestalling disagreement, as when an argument is led by the statement: "No intelligent person would think that X is Y," or "The only proper response is Y"

b) *argumentum ad hominem*. This is an argument which makes either a personal attack, or a special appeal to the other party in the debate. (See further under **ad hominem**.)

c) damning the origin: the technique of quashing an argument by discrediting its source or authority, and highlighting anything about them that can be made out to be reprehensible or ridiculous. It dodges the argument itself.

d) straw man argument. This works by attributing an exaggerated or extreme position to the other party, and attacking it as a way of undermining their credibility. It is often used in political debate.
◊ For further discussion of types of argument, see **argument**.

false analogy

See under **analogy**.

false friends

This translates the French term *faux amis*, meaning words which are common to two languages but with different meanings in each. To an English-speaker it's a surprise to find that in French the verb *assister*, when used with *examen* ("exam"), means to "sit for the exam" not to act as a supervisor for it. Many of the **false friends** among European languages involve words originating in Latin, which each language uses in its own way. But **false friends** are also to be found among words borrowed from European into Asian languages, where they can take on new meanings, as when *siribu* ("silver") becomes the Japanese word for "grey power."

Among the varieties of English used around the world, **false friends** also show up. In American English the expression *table a document* means to close discussion of its contents, whereas in British English it means the opposite: to present it so as to initiate discussion.

false plurals

The assumption that words ending with *s* in English are plural is too familiar to need explaining. No surprise then if it has sometimes been misapplied to loanwords with a final *s* or *z*, and a special singular form been created for use in English. The fruit which we know as the *currant* got its name this way (see **currant**), as did the pea, the cherry and sherry. *Pea* was derived or backformed from *pease*, *cherry* from the medieval form of *cerise*, and *sherry* was *sherris*, an anglicized form of the Spanish name *Xerez*, the town where the liquor was made (now Jerez). See further under **backformation**.

falsehood, falseness or falsity

The word **falsehood** differs from the other two in being applied to particular untruths or untrue statements. It often serves as a formal synonym for a lie. **Falseness** and **falsity** are used of general deceptiveness or lack of genuineness in someone's behavior: the *falseness of their excuses* or the *falsity of their position*. There is little to choose between **falseness** and **falsity**, except that the first is clearly the more common of the two, to judge by databases of current English.

falsetto

For the plural of this, see under **-o**, and **Italian plurals**.

farther or further, farthest or furthest

See **further**.

fatal or fateful

The emphasis in **fatal** is on death (whether actual or figurative), whereas in **fateful** it is on destiny. So **fatal** puts an end to something (a *fatal blow* to their plans) or to someone (a *fatal accident*). **Fateful** is more prospective, anticipating an inevitable future outcome for someone, and at the same time emphasizing the perspective which hindsight gives on it:

> On that *fateful* morning my alarm clock went on strike, and I missed the plane which was to take me to Tokyo to sign the contract.

Fatal is the older word, borrowed from Latin in C15. It could be associated with either death or destiny until the English formation **fateful** made its appearance in C18. Both meanings are blended in the ominous "fatal shore," a convict's reference to Australia in the *Ballad of Van Diemen's Land,* recorded around 1825. Overall **fatal** remains much more common.

father-in-law

See under **in-laws**.

fauna

See under **flora**.

faute de mieux

This apologetic phrase borrowed from French means "for lack of [something] better." It is said in rueful recognition that whatever has been done left much to be desired, lest anyone should think your judgement was defective. Things could be worse however, and once again a borrowed French phrase can say it all: *pis aller*. Literally (and in reverse order) it means "to go worst," but it identifies the last resort – what one must be prepared for in the worst of all possible worlds. If nothing can be done and you can only shrug your shoulders, the verbal equivalent is *tant pis* ("too bad").

faux amis

See **false friends**.

faux pas

Translated literally, this French phrase means "false step," though it's always used figuratively of a breach of etiquette, or of a comment or move which disturbs the smoothness of proceedings. In the plural it remains unchanged:

> In the club his *faux pas* were notorious.

The comparable English idiom is "putting one's foot in it." Its colloquial overtones make it more suitable for informal contexts, while **faux pas** serves for formal ones.

favor or favour

See under **-or/-our**.

fax or facsimile

See under **facsimile**.

fay or fey

Both these smack of older notions of the supernatural. **Fay** is an old-fashioned word for "fairy," and **fey** an adjective which originated as a synonym of "doomed." **Fey** connoted a weird state of excitement and heightened awareness in someone whose death was imminent; and so it has come to mean "under a spell," "lightheaded," and "given to elfish whimsy or eccentricity." In this way **fey** begins to overlap with the adjectival use of **fay**, particularly when used to describe certain kinds of imaginative writing. Shakespeare's *A Midsummer Night's Dream* could thus be regarded as either a *fay tale* or a *fey tale*. And what of Gilbert and Sullivan's *Iolanthe?* Its unlikely fairies suggest that it's more a *fey tale* – but the choice is ultimately up to the critic.

Note that the word **fey** is apt to be misinterpreted as connoting "gay" in phrases such as *a slightly fey young man* – even though the speaker/writer is most probably referring to his mental rather than sexual orientation.

faze or phase

See **phase**.

fecal or faecal, feces or faeces

See under **ae**.

federal or Federal

The question for writers and editors is whether to capitalize this word when referring to national governments and institutions. American style, according to the *Chicago Manual* (2003), is to use **federal** in generic combinations such as *federal government/agency/court/powers*, in keeping with its generally thrifty use of capital letters (see **capital letters** sections 1d and 3). The capitalized **Federal** is of course required in official titles such as the *US Federal Reserve*. Otherwise **federal** prevails, as in the *federal Endangered Species Act* or *federal Bureau of Reclamation,* where the lower case form helps to show that the phrase is not the official name.

Elsewhere the situation is similar. Canadians refer to the *Federal Court of Canada* as such, but write *federal government department names* when they are paraphrases (*Editing Canadian English*, 2000). The Australian government *Style Manual* (2002) has it that the word needs a capital letter in official nomenclature, e.g. *Federal Constitution, Federal Parliament*. Lower case appears in all nonofficial designations and references, such as *the federal department of health, federal–state relations, the federal executive of the Labor party*.

Applications of the word elsewhere in the world have to be decided on their merits. Though *Federal Republic* was the established English translation for the former West Germany, there's no capital letter when alluding to the German *federal chancellor* or to *federal elections* there. Agencies of central government in South America are likewise referred to in lower case – *federal child welfare agency, federal police headquarters* – where the phrase only approximates local nomenclature.

American historical writers sometimes use **Federal** as an alternative to *Federalist* when referring to the northern/Union side in the American Civil War. Both words contrast with the use of *Confederacy* for the southern opposition: see under **confederation**.

Federation or federation

This word is often capitalized when it appears as part of an official name, whether in the *Federation Cup, Police Federation, Engineering Employers Federation,* or less familiar bodies such as the *National Federation of Music Societies* or the one-time *Federation of American Modern Painters and Sculptors*. This doesn't prevent it being used with lower case in references to notional or nonconstituted bodies, such as *a federation of recreation industry unions* or *a Protestant federation across the world*.

For Australians the word **Federation** has particular national significance, and is associated with the year 1901 at which the six former colonies became the unified Commonwealth. The capital letter therefore correlates with its status as a historical event (see **capital letters** section 1f).

feint or faint
See **faint**.

felafel or falafel
See **falafel**.

feldspar or felspar
Both *Webster's Third* (1986) and the *Oxford Dictionary* (1989) recommend **feldspar**, and it's the spelling preferred everywhere by geologists and chemists. It reflects the Swedish origins of the word, coined by D. Tilas in 1740 out of *feldt* ("field") and *spar* ("spat(h))," for a type of gypsum he identified in Finland. **Felspar** represents a mistaken etymology by which the first element was understood as the German *Fels* ("rock"). Though "corrupt," it was at one time the commoner spelling according to the *Oxford*. But true etymology has evidently won out, and **feldspar** is now the dominant spelling in the US as well as the UK, in database evidence from CCAE and the BNC.

fellowship
On whether to double the *p* when this word becomes a verb, see **-p/-pp-**.

female, feminine, feminist or feminazi
These words become controversial in what they express – or seem to express – about a woman's identity.

Female is used as adjective or noun to identify natural gender, as in *a female acrobat* and *the fieldworker was a female*. It contrasts with *male*, in referring to human, animal and plant species, though the two words look alike only because of C14 folk etymology, which respelled the French antecedent *femelle* with *-male* as the second syllable. The use of **female** as a noun became contentious in later C19, because it was thought to degrade women to the level of animals. Meanwhile its use in the jargon of metal trades, where the **female** part (i.e. a socket or bolt) is the one into which another is inserted or screwed, seems not to have occasioned any comment. The BNC provides evidence of now widespread use of **female** as a noun in reference to women, in many analytical contexts where the population is *divided equally* [or otherwise] *between males and females*. The noun **female** is standard in policespeak, as in *accused of killing a white female*. There and elsewhere it avoids reference to and prejudgement about women's age, giving it positive value where nondiscriminatory language is sought.

Feminine has long connoted the social and behavioral attributes of women that were deemed archetypal of their sex, including delicacy, prettiness, refinement of taste and feeling, as well as weakness. The genteel virtues of the word recommend it to those who would emphasize "la différence" and find it

courteous and respectful of women. But those who know or see disadvantage in gender difference are less positive about the word and its connotations. The other familiar use of **feminine** – its application to grammatical gender – is of course neutral and strictly sexless (see **gender** section 1).

Feminist seems very much a contemporary word, though first recorded as adjective and noun in the 1890s. It was and is applied to whoever or whatever advocates equal rights and opportunities for women. In recent usage it connotes also the *female-oriented* critique of society, history or literature, as in the *feminist literary canon*. **Feminist** attitudes are diametrically opposed to those of *male chauvinists*. (See further under **chauvinism**.) Some women (and men) would regard the words **feminist** and **feminine** as mutually exclusive, but the assumption is not shared by all. None are likely to identify with the **feminazi**, the totally negative word used occasionally by those wishing to discredit the **feminist** position, whether reasonable or not.

feminine endings
In English grammar, **feminine endings** are those suffixes that mark a word as female, including *-e, -ess, -ette, -trix*, and combining forms such as *-person, -woman*, discussed as individual entries in this book. All such elements draw attention to *natural gender* or sex (see **gender** section 2), and are therefore increasingly avoided by those aiming for nonsexist language.

In English prosody, **feminine endings** or *feminine rhymes* consist of the two last syllables of a line, with a final unstressed vowel and the stressed one before it, as in the opening couplet of Chaucer's *Canterbury Tales* (c. 1380):
> *Whan that April, with his shoures sote*
> *The droght of March hath perced to the rote . . .*
They contrast with the much more familiar *masculine endings* of Chaucer's next couplet, where the last stressed syllable alone makes the rhyme:
> *And bathed every vein in swich licour*
> *Of which vertu engendred is the flour*
Masculine endings now dominate the rhyming patterns of English poetry.

feminine gender
Grammatical uses of this term are discussed under **gender** section 1.

ferment or foment
Expressions like *fomenting trouble* are the most usual collocation for **foment** meaning "foster," "instigate." It always takes as object a word referring to civil disturbance, such as *discord, revolution, riots, strikes, violence, unrest*. This is nowadays almost the only remaining use for a verb which once had a place in medical practice (there **foment** meant "warm" or "apply a warm poultice [or other substance] to." Shrinking usage of **foment**, coupled with the fact that in standard southern British pronunciation it sounds much like **ferment**, help to explain how the two can be interchanged, as in
> *. . . politicians and warlords who are fermenting this chaos*
> *. . . the sole intention of fermenting a campaign aimed at causing damage*

Examples like these from the BNC show the figurative use of **ferment**, where the latent imagery of brewing works as well as that of putting heat into something. British and American dictionaries all acknowledge this use of **ferment**, alongside its main application to the biological process of *fermentation*. The figurative use is probably helped by the existence of the noun *ferment* and the phrase *in a ferment* meaning "in a state of agitation." There is no comparable noun for **foment**. All this helps to explain why **ferment** is putting pressure on **foment** in expressions like *fermenting/fomenting trouble*, and likely to bubble up on top.

ferret

On how to spell this word when it becomes a verb, see under -t.

fervent or fervid

Both these adjectives derive from the Latin root *ferv-* meaning "glow(ing) hot," and both have developed figuratively, so that they're nowadays applied to intense relationships and attitudes. **Fervent** is the commoner of the two, used of strong commitments to ideals and causes as in *fervent prayer*, and to people as in *fervent admirer*. Though it connotes intensity, **fervent** does not bear the faintly pejorative aftertaste of **fervid**. In *fervid imagination* or *fervid preaching* there's a suggestion that things are overheated and excessive.

fervor or fervour

See under -or/-our.

-fest and fest

This German-derived combining form, probably best known from the *Oktoberfest*, couples with English words or names (*songfest, shooting-fest, Turnerfest*) to provide instant identity for a public event. The earliest American uses, around 1900, make it the snappy title for a planned conference (*talkfest*). But it's also used more informally and offhandedly, as in *gabfest, music biz fest*, and can be applied to more spontaneous concentrations of activity such as the *reefer smoking fest* (a marijuana party). British uses of -fest are less common than American ones, yet *filmfest* and the *footy fest* are firmly rooted in British English.

fetal or foetal

See under fetus.

fetid or foetid

Dictionaries all give preference to **fetid**, which matches the Latin adjective *fetidus*, the word's direct antecedent. In Latin it meant "stinking," as a derivative of the verb *fetere* ("stink"). However variant spellings (both **foetid** and *faetid*) appear in C18, in references to *foetid drugs*, among other things. This usage in prescientific medicine suggests a possible confusion with *fetus/foetus*. See further under fetus.

fetish

This word is used by behavioral scientists (both psychologists and anthropologists) for something apparently ordinary to which some people give extraordinary attention and reverence. Others might call it an obsession.

Elements of language can become "fetishized" in discussions of usage. Particular expressions may be subjected to intense attention, and revered or held up as models of correctness for the rest of the community to observe – such as not splitting infinitives or ending sentences with prepositions (see **split infinitive** and **particles**). The observation of such things becomes the canon of "correctness" for all, irrespective of time and place. **Fetishes** of usage put an arbitrary stamp of "correct" on one expression rather than another, often out of conservatism and sometimes ignorance. Though no longer the focus of English language education, language **fetishes** are still sometimes invoked to pick holes in other people's expression, often as a means of discrediting what they say. Writers and editors who care about communicating need to parry the language **fetish**, and decide when to defy it. This book with its descriptive coverage of usage issues is designed to arm them. See also **shibboleth**.

fetus or foetus, and fetal or foetal

No-one doubts that **fetus** is the standard spelling in American English, and it appears in 99% of all instances of the word in CCAE. But it may come as a surprise that **fetus** is foregrounded in the *New Oxford* (1998), at least as the "technical" spelling. Recent discussions in the British *Lancet* magazine have reinforced the use of **fetus** in British medical and biomedical contexts, and it's comfortably represented in 35% of the word's appearances in the BNC, drawn from 30 different sources. The Canadian preference for **fetus** is clear in the *Canadian Oxford* (1998), whereas Australians still work with **foetus**, according to the *Macquarie Dictionary* (1997).

In fact **foetus** has centuries of tradition behind it. The spelling seems to have originated through misunderstanding – that the word derived from the Latin verb *foetare* ("give birth") rather than the verb *fere* ("conceive"), of which it's the past participle. **Foetus** passed from medieval Latin into Middle English, and has maintained its place in British English, appearing in 65% of instances and almost 4 times as many BNC sources as does **fetus**. It is probably preferred by those who think of it as a simple case of British/American divergence over the use of the *oe* digraph (see further at **oe**). The same applies generally to the use of **foetal** or **fetal**, in *f(o)etal position* etc. In BNC data, **foetal** appears in almost twice the number of sources – though it makes up only a minority (24%) of all instances of the word.

With this duality of usage, writers outside the US (and UK medical circles) have some freedom of choice. They too might prefer **fetus/fetal**, either in terms of etymology or the general principle of reducing *oe* digraphs to *e* – or both. Clearly it isn't a simple British/American divide.

The plural of **f(o)etus** is **f(o)etuses**, as for most other loanwords from the Latin fourth declension. (See further under -us section 2.)

> **International English selection:** The spellings fetus and fetal are to be preferred, for the reasons given above.

few or a few, and several

All are indefinite pronouns and determiners used of a relatively small number, yet there are important differences. Compare:
> *They wrote few letters*

with
> *They wrote a few letters*

The first sentence implies that the number was lower than expected, whereas the second simply notes the small number without any evaluation. In fact it gives no very precise idea as to how many were written: it's simply a casual alternative for "some." The quantity implied by **a few** is always relative to the population referred to. *A few letters* in the mailbox might be half a dozen, whereas *a few spectators* at the match might amount to fifty. Still one should never put too fine a point on it, because the very reason for using **a few** is that it means a vaguely small number. Note that despite the presence of *a*, it always takes plural agreement, as in: *A few buds were beginning to show.*

Several is like **a few** in being non-exact, while differing in its limited numerical range. Dictionaries generally define it as "more than two (or three) but not many." Some (e.g. *Collins,* 1991) suggest that **several** means "more than **a few**" – suggesting a kind of scale between them. The *Longman Grammar* (1999) points rather to a stylistic contrast, based on the fact that **several** occurs twice as often as **a few** in academic texts, and much less in conversation. Despite its non-exactness, **several** seems to be free of the casual and colloquial overtones of **a few**.

fewer or less

These two present themselves as a stylistic choice in one relatively uncommon construction. Compare:
> *... farmers with less financial resources*
> *... farmers with fewer financial resources*

According to prescriptivists, the first construction is wrong because **fewer** must be used with *count nouns* (e.g. "resources"), and **less** only with collective or *mass nouns,* e.g. *farmers with less money.* (See further under **count and mass nouns**). But the prescriptive rule requires us to make a distinction on one side of the comparative paradigm where there is none on the other. We use *more* with both count and mass nouns: *farmers with more financial resources / farmers with more money.* In fact the pressure to use **fewer** with countables is relatively recent. It surfaces first as the stylistic preference of Baker (1770) for **fewer** as the pronoun in *no fewer than a hundred*, and has since then stiffened into a broader grammatical requirement for the determiner (shown in the examples above) – wherever prescriptivists prevail. Meanwhile the use of **less** as the determiner with count nouns goes back a thousand years, by the *Oxford Dictionary* (1989) record.

Apart from its role as determiner/pronoun, **less** is also commonly used as adverb. This is rarely brought into the discussion, but it explains why **less** is sometimes hyphenated with a following adjective in American texts, as in *less-promising results.* It ensures that **less** is read as an adverb qualifying "promising," rather than a determiner indicating a smaller number of "(promising) results." The second meaning can be reliably communicated using **fewer** (*fewer promising results*). But since neither **less** nor **fewer** is quantitively precise, the difference is rather unimportant. This tallies with the fact that speakers are less inclined than writers to use **fewer** as the determiner/pronoun with count nouns, by the evidence of databases. In BNC spoken data the ratio of **fewer** to **less** is half that of the written data; and in CCAE the uses of **less** with countables are typically in quoted speech: "*the less guns you have out there, the less gun-related injuries.*"

In the written medium, the practice of using **fewer** rather than **less** with countables is more visible – although the *Oxford Dictionary* notes the frequent use of **less** with countables in spite of it being "regarded as incorrect." *Webster's Third* (1986) gives "fewer" as one of the definitions of **less**; while the *Random House Dictionary* (1987) comments that **less** is increasingly found with count nouns in all varieties of English, and that **fewer** is becoming a mark of formal style. Data from the *Longman Grammar* (1999) corpus show that **fewer** is rare by comparison with **less** as a determiner, in academic discourse or any other kind.

Exceptions to the imposition of **fewer** are also now recognized, in constructions where **less** is a pronoun, and especially when followed by *than.*
> See for example:
> *Express lane: fifteen items or less.*
> *I live less than four hours drive from the wildfowl marsh.*
> *He smashed his racquet on the ground on no less than eight occasions.*
> *Lager accounted for less than 10 per cent of total beer sales.*

Usage commentators usually note that **less** occurs in expressions involving quantities of money, time, distance, weight etc., where the quantity mentioned may seem to become a kind of collective entity. The acceptance of **less** in this role is reflected in data from both BNC and CCAE, where constructions with *less than* outnumber those with *fewer than* by more than 7:1. Still the shibboleth against **less** shows itself in some odd uses of **fewer** in the BNC, which smack of arbitrary intervention:
> *Fewer than a fifth of the schools kept records ...*
> *An exchange rate of fewer than DM3 to the pound today ...*
> *Opera attracted fewer than 1 per cent (of the population).*

Less than would read more naturally in all of them, and would create no ambiguity.

The pressure to substitute **fewer** for **less** seems to have developed out of all proportion to the ambiguity it may create in noun phrases like *less promising results.* That aside, it was and is essentially a stylistic choice, between the more formal **fewer** and the more spontaneous **less**. **Fewer** draws attention to itself, whereas **less** shifts the focus on to its more significant neighbors.

fey or fay

See **fay**.

fez

This Turkish loanword for a type of hat, reminiscent of what was once national headgear for Turkish men, gives English one of the tiny set of words ending in a single *z*. The plural form is not indicated in the *Oxford Dictionary* (1989), suggesting that it endorses the regular spelling **fezes** found in one of its citations. It does however propose *fezzed* for the adjectival form.

Webster's Third (1986) gives priority to **fezzes** for the plural, while noting **fezes** as well. See further under **-z/-zz**.

fiasco

Literally this is Italian for "a bottle/flask," but in C19 theatrical idiom *far fiasco* meant "be a disaster," hence the meaning "complete failure" attached to **fiasco** as a loanword in English. The image underlying the idiom is uncertain, perhaps that of breaking a bottle, helped by the sound of the word itself (see **onomatopoeia**). But what should the plural be in English? The form **fiascos** is implicit in the *Oxford Dictionary*'s (1989) lack of comment, and it's the only plural used by British writers in the BNC. However *Webster's Third* (1986) gives **fiascoes** priority over **fiascos**, and this accords with its 2:1 ratio in American data from CCAE. It diverges from the usual American preference for the more regular inflection, and from the findings of the Langscape survey (1998–2001), where Americans overwhelmingly preferred **fiascos** – while a proportion of British respondents (24%) were more inclined to use **fiascoes**. Clearly there's room to choose, but no place for "fiasci." See further under **-o**.

fiber or fibre

See under **-re/-er**.

fibula

The plural of this is discussed under **-a** section 1.

fictional or fictitious

The presence of *fiction* in **fictional** reminds us that the creative imagination is at work, as when we speak of a *fictional mid-Victorian poet Randolph Henry Ash,* or of recreating the *fictional journey* of Phileas Fogg in *Around the World in Eighty Days*. **Fictional** creations like these stand in their own right and the fact that they never existed is not an issue or matter of concern.

 Fictitious highlights the nonfactuality of whatever it qualifies. The *fictitious Caribbean island* is no part of the known world, and there's no substance to *fictitious assets such as gold mines*. The spy who double-crosses supplies *a steady stream of fictitious information garnished with sufficient truth to give it credibility*. Yet, as in that example, the boundaries between reality and imagination are often fluid. A TV docudrama may create a *fictitious division* of the British constabulary, and a magazine can flourish on the strength of the *fictitious letters of Mr Denis Thatcher to a golfing friend*. Jane Austen's **fictional** Emma is also the kind of *fictitious Englishwoman who always refers to herself as "one,"* according to one BNC example.
◊ For the distinction between **fictitious** and **factitious**, see under **factious**.

fidget

For the spelling of this word when used as a verb, see under **-t**.

fiefdom or fief

See under **-dom**.

figures of speech

In everyday English the phrase **figure of speech** is used to discount a metaphor or hyperbole: "It's only a figure of speech," people say, when a newspaper editor speaks of "politicians brainwashing the public." The taste or appetite for **figures of speech** has declined, and their range is not as well known as when rhetoric loomed large in the educational curriculum. Yet they remain powerful communicative devices when used occasionally.

 Figures of speech include any unusual way of using words to refer to something, especially those which stimulate the imagination. They work by establishing a likeness between two unlike things – either explicitly, in a *simile:* "My love is like a red, red rose"; or implicitly, through *metaphors* which develop sustained imagery or analogies (see **metaphors**).

 Personification (of abstract concepts) and *anthropomorphism* (of animals) are special kinds of metaphor (see under **personification**). *Metonymy* and *synecdoche* differ from *metaphor* in two ways: they are not usually sustained, and the verbal substitute is closely related to the item it replaces (see further under **metonymy** and **synecdoche**).

 Any **figure of speech** may also gain its effect through exaggeration (*hyperbole*) or through understatement (*meiosis*). The latter term is often replaced by *litotes,* though *litotes* is more strictly a form of understatement in which you assert something by negative means, as in "He doesn't hate us." The intention is to impress by the moderation of the statement.

 Some **figures of speech** work through the arrangements and patterns of words themselves. *Parallelism* involves the repetition of a particular phrase or clause structure with different words slotted in, as in "The bigger they are, the harder they fall." The *chiasmus* exploits the same words or related ones in a symmetrically opposed arrangement (see under **chiasmus**). In an *oxymoron*, words with opposite meaning are juxtaposed in the same phrase (see **oxymoron**). The sound elements of words are exploited through **figures of speech** such as **alliteration**, **assonance** and **onomatopoeia** (see further under those headings).

 Like any kind of ornament, **figures of speech** work best when integrated with the meaning and purpose of the discourse. The overuse of any kind of *metaphor* can result in a ludicrous mix, and an overdose of *litotes* or *alliteration* quickly becomes irritating. In scattered headlines or advertising slogans they may be indulged, but in continuous prose they must be used sparingly for optimal effect.

filet or fillet

See **fillet**.

Filipino

See under **f/ph**.

fill in or fill out

In North American English people **fill out** application forms or personal file documents, whereas in British English they **fill** (them) **in**. Australians have traditionally used the British collocation, but the American one is increasingly familiar. Users of each expression tend to find their own the more rational one to describe what you do when faced with the blank spaces on a form.

fillet or filet

Both these go back to Old French *filet* meaning "thread," and **filet** is the only way to spell the

squarish kind of lace or net, according to dictionaries everywhere. But American dictionaries show that **filet** also varies with **fillet** in the US for referring to a thin strip of material – whether as a hairband, or an architectural fill-in between moldings or the flutes of a column, or other technical uses – and especially in reference to boneless fish or meat, as in *a tender filet of beef*. This last is no doubt influenced by modern French gastronomic terms such as *filet mignon*. In data from CCAE **filet** is used as often as **fillet** in English references to cuts of meat or fish: the *filet of fresh cod / flaky, white-fleshed snapper* or the less attractive *fish filet that's been sitting under the warming light since Memorial Day*. The British meanwhile use **fillet** for their everyday beef steak, or *fillet of fish*, and reserve **filet** for the *filet de boeuf* on the restaurant menu. Australians use **fillet** and **filet** in distinct ways like the British (*Macquarie Dictionary*, 1997), whereas Canadians have the American variation (*Canadian Oxford*, 1998).
◊ For the spelling of **fil(l)et** when it becomes a verb, see under **-t**.

fin de siècle

This French phrase, meaning "end of the century," featured in the title of a novel by F. de Jouvenot and H. Micard (1888). It passed very quickly from being an adjective with the meaning "modern" and "avant garde," to meaning "decadent." The first meaning was there in the Melbourne *Punch* of 1891, in *this fin de siècle ballet*. But by 1908 **fin de siècle** had become retrospective in meaning and associated with "fading glory." At the turn of C21, its use is mostly historical.

All dictionaries present the phrase with its grave accent, though the accentless form would never be mistaken. Hyphens are added to it (*fin-de-siècle*) in *Webster's Third* (1986), presumably because it's usually a compound adjective. Yet as a foreign phrase and often italicized, there's no need, according to the *Chicago Manual* (2003). See **hyphens** section 2c.

final or finale

Both of these serve as nouns referring to the last event in a series, though they are cultural worlds apart. **Final** is the term used in sporting competitions for the concluding match which decides the season's winners. The **finale** is the last movement of a musical composition, or the last item in a stage performance of some kind. Being a loanword from Italian it has three syllables, and the *e* is functional rather than decorative.

fingers and thumbs

Our ability to write – to put pen to paper – is a remarkable fruit of both evolution and our sociocultural history. Both the opposed thumb (which we share with the other primates), and the use of a highly developed written code (which is ours alone), come together as we write. But English is still at sixes and sevens over how to refer to the digits of the hand. Some of the time we speak of having *five fingers,* and talking of a *middle finger* presupposes this too. The traditional marriage service spoke of placing a ring on the *fourth finger.* And nowadays piano music always identifies the fingers to be used by numbers 1 to 5 (the "Continental" system) – reversing an earlier system (the "English" system) by which the thumb was shown with an x, and the fingers as 1 to 4. The etymology of the word *finger* is believed to be related to the number 5.

Yet those who refer to the *first finger* usually mean "the index finger" rather than the thumb; and the question as to which finger bears the wedding ring is usually sidestepped by calling it the *ring finger*. In older tradition it was called "the medicinal finger," because of a superstition that potions should be stirred with it to test for their noxiousness. (The practice linked up with the notion that a nerve ran direct from that finger to the heart – which also explains the choice of finger for the wedding ring.) Contemporary medics and nurses avoid all possible ambiguity by referring to each finger by individual names: *thumb, index finger, middle finger, ring finger, little finger*.

finished with

A curiosity of this idiom meaning "be done with" is the fact that with agent subjects (personal pronouns or names), it can be construed either with the auxiliary *be* or *have*. Either way it remains active in sense:
> When they have finished with you …
> She was finished with planning, with striving.

Both are current in British English, though the construction with *have* is more common than the one with *be,* by more than 2:1 in both spoken and written data from the BNC. This lends no support to the notion that the *be* construction is more common in speech. In their often contracted forms (*the two I've finished with; the ones you're finished with*) the ratio between the two auxiliaries remains much the same. But in American English, the *be* construction is much more frequent overall, lending support to the notion that there is some regional difference about it. The British preference for the *have* construction coincides with higher use of the perfect tenses overall. See further under **have**.

finite verbs

Every fully fledged clause has a **finite verb**. They are the forms of verbs which have a definite tense (either present or past) and mood (indicative or imperative). In the following sentences, all the verbs are finite:
> They give a good performance (present, indicative)
> She gave a good performance (past, indicative)
> Give a good performance (present, imperative)

Finite verbs can be either single words as in those sentences, or the first element of a compound verb phrase, as in the following:
> He was giving a good deal.
> He would have given a good deal.
> He ought to give a good deal.

In compound verbs, the tense and mood are carried by the auxiliary verb(s); and the various parts of the main verb *giving, given, (to) give* are all *nonfinite*. On their own, the nonfinite elements are insufficient to make clauses, and can only be the basis of a phrase:
> Given encouragement …
> Giving no thought for others …
> To give them a chance …

Note that the nonfinite *give* (often called the *infinitive*) is identical with several finite parts of the verb, as shown above in the imperative, and the present indicative with *they*. It would be the same for *I, we* and *you*. In those cases, the finiteness is only evident in the fact that there is a subject directly governing the verb, expressed either as a pronoun or a noun phrase, or else left implicit in the imperative mood.

For many verbs, the past tense (finite) and the past nonfinite form (participle) are identical:

> They supplied the goods quickly.
> They have supplied the goods quickly.

Once again, the finiteness or nonfiniteness can only be seen by referring to the accompanying words. The subject *they* makes *supplied* finite in the first sentence, and the auxiliary *have* makes it nonfinite in the second.

An alternative term for the traditional **finite verb** is *tensed verb*, used in the *Introduction to the Grammar of English* (1984). See further under **auxiliary verbs, infinitives, nonfinite clause, participles** and **phrases**.

fiord or fjord
See **fjord**.

first or firstly
An old and peculiar tradition of style has it that when enumerating items, you should use **first** (not **firstly**), followed by *secondly, thirdly, fourthly* etc. The origins of this are rather obscure. The odd sequence is enshrined in the *English Prayer Book*'s marriage service, which may have lent authority to it. This, coupled with the absence of **firstly** from Dr. Johnson's dictionary, might account for the C19 notion that there was something wrong with it. By 1847 De Quincey calls **firstly** "a ridiculous and most pedantic neologism." But it was no neologism according to the *Oxford Dictionary* (1989), being first recorded in C16 and from time to time after that. De Quincey's view was in fact countered by a contemporary who observed **firstly** being used by a number of authors, "for the sake of its more accordant sound with *secondly, thirdly*." Most usage commentators from Fowler (1926) on agree that **firstly** is perfectly logical as the preliminary to *secondly, thirdly*. Yet the issue refuses to die, at least in academic circles. An obvious and easy alternative is to use *first, second, third* etc.

first cousin
See under **cousins**.

first name, forename or given name
These are three of the several expressions by which we refer to someone's personal name, as opposed to their family name. Formerly it was the *Christian name* (or *baptismal name*), but the religious bias in those phrases is now recognized as something to avoid in multicultural societies. **First name** is the term most widely used in English-speaking countries, although it presupposes the dominant European pattern of naming, in which the given name comes before the family name (*surname*). It creates problems in interactions with those whose culture puts the *family name* first. This includes some European groups:

> Croatian Hungarian Polish Serbian

and many Asian groups including:

> Cambodian Chinese Japanese Khmer
> Korean Laotian Vietnamese

In Arabic cultures of the Middle East, northern Africa, Indonesia and Malaysia, in India, and in the Pacific (Tonga, Maori), the pattern is the same as for English.

The term **forename** is grounded in the same sequential assumptions as **first name**. It neatly complements the French-derived *surname* (literally "extra name," originally either an epithet or a family name). But this hardly outweighs the other consideration, and makes no difference to those for whom the etymology of *surname* is opaque. **Forename** also suffers from being little used in the UK (by BNC evidence) and not at all in the US (in CCAE).

Only the term **given name** avoids the various complications just mentioned. It is transparent and unambiguous in crosscultural use. Despite its extra syllable, it takes up no more space than **first name**, and is increasingly found on official forms of all kinds.
◊ For more about the writing of people's names and titles, see under **forms of address**.

> **International English selection:** Of all the possible terms, **given name** (and *family name*) are most transparent and freest of cultural presuppositions.

---

first person
See under **person**.

First World War
See under **World War**.

fitted or fit
The past tenses of the verb **fit** can be expressed with either **fit** or **fitted**. Overall **fitted** gets a good deal more use in the UK than in the US. The BNC shows the British preference for it, both as simple past tense and as past participle, in examples such as *a garment that fitted me* and *a job for which he was perfectly fitted*. In American English, constructions with **fit** (*garment that fit me / a job he was perfectly fit for*) are in the majority, in data from CCAE. Yet the American scene is somewhat divided, according to *Webster's English Usage* (1989), with evidence to suggest that **fit** is more frequent in the Mid-West. It has also gained ground on the East Coast, according to DARE (vol. 2, 1991), though **fitted** is still strongly associated with New England. Even so, this case makes an interesting counterpoint to the usual finding, that Americans stand firm with the regular *-ed* form. See further under *-ed*.

Fitz-
Surnames with this prefix (the Anglo-Norman form of *fils*, "son") are mostly written without a hyphen: *Fitzgerald, Fitzpatrick, Fitzroy, Fitzsimons*. However some families reserve the right to hyphenate their name, and in that case the following letter is usually capitalized: *Fitz-Gerald, Fitz-Simons* (see **hyphens** section 1c). In a handful of cases (judging by the metropolitan telephone directory) the same name has no hyphen, but still an internal capital letter – *FitzGerald, FitzSimons* – presumably on the analogy of names prefixed by *Mc*. Although the bearers of such names are used to a good deal of variation with their names, they are also highly sensitized to it, so it's as well to check the detail when writing to them.
◊ Compare **Mac or Mc**.

fix, fixed and fixing to
The verb *fix* has found more applications outside Britain than within. In British English its established uses are as a synonym for "fasten" (*fixed to the wall*), and an alternative to "arrange," "settle," as in *date to*

be fixed. The two come together in the idiom *fixed in concrete.*

Elsewhere, in American, Australian and New Zealand English, **fix** also serves as a synonym for "mend" (as in *get the car fixed*), and this usage is now being taken up in Britain, by the evidence of the BNC, where the broken ankle, a broken-down car, and a dysfunctional water supply are among the various items needing to be **fixed.** The compound verb **fix up** is also known in the same sense: *when we've fixed up your plumbing . . .*

Yet another role of **fix** to develop outside Britain is the sense of "prepare," as in *I'll fix you a drink.* This again is associated with American English, but also established in Canadian and Australian. Again the BNC has a sprinkling of it, suggesting that *fix you some tea / a coffee / something for dinner* is not alien to British speakers. In any case, it streamlines the familiar British construction **fix up with** to mean "arrange for," as in *I'll fix you up with a room / a fashion accessory / a job in the organization.*

In American English **fixing to** works like the quasimodal *going to,* speaking of future intentions, as in *He was fixing to get rid of the first one in the divorce courts.* In the US it's traditionally associated with southern speech, and therefore appears more often in the *Atlanta Journal* than the *Christian Science Monitor* or the *Los Angeles Times.* But its users are now to be found in urban as well as rural centres across the South Atlantic and Gulf states (Wolfram and Schilling-Estes, 1998). It also turns up in informal speech further north, and across the Canadian border, to judge by the entry in the *Canadian Oxford* (1998). It has yet to make its mark in British or Australian English.

All these constructions with **fix** are most at home in speech and informal writing. The diversity of applications for both **fix** and **fix(ed) up** means that they can be ambiguous:
> *You and the lady come with me, we'll get you fixed up . . .*
In conversation, the context always narrows down the range of interpretations, but writing has no such aids.

fjord or fiord
These are more and less recent forms of the C17 loanword from Norway. **Fiord,** the then Norwegian spelling, established itself in Britain, and was made the primary spelling in the *Oxford Dictionary* (1989). *Webster's Third* (1986) meanwhile prioritizes **fjord,** which began to be used in C19 English against a backdrop of revisions to Norwegian orthography (through which **fjord** became the standard spelling in Norway, as in Denmark and Sweden). Both **fjord** and **fiord** are current in the US, and about equally used in American data from CCAE. But contemporary British writers clearly prefer **fjord,** by a factor of 3:1 in the BNC. A search of internet documents worldwide (Google, 2003) found **fjord** outnumbering **fiord** by more than 12:1.

The shift from **fiord** to **fjord** can also be seen in the anglicized forms of Norwegian placenames such as *Oslo Fjord, Hardanger Fjord,* the spellings given in both the *Chambers / Cambridge World Gazetteer* (1988) and the *Merriam-Webster's Geographical Dictionary* (1997). New Zealand's *Fiordland* retains the earlier English spelling. See further under **geographical names.**

fl.
See **floruit.**

flack or flak
See **flak.**

flagrant or fragrant
Confusion between **flagrant** meaning "blatant" and **fragrant** meaning "sweet-smelling" goes back centuries. It is evident in medieval manuscripts, and some believe that it originated in popular Latin. The sounds "l" and "r" are easily substituted for each other (as happens in many Southeast Asian languages), and so we sometimes hear of "flagrant perfumes" (not ones that Christian Dior would be proud of) and "fragrant violation of the law" (? confounding the breath analyzer by gargling with eau de cologne).

flagrante delicto
See under **corpus delicti.**

flair or flare
Flair is a recent (C19) loanword from French, meaning "a special skill or aptitude." **Flare** is centuries older, and probably a Germanic word though its origins are obscure. It has developed numerous meanings from the earliest known sense "spread out," and is used to describe shapes: *flared trousers;* sounds: *the flare of trumpets;* movements: *the aircraft flared;* and especially flames: *the tall flare of the refinery.*

Flair was an alternative spelling for **flare** until C19, but since the arrival of the French loanword, each has kept its own regular spelling. Yet there are occasional confusions between them, as in: "He's a brilliant musician – a violinist with flare!" We may presume that he has "fire in the belly."

flak or flack
The spelling **flak** is distinctly un-English, and serves to remind us that it is a German acronym which gained currency during World War II. It originally stood for *Fliegerabwehrkanone* ("aircraft defence gun"), and then referred to anti-aircraft fire from such guns – shells that burst into a thousand jagged pieces. In contemporary civil defence, the *flak jacket* is designed to protect the wearer from hostile fire. **Flak** has also acquired the figurative meaning "damaging criticism," first recorded in 1968 according to the *Oxford Dictionary* (1989). The person who *takes the flak* is on the metaphorical front line, and the image lends itself to the more adversarial types of journalism. In the BNC **flak** is occasionally spelled **flack** (about 1 in 8 instances), a sign of ongoing assimilation. In American English the rate is closer to 1 in 6, in data from CCAE.

American use of the spelling **flack** for "damaging criticism" is intertwined with a quite different use of the word, as an informal term for a press agent or public relations officer. For example:
> *. . . sounded like a flack for the baseball owners*
> *. . . Reagan, once a paid flack for the American Medical Association*
Evidence from CCAE suggests that **flack** may be pejorative for those who "practice the craft of public relations"; and diplomatic relations could indeed

suffer when the spokesperson for the Soviet ambassador becomes the *embassy flack*. Yet with the terms *super-flack* and *chief White House flack*, it identifies an emerging profession – even if *work in the flack factory* is less than glamorous. In that example, we see **flack** extending its use to become a byword for publicity itself, and it also serves as a verb, in:

> *. . . hired a PR firm to flack the thing*
> *Celebrities too often flack so many products that consumers are confused.*

In all this there's other potential confusion when the **flack** (who puts out the publicity) is also the person who takes the **flack** (an alternative spelling for "damaging criticism"). The closeness of the two roles makes a neat pun in:

> *Let him who is without hype cast the first flack.*

But the two roles can be clearly separated if the job is explained as *directing flack and damage control,* or alternatively as being the *community and liaison officer, a kind of flak-catcher.* The spelling **flak** comes into its own here.

The origins of **flack** as a term for a publicity agent are uncertain. Its first recorded appearances were just prior to World War II, and the *Random House Dictionary* (1987) connects it with Gene Flack, a Hollywood publicity agent. But eponymous derivations like this can be difficult to prove. See under **eponyms**, for less contentious examples.

flamingos or flamingoes

Dictionaries recognize both plurals, but **flamingos** is strongly preferred in American English – by more than 10:1 in data from CCAE. In British English, **flamingos** and **flamingoes** are more evenly represented, with a ratio of 3:2 in the BNC. The 1998 Langscape survey found almost three-quarters of respondents preferred **flamingos**, reflecting the larger trend worldwide towards regular plurals for words ending in *-o*. See further under **-o**.

flammable or inflammable

Though these mean exactly the same – "liable to burst into flame" – the first is preferred and to be encouraged wherever public safety is an issue. Apart from being slightly shorter, **flammable** is never subject to the faint ambiguity which dogs **inflammable** – as to whether its *in-* is a negative or intensive prefix (see further under **in-/im-**). It is of course an intensive prefix, just as it is in the related word *inflame*. But with the risk of *in-* being read as a negative in **inflammable** (and failing to serve as a warning of fire), the spelling **flammable** is preferred by all those concerned with fire hazards. The US National Fire Protection Association adopted it in the 1920s, and this has boosted its use generally. In contemporary data from CCAE, **flammable** outnumbers **inflammable** by almost 20:1, and uses of the latter were mostly figurative, noting *inflammable tempers, people* and *remarks*. In other English-speaking countries, the move to replace **inflammable** on warning signs is relatively recent. It proves somewhat less frequent than **flammable** in BNC data, yet its meaning in the 50-odd examples is still almost always "liable to burst into flame." The examples do however come from printed documents, whereas those for **flammable** are more often from spoken sources. The word is presumably still getting around.

flare or flair

See **flair**.

flat adverbs

See **zero adverbs**.

flat or flatly

Both these serve as adverbs, but they combine with different kinds of verbs. **Flatly** usually modifies verbs of saying, as in *said flatly, stated flatly* and especially those with negative implications – *flatly denied/rejected/refused* which it makes more uncompromising. In other special combinations, it expresses monotony, as in a *flatly lit photo* or a *flatly delivered narrative*. **Flat** as adverb combines with verbs expressing:

* downward motion, in both physical and figurative senses: *fell flat, trodden flat, flat broke, go flat out for*
* horizontality, e.g. *lie flat, went flat, held flat*

The musical use in *sang flat* is comparable to the first set. All these uses of **flat** are perfectly idiomatic, but sometimes questioned. See further under **zero adverbs**.

flatulence or flatulency

Only the first is now current, by British and American database evidence. For other similar pairs see **-nce/-ncy**.

flaunt or flout

The overtones of defiance are strong in both of these verbs, though their objects are different. **Flout** means "mock or treat with contempt," especially when it involves defying rules, conventions or the law. **Flaunt** means "display so as to draw public attention to," particularly something over which there might have been some discreetness or sense of shame. But the two often seem to overlap, since *flaunting one's ill-gotten gains* may also mean *flouting the law;* and *flaunting oneself* implies the *flouting of social conventions* – hence the common confusion between them.

flautist or flutist

See **flutist**.

fledgling or fledgeling

Fledgling is the commoner spelling everywhere. In American data from CCAE it stands alone, and it outnumbers **fledgeling** by more than 10:1 in data from the BNC. *Webster's Third* (1986) gave priority to **fledgling**, while the *Oxford Dictionary* (1989) puts **fledgeling** first, presumably because it's the more regular spelling in terms of the rule for a final *e* when a suffix with a consonant is added (see further under **-e**). Yet the *Oxford*'s citations are all for **fledgling**, as Fowler (1926) noted. The *Canadian Oxford* (1998) only lists **fledgling**, whereas the Australian *Macquarie Dictionary* (1997) still registers **fledgeling** as an alternative.
◊ Compare **judgement**.

fleur de lis or fleur de lys

In heraldic French, this means "lily flower," though in horticulture it refers to certain kinds of iris. In its conventional three-headed form it has been emblematic of the French crown since C6, of Florence since C13, and of the Boy Scouts in C20. The *Oxford*

Dictionary (1989) finds **fleur de lis** the prevailing modern spelling, and it's in line with modern French, yet only **fleur de lys** appears in the BNC. *Webster's Third* (1986) also gives priority to **fleur de lis**, although **fleur de lys** has the majority in CCAE, by 10:3. Perhaps the more archaic spelling with *lys* has acquired an antique value, which lends itself to many of the contexts of its use.

flier or flyer
See **flyer**.

floatation or flotation
See **flotation**.

floating hyphens
See **hanging hyphen**.

floor and storey
Does a first floor room allow you to step out into the garden? It depends whether it's the American or British system for numbering the floors, both of which are used elsewhere in the English-speaking world. In American usage, the level at which you enter is normally called the *first floor.* In the British system, the entry level is the *ground floor,* and above it is the *first floor.* Fortunately, in both traditions the first level of the building is the *first storey* – no ambiguity there!
◊ See **storey or story** for the variable spelling of that word, and its plural.

flora and fauna
These two have been coupled together since 1745, when the botanist and naturalist Linnaeus published a *Flora and Fauna* of his native Sweden. In Roman mythology they were the names of divinities who led separate lives, *Flora* as the goddess of flowers, and *Faunus* as the god of agriculture and shepherds. In C20 English **flora** acquired a new realm in references to the micro-organisms that inhabit the internal canals and external organs of animals. In a sense this is a takeover, as it allows the term **flora** to subsume both fungi and bacteria (i.e. both plant and animal life).

Both words are used in modern English as collective words, referring to the whole gamut of plant (or animal) life in a particular location. In such references there's no need to seek a plural form, and writers may choose a singular or plural verb in agreement, depending on whether their discussion focuses on the collectivity of species, or on individual varieties:

> *The flora of our planet is under threat of extinction.*
> *The flora of our planet are under threat of extinction.*

(See further under **agreement** section 1, and **collective nouns**.)

When the **flora** (or **fauna**) of more than one region has to be mentioned in the same breath, a plural form is needed. Writers have the choice of either the regular English forms **floras/faunas** or Latin ones **florae/faunae**. See further under **-a** for the use of each.

floruit
Borrowed by historians from Latin, this word means literally "s/he flourished." When followed by a date or a span of time, it indicates a significant point or period in someone's life, and it provides a historical benchmark for someone whose exact dates of birth and death are not known. The date or time accompanying the **floruit** (abbreviated as *fl.*) may be drawn from circumstantial evidence, such as when the person was appointed to a particular position, or when s/he produced an outstanding literary or artistic work. For William of Ockham (or Occam) the year in which he was put on trial for heresy (1328) is the most precisely known date of his life; and since he managed to escape to Munich and lived in sanctuary for some years after, *fl. 1328* serves to put a date on his career.

flotation or floatation
The spelling **floatation** shows the word's hybrid origins in the English verb *float* and the latinate suffix *-ation*. It was the earlier spelling (dating from the start of C19), and is still occasionally seen, as in the manufacturer's notes for an inflatable product that *stores easy in raft or can be blown up to add extra floatation.* The fully latinized spelling **flotation** appeared later in C19, though never etymologically justifiable, as the *Oxford Dictionary* (1989) notes. In financial reporting it is nevertheless the standard spelling, ubiquitous in references to *stock market flotations* or *public flotation of shares.* These account for more than 95% of its citations in the BNC, though *flotation tanks* and aircraft emergency *flotation systems* apply the newer spelling to the original meaning.

In American English **flotation** is also very much more frequent than **floatation**, in the ratio of 12:1 in CCAE. It commonly appears in references to water safety equipment (*flotation devices/units/systems*), and in technological uses such as *mineral flotation processes.* Financial applications like those exemplified in the BNC data also boost its numbers.

The simple noun *float* serves in British and Australian English as an informal substitute for **floatation** in the financial sense of raising money for a company through an issue of shares. *Float* is also the term used by Australians, Canadians and the British for petty cash used to facilitate transactions at charity events etc. Neither of these uses of *float* is possible in the US, where *float* is bespoken as the term for the monetary value of checks (cheques) outstanding at a particular time.

flounder or founder
Hardly surprising that these get confused when you know that the first may indeed owe its existence to the second. **Founder** meaning "sink to the bottom (of the sea)" is commonly used of ships, or enterprises that come to grief. **Flounder** meaning "move clumsily" often seems to involve struggling close to the ground, as in the fisherman's story from the *Angler in Wales* (1834), in which "man and fish lay floundering together in the rapids" ... and it no doubt got away.

The origins of **founder** are in medieval French, whereas those of **flounder**, first recorded in 1592, are not at all certain. Some scholars have suggested that it is a blend of *flounce* and *founder*: others that it is simply an embellishment of **founder** with *fl,* a sound unit which seems to carry a subliminal meaning of "heavy movement" (see further under **phonesthemes**). In popular etymology however, the verb **flounder** may also owe something to a well-known fish (also *flounder*) that inhabits the sea bottom. The fish itself derives its name from Scandinavia, with cognates in Norwegian and Swedish.

The latter influence seems to be still at work in a memorial plaque set on the wall of a certain men's club:

> IN MEMORY OF FORMER MEMBERS OF THE SPORTS FISHING CLUB, WHOSE BOAT FLOUNDERED ON THE PT. CAMPBELL ROCKS, MAY 16TH 1935.

flout or flaunt
See **flaunt**.

flu
This clipped form of *influenza* (in Italian literally "influence") first appeared in C19 English, and has become fully nativized and accepted. In everyday American English, **flu** has totally replaced the full form, by the evidence of CCAE. In British data from the BNC, **flu** is likewise far more frequent than the full form. *Influenza* maintains its dignity in bureaucratic and medical contexts, but **flu** occurs across a much wider range of prose, in three times as many nonfiction sources (including journalism and other nonfiction intended for the general reader), as well as in fiction. Despite being an abbreviation, **flu** is now rarely punctuated with omission or quotation marks.

fluky or flukey
This colloquial adjective for "chancy" seems to have originated with the noun *fluke* in billiards in C19, and quickly spread to other sports such as cricket and sailing, where luck and skill combine to back the winner. The preferred spelling in both *Webster's Third* (1986) and the *Oxford Dictionary* (1989) is the regular **fluky** (see **-e**). In American English it's clearly in the majority, by 3:1 in CCAE; but in British data from the BNC the majority is just 3:2, and **flukey** is evidently giving it a run for its money.

fluorene or fluorine
The endings make for very different chemicals. **Fluorine** is a nonmetallic element which occurs as a greenish-yellow gas. When impure it is fluorescent. **Fluorene** is a white crystalline hydrocarbon, used in the manufacture of resins and dyes.

flush and hang
See under **indents**.

flutist or flautist
For nonmusical people everywhere, **flutist** is the more accessible term. It has the longer history, dating back to C16 English, and was challenged only in later C19 by the Italianate **flautist**. In North America this never displaced **flutist** as the standard term, and **flutist** still dominates in citations from CCAE, by about 25:1. In Canada, **flutist** is also the standard term, as the *Canadian Oxford* (1998) explains. Yet professional and amateur flute-players in Britain are called **flautists**, and **flautist** reigns supreme in BNC data. Australians likewise use **flautist**, according to the *Macquarie Dictionary* (1997).

flyer or flier
All major dictionaries make these spellings equal, but they are less equal in British than in American

English. The *Oxford Dictionary* (1989) puts **flyer** first, on the strength of "recent quotations," which are indeed spread through C20 and over many of the word's meanings. In BNC data, **flyer** outnumbers **flier** by more than 3:1. Their relative frequencies are more like 3:2 in American data from CCAE, and *Webster's Third* (1986) gives priority to **flier**.

In some applications of the word, **flier** may be preferred, even in the UK. This holds when the reference is to an aviator, especially a *World War II flier*. But the jet-setting passenger may be either a *frequent flyer* or *frequent flier*, depending on the airline; and the metaphorical *high flyer / high flier* can make it either way. The fastest player on the rugby field is the **flier**, but both spellings are used in reference to race horses, pole vaulters and those who fly kites. The use of **flier** to refer to an express train is steadily giving way to **flyer**, even in North America, and rapid transit companies operating taxis, buses and ferries make the most of **flyer** in their business names. The American idiom *take a flyer / flier on,* meaning "take a risk (especially financial)" is also increasingly seen with the *y* spelling:

> I might take a *flyer* at politics again.

Americans are still divided over whether **flyer** or **flier** should be the spelling for the leaflet distributed for political, social or commercial purposes, whereas there's no doubt in Britain that it should be **flyer**, as in *church flyer* or *flyer for the day trip*.

Overall then **flyer** seems to be consolidating and setting itself apart from *crier, drier* etc., which, as the *Oxford Dictionary* notes, are more regular in terms of the rule for turning final *-y* into *i* before a suffix (see **-y>-i-**). Yet the rule makes greater demands on the reader when the word's stem has only three letters; and **flyer** is easier than **flier** if the word has to be understood with little support from the context. For ad hoc and figurative uses, it will be more reliable.

FM
This abbreviation, meaning "frequency modulation," contrasts with **AM** "amplitude modulation" in representing the two kinds of radio transmission now available. Being capitalized abbreviations, they need no stops. See further under **abbreviations** section 2.

focus
This word raises questions of spelling, both as a noun and as a verb. As a noun its plural is usually the English **focuses** rather than the Latin *foci* (see further under **-us**).

When **focus** is a verb with suffixes attached, the preferred spellings in both *Webster's Third* (1986) and the *Oxford Dictionary* (1989) are *focused/focusing,* rather than *focussed/focussing,* in keeping with the broadest principles of not doubling when the final syllable is unstressed (see under **doubling of final consonant**). In the Langscape survey (1998–2001) the form with single *s* (*focused*) was endorsed by just on three-quarters of the respondents. In databases, the doubled forms persist only as minority variants, in the ratio of about 1:9 in BNC data, and about 1:1000 in CCAE.

◊ For ways of maintaining a clear focus in extended writing, see **information focus**.

foetal or fetal, and foetus or fetus
See under **fetus**.

foetid or fetid
See fetid.

fogy or fogey
While **fogy** is preferred in *Webster's Third* (1986) and the *Oxford Dictionary* (1989), database evidence suggests that contemporary writers prefer otherwise. Only **fogey** appears in BNC data, and it's the more frequent of the two spellings in American evidence from CCAE, where both do occur (the raw figures are 14:10). The word's obscure origins would help to explain the lack of conviction about its spelling. It seems to have originated as a nickname for an invalid soldier, and was prefaced by "old" from its first recorded appearances in late C18. Attempts to explain its etymology by reference to "foggy" seem a little far-fetched.

Both *Webster's* and the *Oxford* give the plural of **fog(e)y** as "*fogies* also *fogeys*," and their relative frequencies in the databases confirm that order. **Fogies** is the commoner of the two in both CCAE and the BNC – despite the preference for **fogey** in the singular. Dictionaries usually list the derivatives as *fogyish* and *fogyism,* though they too are subject to the variation between -*y* and -*ey*. See further under -**ey**.

folk or folks
These words diverge in both style and meaning, despite some overlaps.

Folk is the neutral term for an identifiable community of people, e.g. *Derbyshire folk, literary folk, menfolk, middle-class folk, rural folk,* and is usually modified by an adjective, as in these examples. The examples also show that it can be applied as a synonym for "people," and as a nonsexist substitute for "men." But it very often serves as a modifier of other nouns, as in *folk hero, folk memory, folk wisdom,* where it taps traditions in the community; and in *folk festival, folk melody, folk singer,* where it connects with popular cultures of the past.

Folks is sometimes disparaged as oldfashioned or provincial, but it has some contemporary uses. Its connotations are familiar and informal, as when referring to someone's relatives as *his folks, the folks at home,* and also in the unpretentious "just folks." In *old folks* it remains faintly indulgent. Its vocative use, as in *Hi folks* or *Sorry folks* – though long associated with American entertainers – now falls from the lips of British compères and tour guides. They too find it helps to engage with audiences of both genders, in situations where "Ladies and gentlemen" would be too formal.

folk etymology
Popular interpretation of a word's structure and meaning can alter its spelling in the course of time. Loanwords are particularly susceptible to **folk etymology**, as English speakers seek to regularize them in terms of words they are familiar with. So the word *amok* (borrowed from Malay) is reinterpreted and respelled by some as *amuck,* as if it was a composite of the medieval English prefix *a-* (as in *abroad, awry*) and the word *muck*. Like most **folk etymologies,** it only fits where it touches and makes little sense of the word. Obsolete elements of English are also subject to **folk etymology**. Thus *bridegroom* suggests a spurious connection with horses, which

comes from using *groom* instead of the unfamiliar *gome* as its second element. (*Gome* was an alternative word for "man" in early English.) In modern English *colleague* (based on French *collègue*) has acquired an *a*, presumably because of the idea that it's someone with whom you are *in league*. **Folk etymologies** are by definition not true etymologies. See further under **etymology**.

foment or ferment
See **ferment**.

font or fount
Two different words lurk behind these spellings:
1 **fo(u)nt** meaning "fountain, source of water/inspiration"
2 **fo(u)nt** meaning "repository or repertoire of typefaces."

The first and older word, derived from the Latin *fons* ("fountain, spring"), puts the different spellings to different applications. **Font** is the spelling used for the ceremonial *baptismal font* – often the most ancient piece of furniture in English churches. The spelling **fount** survives in poetic diction as a synonym for *fountain,* and in more general use as a figurative word for "source," as in *fount of wisdom.*

The second word, used for a set of printing type, is modeled on the French *fonte* from *fondre* meaning "cast or found (a metal)." It was spelled *font, fond* and even *fund* in C17, but then became confused with the first word **font/fount**. As often, the more radical spelling **font** crossed the Atlantic to become the standard term among printers in North America, while **fount** consolidated its position in Britain. Australians and Canadians both go with **font**; and it's the form used everywhere in the world for the choice of typefaces in computer programs.

> **International English selection:** Since **font** is the spelling used for "typeface" everywhere outside Britain, and inside Britain among computer users, it's the natural choice for international usage.

foolscap
This imperial paper size ($13\frac{1}{2} \times 17$ inches or 343×432 mm) was long known by its distinctive watermark – that of a jester's cap with bells. Its origins are rather obscure, and traditions linking it with Caxton in C15, and Sir John Spielman, a C16 papermaker, cannot be confirmed. The earliest hard evidence of the foolscap watermark is in a C17 copy of Rushworth's *Historical Collections,* kept in the British Museum. The enigma of its origin made it a topic of speculation, and partisan rumor had it that the fool's cap was substituted for the royal coat of arms during the Rump Parliament (1648–53), on the paper used to record the daily records of the House.

foot or feet
Imperial expressions of length, height and depth vary between singular and plural, witness *six foot five* versus *six feet five inches* as the height of the local giant. The first is a conventional, stripped-down expression typical of conversation or no-nonsense reporting, whereas the second elaborates the individual measures to the point of redundancy. When

measurements serve as modifiers of nouns or adjectives, the same variation emerges: *a six-foot pole* versus *she is six feet tall*. As in these examples, the singular is often found in standard sizes, usually hyphenated, as in *two-inch nail, 25-yard line, ten ton truck* – while the plural expression underscores the fact that the measure is specific to the case: *nearly six feet tall and 13 stones when I'm at my best*.

The constructions with *feet* are commoner in American than British English, by the evidence of language databases. Numerical expressions with *feet tall* outnumber those with *foot tall* by almost 10:1 in data from CCAE, whereas it's 5:1 in the BNC. The greater use of the plural unit by Americans reflects their general preference for formal agreement (see **agreement**).

The singular unit is used the world over in imperial and metric expressions that serve as modifiers, e.g. *two hundred-pound weights, a five-kilo pack*. The same quantities are pluralized elsewhere in the sentence, as in *he lifted two hundred pounds yesterday*, or *They bought five kilos of rice*.

footnotes
See **referencing**.

footy or footie
See under **-ie/-y**.

for
This is one of the commonest prepositions, but its role as a conjunction is declining. Nowadays **for** is usually replaced by *because* to express reasons and causes, as in the following:
> They missed the opening ceremony, for (because) the venue had been difficult to find.

Apart from its role as a subordinating conjunction, **for** was once more widely used like a coordinator, alongside other conjunctions:
> For when she called the maid, there was no answer.

This usage now seems rather literary. Though older grammar books class **for** as a full coordinating conjunction, it does not allow deletion of a repeated subject, which is one of the criteria used by modern grammarians (*Comprehensive Grammar*, 1985). Compare *and, but* and **for** in the following:
> He had no transport and came by taxi.
> He had no transport but came by taxi.
> He came by taxi for (he) had no transport.

See further under **conjunctions**.

for ever or forever
The space between *for* and *ever* makes a different meaning for some, but not very many users of English nowadays. The *Oxford Dictionary* (1989) separates them, with **for ever** defined as "for all future time," and **forever** as "incessantly." Compare *It's for ever and ever* with *forever pushing her hair out of her eyes*. It also notes the "chiefly US" use of **forever** in place of **for ever**, and the unspaced form is listed without comment in *Webster's Third* (1986). Yet **for ever** is rare in data from the BNC, and **forever** quite often used where **for ever** might have been expected, by the *Oxford*'s comments. See for example:
> I could stay here forever.
> Christian marriage was forever.
> . . . etched forever in my brain

The tendency to use **forever** instead of **for ever** is as strong in the British database as in the American (CCAE). This process of closing up **forever** matches that of *however, wherever* etc. See further under **-ever and ever**.

for free
Faced with an advertising line like:
> Buy two medium pizzas and get a cup of coffee for free

few customers think they are really getting something for nothing. But they will probably not query the grammar of **for free** either – just accept it as commercial rhetoric. In grammatical terms it makes a full adverbial phrase out of the word **free**, which otherwise seems ordinary and even negligible as the complementary adverb/adjective in *get a cup of coffee free* (see further under **complementation**). The phrase itself is perfectly grammatical if we allow that *free* is a zero adverb, which can combine with *for* just like *for ever, for once*. In contexts other than advertising, people sometimes find **for free** excessive when *free* would suffice. But there are occasions when it prevents ambiguity, as in:
> She and her family gladly work for free at the army base.

For free seems thus able to earn its keep.

fora or forums
See under **forum**.

forbade or forbad
The first of these **forbade** is the preferred form for the past tense of *forbid* in all modern dictionaries, and it's commoner by far in contemporary English databases, both British and American. This is all the more remarkable when one notes the numerous other spellings used over the centuries. The *Oxford Dictionary* (1989) gave preference to **forbad**, which was more consistent with *forbid*, and with the pronunciation.

For the past participle of the same verb, *forbidden* is strongly preferred, as in:
> They had forbidden the students to leave.

The use of *forbid* as past participle now seems a little old-fashioned, if not archaic, as *Webster's Third* (1986) suggests.
◊ Compare **bid**.

forbear or forebear
See under **fore-/for-**.

force de frappe and force majeure
The first of these French phrases, borrowed only in C20, is often translated as "(a) strike force." Though it can be applied almost literally to guerrilla and commando units, the expression has gained world attention as a reference to nuclear capability, and especially the French insistence on their need for an independent nuclear strike force.

Yet even a nuclear **force de frappe** may be less powerful than the so-called **force majeure**, which in traditional legal French meant "a superior force." The concept itself was borrowed from Roman law, where it meant what we now call an "act of God." In modern contract law it covers any one of a set of natural or man-made forces (flood or hurricane as well as strikes, lockouts or a go-slow on the wharf), which may prevent the fulfillment of the contract. There, and in general usage, it implies a force over which the parties referred to have no control.

forceful or forcible

Both these words involve force, but their implications are somewhat different. **Forcible** suggests that either sheer physical force or some other inescapable factor was felt or brought to bear on the situation, particularly when some other means might have been used. The *forcible removal* of interjectors from a meeting implies that the strong arm of the law was exerted against them; and a *forcible reminder* is one which expresses itself through physical circumstances, not the spoken word itself.

Forceful just implies that noticeable energy is or was used in an action or activity, to maximize its impact. It can be physical energy, as in a *forceful blow,* but very often it is verbal and rhetorical, as in a *forceful argument* – or a *forceful reminder.* So either adjective might serve in that phrase, depending on the meaning intended.

forceps

For the plural of this word, see under **biceps**.

fore-/for-

These two Old English prefixes have quite independent meanings, though they are sometimes mistaken for each other. Nowadays **fore-** ("ahead, before") is much more familiar than **for-** ("against, utterly").

Fore- operates in numerous words expressing priority in time or position:

forearm	forecast	forefather	forefront
foreground	foreleg	foreman	forename
foresee	foreshadow	forestall	foretaste
foretell	forethought	forewarn	

For- is fossilized in just a handful of words, including *forbid, forget, forgive, forsake.* Its meaning is no longer separable from such words, and it varied in Old English, being separative, privative or intensive depending on the formation. The lack of transparent meaning helps to explain the confusion with **fore-**, even when it could make a difference.

In principle, **fore-** and **for-** mark the contrast in two pairs of words: compare:

forebear "ancestor"   and *forbear* "hold back"
forego "go before"   *forgo* "do without"

Confusion about the prefix usually means that *forbear* is also used for "ancestor," and *forego* for "do without," and dictionaries do recognize them as alternative spellings. Though it might seem preferable to keep the spellings apart, this doubling up is less problematic than one might expect. The two meanings of *forbear* are distinguished by their grammar, one being a noun, the other a verb. And *forgo* can be spelled *forego* with little chance of misunderstanding, since *forego* ("go before") is very rare as an active verb, and mostly survives in fixed expressions like *foregone conclusion.* On the variable spelling of *foregather/forgather,* see **forgather**.

Note also the difference between *foreword,* a name for the prefatory statement printed at the front of a book, and *forward* meaning "in an onward direction." For the distinction drawn between *foreword* and *preface,* see **preface**.

foreign names

Foreign placenames are discussed under **geographical names**; foreign personal names in **capital letters** section 1; and foreign titles under **forms of address**.

forename or first name

See **first name**.

forestallment or forestalment

Now that *forestall* is everywhere the standard spelling for the verb, **forestallment** has everything to recommend it as the noun. In *Webster's Third* (1986) it holds the floor. Yet **forestalment** is still given as the primary spelling for British English, endorsed by the *Oxford Dictionary* (1989) though it had no more citations than the other. It represents a disused spelling of the verb *forestal* (see further under **single for double**).
◊ Compare **installment**.

forever or for ever

See **for ever**.

foreword or forward

◊ For the uses of these two words, see under **fore-/for-**.
◊ For the difference between a **foreword** and a *preface,* see under **preface**.
◊ For the choice between **forward** and *forwards,* see under **-ward**.

forgather or foregather

These alternative spellings serve to render the Dutch verb *vergaderen* ("assemble") into Scottish English. **Forgather** transliterates it better, since the English prefix *for-* is cognate with Dutch (and German) *ver-*, hence the *Oxford Dictionary*'s (1989) preference for it. **Foregather** is a kind of *folk etymology* (see under that heading), using the prefix *fore-* ("before"), which is more transparent than *for-* (see **fore–for-**). In British English, *foregather(ed)* is now more popular than *forgather(ed)* by the evidence of the BNC; but it makes no showing in the American English of CCAE.

forgo or forego

See under **fore-/for-**.

forgotten or forgot

The verb *forget* takes **forgot** as its regular past tense, and **forgotten** for the past participle, as in:

They forgot the date.   They had forgotten the date.

But dictionaries note in a variety of ways that **forgot** also sometimes serves as past participle. The *Oxford Dictionary* (1989) dubbed it "archaic" and "poetical" while the *New Oxford* (1998) labels it "chiefly US." But there are some citations in the BNC to confirm that it's in contemporary British use as well. Among the spoken data, **forgot** replaces **forgotten** in about 1 in 25 citations, usually following a contracted form of *have,* as in:

I was going to bring a poster for you and I've forgot it.

This makes it no more than a minor spoken variant in Britain, whereas *Webster's Third* (1986) presents **forgot** as the alternative past participle without any stylistic restrictions. To this extent, its status is currently higher in American English.

formal words

A formal choice of words elevates the style of any discourse, as when the sign says PROCEED WITH CAUTION rather than DRIVE CAREFULLY. Or when a public service administrator is said to *oversight* a matter, rather than "keep an eye on it." Formal language sets itself above both standard and colloquial English. It lends dignity, weight and authority to a message.

On the opposite side of the coin, **formal words** put verbal distance between the people communicating, which may or may not be appropriate to the situation. With serious subjects such as religion or law, most people allow that formal language is somehow right, and would feel that a preacher or judge who relied heavily on colloquialisms was behaving unprofessionally. But those who use formal language in ordinary situations are likely to be seen as pretentious and unsympathetic to their audience. This is often an issue in business or institutional letter writing, where the writer must strike a balance between the need to communicate with dignity and seriousness, and the need to speak as pleasantly and directly as possible to the reader. Fortunately English has ample resources to provide for many styles and levels of communication. See further under **colloquialisms** and **standard English**.

format

When it serves as a verb, the inflected forms are *formatted* and *formatting*, everywhere in the world. See further under **doubling of final consonant**, exceptions 3.

former and latter

These words allow writers to refer systematically to a previously mentioned pair of persons or items, so as to distinguish between them:

> *A difference between Morrelli and Friedlander is that the former explains his method while the latter does not.*
> *The former works the soleus (lower) muscle more, while the latter works the gastronemius (upper) muscle.*

As in the first example, **former** refers to the first of the pair, **latter** to the second, and they neatly pinpoint the two people mentioned. The second example shows **former/latter** connecting with the previous sentence in the same way.

Some cautions are in order, however:

1 Like pronouns, **former** and **latter** depend on words that have gone before for their specifics. Those antecedents should not be too far away or readers will have to search for them.

2 Because they identify the members of a pair, **former** and **latter** cannot be used in reference to a larger set of items. Instead *first, second, third respectively* (etc.) should be used. See further under **respectfully or respectively**.

3 Some authorities argue without justification that **latter** should not be used to refer back to a single preceding item. There are of course ordinary pronouns such as *it* and *that* available for this purpose. Yet **latter** by its very bulk draws more attention to itself than *it*, and so is a useful device in longer sentences and denser discussion, provided its antecedent is clear.

forms of address

In spite of the general trend towards informality, **forms of address** are still important in letter writing. Choices have always to be made for the envelope, and within the letter itself (in and above the salutation), for business as well as institutional correspondence. Appropriate titles must be found for both the envelope and the internal address above the salutation, discussed in section 1 below. The salutation itself involves some further considerations, according to whether the writer knows the addressee or not (discussed in section 2).

1 **On the envelope, and the internal address of a business letter** – the title depends on the addressee's qualifications and rank, gender, and in some cases, marital status and nationality. When rank involved is a subordinate step, e.g. *Associate Professor, Lieutenant Colonel,* the title given on the envelope and any internal address is exactly that, whereas the letter salutation by courtesy makes it the higher rank: *Professor, Colonel* etc. The title on the envelope and internal address include the addressee's initials or given name, whereas the salutation inside simply uses the surname.

*Titles for the English-speaking world include:

> *Dr.* for medical practitioners (except surgeons), and holders of university doctorates, Ph.D., D.Sc., D.Litt. etc.
> *Professor* for university professors
> *The Honorable Mr. Justice* for judges
> *Captain/Major/Lieutenant* etc. according to rank, for members of the armed forces
> *Reverend* for ministers of most branches of the Christian church, including the Protestant, Catholic and Orthodox. (For the conventions on combining *Reverend* with other names, see **names** section 2.)
> *Rabbi* for Jewish clerics
> *Senator* for members of the federal upper house in the US, Australia, Canada
> *Sir* for holders of knighthoods
> *Dame* for women who have been made Dame of the British Empire, or admitted to certain other orders of chivalry
> *Lady* for the wives of knights or those knighted
> *Mr.* for men not included in any of the above groups
> *Mrs.* for married women not included in any of the above groups
> *Ms.* for women who prefer a title that does not express marital status
> *Miss,* an older title for unmarried women, and for young girls
> *Master,* an older title for young boys, little used nowadays

The use of stops in *Dr(.), Mr(.)* etc. is discussed in **abbreviations** section 2. For plural addressees with *Dr., Mr., Mrs., Ms.,* see **plurals** section 3.

The convention of addressing a married woman by her husband's name or initials (as *Mrs. J[ohn] Evans*) is disappearing, except in the most formal correspondence. (This once applied to a widow as well as a married woman, and served to distinguish both from a divorcee who used her own given name and initial. The convention is no longer observed.) But letters addressed to married women jointly with their husbands still usually carry the husband's initial or name, as in *Mr. and Mrs. J(ohn) Evans.* The practice of identifying them separately, as in *Mr. J. and Mrs. P. Evans*, is not yet widespread.

*Distinctive titles for European addressees, corresponding to *Mr.* and *Mrs.:*

France	Monsieur	Madame
Netherlands	Meneer	Mevrouw
Germany	Herr	Frau
Spain	Señor	Señora
Italy	Signor	Signora

Note that Italians increasingly use *Mr./Mrs.,* and that the English titles are usual when the addressees are Portuguese, Greek or from Eastern Europe.

*Titles for Asian addressees:

Burma	U	Daw
India – Hindi	Shri	Shrimanthi
India – Sikh	Sardar	Sardarni
Laos	Thao	Nang
Malaysia	Encik	Puan
Thailand	Nai	Nang

As **forms of address** for Chinese, Filipino, Indonesian and Sri Lankan people, the titles of *Mr.* and *Mrs.* should be used.

For more details, see *Naming Systems of Ethnic Groups* (1990).

2 Letter salutations do not necessarily address the recipient in the same terms as those used in the delivery address on the envelope or above the salutation within the letter. In many kinds of correspondence they require an active choice by the writer, and *Dear Sir* can no longer be taken for granted or used with impunity. The salutation should establish an appropriate relationship with the reader, and usually reflects their degree of acquaintance.

a) If the correspondents are at all acquainted, it's likely that first names will be used in the salutation: *Dear John, Dear Helen.* But if the correspondents are not already acquainted, or if the recipient of the letter is unknown, there are a number of options.

b) If only the recipient's name is known, it's conventional to use title plus surname: *Dear Mr. Brown* or *Dear M(r)s. Brown,* depending on gender. The choice between *Mrs.* and *Ms.* in this situation is delicate. Not all women like to be addressed as *Ms.;* and yet with *Mrs.* you imply that the surname following is her married name. (See further under **Miss, Mrs. or Ms.**) If the preferred title is not known, *Dear Patricia Brown* is increasingly used as a semiformal salutation.

c) If only surname and an initial are known, and the gender of the recipient is unknown, the alternatives are to use *Dear P. Brown,* or *Dear Mr./Mrs./Ms. Brown.*

d) If only the gender of the recipient is known, it's still possible to use *Dear Sir* or *Dear Madam,* though they set a formal tone for the letter.

e) If neither gender nor name of the recipient are known, the options are to use *Dear Sir/Madam,* or else some relevant job or role title, such as *Dear Manager, Dear Teacher, Dear Customer.*

f) If the letter is written to a company rather than a particular individual within it, there are two possibilities: either to use *Dear Jeffries Pty Ltd* as the salutation, or just the company name without a preliminary "Dear." The latter often seems appropriate, and is often used in North America.

◊ For further details, see under **first name, letter writing** and **names**, and also the letter formats in Appendix VII.

formula

Americans and the British diverge radically on how to pluralize **formula.** The Latin plural **formulae** is the majority preference of writers represented in the BNC, by a factor of 3:1. American writers are almost wholly behind **formulas**, the regular English plural. For other Latin loanwords of this type, see **-a** section 1.

fornix

For the plural of this word see **-x** section 3.

fortuitous or fortunate

Fortuitous has extended its range in C20 English. Fowler noticed in the 1920s that it seemed sometimes to be a synonym for **fortunate**, and *Webster's English Usage* (1989) provides a number of American citations for this from the end of World War II. *Webster's Third* (1986) registers **fortuitous** as meaning both "happening by chance" and "lucky." But the second meaning is still developing in British English, judging by BNC evidence, and seems rather to represent an intermediate stage of "happening by a good chance." The boundaries between this optimistic sense and the original neutral sense are often ambiguous, and the optimism is often a construct of the context, as in:

> The storm had been fortuitous, an extra.
> It is perhaps fortuitous that Healing appeared when he did, his milling business helping to fill the void.

Other citations in the BNC suggest writers' awareness of the new meaning while attempting to use the old. The author who speaks of *fortuitous good fortune* is presumably trying to keep them apart. In scientific writing, the older sense of randomness is less challenged, and supported by the cool factuality of the context:

> Many modern houses have little fortuitous ventilation because [of] improved standards of insulation.

But the second meaning grows naturally in ad hoc narratives and history, when a strictly **fortuitous** event or observation serves as the foundation for future benefit or progress, as in the first pair of examples. The optimistic meaning "happening by good chance" is now recognized in some British dictionaries, including *New Oxford* (1998), though with a caution that it is "informal." This must reflect the fact that it's subject to doubt, like many items stemming from the Fowler (1926) canon. The BNC citations nevertheless show it being used in a variety of prose contexts, and certainly those intended for a general readership.

Whether **fortuitous** will move further in British English into the semantic realms of **fortunate** remains to be seen, but the chances are that it will, given that it's established in American English. At any rate, this all indicates that **fortuitous** (and *fortuitously*) are increasingly unreliable as ways of referring to pure chance.

forum

This Latin loanword meaning "public arena" came into English in C15, time enough for **forums** to have become established as its English plural. The lack of reference to the Latin plural **fora** in the *Oxford Dictionary* (1989) is its endorsement of **forums**. And in data from the BNC, **forums** is the preferred plural, outnumbering the other by more than 4:1. *International forums, political forums, planning forums, recruitment forums* are some of its numerous applications. The Latin plural **fora** is not however confined to discussions of Roman history. It enjoys scattered use in official documents that speak of *legal and quasi-legal fora* in which individuals may press their cases, and legal writers in the US "persist in using the pedantic *fora*," according to Garner (1998). Other support for **fora** could come from the digital community, where the more formal type of internet discussion is sometimes called a **forum**, and its plural **fora**. Still **forums** is the dominant plural on the internet, found in more than 98% of all instances in a Google search in 2002. See further under **-um**.

forward or foreword

◊ For the use of **foreword** (not **forward**) for the prefatory statement in a book, see under **fore-/for-**.
◊ For the choice between **forward** and **forwards**, see under **-ward**.

forward slash
See **slash**.

founder or flounder
See **flounder**.

fount or font
See **font**.

four, fourteen and forty
The inconsistency in the spelling of these words is a headache for many writers. The spelling of **four** naturally helps to distinguish it from its homonyms *for* and *fore*. To have it also in **fourteen** but not in **forty** seems perverse, especially when records show that it was spelled "fourty" in earlier times, and was only displaced by **forty** in C18. The British *fortnight* (= two weeks) shows the same spelling adjustment, since it's a telescoping of "fourteen nights."

four-letter words
This is a cover term for the group of swear words which refer to intimate bodily parts and functions, especially *fuck, shit* and *cunt*. For some people, *piss, frig, arse* and *turd* might be added to the group, though for others the uses of those words are more diverse, and not necessarily associated with swearing and offensive language. There is no categorical inventory of **four-letter words**, and, despite the examples so far, even the criterion of having four letters gives way. Some would regard *prick* in its taboo sense as a **four-letter word**, because it represents a body part whose name can be used in offensive references to other people. Those seem to be the defining characteristics of **four-letter words**, and serve to distinguish them from other general-purpose swear words, such as *bloody* and *bugger*.

Because **four-letter words** are taboo in many contexts, in printed texts they have traditionally been replaced by a set of asterisks, or hinted at by use of their first letter only, followed by a long dash or three spaces. Other strategies involve using a substitute word which begins with the same sound, such as *sugar* or *shoot* for *shit* (sometimes called *euphemistic dysphemisms*). See further under **euphemisms**, **swear words** and **taboo words**.

fractious or factious
See **factious**.

fragrant or flagrant
See **flagrant**.

franchise
For the spelling see **-ize/-ise**; for the form and meaning, see **disfranchise**.

frangipani or frangipane
The first spelling **frangipani** applies to a tropical tree with strongly scented flowers. The plant is believed to take its name from the C16 Marquis of Frangipani of Rome, who created a famous perfume for gloves. The flower is sometimes spelled *frangipanni* or *frangipane*.

Frangipane is also the word for a pastry tart filled with cream, almonds and sugar. *Larousse gastronomique* (1984) associates it with the first word, and the fact that the Marquis's perfume was based on bitter almonds. Other etymologies connect the gastronomic word with *franchipane*, an old Italian term meaning literally "French bread," but based on Italian use of the second term to mean "coagulated milk."

frantically and franticly
Though *Webster's Third* (1986) and the *Oxford Dictionary* (1989) still list **franticly** as an alternative spelling, it's no longer in use in either the US or the UK, by database evidence. **Franticly** was the earlier spelling (from C16), which has been overtaken by **frantically**, originating in C18. The second spelling conforms to the regular pattern for adverbs derived from adjectives ending in *-ic*. See further under **-ic/-ical**.

-freak
See under **-head**.

-free
This works like an adjectival suffix, to highlight the absence of something undesirable in a commodity or medium:

duty-free goods	*gender-free language*
lead-free paint	*nuclear-free zone*
rent-free accommodation	*trouble-free run*

The regular hyphen in these words suggests that **-free** is not yet a fully established suffix. Yet that status cannot be far off, given that it forms new words so easily. Already it can be seen as complementing *-less*, the suffix long used in words which emphasize the absence of something desirable: *graceless, hopeless, shapeless* etc. See further under **-less**.

frenchification
French culture has always been held in special respect by the English, and innumerable French words and phrases have been borrowed over the centuries. Apart from expressing things for which there was no suitable English word, French expressions often seemed to have a certain something about them, a "je ne sais quoi" which recommended them to the user. Because the Frenchness of such borrowings is part of their value, unusual features of their spelling and pronunciation may be consciously maintained long after they might naturally have been assimilated to

conform with ordinary English words. So *ballet*, as part of high culture, has kept its French pronunciation, whereas *bullet*, borrowed in the same century, has become fully anglicized. The desire to keep French loanwords looking French accounts for the preservation and even extension of their accents. So *creche* and *creme* are often given circumflexes in English, where in French they have grave accents. Other words acquire accents in English which they never have in French: *châlet*, *compôte*, *côterie*, *toupée* (a refashioning of French *toupet*).

This habit of making loanwords more French than the French is also seen in the English addition of an -e to *caviare*, *chaperone* and others. The reversing of earlier anglicized spellings shows the same inclination. So *omelet* was remade as *omelette*, and French -*que* superimposed on the earlier -*ck* in *cheque/chequer* (see **check or cheque**) – at least in British English. Loanwords from classical sources (Greek and Latin) have been refashioned according to French models, as was *program* (respelled as *programme*), *inquire* (as *enquire*), and *honor, labor* etc. confirmed as *honour, labour* etc. The preference for French-influenced spellings intensified in Victorian England, and is enshrined in C21 British English, whereas American English has been little touched by it. Usage in Canada and Australia is mixed, though Australians tend more to the British, and Canadians to the American – except that Canadians have additional exposure to French variants through the official policy of bilingualism.

frescoes or frescos

Both *Merriam-Webster* (2000) and *New Oxford* (1998) put **frescoes** first as the plural of **fresco**; and it's more popular than **frescos** among American and British writers, by about 15:1 in CCAE and 3:1 in the BNC. Yet responses to the Langscape survey in 1998 suggested otherwise, with 70% of respondents (from among hundreds worldwide) indicating their preference for **frescos**. This is in line with the more general tendency to replace -*oes* plurals with -*os* (see further at **-o**). It means there's still room to choose.

freshman, fresher and freshette

The term **freshman** ("novice university student") is strongly associated with North America, and used by students (and administrators), as the first in a series of terms used to identify those in each of the four years of the standard college program:

> *freshman   sophomore   junior   senior*

The term includes both genders of student.

In Britain **fresher** likewise refers to a university student in his or her first year. But it remains informal – not institutionalized in the same way, and mostly used by non-first-year students as a way of identifying those who are a target for orientation or initiation. Again it is gender-free, except when contrasted with **freshette** ("a female first-year student"), a term which enjoyed some vogue in the US and Australia in the middle decades of C20, but is now disused on grounds of gratuitous sexism. See further under **-ette**.

fridge or frig

When you want to reduce refrigerator to a word of one syllable, **fridge** is a good deal more reliable than **frig**, though dictionaries will offer you both. **Fridge** not

only registers the "j" sound unambiguously, but also avoids the risk of a *double entendre* (see **four-letter words**). Why not *frige*, you might ask. It isn't a recognized alternative, perhaps because it suggests a long vowel before the "j" sound, as in *oblige*. The manufacturer who chose *frij* for the name of his portable icebag was up against the same problem, but his distinctive spelling looks distinctly un-English.

friendly or friendlily

Like other adjectives ending in -*ly*, **friendly** challenges us to find an adverb for it. **Friendlily** is registered in *Webster's Third* (1986) and the *Oxford Dictionary* (1989), but it makes no showing in contemporary British or American databases. **Friendly** itself can be used as an adverb according to *Oxford*, as in *treat them friendly* (see **zero adverbs**) – but it sounds awkward. The best alternative is some kind of paraphrase: *in a friendly way*.

frizz or friz

Dictionaries all prefer the spelling **frizz** when referring to the making of a tightly curled hairstyle, while recognizing **friz** as a secondary alternative. The rare homonym **frizz** meaning "fry," listed in *Webster's Third* (1986) and the *Oxford Dictionary* (1989), has only the one spelling.

frolic

For the spelling of this word when it's used as a verb, see **-c/-ck-**.

front matter

See **prelims**.

fryer or frier

When the verb *fry* needs an agent noun ("one who or that which fries something"), the spelling **fryer** is to be preferred. The major dictionaries give it priority, and it dominates in British and American databases. In the BNC it outnumbers **frier** by more than 10:1, and in CCAE, **fryer** is the only spelling to be found in hundreds of citations. **Fryer** evidently resists the change from *y* to *i* which is built into inflected parts of the verb (*he fries*) and the noun (*French fries*). (See further at **-y>-i-**.) **Frier** was also once a variant spelling for *friar*, but ceased to play that role by C18.

fueled or fuelled

American and British English divide over these inflected forms of the verb *fuel*. See under **-l-/-ll-**.

-ful and -fuls

The suffix -**ful** has two functions: to create adjectives, and a special group of nouns. It forms adjectives primarily out of abstract nouns:

> *beautiful   blissful   careful   delightful*
> *doubtful   fearful   graceful   hopeful*
> *pitiful   plentiful   powerful   sinful*
> *successful   thoughtful   wonderful   wrongful*

Yet the stem in some of these words could also be construed as a verb, and in fact a few -**ful** words could only be based on verbs, e.g. *forgetful, thankful, wakeful*.

The special group of nouns created with -**ful** are expressions for measures of volume:

> *armful   bucketful   cupful   handful   mouthful*
> *plateful   spoonful*

These words function as compound nouns, and so their plurals are:

armfuls (of hay)   *cupfuls* (of water)
spoonfuls (of sugar)

According to an older tradition, their plurals should be *armsful, cupsful* etc., because their internal grammar was noun + adjective and the noun should bear the plural marker. But they have long been fully integrated compounds, and "good modern usage" sanctions *armfuls, cupfuls* etc., according to the *Oxford Dictionary* (1989).

fulcrum

Recent dictionaries allow two plurals for **fulcrum**: the Latin *fulcra* and the regular English **fulcrums**. *New Oxford* (1998) puts *fulcra* first, whereas *Merriam-Webster* (2000) makes it English *fulcrums*. As with other Latin loanwords, the conservation of the Latin plural is stronger in the UK than the US (Peters, 2001a). See further under **-um**.

fulfill or fulfil

The first of these spellings is standard in the US, the second in the UK, by the evidence of the BNC and CCAE. In Canada and Australia, both are used, though Canadians are more inclined to **fulfill** and Australians to **fulfil**, by the *Canadian Oxford* (1998) and the *Macquarie Dictionary* (1997) respectively. Worldwide the spelling is a swinger, and the Langscape survey 1998–2001 found **fulfill** in the majority by just 51%, with clear evidence that it was preferred by younger respondents (those under 45). **Fulfill** is easier and more consistent, given the sense connection with *fill* in the second syllable, and the fact that double *l* is always used in *fulfilled* and *fulfilling*. The same considerations apply in choosing between *fulfillment* and *fulfilment*. The variation between the two spellings is a legacy of the more general problem of final *l*. (See further under **single for double**.)

> **International English selection:** The widespread use of **fulfill**, especially among younger people, its consistency with inflected forms, and transparency in terms of derivation, all make it preferable for use in international communication.

full stop, period or stop

The most frequent of all punctuation marks is the **full stop**, its usual name in Britain, though among British editors and printers it's termed the *full point* (see *Hart's Rules* and *Copy-editing*, 1992). Australian usage echoes the British on this, while in North America (the US and Canada) the mark goes by the name **period**. Fowler (1926) used both names, differentiating them by function (he used **full stop** when it marked the boundary of a sentence, and **period** for its role in abbreviating words). But current British practice uses **full stop** for both these functions, or else the short form **stop**, though this also serves as a cover term for any punctuation mark. The terms **full stop / period / stop** are also applied to the mark used in punctuating numbers and dates. All three functions bear close investigation.

1 The full stop/period at the end of a sentence. Stops are used at the end of most types of sentences, whether they are grammatically complete or fragments. The **full stop / period** gives way to an exclamation mark when the utterance it marks is intended by the writer to have exclamatory value (see **exclamations**). If the sentence is a direct question, the **stop** gives way to a question mark:

Why don't you take it?

But in indirect questions, and questions which function as requests or invitations to do something, a simple **stop** is still used.

They asked why I didn't take it.
Do you mind taking it with you.

(For the position of the final **stop** of a quoted or parenthetical sentence, see **quotation marks** section 3c, and **brackets** sections 2 and 3.)

Full stops / periods do not normally appear in headlines, captions or headings, although some editors use them when the heading/caption runs over onto a second line. They are not used in the stub or column headings in tables, nor in vertical lists. See further under **tables** and **lists**.

2 The full stop / period in abbreviated words. In the past **stops** have been the means of marking abbreviated words or sets of them, in both upper and lower case. Current trends are towards removing them from upper case abbreviations, and increasingly when giving people's initials (see **names** section 3). The use of **stops** with lower case abbreviations is an area of great variability (see **abbreviations** section 2). **Stops** are never used in the symbols for SI units (see **abbreviations** section 1).

3 The full stop / period with numbers and dates. Stops serve as a separating device among figures:
a) **in lists.** Successive numbers or enumerating letters are often accompanied by full stops:

1. 2. 3. or 1a. 2a. 3a. or 1.a. 2.a. 3.a.

Brackets 1) 2) 3) are an alternative device, and can be usefully combined with full stops, especially when there are several subdivisional systems of numbering: 1.a.(i), 1.a.(ii). (For the use of single or paired brackets, see **brackets** section 1.) Note that while brackets are effective with lower case roman numbers, they are best avoided with roman capitals because of possible misreading. **Stops** are preferable there: 1.(a) I.
b) **in dates and times of day:**

26.4.89   7.30 pm

c) **in sums of money:**

$24.20 $1.32

d) **as the decimal point:**

0.08%   3.1417

(See further under **numbers and number style**.) A *raised* **full stop / period** – rather than the normal low **stop** – may be used for items covered under (b), (c) and (d).

full verb

This is an alternative term for the *main verb* that complements an *auxiliary verb*, and brings lexical meaning to the verb phrase. See further under **auxiliary verbs**.

fullness or fulness

All modern dictionaries give first preference to **fullness**, and **fulness** is very rare in both British and American databases. **Fullness** was backed by the original *Oxford Dictionary* (1884–1928) on grounds of analogy, in spite of the observed frequency of **fulness** in C19. That principled stand has helped to resolve one of the several points on which English has vacillated between single and double *l*. See further under **single for double**.

-fuls
See under **-ful**.

fulsome
Two contrasting kinds of meaning have been associated with this word from medieval times: "abundant, ample" and "excessive." **Fulsome** may in fact be the coalescence of two separate words, one with positive connotations based on "full," and the other on "foul" with negative connotations. But scanty records leave much in doubt. The *Oxford Dictionary*'s (1989) record of the positive meaning drops out in C16, except for a C19 reference to it as the "original meaning" – suggesting that some still found a duality in the word, despite the dominance of the negative meaning. Since then, the negative meaning is often taken for granted as the only one, though *Webster's Third* (1986) registers the positive meaning as well. Its currency is evident from the intensified criticism of it from mid-C20 (*Webster's English Usage,* 1989), and numerous examples from CCAE and the BNC have **fulsome** applied in positive or at least neutral ways, as in:
> *Green was fulsome in his praise for Barker's determined efforts to reach an equitable settlement.*

Some examples suggest the writer's awareness of the possible connotative problem with **fulsome**, and his/her efforts to make it unambiguously positive.
> *The tribute may sound fulsome, but Modigliani showed exceptional appreciation of his ability.*

As *Webster's Usage* notes, **fulsome** may in fact be more neutral than the C20 debate has allowed. If the "fullness" described is to be seen as good (or bad), this needs to be indicated through accompanying detail. Without it, **fulsome** seems to take on negative connotations by default. It then becomes a kind of *weasel word* (see under that heading).

Fulsome is relatively unambiguous when it refers to sheer size or volume, shown also in current database evidence, both British and American.
> *Fulsome bodies filled the landing*
> *His voice wasn't its usual fulsome boom.*
> *Once the furor has reached its fulsome fury . . .*

Clearly **fulsome** maintains several senses in current English – and this is recognized by *Merriam-Webster* (2000) as well as *New Oxford* (1998).

fun
So many uses of **fun** are predicative (as in *they're fun to be with*) that its attributive use (as in *a fun party*) may come as a surprise. Yet the *Oxford Dictionary* (1989) records it from more than a century ago, with such things as the *fun jottings* of the newspaper columnist, and the *fun room* of a house, where people didn't have to behave with decorum. These applications have however gathered steam more recently, especially since World War II. *Webster's English Usage* (1989) suggests that advertising for such things as *fun furs* and *fun cars* has helped it along, though many of the new collocations are quite general, witness *fun people, fun place, fun time* etc. Examples like these are found in both British and American databases, though they tend to occur in interactive writing intended for a broad public –

hence perhaps *New Oxford*'s (1998) note that this attributive use of **fun** is "informal." Yet some examples like *fun fair* and *fun run* are institutionalized, and could scarcely be rejected from serious prose on grounds of informality. The very new comparative and superlative forms of **fun** (i.e. *funner* and *funnest*) are of course strictly informal.

funereal or funerary
While **funerary** has everything to do with *funerals,* in *funerary monuments/inscriptions/rites/urns,* **funereal** is figuratively removed from them. It connotes a lack of vitality in music (*funereal tune with cumbersome guitars*) or cricket (*funereal pace of his Edgbaston century*); and a darkness of hue in clothing (*dressed in funereal punk*) or in nature (*a funereal sky*). The ceremoniousness of funeral procedures is captured in *funereal Daimler* and the doctor's *funereal tones* when discussing a colleague's latest symptoms. **Funereal** typically has a critical edge, where **funerary** is neutral.

fungus or fungous
The first of these is a noun, the second an adjective. Compare *Fungus was growing everywhere* with *a fungous growth*. **Fungus**, borrowed straight from Latin, still keeps its Latin plural **fungi** in botanical discourse, and more generally, by the results of the Langscape survey 1998–2001, in which more than 90% of respondents preferred it to **funguses**. (See further under **-us** section 1.)
◊ For other *-us/-ous* pairs, see **-ous**.

funneled or funnelled
Funneled is the standard spelling in the US, but very unpopular in the UK by the evidence of the BNC, where all citations were for **funnelled**. See further under **-l-/-ll-**.

furbish or refurbish
See **refurbish**.

furl or unfurl
See **unfurl**.

furor or furore
The older form of this word is **furor**, which is standard in the US. It was replaced in C19 Britain by the Italian **furore** (with a three-syllabled pronunciation), which is now standard in the UK, by the evidence of the BNC. Canadians incline to the American spelling, while Australians embrace both, according to the *Canadian Oxford* (1998) and *Macquarie Dictionary* (1997).

further or farther, and furthest or farthest
These pairs have fallen together in modern English, though their different spellings still seem to suggest different meanings – hence the tradition that **farther** relates to distance in space or time, and **further** to figurative extensions of it. The *far* in **farther** has no doubt helped the notion that it referred to physical space and was the comparative of *far* (pure **folk etymology**). In fact **farther** is simply a C15 respelling of **further**, while **further** itself seems to be a comparative form of the word *forth*.

The idea that **farther** and **further** work in different realms is not sustainable. The *Oxford Dictionary* (1989) comments that C19 usage on this point was often arbitrary; and *Webster's English Usage* (1989) notes that both forms are now freely applied to "spatial, temporal or metaphorical distance." Dictionaries generally give both words as meaning "additional(ly)," although *Merriam-Webster* (2000) notes that **further** is squeezing the other one out of the adverbial role (e.g. *what further annoyed me*). Authorities everywhere agree that only **further** can be used as a conjunct equivalent to "moreover," and as a verb.

Though the use of **farther** is declining everywhere, it persists more strongly in the US than in the UK. The ratio of **further** to **farther** is about 10:1 in American data from CCAE, whereas it's 70:1 in the BNC. The low frequency of **farther** gives it formal and literary connotations, as noted in some British dictionaries. The two forms are more closely matched in the superlative. **Furthest** remains the commoner of the two in the BNC by a factor of 3:1, whereas in CCAE the situation is reversed, with **farthest** turning up more often, by about 2:1. Its use in rhetorical parlance (e.g. *the farthest galaxy*) may help to account for this.

fused participle

For the choice between *They heard him singing* and *They heard his singing*, see under **gerund**.

future tense

English, like other Germanic languages, has no special suffix to add to its verbs to make the **future tense**. Instead it uses auxiliary verbs, or the present tense along with some other indicator of futurity. The best known auxiliaries are *will*, as in *you will receive*, and *shall* as in *I shall retire*. (For the traditional differences between these two, see **shall or will**.)

Modern grammars show that English has various other means of indicating futurity. They include *semi-auxiliaries* and phrasal verbs such as:

> *be going to   be to   be about to   be on the point of*

(See further under **auxiliaries** section 3.) The first of these (*I am going to*) is the most straightforward with no particular implications that limit its use. The second (*I am to*) suggests that the projected event is the result of an arrangement made by other parties, and not something to decide for oneself. The last two (*I am about to / I am on the point of*) show that the projected event is imminent, and not just at some undetermined time in the future. The sense of imminence and immediacy is stronger with *on the point of* than with *about to*.

In certain circumstances, the plain present tense can be used to express futurity. An accompanying adverb (or adverbial phrase) which expresses future time is sufficient in a simple statement, and used very often in conversation:

> *They come tomorrow.*
> *My course finishes in two weeks time.*

In complex sentences (see **clauses** section 3), a plain present tense can be used to express future in the subordinate clause, provided that the main clause has one of the future auxiliaries:

> *I'm going to dye my hair if you do.*
> *Next year we'll celebrate when the yachts arrive.*

-fy

See **-ify**.

G

gabardine or gaberdine

Both spellings go back to C16, when they were alternatives for a loose-fitting overgarment, sometimes called a "smock," sometimes a "cloak." Their application to the closely woven twill fabric dates from early C20, and it's now the dominant meaning. In American English, the standard spelling is overwhelmingly **gabardine**, by the evidence of CCAE. This accords with the fact that *Webster's Third* (1986) associates **gabardine** primarily with the fabric, while **gaberdine** (which it associates with the traditional garment) is hardly ever mentioned. In British English **gaberdine** has also been the C20 spelling for a type of raincoat, made from the fabric of the same name. This has probably reinforced the use of **gaberdine** for the fabric itself, and made it more popular than **gabardine** for that meaning among writers represented in the BNC, in the ratio of 5:2. The British preference for **gaberdine** is in line with the fact that the *Oxford Dictionary* (1989) gives it priority. A regional divergence in spelling thus seems to be opening up. So much for fashion!

The word itself is a curiosity. It has no relatives in English to provide analogies and to pin the spelling down. Its French antecedents *gauvardine* and *galvardine* lend support to **gabardine**, and also show how scholars link it with the old German word *wallevart* ("pilgrimage"). They suggest that the cloak of **gabardine** was the uniform of pilgrims on their travels.

Gaelic

This term is popularly associated with the ancient and modern language of Scotland, though scholars apply it also to the Celtic language of Ireland. See further under **Celtic**.

gaff, gaffe and gaffer

Gaff and **gaffe** represent several different words – two of which are derived ultimately from a Celtic word for "boathook," which appeared in medieval French and English as **gaffe**. It became **gaff** in modern English, and has much of the original meaning when applied to the hooked pole used by fishermen for landing large fish. In another nautical use it refers to the spar on the upper edge of a fore-and-aft sail, as in a *gaff-rigged* boat.

In French meanwhile, **gaffe** continued to refer to a boathook, and it is from nautical accidents (French sailors getting hooked on their own **gaffs**) that the meaning of **gaffe** as "social blunder" is believed to derive. The idiom *make/made a gaffe* came into English in early C20, embodied in the French spelling.

Independent of all this is the slang word **gaff** found in *blow the gaff,* recorded from 1812 on. Its origins are obscure, although **gaff** in this context seems to reflect the meanings "cheat" or "trick" of an identical word

from the underworld. Yet an earlier form of the phrase (*blow the gab*) shows its association with the gift of the gab, and with glib or specious talk. Some dictionaries suggest a link between *blow the gaff* and *gaffe* ("social blunder"), but this is anachronistic by the *Oxford Dictionary*'s (1989) datings.

Gaffer meaning the chief electrician on a movie or TV set owes nothing to either **gaff** or **gaffe**. A contracted form of *godfather*, it earlier developed meanings of its own, including "old man" and "foreman."

gage or gauge

See **gauge**.

Gallic

See under **Gaulish**.

Gallicism or gallicism

In the *Oxford Dictionary* (1989) tradition, this is given a capital letter, and *Webster's Third* (1986) confirms that it's usually so for American English. With or without capital letter, it refers to the elements of French idiom and usage embedded in English. See further under **frenchification**.

Gallup and gallop

The *Gallup poll* was developed by Dr. George Gallup, founder of the American Institute of Public Opinion in 1935. His survey techniques are now vested in the Gallup Organization, which may explain why the word is slow to lose its capital letter, unlike many eponymous words (see further under **eponyms**). The existence of rival pollsters is a challenge to owners of the original concept, and pressure to maintain the capital spills over onto the following word: hence the *Gallup Poll*. The capital letter still stands to prevent **Gallup** being confused with **gallop**, though they sound identical and do indeed merge in folk etymology, on the assumption that the "gallop poll" anticipates a runaway victory for one party or the other.

When suffixes are added to the verb **gallop**, it simply becomes *galloped/galloping* or *galloper,* in all varieties of English – in line with the broadest rules of English spelling. See further under **doubling of final consonant**.

galore

This is one of the few English adjectives which must be used postpositively, i.e. following the noun that it qualifies, as in *bargains galore* or even *reform targets galore*. **Galore** anglicizes the Irish Gaelic *go leor* ("to sufficiency"), an adverbial phrase – which would explain its postpositive use in English. In British data from the BNC it usually qualifies a plural noun, as in the examples just given, but American examples in CCAE have it with singular/collective nouns as well, in *cash/opportunity/talent galore*. Though borrowed in C17, its Irish origins seem always to have raised the question of its acceptability in standard English. Its tone is easy-going and expansive rather than precise, which perhaps goes against it as well. Yet the database evidence comes from written rather than spoken sources, from magazines and newspapers – showing that it's not shunned by those who write for the general public.

gamboled or gambolled
See under -l-/-ll-.

gamey or gamy
See under -y/-ey.

gamut
In the idiom *run the gamut,* this word is sometimes confused with *ga(u)ntlet.* See further under **gauntlet or gantlet.**

ganglion
The plural of this word is discussed under **-on.**

gantlet or gauntlet
The distinction made between these in American English is discussed under **gauntlet.**

gaol or jail
For the choice between these spellings, see **jail.**

gaoler, jailer or jailor
See **jailer.**

garrote, garrotte or garotte
This word for an old Spanish method of execution has acquired a new use in referring to a mugging tactic whereby the victim is half strangled. The spelling is rather variable, and the major dictionaries diverge on first and second preferences. The spellings with two *r*s are prioritized in *Webster's Third* (1986), and **garrote** is the only one to appear in data from CCAE, and closest to the original Spanish verb *garrotear. New Oxford* (1998) however presents **garrotte** followed by **garotte,** in line with their relative frequencies in the BNC: approximately 2:1. Like other loanwords with double consonants, it presents difficulties for English users: see further under **single for double.**

gas
Spellings with double *s* are used with the verb **gas,** whether it's the standard sense (when people are *gassed*),or informal uses (when people are *gassing* at the table or *gassing up* their cars). These spellings prevail in both British and American databases, in line with the standard rule for monosyllabic words (see **doubling of final consonant**).

The noun **gas** varies a little in its plural: usually **gases** but occasionally **gasses** in the US, according to *New Oxford* (1998) and *Merriam-Webster* (2000). Yet **gasses** is used for the noun plural at much the same level in data from the BNC and CCAE (around 2% of all instances). The disinclination to use **gasses** for the noun is perhaps a reflection of the unusual origins of **gas,** as a Dutch transliteration of the Greek word *chaos.* **Gas** as the American abbreviation for *gasoline* is a mass noun, so never pluralized.

gasoline or gasolene
The spelling **gasoline** is preferred everywhere: see **-ine.**

-gate
This fateful suffix originated with *Watergate,* the building that served as headquarters for the Democratic Party, which was burgled for political information in 1972 by persons linked with the Republican Party. The scandal and associated inquiry proved embarrassing for President Nixon, who duly resigned. Since then it has become a formative element in the US and elsewhere for ad hoc words referring to an actual or presumed scandal – especially a coverup – involving the government. The words may include a placename (*Irangate*), a personal name (*Cartergate*), or a common noun (*cattlegate*), depending on the focus of the scandal.

gateaus or gateaux
While dictionaries give priority to the English plural **gateaus,** the French **gateaux** is actually preferred by writers in the UK and the US. Perhaps this helps to maintain its foreignness, and to compensate for the disappearing circumflex. There's little evidence of *gâteau* these days. See further under **-eau.**

gauge or gage
These spellings have been used to distinguish two different words: **gauge** for "measure" or "measuring instrument," and **gage** for the old word "pledge." **Gauge** is an eccentric spelling in terms of English letter-sound correspondences, the only one of its kind. The not uncommon misspelling "guage" (which puts the vowels into the more familiar sequence of words like *language*) appears in about 7% of all instances of the word on the internet, by a Google search (2002). **Gage** is a much more natural spelling for the sound of the word whichever sense is intended, and it was in fact used for both words in past centuries.

The distinction between **gauge** ("measure/r") and **gage** ("pledge") is nevertheless upheld in both *Webster's Third* (1986) and the *Oxford Dictionary* (1989), though they do acknowledge the use of **gage** for **gauge.** *Random House Dictionary* (1987) notes that **gage** is particularly used as the spelling for "measure/r" in technical contexts, and its firm foothold there may help to establish it more generally, as noun and verb. But in CCAE **gauge** occurs about three times as often as **gage**; and in BNC data, **gauge** rules the roost. Its range is enhanced by figurative uses of the verb, as in *Can you gauge what a market's worth,* which make up about 40% of the total instances.

There's little need now to preserve the two spellings, with the uses of **gage** as "pledge" obsolescent, and those of **gauge/gage** increasing with every new measuring device. The acceptance of **gage** for all uses would rid English of one of its anomalies.

Gaulish, Gaullist and Gallic
There are ancient and modern links with France in these words. The first relates to the original Celtic inhabitants of France, to their culture and language, whereas the second relates very specifically to the post-World War II policies of General de Gaulle. Both **Gaulish** and **Gaullist** are subsumed by **Gallic,** which

can be applied to either the ancient or the modern culture of France.

gauntlet or gantlet

The idiom *run the ga(u)ntlet* is probably opaque to most users, and the alternative spellings ultimately connect with two different words. **Gauntlet**, also spelled **gantlet**, is French for "small glove" (i.e. one covering only the wrist). It properly appears in *throw down / pick up the ga(u)ntlet,* the medieval gesture for issuing and accepting a challenge to a duel. The *Oxford Dictionary* (1989) and *Webster's Third* (1986) agree on this. But *Webster's* finds a different etymology for the word in *run the ga(u)ntlet,* in a former Swedish military punishment called *gatlopp* (literally *gata,* "road," and *lop,* "course"), which was anglicized as *gantlope* in C17. It involved two rows of soldiers armed with clubs and other weapons, between which the hapless prisoner had to pass. This likely explanation made **gantlet** the preferred spelling in *run the gantlet* in earlier American dictionaries, although both spellings are allowed. Instances of **gauntlet** outnumber those of **gantlet** in CCAE data by about 5:2.

Figurative applications of *run the ga(u)ntlet* ("go through a testing ordeal") overlap somewhat with those of *run the gamut* ("cover the whole range"), as in:

The farmer has had his good crops and his drought. He has run the gamut.

Gamut, like *ga(u)ntlet,* is a rather obscure word. It comes from medieval music, a blend of *gamma,* the Greek "letter C," the lowest note on the musical scale of Guido d'Arezzo, and Latin *ut,* literally "that," but pointing to the upper end of the scale. The ascending scale is conventionally explained by an acrostic hymn to St. John, whose successive lines give the names of the major tones (*re, mi, fa* etc.). *Gamut* meant the whole musical scale, hence its nonmusical sense of an entire range. Covering the *full gamut* of experience would include the most challenging or threatening part, where you *run the ga(u)ntlet.*

gay

Because the standard use of this word has changed dramatically since World War II, it needs careful handling. The older meaning of **gay** ("lighthearted") is still there in the adverb *gaily* and the abstract noun *gaiety,* but the adjective **gay** now usually means "homosexual." In that sense it can be applied to both men and women, and so if one speaks of either a *gay young man* or a *gay woman,* it is potentially a comment on their sexual orientation, whether or not so intended. But when used as a noun, **gay** regularly means "a homosexual male," as in:

Sydney gays and lesbians are preparing for the annual mardi gras.

The abstract noun *gayness* also connotes homosexuality, though it was earlier just a synonym for *gaiety.*

This newish meaning for **gay** seems in fact to have been around before World War II in American prison and underworld slang, as a reference in Ersine's 1935 *Underworld and Prison Slang* shows us. British evidence from C19 shows that **gay** (as an adjective) had a slang role meaning "licentious or living by prostitution." To say that a woman was "living a gay

life" was to imply that she was "no better than she ought to be."

Gay is not the only English word to develop alternative meanings in the course of time. In this case, the older and newer do not sit comfortably side by side. When the older sense ("lighthearted") is required, either that word or one of its near-synonyms in "elated," "cheerful," "merry" or "in high spirits" is more reliable nowadays, and avoids any possible double entendre.

gelatin or gelatine

For general purposes, **gelatin** is the standard spelling in the US, whereas **gelatine** is preferred in the UK, by almost 3:1 in data from the BNC. Note however the chemists' distinction between *-ine* and *-in* for the naming of chemicals. See further under **-ine/-in.**

gender

Some style guides insist that **gender** is a grammatical term, not to be used in discussing the roles of men and women in ordinary life. Dictionaries often reinforce this view, by labeling the use of **gender** to mean "sex" as colloquial, jocular or "loose." In fact, **gender** is used in serious writing in two ways: as a synonym for *sex* (i.e. physical–sexual identity); and in contrast to it (as one's socially or culturally constructed identity). The first rather than the second sense would seem to be the focus of compounds such as:

gender-bias   gender-marked   gender-neutral
gender-specific

(See further under **sex or gender.**)

1 Grammatical gender. When codifying language, traditional grammarians used the notion of **gender** to classify nouns into groups. Where there are two types, the categories are labeled "masculine" and "feminine"; and where there are three: "masculine," "feminine" and "neuter" (= neither masculine nor feminine). The classification has little to do with male or female. Words for inanimate things may be classed as "masculine" or "feminine," and what is masculine in one language may be feminine in the next: a cloud is masculine in French (*le nuage*) and feminine in German (*die Wolke*). "Masculine," "feminine" and "neuter" are just convenient labels for classes of nouns which take different forms of the definite article and of adjectives. In modern English there are no such classes of nouns. All nouns take the same definite article *the,* and the same forms of adjectives.

2 Natural gender. English grammar makes us conscious of **gender** in the third person singular pronouns, with *he, she, him, her, his, hers.* But here it's a matter of *natural* not *grammatical gender,* since the pronouns are applied according to the sex of the person being referred to. So *she* is used after a reference to "mother," and *he* to a "father." In a language with full-blown *grammatical gender,* the pronoun for "she" would also be used after any "feminine" noun, and the one for "he" after "masculine" nouns.

Because the English pronouns are so firmly associated with *natural gender,* the traditional use of masculine forms to express generic human identity is now felt to be unfortunate and ambiguous, if not sexist. (See further under **he and/or she.**) Ideally

English would have a *common gender* singular pronoun, one which could refer to either a male or female without identifying their sex. The pronoun *it* has only limited uses in references to animals and perhaps babies in scientific or impersonal contexts. This explains why *they,* the *common gender* plural pronoun, is increasingly being used in singular references (see further under **they**).

The quest for expressions which are *common* in gender or *gender-free* has also put the spotlight on the so-called *epicene* words of English, e.g. *athlete, patient, writer.* See further under **epicene**.

genealogy

The first component of this word is Greek *genea* ("race"), hence the spelling of the middle syllable. Not surprisingly, it's sometimes mistakenly spelled "geneology," on the analogy of others based on *-ology.* See further under that heading.

generalizations

See under **induction**.

genitive

In English grammar the **genitive** case is often called the "possessive," and in simple examples such as *the president's house,* the noun marked as **genitive** (by the apostrophe *s*) may be said to own the following noun. But the English **genitive** actually covers a number of relationships other than ownership, witness:

> *a lawyer's answer*   *the dog's footprints*
> *Thursday's program*   *Japan's building industry*
> *Anne's friend*

The examples show the **genitive** used to express a variety of more abstract relationships, including inalienable possession, attribution and association, as well as location in time and space. It often provides a neat expression for a wordier paraphrase. Compare the following paraphrases with their **genitive** equivalents above:

> *the answer characteristic of a lawyer*
> *the footprints left by the dog*
> *the program set for Thursday*
> *the building industry in Japan*
> *a friend of Anne*

(For expressions like *a friend of Anne's,* see **double genitive**.) *Genitive phrases* headed by a verbal noun are potentially ambiguous. *John's appointment* could refer to the person whom John appointed, or to the fact that John himself was appointed. The first meaning with active use of the verb is sometimes called the *subjective genitive,* and the second where the verb is passive, the *objective genitive.* The same expression could also mean "an appointment made for John (at the dentist etc.)." The context should clarify which of the three meanings is meant.

The genitive and the apostrophe

* With plural nouns, the **genitive** is usually shown by the apostrophe alone, as in the *grammarians' term.*
* With proper names and words ending in *s,* both apostrophe *s* and the apostrophe alone have traditionally been used (see **apostrophes** section 3).
* The use of the apostrophe *s* in expressions like *at the hairdresser's* is debatable (see **local genitive**).

Note finally that English possessive pronouns do not take apostrophes, in either **genitive** (or absolute)

forms:

> *my (mine)   your (yours)   his   her (hers)   its*
> *our (ours)   their (theirs)*

For the history of *its,* see further under **its or it's**.

genius

Like many Latin loanwords, **genius** has both Latin and English plural forms (see **-us** section 1), but they are applied to different meanings of the word. The English plural **geniuses** is used with the common human meaning of the word: "an unusually gifted and brilliant person." The Latin plural **genii** is only used in reference to mythical spirits, as in the *genii of the forest.*

genome or genom

This word goes back to the 1930s, though it hardly made headlines before the start of C21. Its original form in German was *Genom* (a blend of *gene* and the last syllable of *Chromosom*), but in current English data, both American and British, the standard spelling is **genome**. Thus English writers prefer to connect it with their own word *chromosome.*

genre

As its French pronunciation suggests, **genre** is a relative newcomer to English. In fact it shares a common origin with *gender:* both derive from Old French *gendre,* meaning essentially "type," though *gender* has acquired new social senses during centuries of use in English (see further under **gender**). **Genre** so far has almost always been associated with types of artistic creation – with works of literature and art in late C18, and music as well as film and photography in C20. In the visual arts, *genre painting* has acquired the specific meaning of "art which depicts scenes of everyday life."

In reference to writing, the term **genre** is variously used. At the highest level, it identifies the archetypal forms of composition, such as poetry, drama and novel. But it's also used to broadly identify the purpose of a work, i.e. as comedy or tragedy, and its substance: fiction or nonfiction. Within any of these categories, **genre** can identify subgroups, such as biography, essays, letters and journalism within nonfiction; and within, say, journalism the subgroups of news articles, editorials and reviews. At these lower levels, individual **genres** still differ in form, purpose and style.

genteelism

As used by Fowler (1926) and others, the **genteelism** is a select expression which substitutes for common everyday vocabulary. So *obtain* is a **genteelism** for *get,* and *purchase* for *buy.* **Genteelisms** are typically longer words of French or Latin origin, and associated with more formal styles of communication. They are gentle euphemisms – not intended to disguise, but to lend a touch of class to a plain reference.

No-one would challenge a **genteelism** which is used in deference to the feelings of others. But when they become the staple of bureaucratic and institutional prose, it's time to rise in ungenteel revolution and campaign against them. See further under **gobbledygook** and **plain English**.

genuflection or genuflexion

Despite academic uses adding to the purely religious, this is a rare word, and its spelling very much a matter of choice. Compare

a certain genuflexion to egalitarian slogans
nervous genuflection to overpraised French
theorists

Webster's Third (1986) and the *Oxford Dictionary* (1989) acknowledge both spellings, though **genuflection** is given priority in the first, and **genuflexion** in the second. They emerge in almost equal numbers from data in the BNC, whereas only **genuflection** appears in CCAE. If **genuflexion** seems slightly older-fashioned, it blends with the sense of tradition required in some contexts. See further under **-ction/-xion**.

genus

This scientific word presents both English and Latin plurals: **genuses** and **genera** respectively. Respondents to the Langscape survey in 1998–2001 showed a slight preference for the English plural. See under **-us** section 3.

geographic or geographical

The shorter form **geographic** occurs more than twice as often as **geographical** in American English, by the evidence of CCAE. **Geographic** is foregrounded in the title of the magazine *National Geographic,* and the *National Geographic Society,* but its use is instantiated in many ordinary collocations. In British English the position is reversed, with **geographical** outnumbering **geographic** by about 5:1, in data from the BNC. Still either may occur in the same collocation: *geographic boundaries / geographical boundaries, geographic location / geographical location,* and the choice may be arbitrary, personal or stylistic, based on the rhythm of the sentence. See further under **-ic/-ical**.

geographical names

The writing of **geographical names** raises several kinds of issues:

* how to capitalize them
* how to abbreviate them
* the choice of anglicized or local forms of foreign placenames
* variable personal names in placenames

The variable use of apostrophes in placenames is discussed under **apostrophes** section 2. For the use of *the* in names such as *The Hague,* see **the** section 4.

1 Capitalizing geographical names. Capital letters are used on all the nouns and adjectives that make up a proper **geographical name**:

Amazon River	*Bay of Biscay*
Bering Strait	*Canary Islands*
Cape of Good Hope	*Cradle Mountain*
Gobi Desert	*Great Dividing Range*
Lake Titicaca	*Mount Cook*

Geographical names like these usually consist of a specific word or words, and a generic word (*Bering* is specific and *Strait* generic). In English the order of the components is mostly fixed by convention – except that references to rivers are quite variable. In North America, *River* is typically the second element (*Colorado River, St. Lawrence River*) whereas in Britain and Europe it can be the first (*River Thames,*

River Rhine). Though the capital letter might seem to make *River* an official part of the name, atlas gazetteers and geographical dictionaries (*Cambridge World Gazetteer,* 1990, *Merriam-Webster's Geographical Dictionary,* 1997) simply list rivers under their specific element, with no suggestion that there is an official order or form. It therefore becomes an editorial matter: the *Chicago Manual* (2003) and the *Oxford Guide to Style* (2002) both recommend capitalizing *River* when it comes after the specific element, and keeping it in lower case when in front: *the river Thames/Rhine.* These practices can be applied equally to English river names and anglicizations of foreign names.

When the geographical reference is a descriptive phrase, not a regular name, the generic element is left without a capital:

the Canberra lake   the Nevada desert

Note also that the generic component has no capital letter when it appears as an abbreviated, second reference, or when it is pluralized in a phrase which puts two or more **geographical names** together: *Amazon and Orinoco rivers.* (See further under **capital letters** section 1e.)

2 Abbreviating geographical names. There are standard abbreviations for the generic parts of **geographical names,** to be used when space is at a premium (for instance on maps), but not normally in running text:

C.	*cape*	*Pen.*	*peninsula*
G.	*gulf*	*Pt.*	*point*
I. or Is.	*island*	*R.*	*river*
L.	*lake*	*Ra.*	*range*
Mt.	*mount(ain)*	*Str.*	*strait*

American style is to put a stop on all of them, as shown; but it would be omitted from some or all of them in British or Australian style (see **abbreviations** section 2).

There are standard abbreviations for whole **geographical names,** such as:

HK   NZ   UK   USA

Within particular continents, abbreviations are available for individual states or countries, for use in lists and tabular material, or for car registration plates and distribution of mail. Two-letter abbreviations for all 50 American states (and the District of Columbia) are listed in the *Chicago Manual,* again written without periods / full stops. In Europe such abbreviations are mostly a single letter, as in *F* for *France, D* for *Germany* etc. Those for Canada are set out in *Canadian English Usage* (1997), and for Australia in the government *Style Manual* (2002).

◊ For the abbreviation of compass points, see **abbreviations** section 1.

3 Foreign placenames – in anglicized or local forms? This is a vexed question in a post-colonial world, when foreign names are no longer preserved in their imperial form. Even in Europe, English-speakers are sometimes surprised to find that "Munich" is *München,* and that "Athens" is *Athinai* to those who live there. Beyond Europe the discrepancies are even more marked, with "Cairo" expressed as *Al Qahirah* and "Canton" as *Guangzhou.* Such differences remind us that **geographical names** are artefacts of different cultures, and those used conventionally in English are a product of history, not always in touch with recent developments in other parts of the world.

Political developments sometimes force us to accept changes in placenames, as when "St Petersburg" became *Leningrad* under the Russian communist regime, and when "Northern and Southern Rhodesia" marked their independence with the names *Zambia* and *Zimbabwe*. In other cases there's a diplomatic imperative to accept a different form of an old name. *Beijing* and *Sri Lanka* are simply local forms of the names we had as "Peking" and "Ceylon," which recommend themselves for reasons of up-to-dateness, as well as the need to shed the trappings of the colonial era. Yet when using the new names in writing, we may need to remind readers of the older form in parentheses, alongside the new one, at least on first mention. The change of the "Gilbert Islands" into the *Kiribati* is not self-explanatory (unless you are a phonetician), and many such changes are strategic, e.g. "Burma" to *Myanmar*. The ultimate reference on all national nomenclature is the United Nations. Newer and older forms of placenames, in English and other languages, are presented in the *Getty Thesaurus of Geographical Names,* at www.getty.edu.

4 Placenames with variable personal names embedded in them. The variable spellings of personal names e.g. *Mackenzie/McKenzie, Philip/Phillip, Stuart/Stewart,* are another detail to reckon with in placenames (see further under **town names**). Further references are the geographical dictionaries and gazetteers mentioned above in section 1, and, beyond them, regional authorities such as the US Board on Geographical Names, Canadian Permanent Committee on Geographical Names, Australian Geographical Names Board.

geological eras
The origins of our planet go back well over 4000 million years, with the evolution of plant and animal life from about 2500 million years ago. The history of human evolution occupies only a tiny fraction of the last 1 million years. For the standard names used in geology and paleontology for the major phases of earth's evolution, see Appendix II.

geometric or geometrical
The shorter form **geometric** is commoner than **geometrical** nowadays, but the difference is much more marked in American than British English. **Geometrical** is still found in more abstract references to complex shapes and designs, in data from CCAE and the BNC, witness:
> *that glowing geometrical L.A. skyline*
> *severely geometrical stage placings*

Geometric meanwhile goes with small physical objects whose function or appearance embodies simple geometry, as in *geometric lock* or *geometric quarry tiles*. These material applications of the word make **geometric** more frequent than **geometrical** by a factor of about 3:1 in BNC data, and about 10:1 in CCAE – where it serves also in more abstract uses. In pure mathematics and science the world over, **geometric** prevails, as in *geometric progression/series*. See further under **-ic/-ical**.

german or germane
These words both refer to relationships: **german** to those of kin, as in *cousin german*, and *germane* to

more abstract logical relationships, as in:
> *His answer was not germane to the question.*

In older usage **germane** could be used in *cousin germane* as well, but this is now archaic. For more about *cousin german*, see under **cousins**.

Note that a link between **german(e)** and *German(y)* is unlikely. Most scholars believe that the name *Germany* is Celtic in origin, whereas **german(e)** derives from a Latin adjective meaning "having common roots."

Germany
After World War II **Germany** was divided into two:
* *Federal Republic of Germany* (BRD) = *West Germany* (*Bundesrepublik Deutschlands*)
* *German Democratic Republic* (DDR) = *East Germany* (*Deutsche Demokratische Republik*)

The first was a member of NATO and the EEC, while the second was a member of the Warsaw Pact and Comecon. This division of Germany put Berlin into East Germany. It too was divided into a Western and an Eastern sector, and, to mark the boundary between them, the Berlin Wall was erected in 1961. The breaching of the Berlin Wall in November 1989 marked the beginning of a new era, and strong pressures for reunification. The two halves were officially reunited in 1990, as the *BRD/FRG* (Federal Republic of Germany).

gerrymander or jerrymander
This word is a blend of *Gerry* (surname of a C19 US senator whose electorate opportunely changed shape in successive elections) and *salamander* (an amphibian whose body shape changes as it matures from the aquatic to the terrestrial stage). In North America, the word is always **gerrymander**, whereas in Britain it's sometimes spelled **jerrymander**, as if it owed something to "Jerry," a derogatory British term for a German.

gerund and gerundive
Both these terms come from Latin grammar. In Latin the **gerund** was a verbal noun, and the **gerundive** an adjective future passive participle which carried a sense of obligation or necessity. The English word *agenda* is a Latin **gerundive**, meaning literally "[things which] should be done."

English grammar has nothing quite like the Latin **gerundive**. Words formed from verbs with *-able* (e.g. *likable*) are as close as we come: they are passive, but do not carry the sense of obligation. There are however equivalents to the **gerund**, in verbal nouns which end in *-ing*, as in:
> *Singing is my recreation.*

Gerunds in English lead double lives, in that they can behave like nouns or verbs (or both). As nouns, they can be qualified by determiners, adjectives etc., and/or followed by dependent phrases.
> *My operatic singing alarmed the dogs next door.*
> *The singing of grand opera caused a violent reaction.*

English **gerunds** also have the capacity of verbs to take objects or subjects, adverbs and adverbial phrases:
> *Singing grand opera was the problem, or rather, the dogs reacting violently to it.*

Does the gerund require a possessive? The last example – *the dogs reacting to it* – exemplifies a construction which has long been a bone of contention in English. Some insist that it should be made possessive: *the dogs' reacting to it;* and Fowler (1926) argued long and hard that without the possessive marker the construction (which he called the "fused participle") was "grammatically indefensible." As with many such issues, it goes back to C18, when the form with the possessive was attacked and defended. According to Webster (in his *Dissertations on the English Language,* 1789) the possessive alone was "the genuine English idiom." But *Webster's English Usage* (1989) shows that the construction without the possessive has been used for centuries. Database evidence shows that both constructions are current in American, British and Australian English (Collins and Peters, 2003), as they are in Canada (*Canadian English Usage,* 1997). The *Comprehensive Grammar* (1985) provides analyses of both constructions to demonstrate their grammaticality.

In fact the two constructions express slightly different meanings. Compare:

> *The dogs reacted to me singing.*
> *The dogs reacted to my singing.*

The first sentence focuses on the verbal fact that I sang, whereas the second seems to imply that it was my way of singing which caused a reaction (making it a noun). Yet those differences intersect with matters of style. The choice of the possessive *my* makes the sentence rather formal, while the use of the object pronoun *me* is acceptable in most everyday kinds of writing. However *my* or other possessive pronouns still seem to be needed when the **gerund** is the subject of the sentence, as in *My singing alarmed the dogs.* The use of *me* there sounds ungrammatical. But when the **gerund** is the object, either construction can be used. The *Longman Grammar* (1999) notes that the second (i.e. verbal) construction is the default.

get, got and gotten

Get is a common and useful verb, especially in informal spoken English. It is an easy synonym for many others, such as *obtain, receive, fetch, buy, take, arrive, become.* Apart from these meanings, it has a number of roles as an auxiliary, both in its present form **get**, and its past **got**, as follows:

1 **Get often works as a substitute for the verb be** in passive constructions:

> *I'm getting married in the morning.*

Compare *I shall be married in the morning,* which is much more formal in style, and ambivalent in its perspective.

Get is also used as a causative verb in:

> *You're getting your suit cleaned for the occasion.*
> *I'm getting her to do it.*

Once again, the alternatives are somewhat formal:

> *You will have your suit cleaned for the occasion.*
> *I have prevailed on her to do it.*

As the examples show, **get** is often used in interactive situations, and is suitable for interactive prose as well as written dialogue. The alternatives are less flexible in style and meaning, and best suited to impersonal and documentary writing.

2 **Got has an auxiliary role in *has got to* or *have got to,*** which substitute for *must* or *ought to* (see **auxiliary verbs** section 3). The *got to* construction is so familiar in speech that the words seem to coalesce, and are sometimes written as *gotta.* This and other grammatical evidence suggests (Krug, 1998) that *gotta* is well on its way to becoming a modal verb – except that its strong associations with casual dialogue tend to keep it out of written discourse. There the construction is normally expressed in its full form.

3 **Got serves as the past tense of get** in all parts of the English-speaking world. It is also the one and only past participle for most in middle and southern Britain, and many in Australia. But for Americans and Canadians, Scots and some others, there are two past participles: **got** and **gotten**, with separate roles: *got is the only one used when obligation or possession (both material and inalienable) are being expressed, as in

> *You've got to come.*
> *I've got a place on the coast.*
> *He hasn't got a chance.*

Diseases whether temporary or more permanent (*got a cold / got high blood pressure*) also combine with **got**, for English-speakers worldwide.

*gotten is commonly found in expressions concerned with changing one's location or state of being, and with achieving or acquiring something:

> *The men had to be gotten out.*
> *The dream had gotten away from me.*
> *The waiting room had gotten twice as crowded.*
> *He had gotten angry.*
> *They had gotten good results by combining the data.*
> *She had gotten a new place on the coast.*

Webster's English Usage (1989) notes a few exceptions, but those represent the dominant patterns of combination. An *Australian Style* survey in 2002 showed that a majority (over 60%) of respondents under 45 would use **gotten** when the verb was intransitive (as in *gotten angry*). The use of **gotten** outside North America seems to be increasing, and it can be heard further south in England than is generally acknowledged. In BNC data, **gotten** appears in over 100 citations, including three quoted in the list above. It no doubt helps to discriminate between those various senses mentioned, and is a useful stylistic alternative in idioms such as *gotten rid of / gotten wind of,* among other examples from the BNC.

Final note: By all the evidence above, **get/got** is a versatile verb; and with its numerous roles it is the staple of daily communication. English databases of printed material show that it occurs much more often in fiction than in nonfiction, though there are examples across all 15 genres of British and American parallel corpora (LOB and Brown). It is rarest in the categories of religious, bureaucratic and academic writing – the genres which can least tolerate informality of style. But it has its place in many English idioms and grammatical constructions, and scarcely needs to be rooted out everywhere like a noxious weed.

gh

This notorious pair of letters represents a bizarre range of sounds in English. At the start of a word, they simply stand for "g," as in *ghost* and *ghastly.* At the end of a word, **gh** never represents "g," and has no sound at all in the following sets:

inveigh   neigh   sleigh   weigh
high   sigh   thigh
bough   plough   sough
dough   furlough   though
through   borough   thorough

In three other sets of words, final **gh** represents "f":

laugh
enough   rough   tough
cough   trough

Note that the word *slough* can be pronounced with "f" or silently, according to its meaning (see under **slay**). Given such bewildering possibilities, it's surprising how few words ending with **gh** have alternative spellings. *Plow* has indeed replaced *plough* in the US and shares the field with it in Canada, but not in the UK or Australia. *Thoro* is still considered informal, as is *thru* (see **through**); and *donut* is only just recognized as a variant of **doughnut**.

The most widely used respelling of **gh** is in *draft*, which has taken over from *draught* in American English, and elsewhere in the world, for some senses of the word (see further under **draft**). Others with small niches are *hi-fi* and *hi-tech* (see under **hi-** and **high-**); as well as *lite* and *nite*: see individual headings.

ghetto

The plural of this C17 Italian loanword was once *ghetti*, but now the choice is between **ghettos** and **ghettoes**. **Ghettos** was preferred by 85% of respondents worldwide to the Langscape survey 1998–2001, and it's given priority in both *Webster's Third* and the *New Oxford* (1998). **Ghettoes** is however relatively more popular in British English than American, appearing in the ratio 2:5 in BNC data, as against 1:10 in CCAE.

Only in C20 has **ghetto** been applied to enclaves inhabited by the rich. Compare its conventional use in:

poverty-ridden ghettos   black ghettoes of LA

with

middle class ghettos   gaijin ghettoes of Roppongi.

As is evident, the plural spellings are indifferent to the two meanings. See further under **-o**.

gibe, gybe or jibe

These spellings are shared by three different words, meaning:

1 "taunt" (noun or verb)
2 "sudden shift in the setting of a fore-and-aft sail from one side to the other" (verb or noun)
3 "accord" (verb), as in *Those numbers don't jibe with what we're seeing.*

The origins of all three are rather obscure. The first may be from French, the second from Dutch, but they have no relatives in English and their spellings were interchanged in earlier centuries. The third appeared from nowhere and made its debut in C19 American English. In a division of labor enshrined in the *Oxford Dictionary* (1989), **gibe** was associated with the word "taunt," **gybe** with the nautical term, and **jibe** was the spelling for the third word.

Usage everywhere now has **jibe** for the first word as well, and it outnumbers **gibe** by more than 3:1 in BNC data. The ratio is more like 5:4 in data from CCAE, where the *easy gibe* complements the *retaliatory jibe*. The stronger American commitment to **gibe** for the word "taunt" may be because of the association of **jibe**

with "accord," as in:

Few accounts jibe with what she observed.
The dollar amounts didn't jibe . . .

In CCAE, **jibe** is used much more often as the verb "accord" than as the noun "taunt." But the American database also shows **jibe** as an alternative spelling for the nautical term (**gybe**), of which there's no sign in the BNC. **Jibe** is thus the most freely used of these spellings, and if it does service for all three words, the contexts always clarify the meaning. In the collocation *jibe at*, **jibe** clearly means "taunt," whereas *jibe with* always means "accord (with)."

In the US, *jibe with* is very occasionally replaced by *jive with*, as in *an aesthetic that may not jive with an American audience*. The word *jive* comes from Black English, and as noun and verb refers to a type of dance music as well as verbal performance art, known as *jive-talk* or *talking jive*. The latter is also a byword for deceptive talk, hence the comment *Don't hand me that jive* and the fictional *caring but don't-jive-me probation officer*. Several strands of its meaning are there in the man who *could jive with dealers in black neighborhoods*. The idea of *jiving with* others suggests accord with them, hence the convergence with **jibe** in the third sense.

gigolo

The plural is **gigolos**, never **gigoli**, because despite appearances it's not Italian but was borrowed from French. Etymologists explain it as a C20 backformation from *gigolette*, the female hired dancing partner. With Continental origins, and only recent use in English, there's no basis for "gigoloes" as its plural. See further under **-o**.

gipsy or gypsy

These are now less equal than they were. See **gypsy**.

given and new

When communicating information we typically advance from the known to the unknown – unless the aim is to surprise or shock. This progress gives the listener or reader a cognitive starting point for whatever is to come. As the discourse proceeds, new information is combined with the old and itself becomes **given**.

The process whereby information passes from **new** to **given** is signaled in various ways in speech and writing. Common to both is the use of pronouns or other substitute words that maintain a reference, as in:

Last week I had a day off. It was the best thing I'd done all year.

The pronoun *it* in the second sentence marks *day off* as now **given**. It effectively backgrounds the item, so that other fresh material can take the stage. Communication would otherwise be choked with cognitively redundant repetition. The move from full to abbreviated references is a similar device to reduce the demands on listener/reader – maintaining the reference while allowing the spotlight to fall on something else:

. . . joined the National Bank. The bank's performance impressed him . . .

While **new**, the *bank* is named in full, but once identified the reference can be cut back to the generic element. Its capital letter is often removed (see **capital letters** section 3), as a further sign of being **given** rather than **new**.

Note that writers can manipulate the presentation of the **new**, to make it appear to be **given**. This is the essence of *begging the question,* in its original sense. See further under **beg the question**.

given name
See under **first name**.

gladiolus
This word has too many syllables for a household word, as Fowler (1926) noted, and the English plural **gladioluses** makes it even longer. This would explain the appeal of the Latin plural **gladioli**, which is just as common in American English and overwhelms the other in British English, by the evidence of CCAE and the BNC. Preference for the Latin plural is of course more common for words ending in *-us* than for other classes of Latin loanwords, as was evident in the 1998–2001 Langscape survey. (See **Latin plurals**, and compare **-us** with **-a**.)

The need to anglicize this classical word has been felt all along. In earlier centuries it was sometimes *gladiole;* and nowadays it sometimes appears as *gladiola*. The latter seems to be a singular, probably derived from the pronunciation of **gladiolus** interpreted as a plural "gladiolas." (For other words formed this way, see under **false plurals**.) *Gladiola* is listed in *Webster's Third* (1986), and its existence is confirmed by a handful of examples in CCAE. The *Canadian Oxford* (1998) also recognizes it (as "informal"), and the Australian *Macquarie Dictionary* (1997) notes it without comment – perhaps because the more iconoclastic form *gladdie* is also current in the antipodes. Though first recorded in Morris's *The Township* (1947), Barry Humphries no doubt deserves the credit for making it known elsewhere. Neither it nor the clipped form *glad* would pass in formal contexts.

glamor or glamour
See under **-or/-our**.

glue
When used as a verb, the inflected forms are *glued* and *gluing*. However the final *e* is retained before other suffixes. See **-e** section h.

glycerin or glycerine
Both spellings are current in American English, by the evidence of CCAE, whereas **glycerine** is the usual spelling in Britain, Australia and Canada. Neither spelling is used by the professional chemist, for whom it's **glycerol**.

GMT
This stands for *Greenwich Mean Time,* the reference point for the world's coordinated time system (see **time zones**). But in international standards, **GMT** has been replaced by *UTC:* see under that heading.

go
This very common verb in English has as its prime function to express motion away from the speaker (cf. *come*), or to express continuous activity. Examples of each are:
> *Go away.   They've gone to the races.*

and
> *The clock is still going.   If all goes well...*
One part of the verb **go** (*going*) also serves with *to* as a way of expressing future intention:
> *We're going to paint the town red.*
(See further under **future**.) This very common structure makes *(be) going to* a kind of auxiliary or modal verb (see **auxiliary verbs** section 3). A sign that its auxiliary function is well developed is the fact that it can combine with **go** itself as the main verb:
> *They're going to go to the races.*
Another sign that *(be) going to* must be counted among the quasi-modals is its assimilated pronunciation in casual speech – rendered by *gonna,* though it could only appear in scripted dialogue.

Go has a place in other English idioms, notably *go and,* which also hovers on the fringe of being an auxiliary, as a way of expressing inchoative action (see under **inchoate**):
> *Caroline wanted you to go and meet people.*
> *I decided to go and see one of the Bond films.*
Go and is at home in informal narrative and scripted dialogue, judging by its distribution in the BNC. In American conversational data from the *Longman Grammar* (1999) corpus, the *and* is frequently dropped, creating combinations like *go see, go get, go look, go do*. In its natural contexts *go and* needs no adapting to "go to," which makes it too purposeful. *Go and* can be turned into the past, as in *went and saw it* (compare *try and,* which is quite fixed). In the present perfect, it can sound rather deprecating, as in *Now you've gone and done it.*

The past tense of **go** (formed with *went*) is eccentric. It seems to have become standard in C15, when the regular *gode* (pronounced with one syllable) was perhaps too much like *God*. Its place was filled by *went,* annexed from the verb *wend,* which then revived an earlier regular past *wended* for its own purposes.

gobbledygook or gobbledegook
While **gobbledygook** is the standard spelling in the US, in the UK it shares the field with **gobbledegook**. American data from CCAE has **gobbledygook** in almost all instances of the word, whereas in the BNC it comes second to **gobbledegook** in the ratio of just on 2:3. British usage may be changing, as reflected in the *Oxford Dictionary's* (1989) preference for **gobbledygook**, whereas *New Oxford* (1998) goes for **gobbledegook**.

Neither spelling can be tied to the word's origins, which are obscure. It may be imitative of the turkey's gobble, or simply a nonsense word for wordy nonsense. It associates with pompous officials and professionals who seem less interested in communicating than in overwhelming their readers with long words. Whether their aim is to impress or cover their tracks, what they offer the reader is verbal fog:
> *The departmental reaction to the municipal government submission on recreational facilities was instrumental in discouraging philanthropic contributions towards them.*
Decoded, this means (more or less):
> *The department was so unhelpful about the council's proposal for a park that people who might have given money towards it have been put off.*

You can just see it happening! Concerted action against **gobbledygook** has been channeled into Plain English campaigns in North America, Britain and Australia. See further under **Plain English**.

God

The capital letter given to **God** is matched in some ecclesiastical traditions by capitalizing the attendant pronouns *He, Him, His* as well as *Thou, Thee, Thine; Me, Mine.* This has been the limit – not normally extended to the relative pronouns *whom, whose.* Both the *Chicago Manual* (2003) and the *Oxford Guide to Style* (2002) recommend against capitalizing any of the pronouns, in keeping with the norms of the Bible and the *Book of Common Prayer.*

goiter or goitre

See under -re/-er.

Gondwanaland

This is the name of the hypothetical supercontinent to which the continents of the southern hemisphere once belonged (Australia, Antarctica and parts of South America and Africa) as well as Arabia and peninsular India. According to the Wegener theory of continental drift, **Gondwanaland** was a single unit from Cambrian times (more than 500 million years ago) until its breakup somewhere between the start of the Permian period and the end of the Cretaceous, probably between 200 and 100 million years ago. (See Appendix II.) The breakup resulted in the formation of three new oceans: the Indian, South Atlantic and Antarctic oceans, and a substantially reduced Pacific Ocean. The evidence for this theory comes from parallel forms of animal and plant life in those now separate continents.

Gondwanaland owes its name to the Gondwana district in southern India, and was coined in the 1880s.
◊ Compare **Laurasia**.

gonorrhoea or gonorrhea

These alternative spellings reflect the regular British–American divergence on using the *oe* digraph. See **oe/-e**.

good and well

Good is first and foremost an adjective, and **well** an adverb. Yet there are idioms in which **good** seems to serve as an adverb too, such as:

It seems good.   *It sounds good.*
You're looking good.

Grammarians might indeed debate the analysis of any of those clauses. Are they instances of subject/verb/adverb or subject/verb/complement, in which an adjective could well appear? (See further under **predicate**.) The question turns on the nature of the verb in those utterances, and the role of copulars, now recognized in the major grammars (see under **copular verbs**). Grammar apart, there's no doubt that they are idiomatic and standard English.

The appearance of **good** and **well** in compound adjectives raises other questions whenever they are compared. Should it be:

more good-looking   *most good-looking*
or
better looking   *best looking*
more well-loved   *most well-loved*

or
better loved   *best loved*
See further under **well** and **well-**.

good day, good morning, good afternoon, good evening and good night

These five greetings are unalike in their applications and tone. Only the second, third and fourth are used both to open and close a conversation, and both stand on the friendly side of formal. **Good day** is nowadays a distinctly formal utterance, mostly used as the final word and to show one's determination to close a daytime conversation. **Good night** also puts the final seal on an (evening) conversation, but can be friendly or formal, depending on the degree of acquaintance.

The boundary between **good morning** and **good afternoon** is set at noon for those who work close to the clock (such as radio announcers), but is otherwise more loosely related to the before-lunch and after-lunch segments of the day. The boundary between **good afternoon** and **good evening** is even more fluid, and is set either by the end of the working day, or the evening meal. All three may serve to open or close a conversation; but their overtones when used at the end are rather detached and businesslike, making them unsuitable for most social situations.

goodbye, good-bye or goodby

Goodbye is the standard spelling everywhere for the word by which we take our leave. In British English the hyphenated form **good-bye** is definitely out of favor, appearing in the ratio of 1:14 in the BNC. **Goodby** is likewise only a minor variant in American English, according to the evidence of CCAE. For more about the formulas used when leaving, see **adieu** and **good day**.

goodwill or good will

All writers use **goodwill** when the word is an adjective, as in *goodwill mission,* and modern dictionaries all propose this form for the noun too, as in the *goodwill between author and publisher.* In older British usage **good will** (spaced) was used for all senses of the noun, or (according to Fowler, 1926) to distinguish the sense of "benevolence" (**good will**) from the "body of customer support built up by a business" (**goodwill**). But the particular sense is usually clear in context; and if not, it's unfortunate to assume that the word's setting will mark the difference, when the settings of compound nouns are so variable. See **hyphens** section 2d.

gossiped or gossipped

See under -p/-pp-.

got, gotten, got to and gotta

See under **get**.

gourmandise, gourmandize or gormandize

The tangle between *gourmand* and *gourmet* pales into insignificance beside these alternatives. Apart from the spelling variation, they represent a noun as well as a verb. The story begins in C15 with **gormandize** as an abstract noun which could mean either "epicurean taste" or "gluttony," and was matched by an identical C16 verb meaning "eat gluttonously." The verb (pronounced to rhyme with "size") could also be spelled **gourmandize**. In C19 **gourmandise** (rhyming with "cheese") was (re)borrowed from French for the epicurean noun, along with *gourmet* for the epicure himself/herself. Derivatives such as *gourmandism* and *gourmanderie* added to the set of abstract nouns in which *gourmand*~ implied good taste – but contrasted strongly with the negative sense of the verb. Since then, attempts have been made to separate *gourmet* and *gourmand* (see next entry), with declining success, and none of the abstract nouns has a secure place in current English. The rare examples (of *gourmandise*) in American and British databases occur in business names.

gourmet or gourmand

The traditional distinction between these – making **gourmet** a term of approval for the connoisseur of fine food, and **gourmand** a negative judgement against someone thought to be a glutton – is increasingly elusive. At bottom both **gourmet** and **gourmand** share a preoccupation with food, and the indeterminacy of some references, e.g. *soirées peppered with gourmand bishops,* leaves some doubt as to which kind of food-lover is intended. Confusion between the two words seems to manifest itself in BNC examples such as the *Relais Gourmand Red Shield [award] for an exceptional restaurant* – unless the backlash against *cuisine minceur* makes it a virtue to provide enormous meals. Erratic use of **gourmand** (e.g. *oysters gourmande*) goes with its increasing rarity in British and American English. In data from the BNC, it's outnumbered by **gourmet** in the ratio of 1:25, and the gap is more like 1:50 in CCAE.

Gourmet is enjoying increased use as a modifier, in examples such as *gourmet food, gourmet dinner, gourmet weekend.* This new grammatical role is perhaps confounding the traditional contrast between the two words, predisposing some writers to use **gourmet** for the adjective and **gourmand** for the equivalent noun. Yet there are many more examples in BNC and CCAE to show **gourmet** in its traditional role as noun: *the wine-conscious gourmet, the cuisine was a gourmet's delight* – though whether it always carries the traditional sense of culinary discrimination is impossible to know. Writers who wish to target that meaning with the noun would be well advised to employ a synonym such as "epicure."

government

Americans usually construe **government** in the singular, whereas the British allow it to take either a singular or plural verb, depending on whether they are concerned with it as a single institution or the individuals within it:

> *The government is planning lavish festivities.*
> *The government are confident that this defence plan will produce . . .*

Grammatically speaking the first represents *formal agreement* and the second *notional agreement* (see further under **agreement**). British use of plural agreement with **government** has been found particularly in reference to the UK administration, whereas singular agreement is applied to foreign administrations (Bauer, 1994).

Pronouns following **government** also vary – either *it/its* or *they/them/their.* Plural pronouns are in fact quite likely to be used, whatever the verb agreement,

in American and British English. This likelihood is enhanced with greater distance between the pronoun and its antecedent, and especially if it extends across a sentence boundary (see Levin, 1998a,b). The pronoun/antecedent relationship is of course not so much one of *agreement* as *reference* (see further under **agreement** and **cohesion**).

On the question of when to capitalize **government**, see **capital letters** section 3.

Governor General and governor-general

This is the title of the Queen's representative, in Canada and Australia. The two forms highlight small differences in usage between them. In Canada the capitalized, spaced form seems to be used officially and more generally, of past and present incumbents. The hyphenated Australian form would be capitalized in references to the present incumbent, but not usually otherwise. Whether capitalized or hyphenated, the plural is officially **Governors General/governors-general**, because the second part of the word is an adjective, strictly speaking. However many would interpret it as a noun, hence the naturalness of **governor-generals** (at least in Australia) which enjoys widespread use, and is recognized in the major Australian and American dictionaries.

In the similar case of *major general,* the plural is always *major generals,* whereas for *attorney-general,* the dictionaries recognize both *attorneys-general* and *attorney-generals,* in that order. (See further under **plurals** section 2.)

goy

This Hebrew word meaning "gentile" is used within Jewish communities to refer to a non-Jew. It has disparaging overtones, as noted in *Merriam-Webster* (2000), *New Oxford* (1998) and the Australian *Macquarie Dictionary* (1997). The *Canadian Oxford* (1998) simply dubs it "slang." In English it's pluralized either in the Hebrew fashion **goyim**, or as **goys**. For other loanwords like it, see **-im**.

graceful or gracious

A different kind of *grace* is acknowledged in these two words. In **graceful** it is an aesthetic grace of form, movement or verbal expression, as in *graceful proportions, a graceful leap* and *a graceful remark.* In **gracious** it's the grace of sympathetic and respectful human interaction, as in:

> *I must decline your gracious offer.*

A *graceful compliment* could therefore be *graciously received,* without any sense of tautology.

Gracious also appears in a handful of fixed collocations, notably *your gracious majesty,* but also as a traditional courtesy for those at somewhat lower levels in society: *your gracious self.* These conventionalized uses seem to hang around the relatively recent phrase *gracious living* (recorded first in the 1930s), where the use of **gracious** rather than **graceful** imbues it a certain irony. It has social pretensions, though it can only connote a lifestyle which has a certain aesthetic charm.

gradable adjective

See **adjectives** section 2 and **absolute** section 1.

graffiti

This indispensable loanword from Italian is strictly speaking a plural, though it couples with either singular or plural verbs in English:

> *Graffiti from floor to ceiling intimidates the visitor.*
>
> *"Russians go home" say the graffiti.*

When linked with a singular verb as in the first example, **graffiti** takes on a collective sense and works like a mass noun. With a plural verb it remains a count noun, as it is in Italian (see further under **count nouns**). The Italian singular form **graffito** is sometimes used in English, to refer to an individual scribble or message in a mass of **graffiti**.

grammar

The deeper secrets of any language lie in its **grammar**, in the underlying rules and conventions by which words combine with each other. This is especially true of English, where word relationships are only occasionally marked in the forms of the words themselves. Many words can work as nouns, verbs or adjectives without showing it in their outward form:

> *in the clear* (noun)
>
> *clear the table* (verb)
>
> *on a clear day* (adjective)

The *grammar of the word,* as well as its particular meaning, only emerges in the phrase or clause in which it is used.

In other European languages, such as German, French, Italian, Latin, the **grammar** is much more on the surface of words, hence all the different forms we have to learn for them. Grammarians would note that for those languages, the morphology of words (i.e. their form and their inflections) is vital to understanding the **grammar**; whereas in English it is the syntax (i.e. the order in which words are combined) which is more important.

1 Regional differences in grammar. In terms of grammatical systems, there are no differences between American and British English. Yet they diverge in many small ways, in the applications of grammatical conventions to particular words and constructions (Algeo, 1988), as documented in individual entries in this book. Divergent applications include the British use of inflected modifiers in compounds and noun phrases such as *cookery book, sailing boat, appointments book, departures lounge, ten-years-old boy, 25–44-aged group* – where Americans would use the base form of noun or verb (see **inflectional extras**). Different levels of usage are noteworthy in widespread American use of the mandative subjunctive, where the British tend to use modalized paraphrases with *should* (see **subjunctive** section 1). In details of morphology and spelling, American English often prefers the more regular and streamlined conventions (in verb forms such as *spelled* [see **-ed**]); and in using English rather than foreign plurals, where British English tends to conserve exotic variants alongside anglicized alternatives: see for example **-um**.

2 "Bad grammar." In one sense, every native speaker of a language knows its **grammar**, learning it intuitively as part of the language acquisition process. Still accusations of "bad grammar" may be flung at native speakers who use nonstandard morphology,

as in:

> *I kep it in the house.*
>
> *Youse had all better be quiet.*

Variant forms like *kep* and *youse* often have a long history of spoken use, but are not accepted as part of the standard written language. "Bad grammar" is also sometimes invoked to censure alternative collocations, such as *different than* (by those who were brought up on *different from*). An unwillingness to recognize variation in the **grammar** of English has resulted in a number of fetishes and shibboleths which are still used to identify "correct" and "incorrect" **grammar**. English **grammar** is nevertheless somewhat flexible from one context to another, and has certainly changed in its details over the course of time. In principle it embraces more than the current conventions of written language.

◊ See further under **clauses**, **parts of speech**, **phrases**, **sentences**, and **syntax**.

gramophone or phonograph

See **phonograph**.

grand prix

How do you make its plural? When the original *Grand Prix de Paris* was set up for three-year-olds at Longchamps racecourse in 1863, it was the one and only. But by 1908 there was a "grand prix" for motor racing, and after that, for the best product at an exhibition . . . etc., etc. To refer to more than one **grand prix**, the French use **grands prix**, and English writers may as well, for lack of a reasonable alternative. Though there are English-style plurals, e.g. **grand prixs** and **grand prixes**, neither is very satisfactory since *prixs* is unpronounceable, and *prixes* adds a foreign syllable to what is still very much a French word. Those reluctant to use the French plural **grands prix** could resort to "big prizes" – an exact translation of the French, but one which loses a lot.

granny or grannie

The standard spelling in both British and American English is **granny**, as one might expect of a well-established family term. See further under **-ie/-y**.

granter or grantor

See under **-er/-or**.

grapheme

A **grapheme** is a unit of a writing system. In English it can be a single letter, like any of those in "cat"; but we also recognize **graphemes** consisting of more than one letter, such as the *th* in "catharsis," and the *tch* in "catch." In languages such as French, the repertoire of **graphemes** is extended by means of accents. Thus *é, è, ê* and *e* are different **graphemes**. Note that **graphemes** are identified by means of chevrons, e.g. <t>, <th>, <tch>.

grave accent

This accent has a number of uses depending on which language it's deployed in. In Italian it marks a stressed final vowel, while in Vietnamese it shows a falling tone. In French it has several functions:

* to mark an open variety of *e*, as in *père*
* to show when a final syllable is stressed as in *déjà*

* to distinguish between homonyms, such as *la* and
là

The **grave accent** tends to disappear quickly from
French loanwords in English, because it's less
important than the *acute accent* in identifying a word's
pronunciation. (See further under **acute accent**.)

The **grave accent** is occasionally used in printing
English poetry, to show when a syllable is to be
pronounced separately, e.g. *time's wingèd chariot*. It
helps readers to recognize poetic meters that depend
on a strict pattern of syllables.

graveled or gravelled
Speaking of road surfaces, Americans generally
prefer **graveled**, where Britons use **gravelled**. (See
further under -l-/-ll-.) Americans also use *gravel* to
mean "irritate," as in *the association with Paramount
has graveled Fox*. This idiom has yet to be seen spelled
with two *ll*s.

gray or grey
See **grey**.

Great Britain
See under **Britain**.

Greek or Grecian
Both as adjectives and as nouns, these have different
meanings. **Grecian**, dating from the English
Renaissance, relates to the ancient culture of Greece,
its art and literature. A **Grecian** is a scholar of
Grecian antiquities. **Greek** is the older word, dating
from C14 and capable of referring to any aspect of
Greece, ancient or modern. A **Greek** is any person of
Greek nationality, from Aristotle to Onassis.

Whether ancient or modern, the language of Greece
is always called **Greek**. *Classical Greek* was the
language of Athens: "Attic Greek." In C20 two varieties
of the language jostled for recognition as the standard:
katharevusa (the "high" variety, with spellings that
link it with the classical language) and *demotike* (the
popular variety, written much more as it is spoken).
Katharevusa was promoted for a while after the
Colonels' coup in 1967, but its role has since
diminished with the use of *demotike* in education, and
for most communicative purposes.

Greek plurals
Some Greek loanwords into English have brought
with them their Greek plurals, e.g. *criterion* whose
regular plural is *criteria*, and *schema,* which has both
a Greek plural *schemata* and an English one *schemas*.
A third group of Greek loanwords with Greek plurals
is little known – except to scholars: *topos* (plural
topoi), though this pattern of plurals is fossilized in
hoi polloi ("the many"), where both article and
adjective show the Greek plural ending.
◊ For words like *criterion*, see further under **-on**; for
those like *schema* see under **-a** section 1.

grey or gray
The use of these spellings is now clearly regionalized,
with Americans strongly preferring **gray**, and **grey**
as the standard form in Britain and Australia.
Canadians are more inclined to **grey** than **gray** (Fee
and McAlpine, 1997).

The choice of spelling for the *Oxford Dictionary* was
apparently in the balance in the 1890s when the chief

editor Murray conducted an inquiry to decide the
issue. Though *The Times* was for **gray**, other printers
and a majority of those he asked voted for **grey**. That
settled the issue for him, in spite of the preference
given to **gray** by previous British lexicographers,
including Dr. Johnson.

The regional preferences for **grey/gray** also
determine the choice of spelling for derivatives such
as *greyish/grayish, greybeard/graybeard* and *grey
matter / gray matter.*

Both spellings are enshrined in proper names:
compare poet *Thomas Gray* with tea magnate *Earl
Grey; Gray's Anatomy* with the *Greyhound Bus*.

griffin, griffon or gryphon
Griffin is standard spelling for both a mythical and a
real animal:
1 the mythical beast with the head and wings of an
eagle, and the body of a lion which was believed by
the ancient Greeks to keep guard over the gold of
the Scythians
2 a type of vulture, at home in southern Europe.
The first item became a feature of the family crests of
many noble families in Europe, and a symbol of valor
and magnanimity. This dignified role probably helped
to generate the alternative spelling **gryphon**
(reflecting its Latin antecedent "gryps"), which was
used in heraldry and other contexts where the link
with tradition was important.

Griffon is used in modern English to refer to a
breed of wire-haired terrier developed in Belgium in
the 1880s. The word is ultimately the French word for
"griffin," though its use may well be ironic. The dog is
rather small and its head is more like that of a monkey
than an eagle. Another sign of irony is the fact that the
French also call it the *chien anglais* ("English dog").

grill or grille
The **grille** is one of a number of French loanwords
which lost its *e* as it was assimilated in C17, and
reappeared with it in C19. By then it was felt
necessary to differentiate the use of the word as "a
decorative grating or set of bars over a window or
opening" from its use in referring to a style of cooking
over a set of metal bars, first recorded in 1766. The two
meanings were distinguished this way in French (by
means of *grille* and *gril*), and their differentiation in
English is another sign of **frenchification** (see
further under that heading). The distinction is
maintained in both American and British English,
with **grill** used for the kitchen or barbecue, and **grille**
in discussions of architecture and automobiles. Hence
both the *Gothic Revival grille* and the *Bentley's
radiator grille*. One further step in frenchification
manifests itself in the upmarket restaurant that calls
itself the *Art Gallery Grille*.

grisly or grizzly
Anything which arouses horror in the beholder can
be **grisly**, as in the *grisly relics of the concentration
camp*. **Grizzly** means "greyish or grey-haired," so that
an elderly person or animal may merit the adjective.

The *grizzly bear* may owe its name to both words. In
a real sense it is a *grisly bear,* formidable in size
(sometimes 2.5 metres) as is implied in its Latin name
Ursus horribilis. However the name could simply be
explained by reference to the bear's color – its fur
being anywhere from creamy brown to near-black, but

often tipped with white. The animal's ferocious embrace is the stuff of popular reporting, and it substitutes for **grisly** in examples from both American and British databases, as in *I'll cut the grizzly ending* (not about a bear attack). Allusive references to *the grizzly* are another symptom of the preoccupation with this animal, turned to good effect in describing a hug *that would have done credit to a grizzly.*

In British English, the word **grizzly** (or *grizzling*) is sometimes used of a whining child. The word is in no way related to ursine terror, but derived from a colloquial verb *grizzle* ("whine"). But just which word is involved in a *grizzly school trip* is a nice question. What exactly did the teachers have to put up with?

groin or groyne

These spellings are usually applied to two different words. The first is anatomical, used to refer to the groove where thighs join the abdomen, a usage which goes back to about 1400. The architectural use of **groin** to mean "a curve or edge where two vaults intersect," dating from C18, seems to be a figurative extension of the use in anatomy.

A **groyne** is a breakwater designed to reduce the sideways movement of sand on a beach, first mentioned in C16. It seems to be quite independent of the first word, though it too is occasionally spelled **groin**.

grotto

This Italian loanword has been used in English since C17, long enough to acquire a plural in **grottoes**. This is still more popular than **grottos** among BNC citations, by about 2:1, and in spite of the more general trend to replace *-oes* plurals. See further under **-o**.

ground or grounds

The word **ground** has numerous physical and figurative meanings: "earth," "soil," "foundation," "position," "area of discussion" etc. It becomes **grounds** in three particular kinds of reference:
1 to the land surrounding a building: the *school grounds*
2 to the sediment or ground-up material associated with a beverage: *coffee grounds*
3 to the basis of an argument, or the reason or motive for an action: *grounds for divorce*

In all three cases **grounds** regularly takes a plural verb, although singular agreement is just possible for the third meaning (see **agreement** section 2).

Some would argue that it's better to speak of the **ground** of an argument or decision when there is clearly only one. According to this principle, one should say:

> The ground of my decision is this. I need the money.

rather than:

> The grounds of my decision are this. I need the money.

But since **grounds** can just as easily be used to mean "basis" as "particular reason," its use in the second sentence seems quite idiomatic. The plural form **grounds** is registered with singular meaning in all the major dictionaries.

groveled or grovelled, and groveling or grovelling

See under -l-/-ll-.

grow

In American English **grow** can take almost any kind of object – no restrictions at all are indicated in *Merriam-Webster* (2000). Elsewhere it has long been confined to agricultural and horticultural produce, as in *growing sheep* or *growing tomatoes* – apart from *growing a beard* or *growing one's hair.* Its application to nonbiological objects, such as a business or the economy, is registered without comment in the *Canadian Oxford* (1998), but still rather new in Britain, judging by *New Oxford*'s (1998) note: "chiefly North American."

groyne or groin

See **groin**.

grueling or gruelling

See under -l-/-ll-.

gryphon, griffon or griffin

See **griffin**.

Guangzhou

See under **China**.

guarantee or guaranty

The older word **guaranty**, dating from the end of C16, seems to have been steadily overtaken by **guarantee**, which came onto the scene about a century later. Fowler (1926) noted that **guarantee** could be used for all senses of **guaranty** except the rather abstract verbal noun meaning "the act of giving security," and even that is now possible, according to the *Oxford Dictionary* (1989). Some dictionaries suggest a distinction based on legal roles: between the **guarantee** who receives an assurance, and the **guaranty** (= *guarantor*) who provides it. But the distinction is confounded by the difficulty of deciding which party merits the label "guarantee" (see further under **-ee**), and the fact that **guarantee** is much more common generally, with its everyday and figurative uses as well as legal ones. They are embodied in thousands of citations in the BNC and CCAE, while **guaranty** has only a sprinkling, and mostly survives in corporate names such as *Morgan Guaranty*. **Guarantee** thus lays claim to all the meanings that were ever those of **guaranty**.
◊ Compare **warranty**.

-gue/-g

Among the various words we owe to the Greeks is the following set:

> analog(ue)   catalog(ue)   demagog(ue)
> dialog(ue)   epilog(ue)   monolog(ue)
> pedagog(ue)   prolog(ue)   synagog(ue)

Apart from *analog* and *catalog*, the **-gue** spellings are standard everywhere in the world, though the shorter spellings *dialog, prolog* etc. are sometimes said to be *the* American spellings. Yet *Webster's Third* (1986) makes it clear that (apart from *catalog*), they are secondary rather than primary spellings, and data from CCAE shows that most are very rare. Only *analog* and *catalog* make a strong showing: with *analog* outnumbering *analogue* by 2:1 (see **analogue**), and *catalog* on level pegging with *catalogue* (see **catalogue**). *Webster's* apart, *catalog* owes its strength to the mail order system, as well as the Library of Congress (see **catalogue or catalog**).

The *-gue* spellings are in fact French forms of the Greek words, mostly borrowed into English during C16 and C17. This helps to explain why they are established in American English – whereas the frenchified spellings of C19 British English have not taken root in the US (see **frenchification**). And though *-g* spellings are accepted alternatives in the US, the shift from *-gue* to *-g* has been less rapid than Noah Webster might have wished, when he tried to usher in "tung" for *tongue* in his dictionary of 1806.

Note that alternative spellings with *-g* are only found for words which end in *-ogue* (not *fatigue, intrigue, colleague,* or *harangue, meringue*), and have at least two syllables (not *brogue, rogue, vogue*).

guerrilla or guerilla

The first spelling is preferred in *Webster's Third* (1986) and the *Oxford Dictionary* (1989); and databases confirm that **guerrilla** is the commoner of the two in both American and British English, by 5:1 in CCAE data, and about 9:1 in the BNC. The two *rs* connect **guerrilla** with its origins in the Spanish word *guerra* ("war"), of which it's a diminutive. **Guerilla** meanwhile reflects the French way of writing the word, exercised through French sources on world news. It also presents a case where a single consonant can easily replace two of the same kind in an isolated loanword. For others, see **single for double**.

guesstimate or guestimate

This colloquial blend of *guess* and *estimate* reminds us that many an "estimate" may be a figure plucked out of the air, rather than a carefully calculated forecast. Dictionaries all give preference to **guesstimate**, and it far outnumbers **guestimate** in British and American databases: the ratio is 4:1 in the BNC and 16:1 in CCAE. The double *s* no doubt helps to prevent readers finding *guest* in the first syllable.

gullible or gullable

The original C19 spelling was **gullable**, which laid bare the word's origins – a combination of the colloquial verb *gull* ("deceive, cheat") and the suffix *-able*. However the latinized **gullible** was probably helped by the prior existence of *gullibility* (recorded in late C18), and has since taken over entirely. In both

meaning and spelling, **gullible** pulls the wool over our eyes.

guy and guys

The archetypal **guy** is male, but the plural **guys** can include both sexes, as often in the vocative form *you guys*. **Guys** is nevertheless exclusively male in older collocations such as *guys and gals,* or *Guys and Dolls,* the title of Damon Runyon's (1932) collection of stories, the basis of the Broadway musical, and movie (1955). In *big guys,* the word also tends to be interpreted as male, though that's a matter of conventional social roles rather than semantics.
◊ Compare **youth**.

gybe, gibe or jibe

See **gibe**.

gymnasium

The plural of this Latin loanword may be **gymnasiums** or **gymnasia** (see under **-um**). **Gymnasiums** is definitely preferred in American English, and **gymnasia** is very rare in CCAE data. British English supports both, though **gymnasia** still has the edge in written sources from the BNC.

gynecology or gynaecology

See under **ae/e**.

gypsy or gipsy

While the *Oxford Dictionary* (1989) gives priority to **gipsy**, others such as *Webster's Third* (1986), *New Oxford* (1998) and *Merriam-Webster* (2000) make it **gypsy**. American data from CCAE offers strong support for **gypsy** (which prevails by more than 30:1), whereas the two spellings are much more evenly matched in Britain. In BNC data, **gypsy** is ahead of **gipsy** in the ratio of 3:2, though **gypsy** is built into significant titles such as the *National Gypsy Council*. As an ethnic name, **Gypsy** is sometimes spelled with a capital letter in running text, as in *the Gypsy minority* (in Prague).

The **gypsy** spelling was backed by Fowler (1926) on etymological grounds: the word is indeed a clipped form of *Egyptian*. But the connection with Egypt is mythical: history traces the migrations of these nomadic people into Europe from northern India. The Romany language associated with **gypsies** is Indo-European rather than Arabic in origin. The spelling **gipsy** would in fact help to quash the spurious connection with Egypt, and it's in line with the general trend to prefer *i* to *y* spellings where there are alternatives (see further under **i/y**). For the moment, however, the tide of usage seems to be against it.

h

The letter **h** is the most unstable letter of the alphabet in terms of pronunciation – and diverse in its written uses. Over the centuries it has come and gone from Latin and French loanwords (see **a or an**). It still slips from common English words such as *he, him, his, her* and *have, has, had*, in the stream of conversation. Much of this *h-dropping* (dropping the **h**) passes unnoticed when it affects the *function words* of the utterance (pronouns, auxiliary verbs etc.; see further under **words**). The chances of it being noticed and censured are much greater when it affects *content* words: *they were all 'ome by then; I felt all 'ot and cold. H-dropping* is now generally associated with a shortage of education and strongly deprecated, but it was once fashionable in pronunciations such as "an 'otel." In North American English **h** is still dropped from *herb* and its derivatives: *herbal, herbicide* etc. English-speakers everywhere omit the **h** from the middle of words such as *shepherd*, and proper names such as *Clapham*.

The lapsing of **h** in medieval French prompted Anglo-Norman scribes to use it in medieval English as an auxiliary letter, and it's the staple of English digraphs such as *ch, gh, sh, th, wh* (see **digraph**). It continues to mark the different meanings and pronunciations of pairs such as *chat/cat, bus/bush*. The pronunciation difference between *wh* and *w* (in *where/wear* etc.) has been contracting in C20 English, especially in southern British English. The change is marked in the *Concise Oxford* (1995), which shows only the "h"-less form for *where, when, which* and others. Its impact on Canadian English is registered in the *Canadian Oxford* (1998). In the US, it's most evident on the east coast, but further south and west the "h" is still regularly sounded in *where, when, which* etc., and both pronunciations are indicated in *Merriam-Webster* (2000).

habeas corpus and sub poena

The somewhat obscure Latin formula **habeas corpus** requires that "you shall produce the person [in court]" (see further under **corps, corpse or corpus**). Several writs in English law begin with it, and it represents an important civil liberty, obliging anyone who holds a prisoner in custody to bring him or her to court, and state the reasons for their detention. The court then examines the law under which the person is held and decides whether imprisonment is justified or not. The process is designed to prevent people being imprisoned by the state without trial. On occasions it's also used to prevent a citizen holding another person captive, and to ensure that custody arrangements for the child of divorced parents are properly observed.

Another Latin phrase which obliges people to appear in court is the **sub poena** ("under penalty"). Once again it's the opening phrase of a writ, one which summons the defendant of a case (and those

nominated as witnesses) to appear before the judge. As a noun and verb *subpoena* is set solid, and usually spelled that way in the US as well as the UK. There's scant evidence of *subpena* in data from CCAE (despite *e* being preferred by Americans for other similar words: see **oe/e**). As a verb, its past form is normally *subpoenaed*, though a case could be made for *subpoena'd* (see further under **-ed**).

háček

This accent, like an inverted circumflex, is used in a few east European languages, including Czech and Croatian. In English it's sometimes referred to as the "wedge." The **háček** is used to extend the number of consonant symbols (or graphemes): e.g. *č* has the sound "tch," while a plain *c* sounds as "s." In Czech where it's most extensively used, the **háček** creates alternative forms for *c, n, r, s* and *z*, upper and lower case, and also for the vowel *e*. The **háček** appears in English writing only in connection with foreign personal names, such as *Beneš, Dubček* and *Dvořák*.

hachure or hatching

Both these refer to lines of shading. Parallel lines of **hachure** were used on C19 maps to show the gradient of a slope, with thick ones for a steep slope and fine ones where it was gentle. (Modern maps use contour lines with the actual heights stated.) **Hatching** refers to the parallel or crossed lines used to show light and shade on drawings, engravings and diagrams. A much older word, it was earlier applied to inlay work in C15, and to engraving in C16. Yet both **hachure** and the anglicized **hatching** derive from the French verb *hacher* ("chop up"). Other related words are *hash* and *hatchet*.

haem-

This prefix is discussed under **hem-/haem-**.

Hague, The

For the use of the definite article, see **the** section 4.

hail or hale

See **hale**.

hairbrained or harebrained

See **harebrained**.

hairdo and do

Dictionaries agree that the plural of the compound is **hairdos**, as is typical of recent nouns ending in *o* from whatever source (see **-o**). It poses few identity problems. They do however arise with the plural of **do** itself, when used to mean "social event," as in *Labour party dos* – where the word looks rather like a Spanish escapee. According to *New Oxford* (1998) it may be pluralized as either **dos** or **do's**, taking advantage of a use of the apostrophe which is now usually reserved for single letters. See further under **apostrophes** section 2.

haitch or aitch
When is a word not a word? Dictionaries do not list **haitch** as a word, or as a way of representing the sound of the eighth letter of the alphabet (at **aitch** or *H*). Though familiar in many varieties of English, "haitch" is frowned upon by those for whom "aitch" is second nature. Its association with Irish dialect / Irish Catholic education would help to explain the censure, as well as its linguistic source. In spoken Irish the letter *h* is used at the beginning of a word to separate adjacent vowels, and it marks the aspiration of consonants after articles and prepositions. Add to this the ill-founded but pervasive idea that using "haitch" means a *lack* of education, and it's clear that social sanctions work against it – as with many a *shibboleth* (see further under that heading).

The pronunciation "haitch" has a certain logic to it, since the letter names of most consonants embody their own sound, often beginning with it ("bee," "cee," "dee" etc.). And since the "dropping" of *h* draws criticism (see **h**), to pronounce it as "haitch" can be seen as exercising extreme care with the name of the letter (see **hypercorrection**). If and when the social prejudice against it can be overcome, **haitch** would stand as an alternative to **aitch** in the dictionaries.

hale or hail
Nearly a score of different words have clustered under these two spellings. **Hale** and **hail** have nine separate entries each in the *Oxford Dictionary* (1989) as nouns and verbs, not to mention others as adjective/adverb. Not all the words are current and some have always been dialect words, but there are enough in general use to give us pause. Of the two, **hail** still has more uses, including:
* "icy precipitation"
* "greeting" as well as "greet or accost verbally"
* "come from," as in *He hails from Amsterdam.*
The surviving uses of **hale** include:
* "haul, pull or drag," as in: *They haled him into court.*
* "healthy" as in the phrase *hale and hearty.*
It too was sometimes spelled **hail**, until C17. This older spelling is enshrined in the Christmas *wassail*, a drinking toast, literally *wes + hail* ("[may you] be healthy").

The megaphone with built-in amplifier is a *loudhailer* in British and Australian English (a *bullhorn* in American and Canadian). Its use in managing crowd movements might suggest "loudhaler," but the standard spelling *loudhailer* makes it simply a device that accosts people noisily.

half-
This is the first element in numerous compound adjectives and nouns. In British, Australian and Canadian English they are typically hyphenated, though there are variations to note in each group:
* in adjectives, **half-** regularly appears with a hyphen, as in:
half-baked	*half-cocked*	*half-hearted*
half-size	*half-timbered*	
  The chief exception is *halfway*, which commonly works as adverb as well as adjective, and is therefore set solid. (See **hyphens** section 2b.)
* in compound nouns, **half-** is usually hyphenated, witness:
half-boot	*half-caste*	*half-deck*	*half-hour*
half-life	*half-light*	*half-mast*	*half-pint*
half-sister	*half-title*	*half-truth*	*half-volley*
  Just a few have **half** set solid, notably *halfback*, *halftone*, *halfwit*. Note also that in American English (and to some extent in Canadian) some of the **half-** compounds are spaced, for example:
half boot	*half deck*	*half pint*	*half sister*
half title			
  The disinclination to use hyphens is typical of American style (see further under **hyphens** introduction section), although American dictionaries do not always agree on individual words. Everywhere in the world it's a fluid area of spelling. The good news is that whether **half-** is hyphened, spaced or set solid, there's unlikely to be any miscommunication.

Half- normally combines with Anglo-Saxon words, or with thoroughly assimilated French ones, as in the examples above. Its counterpart in more formal, latinate words is *semi-* (see further under that heading).

half a or a half
When it comes to ordering a demi-pint in Britain, customers may hesitate over whether to say *half a pint* or *a half pint*, and both are used. In American English these alternatives present themselves in many other constructions, such as:
half a ton	*a half ton*
half an hour later	*a half hour later*
half a dozen	*a half dozen*
candidates	*candidates*
half a century of	*a half century of*
occupation	*occupation*
In spoken English the two constructions are sometimes combined, as in "a half a ton," but this is redundant in writing. To British ears, the forms with **a half** sound less idiomatic, and there's little evidence of them in the BNC, though *a half hour* turns up in attributive uses, as in *a half hour walk*. Other examples such as in *bought a half share in Chrysalis Records*, or *[drill] a half hole in each block* are institutionalized cases (because *half shares* and *half holes* are standard units like the *half pint*). They nevertheless provide models outside the pub for constructions with **a half**.

half-caste
See **miscegenation**.

half of the
Should the following verb be singular or plural? What decides the issue is the noun following **half**. If it's plural, the verb is plural; if singular, the verb is singular:
> *Half of the responses are for it.*
> *Half of his response was unintelligible.*
(See further under **agreement** section 5.)

Note that the word *of* can be omitted, as in *half the response(s)*. See further under **of**.

half past or half after
Though **half after** is sometimes heard in the UK (and the US), the standard written form is **half past**, in database evidence from the BNC and CCAE. **Half past**

is standard also in Canada and Australia. Both *half past seven* and *half after seven* refer unambiguously to the fact that thirty minutes have gone by since the hour mentioned (making it 7.30). The elliptical *half seven,* used informally in the UK (Ritter, 2002), also means 7.30. But to outsiders it's potentially ambiguous, especially if you know the German equivalent (*halb sieben*), which means 6.30.
◊ Compare **quarter**.

half-title

The short title of a book – when printed on the page before the main title page – is its **half-title**. An alternative name among the makers of books has been *bastard title*. (See further under **prelims**.) The name **half-title** is applied also to the titles of individual sections of a book when they appear on a separate page.

hallelujah or alleluia

This Hebrew word of praise is literally *hallelu* ("praise [ye]") *Jah* ("Jehovah"). Apart from **hallelujah** and **alleluia** it is spelled in a variety of other ways, including *alleluya, alleluja, halleluya(h), halleluia,* as often happens with loanwords which cannot be decoded by English users. In Latin the word was **alleluia**, as it was in the earliest English tradition, and it appeared thus in Wyclif's translation of the bible (1394), notably in *Revelation* ch. 19. But in Coverdale's translation of 1535 **hallelujah** appeared in a heading to the *Psalms of Praise*. The legacy of both appears in the Authorized Version of 1611.

During the next 250 years **hallelujah** seems to dominate, replacing **alleluia** in the Revised Standard translation of *Revelation*. Yet it was increasingly associated with dissenting groups of Protestants such as the Salvation Army, witness the term *hallelujah lass*. The exclamation **Hallelujah!** associated with gospel church services contrasts with the formal use of **Alleluia** for the section of the mass immediately after the gradual. The Catholic tradition retains the spelling **alleluia** in the *New Jerusalem Bible* (1985), and it's also enshrined in the Anglican *Book of Common Prayer,* the *English Hymnal* and the *New English Bible* (1961). The preference for **alleluia** among established churches thus seems to complement the use of **hallelujah** within the gospel churches. But both are well represented on the pages of the ecumenical hymnbooks.

hallo

See **hello**.

halos or haloes

Current usage is firmly in favor of **halos**, by the evidence of the Langscape survey (1998–2001), in which it was preferred by over 75% of respondents from round the world. See further under **-o**.

hamstrung or hamstringed

See under **string**.

handfuls or handsful

See under **-ful**.

handicap

When inflected as a verb, the final letter is doubled: *handicapped, handicapping* everywhere in the English-speaking world. See further under **doubling of final consonant**.

handkerchief

The plural is usually *handkerchiefs*. See further under **-f > -v-**.

hang

For idiomatic uses as in *hang in/on/out,* and for the choice between *hanged* and *hung,* see under **hanged or hung**.

hangar or hanger

See under **-ar**.

hanged or hung

The verb *hang* still presents two past forms: **hanged** and **hung**, after centuries of coexistence. **Hanged** is the earlier and authentic form for what was once a regular verb. But **hung**, coined on the analogy of *sing/sang/sung* in northern English dialects, seems to have spread southward during C16. In conservative domains, **hanged** continued as the ordinary past tense, hence its use in the Authorized Version of the bible (Ps. 137: ... *hanged our harps upon the willows*); and in legal English, whence its association with judicial executions. Death by hanging remains the major application for **hanged** in British and American English. Two-thirds of the BNC examples refer to judicial or summary executions:

Malaysia has hanged 90 people under drug trafficking laws.
Anyone found harboring foreigners in Kuwait would be hanged.

The construction is much more often passive (like the second example) than active, as in the first. **Hanged** is also used in ritual killings of other kinds which end in public exhibition of the body, as with the Ku Klux Klan victim *beaten to death, then hanged from a tree*. Contemporary references to the crucifixion vary between **hanged** and **hung**. Compare:

the Jesus crucified or hanged by the Romans
... [the image of] Christ hung on the cross

The death threat or menace of hanging by effigy is expressed as both *hanged in effigy* and *hung in effigy,* the latter increasingly likely, according to *Webster's English Usage* (1989) and data from CCAE. *Webster's* affirms also the tendency of "educated writers and speakers" to use **hung** in reference to all kinds of execution – a natural consequence of its much greater frequency. Research associated with the *Longman Grammar* (1999) found that American news texts were more likely than the British to use **hung** (as opposed to **hanged**) for the past tense/participle. But in reference to suicide, *hanged himself* is still much more frequent than *hung himself* in both CCAE and the BNC. Whether **hanged** or **hung** is used, the construction is rarely ambiguous, because of the accompanying reflexive or the typically passive construction with human subject. Note however the idiom *hung jury/parliament* – which goes home without reaching a final verdict or decision.

When what *hangs* is a material object or the atmosphere, **hung** is always used for the past form, as in:

naked bulbs hung from the ceiling
a map of the Mideast hung on the wall behind

plumes of smoke hung over the evening sky
a cool silence hung over the table

Hung is used everywhere in the numerous idioms associated with *hang* when it means "linger":

* hang around   *he hung around the nightclub*
* hang back   *the family hung back*
* hang in   *...hung in to beat his opponent 6:2, 6:4*
* hang on   *they hung on her every word*
* hang out   *...where my pals hung out*
* hang up   *people get hung up on technicalities*

Note also the use of *hang up* to mean "terminate," in reference to telephone calls (*he hung up on me*), and one's career (*the 72-year-old doctor hung up his stethoscope*). That last idiom, and several others listed above (*hang in/out*, as well as *hang on* in the sense "persist") are labeled "informal" by *New Oxford* (1998). Yet they appear in a range of standard prose styles in the BNC, *not* including the most formal, so that the label "not formal" would more closely describe their usage. CCAE provides evidence of their use in American newspapers.

hanging hyphen

The **hanging hyphen** is not a capital offence but the use of hyphens to save repeating common elements in coordinated structures:

two-, three- or four-weekly visits
micro- and macrolinguistics
businessmen and -women

As the examples show, there's no need to insert a hyphen into compound words which would not normally have them. Another name for the **hanging hyphen** is *floating hyphen*.

hanging indention
See **indents**.

hanging participles
See under **dangling participles**.

Hansard

This is the unofficial name for the daily records of parliamentary proceedings, published by the government in Britain and in Commonwealth countries such as Australia, Canada, New Zealand and Fiji. Their counterpart in the US is the Congressional Record.

The name **Hansard** is a reminder of the long association of the Hansard family with this publication, originally a private enterprise. Some trace the association back to C18 and to Luke Hansard, who published the journals of the House of Commons from 1774. Others give the credit to T. C. Hansard, who was the printer, and subsequently publisher, of the unofficial series of parliamentary debates from 1803 on. Younger members of the family kept it going as an independent publishing enterprise until 1855, but from then until 1890 it depended on government subsidies. During the 1890s and early 1900s **Hansard** records were produced by various commercial publishers; but it did not prove a viable business and in 1909 became the responsibility of His Majesty's Stationery Office.

During C19, **Hansard** records were not verbatim accounts of what was said. Instead, the debates and proceedings were summarized and reported in the third person. Only during C20 were they written with the first person as well, and efforts made to create a "substantially" verbatim record, with only needless repetition omitted and obvious mistakes corrected. The idea of the verbatim record underlies British and Australian use of the verb *hansardize,* to mean "confront a member of parliament with what he is reported to have said" – or "remind [anyone] of their previously recorded opinion."

Hanukkah or Chanukah

These are two of the various spellings for the Hebrew festival of dedication, also called "the festival of lights," which takes place in December. **Hanukkah** is the preferred spelling in North America and Australia, **Chanukah** in Britain.

hapax legomena

This is the plural of **hapax legomenon**, meaning a word recorded only once in a given literature or database. See further under **nonce word**.

harakiri or harikari

This Japanese loanword for a ritual form of suicide by disembowelment (literally "cut belly") stays closest to the original with the spelling **harakiri**. The alternative **harikari**, recognized in the major dictionaries, turns it into a reduplicating word like *walkie-talkie*. (See further under **reduplicatives**.) Though **harikari** may well be more common in speech, only **harakiri** occurs in the written data of BNC and CCAE.

harbor or harbour
See under **-or/-our**.

hard or hardly

Hard can be either an adjective or an adverb:

It was a hard hit. (adjective)
The champion hit hard. (adverb)

Either way **hard** implies putting effort into the task. Adverbial use of **hard** is often associated with verbs of action, and forms compounds with them, as in *hard-earned, hard-fought, hard-won, hard-working*. In this form **hard** is a *zero adverb* (see under that heading).

Hardly is always an adverb. It no longer carries the sense of the adjective **hard**, but means "scarcely, almost not," as in:

They could hardly see through the smoke.

Grammars and usage manuals sometimes refer to it as a negative adverb, although it differs from *not* in being a relative rather than an absolute negative. *Not* and **hardly** contradict each other in very colloquial expressions such as "He can't hardly walk," though not as a case of double negative, as is sometimes said. (See further under **double negatives**.)

Because **hardly** expresses a relative degree or state, it is quite often followed by the comparative conjunction *than*:

Hardly had they gone than we wished them back again.

The use of *than* after **hardly** was often censured by C20 commentators on usage, taking their cue from Fowler (1926) who amplified a query about it in the

Oxford Dictionary (1884–1928). The critics argue that a time conjunction (*when*) is the proper connecter after **hardly**, even though it would sit awkwardly in the sentence above. Alternatively, they suggest that the comparative element should be explicit, and that **hardly** should be replaced by "no sooner":

> *No sooner had they gone than we wished them*
> *back again.*

Doubts about the construction *hardly . . . than* may well have arisen in C19 because both words were developing new roles: **hardly** as a special kind of negative, and *than* as a conjunction when there was no explicit comparison (see further under **than**). The construction may have sounded unidiomatic earlier on. But Fowler himself acknowledged that it was quite common, and by now it's thoroughly established in ordinary usage. It need raise no eyebrows if it appears in writing.

Note that the construction *scarcely . . . than* than has been subject to the same censure as *hardly . . . than,* with the same suggested alternatives: "no sooner" (for *scarcely*) and "when" (for *than*). But there's no reason to use alternatives if they sit awkwardly or alter the meaning. *Scarcely . . . than* has been in use almost as long as *hardly . . . than.*

harebrained or hairbrained

Dictionaries make **harebrained** their preferred spelling, sometimes justifying it with the help of the traditional simile "mad as a March hare." But they also recognize **hairbrained**, suggesting an alternative interpretation of the word in which hair means "very small," as in *hairline* and *hairspring*. Both spellings have centuries of use behind them, as *Oxford Dictionary* (1989) citations show. But at the turn of the millennium, **harebrained** has the upper hand, outnumbering **hairbrained** by 9:1 in BNC evidence, and eclipsing the other entirely in CCAE. The Lewis Carroll effect perhaps.

hark back, harken back or hearken back

This idiom builds on the archaic verb *hark* ("listen"), which in the jargon of hunting was used to urge the hounds to "follow in quest of [something]," hence both *hark after* and *hark back*. The form *h(e)arken* is simply a variant of the same verb, though there's no evidence of its use in hunting. In contemporary British English the form **hark back** is standard, dominating the evidence from BNC while the others are virtually absent. In American English all three are used. Data from CCAE shows that **hark back** is still the most frequent (35 citations), but **hearken back** and **harken back** also make some showing (12 and 8 citations respectively). The latter evidence accords with the preference for **hearken** over **harken** in *Webster's Third* (1986).

harmonium

For the plural see under **-um**.

Harvard system of referencing

This is an alternative name for the *author–date* system of referencing (see **referencing** section 3).

hash

In spite of its many functions, this familiar sign # has yet to be entered in most dictionaries. Computer programmers call it **hash** or the *hash sign* because of its configuration (see under **hachure**), and the name is catching on among editors, though for them it is the "space sign." The *Chicago Manual* (2003) refers to it as the "space mark." Note that while American and Australian editors use # for "space," it has been officially replaced in British editing practice by the sign ⅄ following British Standard 5261, 1976.

In other contexts the **hash** serves as the "number sign" (or "numeral sign"), handy in mathematical tables and computer codes because it can never be confused with the actual quantities in them. As a "number sign" or "unit sign" it's also used in North America and elsewhere to signal an apartment or unit within the block at a particular address. For example:

> *Mr. G Michaels*
> *#3/25 Captain St*
> *SUN VALLEY*

This application of **hash** has something in common with its use in older cartography to mark the site of a village. (There it was called the "octothorp," literally "8 fields.") **Hash** has also been used as the symbol for "pound" in indicating weights, and is sometimes still called the "pound sign" in the US. (Compare the symbol £ which is the "pound sign" in the UK.)

The *hash mark* familiar to American soldiers is different from all the above. It refers to any of the diagonal stripes on the left sleeve of one's uniform, each one representing three years of service.

hatching or hachure

See **hachure**.

hauler or haulier

Americans use **hauler** to refer to a person or company engaged in road haulage, whereas it's **haulier** for the British. **Haulier** is much the older of the two, first recorded in C16, when it referred to a coal miner, and somewhat unusual in that it combines a verb (*haul*) and the suffix *-ier*, which normally combines with nouns (see **-ier** section 2). **Hauler** is quite recent (C19) and formed with the regular agentive *-er*. The verb *haul* itself is a variant of *hale* ("pull, drag"): see further under **hale or hail**.

haute or haut

These are two forms of the French word for "high," closely related to the English word *haughty*. They come into English in a number of phrases, usually associated with the things of high society, such as:

> *haute couture*   *haute cuisine*   *haute époque*
> (high fashion)   (fine food)   (elegant decor –
>   Louis XIV–XVI)

High society is not too far from the *haute bourgeoisie* (strictly speaking the upper-middle or professional class), or the contexts for *haute politique* (the art of high intrigue), which can refer to negotiations conducted by people of high standing, as well as extraordinary wheeling and dealing by those of any class.

In all of the foregoing phrases, **haute** is spelled with an *e* because it accompanies a French feminine noun and must agree with it. When it accompanies a masculine noun, as in *haut monde* ("high society"), it's just **haut**.

have

This is the second most important verb in English, after *be,* and like *be* it is both an auxiliary and a full main verb.

1 As an auxiliary verb the prime function of **have** is to express the perfect aspect of compound verbs, as in:

I have waited
she has been waiting
they had waited

(See further under **aspect**.) These constructions are used in English everywhere, though database evidence shows that they are more popular in British than American English (Hofland and Johansson, 1982). Americans tend to use a simple past tense (*I/she/they waited*) when other elements of the sentence (usually time adverbials) can express the aspect. Compare:

They had waited four hours before seeing a doctor.
They waited four hours before seeing a doctor.

The simple past rather than the present perfect is often found with *just* (see under **just or justly**). Note also that with *yet,* auxiliary **have** is sometimes replaced by *be* (see under **yet**).

Have has other auxiliary or semi-auxiliary functions to express obligation, as in:

They have to come with us.
They've got to come with us.

The latter is the more informal of the two constructions. (See further under **get** section 2.)

Other quasi-auxiliary roles for **have** are as a causative verb, and to express management or facilitation of an action or event:

They're having our house painted.
We'll have them start next week.

See further under **transitive** section 1.

2 As a main verb have carries the sense of possession or attribution, as in:

I have a book about it.
They have the right idea.

But possessive/attributive statements are often expressed with *have got,* in American as well as British English:

I've got a book about it.
They've got the right idea.

Have is then usually contracted, as in these examples. The use of simple **have** to express possession (once a hallmark of British English) is declining in the UK; meanwhile Americans make more and more use of plain *got,* according to the *Longman Grammar* (1999), as in *I got a book about it* (cf. section 1 above). To British ears this might sound like a recent acquisition, though in American English this would be expressed with *gotten: I've gotten a book* (see **get** section 3).

When possessive sentences are made negative and/or into questions, there are several alternatives and some regional preferences, depending on whether the construction involves a definite or indefinite object.

* **With definite objects** they are as follows:

a) *I don't have the book*   *Don't I have the book*
   about it.   *about it?*
b) *I haven't got the book* *Haven't I got the book*
   about it.   *about it?*
c) *I haven't the book*   *Haven't I the book*
   about it.   *about it?*

Construction (a) is typical for American English, and (b) for British, at least in conversation. But the British

do make some use of (a), according to *Longman Grammar* research. Construction (c) is rare except in British fiction.

* **Indefinite objects** allow the same range of alternatives, but there is greater convergence on the last alternative:

a) *They don't have any*   *Don't they have any*
   idea.   *idea?*
b) *They haven't got any* *Haven't they got any*
   idea.   *idea?*
c) *They haven't any idea.* *Haven't they any idea?*
d) *They have no idea.*

The *Longman Grammar* found construction (d) the majority form for the negated indefinite object in both British and American English, and across spoken and written styles. Constructions (a), (b) and (c) are distributed in the same way for indefinites as for definites.

Final notes: combinations with have

  ***have** is often redundant when repeated in successive verb phrases, witness:

I would have liked to have seen the Cook Islands
before the cyclone.

One instance of **have** seems to have prompted another. In conversation one or both would be contracted (to *'ve*), and, in writing, the second one could well be removed. It makes the same point when rephrased as:

I would have liked to see the Cook Islands before
the cyclone.

  ***have** is usually redundant in the construction *had have* that expresses impossible conditions:

If they had've realized how hopeless it was, they
would never have tried to go on.

The use of *'ve* (for **have**) is unnecessary, and the sentence reads better without it:

If they had realized how hopeless it was they
would never have tried ...

  ***have** *is* necessary in combinations with modal verbs such as *could, may, might, should, would.* After them, **have** is sometimes misheard or misconstrued by naive writers as *of,* hence "could of," "might of" etc., and also the occasional "had of." The problem is easily identified by computer grammar checkers, or a simple computer search.

he and/or she

The third person singular pronouns **he** and **she** are one of the few points in English grammar that make us gender-conscious. We are forced to choose between them for any reference to a single human being, and the choice (whether it is **he** or **she**) seems to exclude half the population. Try filling the blank in the following sentence:

Every teacher must ensure that ... can do first aid.

Whether you put **he** or **she**, you seem to imply that teachers are all of the same gender. The same problem affects *his/her* and *him/her*.

On arrival at the hotel, the tourist is expected to
surrender ... passport.

Here again, the choice of *his* or *her* begins to create a gender-specific identikit of the tourist.

In earlier centuries, before the general concern about sexism in language, it was assumed and accepted that *he/his/him* could be both masculine and common in gender (see **gender**). Common gender uses of the pronoun are still to be found in aphorisms, and in quotations from the King James bible:

He who hesitates is lost.

He that shall humble himself shall be exalted.

Such statements make generic use of **he** to refer to every human being, and would be seriously compromised if they applied only to the male half of the human race. Some would argue that the use of *he/his* is also generic in:

The applicant must demonstrate his ability to work independently, and how he would develop the unit if appointed.

However for many people, this use of *he/his* suggests that women are ineligible for the job. Thus in ordinary usage *he/his/him* seems to be losing its capacity to be generic.

Alternatives to "generic" he:

1 **he or she:** *how he or she would develop the unit.* This spells out the fact that both sexes are in the mind of the person communicating, and that no discrimination is intended. Once or twice in a text it's alright, but cumbersome if used repeatedly. In current British and American English, **he or she** is nevertheless strongly favored over options 2 and 3 (in the ratio of 5:1 in both BNC and CCAE).

2 **he/she:** *how he/she would develop the unit.* Both sexes are recognized as in point 1. The stroke puts the alternatives more neatly, in keeping with its regular role (see **solidus**). It has straightforward counterparts in *his/her* and *him/her.*

3 **s/he.** This again is a neat way of showing that both sexes are included, and actually foregrounds the female alternative. It offers no alternative for *his/her, him/her,* at which point the male alternative is again foregrounded. But if the subject pronoun is the only one needed, *s/he* works well.

4 **he** alternating with **she** throughout the text. This is suggested by some as a way of being absolutely even-handed, but it is extremely disconcerting to the reader. The constant switching of gender gives the impression that two different identities are being referred to, when only one generic individual is intended.

5 **it.** An outsider can use *it* and *its* to refer to a baby, though the child's parents are unlikely to do so. The pronoun cannot be used very far up the age range.

6 **they.** This works very well if you turn the whole sentence into the plural:

Applicants must indicate how they would develop the unit.

Nowadays *they* and *them/their* are used increasingly in writing after a singular human referent – as has long happened in speech. To some this is still a grammatical error; but to many it comes reasonably enough, at least after an indefinite word:

Anyone who applies must indicate how they would develop the unit.

Using *they* (*them/their*) after a more specific singular word is more contentious, and may sound awkward or ungrammatical:

The applicant must indicate how they would develop the unit independently.

(See further under **they.**)

7 **you.** In some situations, the indefinite *you* can be substituted. But when repeated, it creates a style which seems to address the reader directly (like the regular pronoun):

When applying you must indicate how you would develop the unit.

(See **you and ye** special uses 1.)

8 Avoid pronouns altogether and rely on abstract nouns:

The applicant must demonstrate an ability to work independently, and present plans for the development of the unit.

This style is impersonal and detached rather than friendly. (See further under **abstract noun** and **person.**)

9 Repeat the words which identify people in terms of their roles, provided this is not too clumsy. The word *applicant* could hardly be repeated within our illustrative sentence, but in successive sentences it can be effective:

The applicant must demonstrate an ability to work independently. The applicant's plans for the development of the unit should also be submitted.

With so many alternatives available within English, there's really no need to invent a new common gender pronoun to replace **he** and **she.** For some however, that's the only way to cut loose from the sexist traditions embedded in English. Among their various proposals are items such as *Co, E, hesh, tey, ther, thon:* see Baron (1986) for scores of others invented since about 1850. Unfortunately most of them require some explanation, and concerted effort to implement them. The most instantly accessible of all such creations is **s/he**, which has been used from time to time in this book.

he or He

Pronoun references to the divinity have conventionally been capitalized in some ecclesiastical traditions, but the practice is declining. See further under **God.**

head

The grammatical uses of this word are shown under **phrases.**

-head and (-)freak

The original use of the suffix **-head** survives only in old-fashioned abstract words such as *godhead* and *maidenhead.* Historically it's a variant of **-hood.** In C20 usage, another **-head** has emerged, in compounds that characterize individuals by their behavior or their appearance – *airhead, skinhead* – or by the substance to which they are strongly attached: *acidhead, beerhead, crackhead.* Such terms are more direct and less flattering than those formed with the Greek element *-phile.* Compare *winehead* and *oenophile,* and see further under **phil- or -phile.**

Words compounded with **-head** are probably less derogatory than those with **(-)freak**, such as *ecofreak, control freak, fitness freak, speed freak.* With them, the person's commitment to a cause or substance is found quite obsessive. Compare **-mania.**

head for and head up

Newer uses of the verb **head** are to be heard and seen, in combination with the particles *for* and *up.* Where *heading for* has been the regular way of indicating a destination or destiny, the passive *headed for* is now used as an alternative, especially for the latter. See for example:

> Banks were headed for a massive government bailout.
>
> The world is headed for a serious energy problem.

These and hundreds of other examples are to be found in CCAE, and the construction evidently originated in American English. But the BNC also contains a modest sprinkling of examples, such as:

> ...promising enough to be headed for a higher grade of cricket
>
> When Blaise dies he'll be headed for a monastery.

On such evidence the passive headed for is beginning to established itself in British English.

The phrasal verb **head up**, used in reference to corporate and institutional leadership, is also gaining ground in British English, from a base in American. See for example:

> ...the appointment of John Trevelyan to head up the BBFC
>
> Coady will head up the new literary group.
>
> ...picking their friends to head up privatised national industries

These and other examples from the BNC show the naturalization of the construction in British English, especially business and sports reporting. As in American English, **head up** is often used in connection with newly forged groups and structures, and therefore not just a wordy alternative to the verb **head**.

heading, headline, header and head

These words all refer to a cue provided for the reader at the start of an item, though they belong to different kinds of documents. **Headings** are a regular feature of nonfiction publications such as textbooks and government reports, where they cue the reader as to the subject about to be discussed. Typically a phrase, the **heading** is set apart by typographic means at the top of a chapter or section. (See next entry for the setting of *headings* and *subheadings*.)

Headlines are the telescoped sentences set in larger, heavier type above newspaper articles, to grab the reader's attention. Some aspects of their wording are distinctive (see **headline language**).

In computer software the term **header** refers to a wordprocessing facility which places selected items at the top of every page of a document – especially the page number and *running head,* i.e. abbreviated chapter or section title.

headings and subheadings

In many kinds of nonfiction **headings** are a boon to readers, in signaling the structure of information in the solid text below, and helping them over the potential problem of not being able to "see the wood for trees." For the writer too, deciding on **headings** and **subheadings** is an important step in getting on top of the material, and being able to present it in manageable blocks. Choosing **headings** also obliges you to think about the order of the blocks – which may come easily if there's a conventional set such as primary/secondary/tertiary (as in education or industry). In more open fields writers have to invent their own series of **headings**, making sure that individually they are suitable for everything under them.

The **headings** correlate with the major structural divisions of any piece of writing. For example (for an essay on the flute):

A   Uses of the flute
B   The European concert flute
C   Music composed for the flute

Within each structural block **subheadings** must be found to label smaller units of discussion, and link up with the major **headings**. Sometimes the main **heading** may need rewording, to enlarge its scope or to make it more specific:

A   HISTORICAL USES OF THE FLUTE
A 1.   Herdsman's pipes in the Mediterranean, and in South America
A 2.   As an aid to courtship in mythology and literature
A 3.   As a professional musician's instrument in ancient Egypt and in medieval Europe

Layout and typography of headings. In a table of contents, **headings** and **subheadings** would be set out as just shown, with **subheadings** indented from the main headings. *Subsubheadings* would be further indented. To enumerate them, a combination of letters and numbers (as above), or just numbers may be used. (See **numbers and number style** section 6.)

Both in the table of contents, and on the ordinary page, **headings** are distinguished from **subheadings** by means of different fonts. So main **headings** may be in bold, and others in normal type, or the main **heading** in caps., and the others using only an initial cap. Most wordprocessors allow you to vary the type size to distinguish the levels of heading, e.g. 12 point for **headings** and the regular 10 point for **subheadings**. Small caps. and italics, if available, serve as further typographic variables to show lower-level **headings**. Letter spacing is also a resource for differentiating the levels of **heading**. Compare U S E S with USES.

With or without flexible typographical resources, the placement of **headings** and **subheadings** on the printed page can be used to distinguish one from another. Main **headings** may be centred, while **subheadings** are flush with the left margin. Additional line space below main **headings** also helps to mark the difference. The first line of text after a **heading** or **subheading** is often set flush with the left margin. But some publishers simply indent it like any other paragraph.

headline language

Newspaper headlines have to say everything in a few words: preferably no more than eight, and ideally less than that. The statements they make are usually elliptical, and some grammatical items such as articles, conjunctions, the verb *be* and verbs of saying, are usually left out. Each is illustrated in turn below:

> BOND TELLS OF MEETING WITH SPY
>
> BULGARIAN LEADERS QUIT, PLEDGE REFORM
>
> COOK MANUSCRIPT STOLEN
>
> OFFICIAL: MANDELA CLOSE TO FREEDOM

As the examples show, verbs are a feature of many headlines, helping to highlight what is happening. They may be finite verbs (*quit, pledge*), participles with the verb *be* omitted (*stolen*), or verbal nouns (*meeting*). Certain short verbs / verbal nouns are regulars in headlines, including:

aid	axe	ban	bar	bid	call
clash	crash	curb	cut	find	flee
leak	pact	probe	push	quite	rise
seek	slam	slash	wed	win	

Words like these suggest decisive action, though they are often matters under discussion which will take time to be acted on. The news is as often about what people say, as what they do. Newspapers have to make the most of it.

headword

In a dictionary, the **headword** is the one which begins each entry, and is then analyzed and defined within it. *Secondary headwords* are those introduced and defined in the middle of the entry. Derivatives of the **headword** are mentioned as *runons* at the end of the entry, without any definitions.

The term **headword** is also used by some grammarians for the *head* of a phrase: see further under **phrases**.

heap(s) of

In both American and British English, **heaps of** serves as a rather vague quantifier of both tangible and intangible things:

> *heaps of freshly caught stone crabs*
> *heaps of money, oil, gas and other resources*
> *heaps of atmosphere*
> *heaps of line-out possession*

As these examples show, the expression becomes informal the more it's associated with intangible objects, which could not conceivably lie around in piles. Its meaning is equivalent to *lots of*. The same is true of *a heap of*, witness:

> *a heap of twisted metal*
> *a heap of laughter*
> *a heap of anecdotal evidence*
> *a heap of trouble*

Again in ranging from tangible to intangible, *a heap of* becomes progressively more informal, the meaning diluted to the point where it's simply a paraphrase for *a lot of*. Expressions at that end of the scale are probably commoner in the US, but they appear also in the UK, by the sprinkling of examples in the BNC. For issues of agreement with the following verb, see **agreement** section 5.

hearken back

See **hark back**.

heaved or hove

In everyday use this word means "lift [something heavy]," and its past tense is **heaved**:

> *... heaved himself out of the chair with difficulty*
> *The door of the cell was heaved open.*

Heaved is also conventional in collocations such as *heaved a sigh (of relief)*.

The past tense **hove** is mostly associated with ships' movements: stopping, as in *hove to;* advancing, as in *hove over the horizon,* and especially *hove in(to) sight/view,* meaning "appeared." These latter idioms are also used figuratively of other things appearing or seeming to appear. Compare:

> *A lone bird hove in sight.*
> *It was 16 days before the old fort hove into view.*

The antecedents of **heaved** and **hove** were among the many variants of the past tense of *heave* in Old English, giving it both regular and irregular forms

which were in general use for centuries. Only in C16 did the regular **heaved** become the dominant form for all non-nautical uses. For other verbs still undergoing this process, see **irregular verbs** section 9.

heavenward or heavenwards

See under **-ward**.

Hebrew

See under **Israel**.

hedge words

One quick way to soften the impact of a statement is to insert a **hedge word**. There are four subtypes, according to the *Comprehensive Grammar* (1985), which presents them under the general heading of *downtoners*:

* approximators   e.g. *almost, nearly*
* compromisers   e.g. *rather, quite* (in British English)
* diminishers (a) e.g. *partly, somewhat* (these modify the force of the following expression)
      (b) e.g. *only, merely* (these confine the reader's attention to a single item)
* minimizers   e.g. *barely, hardly*

These **hedge words** are all from standard English, and there are comparable adverbial expressions in colloquial English: *practically* (approximator); *kind of* (compromiser); *just* (diminisher); *a bit* (minimizer), as used in negative statements such as *He didn't like it a bit*. Note that in positive statements, *a bit* is a diminisher: *I was a bit hasty*. Those examples also show the different positions in which some downtoners may appear. Others have a fixed position, e.g. *enough,* which always follows the word it modifies. Compare:

> *It was rather good.*
> *It was good enough.*

Hedge words curb the assertiveness of a claim, and prevent a style from sounding too arrogant. They put limits on statements which could not be defended in their absolute form. Yet like any stylistic device they offer diminishing returns and become conspicuous (and ineffective) if overused. Even if you "juggle" several of them in the same piece of writing, they eventually draw attention to themselves because they create repetitive phrase patterns. Other strategies are needed, especially ones which help to vary the patterns. Modal verbs such as *can, could, may, might, should, would* help on both fronts, but again must be used sparingly (see further under **modality**). Modal adverbs such as *possibly, probably,* and clausal paraphrases such as *it is possible/probable/likely that* ... provide other ways of hedging a statement. Best of all is to find lexical paraphrases, replacing "rather good results" with *promising results* etc., to extend the verbal range.

◊ Compare **intensifiers**.

Hegira, hegira or hejira

This Arabic word for "emigration, flight" has great significance for the Islamic faith, standing for the flight of Muhammad from Mecca to Medina in 622 AD. When used in reference to that event, or the calendar based on it, **Hegira** is normally capitalized:

> *The coin bears the Christian date 1987 and the Hegira date 1408.*

(See further under **dating systems**.)

When **hegira** refers to any individual's emigration, flight or journey – actual or figurative – it appears with lower case:

> ... *sets forth on a dizzying hegira that ends in Hamburg*
> ... *takes the reader on an intellectually strenuous hegira through four different languages*

The spelling **hejira** occasionally substitutes for **hegira** in any of its senses, as in: *the band's hejira towards the mainstream.*

Neither spelling renders the Arabic *hijrah* exactly, though **hejira** embodies the more authentic consonant. **Hegira**, the form used in medieval Latin, is preferred in *Webster's Third* (1986) and the *Oxford Dictionary* (1989).

helix

The plural of this word is discussed under **-x**.

hello, hallo and hullo

The greeting represented by these three spellings belongs primarily to spoken English, hence the lack of standardization. The *Oxford Dictionary* (1989) notes "the obscurity of the first syllable," and gives priority to **hallo**, apparently because the word is seen as a variant of *halloa* and *halloo*. Dictionaries in North America and Australia prefer **hello**, and it's the most frequent spelling by far in American, British and Australian databases. Americans hardly make any use of either **hallo** or **hullo**, whereas the British maintain a lowish level of both as alternatives.

help (to)

The verb **help** couples readily with other verbs as *bare infinitives* or in their *to*-forms. Compare:

> *A geometric effect was chosen to help break up the space.*
> *Back-row moves would help to break up the pattern of play.*

The choice between the two constructions depends on a number of linguistic factors, one of which is whether **help** is itself preceded by *to*, as in the first of these sentences. The *Longman Grammar* (1999) found that with a preceding *to,* the bare infinitive was very strongly preferred in all genres of writing. It was also the preferred construction whenever there was an intervening noun (phrase), as in *help people break the cycle of poverty*. These two grammatical factors make **help** plus bare infinitive the commoner construction of the two by far in everyday spoken and written English, in both the US and the UK. In British English this represents a shift from earlier preference for **help** plus *to*-infinitive (Mair, 1998). The relatively high proportion (45%) of **help to** constructions found in British academic prose are a sign of its conservatism.

hem-/haem-

This element of ancient Greek, meaning "blood," has been put to use in modern scientific words, especially in medicine and physiology. Some familiar examples are:

> *h(a)emoglobin*   *h(a)emophilia*
> *h(a)emorrhage*   *h(a)emorrhoid*

It also appears as *-(a)em-* when not the first syllable of a word. See for example:

> *an(a)emia*   *hypoglyc(a)emia*   *leuk(a)emia*
> *septic(a)emia*   *tox(a)emia*

British spelling has traditionally preferred *haemoglobin, anaemia* etc. where American and Canadian English uses *hemoglobin, anemia*. In Australia, both spellings are in use for the more familiar words in each set, and major newspapers present *hemorrhage* and *leukemia* while the medical profession is still committed to *haemorrhage* and *leukaemia*. Yet American doctors lose nothing of substance in preferring **hem-** and *-em-*, and some unnecessary clutter is shed from the spelling. (See further under **ae/e**.) The *-em* spelling makes for better spelling/sound regularity in words such as *hypoglycemia, septicemia*, given the general convention that a *c* followed by *a* would be a hard "k" sound. (See further under **-ce/-ge**.)

Some **h(a)em-** words are specialized terms in geology and chemistry, including *h(a)ematite* and *h(a)emat(e)in*. Once again their standard spelling in Britain is with **haem-**, but in North America it's **hem-**, and they are recognized in that form in Australia. The connection with "blood" in such words is remote – which deflates the argument that **haem-** is a more meaningful spelling.

The spelling of the syllable following **h(a)em-** is sometimes in doubt, as to whether it should be *a* or *o*. In most cases it is *o*: *h(a)emoglobin, h(a)emophilia* etc. The chief exceptions are those like *h(a)ematite* and *h(a)ematology*, where the basic element is the combining form *h(a)emat-*, not **h(a)em-**.

> **International English selection:** The spellings with *hem-* and *-em-* are preferable. They are more widely used, and integrate better with the conventions of English spelling, in terms of vowel and consonant–vowel sequences.

hemi-

See under **demi-**.

hence

In abstract argument **hence**, i.e. "from this point," is still a useful word for introducing a conclusion, an alternative to *therefore, thus* etc. There it serves as an adverbial *conjunct* between two sentences (see further under **conjunctions** section 3). But other uses of **hence** in the realms of space ("from this place, from here") and time ("from this time, from now") are very much reduced now. As a time adverb, **hence** is mostly confined to fixed phrases such as: *two weeks hence, six months hence*. When used in references to place, e.g. *go (hence) to Singapore*, it now sounds quite old-fashioned.

The sense of place was once fundamental to **hence**, and it contrasted with *hither* and *here*, as in:

> *Get thee hence!* (from this place)
> *Come hither!* (to this place)
> *I am here!* (in this place)

In spite of those neat distinctions, the system seems to have broken down for **hence**/*hither*/*here* – just as it has for *thence*/*thither*/*there* and *whence*/*whither*/*where*. In each set the third word is the strongest survivor in everyday English. The others have restricted uses, and otherwise seem formal, old-fashioned or archaic. The status of **hence**, *thence* and *whence* seems in fact to have been insecure for centuries. To write *from hence* is strictly redundant (because "from" is part of the meaning of **hence** itself), yet it's on record from C14 on. The King James bible (1611) has numerous instances of *from thence/whence,* including the famous line of Psalm 121: "I will lift up mine eyes unto the hills from whence cometh my help." **Hence**/*thence/whence* linger only as rhetorical variants for *here/there/where* in reference to place.

hendiadys
See under **hysteron proteron**.

hepta-
See under **number prefixes**.

heritage or inheritance
In law, these can both refer to the estate or property which passes to one's legal heirs. But in common usage they diverge. **Inheritance** still has the sense of tangible inherited assets and family property attached to it, hence the *inheritance tax*. One's *genetic inheritance* is also handed down physically. A person's **heritage** is broader and more abstract, often referring to the accumulated culture and traditions which belong to a nation and are the birthright of all its citizens. However the *architectural heritage of the countryside* can too easily become the *heritage industry,* where in BNC citations tourists queue to *buy heritage over the counter,* and cynicism abounds: *this heritage stuff about happy agricultural labourers with straws in their mouths.*

Yet the notion of **heritage** can surmount national boundaries, as in:
> ... Hitler's jack-booted thugs heaping the heritage of the world onto a pyre and gloating as the flames consumed book after book ...

In current usage **heritage** often refers to natural resources which must be carefully preserved for posterity and for humanity as a whole, as in concerns about listing Scotland's Flow country under the *World Heritage Convention,* and the already *betrayed heritage of wild flowers and healthy trees.*

hero
The plural of this word is still **heroes** not **heros**, according to both *Merriam-Webster* (2000) and *New Oxford* (1998). In the Langscape survey (1998–2001) **heroes** was preferred by two thirds of respondents worldwide – which would suggest that **heros** is not beyond the pale. However **heros** was more acceptable to US respondents (57%) than to those from the UK (26%). See further under **-o**.

heroine or heroin
See under **-ine**, and **morphine**.

hesitance, hesitancy and hesitation
These three have all done duty for each other since C17, so there's little to choose between them in terms of meaning. All have been used to express a specific instance or act of *hesitating* as well as the corresponding state or quality. But **hesitation** is by far the strongest of the three in current American and British English. It outnumbers the others by 10:1 in CCAE and the BNC, and presumably gains by being closer in form to the verb *hesitate*. **Hesitancy**

meanwhile has almost eclipsed **hesitance**, by the evidence of the databases.
◊ For other pairs of this kind, see **-nce/-ncy**.

hetero-
This Greek prefix, meaning "different, other," is probably best known in the word *heterosexual*. It's also found in a number of scientific and scholarly words, such as:
> *heterogamous   heterogeneous*
> *heteromorphic   heterorganic*

In such words it often contrasts with a similar word formed with *homo-* ("same"), hence pairs such as *heterorganic/homorganic*. (See further under **homo-**.) In just one pair, *heterodox/orthodox,* it forms a contrast with a different prefix. See further under **ortho-**.

heterogeneous or heterogenous
Biologists use **heterogenous** in the specialized sense of "from outside the body, of foreign origin." But in everyday discourse it's used instead of **heterogeneous** to mean "having a mixture of elements or components, diverse," hence references to the *heterogenous buildings* of a city, or the *heterogenous environment* needed for computer developments. Examples like these emerge in both American and British English, though the evidence of databases (CCAE and the BNC) is that they are not very frequent. The use of **heterogenous** for **heterogeneous** may well be more often heard than seen, because it facilitates pronunciation of what is otherwise a six-syllabled word with compound stress. *Webster's Third* (1986) simply registers **heterogenous** as an alternative form, whereas the *Oxford Dictionary* (1989) dubs it a "less correct" form of **heterogeneous**. There is perhaps potential ambiguity in referring to a *heterogenous electorate:* could it mean that some voters come in from over the electoral border? That may be putting too fine a point on it when the word can always mean "diverse" – its default value, except in biology.
◊ Compare **homogeneous or homogenous**.

heterophones and heteronyms
Heterophones are distinct words with the same spelling but different sound, such as *minute* meaning "very small" and "a sixtieth of an hour." Some linguists including Burchfield (1997) call them **heteronyms**. Whatever the term, they are the opposite of *homophones* (which sound the same), while being *homographs* (written the same way): see further under **homonyms**.

The term *heteronymy* is used differently by others, for alternative words from different origins that refer to the same item: thus *sneakers, plimsoles, gym shoes, trainers* are **heteronyms** for a certain type of soft shoe. As that example shows, **heteronyms** often come from different varieties of English, and they impinge on us as alternative British/American expressions until the immigrant term is assimilated.

hewn or hewed
In British English the past participle of the verb *hew* is still always **hewn**, by BNC evidence, when it appears as part of a fully fledged verb phrase, active or passive:
> *He had hewn down the famous elm tree*
> *A labyrinth of caves is hewn in tiers out of the ravine*

Hewn is also standard in participial or adjectival uses, such as the *seat hewn out of a fallen tree trunk,* or the *newly hewn bomb shelters.*

In American English, **hewn** shares the field somewhat with **hewed**, so that *roughly hewn* may be *roughly hewed,* and a desk may be *hewed from the timbers of the British ship HMS Resolute.* It sometimes appears in full verb phrases: *timber that is being hewed down with an ax.* For all this, **hewn** is still much more common in all the constructions mentioned.

In both varieties **hewed** serves as the simple past tense meaning "cut down." But Americans and Canadians also make figurative use of the verb in the construction *hewed to,* used of stances and political alignments adopted:

> *The court has never hewed strictly to a conservative line.*
> *... suspicion that it* [the proposal] *hewed too closely to Soviet aims*

The idiom suggests active conformity to some preexisting policy, rather than chipping away at the frontier.

hexa-

See under **number prefixes**.

hi- and high-

Hi- is a quasi-prefix of the later C20, standing in for **high-**, and in some cases replacing it as the more common form, witness:

> *hifalutin   hi-fi   hijack   hi-rise   hi-tech*

Both *hi-fi* and *hi-tech* are favored for their simplicity, especially in business, as in *hi-fi set, hi-tech design methods.* To spell them out as *high-fi* and *high-tech* seems rather reactionary if you are going to use them, and *hi-fi* has ousted its rival, by the evidence of American and British databases. But *hi-tech* still shares the field with *high-tech,* in the ratio of 2:3 in BNC citations, and is the minor player in data from CCAE, where the ratio is 1:6. *Hi-rise* appears in real estate / property advertising, but not in the discursive texts of the American and British databases.

The origins of both *hijack* and *hifalutin* are obscure, and the alternative spellings *highjack/highfalutin* show folk etymology at work, trying to inject meaning into the first syllable. But *Webster's Third* (1986) and the *Oxford Dictionary* (1989) both prefer *hijack,* and *Oxford* citations for *highjack* are from back in the 1920s and 30s. Current data from British and American databases is overwhelmingly with *hijack.* The spelling of *hi(gh)falutin* is apparently going the opposite way: there are 5 of *highfalutin* to 1 of *hifalutin* among BNC citations, and in CCAE the ratio is more than 15:1. **High-** no doubt seems right for an "uppity" word.

High- is an element in numerous compound adjectives, and in many neologisms of the *Oxford's* second edition:

> high-brow   high-grade   high-headed
> high-powered   high-rise   high-speed
> high-tone   high-up

It will be of interest to see whether many such words are eventually respelled with **hi-** – a small step in the direction of reforming one of the notorious words with **gh**. (See further under that heading.)
◊ Compare **lo**.

hiatus

For the plural of this word, see under **-us**.

hiccup or hiccough

Dictionaries usually give **hiccough** as a variant of **hiccup**, though there's no support for it in either the word's origin or pronunciation. **Hiccough** is an old folk etymology (first recorded in 1626) which tries to interpret the second syllable. The *Oxford Dictionary* (1989) argues against **hiccough**, but there's evidence of its use in current British English alongside **hiccup**, in the ratio of about 1:5 in the BNC. The ratio is only 1:25 in American data from CCAE, though *Webster's English Usage* (1989) accepts it as having been "in reputable use" for centuries.

Both *Webster's Third* (1986) and the *Oxford* give preference to the regular *hiccuped/hiccuping* over *hiccupped/hiccupping* for the inflected forms, and the spellings with single *p* are much more frequent in CCAE. In BNC data, the two types are about equally used. For the issues underlying these spellings, see **doubling of final consonant**.

hierarchic or hierarchical

The longer form is strongly preferred in both the US and the UK. **Hierarchical** outnumbers **hierarchic** in the ratio of more than 20:1 in CCAE and 30:1 in the BNC. For other examples, see **-ic/-ical**.

hifalutin or highfalutin

See under **hi-**.

highlighted or highlit

The shorter form **highlit** is hardly to be seen in either British or American English, against more than a thousand cases of **highlighted** in both BNC and CCAE. See further at **lighted or lit**.

highly or high

Both these operate as adverb for the adjective *high* (as in *high clouds, a high opinion, to a high degree*), but they pick up different senses. **Highly** is used for the abstract meanings, and it goes with mental process verbs as in: *highly regarded / acclaimed / sought after.* It also serves as an intensifier meaning "to a high degree," as in *highly evocative/competitive/decorative/condensed.* **High** works as adverb in simple physical applications of the word – *flew high over the trees* – and certain mentalistic idioms such as *aim high, hopes ran high.*

hijack or highjack

See under **hi-**.

Hindi and Hindu

A **Hindu** is a person who either speaks a **Hindi** language, or adheres to the Brahmanistic religion of India. **Hindi** is one of the official languages of India, spoken by well over 200 million. *Hindustani* is a form of **Hindi** with elements of Persian, Arabic and Turkish mixed in, used in northern India as a lingua franca for trade and intercultural communication. It was the form of **Hindi** best known to the British in colonial India. Note that **Hindi**, **Hindu** and *Hindustani* all preserve the original Persian word for India: "Hind."

hindrance

This word is correctly spelled without the *e* of *hinder.*
For other examples, see **-er > -r.**

hinging or hingeing

For the choice between these, see **-e** section 1e.

hippie or hippy

Both forms are current for the *hip* person, but
regional preferences are emerging. **Hippie** is
endorsed by more than 9:1 in American data from
CCAE, and *Merrriam-Webster's* (2000) primary
spelling. In British English the field is more divided,
but *New Oxford* (1998) puts **hippy** first, and it
outnumbers **hippie** by more than 2:1 in BNC data.
◊ For other similar pairs, see **-ie/-y.**

hippopotamus and hippo

Dictionaries all give preference to **hippopotamuses**
rather than **hippopotami** as the plural of this word –
pace the comic song "Mud, Glorious Mud" of Flanders
and Swann. **Hippopotamuses** has the support of
scholars as well as those who simply prefer to
anglicize the plurals of well-assimilated loanwords.
Why? **Hippopotamus** is a modern Latin word, coined
around 1600 out of ancient Greek (*hippopotamos,*
plural *hippopotamoi*) – so there's no need to pluralize
it according to the pattern of classical Latin nouns
(see **-us** section 1).

   With its five syllables, **hippopotamus** is
abbreviated to **hippo** in many contexts of writing,
particularly when it comes up in lists of other animals
with shorter names:

> *Africa has a superb array of hoofed herbivores,*
> *including 85 species of antelope, plus zebras,*
> *buffalo, hippos and elephants.*

As the example suggests, the abbreviated form is at
home in both travel writing and science intended for
the general reader. Note that the plural is *hippos* not
hippoes, because it's a clipping as well as a foreign
borrowing. See further under **-o.**

hippy or hippie

See **hippie.**

hire, rent and lease

The oldest recorded use of **hire** is to mean "employ for
wages, recruit," and it has always been used in this
sense in American English. In British English this
use fell into abeyance, but revived after World War II
under North American influence, and is used
especially for ad hoc appointments, as when:

> *The company hired a consultant ornithologist*
> *The Standard hired him as a film critic.*

More than half the BNC citations for *hired* involve
some kind of recruitment.

   Other uses of **hire** continue the world over. The
word is applied to making a payment for the
temporary loan of objects such as boats, caravans,
halls and dinner jackets. The fact that such loans are
short-term helps it to contrast with **rent**, the verb
used for securing a fixed-period tenancy of business or
private accommodation by means of regular
payments. The word **lease** is usually applied to
longer-term arrangements for business premises or
land, and usually implies a formal contract. So **hire,**
rent and **lease** can be distinguished in terms of the

kind of property involved, length of the loan period,
and style of payment.

   The distinctions between the words are
nevertheless increasingly blurred. **Rent** has moved
into the former domain of hire so that we can speak of
renting a truck or renting party gear. And **lease** can
now be used of shorter-term tenancies.

Hispanic

Home base for this adjective is the Iberian peninsula,
so that it designates things Spanish, or
Spanish-speaking, as in *Hispanic civilizations,*
Hispanic heritage. But it is now more prominently
used to refer to things Latin American and to cultural
aspects of the US associated with immigrants of
Spanish or Latin American origin: *the Hispanic city of*
San Antonio Texas. Since the 1970s it has also served
as a noun (*a young Hispanic*), according to *Oxford*
Dictionary (1989) citations, though such usages were
no doubt established earlier in American English. In
the US, **Hispanic** populations are concentrated in
different parts of the country: the so-called *Chicanos*
in southwestern and western states (especially New
Mexico and California), *Cubans* in the southeast
(Florida) and *Puerto Ricans* in the northeast
(especially New York). **Hispanics** are not
uncommonly mentioned in the same sentence as other
disadvantaged groups – which explains why the word
sometimes appears without a capital, if that goes for
the other group(s) mentioned:

> *Four homeboys – two black, two hispanic – quit*
> *the Bronx for a night in Manhattan.*

As a straight ethnic designation, **Hispanic** is
normally capitalized: ... *12 jurors, 10 white, one*
Hispanic, one Asian-American ... in keeping with the
use of initial capitals in ethnic names (see **capital**
letters section 1).

   While the term **Hispanic** is neutral, its various
abbreviations including *spic, spick, spik* and *Spic* are
derogatory (see under **racist language**).
◊ Compare **Chicano** and **Latino.**

historic or historical

The distinction between these two is sharper than for
many **-ic/-ical** pairs. **Historic** is more
self-consciously associated with the making of history,
so that a *historic event* is one which people feel is
particularly significant in the life and culture of the
nation. **Historical** is more neutral, acknowledging
that something belongs to the past, or to the study of
the past, or else that it really happened and is not
fictitious.

   Note that *histrionic* is not related to *history* but
derived from *histrio* ("actor"), hence its connotations
of "melodramatic, artificial" and the implied contrast
with "sincere."
◊ For the question as to whether to write *an* before
historic and **historical,** see **a or an.**

hoard or horde

These words are easily mistaken for each other with
their identical sound and similarity in meanings.
Both can refer to large masses. Yet while a **hoard** is a
collection of inanimate objects stored away, as in a
hoard of old tools, **horde** refers to a large body of
people or animals, as in a *horde of kids,* or *horde of*
mosquitoes. **Horde** often implies some discomfort or
threat associated with that group, although in

colloquial usage it just means "a large number," as in: *golden hordes of tourists*. This rather figurative use is the point at which the line between **horde** and **hoard** becomes harder to draw.

Confusion between the two words has been commented on by usage guides since the 1980s. Ready examples from the databases are *hoards of children / speculators / autograph hounds / gadget-mad consumers;* and in fact 50% of the instances of **hoards** in CCAE refer to groups of people, and more than 30% in the BNC. About half the BNC citations are from transcribed spoken material, but the others come from published texts that would have had editorial scrutiny. Curiously, the confusion seems to work only in one direction: there's no evidence of **hordes** being used where **hoards** might be expected. *Webster's English Usage* (1989) suggests that **hoards** is somehow the more familiar spelling, yet **hordes** is actually more frequent – almost twice as frequent in both BNC and CCAE. **Hoard** is perhaps more English-looking with its *oa* digraph, and it does in fact go back to Old English, whereas **horde** with its seemingly redundant *e* is a C16 loanword from Turkish via Polish. Whatever the incentives for using **hoard** for **horde**, it gets no support from the major dictionaries.

hobo

This word for a vagrant or itinerant worker originated on the western side of the US in late C19, though its etymology (with perhaps Spanish or American Indian roots) is obscure. It enjoyed some vogue in the earlier C20, with the creation of derivatives such as *hoboette* and *hobohemia*, and also spawned a verb, as in *he hoboed to the west coast*. For Americans, the **hobo** was a familar image of the 1930s depression, and their mode of travel – "hopping freights" (i.e. freeloading on freight trains to go anywhere) – became proverbial. Movies, novels and the latter-day *yuppie hobo* perpetuate the lifestyle. In the plural, the word is usually **hobos**, by the evidence of CCAE, though *Merriam-Webster* (2000) puts **hoboes** first. In the UK there's little to go on for the plural (1 instance each way in the BNC), but again **hoboes** is put first in *New Oxford* (1998).

hodgepodge or hotchpotch

See under **hotchpot**.

hoi polloi

See under **Greek plurals**.

holey or holy

The adjective **holey** meaning "full of holes" defies the general rule of English spelling, that a final *e* should be dropped before suffixes (see further under **-e**). Without the *e*, it would of course be **holy**, and indistinguishable from the adjective meaning "sacred." Preservation of the *e* prevents *homonymic clash:* see further under **homonyms**.

holistic or wholistic, holism or wholism

Holistic is closely related in meaning to the English word *whole*, but takes its spelling directly from the Greek element *hol(o)-* ("whole, entire"). It was in fact coined by General Jan Smuts in the 1920s as a philosophical term, and now appears in other academic fields as a synonym for "global." The underlying link with *whole* has naturally helped to generate the spellings with *wh,* which are recognized in the major dictionaries – British, American, Australian and Canadian (for **wholism**). The *Oxford Dictionary* (1989) offers multiple citations of **wholistic** as well as **wholism**; and it treats them as "alterations" of **holistic** and **holism**, with no hint of censure. Current usage however is strongly in favor of **holistic**, in database evidence from the BNC and CCAE.

Holland and Dutch

English treatment of the **Dutch** is a bit casual – at least in the way that the English language refers to them. **Holland** has been used by the English for the homeland of the **Dutch** people since C17, though it is actually the name of two of the twelve provinces (*Noord Holland, Zuid Holland*), and home to just 40% of the **Dutch** population. The official international name for the country is *The Netherlands*, which serves also as adjective, as in *the Netherlands ambassador to the UN*. (See under **Netherlands** for the history of that name.) Yet the term **Holland** persists in English usage, and is still used a good deal more than *(The) Netherlands* in the US, and about as much in the UK, according to database evidence.

The adjective **Dutch** was coined by English-speakers out of *deutsch* (the German word for "German"). Again it seems rather an approximation, despite the fact that the language and people of the Netherlands are Germanic in origin. The term "Pennsylvania Dutch," referring to the US community descended from early German settlers, preserves the older sense of the word.

Negative English attitudes seem to hang around the use of the word **Dutch/dutch**, in various none-too-flattering phrases such as *dutch courage, dutch treat*. Since those expressions owe more to English prejudice than any demonstrable customs of the **Dutch**, there's no reason to use a capital letter in them – though old writing habits die hard. *Webster's Third* (1986) notes that the capital is more likely to be used for the first expression than for the second, but the solitary example in CCAE is for *dutch treat*. Other examples such as *Dutch Treat: bicycling holidays in Amsterdam* may be either a play on the idiom or a reinterpretation of it which implies that it's dying a natural death. See further at **capital letters** section 2, and **throwaway terms**.

home in on or hone in on

The phrase **home in on** originated with pilots finding their direction beacons, or missiles which *home in on the heat emitted from the target satellite*. More figuratively, it's used of narrowing the focus of an inquiry or discussion, as in:

> Several unions homed in on "non-standard" workers.

The relatively uncommon verb *hone* ("sharpen") is sometimes used by mistake in that phrase. *Hone* can be used either literally (of sharpening a blade), or figuratively as in *honing his argument*, i.e. making it more pointed. In this sense it begins to overlap with figurative use of the verb *home,* and may be heard to replace it in **hone in on**. *Webster's English Usage* (1989) notes that **hone in on** seems to be on the increase, though there's little evidence of it in CCAE or the BNC – except in transcribed speech.

home page or homepage
See **homepage**.

homely, homey, homy or homie
Homely, originating in C14, meant "homelike," as it still can when applied to a setting or style of living. In such applications it has positive value, so that *a homely way of entertaining* would connote a lack of pretentiousness and artifice. But when applied to people and their appearance it becomes more ambivalent. In Britain, the phrase *homely girl* may still imply recognition of her practical and domestic skills, whereas in North America it's distinctly unflattering and means she is plain or unattractive.

Hom(e)y, coined in C19, is free of such ambiguity and simply connotes all the familiar and comfortable aspects of home life, as in:

> The food is decent, homey stuff
> Her homey Lancashire friendliness made everyone love her.

The spelling **homey** is strongly preferred, by the evidence of CCAE and the BNC. Yet **homy** is given preference in the *Oxford Dictionary* (1989), and is more regular in terms of the rules for final *-e* (see **-y/-ey**).

In the US and Australia, **homie** is a colloquial abbreviation of "homeboy," i.e. person from one's home town or neighborhood, and by extension a "member of a neighborhood gang."

homeopath and homoeopath, hom(o)eopathy and hom(o)eopathist
Despite the traditional Atlantic divide over the *oe* digraph (see **oe/e**), spellings with **homeo-** seem to have the edge the world over. In the Langscape survey of 1998–2001, a majority of respondents everywhere preferred *homeopathy*. Among Americans the vote was 100%, and 70% even among the British. *New Oxford* (1998) comes out in favor of **homeopathy** and **homeopath**. Fewer and fewer people find any value in preserving the classical *oe* digraph, used to represent a Greek diphthong in such words. The spelling *homeo-* is sufficient to distinguish them from *homo-* (see further under that heading). With its odd sequence of vowels, **homoeopath(y)** defies all the spelling conventions of English, and obscures its own pronunciation.

When it comes to choosing between **hom(o)eopath** and **hom(o)eopathist**, usage everywhere supports the shorter form. Both *Merriam-Webster* (2000) and the *Canadian Oxford* (1998) endorse **homeopath**, and it's the only spelling to be found in CCAE. In British usage as represented in the BNC, **hom(o)eopath** outnumbers **hom(o)eopathist** in the ratio of 4:1. Though both spellings (printed with *oe*) appear as full headwords in the *Oxford Dictionary* (1989), *New Oxford* concentrates attention on **homeopath**, and *homeopathist* is listed only as a run-on (see **ligatures**).

> **International English selection:** The spelling **homeopath** has the weight of usage behind it, even in Britain, and conforms better to the conventions of English spelling.

homepage or home page
Standard dictionaries such as *Merriam-Webster* (2000) and *New Oxford* (1998) allow only **home page** for the introductory page on a website, which acts as its front door and hallway to its resources. But *Wired Style* (1996) sets it solid as **homepage**, and web-users clearly prefer it. A Google search of the internet (2002) found **homepage** outnumbering **home page** by more than 7:1.

◊ Compare **webpage**.

homeward or homewards
See under **-ward**.

homie
See under **homely**.

hommos or hummus
See **hummus**.

homo-
This Greek prefix meaning "same" is used extensively in scholarly and scientific vocabulary as in:

> homocyclic   homodont   homogamy
> homologue   homophonic   homopolar
> homotaxis   homotransplant

A few examples of its use in common words are: *homogenize, homonym, homosexual*.

In one or two words, **homo-** is interchangeable with the look-alike Greek prefix: *hom(o)eo-* or *homoio-*, meaning "similar." So *homotransplant* varies with *hom(o)iotransplant*, and *homothermous* with *hom(o)iothermic*. But *hom(o)eo-* is the only one found in more common items such as *hom(o)eopath* and *homeostatic*. For the tendency to reduce *oe* to *e*, see **oe/e**.

Homo sapiens
This neo-Latin phrase identifies the fully evolved human being, with intellectual powers not shared by animal species. Literally it means "rational human," though the words appear in reverse order, as is usual in scientific nomenclature. **Homo sapiens** contrasts with earlier human species such as *Homo erectus* ("upright man": not stooping like a gorilla), and *Homo habilis* ("skilful man": able to make tools), now postulated as previous stages in human evolution. The initial capital letter conforms to the scientific convention of upper-casing the genus name and lower-casing the species name (see **scientific names**). The initial capital is sometimes dropped (**homo sapiens**) when the expression is used nontechnically as a paraphrase of "human being" or "human kind." For example:

> The biggest threat to both wolf and caribou is homo sapiens.

Its familiarity in American English is evident in the fact that over a third of all examples in CCAE were lower-cased. But the BNC has too few examples of the phrase to show this effect in British English.

Other variants of **Homo sapiens** are ad hoc creations by philosophers of humanity: *homo loquens* ("speaking man": one who has the power of speech), and *homo ludens* ("playful man": the irrepressible joker).

Note that in colloquial usage, *homo* is a derogatory abbreviation for *homosexual* (see further under **homo-**).

homoeopath or homoeopathist
See under **homeopath**.

homogeneous or homogenous

These two have had distinct applications, with **homogeneous** used anywhere to mean "made up of the same kind of elements," and **homogenous** by biologists to mean "of similar structure and/or origin." Amid the difficulty of keeping them apart, biologists have turned to *homologous* (for structure) and *homogenetic* (for origins), and so **homogenous** is free to roam. The convergence of **homogenous** with **homogeneous** has perhaps been helped by the spelling (and pronunciation) of *homogenize,* which means "make homogeneous." The interplay of the two words is recognized by crossreferencing in all major dictionaries – British, American, Canadian and Australian, though *New Oxford* (1998) and the *Canadian Oxford* (1998) still question the correctness of using **homogenous** for **homogeneous.** British/American divergence seems to emerge in the relative frequencies of the two spellings: **homogeneous** is 12 times more frequent than **homogenous** in BNC data, but only 3 times more frequent in CCAE.

homonyms

Words that are alike in form are **homonyms.** They may be alike in sound (*homophones*), such as *bail* and *bale* or *gibe, gybe* and *jibe.* Or they may be identical in their written form (*homographs*), such as *bear* ("carry") and *bear* ("large furry animal"), or *refuse* ("say no to") and *refuse* ("rubbish"). As the latter examples show, *homographs* may or may not be identical in sound. The point is that, although their spelling is identical, they are independent words by virtue of their separate etymologies. (Compare **polysemy**.)

English is well endowed with **homonyms,** partly because of its many one-syllabled words: *I, eye* and *aye.* But there are also plenty of examples with two or more syllables, such as *cellar/seller, gorilla/guerrilla, principal/principle, holy/holey/wholly.* Further **homonyms** are created when ordinary suffixes are added to words, as in *allowed/aloud* or *presents/presence.*

The quantity of **homonyms** in English is sometimes seen as a problem. Scholars in early modern English actually encouraged the use of distinct spellings for *homophones,* as visual reminders of their different meanings. To such efforts we owe the spellings *discreet* v. *discrete, flour* v. *flower,* among others which are maintained everywhere. But the same principle is embodied in others like *check/cheque, curb/kerb,* found only in British English. The different spellings are a two-edged sword: they help the reader, but they impose a heavier burden on the writer to know which goes with which meaning. When surrounding words help to settle the meaning, it seems rather unnecessary to insist on differentiated spellings. American writers who use fewer of them have no obvious difficulties in communicating.

The coincidence of **homonyms** or *homonymic clash* has sometimes seen the extinction of one of the two terms. The Old English word *neat* meaning "ox" has disappeared from modern English under pressure from the French-derived adjective *neat.* A small trace of the lost **homonym** can be found in *neat's foot oil.* **Homonyms** that are subject to some kind of taboo may impact negatively on the other, hence the replacement of *ass* by the Spanish-derived *burro* in

American English, presumably because of the clash with American pronunciation of *arse.*

homous or hommos

See **hummus.**

homy, homey or homie

See under **homely.**

honcho

Based on the Japanese *han cho* ("group leader"), this is used in informal business and corporate reporting to refer to the person in charge. It is still more American than British English, and little represented in BNC except in the slightly redundant phrase *head honcho.* That phrase also appears in a score of American examples in CCAE, and is occasionally paraphrased by *top honcho* or *chief honcho.* But **honcho** is also modified in other ways, as in *network honcho, brand-new Columbia honcho, behind-the-scenes honcho, a crooked, cocaine-snorting honcho,* and thus provides a matrix for relevant information. There's further evidence of its productivity in *honchoette;* and Garner (1998) illustrates its use as a verb (*honchoed, honchoing*) where it means "champion a cause." For the moment it's strongly associated with journalism, and whether the association can be neutralized remains to be seen.

hone in on

See **home in on.**

honi soit qui mal y pense

This ancient French exclamation, literally "shamed be [anyone] who thinks evil of it," is first recorded in English in the medieval poem *Sir Gawain and the Green Knight.* It may be a proverb, though in later tradition it was associated with an act of gallantry by Edward III, founder of the Order of the Garter. As legend had it, he was dancing with the Countess of Salisbury when her garter slipped to the floor. He picked it up, and to save her embarrassment put it on his own leg, saying "honi soit qui mal y pense." Thus interpreted, the statement is intended to call the bluff of those who would entertain scandalous thoughts.

honor or honour

See under **-or/-our.**

honorarium

The receipt of an **honorarium** (fee for professional services rendered) is a paradoxical sign that the recipient is not working in an *honorary* capacity. This puts the word into American newspaper headlines amid public scrutiny of politicians' sources of income, and both Latin and English plurals seem to be used: *honoraria* by the *Washington Post,* and *honorariums* by the *Los Angeles Times.* Both in the US and in UK, **honoraria** appears in a wider range of published materials, by the evidence of CCAE and the BNC. The legal and contractual nature of the word would perhaps explain the tenacity of the Latin plural. For other loanwords of this type, see **-um.**

honorary or hono(u)rable

Different facets of the word *honor* are embodied in **hono(u)rable** and **honorary. Hono(u)rable** serves to express the idealistic side of *hono(u)r,* as in *honorable* *motives* where it applauds high-mindedness in the individual. In this sense it may be spelled **honorable** or **honourable**, depending on one's policy with *hono(u)r.* (Cf. **honorary** below, and see **-or/-our**.) It becomes a courtesy title in *The Hono(u)rable,* used in various institutions, in written references to:

* the offspring of British aristocracy, including the sons of a marquess, earl, viscount or baron; and daughters of earls and below: *The Honourable Diana Spencer.* Other institutional titles precede rather than follow: *Captain the Honourable Christopher Knolly.*
* senior members of the judiciary in Britain, Australia and Canada: *The Honourable Mr. Justice Kirby.* In the US it would be *Honorable Michael Kirby.*
* Cabinet officers in the US, federal ministers in Canada and Australia as well as provincial/state ministers: *The Hono(u)rable Carmen Lawrence.* In the UK, Cabinet ministers are entitled to *Right Honourable,* as members of the Privy Council.
* members (and former members) of the Canadian Senate: *The Honourable Mary Kelly.*
* members of the US Senate, House of Representatives, and State legislatures: *Honorable John Krask.*

All such titles can be abbreviated to *the Hon.*

Honorary also has its official uses, with various implications. The spelling never has a *u,* because of its Latin derivation. An *honorary secretary* is one who works for an organization without receiving any remuneration, and perhaps gains some honor and recognition for it. An *honorary president* is appointed on a rather different basis, as a figurehead with no obligation to help run the organization – as when the Prime Minister's wife is made *honorary president* of a charity. An *honorary degree* has something in common with both uses of **honorary**. It is usually awarded to a distinguished person who does not have to submit to the normal examination procedures; but it also gives recognition to his or her achievements in a particular field. In Latin it is simply said to be *honoris causa* ("for reason[s] of honor").

The Hon. (the Hon.) serves to abbreviate both *The Hono(u)rable* and *the Honorary.* The first underlies *The Hon. Mrs. Anderson Hunt* and *Colonel the Hon. Sir Charles Palmer,* and the second *the Hon. Secretary, Mr. Ken Lucas.* In practice the institutional title always follows directly for *the Honorary,* whereas personal titles or names follow directly, for *The Hono(u)rable.*

honorifics

These are conventional words or phrases used to show respect to the holders of particular ranks or offices. Calling the ambassador "your Excellency," the bishop "His Grace," the judge "your Hono(u)r," the queen "your Majesty" and the pope "His Holiness" are all examples. Some dictionaries also apply the term *honorific* to items such as *Sir, Reverend, Professor,* which might more strictly be called *titles.* See under **forms of address** section 1.

honoris causa

See under **cum laude**.

-hood

This very old English suffix makes abstract nouns out of concrete ones, to create words which identify a state

of being, such as *childhood, manhood, womanhood.* Yet others refer to groups of people with particular status and identity: *brotherhood, knighthood, priesthood.* The most recent formations in these groups are *nationhood* and *sisterhood.*

hoofed or hooved

See under **-v-/-f-**.

hoofs or hooves

See under **-f > -v-**.

hopefully

This word has acquired a new use in C20 English, and especially since the mid-1960s, according to *Webster's English Usage* (1989). It has drawn a remarkable amount of criticism in sentences such as the following:
Hopefully they will go and buy the record.
Objections to this usage are based on the assumption that **hopefully** is and can only be an adverbial adjunct of manner, and so in that sentence it must mean that the record-buyers are *hopeful.* Yet no-one would seriously doubt that the word **hopefully** in such contexts expresses the hopes of the person speaking or writing. It is an attitudinal adverb (or *disjunct*) which contributes interpersonal meaning to the statement (see further under **adverbs** section 1). It takes its place beside numerous others, including:

confidentially	*frankly*	*happily*
honestly	*incredibly*	*luckily*
mercifully	*naturally*	*sadly*
surprisingly	*thankfully*	*unfortunately*

So why the objection to **hopefully**? Perhaps it was the sudden rise of the word in the early 60s, and the critical spotlight put on it by the popular press. Perhaps its frequent appearance as the first word of a clause or sentence (as above) makes it conspicuous and clichéd. Yet despite the continuing resentment of "conservative speakers" (Burchfield, 1996), this use of **hopefully** is very common. Amid hundreds of BNC examples of the word, more than 75% make it an attitudinal adverb. The *Longman Grammar* (1999) finds it in news reports and academic prose, as well as conversation. *Webster's English Usage* believes that the high tide of objections to it in the US was about 1975. High time to cease making a fetish of it!

horde or hoard

See **hoard**.

horrible, horrid, horrendous, horrific or horrifying

All these are related to the word *horror.* Yet "desperate fear" is not always the motive for using them, especially when they are adverbs. In phrases such as *horribly awkward* and *horrendously expensive* they serve only as intensifiers of the following word. As adjectives too, their meaning is beginning to be diluted, as when people talk of a *horrible performance of Beethoven* or having *a horrid day.* In such expressions **horrible** and **horrid** connote a generally negative judgement, and could be paraphrased as "deplorable" and "disagreeable." In colloquial usage there's a persistent tendency for strong words to be overused and to lose their force. It has already happened to *awful* and *terrific,* and the word *formidable* has been diluted in a similar way in French. Fear and terror seem sooner or later to desert the very adjectives which embody them. But if you need a strong word, the last two in the list above, **horrific** and **horrifying**, still connote real *horror*.

hors d'oeuvre(s)

This French phrase, meaning roughly "outside the meal," is well established in English as a way of referring to the preliminary course or the delicacies served with cocktails. **Hors d'oeuvre** is used naturally enough for the first meaning, as in *caviar is the ultimate hors d'oeuvre;* and **hors d'oeuvres** is used regularly for the second meaning in British and American English, as in *they munched hors d'oeuvres and drank champagne.* Some insist that **hors d'oeuvre** should never be pluralized because it's not a noun in French, let alone a count noun (see **count and mass nouns**). But the *New Oxford Dictionary* (1998) and others allow either form for the plural; and **hors d'oeuvres** is in fact the overwhelming choice of writers in the BNC and CCAE, for referring to multiple delicacies on the cocktail plate. See further under **plurals** section 2.

horsy or horsey

Though **horsy** is endorsed by the *Oxford Dictionary* (1989), *Webster's Third* (1986) gives priority to **horsey**; and **horsey** is now the more popular spelling in British and American usage, by the evidence of BNC and CCAE. The trend goes against the more regular spelling convention of dropping *-e* before the *-y* suffix. See **-y/-ey**.

horticulturist or horticulturalist

The shorter form is endorsed in current British and American English. More than 70% of examples in BNC and over 95% of those in CCAE used **horticulturist**. For divergences with other such words, see under **-ist**.

hosteler or hosteller

In British English there are centuries between the ancient **hosteler** who provided accommodation for travelers, and the contemporary **hosteller** who makes the most of youth hostels (= *hostelling*). But in American English **hosteler** is the standard spelling for the person who stays at youth hostels and travels by *hosteling*. The divergence over single and double *l* is discussed under **doubling of final consonant**.

hotchpot, hotchpotch or hodgepodge

These three show how easily a word can transform itself over the centuries. **Hotchpot** originated in C13 English law, as the term for the conglomeration of property which is divided equally between the children of parents who die without making a will. By C15, as **hotchpotch** or **hodgepodge**, it had acquired a use in cookery as a term for a stew of meat and vegetables. Another century and both spellings are also used to refer to any mishmash or miscellany of items.

Nowadays, **hotchpotch** prevails in Britain and Australia as the usual spelling for "mishmash" and "stew," and as an occasional alternative to **hotchpot** for the term in law. **Hodgepodge** gets little use. In North America all three terms are deployed: **hodgepodge** for "mishmash," **hotchpotch** ("stew"), and **hotchpot** is the usual spelling for the legal concept.

hoummos or hummus

See **hummus**.

hove or heaved

See under **heaved**.

however

Versatile and mobile, **however** has two distinct meanings (*indefinite* and *contrastive*), which are not often distinguished in prescriptive comments about it, nor the fact that it has two grammatical roles, as adverb and conjunction. **However** has traditionally been associated with academic and discursive writing, but is also heard now from time to time in conversation. Its role there is beginning to affect its grammar.

1 Indefinite however serves as an adverb or as a conjunction. Compare:
> *However hard they walked, they would not get back before dark.* (adverb)
> *However they went, it would take half a day.* (conjunction)

Either way the position of *indefinite* **however** is fixed. As an adverb (*subjunct*) in the first sentence, it must *precede* the adjective it qualifies; and as conjunction in the second it must appear as the very first word of the clause. Note also that *indefinite* **however** heads a subordinate clause, whereas *contrastive* **however** conjoins main clauses (see below, section 3). This grammatical difference is unmistakable as one reads on in the sentence, and prevents confusion between them.

◊ For a discussion of *indefinite* **however** and **how ever** (spaced), see **-ever**.

2 Contrastive however is first and foremost an adverb, more specifically a *conjunct* or *linking adverb* (see **adverbs** section 1). **However** underscores a point of contrast which is also a link with the previous clause or sentence:
> *We were keen to keep going; they however had had enough.*

However usually follows the contrasting item, and its position in the sentence varies according to the intended scope of the contrast. In that example it creates a sharp contrast between *they* and *we*. Broader or more focused contrasts can be achieved with **however** in other positions:
> *We were keen to keep going.*
> *However they had had enough.*

(contrast between the whole of the first sentence, and the second sentence)
> *We were keen to keep going.*
> *They had had enough however.*

(contrast between the two predicates: *keen to keep going / had enough*) By its mobility as well as its own bulk, **however** helps to draw attention to the contrast. Its three syllables make it a weighty substitute for *but*, and some computer style checkers flag it as "wordy." Used occasionally its effect is powerful.

Note that there is no basis for suggesting that *contrastive* **however** should not appear at the beginning of a sentence – except perhaps through confusion with *indefinite* **however**. In fact almost half of the instances of *contrastive* **however** in BNC informative writing appeared as the first word of a sentence. The *Longman Grammar* (1999) shows that this is the most common position for linking adverbs generally, in speech and in academic prose. Yet *contrastive* **however** also tends to occur immediately after the topic item of the sentence (see **topic**), as in:

> *The Government, however, has "no immediate plans" to change . . .*
> *Under federal law, however, any merger of their operations . . .*
> *Once the centre opened, however, it quickly became apparent . . .*

In this position **however** underscores the preceding phrase or clause quite emphatically, while serving its contrastive and cohesive function (see **coherence or cohesion** section 2).

3 Punctuation with contrastive however. Older books on style often say that **however** should be hedged about with commas, or else a comma and a heavier stop (period/semicolon). The exemplary sentences would then read:

> *They, however, had had enough.*
> *They had had enough, however.*

These days, amid the general trend to reduce punctuation marks, the comma(s) are often left out, especially when **however** is the first or second item in a simple sentence:

> *However they had had enough.*
> *They however had had enough.*

This practice is explicitly endorsed by the *Chicago Manual* (1993). It says that the commas associated with adverbs like **however** (*therefore, indeed* etc.) should be left out when "there is no real break in continuity, and no call for any pause in reading."

But in compound sentences, the punctuation that precedes **however** has important implications for its grammar. Compare:

> *We were keen to keep going. However they had had enough.*
> *We were keen to keep going; however they had had enough.*
> *We were keen to keep going, however they had had enough.*

With the punctuation of the first and second examples, **however** is definitely an adverbial conjunct, working within the confines of its own sentence/clause. The comma used in the third sentence would make **however** a full conjunction. This shift to conjunction is disallowed in prescriptive grammar, for reasons unclear, except that it would enlarge what is usually taught as a closed set of conjunctions. Yet transcriptions of speech from the BNC show that **however** works easily as a conjunction in the flow of discourse:

> *This was a common pattern, however there is one exception.*

The intonation contour would confirm that **however** functions there as a conjunction. The comma reflects that usage in speech transcriptions, and writers may also find occasion for it. Neither the *Oxford Dictionary* (1989) nor *Webster's Third* (1986) allows that *contrastive* **however** can be a conjunction, and yet its currency is implicit in Burchfield's (1996) stern censure of "using *however* as a substitute for *but*." Garner (1998) acknowledges its presence in American English, as well as the fact that it tends to be edited out by composition teachers and professional editors. Some dictionaries, for example *Collins* (1991), do update the record by calling *contrastive* **however** a "sentence connector," a cover term which is designed to "replace the traditional classification of words as adverbs or conjunctions." (See further under **conjunctions and conjuncts**.)

While grammarians and dictionary-makers debate its classification, those anxious about the status of contrastive **however** can always take the precaution of using a semicolon in front of it (or a period / full stop), as shown in the last set of examples above. It's just a game, really!

human or humane

These adjectives both appeal to the better characteristics of mankind. There are loftier principles in **humane**, and a *humane approach* to the prisoners connotes compassion and concern in situations where others might react harshly. The reactions implied in **human** are much more down-to-earth and typical:

> *It was only human to laugh at the situation.*

In their negative forms (*inhuman* and *inhumane*), the two words differ again. *Inhumane* is somewhat formal and detached, pinpointing the lack of compassion, whereas *inhuman* is charged with a sense of outrage, implying the complete absence of any sympathetic traits, to the point of being monstrous:

> *Slave transportation involved the inhuman practice of packing people in between decks, shackled together side by side without head room.*

humanity, humanism or humanitarianism

The last and longest of these abstract nouns is the most straightforward. **Humanitarianism** simply means the philosophy of serving and helping people. **Humanism** is the kind of scholarship which concentrates on the tradition of arts and literature in our culture, and the human values they express. The word is also used to refer to a nontheistic approach to life and our place in the universe, and so the word has negative connotations in fundamentalist theology.

Humanity is first and foremost the abstract noun for the adjective *human* (see **human or humane**), and also the collective word for "people at large" or "mankind." It can be a useful synonym for "mankind" for those who find that word sexist. The plural form **humanities** refers to the scholarly disciplines which are concerned with arts and literature (cf. **humanism**). The word then contrasts with sciences and social sciences.

humbug

This is a two-faced word, much like the meanings it carries. It refers both to the imposter and his/her deceptive talk as well as what is perceived as nonsense. Compare:

> *The dear old humbug lied.*
> *. . . cut through the humbug and pretence of the art world*

The second, abstract use of the noun is much more common than the first, in data from both BNC and CCAE. Critical uses of the word by both understatement and overstatement (*so much humbug, monumental humbug*) are much more common than indulgent ones. American usage highlights the ambivalence of **humbug**, with P.T. Barnum, the self-styled *prince of humbug*, along with the "*Bah, humbug*" of Dickens's Scrooge, reacting ungenerously to Christmas celebrations. An additional use of **humbug** (in the UK, Canada and Australia, but not the US) is to refer to an item of confectionery, e.g. *peppermint humbugs*.

Most dictionaries register the now rare use of **humbug** as a verb. It occurs in only a handful of texts in the BNC and not at all in CCAE. When it does, the final letter is doubled (*humbugged/humbugging*), like that of other compound verbs whose second syllable has a life of its own. (See **doubling of final consonant** note 3.)

The derivative *humbuggery* (first recorded 1831) adds the French suffix *-erie* (see **-ery**) to Anglo-Saxon-looking **humbug** (origin unknown), forming a hybrid which incidentally hints at the taboo as well as meaningless nonsense. This makes it a liability, though in political mud-slinging it lends itself to elaborate putdowns – the suggestion that an opposition speaker must have earned a degree in *advanced humbuggery*.

hummus, hommos or hoummos

For that tasty Arabic food made from ground chick peas and sesame oil, there are multiple spellings in English. The variation between single and double *m*, and the various permutations and combinations of *u* and *o* allow for 18 alternative spellings, sometimes seen on menus and product labels. However the field is narrowed down in published texts, and **hummus** is the commonest by far in both British and American databases (BNC and CCAE). Alongside **hummus**, *Webster's Third* (1986) features **hommos**, which contributes about 1 in 8 of the citations in CCAE. The *Oxford Dictionary* (1989) adds **hoummous**, but it is nowhere to be found in BNC data. There are however a very few examples of *humous* and *houmus*.

One other possible spelling is *humus,* used inadvertently by at least one writer in both BNC and CCAE. This is the actual spelling in modern Turkish, but in English it's to be avoided because of the clash with the (neo-Latin) word for "rotting leaf matter." Most dictionaries trace the gastronomic word to Arabic *hummus,* hence their traditional preference for that spelling in English.
◊ For other gastronomic loanwords with multiple spellings, see **falafel, kebab, tabbouleh, yogurt**.

humor or humour

See next entry and further under **-or/-our**.

humorous, humorist and humoresque

All these are spelled with *humor-*, which is a very good reason for preferring *humor* to *humour* (see **-or/-our**). All are borrowed words, connecting with the underlying Latin *humor* via late C16 French (in the case of the first two) and with late C19 German *Humoreske* (in the case of the third).

humus or humous

In scientific and horticultural prose, there's a grammatical difference between these (see under **-ous**). But both spellings are among the variants for a traditional Arabic dish: see **hummus, hommos or hoummos**.

hung or hanged

See under **hanged**.

hurricane, tornado or cyclone

See under **cyclone**.

hyaena or hyena

See **hyena**.

hydr-/hydro-

Either of these is the Greek element meaning "water," familiar in words such as:

hydrant	hydrate	hydraulic
hydroelectric	hydrofoil	hydrogen
hydrophobia	hydroponic	hydrotherapy

But in the names of some chemical compounds, **hydro-** is a short form for "hydrogen." See for example, *hydrocarbon* and *hydrofluoric acid*.

Note that while a *hydrometer* measures the specific gravity of liquids, a *hygrometer* measures the humidity of the atmosphere. The latter embodies the less well-known Greek element *hygro-* ("moisture").

hydra

The plural of this word is discussed at **-a** section 1.

hydrolyse or hydrolyze

See under **-yze/-yse**.

hyena or hyaena

The classical spelling **hyaena** was introduced in C16, to replace medieval forms such as *hiene*. But it has never been very popular, and the spellings *hyene* and **hyena** suggest that the earlier English form with just *e* persisted and was preferred. Modern dictionaries all give **hyena** first preference.

hype

See under **hyperbole**.

hyper-

This Greek prefix means "over, excessive(ly)," as in:

hyperactive	hyperbole
hypercritical	hyperglyc(a)emia
hyperreactive	hypersensitive
hypertensive	hyperthermia
hyperventilation	

Although **hyper-** is the Greek counterpart of Latin *super-*, the two cannot normally be interchanged because **hyper-** often has negative connotations, and *super-* positive ones (see **super-**). Yet in some pairs of words **hyper-** sets itself higher than *super-*, as in *hypermarket* (clearly one up on the supermarket), and *hypersonic* which is five times faster than *supersonic*. The use of **hyper-** in *hypertext* associates it with the complex structures of electronic documents, hence also *hyperlinks,* for the instant connections between them.

A number of **hyper-** words have been coined as technical terms to contrast with words beginning with *hypo-;* see for example *hyperthermia/ hypothermia*, and further under **hypo-**. Meanwhile in chemistry, the prefix **hyper-** has been decommissioned. It was formerly used in the naming of compounds as *per-* is nowadays, to show that a given element was at its maximum valence (or a relatively high one). See further under **per-**.

Hyper has also established itself as an independent word meaning "overstimulated," "obsessive" or "hyperactive." Here again there's a negative coloring in each of them.

hyperbole or hyperbola

Both these words are modern uses of the Greek *hyperbole,* and originate in the image of throwing a ball high over something. **Hyperbola** is a mathematical term for an off-centre vertical section cut down through a cone to its base. **Hyperbole** is the term given in rhetoric to exaggeration used as a figure of speech. What is said should not be taken literally, but has an emotive or intensifying effect as in the following from a popular song:

> *The future's so bright I gotta wear shades!*

(See further under **figures of speech**.)

The colloquial word *hype* ("publicity designed to create excitement") is thought by some to be an abbreviation of **hyperbole**. Others connect it with *hypodermic* and the drug culture.

hypercorrection

People's anxiety about getting their grammar and pronunciation right can produce expression which is out of step with common usage. The use of "haitch" (rather than "aitch") for the name of the letter *H* suggests a generalized worry about dropping *h*s, resulting in a tendency to "correct" words which do not need it. Saying *between you and I* (rather than *between you and me*) could be explained in the same way (see **between you and me [or I]**). Some uses of *whom* are really **hypercorrection** (see **whom** section 3). The replacement of *cheap* by *cheaply* in idioms such as *bought it cheap* suggests an anxiety about the bare form of the adverb; see further under **zero adverbs**. All these and other phenomena generate expressions which are unidiomatic and awkward – worse than the ones they are designed to "correct." Hall's (1952) title *Leave Your Language Alone* is apt here.

hypercritical or hypocritical

The first of these is easily explained in terms of *hyper-* ("excessively") and *critical:*

> *The reviews were hypercritical of his piano technique.*

Hypercritical is a relatively recent word (only four centuries old), whereas **hypocritical** goes back to Greek theatre. It owes its meaning to *hypocrite,* which in Greek referred to the mime who accompanied the delivery of an actor with gestures. It then came to mean anyone speaking under a particular guise. (See further under **hyper-** and **hypo-**.)

hypernym

This is an alternative name for the superordinate term in *hyponymy*. See under **hyponyms**.

hypertext

See under **hyper-** and **page**.

hyphens

The single most variable element in the writing of words is the **hyphen**, hence the large amount of discussion it generates. **Hyphens** serve both to link and to separate the components of words; and while they are established in the spelling of certain words, they come and go from many others. The use or nonuse of **hyphens** varies somewhat in different Englishes round the world. In the UK under the influence of the *Oxford* dictionaries,

hyphens seem to be used relatively often, and certainly more often than in the US, where according to *Webster's* dictionaries the same words may be set solid, or spaced (if compounds). Canadians and Australians are somewhere between Britons and Americans in their readiness to use **hyphens**.

Though there are few fixed conventions over **hyphens**, authorities do agree on such underlying principles as:

* restrict the use of **hyphens** as far as possible
* shed the linking **hyphen** from the better established formations
* use **hyphens** to separate letter sequences which distract the reader from construing the word correctly

But how to apply these principles to words such as *co(-)operate* and *co(-)ordinate* is still a matter of debate. To resolve the issue, writers are sometimes encouraged to adopt the practices of one dictionary – although dictionaries themselves have mixed policies. Their use/nonuse of **hyphens** with particular words may reflect either typical usage (in so far as they are able to research it), or else editorial policy and their desire to achieve consistency within their own headword list. A further problem is that dictionary lists do not include all possible compounds ("transparent" ones are omitted); nor do they always show what happens to compounds when they are used in new grammatical roles. Many noun compounds which are normally spaced, e.g. *cold shoulder* or *first night,* acquire **hyphens** when they become verbs (*they cold-shouldered him*) or adjectives (*first-night nerves*).

As in these examples, the grammar of words is quite often what helps to decide whether they should be hyphenated or not. This is why grammatical classes and structures are used below in presenting the general practices for hyphenating *compounds*. But when dealing with *complex words,* the legibility of the string of letters is usually the most important issue.

In the following sections we are concerned with the so-called "hard hyphens" (ones which would be used whenever the word appears), and not "soft hyphens" (ones used to show when a word has been divided at the end of a line, because of insufficient space). Questions about soft **hyphens** and where to divide words are discussed at **wordbreaks**.

◊ For the so-called *hanging hyphen* or *floating hyphen,* see **hanging hyphen**.

1 **Complex words** with prefixes are not normally hyphenated, but set solid. See for example:

> amoral   biennial   cohabit
> counterrevolutionary   debrief   dissociate
> excommunicate

In some cases however, as with *co-* and *ex-,* it depends on whether the word is an older or newer type of formation. See further under **co-** and **ex-**.
Other exceptions to that general principle are:

a) using a **hyphen** when the prefix ends in the same vowel as the first letter of the root word, as in:

> anti-intellectual   cf. antireligious
> de-emphasize   deactivate

As these examples show, there's no apparent difficulty when a different vowel follows the prefix, at least in longer and established words. However in short words such as *de-ice* and *re-ink,* a **hyphen** seems desirable to prevent misreading.

b) introducing a **hyphen** in formations which would otherwise be identical with another word. So the **hyphen** in *re-cover* (the furniture) helps to distinguish it from *recover*, just as one in *re-mark* differentiates it from *remark* etc.

c) using a **hyphen** when the following word involves a change in typography, such as capital letters, numbers, to or from italics, or quotation marks:

*anti-Fascist   post-1954   pre-*perestroika
un-"macho"

Complex words with suffixes are almost always set solid, witness:

*advertisement   chauvinism   rationalize
resourceful*

A **hyphen** is still sometimes inserted where the root ends in a vowel and the following suffix begins with a vowel, particularly in formations which are new or not commonly seen in print. So *more-ish* is preferred by some to *moreish* (which violates the general principle of dropping *-e* before suffixes beginning with a vowel; see **-e**). Some writers also prefer a **hyphen** before *-ed* and *-ing* in ad hoc verbs such as *quota-ed* and *to-ing and fro-ing*. Alternative devices are discussed under **-ed** (section 3).

2 Compounds. The use of **hyphens** with compounds at large seems rather unpredictable. Yet within certain grammatical groups, especially verbs, adverbs and adjectives, there are regular principles. Noun compounds (see below, [d]) are the most varied group of all.

a) **Compound verbs** are either hyphenated or set solid, depending on their components. Those consisting of a noun + verb, such as *baby-sit, gift-wrap, red-pencil, short-list* are typically hyphenated. Those consisting of an adverb + verb, such as *bypass, outlast, underrate, upstage* are set solid.

b) **Compound adverbs** are usually set solid, witness examples such as the following:

*barefoot   downstairs   overboard
underground   upstream*

c) **Compound adjectives** are typically hyphenated, but see the exceptions (both set solid and spaced) below. The typical pattern is seen in established cases such as:

*tone-deaf   red-hot   all-embracing
home-baked   icy-cold   labor-saving
nuclear-free open-ended*

Hyphens are also used in ad hoc compound adjectives, as in *open-door policy* and *red-carpet treatment*, to ensure they're construed as intended by the writer. They are also used regularly in compounds which contain numbers written as full words, for example *four-part, two-state*, as well as in fractions used in adjectival roles: *two-thirds majority*. See however the last exception below, when numbers are written as Arabic numerals.

Exceptions to the hyphenated pattern are:

*a few very well-established adjective compounds which are set solid. They usually consist of a simple adverb + verb, such as *everlasting, forthcoming, underdone, widespread*.

*compounds with an inflected adverb or adjective as their first element, which are normally spaced. So there's no **hyphen** in expressions such as the following:

*badly displayed goods
fully fledged scheme*

*higher level units
best known examples*

*adjectives involving *more, most, less, least*. **Hyphens** are only used if there is some danger of ambiguity – for example *more expert staff* could be read as either *(more expert) staff* or *more (expert staff)* – and then only if the sentence cannot be reworded to clarify the issue. Writers should avoid having their meaning hang on a **hyphen**.

*compound adjectives which are institutionalized concepts, such as:

*equal opportunity employer
city council elections
high school teachers
twelfth century manuscript*

*compound adjectives which embrace items with a change of typography, including Arabic numbers, capitals, italics and quotation marks. For example:

*Year 12 students
the US Airforce base
their **haute cuisine** menu
his "do" or "die" attitude*

Style manuals including the *Chicago Manual* (2003) and the *Oxford Guide to Style* (2002) recommend against using **hyphens** in foreign phrases used as compound adjectives, whether or not they are italicized. So there would be no **hyphen** in expressions such as *de facto marriage* or *dernier cri footwear*. Foreign phrases are read as units, and their components do not need to be linked with **hyphens**.

d) **Compound nouns** can be written with **hyphens**, spaced, or set solid, depending somewhat on what they consist of (see below). Yet quite a number of them have different settings according to different dictionaries. Noun compounds, more than any others, are subject to the well-known principle that they begin life spaced, become hyphenated, and are finally set solid. See for example: *dark room, dark-room, darkroom*. However authorities often differ over how well advanced the integration of the two components may be, with British dictionaries often prolonging the use of the **hyphen**, and their American counterparts preferring to join up the components or else keep them spaced.

Of all the major grammatical types, *noun compounds* are least likely to need a **hyphen** (or solid setting) to ensure that their components are read together. The great majority of them have the qualifying component first and the qualified component second, so they can be read like any ordinary sequence of adjective plus noun. Many may just as well be left spaced, and dictionaries the world over show that this is the normal practice with some types particularly:

* those consisting of two polysyllabic words, e.g. *geography teacher, unemployment benefit*

* those whose first component has more than one syllable, e.g. *buffer state, concert pitch, customs house*

* those with strong stress on both components, e.g. *damp squib, green ban, tree fern*

Apart from these considerations, the internal grammar of the compound can often suggest how it's likely to be set, as follows:

i) **those consisting of a simple adjective + noun**, such as *black market, red tape,* are usually spaced. The exceptions are elliptical expressions such as *bigwig, redneck,* which combine to qualify another (understood) entity.

ii) **those consisting of adverb + verb, or verb + adverb,** such as *downpour, runoff,* are usually set solid – except that a **hyphen** is used to separate an otherwise distracting sequence of letters, as in *go-ahead, shake-out.* Hyphens are used as a connecting device when there are inflections on the verbal first element, as in:

goings-on   hanger-on   passer-by
summing-up

iii) **those consisting of verb + noun or noun + verb,** such as *rattlesnake, snakebite,* may go one of two ways. When the verb component comes first and is inflected, the parts are usually left spaced, as in *flying saucer, helping hand, revolving door.* When the inflected verb is the second component, the compound is usually set solid:

mindreader   wordprocessor   glassblowing
sightseeing

iv) **those consisting of noun + noun** can often be left spaced, as in *dial tone, trade union, traffic jam.* But they are set solid when the second component is a common and general word which depends on the preceding word for its specificity. See for example:

policeman   anchorman   chairman
marketplace   birthplace   commonplace
letterhead   bulkhead   figurehead
tigerfish   jellyfish   lumpfish
roadwork   wickerwork   earthwork

The few sets of noun compounds that regularly have **hyphens** are structured differently from all of the above. They are:

* those in which the two components are very much equal terms, e.g. *city-state, owner-operator, secretary-stenographer*
* those with rhyming or reduplicative components, e.g. *culture-vulture, hanky-panky, sin-bin*
* those with a specifying phrase following the head noun, e.g. *ambassador-at-large, mother-in-law, theatre-in-the-round.* Outside the US (in Britain, Canada and Australia), there are more in this category, e.g. *editor-in-chief, lady-in-waiting, prisoner-of-war.*

◊ For the use of **hyphens** in placenames involving French saints, see **Saint** section 1.

hypo-

This Greek prefix means "under" or "lower in location or degree." It appears in scholarly words, and a few which have become generally familiar, such as:

hypodermic   hypoglyc(a)emia   hyponym
hypotaxis   hypothermia   hypothesis
hypoventilation

In the names of chemical compounds, **hypo-** indicates a low valency of the particular element it qualifies, as in *sodium hypochloride,* the active element in household bleach.

What does **hypo-** have to do with the *hypochondriac? Hypochondria* was the medieval name for the abdomen: the soft part of the body beneath the ribs, thought of as the seat of that generalized malaise of people preoccupied with their health.

◊ For **hypocritical,** see under **hypercritical.**

hypocorisms

A **hypocorism** is an affectionate name for a person, an animal or a familiar object, such as *Libby* for *Elizabeth; pussy* for a *cat, potty* for a *chamber pot.* **Hypocorisms** are often associated with talking to children. Yet the familiarity and closeness they express is like that of "familiarity markers" used colloquially among adults, when naming objects, persons and events, for example *brolly, cabby, footy, telly.* The *-y* and *-ie* suffixes are particularly productive in forming **hypocorisms**; others are *-ers* as in *champers* and *-s* as in the *creeps/hots/sulks.* (See further under **-ie/-y,** as well as **-er/-ers** and **-s**). **Hypocorisms** are more common in British than American writing, and in continuous creation in Australia.

◊ Compare **diminutives.**

hypocrisy

To spell this word correctly, think of *hypo-* ("under"), and "crisis." For more about the word's meaning, see under **hypercritical.**

hypoglycemia or hypoglycaemia

For the choice between these, see under **hem-/haem-.**

hyponyms

This is the linguist's word for specific terms (such as *carrot, onion, lettuce*) which are embraced and interrelated through a single cover term: *vegetables. Vegetables* is the *superordinate* term, which serves to identify the class to which the set of **hyponyms** belongs. The classes themselves may be further subdivided, e.g. *vegetables* breaks into *root vegetables* and *green vegetables,* to add an intermediate level of *hyponymy:*

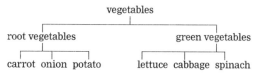

Root vegetables could be further subdivided into roots (*carrot*), bulbs (*onion*), tubers (*potato*), to make each of those a *superordinate* and allow for more **hyponyms** – turnips, parsnips, swedes under *roots.* (Note that linguists sometimes use the term *hypernym* for the *superordinate.*)

The relationship between **hyponyms** and their nearer or more remote superordinates is important in the cognitive structures of thinking and writing. They allow us to move up and down the "ladder of abstraction" in argumentative prose (see further under **abstract noun**). **Hyponyms** also contribute to cohesion in writing. See under **coherence or cohesion.**

hypotaxis

This is an alternative name in grammar for *subordination.* In traditional grammar **hypotaxis** referred to the hierarchical relationship of a subordinate clause to the main clause (see **clauses** section 3). Modern grammarians have extended its use. The *Introduction to Functional Grammar* (Halliday, 1994) has it embrace other constructions which paraphrase subordinate clauses, such as nonfinite clauses and expressions of indirect reported speech. In the *Comprehensive Grammar of English* (1985) **hypotaxis** is also applied to the internal structure of phrases.

hysteron proteron

This phrase, borrowed from Greek, means "the latter sooner," but is put to different purposes in rhetoric and argument. As a figure of speech, **hysteron proteron** reverses the expected order of events: *they died, they starved in their cave*. A somewhat similar displacement is involved in *hendiadys,* which involves altering the normal construction of a phrase, so that "with curious eyes" becomes "with eyes and curiosity."

In argument **hysteron proteron** refers to an inverted form of logic, in which a proposition can only be proved with the help of the proposition itself. In other words it "begs the question." See also **fallacies** section 2.

I

When can **I** be used in writing? It depends on what's being written. Personal letters, diaries and autobiography are the natural medium for **I**, talking about opinions, attitudes and feelings ("I think," "I know," "I feel" etc.). **I** occurs naturally in scripted dialogue and many types of fiction. But in professional writing we conventionally avoid **I** even when expressing individual opinions. Thus a reviewer is less likely to say:

> *I was delighted by the freshness of the performance . . .*

than

> *The performance was delightfully fresh.*

Personal opinion is less obvious in the second sentence, where it's blended into the description with an attitudinal adverb ("delightfully"). It implies that anyone viewing the performance would see it that way, as if there's a weight of opinion behind the comment. By avoiding the use of **I**, the writer masks the subjectiveness of the reaction.

The need to sound authoritative and professional no doubt underlies the convention of avoiding **I** in academic and bureaucratic writing. It also applies in science, though it was not always so. Newton and other pioneering scientists used **I** quite freely. The pronoun was not regularly suppressed in science writing until late C19 (Halliday, 1988), since when an impersonal style replete with passive verbs has been conventional for scientific writers. Yet one school of scientists – the US Council of Biology Editors – has since the 1960s actively encouraged the use of **I**, and others are allowing it back in. In the UK a study of science and engineering writing by Kirkman (1980) found a sprinkling of the pronoun **I** in many of the papers published in academic journals. The study also showed that scientists hardly noticed low levels of **I**, though they reacted negatively to its frequent use, finding it either amateurish or arrogant. Kirkman concluded that "judicious" use of **I** was no problem.

More systematic use of **I** can be found in other contexts. In some government departments, ministerial letters bearing the chief's signature make strategic use of the first person. The motivation may be as much to project the image of a strong executive head as to avoid an impersonal bureaucratic style. Proactive editors of academic manuscripts sometimes make a point of turning every "it was found that" into "I found that," in the interests of readability. This practice can however impair the line of argument which the author has built in (see further under **topic**).

So the reasons for using **I** in writing, or suppressing it, are complex and vary with the context. Writers who avoid it may be adhering to older convention, or trying to divert attention from the lack of evidence for their opinion. Saying "This is not acceptable" sounds much more powerful than "I cannot accept this,"

whether or not there's anything to support it. Let the reader beware!

Grammatical notes: choosing between *I* and *me* **I** is the nominative form of the pronoun, used for the subject of the verb: *I wanted to walk. Me* serves for the accusative, when the pronoun is the object of the verb: *They wanted me to walk.* So far so good. The choice is less obvious when:

*the pronoun complements the subject, after the verb *be*.* Traditional grammarians argued that *It is I* was the only correct form, whereas conversational usage has long endorsed *It's me.* Research associated with the *Longman Grammar* (1999) shows that both appear freely in contemporary news and fiction, but in different constructions. *It's me* is far more common when the pronoun is final (i.e. nothing following it), whereas the opposite holds when the construction has a following relative clause introduced by *who*, as in *it's I who suggested it.* This explains why *It is I* as a simple sentence sounds so very formal.

*the pronoun is used after *as* or *than*.* *Me* appears much more often than I in conversation, where *as/than* take prepositional roles, as in *better than me.* When a verb is added, they become conjunctions as in *X did better than I did*, and the use of I goes with its being the subject of the following clause. Neither construction is common in nonfiction writing, according to the *Longman Grammar* (see further under **than**).

the pronoun is coordinated with another noun, pronoun or name. In theory the choice of I or *me* still depends on the grammar of the clause: *X and I* used for the subject and *X and me* for the object. Compare:

> *John and I liked them*

with

> *They liked John and me.*

Yet in conversation *me* is sometimes used for I when it's the first coordinate of the subject: *Me and my wife were there first.* It often happens when the coordinated phrase is appositional to the clause, as in:

> *You and me, we're a great team.*

In examples like these, the case of the pronoun seems to be neutralized within the phrase (Wales, 1996); and *me* rather than I is used as the conversational option. I is still strongly preferred in all kinds of writing, from everyday news to academic prose, by the evidence of the *Longman Grammar* corpus.

◊ Hypercorrect use of *between you and I* is discussed at **between you and me**. For other issues with the first person singular pronoun, see **me**.

◊ For the ordering of **I**/*me* and other personal pronouns, see **person**.

-i

This suffix has two grammatical roles in English:
* as the plural for Latin loanwords ending in *-us*. See further under that heading.

* as the adjectival suffix on a small set of words (noun or adjective) that refer to people of the Middle East and southern Asia:

Bangladeshi Bengali Iraqi Israeli Jordani Marathi Pakistani Punjabi

The suffix has antecedents in an adjectival ending in both Semitic and Indo-Iranian languages. See further under **Indo-European**.

i before e

The well-known rule of English spelling "i before e except after c" needs some fine-tuning to make it fully reliable. What about *science, conscience, conscientious,* for example? Not to mention *their, height, weight* and *weird* – among others which do not obey the "rule."

Both kinds of exceptions can be accounted for if we add an extra line to the rule:

i before e except after c, when it sounds like "ee"

In this fuller form, the rule doesn't claim to cover any of the exceptional words above, because none of them has the *ie/ei* sounding exactly like "ee." The rule is still a useful guide for spelling words like *ceiling, deceit, receipt* (*ei* after *c*); and for *achieve, belief, grief, niece, piece, relieve, siege* (i.e. because there's no preceding *c*). The only common exceptions to the rule in its fuller form are *seize, leisure* (for many North Americans), and *either/neither* (for those who pronounce them with "ee" rather than "eye"). These variable pronunciations suggest further fine-tuning of the rule:

i before e except after c, when it always sounds like "ee"

Put that way, the only exception is *seize*, apart from chemical terms like *caffeine* and *protein*.

i/y

Large dictionaries register spellings with either **i** or **y** for a handful of English words:

cider/cyder cipher/cypher dike/dyke
gipsy/gypsy kibosh/kybosh pigmy/pygmy
silvan/sylvan siphon/syphon sirup/syrup
stimy/stymy tire/tyre

Usage everywhere converges on the **i** spelling for *cider* and *kibosh*, and the **y** spelling for *gypsy, pygmy, stymie/stymy, sylvan, syrup* (see individual headings). The others vary in spelling in either the UK or the US. Where Americans have settled on the **i** spelling in *cipher* and *siphon* for both noun and verb (by the evidence of CCAE), the British still make use of *cypher* and *syphon*, which appear in 30% to 40% of all instances of those words in the BNC. The American preference for **i** is underscored by two other cases (*dike/dyke* and *tire/tyre*), in which spelling intersects with meaning. The **i** spelling serves in the US to differentiate *dike* ("embankment") from *dyke* ("lesbian"), while British writers tend to use *dyke* for both (see **dike or dyke**). The tables are turned with *tire/tyre* – where the British distinguish *tire* ("become weary") from *tyre* ("rubber wheel cover"), and Americans write both as *tire* (see **tyre or tire**). The net effect is to make **i** spellings more visible in American English.

Other words with **i/y** spelling variation are classical and neoclassical, such as *dyad, dyarchy, dysfunctional, tyro* (see under individual headings). The alternate spellings intersect with meaning for *calix/calyx* (see under that heading).

Alternation between **i** and **y** once affected a very much larger number of English words. In the first century and a half of printing (until mid-C16), **i** was routinely replaced with **y** in words like *ship* (spelled as *shyp[pe]*) because of the flimsiness of **i** in early printers' fonts. Since then, **i** has steadily recovered its ground, and **i/y** alternation persists only in the words mentioned above, and as a regular change before certain suffixes. See further under **-ie > -y-, -y > -i-**.

Note that the equivalence of **i** and **y** is still exploited in surnames like *Smyth* and *Whyte,* though the spelling is fixed for the individuals who bear them. Anyone who writes to them or about them must take care.

-ia

This is a formative suffix in various specialized words (mostly scientific and academic), with singular and collective uses. In the development of scientific nomenclature, it was used in naming medical conditions such as *anorexia, aphasia, hernia, insomnia*; and in myriads of plant names such as *aubrietia, camellia, fuchsia, wisteria*. These and specialized abstract words such as *utopia* and *academia* embody a neo-classical singular (feminine) suffix **-ia**, with roots in both Latin and Greek. Coinciding with this is the classical Latin (neuter) plural suffix, used in academic contexts to form latinate collective nouns: *juvenilia, marginalia, memorabilia, paraphernalia.*

-ian

See under **-an**.

-iana

This suffix is the delight of scholars and antiquarians. It creates a collective term for all the information and material resources on a particular subject, as in *Shakespeariana* or *Australiana*. As these examples show, it's attached to proper names of people, places or institutions. Visually it may overlap with an existing adjective in *-ian*, but the pronunciation marks it as an independent formation. Originally **-iana** referred to the recorded output of an author, as is evident from the C17 publication titled:

Baconiana: certain genuine remains of Sir Francis Bacon, arguments civil and moral

Nowadays the suffix is usually understood to mean publications about a particular author or culture, and is extended to cover archival material and even antique objects.

ibex

For the plural of this word, see under **-x**.

ibid.

This referencing device is an abbreviated form of the Latin *ibidem* meaning "in the same place." Used in footnotes or follow-up references, it directs readers to the same source or place as was mentioned in the preceding reference. It substitutes for the author's name, the title of the book or article, and as much of what follows as would be identical. For example:

1. Hardy, C. "A family line" *American Journal of Genealogy* 3 (1952), p. 85
2. *Ibid.* p. 92

The reference with **ibid**. must come immediately after the full one (if not, the follow-up reference must repeat the author's name or an abbreviated title; see further under **referencing**). **Ibid**. could once appear in the main body of text, but its use has steadily declined and is now confined to footnotes and endnotes.

-ibility or -ability
See -ability.

-ible
See under -able/-ible.

-ic/-ical
Quite a number of English adjectives appear in two forms, for example:

alphabetic/alphabetical	analytic/analytical
astronomic/astronomical	bibliographic/ bibliographical
botanic/botanical	egotistic/egotistical
fanatic/fanatical	geographic/geographical
geometric/geometrical	ironic/ironical
magic/magical	monarchic/monarchical
mystic/mystical	mythic/mythical
obstetric/obstetrical	parasitic/parasitical
parenthetic/parenthetical	philosophic/ philosophical
poetic/poetical	problematic/ problematical
psychic/psychical	rhythmic/rhythmical
satiric/satirical	stereotypic/stereotypical
stoic/stoical	theoretic/theoretical
typographic/typographical	

Is there any reason for preferring one over the other? Often the answer is no. Those paired in that list do not differ significantly in meaning, though one may be more current than the other, as with *botanic(al)* and *poetic(al)*, or enjoy some degree of regional preference (see individual headings). Only for *geographic(al)* and *obstetric(al)* do these preferences run in opposite directions (see individual headings). Other things being equal, the shorter form recommends itself. Yet the extra syllable could enhance the rhythm of a phrase for those with an ear to their prose.

In cases such as *comic/comical, electric/electrical, lyric/lyrical,* the two words have slightly different applications, discussed under their respective headings. Typically the -ic spelling corresponds more closely to the core meaning of the stem, while the meaning of the -ical spelling is rather generalized. Some others show greater divergence, notably *economic/economical, historic/historical, politic/political,* as discussed in their individual entries.

In past centuries (from C15 to C17) there were many more such pairs derived from classical sources – *grammatic(al), identic(al), organic(al), tragic(al)* – where time has selected one or the other for us, but not consistently -ic or -ical, as those examples show. The form with -ical has been the survivor when there was a comparable noun in -ic(s). This explains why we now use *logical, musical, physical, rhetorical, tactical,* all of which had counterpart adjectives ending in -ic in earlier centuries.

Adverbs for -ic/-ical adjectives. The parity of adjectives in -ic and -ical helps to explain why the adverbs for both types end in -ically. So, for example, the adverbs for *organic* and *tragic* are *organically* and *tragically.* Even though the -ical forms of the adjectives have long since disappeared, their ghosts appear in the adverbs. The effect is there even for adjectives which never had a counterpart ending in -ical. So *barbaric, basic, civic, drastic* and others

become *barbarically, basically* etc., and it's as if -*ally* is the adverbial ending for them. This has become the general rule for all adjectives ending in -ic except *public,* whose adverb is still normally *publicly.* (See further under **publicly or publically.**) In centuries past there were others like it: *franticly* and *heroicly* appear in the classics of English literature. But they too now form adverbs with -*ally* (*frantically, heroically*); and with a sprinkling of *publically* in both British and American source material, we may speculate on whether the one remaining exception will be brought back under the rule.

-ic/-ics
Nouns ending in -ic or -ics are very often the names of scholarly subjects:

acoustics	arithmetic	classics	economics
ethics	linguistics	logic	mathematics
music	optics	physics	rhetoric
semantics	statistics	technics	

As the examples show, there are more words of this kind ending in -ics than -ic. Those ending in -ic are much older words going back to the medieval curriculum, whereas those ending in -ics are modern academic disciplines. Yet whether formed with -ic or -ics, the word normally takes a singular verb:

Mathematics has something in common with logic.
Note that this does not apply when the word is modified in some way so as to restrict its field of reference.

His mathematics were those of a shopkeeper.
The mathematics of gambling are based on probability theory.

icon or ikon
The latinized spelling **icon** is given preference in all modern dictionaries, and citations in the *Oxford Dictionary* (1989) show its regular use in reference to a religious image or object of worship. The spelling **ikon** is mostly found in writing concerned with the Eastern orthodox church, and it keeps the word closer to the original Greek (*eikon* transliterates it exactly). The use of **icon** (but not **ikon**) as a computer graphic adds to its range, and to the reasons why it's overwhelmingly preferred by writers in both BNC and CCAE. Derivatives such as *iconoclastic, iconography* and *iconolog* reinforce the position of **icon** as the spelling to prefer. See also **k/c**.

iconify or iconize
These alternatives both refer to the computer facility which deactivates a function and creates a small screen image (*icon*) by which it can be restored. Neither occurs in the reference corpora, but **iconify** was a good deal more frequent than **iconize** (by more than 6:1) in a Google search of the internet in 2002. Perhaps this reflects the power of the *Microsoft Manual of Style* (1998) which recommends against **iconize** and prefers "shrink to an icon" – though the very recommendation suggests that **iconize** enjoys some popularity among software writers. The *Oxford Dictionary* (1989) lists **iconize**, but only with the meaning "form into an image," which died in C17. **Iconify** (with the computer meaning) is the only one registered in *New Oxford* (1998).

identical with or identical to
These days either *with* or *to* may be used. Traditionally it was **identical with**, which was

preferred in the 1950s, according to *Webster's English Usage* (1989). But things have changed, and the use of **identical to** is now so common as to be unremarkable everywhere. In British data from the BNC, **identical to** outnumbers **identical with** by more than 2:1, and in American data from CCAE the ratio is more than 12:1. Similar trends towards using *to* can be seen in other comparative expressions: *compared to* in American English (see **compared with or compared to**); and *different to* in British English (see **different from, different to, different than**).

identify with

This expression has been used reflexively for 200 years, as in

> *He identified himself with the working class.*

But its elliptical counterpart (*he identified with the working class*) seems to have attracted negative attention in the later C20, probably because it was disputed by Gowers in his 1965 edition of Fowler's *Modern English Usage*, and by American commentators from Follett (1966) on. Gowers's objections seem to be that **identify with** belongs in psychology, and that its meaning becomes casual in fashionable idiom. He inserts it into Fowler's list of "slipshod extensions," and crossreferences it to other "popularized technicalities" and "vogue words." Judgements apart, the elliptical construction has become increasingly common since World War II, according to *Webster's English Usage* (1989); and its currency is recognized in both *Merriam-Webster* (2000) and *New Oxford* (1998). The latter updates the *Oxford Dictionary* (1989) where it's still labeled "obs(olete)," with no citation after 1834 – which would explain Gowers's discomfort over its C20 revival.

ideogram or ideograph

Both these are used to refer to the characters of the Chinese writing system, or any other non-alphabetic system such as Egyptian hieroglyphs. In terms of origins and use there's little to choose between them: both originated in philological research of the 1830s, and have remained too technical to make any showing in databases of standard English. But crossreferencing from **ideograph** to **ideogram** in recent British and American dictionaries (*New Oxford*, 1998, *Merriam-Webster,* 2000) suggests that **ideogram** is now preferred. Figurative uses of **ideogram** (but not the other) also help to show that it's the more lively of the two. The *Oxford Dictionary* (1989) presents more than twice as many C20 citations for **ideogram** as for **ideograph**, yet keeps **ideograph** as the main point of reference, as in the first edition.

idiom

This word has been used in two ways in English, to refer to:

1. the collective usage of a particular group, as in *the idiom of sailors*
2. a particular fixed phrase of ordinary usage, for example *a red herring*

The second use of **idiom** is commoner by far nowadays. An **idiom** in this sense is a fixed unit whose elements cannot be varied. Neither *a red fish* nor *a reddish-colored herring* can capture the meaning of the **idiom** *a red herring*. The meaning resides in the whole expression, and cannot be built up or extracted from its parts.

The word **idiom** is sometimes extended to include the conventional and arbitrary collocations of the language. *English idiom* makes it *hit by* (a car) but *hit with* (a hammer) – hence the comment that "hit with a car" is *not idiomatic English*.

idiosyncrasy or idiosyncracy

The second spelling seems more likely, and yet the first is the standard everywhere in the English-speaking world. The element *-crasy* is the Greek word for "mixture," and taken literally **idiosyncrasy** means "one's-own-together-mixing," i.e. that special blend of things that make up a unique entity. Yet **-crasy** appears in no other English word, and not so surprisingly people are inclined to write **idiosyncracy**, with the ending they know from *autocracy, democracy* etc. (see further under **-cracy**). Examples of its use date back to C17, and an article in *Word Study* (1957) reported almost a score from C20, in both academic and general publications, edited in the US and elsewhere. The evidence was powerful and *Webster's Third* (1986) registers **idiosyncracy** as an alternative to **idiosyncrasy**. The *Oxford Dictionary* (1989) acknowledges it with the label "erroneous," though its several citations are from literary and linguistic writing. Here, as elsewhere in British English, etymology holds sway over analogy; while American English allows for analogical reinterpretation and reconstruction.

i.e., ie. or ie

This common abbreviation stands for the Latin phrase *id est* ("that is"), used when offering further explanation or a paraphrase of a previous statement. For example:

> *He came into contact with Free Churches, i.e. ones not tied to either the Church of England or the Roman Catholics.*

Note that **i.e.** is not used to introduce examples, which is the function of *e.g.* (see **e.g.**). These days **i.e.** is usually set in roman, not italics.

The conventional punctuation for **i.e.** is to put stops after each letter, according to both the *Chicago Manual* (2003), and the *Oxford Guide to Style* (2002). In practice this is done more consistently in the US than the UK, by database evidence from CCAE and the BNC. In the latter case, **i.e.** was fully stopped in only about 70% of examples. Among the rest, around 20% had no stops at all (**ie**), and 10% had just one stop (**ie.**).

Traditionally **i.e.** was framed by punctuation marks – preceded by a comma (or else a dash, colon or an opening bracket), and followed by a comma. Yet both Fowler (1926) and Gowers (1965) allowed for discretion, and these days the following comma is usually omitted. About 95% of BNC examples of **i.e.** (and **ie.**) did without it. It was however much more evident when the abbreviation itself was left unstopped: almost half of the examples of **ie** were followed by a comma. The comma thus becomes a curious substitute for the stop that the abbreviation might otherwise have. Some kind of delimiter thus seems to be felt necessary, despite the broader British trend to reduce stops in abbreviations. In both British and American English there is usually some punctuation mark preceding **i.e.** In BNC data this was almost always so with **i.e.**, and held for 85% of examples with **ie.** also.

Like other Latin abbreviations, **i.e.** is increasingly accepted without paraphrase in many kinds of document. Style manuals have traditionally confined such abbreviations to footnotes and parenthetical references, but the *Chicago Manual* (1993) notes their increased use in technical writing of all kinds. The British view as expressed in *Copy-editing* (1992) is also accommodating of **i.e.**, and British editors are cautioned against routine paraphrasing of **i.e.** The Australian government *Style Manual* (2002) echoes the *Chicago Manual* on the now widespread use of the abbreviation; and *Canadian English Usage* (1997) observes it in "running text of all kinds." In BNC data **i.e.** turns up in many kinds of informative and academic prose, and in interactive discourse:

> *Does it complete the nitrogen cycle, i.e. convert nitrate into nitrogen?*
> *These goals will be for weight and also possibly for size, i.e. your "vital statistics."*
> *"I'm surprised that someone like you can have such a fixed view of someone else, i.e. me."*

With **i.e.** established in standard usage, most writers and readers are comfortable with seeing the abbreviation in print. No longer should it be subject to automatic paraphrase by the editor.
◊ See further under **Latin abbreviations**.

-ie > -y-

The letter **i** is regularly changed to **y** in a small group of English verbs: *die, lie, tie, vie*, as well as complex words based on them, e.g. *belie, underlie, untie*. The change happens when *-ing* is added to the stem, as in *dying, lying* etc., and clearly it avoids awkward-looking forms like "diing," "liing" which would result from simply applying the regular rule of removing final *e* before *-ing* (see **-e**). Only recently arrived verbs such as *skiing* and *taxiing* are allowed the double *i*.
◊ For the complementary process, see **-y > -i-**.

-ie/-y

In colloquial references to certain kinds of people, these two spellings often alternate:

> *cabbie/cabby   hippie/hippy   junkie/junky*
> *kiddie/kiddy*

In cases like these, either spelling may be used for the suffix, which is a "familiarity marker," in the terminology of the *Comprehensive Grammar* (1985). The core use of such terms, illustrated by *kiddy*, is *hypocoristic*, i.e. to provide a "pet" name for people within the family circle (see **hypocorisms**). Other examples are *daddy, granny, mummy/mommy*, which would explain why *kiddy* is generally preferred to *kiddie* for this usage in British English, by the evidence of BNC. This leaves *kiddie* free – at least in American English – to serve as the adjective meaning "strictly for kids, childish" as in *kiddie pool, kiddie show*.

Most newer words with **-ie/-y** are outside the family circle, as the other examples show, but they are still apparently motivated by the need to express familiarity. Here the **-ie** ending is usually the commoner of the two, as is true of *cabbie, hippie, junkie* in American English (by the evidence of CCAE), and of *cabbie, junkie* – but not *hippy* – in British English data from the BNC. (Does this make the *hippy* more part of the family, you may ask!) Many words of this kind have only been recorded with **-ie** (*bookie, chappie, groupie, rookie, townie* etc.). The **-ie** spelling allows instant recognition of the fact that

they are colloquial nouns, whereas with **-y** they just could be adjectives (see further under **-y**).

In some cases the use of **-ie** clearly serves to distinguish the colloquial noun from an existing adjective ending in **-y**. See for example:

> *chalkie (Aus/NZ)*   *chalky* "containing
>   "teacher"   or covered with chalk"
> *hippie* "bohemian"   *hippy* "having large hips"
> *junkie* "one addicted   *junky* "valueless"
>   to something"

The **-ie** suffix is no longer restricted to people, but increasingly put to use in familiar names for entertainments, among other things. In *footie/footy* ("football"), *soapie* ("soap opera"), *talkie* ("talking picture," i.e. movie with soundtrack), the underlying compound is trimmed down to its most essential syllable. This makes it less transparent to the outsider, but strong on solidarity for insiders. Many **-ie** words used freely by Australians (e.g. *pokie* for "poker machine") would be opaque to others; and some used by the British would be unfamiliar to Americans – who make least use of this type of word formation.

Personal names with -ie or -y In the spelling of popular names and abbreviations of names there's sometimes a choice between **-ie** and **-y**, as in *Chrissie/Chrissy, Johnnie/Johnny* for example. Celebrated names are nevertheless often fixed, e.g. *Billy Connolly, Willie Carson, Andy Warhol, Nellie Bly*. And whenever such names are actually given names, as often with *Kellie/Kelly, Kerrie/Kerry* among others, the point needs to be checked. The bearer will be very conscious whether the name has been spelled their way or not.

-ienne

This feminine suffix borrowed from French is found in only a few regular English words, such as *comedienne, equestrienne, tragedienne*. All such words were coined in the middle of C19, to provide conspicuously female counterparts to words ending in *-ian* (*comedian* etc.). They have never been very popular, and their extinction is probably assured amid the general drive towards nonsexist language. See further under **inclusive language**.

-ier

This suffix appears on two kinds of English words:
1 a few agent words borrowed from French, e.g. *halberdier, bombardier*. This ending becomes *-eer* in later English formations. See **-eer**.
2 a few English agent nouns, for the person associated with a particular commodity: *clothier, collier, furrier*. This ending was also spelled *-yer*, hence *lawyer*. As the examples show, the stem was normally a noun, but both *haulier* and *sawyer* seem to be based on verbs.

-ies

This string of letters represents two kinds of singular – and two kinds of plural:
∗ for Latin loanwords such as *series* and *species* it is both singular and (zero) plural. See under **Latin plurals**.
∗ for English verbs ending in *y*, such as *carry*, it provides the third person singular: *he/she carries*
∗ for English nouns ending in *y*, such as *berry*(*berries*), *city*(*cities*), it provides the plural:

see **-y > -i-**. A small number of these words have alternative plurals because of their alternative singular forms:

> bogies/bogeys   stories/storeys
> whiskies/whiskeys

See **-y/-ey**, and under individual headings, as well as **plurals** section 1.

if

The ambiguities latent in **if** are easily resolved by intonation in speech, but need careful handling in writing. When **if** is used as a substitute for *whether,* the implicit meaning is "whether or not" – which may be what was intended in:

> *You'll let us know if you're coming . . .*

That sentence could become a question or an indirect command, depending on the intonation. Either way, it seeks to clarify whether people are coming or not, but it's not really clear. The words themselves could be taken to mean that people are expected to reply "if and only if" they intend to come. To prevent misunderstanding (especially over the lack of communication when it was expected), the sentence would be better expressed as:

> *Would you let us know whether or not you're coming?*

This leaves no room for misunderstanding, though the casualness of the original is lost.

If can also be a source of ambiguity when combined in a phrase with *not*:

> *There was a short if not hasty consultation with the coach.*

In such a string of words, *if not* could mean either "short although not hasty," or "short as well as hasty." In other words, *if not* could be either contrastive or additive (see further under **conjunctions**). Writers no doubt use *if not* sometimes to opt out of making a judgement and keep things ambiguous. But if the writer's judgement or meaning are important, *if not* is best avoided.

If and the subjunctive. In conditional clauses, **if** serves to express things which might be. Some are real contingencies, others purely hypothetical. The two kinds of possibility can be distinguished by the choice of verb:

> *If she were more forgiving, they might have reached an agreement.*
> *If he was back from New York he'd lend a hand.*

In the first sentence, **if** is coupled with the past subjunctive *were* to express an impossible condition (see further under **subjunctive**). In the second, the ordinary indicative form of the verb (*was*) is used to express a condition which is a real possibility. This distinction is not always clear-cut however; and the indicative tends to replace the subjunctive in less formal styles, as noted in the *Comprehensive Grammar* (1985). Even the fixed phrase *if I were you* gets casually rephrased as *if I was you*. The absence of past subjunctive forms for any verbs other than *be* is another reason why the distinction is breaking down. The use of *were* after *if he/she/it* is now a matter of formality of style rather than grammar.

-ify/-efy

These verb endings are identical in sound and meaning, yet are attached by convention to different verbs. The less common ending by far is **-efy**, which makes its appearance in only four words: *liquefy,*

putrefy, rarefy, stupefy. But **-ify** is the ending for many, of which the following are just a handful:

> amplify   beautify   clarify
> classify   exemplify   fortify
> glorify   gratify   identify
> justify   petrify   purify
> quantify   simplify   vilify

The reason why words have either **-efy** or **-ify** is a matter of their individual history. In C21 English it seems quite arbitrary, and so the minority group with **-efy** are sometimes spelled with **-ify**. It happens especially with *liquify* (no doubt because of *liquid*). In American data from CCAE, more than 30% of occurrences of the word were *liquify*, and the rate is close to 40% in data from the BNC.

Many dictionaries present *liquify* as an alternative to *liquefy*, whereas only the largest recognize alternatives for the others. *Webster's Third* (1986) registers *putrify* and *rarify,* and the *Oxford Dictionary* (1989) has *stupify* as well, but indicates that all the **-ify** alternatives became obsolescent in the latter half of C19. In fact there's a sprinkling of *rarified* in the reference databases – about 8% and 18% of the total British and American citations respectively. *Stupified* occurs just once in the BNC and is greatly outnumbered by *stupefied*; but CCAE data show that it's relatively more common in American English. No doubt the analogous adjective (*stupid*) – and common pronunciation – seem to support it. The same things apply with *putrify*, but there's too little data to confirm it. The forces of analogy are still evidently at work here, nudging the **-efy** verbs into line with the much larger set formed with **-ify**.

Note that **-ify** is always the spelling for new and ad hoc formations, such as *countrify, funkify, gentrify, yuppify* (not "countryfy" etc.). Here the **-ify** shows the normal change of *y > i* when it becomes bound by a suffix (see **-y > -i-**). It obviously helps to dissimilate the two *y*s (see further under **dissimilate**).

ignoramus

Not a Latin noun, but a verb meaning "we do not know." It was originally (in C16) the formula by which a grand jury declared that there was insufficient evidence to proceed with a bill of indictment. In less than a century it was being used pejoratively of an ignorant lawyer, whence its current application to any person deemed a fool. Should there be more than one **ignoramus**, the plural is properly **ignoramuses**, because of its verbal origins. The use of "ignorami" might indeed suggest an **ignoramus**. (See further under **-us** section 4.)

ignoratio elenchi

See under **fallacies** section 2g.

ikon or icon

See **icon**.

illegal, illegitimate or illicit

All these adjectives imply that things are not done according to law, but their connotations and uses are somewhat different. **Illegal** is the most neutral and widely used of them, and can be applied to any kind of crime from **illegal** parking to the **illegal** slaughter of elephants. **Illegitimate** is best known in the cold phrase *illegitimate child,* i.e. one born outside the laws of marriage. Apart from this **illegitimate** is also used in academic discussion, to describe an argument, conclusion or inference which is unsound by the laws of logic. **Illicit** is applied to activities which are not permitted by law, e.g. *illicit gambling,* an *illicit love affair* or keeping *an illicit still.* Among those who are privy to such things, they are a well-kept secret, and so **illicit** has more than a whiff of enjoying forbidden fruits.

illiterate and illiteracy

Essentially **illiterate** means "unable to read or write." Even in societies with compulsory schooling, there's a small percentage of adults with no command of the written word, and so **illiterate** has some application in that sense.

Yet because reading and writing are taken for granted by the majority, the threshold of "literacy" is often implicitly raised beyond the basic command of letters. Thus *literate* comes to mean "well acquainted with book learning," and **illiterate** "showing little acquaintance with books" or "ill-educated." Only in this second sense can a person's writing be described as "illiterate." Those who use the word this way no doubt count themselves among the *literati* (see **litterateurs or literati**).

Fowler's (1926) use of **illiteracy** – to refer to one of a somewhat arbitrarily chosen set of divergent expressions – is an even narrower application of the word. It makes it a *count* noun (*an illiteracy, illiteracies*), which can be increased and multiplied to suit the commentator. If **illiteracy** in this sense seems less old-fashioned than "vulgarism," the judgement is just as dismissive (see under **vulgar**).

illusion or delusion

See **delusion**.

im-

See under **in-/im-**.

-im

This is the plural suffix for certain loanwords from Hebrew, including the biblical *seraph(im)* and the post-World War II *kibbutz(im).* Another is *goyim,* a plural or collective word meaning "those non-Jewish" (its singular is *goy*).

Note that *cherub* has both Hebrew and English plurals, associated with quite different worlds. The *cherubim* who appeared so often to Ezekiel were divine messengers, while the plump, childlike angels who appear with trumpets aloft in baroque decoration are *cherubs*.

image and imagery

In C21, few would question the use of **image** to mean the "total impression given by a person, institution, company or product etc." This sense was first recorded in 1908, but gained little currency until the late 1950s. After that it enjoyed such a vogue as to raise anxiety in style commentators, hence Burchfield's (1996) equivocal remark that it has "seeped into the vocabulary of every articulate person in the land." We need hardly be surprised at the public person's preoccupation with **image** when the mass media are pervasive in society and culture. Use of the word simply reflects its importance for any person or product whose success depends on mobilizing public opinion.

The **image** generated by publicity, and the **image** which a writer creates are somewhat different. The first is rather abstract, like the sophistication and glamor which is supposed to accompany drinking that glass of wine held by a manicured hand. The poet's **image** is much more tangible, when he says "Drink to me only with thine eyes," and conjures up the very act of drinking and toasting. Another difference is that the **image** of the advertised product is already a composite of ideas, whereas the images raised by a poem or piece of writing usually serve to develop its **imagery** sequentially. Yet both the *publicity image,* and the writer's **imagery** put a particular coloring or set of values on whatever they present, so as to influence people's thinking.
◊ See also **analogy**, and **metaphors**.

imaginary or imaginative

These words express different attitudes to imagination and the products of our imagination. Phrases such as an *imaginative approach* and an *imaginative solution* show that **imaginative** is often a positive quality, and that the imagination is seen as a constructive and creative resource.

The word **imaginary** affirms that something has been imagined and is fictitious, such as an *imaginary conversation* or an *imaginary illness.* The adjective has negative connotations if what is imagined is used to deceive or to manipulate others, but otherwise it's neutral. So David Malouf's novel *An Imaginary Life* (on the life of Ovid) is a perfectly acceptable fiction. The book is also highly **imaginative**, but the author leaves it to readers and critics to apply that word.

immigrant

For the choice between **immigrant** and **migrant**, see **migrant**.

imminent or eminent

See **eminent**.

immoral or amoral

See under **a-/an-**.

impact

This word appeared first in scientific English in the form *impacted* (as in *impacted tooth*), based on the Latin adjective *impactus.* **Impact** as a noun was derived from it late in C18, and is now the commonest form of the word by far. Instances of the noun run into thousands in the BNC, where there are less than 100 of **impact** as a verb. It first appeared in early C20, again in scientific writing, but has since been taken up in the discourse of business and government, as in:

> The housing market impacts on consumer spending in two ways.
> The policy was impacting men and women alike.

These constructions are registered without demur in *Merriam-Webster* (2000) and the Australian *Macquarie Dictionary* (1997); and the *Canadian Oxford* (1998) goes out of its way to note that they are well established despite the objections of some. *New Oxford* (2000) distances itself from them, as "Chiefly American," and warns that some in the UK react negatively to *impact on* as a verb (it doesn't comment on the other construction). Verbal use of *impact on* is evident in a variety of informative British writing in the BNC, suggesting that its currency is growing. The *Oxford Dictionary* (1989) takes both constructions in its stride.

impaired

Used in compounds like *sight-impaired, hearing-impaired, intellectually impaired,* this word provides an oblique reference to a disability. Such compounds are however rather cumbersome, and unclear about the level of *impairment.* See further under **disabled and disability**.

impanel or empanel

These are both used in American English for the legal process of forming a jury. In British English the second spelling prevails. See further under **empanelled**.

impassive or impassioned

These words are almost opposite in meaning, since **impassive** means "showing no emotion," and **impassioned** means "expressing intense emotion." An *impassioned plea* by a speaker implies strong emotional input to the message, and the last thing such a speaker wants to see is *impassive expressions* on the faces of his audience.

Note that *dispassionate* differs from both **impassive** and **impassioned**. It indicates a lack of personal bias when fairness is very important, as in a *dispassionate account of the conflict.*

imperative

This is the grammarian's term for the special form of English verbs which makes a direct command. For example:

> *Go back.*
> *Quick march.*
> *Turn off the lights before leaving.*

As the examples show, the **imperative** has no special suffix, and the subject is not expressed.

Negative imperatives are expressed with the aid of *do not* or *don't* as in:

> *Do not walk on the grass.*
> *Don't look now but . . .*

Note that the abrupt effect of the imperative is softened by combining it with *please* or just *do*.

Please sit down.	*Please put it on.* (polite and detached)
Do sit down.	*Do put it on.* (collaborative and friendly)

◊ For other ways of expressing commands and instructions, see under **commands**.
◊ For the distinction between **imperative** and *imperious*, see under **imperial**.

imperfect

For traditional grammarians this is another name for the *continuous aspect* of the verb. See under **aspect**.

imperial, imperious or imperative

With the decline of empires and emperors, there's less for **imperial** to do – not that *imperialism* is dead. The word remains as a monument to former empires in phrases like *imperial Rome* and *imperial Russia,* and to former emperors in the *Imperial Palace* to be visited by tourists in China and Japan. *Imperial College London* and the *Imperial War Museum* preserve the name despite the commutation of the British Empire into the (British) Commonwealth. In corporate nomenclature such as *Imperial Chemical Industries (ICI)* it's a sign of the longevity of the firm. Most other British **imperial** institutions have disappeared, or been renamed. Gone are the days when *the webs of portly tropical spiders could interrupt an imperial dispatch,* according to a BNC citation. The most widely known surviving **imperial** institution is the *imperial system* of weights and measures, on which see the next entry.

Neither **imperious** nor **imperative** have any connection with empires. Yet **imperious** implies the will to make others do your bidding, as in: *a loud imperious knocking on the ceiling,* or *the sharp, imperious police whistle.* **Imperious** is usually applied to human behavior, **imperative** to circumstances which force us to do something:

> *It was imperative not to get embroiled in politics.*

Note that **imperative** also serves as a noun:

> *In Keynes's view the great imperative was public works.*

For the grammatical use of **imperative**, see under that heading.

imperial weights and measures

The *imperial system* of weights and measures is gradually being replaced by the metric or *international system* everywhere in the English-speaking world. Britain's membership of the EU has accelerated the changeover, and *metres* and *litres* are well represented in BNC data when standard lengths and volumes are quoted, as in:

> *400 metres to the terminal building*
> *the kit (L29.99) covers four to six square metres*
> *one million litres of milk*
> *a lighter car with an engine of less than 6.75 litres*

Still *yards* and *gallons/pints* continue to be used, especially in casual references: *a couple of hundred yards, downed a few pints.* The juxtaposition of metric and **imperial measures**, as in *a capacity of 230 litres (50 gallons),* and of temperatures in degrees Celsius as well as Fahrenheit, are a reminder that the change is still going on.

In the US, change to the *international system* is an "officially recognized goal" (*Chicago Manual,* 1993), most evident in the military, scientific and sporting domains. But in ordinary discourse the imperial *gallon* is used 20 times more often than the *liter,* by their relative frequencies in CCAE; and the *yard* outnumbers the *meter* in a similar ratio. In Canada the metric system is much more fully implemented, being the point of convergence between anglophones and francophones. In Australia the *imperial system* was officially replaced by the metric system back in 1970, and in New Zealand in 1987. Younger people absorb the metric system as part of their schooling, even if their elders still calibrate things in **imperial measures**, putting distances in *miles,* and human weight in *pounds* and *stones.* The key terms of the *imperial system* include:

* for length: *inch foot yard chain furlong mile*
* for mass: *ounce pound stone hundredweight ton*
* for volume: *fluid ounce pint quart gallon*

Some of these linger in common idiom:

> *a six footer   wouldn't budge an inch*
> *miles from anywhere*
> *drinking whisky by the gallon*

Imperial measures persist in a number of specialized fields of sport and industry the world over. A tennis net is set at *3 feet* or *1 yard* (= 0.914 metres) above the ground, and a cricket pitch is still a *chain* or *22 yards* in length (= 20.12 metres). Printers calculate the dimensions of a piece of printed text in *picas*, which measure just on one sixth of an *inch*. The screws used by engineers and carpenters are normally calibrated in terms of so many *turns to the inch*, and by British Standard Whitworth norms, rather than the *ISO-metric* system. The altitudes at which aircraft fly are given in *feet* (e.g. 37 000 feet), and nautical usage maintains its own standard units for depth (*fathom*), speed (*knot*) and sea distance (*nautical mile*).

◊ For the metric system of units, see **metrication**. A full table for converting **imperial measures** to their metric equivalents can be found in Appendix V.

imperiled or imperilled

See under -l-/-ll-.

imperious or imperative

See **imperial, imperious or imperative**.

impersonal style

Writing can seem *impersonal* for different reasons. It may hide the character and attitudes of the writer, so that the information seems detached from both sender and receiver of the message, and shows no human perspective on it:

> *The Library will no longer open on Sundays, as of March 1.*

Impersonal style like that is often produced in the name of an institution, when the writer becomes an official voice, addressing a vast, mixed audience whose reactions are not known.

Writing can also seem *impersonal* when it avoids referring to human participation in the action it describes, as in:

> *It was decided that the meeting should be adjourned.*

This is of course typical of the way in which the minutes of meetings are recorded. It can be frustrating if you want to know who prevailed in the debate. But the impersonal "it was decided" embodies the democratic principle that the majority decides the issue, whether or not there were dissenting votes from influential individuals. In science writing it's also conventional for experimenters to report their work impersonally, on the assumption that what was done (rather than who did it) is what other scientists need to know:

> *A small piece of sodium was added to the flask of water.*

This preference for passive *was added* instead of the active "I [the experimenter] added a small piece of sodium ..." is now being questioned by some scientific bodies (see further under **I**).

For the moment, **impersonal style** serves a number of conventional purposes, bureaucratic and scientific. But in other contexts – where communication needs to be lively, human and sensitive to the individual – the **impersonal style** with its official and academic overtones is to be avoided.

impinging or impingeing

The spelling **impinging** is regular and taken for granted by both *Webster's Third* (1986) and the *Oxford*

Dictionary (1989). Usage from American and British databases confirms that it is standard, and there is no trace of **impingeing** in either CCAE or the BNC. Let no-one say that **impinging** suggests the verb "imping." See further under **-e**, section e.

imply or infer

The distinction commonly drawn between these two words makes them reciprocal. A writer or statement may **imply** something (i.e. convey a suggestion), which readers may or may not **infer** (pick up). But usage commentators note the persistent habit of using **infer** rather than **imply** in sentences like the following:

> *The correspondent inferred in his letter published in June that you were biased.*

This use of **infer**, making it synonymous with **imply**, is recognized in all modern dictionaries although they attach warning labels to it, dubbing it "colloquial" or "loose usage." The Harper–Heritage panel of the 1970s almost all rejected it, and the second edition of the *Oxford Dictionary* (1989) adds a note that it is "widely considered to be incorrect." *Webster's English Usage* (1989) confirms that the stigma developed in the course of C20, and that **infer** was used quite freely in this way earlier on.

The use of **infer** for **imply** may well be a hypercorrection generated by the fine reciprocal line that has been drawn between them. (The same problem besets other reciprocal pairs like *substitute/replace* and *comprise/compose*.) **Imply** is much more common than **infer** according to the evidence of English databases everywhere (by a factor of 4:1 in BNC data). Their patterns of distribution are also very different. **Imply** occurs freely in speech and writing, across all genres of discourse, while **infer** is strongly associated with the more formal styles of bureaucratic, legal or academic prose, and scarce in speech. The relative rarity of **infer** suggests that its use where the "rule" requires **imply** is a sign of writers/speakers overzealous about correctness, reaching beyond the word that comes easily.

Another complicating factor noted by *Webster's English Usage* is the logical use of **infer** with a nonpersonal subject, meaning "indicate" or "have or lead to as a conclusion," a use which originated more than four centuries ago, according to the *Oxford*. Though rare, it's acknowledged in contemporary dictionaries, and exemplified in database evidence such as:

> *The witness gave evidence which inferred that Drew was a violent man*

This use of **infer** stands between the reciprocal uses of **imply** and **infer** distinguished above, and overlaps with the use of **imply** with a personal subject. The shift from nonpersonal use of **infer** ("indicate") to personal use as "imply" is no great move, as the examples show. In conversation and debate many people do not distinguish between these constructions; and in context it's usually quite clear whether **infer** is intended to mean making an active suggestion (="imply"), or a deduction made from something else. As often, the distinction is more important in writing, and writers may be reassured by the general facts of usage outlined above: that the word they need most of the time is **imply**. Like other shibboleths of language, the issue needs to be defused. (See further under **shibboleth**.)

impotence or impotency

See under **potency**.

impractical or impracticable

See under **practical or practicable**.

in-/im-

These two share the burden of representing two meanings in English:

1 "not" as in *inaccurate, indefinite, informal, imbalance, immortal, imperfect* (negative use of prefix derived from Latin)

2 "in" as in *include, income, inroad, imbibe, immigrant, imprint* (intensive prefix based on the preposition/adverb *in*, found in many Indo-European languages including Latin and English)

As the examples show, the negative and intensive uses are indistinguishable. Only by analysing the composition of words can we tell which prefix is there. Doubt as to which prefix is there lies at the heart of the problem with *inflammable* (see further under **flammable**).

In both sets of words, the im- form is used regularly before "b", "m" and "p". The in- form goes with any other consonants except "l" and "r," where the prefixes are il- (as in *illegal, illuminate*) and ir- (as in *irrational, irrigate*). The paired examples again show the negative and the intensive meanings in turn.

◊ For the variation between intensive **in-** and *en-* in some words, see **en-/in-**.

-in/-ine

See **-ine/-in**.

in-/un-

Should it be:

inadvisable	or	*unadvisable*
inarguable	or	*unarguable*
incurable	or	*uncurable*
inharmonious	or	*unharmonious*
insanitary	or	*unsanitary*

For these, and various other negative adjectives, either prefix is acceptable, and there's no difference in meaning. In some cases such as *in-/unarguable* and *in-/unsanitary* there are regional differences (see **inarguable, insanitary**). In others, the prefix is fixed by a mixture of history and convention. The in- prefix is from Latin and generally goes with Latin formations, while **un-** is Old English and goes with English formations, even when the same root is involved. So we have:

incomplete	vs	*uncompleted*
indiscriminate	vs	*undiscriminating*
inedible	vs	*uneatable*

Other points to note from these examples are that the English un- is often prefixed to words ending in *-ed, -ing, -able*, whereas the Latin in- heads words ending in *-te, -ible* and *-ent, (i)al, -ive, -ous*. For the choice between *impractical* and *unpractical*, see under **practical or practicable**.

Note finally the special sets of Latin adjectives which do not use **in-**, but rather *un-, dis-* or *non-*:

unimaginative	*unindustrious*
unintelligent	*unintentional*
disincentive	*disinfectant*
disingenuous	*disintegrate*
nonimperialist	*nonindigenous*
noninfectious	*nonintoxicating*

For some of the *dis-* words, it's arguable that the prefix *dis-* is needed to express reversal rather than straight negation (see further under **dis-**). But in all those examples the complicating factor is that the stem begins with *in-*, and to prefix the negative **in-** would be distracting ("inintelligent," "iningenuous," "ininfectious"). The use of *un-, dis-, non-* helps to dissimilate the prefix from the stem. See further under **dissimilate or dissimulate**.

in back of

See **back of**.

in camera

This Latin phrase was adopted in C19, to refer to legal proceedings conducted as a closed hearing. Literally the phrase means "in [the judge's] chamber," i.e. not in an open court. It is also applied to meetings of committees which are conducted in secret.

in case, in case of, and in the case of

The word *case* in these phrases shows their origin in English law and legal argumentation. But **in case** has become a common conjunction in speech and informal writing, in both the UK and the US:

> *. . . we would be close in case Sir Henry needed us*
> *In case you didn't know, it's National Chip Week.*

In the first example, **in case** expresses an open condition; in the second it's *indirect,* in the terminology of the *Comprehensive Grammar* (1985). In neither is the action directly contingent on the **in case** clause. The prepositional phrase **in case of** can be used to express both contingent and open conditions. Compare:

> *In case of fire, do not use the lift.* (contingent)
> *Bring an umbrella in case of rain.* (open)

The familiar official warning of the first sentence urges action in the event of a fire (i.e. contingent on one), whereas the second is quite open: you should take an umbrella whatever the weather. In British English contingent uses of **in case of** are largely formulaic – *in case of need/accident or injury / damage to property* – and their contingent meaning is often underscored by "only":

> *. . . go out only in case of necessity*

In American English **in case of** is used freely in contingent and in open conditions, so that it's possible to say:

> *Bring an umbrella in case of rain.* (open)
> *In case of rain the game will take place on April 18.* (contingent)

The two uses are usually distinguishable by the internal logic of the sentence, but the second is much less familiar to the British, and they may mistake it when it occurs in mid-sentence, as in the following from American newspapers:

> *Children would be sent home from school in case of nuclear disaster.*
> *. . . hostages to execute in case of an American attack*
> *. . . with the consent of both parents (the custodial parent in case of a divorce)*

Both **in case** and **in case of** are much more freely used in American English than British, by comparative data from BNC and CCAE; and Americans are well accustomed to contingent as well as open senses for **in case of**. There is even some evidence for contingent use of (conjunctive) **in case** in

271

American English, though it is not yet acknowledged in *Webster's Third* (1986). For example:

> *The machine should be turned off in case the red light comes on.*

The sentence makes no sense as an open condition – you would never turn the machine on! But as a contingent condition it is eminently sensible. All this highlights a discrepancy in usage, a point on which American writers must beware, and British readers might recognize that British English is somewhat circumscribed. The conjunction *lest* provides an unambiguous alternative (see **lest**).

The phrase **in the case of** is often censured in style manuals as wordy and overused. In academic prose it's overrepresented, according to the *Longman Grammar* (1999), but less evident in other kinds of writing. Academics may defend it on the grounds that it serves to signal a change of topic in complex discourse, as in the following sentence:

> *In the case of that abusive letter, I would ignore it.*

This upfront use of **in the case of** makes it a *topicalizing* device, a means of spotlighting an item in a series of sentences that would otherwise submerge it. (See further under **topic** and **information focus**.)

in flagrante delicto
See under **corpus delicti**.

in line or on line
When queuing, the British stand or wait **in line**, as do most Americans. But American usage also accommodates **on line**, as in:

> *The public is forced to wait on line outside the building.*
> *The executives don't have to stand on line, and get extra-special treatment.*

This use of **on line** has been associated with New York, but its use in national magazines edited there has probably helped to spread it further afield, according to *Webster's English Usage* (1989). In CCAE there's a sprinkling of it in newspapers from Washington, Atlanta and Los Angeles. Its future prospects are however small, against worldwide usage of **on line** in the cybersense of "accessing electronic systems."

in medias res
This Latin phrase meaning "into the midst of things" refers to the narrative technique of plunging the reader straight into the heat of the action – not working towards it through conventional introductions and setting of the scene. The phrase was coined by Horace (*Ars Poetica* line 148). The technique is quite often used in modern fiction, and is increasingly common in movie-making.

in reference to or with reference to
See **reference to**.

in situ
This Latin phrase means "on site," or less literally "in its original place." It has been used since C19 of on-the-spot forensic inspection or scientific procedure (*in situ water treatment*) as opposed to doing the same in a laboratory. But it's also used more casually, to mean "in the established place," as in:

> *He's still in situ at the Department of Education.*

in toto
Borrowed from Latin, this phrase means "in total," and so "altogether, completely." When coupled with a negative adverb it expresses reservations, as in:

> *She would not support the proposal in toto.*

In toto is also used with verbs of negative implications, such as *deny, disagree, reject*. Because it so often expresses a demurral, the phrase is sometimes thought to mean "on the whole," though that translation shortcircuits its essential meaning.

inadvertent and inadvertently
The spelling **inadvertent(ly)** is standard everywhere, and dictionaries lend no support to *inadvertant(ly)*. Yet both CCAE and the BNC provide a few examples of *inadvertant*, and a Google (2002) search of the internet found *inadvertantly* in 7% of all instances of the word. The vowel in question is of course as indeterminate as that in *dependent/dependant*. See further under **-ant/-ent**.

inapt or inept
See **inept**.

inarguable or unarguable, and inarguably or unarguably
British writers strongly prefer **unarguable** and **unarguably**, by the dearth of evidence of the *in-*spellings from the BNC. Americans meanwhile are at ease with both *in-* and *un-* forms of the adjective and adverb, which are about equally common in data from CCAE.

◊ On the ambiguity of both adjective and adverb, see **arguably**.

incaps
See **capital letters** section 4.

inchoate and inchoative
This indigestible-looking pair have special uses in law and grammar, respectively. Both derive from Latin *inchoatus*, earlier *incohatus*, meaning "just begun" or "hitched up" (*cohum* being the word for a yoke strap). In legal usage **inchoate** refers to a preliminary offense, such as incitement or conspiracy; and to a document which is not yet made specific and operative. In the latter usage it effectively means "not valid," and its legal opposite *choate*, used of a valid document (*choate lien*), confirms that the prefix is understood as a negative rather than an intensive (see further under **in-/im-**). In general usage **inchoate** also seems to be somewhat misunderstood. It is used tautologically as in "inchoate beginnings," and as if the stem had something to do with *chaos*, hence the sense "disorganized, confused, chaotic," as in *apparently orderly systems become inchoate, disorderly*. This sense is questioned in some dictionaries, but accepted straightforwardly in others such as *Webster's Third* (1986) and *New Oxford* (1998). (See further under **folk etymology**.)

Inchoative is used by grammarians to refer to verbal structures that express the notion of an action beginning. Some languages have prefixes for this purpose, but English makes do with catenative verbs such as *begin (to write), start (thinking)*. See further under **catenatives**.

incidentally or incidently

The standard form is **incidentally**, and it outnumbers **incidently** by about 100:1 in both British and American databases. Yet the sprinkling of **incidently** confirms that it is not yet obsolete, as the *Oxford Dictionary* (1989) has it. Rather it persists as an alternative, sustained no doubt by the fact that it seems to correspond better with common pronunciation of the word (with four rather than five syllables). This indeed is how *Webster's Third* (1986) registers it. Historically speaking **incidently** is a legitimate form: *incident + -ly*, reminding us that *incident* once had multiple roles as an adjective, though now confined to law and optics, as in *incident light*.

◊ Compare **accidentally**.

inclose or enclose, and inclosure or enclosure

See **enclose**.

include

Too literal interpretation of this verb has it that its object must be an exhaustive list of the parts of the whole – that it is strictly a synonym for *comprise*. Dictionaries confirm that **include** has always been more flexible. Its object may be only part of the whole, as in:

> Some courses include lectures on theatre history.

At other times it seems to enumerate all parts of the whole:

> ... read Hare's trilogy The History Plays, which include Knuckle, Licking Hitler and Plenty.

The second usage is a good deal less obvious than the first in BNC data, though without background information one cannot always be sure what was intended. What is clear is that **include** does not require full specification of the items *included*.

inclusive language

This is language which raises no social stereotypes in relation to gender, race, age or the perfect body. It avoids terms like *businessman* and *businesswoman* in favor of *executive* or *manager* which are gender-free. It shuns homophobic words such as *dyke* and *faggot*, and those with pejorative implications for members of other races and nationalities, such as *wog* and *Itie*. The use of such words creates instant disadvantage for the people referred to. Governments and public institutions these days affirm the need for **inclusive language** to provide equal opportunity and to ensure that language itself neither raises nor maintains social barriers. Publishers, too, increasingly ask their authors to use **inclusive language** (see Butcher, 1992).

Ways of avoiding sexist language are discussed at **nonsexist language**; and problems and solutions of racist terms under **ethnic**, **miscegenation**, and **racist language**. See also **ageist language**, and **disabled**.

◊ For the backlash against **inclusive language**, see **political correctness**.

incognito and incognita

Borrowed from Italian in C17, **incognito** meant literally "unknown" – as persons traveling in disguise or under an assumed name hoped to be. In Italian the word is masculine, hence the form **incognita** for a female disguising her identity, indicated in some dictionaries. In fact there's no sign of **incognita** meaning "disguised" in either CCAE or BNC – but it does appear as the Latin adjective for "unknown" as in *terra incognita*. This may explain why women and men alike are referred to as being **incognito**, apart from the fact that the word most often serves as an adverb in English, as in *go around incognito*. Its other (minor) role as a noun or noun modifier (meaning "an assumed name/identity") can be seen in examples such as *pierce his incognito* and *carried out incognito tests*. The plural of the noun is **incognitos**.

◊ For other words referring to assumed names, see **nom de plume**.

incompetence or incompetency

In both American and British English **incompetence** appears much more often than **incompetency**. But the latter makes more showing in the US than the UK, by the evidence of CCAE and the BNC. Dictionaries meanwhile continue to acknowledge both forms. There is no differentiation of meaning as for **competence or competency** (see further under that heading).

incredible or incredulous

In formal English, only a person can be **incredulous** (i.e. "unable to believe something"), whereas facts and events are **incredible** (i.e. "unable to be believed"). An Australian television series about bizarre happenings was titled *That's incredible!* But exclamatory usage like this can also be applied to people, as in *You're incredible*, where **incredible** means roughly "amazing or extraordinary," though its connotations of intense surprise outweigh any particular denotation. This sense of that which is "beyond what one might have conceived as possible" is quietly acknowledged in the *Oxford Dictionary* (1989), though labeled "informal" in *New Oxford* (1998). In BNC data, this use of **incredible** is much more frequent than the restrained sense, in both written and spoken sources. The writing that presents it is typically interactive and sometimes extravagant, witness:

> On the windward side you will reach an area of incredible beauty.
> ... the incredible production rate at United Biscuits
> I had been presented with an incredible opportunity.
> The shows in New York were incredible.

Like other words used to express attitude, **incredible** is becoming increasingly uninformative, and leans on others for specific meaning. In easy-going discourse this is no problem, but it doesn't earn its keep in tightly worded prose.

Attitudinal use is also very common with the adverb *incredibly*, in interactive and affective narrative:

> They were incredibly strong.
> I felt incredibly tired.

Again the word has little denotation, and becomes no more than a rather bulky *intensifier*. (See further under **intensifiers**.)

◊ See also **credible or creditable**, and **credulity or credibility**.

incrust or encrust, and incrustation or encrustation

In both American and British English, **encrust** has given way to **incrust**; and **incrustation** to **encrustation**. See further under **en-/in-**.

incubus

For the plural of this word, see under **-us** section 1.

incumbent or encumbent

Only the first of these appears as a headword in modern dictionaries, though the second was used in earlier centuries, and still appears on rare occasions, by the evidence of BNC and CCAE. The reasons are natural enough. Apart from the fact that the prefixes *in-* and *en-* have alternated for centuries in English words (see **en-/in-**), *en-* is the usual prefix in the much more common (and deceptively similar) words *encumber* and *encumbrance*. In fact **incumbent** and *encumber* have quite separate histories. **Incumbent** is formed out of the Latin verb meaning "lean upon," while *encumber* derives from French and means roughly "obstruct." Yet as *the incumbent* of an office, you may be *encumbered* with particular duties, and this coincidence no doubt encourages the identification of the two words.

indefinite article

See under **articles**, and **a or an**.

indefinite pronouns

These include the four sets of compound pronouns *anybody/one/thing, everybody/one/thing, nobody/one/thing, somebody/one/thing,* as well as the simple pronouns *any, each, none, some,* as used in *any of them.* The latter raise issues of agreement because of their indefiniteness (see **agreement** section 3). *Any, each, every, some* also double as *determiners:* see further under **pronouns** and **determiners**.

indention, indentation or indenture

These all originate from the notion of making a notch or toothshaped mark in a document. However only the first two are interchangeable. Both **indention** and **indentation** refer to the practice of *indenting:* leaving a space at the beginning of a line of print. **Indention** is the more widely used term, endorsed in the *Chicago Manual* (2003), the Australian government *Style Manual* (2002), and in the UK by Butcher's *Copy-editing* (1992), although the *Oxford Guide to Style* (2002) prefers **indentation**. (For more about *indenting* practices, see **indents**.)

The term **indenture** was originally applied to legal contracts contained in documents with identical notches cut into the edge. The uniqueness of the notches was intended to prevent false copies of the document being drawn up. Nowadays **indenture** is still a contract or agreement (especially between an employer and an apprentice), but the documents are no longer notched.

indents

The small space set at the beginning of a line of type is an **indent**. A single **indent** marks a new paragraph, and a vertical series of **indents** serves to set off a list of items from the main text. **Indents** are used in almost all print media, fiction and nonfiction; and in newspapers and magazines, whether the text runs across the whole width of the page, or is two or more columns.

The standard **indent** for paragraphs is 1 or 2 ems, varying with the length of the line. For line lengths over 26 picas, the longer **indent** is needed.

Regular indenting may be suspended in certain circumstances:

1 In textbooks and reference works, the line immediately following a heading or subheading is often not *indented,* but set flush with the left margin. This practice is noted in the *Chicago Manual* (1993) as well as the *Oxford Guide to Style* (2002), as is its use at the beginning of a chapter. Yet the decision is partly a matter of looks, and needs to be coordinated with the size and placement of the headings: are they centred, flush with the left margin, or indented? Daily newspapers indent the first line under both headlines and subheadlines.

2 The first line of a block quotation is not usually *indented,* provided it's clearly set off from the main body of the text, either by italics, or change of type size, or by block *indenting.*

3 In fully blocked letter format. See under **letter writing**, and Appendix VII.)

Hanging indention is the reverse of *regular indention:* the first line is flush with the left margin, and the second and subsequent lines in the same unit are all *indented* 1 em, as a block. Note that while *hanging indention* is the term used by British editors (Butcher, 1992), it's *flush-and-hang* in the *Chicago Manual.* The technique is often used in lists and indexes (see **indexing** section 2); and sometimes for setting out a series of points in the body of a text. The runover/turnover lines are also indented.

    1. xxxxxxxxxxxxx
       xxxxxxx
    2. yyyyyyyyyyyy
       yyyyyyyyyyyy
       yy

In statistical tables, *hanging indents* are used in the stub for runover/turnover lines of subheadings. (See further under **tables**.)

For footnotes, standard practice is to use *regular indention.* The number itself is usually *indented* at the start of each note, and the turnover lines go back to the left margin:

    1. xxxxxxxxxxxx
xxxxxxxxxxx
    2. yyyyyyyyyyyy
yyyyyyyyyyyyyyyyyy
yyyyyyyyyy

indenture or indention

See under **indention**.

independent and independence

Dictionaries present these spellings as standard, and instances of *independant* and *independance* are rare in data from CCAE and the BNC. Usage is thus much more streamlined for *independent* than for *dependent/dependant:* see **dependent**.

indeterminate vowel

This is an alternative name for *schwa*: see under that heading.

index

This Latin loanword maintains two plurals: the regular English **indexes** and the pure Latin **indices**. Their use depends on the application, intersecting with regional differences that are quite pronounced. Overall the British are more inclined to **indices**, which is normal in statistical and technical writing, in mathematics, economics and the sciences, and wherever **index** takes on a numerical value:

> *Broadly-based share indices have suffered sharper losses.*
> *... the refractive indices of the organic water-based lens*

Indices is also commonly applied to nonnumerical scales and concepts such as *indices of poverty / physical wellbeing / social change*. Some British prefer **indices** when referring to the **index** found at the back of a book or used as a bibliographical tool, although most would have **indexes** for those purposes.

> *Author and subject indexes are also provided.*

In American English, **indexes** is standard for bibliographic applications, as well as in computer systems, where it serves as verb as well as noun:

> *The software automatically indexes, stores and retrieves digital information.*

This may in the longer run reinforce the use of **indexes** as the regular plural for the noun in British English.

For the moment, **indexes** is more commonly used in American English, applied freely in financial circles to *stock market indexes,* and as an alternative in mathematics and science, or when referring to socio-cultural scales, as in:

> *comparable test scores and other indexes of achievement*

American respondents to the Langscape survey (1998–2001) clearly preferred **indexes** over **indices**, underscoring the opinion of Garner (1998), that the latter was somewhat pretentious.

◊ For other Latin loanwords of this kind, see **-x** section 2.

◊ For information on *indexing* books, see next entry.

indexing

An *index* is an asset for almost any nonfiction book whose material is not already presented in alphabetical order. It helps both committed readers and browsers to access the book's fine detail, and is always a useful complement to the table of contents or chapter headings. By convention and convenience it's the last section of the book – since it cannot be started until the rest of the book has been paginated. The *index* is usually set in slightly smaller type than the main text (e.g. 2 points smaller), and usually in double columns, unless the book is in large format, in which case it may be in three or four columns on a page. *Indexes* tend to be longer and more detailed in academic and technical books, and may indeed be specialized for particular aspects of the book. Hence the varieties of *index* such as: *Index of Names and Places,* and *Subject Index* etc. as well as the *General*

Index. Whenever there's more than one *index,* the most comprehensive one goes last.

The labor of making the *index* may fall to the author of a book, or be done by the publisher or a professional *indexer. Indexing software* is increasingly available for personal computers, which can be used by anyone. But creating the *index* raises a number of questions.

1 What items should be entered in the *index*? The aim is to cover all the key concepts and terms used, as well as any specific references which readers might look for. The *indexer* needs to anticipate the nontechnical terms which browsers might use as their first port of call in the *index.* Established synonyms for concepts (and synonymous phrases), and alternative official and personal names will need to be entered. Crossreferencing within the entries should allow the reader to move from the specific to the general and vice versa. At the same time, the *index* should enable the reader to get information about a topic in one place, as far as possible.

2 How should *index* entries be set? There are two established methods for presenting the entries:

* *broken off*
* *run in* or *run on* (the first term is American style, the second British)

The methods differ in the way they treat subentries. The *broken-off* method has each subentry on a separate line, indented 1 em and with turnovers indented 2 ems. The *run-in/run-on* method blocks all subentries together, indented 1 em, with individual subitems separated by a semicolon:

> *broken off*
> > brackets 102–6
> > > curly brackets 105
> > > round brackets (parentheses) 102–4
> > > slash brackets 104
> > > square brackets (in mathematics) 106, (in linguistics) 105
> *run in/on*
> > brackets 102–6; curly brackets 105; round brackets (parentheses) 102–4; slash brackets 104; square brackets (in mathematics) 106, (in linguistics) 105

On the matter of page spans, see **numbers and number style** section 1. As the examples show, the *run-in/run-on* method takes less space, requires fewer word breaks, and is easy to set. It is however less easy for the reader to consult. The *broken-off* method always takes more space, especially if used for subentries as well as sub-subentries, when the text contracts to the right-hand side of the column. In some indexes the two methods are combined, with *broken-off* setting used for subentries, while sub-subentries within them are run in/on.

3 Should the *indexed* words be alphabetized *letter-by-letter* or *word-by-word*? These alternatives are discussed at **alphabetical order**. The *letter-by-letter* system is more straightforward for the *indexer* or computer to produce. However the reader will locate entries more easily if word-by-word order is used, especially when there are many closely related words.

Indian

This adjective reflects the old Persian word *Hind* for India (see further under **Hindi and Hindu**), and, unqualified, the word's primary reference is still – in most contexts – to the Indian subcontinent and its culture and people. In British English, this is certainly so.

The word **Indian** has however been applied to other peoples in many parts of the globe. During the European colonial era, it was used of the natives of the *East Indies*, and of indigenous peoples in the Philippines. In the same way the Spanish used *Indianos* to refer to the indigenous peoples of the American continent, though this is often explained by the tradition that Columbus believed his first landfall in the Caribbean actually was the East Indies. The inhabitants of the *West Indies* are of course still *West Indians*. The English too used **Indian** for the indigenous people of North and South America, usually with some qualifying word as in *Plains Indians, Amazonian Indians, Mexican Indians*. The term *Red Indians* is also a relic of this, though it smacks of frontier fiction and the Hollywood western.

Within the US, *native American Indians* use the simple term **Indian** as a means of affirming their distinctive culture and social practices. This facilitates its use without qualification in American English generally, in official terms like *Indian reservation, Indian lands, Indian rights. Indian boarding schools* were those to which American Indian children were consigned under earlier government policies of relocation and reacculturation. In Canada the term **Indian** stands alongside *Inuit* and *Metis*, as a way of identifying the three *First Peoples*. Canadian legislation also distinguishes between the *Status Indians* (also called *Registered or Treaty Indians*) and the so-called *Non-Status Indians*. Against those bureaucratic constructs, *Canadian Indians* not unnaturally prefer to use their Aboriginal group names. The term *Amerindian* refers to the original inhabitants of any part of the Americas: North, South and Central.

International English has just a few stock phrases in which the simple adjective **Indian** refers to North American Indians. They include *Indian corn* i.e. maize, *Indian file* (walk in single file as did *American Indians* on the move), and *Indian summer*. This phrase is recorded at regular intervals in C19 America as a way of referring to a period of sunny, stable but often hazy weather at the end of autumn. It is explained through the fact that such weather was typical of the inland areas then inhabited by American Indians, which differed from the changeable cool climate of the coasts settled by Europeans.

indicative

As a grammatical term, **indicative** is applied to verb forms which express factuality, as opposed to those that express the hypothetical (termed *subjunctive*). Both **indicative** and *subjunctive* are a legacy of Latin grammar, but there's little for them to do in English grammar because of the decline of subjunctive forms. See further under **if**, **mood** and **subjunctive**.

indict or indite

In Middle English **indite** was the spelling for two different verbs, meaning:
* "compose or write a literary work"
* "bring a legal charge against [someone]"
The *c* was introduced into **indict** for the legal verb around 1600, as a way of distinguishing it from the other, and as a visual link with its Latin forebear

indictare. The pronunciation has never adjusted to the changed spelling (as with some other respellings of the English Renaissance: see **spelling, rules and reform** section 1).

Both **indict** and the related noun *indictment* continue to be used in law, and outside it, to mean "condemn/ation," as in:

> *a terrible indictment of all those involved in the whaling industry*

Meanwhile **indite** ("compose") has become obsolete. The *Oxford Dictionary's* (1989) last citation was from 1800, apart from two (probably archaistic) instances from the pen of Disraeli. With the start of C21, it's time to reappraise the anomalous spelling of **indict**, given that the need for it has disappeared with the death of the other word. We could well accept the verdict of history, and allow **indict** to revert to **indite**, in keeping with its pronunciation. In doing so we'd rid English of one more trap for the unwary.

indigenous or Indigenous

This word is sensitive for socio-political reasons in English-speaking countries such as Canada and Australia, and now needs a capital letter for some applications. Both *Canadian English Usage* (1997) and the Australian government *Style Manual* (2002) advise this when the term refers to the original habitants of the continent and their descendants, as in *Indigenous people(s) in Canada, Indigenous Australians*. In the same way the phrase *Indigenous peoples* is used to refer to the first inhabitants of lands anywhere in the world, as in *land rights of Indigenous peoples*. The capital letter accords with its use in related ethnic terms such as *Aboriginal*, and, in Canada, *Native*. See further under **capital letters** section 1.

But in its generic senses ("original," "belonging to the place"), **indigenous** needs no capital:

> *Changes to their habitat threaten many indigenous species of bird.*

Occasionally the presence/absence of the capital is critical to meaning. See for example, *indigenous publishing in Australia* (by locally owned publishers – not multinational), which contrasts with *Indigenous publishing* (publishing by Aboriginal groups).

indirect object

See under **object**.

indirect question

See under **questions** section 4.

indirect speech

The differences between *direct* and **indirect speech**, and other ways of reporting what someone has said, are discussed under **direct speech**.

indiscreet or indiscrete

The first is much more likely than than the second, for reasons discussed under **discreet or discrete**.

indiscriminate

See under **discrimination**.

indispensable or indispensible

The first is the standard spelling everywhere, though the second is more in evidence in the US than the UK: see under **dispensable**.

indite or indict

See **indict**.

Indo-European

This term links almost all the languages of Europe with those of Iran and North India into a single family. It represents one of the great linguistic discoveries of C18: that English and Scots and French and Greek, not to mention Russian and Iranian and Hindi, are all derivatives of the same original language, spoken perhaps 5000 years ago, somewhere on the frontiers of eastern Europe and western Asia.

Within the **Indo-European** family, the languages of individual branches are naturally more closely related, as are English and German in the Germanic branch, or Polish and Russian in the Slavic. However the genetic relationship with even the more remote branches, such as Celtic and Indo-Iranian, can be seen when you line up their basic vocabulary. The numbers used for counting in each language provide the most striking evidence of common origin. See for example:

English	Dutch	Italian	Welsh	Russian	Greek	Hindi
one	*een*	*uno*	*un*	*odin*	*heis*	*ekt*
two	*twee*	*due*	*dau*	*dva*	*duo*	*do*
three	*drie*	*tre*	*tri*	*tri*	*treis*	*tin*

Indo-European languages have spread by colonial expansion to all other continents – North and South America, Africa, Australia, New Zealand and the Pacific islands.

Indonesia

The name means "Indian islands" and is a reminder of the vagueness of European geography in the early centuries of colonialism. **Indonesia** was just part of the East Indies, a region stretching from India to Japan.

The present population of **Indonesia**, now well over 150 million, is scattered over more than 13,000 islands, the largest of which are Borneo (in Indonesian, Kalimantan), Celebes (Sulawesi), Irian Jaya, Java, Sumatra, and the Moluccas. The wealth of **Indonesia** attracted the attention of the Portuguese in C16, and then that of the English and Dutch East India companies. **Indonesia** was controlled by the Dutch from C17 until independence in 1949. However the Portuguese continued to govern East Timor until 1976.
◊ See also **Jakarta**.

indorse or endorse

See under **en-/in-**.

indubitably or undoubtedly

See **undoubtedly**.

induce

The verb **induce** has an array of technical and semitechnical uses, which are quite strictly assigned to the noun *induction* or *inducement*. *Induction* is most familiar as a process of argumentation (see next entry), and as a specialist's term in biochemistry, biology, mathematics and engineering (where it is also known as *inductance*). *Inducement* is an everyday term for circumstances (material, financial, psychological, political) that motivate or provide an incentive for a particular action, as in:

> The railways secured huge government land grants as an inducement to build.

> *Despite every inducement, the anxious shag could not be persuaded to get its feet wet.*

In the practice of law, *inducement* is also a technical term for the explanatory material that prefaces the pleading of a case. Here it's an Anglo-Norman *calque* of the Latin *inductio* ("introduction"). See further under **caulk** section 3.

induction

This is the process of reasoning whereby we draw a general proposition or generalization from a series of instances or examples. The *inductive* process underlies much everyday communication, and is easily seen in newspaper headlines such as:

> *RENTS ON THE RISE IN BIRMINGHAM*

A generalization like that is presumably based on evidence gathered by the reporter, and we read on to see what it was. As in that case, the generalization is often stated before the examples that support it. The soundness of the generalization depends on whether it's based on plenty of examples, and on how representative they are. If the headline above was based on a few prices quoted by two estate agents (realtors) in two suburbs of Birmingham, it's potentially misleading and a *rash generalization*.

Inductive generalizations both rash and reasonable are made all the time as people exchange ideas and information. Not often are they "perfect" *inductions,* i.e. ones based on all instances or entities which lend themselves to it. Even a perfect **induction** can only be said to support a general proposition, not to prove it in the philosophical sense of guaranteeing its truth.

Modern science owes a great deal to *inductive reasoning,* and it's the foundation of scientific method. Scientific laws are *induced* from recurrent instances of natural behavior, or tested and confirmed by them. In fact **induction** is the only logical way to validate many a statement. If someone says, *Ash trees grow best in open settings,* the only way to verify the statement is by seeking instances in which this is so, as well as ones in which the opposite holds (e.g. where the tree suffers in dense vegetation). Statements like that, whose validity must be tested *inductively* are called *synthetic statements;* whereas statements which are self-validating (i.e. true by virtue of the way they are formulated) are *analytic statements.* An example of the latter is *No maiden aunt is an only child.* Analytic statements are also a kind of *tautology.*
◊ Compare **deduction**.

industrial or industrious

These adjectives involve two different uses of the word *industry*. Its older denotations of persistent and energetic application to a task are embodied in **industrious** meaning "hard-working," established in English five centuries ago. **Industrial** implies a connection with *industry* in its more recent sense of a manufacturing concern or branch of business. It probably reflects French use of *industriel,* and found ready application in the impacts of the *industrial revolution,* from late C18 on. Two centuries later **industrial** is very much more common than **industrious**, outnumbering it by almost 1000:1 in BNC data. The distance between **industrious** and **industrial** is clear in the ironic fact that *industrial action* means something other than *industrious behavior* on the part of the workers concerned.

-ine/-in

This suffix appears on both adjectives and nouns in English, with variable pronunciation and some variation in its spelling. As an adjective ending it's used to mean "made of," as in *crystalline*, or "associated with," as in *tangerine* (a fruit originally imported from Tangier). The examples show two of the possible pronunciations for this suffix in English, to rhyme with "wine" or "wean." As a noun ending -**ine** has a minor role marking the feminine form of some masculine names, as in *Josephine* and *Pauline*, and in the common noun *heroine*. The latter shows a third pronunciation, rhyming with "win."

In C21 English the spelling -**ine** varies with -**in** in the names of certain household chemicals, notably:

> gelatin(e)   glycerin(e)   lanolin(e)
> saccharin(e)

Americans prefer -**in** for all, by both dictionary and database evidence – except when *saccharine* serves as an adjective ("sugary"), as in *a handful of saccharine songs*. The British agree on *lanolin* and on the different applications of *saccharin/saccharine;* but they like to see -**ine** in *gelatine* and *glycerine* as well (see under **gelatin**, and **glycerin**). Australian preferences are like the British (Peters, 1995), whereas Canadians come closer to Americans in using -**in** for *gelatin:* see *Canadian Oxford* (1998).

The use of -**ine** and -**in** was standardized for professional chemists in C19 by A. W. von Hofmann, whose classification was published in Watts's *Dictionary of Chemistry* (1866) and subsequently adopted by the Chemical Society. Hofmann reserved the -**ine** spelling for alkaloids and organic bases, such as:

> caffeine   cocaine   morphine   quinine   strychnine

He assigned -**in** to neutral substances (including glucosides, glycerides and proteids):

> albumin   gasolin   gelatin   globolin   glycerin

But Hofmann's system stands less clearly than it might (especially for the nonchemist), because -**ine** and -**in** have other uses in chemistry. A number of chemical elements (the so-called "halogens") are spelled -**ine**:

> bromine   chlorine   fluorine   iodine

Meanwhile -**in** is the ending of a number of enzymes and hormones:

> adrenalin   insulin   pepsin   rennin

and of some well-known drugs and pharmaceutical products, such as:

> aspirin   heroin   penicillin   streptomycin

Chemists of course have specialist knowledge and access to chemical formulas which would resolve any question about the suffix. For ordinary users, they are simply fixed elements of the spelling.

For two household chemicals, -**ine** varies with -*ene:* both *gasoline* and *gasolene*, *kerosine* and *kerosene* are registered in dictionaries. American, Canadian and Australian dictionaries all prefer *gasoline* for the first and *kerosene* for the second, and database evidence bears them out – however arbitrary that seems. Contemporary preferences in Britain run the same way, by the evidence of the BNC. Yet the *Oxford Dictionary* (1989) prefers -*ene* spellings in both cases. It gives *gasolene* priority over *gasoline*, apparently for historical reasons; and *kerosene* is preferred on the basis of common usage, although *kerosine* has official backing from technical bodies in Britain and America (British Institute of Petroleum, American Society for Testing Materials, and the American Standards Association). Fortunately the choice of -**ine** or -*ene*

makes no chemical difference for *gasoline* and *kerosene*, whereas with **benzine/benzene** and **fluorene/fluorine** it does. See further under those headings.

inept or inapt

The focus in these adjectives is different, though both imply that something is "not suited or unsuitable" for the purpose in hand. This is more directly expressed in **inapt**, in usages such as: *a more inapt name I cannot imagine*. The word was formed relatively recently in English (only two centuries ago), and has retained the literal meaning of its components. It is largely confined to formal styles of communication.

The much more common **inept** originated in Latin from the same elements, and had already developed the meaning "ineffectual" when it came into English. This is probably the dominant sense in English nowadays, though in particular contexts it can also mean "incompetent" (*inept management*) or "fatuous" (*inept remarks*). The word has a negative value judgement built in, whereas **inapt** is more dispassionate.

inessential, unessential or nonessential

See **nonessential**.

infectious or contagious

For the difference between these, see **contagious**.

infer or imply

See **imply**.

inferable, inferrable, inferrible or inferible

As a derivative of *infer,* this word is straightforward enough. But it's probably more often spoken than written down, hence the uncertainty about how it should be spelled. Dictionaries diverge over the alternatives: whether to dress the word up as English or Latin, and how far to reflect its pronunciation.

The *Oxford Dictionary* (1989) gives priority to the spellings **inferable** and **inferrible**, while *Webster's Third* (1986) has **inferable** followed by **inferible**, **inferrible**. Garner (1998) argues for a shift to **inferable** since mid-C20, and what little evidence there is in the BNC would support this. Neither **inferible** nor **inferrible** appears in BNC or CCAE, nor is there any historical justification for such latinized or "mongrel" forms, as the *Oxford* calls them. Why not keep the word English? (See further at -**able/-ible**.) But both BNC and CCAE provide instances of **inferrable**, which correlates with the more straightforward pronunciation of the word, stressing the second syllable as for *inferred* and *inferring,* and reflected in the doubled *r* (see **doubling of final consonant**).

Either **inferrable** or **inferable** could be justified, depending on whether its stress is like that of *inferring* or *inference*. The first pronunciation is more transparent than the first, but either way the meaning is the same.

◊ Compare the alternatives for **transferable** but not **preferable**: see under those headings.

inferior than

See under **superior**.

infinitives

The basic nonfinite forms of verbs such as (*to*) *ask,* (*to*) *go,* (*to*) *decide* are called **infinitives**. They combine with auxiliaries and other catenatives to form compound verbs and verb phrases:

I will ask	*I wanted to ask*
you may go	*you meant to go*
they couldn't decide	*they tried to decide*

In the first column are the *bare infinitives,* formed without *to.* The **infinitives** of the second column are then the *to-infinitives,* whenever the two kinds have to be distinguished. Alongside simple **infinitives** such as those, *compound infinitives* such as the *perfect infinitive* can be formed with *have,* and the *passive infinitive* with *be:*

I wouldn't have gone	*I'd like to have gone* (perfect)
you will be asked	*you have to be asked* (passive)

Here again the examples show that **infinitives** are not necessarily formed with *to.* Historically it was not part of the infinitive, but was formally attached to it in C18 grammars. Not so surprisingly, the anxiety about *split infinitives* dates from the following century. See further under that heading.

1 Infinitives in other kinds of phrase. The **infinitive** serves as complement to words of other classes than verbs:

* adjectives
   eager to please   easy to undo   ready to go sure to fly
* nouns, especially abstract nouns which embody verbal ideas:
   decision to leave   desire to come
   invitation to abscond

and indefinite or general nouns:

   moment to catch   someone to love
   something to remember   time to reflect
   way to go

Yet another role of the **infinitive** is to serve instead of a verbal noun as the noun phrase/subject of a finite clause:

   To err is human.

2 Infinitives in nonfinite clauses. In their combinations with *modal* and *catenative verbs* (*will ask, wanted to ask*), **infinitives** create one of the most familiar types of *nonfinite clause. Infinitive clauses* formed with *to-infinitives* are very common in fiction, according to the *Longman Grammar* (1999), especially with verbs such as *want, try, seem, begin. Want to* and *try to* are also the commonest catenatives in news reporting and conversation, whereas it's *seem to* in academic prose.

Beyond these complementary uses of **infinitives,** they also form quasi-adverbial *nonfinite clauses* that formulate a purpose:

   We walked fast to beat the rain.
   The teachers brought bags to collect the bottles.

In more formal styles, the *to* is sometimes expanded into *in order to* or *so as to,* but most of the time the **infinitive** with *to* says it all.

◊ See further under **modality, catenatives** and **nonfinite clause.**

inflammable or inflammatory

These both have to do with lighting fires, but the fire lit by something **inflammatory** is purely figurative, as by *inflammatory speech,* whereas what's ignited by an *inflammable liquid* is dangerously physical. The possible ambiguity with **inflammable** has prompted official moves to replace it in public notices. See **flammable**.

inflectional extras

One small point of divergence between British and American English grammar lies in British preference for giving someone's years as *aged 16* where Americans would have *age 16.* The British form is inflected like an adjective (see further under **-ed** section 2), while the American stands like an ordinary numerical compound, as in *grade 7 student* (see **hyphens** section 2c).

This difference affects numerous compound adjectives ending in *-ed.* In British English they are normally inflected, in American English not so. For example:

* *-ed* British: *fine-toothed, golden-haired, matt-finished, snub-nosed, spine-tailed, 10-roomed (house)*
   American: *fine-tooth, golden-hair, matt-finish, snub-nose, spine-tail, 10-room*

It also affects noun compounds with descriptive modifiers. Compare:

* *-ed* British: *barbed wire, iced tea, skimmed milk, striped shirt*
   American: *barb wire, ice tea, skim milk, stripe shirt*
* *-ing* British: *dialling tone, diving school, sailing boat, sparking plug*
   American: *dial tone, dive school, sail boat, spark plug*

Another **inflectional extra** of some British compound expressions but not the American counterparts is the plural *-s.* Where the British use *antiques shop, drugs overdose, departures lounge* etc., Americans have *antique shop, drug overdose, departure lounge.* Those used to the British forms tend to find the American ones curt, although some of them are being adopted in the UK. For those used to the American, the British seem a tad rococo.

Similar differences emerge in pairs such as *cookery book / cook book,* where British English uses a derivational suffix and the American has none. (See further under **suffixes.**) Different conventions for dates, where the British use ordinals (*11th September*) and Americans use cardinals (*September 11*), again show the British preference for suffixes.

◊ for more on the writing of *dates,* see under that heading.

inflections

Inflections are the suffixes which add particular grammatical meanings to words of a particular class (nouns, verbs etc.). Languages such as French, German and Italian have numerous **inflections** for individual classes and subclasses of words. English has relatively few. The most familiar ones are:

* for nouns
   -'s   possessive/genitive
   -(e)s   plural (see further under **plurals**)
* for verbs
   -(e)s   3rd person singular, present tense
   -ing   continuous/imperfect aspect
   -ed   past tense / perfect aspect
       (see further under **irregular verbs**)
* for adjectives and adverbs
   -er   comparative
   -est   superlative

Inflectional suffixes such as these do not change the class of the word to which they are attached, nor do

they effectively form new words. Suffixes which do are termed *derivational* (see under **suffixes**).
◊ For the choice of spelling between **inflection** and *inflexion*, see under **-ction**.

inflicted or afflicted

In passive constructions *inflicted* is sometimes substituted for *afflicted* (not the other way round). This is not hard to explain, given the fact that:
* they are similarly pronounced, differing only in the first unstressed syllable
* their meanings can be almost reciprocal. Compare:
    the plagues inflicted on the Egyptians
    the plagues with which he afflicted the Egyptians
* both **inflicted** and **afflicted** imply negative forces beyond one's control
* *inflict* once meant *afflict*. The *Oxford Dictionary* (1989) has citations from C16 and C17, but notes its rarity with one from C19.

Though far from common, the BNC does contain examples where *inflicted* appears for *afflicted*, as in *citizens had been inflicted with uncanny storms that ripped tiles from roof*. The combination "inflicted with" is the sign of interference between the two constructions, since **inflicted** is normally complemented by *on*, and **afflicted** by *with* (or *by*). But the odd combination hints at supernatural forces punishing the uninsured householder – like the unwary Egyptians.

infold or enfold

See under **en-/in-**.

informal style

We typically use an **informal style** when talking impromptu with others. It consists of relaxed, easy-going language and ordinary colloquialisms rather than scholarly or academic words: *put up with* rather than "tolerate" or "endure"; *get* rather than "purchase"; *trim* rather than "abbreviate." Concrete examples and images come more naturally than abstractions: *tool* rather than "implement"; *job* rather than "appointment"; *date* rather than "engagement." Abbreviated forms of words, such as *mike* for "microphone" and *TV* for "television" are natural elements of an **informal style**, as are contracted forms of phrases, such as: *I'm, they're, wasn't*. The **informal style** allows free and frequent ellipsis of the standard grammatical elements of a clause, so that sentences may be no more than:
    Don't know. A great idea. To show the flag.
Because *informal language* is associated with conversation, its overtones are friendly and expansive, sometimes offhanded. A hundred years ago, **informal style** would hardly have appeared in writing, except in the dialogue of novels, and *informal language* was almost synonymous with *incorrect language*. Nowadays informal features of style are seen as useful resources if used in moderation, especially for writers who want to avoid putting unnecessary distance between themselves and their readers. A few informal touches can help to ensure this, without undermining the purpose of the document or letter. One would of course avoid referring to grave or seriously contentious matters in an informal way. As always, it's a matter of deciding on the appropriate level of formality/informality for the item concerned. See further under **formal words**.

information focus

One of the arts of writing is keeping the reader with you. Amid the flow of words, readers can be distracted or diverted onto marginal things and miss the intended point or emphasis. Not all words in any text are equally important. Those which embody its themes need to stand out against those which are simply the ordinary medium.

There are several ways of spotlighting a word or words in an English sentence. It can be done by means of a focusing device, such as *only, even, also, too, as well*. For example:
    He wished only to publicize the problem. (not to deal with it)
    They had even brought the phone book with them. (How well prepared can you be!)
Less marked versions of the second sentence would be:
    They had also brought the phone book.
    They had brought the phone book too.
    They had brought the phone book as well.
As the examples show, the focusing words sometimes go before and sometimes after the one in the spotlight. *Too* and *as well* usually follow it, whereas the others usually precede. (For more about the position of **only**, see under that heading.) A bifocal spotlight can be achieved when *also* and *only* combine in the correlatives *not only ... but also*, drawing attention to two things of equal importance in parallel structures.

There are less dramatic but more pervasive ways of using English sentence order to provide a particular focus. The reading of any sentence is affected and framed by whatever it begins with, and the effect is cumulative. In a detective narrative, many a sentence will begin by referring to the hero:
    Bond opened the door slowly. He stepped cautiously into the room ...
The repeated and prominent mention of the hero naturally focuses the reader's attention on him. Nonfiction writers can use the start of a sentence to draw attention to a new focus:
    From then on, he presents problems rather than solutions.
Thus skilled writers of both fiction and nonfiction use their sentence openings strategically, to establish, maintain and change the focus. (See further under **topic** and **dangling participles**.) Both phrases and subordinate clauses at the start of a sentence may help to refocus the reader's attention. See for example:
    If any further action is required, we will call a meeting.
Though grammatically subordinate, the clause becomes prominent in its prime position in that sentence. For more about subordinate clauses, see **clauses** sections 3 and 4.

informer or informant

Being similar in meaning and form, these words are sometimes substituted for each other. But because the connotations of **informer** are unpleasant, it's an unfortunate choice of words where the context is meant to be neutral.

Informer has been used for centuries (since early C16) to refer to someone who gives information to legal authorities against another person. The more recent word **informant** was also used this way for about 100 years until later C19. But its common use nowadays is to refer to someone who gives information in response to an inquiry, whether solicited in a casual encounter (e.g. *Which way to the station?*), or in the name of social and linguistic research. **Informant** is definitely the one to use if you wish to avoid depreciating the help received.

infusable or infusible

These two are not simply spelling variants, like other *-able/-ible* pairs. (See **-able/-ible**.) **Infusable** ("able to be infused", of tea, herbs etc.) is an adhoc creation – not registered in the *Oxford Dictionary* (1989) or any other, but perfectly usable and transparent because it conforms to a regular English pattern of word formation. **Infusible** goes back to Latin, and has a place in the largest dictionaries as a technical term meaning "not susceptible of fusion." First used in C16 metallurgy, it has ongoing uses on the frontiers of C21 science.

-ing

This familiar suffix is found on English verbs, adjectives and nouns. For all verbs, regular and irregular, it serves to form the present participle, and appears in many a compound verb:

it was wandering   they had been whistling

These **-ing** forms have long been seconded from the verb to work as adjectives:

a wandering albatross   a whistling kettle

In [*heard*] *the kettle whistling for all it was worth*, the **-ing** word may be seen as adjectival (introducing an adjectival phrase) or participial (introducing a nonfinite clause), depending on your grammar. (See further under **phrases** and **nonfinite clause**.)

The same **-ing** suffix forms verbal nouns in English:

Its whistling interrupted the conversation.

The fact that the verbal noun and adjective/participle are identical has caused a remarkable amount of anxiety in the last 200 years, over constructions in which it could be interpreted as either:

They heard the kettle whistling. (participle)
They heard the kettle's whistling. (noun)

(For more about this controversy, see under **gerund and gerundive**.)

Verbal nouns have been readily formed in English with **-ing** since C13, before suffixes borrowed from French and Latin such as *-al, -ance, -ation, -ence, -ment* were put to the purpose. The long history of **-ing** words has allowed many of them to develop distinctive meanings, shifting away from the verbs on which they are based to materials used in the process, or the object of the process:

bedding   clothing   drawing   dwelling   icing
mooring   roofing   scaffolding   seasoning   stuffing

This transition into full nouns is most obvious when the **-ing** becomes plural, as in:

diggings earnings findings innings   lodgings
makings savings   shavings surroundings takings

The **-ing** suffix is set solid except when attached to a short word ending in *-o*. In cases like *to-ing* and *fro-ing*, the hyphen helps to ensure that they are read as two syllables.

ingenuous or ingenious

These similar-looking adjectives have distinctly different meanings. **Ingenious** means "inventive, clever," while **ingenuous** implies simplicity and a lack of guile or circumspection, so that it can mean "naive" as in *ingenuous acceptance of the contract*, or "candid" as in *an ingenuous smile*. **Ingenious** is far more common than **ingenuous**, by a factor of more than 10:1 in British English, by the evidence of the BNC.

The opposite of **ingenuous** is *disingenuous*, whose connotations are usually negative. A *disingenuous apology* is felt to be false or feigned, and a *disingenuous proposal* is seen as devious, and not be taken at face value. A *disingenuous proposal* might nevertheless be seen as **ingenious**, by those who thought that the end justified the means.

The noun *ingenuity* goes with **ingenious** in terms of meaning, in spite of its original link with **ingenuous**. *Ingenuity* has in fact meant "inventiveness" since C17. A new abstract noun had to be found for **ingenuous**, and *ingenuousness* ("naivety") has been in use since C18.

ingrained or engrained

The first spelling is strongly preferred in both British and American English, by the evidence of databases. **Ingrained** outnumbers **engrained** by 10:1 in the BNC, and more than 30:1 in CCAE. It is one of the few in which *in-* has prevailed (see further under **en-/in-**).

inheritance or heritage

See **heritage or inheritance**.

inhuman or inhumane

See under **human or humane**.

initialed or intialled

The choice between these is discussed under **-l-/-ll-**.

initialisms

For the distinction between *acronyms* and **initialisms**, see **acronyms** last section. Note that **initialisms** are sometimes called *alphabetisms*.

initials

For the question of using full stops when abbreviating a person's given names, see **names** section 3.

in-laws

Dealing with **in-laws** takes some care. The plurals of *brother-in-law* etc. are still formed according to French convention:

brothers-in-law   fathers-in-law
mothers-in-law   sisters-in-law

For other examples, see **plurals** section 2.

But when **in-laws** become possessive, the forms are fully English:

brother-in-law's   father-in-law's etc.

The well-known garden plant *mother-in-law's tongue* is a useful reminder.

inmesh or enmesh

See under **en-/in-**.

inmost or innermost

See under **-most**.

innuendo

In medieval Latin this meant "by intimation" – hence its use in C16 English law to introduce parenthetical notes explaining the defamatory terms used in a case. But it quickly escaped the confines of legal annotation to become a common noun meaning a "deprecatory hint," and acquired not one but two English plurals: **innuendoes** and **innuendos**. The two are more or less equally used by British writers represented in the BNC, whereas **innuendoes** prevails in American data from CCAE. The regular plural **innuendos** gained a two-thirds majority in the world-wide Langscape survey (1998–2001). See further under **-o**.

inoculate

This word was originally a technical term in horticulture, meaning to "engraft a bud into another plant." But it has long been used in medicine, to refer to the practice of immunizing people against a disease, using a dead or weakened virus. In earlier C18, **inoculate** simply implied scratching the patient's skin to implant the protective virus, the technique which Edward Jenner perfected in 1796. The virus used by Jenner was derived from infected cows and called a *vaccine* (*vacca* being Latin for "cow") – hence the term *vaccination*.

In C19 medical practices, both **inoculate** and *vaccinate* came to be applied to any process of immunization that implants a protective form of a virus in a patient, whether by scratching the skin, injecting it under pressure, or consuming it orally.

The different spellings of **inoculate** and *innocuous* ("harmless") reflect their separate origins. **Inoculate** embodies the prefix *in-* ("in, into") and Latin *oculus* meaning "eye" or "bud"; while *innocuous* means "not nocuous or noxious," involving the negative prefix *in-*. (See further under **in-/im-**.) But they impinge on each other in so far as *inoculations* can ensure that future attacks of the disease will be *innocuous*.

inquire or enquire, and inquiry or enquiry

The English-speaking world is at sixes and sevens over the use of these spellings. Some writers use both, giving them different applications: others simply use **inquiry** (and **inquire**) at all times. The distinction maintained by some is that **inquiry/inquire** refer to formal and organized investigations, whereas **enquiry/enquire** are used of single and personal questions. This division of labor was endorsed by Fowler (1926), but gains no support in the *Oxford Dictionary* (1989) which simply presents the two spellings as equal alternatives (**inquire, enquire**; **inquiry, enquiry** in that order) for all meanings. *New Oxford* (1998) distances itself from both Fowler's position and that of the big *Oxford*, proposing instead that there are regional differences, associating the *en-* forms with British English, and the *in-* forms with American. This squares better with actual usage in the US than the UK. American data from CCAE shows that **inquire** and **inquiry** are strongly preferred, and used in 97% and 88% of instances respectively. The facts correlate well with *Webster's Third* (1986), which makes **inquire** and **inquiry** the primary spellings, and **enquire/enquiry** the also-rans.

British data from the BNC presents a complex picture, with **enquire** outnumbering **inquire** by 2:1, while **inquiry** outnumbers **enquiry** in the same ratio. The paradox could be explained by Fowler's semantic distinction, if the verb is more often used for personal/individual questions (=**enquire**), and the noun for nonpersonal/institutional applications of the word (= **inquiry**). Closer inspection of BNC citations shows that the spellings often seem to reflect

the Fowlerian distinction, but it doesn't capture the full range of usage. On the one hand there are examples with **enquire** applied to questions which are societal and intellectual: *a [legal] duty to enquire; enquire about prisoners of conscience; Aristotle did not enquire into the mental process.* On the other, **inquire** is sometimes used for the strictly personal questions: *he doesn't inquire into what it involved; there was no need to humble herself and inquire if he had returned to work.* And though **inquiry** is regularly used of official investigations, **enquiry** sometimes turns up there unexpectedly, as in *Committee of Enquiry, Maria Colewell Enquiry*. Burchfield (1996) also presents nonconforming examples. So while many British writers practice what Fowler preached, some use the two spellings interchangeably, as the *Oxford* still allows.

Elsewhere in the world, there are further intricacies. Australians seem to use **inquire/enquire** interchangeably, but official and house-style dictated uses of **inquiry** make it much the more common in print (Peters, 1995). Canadians prefer **inquire**, but use both **inquiry** and **enquiry**, the latter used particularly for intellectual endeavors as in *scientific enquiry* (Fee and McAlpine, 1997). In fact it's unnecessary to differentiate the spelling for particular applications, because the context normally clarifies what kind of investigation or question is at stake.

Neither **inquiry** nor **enquiry** represents the original form of this word in English. It was borrowed from French as *enquery/enquere*, and was then gradually respelled under Latin influence in C14 and C15. **Enquiry** represents a halfway stage, while in **inquiry** the latinization of the root is complete. Uncertainty about its spelling has no doubt been perpetuated by the general vacillation over **en-** and **in-**. See further under **en-/in-**.

> **International English selection:** Given no consistent ways of differentiating the two spellings, and the fact that differentiation is unnecessary, it makes sense to consolidate the use of one or the other. **Inquire** and **inquiry** recommend themselves as the spellings made first among equals by the *Oxford Dictionary*, and the fact that they are strongly preferred in North America.

inroad or inroads

Dictionaries enter this word in its singular form, but usage in the UK and the US puts it into the plural most of the time. In BNC data **inroads** outnumbers **inroad** by more than 9:1, and the ratio is well over 20:1 in CCAE. **Inroads** is the usual collocation with the verb *make*, and the two go together in 80% of the citations. For example:

> *Northern's faster pack made ever greater inroads.*
> *We all know what inroads a big family makes.*

The particle following is usually *into*, as in *made inroads into Soviet universities*.

With **inroad** the collocation with *make* is less strong – used in about 60% of citations – and the word is more often postmodified:

> *The inroad of foreign capital means some loss of independence.*
> *This case represents a major inroad on the exclusionary rule.*

As the examples show, **inroad** works as a legal and academic term, whereas **inroads** can go almost anywhere.

insanitary or unsanitary

Regional preferences run deep with these. **Insanitary** is definitely preferred by British writers in the BNC, in the ratio of about 4:1; whereas **unsanitary** is overwhelmingly preferred by Americans, on the evidence of CCAE. Otherwise there's little to choose between them. Both are transparent in meaning, and equally well established – with first citations from the same decade (1870s).

inserts

Apart from referring to the loose page(s) inserted into a publication, the term **inserts** is used by some grammarians for the various words or phrases injected into a conversation by those listening. See under **interjections**.

inshrine or enshrine

See under **en-/in-**.

insignia

No-one doubts the significance of **insignia**, but the grammatical status of the word is a little indeterminate. By origin it's the plural of Latin *insigne* meaning "distinguishing mark," first used in C17 English to refer to the badges of office. Latinists would prefer it to be used with a plural verb, as in *no insignia were handed to the person ordained*. But like other Latin loanwords ending in -*a*, it tends to become a collective noun in modern English (cf. *bacteria, candelabra, data*), helped by the fact that **insignia** take different forms in different institutions:

> *Why is the Royal Victorian Order insignia decorated with a rose?*
>
> *... [in camouflage] no rank insignia was visible*

Instances like these with singular agreement are commoner in BNC data than those with plural. In American English this process of anglicization has gone further, and the *Webster's Third* (1986) entry for **insignia** allows the regular English plural **insignias**. CCAE data provide plenty of evidence for it, in examples such as *baseball insignias, gang insignias, school insignias, military insignias* – not to mention *insignias of local motorcycle clubs, insignias from Pepsi, Merrill Lynch and Marlboro*, and *the three-arrowed insignias [used] for "recyclable."* In these various applications **insignia** has become a cover term for ordinary badges of membership and commercial logos, and much less exclusive in its implications.

insistence, insistance or insistency

Though all are listed in major dictionaries, **insistence** is the standard spelling everywhere, by the evidence of the BNC and CCAE. The databases provide no support for **insistency**, and very little for **insistance** (slightly more in American than British English). The -*ence* ending is grounded in Latin, but seemingly arbitrary in modern English. See further under **-ance/-ence**, and **-nce/-ncy**.

inst.

See under **ult**.

install or instal, and installment or instalment

Whether it's computer software, a security system, a bishop or a politician – the verb is normally spelled **install** everywhere in the world, and despite the fact that both *New Oxford* (1998) and *Merriam-Webster* (2000) allow **instal** as an alternative. In data from the BNC, **install** outnumbers **instal** by more than 40:1 (with most examples of **instal** coming from transcribed speech). The gap is almost four times greater in CCAE. **Instal** is thus rare in British English and hardly there at all in American.

This contrasts interestingly with the fact that British writers strongly prefer the spelling **instalment** for all applications of the noun. In BNC data it outnumbers **installment** by more than 50:1. It is a relatively recent (C20) preference, since the original *Oxford Dictionary* (1884–1928) set them as equal alternatives. But *New Oxford* marks **installment** as "US", suggesting the underlying reason for this polarization. *Webster's Third* (1986) meanwhile gives priority to **installment**, and American writers in CCAE support it to the hilt.

The British preference for **instalment** is shared by both Canadians and Australians, according to the *Canadian Oxford* (1998) and the *Macquarie Dictionary* (1997). Yet **installment** has much more to recommend it, being consistent with both the verb **install** and the other relevant abstract noun *installation*.

◊ Compare **forestallment**.

International English selection: **Installment** is the spelling to prefer for the noun because of its consistency with the almost universal use of **install** for the verb.

---

instantly or instantaneously

Both these imply action without delay, but there's a touch of drama about **instantaneously** that's missing from its everyday counterpart **instantly**. While **instantly** is at home in both speech and writing, **instantaneously** is too bulky for casual conversation and much less common even in writing. But **instantaneously** carries the special sense of "happening only a split second afterwards," and so emphasizes the close timing of two events:

> *The pilot touched down and passengers cheered instantaneously.*

Instantly often means just "straightaway," as in:

> *I'd go instantly if I had no appointment this afternoon.*

Thus **instantly** seems to be losing its sense of urgency, just like the adjective *instant*, in unremarkable things such as *instant coffee* and *instant solutions*.

instill or instil

While Americans and Canadians prefer **instill**, British and Australian writers plump for **instil**. Yet the *Oxford Dictionary*'s (1989) citations show that **instil** is a latter-day British spelling, first appearing in C19, with the hardening up of "rules" over final *l*. (See further under **single for double**.) Dr. Johnson used **instill**, which accords better with *instillation* and the word's Latin stem *instillare*. Data from the BNC suggests that the changeover is still going on in the UK, where 1 in 7 are still using **instill**. Among American writers in CCAE, more than 99 in 100 use

instill. The choice between *instillment* and *instilment* naturally turns on one's spelling of the verb.

The particle used after **instil(l)** is normally *in* everywhere in the world, with *into* coming a long way behind. The following examples from the BNC and CCAE show the common pattern:

> *It's the same reaction we want to instil in children.*
> *The fear these smugglers instill in people is incredible.*

But data from the corpora show much less convergence after *instilled*. British writers make almost as much use of *instilled into* as *instilled in,* and rather more use of *instilled into* in passive constructions such as:

> *... the uncompromising principles instilled into her by her Quaker family*

Very occasionally *instilled* is followed by *with* – a faulty construction according to Fowler (1926) and some later usage commentators. Yet both BNC and CCAE provide examples of it such as:

> *... all members of a meritocracy... are instilled with ambition*
> *... several humanitarian arms of the UN have been instilled with a sense of urgency...*

In passive constructions using *with,* the subject is typically human, and the particle following couldn't be *in* or *into.* This is the alternative passive allowable with various ditransitive verbs which have both human and nonhuman objects (direct and indirect/prepositional; see **predicate** section 3). Fowler's examples show he was concerned with "object shuffling" in active constructions, but his criticism has been overgeneralized as if *with* could never combine with the verb **instil(l)**. Perhaps the insistence on using *in* or *into* owes something to the idea that the particle following a Latin verb should match the prefix (as argued for **compared with** and **different from**). At any rate passive use of *instilled with* is grammatically justifiable, and even the active *instil(l) with* seems to accord with dictionary definitions of it as "imbue" or "infuse" – though neither corpus provides any examples.

instinctive or instinctual

Both words are related to *instinct*, but their connotations are a little different. **Instinctive** is the older and much more common word, used since C17 to mean "prompted by instinct." It's often used of actions and feelings which are intuitive, as in an *instinctive liking for her,* where the instinct involved would be hard to identify. **Instinctive** is thus too ambiguous to serve the psychologists' need for an adjective meaning simply "relating to human instincts" – hence the coining of **instinctual** in the 1920s. It remains the more academic and formal of the two words.

institute or institution

Both these can refer to specialized organizations and bodies of people, as well as to an established law or custom. What distinguishes them is the fact that **institution** is usually a generic or abstract term, while **institute** is most often found in the proper names of organizations, witness:

> *Courtauld Institute*
> *British Film Institute*
> *Manhattan Institute for Policy Research*
> *Sicilian Institute of Vine-growing*
> *Catholic Communications Institute*

> *Chartered Institute of Arbitrators*
> *National Institute for Standards and Technology*

As those examples show, **Institutes** often have a very specific educational or professional role, but they also provide social and other support for particular groups, as in:

> *Royal Institute for the Deaf*
> *Women's Institute*
> *City Literary Institute*

Just occasionally, **Institution** is similarly used as part of an organization's name, as for the British *Institution of Engineers,* but more noticeably in the US with the *Smithsonian Institution, Brookings Institution, Hoover Institution* among others, which often feature the name of a benefactor or founder. These are typically long-established entities, whereas more recent foundations in both the US and UK tend to use **Institute**, a trend noted by Fowler in the 1920s. This may be because **institution** also serves as a euphemism for a place of confinement, especially a mental asylum, as when someone is *put in an institution.*

Yet **institution** maintains several other roles. It can refer to a familiar practice, as in:

> *Friday wine-tastings are an institution in their office.*

It also provides the abstract noun for the verb *institute,* as in:

> *The institution of regular on-site meetings kept them better in touch with construction problems.*

Thirdly, **institution** is the generic word for organizations of all kinds, as in:

> *... a risky move for a financial institution*
> *... dissatisfaction with Congress as an institution*
> *IMF officials don't like to think of their institution in such terms.*
> *The family is in deep trouble as an institution*

This allows **institution** to be used as a paraphrase for **Institute**, as when speaking of the *Women's Institute* as a *nineteenth century institution.*

instructive or instructional

We learn something from it, whether the medium referred to is **instructive** or **instructional**. But things **instructional**, such as *instructional materials,* are expressly designed to provide instruction; while those which prove **instructive**, such as an *instructive interview,* are ones which teach us something incidentally. We learn through our own insights from an *instructive experience,* whereas a formal process of education is implied in **instructional**.

instrumental case

Some languages have a built-in way of marking words which express the *instrument* of an action. Modern English no longer has a special suffix for this, and instead uses a phrase beginning with *with:*

> *They cut the bottle with a file.*

In Old English the **instrumental case** was identical with the dative case for nouns, but there were special *instrumental* forms for some of the pronouns, notably the demonstratives and the interrogative. In Latin the *instrumental* was identical with the ablative case. In Australian Aboriginal languages it coincides with the ergative or locative. See further under **cases**.

insurance or assurance
See **assurance**.

insure or ensure
In British and Australian English, these words have different applications. To **ensure** is simply to make sure of something, while **insure** is the business of arranging financial guarantees against loss, theft or damage to your property, or against loss of life and limb. (Cf. **assurance or insurance**.) But in North American English **insure** covers both meanings, and **ensure** is simply a variant spelling.

The British use of the two spellings to distinguish the two meanings is only about a century old. For other cases of variation between *en-* and *in-*, see **en-/in-**.

insurgence or insurgency
Insurgency is the dominant spelling in both British and American English, by the evidence of BNC and CCAE. The data do not show the differentiation proposed by Garner (1998), whereby **insurgence** goes with a specific act of uprising and **insurgency** with a persistent state or condition. See further under **-nce/-ncy**.

integral, integrate and integration
To get the spelling right for any of these, think *integrity*. Its pronunciation helps to ensure you don't write them with *inter-* (that prefix has nothing to do with them). Rather they are all related to *integer* ("a whole, or whole number").

intense or intensive
These have rather different implications. **Intensive** implies sustained and constant attention over a given period, while the word **intense** targets the keenness of that attention at a particular moment. A more important difference is that **intensive** is often associated with organized and institutional activity, as in *intensive search* and an *intensive course*. Whereas **intense** is used to characterize individual behavior and attitudes, as in *intense gaze* and *intense concentration*.

In *intensive care* we would of course hope to find that the patient is keenly watched by the nurse. But from the hospital's point of view it's a matter of the constancy of medical monitoring, rather than periodic visits by the nurse, as in other wards.

intensifiers, amplifiers and emphasizers
An **intensifier** is an adjective or adverb (word or phrase) which amplifies the force of others, pushing them further up (or down) a notional scale. The most familiar example is *very*, as in *a very good product* – which is clearly better than *a good product*. *Very* is thus a *booster*, according to the *Comprehensive Grammar* (1985), rather than a *maximizer* like *absolute(ly), complete(ly), extreme(ly), utter(ly)*, which push the reference to the top of the scale. Compare *an absolute masterpiece / absolutely brilliant*.

These **amplifiers** are somewhat different from **emphasizers** such as *real(ly)*, which underscore the writer's/speaker's conviction about the word or phrase used, as in *a really good speaker* – rather than modifying the notional point of reference on a scale. **Emphasizers** add more to the *interpersonal* aspects of the text (see under that heading), and are available in

various styles. The standard repertoire includes *actually, certainly, definitely, surely*, while their colloquial equivalents (*awfully, incredibly, mega, terrifically* etc.) are subject to fashion, and change from one generation to the next. Swear words such as *bloody, damn(ed)* and others are more durable, but suitable only for very informal styles of writing. In everyday speech, **emphasizers** serve to pinpoint significant words, and give the speaker a few more microseconds of time in which to develop an utterance.
◊ Compare **hedge words**.

intensive or intense
See **intense**.

inter-
This prefix meaning "between, among" is built into hundreds of ordinary words borrowed from Latin, of which the following are only a token:

intercept	*interfere*	*interjection*
interlude	*intermediate*	*interpolate*
interrupt	*interval*	

It also forms new words in English, many of which are hybrid Latin–English:

interact	*interchange*	*interface*
interleave	*interlock*	*intermarriage*
interplay	*intertwine*	*interview*

New, purely Latin formations with **inter-** tend to be longish, academic and institutional words:

intercontinental	*interdenominational*
interdependent	*intergalactic*
interinstitutional	*interpenetrate*
intertribal	

In a few cases **inter-** contrasts with *intra-*, as in:

international	*intranational*
interstate	*intrastate*
internet	*intranet*

See further under **intra-/intro-**.

inter alia
This handy phrase, borrowed from Latin, means "among other things." It indicates that the set of items mentioned is not exhaustive:
> *The figures showed inter alia how audience ratings were going up.*

Inter alia also serves to highlight an item as the most important of a possible set. Notice the much more casual effect of using *etc.* instead:
> *The figures showed how audience ratings were going up etc.*

Because **inter alia** is a neuter plural in Latin, it strictly speaking applies to things rather than people. Parallel forms for referring to people are *inter alios* (again plural, for all-male or mixed groups) and *inter alias* (for an all-female group). None of these phrases is abbreviated, unlike other Latin tags such as *e.g.* or *etc.* Whether to italicize them is a matter of choice. See further under **Latin abbreviations** and **italic(s)**.

intercaps
See **capital letters** section 4.

interdependence or interdependency
Both these originate in the earlier C19, but **interdependence** is far more common in both British and American English. Fowler (1926) preferred it without giving his reasons, as if the meanings of the

two words were indistinguishable. The *Oxford Dictionary* (1989) citations up to about 1900 show that **interdependence** was the more abstract of the two, and that **interdependency** served as a countable noun, as often in such pairs (see further under -nce/-ncy). But the few instances of **interdependency** in the BNC all have it as an abstract, as in *encouraging flexibility and interdependency*.

interjections

Grammars and usage books often give short shrift to **interjections** because they have no place in formal written English. Seen as "natural ejaculation[s] expressive of some feeling or emotion" (to use the *Oxford Dictionary*'s [1989] terms) – or as the tangential comments hurled by an unsympathetic listener at a speaker – they do not seem to contribute to the fabric of discourse. They were however recognized by the earliest Greek grammarians as a special class of words, purely emotive in meaning, which could stand as independent sentences.

The traditional definition is echoed in many grammars and dictionaries, and their examples are confined to words such as *Wow! Ouch! Great! Hell!* But grammarians these days tend to analyze as **interjections** a variety of other words that function as mini-sentences to communicate an attitude or social orientation. These "reaction signals" and "formulae" include:

* reaction signals   *Yes, No, Right, Okay, Thanks*
* expletives   *Damn, Jeez, Shit*
* greetings and farewells   *Hello, Hi, Cheers, Goodbye*

All these, as well as backchannels such as *Mm, Uh-huh,* and pause-fillers such as *Ah, Er, Well,* are now accommodated in the category of **interjections**, by the *Comprehensive Grammar* (1985). The *Longman Grammar* (1999) does likewise, but under the label of *inserts,* to prevent confusion with the traditional **interjection**.

English **interjections** can of course consist of more than one word, and these too are now recognized as members of the same grammatical class. Natural candidates are two-word greetings such as *Good evening,* as well as standardized reactions and formulae like *Hear, hear! Good lord! Bottoms up! Break a leg!* With little or no referential content, they are more like **interjections** than exclamations such as *What a surprise!* – though both are fragmentary sentences (see **sentences** section 2).

Beyond the grammar of **interjections**, their role in interactive discourse is now beginning to be recognized. So whether it's the collaborative *Of course* offered by one person to support another, or the skeptical *Tell us another!* designed to undermine the speaker, **interjections** are an important element of communication. Some now find a place in parliamentary records.

intermezzo

This Italian loanword means literally "interval," though it actually refers to the musical activity that took place in the interval between the major divisions of a theatrical, operatic or musical performance. The lightness of such music is the essence of independent compositions called by the same name. In English the word is usually pluralized as **intermezzi** in strictly musical contexts, but elsewhere **intermezzos.** For more examples, see **Italian plurals.**

international or intranational

See under **inter-**.

international English

Against our heightened knowledge of variation in English around the world, the idea of a region-free, go-anywhere English has much appeal and is increasingly talked about. Its value is obvious for publishers and others who seek to market English language products. What could be better than a type of English that saves you from having to re-edit publications for individual regional markets! Teachers and learners of English as a second language also find it an attractive idea – both often concerned that their English should be neutral, without British or American or Canadian or Australian coloring. Any regional variety of English has a set of political, social and cultural connotations attached to it, even the so-called "standard" forms (see **standard English** and **dialect**). Regional associations can indeed be quite distracting, witness the effect (in translating a Buddhist dialogue) of making the guru say "Sure"! For non-Americans this puts an American accent on oriental wisdom. As that example shows, regional character can come through the printed word, even though it's usually much more muted there than in live speech. As soon as we start to converse, we reveal what part of the world is home.

So the idea of a fully fledged, regionally neutral form of English is somewhat idealistic. We can however get closer to it in the written medium, by identifying the variants of English usage that have the widest distribution. Thousands of words are in fact written in the same way everywhere in the world – like all those used so far in this paragraph. They make up the core of **international English**, though there are subtleties in terms of the set of meanings which are attached to a word in one region but not another – the subject of various entries in this book. Also challenging are words whose spelling or form diverges in British and American English, though an *international* variant can often be found where the sole variant for one variety is a familiar alternative in the other. Consider for example the spelling *catalogue,* which is standard in British English and a common alternative to *catalog* in American English. Spellings and usages such as these which are current on both sides of the Atlantic, are sometimes called "common English" (Benson *et al.*, 1986). They are good candidates for **international English**, since the chances are that the same relativities between variants will hold for Englishes outside the US and UK (e.g. Canada, Australia, New Zealand, South Africa). The *international English selections* presented at the end of various entries in this book recommend themselves for this reason.

International English is harder to maintain in informal style, since many colloquialisms have only local currency. But in standard styles of writing as used in newspaper articles printed in Canberra, New York, Singapore and London, regional identity may not be obvious, provided there are no references to local institutions. Writing that avoids the local and the colloquial may well qualify as "international." See further under **English or Englishes**, and **mid-Atlantic English.**

International Phonetic Alphabet

The **International Phonetic Alphabet** (IPA) is the only alphabet whose symbols have a single, unvarying relationship with particular sounds. This is because they are defined in articulatory terms, i.e. by the speech organs used in producing them. The IPA symbols are indispensable whether we are attempting to describe sounds in a foreign language, or to pinpoint pronunciations of English words. A chart of the symbols used for English can be found in Appendix I.

The symbols of the IPA are mostly drawn from the ordinary Roman alphabet, with permutated forms of them used to extend the inventory. A handful of others come from the Greek and Anglo-Saxon alphabets. Perhaps the most remarkable symbol of all is *schwa* represented by an upside-down, back-to-front *e*, which stands for the indeterminate vowel so often heard in English, and so variously written. See further under **schwa**.

International System of Units

The **International System of Units** translates the *Système International d'Unités*, and the official French title explains why *SI units* has become the English name for the units themselves. *SI units* are the basis of the metric system of measurements, whose implementation is complete in Australia and New Zealand, well-advanced in Canada, and ongoing in the UK and the US (see **metrication**). For the full set of units, see Appendix IV, and see further under **imperial weights and measures**.

internet or Internet

Should this word be capitalized? The global digital network it now refers to grew out of a more local system developed by the US military during the 1970s as part of a defense strategy, which was simply the **internet**. But in the following decade it began to connect with civilian and commercial organizations, and with ever-increasing numbers of participant institutions and global reach, it has become (**the**) **Internet** – the only one in the universe! In corpus data, a small number of writers dare to write it without a capital (around 5% in the BNC, less than 1% in CCAE). Though **Internet** dominates in British and American English at the turn of the millennium, it can only be a matter of time for it to be decapitalized, as noted in the Australian government *Style Manual* (2002). In phrases such as *internet connection* where it becomes a modifier, the lower case form is already more visible. There is no capital on the complementary term *intranet* (a digital communications network using the same technology but confined to a particular institution). Related terms such as *website, web page* do without a capital: see further under **website**.

International English selection: Given that **internet** had no capital letter in the first place, and the generic nature of its use, the decapitalized form makes sense.

---

internet addresses

See under **digital style, line breaks** and **URL**.

interpersonal

Writers do not always think of themselves as setting up a relationship with their readers. They may not know who their readers are likely to be, and tend to forget about them when the subject itself becomes all-consuming. If the writing is technical or philosophical this may not matter, though the style may still seem rather "dry." For writing which is intended as individual or private communication, it's much more of an issue. A shortage of **interpersonal** elements then seems both dry and insensitive to the reader. It could undermine the very purpose of communicating.

The **interpersonal** aspects of language or writing are all those elements which establish a particular relationship with the reader – as opposed to those which express information, or help to structure the text (the referential and textual aspects, respectively). The **interpersonal** effect is strong and direct in the first and second person pronouns (*I, we, you*), and in grammatical structures such as questions, commands and exclamations. Both contribute to a sentence such as:

You really won't believe how great the acting is!

The **interpersonal** dimension in that sentence is also expressed through the use of the contraction *won't* (likewise any word or structure which smacks of conversation); and the word *great,* which invites the reader to share a value judgement. Attitudinal adverbs and intensifiers/emphasizers such as *really* call for a reaction from the reader. Other words which have an **interpersonal** effect are those which mediate degrees of obligation, permission and possibility (modal auxiliaries such as *must, should, can*, as well as the adverbs which paraphrase them: *necessarily, perhaps* etc.). Words which express the writer's judgement on the likelihood of something are again ones which call gently upon the reader.

He's likely to arrive on Friday.

The word *likely* highlights the fact that the statement is an estimate, one which the reader may either accept or re-evaluate. (See further under **modality**.)

Note that some words and expressions combine an **interpersonal** effect with their referential meaning. The word *great* has both when used in reference to someone's acting, though the **interpersonal** effect is hardly there when it refers to the size of a crowd.
◊ See also **textual**.

interpretive or interpretative

The weight of *Oxford Dictionary* (1989) citations suggest that **interpretative** has hitherto dominated the scene; and Fowler (1926) argued from Latin word-forming principles that it was the more legitimate, though he elsewhere argues against unnecessary syllables. American English now clearly prefers **interpretive** – which is not only shorter but more patently linked with the verb *interpret*. According to *Webster's English Usage* (1989) this is a trend of the last few decades, and its strength is measured in CCAE data by the fact that *interpretive* outnumbers **interpretative** by about 10:1. In contemporary British English from the BNC, **interpretative** outnumbers **interpretive** by just on 2:1 – which could mean that **interpretive** is on the rise there too. The older British preference for **interpretative** still seems to be echoed in the

Canadian Oxford (1998) and Australian *Macquarie Dictionary* (1997), both of which give it priority over **interpretive** among the run-ons (see further under **run in or run on**). On the other hand, the order may be merely alphabetical.
◊ Compare **preventive or preventative**.

interregnum

This plural of this latinate word is **interregnums** rather than **interregna**, by what little evidence there is in British and American databases. **Interregnum** is in fact a classical concoction of C16, not an authentic Latin loanword.

interrobang

This yet-to-be-established mark of punctuation could be handy when we need to use a question mark and exclamation mark/point simultaneously. Shaped like a combination of the two‽ the **interrobang** allows us to query and to express incredulity in the same stroke:

> You want the report tomorrow‽

The complex of emotions you may feel at such a moment cannot be adequately expressed through the conventional sequence of ?! or !? and the **interrobang** would be a valuable addition to the punctuation repertoire.

According to the *Random House Dictionary* (1987) the **interrobang** originated in the 1960s as printers' slang. Its potential is discussed in *Webster's Style Manual* (1987), but it makes no showing in the *Microsoft Manual of Style* (1998). Its future no doubt depends on its becoming a standard punctuation item in other wordprocessing packages. Alternative spellings for it are *interrabang* and *interabang*.

interrogative

This is the traditional grammarians' name for the form of verbs that expresses a direct question:

> Are they coming to the barbecue?
> When will he decide?
> Do you like red wine?

In English *interrogative constructions*, the normal subject-verb order is inverted, and the subject *they/he/you* follows the first (auxiliary) part of the verb. Compare the order in *they are coming, he will decide* etc. The third of these sentences shows how a simple verb *like* acquires an auxiliary (*do*) in the **interrogative**. In C16 it too could be made **interrogative** by inverting subject and verb: *Like you red wine?* But modern English always brings in *do* to form the **interrogative** when the verb is not itself an auxiliary.

Modern grammars (e.g. *Comprehensive Grammar*, 1985) apply the term **interrogative** to the particular "sentence function" or "clause type" that expresses a question, rather than the distinctive verb form. (See further under **mood** and **questions**.) This recognizes the fact that an *interrogative construction* can express other speech functions, such as the imperative. In the US and elsewhere, the sentence *Why don't you open the door?* is a polite way of instructing someone to do something.

interrogative words

With these words we signal the start and the focus of a question, as in "Who are you?" or "What's the time?"

Interrogative words include pronouns:

> who what which whom whose

and adverbs:

> when where why how

Both can be used in either direct or indirect questions:

Who's there?	*He asked who was there.*
What do you want?	*They inquired what I wanted.*

Modern grammars such as the *Comprehensive Grammar of English* (1985) and the *Longman Grammar* (1999) use the collective name *wh-words* for both groups.

Note that *wh-words* also serve to introduce several kinds of subordinate clause. *Interrogative pronouns* double as relativizers in relative clauses and complementizers in noun clauses. For example:

> The man who came to dinner went away amused.
> I asked them who else had been invited.

Interrogative adverbs are used as subordinators in adverbial clauses:

> They went where no human being had ventured before.

See **clauses** section 4.

inthrone or enthrone

See under **en-/in-**.

into or in to

Most of the time, the choice between these is straightforward. Compare:

> They went into the theatre.
> They went in to the reception.

The spaced form ensures that the particle *in* is interpreted in relation to the previous verb, and adds a detail of movement that would otherwise be submerged. But in practice the solid form **into** is quite often used where *in to* might be justified, and not too much is lost. The *Oxford Dictionary* (1989) confirms that **into** served both roles in earlier centuries; and even today it is not systematically contrasted with *in to* by all writers – though nice distinctions can be made, as between *tucking someone into bed* and *tucking in to the pancakes*. As that example shows, the need for *in* to might be argued particularly in relation to idiomatic verbs involving *in*. On the other hand, there is no requirement for **into** to refer to physical movement in space, and the object settles what kind of *tucking* is meant in each case. Metaphorical uses of **into** such as *He's turned into a monster* and *She's into astrology* confirm the general tendency to prefer the unspaced form.
◊ Compare **onto or on to**.

intra-/intro-

This prefix meaning "inside" appears in a number of words coined for scientific or institutional usage. The form **intra-** is the more recent one, first recorded in C19, in words such as:

intracranial	intramural	intramuscular
intrastate	intra-uterine	intravenous

A number of **intra-** words are obviously intended as counterparts to those prefixed with **extra-**, witness *intramural/extramural* for instance.

Formations with **intro-** are loanwords from Latin, which mostly date from C17 on, apart from *introduction* which was borrowed in C14. Unlike those prefixed with **intra-**, their second components are not usually independent words in English, and they maintain a classical flavor:

introgression	*introjection*	*intromission*
introspection	*introversion*	*introvert*
introvolution		

Most are specialist words, except for those popularized through psychology such as *introspection* and *introvert/introversion*.

◊ For *intravert* and *intraversion,* see **introvert**.

intra vires

See under **ultra vires**.

intransitive

This is the grammatical name for a verb which does not take an object. See further under **transitive and intransitive**.

intrench or entrench

See under **en-/in-**.

introductions

First impressions are as important in writing as they are in spoken encounters. The first few sentences should combine to convince readers they are in competent hands, and that the writer is in control of the medium.

In nonfiction, the **introduction** needs to identify amd frame the topic to be discussed, with some indication as to the stages in which it will be treated, or the ultimate destination of the argument. The longer the document, the more some sort of map and signposts are needed. A long report may offer its concluding recommendations at the start, and then proceed to show how they were arrived at. The so-called *executive summary* in business documents serves this purpose (see under **reports**).

In fiction the *introductory* chapters serve to set the scene, create a particular tone, and secure the reader's engagement in the imaginative world. Yet engaging the reader's imagination is not unimportant in nonfictional writing. The most effective **introductions** project some lively details of the subject, linking it with the real world and avoiding too many generalizations and clichéd observations.

◊ For the relationship between the **introduction**, foreword and *preface* of a book, see **preface**.

introvert or intravert, and introversion or intraversion

The spellings with *a* are rare variants of the standard forms in *o*, reflecting the indeterminacy of the second syllable. The parity with *extravert/extraversion* no doubt suggests the use of **intravert/intraversion** (see further under **intra-/intro-**). But only **introvert** and **introversion** are recognized by dictionaries.

intwine or entwine

See under **en-/in-**.

intwist or entwist

See under **en-/in-**.

Inuit

See under **Eskimo**.

inure or enure

British and American dictionaries give priority to **inure**, whether the meaning is "become accustomed"

(with negative coloring), or the legal sense "accrue." Compare:

> *He had become inured to long solitary vigils in hotel rooms.*
> *It will not inure to any long term benefit of the plaintiff.*

The use of **enure** is now very limited. It has no currency at all in American English, judging by its total absence from CCAE, and its appearances in the BNC are almost entirely confined to the legal sense. For all common purposes, **inure** is the spelling to use.

invaluable or valuable

See **valuable and invaluable**.

inversion

Any departure from the normal word order used in a clause (subject–verb–object/complement) can be called **inversion**. *Inverting* subject and verb is a regular feature of certain English grammatical constructions, for example:

* in direct questions:
  > *Have you finished?*
  > *Are they on their way?*

* following an adverb which highlights the timing or location of an event at the start of a sentence:
  > *Here comes the bus.*
  > *Now is the time to run for it.*
  > *Down came the rain.*
  > *There stood a surprised passenger.*

* following a negative adverb or adverbial phrase:
  > *No sooner had he reached the bus than he found he'd lost his keys.*
  > *Never had a man felt so embarrassed.*
  > *Under no circumstances could he return home.*

As the last three examples show, **inversion** following a negative adverb/adverbial always requires an auxiliary verb immediately after. Exactly the same construction occurs after *hardly* and *scarcely*. Note that in all these constructions the subject is *inverted* after the auxiliary – whether it's a pronoun or a noun phrase (*Hardly had they / the bus arrived . . .*). But after a simple verb, a pronoun subject cannot be *inverted:* "Here come they" is not acceptable, whereas *Here comes the bus* is fine. Other specialized uses of **inversion** include:

* stock phrases identifying the speaker in dialogue:
  > *"I'd like you to focus on my other side" says he.*
  > *"Here we go again," said the cameraman.*

* clauses expressing an impossible condition may use **inversion** of the subject and verb instead of a conjunction:
  > *Had I known, I'd have been there* (= If I had known . . .)
  > *Were I an expert on computers, I'd have solved the problem.*

All the **inversions** so far, involving subject and verb, can appear in standard written or narrative prose. The **inversion** of object and verb is not often found in writing, but it's common enough in conversation:

> *Avocados they adore. Artichokes they hate.*

Inversions of this kind give special prominence to the object as the *topic* of the clause (see further under that heading). The use of object–verb **inversion** by poets seems to serve the same purpose: *Brothers and sisters have I none . . .* , although one suspects that it's often motivated by the demands of rhyme and metre.

inverted commas

In American English, this term has little currency, judging by its rarity in CCAE. But the British still prefer **inverted commas** to *quotation marks* (or *quote marks*) when speaking about them. In BNC data transcribed from speech, **inverted commas** is well represented, used especially as the oral equivalent of "scare quotes":

I won't be, in inverted commas, a "clergy wife."

Yet the major British style references (*Copy-editing*, 1992, and the *Oxford Guide to Style*, 2002) use the term *quotation marks*, as does the *Chicago Manual* (2003), *Editing Canadian English* (2000) and the Australian government *Style Manual* (2002). See further under **quotation marks**.

inverted pyramid

See under **journalism and journalese**.

investor or invester

In C16 when *invest* meant – more literally – "enrobe," both **investor** and **invester** were used for the noun. The financial sense arrived in early C17, probably based on Italian use of the cognate verb *investire* ("to lay out money on a bargain for advantage"). But according to the *Oxford Dictionary* (1989), **investor** is the only spelling ever used for the noun in its financial sense, first recorded in C19, which accompanies use of the verb in its more generic sense "make financial investments." In theory the noun could be **invester**, as an English derivative of the verb *invest*, but standard spelling keeps it as **investor**, everywhere in the world.

invocation or evocation, and invoke or evoke

For all these issues, see **evoke or invoke**.

inward or inwards

See under **-ward or -wards**.

-ion

This is by far the most common suffix for abstract nouns in English, in spite of its foreign origins. Most of the words embodying it are loanwords from French or Latin, yet many of them are ordinary enough:

action	ambition	decision
instruction	motion	tension

New words are continually being formed, especially from verbs ending in *-ate* (see further under **-ation**).

Though **-ion** forms abstract nouns, many of them (like *action* and *motion*) express the product of the related verb, and so have at least some physical and material properties. Thus not all words with **-ion** contribute abstractions to a text, and don't necessarily contribute to a woolly style – despite this assumption being embedded in certain computer style checkers. In cases like *declassification* or *transmogrification*, the point is taken, but with ones like *action* and *motion* there's no need to seek a simpler synonym.

-ious

This ending is embodied in a very large group of English adjectives – with sometimes ad hoc additions from others that should be spelled *-eous* or *-uous*, because of their different histories, as detailed below. The very many adjectives for which **-ious** is the

regular spelling form several subsets:

* those like *furious, glorious, industrious,* which have related nouns ending in *-y* (*fury/glory/industry*)
* those like *cautious, oblivious, religious,* which have related nouns ending in *-ion* (*caution* etc.)
* those *like audacious, capacious, loquacious,* which have related nouns ending in *-ity* (*audacity* etc.)

Adjectives with **-ious** begin to be recorded in the English Renaissance, though whether they're really English formations is unclear, since many have counterparts in Latin and French. A handful of bizarre later ones like *bumptious, rumbustious, scrumptious* are unquestionably English inventions – words in which the more pretentious latinate **-ious** is juxtaposed to down-to-earth English syllables.

Words with -eous not -ious. The ending *-ious* sounds identical to *-eous*, but the endings are not interchangeable. The words formed with *-eous* (*bounteous, contemporaneous, herbaceous*) are far fewer, and usually distinctive by virtue of their length or specialized character. The oldest group like *bounteous* were French borrowings or based on French or Anglo-Norman models. (Compare Middle English *bounte* with modern *bounty*.) Further examples include:

beauteous	courteous	duteous	gorgeous
hideous	piteous	plenteous	righteous

All have a rhetorical or literary flavor, except perhaps *courteous*. Most of the other *-eous* words are based on Latin and associated with scholarship and science. They include:

erroneous	extraneous	instantaneous
miscellaneous	momentaneous	spontaneous

There are Latin models also for *aqueous, igneous, ligneous, vitreous,* and for the large number of biological names like *farinaceous*. (See further under **-acious/-aceous**.)

Three special cases with *-eous* are *advantageous, courageous, outrageous,* all spelled that way because of the need to preserve a soft "g" in them. (See further under **-ce/-ge**.)

Confusion between -ious and -uous. On occasions *-ious* is used by mistake for *-uous*, so that one hears and sees "presumptious" and "unctious," instead of *presumptuous* and *unctuous*. This problem happens because of the related nouns in *-ion* (*presumption, unction*) from which *-ious* adjectives could be generated (compare *cautious/caution* above).

All adjectives ending in **-ious**, *-eous* and *-uous* are members of the larger set ending in *-ous* (see further under that heading).

ipse dixit

This Latin phrase meaning "he himself said it" was originally used in Greek by the acolytes of Pythagoras to refer to the utterances of the master. In C18 English it became a way of referring to authoritarian statements about the language, alongside its more general meaning of "an assertion made on authority but not proved." The **ipse dixit** rules of C18 grammarians met the cultural needs of the century (sometimes called "the age of correctness"), and were used to condemn the idiom of earlier authors, as well as ongoing changes in English usage. Some of the pronouncements, e.g. those concerning the uses of *shall* and *will*, have been transmitted through English language curriculums of C19 and C20 to become the linguistic fetishes of contemporary English. See further under **fetish**.

ipso facto

Used in argument, this Latin tag means "by that very fact." It draws attention to a point which the speaker/writer claims has a necessary consequence:

The defendant had a shotgun on the back seat of his car and was ipso facto planning for a fight.

There's no necessary connection between that piece of evidence ("shotgun on the back seat") and the interpretation put on it. Yet the use of **ipso facto** presses you to accept the interpretation, and exploits its legal connotations to fend off questions about it. See further under **fallacies** section 2.

Iraq or Irak, and Iraqi or Iraki

Dictionaries all give priority to the Arabic spellings **Iraq/Iraqi**, and British and American databases give them overwhelming support. The anglicized spellings **Irak/Iraki** are registered as alternatives in *Webster's Third* (1986) and the *Oxford Dictionary* (1989), but citational evidence shows that this is mostly an older spelling, used in later C18 and earlier C19. Since 1921, when Mesopotamia became the kingdom and then the republic of **Iraq**, the spellings **Iraq/Iraqi** have become the standard, and **Iraki** is captured in one solitary citation since then. The Arabic form of the word has prevailed in English, despite its rather un-English use of *q* without a following *u*, probably because it's a proper name.

◊ For common nouns in which *q* and *k* vary, see **q/k**.

Ireland and Irish

Only in geography – and jokes – can **Ireland/Irish** refer to the whole of "the Emerald Isle." The 1921 split into *Northern Ireland* (the northeastern segment sometimes called "Ulster") and a larger southern dominion, first called the *Irish Free State,* then *Eire* from 1937 to 1949, and now *Republic of Ireland,* makes for complications in the use of both noun and adjective. References to the government, its people and their language(s), must qualify the name in some way for precise communication.

The official names *Northern Ireland* and *Republic of Ireland* (less formally *Irish Republic*) are neutral and usable anywhere. The use of *Ulster* for *Northern Ireland* is informal and not-so-neutral, suggesting a commitment to the connection with Great Britain, as in *Ulster Defence Association*. The fact that three of the nine provinces once part of *Ulster* now belong to the *Republic* also complicates the use of that name. Neither *Ulster* nor *Eire* (for the *Irish Republic*) are necessarily familiar elsewhere (not in Canada, according to *Canadian English Usage*, (1997).

Names for the people of **Ireland** also present a challenge. *Irish Republican* and *Northern Irishman* mark the difference, though they are not established terms. *Ulsterman* (for the latter) is not entirely accurate or politically neutral, as explained. Both *Irishman* and *Ulsterman* would sound sexist elsewhere in the world, if not at home (see further under **nonsexist language**). That leaves *Irish Republican* and *Northern Irish*.

The original Celtic language of **Ireland** is known to scholars as **Irish**; but in ordinary usage it's *Gaelic*, a reminder of its close similarity to the Celtic language of Scotland. The English of **Ireland** diverges into three varieties, according to McArthur (1992):

* *Anglo-Irish*, developed out of the variety brought by English settlers in C17, and used across most of Ireland by middle- and "working"-class Irish
* *Hiberno-English,* a chiefly working-class variety originating with those whose forebears spoke Irish Gaelic, used by the Catholic population of Ireland (including Northern Ireland)
* *Ulster Scots*, the English associated particularly with Protestants in Northern Ireland, based on the Lowland Scots brought by Scottish settlers in Ulster.

The term *Irish English* is often used to cover all three varieties, though it rides roughshod over significant regional and cultural differences.

ironic or ironical

The first of these is commoner by far, judging by their relative frequencies in British and American databases. In the BNC **ironic** outnumbers **ironical** by more than 8:1, and in CCAE by a factor of more than 20:1 – so the British preference for **ironic** is a much stronger commitment for American writers. But whatever the frequency, the two appear to be interchangeable in meaning and grammar. Either can be used predicatively, as in:

It's rather ironic(al) that . . .

Or attributively, as in:

. . . an ironic smile / an ironical snort

See further under **-ic/-ical**.

irony

This much-used concept originated on the Greek stage, in the duality of meaning created by the character whose words had a simple, immediate meaning as well as another, discrepant meaning for the audience who saw them in the context of the whole play and of the common culture.

From there the notion of **irony** has been extended to the similar effect achieved in modern forms of literature – when there's a discrepancy between the immediate meaning of a writer's words, and the shades of meaning they take on in a broader context. The effect may be gentle as in Jane Austen's works, or biting, as in those of Jonathan Swift. Either way the effect is cerebral, and depends on the comprehensiveness of the reader's response. In this respect **irony** differs from *sarcasm*, which uses taunting words to launch a direct and explicit attack on another person.

Irony is also to be seen in real-life situations and events which turn out contrary to what one might expect. It might for example seem *ironic* to appoint an emotionally unstable person to counsel others with emotional problems.

◊ For the choice between **ironic** and **ironical**, see previous entry.

irregardless

This is a contentious blend of *irrespective* and *regardless,* with the same meaning as either. **Irregardless** has negative affixes at both ends, and thus has a built-in double negative. The effect is redundant rather than rhetorical, as with other double negatives, but it helps to explain objections to it (see further under **double negatives**).

The redundant negative in **irregardless** goes with its use in informal discourse, and the few examples of its natural use in American and British databases (CCAE and BNC) are from transcribed speech or casual journalism. These are greatly outnumbered by examples in which it's the focus of formal linguistic admonition, suggesting that it has become fetishized (see **fetish**). **Irregardless** came into the spotlight in the US amid the emotive public debate that accompanied the publication of *Webster's Third New International Dictionary* in 1961. The dictionary marked the word as "nonstandard," but its presence in the headword list was mistakenly or perversely used by critics to imply that the dictionary endorsed its use, and was out of touch with language standards. The debate gave the word much more attention than it deserves.

◊ Compare **ain't**.

irregular verbs

An important minority of English verbs are irregular in the way in which they form their past tense and past participle. Regular verbs simply add *-ed* for both the past forms, whether they go back to Anglo-Saxon, or are later acquisitions from French and Latin: *want(ed), depart(ed), precipitat(ed)*. The **irregular verbs** are remnants of several groups that existed in Anglo-Saxon, as well as once regular verbs which have developed their own idiosyncrasies over the centuries.

The common **irregular verbs** are grouped below according to the number of changes that their stems undergo to form the past tense and past participle. The great majority are conjugated in exactly the same way for British and American English. But where the paradigms diverge slightly, as when a verb is irregular for Brits but not necessarily for Americans (e.g. *burn*), or vice versa (e.g. *dive*), it appears in the irregular class that covers its changes. Note that the classification is based on spelling, not the sound of the word; and so the doubling of a consonant, the loss of a final *e* or the alteration of a vowel from two letters to one would qualify as a change. All those in bold are discussed further in individual entries in this book.

Irregular verbs by class

1 Those which use the same form for past and present:

burst	cast	cut	hit	hurt	let
put	quit	read	rid	set	shed
shut	slit	split	spread	thrust	

The verbs **bid** meaning "declare (a wager)," and **cost** ("assess the value of") can also be included here, as well as **spit** (for American usage: cf. section 3 below). **Beat** belongs here in terms of its past tense, and informal zero past participle: with the standard past participle *beaten*, it has more in common with section 7 verbs. See also section 7a for *bid* ("utter [a greeting]"). Other verbs of this type appear under section 9.

2a) Those which keep the stem vowel as written and replace *d* with *t*:

> bend build lend rend send spend

Two special cases are *have* and *make*, where *d* replaces other stem consonants.

2b) Those which simply add *t*, such as *deal* and *mean*. This also applies, for some British, Canadian and Australian writers, to a number of other verbs including:

> burn dream lean leap learn spoil

Others in Britain and Australia, and North Americans at large would keep such verbs regular. See further under **-ed**.

3 Those which have a single vowel change for both past forms:

bleed	breed	feed	meet	speed	(ee>e)
bind	fight	find	grind	wind	(i>ou)
cling	dig	fling	sling	slink	spin
stick	sting	string	(i>u)		

Special cases are *win* (i>o), *shoot* (oo>o), *sit* (i>a), *hold* (o>e), *hang* (a>u), all one-off examples of the same kind. In American English *spit>spat* is a further example. Note also *come* and *run*, which form past tenses by changing the vowel to *a*, but revert for the past participle.

4a) Those which change the stem vowel and follow it with *t*:

> *creep feel keep kneel sleep sweep weep* (ee>e)

4b) Those which reduce a double consonant to single and add *t*:

> *dwell smell spell spill*

For *dwell*, this is the dominant pattern worldwide, whereas the other three are kept regular by Americans, Canadians and some Australians. (See under **-ed**.)

4c) Those which change the stem vowel and follow it with *d* :

> sell   tell (e>o)

A similar one-off example is *do* which becomes *did*.

5 Those which change the stem vowel and one or more of the consonants, as well as adding *t*:

bring>brought	buy>bought	catch>caught
leave>left	seek>sought	teach>taught
think>thought		

Special cases of verbs which change vowels and consonants (but do not add *t*) are *stand>stood* and *strike>struck*. The verb *sneak* with its alternative or colloquial past tense *snuck*, used in North America and elsewhere, belongs to the same set.

6 Those with two different stem vowels for the past tense and the past participle:

> *begin* **drink ring shrink sing sink** *spring stink swim* (i>a>u)

Most of these can be found with *u* for the past tense in some linguistic and stylistic contexts: see individual entries. See further under section 9.

7a) Those with a different stem vowel for the past tense, and the present tense vowel for the past participle, with (*e*)*n* added on:

awake	forsake	**shake**	take
wake (a> oo/o >a)			
blow	grow	know	
throw (o>e>o)			

Others of the same kind are *give, forgive* (*give>gave>given*). One-off examples are **bid** ("utter [a greeting]" with *bade/bidden*, **eat** (*ate>eaten*), *fall* (*fell>fallen*), *draw* (*drew>drawn*), and *see* (*saw>seen*).

7b) Those which use a different stem vowel for both forms of the past (past tense and past participle), and add (*e*)*n* to the latter:

break	freeze	speak	steal	weave	(ea>o)
bear	swear	tear	wear	(ea>o)	

Note that for *bear* the past participle is **borne**. Others which belong here are *get* and *forget* (*get>got>gotten*), though the use of *gotten* with **get** is not found in all varieties of English. The verbs *bite* and *hide* are further members of the set.

7c) Those with two different stem vowels for the past tense and the past participle, plus *-en* added on:

> *drive ride rise* **strive** *write* (i>o>i)

Stride has different forms for past tense / past participle in British English, but works with just one (*strode*) in American English. **Strive** is conjugated as a weak verb by some in both the US and the UK (see section 9). The American conjugation of **dive** with *dove* as past tense would fit here, although it has no past participle with *-en*. Other special cases are *fly* (*flew>flown*) and *lie* (*lay>lain*).

8 Those which borrow forms from other verbs to make their past tense (sometimes called *suppletive verbs*). The outstanding cases of this are **go** (*went*) and **be** (*was/were>been*). The verb **be** has more distinct parts than any other English verb. See further at **be**.

9 *Unstable* **irregular verbs** *and hybrids.* Changes are still going on for some verbs with irregular parts. Some with two different forms for the past tense and past participle work increasingly with just one. This is happening with *shrink >shrank>shrunk* (now often *shrink>shrunk*) and almost all section 6 verbs, aligning them with *fling, slink* and other section 3 verbs. These reduced patterns are already quite common in speech, and will no doubt become unremarkable in writing, sooner or later.

Other verbs showing ongoing change are reverting to the regular pattern with *-ed* for the past tense/participle. This is true for verbs such as **bet, knit, shit, sweat, wed, wet.** It can be seen with:

light *(lit)*	now often	*lighted*
shear *(shore>shorn)*		*sheared*
shine *(shone)*		*shined*
shoe *(shod)*		*shoed*
speed *(sped)*		*speeded*
strive *(strove>striven)*		*strived*
weave *(wove>woven)*		*weaved*

In some cases, e.g. *shine, weave,* the regular past form has a slightly different meaning from the irregular one (see under the individual headings). In others (e.g. *strive*) the shift is more advanced in the US than the UK. This also holds for verbs such as **hew, mow,** which have long since acquired a regular past tense, but their *-n* past participle stands firm, at least in the UK.

The number of verbs reverting to the regular pattern is much larger than that going the other way. This opposite process can however be seen with **hang** and **sneak** (for both past forms), and **saw** and **show** (for the past participle only). See individual entries.

irrelevance or irrelevancy

Irrelevancy had a 40 years headstart on **irrelevance** in C19, but the latter has more than made up the ground in the following century. Dictionaries everywhere give it priority, and **irrelevance** outnumbers **irrelevancy** by more than 10:1 in BNC data, though in CCAE it's more like 2:1. Neither database suggests any division of labor that would make **irrelevance** the more abstract of the two (see further under **-nce/-ncy**). Only **irrelevancy** can be made plural (**irrelevancies**), yet both words can be made countable in the singular (*an irrelevancy, an irrelevance*). British writers rarely seem to qualify **irrelevancy**, whereas they give pen to various kinds of **irrelevance** including *(an) expensive /*

humorous/quaint/virtual irrelevance. In American English, either word can be qualified in this way, but the more rhetorical adjectives go with **irrelevance**, witness comments on the *stunning/stupefying/cosmic/terminal irrelevance.* Both trends confirm the statistical fact, that **irrelevance** is the more productive of the two words.

-is

Words ending in **-is** are mostly Latin or Greek loanwords, which continue to behave like foreigners in the way they make their plurals, substituting *-es* for *-is*. It happens whether they are ordinary words like:

> *analysis basis crisis diagnosis emphasis oasis*

Or ones which are mostly at home in fields of science and scholarship:

amanuensis	*antithesis*	*axis*
ceratosis	*ellipsis*	*genesis*
hypothesis	*metamorphosis*	*neurosis*
parenthesis	*prognosis*	*psychosis*
synopsis	*thesis*	*thrombosis*

Note that the plurals of *axis* and *basis* (*axes / bases*) are identical in their written form with the plurals of *axe* and *base*. The context will clarify whether *axes* is the plural of *axe* or *axis;* but with *bases* it's less clear-cut since both *base* and *basis* are abstract enough to fit the same context. (See further under **bases**.)

◊ For the special cases of **chassis** and **metropolis**, see individual entries.

-isation/-ization

These alternative spellings go hand in hand with the *-ise/-ize* option. Your preference for *-ise* entails *-isation* (*civilise>civilisation*), just as *-ize* entails *-ization*. See further under **-ize/-ise**.

-ise/-ize

For the choice between these spellings in words of two or more syllables (e.g. *recognise/recognize*), see **-ize/-ise**.

-ish

This Old English suffix has been used for a thousand years and more to create ethnic adjectives out of proper names. Modern examples are:

> *British Danish English Finnish Flemish*
> *Irish Jewish Polish Swedish Turkish*

A similar and equally old use of the suffix is to create adjectives which connote the qualities of the noun they're based on:

> *bookish boyish childish churlish feverish*
> *fiendish foolish freakish girlish owlish*
> *popish priggish prudish selfish sheepish*
> *stylish waspish*

The examples show that these words are usually built on stems of one-syllable – though *standoffish* proves otherwise. Many such words have negative implications, and writers who are concerned about them in, say, *childish* will resort to the neutral *childlike* instead (see further under **-like**).

In informal language **-ish** is highly productive, adding a tentative quality to the words formed with it. Adjectives like *greenish, whitish, brownish* are not quite the color named in them; and *lowish, tallish, thickish* hint at a particular quality without asserting it. In indicating age or time, we may use **-ish** words to avoid sounding too strict about the matter:

His wife was thirtyish.

Let's have dinner about eightish.

The use of **-ish** after "about" is of course redundant, but its informality and tentativeness are important in some situations.

Islam, Islamism and Islamic

This Arabic word means literally "surrender [to Allah]." As the name of one of the world's major religions, **Islam** is usually referred to in that unmodified form:

the differences between Islam and Hinduism or Sikhism.

Dictionaries register **Islamism** as an alternative, but there's scant evidence for it in the databases. **Islamic** serves as the all-purpose adjective for referring to the political, legal and cultural institutions of **Islam**, as well as the Muslim world generally. It thus comes close to being synonymous with "Arabic."

◊ See also **Muhammad** and **Muslim**.

island or isle

The first and longer spelling is more frequent by far, in both geographical names and common usage. Very few of the countless **islands** named in the index of any atlas are **Isles**, except those belonging to the *British Isles*, witness the *Isles of Man/Wight/Anglesey*, not to mention *Mull/Islay/Skye/Iona*. *Fair Isle* knitted products are a reminder of another in the Shetlands. There is also a sprinkling of placenames with **Isle** in North America, partly thanks to French occupation, as indicated in names such as *Belle Isle, Presque Isle, Isle au Haut, Isle Royale*. **Isle** is also caught up in a few unmistakably English placenames – *Deer Isle, Pine Purple Isle, Isle of Palms*,– reflecting later Anglo-Saxon occupation. **Island** is otherwise the standard geographical term, and the one used in translating names from other languages.

Yet **isle** still serves here and there as a simple paraphrase for **island** especially in American English. *Ellis Island*, the historic gateway for immigration to the US, was also the *Isle of Hope / Isle of Tears*. Some American writers use **isle** as a hyponym of **island**, speaking of the *Isle of Guernsey* among the *Channel Islands*, and *Garden Isle* in the Hawaiian group, though these are unofficial names. Travel writers sometimes use **isle** in reference to that paradisal place for the ultimate vacation in Greece or the Caribbean. The word still lends something to the imagination that **island** cannot. The phrases *desert isle* and *tropical isle* are still found very occasionally among American writers in CCAE, where their British counterparts in the BNC always use *desert/tropical island*.

The fondness for **isle** goes back to the beginnings of modern English literature with Shakespeare's "this sceptered isle" and frequent use of the word in C17 and C18 poetry. Its single syllable lent itself to the demands of poetic meter, as it still does to newspaper headlines – *TRAGEDY ON A CARIBBEAN ISLE* – though its chances of appearing in the news report below are pretty small. In earlier centuries part of the appeal of **isle** was its Frenchness, although its spelling (a C15 respelling of *ile*) represents more antiquarian interests. The silent *s* in **isle** (and in **island**) is the contribution of Renaissance scholars who wanted the word to reflect its origins in the Latin *insula*. They were right about **isle** – but not **island**,

which is a strictly tautologous Germanic compound *ieg land* ("island + land"). (See further under **spelling** section 1.)

-ism

This suffix has come to us through early Christianity in Greek words such as **baptism**. But it's used very freely in modern English to form nouns which embody a particular philosophy or set of principles, or an individual preoccupation or way of life:

absenteeism	*catholicism*	*chauvinism*
colonialism	*communism*	*cynicism*
egotism	*environmentalism*	*existentialism*
fanaticism	*favoritism*	*federalism*
feminism	*hedonism*	*idealism*
imperialism	*jingoism*	*minimalism*
realism	*romanticism*	*welfarism*

The suffix attaches itself to adjectives and nouns, proper as well as common: witness *Calvinism, Darwinism, Platonism*.

The strong feelings embodied in some of these have helped to develop special uses of **-ism** for referring to various forms of social prejudice:

ageism racism sexism

and to conceptualize others in ad hoc names such as:

classism heightism regionism speciesism weightism

(See further under **ageist language**, **nonsexist language**, **racist language** and **regionism** for their linguistic expression.) Words based on **-ism** are not uncommon in medicine, to describe particular conditions such as *astigmatism, monogolism, rheumatism*.

A further role of **-ism** is to refer to the features of a given speech style, especially a distinctive word or idiom:

archaism	*colloquialism*	*genteelism*
malapropism	*neologism*	*provincialism*
solecism	*truism*	*vulgarism*
witticism		

Similar terms are formed with proper names to identify a regional or language-specific expression:

Americanism Gallicism Hellenism Scotticism

They can even get personal, in ad hoc creations such as *a Clive Jamesism*.

Apart from attaching itself to almost anything, **-ism** sometimes assumes a life of its own, as a count noun:

Postwar affluence has fostered hundreds of isms among younger people.

When it stands on its own as an abbreviated word, **ism** is negatively charged.

Israel

This name links both ancient and modern Jewish tradition. Since 1948 it has been the name of the Jewish state in the eastern Mediterranean, established after the horrors of World War II. The land was of course occupied by Jews in biblical times, though the area was then known as Palestine, and while **Israel** was the northern section, Judah was the southern. The word *Israelite* also goes back to biblical times, whereas *Israelitish* is a medieval word. Neither is in common use nowadays except in historical references, and instead the word *Israeli* serves to identify both the citizen of **Israel** and its culture.

The creation of the modern state of **Israel** was the culmination of half a century's work by *Zionists*. The *Zionist* movement was both mystical and practical;

and with its emphasis on Jewish ethnicity and Hebrew culture, it united Jews scattered across Europe. Within contemporary **Israel,** *Zionists* continue to develop the common language and culture, though their emphasis on Jewish nationalism is felt by some to displace the essential Jewish religion.

The words *Jew* and *Jewish* seem to have outlived the pejorative associations which hung around them through centuries when anti-Semitic attitudes prevailed. *Jewish* now serves to mark the religious identity of *Israelis* and others round the world, and thus corresponds to Christian, Buddhist etc.

The word *Hebrew* is used to name the official language of modern **Israel.** Again it's a link between past and present, being the name of the ancient Semitic language of the scriptures, as well as its updated and expanded counterpart. Yiddish is used more informally among Jewish emigrants from eastern Europe. It is a dialect of German, with elements from Slavonic languages and Hebrew added in.

-ist

This suffix is ultimately Greek, but is much used in modern English to mean "someone who specializes in." The word *specialist* itself is a familiar example, and words with **-ist** appear in almost any trade, profession or recreation. Many of the words are Latin and French loanwords, but others are simple English formations:

archeologist	artist	botanist
cartoonist	chemist	columnist
dentist	diarist	economist
flautist	harpist	humorist
organist	pianist	soloist
violinist		

Apart from its use to designate fields of expertise, **-ist** also serves to create words which refer to particular attitudes or habits of mind:

anarchist	conservationist	defeatist
escapist	humanist	materialist
nationalist	perfectionist	theorist

Proper nouns as well as common names can provide the base, witness *Marxist* and *Peronist* as further examples.

As with *-ism*, **-ist** attaches itself to both nouns and adjectives, and this sometimes results in double coinings. For example:

agriculturist	agriculturalist
constitutionist	constitutionalist
conversationist	conversationalist
educationist	educationalist
horticulturist	horticulturalist

The longer (adjective-based) forms are preferred in all varieties of English for *constitutionalist* and *conversationalist,* but there are divergences over the other pairs. See under individual headings.
◊ For the distinctive pursuits of the *naturalist* and the *naturist,* see **naturalist.**

isthmus

This word is a C16 hybrid – Greek in origin but Latin in form – which is why its plural in English is *isthmuses* rather than something more classical. See further under **-us.**

-istic/-istical

Adjectives ending in **-istic** sometimes have alternatives with an extra syllable: for example

logistic/logistical. The choice between them is often arbitrary, and may as well be made on the basis of its effect on the rhythm of the phrase it appears in. The **-istical** form is however always the one on which the associated adverb is based. See further under **-ic/-ical.**

it

This small, hollow word is an important functionary in nonfictional writing, and commoner than any other personal pronoun by a good deal. Like other pronouns, it typically substitutes for some other noun as in:
Choose your plan and stick to it.
In cases like this, **it** borrows its meaning from whatever it refers back to, and forms a cohesive link with it. (See further under **coherence or cohesion.**)

But elsewhere **it** is simply a slot-filler in the syntax of the clause. In statements like *It was raining* or *It's almost midnight,* **it** serves as the grammatical subject without referring to anything in particular. Modern grammarians emphasize its emptiness, calling it a "dummy" subject (*Longman Grammar,* 1999) or "prop **it** " (*Comprehensive Grammar,* 1985).

Other structural uses of **it** are as the anticipatory device for *extraposed constructions,* for example:
It was important to reach agreement.
It was agreed that the meeting should be adjourned.
Set phrases like *it was important/impossible to* and *it was agreed/found that* are among the commonest four-part "lexical bundles" in academic prose, according to the *Longman Grammar.* They are the stuff of the impersonal and often passive style found in reports and formal documents – not their most appealing feature. They make for repetitive and rather weak sentence openings, effectively delaying the topical item, rather than contributing to meaningful topical progression (see further under **topic**).

But **it** is also a strategic device for altering the focus of discourse, in cleft sentences like the following:
It was only last Christmas that we decided to go.
There **it** picks out as its complement one particular constituent from the following clause, making it the topic of interest and subordinating the rest. (See further under **cleft sentences.**) *Cleft* **it** cannot however be used very often, or it becomes a mannerism. In any case **it** needs watching when it turns up at the start of adjacent sentences. With its multiple roles and no intrinsic meaning, it too easily becomes ambiguous.
◊ For the distinction between *it's* and *its,* see **its or it's.**

Italian plurals

Italian loanwords are better assimilated than most and pose few problems for English users. In ordinary usage they all take English plurals in *s* – witness *maestro(s)* and *studio(s); opera(s)* and *regatta(s).* Their Italian plural endings in *i* and *e* respectively are never seen. Even in specialized fields such as art and architecture, Italian technical terms such as *fresco, loggia, pergola* and *portico* are given English plurals. In literature and music, the same is true for loanwords ending in *a,* such as *aria, cadenza, cantata, stanza.* But musical words ending in *o* are sometimes embellished with **Italian plurals** in concert program notes:

concerti	contralti	crescendi	diminuendi
libretti	soprani	virtuosi	

They suggest the writer's relish of their foreign origins. For musicians and many a music lover however, the Italianness of the words is irrelevant to their pleasure, and, like the general public, they pluralize all such words with *s*.

See further under -**a** section 1, and -**o**.

italic(s)

Nowadays the sloping forms of **italic** type serve only to contrast with the ordinary upright roman – though they were once the regular medium for printing. Wordprocessors now offer them as a supplement to the main font, though their availability on the printer may be the key to whether they can be part of your repertoire. *Italic characters* are not part of the basic ASCII font used for internet transmission, and quote marks may be needed to highlight the occasional word. In handwriting, and on typewriters and wordprocessors where **italics** are not available, underlining serves the purpose.

As the alternative typeface, **italic** helps to make a word or string of words stand out from the carrier sentence. But on the computer screen it's less distinct than on the printed page because of lower resolution (Whitbread, 2001). Webdesigners and the authors of electronic documents therefore minimize the use of **italics**, and use boldface or color contrast instead. Underlining is not recommended because of its use in hyperlinking.

Like any contrastive device, **italics** work best when used sparingly, and are not very effective for whole sentences. Their use also raises certain questions and anomalies, which are dealt with in the final section of this entry. Note that **italic** (noun, singular) is the standard term for the font in the UK (*Copy-editing*, 1992; *Oxford Guide to Style*, 2002). But elsewhere – in the US, Canada and Australia – the plural **italics** is used.

Common uses of italics

1 **With English words:**
(a)   to emphasize a particular word in its context:
       That's not a *rhetorical* question!
(b)   to draw attention to an unusual word or one being used in an unusual way, such as an archaism, malapropism or neologism.
(c)   to highlight technical terms or words which are themselves the focus of discussion. Technical terms are usually italicized for first appearance only, whereas those under discussion would be italicized regularly.

2 **With foreign words.** Italics are often used to highlight borrowed words and phrases which are not yet fully assimilated into English. However judging the extent of their assimilation is a vexed question, and one on which it's difficult to be consistent. Dictionaries themselves wrestle with the problem, and their conclusions are sometimes inscrutable. Why should *a fortiori* and *carte blanche* have **italics** but not *a posteriori* and *carte-de-visite* (in the *Oxford Dictionary for Writers and Editors*, 1981)? Instead of providing a canon of words to be italicized, other authorities leave it to individual writers and editors to decide, depending on the readership. The *Chicago Manual* (2003) advises against *italicizing* any familiar foreign words when they are used in an English context. But if the loanword needs its full quota of accents or diacritics, e.g. *pièce de résistance, vis-à-vis*, it probably needs **italics** too (Bliss, 1966). Once the accents disappear, as in *debris* and *debut* (formerly *débris* and *début*), they might as well be printed in roman. Any reduction in the number of accents, as from two to one in *resumé*, is also grounds for not using **italics**.

3 **With Latin abbreviations.** These are no longer set in **italics**, though special exceptions are made by some editors (see under **Latin abbreviations**).

4 **With individual letters.** Italics are one way of setting off single letters against accompanying words, e.g. "minding your *p*s and *q*s." (For other ways, see under **letters as words**.)

5 **With the titles of compositions.** By general agreement you *italicize* the titles of books, periodicals and newspapers, of plays, films, works of art (including sculpture), and opera and music:

> *Angela's Ashes*
> *Radio Days*
> *Six Degrees of Separation*
> *The Creation*
> *The Phantom of the Opera*
> *The Statue of Liberty*
> *The Independent*
> *Time*

An important exception is the bible and its various books, and other sacred texts such as the Koran, which are always in roman.

In the mass media, **italics** are now used generally for the titles of both TV and radio programs. But when it comes down to the names of individual segments or episodes, many style manuals recommend using roman font plus quote marks (*Chicago Manual*; *Oxford Guide to Style*, 2002; Australian government *Style Manual*, 2002). This practice is analogous to the distinction made traditionally between the title of a book and the names of individual essays or poems within it. Yet the *Chicago Manual* also advises that **italics** can be used for both the larger work and the items within, when the two are juxtaposed repeatedly in critical writing. In any case, the distinction is not always easy to make.

6 **With official names:**
a)   the official titles of legislative acts and statutes are set in roman (e.g. the Copyright Act, the Constitution) in the UK, Canada and the US. But Americans do use **italics** when referring to them in their published form, according to the *Chicago Manual*. Australian style, by contrast, uses **italics** for both full and abbreviated references to acts and statutes, according to the government *Style Manual* – except that the titles of Bills before parliament are styled in roman.
b)   the official names of court cases are *italicized,* as in *Kramer v. Kramer.* British style is to put the *v.* separating the names in roman (see *Copy-editing*); whereas Australian government style prefers **italics**. North American style allows either **italics** or roman (*Chicago Manual; Editing Canadian English*, 2000), provided it's consistent within the text.
c)   the names of trains, ships, submarines, spacecraft and other special vehicles are *italicized:*

> *Flying Scotsman*
> HMS *Frolic*
> CSS *Shenandoah*
> *Challenger*

Note that the prefixes are not *italicized*.

d) the Latin names of plants and animals, both genus and species (as well as subspecies and variety), are *italicized,* as in:

> *Nyssa silvatica Falco peregrinus*

But when the generic name is used as the common name, as for example with "camellia" and many other plants, it's printed in roman.

7 With performing directions. In the texts of plays or movie scripts, stage directions are printed in **italics** to separate them from the dialogue. In musical scores, **italics** are likewise used for references to the dynamics of performing, to separate them from the words of the score.

Questions and conundrums with italics. *Italicized* words raise the question as to what to do when they need to be made plural or possessive. Should the apostrophe *s* or plural (*e*)*s* ending be in **italics** or roman? The traditional answer for the possessive ending has been roman, and this is still preferred by the major style guides. When it comes to plural endings, the *s* goes into **italics** when attached to a foreign word, e.g. several *touchés,* but stays in roman if it's a title, e.g. two *National Geographic*s.

Any punctuation mark immediately following an *italicized* word is usually in **italics** too, for the congruity of line. This is of course less important for a full stop than for a semicolon or question/exclamation mark. Note however that accompanying brackets, whether square or rounded, are still in roman.

Finally, how can items normally *italicized* be identified within *italicized* titles or headings? **Italic** within **italics** is somehow needed. Lacking that, editors and writers resort to quotation marks, go back to roman, or stay with **italics** for it (thus leaving it undistinguished). Quotation marks are usually given to titles within titles, and roman to Latin biological names. But *Copy-editing* notes the rather self-conscious effect of giving quotation marks to foreign words in titles or headings, commenting that it's best to leave them in **italics** just like the rest.

-ite

Though ultimately from Greek, **-ite** is a lively suffix – whether you think of *socialite* or *dynamite.* It serves in both common and scientific usage to make nouns which refer to someone with a particular affiliation, and to form the names of certain minerals and chemical substances.

In common usage **-ite** normally attaches itself to proper names. Cases such as *socialite* and *suburbanite* are the exception. Much more often it picks up a place name, as in *Brooklynite, Canaanite, Muscovite;* or that of a notable person, as in *Ibsenite, Thatcherite, Trotskyite;* or that of a party or movement, as in *Labourite* and *pre-Raphaelite.* The suffix sometimes seems derogatory, though not all the examples given would show this. At any rate, the **-ite** word tends to be used by those opposed to the person or party named, while supporters and adherents are unlikely to apply it to themselves. *Darwinite* is probably less neutral than *Darwinist* or *Darwinian.* (See further under **-an** and **-ist.**)

In scientific usage, **-ite** has several functions. In geology it serves as a regular suffix for naming minerals, such as *anthracite, dolomite, malachite;* and for the names of various fossils: *ammonite, lignite, trilobite.* In chemistry it's used for naming explosives such as *dynamite* and *melinite,* as well as the salts of

certain acids (those whose names end in -*ous*), for example *nitrite* and *sulfite.* The fictional name *kryptonite* (the only substance that can reduce Superman to a trembling heap) seems to carry the aura of several of these scientific uses.

Itie, Eyetie or Eytie

See under **Eyetie.**

-itis

This is essentially a medical suffix, creating nouns which mean "inflammation of . . .", as in:

> *appendicitis bronchitis gastroenteritis mastitis tonsillitis*

It also enjoys some popular use in coining words which refer to pseudo-diseases, such as *Mondayitis.*

its or it's

Separated only by an apostrophe, there are few pairs in English which cause as much trouble as these. The usual problem is that **it's** is put where **its** is needed – people insert the apostrophe just in case.

Its without the apostrophe is a possessive pronoun/determiner, pure and simple, as in *left the dog on its own.* Like the other pronouns in those roles (*his, hers* etc.), **its** has no apostrophe. What confuses the issue is the fact that nouns *do* have apostrophes when they are possessive, as in the *dog's breakfast* or a *baker's dozen,* suggesting that **it's** is the possessive pronoun for *it.* The mistake is common in unedited writing, on paper or the internet, but can also be seen in small press outputs, circular advertising and occasionally in major newspapers (Wales, 1996). In fact **it's** was used interchangeably with **its** for the possessive pronoun until around 1800, according to the *Oxford Dictionary* (1989).

It's with the apostrophe is a contraction of *it is,* or occasionally of *it has.* The apostrophe is a mark of omission, not possession (see further under **apostrophes**). Note that because it consists of a pronoun plus a verb, the contraction is often used to introduce statements:

> *It's true. It's unexpected.*

(Compare *its truth, its unexpectedness* when the possessive pronoun/determiner is needed to preface a noun.) **It's** replaced *'tis* as the regular contraction for *it is* during later C18 – having previously been regarded as "vulgar," i.e. the nonliterary contraction. When contracted **it's** began to appear in writing, the possessive pronoun had to be distinguished from it, hence the insistence on writing it without an apostrophe.

From its debut in early C19, contracted **it's** has become increasingly common in everyday writing (see **contractions** section 2). It compacts the space occupied by the functional words of the sentence, and like French *c'est* ("it is") enhances the flow of expository prose. **It's** therefore appears from time to time in the text of this book.

-ity

This is the ending of many an abstract noun which embodies the quality of a related adjective. As *ethnic* is contained in *ethnicity,* so *circular* is in *circularity,* and *readable* in *readability.* Many other nouns ending in **-ity** are not really English formations but words borrowed direct from French (e.g. *falsity*) or modeled on Latin (e.g. *sincerity*); and in some cases (e.g.

atrocity, hilarity) the abstract noun was current in English quite a while before the related adjective. But their large numbers have helped to foster English formations of the same kind.

The most productive types in modern English are those like *readability*, based on adjectives ending in *-able* (*accountability, respectability*) or *-ible* (*compatibility, feasibility*). (See further under **-ability**.) Such words are surprisingly popular, in spite of all their syllables: the earlier *unaccountableness* has given place to *unaccountability*, *unavailableness* to *unavailability* and so on. The inventory of **-ity** nouns is 33% longer than that of those ending *-ness*, according to the *Longman Grammar* (1999). Nouns ending in *-ity* outnumber those ending in *-ness* by more than 4:1 in newspapers and 9:1 in academic writing. See further under **-ness**.

-ive

Thousands of English adjectives bear this suffix. It originated in Latin, but is an element of both Latin and French borrowings, and has been thoroughly assimilated. The following are only a token of the innumerable familiar words with it:

active	*attractive*	*collective*
competitive	*convulsive*	*creative*
decisive	*exclusive*	*impressive*
impulsive	*permissive*	*persuasive*
repulsive	*retrospective*	*speculative*
submissive	*subversive*	

Some **-ive** adjectives have also established themselves as nouns, witness:

collective   imperative   native   representative

Adjectives in **-ive** are often members of tightly knit sets of words, with adjective/verb/noun members:

active	*act*	*action*
collective	*collect*	*collection*
decisive	*decide*	*decision*
persuasive	*persuade*	*persuasion*
repulsive	*repel*	*repulsion*
submission	*submit*	*submission*

The same kind of network is evident with words ending in *-ative/-ate/-ation*. (See under those headings.)

-ix

This is a feminine suffix in Latin. See further under **-trix**.

-ization/-isation

For Americans and Canadians, **-ization** is standard, and it's built into the titles of international agencies such as the *World Health Organization*. But both spellings are used in the UK, and BNC data shows *organisation* occurring in almost twice as many texts as *organization*. In Australia, the government *Style Manual* has long recommended *-ise* spellings and hence *-isation*. The choice between **-ization** and **-isation** depends on the same issues as those discussed in the next entry (**-ize/-ise**).

-ize/-ise

In American English, spellings with **-ize** are standard for the many verbs with that ending, whether they're as old as *baptize* or as recent as *energize*. The same holds in Canada. But in British English, it's possible to use either **-ise** or **-ize**, and the arguments are almost equally balanced. *New Oxford* (1999) gives priority to **-ize** spellings, in keeping with the Oxford tradition, while BNC data shows that the **-ise** spellings are actually more popular with contemporary British writers – witness the following frequencies:

realise	3898	*realize*	2234
recognise	3641	*recognize*	2104
organise	1273	*organize*	824
emphasise	964	*emphasize*	661

In these cases and others like them, the **-ise** spellings outnumber those with **-ize** in the ratio of about 3:2. In Australian English, the difference is still greater (often 3:1, by frequencies in the ACE corpus), and the tendency has been reinforced by official endorsement of **-ise** by the Australian government *Style Manual* since 1966. The *Australian Oxford* (1999) prioritizes the **-ise** spellings. Choosing between the two was clearly vexing for Fowler (1926), and many of the issues are still with us. The preference for **-ize** may be underpinned by linguistic factors, such as:

* (*phonological*) **-ize** seems to represent better the "z" sound of the suffix. This point is somewhat undermined by the fact that in *rise* or *applies*, the letter *s* also represents "z." But at least *z* represents just one sound rather than two. Arguably it helps to take some of the load off the letter *s*.

* (*etymological*) **-ize** correlates better with antecedents of the suffix in Greek (*-izein*), and in late Latin (*-izare*). Scholars have in the past tried to give **-ize** to words which go back to Greek or Latin, and thus distinguish classical loanwords from similar ones borrowed from French with **-ise**. Yet often it proved impossible to know whether the source was French or classical. This impasse prompted the present-day resolution of the problem – to use either **-ize** or **-ise** for all. Either way, it downplays what's known about the etymology, and the trained etymologist will find **-ise** anachronistic in classical examples, and **-ize** unsatisfactory in French loanwords. These loans are in fact a minority in comparison with modern English formations with **-ize/-ise** – which outnumber all other verb coinings, in both academic prose and conversation (*Longman Grammar,* 1999). For new derivatives, the spelling of the suffix is arbitrary.

There are reasons both practical and etymological for choosing **-ise**, as Fowler found. If we apply the **-ise** spelling to all susceptible words of two or more syllables, we are left with a single exception: *capsize* (see under that heading). But if you choose **-ize,** the list of exceptions which need the alternative spelling is as least as long as the following:

advertise	*advise*	*apprise*	*chastise*
circumcise	*comprise*	*compromise*	*despise*
devise	*excise*	*exercise*	*franchise*
improvise	*incise*	*revise*	*supervise*
surmise	*surprise*	*televise*	

Apart from these, which are all verbs, the problem arises with other words such as *enterprise* and *merchandise,* which are acquiring verbal roles (as in *enterprising, merchandising*). Etymology dictates that **-ise** should be used in such words, and the policy of using **-ise** everywhere makes them part of the general pattern. With an **-ize** policy they are yet more special cases. The argument of fewer exceptions would explain why British English has inclined to **-ise** during C20. Fowler observed it in a majority of

English printers in the 1920s; and BNC data shows it in the 1990s

But the "fewer exceptions" argument loses some of its force in the US, where dictionaries already allow some of the words in Fowler's list to be spelled with -ize (e.g. *advertize, apprize, comprize*), and where *-yze* is used instead of *-yse* in *analyse* etc. (see further under **-yze/-yse**). If and when all such words can everywhere be spelled with *z*, the chief argument for choosing **-ise** would evaporate. Even now the regional distribution of **-ize** spellings makes it the better option for all but Fowler's exceptions. It is more broadly based than **-ise,** as the standard spelling in North America and the alternative spelling of a still largish community of writers/publishers in Britain, and some in Australia. Scientists the world over tend to use **-ize**, according to the *CBE Manual* (1994).

International English selection: The systematic use of **-ize** spellings recommends itself on distributional and phonological grounds, despite some exceptions, as discussed.

---

jacketed

The *t* remains single when this word becomes a verb. See under -t.

Jacobean, Jacobite, Jacobin and Jacobian

The first three words relate to different historical periods, and to a different *James* or *Jacques* (since the Latin *Jacobus* underlies both the English and French names). The fourth embodies the name of *Jacobi,* the C19 German mathematician.

Jacobean relates to the history and culture of James I's reign in England (1603–25), particularly its literary and architectural heritage. The spelling cannot be varied with -*ian* (unlike other words ending in -*ean*: see under -**an**) because of the mathematicians' claim on **Jacobian** – not that anyone is likely to confuse *Jacobean tragedy* with the *Jacobian (determinant)* in equations.

Jacobite connects with James II, who abdicated / was overthrown in 1688, and whose descendants and supporters led unsuccessful *Jacobite rebellions* in 1715 and 1745. The suffix seems to carry the negative or alien associations of some other similar formations with proper names (see further under -**ite**). The suggestion (noted in Gowers, 1965) that **Jacobite** could also be used for "devotees of the [American] writer Henry James" would be most likely to come from the pens of James's detractors.

Jacobin is French in origin, connecting with the radical *Jacobin revolutionaries* who originally met in the Dominican convent near the church of *St-Jacques* in Paris. Led by Robespierre, the **Jacobins** instituted the Reign of Terror (1793–4), executing thousands of people on grounds of treason.

jail or gaol

No English spelling is more perverse than **gaol**. With its peculiar sequence of vowels, it has been misspelled as "goal" for centuries, according to the *Oxford Dictionary* (1989). **Gaol** was borrowed from Norman French in C13, and its spelling has been protected in English statutes and the legal code. The *County Gaol* was a conspicuous Victorian institution, and *HM Gaol* still makes the backdrop for the occasional television show filmed on location. But C20 British writers use **jail**, which outnumbers **gaol** by about 5:1 in BNC data. The *Oxford Dictionary* has always given priority to **jail**, borrowed from Central French and used in English since C17. **Jail** has spelling analogues in *bail, fail, hail* etc., and is the standard spelling in North America and Australia.

jailer, jailor or gaoler

The choice between these depends first on whether you prefer *jail* or *gaol*. For Americans, Canadians and Australians, it must be the first (see previous entry). In the UK the scene is still somewhat divided, and the BNC actually provides more citations for **gaoler** than

jailer (jailor), though this is presumably a legacy of past preference for *gaol*. On the choice between **jailer** and **jailor**, dictionaries all give priority to **jailer** (i.e. the English rather than the Latin/French suffix: see further under -**er/-or**). There's scant evidence for **jailor** in either BNC or CCAE.

Jakarta or Djakarta

The simpler spelling with just **J** is the usual one nowadays for the capital of Indonesia. In colonial times the city was *Batavia,* but it became **Djakarta** after the departure of the Dutch in 1949, and was then officially modified to **Jakarta** in the early 1970s. *Merriam-Webster* (2000) endorses **Jakarta**, and it's strongly backed by data from CCAE, where it outnumbers **Djakarta** by about 100:1. The ratio is the same in the BNC, but *New Oxford* (1998) still makes **Djakarta** the primary spelling.

The second city of Indonesia has also seen adjustments to its name: once *Djokjakarta* or *Djogjakarta,* the official spelling nowadays is *Yogyakarta.*

Jap or Japanese

The use of **Jap** for **Japanese** is rarely an innocent case of shortening. The word had derogatory implications from the beginning of C20, according to *Webster's English Usage* (1989), and these intensified during World War II. The full form **Japanese** is neutral and free of racist connotations. (See further under **racist language**.)

jargon

This is the technical vocabulary of a special group. You have to be a sailor to know what a *broad reach* is, or a wine connoisseur to comment on *oxidization* in the wine. Those able to use **jargon** with confidence enjoy a sense of solidarity with others who do the same. **Jargon** is thus inclusive in its effect for some – and very exclusive for others. Its power to exclude is what gives **jargon** its negative connotations. The word is quite often used to express the resentment felt by those who cannot "talk the lingo" and feel disadvantaged by it:

> I couldn't get a word in. They talked economic jargon all through dinner.

Those who use **jargon** can be unaware of how specialized it is or how dependent they are on it. The **jargon** habit becomes ingrained in writing if you write only for a restricted audience or within a particular institution. In bureaucracies, acronyms can become part of the **jargon**.

Jargon has something in common with occupational slang, though it differs in being standardized. So while the pressure in industrial pipes is measured in *kilopascals* (according to the **jargon**), it's a matter of so many "kippers" in the slang of those operating the plant. **Jargon** takes itself seriously, whereas slang can be playful or at least offhanded.

jaw's harp, jaws harp or jew's harp

These are all names for a small folk instrument which originated in southern Asia (in India, Borneo and New Guinea) as well as Europe. It has little in common with a harp, and consists of a single strip of vibrating metal, set in a frame which is held between the teeth, and plucked with a fingertip. The mouth itself acts as resonator, and as modifier of the pitch. Thus the plain names **jaw's harp** or **jaws harp** highlight the method of playing, as for other instruments, e.g. *viola da gamba* ("viol for the leg"). *Grove's Dictionary of Music* (1879–89) speculated that **jaw's harp** was the original name, and that **jew's harp** was a corruption of it. Yet things seem to be the other way round. The instrument was in fact known as a **jew's harp** or **jew's tromp** from C16 on, centuries before the first reference to the **jaw's harp** in *Grove's Dictionary*. The Jewish element is built into the English name for the instrument as well as one of the German ones (*Judenharfe*). Yet the instrument has no special connection with the Jews; nor is it necessarily a poor man's means of making music. Some of the **jew's harps** exhibited in museums are exquisitely worked in silver. Still **jew's harp** probably originated as a "throwaway name," in times when people were less concerned about racist language. See further under **throwaway terms**.

je ne sais quoi

This French phrase means literally "I do not know what," but in English it refers to a special, indefinable quality:

Their house has a je ne sais quoi about it.
The phrase puts on airs. Yet it may have its place when you're writing of a quality which can't quite be pinned down.

jelly or jello

In Britain and Australia **jelly** is a dessert, gelatinous, transparent and brightly colored, which tends to be served at children's parties or as hospital fare. In North America the same food is called **jello**, a name derived from the trademark *Jell-O*. Americans (and Canadians) need the additional term because **jelly** itself is used for a very thin, transparent type of jam. At the opposite end of the scale are *conserves* – jams which are almost solid fruit.

jemmy or jimmy

See **jimmy**.

jerrican, jerrycan or jerry can

Dictionaries are quite unsure about the spelling of this word for a portable container for liquids, approximately 5 gallons or 20–23 litres in capacity. The *Oxford Dictionary* (1989) gives priority to **jerrican** while *New Oxford* (1998) prefers **jerrycan**. American dictionaries also diverge: **jerrican** is given priority in *Webster's Third* (1986), and **jerry can** in *Random House* (1987). Other variants registered are *jerry-can* and *jerican*. The field is left open by the dearth of citations in both American and British corpora – less than a handful of each. Two of the three BNC citations capitalize **jerry can** as *Jerry can* (yet another variant) which makes no bones about the fact that it owes its name to a German prototype, first deployed in World

War II. At least there's no doubt that writers are free to choose the spelling for it.

jerrymander or gerrymander

See under **gerrymander**.

Jew and Jewish

See under **Israel**.

jewellery or jewelry, and jeweller or jeweler

Though **jewelry** is the older spelling by four centuries, **jewellery** (dating from C18) is now dominant in British English, by the evidence of the BNC. The changeover seems to have taken place during C20, judging by Fowler's (1926) reference to **jewellery** as the "commercial and popular form," and **jewelry** as the "rhetorical and poetic." Gowers in 1965 says that the longer form is "more usual." But **jewelry** has remained standard in American English, and there's scant evidence of the longer spelling in CCAE. Canadians use both spellings with about equal frequency, according to *Canadian English Usage* (1997), whereas Australians clearly prefer **jewellery**.

No surprises then that the retailer of *jewels* is usually spelled **jeweller** in UK, while **jeweler** is standard in US. Both spellings conform to the local preferences on whether to double the final *l* before adding a suffix (see under **-l-/-ll-**). Here Canadian spelling falls into line with the British, according to *Canadian English Usage*, as does the Australian (Peters, 1995).

Jewess

This word smacks of both sexism and racism. Its sexism lies in the fact that English terms referring to a person's religion or ethnicity are normally gender-neutral, witness *Christian, Hindu, Moslem; Arab, Chinese, Malay*. So the use of the feminine suffix with **Jewess** is gratuitous if religion or ethnicity are the issue. That apart, it still carries the kinds of social prejudice that *Jew* and *Jewish* used to carry (see further under **Israel**). *Webster's English Usage* (1989) queries whether it may be less offensive in American than British English. But *Webster's* examples are almost entirely from Jewish writers, which would only show that it is one of those terms that can be used innocuously by insiders but not the outsider. (See further under **racist language**.) Its scarcity in both BNC and CCAE (no more than a dozen examples in each) correlates with its perceived potential to offend.

jew's harp, jaw's harp or jaws harp

See **jaw's harp**.

jibe, gibe or gybe

See **gibe**.

jihad or jehad

Whatever dictionary you consult, the first spelling for this word for a Muslim holy war is **jihad**. The *Oxford Dictionary* (1989) made it the primary spelling – no doubt because it transliterates the Arabic original exactly, and in spite of the fact that almost all of its citations (from C19) were for **jehad**. But **jihad** is the only spelling in the BNC, in generic references to the "Holy War" as well as to *Islamic Jihad*. **Jehad** gets no more than a crossreference in *New Oxford* (1998). In

American English the facts are likewise. **Jehad** is no longer current, by the evidence of CCAE, and acknowledged in *Merriam-Webster* (2000) only as a crossreference.

jimmy or jemmy
Burglars in North America are conventionally armed with a **jemmy**, whereas in Britain and Australia it's a **jimmy**. Both words are derived from the name *James*. The verb derived from the name of the instrument (*jimmy/jemmy open*) is spelled accordingly.

jive or jibe
See under **gibe**.

job titles
The terms used to designate professions and occupations are curiously fuzzy, whether you take an international or local perspective. Generic words such as *attorney, chemist, clerk, educator, engineer, lawyer, jurist, optician* are applied in different ways in North America, the UK, Australia and New Zealand (see for example **educator, lawyer, optician**). None of them translates very well from one region to another.

Within any country, occupational classifications are often rather broad and non-specific. Very different kinds of work may be done by bearers of the title *assistant, clerk, officer, secretary* etc., depending on the institution and the level of seniority. The thrust to replace sexist **job titles** with ones which are gender-free has produced some very abstract alternatives, e.g. *server* for "waiter/waitress" in Canada (*Canadian English Usage*, 1997), and *cleaning operative* for "cleaning lady" in Australia (Peters, 1995). See further under **man**.

Where people are free to choose their own **job titles** (in private industry, and among the self-employed), you might expect them to be as specific as possible. But for some it's tempting to find a euphemism to dignify the job with a formal name – and who are we to object if the makeup artist prefers to style herself a "cosmetologist," and those who install burglar alarms as "security executives"? If such names seem inflationary, they are susceptible to devaluation, like any overpriced currency.

Jogjakarta or Jokjakarta
See under **Jakarta**.

jokey or joky
See **-y/-ey**.

Jonathan or Jonathon
The first spelling is traditional for this Hebrew name, borne by **Jonathan** the friend of the biblical King David (I Samuel 18), and many others since him. **Jonathon** is a recent variant, borne by individuals christened under the influence of the new suffix *-athon*, which is a formative element in a number of recent English words (see **-athon**). **Jonathon** is certainly being seen in both American and British English. Database evidence suggests that it's rather more common in the UK, since **Jonathon/Jonathan** occur in the ratio of about 1:35 in CCAE and 1:8 in BNC. More than half of the 200-odd examples in the BNC are embedded in transcriptions of speech, showing that **Jonathon** is the intuitive spelling for many transcribers – though not its correctness for the

person referred to. Some of the instances in written texts are definitely mistakes by the writer/editor, witness opera director and connoisseur *Dr Jonathon Miller*, and publisher *Jonathon Cape*. Yet *Jonathon Porritt* (of Friends of the Earth) is correctly identified with *-athon*. Clearly it's a detail on which editors have to check with the person, as with *Philip/Phillip, Geoffrey/Jeffrey* etc.

With lower case, **jonathan/jonathon** are also alternative spellings for a red-skinned type of apple, helped by "greengrocer's spelling" (analogous to "greengrocer's punctuation": see **apostrophes** section 4). This application of the name originated in the US in the 1870s. Most dictionaries associate it with Jonathan Hasbrouk, an American jurist who died in 1846. But it may owe something to generic use of the name in C19 to mean "an American" – especially one from New England.

journalism and journalese
Journalists are mass producers of words against deadlines. Small wonder then that what they write can sound pedestrian and predictable. Small miracle if they succeed in stimulating readers with the freshness and insightfulness of their writing. The best **journalism** is interesting and original in its expression, making readers more aware of the resources of the common language. It is achieved most often in the personal editorial columns of newspapers, by *journalists* who enjoy the privilege of a guaranteed number of words in which to develop their thoughts. (Cf. the *inverted pyramid* below.)

Bad **journalism** is hack writing with a witch-like power to turn anything into stereotyped dross, partly because it depends so heavily on cliché (see further under **clichés**). Predictable as the style is, it almost "writes itself." Even the awkward three- and four-letter words which are the staple of headlines (such as *ban, bid, leak, wed* etc.) seem curiously natural in it. This is **journalese** at its worst. (See further under **headline language**.)

Other hallmarks of **journalese** are the lumpish sentences with overweight beginnings:

> *St Edmund's Catholic Church Youth Orchestra organizer Jane Filomel . . .*
> *Keen amateur sports fisherman and union Vice President Jeff Bringamin . . .*

The vital information is all there at the start, but so condensed (shorn of articles such as *the, a* and connecting words) that it can generate its own ambiguities. However capacious the noun phrase is, there are limits on what it can effectively put across (see further under **adjectives** and **noun phrase**).

The *inverted pyramid* (or triangle) undoubtedly puts pressure on journalists to present everything "up front." This conventional structure for news articles probably dates back to tabloids of the early C20 (Ungerer, 2002), but gradually spread to quality newspapers in the 1930s. It requires the first, summary sentence to provide the essence of the whole event. This is followed by background information, and details which are increasingly marginal in importance. Readers are often conscious that they get less and less, the further they go in an article.

> SUMMARY LINE ON EVENT
> BACKGROUND DETAIL
> BACKGROUND D'L
> B'GROUND

The *inverted pyramid* is certainly not intended to frustrate the thorough reader. Rather it's to ensure that only less essential details will be omitted, if the *journalist*'s report is cut short by the subeditor through lack of space on the page.

judgement or judgment

In British English, both spellings have their place. **Judgement** is given priority in the *Oxford Dictionary* (1989), which argues against the "unscholarly habit of omitting the *-e*," while allowing that **judgment** tends to appear in legal contexts. *New Oxford* (1998) also endorses **judgement**, and its wide popularity is confirmed in BNC data, where it appears in twice as many source texts as **judgment**. It is of course the more regular spelling, maintaining the *-e* of the verb's stem before the suffix *-ment* (cf. *advertisement* and others presented at **-ment**). Yet **judgment** has been in general use since C16, and was the spelling enshrined in the Authorized Version of the bible (1611). This early use helps to explain why it's the standard spelling in American English. **Judgment** takes priority in *Webster's Third* (1986), and dominates in data from CCAE, outnumbering **judgement** by more than 30:1. In Canada **judgment** is also the commoner spelling of the two, according to *Canadian English Usage* (1997), though both are in use. Australians however are more inclined towards **judgement** (Peters, 1995).

> **International English selection:** The spelling **judgement** is preferable for reasons of orthographic regularity, and its consistency with analogous words such as *abridgement,* *acknowledgement* and *lodgement*. Arguments based on its distribution are not so clear-cut, but **judgement** is the majority spelling in some English-speaking countries, and the minor variant at least in others.

judicious or judicial

Though both link up ultimately with the work of judges, these words have distinct meanings. **Judicial** connects with the official role of the judge in phrases like *judicial hearing* and *judicial procedure*. It implies something done by a judge, or associated with the courts. **Judicial** is strictly neutral in its implications, whereas **judicious** is discreetly positive. It connotes sound judgement in any field of activity, from a *judicious comment* by a teacher, to a *judicious withdrawal* by an army commander. In principle, a *judicial judgement* is also **judicious**, but if the law is (sometimes) an ass, this cannot be taken for granted.

jujitsu or jujutsu

In Japanese, the gentle art of self-defence is **jujutsu**, which is registered alongside the anglicized form **jujitsu** in *Merriam-Webster* (2000) and *New Oxford* (1998). But **jujitsu** is the only spelling supported by data from CCAE and the BNC. It reflects the English tendency to dissimilate adjacent syllables in loanwords: see further under **dissimilate**, and compare **harakiri**.

junction or juncture

These words have common origins in the Latin verb for "join," but only **junction** is widely used in this sense. **Juncture** is mostly confined to the rather formal phrase *at this juncture*, meaning "at this critical moment" (or more loosely "as things come together like this"). **Junction** is much more common and familiar from being used to refer to the place at which roads, railway lines or wires come together. The uses of **junction** start up late in C18 (two centuries after **juncture**) and gather steam with the industrial revolution.

junketing

The spelling of this word is discussed at **-t**.

junkie or junky

See under **-ie/-y**.

jurist or juror

Both these have to take the law seriously. For the **jurist** it is a profession, for the **juror** an occasional commitment. The **juror** is an ordinary citizen, one of the group selected from the community at large to hear the proceedings of a trial, and to cast final judgement on it. The **jurist** is an academic expert on law, a scholar and/or writer in the field. In North America, judges and lawyers are also referred to as *jurists,* hence references such as *Judge MLR, the chief federal jurist in Los Angeles.*

juristic or juristical

Only **juristic** appears in database evidence from BNC and CCAE, though both British and American dictionaries allow **juristical**. See further under **-istic/-istical**.

just or justly

As an adjective, **just** means "fair, impartial or right." The related adverb is **justly**, as in:
> *The commissioner dealt justly with their complaints.*

However **just** has other uses as an adverb in its own right. It carries several meanings, including "exactly," "by a near thing," "very recently," "only" and "really" according to context, as in the following:
> *It's just what they wanted.*
> *The food lasted just long enough.*
> *They've just arrived.*
> *It's just an ordinary day.*
> *The idea was just brilliant.*

In the first three sentences, **just** has an important interpersonal role expressing immediacy (see **interpersonal**). In the last two, **just** could be seen as a *hedge word* and a kind of *intensifier* (see under those headings). Some might argue that it's redundant in such sentences, though it does contribute to their rhythm and emphasis. The examples also show that **just** works as a discourse marker, spotlighting the word or phrase following (see **information focus**).

Using **just** with verbs raises a small point of style. British usage avoids putting **just** with the simple past form of verbs when it means "recently," and prefers the compound form with *has/have* – at least in writing. It would be:

>*It has just come through*   not
>*It just came through.*

Yet the latter idiom (without the auxiliary *has/have*) is well established in North America and Australia. Even in Britain, the simple past verb can be used with **just** in any of several other senses. See for example the use of **just** = "only"

in:

>*For the British champion it's a lean year – he just won two events.*

The meaning of **just** is intricately bound up with its context, so it seems unproductive to insist on using it to decide the form of the verb.

◊ For more on the choice between simple past and perfect verbs, see **aspect** section 2.

K

k/c

Many loanwords beginning with a "k" sound may be spelled with either **k** or **c**. The **k** often comes with words of Greek, Arabic or Hebrew origin, and sometimes Chinese. Whatever the source, the **k** tends to be replaced by **c** as the word becomes assimilated into English. Among the following, only those in roman are more likely to have **k** spellings nowadays:

kabala	*kadi*	kaftan
kaliph	*kalpak*	*kalsomine*
karat	*kathode*	*kation*
kephalin	*keramic*	keratin
ketchup	kleptomaniac	*kola*
konk	*kosh*	kosher
krimmer	kris	*krummhorn*
kumquat	*kyanite*	kymograph

Note that other letters also vary the spelling of some of those words. See under separate headings for **cabala, caliph, carat, ketchup** and **kosher**.

The tendency to replace **k** with **c** can be seen also in the middle of a word: *ikon/icon, okta/octa, skeptic/sceptic;* and at the end: *disk/disc, mollusck/mollusc.* All are discussed at individual entries.

◊ For variation between **k** and *q(u),* see **q/k**.

kab(b)ala, cab(b)ala or qabbalah
See under **cabala**.

kabob or kebab
See under **kebab**.

Kaffir, Kafir, kaffir or kafir
In the past, **Kaffir** could be used as a neutral reference to the Xhosa people of South Africa, and their language. But under apartheid it became a generalized ethnic insult ("Hey Kaffir, get out of the way"), and within South Africa its use is now an actionable offence. Expressions like "kaffir lie" are also unacceptable. There are however some ongoing uses of **Kaffir**, in the various compounds for things native to South Africa – flora such as the *Kaffir lily / melon / lime leaf,* not to mention *kaffir corn* (a type of sorghum, and the staple of *kaffir beer*). The so-called "Kaffir Circus" deals in South African mining stocks. In American English **Kaffir** can also be spelled **kafir**.

Kaffir/Kafir is a derogatory word in Islamic culture for a non-believer: it originates in Arabic *kafir* ("infidel"). *Kafiristan* was formerly the homeland of a non-Islamic people in the northeastern mountains of Afghanistan bordering Pakistan (an area now called *Nuristan*).

Kampuchea
See **Cambodia**.

karat or carat
See **carat**.

kebab, kabob, kebob or kabab
Arabic **kabab**, meaning "roast meat" was introduced into English in the later C17 as "cabob." In the early C19, it was replaced by the Turkish equivalent **kebab**, and this is the primary spelling in *New Oxford* (1998), and the only one to be found in BNC data. In American English the more Arabic form **kabob** is still given priority in *Merriam-Webster* (2000), though data from CCAE shows that many Americans have also adopted the Turkish spelling (**kebab** prevails over **kabob** by almost 3:1). The trend is clear, whether the dish referred to is *shishkebabs* (small pieces of meat roasted on individual skewers), or *doner kebab* (slices of meat cut from a large cylinder of it, cooked on a vertical spit).

keep from
In everyday English this can be used in two ways:
> We can't keep him from speaking out. ("prevent")
> He couldn't keep from speaking out. ("restrain oneself or avoid")

Both constructions are current in contemporary American English, though the currency of the second (intransitive) construction in British English was queried by Burchfield (1996). If there's any doubt, the BNC provides more than 25 lively examples from a range of writing in which people *keep from panicking / crying / being submerged, slipping on the steep slope* – among other actions on the brink. But hundreds of examples in CCAE confirm that the construction is much more common in American English.

kelim or kilim
See **kilim**.

Keltic or Celtic
See **Celtic**.

Kelvin
See under **Celsius**.

kenneled or kennelled
For the choice of spellings when *kennel* becomes a verb, see under **-l-/-ll-**.

keramic or ceramic
See under **k/c**.

kerb or curb
See **curb**.

kerosene or kerosine
This is the standard word for paraffin in the US, Canada and Australia, but its spelling is not quite standardized. See further under **-ine**.

ketchup, catsup or catchup

This Chinese loanword was *koetsiap* ("seafood sauce") in the former Amoy region, and *kechap* in Malaya, for which the closest approximations respectively are **catsup** and **ketchup**. But the earliest English form of the word was **catchup**, where folk etymology is visibly at work, trying to make sense of an inscrutable foreignism (see further under **folk etymology**). **Ketchup** is the primary spelling in the UK, according to *New Oxford* (1998), and there's scant evidence in the BNC of either of the others.

In the US, usage has been more divided, helped perhaps by the fact that the two major manufacturers (Heinz and Del Monte) were committed to **ketchup** and **catsup**, as *Webster's English Usage* (1989) notes. Dictionaries too diverge. *Webster's Third* (1986) still gives priority to **catsup**, while *Merriam-Webster's* (2000) makes it **ketchup**. But whatever their brand or dictionary loyalty, American writers now clearly prefer **ketchup**, which outnumbers **catsup** by 4:1 in CCAE data. **Catchup** meanwhile is used much more literally in the sports idiom *play catchup*, meaning "trail their opponents' higher score."

key or quay

See **quay**.

kibbutz

When written down, this Hebrew loanword is usually pluralized in the regular Hebrew way as **kibbutzim** (see further under **-im**). This is confirmed in evidence from both American and British databases. Yet in conversation **kibbutz** can easily acquire the English plural "kibbutzes," so we need not be surprised to see it in print in due course.

kibosh or kybosh

Putting the kibosh on a plan is a widely known English idiom of uncertain origin, according to most standard dictionaries. A likely explanation from *Brewer's Dictionary of Phrase and Fable* (1981) is that it is Celtic (in Gaelic the *cia bais* is the "cap of death" put over the face of the deceased; in Irish it's *cie bais*). The *Oxford Dictionary*'s (1989) first record of the idiom comes from Dickens, in the form *put the kye bosk on*. It then appears in the more familiar forms **kybosh** (mostly in British English) and **kibosh** (in American). But **kibosh** seems now to be preferred in British English as well, by the evidence of the BNC.

kiddie or kiddy

See under **-ie/-y**.

kidnapped or kidnaped, and kidnapper or kidnaper

In British English the spellings are always **kidnapped** and **kidnapper**. In American English both spellings are current, but still those with two *p*s have more adherents (in the ratio of 2:1 in CCAE). The spelling with single *p* is the more regular of the two, given that the first syllable carries the stress. See further under **-p/-pp-**.

kilim or kelim

Both spellings are used for this word for a rug woven without pile, originally from the Middle East. In Turkish and Persian it is **kilim**, and that spelling is endorsed in English dictionaries everywhere. Yet **kelim** is also seen in advertising; and in BNC evidence it's on a par with **kilim**, in terms of the number of British sources containing it. But in American data from CCAE, **kilim** clearly outnumbers **kelim** by 16:1.

kilo

This Greek prefix meaning "1000" is one of the key elements of the metric system (see **metrication** and Appendix V). Note however that in the computer term *kilobyte*, **kilo** equals 1024. This is because computer systems are essentially binary (not decimal), and 1024 is 2 to the power of 10.

kimono or kimona

This Japanese loanword is normally spelled **kimono** in both American and British English. *Webster's Third* (1986) gives **kimona** as an alternative spelling, and it goes with the alternative pronunciation – ending in a schwa (indeterminate vowel) rather than "o." But there's scant evidence of **kimona** in CCAE, and none in the BNC.

kind and kindly

Both these can be adjectives, with only a little difference in meaning between them. Both imply sympathy in the person to whom they are applied, but while **kindly** refers to a generally benign disposition, **kind** can be related to specific action. Compare:

> *He took a kindly interest in my welfare.*
> *They were kind enough to drive me home.*

As an adverb, **kindly** expresses the meaning of **kind**, and so *They kindly drove me home* paraphrases the second example exactly. The adjective **kindly** has no accepted adverb because of the awkwardness of a formation like "kindlily." Instead we say "in a kindly way."

Kindly also has formulaic roles, in courteous acknowledgements of someone's actions:

> *While I'm away, the Fathers of the Priory are kindly looking after things.*
> *The author has kindly agreed to give a lecture*

And in polite requests and commands, where it's synonymous with "please":

> *Kindly take your seats.*
> *Would you kindly take your feet of the chair.*

In these its function is definitely **interpersonal**. See further under that heading.

kind of

Singular and plural notions come together in **kind of**. It involves a particular class of objects as well as various examples we know. In formal English either the singular or plural is maintained through the sentence, in extended patterns of agreement expressed in the pronouns, nouns and verb:

> *This kind of problem is one to avoid.*
> *These kinds of problems are ones to avoid.*

The second type of sentence with plural agreement turns the observation into a sweeping statement, overstocked with sibilants – which may explain why writers represented in the BNC make much less use of it than the first type, couched in singular agreement. (See further under **agreement**.)

In yet other constructions with **kind(s) of**, plural and singular combine but with different communicative intent:

These kinds of problem are to be avoided.

These kind of problems are to be avoided.

The first sentence entails an abstract/noncountable use of the following noun ("problem"), and helps to synthesize the discussion in argumentative and persuasive writing (see **count and mass nouns**). The second is simply a more relaxed form of the full plural construction, and tends to appear in interactive writing and live speech.Objections to *these kind of* have been stronger in the US than the UK, where Gowers (1965) felt it was one of the "sturdy indefensibles." Yet its frequency in American English is probably not very different from that of British English. The ratio of *these kind of problems* to *these kinds of problems* is 1:3 in BNC data, and 1:4 in CCAE. Much less visible than either is the combination *this kind of problems,* found only very rarely in impromptu speech.

   Impromptu speech is also the home of a very different use of **kind of**, as a hedging device:

It was kind of scary.

Sergei and I are kind of symbols.

It's kind of evolved.

As the examples show, **kind of** can be used to hedge almost any element of a sentence – adjectives, nouns and verbs. Its informality is underscored in the merged form *kinda,* with the same hedging functions:

They're feeling kinda hungry.

Kinda is actually more common in fiction writing than in the speech transcriptions of the BNC. Like other nonstandard spellings, it lends informality to dialogue or narrative. The fact that it's used in more than 80 British texts makes it more than an occasional Americanism. The extended form of this idiom *kind of a* (mostly used before nouns), can also be found in BNC data:

a modest kind of a funeral

a still, silent kind of a winter day

into kind of a pre-60s effect

Again the phrase smacks of laid-back conversation, not pressing the description too hard. The grammar is no more or less explicable than that of indefinite structures that are standard idiom, such as *what kind of a / some kind of a / any kind of a.* See further under **hedge words**.

◊ Compare **sort of**.

kinesthetic or kinaesthetic, kinesthesia or kinaesthesia

See under **ae/e**.

kitty-corner, cater-corner or catercornered

This handy North American expression is hardly known in Britain, in any of its forms. See **cater(-)corner**.

kn/n

The **kn-** spelling is essential in various English words to prevent the convergence of homonyms. See for example:

(k)nave   (k)new   (k)night   (k)nit   (k)nob

(k)not   (k)now

However in some cases the **kn** may be variable. See for example **knick(-)knack**.

knelt or kneeled

The irregular spelling **knelt** is much more frequent than **kneeled** in British English. In BNC data, the relatively few examples are mostly associated with religious or ritual(ized) activity. In American English – where regular spellings are often preferred – **kneeled** gets rather more use. Yet **knelt** still outnumbers **kneeled** by around 5:1 in data from CCAE. See further under **-ed/-t**.

knick(-)knack, nick(-)nack or nic(-)nac

The excess of *k*s in the first spelling is enough to drive anyone to **nic-nac** – though dictionaries show that **nick(-)nack** is the more popular alternative. They also register the compromise spelling **knicknack**. The word's origins are pretty obscure, and it lacks lexical relatives to tie the spelling down. This leaves us with the sounds of the word to decide the spelling. The chiming vowels put the word into the class of playful *reduplicatives* (see further under that heading).

knifed or knived

See under **-v-/-f-**.

knit or knitted

Both these serve as past forms of the verb **knit**, but the uses of **knit** are far fewer. It survives mostly in collocations such as *close/closely knit,* as well as *loosely/tightly knit.* The regular **knitted** is always used for knitting with yarn or something like it (*knitted leggings*), and most likely for the occasional figurative uses:

The court is knitted together by blood and marriage.

... brows knitted together in a permanent frown

In the second example, a British writer might still use **knit**, but for Americans and Australian writers, **knitted** would come naturally (see Peters, 1995).

knock up

In informal British English, this phrasal verb has several meanings, including "improvise" (*knock up an outfit*), "create on the spur of the moment" (*knock up a gourmet dinner*) and "rouse, alert" (*knock up the girl at the Post Office*). The last construction (when the verb takes a human object) has the potential to mislead American readers, for whom **knock up** is slang for "make pregnant."

knowledgeable or knowledgable

This word is at the crossroads of two spelling rules, and large dictionaries allow both **knowledgeable** and **knowledgable**. According to the rules for stems ending in *e* (see **-e** section 1) it should be **knowledgable**. Yet those concerned with keeping a *g* "soft" (see **-ce/-ge**) would have it as **knowledgeable**. **Knowledgable** is somewhat better patronized in the US than in the UK, yet the majority of writers everywhere prefer **knowledgeable**, by the evidence of the reference databases.

KO

See under **OD**.

konk or conk
See under k/c.

kopje or koppie
Outside South Africa, the Dutch-looking **kopje** ("a small hill") is still the best-known spelling for this word. But within South Africa it has long been anglicized to **koppie**.

Koran, Quran, Qu'ran or Qoran
In both British and American English, the Islamic holy book is normally spelled **Koran**, according to the evidence of BNC and CCAE. The early spelling **Qoran** has been totally eclipsed, but the modern Arabized form **Quran**, or more correctly **Qu'ran**, is very occasionally seen.

kosh or cosh
See under k/c.

kosher or cosher
The Yiddish word **Kosher** meaning "in accordance with proper Jewish practices" has become a colloquial word for "genuine," usually written without a capital letter. In the past it was also **cosher**, but this seems to have been eclipsed by **kosher** in C20. **Kosher** is the only spelling represented in data from BNC and CCAE. There's no sign in the American database of *kasher,* the Hebrew form of the word given as an alternative in *Webster's Third* (1986).

kowtow
This Chinese loanword has been abstracted away from its physical origins in *k'o t'ou,* literally "knock [the] head [on the ground]," and also from C19 spellings *kootoo* and *kotow.* The standard spelling **kowtow** still confirms its foreignness – though the obsequious behavior it connotes is recognizable close to home, whether one is seen to *kowtow to bankers / proprietors / the government* or anyone.

krona or krone
Both these refer to Scandinavian units of currency. In Sweden it's the **krona**, spelled the same way whether singular or plural. But in Norway and Denmark the currency unit is the **krone**, which becomes **krone** in the plural.

kudos
In American usage this word is sometimes interpreted as a plural – from which a singular **kudo** is then backformed (see **backformation**). Though far from common, there are a couple of examples in CCAE, such as *the one kudo he gets...,* to prove that it does exist. This doesn't make it sophisticated style.

kumquat or cumquat
This Cantonese loanword for a mini-orange can be spelled either way, according to both American and British dictionaries. But database evidence from CCAE and the BNC runs strongly in favor of **kumquat**. See further under k/c.

kybosh or kibosh
See under **kibosh**.

-l/-ll

The choice between one and two ls in uninflected verbs such as *distil(l), enrol(l), enthral(l), fulfil(l), instil(l)* is discussed under individual headings. See also **forestallment**, **install** and **single for double** for further cases.

-l-/-ll-

Deeply embedded in English there are rules about doubling the final consonant of a word before you add a suffix beginning with a vowel (see **doubling of final consonant**). The rules are applied with reasonable consistency to most consonants, but l is hauled out for special treatment in British English in words such as *traveller, modelling, totalled,* creating anomalies which are largely shared by Australian and Canadian English. Approximately 80% of instances in Australian internet documents follow the British pattern (Peters, 1999b). In Canada final l is doubled more often than not, according to the *Canadian Oxford* (1998), though the pattern varies from east to west, and between book publishers and the press (*Editing Canadian English,* 2000), where the first have been more committed to doubling than the second. In American English the regular spellings *traveler, modeling, totaled* are preferred in all dictionaries, and are clearly supported responses gathered in the Langscape survey (1998–2001). Research by Sigley (1999) based on comparative corpora from the 1960s and 1990s showed that the American endorsement of single l had strengthened from 89% to 94%.

The use of double l in *traveller* etc. in British style seems all the more erratic when you compare its non-use before other verb suffixes such as *-ize* (*equalize, finalize, generalize*). Add in nouns such as *medal(l)ist* and *panel(l)ing* which vary over doubling the l, while others like *specialist* or *federalism* never do. Some adjective suffixes such as *cruel(l)est, marvel(l)ous, wool(l)en* show variation, but everyone uses *devilish.* As these examples show, there is no consistency even in reserving double l for use before inflectional suffixes on verbs and adjectives, and leaving single l before derivational ones (see **suffixes**). Often it comes down to conventions for individual words. Word history may dictate the spelling, as with *crystalline, crystallize* and *tranquil(l)ize.* (See under **crystallized** and **tranquilizer**.)

In American English all such words can be spelled with a single l, and inconsistencies are minimized. Yet because single spellings are identified with the US by regional labels in most non-US dictionaries (*Canadian Oxford, New Oxford,* 1998; *Macquarie Dictionary,* 1997), little attention is paid to their merit in terms of regularity. The single l spellings embody some of the most widely accepted principles of English spelling. Those who exempt words ending in l from the general rule make a rod for their own backs with any new words of this kind. New verbs are continually being

formed from nouns and adjectives ending in l, to test our spelling principles. Should they be:

initialed	or	*initialled*
trialed	or	*trialled*
credentialed	or	*credentialled*

Even those who use British spelling may find that what seems "right" in *travelled* isn't necessarily so in less familiar words. The longer the stem, the more cumbersome the double l seems. When it comes to *paralleled,* most British writers stay with single l (see **parallel**). Internet respondents to the Langscape survey (1998–2001) were systematically more inclined than their paper-based counterparts to use single l spellings.

Because this is such a productive point of English word formation, it seems important not to perpetuate and proliferate anomalies. Already it affects as large a set of verbs as the following:

apparel	*barrel*	*bevel*	*bowel*	*cancel*
carol	*cavil*	*channel*	*chisel*	*counsel*
cudgel	*devil*	*dial*	*dishevel*	*dowel*
drivel	*duel*	*equal*	*fuel*	*funnel*
gambol	*gravel*	*grovel*	*gruel*	*jewel*
kennel	*label*	*laurel*	*level*	*libel*
marshal	*marvel*	*medal*	*metal*	*model*
panel	*parcel*	*pencil*	*peril*	*petal*
pistol	*pummel*	*quarrel*	*ravel*	*revel*
rival	*shovel*	*shrivel*	*signal*	*snivel*
spiral	*squirrel*	*stencil*	*swivel*	*symbol*
tassel	*tinsel*	*total*	*towel*	*trammel*
trowel	*tunnel*	*weasel*	*yodel*	

Derivatives of all those such as *bedevil, disembowel, empanel* are also affected. The broadest rule of English spelling leaves all such words with a single l, and has been adopted in this book.

> **International English selection:** The practice of using single l at the junction between verb and suffix when there is no stress on the final syllable of the stem is familiar throughout the world as the US spelling. It is more regular than the double l, and natural for new and uncommon words. These are good reasons for using it in established words as well.

labeled or labelled, labeling or labelling
Whether to double the l is discussed under -l-/-ll-.

labor or labour
The choice between these is discussed at **-or/-our**.

Labour or Labor
In both Britain and New Zealand the **Labour** parties use the spelling with *-our.* In Australia, the comparable party has always spelled its name **Labor**. The spelling goes back to the roots of the labo(u)r movement in C19 Australia, and disregards the fact that the use of *-our* spellings has firmed up there since then. See further under **-or/-our**.

lack for

The verb *lack* has always taken a direct object as in:
> *For most of the game, Spurs lacked enthusiasm.*

This transitive construction is matched by the intransitive **lack for**, at least in negative statements such as:
> *They don't lack for activities and leisure pursuits.*
> *With IB and DJ, they will not lack for high-class cricketers.*
> *One could never lack for advocates in Rome.*
> *No-one could say the old baggage lacked for courage.*

The **lack for** construction seems to have originated in American English in late C19, and to have crossed the Atlantic during C20. British examples like those just quoted are to be found in both written and spoken sources of the BNC. There's no suggestion in *New Oxford* (1998) that it still has an American flavor.

lackey or lacquey

Dictionaries all make **lackey** the primary spelling, and it was indeed the first to be recorded in C16 English. Some also record **lacquey** as an alternative or archaic variant, a spelling that connects with its French antecedent *laquais* ("footsoldier"). Both spellings flourished in C17 and C18, but **lackey** seems to have become dominant during C19 for both noun and verb. Perhaps the French spelling seemed out of keeping with the servile implications of the word in English (see further under **frenchification**). With no examples of **lacquey** in the reference corpora, C21 dictionaries can safely discard it. R.I.P.

lacquer or lacker

The spelling **lacquer** is given preference in all dictionaries, though the dated **lacker** is closer to the word's origins in the obsolete French word *lacre* ("sealing wax"). The word was mistakenly associated with the French *lacque* ("lake"), and respelled as **lacquer** during C17. **Lacquer** has steadily gained ground since, and it's the only spelling now used in English worldwide, by the evidence of the BNC and CCAE.

lacuna

The plural of this word is discussed under -a section 1.

laden or loaded

In a few contexts either of these words would do, though they differ in their connotations. Compare the difference in:
> *The table was laden with fine food.*
> *The table was loaded with fine food.*

In both cases there is a wonderful excess, but the word **laden** makes its appeal more aesthetic. **Loaded** has strong physical connections with the noun *load*, and with it you can almost see the table straining under the weight of goodies piled on it.

Laden is the last remnant of an old verb *lade*, which otherwise appears only in the fossilized phrase *bill of lading*. It is increasingly a literary word, as is clear when we compare *laden with cares,* and *loaded with responsibilities*. **Loaded** is common and usable in many kinds of context, whether it's a matter of carrying a load of ammunition, money, responsibilities, or in the colloquial sense "under the influence" (of alcohol or drugs), used mostly outside the UK in North America and Australia.

lady or woman

Several kinds of social change since World War II have impacted on these words, among them the liberation of women's roles in society, democratization of the work force, and movements against sexism in language. All have helped to destabilize the choice between **lady** and **woman**. The values of courtesy and respect that have been invested in **lady** to underscore "la différence" are now set against the view that these may serve to disempower women in an unhelpful gender divide. Add to this some skepticism on either ideological front about the motives of the other, and differing reactions from older and younger users of the language, and you have a recipe for hesitation. There are still formal and conventional uses of **lady** which are uncomplicated, but many call for second thought.

The word **lady** comes in fact from humble origins in Anglo-Saxon, originating in the kitchen as (literally) "one who kneads the loaf." A thousand years later it was "my lady" to whom tea and scones were served in the drawing room. Genteel connotations are there in its more generic use as well: *She received the unexpected guest like a lady.* The social graces attached to the word are of course underpinned by continuing use of **Lady** as a courtesy title for women at certain levels of the aristocracy in Britain, women who are the wives or widows of baronets or knights, and otherwise for those below the rank of duchess, according to *Debrett's Correct Form* (1992). In other countries such as Australia and New Zealand where knighthoods have been awarded on the basis of distinguished public service, the title **Lady** is given to the wife of the recipient.

Lady is also caught up in courtesy titles used for women in other hierarchies. Thus *Lady Mayoress* is used of the wife of a mayor, or (if female) the mayor herself:
> *She will make an excellent Lady Mayoress and Chair of this Council.*

In Canada *My Lady* has been the conventional form of address for female justices of the superior courts.

Ceremonial uses of **Lady** like these are uncontentious, as is its plural use in the formula *Ladies and Gentlemen,* used in polite address to a mixed audience. This socially unrestricted use of *ladies* is matched in the use of the singular **lady** (without capital) to women of any class or status whose names are unknown – in public situations when they become the focus of attention:
> *Give your seat to the lady.*
> *Would this lady like to join in?*
> *Come in, young lady.*

In examples like these, politeness is central to the use of the word, in both second and third person applications. That politeness may however be blended with heavy irony, as in *Look where you're going, lady!*

In occupational titles, the so-called "polite" uses of **lady** are increasingly questioned. Terms like *cleaning lady/tea lady* are too obviously euphemisms for the person who performs menial tasks in homes and offices. To feminist ears the titles also sound patronizing. Either way job-centred terms such as *cleaner* and *tea attendant* are preferable and more neutral. There are similar concerns over the use of **lady** in professional titles such as *lady dentist, lady doctor,* though these are also driven by the fact that the gender reference is gratuitous, when for most professional purposes the term *dentist, doctor* says it all. Steady increases in the proportion of women among the ranks of medicos make it no longer remarkable, and drawing attention to their gender seems to perpetuate older assumptions about gender-roles – about who does what in "normal" society. The same kind of problem can be seen even in polite reference to the fact that sandwiches for the church meeting were made by the *local ladies*. Perversely perhaps, the term may seem to imply that this is the proper role of women (to provide services), while their presence as members of local committees and boards is glossed over.

These days, **lady** and **ladies** are subject to multiple interpretations, and on the printed page there is no face to show the actual intent (benign or otherwise) of the person communicating. Writers wishing to use it need to be very sure of their readers. In American English **lady** is becoming something like a "skunked" word, according to Garner (*Modern American Usage,* 1998), i.e. one whose interpretation is so polarized and disputed that the only safe tactic is avoidance.

In contrast, **woman** is increasingly assured among the set of terms available to refer to female human beings. In older usage it was socially differentiated from **lady**, and its lower class associations are still there if applied to one's hired domestic help: *My woman comes on Tuesdays and Thursdays*. The implicit social gradient probably lingers most strongly in British usage. But in more egalitarian contexts everywhere, **woman** is usefully straightforward – unencumbered by genteelism and decadent social assumptions. Research by Holmes and Sigley (2002) based on comparative corpora shows a doubling of the usage of **woman** between the 1960s and the 1990s in written American English, and comparably high levels in Australian and New Zealand data.

In major sports competitions, the "ladies singles" or "ladies open golf tournament" are now often referred to as *women's events*. For feminists **woman** is the preferred term whenever it's felt necessary to refer to gender, as in *women writers, women in publishing* (see Maggio, 1988). However, the principle of avoiding gender specification in professional titles still applies, as with **lady**. (See further under **nonsexist language**.)

laid or lain

These belong to different verbs: *lay* and *lie* respectively. The overlapping parts of these verbs are a source of much confusion, as discussed under **lie or lay**.

lairy, leary or leery

See **leery**.

laissez faire or laisser faire

This phrase, borrowed from C18 French, means literally "let (them) do [whatever]." It stands for the longer phrase *laissez faire et laissez passer,* which was the maxim of the French free-trade economists. Nowadays it's used to refer to any noninterventionist policy of a government or an individual. When used as an adjective, as in a *laissez faire approach to gardening,* it does not need a hyphen because it's a foreign phrase. (See **hyphens** section 3c.) In current

French the same phrase is **laisser faire**, but English writers rarely amend the traditional **laissez faire** to conform. In BNC data **laissez faire** outnumbers **laisser faire** by more than 18:1.

lama or llama

Both are associated with high altitudes, but the man and the beast are kept well apart by the distinct spellings of these words. **Lama** is a Tibetan word for a priest or monk associated with *Lamaism*. The word **llama** comes to us via Spanish from the Quechuan Indians (peoples of the South American Andes) who used the animal as a beast of burden, and as a source of food and fibre.

lamé

Speaking of *silver lamé,* is it safe to leave the accent off **lamé**? See under **accents**.

lamina

The plural of this word is discussed under **-a** section 1.

landslide or landslip

The first is now preferred everywhere. **Landslip** was the earlier term for a devastating movement of earth, originating in C17 Britain, while **landslide** was coined independently in mid-C19 America. In American usage **landslide** quickly developed the figurative sense of an overwhelming election victory, and this was its meaning when first recorded in British sources in 1896. The geological meaning reached Britain not long after, and has taken over from **landslip** as the common term. In BNC data **landslide** in the geological sense appears in more than twice as many sources as **landslip**, though the latter survives in legal and technical texts. In Canada and Australia **landslide** is the standard term for the earth movement as well as decisive election results, and **landslip** has no currency.

landward or landwards

See under **-ward or -wards**.

Langscape survey

The Langscape project (1998–2001) was a joint venture of *English Today* and Cambridge University Press, designed to survey the attitudes of English-users to questions of usage. It took the form of a series of six questionnaires on matters of spelling and word form, capitalization, punctuation and grammar. Hundreds of survey questionnaires were returned in print and electronic form, from English-users around the world, men and women of all ages. Interim reports were published in *EnglishToday* (nos. 56–60 and 62) and two final reports (descriptive and quantitative) in *English Today* 63 and 65.

language academy

The English-speaking world has never succeeded in establishing an authoritative body like the *Académie Française* to guard the language. Attempts to create a **language academy** in C17 and C18 Britain foundered for political reasons; and the American Academy of Language and Belles Lettres, founded by New York businessman William Cardell in 1820, lasted less than two years. Thomas Jefferson was invited to become its president, but declined, noting the dangers of trying to "fix" the language. The proper role of the **language** academy is always a matter of debate, as well as its membership and their terms of office (Peters, 1992). (Should the academy's members be there for life, like the so-called "immortals" of the French academy?) Both membership and function have been key issues for the English Academy of Southern Africa founded in 1961, which reconstituted itself in the 1990s so as to represent a broader range of linguistic interests (see under **South African English**).

In the absence of a **language academy** for English at large, the language has maintained its boundaries by consensus, and by reference to local or imported written authorities. These change generation by generation, allowing for continuous updating of usage norms and using newly developed linguistic tools. It may not be a bad alternative.

language databases
See **English language databases.**

languid or languorous
Both these suggest a lack of energetic activity. But while **languid** usually implies that it is unfortunate, **languorous** can imply that there's something rather appealing about the slow pace. Compare the following:

There was a languid smile on the patient's face.
At low tide the languorous movement of the wave hardly rippled the surface of the pool.

Note that while the *u* in **languid** confirms the "g" sound preceding it, in **languorous** and **languor** it is really superfluous. The word was spelled **langor** for centuries in Middle English, and the *u* was inserted only in C17, to make it match its Latin forebear.

lanolin or lanoline
In general usage **lanolin** now seems to be preferred, everywhere in the English-speaking world – despite the British preference for *-ine* in other everyday chemical terms whose endings vary on this (see further under **-ine/-in**). Yet while **lanolin** appears on the product label, **lanoline** may still be found in the fine print when the substance is listed as a pharmaceutical ingredient. This is the chemist's distinctive use of *-ine* versus *-in* (see **-ine/-in**), which breaks down where common household substances are concerned.

large and largely
There's no simple relationship of adjective and adverb between these. While **large** is the all-purpose adjective of size, as in *a large apple/book/ room/building,* it also serves as its own adverb in verbal collocations such as *bulk large, grow large, loom large* and the idiom *writ large.*

Largely is exclusively an adverb, but has lost its connections with physical size or extent and gained a figurative role as in:

Health campaigns have largely failed to change behaviour.
You will be largely responsible for yourself.

These show its typical use as a synonym for "mostly" or "chiefly." Grammarians would debate whether it is a *degree adjunct* or a *focusing* device (see **adverbs** section 1), and there's room for either interpretation. Just sometimes a potential link with **large** also seems to be there, as in *Dwarf tulips are largely represented by the kaufmannia types* – unless you know your tulips.

large-scale
See **scale.**

largesse or largess
The French pronunciation of this word, with stress on the second syllable, seems to have supported the French spelling **largesse** for centuries after it might have been fully anglicized. First borrowed in C13, it had acquired the English spelling **largess** by C16, which explains how that became the dominant spelling in American English, and still is, according to *Webster's Third* (1986) and Garner's *Modern American Usage* (1998) – in spite of the French stress pattern. But **largesse** has its following among American writers, and appeared in almost 40% of instances of the word in CCAE. Meanwhile British use of **largesse** was probably boosted in C19 by the taste for things French (see further under **frenchification**). The *Oxford Dictionary* (1989) still has the two spellings ordered as **largess, largesse,** but *New Oxford* (1998) prioritizes the second. There's ample support for this in BNC data, where instances of **largesse** outnumber those of **largess** by more than 25:1.

larva
The preferred plural for this word is still Latin **larvae** rather than English **larvas,** by the result of the Langscape survey (1998–2001), in which it was endorsed by 87% of respondents overall. See **-a** section 1, for further discussion.

larynx
For the plural of this word, see **-x** section 3.

lasso
Like other nouns ending in *-o,* **lasso** has had two plurals: **lassos** and **lassoes.** But the *-oes* plural is disappearing, as for most other words of this kind (see **-o**), and dictionaries everywhere make *lassoes* their second choice. They pass over what to do when **lasso** serves as a verb meaning "catch with or as with a lasso," where the third person singular present tense poses the same question. When they need it, American writers in CCAE again keep it simple:

. . . the tow boat finally lassos us
the cowboy who lassos dreams
PDQ lassos laughs with "Oedipus Tex"

Among these new figurative uses of the verb, *lassos* outnumbers *lassoes* by more than 4:1. The past form remains *lassoed.*

last or lastly
When enumerating a series of points, the old convention had it that you should begin with *first* not *firstly,* and end with *last* not **lastly.** In between, however, you would use *secondly, thirdly, fourthly* etc. The rationale for this is obscure, and though it was certainly being challenged last century, it's still around this century. Fowler thought of it as "harmless pedantry": see further under **first or firstly.**

last or latest
These words are often synonyms in informal language, yet they can also contrast in meaning. When they do contrast, **last** means "final, the one after which there can never be any more"; while

latest just means "the most recent." The two meanings are enshrined in *your last chance* and *the latest fashion*. On this basis, someone's *latest book* is not necessarily their *last book*. Yet the distinction is often blurred in comments such as:

I like this book better than his last one.

Out of context that sentence is ambiguous. Does it mean:

I like this latest book better than his previous one

or

I prefer this earlier book to his final publication.

No doubt your knowledge of the author referred to and his various books would help to clarify the comment.

Last often equals **latest** in references to time:

Last Thursday they signed the contract.
During the last month we have taken on two new editors.

In official letter writing, **last** is routinely used this way:

As I said in my last letter...

In such cases both idiom and context clarify the meaning, and there's no reason to modify them. But in decontextualized writing the difference between **last** and **latest** needs to be watched. *The latest software from X* suggests ongoing progress whereas *the last software* could suggest that the company has wound up.

late

The quasi-legal phrase **the late** is a discreet reminder to readers that the person referred to has recently died, in case they are unaware of it. See for example *the late Italian film director, Federico Fellini*. Just how long we should continue to use it after someone's death is a matter of individual judgement. Quotations in *Webster's English Usage* (1989) suggest anything from ten to fifty years. Comments on the "ever-to-be-lamented death" of Lord Nelson by C19 newspapers could be taken to extend the period even further. It seems a little superfluous to prolong use of *the late* for those whose deaths are well known, except that it serves as a mark of respect, as for *the late Rev. Martin Luther King*.

The late is sometimes used to mean that a person's term of office has ended, as in *Chaudry, the late prime minister of Fiji*. Dictionaries in Britain, Australia and North America all recognize this usage, though it bears some risk of misinterpretation. If the person mentioned is remote or little known, it is more likely to be taken as an allusion to his death rather than his retirement or removal from office. The point intended can be made more reliably with the adjective *former* or the prefix *ex-*, as in *ex-prime minister Chaudry*.

lateish or latish

See **latish**.

latex

For the plural of this word see **-x** section 2.

Latin abbreviations

Scholarly writing has transferred a number of **Latin abbreviations** into common usage, and others have gained currency through the conventions of letter writing. Some of them, like *e.g., i.e., etc.* are very well known; others like *ibid., loc.cit., op.cit.* are rare except in academic publishing, and are steadily being replaced (see under individual headings). But many still serve as useful shorthand, as the translations in the list below can show:

c. or *ca.*	*circa* "about, approximately" (with dates)
cf.	*confer* "compare"
c.v.	*curriculum vitae* "profile of [one's] life"
e.g.	*exempli gratia* "by way of an example"
et al.	*et alii* "and other persons"
et seq(q).	*et sequen(te)s* "and the following [page/s]"
etc.	*et cetera* "and so forth"
fl.	*floruit* "s/he flourished"
i.e.	*id est* "that is"
inf.	*infra* "below"
inst.	*instante* "in the present [month]"
NB	*nota bene* "take good note"
pro tem.	*pro tempore* "for the time being"
prox.	*proximo* "in the next [month]"
PS	*post scriptum* "[something] written afterwards"
QED	*quod erat demonstrandum* "[that was the very point] which had to be demonstrated"
q.v.	*quod vide* "have a look at that"
RIP	*requiescat in pace* "may s/he rest in peace"
sup.	*supra* "above"
ult.	*ultimo* "in the last [month]"
v.	*vide* "see"
v. or *vs.*	*versus* "against"
viz.	*videlicet* "namely"

Latin abbreviations are given stops according to whatever editing principle you use for English ones (see **abbreviations** section 2). In the list above, stops are reserved for lower case abbreviations, or rather the shortened words within them (e.g. *al.* but not *et*). When both words in the abbreviation are shortened it's still usual to give each of them a stop, although the practice of working with just a final stop, as in *eg.* and *ie.,* is on the increase.

In older publications, Latin abbreviations were italicized like other foreign loanwords, but the tendency nowadays is to put them in roman. This is recommended for all by the *Chicago Manual* (2003); and by the Australian government *Style Manual* (2002) and *Editing Canadian English* (2000). However British style manuals encourage editors to use roman only for the commonest abbreviations, and italics for the rest. What is "common" then becomes the issue. In *Copy-editing* (1992), the set is defined as consisting of *e.g., i.e., etc., viz.;* whereas *Hart's Rules* (1983) had it include others as well, notably *cf., et seq., q.v.* The question of whether to italicize *v.* when referring to legal cases is discussed under **italic(s)** section 6b.

◊ For the question as to where **Latin abbreviations** like *e.g., etc., i.e.* are appropriate, and what punctuation to use with them, see under the individual entries.

Latin America

This phrase is a reminder of how much of the "New World" is not English-speaking. **Latin America** includes all the countries of North and South America in which Spanish or Portuguese is the official language. Almost all the independent states of South America come under that heading, except Guyana and

Surinam, and the whole of Central America including Mexico.

Latin plurals

English has borrowed words from Latin for over 1500 years. The older loanwords, like *cheese* and *oil,* have long since been assimilated and acquired English plurals. But younger loanwords (those borrowed from the Renaissance on) tend to keep their Latin plurals, at least as alternatives to regular English ones.

The Latin plurals in English are of five major kinds, for words ending in:

-a	e.g. *formula*
-is	e.g. *axis*
-us	e.g. *fungus, corpus, hiatus*
-um	e.g. *atrium*
-x	e.g. *appendix*

Details on forming the plural for each type are discussed under the relevant ending (**-a**, **-is**, **-us**, **-um**, **-x**). One other group to note are words like *series* and *species,* which have zero plurals in Latin. They too are maintained in English, so that the words remain the same whether singular or plural. Compare:

> *the latest series to be proposed*

with

> *three new series since 1980*

See further under **zero plurals**.

latinization

The influence of Latin is far greater than that of any other language from which English has borrowed. Along with hundreds of thousands of Latin loanwords came exotic patterns of spelling and affixation, now embedded as alternative systems in English (see for example **ae/e** and **Latin plurals**). Some of these were actively affirmed in Renaissance English (see **spelling** section 1), and their effect is still felt in such things as the variation between *inquire* and *enquire,* where the process of **latinization** is incomplete (see under **inquiry** and **en-/in-**). In scientific discourse, especially life sciences and mathematics, Latin influence is still visible in the preferred plurals for many neoclassical nouns, which resist assimilation to the English pattern (Peters, 2001a).

Examples of affirmative **latinization** can be found in less specialized vocabulary. *Flotation* is a respelling of *floatation,* formed in English, and has all but replaced it (see **flotation**). English suffixes with Latin counterparts may be replaced by them, which explains the variation in words such as *convener/convenor, deductable/deductible* and others. All these were formed in modern English, but they have been, are being, or tend to be respelled with the Latin suffix – especially in North America – as if they had much longer pedigrees (see further under **-er/-or** and **-able/-ible** and individual headings). This use of latinate spellings in English formations shows the power of linguistic analogy, and the long shadow of our classical heritage.

Latino and Hispanic

Latino is a relatively recent term (first recorded in 1946) for Latin-American inhabitants of the US or Canada. Like other ethnic terms, it is normally capitalized. In many applications it overlaps with **Hispanic**, though the latter includes Spanish-speaking people from any quarter, not just Latin America. In data from CCAE, the two terms are more or less equally common overall, and often used interchangeably as adjective and noun, compare:

> *Hispanics are angry because these errors come at a time when many Latino groups have made a concerted effort to register . . .*
> *. . . urging Latinos to bypass voting for certain Democrats because they feel the party snubbed Hispanic candidates*

Latino is nevertheless the commoner term on the west coast (and for the *Los Angeles Times*), whereas the major east coast newspapers (*Christian Science Monitor, Washington Post*) seem to prefer **Hispanic** (see under that heading). In New York, **Hispanic** provides a superordinate for Caribbean immigrants including Dominican, Salvadorean and Puerto Rican. But in the southwest it naturally includes those from Mexico, as in:

> *an exhibition of Hispanic artists: altarpieces by 12 Chicano, Latino and Caribbean artists.*

Latino as a singular noun is gender-neutral, and the plural **Latinos** refers to both men and women of Latin-American origin. Compare *Latina* (the Spanish feminine form), which is used only of a woman. Its plural is *Latinas.*

latish or lateish

Dictionaries all prefer the first spelling, which has been on record since C17. What is more, it's perfectly regular (see further under **-e** section 1). The BNC has few examples, among which 4 out of 5 are for **latish**.

latter

For the use of this word, both alone and in tandem with *former,* see **former and latter**.

latterly and lately

This curious adverb, based on a comparative adjective, highlights the last or most recent phase in a nonfictional narrative:

> *. . . because of its slow growing (and latterly falling) population*
> *Latterly it was to Eaton Square, where friends continued to gather . . .*
> *I was a member, and latterly chairman of the Commission.*

The word often seems to entail a sense of where we are now in history, and in some examples to replace the more conversational **lately**. For example:

> *There have latterly been some notable donations . . .*

The first record of **latterly** is from C18, which might explain why it's much less popular in the US than the UK. At any rate, it appears in just 2 American sources in CCAE, compared with around 200 in the BNC.

laudable or laudatory

If the verb *laud* ("praise") were still in common usage, these adjectives would never be confused. As it is, *laud* is now closely tied to religious usage (apart from the quasi-religious idiom "lauded to the skies"), and is not familiar enough to many people to help decode the adjectives.

Laudable is the passive adjective "able to be praised" or "worthy of praise," as in *a laudable undertaking*. The word is something of a two-edged sword, since it expresses respect for the aims of an enterprise while hinting that it may not succeed. **Laudatory** means "full of praise," and so is applied to words, speech or documents which commend someone's work: *a laudatory reference on the applicant's achievements.*

laudanum
See under **morphine**.

laudatory or laudable
See **laudable**.

laundromat or laundermat, launderette or laundrette
These two types of word for a public coin-operated laundry turn up together in an American review of the British movie *My Beautiful Laundrette,* in which "two young men take over a Laundromat in England." As the review implies, the common term in the US is **laundromat** or **laundermat,** and **laund(e)rette** in Britain. **Laundromat** was the trade mark (1943) of the commercial-sized washing machines at the heart of the business, and some writers capitalize the word even in generic references: *we can always work at a Laundromat.* But less than half of the 120 instances in CCAE carry a capital. **Laundermat** is a rare alternative, never capitalized. In Canada and Australia, where **laundromat** is also the standard term, the word appears without capital in the *Canadian Oxford* (1998) and the Australian *Macquarie Dictionary* (1997).

Despite appearances, **launderette** is not a French loanword (since the French use *laverie automatique* for the same business). **Launderette** was coined in post-war England (1949), with deliberate ambiguity no doubt in the suffix *-ette,* which could be interpreted as either "small" or "[substitute] female" in this context (see **-ette**). It has become the standard term for those seeking automated help with their washing, written without a capital as far as the *Oxford Dictionary* (1989) is concerned, and not normally capitalized by writers in the BNC. The two-syllabled form **laundrette** occurs a few times – apart from its appearances in the title of the movie mentioned at the start of this entry. But it's very much the minority form, with only 1 instance to every 12 of those of **launderette.**

Laurasia and ``Laurasian English"
The hypothetical supercontinent of the northern hemisphere (which combined North America and Europe, as well as much of Asia north of the Himalayas) is **Laurasia.** It could provide a name for that notional supra-regional variety of English of the northern hemisphere, consisting of the common elements of British and American English – otherwise variously called *mid-Atlantic English* or *common English.* See further under **international English.** The first element of **Laurasia** comes from *Laurentia,* used since the 1930s to refer to the geological precursor of America.
◊ Compare **Gondwanaland.**

lawful or legal
See under **legal, legalistic, legitimate or lawful.**

lawyer, attorney, barrister, counsel, solicitor or notary public
The most general term for one who practises law in Britain, Canada and Australia is **lawyer.** In the US

too, **lawyer** is widely used in nonlegal contexts, but gives way to **attorney** or *attorney at law,* in legal practice. The *attorney general* is the highest legal authority in the US, and elsewhere in the English-speaking world (Canada, the UK and Australia). But **attorney** is otherwise mostly confined to institutionalized phrases such as *power of attorney.*

Outside the US, practising **lawyers** may be either **solicitors** who take on cases for clients, or **barristers,** those called to the bar to act in court. But within the court itself, the **barrister** is usually referred to as **counsel** (in Canada also **counsellor**), as also in the US.

The term *notary* has a historical ring to it for Australians and the British, but continues in North American usage. The **notary public** is authorized to attest and certify legal documents such as contracts (including marriage certficates), deeds and affidavits, either as a public officer or in relation to private cases. An American **lawyer** is often also a **notary public,** and Canadians called to the bar are simultaneously sworn in as **notaries public** – except in Quebec where the roles are distinct.

lay
This is the present of one verb and the past of another. See **lie or lay.**

lay of the land
This is the standard American term for what in Britain is the **lie of the land.** Database evidence bears this out. Among American writers in CCAE all but one uses **lay of the land.** In the BNC all but one British writer uses **lie of the land.**

lay-by
In British English **lay-by** (plural **lay-bys**) means an area beside a highway where vehicles can pull off and park out of the stream of traffic. The word was earlier used for railway sidings and side-canals in other transport systems. On newer highways the **lay-by** is usually not just a side lane, but a small landscaped area which serves a variety of social and other respite functions: *at lunchtime they pulled in to a lay-by for a picnic.* Elsewhere in the world the **lay-by** is a *rest area,* also called a *rest stop* in the US and Canada.

In Australian English, **lay-by** refers to a system of buying goods under an installment plan. It can be used of the article bought, and even as the verb for buying it: *I'll lay-by it for Christmas.*

layman, layperson, lay person and laity
The term **layman** has been put under the spotlight, along with other generic compounds ending in *-man,* as being susceptible to sexist interpretation, whether or not that's the intention. (See further under **man** and **-person.**) But unlike *policeman, businessman* etc. it can scarcely be seen as a source of discrimination against women in the workplace. It might indeed seem to discriminate in their favor whenever the phrase *to the layman* means something like "to the untrained." Either way the nonsexist alternative **layperson** would serve, though it has yet to prove popular with British or American writers represented in the BNC or CCAE, where the ratio of **layman** to **layperson** is about 18:1 and 12:1 respectively. **Layperson** is however recognized in this generic sense in *New Oxford* (1998), *Canadian Oxford* (1998) and the Australian *Macquarie*

dictionary (1997). The Australian government *Style Manual* (2002) notes that **layperson** is in fact one of the best established *-person* words in the set (see further under **-person**).

In its traditional sense, the generic **layman** stood for the **laity**, i.e. the nonclerical population associated with the Church. Both words embody the French *lai*, derived from the Late Latin adjective *laicus*, ultimately Greek *laos*, meaning "people." This makes *lay people* a kind of tautology, though the terms **lay person** and "people person" are clearly distinct. There is indeed scope to distinguish between **lay person** and **layperson**, where the spaced form of the compound could refer strictly to a member of the Church, and the solid form to the nonprofessional in any field – of law, medicine, architecture etc. But distinctions based on space are always fragile, and the dictionaries that register both terms simply make them alternatives. This accords with the mixed evidence of the British and American databases, where **layperson** is occasionally used to refer to a nonclerical adherent of a church: *a layperson with Methodist seminary training;* and **lay person** in reference to other non-professionals/specialists, as in *a panel of four doctors and a lay person*. Still for secular references, **layperson** and **layman** are the usual choices.

-le

Several groups of English words end this way:
1 A largish group of two-syllabled verbs (or verb-related words) which express a quick, light movement or sound that repeats itself. The following are just a token:

bustle	*drizzle*	*fizzle*	*giggle*	*gurgle*
nibble	*rustle*	*scramble*	*scuttle*	*shuffle*
sizzle	*trickle*	*twinkle*	*whistle*	

The source of such words is something of a mystery. In odd cases like *dazzle* we seem to have a diminutive form of *daze*, but the roots of most of the list above are obscure and unparalleled elsewhere. The consonants in them often seem to suggest the process they refer to, as if some kind of sound symbolism is at work. (See further under **phonesthemes**.) Some have a playful character, witness *bamboozle* and *boondoggle* (rare examples with three syllables), not to mention *boggle, bungle, puzzle*.
2 Two small groups of nouns. In some **-le** was once a diminutive, as shown by *speckle* and *nozzle*. But in others it was used to mark the physical object associated with a particular verb:

prickle	*spindle*	*spittle*	*treadle*

3 A handful of abstract words all inherited from Anglo-Norman. They include *participle, principle, syllable* (see further under **principal or principle** and **syllable**). The **-le** ending provides an alternative spelling for a few words ending in *el:* see **mantle or mantel**.

lead or led

Written down, the letters **lead** could be a noun meaning a heavy metal, or a verb meaning "conduct" – though the grammar of surrounding words usually leaves no doubt as to which is intended. What more often causes trouble is the fact that the past form of the verb **lead** is **led**, which sounds exactly the same as the noun. Confusion of sound and spelling has many a writer inadvertently putting **lead** where **led** was intended. It is a point to watch.

leaders

In older punctuation, **leaders** were the series of dots used singly or in groups to guide the eye across the page. They were used in the stub of a table, to draw readers to the right line within the columns, and to indicate empty cells in the table. These days an *em rule* is generally used to mark an empty cell.
◊ Compare **ellipsis**.

leading question

A **leading question** is one which foists its own assumptions on the person responding:
So you knew there were drugs in the refrigerator?
Thus a damaging piece of information is thrust into the discussion in the guise of a question. The question itself seeks a yes/no answer, and people being questioned like this can all-too-easily compromise themselves, whichever way they respond. The most notorious use of **leading questions** is in courts of law, although the defense lawyer is entitled to object to "leading" the witness or defendant in this way.

The term **leading question** is also used more loosely to refer to any embarrassing or pointed question. So a government minister being asked about a confidential decision may resist by saying "That's a leading question." Yet it wasn't, strictly speaking, unless the reporter's question embodied the very information it purported to seek.

leaf or page

See under **page**.

leafed or leaved

The choice between these is discussed under **-v-/-f-**.

leaflet

Paper-based publicity has been a force to reckon with since **leaflet** was first recorded as a noun in 1867. Almost a century later (1962) it takes on a new grammatical role as a verb, as in: *we are going to be leafleting thousands of people*. As in that example, the inflected forms do not require the final *t* to be doubled, and both *Webster's Third* (1986) and the *Oxford Dictionary* (1989) present them as *leafleting, leafleted*. The extra *t* sometimes seen in "leafletting" is superfluous: see further under **-t**.

leaned or leant

Leaned is to be preferred. It is the more regular form; and it avoids one of the possible problems with **leant** – being confused with *lent*, the past tense of *lend*. In fact **leaned** is the preferred spelling for the majority of British writers (more than 4:1 in the BNC) and for all American writers in CCAE. See further under **-ed** section 1.

leaped or leapt

Both spellings are used in American and British English, but the relativities work in opposite directions. In the US the more regular spelling **leaped** is commoner by a factor of 5:1, according to CCAE data. In British data from the BNC, **leapt** is ahead by a similar ratio. See further under **-ed** section 1.

learned or learnt

In English worldwide, **learned** is the commoner form, yet there's a substantial difference between

American and British. Database evidence shows that
the less regular **learnt** is as rare as hen's teeth in
American English, but an alternative to reckon with
in British. In BNC data the ratio between **learned** and
learnt is about 5:2. For the two-syllabled adjective of *a
learned man,* **learned** is of course the only possibility,
but its input to the BNC total for **learned** is slight. See
further under -**ed** section 1.

leary, leery or lairy
See **leery**.

lease, rent or hire
See **hire**.

leastways or leastwise
See under -**wise** or -**ways**.

Lebanon, the
See **the** section 4.

leery, leary or lairy
Three different words, all of slang origin, underlie
these spellings:

1 **leery** (or **leary**, rhyming with "weary") meaning
"knowing, sly"
2 **leery** (or **leary**, also rhyming with "weary")
meaning "distrustful"
3 **leery** (or **lairy**, rhyming with "hairy") meaning
"flashy [in dress]."

The first **leery** connects with **leer**, a verb/noun of
somewhat obscure origin, probably connected with
Old English *hleor* ("cheek"), suggesting a sideward
glance across the cheek that makes the beholder
uneasy. It implies knowing something of which the
beholder is innocent or unaware. This usage survives
only in colloquial expressions like *a leery grin,* of
which there are few examples in the BNC.

The second **leery** ("distrustful, wary") is widely
used in the US and first recorded there in the 1890s,
according to Barnhart (1987). But it seems to
complement the sense of the first **leery**, and
dictionaries usually present it as a questionable
extension of it. (See **reciprocal words** for other
examples where word senses can switch over.) **Leery**
in this second sense commonly appears in the phrase
leery of, and in a range of written styles in CCAE. Its
productivity can be seen in a growing range of
constructions in American English. Alongside *leery of*
we find *leery about,* and on rare occasions it's coupled
with *to* or *that* (i.e. a finite clause). Other developments
are to be seen in absolute constructions such as:

I was a little leery at first
... has a way of making you leery.
*While optimism about Brazil has never been
higher, some experts remain leery.*

Most uses (like all those noted so far) are predicative,
but there are very occasional attributive uses (see
adjectives section 1). Examples from CCAE include *a
leery attitude/the leery merchant,* and creative
compounds such as *the libel-leery editor* and
investment-leery companies. All this confirms that
leery is standard usage for American writers,
whereas in Britain it remains slang, and scarce in
BNC data.

The third **leery** originated in Cockney slang, and
has provided Australians with the noun *lair* ("a
flashily dressed young man"), and the verb *lair up*

("dress up in bad taste"). This use of **leery (lairy)** is
unknown in North America.

LeetSpeak or l33tsp34k
See under **SMS**.

Left and leftist
A capital *L* turns the common adjective **left** into a
broad term for those whose political persuasion runs
counter to the conservative establishment, either by
being more radical or more socialistic. This usage
derives ultimately from the arrangement of seats in
the French National Assembly, where the nobles sat
on the president's right, and the members of the third
estate (representatives of the common people) on the
left. The term **Left** has long since ceased to be simply
a term for the Opposition, since **leftist** governments
take office from time to time. But **Left/leftist** do still
seem to imply a dichotomy of the political scene,
which glosses over the specifics of the alternative
platform. **Leftist** first appeared in the 1920s, often
juxtaposed with "communist," which has tended to
demonize the word – apart from whatever linguistic
disadvantage it suffers through **Left** being the
antithesis of *Right.* The generalized negative still
seems to linger in political reports on how the *rightist
military fought the leftist opposition* (in Chile), or
Germany's *eco-leftist Greens.* The latter does at least
identify a more specific aspect of the **Left**'s position.
But free-handed use of **leftist** seems to go with
simplistic adversarial reporting of political situations
at home and overseas. The fact that **leftist** appears 4
to 5 times more often than *rightist* in CCAE and BNC
shows the asymmetry inherent in the use of such
words.

The **Left** (and *Right*) of politics are regularly
capitalized, whereas the *left/right wing* would not be,
according to the vast majority of respondents to the
Langscape survey (1998–2001). The derivatives **leftist**
(and *rightist*) do without them, as shown
overwhelmingly in data from CCAE and the BNC, and
in accordance with *New Oxford* (1998) and
Merriam-Webster's (2000).

legal, legalistic, legitimate or lawful
All four adjectives take the law as their starting point,
but their connotations are rather different. **Lawful** is
now rather formal and old-fashioned, being caught up
in fixed phrases such as *lawful wife* or *lawful business.*
It is often a reminder of traditional rights inscribed in
the common law of the land. **Legal** is much more
widely used to refer to any provision written into law
(e.g. *legal access*), where a frontier between what's
legal and *illegal* is being defined. Other general uses
of **legal** are its association with the administration
and profession of law, as in *a legal conference, a legal
issue.*

Legalistic has a negative coloring. It implies an
overemphasis on the letter of the law, and a narrow
interpretation of it, with too little attention to its
broader purpose or how people are affected by it.
Legitimate has as many uses outside the law as
within it. It can relate things to principles of logic and
reasoning, as in a *legitimate answer/argument/
conclusion;* and its legal uses mostly relate to
birthright, as in *legitimate child/heir.* For the use of
legitimate as a verb, see **legitimate, legitimize or
legitimatize**.

legislation or legislature

Both nouns relate to law-making. The **legislature** is the body which drafts and approves the laws of a country or state. In many Anglo-Saxon countries the **legislature** is bicameral, i.e. consists of two chambers. The British House of Commons and the House of Lords form the **legislature** in the UK; and in the US it's the House of Representatives and the Senate, which together make up the Congress. Canada has a House of Commons and a Senate, and Australia a House of Representatives and Senate. In the US, Canada and Australia, each state or province also has its own **legislature,** some of them bicameral, some unicameral. **Legislation** is a collective name for any act of law set up by one of the **legislatures.**

legitimate, legitimize or legitimatize

Dictionaries do not distinguish these verbs in terms of meaning, though their crossreferencing makes **legitimate** the key to them all. **Legitimate** is indeed the oldest of the three, dating from C16. But Fowler (1926) noted that it was being challenged by the other two, and *Webster's English Usage* (1989) notes the strength of **legitimize** since then. According to its sources **legitimize** has been about as common as **legitimate** (verb) since the 1970s. The trend has continued in the US, judging by the ratio of the two in CCAE, where **legitimize** outnumbers **legimate** by about 4:1. In the UK, the ratio is a little closer, judging by BNC data in which instances of **legitimize** (including *legitimise*) outnumber those of **legitimate** by more like 5:2. Neither database provides any examples of **legitimatize** or (*legitimatise*), which seems to have fallen by the wayside.

leitmotif, leitmotiv or leitmotive

See under **motif or motive.**

lemma

The plural of this word is discussed under **-a** section 1.

lend or loan

These are sometimes interchangeable, sometimes not. Only **lend** carries the figurative senses of adding or giving, as in *lend strength to the cause* or *lend color to an otherwise routine event.* But for other senses, as when property or money pass temporarily from one owner to another, either word could be used:

> *I'm happy to lend him my car.*
> *I'm happy to loan him my car.*

In American and Australian English, the verb **loan** is readily used as an alternative to **lend** in such applications – but not so much in contemporary British English. The word was used in Britain up to C17, but a curious resistance seems to have developed there during C18 and C19, when the *Oxford Dictionary* (1989) citations are all from the US, and the word somehow acquired provincial associations. Fowler (1926) noted that it had been "expelled" from southern British English, but that it was still used "locally in the UK." Yet Gowers writing after World War II found it returning to British government writing (1948, 1954), and weighs in against it in his 1965 edition of Fowler as a "needless variant" (1965). This seems to be the basis on which British usage commentators argue that **loan** must be used only as a noun (except in banking and finance), and **lend** as a verb. Some

British dictionaries (*Collins,* 1991) and the *Canadian Oxford* (1998) still echo the inhibition, while data from the BNC shows that many British writers are comfortable with it. Among hundreds of examples, anything from crockery to the machete, from a video to a recording studio can be *loaned* – even people such as the *schoolmaster to act as escort* or the *photographer from American Vogue.*

While **loan** as noun or verb can be standard usage for English writers in many places, **lend** is still largely restricted to a single (verb) role, at least in written English. In very colloquial conversation, it is also used as a noun, as in:

> *... if I can have a lend of his dishcloth to wipe my fingers*

But the BNC's handful of examples all come from spoken sources, and there are none in CCAE.

Just why some words can appear in *have a ...* constructions in standard usage, and others not, is quite arbitrary. (See further under **light verb.**) English allows many conversions of verbs into nouns (see **transfers**), yet there's still a stylistic question mark about **lend** as a noun. It seems especially odd when both **loan** and **lend** derive from the same Old English word for "loan," which was both a noun and a verb. **Lend** is a mutant of the older verb, formed in a southern dialect of Middle English, with a change of vowel and an extra consonant added on.

lengthways or lengthwise

See under **-wise or -ways.**

leniency or lenience

Fowler (1926) thought that there was a distinction opening up between these, with **lenience** referring to a *lenient action,* and **leniency** to a *lenient disposition.* But dictionaries do not support this, and simply juxtapose them or crossreference one to the other as equivalents. *New Oxford* (1998) and *Canadian Oxford* (1998) give priority to **lenience,** whereas in *Merriam-Webster's* (2000) and the Australian *Macquarie* (1997) it's **leniency.** The database evidence points to international convergence on **leniency,** which is used in more than 90% of instances of the word in both CCAE and the BNC.
◊ For differences in other pairs like this, see **-nce/-ncy.**

lesbian or Lesbian

The use of this term to refer to a female homosexual goes back to 1890, and for decades it was written as **Lesbian,** showing its origins as a geographical adjective, meaning "of or from the Greek island of Lesbos." (Why Lesbos? It was the home of the ancient Greek poet Sappho, who surrounded herself with a circle of women who were said to have engaged in homosexual practices.) Dictionaries everywhere now list the word without a capital letter, and **lesbian** is the only form of the common noun in data from BNC and CCAE.

less or lesser

The difference between these has exercised many a language watcher. **Less** is a comparative form of *little,* which makes **lesser** with *-er* a kind of double comparative. Both can appear before nouns, and older dictionaries classified both primarily as adjectives. Contemporary grammars distinguish more effectively between them, classing **less** as a determiner and pronoun, as well as adverb (see **determiners**).

Less serves as determiner in examples like *less exposure* or *less demand for premium beef,* where it means "smaller in amount." This is uncontentious, whereas its use to mean "fewer in number," as in *there were less objections,* is still contended, despite being common in informal English (see **fewer or less**). Like many determiners, **less** is also a pronoun, as in *less of a problem.* Its other major role is as comparative adverb, and so it can modify adjectives (*a less negative reaction*), other adverbs (*less rapidly*) and verbs (*worried less than before*).

Lesser is almost exclusively an adjective, meaning "smaller in status, significance or importance." This is its meaning in *a lesser god* and *the lesser demands of the weekend,* as well as *Lesser men would have rushed for the exit.* Very occasionally **lesser** works as the adverb in compound adjectives: *the lesser known town of Okayama.* Note that it's not strictly necessary to hyphenate such adjectives because the *-er* ending (like *-ly*) ensures correct reading of the compound: see further under **hyphens** section 2c.

-less

This suffix, meaning "without or lacking," is the formative element in many an adjective. It is enshrined in clichéd phrases such as *bottomless pit* and *a hopeless case,* and in paired adjectives like *cheerless/cheerful* and *graceless/graceful* which pinpoint the absence or presence of something. Note however that some such "pairs" no longer pair up exactly in meaning.

faithless (not keeping faith)	*faithful* (loyal)
pitiless (showing no pity)	*pitiful* (calling for sympathy)
shameless (having no scruples)	*shameful* (very regrettable)
soulless (inhuman)	*soulful* (with deep feeling)

Not all **-less** adjectives have counterparts in *-ful.* Ones like *fatherless, headless, homeless, toothless* and *wireless* (originally an adjective) show how **-less** highlights an abnormal state of affairs, and we do not need a *-ful* adjective to describe the normal state of having a father, a head or teeth. Note also that a very small number of **-less** adjectives are based on verbs rather than nouns, e.g. *ceaseless, tireless,* and they too have no counterparts ending in *-ful.*

lest

In the US, **lest** has been in continuous standard use through to the present day. In the UK it was on the stylistic margins in mid-C20, as shown by parallel databases of the 1960s, where it was five times more common in American than British English. It probably was "formal or archaic" then, as the *Comprehensive Grammar* (1985) declared. But BNC data from the 1990s shows a sea change in the UK, with hundreds of examples of **lest** from a variety of written texts. So its stylistic status in British and American English is much the same at the start of C21.

Lest appears in two kinds of construction, to express:
1 a fear of some kind:
> *... anxious lest Mitzi upset coffee over them both*
> *... feared to probe too deeply lest it should be disillusioned*

> *... worried lest pushing things too far led to quotas*
2 a negative purpose
> *Liberal commitment must also be tested, lest it become an orthodoxy.*
> *... passed the elephant house lest the irreverent onlooker should make comparisons*
> *... declined to give his view lest the debate became a test of loyalty*

The three examples of each show constructions with (i) the (present) subjunctive, (ii) the modal *should,* and (iii) the (past) indicative, which are found in that order of frequency in BNC examples. The modals *might* and *would* are sometimes used instead of *should.* The use of the present subjunctive with **lest** is one of the several constructions in which it has apparently revived in British English at the turn of the millennium (see **subjunctive**).

In American English **lest** is used to express negative purposes and fears or concerns, just like those illustrated above. The CCAE data is however remarkable in that there are many examples where **lest** begins a sentence:
> *Lest anyone think that ...*
> *Lest it be assumed that ...*

This very prominent use of **lest** might help to explain the idea that the conjunction is more American than British. At any rate such caveats are commonplace in ordinary American newspaper writing, whether or not they sound formal to British ears. But if **lest** seems to come up too often, writers can always vary it with *in case* to express a negative purpose or condition. See further under **in case.**

let us or let's

The difference between these is largely a question of formality, as often with contractions. Compare the ceremonious *Let us pray* with the informal *Let's pray for rain.* The uncontracted **let us** is useful in formal documents when writers want to maintain an authoritative tone while involving readers in the discussion:
> *Let us now turn to the issue of accountability.*
Compare *Let's now turn to ...,* which minimizes the distance between writer and reader.

Let us and **let's** both invite readers to join the writer in the activity proposed, i.e. they involve you and us. This sets them apart from similar constructions exemplified in *Do let us pay our way,* where let stands as an independent verb meaning "allow," and *us* does not mean "you" as well. The *us* in such a construction cannot be contracted without changing the meaning. Compare *Do let's pay our way.*

The pronoun used after *let* is always an object pronoun. In **let us** this is obvious, but not so much in *Let George and us decide.* Speakers are sometimes tempted to use *Let George and we decide,* thus changing the construction in midstream.

In its negative form this idiom becomes either *Let us not (go into that), Let's not (go into that)* or *Don't let's (go into that).* Once again they represent degrees of formality. The first has a slightly rhetorical flavor, which might be suitable for a formal document. The second is broadly useful for writing and conversation. The third is definitely chatty. *Webster's English Usage* (1989) notes also *let's don't* as an American variant, though it goes with spoken rather than written discourse.

letter writing

The questions asked about **letter writing** often focus on format and the formalities. Those things need attention but are really secondary to what the writer actually says and does through a letter. They are the primary substance of communication, through which a relationship is set up or fine-tuned.

Letters are one of the few writing mediums in which you normally communicate with a single individual, either an acquaintance, or someone with a particular role. What you write in personal letters is a way of maintaining a particular relationship, whether intimate or more distant.

When corresponding in the name of an institution to an unknown person, ideally you're also establishing a basis for good relations with them. Institutional letters need to be positive in their tone as far as possible, and to offer a constructive exchange of information or points of view. Avoid correspondence clichés and stereotyped phrasing (see further under **commercialese**). Correspondence which sounds like a form letter (or something drafted by a machine) is liable to alienate the reader.

Letter formats matter most for institutional letters. For personal letters, do as you please, guided only by the level of formality in the relationship. But with institutional letters there are format decisions to make, such as whether to use semiblocked or blocked presentation, and open or closed punctuation. Both these types are illustrated in Appendix VII. The blocked presentation with open punctuation requires fewest keystrokes and is therefore the most cost-effective. Starting everything at the left-hand margin is easy to explain and implement. Yet questions about the look and readability of the letter also arise, especially in longer letters with extended narrative or discussion. Letter writers can and should adapt the standard blocked format in the interests of clear and attractive communication.

The conventions for beginning a letter are also set out in Appendix VII. The salutation itself varies according to whether or not you know the recipient's name. (See **forms of address** section 2.) The closing for most institutional letters these days is "Yours sincerely." It can be used in any situation where the addressee is named in the salutation, and even when that person can only be addressed through their role ("Dear Manager" etc.). "Yours faithfully" is used only when the sender particularly wants to maintain a formal distance from the person addressed, and to emphasize that the correspondence is a matter of duty. See further under **Yours faithfully**.

letters as words

How to set isolated letters in print raises some questions, because they're very slight, especially in lower case. Italics are recognized as the most effective device by the *Chicago Manual* (2003), despite the occasional use of roman. Usually the roman is supplemented by something else. *Copy-editing* (1992) notes the practice of using roman with inverted commas round the letter, and certainly "g" is more distinctive than just g. Whenever the letter is made plural, an apostrophe inserted before the *s* serves instead of inverted commas, and this too makes the roman acceptable, as in "dotting the i's and crossing the t's." Yet even the apostrophe is unnecessary if

italics are used and the plural *s* itself is in roman, as in:

> *Dotting your i*s *and crossing your t*s.

Upper case letters take care of themselves in roman:

> *She had a curious record of three* As *and two* Fs.

Other conventions with single letters:

* the letters used for enumerating a series may be either italics (*a*) (*b*) (*c*) or roman (a) (b) (c)
* when indicating musical notes, a roman capital is used: *middle C, the key of D minor*. In the US, *major* and *minor* key signatures are sometimes distinguished by the use of upper case for the first and lower case for the second (*Chicago Manual*). The practice is rare in the UK (*Oxford Guide to Style*, 2002).
* letters used to represent hypothetical parties in a discussion or points in a description are capitalized, as in:
  > *If A sues B for breach of contract . . .*
  > *Let C be a point midway on the hypotenuse.*
* letters used to designate shapes are capitalized, as in:
  > *an I-beam   a J-curve   a U-turn*
  > *a V-shaped valley*

For the printing of initials in personal names, and the punctuation associated with them, see under **names**.

leukemia or leukaemia

Despite the traditional British/American divide on the use of the *ae* digraph (see **ae/e**), almost a third of the British respondents to the 1998–2001 Langscape survey voted for **leukemia**. Their vote constituted 31% of the more than 700 British responses, showing the way of the future. The *New Oxford* (1998) gives them equal status as headwords (**leukaemia or leukemia**). The American preference is unequivocally in favor of **leukemia**, backed by 94% of respondents to the Langscape survey. In Canada **leukemia** is also standard, according to the *Canadian Oxford* (1998). Australians meanwhile partake of the British duality, and **leukaemia** is made equal with **leukemia** (in that order) in the *Macquarie Dictionary* (1997).

leveled or levelled

The choice between these is discussed at **-l-/-ll-**.

levy and levee

These represent the same underlying French and Latin root *lev-* ("raise/rise"), borrowed into English for quite distinct purposes. **Levy** borrowed in C15 was the tax or manpower raised by government decree. The more French-looking **levee** was used in C17 English to mean a reception held by the king while he got up and was dressed for the morning. It was strictly for men, and this is still central to the word, though the court reception it refers to is now in the early afternoon. Quite independently, **levee** was borrowed into C18 American English, for the embankment raised along a river either by human efforts or natural processes. It is known but little used in Britain. In the BNC, examples of **levee** in the geological sense are confined to two texts – apart from a sprinkling of references to the Led Zeppelin composition "When the Levee Breaks." All three words are pronounced the same way, stressing the first syllable.

lexical verb

This is another name for the *main verb* of a clause. See under **auxiliary verbs**.

liable, likely and apt (to)

The meaning of **liable** varies according to the preposition following it: *for* or *to*. *Liable for* is a legal and quasi-legal phrase meaning "financially responsible for." *Liable to* is everyday English meaning "given to," as in *liable to fainting fits;* and also "likely to," as in *liable to go brittle*. Note that its use overlaps with *likely to*, but that *liable to* normally refers to a negative event as a general possibility, whereas *likely to* predicts either good or bad events on the strength of a specific past event. Compare for example:

> *That horse is likely to win tomorrow's race.*
> *In the pack that horse is liable to bolt.*

Apt to followed by a verb provides a usable alternative for many contexts, not just the colloquial:

> *Employers are apt to underestimate the value of direct discussion . . .*
> *Unorthodoxies are apt to creep in from below.*

The idea that *apt to* can only be used of people is not borne out by BNC evidence, where about a third of all instances have inanimate subjects, like the second example above.

libeled or libelled

The choice between these is discussed under -l-/-ll-.

libelous or libellous

According to the *Oxford Dictionary* (1989) record, this word has been spelled **libellous** since C17, and it continues as standard British English. Writers represented in the BNC prefer it by more than 10:1. But in American English **libelous** is the primary spelling, according to *Webster's Third* (1986), and it carries the day in CCAE by more than 100:1. The spelling **libelous** better represents both pronunciation (stress on the first syllable) and the word's origins in English (*libel* + *-ous*). See further under -l-/-ll-.

liberality, liberalism or Liberalism

These three nouns all express different aspects of the adjective **liberal**: its material, intellectual and political manifestations. At bottom the word embodies the Latin root for "free," so that it can imply being free and generous with your goods (**liberality**), or being open-minded in your thinking and seeking to avoid imposing your own values and principles on others (**liberalism**). The latter meaning is theoretically the basis of political **Liberalism** – a noninterventionist style of government. The capital *L* is always used when alluding to the policy of Liberal parties, past or present, in Britain, Australia or Canada.

libertine or libertarian

Both words have to do with freedom. But while **libertines** vote it all in their own direction and allow themselves every sexual licence, a **libertarian** argues for the rights of others to express themselves as they choose. In theological contexts a **libertarian** is one who maintains the doctrine of free will.

libretto

For the plural of this word, see **Italian plurals**.

license or licence

In British English, the choice between these spellings is a matter of grammar. The verb is **license**, as in *licensed to drive a truck,* while **licence** is the noun: *a driving licence* (see further under **driving licence**). In American English, **license** is used whatever the grammatical role, and it outnumbers **licence** by about 150:1 in data from CCAE. Australian usage is in line with British, while Canadian is somewhat mixed – sometimes using **license** for the noun (*Canadian English Usage*, 1997), while **licence** is also used for the verb, according to the *Canadian Oxford* (1998).

The advantage of using **license** across the board is clear when the verb is used adjectivally, as in *licensed premises*. At that point other Englishes are quite unsure whether this is a verb or a noun derivative. (It could be seen as based on the noun *licence* plus *-ed* [see under **-ed** section 2], which would justify *licenced premises*.) In fact most British writers plump for *licensed premises* rather than *licenced premises*. The first reigns supreme in written texts in the BNC.

licenser or licensor

For the choice between these, see under **-er/-or**. Either way it's based on the verb form – on which see previous entry.

licorice or liquorice

The spelling of this dark confectionery is still rather unsettled. The *Oxford Dictionary* (1989) lists eighteen different spellings for it since C14, none of which is exactly **licorice** or **liquorice**. Common pronunciation still has the final sound as "sh," and this shows in most of *Oxford*'s older spellings. Yet modern English has it as either **licorice** or **liquorice**, American dictionaries preferring the first, and British ones the second. Contemporary corpus data show an almost absolute divide, with 100% of American writers in CCAE using **licorice** and about 90% of BNC writers using **liquorice**. The *Canadian Oxford* (1998) and the Australian *Macquarie Dictionary* (1997) side with *Merriam-Webster*'s (2000) in giving preference to **licorice**.

The spelling **liquorice** embodies folk etymology – a spurious connection with *liquor*. The word was originally Greek *glycyrrhiza* meaning "sweet root," which became *liquiritia* in medieval Latin and *licorice* in Old French.

lie or lay

The reason why people confuse these verbs is clear enough when you set their principal parts side by side:

lie (1)	"tell lies"	lied (past tense)	lied (past participle)
lie (2)	"be in a horizontal position"	lay	lain
lay	"put, place, set down"	laid	laid

The different meanings of **lie** (1) and **lie** (2) keep them apart. But **lie** (2) and **lay** overlap in meaning and form, the past tense of one being identical with the present of the other.

The essential difference between **lie** (2) and **lay** is that **lay** takes an object, i.e. you "lay something." See for example:

It lays eggs.
They lay the groundwork for the future.
In grammatical terms **lay** is a transitive verb, whereas **lie** (2) is intransitive – doesn't take an object (see further under **transitive**). Without that point they are not easy to separate. Compare:
They lay the groundwork for the future (= **lay** transitive, present tense)
They lay on the ground while bullets whistled overhead (= **lie** intransitive, past tense)
The transitive/intransitive distinction and the difference in tense serve to distinguish the two uses of **lay**.

Despite these grammatical distinctions, the colloquial trend is to use **lay** (and *laid*) where conventional grammar would have **lie** (and *lay/lain*). It happens in the present tense with the casual
If you lay down for a while. . .
instead of
If you lie down for a while
In the past tense, the colloquial *They laid on the ground* comes up instead of *They lay on the ground*. For the past participle you'll often hear *I had just laid down when the phone rang*, rather than *I had just lain down when the phone rang*. In fact *lain* has been falling into disuse since C18. The grammarian Campbell corrects *laid* to *lain* in the 1770s, attributing the mistake to French influence. Whatever the cause, the use of *lain* has steadily contracted since then. In standard C20 databases of 1 million words of British and American English (LOB and Brown), it occurred only 6 times in the first and not at all in the second. *Lain* survives now only in the most formal or literary style, and *been lying (down)* takes its place in everyday prose.

The use of **lay** as the present of **lie** (and *laid* instead of **lay** [past] and *lain*) is common in casual talk in all English-speaking countries. Yet the standard forms **lie/lay** are still expected in the written medium – certainly in edited writing. We may speculate on when the pressure of usage will allow their replacements (**lay**/*laid*) to prevail in writing; but for the moment they remain markers of colloquial style. In the longer run they spell the doom of **lie** (2).

lie of the land or lay of the land
See **lay of the land**.

ligatures
A **ligature** is a written or printed character which embodies more than one letter. They come from two sources. In the earliest printing fonts, a small weak letter was often cast with a taller one to ensure that it stood in place during the printing process. **Ligatures** of *c* and *t* (ct) or *s* and *t* (st) were still quite common in C18. The other source of **ligatures** was the special vowels of Latin in which *a* and *e* or *o* and *e* were joined as a single character, although Fowler argued against them (see further under **ae/e**). In modern typesetting, two- or three-letter **ligatures** are occasionally used, as for *ff, fi, fl, ffi, ffl*.
◊ Compare **digraph**.

light verb
Verbs like *take, have, make, do* and especially *give* are the staple of many ordinary idioms such as

have/take a guess	*make a start*
do a run	*give a nudge*

In such constructions the **light verb** (sometimes called *delexical verb*) has little inherent meaning. It simply registers the fact of the action (and its present or past tense), while the particular action is expressed via the noun – which is itself a transferred verb (see further under **transfers**). The noun is almost always prefaced by *a*. Some constructions are found with both *have* and *take*, like the example above, and in such cases British English is more inclined to *have* and American to *take*, according to the *Comprehensive Grammar* (1985). In Algeo's research (1995) the difference proved to be a matter of relative frequency rather than an absolute divide.

lighted or lit
These are alternative forms for two different verbs:
1 **light** "ignite" or "illuminate," based on the noun *light*
2 **light** "get down [from a horse, vehicle]" or "land [on]"/ "hit upon," based on the adjective *light*.
Both verbs date back to Old English, and are among the few regular ones that have developed irregular parts in modern English (see section 9 of **irregular verbs**). **Lighted** was the original past form in each case, which was challenged by **lit** in early modern English, in C16 for **light** (1), and in C17/C18 for **light** (2). In modern use **lit** has overtaken **lighted**, though in differing degrees in different places.
Overall the use of **lit** outweighs **lighted** by about 2:1 in American data from CCAE, whereas in the BNC the ratio is more like 10:1. Despite its dwindling numbers, there are citations for **lighted** in all the same uses as **lit**:
light (1)
verb past: *the tramp might have lighted (lit) a fire*
past participle: *the windows were lighted (lit)*
attributive: *with lighted (lit) cigarettes*
verb figurative: *her pale uninteresting face lighted (lit) up*
light (2)
verb figurative: *the author has lighted (lit) on important new material*
But in BNC data the two forms are neck and neck only for that last construction, where *lighted on* and *lit upon* seem to be the preferred collocations – perhaps for reasons of rhythm. Otherwise **lit** prevails in the numbers stakes by huge margins.
Americans are comfortable with either **lighted** or **lit** in all constructions, and likewise Canadians (*Canadian English Usage*, 1997). Australians agree for the attributive use (Peters, 1995), but they prefer **lit** when the word is part of the verb phrase.
Lit has taken over in some compound verbs. Database evidence shows *floodlit* to be strongly preferred in both British and American English; and *spotlit* has a comfortable edge over *spotlighted* in the BNC. However in American data from CCAE, *spotlighted* dominates, and *highlighted* is preferred overwhelmingly in both databases. The verb *moonlight* uses *moonlit* and *moonlighted* for the different senses of the word (the literal and the figurative). See **moonlight**.

lightning or lightening
The word **lightning** has been associated with the enormously bright discharge of electricity in the sky since C14. It originated from the verb *lighten* ("light

up"), and was still occasionally spelled with an *e* until C18. Nowadays it's still sometimes pronounced as if the *e* were there; but the absence of *e* in **lightning** helps to differentiate it from words derived from either of the two verbs spelled as *lighten* (*lighten* [1] "make brighter" and *lighten* [2] "reduce the weight of"). Compare:

> *Thunder and lightning marked the change of season.*
> *Fireworks lightening the sky were seen miles away.*
> *Some way of lightening their load must be found.*

likable or likeable

See under **-eable**.

like

Like is arguably the most versatile four-letter word in the English language. Or rather, it's the coincidence of two words, one of which is the root of the verb "be favorably inclined to" and the associated noun, as in *their likes and dislikes*. The other **like** ("similar(ly)") is the source of the adjective, adverb, preposition, conjunction, and a noun found in set phrases: *the like, the likes of* (see **like[s]**). **Like** also serves as an interjection or pause-filler for some hesitant speakers: *I wanted, like, to come and help.* For younger English-speakers in both the US and the UK (Levey, 2003), **like** has also become a device for quoting someone's words, as in *He's like "Who do you think you are!"* which is beginning to be recognized in C21 dictionaries. But for writers, the main issues with **like** are its roles as preposition and conjunction, which have been the focus of persistent usage critiques.

1 Like as a preposition. While there are no strictly grammatical objections to using **like** as a preposition, concerns about its potential ambiguity have made it untouchable for some. The problem turns on a perceived difference between the use of **like**:

a) in idioms and similes such as *writes like an angel, built like a tank,* where **like** is said to indicate "resemblance," and

b) when it introduces an example or two, as in *great artists like Rembrandt* or *everyday chores like shopping and housework.*

Yet usage commentators are hard put to find serious examples of ambiguity between these uses of **like** (Burchfield, 1996); and even the more conservative American commentators (Follett, 1966; Bernstein, 1971) are disinclined to worry about it. In fact both uses establish a kind of archetype, the first by reference to the verb phrase, the second to a noun phrase. Distinguished thus by their grammar, there's no problem in their both using **like** – and no need to paraphrase the first with "as" and the second with "such as", as is sometimes recommended. The results of intervention can produce odd and misleading expressions as in "cleans itself as a cat" and "delicate problems as this are pivotal," noted in *Webster's English Usage* (1989). **Like** would be preferable in each case.

On the stylistic front, **like** requires some care in comparative statements, to ensure that the items being compared are properly paralleled. The first sentence in the following pair achieves this, but not the second:

> *Like Jane Austen, he creates characters from real life.*
> *Like Jane Austen, his characters are created from real life.*

Author is compared with author in the first, tightly worded sentence, whereas the second is loosely constructed and oblique in its comparison. Note also that when the comparison centres on a negative statement, the position of the phrase with **like** affects the meaning. See for example:

> *Like Raymond, he would never react.*
> *He would never react like Raymond.*

The first sentence is about no reaction at all, whereas the second is about a particular kind of reaction. The **like** phrase in the second affects the scope of the negative. See further under **negatives** section 2.

Comparisons with *unlike* raise the same issues as **like**, especially when linked with a negative statement:

> *Unlike his predecessor, Rick didn't want a huge office.*

Sentences like that are an obstacle course for the reader. (See further under **double negatives**.)

2 The use of like as a conjunction develops quite naturally out of its role as a preposition. Compare:

> *The dogs were howling like wolves to the moon.*
> *The dogs were howling like wolves do to the moon.*

We accept the parallel roles of preposition and conjunction with other words such as *before, since, than,* so why not **like**? Shakespeare did not shrink from using **like** as a conjunction, nor did other writers up to and including Darwin. The *Oxford Dictionary* (1884–1928) noted that **like** was used as conjunction by "many recent writers of standing," in spite of being "generally condemned as vulgar or slovenly." The evidence of its use abounds. Grammarian Otto Jespersen (1909–49) listed examples from well-published C20 writers such as Wells, Shaw and Maugham. The BNC provides hundreds of examples from written sources of the 1990s. Yet smaller British dictionaries such as *Collins* (1997) and *New Oxford* (1998) still keep conjunctive **like** at arms' length, with the label "informal" or "unacceptable in formal English." In American English it's widely used, and there are thousands of examples in CCAE data from both high- and lower-brow newspapers as well as novels and conversation. American dictionaries record it with no restrictive label. Elsewhere the reaction is mixed. Canadians find it somewhat informal, according to *Canadian English Usage* (1997); but the Australian response is more accommodating. It turns up in various kinds of Australian nonfiction as well as fiction (Peters, 1995), and is only conspicuous by its absence from academic and bureaucratic prose. The climate of opinion is still the chief variable, rather than different degrees of use in different places.

Among the various constructions with **like**, Burchfield (1996) thought that some were more acceptable than others – that its use to mean "(just) as" was better established in the UK than "as if." Examples of each from the BNC are:

a) *I would wear a dhoti like they do in India.*
b) *He starts giving out detentions like they were past their sell-by date.*

The "as if" meaning is frequently blended with copular verbs such as *look, feel, sound:*

> *It hardly looks like they tiptoed.*
> *My legs felt like they had been welded together.*
> *Should they sound like they have sand in them?*

The BNC contains hundreds of examples of these constructions, making "as if" the commonest sense of conjunctive **like** in British English, as in American (Peters, 1995).

With all this evidence of conjunctive use, **like** seems to have regained much of the ground lost to prescriptivist objections of C19 and C20. They were not in fact endorsed by Fowler (1926), who distanced himself from condemnation at the start with "if it is a misuse at all." He invites "the reader who has no instinctive objection to the construction [to] decide whether he shall consent to use it in talk, in print, in both or in neither." There never was a general principle as to why **like** could not be used conjunctively, and it is now strongly supported by corpus data from around the English-speaking world. Fowler would have smiled.

-like

For a thousand years and more, this English suffix has been used to create adjectives which express similarity with something or someone named. For example:

> businesslike childlike craterlike godlike
> ladylike lifelike statesmanlike warlike

Established words with **-like** are normally set solid, whereas ad hoc formations are usually hyphenated:

> a rock-like resistance
> a home of mansion-like proportions

Note that some words ending in **-like** have counterparts ending in *-ly*, witness *godlike/godly*, *statesmanlike/statesmanly*. In such pairs the one with **-like** is more literal and neutral in its meaning, while the one with *-ly* is more figurative and commendatory. ◊ Compare **-ish**.

likeable or likable

See under **-eable**.

likelihood or likeliness

These abstract nouns for the adjective *likely* both originated in C14, but **likelihood** seems to have prevailed in C18, when the *Oxford Dictionary*'s (1989) record for **likeliness** ends. That isn't quite the end of the story, since **likeliness** makes a couple of rare appearances in the BNC and CCAE. But **likelihood** is a thousand times more common in modern English.

like(s)

Phrases such as *the like* or *the likes of* which use the comparative noun **like(s)** are stylistically marked one way or another. *The like* serves as a rather formal alternative to *etc.*, as in *the guaranteed incomes of doctors, lawyers, and the like.* By contrast, *the likes of* appears in informal or off-handed references to a person or persons:

> She won't look at the likes of me.
> . . . small-fry agitation from the likes of the progress association

likewise

As an adverb this can mean either "similarly" or "also." The two uses are illustrated in:

> We ask you to do likewise.
> Ted and his comrades were got rid of, likewise Tony and his.

The second usage makes **likewise** an additive word, and from there it is only a small step to becoming a full conjunction:

> You don't have to play tennis to suffer from tennis elbow, likewise carpal tunnel is not caused by vibrating hand tools.

Purists object to this, as they do to allowing conjunctive use of other connective adverbs such as *however, plus, therefore* (see **conjunctions** section 2). The problem is easily averted with the help of a semicolon, as in:

> You don't have to play tennis to suffer from tennis elbow; likewise carpal tunnel is not caused by vibrating hand tools.

Either a semicolon or a full stop (followed by a capital letter) makes unobjectionable grammar there. That so much should hang on the punctuation mark makes it a fine point indeed.

limy or limey

See under **-y/-ey**.

linage or lineage

Both spellings are used for the (two-syllabled) printer's word meaning "number of lines printed on a page," but **linage** is greatly to be preferred. It is the more regular spelling (see **-e** section 1). It also avoids a clash with the quite independent word **lineage** with three syllables, meaning "ancestry or descent".

line

For the choice between *waiting on line* and *waiting in line*, see under **on-line**.

line breaks

The end of the line often comes up inconveniently, requiring breaks within words or strings of numbers. Principles for the division of words at the ends of lines are described under **wordbreaks**, and those for numbers under **numbers and number style** section 1. See also **turnover or runover lines**. ◊ For the question of where to divide long internet addresses, see under **URL**.

liney or liny

See under **-y/-ey**.

lingua franca

This Italian phrase refers to a hybrid and usually restricted language (with small vocabulary and syntactic resources), which is used for communication between people who do not understand each other's native language. The expression means "Frankish tongue," though the original "lingua franca" embodied elements of Italian, French, Spanish, Greek, Arabic and Turkish, and was used for trade purposes in the ports of the eastern Mediterranean. It has since been applied to trading languages, and pidgins all over the world. (See further under **pidins and creoles**.)

Lingua franca is also used simply to refer to any language which serves as a common medium for communication, as in:

> Latin was the lingua franca of European scholars until the seventeenth century.

Those with a knowledge of Italian may pluralize **lingua franca** as **lingue franche**, but its normal plural in English is **lingua francas**.

linguist

This word was first used in English (in 1550) to mean "someone who speaks a number of languages," and for many people this is still the only meaning. Almost anyone with a facility for languages can be a **linguist** in this sense. The other meaning of **linguist** is very strongly associated with *linguistics* (= the systematic study of language), and **linguists** of this kind are usually professionals or specialists in the field. The word **linguist** was used occasionally this way in earlier centuries, but the usage has only become common with the growth of the subject in C20.

linking verbs

See **copular verbs**.

liquefy or liquify

See **liquify/liquefy**.

liqueur or liquor

The first word **liqueur** is much more specialized. It refers to the sweet, flavored spirit often drunk – along with coffee – at the end of a meal: *coffee and liqueurs*. The second word **liquor** is the general word for spirits and for alcoholic drink, as in *He can't hold his liquor*. In technical uses in industrial and pharmaceutical chemistry **liquor** normally refers to special solutions, although in brewing it's simply water.

    Liquor is centuries old in English. For Chaucer it was *licour*, but was respelled as **liquor** in C16 to show its Latin ancestry. **Liqueur** is the French form of the same Latin word, borrowed into English in C18.

liquidate or liquidize

The verb **liquidate** has only a figurative connection with *liquid*. In political contexts, it has sinister overtones as a euphemism for "execute" or "wipe out":

    Dissidents were all liquidated or driven into exile.
This usage is believed to have come from the equivalent Russian word "likvidirovat." The first English use of the word in this sense dates from the 1920s, after the turbulent years of revolution. The financial uses of **liquidate** are much older, dating from C16. They relate to *liquidity* rather than *liquid*, whether the procedure referred to is to "settle or pay [a debt]," "convert into cash" or "reduce [accounts] to order by deducing the amount owed or due." The more recent **liquidize** (or **liquidise**), coined in C19, has a direct connection with *liquid* and means "turn into liquid form." It's often associated with food preparation, when the recipe instructs you to:

    Liquidize the carrots and add them to the soup.
In scientific and industrial processes, **liquidize** is replaced by **liquefy/liquify**.

liquify or liquefy

Though dictionaries all give first preference to **liquefy**, **liquify** is a common alternative spelling in both British and American sources. See further under -ify/-efy.

liquor or liqueur

See **liqueur**.

liquorice or licorice

See **licorice**.

lists

Setting out a **list** always calls for some decisions. First of all, should it be set out horizontally or vertically? The two systems entail different punctuation practices, and details of layout are an issue with *vertical lists* but not *horizontal lists*. In both, but especially in *vertical lists*, it's important that the items listed are parallel in their wording, and that a consistent style is maintained all through.

1 Horizontal lists are best suited for items that consist of one or two words. Those in the **list** following vary somewhat, and are close to the limits of what can be comfortably presented along the line:

    There are seven major newspapers in Australia:
    the Adelaide Advertiser, The Age, *the* Australian,
    the Brisbane Courier-Mail, *the* Canberra Times,
    the Sydney Morning Herald, *and the* West
    Australian.
(For questions about the serial comma there, see under **comma**.) Such a **list** could be preceded by abbreviations *e.g., i.e., viz.,* or the words that paraphrase them, prefaced by a comma (see **e.g.**). But there's no punctuation at all when the **list** is the object or complement of the preceding verb, as in: *Australia's seven major newspapers are the Adelaide* Advertiser, The Age, *the* Australian, *the Brisbane* Courier-Mail . . .

    The commas separating the items in those **lists** could be replaced by semicolons. Semicolons are essential when you need two grades of punctuation in a **list**, as in the following:

    Australia's major newspapers are as follows: in
    NSW, the Sydney Morning Herald; *in Queensland,*
    the Brisbane Courier-Mail; *in Victoria,* The Age.
(See further under **semicolon**.)

2 Vertical lists can be used for both shorter and longer items, and are generally necessary for the latter. They are much more often used in nonfiction than fiction or essays, so the decision to turn a set of items into a *vertical list* depends also on the genre. In informative (or instructional) writing, that **list** of newspapers could very well be presented vertically for ease of reference. In electronic documents designed for screen-reading, vertical listing is encouraged to promote scannability (see **digital style**).

There are seven major newspapers in Australia:
* *Adelaide* Advertiser
* The Age
* *Australian*
* *Brisbane* Courier-Mail
* Canberra Times
* Sydney Morning Herald
* West Australian

Note the introductory colon preceding the **list**, and the absence of punctuation in the **list** itself, particularly when the items are prefaced by bullets. However a semicolon is conventionally placed after each item (and a full stop after the last one) when the items listed have internal punctuation or are substantial parts of sentences:

    Australia's major metropolitan newspapers are as
follows:
    in NSW, Sydney Morning Herald;
    in Queensland, Courier-Mail;
    in South Australia, the Advertiser;
    in Victoria, The Age;
    in Western Australia, the West Australian.
The **list** also shows how the repetition of a small word ("in") can serve as a listing device. In the same way

"to" is often used to preface each of a set of objectives. The items do not need to be capitalized.

Numbers and/or letters give more specific enumeration to a *vertical list,* as in the example below. They may be used alternately to distinguish the headings, subheadings etc.:

> *Australia's metropolitan newspapers are as follows:*
> 1. *Victoria*
>   a) The Age
>   b) Herald-Sun
> 2. *New South Wales*
>   a) Sydney Morning Herald
>   b) Telegraph-Mirror

Note that a closing bracket is all that's needed with the enumerators in a *vertical list,* whereas they must be enclosed in a pair of brackets in a *horizontal list.* (See **brackets** section 1a.) The items in any *vertical list* should be worded in parallel, as in the second **list** above where each item begins with "in" and the name of a state. The **list** is then much easier to read. Nonconforming items need to be reworded to match up with the rest (so as to make them all verbs, or all nouns preceded by "the," etc.). Consistency of wording in a *vertical list* is as important as consistency in the enumeration or punctuation.

◊ For the styling and setting of more extended *vertical lists,* see **numbers and number style** sections 6 and 7.
◊ For information about the indenting of items and runover lines, see *hanging indention* under **indents.**

lit or lighted
See **lighted.**

lite
This 1950s respelling of *light* has found a useful role for itself in identifying low-fat or low-sugar foods, and low-calorie drinks, especially *lite beer*. **Lite** also appears as a kind of suffix to refer to products that are lighter in weight than the standard: hence the types of footware named *Trek Lite, Tennis Lite*. Cutdown versions of software packages identify themselves in the same way: *NetWare Lite, Z-Mail Lite*.

In North American English **lite** also has a generic role in referring to things deemed light-weight in terms of content and investment, as in references to the space program, where ... *shuttle "lean" is in danger of becoming shuttle "lite"* – *threatening the safety of the entire shuttle program*. The phrase *News Lite* expresses concern about the excess of "soft news" i.e. personal news used to fill news programs, and the juxtaposition of *lite beer, lite acting, lite thinking* suggests a critical view of the commodification of art and public life. Yet **lite** is also used less judgementally, to calibrate levels of entertainment, as in *nightclub lite, lite rock,* and the *Lite Chekov* provided by a local repertory group. All these uses found in data from CCAE show that **lite** has a life apart from commercial nomenclature in the US, whereas it's still confined to commerce in the UK, by the evidence of the BNC. Its generic uses make **lite** one of the very few respellings of a *gh* word to find a place in common usage. See further under **gh** and **spelling, rules and reforms** section 5.

literally
This word has a split personality: plain-speaking and tantalizing. In its primary sense, **literally** urges you to take a fact "according to the letter," i.e. word for word or exactly as the utterance has it. Yet for most of the last two centuries it has also been used to underscore figures of speech or turns of phrase which could never be taken at face value: *They were literally green with envy*. In cases like that, **literally** defies its literal sense and seems to press for factual interpretation of the idiom, however far-fetched. Readers are tantalized – caught between the urge to believe and disbelief. This use of **literally** is recognized in all major dictionaries, though some add cautionary labels or usage notes. *New Oxford* (1998) makes it a stylistic offence: "deliberate non-literal use [of **literally**] for added effect is not acceptable in standard English." Examples of such use are readily found in BNC data, not in the most formal prose, but in interactive discourse both written and spoken, where writers/speakers are very audience-aware, and rhetoric overlays content. In media discourse, **literally** lends impact to quantitative statements (*literally hundreds of calls*) which do not bear scrutiny. It adds a hyperbolic edge to clichés, as in: *His death quite literally shattered the minister.* Yet sensational examples like this don't outnumber those of a more measured kind in the BNC; and it seems odd to censure the word on the basis of its less responsible users. In grammatical terms it's an intensifier or *emphasizer* like "really" – whose use as such is registered without comment in the dictionaries. *Webster's English Usage* (1989) leaves **literally** to the writer's discretion, as do *Webster's* dictionaries. Skilled writers anywhere can capture its essential meaning in serious or playful ways, as in the following from the BNC:

> *The glider pilot literally has the life of the tow pilot in his hands.*
> *Yeast is made up of millions of tiny fungus cells which literally go berserk when confronted by a liquid rich with sugars.*

Despite clichéd use, **literally** still invites readers to savor the aptness of the writer's terms of reference.

litotes
See under **figures of speech.**

litre or liter
The choice between these spellings is a matter of British or American preference (see **-re/-er**). Australia goes with **litre**, as does bilingual Canada, for whom it serves as the point of convergence with French. For the place of **litres** in the metric system, see under *volume* in Appendix V.

litterateurs or literati
These loanwords make people much more than literate – "men and women of letters," as the English phrase goes. **Literati**, borrowed from Latin, indicates that they are of a scholarly or literary bent, while the French **litterateurs** implies that they are writers of literary or critical works. The word **litterateur** is masculine in French, its feminine counterpart being *litteratrice*. But **litterateur** usually serves for both genders in English, what with the decline in general knowledge of French, and the preference for nonsexist terms. The use of **litterateur** without an accent is another sign of its assimilation in English.

livable or liveable

The first is more regular. See under -e and -eable.

llama or lama

See lama.

Lo or lo

As an exclamation, **Lo/lo** belongs to older literary style:

> Lo hear the gentle Lark. . .
> And lo, the angel of the Lord came upon them. . .

But in everyday discourse it still appears in the phrase *lo and behold,* used to draw attention to an observation:

> Lo and behold, this gives the accrual accounts deficit of $5.149 bn.

The capital letter goes with the position of the word in the sentence, as the examples show.

Compare **Lo/lo** as ad-speak for "low-priced," in the *Bi-Lo* supermarket chain and other brand names. In product labels it sometimes carries other senses of "low," as in *lo-cal* ("low calorie"), and on the TV set with *Lo, Mid and Hi controls.* **Lo** ("low") makes little showing yet in noncommercial writing. The solitary case of *living the lo life* in the BNC doesn't make up for the dearth of examples in both British and American databases.

◊ For other trimmed spellings, see **spelling, rules and reforms** section 5.

loaded or laden

See laden.

loafed or loaved

See under -v-/-f-.

loan or lend

See lend.

loanwords

English has borrowed words from other languages throughout its recorded history. In earlier centuries the words came from Latin and other European languages; and since the beginning of the colonial era, they are from languages of all around the globe. **Loanwords** often bring with them unusual spellings, such as the *kh* of sheik(h), or the accent of French *garçon.* These "foreign" features are slowly modified (*kh* becomes *k*, and French accents disappear), as the words become assimilated in English. In the same way, the foreign plural which comes with a borrowed noun (e.g. *kibbutzim*) is gradually replaced by an English plural with *s* (*kibbutzes*). These processes of assimilation are quite natural, and there's no reason to preserve the foreign features of **loanwords** in English, or to continue to set them in italics once they are visibly anglicized. See further under **italic(s)**.

loath or loth

All dictionaries prefer the first spelling for the adjective meaning "reluctant", even though it's more easily confused with the verb *loathe.* Note also that *loath* is the first element in *loathsome* ("horrible"), though its pronunciation and sense link it with "loathe."

LOB

These letters stand for the *Lancaster–Oslo/Bergen* corpus of British English. See under **English language databases**.

lobbyist or lobbyer

Among those who haunt the corridors of power, the **lobbyist** has been recognized by that name since the time of the American Civil War. The verb *lobby (for)* was recorded a little earlier that century, whence **lobbyer**, which the *Oxford Dictionary* (1989) also registers from the 1860s. But by 1900, **lobbyist** seems to have become the standard term, and neither **lobbyer**, nor "lobbier" noted in Garner (1998), makes any showing in databases of current British or American English.

local genitive

Expressions like *at the printers* and *to the cleaners* are sometimes taken to be ellipses of *at the printer's shop / to the cleaner's shop,* and therefore in need of an apostrophe: *at the printer's, to the cleaner's.* This makes them examples of the **local genitive** (*Comprehensive Grammar,* 1985). Yet *the printers / the cleaners* and other such phrases often seem grammatically ambivalent, and able to be construed with a plural or singular verb (see **agreement** section 2). Seen as plurals, there's no need to postulate ellipsis in *at the printers / to the cleaners,* or to insert an apostrophe. Alternatively, the *s* could be regarded as a special *collective* marker: see under **-s**.

locative

This is a traditional grammar term for English adverbs/adverbials that indicate where an action takes place: *New drugs are being developed overseas.* Like *overseas* in that example, they are typically adjuncts in the clause, but they can also serve as subject (*The car seats five people*) or object (*The chicken crossed the road*).

In other languages, **locatives** are associated with nouns, and are one of the regular **cases** (see further under that heading).

loc.cit.

In scholarly referencing this abbreviation stands for the Latin phrase *loco citato* ("in the place just cited"). It saves the writer having to repeat the exact page or the title of the work, once they have been identified in a preceding footnote. For example:

1. G. Blainey *The Tyranny of Distance* p. 56
2. R. Hughes *The Fatal Shore* p. 17
3. Blainey, loc.cit.

Footnote 3 thus refers to exactly the same page as footnote 1, and further details can be recovered there.

The use of scholarly Latin abbreviations is declining, and instead writers use the author's surname and/or a short title (depending on whether the author's name is given in the running text), and only repeat the page number.

◊ Compare **op.cit**.

locum tenens

This handy Latin phrase means literally "place holder." In English it's applied to the person who keeps up the business or practice of a professional, such as a doctor, pharmacist or lawyer, while s/he goes away for a short period. Borrowed in C17, it has been thoroughly anglicized: often abbreviated to *locum,* and pluralized as *locums,* rather than according to Latin principles as *locum tenentes.*

locus
For the plural of this word, see **-us** section 1.

lodgement or lodgment
Lodgement is the more regular spelling and commoner in British English, by BNC evidence. Corresponding data from CCAE shows the American preference for **lodgment**.
◊ Compare **judgement or judgment**.

logistic or logistical
See under **-istic/-istical**.

logogram, logograph, logotype and logo
The *Oxford Dictionary* (1989) shows a great deal of overlap between these, and with the now obsolete word "logogriph," meaning a type of word puzzle. Both **logogram** and **logograph** have been used as names for the puzzle. That apart, **logogram** and the obsolescent **logograph** both mean/meant the symbol for a word or phrase, as & is for "and" and % for "per cent."

From a background in printing, in comes **logotype**, meaning a single piece of type with more than one character on it. **Logotypes** put together common sequences of letters, such as *in, on, se, th.* (They differ from *ligatures,* in which sets of letters may be combined for reasons of spacing: see **ligatures**.)

In C20 English, both **logotype** and **logogram** have been applied to the distinctive sign or symbol representing a company name, though this meaning is now firmly attached to **logo**, first recorded in 1937. **Logo** is obviously an abbreviation, yet it's unclear whether it derives from **logogram** or **logotype**, and with a dearth of citations from mid-century, the *Oxford* allows either. **Logogram** would have the edge in terms of meaning, but relationships within this set of words have always been a tangle.

-logy
See under **-ology**.

lollipop or lollypop
Everywhere in the world, **lollipop** is the standard spelling for the type of confectionery that is licked from the end of a stick – or things that resemble it in shape, such as the sign carried by the *lollipop man/lady* to escort children across busy streets. American English also allows **lollypop**, but it's rare by the evidence of CCAE.

longways or longwise
See under **-wise or -ways**.

look
The verb **look** is about seeing as well as being seen:
> She looked keenly at him.
> He looked puzzled.

These contrasting perspectives take different grammatical complements: the first **look** is an ordinary verb of action, which takes an adverb or prepositional phrase, the second a *copular verb,* usually followed by an adjective or adjectival phrase.

The second construction makes *it looks good* perfectly good English, as is *you're looking good!* – though it's a different kind of complement from *you're looking well!* There *well* is an adjective meaning "healthy," rather than the familiar adverb which substitutes for *good* in other contexts.

loony or loonie
English speakers everywhere know **loony** ("insane"). Only in Canada does it contrast with **loonie**, the informal term for the 1 dollar coin, introduced in 1987. The coin features a Canadian *loon,* an aquatic diving bird with a yodel-like call. The spelling for the coin varied at first between **loony**, **looney** and **loonie** (*Canadian English Usage*, 1997), but seems to have settled on the last. At the same time its meaning has developed so that it becomes the general word in financial reporting for the Canadian dollar, contrasting with the US "greenback." **Loonie** and **loony** form one of the relatively few such pairs with different meanings (see further at **-ie/-y**).

The words' origins are remote from each other. **Loony** ("insane") is an anglicized abbreviation of the latinate *lunatic;* whereas the *loon* from which **loonie** is derived is a reshaping of *loom,* an obsolete name for the bird, based on Old Norse *lomr.*

loose, loosen or lose
The word **loose** is most familiar as an adjective meaning "slack or not tight" and "free or not tied up." Examples of its use are to be found in *a loose end*, and *Let the dogs loose.* The latter idiom has effectively taken the place of the verb **loose** ("set free"), which was in use in older English, but rare nowadays. The verb **loosen** ("make less tight") is by contrast very much in use, as in *He loosened his grip on the rope.*

For centuries the verbs *unloose* and *unloosen* have doubled for **loose** and **loosen**. Their negative prefixes do not reverse the meaning of the root (see further under **un-**). *Unloose* is increasingly rare however, which explains why *unloosen* seems to do service for both, as "make less tight" and "untie."

"Loose" is also a common misspelling for the quite independent word **lose** meaning "suffer a loss" or "fail to keep." While **lose** comes from Old English, **loose** is a Scandinavian loanword, but their spellings were unstable until C18. **Lose** has remained a spelling headache, because of the lack of spelling analogies for it apart from the pronoun "whose."

lose out
Anxieties about **lose out** probably go back to Orwell (writing in *English People*, 1947) who used it to support a gross overstatement that "American[s tend] to burden every verb with a preposition." In Burchfield (1996) it becomes a "slightly risky phrasal verb." But we should ask whether *lose* on its own would serve the purpose in examples like the following:
> British children lose out in critical areas of education.
> Neither group of islands will lose out from this arrangement

Lose out is effectively an intransitive verb meaning "be disadvantaged," whereas *lose* itself is usually transitive. Being intransitive, **lose out** appears freely at the end of a sentence:
> Our viewers will not lose out.

Its prominence at the end of the sentence, plus the fact that it looks like a "preposition" ending a sentence, would help to explain that ill-defined nervousness about using it (see **prepositions** section 2). Its origins in C19 America would also explain British resistance to it in some quarters. The BNC nevertheless contains over 250 examples of **lose out** / *lost out,* suggesting that it would be hard to give up.

loth or loath

See **loath.**

lots and a lot

These phrases serve their purpose when all you want is an approximate largish number or quantity. Both occur freely in BNC data, **lots** over 4000 times, and **a lot** more than 13,000 times. They appear in many kinds of prose, though not the most formal or academic. At home in interactive discourse, they come up in dialogue as well as unpretentious informative writing:

We have sent lots of messages that we were outraged.
Tests show that eating lots of fibre has as much chance of prolonging your life as wearing a wig.
You went to a lot of trouble over the meal.
It works in a lot of circumstances that defy the standard solution.

As the examples show, both **lots** and **a lot** combine with plural count nouns or singular mass nouns. **A lot** also has a modest adverbial role:

It's been on my mind a lot recently.

A lot and **lots** are labeled "informal" in modern British dictionaries, which seems to underrepresent the range of texts in which they currently appear. But if we assume three levels of style, including a stylistically neutral "common" category between formal and informal (as did the original *Oxford Dictionary,* 1884–1928), the status of **a lot** and **lots** can be better explained – as acceptable in informal and standard writing, but not the most formal. American dictionaries put no stylistic restrictions on them.

Lotta as a merged form of "lot of" is unquestionably nonstandard in terms of writing, and serves to represent nonstandard speech even though the assimilation it represents is very common and widespread. Both BNC and CCAE provide scores of examples: *a lotta trouble, whole lotta action, lose a lotta business, save a whole lotta embarrassment;* and it features in the titles of rock 'n' roll songs such as "Whole Lotta Love" and "Whole Lotta Shakin' Goin' On," which again help to connect it with counterculture. *New Oxford* (1998) registers it as a conventional nonstandard spelling, but not *Merriam-Webster* (2000).

◊ For the merged spelling of **a lot**, see under **alot.**

lotus

The latinate spelling disguises the Greek origins of this word (*lotos*), an exotic flower whose symbolic value and psychogenic properties are better known than its botanical identity. Because **lotus** has no roots in Latin, its plural has always been English (**lotuses**).

loud or loudly

Dictionaries these days all allow that **loud** can be either an adjective or an adverb, in certain contexts.

So apart from qualifying a noun as in *a loud voice,* it can modify a verb as in:

Don't shout so loud!
They turned the radio up loud.

In the second case at least, **loud** seems to be the only possible word, and in the first it serves to make the imperative rather curt. Compare the more polite

Don't shout so loudly.

Loud is also established as an adverb in idioms such as *read / say / laugh out loud,* where it replaces *aloud.* In BNC data, *out loud* appears more than 30 times as often as *out aloud,* and in CCAE *out loud* reigns supreme. The data show an increasing range of verbs coupling with *out loud,* beyond the familiar ones noted above:

Nowadays people can speculate out loud.
. . . tortured himself out loud
He supposed out loud that 90 percent . . .

In expressions like these, from both British and American English, the adverb **loud** refers to the physical production of sound in a situation, where **loudly** can be more detached and figurative, implying a social judgement about the use of voice:

They complained loudly about their poor accommodation.

loudhailer or loudhaler

The first is the only spelling registered in dictionaries for the hand-held loudspeaker used in crowd control. See further under **hale or hail.**

lounge

In all varieties of English a **lounge** is a room designed for comfortable sitting and relaxing. It may be a public space, as in a hotel, theatre or an airport, or in a private house. Alternative names for the private **lounge** room are *sitting room* (in the UK and Canada), and *living room* (in the US, UK and Australia). *Drawing room* and *parlo(u)r* generally sound dated.

Americans also use the word **lounge** for a piece of furniture on which "one person may recline or several sit," according to *Webster's Third* (1986). The standard **lounge** in this second sense has a headrest at one end, which may or may not extend along the back. For Australians too, **lounge** can mean a piece of furniture on which several people sit, though it has armrests at both ends and a fully upholstered back. For *lounge chair* and *chaise lounge,* see **chaise longue.**

lour or lower

In conventional expressions such as *louring sky / lowering sky,* the spelling of this ominous verb can go either way. Both spellings are recognized in the major dictionaries: the *Oxford Dictionary* (1989) prioritizes **lour**, while *Webster's Third* (1986) makes it **lower.** But the second spelling can be confused with a different verb meaning "move down," in less familiar examples. The danger of confusion is there even in *lowering cloud,* and imminent when **lour/lower** is pronounced so as to rhyme with "blower" (rather than "flower"), as sometimes happens according to *Webster's.* **Lour** is unambiguous, whatever the collocation.

louvre or louver

See **-re/-er.**

lovable or loveable

See **-e** and **-eable.**

low and lowly

These work as independent words, and do not correspond as adjective and adverb of the same word. **Low** is first of all an adjective or adverb meaning "not far off the ground," as in *a low wall* and *the plane flew low over the city*. It works more figuratively in *a pretty low thing to do* or *they would lie low for a while,* where it again can be seen as adjective and adverb.

Lowly is normally an adjective meaning "humble," as in *of lowly origins*. Just occasionally it's pressed into service as an adverb, as in:

> *He began lowly in this organization.*

Yet there's a certain ambiguity and discomfort about it – which is easily avoided by paraphrase: *He began at a low level in the organization.*

Low Countries

This phrase is still sometimes used by English-speakers as a collective reference to Holland, Belgium and Luxemburg. See further under **Netherlands**.

lower or lour

See **lour**.

lower case

Lower case letters are the ordinary, small letters of type, the opposite of capital letters, also known as *upper case*. In scholarly tradition the *lower case letters* are *minuscules* and contrast with the *majuscules*. But in general usage, it's the printer's terms **lower case** and *upper case* which have prevailed. Those terms are a reminder of the way the elements of type were stored in boxes in two large sets, with the capital letters in the higher rows – at more of a stretch of the printer's arm but needed less often. The small letters were in the more accessible lower rows, being needed all the time. ◊ On the various kinds of words that may begin with an *upper case* letter, see **capital letters**.

luck in, into, on, upon or out

The verb *luck* is surrounded by a tangle of phrasal verbs. The oldest of them **luck (up)on** meaning "meet [someone] by chance" has been used since C17; but its role is now challenged by **luck into**, originally referring to the lucky acquisition of something, and now also used in reference to people, witness:

> *In the oil business he lucked into some money.*
> *Baker lucked into a big-name master of ceremonies.*

Luck out is a further contender in American English, appearing in the 1950s with the meaning "be lucky," as in:

> *I lucked out with really good people both times.*

This is its regular use in CCAE data, in a variety of spoken and informal written contexts. It puts **luck out** in parallel with **luck into**, both signaling good fortune.

Yet those unfamiliar with the idioms sometimes take them to be opposites, and assume that **luck out** means "run out of luck." The journalist who wrote of someone who "bad-lucked out of the prize winnings" was taking no chances. Some Canadians use **luck in** instead of **luck out** for this reason, according to *Canadian Oxford* (1998). Outside North America the idioms have yet to catch on. There are no examples in the BNC; and Australians – like Canadians – are still

coming to grips with their overlapping senses. For the moment then, **luck into** and **luck out** are unreliable elements in international communication.

lucre

This is one of the few words ending in **-re** that don't change their spelling in crossing from British to American style. See further under **-re/-er**.

luge, sled or toboggan

See under **sled**.

lunch or luncheon

Lunch is the standard word for the ordinary midday meal, everywhere in the world. **Luncheon** makes it a special occasion, typically run by an establishment group for some formal purpose, and attended by a distinguished guest who does the honors – handing out the English Tourist Board awards (in UK), or the National Retailers' equivalents in the US. In American English, a midday press conference can also be called a *press luncheon / media luncheon,* and the word seems to be more generally democratized than in Britain. The idea of a *pot-luck luncheon* (for American school children) might seem oxymoronic, though it goes with instruction in nutrition, and thus clearly differs from **lunch** spent milling in the playground. Democratization of the word **luncheon** can nevertheless be seen in British English concepts such as the *luncheon voucher* and the less-than-distinguished *luncheon sausage*. ◊ Compare **dinner**.

lunging or lungeing

The first spelling is the more regular of the two (see **-e** section 2e), and the only one to appear in current English, by the evidence of the BNC and CCAE.

lustre or luster

See under **-re/-er**.

lusty or lustful

A positive energy often goes with the use of **lusty,** whether it's *lusty singing,* the *lusty cry of a new-born baby,* or the *lusty 150 bhp* developed by a car engine. These more or less innocent uses of **lusty** shade into others where its connections with the word *lust* ("sexual desire") come to the surface, as in *lusty heterosexual students* or *his young, lusty brother.* At this point **lusty** means much the same as **lustful** i.e. "full of lust, lecherous," as in *lustful glances, his lustful urgent breath* or *the lustful invitations of Venus.* But as the examples show, **lusty** tends to mean **lustful** only when applied to people. With other referents such as *lusty speculation* or *a lusty performance* it's quite safe. A *lusty meal* could only mean "hearty."

luxuriant or luxurious

In spite of their similarity, these are used very differently. **Luxuriant** refers to abundant natural growth, either in the environment – *a luxuriant canopy of creepers in the rainforest* – or on the human head: *After six weeks he sported a luxuriant beard.*

Luxurious always relates to the man-made environment, and has strong links with the noun *luxury*. See for instance:

> *With their winnings they rented a luxurious hotel suite.*

-ly

This ending serves both adjectives and adverbs in English. It is better known as an adverb suffix, as in *coolly, excitingly, quietly, smoothly*, where it has clearly been added to a simple adjective (*cool* etc.). Adverbs with **-ly** often show some of the standard spelling adjustments of English, such as losing the final *-e* of the adjective in cases such as *simple<simply*. For the change from *y* to *i* in cases such as *merrily*, see under **-y>-i-**. Note also that adjectives ending in *-ic* usually add *-ally*, as with *organic<organically*. See further under **-ic/-ical**.

In earlier centuries **-ly** was also often used to form adjectives from nouns, as with *friendly, leisurely, lovely, scholarly*. Sometimes an existing adjective formed the base, as in *deadly, elderly, kindly, sickly*. Such words are well established, and can be compared by just adding *-er* or *-est*, e.g. *friendlier/friendliest*, at least when they begin with no more than two syllables. (See further under **adjectives** section 2.) Note that adjectives ending in **-ly** do not usually convert to adverbs by adding another **-ly**. The awkwardness of formations such as *friendlily* is obvious, and so it's normally replaced by a paraphrase: *in a friendly way*.

A distinctive group of adjectives with **-ly** are those designating points of the compass, such as *easterly, northerly* etc., and those referring to intervals of time, including:

> *daily   hourly   monthly   nightly   quarterly*
> *weekly   yearly*

These serve as adverbs as well as adjectives.
◊ Adverbs which operate both with and without an **-ly** ending (such as [*Go*] *slow/slowly*), are discussed under **zero adverbs**.

lyric or lyrical

The shorter adjective is closer in meaning to the origins of both words in the Greek *lyre,* and the song-like verse associated with it. So **lyric** usually collocates with things literary or musical, as in *lyric poetry* or *a lyric soprano*. **Lyrical** usually implies the graceful expression of emotion associated with lyric verse, as in:

> *She gave a lyrical account of the experience.*
◊ For similar pairs of words, see **-ic/-ical**.

lyricist or lyrist

Lyrist is the older of these, dating from C17 when expertise in playing the *lyre* was a familiar form of musicianship. Early in C19 it was also applied to the writer of *lyric* poetry. Later that century, the words associated with popular songs began to be called *lyrics*, and their authors referred to as the **lyricist**. Dictionaries allow the interchange of **lyricist** and **lyrist**, yet data from CCAE and BNC show that only **lyricist** is in current use, almost always applied to the author of *lyrics* for musicals or recordings – the heirs of Ira Gershwin rather than Shelley and Keats.

-lyse/-lyze

See under **-yze/-yse**.

-m/-mm-

The final **m** of verbs like *dim, trim* is doubled before
-ed and *-ing: dimmed, trimming.* The same holds for
verbs with two or more syllables such as *diagram,
monogram, program* (*diagramming, monogrammed*
etc.) even though the syllable ending in **m** is
unstressed – probably because that syllable is
identical with an independent word (see under
doubling of final consonant).

◊ For more on *program* as a verb, see under **program
or programme**.

ma'am or mam

See under **madam**.

Mac or Mc

How do you write the name of a well-known
hamburger restaurant chain?

McDonald's MacDonald's Macdonald's

The first spelling is the one used by the company,
although the second or third spellings are also used by
many people with the same surname – as a glance at
the metropolitan phone book will confirm. Apart from
those three spellings, there are two other ways of
writing Celtic surnames of this kind: *Mcdonald*
(which is rare by comparison with the other three
above); and *M'Donald*, used in C19. *M'* can still be seen
in the names of Walter Scott's characters, and
sometimes in references to *M'Naghten rules* (a legal
plea which seeks to defend someone on the basis of
diminished responsibility).

Ultimately, the decision about how to spell these
surnames rests with the individual. Individual
choices put contrasting forms of **Mc** and **Mac** together
on the cover of a book, when authors surnamed
McLeod or *MacKenney* are published by *Macmillan*.
Yet there are some general trends towards one or the
other spelling, in that Irish surnames seem to stay
with **Mc**, as in *McConnochie, McElroy, McEvoy;* while
Scottish names more often convert to **Mac** (with or
without a following capital), and hence may appear in
two or three forms, as in the *McDonald's* example.
Other things being equal, the commoner the name, the
more chance of it being **Mac**. And **mac** (with no
capital letter) is the spelling found in common words
derived from **Mc** surnames, such as the verb
macadamise (named after John McAdam 1756–1836).
(See **capital letters** section 2, and **eponyms**.) In
mackintosh, the common spelling for a "raincoat,"
assimilation has gone one stage further with the
insertion of the *k* to conform with standard *c/ck* rules.
(See further under **mackintosh**.)

1 Geographical names based on Celtic surnames are
regularly written with **Mc** in the US, spellings set by
the US Geographical Names Board. Elsewhere in the
world where pioneering Celts have implanted their
names, it may be either **Mac** or **Mc**. In Canada the
spelling of *Lake McKenzie* (Ontario/Saskatchewan)
contrasts with the *Mackenzie River* (in the NorthWest
Territories). Australians too cope with a varieties of
Macs and *Mcs,* as for example with the *McGregor
Range* in SW Queensland, *MacGregor* as a suburb of
Brisbane, and *Macgregor* (ACT), all of which invoke
the name of Sir William MacGregor, Governor of
Queensland 1909–14. The variant spellings owe as
much to the vagaries of tradition as to the particular
person being commemorated. The benefits of
standardizing geographical names with the Celtic
prefix – as in the US – are clear.

2 Indexing names with Mac and Mc Both personal or
geographical names with **Mac/Mc** raise questions of
alphabetization, and how to integrate them with other
names in an index. One system (A) is to list them as if
they were all **Mac**, but with their individual spellings
indicated; a second system (B) lists them according to
their individual spellings. In either case, they are
integrated with other names, and medial capitals are
disregarded. When there are several cases of the same
surname with **Mac** or **Mc**, the order depends on the
initial of the first given name.

A	B
Maas Y	Maas Y
Mabey L	Mabey L
McAdam H	MacAndrew S
MacAndrew S	Macarthur A
Macarthur A	MacArthur W
McArthur J	Mace R
MacArthur W	Macfarlane M
Mace R	McAdam H
Macfarlane M	McArthur J
McFarlane P	McFarlane P

Systems A and B are both recognized in the *Chicago
Manual* (1993) and *Copy-editing* (1992). Though both
incline to System B, *Copy-editing* makes it clear that
System A is more helpful to those unsure of the exact
form of the prefix for a particular name – which is why
it's used in telephone directories and atlas gazetteers.
System B is preferable in book indexing, where it
reflects the actual forms of names used in the text.

A third system, sometimes used in short indexes, is
to group the *Macs* and *Mcs* together at the start of the
letter *M*,which is visible from where **Mac** and **Mc**
would otherwise come up.

macaroni or maccaroni

Database evidence shows that **macaroni** is the
standard English spelling today, though the original
Italian **maccaroni** was used for centuries and is still
recognized as an alternative in some dictionaries. The
Italians themselves now use *maccheroni*, but this has
made no headway in English.

mackintosh, macintosh and Macintosh

Dictionaries allow that the British term for the
generic "raincoat" may be spelled with or without a *k*.
But the spelling **mackintosh** is the only one to appear
in scores of examples in the BNC – without a capital

letter, like other *eponyms* (see under that heading). The word immortalizes the name of Charles Macintosh (1766–1843), an industrial chemist whose discovery of the process of waterproofing was patented in "macintosh cloth."

In the late C20, the name **Macintosh** was trademarked for a type of personal computer originating in northeastern USA. With its apple logo, it plays on the name of a late-ripening American apple, known as the *McIntosh (red)*. The apple owes its name to a Canadian fruit farmer John McIntosh (1777–1845). ◊ For more on the instability of names with this Celtic prefix, see **Mac or Mc**.

macro-

This Greek prefix means "large or large-scale." It has been in service in English only since the 1880s, but the *Oxford Dictionary* (1989) has columns of new technical terms coined with it. Such words are often the opposites of ones formed with *micro-*, as for:

macrobiotic	microbiotic
macrocosmic	microcosmic
macroeconomics	microeconomics
macroscopic	microscopic
macrostructure	microstructure

Macro- usually combines with classical roots to form scholarly words. On this it differs from *mega-*, another newish Greek prefix meaning "large," which combines with simple English roots as well. See **mega-**.

mad

This word has covered a range of mental states from insanity to (foolish or excessive) enthusiasm to anger since the 1300s. But there are latter-day questions about its use – especially in British English. The use of **mad** to mean "insane" is not in question, whereas its use to mean "angry" was labeled "colloquial" in Worcester's *Dictionary of the English Language* (1860), as well as the first *Oxford Dictionary* (1884–1928). A century later, the stylistic questions have faded in the US, while they have intensified in the UK. The *New Oxford* (1998) adds the label "informal" to **mad** meaning "carried away with enthusiasm" as well as **mad** meaning "angry." Meanwhile *Webster's Third* (1986) and *Merriam-Webster* (2000) present all uses of **mad** as stylistically unmarked and uncomplicated. Garner (1998) also affirms their acceptability.

The stylistic dividing line between **mad** = "insane" (standard) and other uses of **mad** (informal) is problematic in at least two ways. The distinctions between madness, passion and obsessiveness are blurred in many idioms:

It drives men mad but it's the sensible thing to do.
What makes me mad is the flippant desire to dismiss it as dead.
Is not this bureaucracy gone mad?

These idioms, and collocations such as *mad panic/rush/scramble*, and compounds such as *money mad, aeroplane mad, music mad*, all help to diversify the uses of **mad**, to mean something other than "insane." They share the field with the sense "insane" in about half the instances of **mad** in BNC written sources. The fact that they appear in the same kinds of sources makes it rather arbitrary to say that one use is standard and the others informal. In any case **mad** is not the formal/professional term for "insane" used by psychiatrists.

Close inspection of the *Oxford Dictionary*'s (1989) note on **mad** = "angry" is also revealing. Alongside the label "colloquial" it notes that "in many dialects in GB and US [this is] the ordinary word for "angry." The stylistic label thus turns on regionally preferred usage, and cannot be regarded as an international position. Data from CCAE shows that **mad** = "angry" is the dominant sense in the US, and it appears in many standard kinds of writing:

Customers get mad at the credit company.
Salas didn't get mad, he got even.
Two of the largest [theater] chains are already mad at Disney.

The anger is underscored in expressions like *hopping mad, boiling mad, steaming mad, fighting mad, kicking mad* etc. Meanwhile in British English data from BNC, **mad** = "insane" is probably the most frequent of the three meanings – if we regard all uses of idioms like *drive mad / gone mad* as belonging to the "insane" set. This trans-Atlantic difference may well explain the intensifed comment on other uses of **mad** in recent British dictionaries. Yet British writers represented in the BNC do not share the dictionaries' inhibitions, and are finding productive uses of **mad** in interactive writing.

The idiom *like mad* has all the wild fuzziness of **mad**, and serves to intensify rather than clarify the process it refers to:

People are spending like mad.
Schools are competing like mad for pupils.

If the rhetorical effect is all that counts, *like mad* will do. It does however suggest a gap in analytical thinking.

madam, madame, ma'am and mam

These are all English renderings of the French expression *ma dame*, literally "my lady," though as **Madame** it's the common French word for "Mrs." In English **Madame** and **madam** have quite different applications.

Madam can be used freely as a polite way of addressing a woman whose name and status are unknown. "Would madam like to see the menu?" could be used by the waiter in an expensive restaurant; or the suggestion that "Madam might like to try a larger size," by an assistant in an upmarket department store – at least in the UK. **Madam** also appears in the salutation of letters addressed to unknown female recipients, though there are other options (see **forms of address** section 2e). The title **Madam** lacks a plural of its own, though *Mesdames* would fill the need (see **plurals** section 3). The plural **madams** goes with **madam** as a common noun, in which case it means either:

* a bossy woman: *She's quite a madam to deal with.*
* a woman in charge of a brothel: *She had no prospects other than to graduate from tart to madam.*

The word **Madame** is used in English to preface the name of a celebrated Frenchwoman, especially one associated with the arts – *Madame Pompadour, Madame de Staël, Madame Tussaud* – or created by artists: *Madame Arcati, Madame Butterfly, Madame Sosostris*. It also serves as a courtesy title for female foreign dignitaries from any part of the world (*Madame Phiroun, Secretary-General of the Cambodian Parliament*), and for the wives of male dignitaries: *the Dutch ambassador Jan Peeters and*

Madame Peeters. The English plural for **Madame** is like the French: **Mesdames**.

The contraction **ma'am** (rhyming with "ham") continues to be used in the US, in responses to instructions and questions posed by a woman: "Yes, ma'am, the docket's inside." **Ma'am** was once heard across the country, but according to DARE (1996), its stronghold is now the South and South Midland areas, in terms of frequency and range of uses. Garner (1998) associates it also with the Midwest and West. *Webster's Third* (1986) notes that it may also be written as **mam**, but there's no evidence of this in CCAE.

In the UK, **ma'am** (rhyming with "harm") is also widely used in courteous address to women but it emphasizes difference in social status:

> *Special delivery, ma'am.*
> *"Your little fellow's all right, ma'am?" the farmer addressed Biddy.*

Female police officers above the rank of sergeant are addressed as **ma'am**, and women of any rank to which one is junior, in the armed services. **Ma'am** (rhyming with "ham") is the correct form of address when meeting the Queen or other female members of the royal family (Simpson, 2001). **Mam** can be used as an alternative to **ma'am** in direct address: *Welcome, sir; welcome, mam.* Note that it's also a familiar or dialect word for referring to "mother" as in: *He'd get his mam to do them.*

◊ For non-European courtesy titles, see **forms of address** section 1.

mafia, Mafia or Maffia

Italians write this as **Maffia**, but spellings with one *f* are standard in English – whether the reference is to (i) the Italian organized crime network, or (ii) its analogues elsewhere, or (iii) less sinister power networks in other domains. Yet while the first is clearly distinguished by the use of a capital letter, dictionaries diverge slightly on the second group. According to *New Oxford* (1998) the capital letter is also applied to *Mafia-like* organizations operating in the US – but not elsewhere in the world. BNC data confirms that both Italian and US *Mafias* are regularly capitalized; however beyond them there's much variation:

> *Columbia's cocaine mafia*
> *the building boom organised under the power of the [Brazilian] Mafia*
> *a [Bombay] hawker has to pay off the local mafia don*
> *what he called the "Scargill Mafia"*

The quotation marks of the last example are a reminder that the line between **mafia** in the second sense (criminal activity, actual or imputed) and the third (sheer power) may reflect one's socio-political persuasion. References of the third type are usually left uncapitalized, as in *the British literary mafia, a great medical mafia, the sex magazine mafia.* The lower case *m* helps to identify these as figurative uses.

In American English the pattern is similar, according to *Merriam-Webster* (2000), except that the capital letter is extended to all *Mafia-like* criminal organizations in the second set. CCAE data confirms that **Mafia** (with capital letter) is used for the Italian/Sicilian crime syndicate and its analogues in US cities such as New York, Chicago and Los Angeles. But look-alike operations elsewhere are as often lower-cased in the data (*the Russian/Turkish/Albanian mafia*). Perhaps this is a way of playing safe when the criminality of these more remote operations has still to be demonstrated in courts of law. It has the disadvantage of not distinguishing the dubious from clearly figurative applications of the word, as in *"rain-forest mafia," Hollywood's "Irish mafia."* But with only two options (to capitalize or not to capitalize), it recommends itself in legally sensitive publications.

magic or magical

These coexist as adjectives, **magic** generally serving as a definitive adjective, and **magical** as an evaluative one (see **adjectives**). **Magic** appears in common collocations such as *magic wand, magic lamp, magic touch* as well as the *magic formula/potion/spell/words* which are the presumed instruments of **magic**. Compare the more abstract uses of **magical**, which implies the pleasure and delight of something, as in *magical moments,* or else their unreality: *no magical solutions.* The two adjectives sometimes seem to coincide, as in *magic powers/magical powers.* Even there the second suggests something more elusive than the first. This is also true of *magic charm/magical charm,* when referring to a talisman. When referring to a person's charming manner, only **magical** will do.

magistracy or magistrature

Some dictionaries present these as alternatives for referring to the collective body of *magistrates* or their office and authority. But **magistracy** is the only one to appear in contemporary databases of American and British English (CCAE and the BNC), suggesting that **magistrature** has slipped out of common usage.
◊ Compare **candidacy and candidature**.

magma

For the plural, see **-a** section 1.

magnitude

This weighty word indicates precise measurements of quantity in mathematics, astronomy (the brightness of stars) and geology (the strength of earthquakes). The *order(s) of magnitude* are also precisely defined. But in nonspecialist discourse, **magnitude** connotes relative importance and vast size rather than any mathematical reference point:

> *... the sheer magnitude of the task facing it*
> *We are in the presence of a disaster of the first magnitude.*
> *Language evolves at a rate which is orders of magnitude faster ...*
> *The problems associated with the British atomic bomb were of a different order of magnitude.*

These rather portentous uses of **magnitude** have little appeal for those who prefer mathematical terms to be used in the service of science rather than rhetoric. Not that rhetoric itself is reprehensible – but it is subject to the law of diminishing returns for the extravagant cliché.

magnum opus

This Latin phrase, meaning "great work," is applied in English to the major literary or artistic composition by a particular person. However it often seems to imply that the work is more remarkable for its size than anything else. (The French phrase *chef d'oeuvre* is not equivocal in this way.) In earlier centuries the phrase **magnum opus** appeared as *opus magnum,* and both word order and meaning were then more closely aligned with Latin.

maharajah or maharaja
The second spelling was recommended by both *Webster's Third* (1986) and the *Oxford Dictionary* (1989), no doubt for reasons of etymology, since **maharaja** is an exact match for the Sanskrit *maha raja* ("great king"). Yet the *Oxford* citations also show the first spelling **maharajah** in regular use since the word made its debut in English (1698). Late C20 citations from British and American databases run strongly in favor of **maharajah**, which outnumbers **maharaja** by more than 4:1 in the BNC, and 2:1 in CCAE.

The wife of a **maharaja(h)** is a *maharani,* sometimes spelled *maharanee,* like other Hindi words ending in that sound. (See under **-ee**.) But once again, *maharani* is closer to the word's origins as *maha rani* ("great queen").

Mahomet
See under **Muhammad**.

maiden name
With its possibly sexist implications, the term **maiden name** is marked for replacement by others such as "birth name" and "former name." But neither of those makes clear the issue (that of a woman's name prior to marriage), and a term such as "pre-marriage name" has still to be invented for the purposes of official forms. In running text the French loanword *née* lends itself to the cause, as a neat way of indicating the woman's prior name. See **née**.

main clause
A **main clause** (or *principal clause*) is not grammatically dependent on any other in the sentence, and may indeed stand alone. A single **main clause** with one or more *dependent* (or *subordinate*) clauses forms a *complex* sentence. Two or more **main clauses** in the same sentence create a *compound* sentence. See further under **clauses**.

main verb
In compound verbs, the **main verb** combines with one or more *auxiliary* verbs, to form a finite verb phrase. See further under **verbs** and **auxiliary verbs**.

maintain and maintenance
See under **-ain**.

Majorca or Mallorca
These both refer to the largest of the Balearic Islands in the western Mediterranean, **Majorca** being the English name for it, and **Mallorca** the Spanish.

majority
When used to mean "larger number of people," **majority** can take either a singular or plural verb in agreement:
> *The majority of the party is/are still behind it.*
> *The silent majority is/are still a force to reckon with.*

Constructions with the plural are more common in Australia and Britain than in American English (see further under **collective nouns** and **agreement** section 1).

Apart from the question of agreement, a curious restriction on the use of **majority** seems to have evolved during C20, by which only the first two of the following sentences is acceptable as "good standard English" (*New Oxford,* 1998):
> *The majority of perennials flower during this period . . .*
> *The majority of people who have a church wedding . . .*
> *The majority of driving is done on motorways . . .*

The difference between the first two and the third is clearly not a matter of a plural versus a singular noun after **majority**, but rather whether the following noun is inherently countable. Collective nouns like "people" are, whereas mass nouns like "driving" are not. Gowers (1965) revising Fowler underscored the point that the item after *majority of* had to be "numerical" – disallowing the third type of construction, as well as the fact that dictionaries all define **majority** as "the greater number or part." The definition allows for all three constructions illustrated above, and the *Oxford Dictionary* (1989) embraces them without comment. In fact most British writers represented in the BNC use *majority of* with plural nouns, yet there is a sprinkling of instances with a following collective or mass noun, like those illustrated above. They are rather more common in American English, by the evidence of CCAE. Parallel constructions such as *the majority of the public / the majority of public opinion,* and *the majority of the money / the majority of its funding* show free use of collective and mass nouns, alongside constructions with plural nouns. American commentators are not fussed about the issue. *Webster's English Usage* (1989) sees the construction with mass nouns as a "reasonable extension" of those with a countable entity, and Garner (1998) makes no reference to it.

Grammar apart, constructions with **majority** may seem a little heavy for the discourse. In sentences like those quoted above, *most* is normally enough to make the point. But that's a matter of style, not correct usage, and there is no danger of misunderstanding.

majuscule
See **lower case**.

mal- and male-
Both these prefixes contribute negative meanings to English words. In the cases of *malediction, malefactor, malodo(u)r, maltreat,* it means "bad" or "evil." With *maladministration, malformed, malfunction, malnutrition, malpractice,* it means "corrupt" or "defective." Always it bodes ill.

Male- is the original Latin form of the prefix, and so examples like *malediction* and *malefactor* are really Latin compounds. **Mal-** is the French form of the same prefix, appearing in a few loanwords, and others created in English during the last four centuries. In C17 the French prefix was sometimes overwritten with the Latin, so **mal-** was written as **male-** in *mal(e)government* and *mal(e)practice.* But in modern English the French form of the prefix prevails in such words, and it's the only one used to form new ones.

malapropisms

A **malapropism** is the faulty use of a word which shows that the writer/speaker has confused it with another similar one. See for example:

> *The book I eluded to a little while ago . . .*
> *The ship floundered on the reef . . .*

The distinction between *elude* and *allude*, *flagrant* and *fragrant*, *flounder* and *founder*, and many others are detailed in this book. In serious prose they're an unfortunate distraction. But their incongruity has its funny side, and comedy writers from Shakespeare on have exploited their effect for amusement. Some of the most memorable examples were uttered by Sheridan's character Mrs. Malaprop, in exchanges such as:

> *[What's the matter?] . . . Why murder's the matter!*
> *He can tell you all the perpendiculars . . .* [from *The Rivals*]

Mrs. Malaprop's name has become the byword for this kind of word play, though her name itself derives from the French phrase *mal à propos* ("not to the point").

Malaya, Malaysia and Malay

Malaya is a geographical term referring to the southern end of the *Malay Peninsula*, which now forms part of the *Federation of Malaysia*. **Malaysia** is the name for the political unit formed in 1963 out of the mainland **Malay** states, as well as those in North Borneo (Sabah and Sarawak) and Singapore. (Singapore left the federation in 1965.)

Malay is strictly speaking an ethnic term for the indigenous people of **Malaya** and the *Malay Archipelago*, and parts of Indonesia. The population of **Malaysia** itself is only about half **Malay**. The other major community blocks are the Chinese (35%) and the Indian (10%).

malevolent, malicious, malignant or malign

These words point to an area of meaning which is well supplied with adjectives. All imply a negative disposition or orientation to others, and dictionaries quite often give them as synonyms for each other. There are however some differences, in that **malicious** and **malevolent** are always associated with people and their behavior (*malicious intent, a malevolent smile*), whereas **malignant** and **malign** (as an adjective) are often applied to forces and circumstances. Further differences are that **malevolent** implies general ill-will towards another, while **malicious** suggests that the feeling is channeled into spiteful words or actions.

Malignant is most often used of relentlessly destructive forces, as in the medical phrase *malignant tumor*. **Malign** has also been used this way in the past (*malign syphilis*), but nowadays it most often serves as a verb meaning "speak unfavorably of," shown in *He maligned all the people he worked with*. The influence of the adjective **malign** is still to be found in its opposite *benign*, which serves as the antonym to **malignant** in *benign tumor* etc.

malignancy or malignance

Though many dictionaries allow either, **malignancy** is very much more common than **malignance**, in both British and American English, by the evidence of BNC and CCAE. For other pairs of this type, see **-nce/-ncy**.

Mallorca or Majorca

See **Majorca**.

man, man- and -man

For over a thousand years, **man** has carried two meanings:
1 "person, human being"
2 "adult male"

The first meaning embraces the second, except where the context dictates otherwise. As often in language, the ambiguity of any particular word is resolved by others in the context. All this was taken for granted until the latter decades of C20, when feminist concerns were raised as to whether **man** was really being taken in its first, generic sense as often as was assumed. The debate drew attention to some of our oldest compounds, such as *mankind* and *manslaughter*. Were they interpreted in broad human terms or as "men only" references? Would it be a surprise to hear that a *man-eating shark* has taken a woman who was diving in the coral reef; or that a woman has fallen down a *man-hole?*

Doubts about individual **man-** compounds are reinforced by the large set where **-man** is the second element, as in *businessman, policeman, salesman*. Outside the specific contexts in which they actually refer to **men**, such words are thought likely to endorse and perpetuate sexist ideas about social and occupational roles, and to make being a *businessman* an exclusively male preserve. Of course those who use such words may not be male chauvinists: sexism may very well be in the eye of the beholder. Some women indeed prefer to be called *chairman*, because it's the usual way to refer to the role they are taking on. Yet many people feel we should avoid any expressions which raise such questions, and look for synonyms and paraphrases.

For individual job titles there are usually alternatives which focus on the job and bypass the sex of whoever does it. So for example:

	can be replaced by
businessman	*executive, entrepreneur*
cameraman	*camera operator*
chairman	*convener, coordinator*
draftsman	*drafter*
fireman	*firefighter*
first-aid man	*first-aid attendant*
foreman	*supervisor*
insurance man	*insurance agent*
juryman	*juror*
linesman	*lines worker*
mailman/postman	*mail deliverer*
newsman	*reporter, journalist*
policeman	*police officer*
railwayman	*railway worker*
repairman/ serviceman	*repairer*
salesman	*shop assistant, sales clerk*
serviceman	*member of armed forces*
spokesman	*representative (of)*
sportsman	*athlete, player, competitor*
storeman	*stores officer*
weatherman	*weather officer*
workman	*worker*

In some of those cases, there is an exact female counterpart to the male term, as with *businessman/businesswoman*, and the latter could be used when it seems important to identify the gender of the person concerned. Yet as a generic term, *businesswoman* is no less sexist than *businessman*. Better than either term would be one which covers both sexes, and satisfies the broadest principle of nonsexist language (see **inclusive language**). Some advocate the use of words ending in *-person* (e.g. *chairperson*), although they work better in some cases than others (see under **-person**). Note also the need to avoid **-man** in some nationality words such as *Englishman*. You could use either *English person* (if the reference has to be singular), or *the English* (for the plural/collective).

When **man-** is the first element of the compound, satisfactory alternatives and paraphrases are not so easy to find. The following substitutes seem rather cumbersome and less precise:

manhours	working hours
mankind	the human race, humanity
man-made	artificial, manufactured
manpower	the work force

We might also ask whether the original word really works to the disadvantage of women. Do such generalized concepts prejudice women's chances of getting a particular job? The same may be argued in connection with certain conventional phrases containing **man**. Do they need to be paraphrased away?

every man for himself	everyone for themselves
man in the street	average person
no man's land	uncontrolled or ambiguous area
to a man	to the last person

Idiomatic expressions lose their vital connotations in a paraphrase.

The hunt to eradicate **man** from the language is sometimes taken to strange extremes by those who find sexist problems in words such as *manicure, manipulate, manoeuvre, manual, manufacture, manuscript*. The first element in all those words is the Latin root *man(u)* ("hand"). The words have nothing to do with **man** ("adult male").

manakin

See **mannequin**.

Mandarin, mandarin or mandarine

The word **Mandarin,** used to refer to officials of the former Chinese Empire, seems to have been coined in Chinese pidgin out of Portuguese *mandarim* (literally "they command"). The Portuguese themselves had borrowed and reinterpreted it from Malay and Indian sources (ultimately it's Sanskrit *mantrin,* "counsellor"). In current English the word had three distinct uses:

1 The capitalized form **Mandarin** now generally refers to the official language of the Republic of China, written as characters in the traditional way (not in alphabetic form). It was and is the language of northern China, as well as the Chinese bureaucracy and government.

2 In lower case, **mandarin** is used figuratively for high-ranking persons in any bureaucracy, or individuals who exercise influence in the intellectual sphere: *Armed with the classic mandarin's pedigree, he joined the Treasury in 1961.*

3 Both **mandarin** and **mandarine** are used to refer to a small tangerine-like fruit. The name is borrowed from French, when *mandarine* was short for "Chinese [orange]." In other European languages, the orange is a "Chinese apple": witness German *Apfelsiene,* Dutch *sinasappel*. In British English the fruit is occasionally spelled **mandarine**, in line with the French, but usually it's **mandarin**, as elsewhere in the world. See further under **-ine**.

mandatory, mandatary, and mandative

The first spelling **mandatory** is the common adjective meaning "obligatory," as in a *mandatory repatriation* or *mandatory comprehensive secondary education*. **Mandatary** translates the Latin *mandatarius* ("agent") in legal usage, and also serves to refer to a nation that holds a *mandate* over another, as decreed by the League of Nations after World War I. Thus the noun **mandatary** contrasts with the adjective **mandatory** – in theory. But the second is very much commoner than the first, which explains why **mandatory** is sometimes found for the noun, according to *Webster's Third* (1986) and the *Oxford Dictionary* (1989).

Mandative is mostly used by grammarians, to refer to the construction used after a persuasive word (verb, noun or adjective) which expresses the obligation in it. For example:

I insisted that he explain things fully.
Their demand that it be sent by return mail was unrealistic.
It is vital that she speak for them.

The verbs *explain, be, speak* in those sentences are *mandative subjunctives*. See **subjunctive** section 1.

manège or ménage

See **ménage**.

maneuver or manoeuvre

See **manoeuvre**.

mango

For the plural, **mangos** was strongly preferred over **mangoes**, by 72% of all respondents to the Langscape survey (1998–2001). See further under **-o**.

-mania

This Greek root means "madness," but in English its meaning is more often "obsession" or "compulsion," as in

kleptomania   megalomania   pyromania

Words like these imply a deluded or perverse mentality rather than one which is disordered. Perfectly sane people can suffer from *regalomania* ("an obsession with rules and regulations").

The meaning of **-mania** can be positive, as with *bibliomania,* where it simply refers to a passion for something. This is also shown in other recent formations with English roots, such as:

balletomania   discomania   videomania

Older words with **-mania** generate nouns ending in *-maniac* for referring to the person with the obsession or compulsion, as in *kleptomaniac* or *pyromaniac*. But for the newer, less pejorative words with **-mania** there are various counterparts:

balletomania >	balletomane
bibliomania >	bibliophil(e)
discomania >	discophil(e)

See under **phil-** or **-phile**.

manifesto

In British English, as in American, the plural of this word is now usually **manifestos**, which outnumbers **manifestoes** by almost 9: 1 in BNC data. For the declining use of *-oes* plurals, see **-o**.

manikin

See **mannequin**.

manila or manilla

Contemporary dictionaries prioritize the spelling with one *l* for all references to the fibre products (rope, envelopes, folders etc.) originally associated with the capital of the Philippines (see next entry). For *New Oxford* (1998) **manila** is the only spelling, whereas both *Webster's Third* (1986) and *Merriam-Webster* (2000) note **manilla** as an alternative. Paradoxically **manilla** is very little used in American English, by the evidence of CCAE; whereas the two spellings share the field in British data from the BNC, and **manilla** is actually a good deal commoner in transcribed spoken texts. This makes it the more intuitive British spelling, and it was in fact preferred by the *Oxford Dictionary* (1884–1928). That apart, the similarity with "vanilla" and the bland color of *manil(l)a paper* may prompt the use of **manilla**. For more on the issue of single or double consonants in foreign loanwords, see **single for double**.

No capital letter is needed when **manil(l)a** is used in reference to fibre products, pace *New Oxford,* since they have long since become generic, and all BNC citations are with lower case initial. *Merriam-Webster* indicates a capital for *Manila* = "hemp" but not paper products, again an unnecessary distinction not supported by CCAE.

Manila or Manilla

The first spelling with one *l* is gazetted for the capital of the Philippines. Very occasionally a second *l* slips in, and American dictionaries allow **Manilla** as an alternative to **Manila**, though there's scant evidence of its use in CCAE, apart from sporting references to the "Thrilla in Manilla."

Manila is also the official spelling for US towns in Arkansas and Utah, whereas others in Iowa and Australia (New South Wales and Queensland) use **Manilla**.

mannequin, mannikin, manikin or manakin

All these derive from the Dutch *manneken* ("a little man"), but their spellings put them in different worlds. The frenchified spelling **mannequin** is the one associated with fashion and the displaying of clothes to public gaze. It may refer either to a shopwindow dummy or a live model who parades up and down the carpeted catwalk.

A **manikin** is a small model of the human figure, as used by an artist, or in the context of teaching anatomy and surgery. Very occasionally it's used to refer to a small human (or quasi-human) figure: a pygmy or a dwarf. Alternative spellings are **mannikin** and **manakin**. Note however that **manakin** is also the name of a small brightly colored bird of Central and South America.

manoeuvre, manoeuver or maneuver

The spelling **manoeuvre** seems to have an excess of vowels, but it's the standard spelling for this French loanword in Britain and Australia, and more common in Canada than the other spellings, according to *Canadian English Usage* (1997). The spelling seems less awkward if you keep *hors d'oeuvre* in mind when writing it.

Maneuver is standard in the US, making it a good deal easier for Americans to put on paper. However the use of *e* for *oe* will not appeal to those who associate this spelling convention with words of Greek origin, such as *am(o)eba* (see further under **oe**). The use of *-er* instead of *-re* is again the regular American pattern for such words: see **-re/-er**. In Canada a hybrid spelling **manoeuver** is occasionally seen (*Canadian Oxford,* 1998).

When **manoeuvre** becomes a verb, the forms with suffixes are *manoeuvred* and *manoeuvring*. As an adjective it is *manoeuvrable*. For **maneuver**, the corresponding forms are *maneuvered, maneuvering* and *maneuverable*.

mantle or mantel

The first of these is a word for an old-fashioned garment, a loose, sleeveless cloak. By extension it also applies to any covering, such as the **mantle** on a portable gas lamp, or a blanket of snow over the earth. The metaphorical **mantle** which passes from one person to another is a symbol of authority – recalling the biblical story of how Elijah's **mantle** was passed down to Elisha.

A **mantel** is a shelf over a fireplace, often spelled out as a *mantelpiece* (or *mantelshelf*). However the spellings **mantle** and *mantlepiece* are also sometimes used with this meaning, less often in British English (ratio of 1:10) than American (3:10), by the evidence of BNC and CCAE.

Look back into their history and you find that both words derive from the Latin *mantellum* ("cloak"). The word was used in Old and Middle English with various spellings and meanings, and only in C17 did **mantle** become the regular spelling for the garment or covering, and **mantel** for the structure around a fireplace.

Maori

The indigenous people of New Zealand are now referred to as **Maori**, whether singular or plural. This reflects the fact that there is no *-s* plural in the **Maori** language. Other **Maori** loanwords are also left unmarked in the plural, thus *They heard several haka; there were once thousands of moa in the South Island.* See further under **New Zealand English**.

marijuana or marihuana

Dictionaries everywhere give first preference to **marijuana**, and it's the commoner spelling by far in American and British databases – almost to the exclusion of **marihuana**. The latter represents the word's pronunciation more satisfactorily if you are unfamiliar with Spanish pronunciation. Yet **marijuana** is closer to the etymology of this curious word, as far as it's known. Originally an American Indian word, the Spaniards could only interpret it as *Maria Juana* ("Mary Jane"), and this folk etymology

is still written into **marijuana**. See further under
folk etymology.

marquess or marquis

The *Oxford Dictionary* (1989) notes an early C20 trend
to replace **marquis** with **marquess**, based on
newspaper evidence. This now seems to apply mostly
to current British incumbents in the UK, but not their
historical or continental counterparts, by the
evidence of the BNC. The *Marquis de Sade* has not
become a **marquess**. American writers, more remote
from the latest trends in aristrocratic titles, continue
to use **marquis** for current British incumbents as
well as others, and it outnumbers **marquess** by more
than 16:1 in CCAE data.

In English the wife or widow of a **marquess/
marquis** is a *marchioness,* a term which goes back to
medieval Latin. In French she is a *marquise*.

marshal, marshall and Marshall

As a proper name, **Marshall** almost always has two *l*s
– witness geographical and historical names such as
the *Marshall Islands* and the *Marshall Plan*, as well as
the countless *Marshalls* in the metropolitan phone
directory. There are columns of surnames with two *l*s,
and only a handful with one *l* .

But as a common word (verb or noun), or as part of
a title, **marshal** normally has only one *l* . See for
example:

> *GW started to marshal his thoughts.*
> *Pick up your competition shirt from the beach
> marshal.*
> *Field Marshal Montgomery wrote breezily . . .*

After centuries when either spelling was acceptable,
the spelling **marshal** seems to have become dominant
in C19, according to *Oxford Dictionary* (1989) citations,
and in current British data from the BNC, there's
scarcely a **marshall** to be found. *Webster's Third*
(1986) allows Americans both spellings, yet usage data
from CCAE makes **marshal** the preferred spelling (by
about 5:1) for both verb and noun: *to marshal votes;
state/city fire marshal*.

Regional differences with **marshal** are most visible
in the spelling of inflected verb forms, where the
British have *marshalled/marshalling* and Americans
prefer *marshaled/marshaling*. See further under
-l-/-ll-.

martin or marten

The spelling **martin** refers to a small insectivorous
bird, such as the *house martin* or the *tree martin*. The
bird's name is believed to echo the personal name
Martin.

Marten is the spelling for a small carnivorous
animal like a weasel. It is native to North America and
hunted for its fur, often referred to as "sable." **Marten**
seems to be an adaption of the French word *martre*.

marveled or marvelled, and marveling or marvelling

The inflected forms of *marvel* may be spelled with one
or two *l*s, depending on your regional affiliation. In
American English *marveled/marveling* are preferred
by a large margin in CCAE data (more than 8:1),
whereas British preferences as shown in the BNC are
solidly with *marvelled/marvelling* (no trace of the
single *l* spellings). See further under **-l-/-ll-**.

marvelous or marvellous

The choice between these still turns on regional
preferences for single or double *l*. British preference
for **marvellous** runs deep, by 9:1 in responses to the
Langscape survey of 1998–2001, while Americans are
equally committed to **marvelous,** also by a factor of
9:1.

masculine gender

See under **gender**.

mass nouns

See under **count and mass nouns**.

masterful or masterly

Showing who is *master* and showing that you are a
master at something are clearly different. But there's
no simple dichotomy between **masterful** and
masterly that lines up with it, pace Fowler (1926), who
believed that **masterful** expresses the first meaning
(that you're in command of a situation), and that
masterly is to be deployed when great skill has been
demonstrated. Dictionaries register **masterful** in
both senses, and data from the BNC has it used about
as often in one sense as the other. Compare:

> *D would clamp a masterful hand on A's shoulder.*
> *He writes with masterful facility.*

Masterful appears in collocations where **masterly**
might have been expected, by Fowler's dichotomy, for
example in *masterful skill/performance*, as well as
masterful understatement.

The wider scope of **masterful** is ensured by the fact
that it's the only one of the pair which can serve as an
adverb: *masterfully*. **Masterly**, like other adjectives
ending in *-ly*, cannot satisfactorily add on the
adverbial *-ly* suffix, and so **masterfully** has to do
service for both adjectives. In *He had marginal talent
which he exploited masterfully,* we assume the adverb
means "in a masterly way."

Masterly and **masterful** are sometimes the focus of
feminist critiques of language, at which point
adjectives such as "skilled," "accomplished,"
"excellent," "consummate," "powerful,"
"authoritative" are suggested as alternatives (Maggio,
1988).

matey or maty

When excess chumminess is the issue, the adjective is
always **matey** – and the spelling refuses to conform
with the standard rules for words derived from stems
ending in *e* (see **-e**).

Mathew or Matthew

See **Matthew**.

maths or math

The first is the usual British abbreviation for
mathematics, the second is standard in American
English.

matrix

The plural of this word could be either Latin **matrices**
or English **matrixes** – and surprisingly perhaps, the
Latin has prevailed. *Webster's Third* (1986) endorses
matrices; and though the *Oxford Dictionary*
(1884–1928) gave priority to **matrixes**, the order was
reversed in the 1989 edition, on the strength of

numerous citations from mathematics and various new technologies including photography, computing and broadcasting. Most people are touched by one or other of those domains, and no strangers to **matrices** as the technical form of the plural. At any rate **matrices** reigns supreme as the plural of **matrix** in both British and American databases. **Matrixes** may be more often said than written, but there's scant evidence of it.

matte, matt or mat
British English often differentiates meanings with different spellings where American English makes do with one. So the British use **matt** (or **mat**) to refer to a non-shiny surface; and **matte** for
* the photographic and cinematographic technique of masking out part of the image on a frame or frames, so as to superimpose something else there
* the foundation layer in facial makeup
American English uses **matte** for all these meanings, by the evidence of CCAE:
> *The airport is covered in matte-finish steel.*
> *...awkward faking in the matte shot of Q and the fish in the same frame.*
> *Her matte cheeks were streaked with tears.*

Matte is the primary spelling in *Merriam-Webster* (2000), although *Webster's Third* (1986) foregrounded **mat**, in line with earlier usage in both the US and UK. This reflects the word's origins in French *mat* meaning "dead," as it was borrowed in C17. The spelling **matte** is of course the feminine form of the same adjective, borrowed in C19.

The noun **mat** ("carpet") is quite independent, rooted in earlier English *matt(e)* which probably came from Late Latin *matta*.

Matthew or Mathew
The spelling with two *t*s reflects the Latin antecedent *Matthaeus,* where the French form *Mathieu* had only one (Reaney, 1967). Database evidence from both the US and the UK shows that **Matthew** is a good deal commoner than **Mathew**, as a given or family name (*Matthew(s)* v. *Mathew(s)* etc.). The difference is more than 4:1 in CCAE and almost 30:1 in the BNC.
◊ See further under **single for double**.

maty or matey
See **matey**.

maunder or meander
Similar looks and uses have brought these together, though their origins are quite distinct. **Meander** is associated first and foremost with the winding course of a river, and was the Greek name for a Turkish river which flows into the western Mediterranean. The river is now known as the *Menderes*. **Maunder** means "talk in a rambling way, or act idly," as in *maundering through the interview*. It probably comes from medieval French *mendier* ("beg"). Both words can be used to mean "wander aimlessly," so you could say either:
> *Tourists meandered through the market stalls*
or
> *Tourists maundered through the market stalls*
There are still somewhat different implications. The first makes it a natural leisurely movement, where the second is rather pejorative.

mausoleum
The archetypal **mausoleum** was the tomb of the Greek king *Mausolus,* built at Halicarnassus in the fourth century BC, and so large that it counted as one of the "seven wonders" of the ancient world. In English **mausoleum** has two plurals, the latinate **mausolea** and the anglicized **mausoleums**. The first is used in antiquarian discussions of other largish tombs in the ancient world, the second for their modern analogues
> *...a sombre collection of blackened Christian mausoleums and monuments.*
◊ For more on the plurals of Latin words ending in -**um**, see under that heading.

maxi-
This prefix of the 1960s is derived from Latin *maximus* ("greatest or largest"). In English it usually means "large-sized", as in:
> maxibudget maxisingle maxiskirt
> maxi-taxi maxiyacht
Although they are hybrid Latin/English formations, new words with **maxi-** quickly lose their hyphens. In some examples the **maxi-** word is obviously coined to match a similar word with **mini-**. So *maxi-taxi,* first recorded in 1961, seems to parallel *minicab* (1960); and *maxiskirt* (1966) appeared just a year after *miniskirt. Mini-* is also a relatively new prefix: see **mini-**.

maxim
See under **aphorism**.

maxima cum laude
See under **cum laude**.

maximum
In scientific use, as when referring to the highest temperatures recorded, the plural is **maxima**. Elsewhere the anglicized plural **maximums** comes naturally.
◊ For more on the plurals of Latin loanwords ending in -**um**, see under that heading.

may or might
The choice between these two *modal* verbs is usually a matter of perspective rather than right or wrong. In simple statements this is certainly so. Both *they may come* and *they might come* are grammatically acceptable, and differ only in the fact that **might** makes the statement more tentative and the possibility more remote. The difference is more marked in polite questions:
> *May I have a cup of tea?*
> *Might I have a cup of tea?*
In British English the first has long been standard polite form, and so the second seems overanxious to let the other party determine your right to the simplest of drinks. (In fact, even *May I* can sound overpolite, and *Can I* takes its place: see **can or may**).

Grammatical issues weigh more heavily in the compound verb phrases *may have* and *might have*. Here the choice is sometimes argued as a matter of tense, given that **might** is historically the past tense of **may** and therefore appropriate alongside other past tense verbs:
> *Whatever he may have said, he is basically loyal.*
> *Whatever he might have said, he was basically loyal.*

The here-and-now perspective of the first sentence contrasts with the all-in-the-past of the second. The verb tenses are consistent in each, shifted back from present to past, and present perfect *may have* to past perfect *might have,* if you wish. See further under **sequence of tenses**.

But the use of *might have* in that second sentence also affects the meaning, making the possibility of disloyal comments more remote than with *may have.* Because **might** seems to foreclose on such possibilities, it is argued as the only logical choice in contexts such as the following, where the use of *may have* would be ruled ungrammatical:

> *The girl may not have survived if the operation hadn't been performed.*

Clearly the girl did survive, and *might (not) have* would have signaled the positive outcome up front. The writer's choice of *may have* leaves the outcome briefly in doubt, thereby involving readers in the tension of the situation, though the meaning is the same in the end. This use of *may have* rather than *might have* is most often noted in news reporting, both in the UK (Burchfield, 1996) and the US (*Webster's English Usage,* 1989). In the context of current affairs, *may have* lends a sense of immediacy which is valued more highly than other considerations. A polished sequence of tenses is a nicety, if not a distraction from the realities of the event. Readers with a firm grammatical training still tend to find *may have* awkward and/or reprehensible; yet for many, **may** is the modal verb of choice in these contexts, and unremarkable.

Contemporary grammarians maintain that the tense distinction between **may** and **might** (and between *may have* and *might have*) has been largely neutralized (*Comprehensive Grammar,* 1985). The *Longman Grammar* (1999) regards these and other modal verbs as unmarked for tense, because their use so often reflects speaker/writer stance rather than time in the world being referred to. That apart, **may** is overall much commoner than **might** in nonfictional writing, according to *Longman* research, and becomes the unmarked choice between the two modals. Thus a complex of issues underlies the use of *may have* where *might have* could otherwise have appeared. Its use in formal prose remains answerable to questions of grammatical logic, but it can be rationalized in interactive styles of writing.

◊ For more on the uses of these verbs, see under **modality**, and **can or may**, and **could or might**.

◊ For *may of* and *might of,* see **have** ("Final notes").

May Day or mayday

With its capital letters and a space between the words, **May Day** (May 1) is celebrated in the northern hemisphere as the first day of spring. But the traditional games and dancing and celebration of nature have given way, in the last century, to parades celebrating the international labor movement.

Without capitals or space, **mayday** is the international distress call used by ships and aircraft to radio for help. The rhyming syllables represent the French cri de coeur *m'aider* – or *m'aidez* – ("help me)". The English spelling is a neat example of *folk etymology* (see under that heading) – but it ensures that we get the pronunciation right when in dire straits.

maybe or may be

The space makes all the difference. **May be** with space between the words is a compound verb, as in *It may be vital,* where *may* is the auxiliary verb (see further under **auxiliary verbs**).

Maybe is an adverb meaning "perhaps." It has a slightly informal character in British English, perhaps because of its frequent occurrences in conversation and "thinking aloud":

> *Maybe they'll arrive tomorrow.*

In BNC data **maybe** occurs about three times as often in spoken texts as in written ones. This does not prevent it from appearing in various kinds of writing, except the most formal. Burchfield (1996) suggests that **maybe** has made a comeback in British English vis-à-vis *perhaps,* and relatively speaking there's something in this. In BNC data the overall frequencies of *perhaps* and **maybe** put *perhaps* ahead by a factor of 3:1 – whereas it was 5:1 in corpus statistics from the1960s (Hofland and Johansson, 1982). So **maybe** is not so far behind as it was, and being so often at the start of a sentence (about 40% of the time, in BNC data), it impacts more strongly on the reader/listener than it might otherwise. In American English the gap between the two has also narrowed over the last decades of C20. In the 1960s *perhaps* outnumbered **maybe** by a little over 2:1; they are now almost 1:1 in data from CCAE. **Maybe** is increasingly popular everywhere, and usable in all but the most formal kinds of writing.

Mb, MB, mb or mbyte

See **megabyte**.

me

The pronoun **me** comes very close to us all, though grammarians and other language commentators of the past have made us rather self-conscious about it. People sometimes replace it with *myself,* as if to avoid putting the spotlight directly on themselves:

> *The chairman appointed myself to that position.*

There is no need to do this. In fact we draw less attention to ourselves by using the ordinary **me**:

> *The chairman appointed me to that position.*

Anxieties about **me** probably stem from two constructions which are censured by the grammarian, though they are quite common in informal dialogue. One is the use of **me** instead of *my* as a possessive adjective (especially by young people), as in:

> *I rode up there on me bike.*

Written down, this **me** seems ungrammatical (a first person pronoun where a determiner should be used). In fact it looks worse than it usually sounds – like *my* with a shortened vowel or *schwa* (see further under that heading). When scripting informal dialogue there may be good reason to write **me** or *m'* instead of *my,* though it would be out of place or substandard in most other kinds of writing.

The other informal construction uses **me** after *and* for a coordinated subject, as in:

> *Jim and me left before the rest.*

Here **me** substitutes for *I,* and in standard grammar it would be *Jim and I left before the rest.* But in easy-going conversation some speakers use the object pronoun **me** whether its role is subject or object. This would reflect the more general trend among world Englishes (Wales, 1996) to use the object pronoun for all cases (see further under **cases**). But there's a curious counterpoint in the way *I* is sometimes used instead of **me** when coordinated as the object of a preposition, e.g. *for you and I, like you and I, between you and I.* It may be a form of hypercorrection (see **between you and me (or I)**).

Whatever the vagaries of **me** in casual speech, its use in writing is still complementary to *I*, as object and subject pronoun respectively. In noncoordinated constructions, the use of **me** is stable, and the *I/me* distinction is matched by *we/us, he/him, she/her, they/them,* though absent from *you* and *it.* For the moment there are more English pronouns with the subject/object distinction than without it.
◇ See further under **I** ("grammatical notes").

mea culpa

This Latin phrase meaning "by my fault" comes from the confession at the beginning of the mass. But it has long been used in secular English to mean simply "I am to blame" whenever we feel the need to admit responsibility for a problem – whether it's the mismatched cutlery on the table or the mistaken information which has made everyone late for dinner. Its Latin dress still makes it a rather earnest admission, and neither it nor *peccavi* ("I have sinned") can be used very lightheartedly.

meagre or meager

Regional preferences are as you might expect. **Meager** is strongly preferred in American English (by more than 20:1 in CCAE data), whereas **meagre** outnumbers it by 200:1 in data from the BNC. See further under **-re/-er**.

meander or maunder

See **maunder**.

meaningful

Overworked words lose their cutting edge, and the meaning of *meaningful* is threatened in this way. Even worse, *meaningful* tends to devalue the words it's combined with. In clichés such as *meaningful dialogue, meaningful discussions, meaningful negotiation,* we begin to wonder what the opposite ("meaningless" dialogue/discussions/negotiation) might be. Can anything be discussed or negotiated without some meaning being exchanged? And does **meaningful** mean much in *meaningful experience* or *meaningful relationship?* In many cases it's redundant, or simply substitutes for "important" or "worthwhile" – which more clearly express the value judgement. If **meaningful** is a synonym for "significant," then the actual significance should be explained. If we take the load off **meaningful** by these various means, it has a better chance of retaining its essential denotation – "full of meaning" in expressions such as *meaningful look, meaningful smile, meaningful pause* – and of being a **meaningful** component of English.

means

This word looks plural, yet it can combine with either a singular or plural verb, depending on the meaning. When it means "resources or income," it's always plural:

> *Their means were never large enough for her dreams.*

When it means "method of doing something," it can be either singular or plural, according to whether one or several methods is at stake:

> *His ultimate means of gaining public attention was to fake disappearance.*
> *We've tried all the means that are available to ordinary citizens.*

As the last example shows, the use of words such as *all, many, several* (or any plural number) confirms the need for a plural verb; and the use of *a, any, each, every* would show where a singular verb is needed.

measles

Should it be *Measles is rampant at the school* or *Measles are rampant . . . ?* See **agreement** section 2.

medalist or medallist

While **medalist** is strongly preferred in American English, it's **medallist** in British English. The preferences are overwhelming in database evidence from BNC and CCAE. Yet in the Langscape survey 1998–2001, **medalist** was endorsed by a small majority even in the UK (55%), by 56% of Asian respondents and 67% of those in Europe – suggesting the way of the future. The practice of doubling the *l* is in any case less strong for derivatives like **medal(l)ist** than for inflected parts of the verb. See further under **-l-/-ll-**.

> **International English selection:** Medalist is to be preferred on grounds of its greater regularity and wider distribution worldwide.

media and medium

In English **media** has long been used as the plural of the Latin *medium* ("a vehicle or channel of communication"), especially in reference to the various forms of visual art, such as fresco, mosaic, relief, oil-painting, charcoal, gouache. But in C20 it has been largely overtaken by the use of **media** to refer to the channels of mass communication, such as radio, TV and newspapers. *The media,* first recorded in the 1950s, is now a byword for the *mass media* at large. This collective usage of **media** not unnaturally couples with a singular verb from time to time, as in:

> . . . *fears which the media has shamelessly played on*

The same idea could equally be put as:

> . . . *fears which the media have shamelessly played on*

In BNC data, the two types of agreement are about equally common overall, and in spoken data the singular dominates. An *Oxford Dictionary* (1989) citation from 1966 noted the use of **media** as a singular noun "spreading into upper cultural strata" – a not-entirely neutral observation. The dictionary still labels such usage "erroneous," though it makes **media** a headword in its own right. *New Oxford* (1998) moves things along one step with a usage note saying that **media** "behaves as a collective noun," and is "acceptable in standard English with either singular or plural." *Webster's Third* (1986) lists it under *medium,* but allows that it is "sometimes singular in construction." In CCAE the ratio of singular to plural is about 2:3. Yet neither the American nor the British database provides many instances that are clearly singular or plural. Over 80% of examples are indeterminate in number, many because they are attributive, as in *media coverage, a media event, the media industry.*

This large-scale indeterminacy paves the way for the use of **media** as a count noun, as in *a new recording media,* and the corresponding English plural **medias,** both noted in *Webster's English Usage* (1989). There are grains of evidence for both in CCAE: several examples of the type *a media given over to press agentry,* and *the network news medias.* Only the second type appears in the BNC (e.g. *Ethernet medias*). So neither is well established in print, nor yet registered in *New Oxford* (1998) or *Merriam-Webster's* (2000).

Media as *mass media* is thus on the cusp of switching from the Latin paradigm in which it was plural, to English uses in which it's singular – a collective and even a countable noun. Dictionaries have been rather slow to endorse these developments, though the collective use of **media** supports plural as well as singular agreement, and thus embraces the traditional use. (See further under **collective nouns.**)

Part of the fallout from this grammatical shakedown is that **medium** takes over the English plural **mediums** for all its purposes:

* the occult: *manipulating spirits and demons with the help of exorcists and mediums*
* in the arts: *acrylic mediums, water-based painting mediums; the more inventive mediums of children's literature*
* general, as in *mediums of exchange; water is the most forgiving of mediums to fall into*
* ad hoc, in reference to the *medium-sized: mediums priced at 120p.*

Though dictionaries still allow **media** as the plural for all but the first of those uses, **mediums** helps to distinguish them all from specific references to the *mass media.* The two plurals are now more strongly differentiated than for most other Latin loanwords ending in *-um.* See under that heading.

medieval or mediaeval

The first of these has now largely eclipsed the second, even in British English. It was endorsed by more than 70% of UK respondents to the Langscape survey 1998–2001. **Medieval** outnumbers **mediaeval** by more than 20:1 in data from the BNC. See further under **ae/e.**

medio-passive

See **middle voice.**

mediocre

This word is spelled the same way everywhere in the English-speaking world. Even in North America the *-re* is standard spelling, never replaced with *-er:* see **-re/-er.**

The word **mediocre** ("middling") is taken very literally by some as the mid point of a scale. They therefore argue that it cannot be qualified by words such as "rather" or "very": something either is or is not "in the middle." (See **absolute** section 1.) For most people **mediocre** is more general in its meaning, just "ordinary and unremarkable," and there's no problem in qualifying the word with adverbs of degree. But it has become rather pejorative in most applications. Calling the recital "a mediocre performance" now seems to mean it was actually below average, i.e. "inferior."

medium

Should the plural of this word be **media** or **mediums**? See **media.**

meet (up) (with)

For centuries the verb *meet* has worked simply and effectively, with no extra particles:

> *We met the director in her office.*
> *They met at the bar after work.*

In grammatical terms the first sentence is transitive, the second intransitive (see further under **transitive**); but each is self-sufficient. The very simplicity of this seems to make English-speakers want to add to it, and many are inclined to use **meet with** as the transitive form, and **meet up** as the intransitive:

> *We met with the director . . .*
> *They met up at the bar . . .*

Between the first and second set, there are perhaps some subtle differences: a certain formality about **meet with** and a sense of the importance of the encounter; while **meet up** seems to connote a more ordinary get-together, even by chance. These differences in connotation may justify their use on occasions, though **meet** itself would also be sufficient.

British usage commentators sometimes present a different argument for avoiding **meet with** in the sense of "come into the presence of." They find it unfortunate that this coincides with **meet with** in the sense "incur or experience," as in:

> *I hope it meets with your approval.*
> *She met with huge resistance.*

Yet dictionaries allow both kinds of meaning for **meet with,** and the distinction is clear from whether the object of **meet with** is animate (as with "director") or abstract (as with "approval" and "resistance"). The two meanings are about equally common in data from the BNC.

As if this were not enough, **meet** is quite often accompanied by *up* as well as *with,* when it perhaps means no more than **meet** in its simple, transitive sense of "encounter or come together with." See for example:

> *. . . no lack of opportunities to meet up with your contemporaries*

Perhaps there's something more purposeful about **meet up with** than just **meet,** to justify the extra words. At any rate the usage is widespread – far from confined to American English, where it originated last century. There are scores of examples in the BNC, in both written and spoken texts; and it's acknowledged in Canadian and Australian dictionaries. Although the use of two particles (*up, with*) after a simple verb may seem excessive, we take it for granted in quite a few other verb phrases, such as *come up with* and *walk out on* (see further under **phrasal verbs**). Their flavor is slightly informal, but they are established idioms.

mega-, megalo- and mega

Derived from Greek, this prefix means "huge." In physical measurements, such as those calibrated in *megahertz, megatons, megawatts,* **mega-** means exactly "1 million or 10^6." It takes its place among the standard metric prefixes, represented by the symbol *M* (see Appendix IV). In the computer term *megabyte,* **mega-** equals 2^{20}.

In other scientific and scholarly words, **mega-** just means "impressively large," as in:

> megafauna   megalith   megaspore
> megastructure

Megapod meaning "having large feet" can be applied generally in zoological description; whereas *macropod* (again literally "having large feet"), is strictly the term for members of the kangaroo family. (For other uses of **macro-** see under that heading.)

Megalo- is an older form of **mega-**, which combines only with Greek words, as in *megalomania, megalopolis, megalosaur*. The older *megalocephalic* is being replaced by *megacephalic*.

In the past, the words coined with **mega-** were scientific and scholarly. A few of them have however taken root in everyday English, as when the technical term *megaton(s)* provides a hyperbolic word for "a huge load of": *megatons of work to do*. Since World War II **mega-** itself has taken off as an intensifying prefix meaning anything from "vast in numbers" to "awesomely great or large," as in:

> megabucks   megadeal   megadeath
> megadose   megaflop   megahit
> megamerger   megastar   megastore

In words like these **mega-** clearly lends itself to reporting on the spectacular, and to promotion of larger-than-ever businesses. These ready applications are the launching pad from which **mega** becomes a word in its own right, a powerful adjective or adverb to be flung around in casual conversation:

* adjective
    a mega prize
    see mega forests instead of trees
    the mega money need to gain a foothold
* adverb
    to think mega
    mega rich
    mega lively hotel

These new grammatical roles are recognized in *New Oxford* (1998), *Canadian Oxford* (1998) and the *Macquarie Dictionary* (1997), though labeled "informal" or "colloquial." Despite its meteoric rise, **mega** as a popular intensifier could suffer the fate of any overused word – a rapid decline into merely sounding dated (see further **intensifiers**). Meanwhile, the stable uses of **mega-** in science and scholarship go quietly on.

megabyte

The computer industry and computer magazines have still to reach consensus on how to abbreviate **megabyte**. The most common forms are *MB* and *Mb*, while *M*, *Mbyte* and *megs* are among the alternatives. Database evidence from CCAE puts **MB** way ahead in American usage, which may have something to do with the fact that it's recommended by the *Microsoft Manual of Style* (1998). In British data from the BNC, **Mb** leads from **MB** by about 2:1, with **mb** a long way behind. Note that the use of *M* and *mega* itself is somewhat contentious: see under **bytes**.

meiosis

See under **figures of speech**.

Melanesia

See under **Polynesia**.

melodious or melodic

For musicologists and others, **melodic** is the one to use when you're talking technically about the structure of music, and distinguishing the melody component from rhythm and harmony. But for other general purposes, **melodic** and **melodious** are synonyms. Both can be applied to a tune or pattern of sound which appeals to the ear:

> *He was in full melodic voice*
> *... the melodious chant of the monks*

Effectively **melodic** has more applications than **melodious** – which would explain why it's the commoner of the two, by a factor of 5:1 in BNC data. Apart from its use as banter in "I heard your melodious voice," **melodious** has a somewhat literary flavor these days, which also helps to account for its decreasing use.

melted or molten

In current English we conventionally speak of *melted butter* and *melted ice*, but *molten lead* and *molten lava*. The twin adjectives are reminders of the fact that there were once (in Old English) two verbs relating to the process of becoming liquid. They merged in Middle English, and both **molten** and **melted** were used as past participles for the verb *melt* in early modern English. The regular form **melted** eventually prevailed, as often when regular and irregular forms compete (see **irregular verbs**); and **molten** was confined to the adjective role, especially to phrases in which it combined with metals or other substances that are liquefied only by great heat. Earlier authors could write of "molten passions," but that's probably too much hyperbole for C21 taste. We do however make figurative use of **melted**, as in "At those words he melted," to express a much gentler human emotion.

membranous, membraneous or membranaceous

Shorter is definitely better. **Membranous** is the only one of the three to occur more than once in BNC data, and is found in a variety of scientific texts, both biological and medical.

memento or momento

The Latin imperative **memento** ("remember!") has been used in English for a token of remembrance since C18. Just occasionally it's written as **momento**, a variant now registered in *Webster's Third* (1986) and the *Oxford Dictionary* (1989), though it first appeared in the middle of C20, according to *Webster's English Usage* (1989). No doubt **momento** has been downplayed because the spelling obscures the Latin root *mem-* ("remember") in the first syllable. It nevertheless reflects the way the syllable is pronounced in English – often with an indeterminate vowel. **Momento** also suggests folk etymology at work, aligning the word with *momentous* and the special *moment*, rather than the means of *remembering* or *commemorating* something. (See further under **folk etymology**.) But **momento** is still far from common in either British or American English, occurring in only about 10% of all instances of the word, by the evidence of BNC and CCAE.

The plural of **memento** is usually **mementos** (not **mementoes**), by a majority of 72% in the Langscape survey 1998–2001. See further under **-o**.

memento mori

See under **danse macabre**.

memorandum and memo

Both these refer to a genre of inter-office communication in government and industry, one which is more public and less personal than letters. In official references to such documents (both inside and outside the bureaucracy), **memorandum** is the standard form. It lends quasi-legal status to documents in *Memorandum of Agreement* and *Memorandum of Association*. In keeping with these formal roles, its plural is usually the Latin *memoranda* rather than the anglicized *memorandums*. *Memoranda* was supported by two thirds of those responding to the Langscape survey 1999–2001, and it's strongly endorsed in database evidence from the US and the UK. CCAE has it in 73% of all instances of the word, and the percentage rises to 95% in the BNC. See further under **-um**.

The abbreviated form **memo** nevertheless has a life of its own, going back over a century, according to the *Oxford Dictionary* (1989). In BNC data it occurs in 150 different texts – a variety of nonbureaucratic documents intended for the general public:

Each time a memo was fired off and the problem was solved.

Diligent searching had unearthed a memo sign by Dr S...

Both *New Oxford* (1998) and *Merriam-Webster* (2000) make the plural **memos**, as is usual for abbreviated words ending in *-o* (see under **-o**).

◊ For the format of **memos**, see Appendix VII.

ménage or manège

These French loanwords refer respectively to the management of one's house and the management of one's horse, so they are not to be confused. Without their accents, they are easily mistaken for each other. One way to remember the difference is that **ménage** is like *menial*, and involves the humdrum business of running a household; whereas **manège** which embodies the Latin root *manus* ("hand") has to do with handling a horse.

Ménage also refers to the structure of a household, and the people who comprise it. So the *ménage à trois* (literally "household with three") is a discreet way of referring to a nonstandard household of three persons – a husband, wife, and a third who is the lover of one of them.

mendacity or mendicity

These two are dangerously alike. **Mendacity** refers to the falseness of something, or a particular falsehood. A *mendacious report* embodies false and deceptive statements. Those accused of **mendicity** have the consolation of knowing that they are poor but honest about their condition. **Mendicity** is a formal word for begging, and a way of life for a *mendicant* ("beggar").

Menorca or Minorca

See **Minorca**.

-ment

This suffix, borrowed from French and Latin, forms many an English word. It makes nouns out of verbs, especially those which are French in origin. Here is a sample of them from the letter *A*:

accomplishment	advertisement	agreement
alignment	amusement	announcement
arrangement	assessment	

Only a handful of **-ment** words are formed with English verbs, including *catchment, puzzlement, settlement,* and a special subgroup prefixed with *em-* or *en-*: *embitterment, embodiment, encampment, enlightenment, enlistment.*

Most words ending in **-ment** can express the action of the verb they embody, as well as the product which results from the action:

the development of the program	*a new housing development*
an investment in their future	*devaluing our investments*

The spelling of words with **-ment** usually means leaving the verb intact, as in all the examples so far. Verbs ending in *-e* retain it, in keeping with the general rule before suffixes beginning with a consonant (see under **-e**). Note however that when the verb ends in *-dge*, two spellings are possible, as with *abridg(e)ment, acknowledg(e)ment, judg(e)ment, lodg(e)ment.* In the Langscape survey (1998–2001) the spellings with *-dge* were endorsed by a majority worldwide, but not the American respondents, with whom *-dg* spellings are at least as popular. (See further under **abridgement**, **acknowledgement**, **judgement**, **lodgement**. For the spelling of *argument*, see under that heading.)

Note also that **-ment** words based on verbs ending in *l* may have one or two *l*s before the suffix, as with *enrol(l)ment* and *fulfil(l)ment*. In Britain such words often have only one *l*, because of the current British spelling of the simple verb (*enrol, fulfil*). In North America the two *l*s of the simple verb carry on into the words with **-ment**. However the spellings *forestalment* and *instalment* reflect outdated spellings of the verb even in Britain. See further under **forestallment** and **installment**.

merchandise or merchandize

Borrowed from French in C13, **merchandise** added to itself a verb role in C16 and C17 English, meaning just "buy, sell." In C20 it has resurfaced in the more formal sense of "put on the market via publicity," primarily as the verbal noun *merchandising*:

We'll do the ticketing, the merchandising, the sponsorships, the TV rights...

It is also often used as a verbal adjective, in *merchandising campaign/director/machine/rights*. It rarely appears yet as a simple verb, but that is presumably only a matter of time.

Both *Merriam-Webster* (2000) and *New Oxford* (1998) allow that the verb may be spelled as **merchandize**, making it part of the large set of verbs ending in *-ise* which can also be *-ize* (see **-ize/-ise**). This option is rarely taken up in either American or British English, by the the evidence of CCAE and the BNC.

merino

For the plural of this, see **-o**.

meronymy

See under **metonymy**.

Mesdames

See under **madam** and **plurals** section 3.

Messrs(.)

Conventional titles such as *Mr. (Mrs., Ms.)* are normally used in the singular, but just occasionally a plural is needed to refer to the two or more male principals of a company. At such times, English looks to French to fill the gap, **Messrs** being a contracted form of *messieurs*. The word most often appears in

* correspondence, as in *Messrs Smith & Jones, Solicitors*
* news reporting, as in *Messrs Mondale, Foot and Kinnock,* where it provides a common title for a diverse set of male political leaders.

As shown in these examples from the BNC, the word is never stopped, because it's a contraction. (See **contractions** section 1 and **abbreviations** section 2b.) In American English, meanwhile, the word appears with a full stop as **Messrs.**, in keeping with standard American practice for all abbreviations and contractions.

mestizo
See under **Metis**.

meta-
Derived from Greek, this prefix essentially meant "with, beyond or after" (in space or time), and often involved a change of place or condition. The idea of change is the one in *metamorphosis,* as well as *metaphor* and *metathesis;* and the meaning "after" is the original one in *metaphysics*, though in modern English it has been reinterpreted there as "beyond, transcending."

All these kinds of meaning are to be found in modern formations with **meta-**. In anatomical words such as *metacarpus, metatarsus, metathorax*, **meta-** means "beyond" in a simple physical sense. *Metabolism* and *metachromatism* build on the idea of change. And the most widely used sense of all, "transcending," is exemplified in new words such as *metalanguage, metapsychology, metempirics.*

metadata
The information that identifies the contents of an internet document, its source and physical properties, is its **metadata**. This is coded into a header on the homepage (and other pages within), to enable search engines to find them for relevant purposes. See further under **page**.

metal or mettle
These two spellings have evolved from one and the same word, to distinguish its concrete meaning from the more abstract one. The spelling **metal** remains close to the form and meaning of the original Latin and Greek word *metallum/metallon*. The word's more abstract and figurative meaning, "spirit, strength of character," began to appear in late C16, and by the beginning of C18 this sense was regularly written as **mettle**. The English spelling masks both its classical ancestry and its physical connections.

metallic and metallurgy, metal(l)ed, metal(l)ize and metallise
Everywhere in the English-speaking world, **metallic** and **metallurgy** are spelled with two *l*s. Both words were borrowed ready-made from French, and so are unaffected by the variation between single and double *l*.

The word **metal(l)ed**, usually in *metal(l)ed road/highway* etc. is spelled with two *l*s in British

English and one in American, in keeping with the usual regional divergence for verbs based on words ending in *l*. (See -**l-/-ll-**.)

The verb **metal(l)ize** diverges in the same way, with **metalize** used in the US, and **metallize** (or **metallise**) in the UK. In this three-way split, Canadians prefer **metallize**, according to the *Canadian Oxford* (1998), whereas Australians go for **metallise** (*Macquarie Dictionary,* 1997). See further under -**ize/-ise**.

metaphors and similes
Metaphors are non-literal uses of words, and a life-force of language. They lend vitality to routine commentary on anything, as when a golfing shot is said to be "rocketing its way to the ninth green." The *metaphorical* word "rocketing" brings lively imagery to bear on an ordinary subject. **Metaphors** help to extend the frontiers of words, beginning as fresh figurative uses, and ending up as permanent additions to the word's set of meanings. The notion of seeking one's "roots" and discovering unknown "branches" of one's family are thoroughly established, and to understand them we do not need to invoke the "tree" metaphor on which they're based.

When **metaphors** like these become ordinary elements of the language, they are sometimes referred to as *dead metaphors*. Yet even dead metaphors have a phoenix-like capacity to revive, as when President Gerald Ford declared that "solar energy is something that cannot come in overnight." The imagery in familiar **metaphors** is latent rather than dead.

A *mixed metaphor* involves using two (or more) divergent metaphors in quick succession. Between them they create a dramatically inconsistent picture, as when someone is said to "have his head so deep in the sand he doesn't know which side of the fence he's on" – to quote Australian state premier Bjelke-Petersen, who knew how to use the *mixed metaphor* (or "mixaphor") to divert and disarm those interviewing him.

Metaphors, like most stimuli, need to be indulged in moderation: not too many at once, and none exploited too hard. An *extended metaphor* can work well provided it's not used relentlessly. The effectiveness of the *metaphor* in the following passage begins to flag after the third or fourth attempt to extend it:

> *The boss entered them for all kinds of new competitive activities. They were spurred into presenting themselves at the starting gate for every government grant (whether it was the right race or not), and feeling thoroughly flogged, they yearned for green pastures . . .*

Like the hard-worked public servants of that example, **metaphors** can be overextended. They then become too obvious, and run the risk of parodying themselves.

Metaphors and similes. Metaphors work best allusively, likening one thing to another by passing implication. Their contribution is much less direct and explicit than that of **similes**. Compare:

> *The ball rockets its way to the ninth green.*
> *The ball goes like a rocket to the ninth green.*

In **similes**, the comparison is spelled out in a phrase beginning with *like* or *as,* and the image it raises is set alongside the statement, not integrated with it as in a **metaphor**. But **similes** do allow for more complex comparisons which cannot be set up in a single word. For example:

> *Conversing with him is like wrestling with an octopus. He weighs in with one heavyweight topic after another.*

Similes, like **metaphors**, can become regular idioms of the language:

> *built like a tank   mad as a hatter*
> *charge like a wounded bull*

Some **similes** are common to all varieties of English, others reflect the regional context, e.g. the Australian *mad as a cut snake.* Everywhere they lend color to everyday talk.

◊ For the difference between **metaphors** and *metonyms,* see **metonymy**.

meteor, meteoroid or meteorite

These words are sometimes interchanged, yet they refer to different phases in the life of a celestial object. It begins as a **meteoroid**, an inert mass of mineral traveling in space far from the earth's orbit. When drawn into the earth's orbit and through earth's atmosphere, it becomes white-hot and is seen as a fiery streak through the heavens. In this form it's called a **meteor** or "shooting star." Small **meteors** burn up to nothingness in the skies, but larger ones shoot through to the earth's surface, sometimes creating a great cavity in it. The cold and once again inert mass which remains is the **meteorite**.

meter or metre

See **metre**.

Metis and metis

In Canada, this term indicates a person of mixed European and Aboriginal Indian ancestry. Derived from older French *métis* ("mixed"), it keeps the long *e* in English pronunciation but loses the accent when written down. The word is invariable, whether used in the singular, plural or as an attributive: *She represents Metis tradition.* Used in reference to the distinct socio-cultural group, it's always capitalized.

In the US, **metis** without a capital letter is used to refer to people with mixed Amerindian and European ancestry (especially French/Indian). In northern and central US it takes the place of *mestizo,* which is used in the south and west of the country. *Mestizo* derived from Spanish and **metis** from French are cognates going back to the same late Latin word *mixt(ic)us.*

◊ For other issues in referring to people of mixed ancestry, see **miscegenation**.

metonymy and meronymy

Metonymy is a figure of speech in which you name something by something with which it is regularly associated. So *the bar* comes to stand for the legal profession, because of the railing in a courtroom which divides the public space from the area reserved exclusively for legal personnel. *The press* stands for journalists and reporters whose writing is made public by the newspaper press. A *metonym* thus often stands for an institution of some kind. They can also be used in reference to familiar practices. In the phrase *on the bottle, the bottle* is a *metonym* for heavy consumption of alcohol, just as *(tied to) the kitchen sink* represents the (typically) female domestic duties.

Metonymy (which works by associated objects) should be distinguished from **meronymy**, the figure

of speech which names a part of something as a way of referring to the whole. Thus the "roof over our heads" is a *meronym* for "house." In traditional rhetoric this was called *synecdoche.* See further under that heading.

metre or meter

These different spellings mean several different things, unlike other -**re**/-**er** pairs (see under that heading).

A **metre** is first and foremost a measure of length, the standard SI unit for it, and the one from which the *metric system* itself takes its name (see Appendix V). The spelling **metre** is used everywhere except in the US, where it's **meter**. **Metre** (US **meter**) is also the word/spelling for a particular rhythmic pattern in poetry. Both words come from the Greek *metron* ("a measure").

The word **meter** ("measuring instrument") is a native English word, based on the verb *mete* ("distribute or give out"), which once meant "measure." This then provides a contrast between *gas meter* and *poetic metre,* except in American English, where the same spelling **meter** is used for both.

-metre or -meter

Is a *micrometre* the same as a *micrometer?* Not at all. A *micrometre* is one millionth of a metre, whereas *micrometer* is a special instrument for measuring minute lengths. Having said that, both would be *micrometer* in the US.

In Britain, Canada and Australia, the spelling -**metre** is attached to words that are units of length within the metric system, like *millimetre, centimetre, kilometre* (see Appendix V). In the US, -**meter** is the standard spelling.

Everywhere in the English-speaking world, the spelling in -**meter** is used for:

1 measuring instruments, such as:

> *altimeter   barometer   odometer   speedometer thermometer*

2 poetic metres, such as:

> *hexameter   pentameter   tetrameter*

The use of -**meter** for the second set with (poetic) *metre* is an anomaly for those using British, Canadian and Australian English. In American English *hexameter* and poetic *meter* are happily consistent (see previous entry). It would be better still if -**metre**/ *metre* were used by all for poetic metres and units of measurement, and -**meter**/*meter* for measuring instruments, in accordance with their etymologies. But that would be language engineering!

metres square or square metres

See under **square metres**.

metric or metrical

The word **metric** is usually associated with the SI units of the *metric system;* whereas **metrical** is the adjective associated with poetic metres. In the past **metric** could also be used for the latter, helped no doubt by the fact that the noun *metrics* also referred to poetic metre. So like some other -*ic*/-*ical* pairs, the two adjectives have acquired distinct areas of meaning. See -**ic**/-**ical** and **metre or meter**.

metrication and the metric system

The **metric system** of measurement was instituted in France late in C18, and originally standardized by reference to physical objects kept in Paris, such as the platinum-iridium bar for the metre. Following the international metric convention 1870–5, many nations in continental Europe and South America went metric. But English-speaking nations have moved much more slowly, and progress is still uneven in different parts of the world.

∗ In Britain the process of **metrication** began officially in 1965, and though the currency is fully decimalized, metric and imperial measures continue to coexist in many domains. The "pint" of beer is dispensed as a fraction of a litre, and goods sold by weight are costed by the kilo – though imperial measures die hard with some retailers. Most road signs give distances in miles, while the permitted lengths of vehicles are in metres. British engagement with the EU has provided greater incentives for **metrication** than ever before, though there are still strong feelings about abandoning "good old British feet" in favor of the metre.

∗ In the US, public use of metric measures is still not conspicuous, despite being legalized by Act of Congress in 1866. Attempts in the 1890s to make it the official system were resisted, especially by the manufacturing industries; and only now with the adoption of the **metric system** by the US Army and Marine Corps, and by NASA for their weapons and equipment, is there some pressure for a general change. The US Metric Board, set up in 1975, has responsibility for developing a national conversion program.

∗ In Canada the **metric system** was officially adopted in 1971, and is well supported in government, business, science and education, even if older Canadians feel a little disoriented. It was always a natural in Quebec.

∗ In Australia, the **metric system** was implemented very systematically following the Metric Conversion Act (1970), and there are now few remnants of the imperial system except in very specialized fields (see **imperial weights and measures**).

∗ In New Zealand, the *Weights and Measures Act* (1987) established the use of SI units of measurement: see next section.

1 **The metric system** is essentially the one based on the seven key units of the Système International (SI) des Poids et Mesures ("international system of weights and measures"). They are:

metre	for	length
kilogram		mass
second		time
ampere		electric current
kelvin		thermodynamic temperature
candela		luminous intensity
mole		amount of substance

From these SI base units, others – either decimal fractions or multiples of them – are named, such as the *millimetre* and *kilometre*.

Apart from those, there are:

a) two *supplementary units,* namely the *radian* (a unit of plane angle) and the *steradian* (a unit of solid angle); and

b) the so-called *derived units:* ones whose values are a product of certain base units. The standard unit of area is the metre squared, while that of density is based on kilograms per metre cubed. Derived units with special names (such as the *joule* which calibrates energy, and the *watt* which calibrates power) are also

calculated from a formula involving the base units. For the *watt* it's 1 kilogram metre squared per second cubed. The non-SI units employed within our metric system are also defined in terms of metric units. Thus the *litre,* our measure of liquid volume, is defined as $10^{-3}m^3$; and the definition of *bar,* used in measuring pressure, is 105 pascals. Other familiar non-SI units are the *hectare, tonne, day, hour, minute* and the *degree Celsius*.

All the units mentioned so far are in general use, but a few others have become officially "declared units" for limited uses only. Examples are the *knot* and the *nautical mile,* for marine and aerial navigation as well as meteorology; the *tex* (a measure of linear density), used in measurements of yarns, fibres and cords; and the *kilogram per hectolitre,* used in measurements of grains and seeds.

2 **Writing metric units.** Both base and derived units in the **metric system** have official symbols, many of which are written with a capital letter because they are proper names. This applies to units such as the *ampere* (A), the *joule* (J) and the *watt* (W), as well as our scales of temperature: *Kelvin* (K) and *Celsius* (C). By convention the symbol for litre is L (also a capital, to make it more conspicuous than an ordinary lower case *l* would be). Other metric items written with upper case are the symbols for prefixes which express multiples of any base unit, including *mega-* (M), *giga-* (G), *tera-* (T), *peta-* (P), *exa-* (E). (The symbols are all listed in Appendix IV.)

Metric symbols are never pluralized, whether they are upper or lower case. See for example:

> The generator's output is 600 MW (= megawatts)
> The walk is 14 km over rough ground (= kilometres)

But when metric units appear as full words, they're almost always lower case (e.g. *watt, metre*), the only exception being *Celsius.* As full words they should be pluralized like ordinary English nouns with an *s* (e.g. *watts, metres*), except in the cases of *hertz, lux, siemens* which have no marked plurals. (See further under **zero plurals**.)

Other points to note are:

a) either full words, or symbols (not a mixture of them), should be used in any expression: either *kilometres per hour* or *km/h*, but not *km/hour* etc. The symbols lend themselves to use in tables and diagrams, and the full words are most likely in discursive text.

b) only one unit should be used in expressing quantities, i.e. not both metres and kilometres. The writer chooses the unit so as to ensure as far as possible that the numerical values are between 0.1 and 1000. So working in metres makes best sense if you're comparing distances such as *75.2 m* and *106.5 m*. (In kilometres they would be *0.0752 km* and *0.106 km* respectively.)

c) between the figure and the abbreviated unit of measurement, a space is needed.

metro and Metro

In both British and North American English, the term **metro** can be used of any underground urban railway system like the archetypal **Metro** in Paris. Note that in Canada, **Metro** is also a way of referring to downtown Toronto.

metronymic

See under **patronymic**.

metropolis

Though Greek in origin, this word was mediated through Late Latin to modern Europe. This explains why its plural has always been **metropolises** since it was recorded in English in C16.

mews

Fashionable living in London may begin with an address involving **Mews**, tucked in behind the main street, and originally the stables of fine houses. The word has nothing to do with cats, but rather birds of prey, since their cages were originally **mews**, literally the place where hunting hawks were "mewed," i.e. "kept while moulting." Though plural by origin, **mews** is almost always construed in the singular: *an eighteenth century mews; a mews off Cromwell Road,* by the evidence of the BNC.

miasma

In Greek, **miasma** is associated with "pollution," and its earliest associations in C17 English were with the disease-bearing vapors from putrid marshes. Its plural then was *miasmata.* Nowadays **miasma** is applied to noxious smells such as the *miasma of stale alcohol,* and more abstractly to a noxious atmosphere or climate of opinion, as in a *miasma of McCarthyism/mediocrity/post-occupation guilt.* Some writers use it to refer to verbal fog, as in *legal miasma* or *a miasma of fact and fantasy.* These latter-day uses rarely require a plural, but then it's always **miasmas,** by the evidence of both CCAE and the BNC.

◇ For the plurals of other Greek loanwords, see **-a** section 1.

micro-

Derived from Greek, this prefix means essentially "very small, minute," as in *microcosm, micro-organism, microprint, microprocessor.* In C20 scholarship, science and technology, **micro-** has developed a set of new meanings:

1 "small in scale or focus," as in:
    microclimate microeconomics microstructure
2 (within the metric system) "one millionth" of a given unit, as in:
    micrometre micro-ohm microsecond microvolt

Note that *microwaves* are not a precisely defined element of this kind. They have traditionally been explained within a range of wavelengths, and the range itself has been shifting down the scale in dictionary definitions since the 1970s, from between 100 cm and 1 cm (*Webster's Third,* 1986) to between 30 cm and 1 mm in the *Oxford Dictionary* (1989). Whatever, the niceties of their length, *microwave ovens* are familiar in the kitchen nowadays, and the abbreviation **micro-** begins to embody the meaning "microwave," as in *micro-oven* (NOT a very small oven).

Other new meanings for **micro-** have developed out of its use to mean "amplifying what's very small," as in *microphone* and *microscope.* From the latter the prefix has come to mean "associated with the microscope," as in *microbiology, microphotography, microsurgery.* The *microdot, microfiche* and *microfilm* all depend on magnifying processes to yield the

information stored on them; and through this **micro-** has come to refer generally to the vehicles on or in which vast amounts of data are stored, such as the *microchip* and the *microcomputer.* The last word, abbreviated to *micro,* also stood alone as a way of referring to the "personal computer," while they still contrasted with the large mainframe computer. But computer power being what it is – now almost in inverse ratio to the size of the machine – *micro* in this last sense no longer seems apt.

Micronesia

See under **Polynesia**.

mid-Atlantic and mid-Atlantic English

For Americans the term **mid-Atlantic** tends to refer to the coastal states between New York and West Virginia. Others use it for a geographical location in the middle of the Atlantic ocean, as for the *Mid-Atlantic Ridge.* The term is also used notionally, as in **mid-Atlantic English**. In the UK this can refer to the pseudo-American accent used by British disk-jockeys and pop-singers. But among teachers of English in Europe, it constructs a kind of English common to Britain and North America – an amalgam of the two supervarieties which are increasingly in competition as models. Just what **mid-Atlantic English** would consist of is unclear, however. Discussions tend to concentrate on how to minimize the differences between British and American accents (Modiano, 1998), while the larger issues of how to bridge gaps in vocabulary, semantics and idiom still have to be worked out. For English-speakers and English-users in Asia and the southern hemisphere, **mid-Atlantic English** doesn't quite sound like a lingua franca for the world, since southern and eastern hemisphere preferences are not apparently taken into account. The notion of *international English* has more relevance and appeal. See further under **international English**.

mid-caps

See **capital letters** section 4.

middle voice

This term is sometimes borrowed from the grammar of Greek to describe English verb constructions in which the action affects the verb's subject rather than its object. For example: *the movie is screening in downtown cinemas.* The English **middle voice** often appears where you might expect the passive construction and effectively makes it active but intransitive. Its mixed status is captured in the alternative name *medio-passive.* It coincides with what some linguists call *ergative* constructions. See further under **active verbs**, **ergative** and **transitive and intransitive**.

might or could

See under **could**.

might or may

See under **may or might**.

mighty

In British English this is typically an attributive adjective, as in *the mighty River Ganges, under the mighty oaks,* and a noun, as in *How are the mighty fallen!* In North American English **mighty** also has adverbial uses as an intensifier:

"*That's mighty nice of you!*"

migrant or immigrant

In many parts of the world, these two words distinguish the temporary resident from one who has sought permanent residence. **Migrant** appears in expressions such as *migrant labor, migrant workers from the Middle East,* where returning to their homelands is assumed. The **immigrant** meanwhile has negotiated his/her rights to stay in their adoptive country.

In Australia and New Zealand the two terms converge, and **migrant** is the standard term for someone who has *migrated* from another country on a permanent basis. This is the sense enshrined in the Australian *Adult Migrant Education Service.*

mileage or milage

The first of these spellings is given priority in all modern dictionaries. The second is however a recognized alternative, and certainly the one we might expect by all the general spelling rules which apply to roots ending in -**e** (see further under -**age**). But introduction of the metric system guarantees the word's obsolescence as an everyday measurement, and, in its residual other uses, the irregular spelling is not subject to review. **Mileage** vastly outnumbers **milage** in BNC data, and is unchallenged in American data from CCAE.

Measurements apart, **mileage** has acquired other uses, as when it stands for the word "distance" or "performance over a distance," as in *What's the mileage to Chicago/Edinburgh/Toronto/Perth?* Even where distances are measured in kilometres, **mileage** still expresses the concept because of the lack of any term like "kilometrage." **Mileage** has a place in casual idiom, as in *He gets a lot of mileage out of that story* – where it's unllikely to be replaced by **milage**.

milieu

Borrowed from French in C19, this can be pluralized as either **milieus** or **milieux** in American English, the first being slightly more common than the second in data from CCAE. But British data from the BNC shows a clear preference for the French plural **milieux**, which outnumbers **milieus** by more than 3:1.

militate or mitigate

Confusion between these two – **mitigate** used instead of **militate** – is a persistent malapropism of contemporary English. **Mitigate** means "make less harsh," in either a physical or a figurative sense:

to mitigate the effects of drought

It might help to mitigate the boredom.

Militate means "be a force," or "work," usually against something. The word is related to *military,* and once meant literally "serve as a soldier, go to war." Its current, metaphorical sense is shown in:

Inequalities of power may militate against any real negotiation.

But instead, you may see or hear:

Inequalities of power may mitigate against any real negotiation.

This presents a clash of idiom as well as problems of meaning, since in some contexts **mitigate** means almost the reverse of **militate** – to soften rather than

intensify an effect. Faulty use of **mitigate** is usually rather obvious, by the use of *against* following it (or just occasionally *for* or *in favor of*). No following particle is needed, because **mitigate** is a transitive verb. See further under **transitive and intransitive**.

millenarian, millenary and millen(n)ium

In Christian tradition, *The Millennium* heralds the thousand-year reign of Christ on earth, anticipated at the end of the bible (Revelation 20:6–7). From this, **millennium** has developed the more general sense of a future "golden age," in which every human ideal is realized. The latter meaning is at the heart of **millenarian**, both adjective and noun, which are used respectively to describe anything relating to the **millennium**, and a believer in it. The word **millenary** can substitute for **millennium** as well as **millenarian**.

The single *n* in **millenarian** and **millenary** goes back to the classical Latin adjective *millenarius,* on which both words are based. **Millennium** with two *n*s is a neo-Latin formation dating from C17, formed from *mille* ("a thousand") and -*ennium* meaning "a period of years" (cf. *biennium, triennium*). But the discrepancy between Latin and neo-Latin has helped to foster **millenium**, which appears in about 15% of all instances of the word in the BNC, and in 5 out of 11 of the *Oxford Dictionary* (1989) citations, though the dictionary does not acknowledge it as an alternative. According to *Webster's English Usage* (1989) it's one of their "best attested spelling variants," though not recognized in *Webster's Third* (1986). It does appear as the sole headword in several smaller dictionaries, including two by Longman in 1978 and 1981, according to Kjellmer's research (1986) – probably not intentionally, but that's part of the point. If other dictionaries do not yet recognize **millenium** as an alternative, we might well ask why not? Etymology is of course with **millennium**, but the strength of analogy is with **millenium**.

In principle, the plural of **millen(n)ium** can be either the latinate **millen(n)ia** or the anglicized **millen(n)iums**. Yet database evidence shows that in the UK as well as the US, **millen(n)ia** outdoes **millen(n)iums**. In BNC data the ratio is more than 20:1, whereas in CCAE it's around 6:1. See further under -**um**.

millepede or millipede

See next entry.

milli-

This prefix is derived from Latin *mille* ("a thousand"). In the metric system however it means "a thousandth part," as in *milligram, millimetre, millisecond,* and this very precise meaning is the one most widely known and used.

A different and rather less precise meaning is the one attached to **milli-** in biological words such as *millipede* and *millipore,* which refer to creatures with supposedly 1000 feet and 1000 pores. Alternative spellings *millepede* and *millepore* help to connect the words with the whole thousand, rather than the thousandth part. There seems little point however, when the figure is very wide of the mark: a *millepede* has up to 400 feet (200 pairs of legs) but nowhere near 1000. Though the *Oxford Dictionary* (1989) gave priority to *millepede* over *millipede,* the order is

reversed in both *New Oxford* (1998) and *Merriam-Webster* (2000). In fact *millipede* is the only spelling to be found in either BNC data or CCAE.
◊ Compare *centipede,* under **centi-**.

milliard

In the UK **milliard** has been used to refer to "a thousand million," by those who wished to avoid using the term *billion* for this purpose (wanting to reserve *billion* for "a million million"). But it has never had much currency, and its occurrences in BNC data can be counted on the fingers of one hand. The so-called "American" *billion* is now firmly established in Britain, Australia and elsewhere (see under **billion**), and the raison d'être for **milliard** has disappeared.

millipede or millepede

See under **milli-**.

mimic

For the spelling of this word when used as a verb, see **-c/-ck-**.

mini-

This C20 prefix is believed to be an abbreviation of *miniature* (on which see next entry). Its earliest use in the US in the 1930s was to name new and more movable or portable instruments, such as the *minipiano* and the *minicam(era)*. They were followed by the *minicar* (1945) and the *miniprinter* (1950). But it was during the 1960s that **mini-** "took off," since when it's been used to name new vehicles (*minibus, minivan*), garments (*minicoat, miniskirt*) and sports (*minigolf*), as well as less material items such as the *minibudget* and the *miniseries*. New formations sometimes carry a hyphen, which is quickly shed once the word becomes established.

miniature

The spelling of **miniature** connects it with its Latin antecedent *miniare* ("paint red"), which is based on *minium* ("red lead"). The tiny decorations and illustrations in medieval manuscripts were often done with red ink, and from this comes the prime meaning for **miniature** nowadays: "very small scale [reproductions]". The word is often pronounced with three syllables, hence the deviant spellings "minature" and "miniture," neither of which is sanctioned by dictionaries.

minimal or minimum

Most of the time, these words simply complement each other: **minimal** is the adjective and **minimum** the noun, and it's a matter of grammar which you use to express "the least possible." Yet like many a noun, **minimum** can be pressed into service as an adjective, taking the place of **minimal**:
It was done with minimum effort.
Compare *done with minimal effort,* which is a little more literary in style. Note also that **minimal** often has a negative cutting edge to it, which **minimum** as an adjective does not. Compare:
They gave minimum time to their patients.
They gave minimal time to their patients.
The first sentence notes that the amount of time given to patients was only as large as was absolutely necessary, whereas the second seems to say that this was negligible and reprehensible.

In British English, **minimum** is usually pluralized as **minima**, whether in scientific, mathematical, financial or legal contexts:
a north-east south-west trending belt of inversion maxima and minima
redundancy payments above the statutory minima
Common usage does however allow **minimums**, as in *the bare minimums*. In American English there's little use of **minima** by the evidence of CCAE, and **minimums** serves in all but the most specialized scientific contexts.

minimize or minify

Not all dictionaries agree that these are synonyms, pace Fowler (1926), who argued that **minify** was a "needless variant." While **minimize** means "make as small as possible," **minify** can also mean "reduce in importance or value," a meaning which Theodore Bernstein (1965) found worth preserving. In frequency they differ sharply. **Minimize** is quite common and **minify** very rare, appearing only twice in CCAE, and not at all in the BNC. Whether this reflects Fowler's influence on both sides of the Atlantic – or the fact that he was flogging a dead horse – is an open question.

miniscule or minuscule

See **minuscule**.

Minorca or Menorca

The English name for the second largest Balearic island in the western Mediterranean is **Minorca**, whereas its Spanish name is **Menorca**.
◊ Compare **Majorca or Mallorca**.

minority

Two different uses of **minority** can confound its meaning:
The motion was lost by a minority of three.
Does this mean that out of say 25 people, only 3 voted for it? Or that the number of people voting for the motion was 3 less than the number who voted against it, so that the vote ran 11:14 against?

According to the second interpretation **minority** means "the shortfall between the votes for and against." In the first, **minority** just identifies the smaller set of voters, in contrast with the majority. This is certainly the meaning in:
A minority of members wanted more frequent meetings.
In phrases like this one, **minority** means "less than half," and so in a group of 25 could be any number from 12 down. The inherent vagueness in this use of **minority** makes some people qualify it, as in "a small minority" or "a large minority." Yet expressions like those are problematic in other ways: the first seems tautologous and the second contradictory.

Problems like these with **minority** (and *majority*) mean that it's best to paraphrase them whenever precision counts. For example:
The motion was lost by a vote of 11 to 14.
(instead of "a minority of three")
Only about a third/quarter (etc.) of the members wanted...
(instead of "a small minority")
Just under half the members wanted more meetings...
(instead of "a large minority")

The use of **minority** with noncomposite items, as in "a minority of her time," is sometimes challenged, echoing a reaction to the same kind of construction with *majority*. For a discussion of this, see **majority**.

minus

This Latin loanword meaning "less" has long been used in discursive arithmetic to express negative operations, values and quantities, as in:

> *What's the square root of minus 16?*
> *... temperatures from minus 253 °C*
> *... to deposit the funds minus a 10 per cent cut for his relatives*

Quantitative uses of **minus** like these are established and uncontroversial. Yet recent usage in which it expresses absence or negativity is queried in some dictionaries:

* prepositional use of **minus** (meaning "without"). This is taken on board by American, Canadian and Australian dictionaries without reservations, but labeled "colloquial" by the *Oxford Dictionary* (1989) and "informal" by *New Oxford* (1998). Just how informal is it for British writers? In BNC data it's by far the commonest of the new uses of **minus**:

> *It comes into flower, minus its leaves, in October.*
> *She arrived minus dogs this time.*
> *... the New Historicists minus the ideological change*
> *... their corpses – minus their shoes and socks – were found by the station manager*

The examples show some of the various writing styles in which **minus** (= "without") can appear, both narrative and informative. Its wide distribution in British texts – not at all confined to spoken texts – suggests that it is close to standard in British usage, and usable in all but the most formal style.

* adjectival uses. Arithmetic or quasi-arithmetic uses of **minus**, as in *on the minus side* (i.e. "negative"), are standard and unlabeled in all dictionaries. The *Oxford Dictionary* stands alone in labeling the extended senses of "lacking"/"nonexistent" as "colloquial," but other dictionaries take them as standard.

* as a noun meaning "deficiency," "deficit," "disadvantage," **minus** is entered with no restrictive label in any of the reference dictionaries. This sense is typically found in the plural, as in:

> *... nothing but political minuses in this*

Very often **minuses** is coupled with *pluses: Other top teams have their pluses and minuses.*

All this shows that the extended uses of **minus** are well established as standard usage almost everywhere. Except in formal British writing, they need no second thought.

◊ Compare **plus**.

minuscule or miniscule

Several factors combine to make this word's spelling rather insecure. Standard pronunciation leaves the second syllable rather obscure (an indeterminate vowel [*schwa*]); and the Latin diminutive ending *-usculus* is rare in the everyday vocabulary of English. Add to this the fact that its meaning "very small" connects it with the lively prefix *mini-*, and it's clear why **miniscule** has become a strong challenge to the etymological **minuscule**. The *Oxford Dictionary* (1989) records 7 citations for **miniscule** since 1898, and *Webster's English Usage* (1989) notes increasing

use of it since the 1940s, in parallel with the growing use of *mini-* as a prefix. **Miniscule** makes up almost 20% of all instances of the word in both CCAE and the BNC. The proportion worldwide is larger: an internet search by Google in 2002 found it in more than 35% of all instances of the word.

Whether **miniscule** is an acceptable alternative is still a matter of opinion. The *Oxford Dictionary* dubs it "erroneous," as does *New Oxford* (1998); whereas both *Webster's Third* (1986) and *Merriam-Webster* (2000) have it as an allowable alternative. *Canadian English Usage* (1997) is ambivalent, finding it very common but unacceptable. Studies of Australian data find that **miniscule** dominates, hence the *Macquarie Dictionary*'s (1997) comment that it is "etymologically incorrect but very frequent." Lexicographers have always been inclined to resolve issues of spelling in the light of etymology – in the absence of wide-ranging evidence of usage. But computer-based data on usage now provides an alternative and powerful reference point. It makes **miniscule** a legitimate variant – while not displacing the traditional spelling **minuscule**.

◊ For the uses of *minuscule letters,* see **lower case**.

mis-

This prefix, meaning "bad or badly," occurs in many an English verb and verbal noun, witness:

misadventure	misalliance	miscarry
misconduct	misdeed	misdeliver
misfit	misgivings	mishit
mislay	mislead	mismanage
mismatch	misnomer	misprint
misrepresent	misspell	mistake
mistrial	misunderstand	

Mis- is actually a coalescence of prefixes from two different sources:

1. **mis-** which goes back to Old English, and is found in other Germanic languages (in modern German *miss-*)
2. *mes-* an early French prefix derived from Latin *minus* ("less").

Both imply that a process has gone wrong, and the use of the older English **mis-** was reinforced by the arrival of French loanwords with *mes-* from C14 on. For a while the two prefixes were interchanged in a number of words, but by C17 **mis-** was the standard spelling for all. For Shakespeare and his contemporaries it was a very popular formative for new words.

Some English words formed with **mis-** are matched by ones coined with the negative prefix *dis-*, for example *miscount/discount, misinformation/ disinformation, misplace/displace, mistrust/distrust*. Only in the case of the last pair do the two words converge in meaning (see **distrust**). With *misinformation/disinformation* the sources of the faulty information are different (see **misinformation**), and the others present quite divergent meanings:

miscount "count incorrectly"	*discount* "take no account of"
misplace "put in the wrong place"	*displace* "move out of place"

◊ Compare **dis-**.

miscegenation

One of the most delicate questions of usage is how to refer to people of mixed race, which can be a matter of embarrassment, and worse – of condemnation. The

word **miscegenation** may itself have fueled the problem, since its first element is easily misconstrued as *mis-* ("bad, faulty"; see previous entry). That element is in fact the Latin root *misce-* ("mixed"), which is neutral in meaning. To skirt around the problem, less formal words have been coined on all continents, some of them euphemistic, some offhanded.

Settlers in Canada, Australia and other parts of the British Empire shared an array of such words: *colo(u)red* (from South Africa); *half-caste* (from India); and *half-blood, half-breed, half-white, mixed blood* (from the US). Other terms such as *metis* (from French), *ladino, mestizo, mulatto* (from Spanish colonial territories) were also familiar, especially in North America (see individual entries on **colo(u)red** and **Metis and metis**). Terms such as *quadroon* and *octoroon,* with their built-in genetic analysis, do not appear to have been widely used.

Most of the disadvantages of these words are avoided with terms such as *part-Indian, part-Aboriginal* and so on. They do not pretend to precise mathematics, nor do they invoke agricultural analogies of breeding, and their tone is neither patronizing nor off-handed. They are suitably neutral for situations where complex ethnic origins and culture need to be acknowledged. The straight ethnic or geographical term (e.g. *Eurasian*) seems to best preserve the dignity of the individual – as when avoiding *racist language.* See further under that heading.

miscellanea and miscellaneous

Miscellanea is a Latin plural (see -a section 2), literally "miscellaneous articles," and like *data* and *media* it raises questions of agreement in English. It normally refers to a literary collection and is not unnaturally given a singular pronoun and verb:

> *This miscellanea is a great advance over the others.*

However the cognoscenti would construe the same sentence in the plural:

> *These miscellanea are a great advance on the others.*

The first may seem awkward; the second, pretentious. The word *miscellany* provides an escape route from both. It means the same and is unquestionably singular.

The adjective **miscellaneous** is spelled with *-eous* rather than *-ious* because of its connection with **miscellanea**. For other adjectives ending in *-eous,* see **-ious**.

mischievous or mischievious

Mischievous is the standard spelling for the adjective associated with *mischief.* The spelling **mischievious** reflects a not uncommon pronunciation of the word which alters the stress and gives it four syllables. It dates back to early modern English, according to the *Oxford Dictionary* (1989), but somehow became marginalized after 1700, and is now only "dialectal, vulgar or jocular." Despite this, **mischievious** still occasionally gets into print. There are a couple of instances in the BNC, and a Google search of the internet in 2002 found it in about 5% of all instances of the word. Australian surveys of pronunciation in 2000 show that "mischeevious" is used by about 25% of the population, which no doubt impacts on the spelling. But **mischievious** has no status where dictionaries

are concerned, and isn't registered (even as an erroneous variant) in *New Oxford* (1998) or *Merriam-Webster* (2000).

misdemeanor or misdemeanour
See *-or/-our.*

misinformation or disinformation
Formed centuries apart, these present quite different perspectives on faulty information. The C16 **misinformation** implies that it was supplied by accident, whereas **disinformation**, coined in C20, makes it a deliberate strategy, as in counterespionage.

Miss, Mrs(.) or Ms(.)
Both **Miss** and **Mrs.** are abbreviations of *Mistress,* which was once the general title for a woman. **Mrs.** is the earlier abbreviation, which in C17–18 could be applied to any adult woman, irrespective of whether she was married or not. Only in C19 were **Mrs.** and **Miss** used to identify different kinds of marital status, and the importance of the **Miss/Mrs.** distinction in Victorian England goes without saying. But the use of titles marking marital status is no longer in favor – except with older people – for various reasons. To some the distinction is invidious, because of the spinsterly associations of **Miss**; to others gratuitous and/or sexist. The alternative title **Ms.** is maritally neutral, and recommends itself to many women as well as institutions and the news media that refer to them. Coined in the 1930s (Baron, 1986), **Ms.** was taken up by American business organizations in the 1950s, hence its early connotations of "career woman." Its feminist associations with the "liberated woman" probably owe more to the *Ms.* magazine launched in 1972. But these colors have faded as more and more women of many lifestyles adopt the title (see **forms of address** section 2).

In American style all abbreviations with lower case letters are given stops, and the *Chicago Manual* (2003) uses **Ms.** and **Mrs.** alongside **Mr.**, whenever titles are given. British style is to omit the stop with **Mrs** and **Ms** because they are deemed contractions rather than abbreviations (see **contractions** section 1). On this Canadians do likewise, according to *Editing Canadian Usage* (2000), as well as Australians (*Style Manual,* 2002).

Note that **Ms.** is normally written with capital *M* and lower case *s,* which distinguishes it from the abbreviations for "manuscript": *MS* or *ms.* (see further under **MS or ms**).

◊ For the plurals of **Mrs.** and **Ms.**, see **plurals** section 3.

misspelled or misspelt
See under -ed.

mistakable or mistakeable
See under -eable.

mistrust or distrust
See **distrust**.

mitigate or militate
See **militate**.

mitre or miter
See -re/-er.

mixed metaphors

See under **metaphors**.

moccasin or mocassin

The *Oxford Dictionary* (1989) records more than twenty spellings for this American Indian loanword, of which **moccasin** and **mocassin** are presented as alternatives in *Webster's Third* (1986). **Mocassin** was popular in C19, according to *Oxford* citations – whether referring to the shoe, the flower or the water snake that go by the same name. It comes closer to the Algonquian word from which it derives, rendered as *mokussin* in the Narragansett language, and *mohkisson* in Massachusetts. But for English writers there's no motivation for the pattern of single/double consonants; and **moccasin** is just as plausible. It features in various American placenames from Georgia to California, including *Moccasin Lake,* the *Moccasin Bends* (of the Tennessee River), and *Moccasin Creek State Park*. **Moccasin** is now clearly the dominant spelling for the common word in both British and American English, by the evidence of the BNC and CCAE.

◊ For other loanwords in which the doubling of consonants is unstable, see under **single for double**.

modality and modal verbs

What is **modality**? It depends who you ask. Grammarians differ in their definitions of it, though most would agree that it's the factor which differentiates the first sentence below from the two following:

> *The books are coming tomorrow.*
> *The books should come tomorrow.*
> *You should check in the morning.*

The sentences all contain auxiliary verbs (*are/should*). But while the auxiliary *are* indicates purely grammatical things such as the verb's tense and number, *should* expresses something of the writer's or speaker's attitude to what's being stated. The second sentence shows the degree of confidence she expects others to have in it, and the third what she expects others to do about it. These extra dimensions of linguistic communication are what is now generally called **modality**. The two major kinds of **modality** shown in the second and third sentences above are distinguished by grammarians as the *epistemic* (concerned with the truth of a proposition), and the *deontic* (expressing permission or obligation). See further under **deontic**.

The **modal verbs** form a large subgroup of auxiliary verbs. They are capable of expressing more than one kind of **modality**, depending on the sentence they occur in and the broader context of communication. Is it an exchange of information, or are people formulating actions in words, e.g. making offers or issuing commands? The sense of the **modal verb** and its force is interconnected with the use of the first, second or third person (see further under **can or may, could or might**). The verb *must* can express obligation or inclination with the first person, as in *I must send them a letter;* and necessity or prediction with the third, as in *He must come soon.* Contexts often determine the sense, though it may not be clear-cut. Complementary senses, such as *permission/ possibility, obligation/necessity* and *inclination/ prediction* are therefore grouped together in the table below. Even so the boundaries between some senses e.g. *possibility* and *prediction* are indeterminate.

The table shows the range of uses of the *central modals,* and their approximate force from strong to weak (Halliday, 1994), again with the caveat that this is often context-dependent. The relative frequencies of the commonest **modal verbs** are indicated in terms of ratios, based on statistics from the *Longman Grammar* (1999) corpus. The frequencies of some are affected by the parallel use of *quasi-modals,* e.g. *be going to* alongside *will,* especially in conversation (see further under **auxiliaries** section 2, and **future tense**). The uses of **modal verbs** shown in the table are those associated with main clauses: others may be found in subordinate clauses. For example, the sequence of tenses in a particular sentence may dictate the choice (see under **sequence of tenses**). Compare: *I will come* with *I said I would come.* However discourse orientation can override the conventional sequence (see **may or might**).

Modal verbs are fluid rather than fixed in meaning, and most have changed and extended their meanings over the centuries. Yet they are more rigid than any other kind of verb in their form: one serves for all persons e.g. *I/you/he/they must.* There's no regular adjustment for tense even though there were once present/past contrasts among them (as with

	can	could	may	might	must	shall	should	will	would
permission	+	−	−						
possibility	*	+	+	−					
ability	*	+							
relative freq.	10	7	4	2.5					
obligation					*	−	+	−	
necessity					*		+		
relative freq.					3.5		4.2		
inclination					−	+		*	−
prediction					−	+		*	+
relative freq.						1		15	12
habit/frequency					−				−

Note: Legend on relative force: * connotes strong, + moderate, − weak, to be read horizontally. Relative frequencies are given only for the most frequently used modals/senses in each set. Those without frequency ratios are very minor uses.

shall/should, will/would). They have no infinitive forms.

British and American uses of the **modal verbs** diverge a little, but the differences are relative rather than absolute. See under **can or may**, **could or might**, **may or might**, **shall or will**, **should or would**.

◊ For the use of double *modals* such as *might could,* see **double modal**.

◊ For the connection between **modality** and grammatical *mood,* see under **mood**.

Using modals in communicating. In writing as well as speaking, the various shades of **modality** are enormously important. Speakers express and control relationships with each other through them; and writers use *modals* as a way of fine-tuning the factuality and the force of the statements they make. *Modals* are often used to modify claims which could be challenged or prove difficult to substantiate, as in:

The number of applicants may go down next year.

Inexperienced writers sometimes rely too much on **modal verbs** to cover themselves. Yet whether they use the same *modal* repeatedly, or "juggle" the set of *modals* that express possibility, it becomes conspicuous because the *modal* is always the first item in the verb phrase. A better stylistic strategy for remaining tentative is to include also *modal* adverbs expressing degrees of certainty (*likely, perhaps, possibly, probably* etc.) as well as *downtoners*. (See further under **hedge words**.) Rewording the tentative statement is better still, so that the terms in which it's expressed are themselves appropriate and do not need to be toned down.

modeled or modelled, modeling or modelling

Americans and the British are strongly divided on whether to use one or two *l*s in the inflected parts of the verb *model*. British writers in the BNC are committed to double *l* spellings, where their American counterparts in CCAE overwhelmingly use the single *l*. Elsewhere things are less polarized. Canadians are more inclined to **modelled/modelling**, according to the *Canadian Oxford* (1998), but **modeled/modeling** are accepted variants. Australian usage by and large goes for the double *l* spellings: usage research for the government *Style Manual* (Peters, 1999b) showed that the single *l* spellings constituted about 20% of all instances of the word. See further under **-l-/-ll-**.

modifiers

This term is used in two ways in English grammar:
1 to refer to whatever qualifies the head of a noun phrase, either as premodifier or postmodifier (see under **noun phrase**)
2 to refer to words or phrases that soften the impact of others, such as *rather, somewhat, a bit*. Some grammarians call them *downtoners*, others *hedge words* (see under that heading). Compare **intensifiers**, words or phrases which reinforce or emphasize the force of others.

modus

This Latin word meaning "way" is caught up in a number of phrases used in English. Two familiar examples are *modus operandi* ("way of working or proceeding"), and *modus vivendi* ("way of life or

living"). Both also have specific meanings in law. A *modus operandi* is the characteristic way in which a criminal works; and *modus vivendi* is used of an interim working arrangement which precedes a legal settlement.

In logic the phrases *modus ponens* and *modus tollens* refer to two different kinds of reasoning. See under **deduction**.

Mohammed

See **Muhammad**.

Mohave or Mojave

When referring to the AmerIndian people associated with the Colorado River region of the US, either **Mohave** or **Mojave** may be used, though dictionaries all give priority to the first spelling. Where placenames are concerned, there are local differences. **Mohave** is used on the Arizona/Nevada frontier, for *Lake Mohave* and the *Fort Mohave Indian Reservation*. Further west it's **Mojave** (the Spanish form of the name) for the California town and the *Mojave River,* as well as the *Mojave Desert* – though *Merriam-Webster's Geographical Dictionary* (1987) also allows *Mohave Desert*. Yet CCAE data show that **Mojave** is the commoner spelling by far, outnumbering **Mohave** by more than 16: 1 in references to the desert and its resources.

◊ Compare **Navajo or Navaho**.

mold or mould

See **mould**.

mollusk or mollusc

Both spellings are recognized everywhere, but there are strong regional preferences. **Mollusk** is shown as the primary US spelling in *Webster's Third* (1986), and its position is confirmed in CCAE data, where it prevails over **mollusc** in the ratio of about 12:1. **Mollusc** is given priority in the *Oxford Dictionary* (1989), and it's the only spelling to be found in the BNC. In C18 the spelling was neither of these, but *mollusque*, reflecting its French background. But the Latin stem *mollusc-* seems to have prevailed in C19 British respellings of the noun, and everywhere in the adjective. In *New Oxford* (1998) *molluscan* is the only form registered, and even *Merriam-Webster* (2000) puts *molluscan* ahead of *molluskan*. This may reflect the preference of scientists, who are chief users of the word; it also allows those who prefer **mollusk** to use the analogous *molluskan*.

molt or moult

See **moult**.

molten or melted

See **melted**.

momentary or momentous, and momentarily

The adjectives **momentary** and **momentous** express very different meanings of the word *moment*. **Momentary** is strictly concerned with time, as in *a momentary lapse of memory,* while **momentous** picks up the idea of importance ("an event of great moment"), and is usually found in phrases such as "momentous event" or "a momentous occasion." The corresponding adverbs **momentarily** and *momentously* contrast in much the same way, with their respective emphasis on time and importance.

But for **momentarily**, referring to time has its complications. Fowler (1926) found it in competition with *momently* over two perspectives on the passing *moment;* and he tried to insist that **momentarily** meant "for a brief span of time," and *momently* "from moment to moment." Compare:

The dancer pauses momentarily in a pose.

Their excitement increased momently.

The distinction is somewhat academic with the disappearance of *momently* from current British and American English (by the evidence of both BNC and CCAE). Yet there is perhaps some fallout in the fact that the sense "from moment to moment" is not given to **momentarily** in either *New Oxford* (1998) or *Merriam-Webster* (2000). The dictionaries agree that **momentarily** still means "for a brief span of time," and databases show that this is the dominant meaning everywhere.

Dictionaries also register a new meaning for **momentarily**, that of happening "at any moment." For example:

Beijing lacks only the formal approval of the board, which could come momentarily.

The meaning originated in 1928 in the US, according to the *Oxford Dictionary* (1989), and it maintains its place in American and Canadian English, while there's scant evidence in the BNC of its use in British English. This explains why American pilots can safely advise passengers that "this aircraft will be taking off momentarily" – while alarming or amusing those who take **momentarily** to mean "for a moment" (it seems they're not going anywhere fast!). But North Americans and others who use both the current senses of **momentarily** would associate them with different kinds of discourse. The number one sense ("for a moment") goes with narrative and retrospective comment, whereas the second "(at any moment") goes with prospective statements.

momento

See under **memento**.

monarchal, monarchial, monarchic or monarchical

Dictionaries find small differences in these four forms of the word: that while **monarch(i)al** means "relating to a/the monarch," **monarchic(al)** can express a connection with either *monarch* or the *monarchy*. But like many such pairs, **monarchic** and **monarchical** do not differ in meaning (see further under **-ic/-ical**). And since the second pair embrace the meaning of the first, it's no surprise that occurrences of **monarchic(al)** considerably outnumber those of **monarch(i)al**, by more than 4:1 in both BNC and CCAE. *Merriam-Webster* (2000) gives preference to **monarchical** over **monarchic**, which corresponds exactly with their relative frequency in both American and British databases, where the first again outnumbers the second by more than 4:1. Fowler declared **monarchial** to be a superfluous variant of **monarchal**, though only the first makes a (small) showing in BNC data. Both forms appear in CCAE, but also in such small numbers that they hardly count. All this tends to make **monarchical** the lone

survivor of a diversified set of adjectives, whose raison d'être has declined with the reduced status and functions of *monarchy* everywhere.

monetize or monetarize

The standard form is **monetize** or **monetise**, matching the French verb *monetiser.* These are the only spellings registered in *New Oxford* (1998) and *Merriam-Webster* (2000). Garner (1998) notes also the use of **monetarize** (backformed from *monetarism*), but it's relatively scarce in CCAE (only 1 in10 relative to **monetize**). These usage figures suggest that few writers are tempted by the alternative form, and de facto share Garner's view that **monetarize** is a "needless variant."

money, moneys or monies, and moneyed or monied

In ordinary usage **money** is a mass noun with a collective sense, and there's no need to pluralize it:

All the money they earned was pooled.

But in law and accounting, **money** is a countable noun which can be pluralized to express the idea of individual sums of money. (See further under **count and mass nouns**.) For example:

We cannot reclaim any moneys already paid to you.

The regular spelling **moneys** is given preference over **monies** in all dictionaries, in line with other words ending in *-ey* (see under **-y>-i-**). Yet general usage in both the UK and the US is clearly in favor of **monies**, and it's no longer the unusual spelling of legal and financial documents. In BNC data **monies** appears in about 75% of all instances of the word, and in CCAE it's close to 95%.

When **money** becomes a verb, the dictionaries' preferred spelling is once again the regular **moneyed**, and this does have majority support over **monied** among both British and American writers, by about 3:2 in data from the BNC and CCAE. Since **moneyed/monied** (as in *the moneyed classes*) tends to appear in conversational data, rather than the nonfictional prose inhabited by **monies/moneys**, the inconsistency is rarely a problem.

-monger

This is a fossil of an Old English agent noun *mangere*, based on the verb *mangian* ("(to) trade"). Its older, neutral sense survives in British *ironmonger* and *fishmonger*. But new metaphorical formations usually have negative overtones: witness *scaremonger, warmonger,* etc.

mongoose

Should you encounter not one but two of these small ferret-like animals, native to India, the plural to use is **mongooses**. (Neither the animal nor the word has any connection with *goose*, so "mongeese" is unthinkable.) The word **mongoose** originated as *mangus* in the Marathi language of western India. Its respelling clarifies the pronunciation, but looks like *folk etymology* at work. See further under that heading.

mono-

This Greek prefix meaning "one or single" is derived from loanwords such as *monochrome, monologue, monopoly, monotony.* New words formed with it are usually technical, though the items named may be familiar enough:

monofilm	monocle	monohull
monorail	monoski	monotype

Most other words formed with **mono-** are scholarly, like *monogamy, monograph, monolingual, monosyllabic;* or scientific names for chemicals like *monoxide* and *monosodium,* or for broad groups of plants and animals such as *monocotyledons* and *monotremes.*

In strict scientific nomenclature the prefix **mono-** ("one") is the counterpart of *di-*, the Greek-derived prefix for "two":

monocotyledon	dicotyledon
monoxide	dioxide

Bur elsewhere **mono-** complements *bi-*, the Latin prefix for "two":

monocular	binoculars
monogamy	bigamy
monolingual	bilingual

As the examples show, **mono-** combines with any kind of root, not just Greek ones. It therefore competes with the Latin prefix *uni-* ("one") for new coinings: see **uni-**.

monogram or monograph

Monogram is a classical loanword of C17, meaning "single letter." It refers to the single figure made up of interwoven letters – usually a person's initials. These may be printed as personal identification on stationery, or stitched onto garments. **Monograph** is a C19 formation from the same Greek roots as the other word, though it means a single piece of writing. The typical **monograph** is a treatise on one particular subject or branch of it, and published as a single volume. In both those respects a **monograph** contrasts with the scholarly journal.

monologue or soliloquy

Both these are sustained utterances by a single speaker. A **soliloquy** is a speech effectively addressed to oneself, whereas a **monologue** is normally part of a larger dialogue, though the rules of turn-taking have been temporarily suspended.
◊ For the choice between **monologue** and *monolog*, see **-gue/-g**.
◊ For the plural of **soliloquy**, see under **-y>-i-**.

monotransitive

See under **transitive**.

mood

In the grammars of Latin and Greek, **mood** referred to the different forms of the verb used according to whether a fact or hypothesis was being expressed. The term was borrowed by traditional grammarians for English, as a means to distinguish the indicative, subjunctive and imperative forms of verbs:

* *indicative* (making factual statements) *They* are *there.*
* *imperative* (issuing commands) Be *there!*
* *subjunctive* (expressing wishes or hypothetical statements) *If only I were there.* Were *I there it would all be easier!*

Some grammarians would include the interrogative (where the verb is inverted: Are *they there?*). A few also count the infinitive among the moods of English (e.g. [to] be).

Nowadays the usefulness of the notion of **mood** for English is seriously questioned. Except with the verb *be*, the different forms of verbs do not correspond in a regular way to the expressive functions of clauses and sentences. In fact the expressive function seems much more important, and the set of clause functions now usually recognized (in the *Comprehensive Grammar,* 1985, and the *Longman Grammar,* (1999) is:

> declarative imperative interrogative exclamative

The meanings expressed through the different **moods** of the verb in classical languages are typically expressed through auxiliaries and modal verbs in English. Thus *modality* and *sentence functions* are more useful concepts for describing English grammar than **mood**.
◊ See further under **auxiliary verbs**, **modality** and **sentences** section 1.

moonlit or moonlighted

The light of the moon makes for a *moonlit garden/ hall/night/stroll* in many a romantic novel in both American and British English. **Moonlit** is the only spelling used for this sense in data from CCAE and the BNC, and it's the traditional way of forming the word's past tense or participle (see **lighted or lit**). Its use is reinforced by the need to reserve **moonlighted** for the past of the compound verb *moonlight* ("work as a second job"), first recorded in 1957. *Moonlighting* in the past tense is always spelled **moonlighted** in both the US and the UK, witness:

> ... *a police officer who moonlighted as a hotel security guard*
> ... *he moonlighted as a lion tamer to make ends meet*

The two forms **moonlighted** and **moonlit** distinguish thus between hard work and serious play carried out in the darker hours.

mopey or mopy

See **-y/-ey**.

mora

For the plural of this word, see **-a** section 1.

moral, morals, morality and morale

The adjective **moral** has two major senses, the older and more central of which is "discriminating between right and wrong." This is also enshrined in the plural form **morals**, and the C14 noun **morality**. The *morality plays* and other improving literature gave rise to the notion of the *moral of the story,* the *moral lesson* which it embodies.

In another strand of meaning, **moral** means "confident of the rightness of one's position" as in *moral victory,* and can become *moral support* when lent to others. This sense connects with the noun **morale**, borrowed from French as **moral**, but respelled with the extra *e* in C18. In American English, **moral** can still be used as a noun instead of **morale**, and **morale** for **morality**, according to *Webster's Third* (1986), but there's scant evidence of either in data from CCAE. Rather, **moral** is firmly connected with **morality**, and **morale** with "confidence in one's position." Compounds such as *morale-booster* and *morale building* put **morale** into a quasi-attributive role, which could eventually lead to revised spelling for the adjective in "morale support."

moratoriums or moratoria

The plural of **moratorium** may be either **moratoriums** or the latinate **moratoria**. The British prefer to say **moratoriums** and to write **moratoria**, by the evidence of the BNC. Americans meanwhile use **moratoriums** for both kinds of discourse, and there's little evidence of **moratoria** in data from CCAE. See further under **-um**.

more than one

Should it be "More than one is . . ." or "More than one are . . ."? Despite the plural implications of the phrase, most writers take their cue from the last word *one,* and construe it in the singular, as in *proximity agreement* (see **agreement** section 5). For example:

> Apply one coat [of paint] only, as more than one encourages flaking.
> More than one sceptical colleague has been admonished.

In some examples like the first, **more than one** effectively means "the second," so that the choice of singular verb is reinforced by *notional agreement.* The second example suggests "at least two"; but the plural possibilities are still reined in by the singular verb, and the proximity of *one* helps to account for it.

morphemes

See under **morphology**.

morphine, morphia, laudanum, heroin and opium

The soothing effects of the **opium** poppy have been known for thousands of years. It was prescribed by Greek and Roman physicians, and remained an effective pain-reliever for more than two millenniums. **Laudanum** was an early modern medicinal preparation from **opium**, which owes its name to the Swiss physician Paracelsus (1493–1541) – probably an adaption of *labdanon* or *ladanon,* i.e. gum resin from the "rock rose." It was prepared as an alcohol solution and taken orally. **Morphine**, developed in early C19, is a chemical extract of **opium**, a crystalline alkaloid which is its most important narcotic; and **morphia** was an alternative name for it in the first century of its use. Both words had some currency, and the problems of *morphine addiction* could be called either *morphinomania* or *morphiomania.* However **morphine** seems to have had the edge, judging by the large number of derivatives from it, and it became the dominant form in C20 English.

Apart from their medicinal uses, **opium** and its relatives have long been misused as "pick-me-ups," and *opium addiction* is one of the recurring motifs of modern history both in the East and the West. **Opium**, **laudanum** and **morphine** were all available without doctor's prescription in C19 Europe and America, and only in the following century did governments legislate against it. In its simple form, **opium** is still eaten or smoked in various parts of Asia. Its newest and most powerful form **heroin** ("the drug that makes you feel like a hero") was developed in pharmaceutical laboratories in the West, and is taken by intravenous injection. The name **heroin** is nevertheless reserved for nonmedical uses of the drug.

morphology and morphemes

The **morphology** of words is their form or structure, and the meaningful units of which they consist. The word *meaningful* has three such units or **morphemes**:

> mean + -ing + -ful

Morphemes may be roughly divided into the *free* and the *bound*, the first being independent units, able to stand without any attachments; whereas the second must be attached to a free **morpheme**. (So in the case of *meaningful, mean* is a free morpheme, and the other two are bound.) In English the various prefixes and suffixes are all bound morphemes, and they usually fit the definition just given. Some affixes such as the prefix *ex-* and the suffix *-able* do nevertheless seem to be capable of standing alone. Still it can be argued that they have somewhat different meanings when standing as words and when functioning as affixes, and this makes them different **morphemes** which coincide in form.

More debatable is the question as to just how free some of the "free" **morphemes** are, when the basic stem to which suffixes are attached cannot itself stand alone. What about the stem of the word *driving?* There *driv-* must be the "free" **morpheme**, even though it never stands alone in exactly that form. The linguist's way out of this dilemma is to regard *driv-* as a variant (or visual *allomorph*) of *drive,* which is unquestionably free.

mortgagor or mortgager, and mortgagee

In legal contexts, **mortgagor** is the standard spelling, and the only spelling in general use in the US and the UK, by the evidence of CCAE and the BNC. Though **mortgager** is more regular in its spelling (see under **-ce/-ge**), and on record since C17, it seems to have disappeared. The *-or* ending is no doubt supported by the fact that it's first and foremost a legal word. See further under **-er/-or**.

When arranging the finance for a new home, some buyers are surprised to find that they are the **mortgagor** and the bank or building society is the **mortgagee**. The surprise probably has something to do with the idea that the suffix *-ee* connotes someone who is on the receiving end of an action (as with *employee/employer*). In fact not all *-ee* words are passive expressions (see further under **-ee**). Add to this the obscurity of the verb *mortgage* itself. Its meaning is still a little elusive, even when one knows that the first syllable is the Latin/French word for "dead" and the second means "pledge." The *Oxford Dictionary* (1989) offers its best help in a quotation from a C17 lawyer, who explains that the property involved in a *mortgage* is a pledge which is "dead" to the provider of the *mortgage* if the owner repays the loan on time; and "dead" to the owner if he cannot. The **mortgagor** executes the "dead pledge" one way or the other.

mortise or mortice

The spelling **mortise** has been in continuous use since the word came into English in C15. Fowler (1926) backed it, and it's given preference over **mortice** in the *Oxford Dictionary* (1989) as well as *Webster's Third* (1986). **Mortice** appears in C18, and is preferred in dictionaries of architecture and building, perhaps because of the spelling of other terms such as *cornice* and *lattice*. In general British English represented in

the BNC, **mortise** prevails in written references to such things as *mortise deadlocks* and *mortise-and-tenon joints,* although **mortice** is common in the transcribed speech, suggesting that it may be the more intuitive spelling. But in American English it is always **mortise,** by the evidence of CCAE.
◊ Compare **vice** or **vise.**

Moslem
See under **Muslim.**

mosquitos or mosquitoes
The plural of **mosquito** should be **mosquitos** rather than **mosquitoes,** according to the majority (57%) of those responding to the Langscape survey (1998–2001). Among American respondents, the vote ran higher (71%), whereas among the British it was borderline (49%). But a general trend away from *-oes* plurals is clear in the northern hemisphere: see **-o** section 1.

most or mostly
As adverbs these two are never interchangeable, despite their similarity. **Mostly** is much less common and more elusive, used as
* an adverb of degree, meaning "for the most part" (*children are mostly friendly*), or
* a focusing adverb, meaning "chiefly, largely" (*the routes are mostly concentrated on the left side of the crag*). (See further under **adverbs** section 1.)
The two meanings can be difficult to separate, and **mostly** could be either in examples like:
> *The doctor was mostly concerned that I should have some time off.*
Most is a common intensifier meaning "very," used in:
* verb phrases where it modifies a past participle, as in:
> *The doctor was most concerned that I should have time off.*
* superlative constructions for many adjectives with two or more syllables, such as *most vibrant, most beautiful* (see **adjectives** section 2).
Most also works as shorthand for *almost* before indefinite determiners (especially *any* and *every*) and in indefinite compounds, for example *most anyone/everyone, anything/everything, anywhere/everywhere,* and *anytime.* Americans also use it before *all* and in the phrase *most always.* This use of **most** originated in the US, and after more than a century of debate is standard American idiom, according to *Webster's English Usage* (1989). In the UK it's little used, given the handful of examples in BNC data. Canadians use it, though it's labeled "informal" by the *Canadian Oxford* (1998); and Australians also use it, though with some sense of its American origins, according to the *Macquarie Dictionary* (1997). All this makes it not quite international English idiom, but moving in that direction.

-most
This Old English suffix means "in the extreme," but is only found in adjectives of location:

foremost	*hindmost*	*innermost*
outermost	*topmost*	*uppermost*

and of direction:

easternmost	*northernmost*
southernmost	*westernmost*

The suffix actually consists of two superlative elements from Old English: *-ma* and *-est,* the combination of which was later reinterpreted as *-most.* A comparative element has since been added in to some words, witness *innermost,* which has largely eclipsed the earlier *inmost,* by the evidence of the BNC. But *uttermost* is a long way from replacing its counterpart *utmost,* appearing in the ratio of only 1:25 in the BNC.

mot juste
See **bon mot.**

mother-in-law
See **in-laws.**

motif or motive
Either of these can be used if it refers to a dominant theme in literature or art, but only **motive** means the "goal or incentive which prompts a person's action."
Both words derive from the Latin verb for "move," and their spelling and meanings have both shifted in the course of time. **Motif** was first borrowed into C14 English from French, meaning something like "that which creates a moving impression on the mind." In less than a century it was being respelled **motive,** in line with its Latin ancestor, and acquiring new meanings such as "argument" and "whatever spurs someone into action." In French it remained **motif,** and acquired the further meaning of "dominant artistic theme," which came into C19 English as a fresh loanword. Quite soon however, it too could be spelled **motive,** though this remains the secondary spelling. Note that **motif** is pluralized simply by the addition of *s* (**motifs**). Not having Anglo-Saxon origins, its final letter makes no change from *f* to *v,* as in *leaf* etc.
The German loanword *Leitmotiv* ("leading theme") can also be written in several ways. While *Leitmotiv* is the standard German form, *Leitmotive* and *Leitmotif* also occurred in C19 English, and increasingly the initial capital has been replaced by lower case. In both the UK and the US *leitmotif* seems now to be the dominant form, ahead of *leitmotiv* by more than 2:1 in BNC data, and more than 8:1 in CCAE.

mottos or mottoes
How should the plural of **motto** be spelled? **Mottoes** still seems to be preferred by American and British writers, and has a substantial majority in data from both CCAE and the BNC. Yet **mottos** was endorsed by 85% of respondents to the Langscape survey (1998-2001), including hundreds of British and Americans. This is in line with the worldwide trend for the plurals of borrowed words ending in *-o* : see **-o** section 1.

mould or mold
These alternative spellings apply to three distinct words, for "fungus," "shape" (as noun and verb), and the rather archaic "earth," still found in *leaf mo(u)ld.* The third goes back to Old English *mold,* which gives the spelling **mold** the better pedigree by far. **Mould** dates only from C17. Obscurities in the origins of the first two words have left them taking on the spellings of the third by default.
Mould is now the standard British spelling for all three words, and it dominates the BNC data with only rare instances of **mold** for the sense "shape." But in American English **mold** is standard, outnumbering

mould in CCAE data by more than 12:1. Canadian usage tolerates both **mould** and **mold**, though the first is more visible, in the judgement of *Canadian Oxford* (1998). Australians mostly use **mould**, like the British (see the *Macquarie Dictionary*, 1997).

The spelling of all derivatives of **mo(u)ld**, including *mo(u)ldboard, mo(u)lder, mo(u)ldy*, will also depend on which regional tradition you are working with.

moult or molt

This word originated in medieval times as *mout*, probably based on the Latin stem *mut-* ("change"). But the source has been modified in both the current spellings. American English uses the C16 **molt**, whereas British, Canadian and Australian English use **moult**, first recorded in C17.

mouse

The plural of **mouse** is **mice** if you're referring to more than one rodent. But among computer users it's often **mouses**, when referring to the manual aids used to direct the cursor on screen. *Wired Style* (1995) prefers **mouses** and dictionaries including the *New Oxford* (1998) and the Australian *Macquarie* (1997) acknowledge it as an alternative for that purpose.
◊ On the choice between *mousey* and *mousy*, see **mousy**.

moustache, mustache or mustachio

The standard British spelling is **moustache**, used overwhelmingly in BNC data. In the US, **moustache** and **mustache** divide the field in the ratio of about 1:4, by the evidence of CCAE. Both **moustache** and **mustache** reflect the French source word, whereas **mustachio** is a curious blend of Italian *mustaccio* and Spanish *mostacho*. **Mustachio** (or **mustachios** – identifying the two parts of a longer **m(o)ustache**) appears only very rarely as an alternative to the other two in either British or American data. More often it in appears in adjectival form as *mustachioed*, as in:
> Rows of mustachioed men looked down from their perches along the walls.
◊ For the derivation of the adjective *mustachioed*, see **-ed** section 2.

mousy or mousey

To be likened to a *mouse* is unflattering for men as well as women, and more often said than written. But the *Oxford Dictionary* (1989) has citations for **mous(e)y** since 1812 – decades long enough for it to work without an *e*. **Mousy** is the more regular spelling foregrounded in dictionaries (see **-e**). Yet **mousey** is the preferred spelling of more than 75% of citations in data from both BNC and CCAE. Other research (Sigley, 1999) suggests that the late C20 reversion to *-ey* spelling among informal adjectives is stronger in British than American English. See further under **-y/-ey**.

mouthful

The plural form of this word is discussed under **-ful**.

movable or moveable

Movable is the more regular of the two (see **-e**), and dictionaries everywhere give it priority. In both American and British English, **movable** is clearly in the majority, by 3:1 in CCAE data, and 2:1 in data from the BNC. **Moveable** has its special domain in the field of law, as in *moveable assets*, yet BNC data show that it's being harnessed for other ordinary purposes, as in *moveable furniture/walls* as well as *moveable feast*. The tendency to reinstate **moveable** in late C20 British English is visible in other words of this kind: see **-eable**.

mowed or mown

Both these serve as past participles for the verb *mow*. The *Oxford Dictionary* (1989) gives preference to the older **mown**, while other dictionaries in the UK and the US make it **mowed**. The alternatives remind us that the verb *mow* is still evolving into a regular verb. In Old and Middle English it was irregular, but began to acquire regular parts (**mowed** for past tense and past participle) in C16, and the transition further advanced in the US. **Mown** is used for only about 25% of past participles in CCAE data, whereas in the BNC it appears in more than 90% of instances. British writers typically use **mown** for both *new mown grass* and for figurative applications, such as *mown down by gangsters' bullets*. The American equivalents are *freshly mowed grass* and *worshipers mowed down in a Hebron mosque*. As often, American English is readier to endorse the regular patterns of spelling and word formation. See further under **irregular verbs** section 9.

Mr(.)

This has been used as a courtesy title for decades, replacing the earlier *Esq*. It lends dignity to the names of ordinary citizens, and in press reporting it is still conventional to preface the names of both famous and unknown men with **Mr**. For example:
> When both the Minister for Justice, General McEoin, and the Attorney General, Mr. Charles Casey, made it clear that they considered the legislation inopportune...
> Mr. Murray now wants to give away the Smugglers' Kitchen.
> [The] Academy assistant manager promised to look into Mr. Doblin's case

Several groups are however exempt from this general practice. The first example above shows how persons with a title of their own do not have it replaced by **Mr**. Others exempted are those with a claim to fame in the worlds of sport, entertainment or the arts. For them, adding **Mr**. (and removing the first name) may compromise their identity: witness *Mr Woods* for *Tiger Woods*, *Mr Cook* for *Alistair Cook*, *Mr Hockney* for *David Hockney*. Historical figures are identified without **Mr**. – as are boys, for whom it would seem inappropriate. Those charged with criminal offences are a further category of exception. Most newspapers refer to them by surname only – except the *New York Times*.

Note that **Mr**. normally appears as **Mr** in British style, because it's regarded as a contraction, rather than an abbreviation. See **contractions** section 1.
◊ For the use of **Mr(.)** in letter writing, see under **forms of address** sections 1 and 2.

Mrs(.), Miss and Ms(.)

See under **Miss**.

MS(.) and ms(.)

The abbreviation for "manuscript" can be set either in full caps as **MS** or lower case as **ms**, though dictionaries give priority to the first. They give stops to both **MS**. and **ms**., though this strictly depends on your policy for punctuating abbreviations (see **abbreviations** section 2). The plural forms are **MSS** and **mss**, with or without stops.

While **MS(.)** and **ms(.)** are the forms listed in standard dictionaries, *Ms* is also occasionally seen for "manuscript." Whether it represents an accident of typesetting or a decision of the editor is a further question. Set that way, it coincides with the common title for a woman, though the likelihood of their being confused seems remote. See further under **Miss, Mrs(.) or Ms(.)**.

muchly

The *-ly* is not needed to make an adverb of *much* (see **zero adverbs**). Yet from time to time **muchly** turns up in impromptu speech as in "his muchly appreciated article," or as playful variation on plain idiom: "Thank you muchly." In print these are very rare, but they have little reason to appear there. Garner (1998) classes **muchly** as nonstandard American English; whereas Burchfield (1996) simply says that in British English its status has slipped and one no longer takes it seriously.

mucus or mucous

See under **-ous**.

Muhammad, Mohammed or Mahomet

These are the three most widely used spellings for the name of the founder of Islam – though there are others on record which vary the vowels, the use of double or single *m* and the choice of *d* or *t* at the end. The variability of the vowels results from the fact that traditional Arabic script registered only the consonants of a word: and the vowels vary with the different forms of spoken modern Arabic which supplied them.

The earliest European spelling was **Mahomet**, used from C16, and this survives in C19 English literature. The form **Mohammed** gained currency in C17 and C18, and was the primary spelling well into C20. **Muhammad** is now felt to best represent the Classical Arabic form of the name, and it's the spelling given priority in *Webster's* (1961) and the second edition of the *Oxford Dictionary* (1989). But database evidence suggests that **Muhammad** is better established in the US than the UK. **Muhammad** appears in the majority of instances in CCAE data, whereas in the BNC it makes only about one third of the total. In both databases the frequency of **Muhammad** is boosted by various references to *Muhammad Ali* (once Cassius Clay, world heavy-weight boxing champion). The changed spelling of his name is symptomatic of the general change, whether in reference to the prophet or not. But in the transition, **Mohammed** remains the given name for many prominent Muslims, and continues in the names of historical personages, e.g. *Mohammed II, Sultan of Turkey 1145–1181*.

mulatto

This, the Spanish/Portuguese word for a young mule, is scarcely polite as a reference to someone of mixed race, though dictionaries do not actually label it "derogatory." Alternative expressions are discussed under **miscegenation**.

◊ For the plural (**mulattos** or **mulattoes**), see under **-o**.

multi-

This prefix meaning "many" is derived from Latin loanwords such as *multifarious, multiply, multitude*. Since C19 it has helped to create various technical words, including:

multicellular	multilaminate
multimeter	multipartite

as well as ones which are part of our common vocabulary:

multicolored	multicultural
multifaceted	multigrade
multilateral	multilingual
multimillionnaire	multinational
multiplex	multipurpose
multiracial	multistorey

Further development of the prefix can be seen in compound adjectives, such as *multi-handicapped* and *multi-tasking* (abilities), where **multi-** is an abbreviation of either *multiple* or the adverb *multiply*. The hyphen is a useful indicator of this extended meaning. But note that some dictionaries and writers, especially in the UK, are inclined to use hyphens in other words from the list above. There's little need for a hyphen in any of them, because the stem begins in each case with a consonant. The *New Oxford* (1998) gives hyphens only to words such as *multi-ethnic*, where the stem begins with a vowel.

multicultural

See under **ethnic**.

multiple punctuation

When two punctuation marks coincide at the end of a sentence, do you need both? The general principles are:

* if the marks are the same, only one is needed
* if they are different, the stronger or "heavier" one takes precedence

A question mark thus supersedes a period or stop used to mark the end of a sentence or quotation:

> He asked "Do you want a lift?"
> What did they mean by "Further information is needed"?

In each case, the question mark takes over from the final period/stop which might have appeared on the other side of the quote marks. On occasions when the exclamation and question mark coincide, the *Chicago Manual* (2003) recommends using the mark more appropriate to the (communicative) context, hence the exclamation point in *You ask me why am I here!* However when two marks of "equal strength" are needed (Ritter, 2002), both punctuation marks may be used (?!). The alternative would be to use an *interrobang* (see **interrobang**).

When **multiple punctuation** involves an abbreviatory stop, it yields to the period that ends a sentence, but is retained alongside other marks. Compare:

> We need food and drink etc.
> Food and drink etc., are what we need.
> Did you say "food and drink etc."?

(See further under **quotation marks** section 3c.)
◊ For **multiple punctuation** with parentheses, see **brackets** section 3.

multiplier symbol, point, period or dot

In mathematical scripts, the symbol for multiplication can take several forms, that of $\times$, of a raised dot $\cdot$ or a dot like a period/full stop on the line of print.

$$k \times g\,(a + 3) \quad k \cdot g\,(a + 3) \quad k.g\,(a + 3)$$

The second symbol has no standard name, and it's variously called the *multiplication point* or *medial point* (Butcher, 1992), *multiplication dot, raised dot, multiplier sign* (*Chicago Manual*, 1993) or the *raised period, centered dot* (*CBE Manual*, 1994). The third symbol also lacks a name, and when used with numbers could all too easily be misread as a decimal point (see under **numbers and number style**). The Royal Society recommends against it and in favor of the raised dot.

mumps

Though it looks like a plural word, it takes a singular verb. See under **agreement** section 2b.

Muslim or Moslem

The spelling **Muslim** is preferred by English-speaking followers of Islam, and the only correct one for the so-called *Black Muslims*, that is the "Nation of Islam" in the US. Scholars also recommend **Muslim** as the best transliteration of the Classical Arabic, hence the *Oxford Dictionary*'s (1989) note that **Muslim** is "now the preferred form." But the *Dictionary* still presents **Moslem** first, as in its first edition, and *Webster's Third* (1986) does likewise. The switchover from **Moslem** to **Muslim** is slightly less advanced in the US than the UK, judging by the fact that the two spellings appear in equal numbers in CCAE, whereas the data from BNC are weighted in favor of **Muslim**, by a factor of 2:1. The direction is clear, and both *Merriam-Webster* (2000) and *New Oxford* (1998) now recommend **Muslim**.

must

This modal verb usually bears a strong sense of obligation and/or necessity, whether in written or spoken discourse:

> *Candidates must demonstrate their command of a language other than English.*
> *You must come with me.*

Much less common is the use of **must** to express likelihood:

> *That must be Leslie.*
> *The sun must rise.*

British writers and speakers make somewhat more use of **must** than their American counterparts, according to the *Longman Grammar* (1999). See further under **modality**.

mustache, mustachio or moustache

See **moustache**.

mutatis mutandis

Equivalent English for this compact Latin phrase is "changing those things which need to be changed." In effect it means that when a rule or principle from one case is being applied to another, the appropriate adjustments have been made.

mutual

See **common or mutual**.

Myanmar

See **Burma**.

myriad and myriads

Though in Greek it meant "ten thousand," this word in English now means an indefinitely large number. Its grammatical status is also somewhat indefinite, and it's variously used as a noun and as a kind of determiner.

* as noun, myriad is usually construed in the singular with the indefinite article, as in *a myriad of papers,* but sometimes with other determiners, as in *the myriad of books written about her,* and *their myriad of products.* The plural form **myriads** is also found, as in *myriads of tiny shells,* more in British than American English, by the evidence of BNC and CCAE.

* as determiner, myriad combines with other determiners, as in:

> *a myriad pine needles*
> *the myriad administrative changes*
> *your myriad younger readers*
> *its myriad problems*

as well as appearing on its own:

> *... chased by dolphin and myriad seabirds*

The use of **myriad(s)** often seems faintly rhetorical – geared to impress with the vast and countless numbers of something. It therefore couples rather strangely with an ordinary finite number, as when *De Koonig's myriad subjects* turn out to be no more than those of the 76 paintings exhibited. The suggestion that *pregnant women have a myriad choices for exercising* sounds more than a little far-fetched, and dilutes the force of the word. Dictionaries don't yet suggest that the word just means "many."

myself

This reflexive pronoun is sometimes used as a rather self-conscious replacement for *me* or even *I*. The effect is not always the one intended (see under **me**). Others use **myself** to underscore a personal reference, as discussed under **self**.

mystic or mystical

The word **mystic** is both noun and adjective, as in *a sixteenth-century mystic* and *mystic transcendentalism*. As in these examples, the adjective **mystic** often reflects the sense of the noun, although it sometimes appears with the more general meaning usually associated with **mystical** ("metaphysical," "mysterious"), as in *it had an almost mystic effect on me*. But the borderland between the two adjectives is fuzzy, and **mystical** claims much of it, as in

> *an almost mystical appeal*
> *his brand of mystical atheism*

Mystical is far commoner than **mystic** (as adjective) in both American and British English, by the evidence of CCAE and the BNC. Like other *-ic/-ical* pairs, they still seem to be negotiating the semantic space between them. See **-ic/-ical**.

mythological, mythic and mythical

All these adjectives connect with *myth*, but their implications are a little different. **Mythological** relates to a body of myths, or study of them, as in "mythological elements in ancient history." **Mythic** essentially means "dealt with in a myth," as in *mythic* *animals and anthropomorphic deities.* Yet either word would work in a sentence such as the following:

> *Prometheus was a mythic/mythological king of Greece.*

Both **mythic** and **mythical** can carry the sense "existing only in myth, fictional," but this is rather more the domain of **mythical**, as in:

> ... *the mythical Welsh seaside town in "Under Milk-Wood"*

In British English, **mythical** is a good deal more common than **mythic** (in the ratio 5:2 in BNC data), whereas they appear in almost equal numbers in the American English data of CCAE. Like many *-ic/-ical* pairs, they share a good deal: see **-ic/-ical**.

-n/-nn-

Words ending in **-n** behave like others with one final consonant when suffixes are added. When the suffix begins with a vowel, the **-n** is doubled only if two conditions are met:
1 the vowel before the **-n** is spelled with just one letter: compare *grinned* with *gleaned*
2 the syllable ending in **-n** bears the word's stress
So any word of one or more syllables that meets these conditions will have a double **-n**: for example, *planned*, *beginner*. The spellings most in doubt are inflected verbs derived from nouns with two or more syllables, e.g. *button, toboggan*. Yet by the principles just mentioned, such words can only be spelled with one *n*, as follows:

> buttoned   hyphened   pardoned   sequined
> tobogganed   turbaned

Anomalies and exceptions are:
* loanwords with variable stress, such as *chagrined*, which will be irregular for those who stress the second syllable
* compounds like *sin(-)binned*, whose second component seems to dictate the spelling of the inflection

For other sets of words affected by doubling, see **doubling of final consonant**.

naive, naïve, and naïf

This French loan comes into English in both masculine and feminine forms: **naïf** and **naïve**. The two are acquiring distinct grammatical roles, in which the French gender distinction is neutralized. So **naïve** or rather **naive** is used for the adjective in reference to both men and women. The accent-free spelling is fostered by the lack of dieresis on many typewriters and wordprocessors; and three quarters of all instances of the word in BNC data were without it. So **naive** stands as the primary spelling for the adjective in reference dictionaries such as *New Oxford* (1998) and *Merriam-Webster* (2000), the *Canadian Oxford* (1998) and the Australian *Macquarie* (1997). Both *Webster's Third* (1986) and the *Oxford Dictionary* (1989) preferred the accented French spelling.

Meanwhile the masculine form **naif** is increasingly used in both British and American English for the noun meaning "an innocent," again for both women and men. See for example:

> *Linda P is a fresh-face naif . . .*
> *. . . the rich naif played by Henry Fonda*

Naif still occasionally finds uses as an adjective, in examples which suggest lingering deference to its masculine gender in French. This would explain examples such as *Yankovic plays the naif George Newman,* as well as *naif art* (in English usually *naive art*) and the loanword/compound *faux-naif* (usually predicative; see under **adjectives**). But the role of **naif** as gender-free noun is well recognized in current dictionaries.

naivety or naïveté

These two spellings represent the opposite ends of a scale from least to most French. There are permutations and combinations of the two variable items in between: forms with or without the dieresis; and with *é*, plain *e* or *y* as the last syllable – though all are compromises on linguistic consistency. Surprisingly perhaps, the trend to replace the French *é* with *y* is stronger in British English than American. In data from the BNC **naivety** outnumbers **naïveté** by almost 4:1, and the latter is absent from *New Oxford* (1998). This coincides with a note in *Merriam-Webster* (2000), that **naivety** is "chiefly British." The American preference is clearly for **naïveté**, which outnumbers **naivety** by more than 100:1 in data from CCAE. Canadians also prefer **naïveté**, according to the *Canadian Oxford* (1998), whereas Australians are for **naivety**, and the French forms are little used by their position in the *Macquarie Dictionary* (1997) sequence of alternatives.

The dieresis in **naïvety** is steadily disappearing, as from **naïve** (see previous entry), and all dictionaries put **naivety** ahead of **naïvety**. But where **naïveté** is the preferred form (in the US and Canada), the dieresis is part of the primary spelling. If you're going to use the French form, there can be no compromises.

name–year system

This is an alternative name for the **author–date** system of referencing. See **referencing** section 3.

named after or named for

These are sometimes said to be distinctively British and American idioms for commemorative naming – that British English prefers **named after**:

> *the Wright amendment, named after a former speaker . . . Jim Wright*
> *a Cairn Terrier named after Fletcher Christian*

whereas American idiom uses **named for** for this purpose:

> *the new gun law, named for James Brady*
> *the Axel jump was named for its inventor Axel Paulsen*

Usage data show that the divide is not so absolute. Though **named after** is far more common than **named for** in BNC data, by about 10:1, the latter is clearly not unknown. Americans make substantial use of both idioms, while favoring **named for** over **named after** by about 3:2 in data from CCAE. Canadians prefer **named after**, according to the *Canadian Oxford* (1998), as do Australians (*Macquarie Dictionary*, 1997).

In all the examples so far, being **named after/for** involves the proper name of a person. But the data show other kinds of proper names invoked in such naming. Some instances refer you to a placename:

> *the Pugwash conference – so named after the site of their first meeting in Nova Scotia.*

Some explain a name by reference to commercial products (*named after a bar of soap*), or the titles of songs or books (*each ... named for a different book in the bible*). Yet other names come from mythical animals or successful race-horses. Beyond all these are names that connect with generic elements, for example:

> *Copper Canyon – named for the minerals mined there*
> *The redstart, named for its strikingly red tail, is mainly a woodland bird.*

These examples, among others from both CCAE and the BNC, show the further reaches of the idiom, indicating other than commemorative reasons for choosing a name.

names

What's in a name? Plenty – though our answer to Shakespeare's question focuses on whether the form of the **name** is right for the person concerned. Individual family decisions as well as cultural elements are embedded in people's nomenclature, and both courtesy and diplomacy may be at stake in getting them right. No-one is so aware of the mistreatment of a **name** as its owner.

The sections following concentrate on personal **names**, titles and initials, all of which raise issues of style. The writing of institutional **names** is discussed under **capital letters** (sections 1 and 3), and **geographical names** are examined under their own heading.

1 Order of names. In western culture a person's given **name** comes first and so is their "first name." Many Asian and some East European **names** are ordered the other way, with the family name first and the given name(s) after it. (For specific nationalities, see further under **first name or forename**.) Asians and others may nevertheless invert the customary order of their **names** to comply with Anglo-Saxon and West European practice. It will not be obvious with, say, a Japanese **name** unless you're familiar with Japanese given **names**. Note also that Spanish Latin American **names** normally comprise three units: a given **name**, the family **name** (patronymic), and mother's family **name**. For men and unmarried children the **names** appear in that order, though after being introduced they drop the third and use the first two. Spanish women after marrying are known by four **names**: their given and family **names**, followed by *de* and their husband's two surnames. However once introduced they would be called by their husband's family **name**, like married women in the English tradition.

2 Titles and names. Most **names** are preceded by some sort of title. Those for a number of different nationalities are listed under **forms of address**. Beyond the choice of title there are questions about how it combines with the rest of the **name**. The title is generally used in full if followed by the surname alone. For example:

> General Monash   Professor Waterhouse
> Senator Button

The title may be abbreviated if followed by initials or a given name:

> Gen. John Monash   Prof. E.R. Waterhouse
> Sen. J. Button

The title *Reverend* has been subject to different conventions of style. According to the highest Anglican tradition, it must always be followed by initials or a given **name**, never just *Reverend Marshall*. Fowler (1926) likens it to the structure of **names** titled with *(the) Hon.* and *Sir,* which helps to explain the force of tradition behind it in Britain. He does nevertheless allow for *Reverend Dr.* (or *Mr.) Marshall,* when the cleric's name or initial are not known. Gowers (1965) noted lapses in these conventions ("especially in Scotland and Ireland"), and thought that the style *Reverend Marshall* was on its way to acceptability. This is so in the "lower" Protestant churches, according to *The Right Word at the Right Time* (1985). Yet in more encompassing data from the BNC, instances of *Reverend* plus surname make up only about 15% of the total. There are alternative views and practices in the US also. The *Chicago Manual of Style* (1993) affirms the high Anglican convention; but with other churches there's no such prescription, as *Webster's English Usage* (1989) noted. The variation shows up in CCAE data, in examples of "high" and "low" church styles. Christian names are there in *Reverend Martin Luther King, Reverend Jesse Jackson* and some less widely known (e.g. *Reverend John Pinkerton, Reverend William Borders*), but absent from numerous others who are simply *Reverend Johns, Reverend McLean, Reverend Morton* etc. On rare occasions these are second references to the persons concerned, and abbreviations of the full form given earlier – but mostly not. Rather they suggest that *Reverend* is being used like other professional titles (*Professor, Dr*), and put with the surname alone. The transition is restrained by tradition within the Anglican church of Canada (*Canadian English Usage,* 1997) and Australia (*Style Manual,* 2002), but accepted within other Protestant denominations.

◊ For the abbreviations *Rev.* and *Revd.,* see under **Reverend**.

◊ For the use of stops in *Rev(.), Gen(.)* and other abbreviated titles, see **abbreviations** section 2.

3 Initials. The practice of using initials to represent given names has been more common in Europe than in America or Australia. Various celebrated names are rarely given in any other form: *C. P. E. Bach, T. S. Eliot, C. S. Lewis, P. G. Wodehouse.* In bibliographies and referencing systems (*author–date, Vancouver*), the use of initials is well established (see **bibliographies**). Both the *Chicago Manual of Style* (2003) and *Copy-editing* (1992) use stops after each initial, as well as space, as shown in the names above. But in common usage the space between initials is being whittled down (*C.P.E. Bach, T.S. Eliot, C.S. Lewis, P.G. Wodehouse*), making the spacing exactly like that used in initialisms (see **acronyms** last section). This was the style endorsed by a majority of respondents (68%) in the Langscape survey 1998–2001. Stops too are often omitted – as in *C P E Bach* – in lists of names in newspapers, journals and directories. In Britain this is now standard style for correspondence (Todd, 1995), and it's endorsed in the Australian government *Style Manual* (2002). Unpunctuated initials need not keep a space between each letter, and evolve naturally enough into *CPE Bach* etc. This was endorsed only by a third of respondents to the Langscape survey mentioned before, but it is standard in the Vancouver referencing system (see under **bibliographies**). *Chicago Manual* (2003) accepts this style with neither stops nor space when naming public figures such as *JFK* and *FDR,* but not more generally. Presidents seem to be special cases, as also *Harry S Truman,* where the *S* is unstopped because it doesn't stand for one particular name. (Truman's parents wanted the letter to invoke a name belonging to each of his grandfathers: *Solomon* and *Shippe.*) The practice of using an initial as well as a given **name**, as in *J. Arthur Rank, Dwight D. Eisenhower* is more widespread in the US than the UK. ◊ For the convention of addressing a married woman by her husband's initials, see under **forms of address** section 1.

4 Surnames. Getting a surname exactly right may require checking with *Who's Who,* a dictionary of biography, or the telephone directory. There are permutations and variants of most English surnames (e.g. *Haywood/Heywood, Matthews/Mathews, Philips/Phillips, White/Whyte*), apart from the rather fluid spelling of foreign **names** on the way to being anglicized. Following the initial capital there may be internal capitals in surnames beginning with *Fitz-* and *Mac* or *Mc* (see under those headings). Capitals are also an issue with the particles *da, de, van, von* etc., which begin numerous Italian, French, Dutch, German and other European names. (See **capital letters** section 1.) Note also the use of space, and hyphens, in compound surnames such as *La Nauze* and *Lloyd-Jones.*

5 Roman numerals. Postnominal enumerators such as *III, IV, V* and the designations *Jr.* and *Sr.* have been used in American families to differentiate older and younger bearers of the same **name**, as with *Joseph Kennedy Jnr.* and *Joseph Kennedy III.* The original convention had these designators updated once the first bearer of the **name** had died, so that *JK III* then became *JK Jr.* etc. But the convention stopped with some celebrated figures such as *Adlai Stevenson III,* whose numeral was never updated. This fixed style has created an alternative custom in some American families, according to the *Chicago Manual* (1993). The enumerators have never been set off with a comma, and this is now the normal style for *Jr.,* as illustrated above. Note also that *Jr.* (and *Sr.*) carry a full stop, like most American abbreviations. See **abbreviations** section 2.

Nanking or Nanjing
See under **China.**

narcissus
The *Narcissus* of Greek myth gave his name to the flower, which came into English via Latin. Its plural can be either **narcissi**, or the English **narcissuses**, given that many Latin plant names attract English plurals in ordinary usage (see under **-us** section 1). Yet **narcissuses** presents a rapid set of *ss* to be uttered, and though this hardly affects the printed page, it seems to combine with traditional latinity to support **narcissi** as the preferred plural. Both *Oxford* (1989) and *New Oxford* (1998) endorse it as the primary form, and it is indeed the only plural to be found in the BNC. In American data from CCAE, both **narcissi** and **narcissuses** occur, in the ratio 3:1 – and the first is given preference in *Merriam-Webster* (2000). *Webster's Third* (1986) prioritized **narcissus** itself to be used as a *zero plural* (see under that heading), and both databases provide examples:

> *simple to grow scented [plants] include lilies, carnations, narcissus, friesias*

In CCAE the zero plural **narcissus** is almost as common as **narcissi**.

narrative
An ancient form of art and entertainment, **narrative** comes naturally to most of us when we have something to tell. The habit of recounting things in the order in which they happened, i.e. in chronological order, is what many people resort to in impromptu discussion, when they have to explain such things as how a meeting turned out, or what caused the accident. Making the order of a **narrative** match the order of happening is the simplest way for the speaker to relate the story, and for the listener to digest it – as long as there's time for the whole of it.

In documentary writing, **narrative** is definitely less satisfactory. Readers usually want to know more than what happened to get a perspective on it, and some insights out of it. The writer's point of view comes through more clearly if only significant events are told, and this selection would be structured argumentatively rather than chronologically. See further under **persuasion.**

naturalist or naturist
There's a dramatic difference between these two. The **naturalist** is primarily a student of *nature* and its flora and fauna, though the term is also applied to those concerned with *naturalism* in art, literature or philosophy. A **naturist** is one who advocates or practises nudism. **Naturist** is thus what "insiders" would call themselves, whereas outsiders typically use *nudist.* In the US, *nudist* is far commoner than **naturist** – by more than 7:1 in data from CCAE. But in the BNC the ratio is roughly 3:2 – suggesting that more practitioners of *naturism* get into print in the UK than the US.

naught or nought
Though both mean "nothing," these two have slightly different origins: **naught** is a compound of Old English *na* ("no") + *wiht* ("thing"), and **nought** of *ne* ("not") + *owiht* ("anything"). In British English the first is a good deal more current than the second, by the evidence of the BNC. **Naught** mostly survives in phrases such as *come to naught, set at naught, all for naught,* which have a slightly old-fashioned ring to them. **Nought** is in fact taking over from **naught** in some of those phrases, for example:

> *peace negotiations came to nought*
> *not for nought did he train in the jungles of Borneo*

But **nought** also has a working life as a reference to the number 0 in arithmetic, and elsewhere when numbers are being quoted:

> *worth nought out of ten*
> *If nought is divided by nought, is the answer infinity?*

Even so **nought** is replaced by *zero* in some numerical roles (*temperatures well below zero*), and in its descriptive functions in the domains of finance (*zero dividend, zero risk*), sport (*zero points score*) and science (*zero concentration, absolute zero*). BNC data has *zero* outnumbering **nought** by about 4:1 in current British English. (See further under **zero.**)

In American English, **naught** has survived better than **nought**, by a factor of almost 15:1 in data from

CCAE. Most occurrences of **naught** are in phrases such as *all for naught, it wasn't for naught, went for naught, naught had been lost,* which seem to appear in ordinary usage – rather than self-conscious styles of writing. On its few appearances, **nought** appears in those phrases, but never as a number. This is where Americans prefer *zero,* and it outnumbers **naught/nought** in CCAE data by about 350:1.

Canadians find both **naught** and **nought** rather archaic, according to *Canadian English Usage* (1997), but like Americans, they are more used to the first than the second. Australians, like the British, make some numerical use of **nought** alongside *zero,* but very little of **naught**.

nauseating, nauseous and nauseated
Older dictionaries held that both **nauseating** and **nauseous** meant "causing or engendering nausea," and **nauseated** "affected with nausea." But all current dictionaries allow that **nauseous** now most commonly means what **nauseated** has always meant. Its most common collocations in BNC data both written and spoken are *feel(ing) nauseous* and *felt nauseous,* and this is now acknowledged as the dominant sense by British and American authorities (Burchfield, 1996, and *Webster's English Usage,* 1989). In British data **nauseous** means "affected with nausea" in about 65% of instances, whereas in American data it's more than 85%. Older usages such as *the nauseous odor of popcorn* and the figurative *nauseous repetition of the phrase* are in the minority. *Webster's English Usage* documents the rise of **nauseous** meaning "nauseated" in post-World War II America, but there's little to show for it in the UK, and Gowers's edition of Fowler (1965) has no reference to it. Yet the *Oxford Dictionary* (1989) has C17 citations of **nauseous** used to mean "inclined to nausea," labeled "obsolete" – which perhaps diverted researchers from updating the entry for the second edition. The current use of **nauseous** may thus be a kind of revival rather than innovation. All this makes **nauseous** more often a synonym for **nauseated** than for **nauseating,** and **nauseated** becomes the least common of the three words in current English.

Navajo or Navaho
The original name of this American Indian nation was something like *Navahu,* meaning "large field," and the spelling **Navaho** stands relatively close it. This would explain why *Webster's Third* (1986) made it the first of the alternatives, although the Spanish-style **Navajo** had also been used for three centuries, by the *Oxford Dictionary* (1989) record. Database evidence shows that **Navajo** is now the preferred spelling of both British and American writers. **Navajo** outnumbers **Navaho** by more than 2:1 in BNC data, and by 14:1 in CCAE. Both *New Oxford* (1998) and *Merriam-Webster* (2000) make **Navajo** the primary spelling.
◊ Compare **Mohave or Mojave**.

NB
These letters represent the Latin imperative *nota bene* ("note well"). Since its first appearance in C17 scholarly writing, it has become one of the most familiar abbreviations. Its tone is almost confidential, and definitely less formal than the word *Note* itself. It normally appears in capitals as the first item in a sentence, with the next word also capitalized:

NB The keys are under the doormat.
Like other fully capitalized abbreviations, it often appears without stops. See **abbreviations** section 2.

-nce/-ncy
Words which are identical but for these endings often seem to offer us a choice. Should it be *complacence* or *complacency, compliance* or *compliancy?* Many others raise the same question, although usually one is a good deal more frequent than the other. In the list below, the one in italics is far more common in database evidence. More often than not it's the word ending in **-nce** which dominates, but not always.

> *brilliance*/brilliancy
> *competence*/competency
> complacence/*complacency*
> *compliance*/compliancy
> *concomitance*/concomitancy
> *concurrence*/concurrency
> *consistence*/consistency
> *consonance*/consonancy
> *convergence*/convergency
> *dependence*/dependency
> hesitance/*hesitancy*
> *insistence*/insistency
> insurgence/*insurgency*
> lenience/*leniency*
> malignance/*malignancy*
> *permanence*/permanency
> *persistence*/persistency
> *recalcitrance*/recalcitrancy
> *relevance*/relevancy

With *ascendance/ascendancy/ascendence/ascendency* there are four choices (see further under **ascendant**). For the choice between *dependence/dependency* and *dependance/dependancy,* see **dependent or dependant**.

Many of the words listed embody abstractions that are on the margins of common usage, mostly invoked in formal and theoretical writing. One may have an old-fashioned ring to it, as with *brilliancy* and *consistence,* while the other *brilliance/consistency* is the standard word. As those examples show, it's impossible to predict which of the pair is likely to be the "ordinary" member.

The lack of clear distinction between the two endings is at least partly due to the fact that the abstract/concrete relationship between them is changing. Historically it was **-nce** which was the more concrete of the two, because it was the verbal noun, and the verb element can be seen and felt in some like *compliance* and *convergence.* However many **-nce** words were formed in French from verbs which have not come into English. They therefore seem quite as abstract as those ending in **-ncy,** which represent Latin abstract nouns ending in *-ntia,* and express the state or quality of a related adjective.

In contemporary English, the **-ncy** word is often more specific than the **-nce** one. This shows up in the contrast between *emergence* and *emergency,* or between *dependence* and *dependency* (when the latter is used to mean "dependent territory"), and between *excellence* and *(your) excellency.* Other **-ncy** words with quite specific meanings are *constituency* and *vacancy.* When both **-nce** and **-ncy** words are current, it's the **-ncy** one which can become plural, as with *competence/competencies, irrelevance/irrelevancies, insurgence/insurgencies.* In grammatical terms, the

-ncy word is a *countable* noun, while the -nce one is a *mass* noun (see further under **count nouns**). All this shows that the older distinction between the two groups is breaking down and being replaced by a fresh paradigm. We are caught between the two paradigms with the less common pairs.

né

See under **née**.

ne plus ultra

This Latin phrase means literally "no more beyond." It refers to the furthest point of achievement in anything, the acme of perfection. In ancient tradition it had a geographical meaning, "the furthest limits [of navigation]", and was the message inscribed on the Pillars of Hercules in the Straits of Gibraltar, to discourage seamen from venturing beyond the safety of the Mediterranean. There's a play on both meanings in the *Plus ultra* on the Spanish royal coat of arms. This was Charles V's modification of the original phrase, amid the triumph of the discovery of America.

Neanderthal or Neandertal

The archetypal European human was named after the West German valley (**Neanderthal**) in which s/he was found in mid-C19. Since then the German word for "valley" has been trimmed from *thal* to *tal* – hence the alternative spelling **Neandertal**, found by Google (2003) in about 10% of all instances of the word in English texts on the internet. But it's more acceptable in American than British English, judging by the fact that *Merriam-Webster* (2000) registers it as an alternative but not *New Oxford* (1998).

Neanderthal itself has acquired new uses: in describing uncouth persons e.g. *your Neanderthal friend;* and in criticism of backward views or primitive facilities: *a neanderthal attitude, neanderthal plumbing, neanderthal armed forces.* As the examples show, the word often appears without a capital letter when used abstractly.

nebula

This astronomical term borrowed from Latin can be pluralized in the regular English way as **nebulas**, or according to its latinate origins as **nebulae**. Scientists might be expected to prefer the latter, but so did almost 75% of respondents to the Langscape survey 1998–2001. For the plurals of other loanwords of this kind, see **-a** section 1.

necessities or necessaries

Are these synonyms? Fowler (1926) believed so, and his point seems to be confirmed by dictionaries: among various definitions they do allow that both can mean "things necessary or indispensable." **Necessities** is the commoner of the two by far in database evidence, and thoroughly established in phrases such as *the necessities of life. The necessaries* seems less natural, perhaps because it's uncomfortable as an adjective which has been converted into a noun and then pluralized.

née and né

Née is the feminine form of the French word meaning "born." It was borrowed into C18 English to preface a woman's maiden name, as in *Agatha Christie née Miller.* As in that case, the **née** links the woman's married name directly with the other, and her given name is not repeated. The juxtaposition of the two surnames helps those who know her only by one of them.

The masculine counterpart **né** made its debut in American English in the 1930s, and is beginning to be seen in Britain. It matches **née** as a way of juxtaposing a man's given and family name with an assumed professional name, for example *Tab Hunter, né Arthur Gelien.* Its more remarkable function is to indicate the changed name of a place or institution, for example *Sri Lanka né Ceylon.* Yet American writers also tend to use **née** for both these additional functions, as in the following from CCAE:

> *Harry Ross (née Rosenzweig)*
> *Chevron Corp, née Standard Oil of California*
> *. . . taken the lead from the Los Angeles née Oakland Raiders*
> *the Historical Society of Washington née the Columbia Historical Society*

The general preference for **née** rather than **né** can perhaps be explained by the fact that two letters put it below the common threshold for content words in English (see under **words**). Three letters are also safer when, as often, the accent cannot be printed (*nee*). The French genders vested in **née** and **né** have evidently faded, as in some other French loanwords e.g. *employee, naive, plaintiff.*
◊ Compare **alias and aka**.

need

This verb has three roles in contemporary English: as a main verb, a semi-modal, and a catenative:

> *She needs a holiday (main verb)*
> *She needn't take it now (quasi-modal)*
> *She doesn't need to take it before Christmas (catenative)*

As a main verb in the first sentence, *needs* takes an *s* ending for the third person singular present tense, and its own object. In the second sentence *need* as semi-modal has no *s* ending, and a bare (*to*-less) infinitive to extend its meaning. Note also that the negative *n't* is attached directly to it – another feature of auxiliaries. The third sentence is a kind of compromise between the first two. **Need** as catenative takes an infinitive with *to* (see **catenatives**). The negative is formed in the normal way for main verbs, i.e. with the help of the verb *do* and the negative attached to it.

The use of **need** as a quasi-modal is probably not as common as it used to be. Nowadays it's largely confined to negative statements like the one above, or those with negative implications expressed through *hardly, only, scarcely* etc. Research for the *Longman Grammar* (1999) shows this usage now mostly in academic writing, and in British – but not American – fiction. The non-modal form with *do* support prevails in other kinds of discourse, in 90% of instances of **need** as main (and catenative) verb.

negative concord

This is an alternative term for double or multiple negation within the same clause. It covers the stereotypical *You ain't seen nothing yet,* as well as the lively examples published by Labov (1972):

> *Ain't nobody know about no club.*
> *We ain't write over no streets nothing.*

In each case the repetition of the negative by alternative means in close proximity helps to underscore the force and/or defiance of the utterance. Though **negative concord** is socially stigmatized in both American and British English, it has a long history of use and survives in casual conversation. Double or multiple negation is not censured when it occurs through repetition or reformulation of the negative in independent phrases, as in *No, not that one,* or at different levels in the grammatical hierarchy: *a not unacceptable solution.* See further under **double negatives.**

negatives

In English, *negation* may be expressed in several ways:
* through whole words
not	*never (adverbs)*
no	*(adjective)*
none	*(pronoun)*
nobody	*no-one nothing (nouns)*
* through phrases embodying those words, such as
  not at all   under no circumstances   by no means
* through prefixes such as *a-, dis-, in-, non-, un-,* and the suffix *-less* (see under each of those headings)

Negation is also implied in a number of other words, including *unless* (conjunction), *without* (preposition), *few, little* (adjectives/pronouns), and *barely, hardly, only, rarely, scarcely, seldom* (all adverbs).

When a **negative** or *quasi-negative* adverb is the first word in a sentence or clause, the next item must be an auxiliary, followed by the subject:

Never would she believe that it was over.
Hardly had they arrived when the telephone rang.
Seldom did he speak of his former life.

This *negative inversion* also applies to adverbial phrases. See further under **inversion.**

1 Communicating with negatives. A single **negative** causes few problems. But when two or more are combined in the same sentence or clause it can make difficulties for the reader. This is the real problem with the so-called "double negative," though not the kind which has been the traditional target of criticism. (See further under **double negatives.**) When formulating questions, even single **negatives** can complicate things unnecessarily and make it hard for anyone to know how to reply:

Were you not driving in excess of 140 kilometers per hour?
Are you an unlicensed driver?

If you wanted to say (in answer to either question) that your behavior was perfectly legal, you would have to use two or three **negatives:**

No, I was not...
No, I am not unlicensed...

Removing the **negative** element from the original question helps to guarantee a more reliable answer.

2 The scope of negatives. A **negative** word has considerable reach both within its own clause and beyond it. When attached to a verb which expresses a mental process, it immediately affects the clause depending on it. In fact it's more idiomatic to say *I don't think he speaks well* than *I think he doesn't speak well.* Note also the way in which a **negative** can dominate a whole sentence and forge a cohesive link with the next sentence:

We didn't laugh because he fell into the water. The whole ceremony was so ridiculous that we were bursting at the seams...

The scope of such a **negative** could be limited by a strategically placed comma. With it, the meaning of the sentence changes dramatically:

We didn't laugh, because he fell into the water. He might have been crushed against the wharf...

The extent of the **negative** is also the basis of choosing between *nor* and *or* later in a sentence. See under **nor.**

negligible or negligent

Both these adjectives have a lot to do with putting things out of one's mind. **Negligible** is the one to apply to things which are so small that they can be discounted: *a negligible amount of makeup on her face.* **Negligent** is applied to the conduct of people who do not attend to things in the usual or proper way. The word embodies more or less criticism, depending on whether the word expresses legal sanctions or not. In *negligent driving* its censure is much heavier than in *a negligent attitude to the garden.* In general usage **negligent** sometimes seems to connote something as light as nonchalance – as if some forms of **negligence** are **negligible.** So if neglect and failure to attend to things are really the issue, you may need to use *neglectful* rather than **negligent.**

The word *négligée* (the slightest form of dress known to man or woman) embodies the same stem as **negligible** and **negligent.** Both its accents and the second final *e* are often neglected.

negress or Negress

Race and gender are stamped too heavily on this word to make it acceptable in print nowadays – except when rendering the utterances of racist/sexist characters. In any case, the *-ess* suffix is falling into abeyance (see **-ess**), so that the word seems dated. The word is little used in current American or British English, by the few examples in CCAE and BNC, most of which are from historical texts. In both databases it's usually **negress** rather than **Negress.** But the capital letter now used to respect racial and ethnic terms (see under **capital letters** section 1) only underscores its explicitness about race.

Negro or negro

Strong associations with colonialism, and with Afro-American slavery have made **Negro/negro** a touchy term. The struggle for emancipation goes on in the struggle for equality, whatever the differences between *the American "Negroes" of the 1930s and 40s, and Afro-Americans in the 1990s,* as one citation from CCAE has it. **Negro** remains the "outsider" term, and all the more so with the affirmation of *Black* in the last few decades (see under **black or Black**). This explains the discomfort of a speaker reported in CCAE:

"The mayor...went on preaching...about what was good for Negroes. (He didn't say Negroes. He said blacks, but I don't like the word blacks, never did. You can call me old-fashioned if you like.)"

The political and social implications of using the word **Negro** have still to be reckoned with. In database evidence **Negro** is usually capitalized in reference to a person, though this adds little by way of respect (see under **capital letters** section 1). But more generic uses e.g. *negro spiritual, negro slaves* can appear in lower case.

The plural of **Negro/negro** is almost always **Negroes/negroes,** in keeping with its being an older loanword whose usage is tied to the past rather than the present. See further under -o.

neighbor or neighbour
See -or/-our.

neither
This word plays several parts in English:
* *pronoun,* as in *Neither of the two is perfect*
* *determiner,* as in *Neither player could serve reliably*
* *conjunct,* as in *They couldn't speak. Neither could I*
* *conjunction,* as in *They didn't apologize, neither did they offer help*

Neither raises questions of agreement, both as a pronoun, and when as a correlative conjunction it serves to create a compound subject for the clause. These, and the correlation of **neither** with both *nor* and *or,* are discussed below. The inversion of subject and verb following **neither** as conjunct (illustrated above) is discussed under **inversion**.

1 As a pronoun, neither is often the focus of grammatical comment. When translated as "not either" it sounds like a singular pronoun and seems to require a singular verb – as it has in the example above. This is the only correct form, according to some usage commentators; yet the *Oxford Dictionary* (1989) demonstrates the acceptability of plural agreement with a set of citations from C17 on. *Webster's Third* (1986) and *Merriam-Webster* (2000) draw attention to the fact that it often happens after a "periphrastic genitive" (with the preposition *of*), as in the following:

Neither of the movies are what you'd call exciting.

The plural verb is hardly surprising, seeing that **neither** can very well mean "not this one, nor that one" in such a context, and the sentence effectively reports on two items at once. It can therefore be justified as *notional agreement* – or as *proximity agreement* following "movies." (See **agreement** sections 1, 4 and 5.) Plural agreement after *neither of* is strongly associated with spoken discourse. In BNC it's used in 75% of all instances from transcribed speech, but only about 20% of instances from written texts.

2 Neither with nor. Questions of agreement also come up when **neither** is paired up with *nor* as a correlative conjunction. Again the traditional view was that the following verb should be singular, and yet research for the *Longman Grammar* (1999) shows that the use of a plural verb is quite common. In fact singular and plural agreement have slightly different effects. Compare:

Neither director nor producer has much experience.
Neither director nor producer have much experience.

The singular verb seems to particularize while the plural one generalizes. The use of a plural verb there is as natural as it would be in a matching positive statement: *Both director and producer have plenty of experience.*

The plural verb is sometimes used as the way out of another dilemma with **neither**–*nor* constructions: what to do when the items paired are different grammatical persons, as in:

Neither John nor I ... ready to leave.

Some would argue that the verb should agree with the nearest person (in this case *I*), and so it should be *am*. Others would feel that here again the plural *are* seems quite natural. Or could it be *is*? (See further under

agreement section 4.) Note that with any verb other than *be,* the alternatives are reduced to two, and so rewording the sentence reduces the problem.

3 Neither with or. In formal writing, **neither** always combines with *nor* (not *or*) in coordinated subjects like the ones in the sentences above. But in more informal discourse, *neither X or Y* is used, and thanks to the *Oxford* citation record, has been captured in print since C16. In contemporary English data from the BNC, there are about 100 examples from both written and spoken sources:

... can bring about neither equity or development
Neither Ari or Nathan had seen a place like it.

... neither exclusively tough or exclusively tender
Merriam-Webster (2000) notes that **neither** followed by *or* is "neither archaic nor wrong," but that *nor* is more usual. This certainly holds true by their relative frequencies in the BNC, where instances of *neither–nor* outnumber those of *neither–or* by more than 20:1. Yet *neither–or* is a legitimate construction. It actually extends the negative scope of **neither** over both or all the alternatives mentioned. See for example:

Neither the French, the Austrian or the Prussian embassies were willing ...
The movie contrives neither to inform, excite, entertain, titillate or engage the eye ...

Provided the alternatives match each other syntactically, the negative parallelism of *neither–nor* is still achieved with *neither–or,* and it underscores the set rather than its members. The *neither–or* construction is likely to become more rather than less frequent, given the general decline in the use of *nor.* See further under **nor**.

4 Neither with more than two alternatives. This has just been illustrated by-the-by with *neither–or,* and constructions with three or more alternatives strike at the heart of another prescription attached to **neither**: that it meant "not either one [of two]," and should therefore always introduce a pair of items. The great majority of examples from the BNC and CCAE do consist of two, yet there are others in which **neither** spells out three alternatives, as in:

I was neither Jew nor English nor white.
Neither pianist, nor orchestra nor dancers indulge in virtuoso passages ...
... neither the police, the Army, nor the ranchers are venturing out ...
Neither Chrysler, Ford, nor General Motors adapted quickly.

While the negative force of **neither** is at its strongest with two alternatives, there's no doubt that it can introduce a larger set.

nem. con.
This abbreviates the Latin phrase *nemine contradicente,* which means "with no-one speaking against [it]." When noted in the minutes of a meeting, it emphasizes that all the votes registered were in favor of the motion. It does not preclude the possibility of abstentions, however, so that **nem. con.** does not necessarily mean a unanimous vote.

neo-
Derived from Greek, this prefix means "new." **Neo-** appeared first in mid-C19, and gained popularity in both scholarly and general use.
* In chemistry **neo-** has been used to name newly discovered forms of chemicals, such as

neodymiuim, neomycin, neoprene; while in geology (and archeology) it marks the latter end of one of the classical periods, as in *Neocene, Neolithic, Neozoic.*

* In medicine **neo-** means "new or fresh" in *neonatal, neoplasm.*
* In the humanities (and in general usage), **neo-** helps to name new or recently revived practices and philosophies, especially those identified with a particular leader, thinker, group or style:

     Neo-Darwinian   Neo-Fascist   Neo-Gothic
     Neo-Lamarckism   Neo-Nazi

It can be attached in the same way to any proper name to create a nonce word, as in *neo-Thatcherism* or to ordinary words, as in *neoclassical, neocolonial.* In recent uses to form *neophilia* ("passion for things new") and *neophobia* ("fear of things new"), **neo-** seems nicely ironic.

The setting of words with **neo-** is quite variable. Nonce words and those where the proper name is still crucial often capitalize **Neo-** as well as the name, with a hyphen between them, as shown in all the established examples. But established ones slowly advance from the hyphenated setting to a more integrated state, as with *Neo-Platonism* to *Neoplatonism* to *neoplatonism.* Dictionaries differ in their treatment of words in that group, though they usually concur about those formed with common words – which are integrated except when they contain a difficult sequence of vowels, as with *neo-impressionism.* Terms used in specialized fields such as chemistry and medicine are always fully integrated in lower case, while those in geology and archeology have a single capital.

nerve-racking or nerve-wracking

See under **r or wr.**

-ness

This Old English suffix forms abstract nouns out of adjectives, for example:

     darkness   feebleness   freshness   goodness
     kindness   politeness   tenderness   usefulness

It takes verbal adjectives, either present or past participles in its stride:

     contentedness   drunkenness   willingness

as well as compound adjectives:

     kindheartedness   levelheadedness
     longwindedness   shortsightedness
     straightforwardness

and hyphenated compound adjectives:

     matter-of-factness   up-to-dateness

Note that adjectives with a final *y* normally change it to *i* before **-ness,** as with *prettiness, readiness, weariness.* The best known exception is *busyness* (from *busy*), where the *y* must remain so as to distinguish the word from *business.*

Because abstract nouns are so readily formed with **-ness,** there are numerous doublets with abstracts borrowed or made according to French or Latin patterns, ending in *-cy, -ion* and *-ty:*

     abstractness/abstraction
     accurateness/accuracy
     acuteness/acuity
     capaciousness/capacity
     conciseness/concision
     considerateness/consideration
     crudeness/crudity

     enormousness/enormity
     falseness/falsity
     ingenuousness/ingenuity
     notoriousness/notoriety
     preciseness/precision
     sensitiveness/sensitivity
     tenseness/tension
     turgidness/turgidity
     vacuousness/vacuity

The words formed with **-ness** always have a strong link with the adjective, whereas the other member of the pair has usually developed additional meanings. It means that there's room for both, though there may also be some overlap between them. See further at **acuity, conciseness, enormity** and **ingenuous.**

net or nett

The French adjective *net* ("neat," "clean") was borrowed with that meaning into C14 English. The accountancy meaning "not subject to further deductions" had been added to **net** by C16, as well as the alternative spellings **nett** and *nette,* the feminine counterpart to masculine **net** in French. The longer spellings were perhaps thought necessary to distinguish the adjective from the Old English noun **net,** meaning "any thing made with interstitial vacuities," as Dr. Johnson (1755) so unforgettably put it. The simple spelling **net** has nevertheless won out for the adjective, and there's no mistaking it because of the collocations that it regularly appears in: *net assets, net income, net loss, net profit, net sum* – all connecting it with the balance sheet. The image lends itself to metaphor, as in *net immigration* or *the net effect in terms of the streetscape.*

Dictionaries all give priority to the spelling **net,** though the earlier **nett** remains a recognized alternative in British English. In BNC data, **nett** is quite rare, occurring scarcely 1 in 100 times by comparison with **net,** and mostly in transcriptions of speech rather than edited prose. It has no role at all in American English, by the evidence of CCAE.

Netherlands

The Netherlands is the official name for what the English have long known as *Holland.* It means literally "low(-lying) lands," and much of the land was and is below sea level, continually threatened by flood tides until a protective wall of dikes was completed in the 1970s.

In earlier usage, the term **Netherlands** referred not only to Holland, but also to Belgium and Luxemburg. The British translated it as *Low Countries,* and have used that phrase to group the three countries together since C16. But Belgium claimed its independence in 1830, and Luxemburg did the same in 1890, so the name *The Netherlands* was left as the official name for Holland alone. (See further at **Holland.**) A fresh term *Benelux* was coined in 1948 to refer to the three countries as a customs union, and this name is the one now used for the three as a unit within the European Union.

In English-speaking countries both **Netherlands** and *Holland* continue to be used, with the balance tipping in favor of *the Netherlands* in both British and American English, by the evidence of the BNC and CCAE. The definite article was once part of the official title, and capitalized in mid-sentence, as it still sometimes is:

...the national anthems of The Netherlands, the
USSR and Britain sounded through the theatre
But the convention was also challenged by the
editorial practice of lower-casing *the* in titles that
occur in mid-sentence (see **the** section 4). The extra
capital letter is given to *The Netherlands* in only about
one third of instances in the BNC, and rarely in
CCAE. The article itself is sometimes omitted in the
interests of streamlined syntax, as in *a*
Netherlands-based company.

nett or net
See **net.**

neuralgia, neuritis or neurosis
All three are based on the Greek root *neur-* meaning
"nerve" and connote problems with nerves.
Neuralgia means literally "nerve pain," while
neuritis is "inflammation of the nerve." However the
two words are usually distinguished in terms of the
type of pain associated with each, **neuralgia** with
sudden sharp pain along the course of the nerve, and
neuritis with a more generalized and continuous
pain. **Neurosis** involves emotional and psychological
disturbance, often manifested in anxiety and
obsessive behavior.

neuter
This means literally "neither." For grammarians it
means that a noun is neither masculine nor feminine,
but a member of a third, catch-all class. In Latin *neuter*
words were nonhuman and usually inanimate, but in
German they are sometimes human, as with *Fräulein*
("miss"), *Mädchen* ("girl") and other diminutives. See
further under **gender.**

New Englishes
This term was coined in the 1980s to refer to varieties
of English used in communities of
non-native-speakers of English, so typically in
bilingual or multilingual contexts, as in India,
Singapore, Nigeria. See further under **English or**
Englishes.

New Guinea
See **Papua New Guinea.**

New Zealand
The largest islands in the South Pacific were
christened "Nieuw Zeeland" by Abel Tasman in 1642,
a name which was subsequently anglicized as **New**
Zealand. It remains the international name, though
internally **New Zealand** stands alongside the Maori
name *Aotearoa,* meaning "land of the long white
cloud" (originally applied to the North Island). The
double-barreled *Aotearoa New Zealand* is used in
government correspondence and in the media for the
first reference, but it can be abbreviated to **New**
Zealand or *Aotearoa* for second and subsequent
reference, depending on the context, according to the
New Zealand government *Style Manual* (1997).

New Zealand English
Two kinds of English have contributed to **New**
Zealand English. One is Scottish English, which can
still be heard in the Southland of the South Island,
where Scots settled in numbers during C19. Many
other settlers came from Australia, hence the

underlying similarities between Australian and **New**
Zealand English. The two share numerous
colloquialisms and other words that set both apart
from British and other varieties. Occasionally the
New Zealand record predates the Australian on
particular words – allowing the question as to which
side of the Tasman Sea they originated on, although
reverse immigration from New Zealand to Australia
gathered steam only in the latter decades of C20.
There's no question of the many distinctive New
Zealandisms coined since settlement, such as *section*
("block of land"), *bach* ("a small weekend house"),
aerial topdressing ("cropdusting"). Maori loanwords
naturally make up the largest group of local terms, for
trees and shrubs such as *kauri* and *kowhai,* birds such
as *kiwi* and *kakapo,* and animals such as the
dangerous *katipo* spider.

With a smaller and more homogeneous population
than Australia, New Zealand's usage norms have
remained more like those of British English. This is
not unrelated to the fact that its language references
have until recently been imported. The earliest
New Zealand dictionaries, Orsman's *Heinemann New*
Zealand Dictionary (1979, 1989) and Burchfield's *New*
Zealand Pocket Oxford Dictionary (1986) were based on
wordlists provided by the European publisher. With
the second edition of the *New Zealand Pocket* (1997)
and the large *Dictionary of New Zealand English*
(comprising New Zealandisms alone), the elements
of the New Zealand variety are much more fully
codified.

New Zealand English grammar distinguishes
itself from British and American in terms of relative
frequencies rather than absolute differences. In the
details described in Hundt's research study *New*
Zealand English Grammar (1998), it's usually closer to
British than American, and hardly distinguishable
from Australian. The national editorial style is
outlined in *Write Edit Print: Style Manual for Aoteoroa*
New Zealand (1997), based on the Australian
government *Style Manual,* but with input from the
Maori Language Commission on acceptable printed
forms for Maori words.

newspapers and news reporting
No generalization about **newspapers** could capture
the wide range of writing in them. Their prose styles
range from the clichéd to the creative, and from
authoritative to sensation-seeking to cosy intimacy.
The style can be commonplace and pedestrian in
work-a-day **news reporting,** or stimulating and
original in house editorials, reviews and opinion
columns. The signed articles of well-known writers
and journalists from Clive James to William Safire are
analogues of the C19 literary essay. The wholesale
critics of newspaper writing tend to generalize on the
basis of the less creditable journalism of low-brow
"tabloids." Yet the broadsheet newspaper doesn't
guarantee you sophisticated journalism, and the more
convenient tabloid format is also used by "quality"
newspapers in many English-speaking countries,
especially for their overseas editions.

The sheer variety of writing that appears in
newspapers is one reason for their great value in
language research. Journalistic innovations that
persist are read by very large numbers of people and
evolve rapidly into accepted idiom. This is why
language databases such as the British National

Corpus (BNC) and the Cambridge International Corpus (CCAE) contain substantial quantities of **news reporting** and other journalism, as a way of capturing neologisms and new idioms.

◊ For aspects of news language, see further under **clichés**, **headline language** and **journalism**.

next or this

The word **next** sometimes raises doubts when it refers to dates in the future, as in *next Friday* or *next weekend*. In principle it means "nearest in time." But many people draw a distinction between **next** and **this**, using **this** to mean "during the current week" and **next** "in the week which has yet to begin." So on Thursday the "next weekend" would be the one in ten days time, and "this weekend" would be the one only two days away. Like the distinction between **this** and *that*, **this** is closer to the speaker/writer's standpoint, and **next** is further away.

The time distinction between **next** and **this** is drawn by northerners rather than southerners in Britain, according to Burchfield (1996). Yet the much greater frequency of *this weekend* over *next weekend* in BNC data (of the order of 4:1) suggests that plenty of writers prefer the first for immediate time reference, and are not using *next weekend* for any future reference. The ratio between the two expressions is much the same for American users, by the evidence of CCAE. A survey of more than 550 Australians conducted in 1995–6 by *Australian Style* found generational differences: that older Australians (45+) were much less inclined to make the distinction than younger ones, and would simply use **next weekend** (on a Thursday) for the weekend immediately following. (Dare one suggest that younger people plan further ahead?) Whatever one's age, the only safe course is to make a point of giving the actual dates of any arrangement involving the word **next**. This is the advice of *Canadian English Usage* (1997), where both systems are in use, as in Australia, Britain and the United States.

nexus or nexuses

In Latin the plural of **nexus** was the same, i.e. a *zero plural* (see under that heading). In current usage the zero plural shares the field with the English plural **nexuses**, which was endorsed by almost half (46%) of those responding worldwide to the Langscape survey (1998–2001). This correlates with the mixed recommendations of dictionaries: **nexuses** is given priority in *Merriam-Webster* (2000) and the *Canadian Oxford* (1998), where **nexus** is preferred by *New Oxford* (1998) and the Australian *Macquarie* (1997). There is no case for "nexi." See further under **-us** section 2.

NGO or quango

See **quango**.

nice

The battle to defend the precise meaning of this word was lost some time ago, perhaps in Jane Austen's time when one of her characters in *Northanger Abbey* exclaims that **nice** "is a very nice word indeed! It does for everything." It is of course a commonplace of conversation, a word expressing favorable judgement without putting too fine a point on it. This strikes at the heart of those who would wish to conserve the use

of **nice** to mean "fine, discriminating" – which can still be done in phrases such as a *nice distinction* or *nice judgement*. But the finer meaning hangs on the collocation, rather than the word itself. In data from the BNC **nice** is only rarely used in the sense "fine, discriminating." Even in written texts, the commonplace meaning is exploited in the vast majority of citations:

> *a multitude of nice misguided types who seek to* . . .
> . . . *nice letters praising Steffi*
> *It would be nice if there were pressure groups.*

Nice thus serves the interim needs of the writer who wants to be tactful and put a positive spin on the statement. Equally it's unsuitable for serious prose analysis.

Writers who use **nice** to mean "fine, discriminating" are very much in the minority in BNC data. Examples such as a *nice matter of judgement, F's nice example, nice verbalism* demonstrate their intent, evident in perhaps 15% of instances overall, at a conservative estimate. Yet the examples are often faintly ambivalent, the further their wording is from the regular collocations. **Nice** has a long history of shifting its ground. From its origins in Latin as *nescius* meaning "not knowing, unaware," it has evolved in English to mean almost the opposite in "discriminating," and the *Oxford Dictionary* (1989) documents a trail of obsolete meanings in between. The word seems to resist being pinned down for too long.

nickel or nickle

In North America, the **nickel** has always been small change, hence the rather dismissive phrase *nickel-and-dime* meaning "involving only small amounts of money" and hence "petty, trivial." It takes on verbal form in *nickel-and-diming* (with or without hyphens), which is used literally to mean "put under cumulative financial stress through small expenses," and more figuratively as "wear down or defeat through small incursions." The verb appears both as *nickeled-and-dimed* and *nickel-and-dimed:*

> *The regulatory unit has been nickeled and dimed to death already.*
> *Montana nickel-and-dimed his way through the defense.*

Idioms like these move the word away from its metallic base in **nickel**, and would explain why **nickle** may seem just as good a spelling. It is a recognized alternative in both *Webster's Third* (1986) and *Merriam-Webster* (2000), though supported by relatively few examples in CCAE, only about 1 in 300.

The metal itself was inauspiciously named by German miners: it was *Kupfernickel* ("copper devil"), because it looked deceptively like copper. It is the major ingredient in what the English call "German silver," but Germans return the compliment by calling it "English silver." (See further under **throwaway terms**.)

When used as a verb ("apply nickel plating to") **nickel** behaves like any other ad hoc verb ending in *l* – tending to double the *l* (as *nickelled*) in British spelling, but not in American, where it remains *nickeled*. (See further under **-l-/-ll-**.)

nicknack or knickknack

See **knick(-)knack**.

nigger, Nigger or Nigga

Agatha Christie's detective novel *Ten Little Niggers* (1939) stands to show how things have changed. No publisher could approve such a title now, even though it invokes a relatively innocuous children's rhyme. Idioms such as *nigger in the woodpile* and *work like a nigger* are usually edited away. Dictionaries such as *New Oxford* (1998) and *Merriam-Webster* (2000) emphasize the offensiveness of **nigger,** which as Landau (2001) suggests, has probably intensified in the US since the O.J. Simpson trial (1994). Its shocking negativity is often the focus of citations in American and British databases:

> *A nigger wouldn't know one name from another, would he?*
> *They used to call me "nigger lips" in high school.*

Whether quoted or not, the word is frequently enclosed in quotation marks as writers distance themselves from it (see *shudder quotes,* in **quotation marks** section 1). The capital letter is occasionally used in British examples in the BNC, but rarely in American. Neither quote marks nor capital letter are used when its use is attributive, as in *nigger lawyer, nigger talk.* The nonstandard spelling *Nigga* (plural *Niggaz*) is used in self-reference by some Afro-Americans as a solidarity name, but would be offensive coming from outsiders.

The word originated in C16 as *niger,* a remake of French *nègre* ("negro"), but both "colloquial" and "contemptuous" in English, according to the *Oxford Dictionary* (1989). In direct address, **nigger** has always been inflammatory, whereas its use in idiom and offhanded third person references were tolerated on the printed page. They too now look rather uncomfortable.

Note that the adjective *niggard(ly)* ("stingy") has nothing to do with **nigger.** It seems to be based on an Old Norse root, appearing as *nygg* ("mean") in Swedish dialect, and in Norwegian as the verb *knika* ("pinch, be mean").

nil

Apart from its use in sports reporting (*North scored three tries to nil*), this word has its base in bureaucratic and scientific analysis:

> *Employment opportunities are almost nil.*
> *Facilities for residential care outside hospital are still nil.*
> *Fat content per serving – nil.*
> *A maximum velocity at the equator reduces to nil at the poles.*

But in British English **nil** is also freely used in everyday discourse:

> *the Parish population had sunk to nil*
> *the artistic loss to the world will be nil*

Examples like these, where **nil** appears in more and less formal estimates, abound in the BNC. In American English **nil** is rather less popular, by the evidence of CCAE, but still tends to collocate with estimates of probability, as in British English:

> *The chance of manufacturer error is almost nil.*
> *The government's prospects for wiping out X are seen as nil.*

◊ Compare the uses of **naught or nought,** and **zero.**

nil desperandum

This Latin phrase rolls off the tongue with the advice "never despair." It was borrowed by C17 Englishmen from Horace's *Odes* (I vii line 2), and has been uttered in much less literary contexts to encourage others to "keep their spirits up."

nil nisi bonum

See **de mortuis.**

nite

As a rational respelling of *night,* **nite** has been on record since the 1930s, but is still waiting in the wings. The *Oxford Dictionary* (1989) finds it a "widespread vulgarism" especially in *nite spot,* but the BNC has no examples of its use except in signs (*Late Nite Lounge*) and in transcriptions of casual speech. In American data from CCAE, almost all examples are from business names, *Nite Owl Printing, Happy-Nite Escort Service,* or the names of tours, songs and entertainment: *Moms' Nite Out, Gentle is the Nite, Saturday Nite Alive* (at the United Methodist Church), *nite-glo* (a show of hot-air balloons, stunt pilots and skydivers after dark). The variety of applications show that **nite** entertainment is not necessarily risqué in the UK. But it's normally embedded in proper names, usually capitalized, and never seems to be used in ordinary prose as a substitute for *night.*
◊ For other respellings of this type, see **spelling, rules and reforms** section 5.

nitroglycerin or nitroglycerine

Dictionaries register both spellings, and American English uses both, by the evidence of CCAE. In British data it's usually **nitroglycerine.** These divergent patterns match up with those for *glycerin/glycerine* in each case (see **glycerin**). Chemists the world over prefer **nitroglycerin,** given that *glycerine* is a neutral substance: see **-ine/-in.**

no

This small word has considerable power as an absolute negative. It has several grammatical roles:
* determiner, as in *no bird sings*
* adverb, as in *worked no better*
* interjection or reaction signal, as in *No, that's impossible*
* noun, as in *They would never take no for an answer*

Note that when **no** means "a vote cast against a motion," the plural is **noes.** There's no need for quotation marks when **no** serves as a noun, or when it appears as part of an indirectly reported utterance:

> *She said no, she could only do it later.*

For the scale from direct to indirect speech, see **direct speech.**

Constructions with **no** as determiner are equivalent to indefinite ones expressed with with *not ... any: they had no money* can be paraphrased as *they did not have any money.* (Compare *they did not have the money,* the definite construction, which cannot be paraphrased with **no.**) The **no** construction prevails across the board in indefinite constructions in written texts from both British and American English, according to the *Longman Grammar* (1999). But the researchers also found that *not ... any* was the preferred form in conversational English in the UK, making it very familiar to British ears. See further under **not.**

No(.)/no(.)

For Americans, this abbreviation for Italian *numero* ("number") needs a stop (**No.**), just like any other (see **abbreviations** section 2a). For British writers it's strictly speaking a *contraction,* which would not normally carry a stop in British style (see **contractions** section 1). Yet the *Oxford Dictionary for Writers and Editors* (1981) presents it as **No.** – perhaps to avoid confusion with the common word *No/no* (see previous entry). In practice this is unlikely because the abbreviation is regularly followed by a number (*No 1*), and its distinctive function is clear in context. British writers are in fact divided on the issue, and **No.** and **No** share the field almost equally in data from the BNC, whether it's *Symphony No.1* or the *No 1 seed* in tennis. When **No(.)** needs a plural, the British scene is again divided, though **Nos** is rather more popular than **Nos.**, judging from the number of BNC texts in which it appears. Neither is ideal (see **abbreviations** section 2). American writers just write **Nos.**, as in *Lexington Avenue Nos. 5 and 6.*

Singular forms rarely appear in lower case, in either American or British data. But the plural forms can, especially in reference to the serial numbers of publications. Still **nos.** is three times as frequent as **nos**, in data from the BNC.

no one and no-one

See under **nobody**.

noblesse oblige

This French phrase means literally "[one's] nobility obliges [one]" i.e. there are obligations and duties incumbent on those of noble rank. When first used in C19 English, it was with the implication that the aristocracy should conduct themselves honorably and give generously. Nowadays it's used more widely, and said of other kinds of status and privilege that have duties attached to them:

> *The students' 40 hours of community service (in order to graduate) may be seen as noblesse oblige . . .*

nobody, no one, no-one and none

The first three take singular verbs in agreement with them:

> *Nobody / no-one has arrived yet.*

This is only natural, given the singular elements *-body* and *-one*. **None** is variable, and may take either singular or plural. Compare:

> *None of the mixture is left.*
> *None of the ingredients are expensive.*

The plural verb in the second example shows the not untypical *proximity agreement* when the *of-*phrase finishes with a plural noun. (See further under **agreement** sections 3 and 5.) In BNC data the plural occurred in about 1 in 3 examples following a plural noun. Pundits of the past argued against the latter, apart from Fowler (1926), who commented that it was a mistake to suppose that **none** "must at all costs be followed by a singular verb." The *Oxford Dictionary* (1989) also notes that **none** as the plural of **no one** is commonly found with a plural verb.

The setting of **no one** has been much debated. The original *Oxford Dictionary* had it as two words, arguing that it was somehow analogous to *every one*. Fowler found it more like *everyone,* but because *noone*

was liable to be misread, preferred **no-one** as "the right compromise." Gowers (1965) reversed Fowler's recommendation, saying that **no one** "has more backing than **no-one,** and is recommended." These contrasting views are still reflected in the mix of practices shown in the BNC. Overall there are a good many more instances of **no-one**, which outnumbers **no one** by about 3:2; yet there are rather more writers using **no one**. In American English data from CCAE, **no one** is commoner by far, and the only form registered in *Webster's Third* (1986).

In the choice between **no-one** and **nobody**, the data show that both Americans and the British prefer the first (by about 3:2). See further under **-one**.

nom de plume or nom de guerre

These French phrases both refer to assumed names. **Nom de plume** ("pen name") is not in fact borrowed from French but was coined in C19 English, for the name assumed by an author to hide his or her identity. The French themselves use **nom de guerre** ("war name"), i.e. the name you soldier under. It includes pseudonyms adopted for any strategic purpose, not just getting books published.

Other ways of indicating pseudonyms and changed names in English are **aka**, **alias**, **incognito**, **née** and **né** and **sobriquet**. See under those headings.

nominal

In grammar **nominal** means "relating to the noun," and so *nominal phrase* is an alternative name for the *noun phrase* (see further under that heading). A *nominal style* is one which relies heavily on nouns, especially abstract ones, and invests relatively little meaning in its verbs. The verbs are typically copular – the verb *be* or others which string the noun phrases together, but do not lend any dynamic to the message. (See further under **verbs**.)

The *nominal style* creates sentences like the following:

> *Recent expansion of the company's offices in all major cities requires the installation of new communication systems . . .*

Amid the dull sequence of nouns, verbs are conspicuous by their absence, and the only one used (*requires*) is itself rather abstract. Compare a *verbal style* version of the same sentence:

> *The company has recently expanded its offices in all major cities, which means we must install new communication systems . . .*

The *verbal style* style relies less on nouns generally, and replaces some of the abstract nouns with equivalent verbs. It is usually less impersonal and makes livelier reading.

To turn verbs (such as *expand, install*) into abstract nouns (*expansion, installation*) is to *nominalize* them. *Nominalizations* have their place in official and theoretical prose (see **abstract nouns**). But they are also addictive, being easy to construct into passable phrases and sentences. This is why they are the staple of institutional writing, despite being the reverse of reader-friendly if used continuously. To kick the **nominal** habit – play down the nouns and make more of verbs – demands more versatility, and sharper thinking. It forces writers to identify a suitable subject for every verb, as well as its tense, aspect and modality. The reward is being better read.

nominative

This is the grammatical name for the case of the subject of a clause. It was important in the grammar of ancient languages such as Greek and Latin, as well as Old Norse and Old English, where nouns acting as subjects had a distinctive form. In modern languages such as German, and in Aboriginal languages, the term **nominative** is used for the same reason. But in modern English the nouns are the same whether subject or object of the clause: there's no external marking to show the **nominative** as opposed to the accusative case. This is why the *Comprehensive Grammar* (1985) prefers the terms "subjective" and "objective," stressing function rather than the form of the word. Yet most English pronouns do have different forms for subject and object (*I, me; we, us; who, whom* etc.) and the traditional term **nominative** is used for them in the *Longman Grammar* (1999). See further under **cases**.

-nomy and -nymy

See -onymy.

non-

Since C19 **non-** has become the most freely used negative prefix in English. Originally and for centuries it was used in law, in formations like *non-parole*, but it's now firmly embedded in everyday English. It is pressed into service in nonce words, apart from being the formative element in many established words. Dictionaries list only a quota of them.

Examples from the start of the alphabet show how often **non-** creates new adjectives and nouns from the existing word stock:

nonactive	nonarrival
nonbeliever	nonclassifiable
noncriminal	non-English-speaking
nonexistent	nonfiction

Many **non-** words come into being to show recognition of a problem, and raise hopes of a solution:

nondutiable nonnuclear nonsexist nontoxic

Advertisers find them useful for highlighting the virtues of their product, witness *nonskid tyres, nonslip soles, nonstop entertainment*. Examples like these gain verbal force from the fact that the word with which **non-** combines (*skid, slip, stop*) could be a verb rather than a noun.

1 **Should non- words be hyphenated?** Dictionaries agree on one point: that **non-**words formed with a proper name, e.g. *non-European* must have a hyphen, in keeping with a general rule of editing (see **hyphens** section 1c). For the rest there's no consensus. The *New Oxford* (1998) and *Canadian Oxford* (1998) give hyphens to all, whereas *Merriam-Webster* (2000) sets them all solid, in keeping with the *Oxford/Webster* divergence on hyphens generally. The Australian *Macquarie Dictionary* (1997) exercises its discretion, streamlining the hyphen from many **non-** words, and keeping it in those which might otherwise challenge the reader. Writers can take their cue from a particular dictionary (as far as it goes), or decide for themselves how essential the hyphen is to decoding the word in its context. If *nonmatching socks* are mentioned in the context of pairing them up, the word's meaning is probably clear and not likely to be misconstrued without a hyphen. The fact that *nonmatching* has not been used before, or if so, never recorded in dictionaries, is neither here nor there.

2 **Non- and other negative prefixes.** Words prefixed with **non-** are particularly useful for drawing attention to the word they're coupled with, and expressing its exact opposite. No doubt this is why new words are created with **non-** alongside older negative words, especially those whose meanings have diverged from being a strict opposite of the base word. This is the raison d'être for *nonappearance* and *disappearance*, for *nonedible* and *inedible*, for *nonproductive* and *unproductive*. The difference is perhaps clearest when we compare *non-American* with *un-American* or *non-Christian* with *un-Christian*. The words with **non-** simply denote the fact that something/someone has no connection with the US or with Christianity. The words with *un-* have a range of emotional connotations, suggesting alien values, loyalties, cultural and ethical practices from which "true" Americans/Christians would distance themselves. History has shown how dangerous such words can be, with the persecution of supposedly *un-American activities* by McCarthyist forces in the US in the 1950s. Words with **non-** are normally more neutral and specific – more literal in meaning than their counterparts with the other negative prefixes.

non compos mentis

This Latin phrase means "not of sound mind." Cicero used it in one of his famous court cases (*In Pisonem* xx 48), though its use in medieval law probably accounts for its currency in modern English. In legal and formal English it still means "mentally incapable"; but when shortened to *non compos* in colloquial usage it can simply mean "vague, distrait," or even "in an alcoholic stupor."

non sequitur

In Latin this means "it doesn't follow." Used in analyzing argument, it means there's a break in logic from the previous sentence or proposition. It may occur in the output of a single speaker/writer, especially one who is keen to express a conviction without too many preliminaries. For example:

Research shows that children who have been taught English grammar do not write better than those who have not. Lesson time would be better spent on other subjects such as social studies.

The second statement shortcircuits the first, not pausing to see what its implications might be. (Is grammar of value only as a means to writing? What things should be taught by direct and indirect methods?) Instead it introduces a new assertion. In the rush of argument the missing link(s) can unfortunately – or deliberately – be overlooked.

The same problem can easily occur in dialogue, as people debate ideas on the run. The term **non sequitur** can then be applied to a false or inappropriate inference drawn by one person from what the other has just said.

nonce word

A **nonce word** is one coined on the spur of the moment. It works in its context but may never be used again. Thea Astley's use of "dactylled" roofs in North Queensland (presumably a reference to the ubiquitous corrugated iron roof) is an example. Strictly speaking a **nonce word** is only used once, though any that appear in print have some chance of gaining currency and ceasing to be **nonce words**. The English term **nonce word** corresponds to what classical scholars called a *hapax legomenon*, a Greek phrase meaning "something said only once" (*hapax* for short). Classical scholars use it to refer to words or a phrase for which there is only one citation in a given author, or literature.

nondiscriminatory language
See **inclusive language**.

none
See under **nobody**.

nonessential, inessential and unessential
Large dictionaries confirm that all three words exist and mean the same thing. Databases (CCAE and the BNC) show they are far from equal in terms of frequency, **nonessential** being far more popular than the others with American writers, and **inessential** with the British. **Unessential** gets little use in either database.

nonfinite clause
This term has been used by modern English grammarians for the various structures which express the same kind of information as a subordinate clause, but do not have all its regular components. Compare:
> *He asked if he could come to the meeting.*

with
> *He asked to come to the meeting.*

The second sentence is very similar in meaning. The point of the *if-* clause is expressed through a **nonfinite clause** (in roman), with a nonfinite form of the verb (in this case, the infinitive). Other types of nonfinite clause work with participles, either the present with *-ing* or the past with *-ed/-en* etc.:
> *Leaving early we miss out on the drinks.*
> *The new recruits, bored by the formalities, had stopped listening.*

Note that **nonfinite clauses** do not usually have their own subject, but borrow it from the adjacent main clause. The rather uncommon cases in which they do express their subject are those where the subject of the **nonfinite clause** differs from that of the main clause, as in infinitive clauses with *for:*
> *His intention was for you to be there.*

And also in certain past participle clauses:
> *That settled they became good friends.*

Nonfinite clauses work as alternatives to all kinds of subordinate clauses, noun, adjectival/relative and adverbial. Stylistically they make for compactness of expression.

nonfinite verbs
In modern English grammar this term covers parts of the verb such as the participles and the infinitive, which do not by themselves constitute a finite verb. See further under **verbs**.

nonplussed or nonplused
All dictionaries give priority to **nonplussed**, and the spelling with two *ss* is quite regular for the pronunciation which stresses the second syllable. (See further under **doubling of final consonant**.) The alternative pronunciation which stresses the first

syllable is recognized in the major American dictionaries, along with the corresponding spelling with one *s*. Pronunciation apart, the spelling **nonplussed** is clearly preferred in both the US and the UK. Among American respondents to the Langscape survey (1998–2001), 67% endorsed **nonplussed**, while for the British it was 88%.

nonrestrictive
This word usually comes up in the discussion of *nonrestrictive relative clauses*. See under **relative clauses** section 4.

nonsense
This word usually works as a mass noun, as in *That's nonsense*. But the *Oxford Dictionary* (1989) records its use as a count noun (*a nonsense*) from C17 on. Countable uses of **nonsense** occur in about 10% of all instances in the BNC, often phrased with the verb *make:*
> *That makes a total nonsense of conservation policy.*
> *...made a nonsense of the enemy's numerical superiority*

Countable uses of **nonsense** are rare in American data from CCAE, and then construed with the verb *be*, as in *That, in my view, is a nonsense*. More often, **nonsense** is used attributively, as in *a nonsense figure/lawsuit/objection/rule*.

nonsexist language
The feminist movement has undoubtedly succeeded in making people more aware of how sexism can be built into language. Most people now think twice before talking about *manning the switchboard* or *mastering the computer;* and reflect on the implications of saying that someone is *bitching about* their colleagues or that the boss is *an old woman*. Expressions like those, which could suggest that it takes men to do the job properly, and that negative human behavior is associated with women, are unsympathetic to half the human race. The users of such expressions may have nothing against women, yet the terms in which they project their ideas suggest stereotypes which either make women invisible, or at worst seem to trivialize and denigrate them. The use of sexist language by men or women helps to preserve its negative stereotypes, and social values which disadvantage women generally – just as cigarette smoking creates an atmosphere that endangers even nonsmokers.

Specific issues include:
* generic use of the pronoun *he* when the reference is to both men and women (see under **he and/or she**)
* exclusive-sounding *man* compounds and idioms. For alternatives, see under **man**.
* gratuitous use of female suffixes, especially *-ess* (see **-ess**). These can be avoided.
* letter writing with *Sir* as the standard salutation. *Nonsexist* salutations and modes of address are presented under **forms of address** section 2.

Solutions to the problems of **nonsexist language** sometimes look like attempts to even the score, as when *frontwoman* is invented to replace *frontman*. Yet *frontwoman* is no less sexist than *frontman*. It may serve the purpose in a given context, but is not a general substitute. At that point an inclusive substitute is needed, and some compounds using *-person* are now quite well established. (See **-person**.)

Better still are terms that emphasize the role or job rather than the gender of the person in it, such as *frontliner.* Gender-free terms alleviate the problems of both sexism and any latent homophobia that may work to the disadvantage of those who would like to do the job. See also **spouse.**

nonstandard

Nonstandard is sometimes used as a label in dictionaries and language references as a way of marginalizing words, idioms and spellings of which the authors don't approve. The label begs the question as to what is *standard,* and seems to imply a uniform measure of what is appropriate. It could mean that the **nonstandard** form is not used in writing, but this is not usually said. It could mean that in statistical terms it's a minority usage, but frequency information is not usually provided. Rather, the term often seems to involve some "ideology of the standard" (Milroy and Milroy, 1985), which is uncomfortable with variation in language. It seeks to identify a single *standard form* wherever alternatives present themselves. Newer forms are typically excluded, and the *standard* is thus liable to become tied to a particular time and style of language. Regional and dialectal variants are downplayed or disregarded. The terms *standard* and **nonstandard** need constant scrutiny, to ensure that they do not shortcircuit the recognition and consideration of alternative forms of expression. See further under **standard English.**

non-U

See **U and non-U.**

nor or or

The use of **nor** is probably declining, even in its core domain of coordinating two negative phrases. Compare:

> *The gallery will not be open on Sundays or public holidays.*
> *The gallery will not be open on Sundays nor public holidays.*

Both sentences are perfectly acceptable English, but the first shows that **nor** is not really needed to extend the negation over to "public holidays." Rather it may seem to overdo the expression of the negative for the purposes of a simple announcement. This use of **nor** for the second coordinate underscores the parallelism of the two phrases, and in the context of fine writing, with more extended coordinates, it would have its place. For example:

> *The word universal is never the name of anything in nature, nor of any idea or phantasm found in the mind...*

Substitute **or** for **nor** in that sentence, and the structure and meaning are still perfectly viable. The negative scope of "never" carries over to the second coordinate (see further under **negatives**). But the use of **nor** helps to reaffirm the negative after a complex phrase, and to lift the latter part of the sentence.

Nor is still most commonly used as a correlative with *neither,* though even there, **or** is occasionally found (see **neither**). It creates negative coordination with other negatives including *no, not* (and *n't*), *never, nothing, nowhere,* as well as words with negative prefixes such as *un-:*

> *He was unable to say why this was necessary, nor why the stamp read "Do Not Bend."*

It would be equally possible to use **or** in that sentence.

The only situation in which **nor** and only **nor** will do is when the second coordinate is a main clause with its own subject and verb. For example:

> *Life would not have been the same without them, nor would it be now...*

The second clause introduced by **nor** has negative inversion, like any main clause. See under **inversion.**

normalcy or normality

Both these make their first appearance in mid-C19, though **normality** seems to have quickly become more common and to have developed more applications. In terms of word structure it's more regular: there are many similar nouns ending in *-ity* made out of adjectives ending in *l,* whereas there are none like **normalcy.** (The nearest analogue is *colonelcy,* based on a noun ending in *l.*) On both counts then **normalcy** is an unusual word, and perhaps that was why President Harding used it in a famous speech of 1920. Unfortunately his use of it drew censorious comments from across the Atlantic, which still echo in the *Chambers Dictionary* (1988) comment: an "ill-formed word." But the *Oxford Dictionary* (1989) has citations both before and after Harding, from both UK and US sources. **Normalcy** is not however very popular with British writers represented in the BNC, and it makes up less than 1 in 20 instances of the noun. In American data from CCAE, *normalcy* and *normality* appears in the ratio 1:2 – so it's still not the majority usage but a well-established alternative.

north, northern and northerly

The geographical differences between these are standard throughout the English-speaking world. **North** and **northern** locate places relatively closer to the *North Pole,* while **northerly** implies an orientation toward the **north** (as in *the northerly aspect of the house*) or, paradoxically, direction from the **north** (as in *a northerly breeze*). Yet while *northerly wind* carries the chill factor in Manchester and Michigan, it brings extreme heat in Melbourne. So **north** and other compass directions are always relative to the writer's point of reference, and should be counted among the *deictic* words of the language (see under **deixis**). Like other compass points, **north** has its political implications, as in the *North–South Center* in Miami, which draws a line between continental North America and the Caribbean Nations. What for Australians is sometimes called the "Near North" is to Britons the "Far East."

In both British and American English, **north/northern** also have linguistic connotations. *Northern dialects* are frequently contrasted with the implicit southern standard in the *Oxford Dictionary* (1989). Just where the boundary lies depends on which vowels and common terms are used as touchstones, but it seems to lie on the southern side of the Central Midlands (Wales, 2000). With speech that neutralizes the distinction between "foot" and "strut" go the stereotypes of working-class England and Scotland, perpetuated in parts of the media despite radical changes in the industrial scene. But the BBC's use of announcers with a variety of accents is helping to break down the assumption that only a southern voice can be cultivated.

In the US, linguistic stereotypes work the opposite way, so that **northern** accents carry prestige and the southern accent is routinely devalued. Again the borderland is fuzzy and depends on whether you use accent or dialect words as the criteria. Carver's "word geography" (1987) puts it further south (along the Ohio River) than Labov (1991), whose analysis of American vowels reaffirmed a "midland" dialect separating **northern** and southern speech, and pushed the **northern** back up into central Illinois and Indiana. Preston's work on "perceptual dialectology" (1996) showed that the stereotypical judgements of good and bad speech are tempered by living on one side of the notional boundary or the other. But those from the Indiana borderland tend to distance themselves from the southern dialect, and seem to take the negative stereotypes about it for granted.

nosey or nosy
See nosy.

nostrums
In spite of its Latin origins, the plural of **nostrum** is always **nostrums** – not "nostra" because it was never a noun in Latin, but an adjective meaning "our [thing]." The word has long smacked of home remedies and quack medicines, and the C18 compound *nostrum-monger* suggests their association with the traveling salesman rather than reputable pharmacy. For Latin loanwords that do go back to classical nouns, see **-um**.

nosy or nosey
Nosy is the regular spelling (see **-e**), and foregrounded in both *Merriam-Webster* (2000) and *New Oxford* (1998). Yet **nosey** has a surprising following, especially in the UK. Among British respondents to the Langscape survey (1998–2001), 64% preferred **nosey**, whereas an equal majority of Americans voted the opposite way for **nosy**. The British trend is in line with Sigley's (1999) research suggesting the deregulation of British spelling. See further under **-y/-ey**.

not and n't
Negation can be expressed in several ways in English, but the lion's share is borne by **not** and its contracted form **n't**. In nonfiction writing **not/n't** is used twice as often as other negatives such as **no, nothing, never**, and in conversation about eight times as often, according to the *Longman Grammar* (1999). Why should this be? It probably reflects the fact (a) that **not/n't** attaches itself to verbs, and (b) that verbs referring to mental processes (*think, like, expect, remember, want* etc.) are common in both positive and negative forms in conversation.

Not/n't also attaches itself readily to auxiliary and modal verbs, as in *don't* (*do not*) and *won't* (*will not*). In such cases the negative is more often contracted than the verb; so *I don't* is a good deal more frequent than *I'd not*, and *I won't* than *I'll not* etc. A general rise in American use of **n't** was found by Krug (1994) in news reporting, which Hundt (1998) confirmed in the particular case of the verb *have*. The verb *be* tends the opposite way, and *it's not* and *we/you/they're not* are far more common than *it isn't*, *we aren't* etc. in speech and everyday writing, according to the *Longman Grammar*. But verb contraction with **not** is strongly associated with personal pronouns in

declarative sentences, while **n't** goes with noun subjects and with question openers. Compare:
> *The dog isn't coming. It's not coming.*
> *Isn't the dog coming? Isn't it hot today?*

Grammar aside, there are local divergences in the use of **not/n't**. The *Comprehensive Grammar* (1985) notes that speakers from Scotland and northern England tend to use **not** forms with contracted auxiliaries (*I'll not, he'd not* etc.) Hundt reports surprisingly high levels of **not** alongside **n't** in New Zealand newspapers, attributable perhaps to the sizable Scottish element in the population – or else their conversational style.

The contracted negative **n't** still tends to be edited out of academic prose, although it is found increasingly in general prose such as news writing. Newspapers of the 1990s in Westergren-Axelsson's (Uppsala) Press Corpus – both quality and popular press – made much more use of **n't** (in *don't* and *won't*) as well as *it's* and *that's* in nonquoted material than their counterparts from the 1960s. The contracted negative is there in many kinds of prose in the BNC, though its overall representation in written material is still much lower than in spoken data: 0.2 per million words compared with 1.2 per million words. (See further under **contractions** section 2.)

Ambiguous uses of not. Depending on its position in the sentence, **not** may create ambiguity. For example:
> *All men are certainly not equal.*

Does this mean that "all men are unequal," or that "not all men are equal?" The question turns on which part of the sentence is covered by the negative –or what its *scope* is. (See further under **negatives**.)

When **not** or its abbreviation **n't** is used in a question, there may be no negation in it at all. *Didn't you write to them last week?* asks the same question as *Did you write to them last week?* In such questions the **not/n't** works simply as a kind of question tag, a telescoped version of *You did write to them last week, didn't you?* It makes a kind of **leading question** (see under that heading).

not about to
See **about and about to**.

not only...but (also)
This correlative pair make for strong affirmations, despite their negative and contrastive ingredients:
> *Ghatak was not only a director, but also a teacher and theorist of cinema.*

Used in tandem, the first statement anticipates a second, and the second affirms the first while adding its own point. They make a double platform in any argument, and elegant parallelism – provided the syntax of the two points is exactly the same. In the next example, this isn't quite so:
> *He sees them as not only strengthening small communities, but also as actually beginning to reverse the population flows from the countryside to the towns.*

The words "as actually" following **but also** impair the parallelism somewhat, and a tighter effect would be gained by omitting them:
> *He sees them as not only strengthening small communities, but also beginning to reverse the population flows...*

More could be done to it, but the sentence does now make the most of the correlatives with the same verbal form (*-ing*) following. The writer may of course prefer not to make too much of the potential for parallelism, feeling that it's a syntactic straitjacket. Data from the BNC shows that **not only** is more often followed by just **but**, which allows greater freedom in the construction of the second point.

> *More than one art historian was not only learned but had an eye.*
> *Not only are customers encouraged to return, but subtle features are identified so that guests feel cared for.*

Not only . . . but also serves in many fully parallel constructions, as a less emphatic alternative to **not only . . . but also**.

not un-/in-

Because they are double negatives, constructions such as these bear thinking about:

> *not unprecedented*   *not unwelcome*
> *not indifferent*   *not impossible*

Those examples are so well established as to be almost clichés, and so they're less demanding of the reader than ones which are freshly coined. The reader has to work harder with ones such as *not unoriginal* or *not incompetent,* to decide where the emphasis lies in them. Instead of negating the other word, **not** tempers its force; and so *not unoriginal* means "having some originality" rather than "most original." Occasional expressions like this can contribute to the subtlety of an analysis, though, as already indicated, they present some obstacles for the reader, and look mannered if used too often. See further under **double negatives**.

notary public

See under **lawyer**.

nothing (to do with)

By itself **nothing** is a singular word, and the verb that follows it directly is naturally in the singular too.

> *Nothing is closer to my heart than that.*

But when **nothing** is separated from its verb, and especially when it is followed by a phrase ending in a plural noun, a plural verb is common enough:

> *Nothing except a few minor criticisms were offered.*

The plural verb "were" agrees with the adjacent noun "criticisms" rather than the head noun **nothing** (making *proximity agreement* rather than *formal agreement*). (See **agreement** sections 3, 4 and 5.)

The idiom **nothing to do with** has conventionally been preceded by *has,* and this is still true in American English. But in British English an alternative form *is nothing to do with* is also in use:

> *This murder has nothing to do with poachers.*
> *Sexual passion is nothing to do with age.*

Is nothing to do with was first noted in the earlier C20 by Fowler (1926) and Jespersen (1909–1949). Its currency in late C20 is vindicated by a total of 66 examples in the BNC, of which just under half appear in written texts, and are therefore as the writer/editor intended. (If all of them came from transcriptions of speech, one could argue that they were rather erratic expansions of *'s nothing to do with.*) Still the form with *is* ranks well behind standard *has* in BNC data, and appears in less than 20% of all instances of the idiom.

notional agreement

See **agreement**.

notorious and notoriety

From its earliest use in C16 **notorious** could mean "well known" for good or bad reasons. In collocations like *notorious gambler/trouble-maker,* the negative values are really expressed through the nouns rather than the adjective. Yet **notorious** now seems to carry a negative meaning by default – "well known typically for some bad quality or deed" (*New Oxford*, 1998). *Merriam-Webster* (2000) notes that the neutral meaning "well known" is rare. For **notoriety**, the neutral meaning is not quite so rare in the UK or the US. It lends itself to situations where "fame" would be inappropriate, as when a company *gained notoriety for backing GP, the failed MGM studio film owner.* Thus a well-publicized failure may amount to **notoriety**, as can unorthodox kinds of celebrity:

> *CF gained notoriety as one of Paris's most flamboyant dress designers.*

In data from the BNC about 10% of examples of **notoriety** referred to reputations made in unorthodox or inverted ways, where the word is neutral rather than inherently negative.

Notoriety can also refer to an individual with a reputation of any kind, as in *a racing/sporting notoriety,* and has been used this way since 1837, by the *Oxford Dictionary* (1989) record. Although there's no indication in either *New Oxford* or the *Canadian Oxford* (1998), it's alive and well in American and Australian English, according to *Merriam-Webster* and the *Macquarie Dictionary* (1997).

nought or naught

See **naught**.

noun clause

A **noun clause** works as either the subject, object or complement of a main clause:

> *What they wanted was a lift to the station* (subject)
> *A lift to the station was what they wanted* (complement)
> *They told us what they wanted* (object)

The first and second types are often used to foreground part of a simple statement: compare *They wanted a lift to the station.* (See further under **cleft sentences**.) However the third type is by far the most common, where the **noun clause** is found after a verb which expresses a mental activity, such as thinking, feeling, knowing or saying.

Noun clauses which detail a mental activity may be introduced by one of the *wh*-words (*what, who, which, when, where* etc.) or by *that,* or by nothing at all. For example:

> *He knows what they're worth.*
> *They believed that the group would come.*
> *They believed the group would come.*

That is often omitted before **noun clauses** in informal writing, and it reflects a very common habit of speech. Just occasionally it leads to ambiguity in writing, because of the absence of intonation to show where the **noun clause** begins. See further under **zero conjunction**.

noun phrase

These phrases are the expanding suitcases of English grammar. In their most basic form they consist of a single word, such as a pronoun or proper name, but more often they consist of an ordinary noun as head with other modifying words on either side of it. The following **noun phrase** shows how the basic head can be embellished:

those very fine old Greek vases   from the site of
                                   an ancient temple
(premodifiers)   head   (postmodifiers)

As the example shows, the **noun phrase** is premodified by determiners and adjectives (one or more). General enumerators like *all* or *some* could come before the determiners: *all those very fine . . .*, while cardinal numbers come between the determiner and the adjectives: *those two very fine old Greek . . .* When there are two or more adjectives, their order is from least to most specific, so that the most definitive one (*Greek*) is closest to the head, and any evaluative ones (*fine*) are further away. Adverbs (such as *very*) come in front of the adjective which they modify.

The example also shows how postmodification often involves prepositional phrases, one after another (*from the site / of an ancient temple*). Just occasionally an adjective or adjectival form of a verb comes immediately after the *head*, as in *fine old Greek vases retrieved from . . .* The postmodification may also involve a relative clause: *old Greek vases that came from the site of an ancient temple.*

Noun phrases are all too easily extended with another and yet another phrase – an unfortunate feature of some of the least readable prose styles. Sentences like the following need to recast some of their **noun phrases** as clauses:

The three new members appointed to the committee for forward planning of the municipality have declared their support for our campaign against the building of highways through nature reserves.

See further under **nominal**.

nouns

The words that express the tangible and visible things of our experience, such as *sand, cliff, sea* are all **nouns,** as are those expressing intangibles such as *love, humor, idealism.* The first type have traditionally been called *concrete nouns* and the second *abstract,* though there's no hard and fast boundary between the two. They represent opposite ends of a semantic scale from highly differentiated things to very generalized concepts. Even among *concrete nouns,* the scale gives us ones which are more general than others: compare *feline, cat, siamese, seal-point.* (See further under **abstract nouns**.)

The terms *common noun* and *proper noun* draw a sharp distinction between general words and very particular names. Effectively *common nouns* refer to a class of entities, objects or persons, e.g. *town, adult,* whereas *proper nouns* single out individual cases, and are therefore capitalized. They purport to be unique names, even if there's more than one *Canterbury* in the world, and more than a few *John Hardys* in any metropolis. (See further under **proper names**.)

Common nouns can be distinguished grammatically in terms of whether they refer to countable things, as do *cliffs* and *cats,* or to noncountable and unbounded things such as *sand* and *idealism.* The first group are *count nouns* which regularly have plural forms, whereas the second, often known as *mass nouns,* are only pluralized under special circumstances. *Mass nouns* do not take the indefinite article (*a/an*). See further under **count and mass nouns**.

Different again are the **nouns** which refer to groups or bodies of people or animals, such as *team, orchestra, committee, mob,* sometimes called *collective nouns.* These too need to be identified for grammatical reasons, particularly questions of agreement. See **agreement** section 1 and **collective nouns**.

nouveau riche

This French phrase, meaning "new rich," was borrowed into Victorian England, when it seemed important to know who belonged to the hereditary aristocracy, and who happened to be just as rich but to lack the pedigree. Those who regarded themselves as having "class" applied the phrase to individuals who (in spite of their wealth) did not. **Nouveau riche** implies an aristocratic disquiet that wealth and nobility might not be indissolubly linked, yet it's not explicitly derogatory like *parvenu* ("upstart"). (See **parvenu or parvenue,** and compare **yuppie**.)

Note that the plural of **nouveau riche** calls for the full French form **nouveaux riches**. Noblesse oblige!

nouvelle cuisine

This is the "new [style of] cooking" emanating from France, which emphasizes the artistic appearance of food on the plate, and relies less for its appeal on richness and quantity. The chef no longer stakes his reputation on generous use of brandy and cream. **Nouvelle cuisine** coincides with the weight-watcher's concerns, and so is often a synonym for *cuisine minceur* ("slim/thin [style of] cooking"). It satisfies the gourmet rather than the gourmand, in the traditional senses of those words (see **gourmet or gourmand**). Both **nouvelle cuisine** and *cuisine minceur* qualify as *haute cuisine*. See under **haute or haut**.

nova

This is astronomical shorthand for *nova stella* (in Latin "new star"), a star which is faint and variable in its luminosity. The word's plural is **novae** (see further under **-a**).

In modern Portuguese **nova** still means "new," and generally has overtones of sparkle – except as the ill-starred *NOVA* car, launched amid skepticism in Brazil because the name could be interpreted as *no va* ("it doesn't go").

nucleus

Borrowed from Latin, **nucleus** still usually takes **nuclei** rather than **nucleuses** as its plural (see under **-us**). More than 90% of respondents to the Langscape survey (1998–2001) endorsed it. **Nuclei** was the only plural used by British writers represented in BNC data, and their American counterparts in CCAE.

nudist or naturist

See under **naturalist or naturist**.

null hypothesis

The **null hypothesis** is a tool of statistical reasoning. It formulates the negative counterpart to the *experimental hypothesis* which proposes that there is significant correlation between two nominated variables in given populations. The **null hypothesis** states that there's no significant correlation between them, and that any suspected or apparent connection is a matter of chance (or else due to skewed sampling or some other flaw in the experiment). If however the statistics show only a very small probability that the connection is due to chance, the **null hypothesis** may be rejected, and the *experimental* (or *alternative*) *hypothesis* affirmed.

◊ For more about deductive reasoning, see **deduction**.

number

To a grammarian, **number** is the concept above and beyond *singular/plural* – the idea that language may refer to one thing or to more than one, and that this distinction is shown in the form of words. In English it's most obvious with nouns, most of which add an extra suffix or change in some way for the plural (see further under **plurals**). Apart from being expressed in nouns, **number** also affects the English pronoun system, in the distinction between *I* and *we*, etc., and in the present tense of all verbs except the *modals*. For example *goes,* the singular form for the third person, contrasts with the plural *go,* and in this case the singular adds the suffix. (See further under **-s.**)

The convention that singular pronouns/nouns go with singular verbs, and plural with plural is fundamental to English syntax. Thus **number** underlies the principle of *agreement* between the subject and verb of a clause, and between pronouns and their antecedents in the same sentence or successive ones. But the application of the principle is not straightforward for several types of word and phrase (see further under **agreement**).

Issues of **number** and singular/plural agreement also come up within the noun phrase itself, especially those involving a possessive or quasi-possessive element. The position of the possessive apostrophe expresses singular or plural (singular before the *s*, and plural after it). But in cases such as *the visitors book,* it seems arguable either way. *Visitors* could be regarded as a plural reference to all those expected to sign *the visitors' book,* or a generic reference in the singular: *the visitor's book.* In the final analysis it makes no difference, hence the trend toward leaving the apostrophe out altogether (see **apostrophes** section 2).

Similar issues arise in reciprocal constructions like the following:

> The students all saw each others messages.
> Married women sometimes use their husbands initials.

In the first sentence, the presence of *each* seems to demand the singular *other's,* while *all* and *messages* suggests the plural form (see further under **other's or others'**). In the second, *their* suggests the need for plural *husbands'* – whereas the singular *husband's* seems more in keeping with the principles of monogamy. The semantics of the sentence are too complex to be sorted out by the apostrophe, and where you place it is entirely arbitrary.

number of

Should the verb after **number of** be singular or plural? The decision rests on whether *the* or *a* precedes *number:*

> The number of applications is small. (singular)
> A number of applications are still to come. (plural)

In grammatical terms the difference is that *number* is the head of the subject phrase in the first sentence, but a premodifying element in the second. (See further

under **noun phrase.**) These complementary patterns of agreement are regularly used in contemporary English. There's scant evidence of the hypercorrect usage "A number of applications is still to come."

◊ Compare **total of.**

number prefixes

English makes use of a full set of **number prefixes** derived from Latin, and a less complete one from Greek:

Latin		Greek
uni-	"one"	*mono-*
bi-	"two"	*di-*
tri-	"three"	
quadr-	"four"	*tetra-*
quin-	"five"	*penta-*
sex-	"six"	*hexa-*
sept-	"seven"	*hepta-*
oct-	"eight"	*okta-*
nona-	"nine"	
deca-	"ten"	*deka-*
cent-	"hundred"	
milli-	"thousand"	*kilo-*

The metric system borrows from both sets: see the list given in Appendix IV. Parallel prefixes from the two sources have been given distinct roles in some disciplines. See further under **di-**, and **octa- or octo-**.

numbers and number style

How to write and print **numbers** is partly a question of what field you're working in. In mathematics, statistics, science, or technical or commercial writing, there's every reason to present **numbers** as *Arabic numerals.* They are by far the most direct and efficient way to communicate quantities. In literary or humanistic writing, the occasional **number** will more than likely be written in words. But in any kind of writing, the following kinds of **numbers** are almost always given as figures:

* sums of money: *$30.65*
* weights and measures: *16 kilometres*
* percentages: *17 percent*
* dates: *22 October 1995* (see further under **dates**)
* times of day: *5.30 a.m., 17 hours.*

Times expressed with *o'clock* are normally written as words (*eleven o'clock* rather than *11 o'clock*) according to the *Chicago Manual* (2003) and the *Oxford Guide to Style* (2002).

Other points of *number style*:

1 **Numbers** as figures. Strings of figures are hard to read, and the maximum number of digits set solid is four. However this only happens in the case of a whole number, as in *The mountain is 2379 m above sea level.* **Numbers** consisting of more than four digits are grouped in threes on either side of the decimal point:

> *1 515 069*
> *15 150.69*
> *1.515 069*

The international standard (ISO 31:1992) recommends using thin space between each set of digits, which helps to prevent large **numbers** being divided at line breaks. This is the preferred style for scientific and mathematical texts in American and British English, according to the *Chicago Manual* (2003) and the *Oxford Guide to Style* (2002). But in the context of nonscientific and "general" books, commas are allowed instead of space to separate the sets of digits in front of the *decimal point*. Those after it are run together:

15,150.69111

This use of commas runs counter to that of the ISO recommendation observed in continental Europe, where a comma is used as the *decimal point* (the *decimal comma*). So *15 150, 69111* would correspond to the number quoted just above. The *decimal comma* has yet to be established in British or American style, and attempts to introduce it into Australian alongside metrication in the 1970s have not succeeded. Only in Canada is the *decimal comma* an option alongside the *decimal point,* following their dual endorsement by the Metric Commission in 1971. But where commas are used to separate groups of integers, the *decimal comma* can only add confusion. All this shows why the use of (thin) space as the separator has much to recommend it.

The *decimal point* is now always set low on the line of type (as recommended by the Royal Society), and can thus be distinguished from the mathematical *multiplication point* or *raised dot.* (See further under **multiplier symbol**.)

2 **In spans of numbers** (i.e. *inclusive numbers*), how many digits should be repeated? This question is usually raised in connection with page **numbers**, and there is less divergence now than there used to be. British style has always been economical, recommending that only the changed digit be given, as in *pp. 32–5, pp. 131–6,* except when the span involves the second decade. The **numbers** there are deemed to be "single rather than compound" (*Oxford Guide to Style,* 2002), and so two digits must be given, as in *pp. 112–17.* In American style (*Chicago Manual,* 2003) two digits are always given in spans below 100 (as in *pp. 32–35*) and above 110 (as in *pp. 131–36*). But in the first decade above each hundred, just one digit is given, as in *pp. 103–5.* (See further under **dates** section 1.)

3 **Numbers** as words. Where **numbers** occur only occasionally in a text, they're usually spelled out as words. Still it depends on how large the **number** is – or rather, what threshold the writer/editor sets for using figures rather than words. Any threshold is arbitrary, and may have to be overridden in context. For nontechnical writing, the *Chicago Manual* (2003) and the *Oxford Guide to Style* (2002) both set the upper threshold for **numbers** as words at 100. Other style guides, e.g. those of newspapers, set the general threshold at 20 or 10, while reserving the right to use words for occasional round **numbers**: *twenty, fifty, a hundred.* Whatever the threshold, there may be anomalies when **numbers** above and below it have to be cited in the same sentence:

There were 19 letters on Thursday, and only eight on Friday (assuming the threshold is 10)

Consistency calls for both **numbers** to be treated the same way in the same sentence – as either words, or figures. If the comparison between the two **numbers** is important, figures speak louder than the words:

There were 19 letters on Thursday, and only 8 on Friday.

Style guides all recommend against using a figure at the start of a sentence:

Nineteen letters came on Thursday and only eight on Friday.

The sentence could of course be reworded to avoid having a **number** as the first item.

The choice between figures and words gives a writer alternatives when there are **numbers** from different sets to express in the same sentence:

The two-day course had 5 participants on the first day, and 12 on the second.

As the examples show, a single threshold for writing **numbers** as words/figures can be difficult to maintain. In practice we may need to write **numbers** of similar size as words or as figures in nonscientific writing. In science and technical writing they would normally all be figures, though the *Oxford Guide* stll suggests a threshold for writing **numbers** as words in technical contexts.

4 **Punctuating number words.** Hyphens are regularly used in the **numbers** from *twenty-one* to *ninety-nine,* according to *Copy-editing* (1992) and the *Chicago Manual* (2003). Contemporary databases show that both British and American writers do this. Yet when it comes to fractions, British writers seem less committed to using the hyphen. Amid hundreds of examples, both *two-thirds* and *two thirds* are used, though the hyphened form appears about three times as often as the other. American writers mostly use the hyphen, in comparable data on *two(-)thirds* from CCAE. This is a little surprising, given that American English generally makes less use of hyphens than the British (see **hyphens**).

Note that when **numbers** are pluralized, they take the same kind of plural suffix as other words with the same final letter: *ones, twos, fours, sixes, twenties.*

5 **Roman numerals** are given in upper case, when they appear as part of a title (*George VI*) or family name (*Adlai Stevenson III*). See further under **names** section 5. But when they refer to such things as the introductory pages of a book, or the subsection of a play, they appear in lower case: *Romeo and Juliet Act iii Scene 2.* Note fhat the volume **numbers** of journals are usually expressed in Arabic **numbers** nowadays, though it was once the convention to give them in Roman numerals.

6 **Enumerating lists of headings and subheadings.** Roman numerals are still widely used in alternation with Arabic ones, and/or with alphabetic letters to enumerate the sections of a document. By using all three, together with strategic use of full stops and single as well as double brackets, a large **number** of different levels of heading can be identified. For example:

Level A	*I*	*II*	*III*	*IV*
Level B	*A.*	*B.*	*C.*	*D.*
Level C	*1.*	*2.*	*3.*	*4.*
Level D	*a)*	*b)*	*c)*	*d)*
Level E	*i)*	*ii)*	*iii)*	*iv)*
Level F	*(1)*	*(2)*	*(3)*	*(4)*
Level G	*(a)*	*(b)*	*(c)*	*(d)*

and so on. If only two or three levels of heading are needed, any subset of those enumerators would do. Many reports simply use *1,2,3* etc. for main headings, and *1.1,1.2,1.3.* etc. for the subheadings.

7 **Indenting enumerators.** Each level of enumeration is indented on the previous one, the amount of indention depending on how many levels have to be catered for. When there are many levels, the standard 1 em is as much as can be allowed, but with only two or three levels, a 2 em indent is manageable and effective:

> 1.
>> 1.1
>>> 1.11
>>> 1.12
> 1.
>> 2.1
>>> 2.11
>> 2.2
>>> 2.21
>>> 2.22.

When Roman numerals serve as enumerators, they are normally aligned on the right-hand side:

> *i)*
> *ii)*
> *iii)*
> *iv)*

This makes for more consistent vertical spacing on the page. (See further under **indents**.)

◊ For the use of different typefaces and settings for each level, see under **headings and subheadings**.

-nymy or -nomy

See **-onymy**.

O or Oh

These are exactly the same sound. But as written exclamations they have different overtones and belong to very different styles. **O** pure and simple is associated with religion and with high literary style:

> *O God our help in ages past*
> *O wild west wind, thou breath of autumn's being*

As in those examples, it prefaces an apostrophe to the supreme being, and supernatural or abstract forces. (See further under **apostrophe**.) The same spelling is the one used in hymnbooks, whether the saints above or below are being invoked. It always appears with a capital letter.

The spelling **Oh** is the ordinary, everyday exclamation which expresses various emotions from surprise and delight to disappointment and regret, depending on the context. It also serves as a pause filler in spontaneous outbursts:

> *I'd be there like a shot, but oh ... who would look after things here?*

Other uses of **Oh** are to be found in the worried expression *Oh dear!* as well as in addressing other people: *Oh Kim, would you put the kettle on.* As the examples show, **Oh** doesn't necessarily have a capital letter, nor is it always followed by a comma or full stop.

Oh/oh sometimes serves as the written form of the number *0*, especially in sets of two or more numbers. It stands for *0* in quoted phone numbers or post/zip codes, for Americans as well as the British (Burchfield, 1996). London newspapers found some support for calling the first decade of C21 "the oh-ohs" – but that "the zeros" was the popular choice. See further at **decades**.

-o

Most words ending in **-o** in English are borrowings made more or less recently from Italian and Spanish, such as *fiasco, piano, merino, mulatto*. A handful come from Latin (*hero, veto*), Greek (*echo*), and from non-European sources (*calico, dingo*). Since about 1700 the assimilation of such words into English involved forming their plurals with *-es,* in parallel with the plurals of words ending in *y,* which still become *-ies*. These spelling adjustments also affected verbs ending in *-o* and *-y* for the third person singular present form: *he/she/it echoes* and *he/she/it replies*. A few monosyllabic English formations ending in *-o*, i.e. *do, go, no* behave the same way as verbs and/or nouns (*does, goes, noes*). While the *-oes* spelling mostly stands firm for verbal use of these words, it is slowly but surely disappearing from the older borrowed nouns, and not being implemented at all in newer loanwords and recent English formations. Let's look first at the nouns.

1 Nouns ending in -o. Although it varies from word to word, the general trend towards using simple *-s* plurals instead of *-es* emerged clearly from the Langscape survey (1998–2001) of more than 1100 people worldwide. It is stronger in the northern hemisphere (putting together results for the UK [488], Europe [251] and the US/Canada [175]) than in southeast Asia and Australia. The simple *-s* plurals were embraced more keenly by the younger respondents (under 45) than older ones. Current usage is thus cutting back on the **-o** words accorded *-es* plurals, from the tally of 29 indicated in *Hart's Rules* (1983). The Langscape survey tested 20 common examples, and of those only 3 were clearly endorsed with *-oes:*

> echoes   heroes   tomatoes

For *volcano(e)s* the result was 50/50. *Potato* – which might be expected to go the same way as *tomato* – was not included in the survey. But simple *-s* plurals were preferred by the majority of respondents for:

> avocados   banjos   buffalos   cargos
> fiascos   flamingos   frescos   ghettos
> halos   innuendos   mangos   mementos
> mosquitos   mottos   tornados   torpedos

This doesn't make the *-es* plural unacceptable for such words, and they continue to be listed in the major dictionaries. It does mean that they look increasingly old-fashioned. Plurals with *-es* are out of place with many kinds of words to which they were never attached, or are not normally now. They include:

* words where the **-o** follows another vowel: *bamboo, embryo, pistachio, portfolio, radio, ratio, rodeo, studio, taboo, video*
* words with four or more syllables: *archipelago, armadillo, diminuendo, generalissimo, manifesto, obligato, peccadillo*
* foreign borrowings: *calico, calypso, casino, flamenco, gigolo, inferno, kimono, piccolo, placebo, poncho, proviso, sombrero, stiletto*
* abbreviations: *auto, curio, hippo, homo, kilo, memo, photo, physio, piano, pro, rhino*
* informal coinages where a longer word or phrase has been cut back and sealed with the suffix **-o**: *ammo* ("ammunition"), *nutso* ("an eccentric"), *weirdo* ("a weird person"). Australian English has a repertoire of words formed with **-o**: for people, *milko* ("milkman"), *wino* ("alcoholic") etc.; and for inanimates, *arvo* ("afternoon"), *compo* ("compensation"). *Ambo* can be "ambassador" or "ambulance", according to context.

Where the plurals of nouns ending in **-o** are reverting from *-es* to the regular *-s*, usage will be variable. Writers and editors may decide the issue word by word, or across the whole set. Either way it's unlikely to impinge on readers, because the words concerned are scattered across many fields, and do not often rub shoulders. Those concentrated in the field of music (*concerto, divertimento, solo, soprano*) can safely be written with just *-s*, unless you prefer to italianize them as *concerti* etc. (see **Italian plurals**). But pity the greengrocer who has to label the more exotic *avocados, babacos, tamarillos* alongside humble *potatoes* and *tomatoes,* for his spelling-conscious customers.

2 Verbs ending in -o. The diminishing use of *-oes* for nouns ending in **-o** does not seem to affect the spelling of the third person singular, present tense, at least in British English. BNC data on *echo* and *veto* for that part of the verb show only the *-oes* spelling, and it is supported by the regular past forms *echoed* and *vetoed*. Since almost half the instances of *echo* are verbal, this would help to explain why the noun plural is still generally spelled *echoes,* according to the Langscape result. Other verbs ending in *-o* (e.g. *embargo, lasso, torpedo*) may be expected to spell the third person singular, present tense with *-oes,* although only the past forms *embargoed, lassoed, torpedoed* are evidenced in the BNC. American English may however be closer to accepting plain *-s* forms for the third person singular, present tense – as well as the plural noun. Data from CCAE provides a handful of examples for verbal use of *echos, lassos* and *vetos,* but only for *lassos* do they make a majority. See further under **lasso**.

> **International English selection:** Given the widespread trend toward regular *-s* plurals for nouns ending in **-o**, it makes sense to standardize on them even for those on which usage is still variable – as is done in this book.

-o-

This is the combining vowel in various compound names, such as *Anglo-Saxon, Franco-Prussian, Graeco-Roman*. It works like a hyphen between them, though a hyphen is also needed because the second element begins with a capital letter. (See **hyphens** section 1c.) When **-o-** serves to combine two common words into a compound, no hyphen is used, as in *gasometer*.

oasis

For the plural, see **-is**.

obiit sine prole

See under **decessit sine prole**.

obiter dictum and obiter dicta

These Latin phrases both mean "said by the way, or as an aside." The difference is simply that the first (with **dictum**) is singular "something said," and the second with **dicta** is the plural "things said." The phrases originate in law, where they refer to incidental remarks uttered by the judge which are not part of the judgement, and therefore not binding. Such remarks contrast with the *ratio decidendi* ("reason for the determination"), i.e. the principle(s) on which the case is decided.

object

An essential yet elusive concept in English grammar is the **object**. It is a key element of clause structure, though not all clauses have them (see **predicate** and **transitive**). Some clauses effectively have two objects of different kinds, one *direct* and the other *indirect*. It takes several definitions to show the range of things a *direct object* can be, let alone the *indirect* kind.

1 Direct objects can be the target, goal or product of the action of the verb:

> *She moved the bed over to the window.*
> *He baked a pizza for lunch.*

The **object** can also express the arena or extent of the action:

> *They could weed the garden.*
> *The students walk 5 km to school.*

The *direct object* is sometimes a person affected by the action, as in:

> *They put their mother into hospital.*

In spite of their variety, these **objects** have one thing in common: they would all be the item identified if you took the verb and asked *what/who?* immediately after.

> *He baked what?* a pizza
> *They put who into hospital?* their mother

The test still works with some of the less obvious kinds of **objects**, which do not fit into any of the categories described so far because the verbs concerned are mental processes. For example:

> *They expected a big majority.*

In these cases the **object** must be seen as the *phenomenon* (Halliday, 1994).

2 Indirect objects only appear when there's already a *direct object* in the clause. They are associated particularly with a group of verbs that express the idea of transmitting something, or making something change hands; and the *indirect object* is the person or thing that receives whatever is being transmitted.

> *They sent the agent a confirmatory fax.*
> *He gave the door a kick.*

As the examples show, the *indirect object* precedes the *direct object*. If the two were in reverse order, the *indirect object* would have to be expressed through a prepositional phrase:

> *They sent a confirmatory fax to the agent.*

Grammarians then debate whether that final phrase is still an indirect object or whether it should be regarded as a prepositional phrase. Traditional grammars took the former view, while contemporary grammars like the *Comprehensive Grammar of English* (1985) and the *Longman Grammar* (1999) regard it as a *prepositional object*.

In traditional grammar the case of the *direct object* is referred to as the *accusative,* and that of the *indirect object* (without any preposition) as the *dative*. They are identical in form however, whether they're nouns or pronouns.

3 The position of the object. In statements, **objects** normally follow the verb, as in the examples above. That order is occasionally altered in conversation, to highlight the **object** in front of both subject and verb:

> *Roses she liked better than anything.*

(See further under **information focus**.)

In questions seeking discursive answers, the **object** is regularly put up front:

> *Which newspaper do you prefer?*
> *What will they do now?*

Final notes:

∗ The verbal **object** can be either a noun phrase, as in previous examples, or a noun clause. Compare:

> *The teachers spoke their mind.*
> *The teachers said what was on their mind.*

(See further under **noun clause**.)

∗ Any noun phrase governed by a preposition is its **object**, in traditional grammar terms: see **prepositions**.

objective case

This is the name given by some English grammarians to the case of words which function as either *direct* or *indirect objects* (see previous entry). In languages other than English, the two kinds of *object* are often distinguished as the *accusative* and *dative case,* because of changes in the form of nouns corresponding to each. See further under **accusative** and **cases**.

objective genitive

For the difference between *objective* and *subjective genitive,* see under **genitive**.

objet d'art

Translated literally from French, this means "object of art." Though it serves as a general heading for things of artistic value, it's very often applied to the smaller objects kept by private collectors as decorative pieces. The term then contrasts with *objet de vertu.* which is used of pieces valued for their antiquity or their craftsmanship. The latter phrase can only be translated as "object of virtue," though it is pseudo-French, coined in English as a counterpart to **objet d'art**. Both expressions make their plurals in the French fashion, as **objets d'art**, *objets de vertu.*

obliged to or obligated to

Obliged and *obligated* both express some kind of moral imperative, and enter into the same kinds of construction:

> The council is not obliged to issue any formal letter of approval.
> IBM's customers will be obligated to make drastic cutbacks.

These sentences illustrate the most usual use of both verbs, as "marginal modals" paraphrasing *must* (see **auxiliary verbs** section 2). In British English **obliged to** is far more common, with hundreds of BNC examples occurring in all kinds of discourse – whereas the dozen or so of **obligated to** are mostly from spoken material. The auxiliary-like role is found in more than 90% of all instances of **obliged to**, and constructions in which it expressed a personal obligation were relatively rare:

> Many are obliged to us for the work they get here.

However the sense of personal obligation remains in the collocation *much obliged:*

> "I'm much obliged" the would-be warehouse-breaker replied, shaking the policeman by the hand.

Americans make much more use of **obligated to** as an alternative to **obliged to**. In CCAE's extensive written data, the two are used almost equally often as marginal auxiliaries, and **obligated to** appears where the British might expect **obliged to**:

> We're obligated to help mankind.
> Crews are obligated to be under way within two hours of notification.

In American but not British English, *obligated* is used to mean "financially bonded":

> All aid for the rebels had already been obligated for other groups.

This sense is also used attributively, as in *obligated parent* (i.e. one legally obliged to provide child support). See **adjectives** section 1.

oblique line or stroke

The **oblique stroke** (/) goes by various names, depending on the context. In technical writing and editing it's the **solidus** (see further under that heading).

oblivious to or oblivious of

In Latin and earlier English, **oblivious** meant "forgetful," and so was only used when the person concerned had indeed forgotten something s/he had previously known: *oblivious of his vow.* More recently its meaning has developed to the point where it is a synonym for "unaware":

> ...oblivious of the confrontation developing ahead of them

This meaning was for a long time censured, and 30% of the Harper–Heritage usage panel still found it unacceptable in the 1970s. However the *Oxford Dictionary* (1989) says that it can "no longer be regarded as erroneous," and simply notes that the newer meaning is often though not always associated with the use of **to** after it. British writers in the BNC mostly use **oblivious** to mean "unaware," but this sense is in no way restricted to **oblivious to**. Most cases of **oblivious of** refer to present rather than past circumstances. Yet **oblivious to** is clearly the more popular collocation, used by almost twice as many BNC writers as **oblivious of**. In American English the shift is still further advanced: instances of **oblivious to** outnumber **oblivious of** by almost 10:1.

observance or observation

These abstract nouns relate to slightly different aspects of the verb *observe.* Its older (C14) meaning "attend to, carry out, keep [a practice]" is the one enshrined in **observance**. The word is often coupled with references to a ritual or tradition, as in *observance of Sunday.* But by C16, *observe* could also mean "regard with attention," and this is the meaning embodied in **observation**:

> Close observation of the fish showed they preferred to feed at night.

Thus the two words represent quite different cultures: **observance** expresses the medieval reverence for tradition, whereas **observation** is the key to modern empirical science.

obsessed

New things are afoot with **obsessed**, alongside the old familiar passive constructions, such as:

> He was obsessed by epistemological questions.
> My dog is obsessed with wood.

Passive uses of **obsessed** still take up more than 90% of all examples in the BNC. Yet the simple active construction has been on record since the 1880s, according to the *Oxford Dictionary* (1989), and does show its face in current British English, as in BNC examples such as:

> The thought of being parted obsessed them.

Nothing new there, however some of the active-transitive uses of *obsess* are reflexive:

> Wayne has more things to obsess him than himself.
> Don't obsess yourself with the idea that...

From these it's only a relatively small step to the intransitive construction (see **transitive and intransitive**). *Obsess* thus becomes a mental process verb like *worry,* as in:

> I went around obsessing about whether or not I seemed like...I'm obsessing when I want to be impacting.

The intransitive use of *obsess,* and this *absolute* use is still rare in British English, by BNC evidence (see **absolute** section 3). It may sound like the cutting edge of idiom. In American English the intransitive is familiar though less common than the transitive, by their relative frequencies in CCAE. Americans make more use of all constructions with *obsess* than the British, and of a variety of intransitive collocations, using *about*, *over* or *on*.

> *She obsesses about an elderly neighbor.*
> *He obsesses over money.*
> *We obsess on our own personal health but we oppose national health.*

The order of these examples shows the relative frequency of the three types of collocation, *about* being the commonest.

These grammatical developments from passive **obsessed** to intransitive *obsess* reflect semantic shifts – or is it the other way round? At any rate external pressures on people can become internal neuroses – hence the idiom: *stop obsessing.*

obstetric or obstetrical
In the US **obstetrical** prevails over **obstetric**, by about 5:2 in data from CCAE. In the UK **obstetric** is dominant, and **obstetrical** makes very little showing in the BNC. See further under **-ic/-ical**.

obverse or reverse
These refer to the two sides of a coin. The **obverse** is the primary face, with the principal design on it, i.e. the one which identifies the nation or person in whose name it is minted. For British coins, this is the side with the Queen's head on it, and the one known as "heads" when tossing a coin. The **reverse** is the other face whose design varies with each denomination. It of course is "tails."

occupant or occupier
These can be synonyms, and dictionaries give "one who occupies" among their definitions for both. Yet there are differences to note: **occupant** often connotes short-term occupancy, and can refer to a variety of locations, from the bus seat, phone box or hotel room to a place in the House of Lords. The **occupier** is usually a longer-term resident or tenant of particular premises, as in:

> *Rate bills are the occupier's responsibility.*

Occupier is also used of the nation-state which *occupies* another, as in *Northern Cyprus now has an occupier.* That apart, **occupier** tends to be used in official and legal texts, whereas **occupant** is at home in general discourse.

The applications just described are those of British English, where both **occupant** and **occupier** are freely used. In American English **occupant** has much greater currency, by the evidence of CCAE, and its range includes that of the longer-term resident or tenant:

> *the only occupant of a red Pontiac*
> *most admired occupant of the podium*
> *a malleable occupant of the prime minister's chair*
> *the owner-occupant must pay fair market rent of the house*

Americans reserve **occupier** for the *occupying power*, as in *working against the enemy occupier.*

ochre or ocher
See under **-re/-er**.

o'clock
Should the time that goes with **o'clock** be expressed in words or figures? See **numbers and number style** introductory section.

octa or okta
See **okta**.

octa- or octo-
These are respectively the Greek- and Latin-derived prefixes for the number "eight." **Octa-** appears in mathematical and scientific terms such as *octagon, octahedral, octamerous, octavalent.* **Octo-** prefaces words in the humanities and in more general use: *octocentenary, octogenarian, octoroon, octosyllabic.* Though etymology dictates one or the other, the two prefixes are hard to distinguish without stress on the second syllable, and large dictionaries allow alternative spellings for *octahedral* (*octohedral*), *octamerous* (*octomerous*) and *octoroon* (*octaroon*). The switch of prefixes is harmless in terms of meaning.

octopus
What should the plural be for this iconic eight-legged animal? By its Latin appearance people have been inclined to make the plural **octopi**, as with other loanwords ending in *-us*. (See **-us** section 1.) Those with superior knowledge would say the plural should be **octopodes**, because the word was actually coined out of Greek elements as "oktopous." **Octopodes** is still foregrounded as the preferred plural in the *Oxford Dictionary* (1989), though neither the dictionary nor *Webster's English Usage* (1989) has any citations for it. What *Webster's* C20 files show is both **octopi** and the regular English plural **octopuses** in scholarly as well as general use, but the latter gaining the upper hand. **Octopuses** was endorsed by almost two thirds of those responding to the Langscape survey (1998–2001). Its dominance is confirmed in data from both CCAE and the BNC, though the scene is a little more diverse in the UK, with **octopi** occurring in 25% of all instances of the word.

octoroon or octaroon
See under **octa- or octo-**.

oculist
For the distinctions between this and other words for related professions, see **optician**.

OD and KO
For the inflected forms of the verb **OD** ("overdose"), the apostrophe provides a consistent solution. Dictionaries all prefer *OD'd* for the past tense / past participle, but note the regular *ODed* as an alternative. For the present participle, they again prefer *OD'ing*, though this time the alternative given by some is *OD-ing*. The regular "ODing" is not registered anywhere, and lends itself to misreading – as could *ODed*. The apostrophed forms work best also for the verb **KO** ("knock out, defeat") as in *KO'd, KO'ing.* See further under **-ed** section 3.

-odd and odd
Minimizing the use of hyphens is more typical of Americans than the British (see **hyphens**), and on the whole it makes for tidier and no less readable text. But in this case it creates a problem. Compare

a table with twenty-odd books in a heap

with

a table with twenty odd books in a heap

In the first, **-odd** works as an approximator, whether the number is in figures or words. In the second it seems to be a fully fledged adjective meaning "peculiar." The hyphen solves the problem in writing, whereas speakers quite often preface the number with *some* to underscore the interpretation of "odd" as **-odd**: "some twenty odd books were on the table." (For the use of *some* as approximator, see **some**.) This use of *some* together with **-odd** is strictly redundant in writing, yet it gets carried over into written texts in both BNC and CCAE:

The liberation army drove out some 2000-odd armed white right-wingers.

In written examples, the numbers to which **-odd** is attached are very often figures, especially in American English. This is however determined by the writer/editor's policy on the writing of numbers. See **numbers and number style** section 3.

odious, odorous, odiferous and odoriferous

The first word is the odd one out. All the rest have something to do with *odors;* whereas **odious** with its roots in *odium* ("hatred," "repugnance") means "offensive." Yet **odious** is sometimes confused with **odorous**, as in "odorous comparisons" (see **malapropisms**). The confusion is no doubt fed by their similar forms, and the fact that both have emotive force. **Odious** is always negative, whereas **odorous** may or may not be, depending on context.

Odorous, odiferous and **odoriferous** all have to do with strong affecting smells, and the number of syllables makes little difference to the meaning. The connotations can be good or bad, witness:

the odorous soft bed of the receding sea

... dredged from odorous mud

Odorous is also used neutrally by chemists, as in *odorous substances.* In British English, **odorous** is the only one of the three "odor" words in regular use, by the evidence of the BNC. Americans meanwhile make roughly equal use of **odorous** and **odoriferous** in CCAE data (**odiferous** remains rare). Again the words can have good or bad connotations, but the latter are definitely more common. Sometimes it's a matter of taste, as with the *odoriferous durian,* that notorious/delectable Asian fruit. What the nose responds to is probably culture-bound, and indeed species-bound. In English it seems that most anything "on the nose" is distasteful. But if the effect needs to be spelled out, there's *malodorous* for the bad smell and *fragrant* for the good.

odor or odour

See under **-or/-our**.

oe/e

The **oe** digraph is one of the eccentricities of modern English. It is built into the spelling of a few common words, such as *shoe, toe, canoe;* and into the plurals of some ending in *-o,* such as *echoes* and *heroes.* In short, everyday words like those, it's a regular part of the spelling. But in longer and less common ones such as *innuendo(e)s* and *memento(e)s,* the plurals are increasingly spelled without the *e.* (See further under **-o**.)

Another set of words in which **oe** is being slowly reduced to one letter (this time to **e**) includes Greek loanwords such as *am(o)eba, diarrh(o)ea, hom(o)eopath, (o)edema, (o)estrogen,* all put to scientific purposes in English but part of the general vocabulary as well. The **oe** digraph is in fact a Latin rendering of the Greek diphthong *oi,* so that its pedigree is a bit limited. The digraph became a ligature in earlier English, and is still printed as such in the *Oxford Dictionary* (1989). But Fowler argued for its being printed as the digraph **oe**, and British English has standardized it that way (see further under **ae/e**). In American English the ligatured **oe** was replaced by **e**, hence the alternative standard spellings.

These regional differences are not absolute, by the evidence of the Langscape survey (1998–2001), and individual words vary somewhat. The expected differences held for *diarrh(o)ea, (o)esophagus, (o)estrogen,* where the **oe** spellings were endorsed by about 90% of British respondents, and the **e** spellings by more than 90% of Americans. Yet a majority of the British (71%) also accepted *homeopathy,* and, more surprisingly, about 80% of Americans were ready to endorse *amoeba* (though this may reflect the fact that it's foregrounded in the *Webster's Third* [1961/86] entry as the scientific name of the genus). Other research shows growing acceptance of *fetus* in British English (Sigley, 1999); see **fetus**. A majority of Australians who have traditionally followed British spelling habits in this area seem ready to endorse both *diarrhea* and *homeopath* (Peters, 1995). Canadians tend to use **e** spellings in most such words, and to see **oe** as British, according to the *Canadian Oxford* (1998).

Whether these shifting preferences will affect others in the same set of words remains to be seen. British writers who accept *homeopathy* might now be content with *homeostatic, homeothermic, homeotransplant.* The Australian endorsement of *diarrhea* could pave the way for *dysmenorrhea, gonorrhea, logorrhea* etc. The more technical words are however often the preserve of specialists, who present concerted professional resistance to "popular" moves for change. Some argue that the **oe** is more etymological and therefore informative, which is dubious on both counts. The **oe** is not the original Greek spelling, as we have seen; and readers without Greek are unlikely to make anything of the spelling of a syllable – much more likely to take the word's sense from the whole.

No-one would turn the clock back on words like *ecology, economic, ecumenical,* all of which originally began with **oe** in English. They show the natural tendency to simplify the ligature to **e** rather than enlarge it to a digraph. It can happen at the start of a word, though some find it a barrier to recognizing the word. The simplification has an obvious value when it reduces odd sequences of vowels in the middle of a word from three to two, as in *homeopathy* and *diarrhea.*

> **International English selection:** The plain **e** spellings recommend themselves instead of the digraph **oe** for general written discourse, for the various reasons discussed. They are established in both US and Canadian English, gaining ground in Australia, and accepted in some cases even in Britain.

Note: oe remains as is when the two letters belong to different syllables, as in words like *coefficient, gastroenteritis, poem, whoever,* and in loanwords from modern German, such as *roentgen,* where the oe represents an umlauted vowel (see **umlaut**).

◊ On the choice between **manoeuvre** and **maneuver,** see **manoeuvre.**

oedema or edema

These present the standard British and American options with *oe* and *e.* Canadians accept **edema,** whereas Australians still use **oedema.** See further under **oe/e.**

oenology or enology

The first spelling is standard in the UK, Canada and Australia. The second is used in the US, as in the American Society of Enology and Viticulture. See further under **oe/e.**

oesophagus or esophagus

British and Australian English use **oesophagus,** whereas Americans and Canadians prefer **esophagus.** In the Langscape survey (1998–2001) **esophagus** was also well supported by two thirds of the European respondents. See further under **oe/e.**

oestrogen or estrogen

In British and Australian English, **oestrogen** is standard, whereas in American and Canadian it's **estrogen.** A majority of the Asian respondents to the Langscape survey (55%) also preferred **estrogen.** See further under **oe/e.**

of and 've

Of is the most common preposition in written discourse, because of its multiple roles in joining words and phrases. Most of these are uncontroversial, and they provide useful alternatives to other constructions.

* Nouns and noun phrases are linked by **of,** as in *cup of tea* and *no hope of a golden handshake.* As in those examples, it connects the syntactic head and semantic anchor with the finer detail of the utterance. **Of** helps to paraphrase possessive expressions, as in *the assistance of the parents* for *the parents' assistance.* On occasions it seems to duplicate the possessive, as in *that friend of Jim's:* see **double genitive.**

* Verbs are linked with their complements, whether they are phrases as in *think of England,* or nonfinite clauses, as in *think of going to England.* For verbs like *convince, inform, persuade, remind, tell, warn* the **of** construction is a nonfinite alternative to other kinds of finite clause:
    The letter reminded us of their coming.
    The letter reminded us that they were coming.

* Adjectives use **of** to connect with their complements, as in *aware/mindful/suspicious of.* Again these can be paraphrased with finite clauses:
    The police were aware of their threat to the neighbors.
    The police were aware that they threatened the neighbors.

* Adverbial expressions of habitual time may be constructed with *of,* for example:
    Of an evening, guests dine by candlelight.

    In Athens, a woman can walk the streets of an evening without fear …
This **of** construction and its genitive equivalent *evenings* (as in *everything tapers off Sundays and evenings*) are both relatively rare in British and American English, by the evidence of the BNC and CCAE. Their place has been taken by adverbial phrases *in the evening* or *in the evenings.* On the fringe in both databases is *on evenings,* a natural extension of *on Saturdays,* but still more American than British idiom. (See **on/in.**)

Other issues with of.

* in noun phrases. The **of** that appears in definite quantitative phrases such as *both of the letters* may be omitted, as in *both the letters.* The same holds for *all of the* and *half of the* (see **half of the,** and **all and all of**). This allows *all/both/half* to be used as *predeterminers* (see under **determiners**), which is not possible for indefinite quantifiers such as *some / several / a few.* **Of** cannot be omitted from phrases like *some of the letters.*

* in verb phrases. **Of** has no place in the verb phrase – though it's sometimes mistakenly used there instead of *have.* No doubt this results from the fact that *have* is commonly reduced to *'ve* in continuous speech, and then sounds identical with *of.* Thus *could of* appears for *could 've, may of* for *may 've, might of* for *might 've, should of* for *should 've, would of* for *would 've.* By the same process *had of* sometimes appears for *had 've,* though there's rarely any need for *had have.* See further under **have** final notes.

off and off of

Off serves primarily as adverb and preposition of removal, as in:
    Take your shoes off.
and
    Take your shoes off the seat.
Off also appears as an adjective, with privative or negative meanings as when the *electricity/game/joke/milk is off.* Idiomatic uses of **off** are also embodied in compounds derived from phrasal verbs, such as *castoff, selloff, showoff, spinoff, turnoff, writeoff.* Gerunds based on such phrasal verbs take other nouns in tow, whereat **off of** is the necessary sequence:
    the selling off of irreplaceable books from the library
    with much showing off of their remarkable crests
While this use of **off of** is unobjectionable, its use as a complex preposition raises stylistic eyebrows, at least in Britain. It probably stems from the *Oxford Dictionary* (1884–1928), which noted that **off of** was "dialectal," and in the second edition (1989) that it was "colloquial and dialectal." The BNC certainly contains far more examples in spoken material (where one's local identity is more readily expressed) than in written texts. Still there's a sprinkling of the complex preposition in printed sources:
    Sinatra stormed off of the set of Carousel.
    Juniors are welcomed on and off of the courts.
    It will take some of the edge off of Gates' competitiveness.
In examples like those, **off** would be sufficient, and one can argue that the **of** is redundant. Yet in American English **off of** appears so often in print that it has idiomatic status, and is not edited out, as in British English. American writers use it freely in

high- and lower-brow journalism in CCAE, as in:
> *. . . keep the pressure off of interest rates*
> *The boat was salvaged off of Ireland.*
> *He shoveled snow off of his narrow driveway.*

Webster's English Usage (1989) expresses reservations about using it in the most formal prose, but there's no doubt that **off of** is thoroughly established.

Both **off of** and **off** tend to attract negative comment when they appear instead of *from,* as in:
> *They downloaded it off of the internet.*
> *I got it off my grandfather.*

Objections against the first sentence are probably fueled by the (relative) informality of style, and the seemingly redundant use of **of** noted before. Sentences of the second type, using **off** for *from,* were barely tolerable in informal speech, according to Mittins *et al.*'s informants (1970), and not at all in writing. The structure is also potentially ambiguous. Does it mean "my grandfather gave it to me," or "I extracted it from my grandfather's keeping"? There's the heart of the problem. Allusive expression is acceptable and probably clear enough in conversation, but in prose it creates ambiguities which are to be avoided.

offense or offence
See under **-ce/-se.**

official or officious
As adjectives, both invoke the word *office,* but their implications are quite different. **Official** implies the proper execution of duties, as in *official appearance,* or the proper expression of an office, as in *official position.* **Officious** suggests intrusive exercise of authority, as in:
> *An officious clerk wanted to double-check my passport.*

Thus **officious** has negative implications, while **official** is neutral.

officialese
This is an institutional written style that everyone objects to. **Officialese** frustrates the reader with long words and interminable sentences, while seeming to emphasize the importance and authority of the office it speaks for. Dissatisfaction with **officialese** helps to explain the appeal of *Plain English,* and why various government departments and private companies are endeavoring to restyle their publications to ensure better communication.

Officialese is above all an impersonal style, the voice of an institution rather than an individual. It is fostered in bureaucracies where teams of people work in succession on the same letter or document. Yet when that same style comes from the pen of a single person writing to another, it can only seem pompous and insensitive. The components of **officialese,** and ways of eliminating them are discussed at **Plain English.** See also **gobbledygook.**

officious or official
See **official.**

offspring
This can refer to one or more than one :
> *That poor child is Mr H's only offspring.*
> *When living things reproduce, the sibling offspring vary.*

As the examples show, the verb will show singular or plural agreement according to the number of progeny.

oftener or more often
Adverbs without *-ly* can be inflected (see **adverbs** section 3). But the periphrastic form **more often** is far more common than **oftener** in both British and American English, by the evidence of BNC and CCAE. See **adverbs** section 3.

ogre and ogreish
In the US **ogre** is the standard spelling, as in the UK. There's no "oger," lest the *-ge* should suggest a soft "g" in the word. (See **-re/-er** and **-ce/-ge.**)

Despite its eccentric looks, **ogreish** is the preferred spelling for the adjective in both *Merriam-Webster* (2000) and *New Oxford* (1998), as in:
> *You see ogreish smiles all over the place these days.*

Ogreish overrides the common English spelling rule of dropping *e* from the stem before adding *-ish* (see further under **-e**). *New Oxford* notes the regular *ogrish* as an alternative spelling, but there's no sign of it in the BNC.

Oh or O
See **O.**

-oid
This suffix is derived from the Greek word *eidos* meaning "shape or form." It creates an adjective or noun which implies resemblance to a known body shape, as in:
> alkaloid   anthropoid   arachnoid
> asteroid   cricoid   rhomboid

Most of the words formed with **-oid** are technical. The majority are based on Greek roots, though a few Latin/English examples have appeared in C20, such as *celluloid* and *humanoid.* The use of *-oid* to refer to alien species in science fiction adds a faintly negative coloring, which is exploited in the disparaging *trendoid.*

OK or okay
This word raises several issues of style, as it appears increasingly in print. **OK** needs no stops, given the trend away from using them in abbreviations consisting solely of capitals (see **abbreviations** section 2). When used in British English, **okay** is much more likely than **OK,** by more than 4:1 in the BNC. In American English the odds are much closer, and in data from CCAE, they appear in the ratio 4:3. As a verb **okay** simply becomes *okayed,* whereas **OK** is usually *OK'd.* (See **-ed.**)

The origins of **OK** have been much debated. It was first recorded in Boston in 1839, and remained an Americanism until the 1920s. Some have sought its etymology in an American Indian language, others in European immigrant languages including French, Finnish, Scots English and especially German. A likely explanation is that the letters stand for "Oll Korrect," a humorous misspelling of *all correct.* A.W. Read's research (reported in the *Oxford Dictionary,* 1989) also suggests that the abbreviation gained rapid acceptance because the initials coincided with "Old Kinderhook," nickname of Martin van Buren (US president 1837–41), who came from the Dutch community of Kinderhook, New York.

okta or octa

Dating only from 1950, this word meaning a one-eighth sector of the sky is used in meteorology and aircraft control. The standard spelling is **okta** in the dictionaries which list it (*Oxford,* 1989, *Macquarie,* 1997), thus modeling it on the Greek number "eight" (see **number prefixes**). The variant **octa** makes it more Latin-looking, though it could be no more than a case of replacing the *k* in a foreign word with *c*: see **k/c**.

older or elder, and oldest or eldest

For the choice of adjective in each of these pairs, see **elder**.

olla podrida

See under **potpourri**.

-ology

This ending is strictly speaking a combination of the Greek combining *-o-* (as in the compound *Anglo-Saxon*) and *-logy,* an element meaning originally "statement, discourse about something," from which it came to mean the "study or science of a subject." Yet so many of our sciences are named with words ending in **-ology** that it seems to be a unitary combining form. It occurs as a word in its own right, in Quinion's dictionary of *Ologies and Isms* (2003).

Some of the many areas of science and scholarship which are established *-logies* are:

biology	campanology	cosmology
criminology	entomology	etymology
geology	histology	ornithology
parasitology	philology	psychology
sociology	theology	zoology

The **-ology** ending is also used in the names of pseudosciences and recreations, such as:

astrology	graphology	iridology
numerology	phrenology	speleology

It contributes to the humor of hybrid formations such as *fruitologist* and *garbologist.*

Olympian, Olympic and Olympiad

The adjective **Olympian** refers first and foremost to *Mount Olympus* in northern Greece, which was the mythological home of the Greek gods. **Olympic** is associated with the plain of *Olympia* in the Peloponnese, west of Athens, where the original *Olympic games* were held in ancient times. Nowadays it's the standard adjective for the modern international athletic contest which perpetuates the tradition. Yet as a noun **Olympian** can refer to either one of the mythological inhabitants of *Mount Olympus,* or someone who has competed at the the modern *Olympic games*. Those who participate in the **Olympics,** and especially those who "bring home gold," do indeed seem to attain the status of demigods via the media.

The associated word **Olympiad** also has both ancient and modern meanings. It originally referred to the four-year interval between the **Olympic** contests; now it usually refers to the actual celebration of the games, as in *the opening ceremony of the XXVII Olympiad.*

ombudsman, ombud, ombudsperson

Swedish *ombud* and *ombudsman* both mean "agent" or "representative." The latter was borrowed into English in the 1960s, with slightly different applications in the UK and the US. In British (and Australian) English the **ombudsman** is an independent official, appointed to take up complaints against government departments by members of the public. In American and Canadian English, an **ombudsman** hears complaints within a particular institution or associated with a particular cause, e.g. *human rights ombudsman.*

In English **ombudsman** looks less than gender-neutral, hence the creation of the more inclusive **ombudsperson** in the 1980s. But it hardly makes a mark in British or American data from the BNC/CCAE. The suggestion that the original Swedish provides its own gender-free term (**ombud**) was taken up in some American universities (Maggio, 1988), but has had little impact elsewhere. Perhaps the **ombudsman's** role is still too new to permit any variation in the form of the word.

omelet or omelette

The first spelling is the older one and to be preferred, according to both the *Oxford Dictionary* (1989) and *Webster's Third* (1986). **Omelet** has been in use since C17; while **omelette** gained currency in C19 Britain. It dominates the C20 citations of the *Oxford,* and is therefore given equal status with **omelet,** but still put second. The *New Oxford* (1998), *Canadian Oxford* (1998) and the Australian *Macquarie* (1997) give preference to **omelette.** See further under **-ette**.

omission mark

The various marks of omission are discussed under **asterisk, carat, karat or caret, dashes,** and **ellipsis** (section 2).

omitted relative

Not the cousin whose name was left off the guest list but the grammatical phenomenon of leaving out the *relative pronoun.* See **relative clauses** section 1, and **that** section 2.

omnibus

In Latin **omnibus** meant "for all," i.e. public rather than private transport, when the idea was somewhat novel. The horse-drawn **omnibus** has had its day, superseded by the motorized *bus.* Yet the word **omnibus** remains as an *archaism* in British narrative (see **archaisms**), and in the phrase "man on the Clapham omnibus," the proverbial reference person for public attitudes:

> *Who knows what uses the man on the Clapham omnibus will find for new technology?*

That phrase may however be reaching its own use-by date, as it begins to be paraphrased by "the man in the Clapham McDonalds."

Omnibus lives on as the word for a compendious book, e.g. *an Agatha Christie omnibus,* which publishes together a series of compositions which have previously appeared separately. The analogue in television is presenting in quick succession the separately screened episodes of a popular program. (If a plural is needed, it would be **omnibuses:** see **-us** section 4.) The sense of "compendious" or "comprehensive" also continues in the adjective **omnibus,** as in *omnibus declaration, omnibus exhibition, omnibus retail outlet.* In American English the *omnibus bill* bundles up together a very large number of legislative provisions as a way of pushing them through Congress.

on/in

British and American English diverge slightly over the use of these prepositions in references to time and space. Americans make use of **on**, in phrases like *on evenings, on weekends* where the British would use *in the evening(s)* and *at the weekend*. American English also uses **on** for locations as in *the museum on Park (Street)*, where British English would use *the museum in Park Street*. The "British" idioms are also current in American English as alternatives.

◊ For the choice between *wait/stand on line* and *in line,* see **in line or on line.**

-on

The **-on** ending is the mark of Greek loanwords or neoclassical formations in various academic disciplines. Those used include:

anacoluthon	asyndeton	criterion
etymon	oxymoron	phenomenon

Because these were borrowed from Greek, they all come with Greek plurals in *-a,* which can be reliably maintained alongside the singular forms in specialist discourse. But *criterion/criteria* and *phenomenon/phenomena* also occur freely in general writing, where their identity as singular/plural is not necessarily understood – nor do the contexts necessarily make it plain. This is why *criteria* and *phenomena* are not uncommonly interpreted as singular forms in current English. See further under **criterion,** and **phenomenon.**

Other Greek-derived words ending in **-on** usually take *-s* plurals in English. This is true of neoclassical scientific and scholarly words such as *automaton, electron, lexicon, neutron, photon, proton, skeleton.* Only *ganglion* is more likely to appear with an *-a* plural.

Many English words ending in **-on** have no Greek connections, or are so fully assimilated that the **-on** works as part of the stem. The following are just a token of these, which always have *-s* plurals:

canon	cauldron	chevron	crayon
deacon	demon	melon	pylon
tenon			

In a small set of C20 formations, **-on** is a suffix meaning "synthetic material," as in *nylon, orlon, teflon.* The suffix originated in *rayon,* the first artificial fibre, whose name is simply French for "ray." The name was chosen because of the sheen on the fabric made with it.

◊ For the suffix in *cyclotron* and *waitron,* see **-tron.**

one

This word has several roles in English, some of which are uncomplicated. Its use is straightforward when it's the first number in a counting system (*one, two, three*), and when it appears as a substitute word for nouns and noun phrases, as in:

I'd like a ticket. This man needs one too.
The children were at school but one of them had gone on an excursion.

The most critical usage questions for **one** are when it's used as a substitute personal pronoun as in:

What can one say to that?

Just which personal pronoun **one** replaces is not entirely clear. Historically it's a third person pronoun,

though the context could make it *I* or *you* (or both of us; Wales, 1996). Often it seems detached, not as ego-centred as *I,* nor as direct in its address as *you.* Sometimes called the *indefinite pronoun,* its very indeterminacy makes it ideal in certain situations. British writers make considerable use of it, but Americans find it rather formal.

Because **one** has no regular place in the pronoun system, it's unclear which pronoun should agree with it. This leaves several possibilities:

One just has to do one's best.
One just has to do his best.
One just has to do her best.
One just has to do their best.

The choice is a mostly a matter of style. The second option using *his* is the oldest, according to the *Oxford Dictionary* (1989), but has been under attack during the last 200 years by usage commentators who preferred the first option with *one's.* It has the virtue of consistency and is gender-free. Yet the repetition of **one** in possessive form draws attention to its awkwardness, and it sounds pompous to American and Australian ears. Neither the second option with *his* nor the third with *her* are usable now, because of their perceived sexism. This leaves us with the fourth option – even though it has been subject to grammatical criticism because it follows the singular **one** with the plural *their.* That kind of agreement is however increasingly common after other indefinite pronouns such as *anyone, everyone, someone,* and avoids gender complications. (See **agreement** section 3, and **they, them, their.**)

Whichever pronoun you choose, it should be used consistently: i.e. *one/one's/oneself* or *one/their/ themself* or *themselves.* Any switching from **one** to *you* or *we* disturbs the expository perspective and cancels its detachment. One should use **one** sparingly!

-one or -body

The alternatives *anyone/anybody, everyone/everybody, someone/somebody, no one/nobody* are in regular use in both the US and the UK, yet the forms with **-one** are a good deal more frequent overall, in data from CCAE and the BNC. The forms with **-body** are most common in conversation, according to the *Longman Grammar* (1999), and used more freely in American than British fiction.

◊ For the spelling of **no-one** – or should it be **no one** – see under **nobody.**

one in, one out of, and one of those

Should it be:

One in five men has a health problem.

or

One in five men have a health problem.

Those who incline to the singular verb want it to agree with the word *one,* whereas those who go for the plural may be influenced by the proximity of the number *five* in that example, and/or the fact that the phrase expresses a ratio, and notionally corresponds to a group within the population of men. (See further under **agreement.**) Plural agreement predominated in data analyzed for the *Longman Grammar* (1999) on constructions with **one in** or **one out of** followed by a number.

The same dilemma comes up in relative clauses following **one of those.** Both patterns of agreement are found in BNC data for *one of those that:*

> . . . *one of those that fits perfectly*
> . . . *one of those that only turn one way*

Likewise singular or plural verbs can be used after *one of those (people) who.* The alternatives also present themselves after *one of the things that:*

> . . . *one of the things that has been most useful*
> . . . *one of the things that are going to disappear*

For most writers the choice depends on whether you're thinking of a single case or general principle. Usage commentators in the UK and the US have been inclined to say it should be plural; and the Harper–Heritage usage panel voted heavily in its favor (78%). Yet *Webster's English Usage* (1989) found ample American evidence for the singular construction, and it's just as common as the plural in British data from the BNC. Writers using the singular take their cue from *one*, whereas the plural-users are responding to *those [people]* or *the [things]*.

◊ Compare **number of**, and **total of**.

on-line, online or on line

All three can refer to digital communication, and this is the only role for the first two. Both British and American English currently prefer **on-line** for the adjective (*on-line services*) as well as the adverb (*services available on-line*), by the evidence of the BNC and CCAE. **Online** is also used this way, but has been commandeered by many a computer network company (apart from *America Online*), and the hyphen marks the generic word, pro tem.

On line is occasionally put to the same purpose as **on-line**, but is built into a variety of other idioms that embody a particular verb or verbs. Thus:

being on line	means	"being on the phone (to)"
coming/going on line		"about to be operative"
waiting/standing on line		"queuing"

In American English *waiting/standing in line* is sometimes used instead of *on line:* see **in line or on line**.

only

This puts a spotlight on its neighbors in a sentence. It usually focuses on the one following, and the point of the sentence changes according to where it's placed:

> *Only the secretary received the letter.*
>> (nobody else got one)
> *The secretary only received the letter.*
>> (did not open it)
> *The secretary received only the letter*
>> (not the cheque)

In conversation the placement of **only** is less critical, because intonation can extend the "spotlight" over several words to the one which matters. (With extended intonation we could make the word order of the second sentence communicate the meaning of the third.) But in writing, **only** must be adjacent to the crucial word or phrase to ensure its full effectiveness. (See further under **information focus**.)

Only has a minor role as a conjunction expressing contrast, in sentences like:

> *He'll certainly come, only don't hold the performance up for him.*

For some, this usage smacks too much of conversation to be suitable for formal writing. It was rejected by 85% of the Harper–Heritage usage panel. Yet its written record began in C14, according to the *Oxford Dictionary* (1989), and *Webster's English Usage* (1989) has enough recent citations to deem it standard. Those who find it too informal may replace it with *but* or *except that,* as appropriate.

onomatopoeia

This unlikely word refers to a figure of speech, as well as one of the ways in which words are formed. In both kinds of **onomatopoeia**, the word or words seem to express the sound of the very thing they refer to or represent. Individual words such as *croak, hiss, miaou, neigh, quack, rustle, splash* probably owe their origins to ad hoc creation of a word on the stimulus of sound. This correlates with the fact that they have no relatives among English words or even in other languages, where the same sounds are represented by different words. Yet within English not only words, but individual sounds are sometimes felt to have equivalents in terms of meaning. (See further under **phonesthemes**.)

Onomatopoeia can also be generated as a *figure of speech* from sets of ordinary words which are strategically put together. Again the words seem to hint at sounds associated with whatever is being described. Poets of all ages have enriched their work with **onomatopoeia**, as did Gerard Manley Hopkins in the opening lines of *God's Grandeur:*

> *The world is charged with the grandeur of God*
> *It will flame out, like shining from shook foil*
> *It gathers to a greatness, like the ooze of oil*
> *Crushed.*

The words provide "sound" support for the two images: that of static electricity breaking out from metal foil when it's shaken, and the viscous spread of a heavy liquid. Apart from the *onomatopoeic* effect of the words, Hopkins makes use of alliteration and simile in those lines. (See further under **figures of speech**.)

Advertisers find uses for **onomatopoeia** in marketing their product, as did the makers of Rice Bubbles / Krispies with their "snap, crackle, pop" slogan. The same effect has been sought when the product is marketed in non-English-speaking countries. So in Sweden it's "piff, paff, puff"; in parts of Germany "knisper, knasper, knusper"; and in South Africa "klap, knotter, kraak." It confirms that the sound effects of words are relative to a particular language, not universal.

onto or on to

The preposition **onto** was used alongside **on to** for more than a century before British usage commentators (Alford, 1863) censured it. The objection seems to be total – that **onto** should never be used. Closer investigation shows that it has its place, but needs to be distinguished from **on to**. The difference betwen them is illustrated in the following:

> *He went on to become a consultant engineer.*
> *Much of the material was passed on to other colleagues.*
> *I journeyed on to Liverpool.*
> *The dog leapt onto one of the machines.*
> *She cleared her desk onto the floor.*
> *The data can be written directly onto the screen.*

As the examples show, **on to** is necessary for phrasal verbs formed with **on**, where **to** introduces a separate constituent. But **onto** is more satisfactory for simple verbs of motion, because **on to** would seem to divide the movement into two aspects. Verbs like *cling/fit/hang/hold/stick* – used in their physical senses – mostly take **onto**. But in BNC data their more idiomatic uses are often **on to**, as in *hold on to audiences.*

Note the use of **onto** in idioms for becoming aware of something or getting in touch with someone:

He put me onto the Legal Section.
Next thing the police will be onto him.
I'll get onto the agent tomorrow.

In American English **onto** is now standard, according to *Webster's English Usage* (1989); and in data from CCAE **onto** and **on to** are matched 1:1. In British usage **onto** also seems pretty secure, with the ratio 3:4 in data from the BNC – despite the *Oxford Dictionary's* (1989) preference for **on to**. The merged **onto** is as natural a combination as *into*. See **into or in to**.

onward or onwards
See under **-ward**.

-onymy or -onomy
These two Greek endings sound exactly alike, though they are of independent origin and embodied in different sets of words. While **-onymy** enshrines the Greek word *onoma* ("name"), **-onomy** is a composite of the combining vowel **-o-** and Greek *nomia* ("law," "system"). The first ending is built into linguistic terms such as:

antonymy	eponymy	heteronymy
homonymy	hyponymy	meronymy
synonymy	toponymy	

All are concerned with naming, or the relationships among words. Most are discussed under individual entries in this book.

The second ending is familiar in tems such as:

astronomy autonomy economy gastronomy

These words refer to domains that are distinct systems or bodies of knowledge. So if *geonomy* or *zoonomy* take you by surprise, you know that they are concerned respectively with geological and zoological systems, not with the naming of rocks and animals.

opacity or opaqueness
These are synonyms according to modern dictionary definitions. Both **opaqueness** and **opacity** work as the abstract noun for *opaque*, in its literal and more figurative senses ("obscure" / "lacking light and openness"). Compare other similar pairs where the noun formed with *-ness* is the more literal of the two (see **-ness**). The two serve equally for the literal sense in:

The fog rolled in with a flannel-like opacity.
. . . qualities of opaqueness and opalescence in the glass

And for the figurative in:

prose of baroque opacity
problems of ambiguity and opaqueness

Though **opaqueness** is just as possible as **opacity** in terms of meaning, there's a substantial difference in their relative frequency. In American as well as British, **opacity** is approximately 10 times more frequent than **opaqueness**, by the evidence of CCAE and the BNC.

op.cit.
This Latin abbreviation is only used in footnotes and endnotes, as a follow-up to a previous reference. It means "in the work [already] cited." **Op.cit.** saves the writer having to repeat the full title of the work referred to, provided it has been cited in full in an earlier footnote:

1. See G. Blainey *The Tyranny of Distance*, p. 31.
5. Blainey *op.cit.* p. 35.

As the footnote numbers show, the reference with **op.cit.** need not follow immediately after the full reference. However the use of **op.cit.** is on the decline, and actively discouraged by some publishers such as the Chicago University Press. Its place is being taken by follow-up references with a short title instead:

1. See G. Blainey *The Tyranny of Distance*, p. 31.
5. Blainey *Tyranny*, p. 35.

Note that if the author's name appears in the running text before the repeated reference, just the book title and the page number would be enough. And if no other work by Blainey is being referred to, just his name and the page number are sufficient.
◊ Compare **loc.cit.**, and see further under **Latin abbreviations**.

opera and operetta
Since its origins in C17, **opera** has developed in scope and variety. There are large differences in scope between the one-hour music dramas of Scarlatti and the *grand operas* of Verdi. In the latter, the whole libretto is set to music, and its serious and heroic subject matter contrasts with that of *opera buffa* (or French *opéra bouffe*) – names for *comic opera* in which the musical climaxes are embedded in recitative. French *opéra comique* combines plain spoken dialogue with the musical highlights, but is not necessarily comic in its substance, witness examples such as *Carmen*. In English the term **operetta** is used for (1) short **operas** of any variety, and (2) *light operas* whose subjects contrast with *grand opera*. *Light opera* in the second sense has much in common with musical comedy. Both deal with humorous or sentimental subjects, and one can hardly distinguish them except that the term *musical comedy* is usually applied to those which were composed more recently in the US, and are familiar through film as well as stage versions.

operator or operative
Both can mean "worker in an industry," according to dictionary definitions, but there the similarity ends. In secondary industry, **operator** may refer to persons with specific skills for a particular machine, e.g. *lathe operator, switchboard operator,* whereas **operative** is used for someone whose skills range over a process, as in *cleaning operative, waste disposal operative.*

Outside the regular work force both words refer to persons with rather more power. **Operator** can be used to refer to the manager of a particular secondary or tertiary industry, as in *mine operator, plant operator, cycle tour operator, photobooths operator.* In colloquial use *an operator* is one who manipulates others:

HB had always been a political giant, a supreme operator.

Operative meanwhile has its own special applications, in reference to a secret agent, or a private detective.

ophthalmic or opthalmic, ophthalmologist or opthalmologist

All these embody the Greek *ophthalma* ("eye"), hence the first and third spellings which are standard for those who specialize in care of the eyes – and the only spellings allowed in *Merriam-Webster* (2000) and *New Oxford* (1998). Yet there's a sprinkling of **opthalmic** in data from CCAE and the BNC; and an internet search (Google, 2003) found **opthalmologist** in 7% of all instances of the word. The spellings with *opth-* reflect common pronunciation of the first syllable as "op-," which is registered as an alternative for both words in North American dictionaries (*Merriam-Webster* and the *Canadian Oxford,* 1998). The pronunciation with "op-," and the nonstandard spelling, are both fostered by the much more familiar Latin stem for "eye": *opt-* as in *optical, optician, optometry.*
◊ Compare **diphtheria.**

opium

See under **morphine.**

opportunity to, opportunity of or opportunity for

Of the several possible constructions after **opportunity**, these three recur most often in both American and British English:
1 *It gave them the/an opportunity to talk.*
2 *It gave them the(an) opportunity of talking.*
3 *It gave them an(the) opportunity for discussion.*
The first construction using **opportunity to** is the most popular by far in the UK as well as the US. It far outnumbers **opportunity of**, by almost 8:1 in BNC data, and more than 30:1 in data from CCAE. This is in line with the observation of *Webster's English Usage* (1989) that the *of* + gerund was more a British construction, though it had been commoner in the US until the 1970s. In Australian English it's now rare (Peters, 1995). The third construction is more flexible than the first two, and permits several kinds of complement: abstract noun, gerund (rarely), and a person or persons, often the subject(s) of a following *to*-infinitive.
> the opportunity for hands-on experience
> an opportunity for gathering intelligence
> a shining opportunity for venturesome British outfits
> any opportunity for me to stand out …
All three constructions (**opportunity to/of/for**) can appear with a preceding definite or indefinite article. They are equally likely with **opportunity to**, whereas *the* is more typical with **opportunity of**, and *a, an* or another indefinite such as *any, no, some* with **opportunity for.**

opposite of, opposite to or opposite from

The choice of word after *opposite* varies according to whether it serves as a noun, adjective or preposition. As a noun it's most often followed by *of*, as in *the opposite of what happens normally.* Yet *to* is increasingly common after the noun (*the opposite to what I expected*), appearing in the ratio of about 1:5 of all instances in BNC data.
As an adjective, *opposite* is usually followed by *to,* very occasionally by *from*:

> Opposite to S's display was an even grander show.
> Opposite from the Butter Cross, the Town Hall is built above a piazza.

The use of *to* after the adjective *opposite* is often felt to be redundant when it refers to spatial locations, and increasingly it's left out, making a preposition of *opposite*:

> Directly opposite the stove is the icon corner …

This use of *opposite* as a preposition is more common in British English than American, by its relative frequency in data from BNC and CCAE – but established in both.

opthalmic or ophthalmic

See **ophthalmic.**

optician, optometrist, oculist or ophthalmologist

The professionals who attend to people's eyesight go by slightly different names, depending on their role and qualifications as well as where they carry out their business. In Britain there are two kinds of **optician.** The *dispensing optician* supplies you with spectacles or lenses, while the *ophthalmic optician* tests eyes and prescribes lenses. In North America and Australia, the latter role is that of the **optometrist,** and **optician** refers only to the dispenser of optical items. **Ophthalmologist** is used everywhere for the trained doctor who specializes in eyes – despite its challenging spelling and pronunciation (see further under **ophthalmic or opthalmic**). The more pronounceable **oculist** was previously used in both the UK and the US as the term for one whose practice included both *ophthalmology* and *optometry.* But it has fallen into disuse with the separation of the two fields.

optimum or optimal

The noun **optimum** is very often used to premodify other nouns, as in:

> The optimum conditions for ballooning are at dawn.

More than 80% of the instances of **optimum** in British data in the BNC were of this "adjectival" kind. The adjective **optimal** could equally have been used:

> The optimal conditions for ballooning are at dawn.

Optimal was once "rare" and belonged to biology, according to the *Oxford Dictionary.* It now appears in hundreds of examples in the BNC, but confined to a narrower range of documents than **optimum** (as modifier), suggesting that its tone is still rather formal. In American English **optimal** is clearly less common than **optimum**, by the evidence of CCAE.

optometrist, oculist or ophthalmologist

See under **optician.**

opus

This is a Latin loanword, whose Latin plural **opera** is maintained by some in English (see under **-us** section 3). The fact that it coincides with the Italian word for a musical form (see **opera**) nudges others in the direction of an English plural: **opuses.** *New Oxford* (1998) and the *Canadian Oxford* (1998) give priority to

opuses, whereas *Merriam-Webster* (2000) and
Macquarie (1997) make it **opera.**

Note that *Opus Dei,* literally "work of God," is the
title of a politico-religious organization aligned with
the Catholic Church, which originated in Spain in
C20. In that application *Opus* always bears a capital
and is never pluralized.

◊ For *opus magnum* see **magnum opus.**

or

The conjunction **or** connects alternatives: *seen or
heard, right or wrong, confirm or deny.* At bottom it's a
coordinator like *and,* and raises similar questions of
agreement with coordinated subjects (see **agreement**
section 4). Because **or** is used much more often in
academic prose than in other kinds of writing,
according to *Longman Grammar* (1999) research,
there's particular pressure to make the "correct"
decision. As often, the issues are not simple, whether
it's the choice between:

* singular or plural verb
* first, second or third person of the verb, with a mix
  of pronouns
* masculine, feminine or neuter gender in the
  following pronoun

1 Singular or plural verb. When **or** coordinates two (or
more) items/people as subject of the sentence, some
style guides say that the verb should always agree in
the singular.

> *Perhaps the father or mother agrees to that.*

The advice seems to make sense when the alternatives
are mutually exclusive. The *Longman Grammar*
found that singular agreement was mostly used with
or – provided the alternates were themselves singular,
as in the previous example. When one or other (or
both) was a plural, plural agreement was regularly
used. For example

> *The rustling of papers or chairs scraping were
> enough to disturb his concentration.*

Plural agreement was used, whether the plural item
came first or second, so that *notional* rather than
proximity agreement is apparently at stake.

2 Person of the verb (i.e. first, second or third) with or.
After a mix of pronouns involving more than one
person, the nearest one determines the choice of verb

> *He or I do this every day.*
> *Are you or he responsible for this?*
> *They believe either you or I am responsible.*

In the first two examples the verb agrees with the
person of the nearest pronoun, but it could equally
be thought of as plural agreement with the notional
pair of pronouns. The third example is less
comfortable, because the verb *be* is involved, and the
verb *am* agrees only with the nearest pronoun, and
so *proximity agreement* is the only form achieved. If
the plural verb *are* is used, it makes for *notional
agreement* but is awkward in terms of *proximity.*
Avoidance may be the best strategy in such cases,
thus:

> *They believe that I am responsible, or that you are.*

3 Gender of the pronoun following or. When **or**
connects male and female nouns or names, the gender
of the nearer one could decide the issue, as in:

> *Every boy or girl must cover her books with plastic
> film.*

The statement seems unfortunately sexist, as does the
following – unless you have a very strong faith in
generic *his:*

> *Every boy or girl must cover his books with plastic
> film.*

In such cases the plural *their* provides *notional
agreement* as well as a gender-free alternative:

> *Every boy or girl must cover their books with
> plastic film.*

Those who still find that sentence grammatically
anomalous would need to reword it.

4 Punctuation with or. This is simply a matter of
whether to put a comma before **or** when it introduces
the last of a series of alternatives. The issue is the
same as for *and* in the same position. See the
discussion of the *serial comma* under **comma** (section
3b).

5 Or as a correlative conjunction. **Or** often appears in
tandem with *either,* and with *neither:*

> *You can go on either Tuesday or Friday*
> *Neither Tuesday or Friday is perfect for me.*

The choice between *nor* and **or** with *neither,* is
discussed at **nor or.**

◊ For the use of **or** in *and/or,* see **and/or.**

-or/-our

These are alternative spellings for a sizable group of
abstract nouns, such as *colo(u)r, favo(u)r, hono(u)r,
humo(u)r.* They form a sharp divide between British
and American spelling, whereas both are used in
Canada and to some extent in Australia. The variation
between **-or** and **-our** goes back to C17 and C18
uncertainties about how to relate these spellings to
word origins. Scholars wanted to use **-or** for words
received from Latin, and **-our** for the French
loanwords. But in many cases it was unclear which
language was the source, and the choice of ending
became arbitrary. C18 dictionaries show a continuing
trend toward **-or** for all of them, and this process was
allowed to run its full course in the United States. In
Britain it was halted by the publication of Dr.
Johnson's dictionary (1755), and, more importantly,
the fact that the dictionary was reprinted with the
spellings virtually unchanged for decades after his
death. Johnson had a mixture of spellings for words in
this group (compare *anterior* with *posteriour*), and his
lack of conviction also emerges in the fact that the
spellings in his correspondence didn't always match
up with those in his dictionary. Yet the words his
dictionary has with **-our** are by and large the ones
which British spelling preserves today. Fowler's
discomfort with them is evident in his *Modern English
Usage* (1926), yet he seems to have been overruled by
his publisher. American spellings with **-or** were
recommended in *Webster's* dictionaries from 1828 on.

In Canada the field is divided. The *Gage Canadian
Dictionary* (1983) recommended **-or,** but *Canadian
Oxford* (1998) prefers **-our.** *Canadian English Usage*
(1997) notes some regional differences, by which those
working in eastern Canada (Ontario and Quebec) and
in British Columbia are most likely to use **-our,** while
those in the intervening prairie provinces generally
use **-or.** The publishing medium also affects the issue,
since most newspapers have **-or** where the major book
publishers use **-our.** Australian usage has mostly
followed the British in C20, though **-or** spellings
appeared in various sources in C19, including
regional newspapers and some legal codes. The **-or**
spelling was adopted by the *Australian Labor Party* at
the turn of the century (see under **Labour**). The **-or**
spellings are more evident in some states than others,

especially Victoria and South Australia, where the major newspapers have continued to use it. Advertising copy often enshrines it in newspapers that use -our in the main text.

The prime reason for preferring -or spellings is still exactly as Fowler suggested: they are more consistent with their common derivatives, for example:

glamo(u)r	glamorous	glamorize
hono(u)r	honorary	honorific
humo(u)r	humorous	humorist
labo(u)r	laborious	laboratory
odo(u)r	odorous	deodorant
vigo(u)r	vigorous	invigorate

Those who use -or can simply maintain it in the derivative words, whereas -our-users have to remember to adjust their spelling habit. The occasional appearances of *glamourous* and *humourist* are a sign of the problem. This is why -or spellings seem both preferable and practical in all the basic words:

arbor	armor	behavior	clamor
color	demeanor	endeavor	favor
fervor	flavor	glamor	harbor
honor	humor	labor	neighbor
odor	parlor	rancor	rigor
rumor	savior	savor	splendor
succor	tumor	valor	vapor
vigor			

The -or also applies to all English and French derivatives, including *colorful, favorite, honorable, misdemeanor* etc., as well as the latinate ones already illustrated.

International English selection: The -or spellings are to be preferred as a consistent pattern for both the basic words and their derivatives – an advantage that should not be sacrificed to regional loyalty. They have therefore been used throughout this book. The fact that -or spellings enjoy some use in Canada, Australia and elsewhere should work to dilute the regional divide.

◊ On the choice between -or and -er in agentive words such as *protester*, see -er/-or.

oratio

This Latin word meaning "speech" is the key to the phrases *oratio recta* ("direct [or quoted] speech") and *oratio obliqua* ("indirect [or reported] speech"). For a discussion of the difference between them, see **direct speech**.

orbited

For the spelling of this word as a verb, see -t.

ordain and ordinance

The spelling difference between these is discussed under **-ain**.

ordered

The standard construction following *was ordered* involves a *to-infinitive*, as in *was ordered to close*. In passive constructions it usually involves *to be* and a past participle, as in:

The incinerator was ordered to be closed immediately.

This double passive (*was ordered / be closed*) gives totally impersonal expression to a legal order. It avoids specifying either who gave the order or who is to carry out the action – but is grammatically cumbersome. American English allows it to be compacted as:

The incinerator was ordered closed immediately.

Many a legal ruling is reported this way in newspapers, and the idiom is well established. A murder suspect *was ordered held without bail,* while one associated with lesser crimes may be *ordered released on his own custody.* This construction is unknown in British English, where both passive and active constructions after *was ordered* are expressed in full with *to-infinitives.*

ordinance or ordnance

Of these two **ordinance** is much more widely used, in reference to an official regulation or rule which is backed by authority. **Ordnance** is a collective word for military equipment and supplies, including weapons. The *Ordnance Survey* maps were so called because they were originally commissioned in connection with moving military supplies around on the ground. ◊ For the relationship between **ordinance** and *ordain*, see under **-ain**.

ordinary or ordinal, and cardinal

In ecclesiastical contexts both the **ordinary** and the **ordinal** are reference books. The **ordinary** gives the order for divine service, whereas the **ordinal** is the directory of church services overall, or the forms of service for *ordination* of members of the clergy. But the term **ordinary** can also be contrasted with **cardinal** among officers of the Church. **Ordinary** then refers to any official (e.g. bishop) in his capacity as an ex officio ecclesiastical authority. **Cardinal** is restricted to members of the privileged Sacred College, ranking next after the Pope.

When it comes to numbers, the contrast is between **ordinals** and **cardinals**. The **ordinals** are the numbers which enumerate an *order,* i.e. first (1st), second (2nd), third (3rd); whereas the **cardinals** are the regular integers 1 (one), 2 (two), 3 (three), used to register how many there are in any set. ◊ For the choice between **ordinals** and **cardinals** in quoting the day of the month, see **dates**.

organdie, organdy or organza

The first two are alternative spellings for a type of muslin, a finely woven cotton fabric. The spelling **organdie** is used in Britain and Australia, and **organdy** in the US and Canada. **Organza** is a similar fabric though with more body and stiffness, made out of silk or a synthetic fibre.

orient or orientate

British English uses both of these verbs referring to direction and goal-setting. Fowler thought that **orientate** was likely to prevail in the more figurative applications, and, in BNC data, many examples of the word relate to goals rather than physical direction. Examples like *market orientated schools* are a good deal more common than ones like *the lift orientated at 50 degrees to the natural slope.* Yet the data on **orient** shows the same distribution: many figurative examples like the *sports oriented motif,* and a few physical ones like *north–south oriented graves.* The main point to note is that **orient** is roughly twice as frequent as **orientate** in this area of British usage. In American English, usage is almost entirely confined to **orient**, by the evidence of CCAE. Canadians too make more use of **orient** than **orientate**, according to *Canadian English Usage* (1997), as do Australians (Peters, 1995).

orphans

For the distinction between **orphans** and *widows* in text formatting, see **widows**.

ortho-

In Greek this meant "straight" or "right." In modern English it's built into a handful of semitechnical terms, including *orthodontics, orthodox, orthogonal, orthography, orthopedics*. Its major role however has been in the creation of specialized terms in physical chemistry.

orthopedic or orthopaedic

See under **ae/e**.

-ose

This suffix is found in a number of formal and chemical words. In general use it's found in adjectives, with the meaning "full of" or "given to," as in *bellicose, comatose, grandiose, otiose* and *verbose*. All such words have a pejorative quality, and connote a certain excessiveness. The identical but strictly independent suffix **-ose** used in chemistry is neutral. It derives from the word *glucose,* and forms nouns that serve as the names of sugars and other carbohydrates, for example *fructose, lactose.*

The adjectival **-ose** sometimes varies with *-ous,* as with *torose/torous;* but in the case of *stratose/stratous* and *viscose/viscous,* there's a contrast in meaning. See further under **stratose** and **viscous**.

o.s.p.

See **decessit sine prole**.

ostensible, ostensive or ostentatious

All these have to do with showing something. The most familiar of them is **ostentatious**, meaning "putting on a display" as a means to show off one's wealth or importance. **Ostensible** and **ostensive** are rather academic words, both associated with the burden of proof. **Ostensive** means "embodying the very thing it's intended to demonstrate," as printing the word BLACK in large black letters shows what "black" means. **Ostensible** means almost the opposite, implying that outward appearances are a false indication of what is underlying. Meanwhile the adverb *ostensibly* enjoys much wider use and currency than all three adjectives put together, by the evidence of the BNC. It nudges readers into questioning whether what's put before them is exactly as it seems.

other than and otherwise

Other is historically an adjective meaning "second" or "alternative," as in *the other lady.* Contemporary grammarians class it as a *determiner* and *pronoun* (see next entry), and it's also on record as an adverb equivalent to **otherwise**. Modern dictionaries recognize *other* in all these roles, although its adverbial use especially in **other than** has been subject to controversy in Britain, following Fowler (1926).

Many constructions with **other than** are uncontentious, when *other* is a (post-posed) adjective or determiner, as in:

> *Kids need heroes other than rock stars.*
> *. . . arranged to take showers at places other than their homes*

These constructions often follow indefinite pronouns such as *anything/anyone, something/someone, nothing/no one.* In British English the idiom *none other than* is a very popular example:

> *Inside was none other than the Queen.*

The adverbial use can be analogous to this, following an indefinite adverb:

> *They might behave somehow other than arrogantly.*

Fowler's objection was to sentences in which there was no preliminary adverb, for example:

> *He refused to discuss it other than to curse.*
> *. . . the wounded man, unidentified other than by his age . . .*

Though these examples may sound awkward to British ears, they are not so unusual in American English, which makes much more use of **other than** altogether, by the evidence of CCAE. British writers would probably want to substitute **otherwise** for *other* in the first of those examples, and *apart from* in the second.

Otherwise raises similar issues. Though formed as an adverb (see **-wise**) it can take on other grammatical roles, especially in the combination *or otherwise* (or *and otherwise*). In *shoot or otherwise put to death,* it remains an adverb. But in *sincere or otherwise* it's effectively an adjective, and in *innocuousness or otherwise* it takes on the role of a noun. All these are standard usage in both British and American English.

Or otherwise can go further still, to substitute for a whole phrase or clause, as in:

> *They may have succeeded or otherwise* (i.e. not succeeded)

This type of sentence is somewhat elliptical, yet not ungrammatical, as Fowler argued. As a tag, *or otherwise* communicates its meaning well enough. It may be off-handed, but not redundant since it hints at other possible outcomes. *Or otherwise* may nevertheless be partly redundant when used after *whether:*

> *They need to know whether the cheque has arrived or otherwise.*

In this case the alternatives are implied in *whether,* and *or otherwise* adds nothing of substance. The phrase can also be partly redundant when used to conjoin clauses:

> *We need to arrive by midnight, or otherwise the hotel will be shut.*

In such a sentence, **otherwise**, or just *or,* would be sufficient.

Apart from these latter examples, constructions with *or otherwise* and **other than** serve their purpose, and are idiomatic and standard in both British and American English. Their grammar is a good deal more flexible than Fowler dreamed of.

other's or other's

The pronoun *other* behaves rather like a noun, in that it can be made plural with *s,* and possessive (singular with *'s,* plural with plain *'*). These options come to a head in sentences like the following: where should the apostrophe be put in them?

> *The group read each others letters.*
> *They took one anothers hand.*

Either **other's**, **others'** or **each others** could be defended. In the first there are multiple participants in "the group," despite the singularity of "each"; and the second expresses mutual action, though "one" is resolutely singular. Style guides take their cue from *each* to argue that the singular possessive form (**other's**) is the only one possible. But this seems a little awkward when the noun following is plural (*letters*) and the wording implies more than a single exchange. In the second sentence either form again seems possible: **other's** because of the singular "hand," or **others'** because of the mutuality inherent in the action. The formal grammar of words and the notional grammar of the underlying semantics are at loggerheads.

◊ For the alleged distinction between *each other* and *one another,* see **each other**.

otherwise

See **other than**.

ought

This word is a lone wolf in English grammar – an estranged relative of the verb *owe*. The chief function of **ought** nowadays is as a marginal modal verb, a substitute for *should* or *must* (see **auxiliaries** section 3, and **modality**). Its place in English is shrinking, and corpus data used for the *Longman Grammar* (1999) shows that its place is strongly challenged by *should* and *must,* as well as *have to* in conversation. Most examples of **ought** were found in British fictional discourse, and though they "accentuate the positive," they highlight the uncertainties about its use in negative constructions and in questions. Older usage phrased them as follows:

> *You oughtn't to work so late.*
> *Ought he to know about it?*

In these examples **ought** is construed rather like a modal, taking the negative particle upon itself in the first, and framing the question without any support from the verb *do* in the second. When **ought** is construed as an ordinary verb, the negative sentence would be rephrased as:

> *You didn't ought to work so late.*

Burchfield (1996) regards it as a relatively recent construction, associated with "sparsely educated speakers," though it may well go back to the roots of **ought** in the lexical verb "owe." The *Longman Grammar* notes that contemporary speakers often bypass the problem by putting **ought** into a subordinate clause:

> *I don't think you ought to work so late.*

This shifts the negation into the higher clause, and **ought** works straightforwardly in the affirmative. If negative statements using *do* with **ought** are difficult, interrogative constructions sound unusable: *Didn't he ought to know??*

Ought seems to have reached the end of an evolutionary phase in which it might have become a fully fledged modal. But the trappings of its older identity as a lexical verb have hung around – in the fact that *to* is almost always there to link it with the following verb, and in the use of *do* support in negative statements. So while **ought** still works

affirmatively as a marginal modal expressing obligation, it's otherwise replaced by modals such as *should* and *must* in nonfiction writing of all kinds, everywhere in the world.

-ous

Many English adjectives end in **-ous**, meaning "full of" or "similar to." The ending came into English with French loanwords such as *courageous, dangerous, glorious, virtuous,* and has since been used to create new adjectives out of English nouns, of which the following are only a few:

> *glamorous* *hazardous*
> *momentous* *murderous*
> *poisonous*

Many such adjectives are formed simply by adding **-ous**, though some modify the stem slightly, by telescoping a letter as in *wondrous,* or respelling the final consonant as in *prodigious.* (See **-er>-r** and **-y>-i-**.) In a few cases, the adjective in **-ous** parallels a noun ending in *-ion* or *-ity:*

> *cautious*   *caution*
> *capacious* *capacity*

(See **-ious** for other examples.) The **-ous** corresponds to latinate adjectives ending in *-ose,* and there are a few parallel formations (see **-ose**).

Some adjectives ending in **-ous** contrast with a semantically related noun ending in *-us,* especially scientific pairs of words such as:

adjective	noun
fungous	*fungus*
humous	*humus*
mucous	*mucus*
(o)estrous	*(o)estrus*
phosphorous	*phosphorus*

In fact the noun/adjective distinction is not systematically observed, partly because the nouns are all much more common. The adjective *fungous* makes no showing in CCAE or the BNC, nor does *humous* – except as an alternative spelling for the Arabic dish *hummus* (see **hummus**). Only for *mucous* are there enough examples in both databases to show understanding of the contrast with *mucus,* although the data also have *mucous* occasionally used as a noun (*full of mucous*). *Phosphorous* too is used as a noun (at least in nontechnical writing), as in *It gives the algae nitrogen and phosphorous.* Half the examples in the BNC and almost all in CCAE used *phosphorous* where *phosphorus* might have been expected. Meanwhile the nouns are often used attributively, as in *(o)estrus cycle, mucus membrane, phosphorus bomb,* and are taking on the categorial role of adjectives (see **adjectives** introduction). *Citrus* never gives way to *citrous* in phrases like *citrus trees* (see **citrus**). There is thus little for the **-ous** adjectives to do.

Note that in the case of *callous/callus,* the adjective and noun have moved apart. See further under **callous**.

out of and out

Most of the time, **out of** is used in the same way in British and American English. The following would be standard for speakers and writers of both varieties:

> *driven out of Africa*
> *step out of the shadows*
> *notes smuggled out of the jail*

Only with *door* and *window* are there differences. Americans are much more likely to use the curtailed form with just **out**, especially in *out the door* and *out the window*. Why these two, both relating to apertures, should be treated differently is debatable. Yet the same ones are catching on in British English, and especially *out the door*, according to research by Estling (1997). She found ample evidence of their use in spoken discourse and in published fiction, though this doesn't yet guarantee their place in British written style generally.

outdoor, outdoors and out-of-door

The first two complement each other as adjective and adverb. Compare:
>   *Enjoy the outdoor life.*
>   *Try to avoid going outdoors in very cold weather.*
Both **outdoor** and **outdoors** are used throughout the English-speaking world, whereas **out-of-door** is an occasional US alternative, as in *a healthy out-of-door appetite.*

outside of and outside

These words form a complex preposition, used in both spatial and more figurative senses:
>   *economic growth outside of London* ("not located within")
>   *little support outside of the catholic community* ("external to")
>   *there's no authority outside of me* ("apart from")
These examples, and hundreds more in BNC data, show that **outside of** is established in British English, and used across a range of prose styles for the general reader. No longer is it confined to American English. It could be edited back to just **outside** in the first and second example above, but there's no doubt that **outside of** is idiomatic for the writer, and probably helps the rhythm of the statement.

outward or outwards

See under **-ward**.

over-

This English preposition/adverb has been used to forms words with two kinds of sense:
* "above" as in *overhang, overpower, overrun, overthrow*
* "excessive" as in *overdone, overdue, overemphasis, oversupply*
Words with **over-** are rarely hyphenated in either British or American English.

overawing or overaweing

Regularity seems to prevail here, with **overawing** endorsed by two thirds of respondents to the Langscape Survey (1998–2001). A Google search of the internet (2003) endorsed it even more strongly, with **overaweing** found in less than 2% of instances of the word. The dominant spelling maintains the general rule for dropping final *e* from the verb stem (see **-e** section 1), though it's not to be taken for granted.

overflowed or overflown

Overflowed is the past form of *overflow*, in both physical and figurative senses:
>   *A drain had overflowed at the end of the road.*
>   *The church overflowed with people.*

As the examples show, **overflowed** serves for past tense as well as past participle.
   Overflown is the past participle of the rare verb *overfly*:
>   *A Peruvian helicopter had overflown Ecuadorian territory.*
The past tense is *overflew,* as in: *Iraqi aircraft overflew Tehran.*

overlay or overlie

These two converge in many of their uses, by virtue of their meaning as well as their grammar. The idea of lying physically over and above is strong in **overlie**, so the word lends itself to scientific description:
>   *the clays which overlie the chalk*
>   *coarse outer hairs which overlie the thick insulating underfur*
The past tense of **overlie** is **overlay**, as in:
>   *The early road clearly overlay a burnt horizon.*
>   *He spoke in a barely audible growl which overlay controlled anger.*
Its past participle is *overlain:*
>   *Organic-rich silt is overlain by glacial till.*
Overlay involves the affixing of a layer or special surface to an object, as in printing and other crafts:
>   *The area was concreted and overlaid with mosaic marble.*
However the verb lends itself to figurative applications, as in:
>   *If we overlay the model that we came up with . . .*
>   *Panama's nationalism is more than usually overlaid with issues of race.*
Note that *overlaid* serves as past participle and as the simple past tense.
   Overlie and **overlay** come closer even than *lie* and *lay* because both are transitive (see **lie or lay**). While most geological examples in the BNC have **overlie**/*overlain,* there are some with **overlay**/*overlaid,* as in *sediments have overlaid the older rocks.* The verb **overlie** is given the meaning "smother by lying on," yet the BNC has *a village woman overlaid her baby last summer.* In figurative uses the two are even harder to separate, and it becomes somewhat moot as to which it should be. One can certainly decide the issue by whether the layer or covering seems to be consciously applied, so you would then speak of the pessimism *overlying* a letter, and of fine words *overlaying* her suspicions. In those present participle forms, the two verbs contrast most clearly. But the other forms are too close for comfort, and crossover (mostly from **overlie** to **overlay**) is the result. It probably reflects the general impact of *lay* on *lie*. Be that as it may, the verb **overlay** is taking on most of the fresh figurative applications in BNC data, and looks likely to eclipse the other, sooner or later.

overlook, oversee and oversight

The first two words are established verbs, with quite different meanings. **Oversee** means "supervise" or "manage," as in:
>   *He was appointed to oversee the building of the factory.*
Overlook can mean quite literally "look over," as in:
>   *Their window overlooked the garden.*
More often it's used in the abstract sense "fail to take into account" as in:
>   *They overlooked the need to check the tides.*

Oversight provides an abstract noun for that second meaning of **overlook**, as in:

> By an oversight we did not send the collateral agreement along with the publishing agreement.

In bureaucratic management, **oversight** is also the noun corresponding to **oversee**:

> He is responsible for the oversight and declaration of expenses.
> Local authority social service departments have oversight of all who need domiciliary care.

The phrase *have oversight* is sometimes compacted into a simple verb, as in:

> The department will oversight the domiciliary care program . . .

This newish use of **oversight** as a verb is also associated with the bureaucracy, in British examples in the BNC, and some from Australia (Peters, 1995). American examples provided by Garner (1998) come from corporation-speak. Dictionaries in the northern hemisphere have yet to recognize **oversight** as a verb, and are perhaps reluctant because of stylistic objections to it. Still it exists by *transfer* (from noun to verb class) like many an English verb (see **transfers**). Its connotations of higher authority and responsibility make it distinct from the verb **oversee**.

overly

This adverb meaning "excessively" seems to have originated in the US in C18. It has steadily gained ground in the UK, by the note in the *Oxford Dictionary* (1989), and by its use in everyday writing in almost 150 BNC texts. It occurs in various kinds of analysis, whether focused on:

> the demise of the overly modest bathing costume

or

> not being overly concerned about the future

Despite suggestions that **overly** is an unnecessary word – which could be replaced by "too" or "excessively" – it fills the niche between them in terms of bulk. **Overly** is equally useful in noun and verb phrases, as shown in those examples, whereas "too" is awkward in the noun phrase, and "excessively" rather an overkill in either. One other alternative is to use the adverbial prefix *over-*, creating compounds such as *overmodest, overconcerned,* though this works better with the second type (adjective / past participle) than the first (a simple adjective). See further under **over-**.

overstatement

For the rhetorical effects of **overstatement** and *understatement*, see **understatements**.

overtone or undertone

Their prefixes make these look like a complementary pair, and we might even expect them to contrast. Yet often there's little to choose between them, when applied to the special effect or characteristics of a piece of communication. Should it be *overtones of arrogance* or *undertones of arrogance*?

Various distinctions have been proposed. Fowler argued that **overtones** were the implications of words, on the analogy of *musical overtones* which are the higher notes produced by a vibrating string above the note actually struck. **Undertones** are explained in terms of an undercurrent, something embedded in an utterance and inferrable from it. This would allow us to draw a distinction between the pervasive quality of a text (its *undertone*), and the more explicit **overtones** of words and phrases in it. How useful and usable such a distinction would be in a given case is another question. Sheer frequency suggests that **overtone(s)** is the more useful of the two, with more than twice as many instances in the BNC, in comparison with **undertone(s)**.

ovum

The plural is **ova**, as for other Latin loanwords used in scientific English. See **-um**.

owing to or due to

See under **due to**.

oxidation and oxidization

The abstract noun for the verb *oxidize* is **oxidation** rather than **oxidization**, according to the major dictionaries. This is confirmed by their relative frequencies in the BNC, where **oxidation** outnumbers **oxidization**/*oxidisation* by about 12:1. **Oxidation** was the earlier word, borrowed from French and first used by English scientists late in C18. It seems to have held its own against **oxidization**/*oxidisation,* which are derivatives of *oxidize/oxidise,* first recorded in earlier C19.

oxymoron

When words incongruous or opposite in meaning are combined in the same phrase, they form an **oxymoron**, a paradoxical *figure of speech* (see further under that heading). Everyday examples are the aphorism *Hasten slowly* and the cliché *thunderous silence.* An American example is the word *sophomore* ("a second-year student"), which is explained by *Webster's Third* (1986) as meaning "wise-foolish." The band *Limp Bizkit* makes the most of the *oxymoronic* effect, whatever the quality of its music.

Like other Greek loanwords ending in *-on,* **oxymoron** has a plural in **oxymora** (see **-on**) as well as an English **oxymorons**. The silence of *New Oxford* (1998) on this issue argues for consent to the English plural, whereas *Merriam-Webster* (2000) specifically mentions **oxymora**. Yet there are no examples of *oxymora* in American data from CCAE, and almost a score of **oxymorons** – suggesting that this is the de facto plural for most writers.

The term **oxymoron** is sometimes stretched in reference to ad hoc and unthinking juxtapositions of words which create a contradiction in terms. For example:

> It's been a night of near misses as far as direct hits are concerned.

Examples like these do not meet the essential syntactic criterion of being within the same phrase (noun or verb), nor do they create any "epigrammatic effect," as *Webster's* defines it. But perhaps they constitute "oxymoronism" – the word coined in 1992 by Australian columnist and playwright Alex Buzo.

Oz

See under **Australia**.

-p/-pp-

Words ending in **-p** generally conform to the common English spelling rules when suffixes are added (inflectional or derivational: see **suffixes**). Monosyllables with a simple vowel double the *p*, witness:

clapping   flipper   floppy   stepped

Words of more than one syllable, including an unstressed one before the **-p**, do not double it:

*chirruped   developer   enveloped   galloping
gossipy   scalloped   walloping*

All these are perfectly regular, throughout the English-speaking world (see **doubling of final consonant**). But the pattern begins to fray at the edges with verbs whose second element coincides with a simple monosyllable. *Hiccup* is regular in American English, while in British its inflected forms may have either one or two *ps*: *hiccuped* or *hiccupped* (see **hiccup**). *Kidnap* and *worship* may be spelled either way in the US, although in the UK and Australia they always have two (see **kidnapped or kidnaped**, and **worshipped or worshiped**). Canadians live with both spellings in each case. Double *p* is in fact the standard spelling everywhere for words such as *handicapped, horsewhipped, sideslipped, workshopped,* and for ad hoc creations such as *fellowshipped* and *membershipped*. Since the ordinary meaning of *ship* is irrelevant to the verbs *fellowship, membership* and *worship,* doubling the *p* seems doubly unfortunate (see **-ship**). By the same token, the double *p* in *horsewhipped, sideslipped, workshopped* etc. probably helps to identify them as compounds. It raises the broader question as to whether spelling conventions are there to represent the sequences of sounds or the internal structure of words. See further **spelling, rules and reforms** section 3.

p.

See **pp**.

pace

As a one-syllabled word this needs no explanation. But the same four letters can represent a slightly cryptic Latin loanword with two syllables and several pronunciations, including "pacy," "pah-chay" and "pah-kay." **Pace** is the ablative form of the more familiar Latin word *pax* ("peace"), so literally it means "with peace." More idiomatically it means "with the permission or pardon [of]" or "with apologies [to]" whoever is named immediately after. It offers a respectful apology for going against whatever the person named has said on the subject being discussed. Its proper use is shown in the following:

An Australian alliance with the USA need not, pace Prime Minister Holt, mean "going all the way."

As the example shows, **pace** is used with the name of a person (or their title) immediately following. It

expresses polite disagreement with some notable statement or opinion expressed by that person. Note that it's not a referencing device like *vide*, or an alternative to *e.g.* for introducing an example. **Pace** may be set in italics as *Webster's English Usage* (1989) recommends, although with a name or title always following, it's unlikely to be mistaken or misread.

◊ For a different use of the same word, in *requiescat in pace,* see **RIP**.

pacifist or pacificist

In British English only **pacifist** is current, by BNC evidence, and it alone is registered in *New Oxford* (1998). In American English both **pacifist** and **pacificist** are current, though the first is very much more frequent in CCAE, by a factor of 200:1. The data challenge Garner's comment (1998) that **pacificist** is "lamentably common" in the US.

paederast

See **pederast**.

paediatrician and paediatrics

See under **pediatrician**.

paedophile and paedophilia

See under **pedophile**.

page, homepage and webpage

Through all the centuries in which books have been the primary mode of publishing, the word **page** has been uncomplicated. Most people simply use it for one of the printed sides of any leaf of a book, as in *The novel takes 300 pages to set the scene*. Those concerned with the making of books may also use **page** to refer to the individual *leaf*. Dictionaries all confirm this additional sense of **page** – and the potential for confusion between the senses.

This pales into insignificance beside the use of **page** on the internet, where it refers to quite variable lengths of text. It can be used for the rather small amount of text displayed on the computer screen at any one time, which varies with the browser, and changes as you scroll forward and backward. More technically, **page** refers to a whole hypertext document, whatever its length and structure, or to indexed sections of it. Their identity as *webpages* depends on being individually indexed with their own *metadata,* for searching by internet browsers (see **metadata**).

Hypertext documents always begin with a **homepage**, the screenful that greets the eyes at the start of a visit to any *website*. It serves as a brass plate or advertising billboard or table of contents or tour guide – or combinations thereof – according to the nature of the site.

◊ On the question of whether **homepage** and **webpage** should be spaced or set solid, see individual entries.

paid or payed

See under **payed**.

pajamas or pyjamas

See **pyjamas**.

Pakistan

This name was coined to unite the predominantly Muslim provinces of western India. The two components of **Pakistan** mean "peace"/"land," but it also works rather like an acronym, with letters from each of the five provinces involved:

Punjab
Afghan province (properly called North West Frontier Province)
Kashmir
SInd (the S and I are reversed)
BaluchisTAN

The name **Pakistan** was taken up after the partition of India in 1947, and applied to the single nation newly created out of Muslim states on both western and eastern sides of India, which were then *West Pakistan* and *East Pakistan* respectively. However the two had little in common apart from their religion. Major cultural differences, and sheer geographical separation prevented any real unification between the two, and, after years of civil war, the two formally separated in 1971. The eastern provinces renamed themselves *Bangladesh*, and the name **Pakistan** reverted to being that of the western provinces alone. Their official name is the *Islamic Republic of Pakistan*.

palate or pallet

See under **palette**.

paleo-/palaeo-

This Greek prefix meaning "very old, ancient" is probably most familiar in *paleolithic*. The words it forms in English are rarely household words, though scholars in both sciences and humanities know it in one or more of the following:

pal(a)eobotany	pal(a)eo-ecology
pal(a)eogeography	pal(a)eogeology
pal(a)eomagnetism	pal(a)eontology

When the following word begins with *o* or *a*, pal(a)eo- often becomes pal(a)e-, as in *pal(a)earctic*. The spelling with the *ae* digraph has prevailed in the UK, and in Australia, while plain *e* is standard in the US and Canada. The general arguments for simplifying it to *e* are set out at **ae/e**. The particular ones in this case are that the *ae* puts too much weight on an unstressed syllable, and makes a monstrous string of vowels – with which a hyphen is mandatory when the following stem begins with *e*, as in *palaeo-ecology* etc. Though the sequence looks less cumbersome with the *ae* printed as a ligature, the facilities to print ligatures are denied to most of us. The pronunciation of **paleo-** is more accurately represented without the *a* in the second syllable, and the word is perfectly recognizable without it. In the Langscape survey (1998–2001), a majority (61%) of the 1160 respondents worldwide endorsed the spelling with just *e* in *paleolithic*.

palette, pallette, pallet or palate

The first three words derive from a diminutive of the Latin word *pala* ("spade"). That flat shape becomes the **palette** on which artists mix their colors, and as **pallette** it was the name for a particular plate of metal in the armpit of a medieval suit of armor. With the spelling trimmed to **pallet**, it was the name of a tool used by the potter to smooth the clay being worked on the wheel. In modern industries, **pallet** is applied to the movable wooden platform on which goods are stored before transportation.

But the spelling **pallet** also represents an unrelated word for a mattress of straw, derived from the French word for straw: *paille*. And **palate** ("roof of mouth"), which is pronounced in exactly the same way as all of the above, is also unrelated, derived from Latin *palatum*.

Apart from their likeness in sound, **palette** and **palate** can almost overlap in meaning when each is figuratively extended. The image of the artist's **palette** is sometimes extended to mean "range of colors," while **palate** is quite often a substitute for "taste," based on the old idea that the taste buds were in the roof of the mouth. So either **palette** or **palate** might be used in an impressionistic comment about the rich tones of a new musical composition. It depends on whether the writer is thinking of the color or the flavor of the music.

palindrome

A **palindrome** is a word or string of them which can be read either forwards or backwards with the same meaning. Words which are **palindromes** include *noon, level, madam*. Longer examples include:

don't nod! (injunction to bored audience)
revolt lover! (goodbye to romance and all that)
step on no pets! (warning as you enter premises of an incorrigible cat breeder)
red rum sir is murder (I'd settle for a beer)

Few **palindromes** get put to a serious purpose. The only well-known exception is *a man, a plan, a canal, Panama!* used, as it were, to hail the work of Goethals, the US army engineer who completed the canal's construction in 1914, after decades of setbacks.

Those addicted to **palindromes** are also conscious of the next best thing, i.e. words or phrases which can be read both ways but with a different meaning each way, such as:

dam/mad *devil/lived* *regal/lager*
stressed/desserts

There is no standard name for them, though one addict has proposed "semordnilap" for reasons which will be apparent.

pallette, pallet, palette or palate

See **palette**.

pan-

This Greek element meaning "all" is embedded in loanwords such as:

panacea	pandemic	pandemonium
panegyric	panorama	pantechnicon
pantheist		

In modern English **pan-** has spawned only a few technical terms, e.g. *panchromatic* for a type of film sensitive to all colors of the rainbow. Its more public use is as an element of proper names, for international institutions such as the *Pan-Pacific Congress*, and *Pan-American* for a former US airline.

pandemic, epidemic or endemic

See **endemic**.

pandit or pundit

See **pundit**.

paneled or panelled, and paneling or panelling

The choice between these is partly a matter of regional identity, with American writers preferring the single-*l* spellings and the British using double-*l*. But the 1998–2001 Langscape survey also showed that electronic communicators (i.e. those who responded and presumably wrote on the internet) were more likely to use the single-*l* spellings. See further under -l-/-ll-.

panic

As a verb, **panic** can be construed in several ways:

I panicked   I was panicking   I was panicked

Whether these all mean the same is debatable. They present different angles perhaps, in that *I panicked* makes the **panic** an event; *I was panicking* dwells on the emotion; and *I was panicked* hints at an external cause. But the three aspects fall together in comments like *I was scared but not panicked*. The passive construction (*be panicked*) is increasingly used to describe a heightened level of anxiety rather than fear of death – more often in the US than the UK, by the evidence of CCAE and the BNC. Yet American and British writers both use *panicked into,* to describe acting under pressures which are scarcely matters of life or death. For example:

My mother was panicked into retiring.
We should not be panicked into top-down solutions.

As a passive adjective, *panicked* covers the range from fear of death (*a horde of panicked civilians*) to loss of income (*panicked investors*) to the social faux pas requiring *a panicked phone call*. While *panicked* adds an emotive edge, it just might be in danger of becoming a cliché.

◊ For other words like **panic** which "double" their final letter with a *k*, see -c/-ck-.

paparazzi

This is the Italian plural for the pushy photographers whose candid shots of celebrities have made them notorious. Its Italian singular is **paparazzo**, also used in English, yet rarely seen because of their habit of working in groups. This is sometimes underscored in references to *a horde of paparazzi* or *thousands of paparazzi*. It remains implicit in *the paparazzi,* the phrase in which the word is couched in two thirds of BNC examples and all those in CCAE. Whatever the phrasing, **paparazzi** is normally construed in the plural:

There were paparazzi present for each drink and each kiss.

The smallest hint that it could turn into a countable noun is there in:

JP is a low-life "shutterbug" – that's paparazzi to you . . .

The corollary would be an English plural "paparazzis." There are no signs of this in the BNC or CCAE, though Garner (1998) reports a few American examples.

papaya, papaw or pawpaw

See **pawpaw**.

Papua New Guinea

Both culturally and linguistically **Papua** and **New Guinea** are separate entities, and they were managed by different colonial powers until the end of World War I. In C19 **Papua** was administered by Britain, and **New Guinea** by Germany. However **Papua** was ceded to Australia in 1905, and **New Guinea** became Australia's mandated territory by resolution of the League of Nations after World War I. Australia has since then administered the two together, and they were forged into a single unit through independence in 1972, with the double-barreled name – but with no hyphen. Citizens refer to themselves in full as *Papua New Guineans*, though those from **Papua** have been known to describe themselves as just *Papuans*. Fortunately the whole nation is united by the use of a common lingua franca: *tok pisin* (also known as *New Guinea pidgin* or *Neo-Melanesian*). In it, **Papua New Guinea** is called *Niugini*, a neat and distinctive title. For more about *New Guinea pidgin*, see **pidgins**.

As a geographical term, **New Guinea** refers to the whole island, and therefore includes not only **Papua New Guinea**, but also *West Irian*, or *Irian Jaya* – once a Dutch territory, but now part of Indonesia.

papyrus

For the plural of this word, see **-us** section 1.

para-

These letters represent three different prefixes, one Greek, one derived from Latin and a third which has evolved in modern English. The first, meaning "alongside or beyond" is derived from Greek loanwords such as *paradox, parallel, paraphrase, parasite*. Fresh uses of it are mostly found in English scholarly words such as:

par(a)esthesia   paralanguage   paramnesia
paraplegic   parapsychology   parataxis

Note that before a word beginning with *a*, the prefix becomes just *par-*.

The second prefix involving the letters **para-** comes to us through French loanwords such as *parachute* and *parasol*. They embody an Italian prefix meaning "against," a development of the Latin imperative *para* – literally "be prepared."

Parachute is itself the source of the third meaning for **para-**, found in recent formations such as the following:

parabrake   paradropper   paraglider
paratrooper

All such words imply the use of the *parachute* in their operation.

Paramedic may involve either the first or the third use of **para-**. When referring to the medical personnel who provide auxiliary services besides those of doctors and nurses, it belongs with the first set of scholarly words above. But when it's a doctor or medical orderly in the US armed forces, who parachutes in to wherever help is needed, the word is clearly one of the third group.

parable

A **parable** uses a simple story to teach a moral truth. The word has strong biblical associations, as the word applied in New Testament Greek to the didactic stories of Jesus Christ. But the definition applies equally to Aesop's fables. A **parable** differs from an allegory in that the latter is concerned with more than a single issue, and often involves systematic linking of the characters and events with actual history. See further under **allegory**.

paradigm

This word is widely used to mean "model," though its older use is as a "model of thinking," an abstract pattern of ideas endorsed by particular societies or groups within them. The term has been applied to the medieval assumption that the sun revolved around the earth, which has now been replaced by the opposite cosmological **paradigm** – that the earth revolves around the sun. Sociologists use the phrase *dominant paradigm* to refer to a system of social values which seems to set the pace for everyone. Rebels try to expose it with the slogan *Subvert the dominant paradigm.*

Paradigm is also a synonym for the word "model" in a different sense, that of "exemplar," used in many kinds of prose from the religious to the secular, for people and institutions:

> *Christ, the paradigm of perfect humanity . . .*
> *the paradigm for the village school*
> *He was hardly the paradigm of the bookish politician.*
> *Japan is many people's paradigm of how finance should serve industry.*

This use of the word makes a tautology of the phrase *paradigm case*, as some have argued. It is nevertheless fully recognized in the *Oxford Dictionary* (1989).

The word **paradigm** has long been used in grammars to refer to the set of different word forms used in the declension or conjugation of a particular word. The often-quoted **paradigm** for the present tense of the Latin verb *amare* ("love") is:

amo	"I love"
amas	"you love" (singular)
amat	"he/she/it loves"
amamus	"we love"
amatis	"you love" (plural)
amant	"they love"

For a given context you select the form of the word you need. This idea of selecting one out of a vertical set of options has been extended in modern linguistics to refer to the alternative words or phrases which might be selected at a given point in a sentence. See for example the various paradigms in:

Several	*new staff*	*begin*	*on Monday.*
A few	*employees*	*commence*	*next Monday.*
A number of	*assistants*	*start*	*next week.*

The use of **paradigm** in this last sense is the basis on which linguists speak of the *paradigmatic axis* of language, as opposed to its *syntagmatic axis*. For more about the latter, see under **syntax**.

paradise

When things are so good it seems like heaven, there are plenty of adjectives to express the feeling. In fact there's a confusion of choice:

paradisiac	*paradisaic*	*paradisic*
paradisiacal	*paradisaical*	*paradisical*
paradisial	*paradisal*	
paradisian	*paradisean*	

Though the major dictionaries give separate entries to several of these, their crossreferencing shows which is preferred: *New Oxford* (1998) makes it *paradisal* and *Merriam-Webster* (2000) *paradisiacal*. This accords well with corpus data for British and American English respectively. For writers in the BNC it's clear

that shorter is better, and *paradisal* outnumbers its nearest rival (*paradisiacal*) by 3:1. American writers are more pluralistic, but the majority prefer *paradisiacal,* by the evidence of CCAE.

paragraphs

For those who cast a casual eye down the page, **paragraphs** are just the visual units that divide up a piece of writing. *Paragraph breaks* promise relief from being continuously bombarded with information. The start of each **paragraph** is still marked by an indent in most kinds of writing and (print) publishing. But in business letters and electronic publishing the trend is to set even the first line of each **paragraph** out at the left hand margin (= "blocked format"). See further under **indents**, **letter writing** and Appendix VII.

For the reader, **paragraphs** should correlate with units of thought or action in the writing. They should provide digestible blocks of information or narrative, by which the reader can cumulatively absorb the whole. Ideally (at least in informative and argumentative writing) the **paragraph** begins with a *topic sentence*, which signals in general terms whatever it will focus on. The following **paragraph** shows the relationship between topic sentence and the rest:

> *In Sydney it's commonly said – and perhaps believed – that Melbourne is the wetter place. The facts are quite different. Sydney's rainfall in an average year is almost twice that of Melbourne, and in a bad year, a lot more. Suburban flooding is a much more frequent problem in Sydney than in Melbourne . . .*

The first sentence says what the **paragraph** is about, the notion that Melbourne is a wetter place (than Sydney). Note that the second brief sentence in fact combines with it to show what the **paragraph** is intended to do, and also works as a kind of topic sentence. Following the statement of the topic, there are specific points to back it up, and so a **paragraph** forms a tightly knit unit around a particular idea.

Readers (especially busy ones) appreciate having topic sentences that flag the point or content of each **paragraph**, and thus outline the structure of the argument.

1 How long should paragraphs be? What is considered normal in length varies with the context. Many newspapers use *one-sentence paragraphs* in their ordinary reporting – presumably because they are conscious of the visual effect of longer ones, and are less concerned about giving their readers information in significant units. In scholarly writing and in institutional reports, **paragraphs** are often quite long – as if shorter ones might imply only cursory attention to an issue. For general purposes, **paragraphs** from three to eight sentences long are a suitable size for developing discussion, and some publishers recommend an upper limit of five or six sentences. **Paragraphs** which threaten to last the whole page certainly need scrutiny, to see whether the focus has actually shifted and a new **paragraph** is needed.

2 Continuity of paragraphs. Paragraphs need to be in an appropriate order for developing the subject matter. The connections between them can then be made unobtrusively – often embedded in the topic sentence. In the following example, a small but sufficient link with what's gone before is provided by means of the word *different:*

> *A different approach to marketing fiction*
> *paperbacks might be to develop automatic*
> *vending machines for them, to be installed at*
> *railway stations, bus terminals and airports ...*

The word "different" reminds readers that at least one other "approach" has already been discussed, and cues them to expect a contrasting strategy now. It thus achieves two kinds of cohesion with what went before. For a range of other *cohesive devices,* see under **coherence or cohesion**, and **conjunctions**.

Writing guides sometimes advocate including a cohesive or transitional device at the end of each **paragraph**, as well as at the beginning of the next. This becomes very tedious if done over every *paragraph break* – and is not necessary if there's adequate cohesion at the start of new **paragraphs** with what has gone before.

parakeet or parrakeet

Some dictionaries present these as alternative spellings for the colorful tropical bird, but usage in both the US and the UK seems to have swung strongly behind **parakeet**. It is the only spelling in data from the BNC and CCAE, and foregrounded in *New Oxford* (1997), *Merriam-Webster* (2000), the *Canadian Oxford* (1998) and the Australian *Macquarie* (1997).

The spelling **parrakeet** preferred by *Webster's Third* (1986) would underscore the word's connections with *parrot* and French *perroquet*. Other possibilities however are the Spanish *periquito*, or Italian *parochetto*. Both French and Spanish explanations make **par(r)akeet** a diminutive of the name *Peter* (French *Pierre,* Spanish *Pedro*). Whatever the source, the alternative spellings with single/double consonants are symptomatic of it being an isolated loanword in English: see **single for double**.

parallel

This word is well endowed with *l*s, and so the final *l* is not normally doubled when suffixes of any kind are added to it. Hence *parallelism* and *parallelogram,* as well as *paralleled* and *paralleling*. Spellings with one *l* are endorsed in current American, Canadian and British dictionaries; although *parallelled* and *parallelling* would be in line with conventional British doubling of final *l* (see under **-l-/-ll-**). Fowler (1926) however weighed in against subjecting **parallel** to the doubling rule, and most British writers agree with him, judging by the fact that *paralleled* outnumbers *parallelled* by more than 25:1 in the BNC.

parallel constructions

Presenting comparable or contrasting thoughts in a **parallel construction** is an effective way of drawing attention to their similarities and differences. Many ordinary observations become memorable sayings or aphorisms with the help of parallelism:

> *Least said soonest mended.*
> *Run with the hare and hunt with the hounds.*

Identical grammatical structures bind together the two contrasting parts of these sayings, with telling effect.

Any writer can create **parallel constructions** to draw attention to ideas which complement or contrast with each other. See for example:

> *The traveller doesn't need to go outside*
> *Australasia for sightseeing, or to see the best, get*

> *the best or do the best this planet affords ...* (G. D.
> Meudell)

Whatever the validity of the view, it gains rhetorical force from the three parallel points, grammatically matched so that all can be read in connection with the final clause.

Parallel constructions do have to be exactly matched. Sentences whose grammar nearly matches – but not quite – make difficult reading:

> *The speaker was not able to hold their attention,*
> *nor his jokes to amuse them.*

In that example of *faulty parallelism,* the use of correlative *not–nor* cannot make up of the lack of a plural verb in the second statement (it cannot be borrowed or "read" from the first statement). The benefits of parallelism are easily compromised by noncorrespondence of the two parts, and the result is stylistically worse than if there had been no hint of parallelism at all. But with some simple changes, the parallelism is secure:

> *The speaker was unable to hold their attention, or*
> *to amuse them with his jokes.*

Correlatives such as *not–nor, neither–nor* can be used to create **parallel constructions** in the negative. Positive sets can be phrased with *either–or* when the points are alternatives; and with *not only – but also* or *both – and* when one point is added to another. See further under individual headings.

paralyze or paralyse

Americans make **paralyze** their standard spelling, where the British have **paralyse**. There are however a few examples of **paralyze** (and its inflected forms) in the BNC, scattered over written and spoken texts. See further under **-yze/-yse**.

paranoid, paranoiac and paranoic

All three serve as nouns and adjectives to describe someone suffering from *paranoia,* either in the clinical sense of a severe mental disturbance, or the ordinary sense of an anxiety that makes someone hypersensitive or suspicious. Psychiatrists prefer to keep **paranoiac** for the clinical meaning, and leave **paranoid** to the general public for the ordinary meaning – a distinction reflected in some dictionaries. Database evidence from the US and the UK shows rather that **paranoid** is far commoner than **paranoiac** (by about 20:1 in CCAE and the BNC). They also show that **paranoiac** is used nonclinically more often than not, as in:

> ... *the almost paranoiac feeling that machines*
> *will take over ...*

Paranoic is the least common of the three words, and almost always nonclinical in its application:

> *"They're paranoic here about secrecy," a Palace*
> *source said.*

For the adverb, dictionaries register **paranoiacally** as well as **paranoically**, but there's scant evidence of either in the databases.

paraphernalia

This cumbersome Latin loanword for a mix of objects, more (or less) physical, is plural in form. But in English **paraphernalia** is often collective in sense, whether it refers to a mass of equipment, as in *the paraphernalia of an intensive care unit,* or the trappings of an institution, as in *the paraphernalia of capitalism – banks, mortgages.* Collective uses of

paraphernalia foster its construction in the singular: *there was drug paraphernalia all over the house,* and both *New Oxford* (1998) and *Merriam-Webster* (2000) allow for singular or plural agreement. See further under **collective nouns**.

paraphrase

A **paraphrase** finds an alternative way of saying something. Dr. Samuel Johnson demonstrated the art of it when, according to Boswell, he first commented that a contemporary drama "has not wit enough to keep it sweet," and immediately afterwards turned it into:

> *It has not vitality enough to preserve it from putrefaction.*

In that famous case, the **paraphrase** has also effected a style change, from plain Anglo-Saxon language to rather formal latinate language. The stylistic change could of course go in the opposite direction – further down the scale of informality:

> *Not enough spark to keep it lively.*

People use **paraphrases** for any of a number of reasons. A style may need adapting to communicate with a different audience from the one originally addressed. So a technical document may need extensive *paraphrasing* for the lay reader. A piece which is written for silent reading may need to be revised for a listening audience.

Paraphrase works best with whole phrases and ideas, not by finding new words for particular slots in the old sentence. (The example quoted from Johnson above is rather limited in this respect.) By totally recasting the sentence you can achieve a more consistent style, and more idiomatic English.

parasitic or parasitical

The first is far more common than the second in the US and the UK. **Parasitic** outnumbers **parasitical** by 12:1 in data from CCAE and the BNC. There are relatively more instances of **parasitical** in spoken discourse, but writers clearly find **parasitic** long enough. See further under **-ic/-ical**.

parataxis

This is an another term for grammatical *coordination.* See under **clauses** section 2.

parcel

For the spelling of this word when verb suffixes are added to it, see **-l-/-ll-**.

parentheses

This is the standard name for *round brackets* in the US and Canada, and increasingly in Australia (see **brackets** section 1a). In the UK **parentheses** is still mostly a technical term, by BNC evidence, where it appears in scientific and bureaucratic documents. But overall British writers are about three times more likely to use *in brackets* than *in parentheses.*
◊ For the punctuation associated with **parentheses,** see **brackets** sections 2 and 3.

parenthesis

This is a grammatical term for a string of words interpolated into a sentence but syntactically independent of it:

> *The old woman had managed (heaven knows how) to move the cupboard in front of the door.*

The brackets (or *parentheses,* see previous entry) put bounds on the *parenthetical* comment. A pair of dashes would also have served the purpose. Paired commas are sometimes used but are not ideal: they imply a closer interrelationship between **parenthesis** and the host sentence than there actually is. For other punctuation associated with *parentheses,* see **brackets** section 2.

Because a **parenthesis** interrupts the reading of the host sentence, it should not be too long, nor introduce tangential material which could and should be kept for its own sentence. In examples like the one above, the **parenthesis** is brief and simply adds in an authorial comment on the main point.

parenthetical or parenthetic

The longer spelling is more popular than the shorter one, in both British and American English. But while **parenthetical** is the only spelling to be found in CCAE data, it shares the field with **parenthetic** in data from the BNC, where the ratio between them is more like 5:2. See further under **-ic/-ical**.

parlay or parley

In North American English, **parlay** is a kind of wager which doubles the previous winnings. The risks involved are worlds apart from those of the **parley**, a discussion between warring parties to decide the terms of surrender.

Both come into English via French, but where **parley** derives from standard French *parler* ("talk"), **parlay** is a French remake (*paroli*) of Neopolitan Italian *paralo* ("a pair").

parliament

The pronunciation of this word confounds its spelling, which has been quite variable even up to a century ago. In earlier times the second syllable was spelled with just *a*, just *e* and just *y* or *i*. The standard spelling comes from Anglo-Latin *parliamentum* (with the Middle English *parli* written into the Latin root *parla-*). The Anglo-Latin spelling began to be recorded in English documents from C15, and became the regular spelling in C17.

parlor or parlour

See under **-or/-our**.

parody

A **parody** is a humorous or satirical imitation of a literary work (or any work of art). It usually keeps the form and style of the original work, or the genre to which it belongs, applying them to rather different subject matter. Its purpose may be to debunk the original, or to express a fresh comment through it. In the example below, Dorothea Mackellar's passionate poem about the Australian landscape is reworked as a satirical commentary on suburban development. Mackellar's original version appears on the left, and the **parody** by Oscar Krahnvohl on the right:

I love a sunburnt country	*I love a sunburnt country*
A land of sweeping plains	*A land of open drains*
Of rugged mountain ranges	*Mid-urban sprawl expanded*
Of droughts and flooding rains	*For cost-accounting gains*
I love her far horizons	*Broad, busy bulldozed acres*

I love her jewelled sea

Her beauty and her terror
The wide brown land for me

Once wastes of ferns
and trees
Now rapidly enriching
Investors overseas.

Taken on its own, Krahnvohl's verse is a vigorous satire of urban expansion at the expense of environment and community. Taken alongside Mackellar's original, it gathers extra emotional force, pointing up the betrayal of those who delight in the natural landscape. As often, the **parody** highlights contrasting value systems.

paronomasia
This is a learned word for punning. See further under **puns**.

parrakeet or parakeet
See **parakeet**.

parricide or patricide
While **patricide** is strictly "killing one's father," **parricide** covers the killing of a parent or other near relative, according to both *New Oxford* (1998) and *Merriam-Webster* (2000). In older usage **parricide** could also mean the killing of one's ruler (thought of as a father figure) as well as the crime of treason against one's country; see *Oxford Dictionary* (1989) and *Webster's Third* (1986). This wider range of uses would explain why **parricide** is more common in BNC data than **patricide** and *matricide* put together.

Yet American writers are less inclined to use **parricide**, by the evidence of CCAE, where **patricide** outnumbers **parricide** by almost 2:1. Since *matricide* is also in use, this suggests that Americans prefer the more specific terms. **Patricide** is of course more transparent than **parricide**, because of the root (Latin *pater,* "father") that it shares with *patriarch, patrimony* etc. **Parricide** meanwhile is isolated, probably based on the same root as *parent,* but visually disguised by the double *r.* In Latin the word was often spelled with just a single *r,* and in Roman law *par(r)icidium* included the killing of either father or mother.

pars pro toto
This Latin phrase, literally "part for the whole," is an alternative name for *meronymy* or *synecdoche.* See further under **synecdoche**.

part or parting
The division of the hair on one's head is a **part** in North American English (both the US and Canada), whereas in the UK and Australia it's the **parting**. All other uses of **part** and **parting** are shared.
◊ For other examples, see **inflectional extras**.

part of
In older usage, the idiom *on the part of* was used to mean "on behalf of" or "as the representative of," as in:

> *The mortgagee shall perform all covenants and agreements on the part of the lessee.*

In contemporary English, it usually means "emanating from," and the source mentioned acts on its own behalf, not for another party. For example:

> *There have been changes of mind on the part of the local authority.*
>
> *. . . unacceptable behavior on the part of cadets*

Data from the BNC and CCAE suggest that this second use is a good deal more common in American than British English.

participles
In traditional grammar terms, English has two **participles**, traditionally called *present* and *past.* The *present* ends in *-ing,* and the *past* in *-ed* for regular verbs, but with *-en* or *-n* or a change of stem vowel for others (see **irregular verbs**). The following show the various forms:

* present: *rolling taking blowing ringing*
* past: *rolled taken blown rung*

The names *present* and *past* are misnomers, since either **participle** can occur in what is technically a present or past tense. In *we were rolling,* the *present participle* combines to form the past continuous tense, and in *we have rolled* the *past participle* contributes to the present perfect.

What the **participles** really do in English is create different aspects for the verb, either *imperfect* (also known as *continuous* or *durative*) or *perfect* i.e. completed (see further under **aspect**). The **participles** also contribute to the active/passive distinction, in that the *present participle* is always active, and the past one is normally passive (see further under **voice**). The two kinds of **participle** are frequently used as adjectives in English, as in *a rolling stone* and *a rolled cigarette.* Each type is also capable of introducing a nonfinite clause, witness their role in the following sentences:

> *Rolling towards them, the tyre loomed larger every second.*
>
> *She found the papers rolled up in a cardboard tube.*

See further under **nonfinite clause**.

The *-ing* ending of the *present participle* makes it identical with the English verbal noun, though they have separate origins. The coincidence between them in some constructions has fueled grammatical controversy for more than two centuries. See further under **gerund and gerundive**.

particles
The term **particle** has been used to label various kinds of words which are difficult to categorize among the standard grammatical word classes (see **parts of speech**). **Particle** is often applied to the adverb-cum-preposition which is attached to simple English verbs, and becomes integral to their meaning, as with *take up, write off* and many more. (See further under **phrasal verbs**.) It also serves to refer to the much censured "preposition" which can occur at the end of a sentence: see **prepositions** section 2.

partly or partially
Similar, yet not identical in their grammar, these have exercised usage commentators from Fowler (1926) on. Both are adverbs meaning "in part," and can substitute for each other as subjuncts and downtoners, as in *a partly/partially demolished building.* (See further under **hedge words**.) **Partially** is in other ways more limited, used mostly to modify verbs or verbal derivatives (as in the previous example), but sometimes adjectives and other adverbs, as in:

> *Efforts to reduce residues in pork products had been partially successful.*

Partly is more versatile, able to replace **partially** in all those roles, and to modify whole phrases, witness:

> *It was partly their responsibility.*
> *This he did with difficulty, partly on account of his bad eyesight.*

Examples like this show **partly** functioning as a *disjunct,* in addition to its roles as subjunct. (See further under **adverbs** section 1.)

Note also that **partially** is stylistically somewhat formal, as *Webster's English Usage* (1989) comments. This, plus the wider range of uses for **partly,** give it much greater currency than **partially** – at least in British English. In BNC data, **partly** outnumbers **partially** by more than 4:1, whereas it's 2:1 in data from CCAE.

partner

This useful word lends itself to relationships of many types and durations. Just what kind of *partnership* is involved can be made plain in context:

> *A partner catches and returns it, and the throw is repeated ten times . . .*
> *He steps on his partner's toes.*
> *. . . meeting a partner's parents for the first time*
> *We want a minority partner.*
> *Our Japanese partner has no right to increase its shareholding.*

Yet **partner** lends itself equally to contexts where the exact nature of relationship is not to be specified, and can be deliberately ambiguous. Business and personal relationships are intertwined in the tantalizing advertisement for sophisticated conference accommodation:

> WHAT WILL YOU DO WHILE YOUR PARTNER IS MEETING HIS PARTNER?

Partner covers a variety of live-in relationships, as in the following comment:

> *If you're an experienced homicide investigator and the woman turns up dead, until you cross him off the list, the partner, be it a boyfriend, a former husband or husband, is always considered technically if not legally a suspect.*

Both married and unmarried relationships are thus covered by **partner,** and straight as well as gay ones. ◊ Compare **spouse.**

parts of speech

This is the traditional term for what are now usually called *word classes.* Either way they are the eight groups by which words may be categorized, according to their roles in sentences:

> nouns   adjectives   verbs
> pronouns   prepositions   conjunctions
> interjections   adverbs

These grammatical classes have long been the basis of dictionary classifications of words, with the addition of *articles* (*definite* and *indefinite*).

Modern English grammars such as the *Comprehensive Grammar* (1985) and the *Longman Grammar* (1999) have updated the **parts of speech** in several ways. They use the broader class of *determiner* to include both articles and certain kinds of adjectives (see **determiners**). Numerals also function as *determiners,* but are made a separate class because their other role is like that of noun or pronoun at the head of a noun phrase. There are separate classes for three types of verb (*primary, modal, full* or *lexical*), because of their distinctive roles in syntax (see

further under **auxiliary verbs**). Both the grammars mentioned would expand the class of *interjections,* so as to include a wider range of lexical items like "yes," "cheers," as well as nonlexical noises such as "hmm" and "uhhuh," which are important in spoken interaction. The *Longman Grammar* rechristens the class as "inserts," to escape the constraints of the term *interjection* (see **interjections**). Grammarians and linguists also draw attention to the divide between two broad classes of words: the "closed" and "open" sets. The first set consists of classes whose membership is relatively fixed: *determiners, pronouns, prepositions, conjunctions, auxiliary verbs.* The second includes *nouns, adjectives, adverbs, full/lexical verbs,* whose membership is open-ended and continually being expanded. The "closed"/"open" distinction correlates with that of *function words* versus *content words* (see under **words**).

The English language challenges the traditional **parts of speech** in other ways as well. Words can clearly belong to more than one class, for example *down,* which can be a noun, adjective, verb, adverb or preposition, depending on the verbal context. It proves more useful to think of word classes as representing the set of grammatical functions which a word may take on, rather than pigeon-holes for classifying words. In Latin and Greek, most words had a single function and could be seen as belonging to a particular class; whereas in English their classification varies with their function. It makes less sense to say that English words "belong" to particular classes. But the functions of English *word classes* can still be discussed under the familiar headings of noun, verb etc.; and it's still conventional to talk of words being converted or transferred from one class to another when they take on new grammatical roles. In fact this usually means an additional rather than a substitute role. See further under **transfers.**

parvenu or parvenue

In French **parvenu,** meaning "social upstart," is inflected according to gender (**parvenu** being masculine and **parvenue** feminine), and pluralized with *s,* as appropriate. But in both British and American English **parvenu** is by far the commonest form in database evidence – not that men present the most frequent or obvious cases, but rather that the word has been grammatically neutralized. Examples such as *parvenu bureaucrats* and the *parvenu heroine of the play* from the BNC and CCAE show this in attributive use, as do nonhuman applications such as the *parvenu art of photography. New Oxford* (1998) gives **parvenu** as the only spelling for both noun and adjective, whereas *Merriam-Webster* (2000) maintains separate entries for **parvenu** (noun and adjective) and **parvenue** (feminine, noun and adjective), affirming the original French distinction.

passed or past

These words are identical in sound and origin (both being derived from the verb *pass*), but only **passed** can now be used for the past tense and past participle of that verb. **Past** was used that way until about a century ago, but it's now reserved for all the other uses of the word, as adjective (*past tense*), adverb (*they marched past*), preposition (*It's past midnight*) and noun (*in the past*).

passim

This Latin word, meaning "in various places" or "throughout," is used in referencing when you want to indicate that there are relevant details at many points in the work, too many to make it worthwhile noting them all. Some would say that it's not very helpful to do this: if the references are in just one chapter, it looks rather lazy to say "chapter 6 passim" instead of giving specific page references. **Passim** is however justifiable when referring to a key word which recurs many times on successive pages; or else to an idea whose expression is diffused through the discussion and not in any fixed verbal form.

As a foreign word and/or as a referencing device, **passim** may be set in italics rather than roman. Yet editorial practice is changing on the setting of reference devices (see under **Latin abbreviations**), and the word can scarcely be mistaken for any other when set in roman.

passive verbs

People seem to polarize over *passives;* they're either addicted to them or inclined to crusade against them. But **passive verbs** serve some legitimate ends in grammar and style, and their use can be moderated accordingly.

1 The grammar of the passive. A **passive verb** is one in which the subject undergoes the process or action expressed in the verb, as in:

Several candidates were included on the short list.
Only two have been called for an interview.

As the examples show, **passive verbs** consist of (a) a part of the verb *be* and (b) a past participle. Between them they ensure that the subject is acted upon, and thus a passive rather than active participant in whatever is going on. *Passive constructions* emphasize the process, rather than who is performing the action, and so are called *agentless passives*. It is possible to express the agent of a *passive verb*, but only as a phrase after it:

Only two have been called by the secretary for an interview.

Even in this form, the *passive* seems to downplay the agent, not allowing it to take up the more prominent position at the start of the sentence (see further under **information focus**).

2 Style and the passive. Because **passive verbs** play down the agent (or make it invisible), they are not the stuff of lively narrative when you want to know who is doing what. Used too often, as in some academic and official styles, they make for dreary reading. Yet for institutional communication they're all too useful. In their *agentless* form (without the *by* phrase) they avoid saying who is controlling and managing the situation – which is a distinct advantage if you have to break the news that terminations are on the horizon:

The employment of staff with less than six months service will be terminated.

Such wording is less confrontational and perhaps more tactful than:

We, the senior management, will terminate the employment of staff with less than six months service.

The second version with an *active verb* puts a glaring spotlight on the people who have to do the dirty deed. *Active verbs* must have their agents expressed as the subject: see further under that heading.

◊ For the use of the *double passive* in American court reporting, see under **ordered**.

3 The passive in scientific prose. Apart from its use in official and corporate documents, the *passive* is a regular component of some kinds of science writing. Scientific reports are intended to provide objective description of experimental procedures, in terms of processes rather than people. The *agentless passive* allows the scientist to report that:

The mixture was heated to 300 °C

without saying who actually did it. Who did it is irrelevant (or should be) as far as the scientific process goes. The *passive* also allows scientists to avoid implying any particular cause and effect in their statements, and to concentrate on what happened until they are ready to look for explanations in physical laws and principles. Not all science writers rely on the *passive*, and the pressures just discussed are probably stronger in chemistry than in biology. The Council of Biology Editors in the US has pushed for more direct, active reporting of scientific observations since the 1960s, encouraging their members to counter the ingrained habit of using **passive verbs**. Kirkman's (1980) research into British science and engineering style also showed that less highly passivized writing was greatly preferred by the 2800 professionals surveyed: even reasonably well written texts in the "traditional" passive came a poor second to more direct, active writing.

Final note. The *passive* construction is not a blanket necessity, despite its traditional use in some quarters. It does serve strategic purposes here and there; and it has a place in any writer's repertoire as a resource for altering the focus of discourse and setting up a new topic at the beginning of a sentence. See further under **topic**.

past or passed
See **passed**.

past tense

Most English verbs show whether the action they refer to happened in the past, rather than the present or some indefinite time in the future. This is the point of difference between:

live/lived   send/sent   teach/taught   write/wrote

The **past tense** is often shown simply by the -(e)d suffix, as with *lived* and all regular verbs. Irregular verbs make the **past tense** in other ways, with changes to vowels and/or consonants of the stem, as illustrated by *sent/taught/wrote*. Just a handful of verbs (old ones ending in -*t* like *hit* and *put*) make no change at all from the present to the **past tense** (see under **irregular verbs**).

Only the *simple past tense* is formed by those means. For *compound past tenses*, auxiliaries are combined with one or other participle, and they in fact mark the tense:

was living (past continuous, progressive)
had been teaching (past perfect continuous)
had written (past perfect)

All such compound tenses express *aspect* as well as *tense* (see further under **aspect**).

pasta, paste, pastry, pasty, pâté or patty

All these words for food go back to the Greek word for "barley porridge." They are a tribute to the versatility of European cuisine, and all improve on the shapeless cereal of the original.

In **pasta** the focus on cereal remains, yet this staple Italian food comes in myriads of shapes: cannelloni, macaroni, ravioli, spirelli, tortellini, vermicelli etc. The English word **pastry** embodies the same root, and with the *-ry* suffix transforms the cereal substance into the medium out of which shapely pies and pie crusts can be created.

The traditional English **pasty** features both the **pastry** medium, and its meaty filling, whereas in **paste** and **pâté** the meaning has shifted away from the cereal to the prepared meat. Both **paste** and **pâté** are enjoyed in their own right, though we normally consume them with the help of other cereal items (bread or biscuits).

The English word **patty** sustains both kinds of meaning. What we cook in *patty pans* is again a cereal item, a small pie, tart or cake; whereas the *patties* cooked in a frying pan are a savory item made out of minced meat. **Paté** is often written in English without its circumflex, though the final acute accent lingers to distinguish it from the English word *pate* ("head"), as in *bald pate*. Its origins are obscure, but it may owe something to the word *paten,* the shiny ceremonial dish used in celebrating the Mass.

patella

This Latin loanword meaning a "shallow pan" has two plurals: the anglicized **patellas** and the pure Latin **patellae**. Archeologists who use the word in its Latin sense naturally prefer the Latin plural. But either plural may be used when the word means "kneecap," depending on how specialized the readership is. In prose intended for anatomists, the Latin plural is more likely than the English – but vice versa when the discussion is intended for the general reader. See further under **-a** section 1.

pathos

In the ancient art of rhetoric, **pathos** meant an appeal to the audience's sense of pity and using it to sway them. It contrasted with *ethos,* the attempt to impress the audience through the intrinsic dignity and high moral stance of the presentation. Neither **pathos** nor *ethos* is to be mistaken for *bathos:* see under that heading.

patricide or parricide

See **parricide**.

patronymic

This is a name which identifies someone in relation to his/her father or ancestor. In Britain and North America **patronymics** are most familiar to us in surnames with the suffixes *-son* or *-sen*, or the prefixes *Fitz-, Mac-* or *O'*. In Russian and some Slavic languages, there are parallel **patronymics** for the surnames of sons (*-ov*) and daughters (*-ova*), as there are in Iceland, with *-sonar* for sons and *-dottir* for daughters. The female term equivalent to **patronymic** is *metronymic* rather than "matronymic."

patty, pâté, pasty or pasta

See **pasta**.

paver, paviour or pavior

Both **paver** and **pavio(u)r** have been around since C15, nudging each other for space. The second word seems now to be falling out of use in both British and American English, leaving the field to **paver**, which serves for the person or the machine that does the *paving,* and for the *paving material* itself.

> *The paver probably doesn't have a back yard crammed with a trampoline...*
> *The concrete path paver will lay a continuous 8-foot wide path.*
> *... sweep the sand into the space between the pavers*

The rare examples of **paviour** in the BNC show that it too could mean the person who *paved* as well as the *paving stone,* so it has no advantage over **paver** in this respect. In industrial awards, a paraphrase is used to refer to the person who *paves,* such as *paving plant operator* or *paving and surfacing labo(u)rer.*

pawpaw, papaw or papaya

In British, Australian and Canadian English, all these refer to a large, soft-bodied tropical fruit with succulent orange-colored flesh. **Papaya** is the oldest of the three names, borrowed from Spanish in C15, followed by **papaw** in C16 (also based on Spanish *papaya*); and then **pawpaw** from 1902, which is tending to replace **papaw**. Australian fruit-lovers sometimes distinguish between **pawpaw** (the larger orange-fleshed variety) and **papaya** (the smaller one with bright pink flesh). But **papaya** is the most common form of the word in Britain and elsewhere.

Americans use **papaya** for the tropical fruit in all its shapes and colors, and reserve **pa(w)paw** for a native tree which is a member of the custard apple family. Its fruit is shaped like a stubby banana and rather tasteless.

payed or paid

Paid has always been the standard past tense for *pay,* whether the payment is a matter of money, attention or the loss of some advantage: *They paid for the privilege* could be either the first or third of those. The spelling **payed** is found in these senses only in unedited or rapidly edited texts, in the BNC and CCAE. But when the word refers to the *paying out* of rope or cable, as in:

> *The kite has hundreds of metres of line payed out.*

payed is the accepted spelling, endorsed by the *Oxford Dictionary* (1989) and *Merriam-Webster* (2000).

PC, p.c., pc or pc.

A miscellany of abbreviations converge on these two letters of the alphabet. The upper case abbreviation **PC** has long been used in Britain for "Police Constable" and "Privy Councillor," as well as "Parish Council" and the "Parish Councillor." In Canada it also refers to a "Progressive Conservative." All these – now written without stops – coincide with **PC** as the generic "personal computer," coined in the 1970s to distinguish it from the large mainframe computer.

Lower case **p.c.** is primarily associated with "political correctness," which appeared in the early 90s, shortly after the concept itself (see **political correctness**). In American and Canadian English, **p.c.** also abbreviates *per cent* and *post cibum* ("after meals," used in pharmaceutical prescriptions). In British and Australian English, where stops in abbreviations are disappearing more quickly, **pc** can appear in these various applications without stops.

The hybrid **pc.** is sometimes used as the abbreviation for "price" and "piece," where the single stop shows that the full form is a single word. This is a nicety, but with or without stop, **pc(.)** is unlikely to be misunderstood in its typical context, attached to numerals in a catalogue.

peaceable or peaceful

These are sometimes substituted for each other, but their normal lines of demarcation are as follows. **Peaceable** applies to a person or group of people who are disposed to keep good relations with each other. It can also be applied to human character or intentions. **Peaceful** goes with nonhuman nouns, referring to situations, periods or general activities which are calm and free of disturbance, conflict and noise.

peak, peek or pique

Because they sound alike, these verbs are sometimes mistaken for each other. The four letters of **peak** in fact represent two verbs, one of which ("become sickly") is much less familiar than the other: "reach a climax," as in *the temperature peaked at 38 degrees*. **Peek** is an informal verb meaning "take a quick or furtive look at," as in *peek out of the window,* and by extension "poke out," as in *his toes peeked through the holes*. **Pique** connects with both high and low emotional states. In *piqued their interest* it means "arouse"; and the reflexive *pique oneself on* means "pride oneself on." But the passive *was piqued about* takes on the meaning of "disappointed, resentful," which it shares with the noun **pique** (as in *a fit of pique*).

So far so good, yet the identities of these words are less clear in figurative uses and derived forms. Should it be *peaked* or *peeked* in *The morning sun peeked over La Costa?* It would of course depend on whether you meant sunrise (*peeked*) or midday (*peaked*). *Peaked* in the sense of "off-color" is also potentially confusable with the negative sense of *piqued* ("disappointed") in constructions such as "feeling peaked/piqued." Again the writer's choice impacts on the narrative.

The adjective *peaky* does double service – at least in British English – for both verbs spelled **peak**, and so can mean "sickly" as well as "having peaks." These two meanings are however distinguishable by the fact that the first meaning almost always collocates with either "look" or "feel": *you're looking a bit peaky; whereas the second is often attributive, as in *peaky swirls of cream on the cake*.

peccadillo

The plural of this word is discussed under **-o**.

peccavi

See under **mea culpa.**

pedagogue or pedagog

See **-gue/-g.**

pedaled, pedalled or peddled

See under **pedlar.**

pederast or paederast

Even in British English, **pederast** with just *e* is the standard spelling. Amid a handful of examples of the word in the BNC, it's the only spelling to be found.
◊ Compare **pedophile.**

pediatrician or paediatrician, and p(a)ediatrics

Regional preferences still hold strong in the UK and the US with **p(a)ediatrician** and **p(a)ediatrics**. In British English data from the BNC they are almost always spelled with *ae*, whereas in American English the standard is with *e*. Canadians do as the Americans do, according to the *Canadian Oxford* (1998); and a majority (60%) of the Australian professional writers surveyed in 1991 were also that way inclined – though doctors themselves demurred (Peters, 1995). See further under **ae/e.**

> **International English selection:** The spellings **pediatrician** and **pediatrics** are to be preferred because they enjoy more widespread use around the world.

pedlar, peddler or pedal(l)er

Both the British and Australians apply the first two words to different kinds of trader. **Pedlar** is the older word, applied to an older type of traveling salesman who went from village to village dealing in household commodities, including pots and pans and haberdashery. His business was quite legal, whereas the word **peddler** was and is reserved for those who deal in illegal drugs or stolen goods. (See further under **-ar.**) In the US and Canada, **peddler** is applied to both, as well as to figurative uses: *peddler in pipe dreams*.

A **pedaler** or **pedaller** is one who pedals a bicycle or other pedal-powered vehicle. The choice between single and double *l* is discussed under **-l-/-ll-.**

pedophile or paedophile, and p(a)edophilia

These terms originated in the domain of psychotherapy, but are now in everyday use as ways of referring to sexual attraction to children. They are steadily replacing *pederast/pederasty,* which are more narrowly defined as the sexual engagement of men with boys. The spelling choices between **pedophile/paedophile** and **pedophilia/paedophilia** are still a matter of divided loyalties in the UK and the US. The Langscape survey (1998–2001) confirmed the polarization with all American and Canadian respondents endorsing **pedophile,** and only 11% of the British. **Pedophile** was also preferred by a majority of Europeans responding, but marginal for Asian respondents and favored by only 30% of Australians. (See further under **ae/e.**)

> **International English selection:** The spellings **pedophile** and **pedophilia** have wider currency than those with the classical digraph *ae,* and are therefore to be preferred.

peek, peak or pique

See under **peak.**

pejorative

This un-English-looking word (sometimes misspelled as "perjorative") is used by linguists for several purposes:

1 to refer to affixes which have a derogatory effect on the word they are attached to. This is the effect of prefixes such as *mis-* and *pseudo-*, and occasionally of suffixes such as *-ose* and *-eer*. (See further under individual headings.)
2 to refer to words with disparaging implications, e.g. *hovel, wench*.
3 to refer to the process by which some words acquire negative meanings over the course of time, usually over centuries. **Pejorative** processes can be seen with the word *cretin,* formerly a word for "Christian," and *silly*, which once meant "blessed."

Peking or Beijing

The capital of China is now known worldwide as **Beijing** (see further under **China**). This reformation of the name is not however likely to affect traditional designations such as *Peking Duck*, the *Pekin(g)ese dog* or the *Peking man*. Restyled with "Beijing" the first two would lose something of their cachet, and the third, its credibility as an ancient human species.

penciled or pencilled

When *pencil* becomes a verb, it raises spelling questions. See further under -l-/-ll-.

peninsula or peninsular

Dictionaries advise that there's a grammatical distinction between these two spellings: **peninsula** is the noun and **peninsular** the adjective, as in:

> The Yucatan Peninsula is part of Mexico.
> All peninsular traffic has to exit and return by the same route.

The distinction was carefully observed in references to the *Peninsular War* – fought in the *Iberian Peninsula,* and in the *P&O*'s full name *Peninsular and Oriental Steam Navigation Company*. However in British data from the BNC, **peninsular** is mistakenly used for the noun in almost 15% of instances, in examples such as "Gower Peninsular" and "Malay Peninsular." In standard southern British pronunciation, the two sound exactly the same. The problem does not come to light at all in CCAE.
◊ For the spelling of the adjective, see under **-ar**.

penumbra

The plural of this word is discussed under **-a**.

per

This Latin preposition, meaning "through, by," has a number of uses in English, mostly as a member of stock Latin phrases which are detailed below. **Per** can also be combined with English words of the writer's own choosing for various meanings. When used in recipes, as in *200 gm cheese per person*, it means "for each," and its meaning is similar in price lists: *$25 per 100 units*. In the phraseology of commercialese, to be delivered *per courier* means "by or through the agency of." Some object to such expressions, especially when the English preposition *by* would do. Yet the meaning embedded in *per person* would be hard to express as neatly in other words.

* *per annum* means "by the year," often used after quoting a salary: *$48 500 per annum*. In job advertisements it's usually abbreviated as *p.a.*
* *per capita* means "by heads." Its usual context is in economic writing, when statistics are being presented in terms of the individual:
> The per capita consumption of wine has increased dramatically over the last three years.
* *per cent*. See **percent**.
* *per diem* means "by the day," typically used in calculating the daily cost of living away from home, apart from overnight accommodation itself. In English it also serves as a noun to refer to the allowance conceded by some institutions to traveling employees.
* *per procurationem or p.p.,* as used in correspondence. See individual entry.
* *per se* means "by itself" or "for its own sake." It distinguishes the intrinsic value of something from its ramifications:
> The discovery is of some importance per se, as well as for the directions it suggests for future industries.
In everyday American English, *per se* is increasingly used to question the application of a word:
> This is not cleanup work per se.
> I really don't have a feud per se with him.
As in these examples, the word in question is usually preceded by a negative and followed by *per se*.

per-

Chemists make productive use of this Latin prefix in the names of inorganic acids and their salts, as in *perchloride, peroxide, potassium permanganate*. **Per-** indicates that they have the maximum amount of the element specified in them. It replaces *hyper-* and *super-*, used in this sense in older chemical nomenclature.

per procurationem and p.p.

The former is the full form of a phrase we know better by the abbreviations *per proc., per pro* or just **p.p.** The full Latin phrase means "through the agency [of]," and when followed by capitalized initials it indicates who actually signed the letter, as opposed to the person in whose name it is sent. The usual convention is for **p.p.** and the proxy's initials or signature to appear just above the typed signature of the official sender.

An older convention reported by Fowler and others is for the proxy also to handwrite the official signatory's name, either before the **p.p.** or after their own initials. So a letter going out for James Lombard might be signed in either of the following ways:

> Yours sincerely   Yours sincerely
> *J. Lombard*   pp R.S.M.
> pp R.S.M.   *J. Lombard*
> J. Lombard, Manager   J. Lombard, Manager

More common than either nowadays is the simple use of **p.p.** and the proxy's initials.

The older abbreviation *per pro* (without a stop) was taken by some users to be a combination of two Latin prepositions, and to mean "for and on behalf of." In accordance with this interpretation, they would write it as *per/pro*. With decreasing knowledge of Latin in the community, this variant is disappearing.

◊ For other points of institutional letter writing, see **commercialese**, **letter writing** and Appendix VII.

percent, per cent and %

All these serve to abbreviate *per centum* ("by the hundred") – a pseudo-Latin phrase, probably based on Italian *per cento,* according to the *Oxford Dictionary* (1989). The abbreviation **per cent** saw a rapid rise from mid-C16, and it now stands in its own right without any full stop, and never in italics. Though traditionally written as two words, the standard American form is now **percent** – in principle, as indicated in the *Chicago Manual* (2003); and in practice, in regular use in data from CCAE. The *Oxford Dictionary* observes that **percent** as one word is "now frequent." Yet **per cent** is firmly maintained in the British editorial tradition: the *Oxford Guide to Style* (2002) presents it as the only form, though **percent** occurs in up to 10% of all instances in BNC data. The *Canadian Oxford* (1998) recognizes both **per cent** and **percent**, as does the Australian *Macquarie Dictionary* (1997). In Australian corpus data, **percent** appeared in about 20% of instances (Peters, 1995). The merged form shows the natural tendency for well-used Latin phrases: compare *postscript* and *subp(o)ena.*

The numbers accompanying **percent** are normally printed as figures, i.e. *10 percent,* according to the *Chicago Manual* (2003). In newspaper data from CCAE, figures are almost invariably used, for small or large percentages, i.e. whether below or above the general threshold for numbers as figures (see **numbers and number style** section 3). British newspaper data also show regular use of figures with **per cent**. But in other kinds of everyday writing in the BNC, figures and words appear about equally. Words are typically used for round numbers such as *ten per cent, fifty percent,* and also for non-round numbers that come at the start of a sentence: *Twenty-eight percent were putting off-farm income into their farms.* Either way, a space is left before **percent / per cent**.

The **percent** sign **%** is now freely used in most kinds of nonfiction, including humanistic writing that contains many percentage figures (*Chicago Manual,* 2003). The *Oxford Guide to Style* notes also its use in statistical writing in the social sciences. The symbol is always set solid with the preceding number, as in *10%*. When used in tables, the **%** sign need not be printed with every number in a column of percentages, but at the top of the column. Should the figures in the column add up to something other than exactly *100%*, the total at the bottom should be left as *99.4%* or *100.2%*, not rounded off (Butcher, 1992).

When used in continuous text, a percentage figure may take either a plural or singular verb in agreement, depending on what's under discussion. Is it plural or a mass noun? The two patterns work as follows:

Of the students who came, 10 percent were unprepared.
In the end 10 percent of the wool was rejected.

percentage

This is the fully formed abstract noun for *percent,* meaning "proportion calculated in terms of a notional population of 100." It lends itself to specifics such as a rise of *two percentage points* in interest rates or the *high percentage of silicone* in a waterproofing agent. As in these examples, **percentage** is normally quantified or qualified in some way, to pin its meaning down. The word otherwise can only mean "an unspecified proportion," as in:

A percentage of the school went to the races.

Does that mean *95 percent* or *10 percent?* The statement begins to be useful with the addition of an adjective:

A large/small percentage of the school went to the races.

Percentage is also used figuratively to mean "advantage," a sense derived from its use in specifying profit margins. For example:

There's no percentage in rushing back to the office.

When used in this sense, **percentage** is often preceded by a negative (*no,* as in that case) or by indefinites, such as *any* or *some.* Such usage is still "informal," according to *New Oxford* (1998) and the *Canadian Oxford* (1998), and "colloquial" for the Australian *Macquarie Dictionary* (1997), but *Merriam-Webster* (2000) registers it without demur.

perceptibly or perceptively

The adverb **perceptively** means "showing fine perception," implying the exercise of intelligence and critical judgement, not just powers of observation. **Perceptibly** is more closely related to what is observable. It means "able to be perceived" as in:

He was perceptibly distressed by the things that were said there.

Just how obvious an effect is, when it's described as "perceptible," can only be assessed in context. Both the adverb **perceptibly** and the adjective *perceptible* cover a wide range from the conspicuous to the barely noticeable.

perfect aspect

See under **aspect**.

perfectible or perfectable

Either spelling makes you capable of *perfection* in American English, according to *Webster's Third* (1986); and both are there in very small quantities in CCAE data. In British English it has to be **perfectible**, the only spelling to appear in BNC data, or to be registered in *New Oxford* (1998). See further under **-able/-ible**.

perhaps or maybe

See **maybe**.

peri-

This suffix, meaning "around," is embodied in Greek loanwords such as *perimeter, periphery, periscope, peristyle.* As these examples show, it's most often used in the dimension of space, and recent medical terms use it to describe a bodily structure in terms of the organ it lies around, as with *pericardium* and *periodontal.* Just occasionally it has formed words in the time dimension, as with *perinatal,* used in relation to the latest stage of pregnancy and the earliest weeks after giving birth.

period

In both the US and Canada, the term **period** is applied to the (full) stop used in word and sentence punctuation. (For a discussion of those functions, see **full stop**.) In North America **period** is also the word for the decimal point: see **numbers and number style** section 1.

◊ For issues relating to periods of time, see **dating systems**.

periodic or periodical

As nontechnical adjectives meaning "from time to time," these are interchangeable, as in *periodic/periodical payment* and *periodic/periodical outbursts*. But **periodic** is now much commoner than **periodical**, by a factor of about 10:1 in BNC data and 15:1 in CCAE. **Periodic** is also the regular form of the adjective in scientific contexts, including the *periodic table* which sets out chemical elements according to the *periodic functions* of their atomic weights.

More important for **periodical** is its role as a noun meaning "serial publication," i.e. magazine or journal, which accounts for about two thirds of all its occurrences. Note that with this meaning it can also be an attributive adjective, as in:

Thousands of newspaper and periodical articles are indexed there.

For librarians the **periodical** contrasts with the monograph (see under **monogram or monograph**).

perjurer or perjuror

Dictionaries all agree that the only acceptable spelling for one who commits *perjury* is **perjurer**. This is because it's an English formation based on the verb *perjure,* and not related to *juror,* which is a French loanword.

perma-

This prefix, newly derived from *permanent,* was put to formative use in C20, witness *perma frost* from the 1940s, and more recently *permapress* ("permanent press") and *permaculture* (that type of agriculture which is self-sustaining and does not require regular plantings).

permanence or permanency

The first is far more common than the second: see under **-nce/-ncy**.

permissive or permissible

These adjectives express complementary notions in society's control of its members. **Permissive** is the hands-off approach, tending to permit anything, as in *permissive parents.* **Permissible** implies statutory limits on what is permitted, as in *permissible levels of radiation.*

pernickety or persnickety

Dictionaries all say that this fussy word comes from Scotland, but beyond that nobody knows – so there's nothing to tie it down, one way or the other. The British prefer **pernickety**, by the evidence of the BNC, whereas Americans represented in CCAE stand united on **persnickety** – with a hint of the disdainful *sniff* embedded in it.

perpetual calendar

This remarkable tool allows us to know exactly what day of the week any date in the past or future might be. Both historians and astrologers are interested in what day of the week people are born on; and those making forward plans for celebrations may be interested in what day of the week Christmas Day will be in the year 2006 or 2010.

The calendar was originally developed within the Christian church as an aid to knowing what days of the week the fixed saints' days fell on, and how they related to Easter in a given year. It can be calculated from the date of the first Sunday in the year, which provides a dominical letter i.e. a "Sunday letter" for each year. If the first Sunday is actually January 1, the dominical letter for the year is A. If the first Sunday is January 2, the dominical letter is B; and so on, through to G. Put the other way round, we have a scheme for checking the rotation of days of the week against fixed dates. So:

Dominical letter			
A	January 1	=	Sunday
B		=	Saturday
C		=	Friday
D		=	Thursday
E		=	Wednesday
F		=	Tuesday
G		=	Monday

In leap years two dominical letters apply: one for January and February, and the second for March to December. The dominical letters, and their numerical equivalents, are shown in the table in Appendix III, along with a segment of the calendar for the years 1901 to 2008.

◊ For more about the development of the European calendar, see under **dating systems**.

perquisite or prerequisite

See **prerequisite**.

persistence or persistency

The first is far more common: see **-nce/-ncy**.

persnickety or pernickety

See **pernickety**.

person

For grammarians, the concept of **person** separates the person speaking (*first person*), the one spoken to (*second person*), and the one spoken about (*third person*). These differences can be seen in the English *personal pronouns*:

* *first person*	I (me, my, mine)	we (us, our, ours)
* *second person*	you (your, yours)	
* *third person*	he (him, his)	they (them,
	she (her, hers)	their,
	it (its)	theirs)

The only other point in English grammar where **person** makes a difference is in the present tense singular of most verbs. The *third person* has an *-s* suffix, while the *first* and *second* do not. Compare: *I believe, you believe* with *s/he believes.* However with the verb *be,* all three persons are different: *am, are, is.*

When the *first person singular* is used in the same phrase as one of the other two, politeness dictates that it comes second, as in *he and I, you and I/me.* The same applies when a noun (= *third person*) is mentioned with the *first person,* as in *her mother and I.* These conventions apply in standard written texts, although they may be relaxed in conversation (Wales, 1996). They also tend to be set aside when *I* is coupled with a bulky coordinate, as in *I and other members of the Board.* The *first person plural* pronoun *we/us* usually comes first (Strang, 1962), as in *we and they, we and their parents.*

First- or third-person style. When writing, the choice of **person** has a pervasive effect on the style. The *first person* singular (*I*) engages readers closely in what's being described, and provides or simulates direct experience of it. The *first person* plural (*we*) also tends to involve the reader, suggesting a kind of solidarity between writer and reader which can be played on when seeking to persuade. The *third person* tends to put distance between writer and reader, in both fiction and nonfiction. A *third person* narrative, written in terms of *he/she/it/they*, seems to set both writer and reader apart from whatever's being described. Continuous use of the *third person* in nonfictional writing can seem very impersonal – which may or may not be the intention. See further under **I**.

-person

This has long been used as a gender-free combining-form in expressions for the numbers of people involved, as in:

> *a two-person room*
> *a 50-person waiting list*
> *a 15 000-person retirement community*

In the quest for inclusive language, **-person** has also been used in some quarters as a way of avoiding the invidious choice between *-man* and *-woman,* when one wished to avoid preempting the sex of possible incumbents of a position. This is not a trivial matter in, say, selecting someone to chair a committee, where using either *chairman* or *chairwoman* may seem to preempt the issue. (See further under **nonsexist language**.) Several formations with **-person** are more or less current in most varieties of English, including:

> *anchorperson   businessperson   chairperson*
> *layperson   newsperson   salesperson*
> *spokesperson   sportsperson   tradesperson*

Of these, *chairperson, salesperson* and *spokesperson* are well established in both British and American English, and Americans use all the rest to some extent, by the evidence of CCAE. British use of *businessperson, layperson, sportsperson, tradeperson* shows up in BNC data, but not of *anchorperson* and *newsperson* (both media-oriented terms).

The currency of these terms with **-person** goes against the view of Maggio (1988) that they were "a last resort." They have proved more durable than expected, and the suffix is still clearly productive. The only inherent problem is if **-person** gets used more often to paraphrase words ending in *-woman* than ones ending in *-man*. People then tend to see **-person** as a thinly veiled substitute for the female term only, and it too acquires sexist connotations. An alternative strategy with job titles (where it matters most) is to use occupational and structural titles that highlight the role or occupation and make no reference to gender. See further under **man, man-** and **-man**.

persona

This Latin loanword has two plurals: the anglicized **personas** and the pure Latin **personae**. In British English **personae** is used much more than in American for the identities projected by authors in their writing, or the roles of public figures – by the evidence of the BNC and CCAE. Typical examples are:

> *. . . the personae of Arthur Ransome, E Nesbit and Enid Blyton*

> *. . . one of the nation's most trusted television personas*

In both American and British texts, the plural **personae** appears in fixed phrases borrowed from Latin, as one might expect: in *personae non gratae* (see next entry) or *dramatis personae*, the characters listed to appear in a play. See further under **-a** section 1.

persona non grata

In Latin this phrase means "unwelcome person." It has an official use in diplomatic circles, referring to representatives of foreign governments who are unacceptable in the country to which they have been accredited. But it's also used freely in many contexts to refer to someone who has lost their welcome there. The phrase was originally used in English in its positive form *persona grata*, but the negative form is now the one most widely known and used, especially in nondiplomatic contexts. Even so, it resists assimilation and its plural is still inflected as in Latin: **personae non gratae**. See further under **-a** section 1.

personal or personnel

The first word is a common adjective meaning "belonging to the particular person," whose use is illustrated in phrases such as *personal column, personal computer, personal effects, personal space*. The word **personnel** is used in companies and government departments as a collective noun for all those employed there. It may take either singular or plural verbs in agreement (see under **collective nouns**).

Like many an English noun **personnel** occasionally serves as an adjective, as in *Personnel Department*, and the *Personnel Officer* who heads it. Used in this way, it comes close to the domain of **personal**. Compare *personal development* with *personnel development*. Both are possible, though the first is about maximizing individual potential, and the second represents the management's concern with staff training.

personal pronouns

These are the set of pronouns which stand in place of nouns referring to person(s) or thing(s):

> *Has Lee brought the letter? No, he faxed it yesterday.*

For the full set of **personal pronouns**, see under **person**. Other kinds of pronoun are presented under **pronouns**.

personification

This is a literary device and figure of speech which imputes a personal character to something abstract or inanimate. Poets personify the great abstracts of our experience, as did Shakespeare in the simile:

> *Pity like a naked newborn babe striding the wind . . .*

In such lofty rhetoric the abstract is given human identity, and demands a human response from us. The use of *He* (*His, Him*) to refer to God in hymns and religious discourse is also a form of **personification**. Yet the use of *his* (with nonhuman subjects) in literature up to and including C17 is not necessarily **personification**, because until then *his* served as the possessive for both *he* and *it*. The neuter pronoun *its* appeared first at the end of C16, and was not in regular use until about 1675. This explains its absence from

the Authorized Version of the bible, and from Shakespearean texts until the Folio editions of 1623.
Anthropomorphism and personification.
Anthropomorphism is a similar device, which gives human form and attributes to the nonhuman, whether a deity, an animal or an object. In ancient art the gods were anthropomorphized, and so Athena, goddess of wisdom and justice, was depicted holding balanced scales, and Diana, goddess of the moon, appears as the huntress with bow and arrow in hand. A modern example would be the way a successful yachtsman might describe his boat as "dancing her way to the finishing line."

personnel or personal
See **personal**.

persuade or convince
The verb **persuade** has long been complemented by two kinds of grammatical structures: either the infinitive (implying an action), or a finite clause (implying a change of mind):
She persuaded me to give up smoking.
She persuaded me that I should give up smoking.
Until C20, only the second kind of structure was used with **convince**:
She convinced me that I should give up smoking.
The other construction, in which **convince** implies mobilizing action, appeared in American English during the 1950s:
She convinced me to give up smoking.
It raised some hackles, reviving questions which had earlier been asked about how **persuade** should be construed, according to *Webster's English Usage* (1989). But it concludes that *convince to* is now "fully established idiom," and this view is implicit in contemporary British grammars such as the *Comprehensive Grammar* (1985) and the *Longman Grammar* (1999), both of which present the construction with no comment to suggest its illegitimacy. Still it's probably newer to British ears than American. In BNC data *convince to* occurs in the ratio of about 1:12 to *convince that*, whereas it's 1:2 in CCAE.
Note finally that both **persuade** and **convince** can be followed by *of:*
He persuaded me of the need to give up.
He convinced me of the need to give up.

persuasion
The desire to persuade or convince the reader is often a motive for writing, one which calls for special attention to writing technique. Keeping readers with you is all-important, anticipating their attitudes and reactions, and managing the subject matter so that your point of view becomes not just plausible but compelling.
We sometimes think of politicians and advertisers as the archetypal persuaders, yet the arts of **persuasion** were highly developed as *rhetoric* in ancient courts of law. Then and now, **persuasion** depends on getting listeners or readers on side, by an appeal to emotion or reason. Emotion has always been the more direct method – trying to arouse the audience's anger and/or sympathies as an appeal to their better instincts (see further under **pathos**). The emotional appeal may also target instincts lower

down the body – gut feeling or the hip-pocket nerve. Then and now, persuaders knew the power of appealing to self-interest, with the *argumentum ad hominem* (see **ad hominem**).
Persuaders with more respect for the intelligence of their audience are more likely to invoke reason and logic on their side, and to use the force of argument in **persuasion**. Classical rhetoric too recognized the place of induction and deduction in constructing an argument; and with less formal logic, today's persuaders may compile a convincing list of examples to make a general point, or get us to endorse a premise which leads to an inescapable conclusion. (See further under **induction** and **deduction**.) Either way they are not simply giving us loose information or an extended narrative, but selecting and structuring a telling set of points for maximum effect. The ultimate key to **persuasion** is in getting the audience or reader to share your value system – to agree that something is worthwhile, or to be condemned. This often comes back to using evaluative words which embed those values in whatever is being talked about. Environmentalists evoke the common concern with preserving natural resources, and so words like "natural," "renewable resource" and "rainforest" are positively charged, while "exploitation" and "pollution" carry negative values. Such values can be shared by many people these days, whether they look to nature for recreation or for raw materials. Advertisers often try to persuade by appealing to the social values latent in their readers, their concern with self-image and social status. So words like "luxury," "glamorous" and "sophisticated" are used to tap that value system, and help consumers reach for their wallets.

pertinence or pertinency
When juxtaposed in dictionaries, the abstract nouns for *pertinent* always appear in this order. This is not simply a matter of alphabetization, but the fact that **pertinence** is very much more frequent than **pertinency** in both British and American English, by the evidence of the BNC and CCAE. Neither database has more than a solitary instance of **pertinency**, whose use seems to have declined steadily since C19, by *Oxford Dictionary* (1989) citations. **Pertinence** now carries the weight of usage, like the *-nce* form in most other pairs of this kind. See **-nce/-ncy**.

perverse or perverted
The second adjective makes a much more serious charge than the first. **Perverse** just implies that something defies convention and normal practice, as in:
He took a perverse interest in watching the film credits to the very last name.
The habit described could never be thought of as morally reprehensible, whereas **perverted** does imply an infringement of the common moral code, as in:
He took a perverted interest in nude photos of children.
Perverted is of course part of a verb, which also refers to a serious moral and/or legal matter, witness the charge of *perverting the course of justice.*
When it comes to abstract nouns, either *perverseness* or *perversity* serves for **perverse**.
Perversion is reserved for **perverted**.

petaled or petalled

When *petal* becomes an adjective (see **-ed** section 2), it raises spelling questions like those of verbs ending in *l*: see **-l-/-ll-**.

petitio principii

See **beg the question**.

petrol or petroleum

These are not synonyms because they refer to products from different stages of the oil-refining process. **Petroleum** is the natural raw material, also known as "crude oil," "rock oil" and "black gold." Stage by stage in the refining process, **petroleum** yields various fuels, including kerosene (also known as "paraffin"), diesel, *liquefied petroleum gas* (LPG) and **petrol** itself. While **petrol** is the standard name in Britain and Australia, the same fuel is sold as *gasoline* or *gas* in the US and Canada. See further under **gasoline**.

ph or f

See **f/ph**.

phalanx

In anatomy, **phalanx** can refer to a bone of either finger or toe, with the classical plural **phalanges** (see further under **-x** section 2). But everyday use makes more of another ancient meaning of **phalanx** as a "closely packed body of people." This use of **phalanx** harks back to the protective battle formation used by the Greeks and Macedonians, when contingents of soldiers massed under overlapping shields. Its modern English analogues can be found everywhere, in *a phalanx of tourists / senior management / small boys*. The word is now also applied to inanimate structures, in contexts from chess to architecture:

> *a powerful phalanx of black pawns*
> *the blast from a phalanx of heaters*
> *a phalanx of elegant apartment blocks*

The plural for all these latter day uses of **phalanx** is **phalanxes**.

phallus

This Graeco-Latin hybrid from C17 still takes both Latin and English plurals: **phalli** and **phalluses** (see further under **-us** section 1). Database evidence from the US and the UK show that **phalli** is mostly confined to science and classical scholarship, while **phalluses** turns up in anthropological and general writing:

> *surreal, semihuman creatures possessed of large phalluses, pendulous breasts and extra sets of hands or eyes.*

pharmacist, druggist or chemist

Americans use the term **druggist** for the trained maker and dispenser of pharmaceutical remedies. It is a C17 respelling of the French *droguiste,* never to be confused with *drug dealer.* The **druggist** may own a *drug store,* which retails medicines and other goods more or less closely associated with health care: *soaps and talcum powders, bath salts and loofahs,* as the advertisement says, not to mention household wares, food and soft drinks. Canadians use **druggist** as well as **pharmacist**, which is the standard professional term now in Britain and Australia. The long-standing alternative in British English – and still to some

extent in Australia – is **chemist**, short for *dispensing chemist*. **Chemist** in this sense often comes up amid references to other health professionals, as in:

> *Ask your school nurse, doctor or chemist for a suitable treatment.*

or alongside other retailers:

> *Between the baker's and the grocer's was a chemist's.*

The context thus makes it clear that the *local chemist* is what's meant, not the type of **chemist** who works as a *chemical scientist* at a university or research laboratory. These academic and industrial applications of the term **chemist** are shared by English-speakers throughout the world.

phase or faze

Despite their separate origins and distinct meanings, these sometimes tangle with each other, helped by the interchangeability of *ph/f* and *s/z* in some other English words.

Phase began life in English as a noun, but has since World War II become an administrative verb meaning "carry out in stages." Its most frequent use is in phrasal verb constructions (*phase in,* and especially *phase out*) which are usually passive:

> *Tax relief on company cars would be phased out.*

Other constructions, notably *phase down* and *phase back* also express this sense of "planned cutbacks," as does the adjective *phased* in examples such as *phased reduction* and *phased divestiture*. Given that all these uses of **phase** are impersonal, it seems surprising that it could be mistaken for **faze** meaning "disconcert," which is almost always used of people, as in

> *Nixon isn't fazed by such name-dropping*

Faze seems to be a C19 American variant of an old dialect verb *feeze/feaze* meaning "daunt, frighten off," recorded in various other spellings as well. The instability of its spelling, and the occasional use of **phase** for **faze** was first commented on in the 1890s, according to *Webster's English Usage* (1989). The fact that both are used in passive constructions (as shown above) would help to explain the substitution. In data from CCAE about 1 in 10 examples of *fazed* appear as *phased:*

> *He doesn't seem phased by the lack of commercial success.*
> *Hardly phased by the disaster, Seattle entered a long period of prosperity.*

The use of *by* following *phased* helps to show that these are variants of **faze**, as does the negative or quasi-negative that typically goes with them, whether in passive or active constructions: *None of the drawbacks phased Benson.*

American authorities are divided about whether to accept **phase** for **faze**. While *Webster's Dictionary* (1961) presents **phase** as a possible variant, *Webster's English Usage* (1989) is not so inclined, and Garner (1998) regards it as a "blunder." Administrative use of the verb **phase** probably expanded dramatically in the decades between, and the usage commentators note further dimensions of the problem in very occasional uses of "unphased by," and of **faze** being used for **phase**, as in "fazed out." These add to the argument for keeping the two spellings apart and attached to separate words. A "fazed withdrawal" – as opposed to *phased withdrawal* – could make bad PR for a military operation!

In British English there's little recent evidence of the interchanging of **phase** and **faze**. BNC data provides one example in a transcript of speech:

the perceiving person is much less phased by this . . .

The only citations in the *Oxford Dictionary* (1989) are American ones from C19. The fact that it labels them "erroneous," and that *New Oxford* labels **faze** "informal" would help to explain British caution in writing the word. Yet the BNC has rather more examples of **faze** in written sources than in transcribed speech. Its relatively recent importation to the UK (in the 1970s) – well after its formative stages in the US – would also account for its more stable spelling in British sources.

PhD, Ph.D or Ph.D.

How many stops does this hard-won abbreviation need? The stopless form **PhD** is usual in British and Australian English, and is recommended by *Scientific Style and Format* (1994) for scientists the world over. *Merriam-Webster* (2000) also presents it as **PhD**, as does the *Chicago Manual* (2003) – while acknowledging the traditionalists' preference for **Ph.D.** (see **abbreviations** option a). The fully stopped form is also endorsed by the *Canadian Oxford* (1998). No-one owns the inbetween form **Ph.D**, an unhappy compromise.

phenomenon and phenomena

These are, respectively, the singular and plural of a classical loanword, presented in all dictionaries as the standard forms (see further under **-on**). The word is ultimately derived from a Greek verb *phaino* ("show"). But grammatical transformations mask its origins, and probably underlie uncertainties about its plural form that date from its debut in C16 English. **Phenomena** has occasionally been used as the singular from 1576 on, by the *Oxford Dictionary* (1989) record; and usage notes in many dictionaries register it as a current tendency, especially in spoken discourse. Editorial intervention probably helps to reduce its appearances in writing.

Both plural and singular examples of **phenomena** can be found in BNC data as well as CCAE, in news and sports reporting. A certain number are directly marked with plural or singular determiners, as in:

these phenomena	*many uninteresting*
	phenomena
a nation-wide	*the origins of this*
phenomena	*phenomena*

The marking of plural (or singular) is sometimes there in the form of a present tense verb:

when such celestial phenomena as comets are predicted
the phenomena reminds her of an episode of "MASH"

In many examples however, **phenomena** is indeterminate in its grammatical number:

a clearer view of the phenomena they are investigating
the state has experienced the same phenomena

Phrases like *natural phenomena* and *psychic phenomena* often seem to be collective concepts, rather than countable plurals. Thus ambiguous usage contributes to the uncertainty as to how **phenomena** should be construed. Research by Collins (1979) among young Australian adults showed that between

80% and 90% would think of **phenomena** as a singular. That they (and other young people) do so can be seen as dereliction of grammar and/or the process of assimilation at work. British and American dictionaries diverge on this: *New Oxford* (1998) makes no bones about calling it a "mistake"; whereas *Merriam-Webster* (2000) reports the more complex view that it's "still rather borderline." The assimilative process is no doubt further advanced in the US, as well as attitudes to it. The larger step in assimilation (the use of **phenomenas** as a countable plural) is not visible for British or American English in data from either the BNC or CCAE.

The anglicized plural **phenomenons** is registered in *Webster's Third* (1986), and associated particularly with the use of **phenomenon** to mean an "outstanding person" and used by publicists and media in the marketing of both persons and products. There are half a dozen examples in CCAE, such as:

It was one of the publishing phenomenons of the 1980s.
All of these phenomenons – Roosevelt, Reagan, Abbie etc. – affect us. They become our cultural icons.

There's no such evidence of **phenomenons** in BNC data, nor does it reign supreme in this niche of American English. Counter examples using **phenomena** can also be found in CCAE:

Kylie became one of the entertainment phenomena of the 1980s.
Danzig [a band] is unusual among metal phenomena in that it's not just a boys' club.

Overall then, **phenomena** seems to be consolidating its position for plural uses, apart from extending its influence into the singular.

phil- or -phile

This Greek root means "loving," and it serves as either first or second element in a number of loanwords and neo-Greek formations including:

philanthropy philharmonic philologer philosopher

and

Anglophile audiophile bibliophile zoophile

In modern usage its meaning is quite often "collector (of)," as in *philatelist, phillumenist* and *discophile*. Note that the words ending in **-phile** are sometimes spelled without the final *e*, and both *bibliophile* and *bibliophil* are recognized in the *Oxford Dictionary* (1989). The abstract noun associated with **-phile** is usually *-philia*, as in *audiophilia*. In a few older cases it can also be *-phily*, as with *bibliophilia* or *bibliophily*, but the *-philia* form is more common.

Philip or Phillip

Both spellings are well used in English proper names, as first name or surname, and in placenames. The original Greek name consisted of *phil-* ("loving") and *(h)ippos* ("horse"). So by rights the name should have one *l* and two *ps* – as it does in *Philippines*. *Philip of Macedonia,* and all the kings of Spain and France had the name as **Philip**, in keeping with the Greek source. In database evidence from both the US and the UK, **Philip** is the commoner form of the given name, by about 3:1.

Phillip is equally well established in English. It shows the doubling of a consonant that has been a headache in English orthography since C18.

(Dr. Johnson's difficulties with it are noted under **single for double**.) Many an Anglo-Saxon surname has been spelled **Phillips**, and it's about twice as common as **Philips** in BNC data. It gave us the *Phillips head screw* (named after a Brit) and the *Phillips curve* in economics (after a New Zealander). Many American and Australian placenames embody the surname with two *l*s, for example:
(in the US) *Mount Phillips   Phillipsburg* (Kansas)
Phillips County (in Arkansas, Colorado, Kansas, Montana)
(in Australia) *Phillip Island   Port Phillip Bay* (Vic.)
Phillip (ACT)   *Phillip Creek* (NT)
Yet **Philip** also appears in a few American placenames, most notably in Montana where *Philipsburg* contrasts with the city in Kansas; and in Dakota, with the city of *Philip*. The spellings are no doubt historically justified in each case, but the effect is arbitrary for those distanced in time and space.

There are several kinds of reference to help with the **Philip/Phillip** problem:
* for *placenames*   a large atlas or gazeteer
* for *historical names*   dictionaries of biography
* for *surnames of living*   telephone directory or
  persons   institutional websites
The spelling for those who have **Phil(l)ip** as a first name may still be elusive, and need to be checked for the person concerned.

Philippines

This nation of many islands (over 7000, of which only about one tenth are inhabited), was named by the Spaniards in 1521 in honor of *Philip II* of Spain. Until 1898 it was ruled by Spain, but then came under US control as part of the treaty which ended the Spanish–American war. After a brief period of Japanese control from 1942 to 1945, it became an independent republic in 1946.

The English spoken in the **Philippines** has a noticeable American coloring, a legacy of the American presence in the first half of C20. But the national language is *Pilipino,* an Austronesian language based mainly on Tagalog. The citizens of the **Philippines** are called *Filipinos* (see further under **f/ph**).

Phillip or Philip
See **Philip**.

philtre or philter
When you need a literary word for a liquid aphrodisiac, this may come in handy. It adjusts the second syllable to comply with conventional British or American spelling: **philtre** in the UK, Australia and usually in Canada, and **philter** in the US. See further under **-re/-er**.

-phobia and phobia
This Greek word element, meaning "morbid or irrational fear," is embodied in ordinary words such as *claustrophobia,* as well as more specialized formations such as *Anglophobia* and *Judophobia,* where it generally means "antipathy (to)." The first meaning is uppermost in modern English naming of very specific and sometimes bizarre anxieties: *arachnophobia* ("fear of spiders"), *galeophobia* ("fear of sharks"), *triskaidekaphobia* ("fear of the number 13"). The spawning of such terms made **phobia** an

independent word by early C19, hence the "phobia of inns and coffee houses" recorded in the *Oxford Dictionary* (1989). A further sign of its independence is the fact that **-phobia** can now combine with words from languages other than Greek, as in *taxophobia* (to refer to the collective anxiety of the electorate about increased taxes).

A person suffering from or obsessed with a **phobia** is a *-phobe* or *-phobic*, as in *claustrophobe/phobic*. Words formed with *-phobic* also serve as adjectives, for referring to the **phobia**, or something that produces it: *claustrophobic sensation, a claustrophobic cabin.*

phonesthemes
This is the technical name for sounds (usually pairs or sequences of them) which seem to express a particular quality whatever words they appear in. The most noticeable examples are the initial consonant sounds, and those the syllable ends with. The letter *s* is involved in a number of the classic examples. It seems as if "sk" at the start of words such as *scoot, skip, scuttle* expresses the quick movement implied in all of them, while "sl" suggests either a falling or sliding movement as in *slip, slither, slouch,* or something slimy or slushy, as in those words and in *sludge, slobber, sloppy.* "Sp" seems to represent a quick ejective movement in *spit, spatter, spout, spurt;* and "sw" a swaying or swinging movement, as in both of those and in *sweep, swirl, swagger*.

The closing part of a word also seems to be suggestive of the meaning itself in various cases. Words ending in "ip" often suggest a brisk, quick movement, as with:
       clip flip nip rip skip tip whip
The "le" suffix seems to bring a sense of light movement or sound to most words it's attached to, witness:
       crackle crinkle fizzle   giggle   prattle
       rustle   scuffle trickle twinkle   whistle
(See further under **-le**.)

A further example is in words ending in "ump," which are often associated with heaviness and falling weight. For example:
       clump dump hump lump   plump slump
       thump
In some words, the effects of **phonesthemes** at both the beginning and the end of the word are felt, as with *slip* and *slump* from the examples above.

Some of the **phonesthemes** shown above are older than English itself. In other Indo-European languages, words beginning with "sp" also connote senses such as "spit out" or "reject." Yet this kind of sound symbolism also depends on there being a sufficiently large group of such words in a language at any one time. Words embodying **phonesthemes** (like any others) adapt their meanings over the course of time, and may thus dilute the collective effect. And of course there are always other words which coincidentally have the same initial or concluding letters, but whose etymology and current meaning go against the common sound symbolism. Words like *space, spade, spectrum* could hardly be said to embody any of the sound effects attributed to "sp," let alone words like *spare, special, speculation.*

So **phonesthemes** are one of the latent aspects of words, useful to poets for *onomatopoeia,* and to advertisers in promoting their products, but not a

powerful force in ordinary prose. See further under
onomatopoeia.

phoney or phony
See **phony.**

phonograph and gramophone
The world's first two means of recording sound were
distinguished by these names. American Thomas
Edison gave the name **phonograph** to the cylindrical
instrument which he invented in 1877, which was soon
rivaled (in 1887) by the **gramophone** system of
Berliner, a German immigrant, who succeeded in
recording and reproducing sound on a revolving disk.
Americans then applied the earlier term **phonograph**
to Berliner's invention, and the records used on it
were also known as **phonograms**. But in Britain the
term **phonograph** went out with cylinder recordings,
and the revolving disk system was always known as
the **gramophone.** In the second half of C20, both
terms were displaced by *record player, hi-fi* and *stereo* –
and now by the *CD player* with laser technology, which
is used worldwide. See further under **disc or disk**.

phony or phoney
This word was first recorded in the US in the year 1900,
and entered the headword list of *Webster's Third* (1986)
as **phony**. In British sources its record begins with
the so-called "Phoney war" of 1939 which escalated
into World War II; and the *Oxford Dictionary* (1989)
gives priority to **phoney**. Contemporary databases
confirm the British–American divide. In BNC data
phoney outnumbers **phony** by 8:1, while in American
data from CCAE the ratio is more than 30:1 in favor of
phony. The two spellings are about equally used in
Canada and Australia, according to *Canadian English
Usage* (1997) and the *Macquarie Dictionary* (1997).

The word's variable spelling goes with its uncertain
origins, although most authorities are inclined to a
connection with the Irish word *fawney*, used to refer to
cheap jewellery, and to the ring used in confidence
tricks. If so the respelling of the word with *ph* is itself
phony, but we can hardly propose a return to *f* there.
We can however give preference to **phony** as the
spelling which avoids any spurious connection with
the telephone!

The stylistic status of the word seems to be rising.
Webster's English Usage (1989) demonstrates its
appearances in increasingly respectable American
sources after 1960. Most BNC examples come from
written rather than spoken texts – not the most formal
kind of writing, but certainly intended for a wide
British readership.

phosphorus or phosphorous
See under -ous.

phrasal and prepositional verbs
Many English verbs express their meaning with the
aid of a following particle, as in *blow up* ("explode"),
give off ("emit"), *turn down* ("reject"). They are some
of the innumerable *multiword verbs* now recognized
by English grammarians (*Comprehensive Grammar,*
1985, and the *Longman Grammar,* 1999). Both **phrasal
verbs** and **prepositional verbs** consist of a lexical
verb plus a closely associated adverb/preposition,
whose meaning and grammatical status is neutralized
within the larger semantic unit, as the "translations"

above show. This integrated unit of verb plus particle
is syntactically different from constructions in which
the same verb takes a prepositional phrase as
adverbial adjunct. Compare *turn off* (meaning
"extinguish") as in *he turned off the light* with *he
turned off the highway,* which indicates a direction
relative to the noun "highway." In the first case *off* is
semantically merged with the verb, in the second it
works independently as head of the following phrase.

Phrasal verbs can be transitive or intransitive,
according to the idiom. Compare *they set off together*
with *they set off the alarm*. The transitive *phrasal verb*
allows its object to come either before or after the
particle: *they set the alarm off* is just as acceptable as
the other version of that sentence. With such
flexibility, **phrasal verbs** are much used in
conversation and in fiction, but rather less so in
newspapers or academic writing, according to
Longman Grammar research. Many are formed with
high-frequency verbs such as *take, get, put, come, go,
set;* others are one-offs, such as *freak out, hype up, write
off.* The verbs involved are typically monosyllabic, and
sometimes colloquial, which helps to explain why
they are often felt to be "informal." The criticism of
phrasal verbs by commentators such as Gowers
(1965) was more specifically aimed at "redundancy" in
examples such as *drop off, lose out, pay off,* where the
verb alone could perhaps express the meaning. Yet
there are often subtle differences (see **lose out**).

Prepositional verbs are not usually objected to,
and are in fact three to four times more frequent than
phrasal verbs in the *Longman Grammar* corpus.
Examples like *account for, consist of, refer to, start with*
show that they are the staple of argument and
discussion, and found almost as often in academic
discourse as in conversation. They are differ from
transitive **phrasal verbs**, in not allowing an object to
come between the two parts – thus *to account for the
discrepancy* not "to account the discrepancy for." Yet
like the **phrasal verb**, the **prepositional verb** keeps
its two elements together when the object is preposed,
as in *something to account for.* The objects of
prepositional verbs are technically *prepositional
objects* (see **transitive and intransitive** section 3).

The strongest objections are usually reserved for
what grammarians call *phrasal-prepositional verbs,* a
combination type involving two particles:

check up on	come up with	face up to
get out of	look down on	meet up with
walk out on		

Like **phrasal verbs,** they mostly express activities,
and are most commonly used in conversation and
fiction. Again this makes them spontaneous or
informal in style, and the question of redundancy
returns. In fact the second particle usually lends a
quasi-transitivity to the intransitive **phrasal verb**, as
in *check up on, get out of, meet up with,* and fine-tunes
the positioning of the narrative. (See for example
meet (up) (with).)

The choice of prepositions after verbs, and their
presence or absence, is sometimes a matter of dialect
difference. See **prepositions** section 1.

phrases
A **phrase** is often thought of simply as a multiword
unit, contrasting with the single word. So *quick as a
flash* is a **phrase** consisting of four words. But for the
grammarian a **phrase** is a unit of a clause. It may

consist of a single word (such as a name or pronoun) or of several words. In English we distinguish five types of **phrases**, according to the grammar of the key word or *head:*

* *noun phrase*   with a noun or pronoun as head: *their pet cat / it*
* *verb phrase*   with a verb as head: *was lying / lay*
* *prepositional phrase* with a preposition as first word: *on the bed / there*
* *adjectival phrase*   with an adjective as head: *very well-bred / elegant*
* *adverbial phrase*   with an adverb as head: *deep asleep / sleepily*

See individual headings for more about each.

pica

This word has several meanings in relation to type:
1 For typewriters it is a type size yielding 10 characters to the inch, also known as *ten pitch.*
    —This is in typewriter **pica**.
2 In typesetting the 12 point typesize has been called **pica**.

—This is in typesetter's **pica**.

3 In typesetting, the **pica** is also a unit of linear measurement, equal to just on 4.21 mm or one sixth of an inch, and used to measure the column of print as well as the dimensions of graphics.
    The *point* used in measuring the size of a font is one twelfth of a **pica**, i.e. one seventy-second of an inch. *Point* in this technical sense is often abbreviated as *pt.* (American style) or *pt* (British style), as in *12 pt(.)* type. See further under **contractions** section 1.

picket

For the spelling of this word when used as a verb, see **-t**.

picnic

When it becomes a verb, a *k* has to be added. See **-c/-ck-**.

pidgins and creoles

New languages for old! A **pidgin** is an ad hoc system of communication, put together from existing languages under special circumstances. It typically happens when groups of people who have no language in common try to communicate with each other, using whatever words they hear being used around them. **Pidgins** often develop for the purposes of trade, as did "Bazaar Malay," and the "Bamboo English" used in Korea; but they are also associated with colonial plantations, which employed workers (or slaves) from diverse other places. American "Black English" and New Guinea Pidgin are both thought to have originated this way.
    Pidgins consist of a very basic inventory of words, which work without suffixes and prefixes. Any single word has to do service for a wide range of meanings, witness the use of *arse* in New Guinea Pidgin to mean "foundation, basis," and *mary* as the common noun for "woman, wife, girl, maid." **Pidgin** sentences have the simplest grammatical structure and subordination is rare. Both words and grammatical structures are drawn from the dominant language in the context, typically the language of the colonialist,

hence the development of "English-based pidgins," "French-based pidgins" etc.
    Pidgins begin life as very restricted languages, sufficient for communication between peoples who have few dealings with each other. But as people resort to **pidgin** more often and the topics of conversation increase, it develops as an *elaborated pidgin* and then into a lingua franca for people in linguistically diverse regions. This was how New Guinea Pidgin grew from its plantation origins to become the lingua franca of the New Guinea region, and now one of the official languages of Papua New Guinea. In fact it has become the native language of many New Guineans, at which point its status is strictly speaking that of a **creole**, no longer a **pidgin**.
    Creoles operate as fully-fledged languages in bilingual or multilingual communities. The Caribbean is the home of several, including Haitian Creole based on French, and Jamaican Creole based on English. The **creole** maintains a mix of elements from local languages, but over the course of time tends to add in lexical and grammatical features of the standard language on which it's based (English, French etc.), in the process known as *decreolization*. American Black English is believed by many to be the *decreolized* product of **pidgins** used among plantation slaves (see **Black English**).
Final notes: the word **pidgin** is sometimes (rather distractingly) spelled "pigeon," though the word is more likely to be derived from business than birds. **Pidgin** is arguably a reduced form of the word "business," as spoken by those whose language had fewer consonant sounds than English and no "s" sound (rare in languages of the Pacific region). The connection with "business" is eminently likely, seeing that **pidgins** are often associated with trading. The word **creole** is borrowed from French, though ultimately it's a Spanish and Portuguese word meaning "native to the locality."

pièce de résistance

Two of the three words look English, but they shed little light on the meaning of this French phrase. English-speakers use it to mean the "most important item in a collection or program of events," an extension of its original use in reference to the most substantial dish in a meal. The phrase complements *chef d'oeuvre:* see under that heading.

pied à terre

This in French is literally "foot on the ground." But in English it refers to a lodging in the city which serves as temporary accommodation for someone whose normal place of residence is out of town, or in another city.

pigmy or pygmy

See **pygmy**.

pimento or pimiento

Should it be *pimento-stuffed olives* or *pimiento-stuffed olives?* These are the Portuguese and Spanish forms of the same word for "pepper," borrowed into English two centuries apart for different applications. **Pimento** is the Portuguese form, first used in late C17 English for the spice made from the dried berries of the tropical American tree *Pimenta droica* or *Pimenta officinalis,* also known as "allspice." **Pimiento**, the

Spanish form, was borrowed by English-speakers for the fruit of the shrub *Capsicum annuum*, which is enjoyed for its pungent sweetness, whether eaten red or green. Alternative names for it are the "bell pepper," "sweet pepper" and "capsicum" itself. By rights then you'd expect *pimiento-stuffed olives;* and *ground pimento* to be prescribed in spicy Jamaican dishes. But the names are not uncommonly substituted for each other in both British and American English. Most often it's **pimento** being used for **pimiento** (as in *chopped pimento*), but now and then the reverse happens, when the recipe calls for *a quarter teaspoon of pimiento*. As long as the cook knows which is meant, there's no problem.

pinky, pinkie and pinko

In both American and British English the spelling **pinky** is used for the adjective meaning "a shade of pink," as in *the pinky hue of the eastern sky.* But both **pinky** and **pinkie** are used for the noun referring to the smallest finger, probably based on the Dutch word *pinkje* ("small"). The British seem to prefer **pinkie** for this, by the evidence of the BNC, whereas **pinky** has the edge over **pinkie** in American data from CCAE. While British writers note the *pinkie-ring,* their American counterparts tend to write of the *pinky-ring.* All these uses of **pinky/pinkie** are standard and can be used in a wide range of written discourse.

The noun **pinkie** has some more specialized and informal uses, according to the *Oxford Dictionary* (1989). It serves as the name of a small marine fish, as well as the maggot of the greenbottle fly used as fishing bait, as in *took small carp on pole and pinkie.* In Britain **pinkie** has been a term for cheap red wine, a usage that continues in Australia. Also derogatory is **pinko**, which has been applied in Britain and North America to putative communist sympathizers, but now more generally to persons whose politics or social mores are well to the left of the speaker, as in *pinko liberal vegetarian* or *pinko student demonstrations*. For obvious reasons, none of these latter usages appear very often in print.

pique, peek or peak

See under **peak**.

pis aller

See **faute de mieux**.

piscina

The plural of this word is discussed under **-a** section 1.

pistol or pistil

The first is the spelling for a small fire-arm, a Czech word mediated through German and French in C16. The second is one of the reproductive structures of a flower, going back to Latin *pistillum.*

pitiful, pitiable or piteous

All these revolve around a sense of pity, and the first two are interchangeable in some contexts. In *a pitiful sight* and *pitiable squalor,* either adjective could be used, though the chances are that it would be the first, which is much the more common of the two, in BNC evidence. **Piteous** stands apart, and is nowadays mostly used to describe vocal sounds, as in *a piteous cry,* where it also implies weakness and faintness.

Both **pitiful** and **pitiable** can imply a certain contempt for the condition they describe. *A pitiable effort* or *a pitiful attempt at good relations* carries negative judgements, rather than pity for what is observed. Thus the connotations of **pitiful** and **pitiable** are becoming what they already are for *miserable* and *wretched*. This use of **pitiful** is underpinned by the adverb *pitifully,* which is again much more freely used than *pitiably,* by a factor of 20:1 in data from the BNC.

pixil(l)ated or pixelated

One of these is a good deal older than the other – unsurprising when you know that **pixilated** embodies the word *pixie* and **pixelated** the word *pixel* (a term coined by computer specialists which blends *pix* "pictures," and *el[ement]*).

Pixil(l)ated first appears in C19 print, probably as a learned variant of *pixie-led* which goes back at least two centuries further, and incidentally provides the first citations for *pixie*. With the rise of **pixil(l)ated**, *pixie-led* disappears, and the word's meaning begins to extend, from the sense of "eccentric, whimsical" to "confused" and so to "tipsy." The awkward movements of the **pixil(l)ated** (in the last sense) would then explain the use of **pixil(l)ation** for a theatrical and especially filmic technique developed in the 1940s, which makes an actor move in a jerky way as if s/he were a celluloid animation. The spellings with one *l* are of course the standard American forms of these words, while those with two *l*s are British (see -l-/-ll-).

Enter **pixelated** and the computer technique of the 1980s for atomizing images into minute elements from which they can be recreated and manipulated. For some, this manipulation of images is analogous to the filmic technique of **pixilation**, and **pixelated** becomes **pixilated**. The convergence of the two words is no doubt helped by the fact that film-makers can and do contribute to the design of websites and electronic documents. It would of course be neat if **pixelated** were used for any kind of image manipulation, and **pixil(l)ated** for the older meanings ("whimsical," "tipsy"), but language is not necessarily like that. For the moment *New Oxford* (1998) lists both technical and nontechnical meanings for **pixil(l)ated**, whereas *Merriam-Webster* (2000) separates them under **pixilated** and **pixelated**, according to the history just described.

placenames

See **geographical names**.

placenta

For the plural of this word, see **-a** section 1.

plagiarism

Plagiarism involves passing off someone else's writing as if it were your own – whether done on the grand scale by taking over a whole publication, or by "borrowing" sections, paragraphs or sentences. Any verbatim quotation of a sentence or more which originates from another writer, and which is not acknowledged to be theirs, is an act of **plagiarism**. For professional writers, it's a crime, and for student writers, a dishonest and reprehensible practice, whether it involves borrowing from fellow students, or from published sources in print or on the internet. It shows a disinclination to engage the mind in writing for oneself, a combination of intellectual laziness and intellectual theft. Proper quotation and acknowledgement of sources are a part of good scholarly practice, and a way of avoiding **plagiarism**.

plain or plane

These words can have quite similar meanings, and in fact they derive from the same source, the Latin adjective *planus* ("flat or level"). The different spellings became attached to their different uses in C17. The spelling **plane** became the one for mathematical and technical nouns, including the *vertical plane*, the *(aero)plane,* and the *plane* used to smooth wood in carpentry. The same word serves as an adjective in *plane geometry*.

The other spelling **plain** is used as a noun in geographical analysis of landscapes, as in a *well-watered plain*. It also serves as a general-purpose adjective meaning "simple, unadorned." *Plain English* aims to be just that, not complex and convoluted (see under that heading). *Plainsong* (the earliest kind of church music) was sung in unison without any accompaniment. So spelling distinguishes a *plain surface*, i.e. one without any decoration, from a *plane surface*, one which may be a subject for discussion in geometry or mathematics.

Doubts about which spelling to use may arise in figurative expressions, such as *the moral plane*. The spelling there confirms that it's a metaphor from mathematics. But when it's a matter of *one plain one purl* (in knitting), the *plain stitches* make the ordinary texture of the fabric.

The *plane tree* stands apart from all these uses of **plain/plane**. It owes its name to a different source altogether, the Latin word *platanus*.

Plain English and plain language

Being "plain" is not often a virtue, let alone a rallying call. But if you have been confounded by turgid bureaucratic prose, disarmed by tortuous questions on official forms, and appalled by the prevarications of government communications generally – the word speaks for itself. Those familiar problems were, and still are, the stimulus for **Plain English** action.

The **Plain English** movement gained momentum in the US in the 1970s, its profile raised through the "Doublespeak Awards" of the National Council for the Teachers of English (see **doublespeak**). President Carter took up the cause, and in 1978 ordered that all government documents should be written in **Plain English**. In the same decade, the Law Reform Commission of Canada began reviewing all federal laws and recommending **Plain English** improvements. In Britain, the *Plain English Campaign* took off in 1979, with the much publicized shredding of unreadable official forms in the Houses of Parliament. By 1982, the British government had officially embraced it, obliging bureaucracies to review and revise their documentation, with changes to over 21 000 forms. The Australian government endorsed **Plain English** in legislation in 1984. The fact that **Plain English** is enshrined in legislation helps to explain the initial capital letter, as well as its quasi proper name status. Some paraphrase it as **plain language**.

Apart from challenging bureaucratese, the **Plain English** movement has put the spotlight on impenetrable legal prose, in legislation as well as private legal documents. A good deal of **Plain English** energy has gone into revising insurance documents, because policy-holders need to understand their rights and responsibilities. Lawyers have not been altogether enthusiastic about **Plain English** revisions to their texts, for better and worse reasons. Jurists working with **Plain English** documents could provide legal interpretations in half the time, according to research by the Law Reform Commission of Victoria (Australia), published in 1987. Yet the warning that legal provisions may be altered by **Plain English** revision still needs to be heeded. Collaborative work between lawyers and **Plain English** writers is the obvious answer.

Despite the name, **Plain English** is only partly about language (on which see below). It also emphasizes the importance of document design. Any document needs clear layout, in sections and paragraphs that express the structure of the information, and with effective headings and subheadings to identify local content. Adequate white space between sections and in lists also makes the information more accessible. Where language comes in, it's broadly a matter of seeking simple, everyday words whenever possible, and speaking more directly to the reader. Sentences need to be shorter and less intricate, with punctuation that ensures reliable reading. An average of 20 words is recommended, though individual sentences will of course vary around that. The most important principle of **Plain English** is to keep the reader in mind as you write. Think of yourself as communicating to someone across the table, and of how each sentence sounds. Your writer's "ear" should react whenever sentences leave the reader gasping for breath.

1 **Language elements of Plain English: what to avoid:**
*wordy phrases. Many formulaic phrases in official prose can be paraphrased more simply: "in the event of" often amounts to just plain *if,* and "in respect of" to *about.* High density phrases such as "new employees health and welfare committee" are ambiguous and hard to decode, and can be accessed more easily if unpacked as the "committee on the health and welfare of new employees." Note that **Plain English** doesn't necessarily mean restricting the number of words, especially when expressing something complex.
*passive constructions that make for roundabout expression. "The motion was supported by all members of the committee" communicates more directly and succinctly as "the committee voted unanimously for the motion." Passive constructions may still be useful from time to time in maintaining topical progression at the start of sentences (see further under **topic**, and **passive verbs**).
*double or multiple negatives (see **double negatives,** and **negative concord**).
*double-pronged questions. Most people have to think twice at least when asked:
"Are you over 21 and under 65?"
The answers will be more reliable if you ask the two questions separately, or else reword them into a single question:
Are you between 21 and 65 years of age?
A simple yes or no can be given to that question.
2 **Adapting to the communicative context with Plain English.** The *Plain English movement* is sometimes criticized as attempting to provide a "one size fits all" answer to communication problems. Its most

committed practitioners never suggest that, and take care to say that **Plain English** intervention will vary with the context. Technical jargon is alright for specialist readers, but not the general public. The average paragraph length will probably be longer in a discussion document than, say, in business letters. Imperative verbs can be effective in household or technical instructions, but in advisory documents they sound rather too curt. The use of second person (*you*) may make advice clearer, but too much direct address can suggest heavy-handed control (see under **you**). **Plain English** revisions often affect the tenor of the text, and so revisers must always consider whether this is intended. Is the revision meant to be friendlier (or less so) than the original, or to keep the same distance from the reader?

3 **The benefits of Plain English.** In the end **Plain English** can do more than clarify communication – though that itself is a substantial benefit. It also reduces reading errors, as well as complaints and law suits relating to official documents. Apart from saving time and energy and money on all those fronts, it helps citizens to better understanding of government procedures and policies, and of their own rights.

plaintiff and plaintive

Plaintive is an adjective meaning "sad, mournful," as in the *plaintive cry of the seagull.* **Plaintiff** is a noun referring to the person who raises legal action against another party in a criminal case. (The other party is the *defendant.*) Both words derive ultimately from the French adjective *plaintif* meaning "complaining," where the form ending in *f* is masculine and the one with *ve* feminine. In English the gender distinction does not apply, and the woman who raises a law suit is still a **plaintiff.**

plane or plain

See **plain.**

planetarium

This is a neoclassical creation of C18, with a Latin plural **planetaria** as well as the English **planetariums.** The second is given priority in both *New Oxford* (1998) and *Merriam-Webster* (2000), and is the only one to appear in data from the BNC or CCAE. See further under **-um.**

plateau

British writers still tend to pluralize this C18 French loanword in the French fashion. **Plateaux** appears more than twice as often as **plateaus** in data from the BNC, whether the word refers to a geological formation or a statistical shape. Americans regularly use the *-s* plural, judging by the total absence of the *-x* plural from CCAE. **Plateaus** is everyone's choice when **plateau** is a verb, as in *the mortality plateaus out.*

For other French loans of this kind, see **-eau.**

platefuls or platesful

See under **-ful.**

playwright, playwrighting and playwriting

The writer of plays is definitely a **playwright**, where the second element of the compound is the Old English word for "worker," which survives also in

wheelwright and in surnames such as *Cartwright.* But the word for the activity itself is a-changing. According to the *Oxford Dictionary* (1989) it's **playwrighting,** on record since 1896, whereas *New Oxford* (1998) has only **playwriting.** *Webster's Third* (1986) allows both forms of the word, in that order, while *Merriam-Webster* (2000) puts **playwriting** ahead of **playwrighting.** Database evidence shows that **playwriting** is a good deal more popular than **playwrighting** in both the UK and the US, by a factor of about 4:1 in the BNC as well as CCAE.

pleaded or pled

The verb *plead* is one of those old irregular verbs which has reverted to being regular, in most parts of the world. **Pleaded** is given as the primary spelling for the past tense / past participle in all modern dictionaries, British and American, Canadian and Australian. **Pled** is noted as the second option, but databases show that it has little currency now in either British or American English, and little use except in legal formulas such as *pled (not) guilty.* Even there *pleaded (not) guilty* is more than three times more frequent, in data from the BNC. **Pleaded** stands alone in nonlegal uses of the verb, as in *Everyone pleaded for compromise.* The use of **plead** (to rhyme with "led") as the past form died out in C19.

plein air

This French phrase means "open air," although unlike *al fresco* it doesn't refer to anything outdoors. Instead **plein air** is used in analyzing landscape painting that creates the effect and atmosphere of outdoor light, particularly the work of impressionist painters. Note that there's no need to hyphenate **plein air** when it serves as a compound adjective: *a plein air depiction of the haystack.* See further under **hyphens** section 2c.

plentiful or plenteous

Both mean "abundant," but **plenteous** now sounds old-fashioned, and is confined to literary and religious diction. **Plentiful** enjoys wide currency, whether it's a matter of the *plentiful supply* of trout in mountain streams, or of good quality bananas at the markets.

plenty

This French loanword came into C14 English as a noun meaning "fullness." Since then **plenty** has been quietly evolving into a quantifier, to the consternation of critics from Johnson (1755) on. While some of the mutants are colloquial and/or regionally restricted, others are now standard English everywhere. The latter include its use as a pronoun in *we have plenty,* and the phrase *plenty of,* where it works as a *complex determiner* (see under **determiners**). Like most general quantifiers, *plenty of* may take a singular or plural verb in agreement, depending on the noun involved. Compare:

Plenty of time was allowed.
Plenty of laughs come with them.

The combination of **plenty** with *more* as in *plenty more (examples)* is also standard anywhere in the world. Beyond that, **plenty** is sometimes used as a determiner on its own, as in *there's plenty work to be done* – at least in colloquial American English. Its use may nevertheless be declining, given that the latest citations in *Webster's English Usage* (1989) are from the 1950s.

Plenty can also be an adverb, as in *The water's plenty hot enough.* Constructions like these, where **plenty** modifies a quantifiable adjective, could be used anywhere in the world. They are however labeled "informal" or "colloquial" by dictionaries such as *New Oxford* (1998), *Canadian Oxford* (1998) and the Australian *Macquarie Dictionary* (1997). The note in *Merriam-Webster* (2000) focuses rather on the loss of precision when **plenty** is replaced by other adverbs. American English goes further with adverbial **plenty**, using it to modify participial adjectives, e.g. *He was plenty scared;* as well as verb phrases such as *having practiced plenty,* and *he got around plenty. Webster's English Usage* notes adverbial **plenty** as common in American speech and writing, except of the "starchier" sort.

pleonasm
This means using a combination of words which overlap or duplicate each other in meaning. In some cases it may be viewed negatively, as overwriting or redundancy; in others it seems acceptable either because it's the established idiom, or because it lends intensity to whatever is being said.

1 The negative side of pleonasm is usually referred to as "redundancy" or "tautology." (Note that for philosophers the word *tautology* is neutral in meaning. See under **induction**.) Samples of redundancy are all too common in officialese, in the unnecessary abstract nouns:
> the weather *conditions for the race*
> problems *in the classroom situation*

Redundancy is particularly common in impromptu public speaking by politicians and radio announcers, as they try to maintain continuous output with not quite enough ideas for their rate of speaking, as in phrases like:
> the two *twins*   new *innovations*   revert *back*

More conspicuous examples are the focus of pompous or ponderous statements such as:
> *Traditionally, most of our imports have come from overseas.*

In all such cases, the redundant word weasels meaning out of the other one.

2 Acceptable pleonasms. Numerous time-honored English phrases are strictly tautologous, witness:
> free *gifts*   grateful *thanks*
> past *history*   usual *habit*

Though the adjective adds little to the noun in such expressions, they are sanctioned by usage, and in some cases by the highest authorities in the land. Many **pleonasms** come from law and religion:
> last *will and testament*   null *and void*
> join *together*   lift *up*

Such expressions do have a function in their original context, in their rhetorical effect and in providing synonyms for less familiar words. Rhetorical emphasis is certainly part of the effect in the very common speech-maker's line:
> *I have one further point to add.*

The doubling up of "further" and "add" draws attention to the start of a new structural unit in the text, and underscores the final argument. Why should we quibble at that, any more than we do at Shakespeare's dramatic use of tautology in "the most unkindest cut of all?" The double superlative, like the double negative, may be condemned as tautology, or recognized as a resource for intense expression. If you're aiming at hyperbole, **pleonasm** helps to create it in:
> *What wasteful superfluous trivia I had rammed into my head as a kid!*
> *As an example of bogus semiotic pseudo-scholarship, this book is priceless.*

See further under **hyperbole** and **figures of speech**.

plethora
Derived from Greek, **plethora** was once a medical term meaning the "oversupply of blood." In current English it can refer to an oversupply of anything, or else a "rich abundance," according to larger dictionaries. In data from the BNC, the negative use of **plethora** is more common, yet the fact that it's often accompanied by other negative words suggests that its own negativity is now not so strong, and that its meaning is becoming neutralized. See for example:
> ... *the plethora of spurious genealogies that litter the later literature*
> *There has been a plethora of books on country houses, but PM and BD have found a new approach.*

As in these examples, **plethora** can take a plural or singular verb. When it follows a countable plural (as in the first), it will be plural: but proximity to **plethora** itself (as in the second) may make it singular (see **agreement** section 5). The use of a mass noun following **plethora** also prompts a singular verb: *The plethora of published research is testimony to this.*

As a classical abstract noun, **plethora** meant "fullness" and had no plural. In current English it's sometimes pluralized as **plethoras**, though this is spoken rather than written usage. There are no examples in either BNC or CCAE.

plough or plow
British and Australians are committed to **plough**, whereas Americans and Canadians mostly use **plow**, following Noah Webster's spelling reforms. This clear divide is borne out by data from both BNC and CCAE. It impacts not only on the **plough/plow** used in agriculture, snow-clearing and land management, but wherever the verb is used in more abstract ways. Thus we may *plough/plow back* a resource, *plough/plow through* a heavy document, and decide to *plough/plow on* or *ahead* in adverse circumstances. For non-Americans **plow** is a shock to the system, but also proof of the fact that English can survive spelling adjustments. Depending on your point of view, it lends hope for other words like **plough**. See under **gh**.

plummet
For the spelling of this word when used as a verb, see **-t**.

pluperfect
The past perfect tense is also known as the **pluperfect**. Compare *had arrived* (past perfect) with *have arrived* (present perfect) and see further under **aspect**.

pluralia tantum
This is grammatical Latin for English nouns which look like plurals because they end in *s*, but whose meaning (in that form) is collective or composite.

Some consist of a variety of elements, others are an accumulation of the same kind of element. Examples include:

alms	*amends*	*arrears*
credentials	*dregs*	*earnings*
headquarters	*looks*	*outskirts*
premises	*regards*	*remains*
surroundings	*thanks*	

Membership of the group varies somewhat with the variety of English. *Brains* (as in *use your brains*) is there for British English, but not American. *Accommodations* is an example for Americans, but not most British.

Some grammarians (Wickens, 1992) extend the term **pluralia tantum** to include words ending in *s* which refer to a single object consisting of two parts, notably tools and instruments such as *scissors, spectacles;* and garments such as *jeans, trousers*. Others keep them separate: they are "bipartites" for Huddleston and Pullum (2002), and "summation plurals" for the authors of the *Comprehensive Grammar* (1985). Issues of verb agreement for all groups are discussed at **agreement** section 2.

plurals

Plural forms of words contrast with singular ones, to show that more than one item or person is meant. In English the difference is regularly marked on nouns and most pronouns, but only to a limited extent on verbs. (For more about the grammatical interplay between them, see **number**.) In this entry we concentrate on the **plural** forms of nouns and noun compounds, as well as proper names, titles and national groups. For the **plural** forms of numbers and letters, see **letters as words**, and **numbers and number style**.

1 Plurals of common nouns. The letter *s* is the standard English plural suffix, used with the oldest words of the language, well-established borrowings and all new coinings. Being the default pattern, it's often left unsaid in dictionary entries, and only the nonstandard **plurals** of nouns are indicated. These nonstandard patterns and the words that take them include:

a) -es **plurals,** associated with several groups of nouns:

* those ending in an "s," "z," "tch," "dg," "sh" or "ks" sound such as

    kisses, quizzes, batches, ridges, dishes, boxes
* those ending in plain *y* (as opposed to a vowel plus *y* [-*ay* etc.]) where the *y* changes to *i* before adding -*es*, as in *allies, cherries*. See further under -**y** and -**y** > -**i**-.
* some of those ending in *f* (or *fe*), which changes to *v* before adding the -*es*, as in *loaves, wives*. See further under -**f** > -**v**-.
* some of those ending in *o*, such as *echoes*. See further under -**o**.

b) internal vowel changes for the **plural,** found in some very old words such as *man>men, woman>women; foot>feet, goose>geese, tooth>teeth; louse>lice, mouse>mice*. Note the change of consonant as well in the last pair.

c) -(r)en **plurals,** found in just three words: *children, oxen, brethren*. The third is an old **plural** of *brother,* used only in restricted contexts these days. See **brethren**.

d) zero **plurals** (i.e. no change at all from singular to **plural**), as with *aircraft, apparatus, sheep*. See **zero plurals**.

e) Latin **plurals** for loanwords from Latin (some also have English plurals in -*s*). See under -**a**, -**is**, -**um**, -**us**, -**x**.

f) Greek **plurals** for loanwords from Greek (some also have English **plurals** in -*s*). See under -**a** and -**on**.

g) French **plurals** in -*x* for loanwords from French ending in -*eau, -ieu, -iau* (some also have English **plurals** in -*s*). See -**eau and -ieu**.

h) Italian **plurals** for loanwords from Italian (most if not all have English plurals in -*s* as well). See under **Italian plurals**.

i) Hebrew **plurals** in -*im* for a few recent loanwords from Hebrew. See under -**im**.

2 Plurals of compounds. Ordinary English compounds are pluralized simply by adding *s* at the end, whether they are set solid, spaced or hyphenated:

baby-sitters	*breakdowns*
forget-me-nots	*geography teachers*
go-betweens	*grownups*
handouts	*shop assistants*
tip-offs	*wordprocessors*

The chief exceptions are compounds in which the key noun comes first, as with:

ambassadors-at-large	*goings-on*
grants-in-aid	*passers-by*
rights-of-way	*sisters-in-law*

The traditional **plurals** for some legal and historical terms also have the -*s* attached internally:

attorneys-general	*courts martial*
heirs apparent	*judges advocate*
poets laureate	*sergeants major*

Titles like these originated in French where nouns normally precede adjectives, and so the first word (the noun) naturally takes the **plural** inflection, rather than the adjective which comes second. These **plurals** have lasted for centuries in English official usage; but those in everyday use also have anglicized equivalents, e.g. *court martials, sergeant majors,* which add the **plural** inflection at the end, as if they were ordinary compounds. (For the plural of *Governor General / governor-general*, see under that heading.)

Other foreign compounds, especially those from modern French, raise similar issues. A few are pluralized in the French way, for example *aides de camp, objets d'art, pièces de résistance*, no doubt because their structure is clear even in English, and we recognize that the key noun comes first. In cases where the phrase is not transparent, the **plural** *s* is simply added to the last word:

cul-de-sacs	*hors d'oeuvres*	*roman à clefs*
vol-au-vents		

These seem pretty strange if you know the French words, but it's a sign of their assimilation into English (see individual headings). The **plural** of *grand prix* poses its own particular problems in English (see **grand prix**).

The tendency to just add an *s* at the end is even stronger with Latin compounds, witness *postmortem(s), pro forma(s), curriculum vitae(s)*. See further under those headings.

3 Plurals of proper names and titles. On the somewhat rare occasions when we need to pluralize personal names, we usually add an *s* or *es* in accordance with the general rules for nouns:

The Smiths and the Joneses are on our list.

Note that names ending in *y* never have it changed to *i*:

McNallys are on the list too.

When two people share a surname and title, either title or name may bear the plural marker:

> Misses Smith   Messrs. Smith
> Miss Smiths   Mr. Smiths

The pluralized title still appears in any formal or corporate address (e.g. on envelopes), whereas the pluralized name is more likely elsewhere. When the surnames are different, the only option is to pluralize the title: *Misses Smith and Jones; Messrs. Smith and Jones.* Note that there's no **plural** for the title *Mrs.*, unless we use *Mesdames. Ms.* can be pluralized as *Mss.* or *Mses.*, but neither is much used yet. The **plural** of *Dr.* is simply *Drs.*

4 Plurals of national groups. The names of national and tribal groups are now usually made in the regular way with *s*: *growing numbers of Khmers* (not *Khmer*). Increasingly people feel that using the *zero plural* (*Khmer*) is unfortunately like the standard **plural** for various groups of animals (see further under **zero plurals**). The only national names to keep their *zero plurals* are ones ending in sibilants, notably *-ese* and *-ish*: *the Japanese, the British.*

plus

From its home base in mathematics, **plus** has been annexed into ordinary usage, as in *total cost plus postage.* The example shows how **plus** has extended its scope in constructions that are not explicitly quantitative, and from there into specifying any kind of additional factor, whether it belongs to the same genre or not:

> *This led her into masterpieces like G and L of S, plus a fistful of failed marriages.*

This prepositional use is accepted by current dictionaries such as *New Oxford* (1998) and *Merriam-Webster* (2000), as are its extended uses as noun and adjective (*in the plus, on the plus side*). **Plus** is sometimes used *postpositively,* especially following numbers as in *the 60-litre plus range,* but also in verbal estimates: *"Jeremy has his talent plus" said Lucy.* Although there may be an informal feel to these constructions, they appear freely in many kinds of writing. There are over 6000 examples in written sources in the BNC and more than twice that in CCAE.

The only use of **plus** which seems to be queried by dictionaries and usage commentators is its appearance as a conjunct or conjunction, illustrated below:

> *I have a high-powered job. Plus I have just signed on a major new client.*
> *I have a high-powered job, plus I have just signed on a major new client.*

Punctuation is all that distinguishes the two uses. The first example makes **plus** a conjunctive adverb meaning "as well," which is unproblematic because that word class is relatively open-ended. But the second sets it up as a conjunction, and implicitly challenges the closed set of words normally called "conjunction." (See further under **conjunctions**.) Both kinds of use have been noted in American English since the 1960s, according to *Webster's English Usage* (1989), though not in formal contexts. The *Oxford Dictionary* (1989) documents the "quasi-conjunction" from 1968 on, and labels it "informal." So conjunctive **plus** is still establishing its credentials in written English in both the US and the UK, whereas its other uses as preposition, adjective and noun are accepted.

For the plural of *plus, pluses* is strongly preferred over **plusses**. The first outnumbers the second by more than 10:1 in both British and American databases.

p.m. or pm

This is the standard abbreviation for times of day which fall between noon and midnight. It stands for Latin *post meridiem* ("after midday"). Full stops are not essential with it, since it cannot be confused with any other word, and its time function is made clear by the numbers (between 1 and 12) which precede it. However some writers and editors would use stops with it, in accordance with their general policy on lower case abbreviations, and their treatment of its counterpart *a.m./am* (see **abbreviations** section 2). In British data from the BNC there were almost equal numbers of **p.m.** and **pm**, whereas the second is still strongly preferred in American usage, by the evidence of CCAE, despite their general preference for retaining stops in abbreviations. There was no widespread use of PM, the other American alternative (compare **a.m.**).

Note that **p.m.** times begin immediately after noon, and so the first minute after 12 noon (= 12 a.m.) is 12.01 p.m. This naturally means that 12 midnight is 12 p.m., and the first minute of the next day is 12.01 a.m.

By using **p.m.** you indicate clearly to readers that you're not working with a 24-hour clock. This may be important in talking travel arrangements with those who are unused to 24-hour schedules. But in international travel, "arriving at 6.30" would always mean a morning arrival, and the equivalent evening arrival (= 6.30 p.m.) would be specified as 18.30.

pocketfuls or pocketsful

For the choice of plurals, see **-ful and -fuls**.

podium

In most halls, there's only one **podium** on which to elevate performers or dignitaries. When the word needs a plural, **podiums** is more likely than *podia*, according to both *Webster's Third* (1986) and the *Oxford Dictionary* (1989).

poetic or poetical

In the past these two shared the adjectival role in relation to *poetry,* but **poetic** now has the lion's share of the business, in both American and British English. What was once *poetical diction* is now *poetic diction*, and *poetic justice* is now the only possibility. For similar pairs, see **-ic/-ical**.

point

For the use of this word in measuring typefaces, see under **pica**.

poky or pokey

British and American English are diverging in the use of these spellings and the meanings attached to them. The British use **poky** to mean "small and cramped," as in *a poky little flat,* and they strongly prefer the spelling **poky** to **pokey**, by a factor of 10:1 in data from the BNC. Americans meanwhile prefer **pokey** for the spelling, and typically use it to mean "slow-moving." Examples in CCAE range from *pokey local traffic,* to *pokey service* in a restaurant, to a *pokey disk drive* on the computer. **Poky** too is used for this meaning in about 30% of cases, but less than you would expect when it's given as the primary spelling in *Merriam-Webster* (2000). Also curious is the fact that the dictionary foregrounds the sense "cramped," which in CCAE data can only be seen in *the pokey,* a slang term for "jail." Canadians live with both American and British senses of **pok(e)y**, according to the *Canadian Oxford* (1998). Australians also have *pokie,* an informal word for the *poker machine,* which usually appears in the plural, as in *playing the pokies.*

polarity

Language, like a magnetic field, may be charged either positively or negatively. This **polarity** is rarely an issue in statements about the way things are, because the facts of the situation decide whether it should be positive or negative. Either:

> *Schools reopen next Monday*

or

> *Schools do not reopen next Monday – not until the week after.*

But when posing questions we quite often seek to know whether something is or is not:

> *Has the minister overlooked the matter?*
> *Would they prefer coffee?*

In such questions, the **polarity** has yet to be established, and they are in fact known to many as *polar questions.* Because they require either yes or no for an answer, they are also known as *yes/no questions.* (See **questions** section 2.)

The **polarity** of a statement affects that of the *tag question* that echoes it. Compare the following:

> *You'd like to come, wouldn't you?*
> *You wouldn't want to come, would you?*

As these sentences show, a positive statement is normally followed by a negative tag question, and vice versa.

polemic or polemical

These two complement each other, with **polemic** working as the noun (*a largely ill-informed polemic*) and **polemical** as adjective (*N. writes with a polemical edge*). Very occasionally **polemic** is also an adjective, but it happens in less than 10% of all instances in British data from the BNC, and only slightly more in American source material in CCAE.

police

Because this word is a collective noun, and regularly takes a plural verb, it leaves the question of its singular in doubt. *Policeman* and *policewoman* are well-established terms but neither is gender-free. When this is needed, *police officer* serves for both sexes and for persons of any rank, because **police** are not divided into officers and rank-and-file, like the defense forces. Any "policeperson" can be addressed as "Officer." In American English *police officer* is the most frequent term by far, by the evidence of CCAE, used for men and women in the service. In British English too, *police officer* serves for both sexes, yet *policeman* outnumbers it by a factor of 3:1 in data from the BNC. For some, *policeman* remains the generic term, as in *a policeman's lot.* There's no sign of *policeperson* in either database.

political or politic

These two have diverged, so that **politic** is now confined to the meaning "judicious, prudent in public affairs," and **political** covers the broad range of "belonging to the state or government or a power group and its policies." **Politic** once covered that ground too, as fossilized in the *body politic.* But the area was taken over by **political** by mid-C18.

political correctness

The term **political correctness** gained currency in the mid-1980s, in the backlash against pressures to avoid sexism and other kinds of noninclusive language. It expresses resistance to any affirmative action against language bias, and projects it as a kind of language police state. The putative curbs on freedom of expression are played up, and the intended goals of better social integration are played down. It insists on the individual's right to continue using modes of expression which have been unexceptionable in the past.

For liberal-minded linguists, it poses a dilemma: testing their social conscience as well as the tenet that language norms are made by the community and cannot be imposed (see **Whorfian principle**). Yet the longer-term effects of highlighting language bias do seem to be reduced use of sexist and racist terms in print in late C20 English. This has been underpinned by the articulation of nonsexist/inclusive language guidelines in publishing houses, media outlets and institutions – though skeptics would question their impact on private discourse and on community thinking.

Whatever the depth and breadth of socially motivated language reforms, the phrase **political correctness** is here to stay. It can now express resistance to affirmative action in other arenas than language, in the US and the UK:

> *It's only recently that political correctness has demanded that fathers be not at the birth.*
> *In an act of knee-jerk political correctness, the University has sold all its Microsoft shares because it is doing business in South Africa.*

Other signs of the productivity of the phrase are spinoffs such as *politically correct* and *politically incorrect.* These too are frequently used outside the realms of language, as in *a politically correct mix of ethnic groups,* and *the most politically incorrect artist.*

Because of its bulk, **political correctness** tends to be abbreviated in casual conversation. On its rare appearances in print, the abbreviation may be seen in lower case, according to *New Oxford* (1998) – as in *applauded for p.c. effort* from the BNC. In American English upper case is usual, according to *Merriam-Webster* (2000). Either way, with or without stops, it coincides with several other abbreviations based on the same letters (see separate entry on **PC, p.c., pc or pc.**). The *Oxford Dictionary of New Words* (1998) documents the form *non-PC* in an American advertisement, but neither this nor other derivatives such as *PC-ness* can be found in the BNC or CCAE.

pollex

For the plural of this word, see **-x** section 3.

poly- and poly

This Greek-derived prefix has taken off in new directions from its core sense "many," found in Greek loanwords such as:

polygamy   polyglot   polygon   polymath
polyphonic   polysyllabic

The first modern English applications of **poly-** were in chemistry, in the names of new compounds:

polyester   polymer   polythene
polyunsaturated

But as chemical terms such as these became household words, **poly-** itself acquired new meanings. *Polyunsaturated* helped to form a second generation of words such as *polymeat* and *polymilk* – where **poly-** means a relatively high level of *polyunsaturated fat*. A different set of derivative words connect with *polyester,* and it gives its meaning to the prefix in *polycotton, polyviscose, polywool* – textile blends containing *polyester.*

In contemporary English **poly-** has also become an independent word, with more than one application. For the British its most familiar use has been as an abbreviation for *Polytechnic,* hence the juxtaposition of *university, poly or college.* Americans also know this use, in sports reporting that refers to the *Brooklyn Poly, Cal Poly* or other teams associated with a *Polytechnic.* **Poly** is now used in both varieties of English as shorthand for *polymer/polythene,* and appears on the labels of household products such as the *poly brush, poly-coated (board), poly wrap.* These uses of **poly** as a noun require a plural, which is always **polys,** by the consensus of both current dictionaries and the reference databases.

Polynesia

Together with *Melanesia* and *Micronesia,* **Polynesia** provides a geographical term for various groups of Pacific islands, as well as an ethnic or anthropological term for their diverse inhabitants.

Polynesia is the broadest of the three, covering the islands from Hawaii in the north to New Zealand in the south, and including Samoa, Tahiti and Tonga. The *Melanesian* group are west of **Polynesia**, and include Fiji, New Caledonia, Vanuatu and the Solomons. *Micronesia* embraces a set of small islands east of the Philippines, the best known of which are the Mariana, Caroline and Marshall islands, as well as Kiribati and Nauru.

The three words were coined by the French explorer Dumont D'Urville in the 1820s. All contain the Greek root *-nes-* ("island"), and so **Polynesia** is the "many-island group," *Micronesia* is the "tiny-island group", and *Melanesia* the "black-island group." The last group may be so named because of the skin color of their inhabitants, or perhaps because of the dark profile of the islands as seen from sea level.

polysemy

Many words have more than one meaning, and **polysemy** ("multiple meaning") is the normal state for all our common words. Dictionaries have to enumerate a set of definitions, not just one for each of them. So to talk in terms of the "true meaning" of a word is rather a misconception. Only new words, and especially scientific and technical ones, have a single meaning, and even they tend to gather new meanings around themselves as they gain wider currency.

Scientists sometimes lament the fact that "their words" are used differently by others – that expressions like *calorie, paranoia* and *quantum leap* have developed nontechnical meanings. It simply shows **polysemy** working in the usual way.

Some words develop meanings in so many different directions that they might seem to have come from quite independent sources. Thus *tank* ("armored vehicle") and the *tank* where farmers in various English-speaking countries store water are one and the same word, though there's no obvious connection between them. Cases of **polysemy** like that need to be distinguished from *homonymy,* where two or more words two from quite separate sources coincide, as with the *lock* on the door and *lock* of hair. See further under **homonyms.**

pommel and pummel

In origin these are one and the same, referring to a knob that projects from the top of a sword or the rounded peak of a saddle, hence also the *pommel horse* used in gymnastic routines. **Pommel** goes back to C14, and began to be used as a verb for punching with one's fists in C16. **Pummel** emerged at about the same time as an alternative. But in C20 English the two spellings have become attached to noun and verb respectively. This happened sooner in the UK than the US, judging by the fact that **pommel** is still represented as the spelling for noun or verb in *Merriam-Webster* (2000) – though there's scant evidence of **pommel** as a verb in CCAE.

Meanwhile **pummel** as verb has extended its range considerably. In British English it can be used to describe physical punching, as in *pummelled the pillows* as well as assaulting the ears, for example the *pummelling bass* in a band. The further reaches of **pummel** can be seen in American English, where it's also used figuratively with the sense "give/take a beating," of a *region pummeled by war* or a *show pummeled by the critics.* Finance reporters use it to dramatize events in the day's trading, such as *the pummeling of the greenback in international currency markets.*

As the examples show, Americans have *pummeled/pummeling* as the inflected forms, whereas the British use *pummelled/pummelling:* see **-l-/-ll-.**

poncy or poncey

See under **-y/-ey.**

-ponic

The agricultural term *geoponic* ("relating to the science of agriculture") is the source of this late C20 suffix, now found also in *hydroponic* ("relating to the cultivation of plants in liquid"). The second element is ultimately derived from the Greek verb *ponein* ("labor"), but those without Greek will perhaps associate it with the more familiar ending *-onic,* found in words such *electronic.*

popular, populous and populist

People or the public are at the heart of all these adjectives, but the different suffixes make for quite different perspectives. **Populous** is the least common and most neutral of them, used to refer to the sheer numbers of people, as in *Los Angeles is the most populous county in America.* **Populist** puts a negative cast on appealing to public sentiment for strategic advantage: *The Gallery is bowing to populist pressures.* **Popular** complements it with the sense of being favored by the general public. It's the commonest of the three, capable of carrying positive or negative values, according to whether one relishes a large following or takes an elitist stance against it.

portentous or portentious

North American commentators note that **portentous** (and *portentously*) sometimes appear as **portentious** (and *portentiously*). In CCAE there's one solitary example, suggesting that editors are still nipping it in the bud.

portico

This C17 Italian loanword has long had an English plural. Spelling it as **porticoes** is still rather more popular than **porticos**, in both British and American English, by the evidence of BNC and CCAE. For other words of this kind, see **-o**.

portmanteau

The plural of this word is discussed under **-eau**.

portmanteau words

This is Lewis Carroll's term for words which are blends of the beginning of one and the end of another. Few of those which he himself coined have been taken up in general usage, apart from the verb *chortle,* a blend of "chuckle" and "snort." The **portmanteau words** which do gain currency are typically nouns or verbs referring to something new or newly identified in our times:

> breathalyser brunch cultivar electrocute
> guesstimate heliport telecast

In examples like those the two components are still recognizable enough to contribute to the meaning of the word. This also seems important in the survival of a blend, and explains the rapid demise of rather obscure ones such as *catalo* (cross between "cattle" and "buffalo") and *incentivation* (a blend of "incentive" and "motivation"). But well-chosen **portmanteau words** can provide both name and slogan for a new product, witness:

> Everlastic Glampoo Soyamaise Sunbrella

possessive adjective

Older grammars of English use the term **possessive adjective** for the form of a personal pronoun which precedes and modifies the noun. Examples include *my, your, his, her, its, our, their.* In modern English grammars, the **possessive adjectives** are regarded as one of the groups of *determiners* (see further under that heading and also **possessive pronouns**).

possessive case

This is the expression used in some traditional grammars for what others know as the *genitive case.* The name *possessive* is not however ideal for the English genitive since that case expresses other relationships than that of possession or ownership. For the full range of uses, see under **apostrophes** and **genitive**.

possessive pronouns

In traditional grammar this term includes the *possessive adjective/determiner* (*my, your, his* etc.) as well as the "true" pronouns:

> mine yours his hers its ours theirs

These refer to an item already mentioned, and are often the sole item to express the subject, object or complement of a verb:

> *Mine is the one on the left.*
> *They put yours on the other side.*
> *Which one is theirs?*

Their capacity to stand alone is recognized in modern grammars by the name "independent possessive" (in the *Contemporary Grammar of English,* 1985) and "absolutes" (in the *Introduction to the Grammar of English,* 1984). Note also *whose,* which is the independent possessive form of the relative/interrogative pronoun, as in *Whose is this?* See further under **interrogative words**, and **who and whose**.

post-

This prefix, meaning "after," was a preposition in classical Latin. In Anglo-Latin its life as a prefix began in words like *postponere* and *postmeridianus,* which have found their way into English as *postpone* and *postmeridian.* In modern English **post-** mostly helps to form adjectives which designate a period in time:

> postclassical postdoctoral postglacial
> postgraduate posthumous postmedieval
> postnatal postprandial

As these examples show, the prefix **post-** normally combines with scholarly, latinate words. The most notable exceptions are *postwar* and *postmodern.* In technical terminology **post-** often creates antonyms for a more familiar word prefixed with *pre-,* for example *postfix, postlude, postposition.* Entirely different is the **post-** of expressions such as *postman* and the British *postcode.* This is a French loanword (*poste*), based on Italian (*posta*), which is ultimately derived from Latin *posita* ("placed").

post hoc

This Latin phrase means literally "after this." It abbreviates the longer phrase *post hoc ergo propter hoc,* meaning "after this therefore because of this." It identifies the fallacy of concluding that an event was caused by whatever preceded it – mistaking sequence in time for a causal relationship. For example, if you pray for a taxi and one comes around the corner immediately after, you might be deluded into thinking that it was prayer-controlled rather than radio-controlled.

post mortem, post-mortem and postmortem

In Latin **post mortem** means "after death," but in English it's used specifically for the *post-mortem examination,* i.e. an autopsy performed on a dead body to establish the cause of death. Both **post-mortem** and **postmortem** are used instead of the full official phrase, the latter showing the typical solid-setting of emerging compound nouns (see **hyphens** 2d). Dictionaries generally prefer the hyphened form for all uses of the word, and it's given priority in *New Oxford* (1998) as well as *Merriam-Webster* (2000). This agrees with database evidence, where **post-mortem** outnumbers **postmortem** by about 4:1 in both BNC and CCAE. Perhaps the string of consonants in the non-hyphened spelling still seems intimidating, even after more than 200 years of use. The fact that it now has many nonlegal uses (as in *an election postmortem*), should help the process of assimilation.

postdeterminer
See under **determiners**.

postmortem
See **post mortem**.

postnominal
Adjectives placed after the noun they qualify are said to be **postnominal**. A few such must always appear in that position, for example *galore*, and *elect* in *president elect*. For some adjectives, going **postnominal** is an option. Compare *There's enough time for coffee* and *There's time enough for coffee*. The **postnominal** adjective is used *postpositively:* see next entry.

postpositive
This is the grammarians' term for the placement of a word after rather than ahead of the word it modifies. Thus *ago* in *four weeks ago* is **postpositive**, as is *not* in *let's not drive there*, and *aboard* in *the loss of all aboard*. Some larger structures can be *postposed*, as in *He wrote reports as clear as any I have read* – where the comparative phrase modifying *reports* is delayed so as to connect with the comparative clause.

postscript
In anglicized form this is the Latin phrase *post scriptum* or *post scripta*, literally "thing(s) written afterwards." Since C16 it has been used to preface anything added after the final signature on a letter. These days it applies also to something added to a book after the end of the main text. At the end of letters, it's always abbreviated to *PS*. It appears in capitals, with no full stops nowadays (see further under **abbreviations**). If something further is added, it can be prefaced by *PPS* ("post postscript").

potato
Database evidence from CCAE and the BNC shows that **potatoes** is still overwhelmingly preferred as the plural. See further under **-o** section 1.

potency or potence, and impotence or impotency
Usage has settled on **potency** rather than **potence**, by the evidence of both American and British databases. But the opposite holds for its antonyms. **Impotence** vastly outnumbers **impotency** in BNC data; and in CCAE **impotence** also has a clear majority, though about 25% of all instances of the word are spelled **impotency**. For other similar pairs, see **-nce/-ncy**.

potpourri
This French phrase means (in reverse order) "rotten pot." However we have to dig deeper into the Spanish phrase *olla podrida* which it imitates, to unearth its meaning. In Spanish it was a culinary term for a miscellany of foods stewed until they were "rotten," i.e. broken down into small pieces, but had developed a wonderful flavor. This at any rate is the Spanish

explanation of that otherwise rather puzzling phrase, and shows how the French, and the English, could come to use it for something attractive, especially the mixture of dried petals and spices kept as nature's own deodorant.

Both the Spanish *olla podrida* and the **potpourri** can be used in reference to any collection of assorted items, and so to such things as a miscellany of musical or literary pieces. The extension of meaning is like that of *hotchpotch* though the overtones are rather more aesthetic: there's a little *je ne sais quoi* in **potpourri**. See further under **hotchpot**.

potter or putter
British English uses **potter** to refer to gentle rather nonpurposive activity, and **putter** for the slow movement of a vehicle. In American English both meanings are loaded onto **putter**, so that both people and vehicles do it. Compare:

> *He puttered around his West Hollywood hotel room.*
> *Another tug puttered off through the night.*

poule de luxe
See under **cocotte**.

pound or pounds
Which should it be in *a two-hundred-and-fifty-pound(s) weight-lifter?* See final note under **foot or feet**.

pp. or p.p.
The stops show that these are two different abbreviations.
1 With just one stop **pp.** means "pages," as in *pp. 115–17* used in referencing, whenever a series of pages is the focus of a footnote or reference. In bibliographies it serves to show how many pages there are in the journal article or chapter of a book being cited. When referring to a span of pages, **pp.** appears before the numbers, but when the total number of pages in the book is to be shown, it comes after: *140 pp.* Note that **pp.** is increasingly being omitted before spans of numbers, in running references (see **referencing** section 3).
2 In official letter writing, **p.p.** with two stops may be used near the typed signature to indicate that the letter is being signed and sent by proxy. See further under **per procurationem**.

practical or practicable
Is a **practical** suggestion the same as a **practicable** one? It could be, though the two words focus on slightly different things. A *practical suggestion* is one which comes to grips with the situation, while a *practicable suggestion* is one that's feasible and could be put into *practice*. The tone of the two words is different, in that **practical** comments and commends in a straightforward way, while **practicable** is more detached and academic in its assessment. In British (BNC) database evidence, the ratio between **practicable** and **practical** is about 1:13, whereas in CCAE **practicable** is much rarer, appearing in the ratio of 1:70. This suggests that **practical** tends to serve for both words in the US.

The two words have several opposites. For **practicable** the antonyms are *impracticable* and *unpracticable*. Fowler's choice (1926) was *impracticable,* which overwhelms the other in contemporary British and American writing, on the evidence of the BNC and CCAE. For **practical** there are two kinds of antonym with different applications: (1) *theoretical,* and (2) either *impractical* or *unpractical.* Fowler put his weight behind *unpractical* and dismissed *impractical,* and the latter was labeled "rare" in the original *Oxford Dictionary.* But at the turn of the millennium *impractical* is strongly preferred in both British and American databases, and the label has been removed from *Oxford*'s second edition (1989). Those who use both *unpractical* and *impractical* sometimes apply the first to people (*an unpractical person*), and the second to inanimates (*an impractical scheme*). For those who use only *impractical,* this division of labor does not exist; and only 2 out of the 9 instances of *unpractical* in the BNC refer to people. So *impractical* and *impracticable* have won the day, and British writers make considerable use of both. Their American counterparts incline much more toward *impractical* – limiting the options, as with **practical.**

practice or practise

The choice between these depends first on which variety of English you're writing, and secondly on grammar. In British and Australian English, **practice** is the standard spelling for the noun, and **practise** for the verb. Complementary spellings with *-ce/-se* are used elsewhere in English to distinguish nouns from verbs, although in most such cases they match up with different pronunciations (see under *-ce/-se*). American English uses **practice** for the verb as well as the noun – a preference which reflects their common pronunciation, and is in keeping with the more general American avoidance of *-ise* as a verb ending (see *-ize/-ise*). In data from CCAE there's only a handful of cases of **practise,** against thousands of **practice.** Canadian usage is very mixed, according to *Canadian English Usage* (1997): many writers use the British system while the press tends to go with the American.

The alternative ways of dealing with this word pose more problems for the British than the Americans in expressions where the word's grammar is debatable. Compare:

British	American
golf practice	*golf practice*
they practise on Saturdays	*they practice on Saturdays*
a practice?practise range	*a practice range*

In the third example, is it a noun or a verb? Compounds like this more often consist of noun + noun, yet verb + noun is a possibility: compare *dance party.* At the best British golf clubs there's a dilemma, where for Americans there is none.

The spellings **practice/practise** hint at the separate C14 origins of the two, **practice** in the noun *practic,* and **practise** in the verb *practisen,* with stress on the middle syllable. The *Oxford Dictionary*'s (1989) many alternative spellings recorded from the next two centuries suggest that the verb took on the early stress of the noun, and its second syllable was then pronounced like that of "service." At the same time the noun's pronunciation and spelling were changing to match the verb, in forms such as *practis/practys.* Shakespeare, like many in C16, used **practise** for both. This complex past underlies the divergences of the present, where American English runs with a

single spelling and British uses two. As elsewhere, British English works with fine distinctions where American English looks for the larger patterns. See further under **spelling, rules and reforms.**

pre-

This well-worked Latin prefix means "before." In many words including most modern formations, it means "prior in time"; but in older loanwords and a few modern technical words, it can mean "standing in front." We derive it from numerous Latin loanwords such as:

> *preclude*   *predict*   *prefer*   *prefix*
> *preliminary*   *prepare*   *prevent*

In modern English it teams up easily with words of both French and Anglo-Saxon origin to make new ones:

> *predate*   *predawn*   *predestined*   *preheat*
> *prejudge*   *prepaid*   *preschool*   *preshrunk*
> *prestressed*   *preview*

The examples show **pre-** as a formative element in many common nouns, verbs and adjectives, though it also combines with proper names to identify a historical or geological period by the one adjacent to it. For example: *pre-Cambrian, pre-Christian, pre-Shakespearean, pre-Raphaelite.* In those cases there's a hyphen between **pre-** and the next word, because of its initial capital. Hyphens are not otherwise needed, except perhaps when **pre-** is attached to a word beginning with *-e* or another vowel, e.g. *pre-empt, pre-eminent, pre-exist* and *pre-arrange, pre-industrial, pre-owned.* At this point British writers are more inclined to use a hyphen than their American counterparts, and so *New Oxford* (1998) hyphenates all those examples where *Merriam-Webster* (2000) has them set solid, except for the last. Yet even British writers and dictionaries have *preadolescent, preoccupied, preordain,* suggesting that well-established derivatives with **pre-** do not need hyphens even when vowels are juxtaposed. The context of occurrence often helps to prevent misreading. When elections are in the air, the *preelection campaign* is unlikely to miscue the reader.

Because **pre-** means the same as *ante-,* the two prefixes present a few corresponding pairs:

> *predate/antedate*   *precedent/antecedent*
> *prenatal/antenatal*

In each case the word with *ante-* is more restricted in meaning or its context of use. Overall there are many more words with **pre-,** no doubt because of the risk of confusing *ante-* with the very different *anti-.* (See **ante-/anti-.**)

Pre- serves as the contrasting prefix to *post-,* as in *prewar/postwar.* See further under **post-.**

precede or proceed

A mistaken choice between these verbs can easily sabotage the meaning, because **proceed** means "go ahead, advance" while **precede** means "go before," "introduce." Compare:

> *Please proceed to the front of the queue.*
> *A long queue of passengers preceded me to the check-in.*

Grammarians would note that **proceed** is always intransitive, whereas **precede** can be either transitive or intransitive. Since only transitive verbs can work in the passive, **precede** is the only possibility in constructions like:

> *I was preceded by a long queue of passengers.*

(See further under **transitive**.)

For the difference in the spelling of the second syllable of each word, see under **-cede/-ceed**.

precedence or precedent

These differ in meaning and in the grammar of their use. **Precedence** is an abstract noun meaning "priority in rank or importance," most often used in idioms such as *give precedence to,* or *take/have precedence over.* **Precedent** is a countable noun meaning a "model or example from the past," which is used in idioms such as *set a precedent, no precedent for* or *find a precedent for* (something). As the phrases show, the words use different prepositions in collocating with what follows. This serves to differentiate them, even when they come close to each other, as in:

> *The prime minister has precedence over others in speaking.*
> *The office of the prime minister has its precedent in the chancellor of Tudor times.*

Dictionaries note *precedency* as an alternative to **precedence**, but it hardly appears at all in databases of current British and American English.

For other pairs of this kind, see **-nce/-ncy**.

preciousness or preciosity

Like the adjective *precious,* the English abstract noun **preciousness** can be either positive or negative. Compare:

> *... the preciousness of the freedom to speak*
> *Her lyrics suffer from preciousness*

Preciosity, borrowed from French, carries only the negative sense "overrefinement."

precipitate or precipitous

Both adjectives can embody the idea of rushing headlong, though **precipitate** originates in the time dimension, and **precipitous** in space (like *precipice*). Archetypal examples of each are *a precipitate strike* and *precipitous canyons.* Yet **precipitous** is increasingly used in more figurative ways which bring it close to **precipitate**. When financial reporters write of a *precipitous decline* in the value of shares, they are no doubt thinking of the way the trend would appear as a line on a graph, a sharp fall which when plotted against time means a rapid event. Thus **precipitous** comes to mean "sudden and dramatic," and to serve instead of **precipitate** – as in almost 20% of instances in the BNC. The scope for using it this way, and in talking about *precipitous action* (i.e. not necessarily related to statistical trends) is taken much further in American English. Close to 80% of examples of **precipitous** in CCAE express the temporal meaning, and it's registered in both *New Oxford* (1998) and *Merriam-Webster* (2000).

The trend toward using **precipitous** instead of **precipitate** for "sudden and dramatic" correlates with the fact that **precipitate** itself is now more often used as a verb than adjective (in about 60% of instances in the BNC and 80% in CCAE). In this way they complement each other grammatically, with **precipitate** as verb (or noun), and **precipitous** the adjective for spatial, temporal and other figurative senses. Realignments like this are the stuff of English language history.

précis

A **précis** is a summary version of a document (see further under **summary**). The word comes from French with an acute accent which is disappearing in English. In other ways it's only half assimilated. It remains the same when used in the plural (i.e. has a zero plural); and though it takes regular English verb suffixes, as in *precising* and *precised,* they are pronounced in the French fashion, without the "s" sound. On the last point compare other French loanwords such as *debut:* see under **-t**.

precision or preciseness

Though **preciseness** has the longer history as an abstract noun for *precise* (by about two centuries), it has been overtaken by **precision** since C18. Database evidence from both the US and the UK show that **precision** is very strongly preferred.

Compare **conciseness or concision**.

predeterminer

See under **determiners**.

predicate

This traditional grammar term still has a useful role in identifying the elements of a clause which complement the subject to form a statement. (In *transformational grammars* the **predicate** is called the *verb phrase*, which conflicts with other important uses of that phrase. See under **verb phrase**.) Together the subject and **predicate** (italicized in the following examples) embody the heart of a clause, as in:

> Empty vessels *make the most sound.*
> Actions *speak louder than words.*
> The pen *is mightier than the sword.*

In statements the subject usually precedes the **predicate**, though some (or all) of the **predicate** comes first in certain questions, negative statements and other inversions (see under **inversion** and **subject**). Further points about the **predicates** of positive statements are discussed below.

1 The predicate always contains a finite verb, and, depending on the nature of that verb, another component. Some grammarians simply call it the "complement," but many others including the *Comprehensive Grammar* (1985) and the *Longman Grammar* (1999) identify three different kinds of complement to the verb, namely (a) *object,* (b) *adverbial,* (c) *complement* (in a more restricted sense). The three types are illustrated by our three proverbs:

a)
> *Empty vessels make the most sound.*
> subject/verb/object (SVO)

Objects are often needed with a verb of action to complete its sense (see further under **transitive** and **object**). The *object* may be a noun phrase, as in that example, or a pronoun.

b)
> *Actions speak louder than words.*
> subject/verb/adverbial (SVA)

Some verbs of action take an *adverbial* which details it in terms of the manner, place or time in which it takes place. The *adverbial* may be only a single word, or a phrase (usually an adverbial or prepositional phrase). The term *adjunct* is used for this component by grammarians such as Halliday (1985) and Huddleston and Pullum (2002).

c)

> *The pen is mightier than the sword.*

subject/verb/complement (SVC)

Complements in this restricted sense typically come after the verb *be* or another copular or linking verb, and help to detail the subject of the clause. (See further under **copular verbs.**) They are typically noun phrases, adjectives or adjectival phrases, as in the example. Some English adjectives, e.g. *ahead, asleep, awry* can only appear *predicatively* (see **adjectives** section 1).

2 Occasionally a predicate consists of a verb alone, as in:

> *The telephone rang.* (SV)
> *He had been sleeping.* (SV)
> *The younger staff would come.* (SV)

As these examples show, the verb component may be a simple verb, or a combination of auxiliaries and main verb forming a verb phrase. For further extensions of the verb phrase by infinitives, as in *They managed/intended to come,* see **catenatives.**

3 Three-part predicates are required for three groups of verbs to complete the clause. They create the **predicate** patterns VOO, VOA, and VOC, illustrated in the following:

> *They gave him oxygen.* (SVOO)
> *They put him in an ambulance.* (SVOA)
> *They made him a hero.* (SVOC)

The first group are *ditransitive* verbs, which require OO (i.e. both *indirect* and *direct objects*), because they involve transmitting something to someone. The second group of *complex transitive* verbs are those with the pattern OA, which typically place or locate an *object,* and the *adverbial* shows where. The third group with the pattern OC includes verbs that confer a status (notional or actual) on the *object,* using an extra *complement* to express it. As in SVC clauses, the *complement* is often an adjective: *They thought/called it miraculous.* A rare variant of SVOC is the SVCC pattern, as in *That house is worth a million.*

Final note on predicates. The patterns described above show the obligatory elements of the **predicate,** without which the clause would be incomplete. However English clauses often include other optional elements, particularly *adverbials,* as in *They immediately gave him oxygen* (SAVOO). Additional *adverbials* may precede or follow the obligatory elements of the **predicate.**

predominant or predominate, and predominantly or predominately

Both **predominant** and **predominate** have served as adjectives in English since late C16, though the first has occupied centre stage and is far more common. In databases of American and British English, instances of **predominate** as adjective can be counted on the fingers of one hand (the spelling is almost entirely used for the verb). But as *Webster's English Usage* (1989) noted, the equivalent adverb **predominately** is also current and somewhat more common than the adjective. The ratio of **predominately** to **predominantly** is about 1 in 20 in CCAE and about 1 in 50 in the BNC – though two thirds of the cases of **predominately** are from transcriptions of speech where there's little to separate the two. It is also possible that writers and editors have long been inclined to make the adverb match the dominant

form of the adjective, and assumed that the minority form was a mistake.

preface

Between the title page of a book and the start of the main text, there may be any or all of the following: *foreword, preface, introduction.* The boundaries between them, and their location, vary with the publisher and the publication.

An *introduction* by the author is these days often as long as a chapter of the book itself; and when it outlines the book's structure and contents, it may be treated as the first segment of the main text and paginated in arabic numbers with the rest. However when the main text is a reference book, such as a dictionary, even long introductory essays are paginated in lower case roman numbers, and made part of the preliminary matter. (See further under **prelims.**)

The *foreword* and/or **preface** are always paginated in roman. In older bookmaking practice they would both precede the table of contents, and this is still recommended by the *Oxford Dictionary for Writers and Editors* (1981). The reverse is recommended in *Copy-editing* (1992) and the *Chicago Manual* (2003). Their rationale is that the table of contents should come first, so that a reader can immediately locate all the components of the book, and then begin to read more discursively. A possible compromise is to put the *foreword* before the table of contents and the **preface** after it. This seems a sensible compromise if, as often, the *foreword* is brief (only two or three paragraphs), and is written by someone other than the author – usually a celebrated person whose name lends distinction to the volume. The **preface** is usually written by the author (or editor, if the work is an anthology), and may amount to two or three pages. It typically explains how the book came into being, and acknowledges the contribution of others to it. Sometimes the acknowledgements are made on a separate page, with their own heading.

In subsequent editions of the book, the *foreword* is likely to remain unchanged. But the **preface** may be modified, or complemented by a separate "Preface to the second edition."

Dictionary definitions of *foreword* often make it synonymous with **preface,** and it seems to have originated that way in C19, amid moves to replace latinate words with home-grown Anglo-Saxon ones. To some users they are synonyms, though, as shown above, those who are involved in the making of books see them as having different functions.

preferable

The standard spelling is **preferable,** whatever the pronunciation. "Preferrable" would seem apt for those who stress the second syllable, but neither it nor "preferrible" have been used since C18, according to the *Oxford Dictionary* (1989).
Compare **inferable.**

prefixes

The meaningful elements we attach to the beginnings of words are **prefixes.** Their distinctiveness can be seen in sets of words like the following:

> *antiwar   postwar   prewar*
> *inactive   proactive   retroactive*

Most of the **prefixes** used in modern English are of classical and especially Latin origin, as are all of those just illustrated. The best known **prefixes** from Old English are *be-* as in *befriend* and *un-* as in *unlikely*.

Prefixes do not usually affect the grammar of the word they are attached to (as suffixes often do). The only **prefixes** which move words from one grammatical class to another are *a-* as in *awash* (verb to adverb), *be-* as in *befriend* (noun to verb), and *en-/em-* as in *enable, empower* (adjective or noun to verb). Very many others modify the meaning, not the grammar of the word.

The kinds of meaning added by **prefixes** can be seen under several headings. There are **prefixes** of time and order (*pre-, post-*), of location (*sub-, super-*), of number (*bi-, tri-*), and of size or degree (*macro-, hyper-*). Others express the reversing of an action (*de-, dis-*), its negation (*un-/in-*), or a pejorative attitude to it (*mal-/mis-*). English words may take **prefixes** from one or two of those groups, but that's the limit, witness: *polyunsaturated, unpremeditated, antidisestablishment.*

Prefixes are generally set solid with the rest of the word. Hyphens appear only when the word attached begins with (1) a capital letter, as with *anti-Stalin,* or (2) the same vowel as the prefix ends in, as with:

   anti-inflationary de-escalate micro-organism
Yet in well-established cases of this type, the hyphens become optional, as with *cooperate, coordinate* and their derivatives. (See further under **co-**, and **hyphens** section 1.)

Compare **suffixes**.

prelims.
Publishers and printers use this colloquial abbreviation for the *preliminary matter* of a book, more formally known as the "front matter." The term **prelims.** covers:
   half-title page
   title page
   imprint page
   dedications page and/or epigraph
   table of contents
   table of figures and diagrams
   list of contributors
   foreword, preface and acknowledgements
   list of abbreviations
   maps providing location for the text overall
The typical order of appearance is as above, though the location of foreword and preface varies somewhat with the publisher. (See further under **preface**.)

Compare **endmatter**.

premier or premiere
These are the masculine and feminine forms of the French adjective meaning "first," borrowed centuries apart (C15 and C19). **Premier** is the earlier loan, now an alternative term for "prime minister" in the UK; and in Australia and Canada, a term for the head of an individual state, province or territory. In official titles the word is always capitalized. Compare *the Premier of Queensland* with *the Quebec premier.* In sporting contexts the **premier(s)** are the winning team in the season's competition: *The Panthers are premiers again.* The ranking associated with this use of **premier** is exploited by advertisers in promoting

products, as in *the premier beer style, Ghana's premier hotels, the premier wilderness organization in Scotland.*

Premiere (originally *première*) is a recent loanword, taken up in artistic circles. It refers to the first performance of a play or musical composition, or the first showing of a newly made film. Increasingly it's used as a verb, transitive or intransitive:
   ... the Grand Theatre Leeds, where the ballet was premiered...
   The film premiered in New York this week.
The use of **premiere** as a verb dates from 1940, according to the *Oxford Dictionary* (1989), and there are more than 40 examples in data from the BNC. In CCAE there are hundreds, showing its appeal to entrepreneurs and institutions wanting to add a touch of first-night glamor to whatever they are launching. The usage panel of the *American Heritage Dictionary* (1969–2000) has only gradually accepted the use of **premiere** as a verb, and is still reluctant to have it applied outside "the entertainment industry." Do television programs and computer games come under that heading, you may ask. The launch of a new degree program by a college probably doesn't, and only 25% of the panel accepted the use of of **premiere** in that context. But useful words have their own momentum. *Webster's English Usage* (1989) concludes that the verb **premiere** has outgrown whatever qualms there have been about it.

With its new grammatical roles in English, **premiere** is well assimilated – hence the disappearance of the grave accent from both noun and verb in *New Oxford* (1998) and *Merriam-Webster* (2000).

premise, premiss and premises
In philosophy and logic, the first two spellings refer to a basic argument or proposition. **Premiss** is the older spelling, dating from C14, and the one recommended by the American philosopher C. S. Peirce in C19. But philosophers since then have varied, and the alternative form **premise** (dating from C16) is the one used by ordinary citizens concerned about the grounds of an argument. In American data from CCAE, **premise** is the only spelling to be found; and BNC writers using **premise** outnumber those using **premiss** by more than 10:1.

The plural form **premises**, encountered in reference to real estate and legal rights over it, is from exactly the same source. The very different contexts of use mean there's unlikely to be any confusion, especially when the *premises of an argument* are abstract, and the **premises** which are the subject of a lease are concrete – or at least very tangible. **Premises** usually takes plural verbs and pronouns in agreement, even when referring to a single house:
   Those modest premises were all I could afford.
See further under **agreement** section 2.

premium
This C17 Latin loanword has long had *premiums* as its **plural**, according to the *Oxford Dictionary* (1989).

prepositional phrases
These consist of a *preposition* followed by a noun, noun phrase or pronoun, as in:
   after dinner after a long evening after you
They may forge a link with the verb of a clause, with another prepositional phrase, or with a noun or

adjectival phrase. All four are illustrated and italicized below:

1 The delegation left *for the Caribbean.*
2 At the last session *for prospective candidates,* they met her.
3 The search *for meaning* goes on and on.
4 Thankful *for their help,* they forgot the previous disagreement.

The examples also show the various ways in which **prepositional phrases** may function in a sentence:

* as adverb (sentence 1) (see further under **predicate**)
* as an extension to the adverb (sentence 2)
* as postmodifier of the noun phrase (sentence 3)
* as postmodifier of the adjectival phrase (sentence 4)

For the term *postmodifier,* see under **noun phrases.**

prepositional verbs

See under **phrasal verbs.**

prepositions

The basic role of a **preposition** is to detail the position of something, its physical location or direction, or a more abstract relationship to other things. The most common **prepositions** are:

about	*above*	*across*	*after*	*along*	*around*
as	*at*	*before*	*below*	*beside*	*between*
by	*down*	*for*	*from*	*in*	*into*
like	*near*	*of*	*off*	*on*	*onto*
over	*past*	*since*	*till*	*than*	*through*
to	*under*	*until*	*up*	*with*	*without*

English also has a number of *complex prepositions* with two or more elements, such as:

because of	*in front of*	*instead of*
on top of	*out of*	*due to*
in regard to	*next to*	*owing to*
with reference to	*in accordance with*	

Within sentences, **prepositions** typically lead in a noun, noun phrase or pronoun, and with it form a *prepositional phrase.* It may serve one of several functions in a clause (see **prepositional phrases**).

Many English **prepositions** double as adverbs, as a glance at the list above would confirm. The similarity in their roles is clear in the following:

They went up the stairs as the lift was going up.
        (preposition)   (adverb)

The very same word *up* can be an integral part of the meaning of a verb, as in:

He ran up a big bill.

Compare:

He ran up a big hill.

In the second sentence, *up* is an ordinary **preposition** heading a *prepositional phrase* ("up a big hill"). In the first, it works as part of a transitive phrasal verb "ran up," with "a big bill" as the object. (See further under **phrasal and prepositional verbs.**)

Other issues with *prepositions*

1 **Prepositions** and collocations. Convention dictates that certain verbs and related words are followed by particular **prepositions**/particles. Words like *compare/comparison* take either *with* or *to,* and *differ/different* may take *from, to* or *than,* depending on the context, and which part of the English-speaking world you belong to (see **different from**). In Britain you *fill in* a form, whereas in the US you would express it as *fill out.* Note also the fact that, in American English, no **preposition** at all is needed

with some verbs which do require one in British English. Compare:

British	American
cater for a party	*cater a party*
protest against the war	*protest the war*
provide us with a plan	*provide us a plan*
wrote to his MP	*wrote his Congressman*

2 Ending sentences with **prepositions.** The prescriptive "rule" that **prepositions** should never appear at the end of a sentence flows from the idea that they are always "preposed" to a noun/pronoun, as indeed they are in *prepositional phrases.* It disregards that fact that **prepositions** can also be semantically attached to verbs, e.g. *get off, play up, take on,* as we have seen (see further under **phrasal and prepositional verbs**). This means that they operate in relation to what has gone before rather than what follows (hence the value of calling them *particles,* which is more neutral than *preposition* as to the direction of attachment). But the narrow understanding of **prepositions** led C18 grammarians to think they could never be the last word of a sentence, and their "rule" has been vigorously taught until well on in C20. It obliged writers to recast any sentence with a final **preposition** so that the offending item appeared earlier in the sentence. Compare:

Which result were you relying on?

with

On which result were you relying?

And *I wonder which train he was waiting for.*

with

I wonder for which train he was waiting.

The effect of observing the rule is an overly formal and sometimes unidiomatic sentence. Churchill threw his considerable weight into the scales against it, saying it was "a form of pedantry up with which I will no longer put." Yet the old rule lives on in some computer grammar checkers. Modern grammarians refer to the final **preposition** as being *stranded;* and *stranded prepositions* occur freely in interrogative and relative clauses, according to the *Longman Grammar* (1999), in all kinds of discourse except academic prose. As the final word on this issue, we might note that a **preposition**/particle can make a rather limp ending to a sentence. Still this is a matter of style, not bad grammar.

prerequisite or perquisite

A **prerequisite** is a prior condition:

Four years experience is a prerequisite for the program.

A **perquisite** is a benefit or privilege attached to a position, as in *the perquisites of office.* These days the *perquisites* might include any additional income beyond the fixed wages or salary, and so may refer to anything from tips to the use of a company car. The word **perquisite** now sounds formal or old-fashioned, and has long been abbreviated to *perk,* first recorded in 1869. *New Oxford* (1998) labels *perk* "informal" – though this may have more to do with the informality of some of the arrangements it connotes. The word is usually used in the plural. In BNC data *perks* occurs freely in administrative and financial writing:

The perks took the form of discounts on quarterly bills.

Shareholder perks are primarily a marketing exercise.

Perks is used in the same way in American data from CCAE, and has no restrictive label in *Merriam-Webster* (2000).

prescribe or proscribe
These both involve the exercise of power and authority. Those who **prescribe** set out rules or a course of action for others to follow, whether it is the judge prescribing the terms of settlement for a case, doctors prescribing medicines, or educators prescribing syllabuses. Those who **proscribe** are public authorities through whom particular practices may be banned:

> *Smoking is now proscribed in most government buildings.*

As those examples show, **proscribe** involves a negative force, while **prescribe** implies a very positive kind of directive. The contrast is perhaps clearest if we compare *prescribed books* (those which a student must read) with *proscribed books* (those banned by the authorities to make it impossible for people to read them).

prescriptive or descriptive
For the difference between **prescriptive** and **descriptive** approaches to language, see **descriptive**.

present tense
The simple forms of English verbs such as *smile, walk, discuss,* tend to project events as if they are happening in the here and now – or at least as if there's no time limit on them. Compare the forms *smiled, walked, discussed,* in which the action is set in the past and confined to it. Thus English verbs are said to express either a *present* or a *past tense,* the latter being marked by the added *-(e)d,* or some other change to the simple form. (See further under **past tense** and **principal parts**.)

But in certain contexts the **present tense** can express both future and past time. See for example:

> *My new job starts tomorrow.*
> *If it rains, they will reschedule the event.*
> *After all that he reappears with a grin as if nothing had happened.*

In all such sentences, the tense is expressed through something other than the simple verb. In the first sentence, it's the adverb *tomorrow;* in the second, the conditional *if* and the *will* of the main clause both put *rains* into the future. In the third, the narrator heightens the drama with the use of *reappears,* but the other verb makes it clear that the overall context is in the past. This dramatic use of the **present tense** is known as the "historic present" or the "narrative present." Note also that the **present tense** serves to describe ongoing habits and customs, and to make generalizations. For example:

> *We go to the markets most Saturdays.*
> *The boss likes to have flowers in the office.*
> *The rains come with the changes of season.*

Compound present tenses. In ordinary conversation, and in some kinds of writing, the *present continuous* rather than the simple **present tense** may be used to project what is happening here and now:

> *After weeks of drought the rain is coming.*

The *present continuous* creates a span of time in the present, whereas the *present perfect* marks a moment in it, at which writer and reader can share a retrospective view:

> *Now that the storm has passed we can reconnect the computer.*

For more about the *continuous* and the *perfect,* see **aspect**.

pressured, pressurized or pressurised
American English uses **pressured** to refer to people under stress, and the verb *pressurize* for technological applications of *pressure,* as in *pressurized cabin, pressurized water reactor.* Yet in recent British English, *pressurize/pressurise* has come to be used of people under psychological *pressure* to do something:

> *She would not be pressurized to publish things against their judgement.*

This human use of **pressurized/pressurised** was first recorded in 1956 according to the *Oxford Dictionary* (1989), and is now freely used alongside **pressured**. In BNC data, human uses of **pressurized/pressurised** and **pressured** are represented in the ratio of about 2:3, whereas in CCAE **pressurized** still usually means an engineered system. Just occasionally it's extended to refer to a working context (*a competitive, pressurized situation*), but rarely applied to the individual.

For the **pressurized/pressurised** spelling difference, see **-ize/-ise**.

presume or assume
See **assume**.

presumptuous or presumptive
In the past, these words were occasionally interchanged, but nowadays they are associated with different aspects of the verb *presume.* **Presumptive** represents its more neutral sense of being based on a *presumption,* as in *presumptive title* and *heir presumptive.* It occurs much less often than **presumptuous**, a negatively charged word which represents the sense of "presuming too much" or "taking unwarranted liberties."

Presumptuous is sometimes pronounced and spelled "presumptious," a spelling recorded up to C18 (*Oxford Dictionary,* 1989), and still fostered by its connection with *presumption* (see **-ious**). A search of the internet (Google, 2003) found it in about 5% of all instances of the word.

prêt-à-porter
This French phrase means "ready to wear," and refers to garments which are mass-produced in standard sizes for retailing, instead of being made for the individual by a tailor or dressmaker. However inspired their design, clothes bought *prêt-à-porter* are unlikely to qualify as *haute couture* ("high fashion"). See further under **haute**.

pretense, pretence, pretension or pretentiousness
These overlap considerably, in spite of their different appearances. The first two are simply alternative spellings, **pretense** being used in the US, and **pretence** in the UK. (See further under **-ce/-se**.) As far as meanings go, we might note that **pretense/pretence** is the abstract noun for the verb *pretend* when it means "feign, put on," as in:

> *They made a pretence of sympathy.*

Pretension picks up the sense of "lay claim to" which is also part of the scope of *pretend:*

> *He had no pretensions to becoming president.*

Pretentiousness embodies the sense of showing off, either socially or intellectually, *pretending* to sophistication which isn't quite there:

> *The pretentiousness of his conversation drove his colleagues to despair.*

Still the major dictionaries all allow that **pretense/pretence** is sometimes used instead of both **pretension** and **pretentiousness**, and **pretension** for **pretentiousness**. None of them is very flattering.

pretty

As an adjective this word is uncomplicated. But its status as an adverb as in *pretty run down* or *a pretty good case* is still queried – in terms of style rather than grammar. There's no question that it works as an "amplifier" and "downtoner" (see further under **intensifiers** and **hedge words**). But the idea dies hard that **pretty** as an adverb is somehow "informal." It bears the label in the *New Oxford* (1998), although not the *Oxford Dictionary* (1989), which shows that it has been in literary use since C16. In current British English it occurs freely in everyday factual and interactive writing, judging by the more than 5000 examples in the BNC:

> *This is pretty low for speculative investment.*
> *The exhibition illustrates some pretty horrific mistakes that we made.*

Merriam-Webster (2000) comments that **pretty** is neither "rare nor wrong in serious discourse," though "common in informal speech and writing." Research by authors of the *Longman Grammar* (1999) shows that **pretty** is indeed very common in American conversational English, much more so than in British English, by a factor of 4:1. Where Americans say *pretty bad/easy/interesting,* the British say *quite bad/easy/interesting.* In American English **pretty** works as both intensifier and downtoner, whereas British usage seems to make more of the latter (both uses are nevertheless registered in British dictionaries). Having a double role may of course make for ambiguity, which can be a problem as well as a resource. The indeterminacy of **pretty** as a modifier may well prevent a rush to judgement by speakers or writers, and allow them to negotiate or fine-tune their argument as it develops. This would explain the uses of **pretty** in both speech and interactive or discursive writing – and its absence from academic texts, according to the *Longman Grammar.* Pragmatics are at issue rather than style.

 Compare **quite.**

prevent (from)

Following the verb **prevent**, there are two possible kinds of construction:

> *prevent them from contacting the source*
> *prevent them contacting the source*

Research by Mair (1998) shows that the second construction is relatively recent, established in late C20 British English, but not yet in American English. There is little sign of the gerundial equivalent *prevent their contacting the source:* see further under **gerund and gerundive.**

preventable or preventible

The older spelling by far is **preventable** (dating from 1640), and it's given priority in the *Oxford Dictionary* (1989) and all current dictionaries. It is the only spelling to be found in BNC data, and overwhelmingly preferred (by almost 250:1) in CCAE. **Preventible,** dating from 1850, may nevertheless seem more consistent with related words such as *preventive* and *prevention.*

preventive or preventative

The primary spelling in both *Webster's Third* (1986) and the *Oxford Dictionary* (1989) is **preventive,** preferred because of its better formal relationship with *prevention.* Americans are strongly behind it, and in CCAE it appeared in almost 90% of all instances of the word. But **preventative** has increasingly challenged it in British English since C18. In data from the BNC, **preventive** still predominates in terms of overall frequency, yet a significant number of texts (40%) use **preventative** rather than **preventive.** The two share various common applications, in *preventive/preventative medicine* and *preventive/preventative measures,* and both are very occasionally used as nouns, as in *noise-preventive* and *an excellent preventative of disbelief.*

pricey or pricy

In both American and British English, **pricey** seems to be strongly endorsed. Both *Merriam-Webster* (2000) and *New Oxford* (1998) give it priority, and it's overwhelmingly preferred in data from CCAE and the BNC. Yet **pricy** is the more regular spelling (see -e), and gained 40% of the vote in the Langscape survey (1998–2001), when **pricy/pricey** was presented along with other words of the same type.

prima donna, diva and prima ballerina

In Italian **prima donna** means "first lady," though it's associated with the operatic stage rather than the White House. The term was and is given to the principal female singer in an opera company, though it's now also applied to a temperamental, conceited and autocratic person of either sex. In fact those negative connotations are on record from mid-C19, and probably help to explain the arrival in the 1880s of **diva,** another Italian loanword for a great female singer, meaning literally "goddess" and still a term which registers admiration.

 In English both **prima donna** and **diva** are pluralized in the regular way with *s,* though the Italian plurals **prime donne** and **dive** are sometimes used for their foreign cachet. Perhaps they help to bypass the negative associations of **prima donna,** which are now firmly built into the English language in derivative words such as *prima donna-ish* and *prima donna-ism.*

 A **prima ballerina** is the matching term in a ballet company identifying the leading female dancer, or one of the highest rank. The only title above that is *prima ballerina assoluta,* a title so rarefied it was only given twice in the history of the Russian Imperial Ballet. The expression **prima ballerina** is normally given an English plural, helped by the fact that the word *ballerina* itself is pluralized that way. Yet **prima ballerina** too is developing more general senses. The

Oxford Dictionary (1989) records both "important or self-important person" and "leading item in its field," both since 1950. It also recognizes the Italian plural **prime ballerine**, which here again may serve to designate outstanding dancers, and distinguish them from leading persons or items in other fields.

prima facie
This well-assimilated Latin phrase means literally "by the first face." Less literally it means "at first sight" or "on the face of it," as applied since C15 in English law, where *a prima facie case* is one for which there is sufficient evidence to justify further investigation or judicial proceedings. Similarly it's used in scholarly argument of data which looks significant but requires further investigating. Note that there's no need to hyphenate *prima facie* when it serves as a compound adjective. See **hyphens** section 2c.

primaeval or primeval
See **primeval**.

primary auxiliaries
See under **auxiliary verbs**.

primeval or primaeval
The preferred spelling among both US and British writers is **primeval**. In BNC data, only a small minority of writers (about 10%) spelled it **primaeval**, and none at all in CCAE. Though less common than *medi(a)eval*, its digraph seems to be disappearing faster. See further under **ae/e**.

primus inter pares
This Latin phrase means "first among equals." It may be used to identify someone who is the spokesperson for others of equal status; or to suggest that the person who is technically the leader has no special authority over those with whom he is associated.

principal or principle
Most adults cope with one-syllable homophones such as *cede* and *seed*, but three-syllabled ones like **principal/principle** get the better of many. The words do however differ in meaning and function, and we can thus distinguish them.

Principal is an adjective borrowed from Latin meaning "chief, most important." It has acquired many more meanings as a noun in English, in reference to the head of a school or college, the leader of a section of an orchestra, and those who are the key agents in a law case. In law it refers to the real assets of an estate (as opposed to the income they earn), and it's used more generally in financial calculations, to distinguish the capital sum from any interest or profit associated with it.

Principle is an abstract word meaning "rule" or "formative characteristic," as in:
Those groups work on a principle of collaboration.
The underlying principle of the design is inspired.
Because **principle** is an abstract, there are modifiers before and/or after it to specify its meaning. This helps to distinguish it from **principal** as a noun, whose meaning is specific enough in most contexts to need no elaborating.

The problem with these words arises from the fact that English preserves the word **principle** and certain others in forms which were peculiar to northern French and Anglo-Norman (see -le section 3). The standard French for **principle** is "principe," which does not make a homophone for **principal**.

principal clause
See **clauses** section 3.

principal parts
These are the alternative forms of a verb which serve to make the present and past tenses, from which all other forms can be inferred. So for the verb *speak*, the **principal parts** are *speak/spoke/spoken*. The first one of the set provides the necessary stem for *speaks* (3rd singular, present tense) and *speaking* (present participle); and the others provide the past tense and past participle respectively. Although it's customary to give three **principal parts**, this is only essential for irregular verbs. Most regular verbs have just two distinct forms: e.g. *laugh* (present) and *laughed* (past), because the past participle is identical with the ordinary past tense. See further under **irregular verbs**.

principle or principal
See **principal**.

prise or prize
These spellings represent quite a clutch of different words, both nouns and verbs. In British, Canadian and Australian English the verb **prise** ("lever off") is distinct from the verb **prize** ("value greatly"). The noun is always **prize**, whether it refers to a special award, or to something captured by strenuous effort. In the US the first verb is usually spelled **prize** as well – which is a straightforward way out of the problem of knowing which spelling to use for which meaning. It coincides also with the standard American use of *-ize* in the choice between *civilize/civilise* etc. (See further under **-ize/-ise**.)

The use of **prize** for the noun is itself an amalgamation of two once separate words – extensions of different roots. The sense of "special award" comes from the medieval "pris" and Latin *pretium* (which also gives us *price*); and the sense of "something captured" is from "prise," part of the French verb meaning "seize" (the source of the English verb **prise**). Meanwhile the verb **prize** ("value greatly") is an alternative form of the word *praise,* based on Old French *preisier/prisier.*

While **prize** is the regular American spelling for all the nouns and verbs mentioned above, *pry* occasionally serves as an alternative for the verb "lever off." See further under **pry**.

pro- and pro
English embraces both older and newer uses of this Latin prefix-cum-preposition. As a prefix it means "forward" or "in front of [in time or space]," as in:
proceed progress project promote propose
In these old loanwords **pro-** is always set solid.

Another older use of **pro-** is to mean "substitute for," which has come down in words such as *proconsul* and *pronoun,* and has generated new formations such as *pro-vice-chancellor*. New words formed this way are hyphenated.

A similar but recent use of **pro-** is to be found in words like *pro-American, pro-communist, pro-Israel,* where it means "in favor of." In such words it's always hyphenated, whether the following item bears a capital letter or not. This meaning corresponds quite closely to one associated with **pro** as a preposition in Latin – which perhaps explains both the hyphen and the fact that they can be formed ad hoc with almost any raw material: *pro-daylight saving.*

Pro has additional roles as an independent word in English. In *pros and cons* it refers to arguments in favor of a proposition, a direct use of the Latin preposition. Note that **pro** also stands as an abbreviation for two English words: (1) professional and (2) prostitute.

pro forma

In Latin this means "as a matter of form." It refers to documents required by law or convention, as in *pro forma letter* and *pro forma invoice.* Nowadays it often serves as an abbreviation for the invoice itself, as in:

A pro forma will be sent with the goods.

The Latin abbreviation no doubt helps to avoid the unwelcome word *invoice.* To pluralize **pro forma,** use **pro formas,** as for other foreign compounds. See further under **plurals** section 2.

pro rata, pro-rata and pro-rate

This medieval Latin phrase meaning "in proportion" is mostly found as an adverb or adjective in English, as in:

Funding will not increase pro rata.

. . . a scheme of pro-rata payments to creditors

The spaced form **pro rata** is more common overall in Britain and the US. Yet BNC evidence shows that British writers are more inclined to use it for the adverb (as in the first example), and make equal use of the hyphened form (**pro-rata**) for the adjective.

In American and Canadian English (but not British or Australian) the phrase has been anglicized in the verb **pro-rate,** for example:

to pro-rate the property tax bill between buyer and seller

pro tem

In abbreviated form this is the Latin *pro tempore* ("for the time being, temporarily"). As an informal expression for an interim arrangement, it can be used in almost any situation. Compare the formal phrase *locum tenens,* used of a carefully arranged professional replacement. See further under **locum tenens.**

problematic or problematical

Writers everywhere prefer the shorter form. In data from both BNC and CCAE, **problematic** outnumbers **problematical** by about 6:1. See further under -ic/-ical.

proboscis

In scientific use this classical loanword (from Greek via Latin) refers to a large facial organ used for feeding purposes, like the elephant's trunk, or to the sucking organ of certain insects and worms. In English its usual plural is the anglicized **proboscises** – which is either specified in the dictionary entry, or endorsed by the lack of any other specification. Neither *New Oxford* (1998) nor *Merriam-Webster* (2000) suggest the Greek plural **proboscides.** The need for any kind of plural is remote when **proboscis** is used to caricature a human nose.

proceed or precede

See **precede.**

proclaim and proclamation

See under -aim.

Professor and Prof(.)

This academic title resists abbreviation, in correspondence, and in running text. Letter writing conventions have **Professor** followed by initials on the envelope: *Professor S.R. Herman;* by the given name(s) in the superscription inside: *Professor Susan Herman;* and by the surname in the salutation: *Dear Professor Herman.* (See Appendix VII for letter formats.)

Data from texts in the BNC and CCAE provide thousands of examples of **Professor** and only a few hundred of **Prof(.)** in each case. The two do not usually appear in the same text (with **Prof[.]** abbreviating an earlier use of **Professor**). Instead the academic title/name is abbreviated in the same way as in letters: from *Professor David Stuart* (or *David Stuart, Professor of Engineering*) to *Professor Stuart.* Initials are rarely found with the title in running text. Note that the second style with title following is likely to be fully capitalized in British English, and lower-cased (*professor of engineering*) in American English.

When **Prof(.)** is used to save space or avoid formality, the use/non-use of a stop goes with one's general policy on abbreviations (see **abbreviations** options a–d). Consistency with other titles such as *Mr(.)* and *Dr(.)* is also an issue where they are juxtaposed in lists or documents.

profited

For the spelling of this word when used as a verb, see -t.

pro-forms

Grammarians use this term to cover the various words that substitute for others in a text, including pronouns and pro-verbs (especially *do*), as well as *one* and *so.* See further under individual headings.

progeny

Depending on the application, **progeny** ("offspring") may be construed as plural or singular:

All the progeny of the wasp then perish

He became semi-divine, the progeny of a tribal king and the female deity.

In BNC data the two applications are about equally common.

prognosis

Originally Greek, **prognosis** comes via Latin into English, and maintains its Latin plural **prognoses.** See further under -is.

program or programme

Program is the standard spelling in the US for all uses of the word. In the UK **program** is reserved by many for computer uses, and **programme** applied in all other contexts. In fact **program** was endorsed by the original *Oxford Dictionary* on two grounds:

1 **Program** was the earlier spelling, used in the word's first recorded appearances in (Scottish) English in C17, while the spelling **programme** made its appearance in C19. (We may speculate on whether it was motivated by the desire to "improve" the Scots

form or to "frenchify" it – or both. See further under -e.)

2 **Program** is analogous with *anagram, diagram, histogram, radiogram, telegram* etc., while there are no analogues for **programme**. Fowler quietly endorsed those points in 1926, but his reviser Gowers (1965) made haste to affirm the British preference for **programme** – which suggests that it may have crystallized only by mid-century. Yet in BNC data, approximately one third of all uses of **program** are not computer-related, raising the question as to whether the British preference is beginning to change (or never was as firm a distinction as has been claimed). In Canada, **programme** is used by the federal government to embrace French interests, whereas Canadians more generally use **program**, according to *Canadian English Usage* (1997). Australian government style has endorsed **program** for all purposes since the 1960s.

When **program** serves as a verb, the final *m* is normally doubled before suffixes, as in *programmed, programming* and in *programmer*. In the US the words are sometimes spelled with a single *m*, but this is not very common, even though it conforms to more general American habits of spelling. The fact that the second syllable is a separable unit may help to explain why. See further under **doubling of final consonant**.

prolegomenon
This makes a weighty alternative to "introduction." Being originally Greek, its plural should be **prolegomena** (see **-on**). No excuses for those who wish to use the word.

prologue or prolog
See under -gue/-g.

promptness or promptitude
Both are current as abstract nouns for *prompt*, but **promptness** is clearly preferred in both British and American English, by about 3:1 in BNC data, and 10:1 in data from CCAE.

pronounce and pronunciation
The spelling difference between these is a common problem, and inexpert writers sometimes impose the *-oun* of the verb on the second syllable of the noun ("pronounciation"). It was until C18 a recognized alternative spelling. But nowadays only **pronunciation** will do, making the word's stem as Latin as the suffix. The spelling of the verb **pronounce** is Anglo-Norman, and a reminder that it was used in English rather earlier than the bookish noun. Other words related in exactly the same way are *denounce/denunciation* and *renounce/renunciation*.

pronouns
A **pronoun** is a small functional word which stands instead of a noun, noun phrase, or name, as *she* may substitute for "Agatha Christie," or *this* for "the camera I have in my hand." There are several kinds of **pronouns**:
* personal   *she, he, you* etc.
* possessive   *hers, yours* etc. (see further under **possessive pronouns**)
* reflexive   *herself* etc.
* demonstrative   *this, that, these, those*
* indefinite   *any(one), each, everyone, some(one)* (see **indefinite pronouns**)
* interrogative   *who, which, what, whose, whom*
* relative   *that, who, which, what, whose, whom*

Pronouns usually stand for something which has been mentioned already, though just occasionally a narrative may begin with a **pronoun** and proceed to explain:

> *He turned out to be the best friend I ever had. We shared a long flight to New Zealand, and after that...*

Whether the **pronoun** anticipates the details (as in that example) or harks back to something detailed earlier, it helps to provide cohesion. (See further under **coherence or cohesion**.)

Many **pronouns**, especially those from the demonstrative and indefinite groups, also function as *determiners*. See further under that heading.

proofreading
This is an essential part of checking your own writing, or preparing anyone else's for printing. It involves reading at more than one level – firstly at the level of ideas and how those ideas are expressed, and secondly at the level of spelling, punctuation and typesetting. This means at least two readings of the MS, since the people who can reliably read on both levels at once are as rare as hen's teeth.

The standard *proofreading marks* used to indicate settings and changes to the typesetter are listed in Appendix VI.

propellant or propellent
The original *Oxford Dictionary* preferred **propellent** for the noun and the adjective, but its second edition (1989) acknowledges a swing of the pendulum to using **propellant** for both. In BNC data, **propellant** is the only spelling of the word, almost always used as a noun. In American English **propellant** is also the dominant spelling, outnumbering **propellent** by more than 20:1 in data from CCAE. Again it serves for noun (*a propellant in aerosol cans*) as well as adjective (*solid-propellant booster rockets*). The only uses of **propellent** were nouns, pace *Merriam-Webster* (2000) and *New Oxford* (1998), which suggest that it survives for the adjective. This consolidation of the *-ant* form can be seen in several similar words: see further under **-ant/-ent**.

propeller or propellor
The English form **propeller** dominates in both British and American English, by the evidence of BNC and CCAE. Instances of **propellor** can be counted on the fingers of one hand.

proper names
A **proper name** designates a unique person or entity, such as *Stephen King, Capetown* or the *University of Canterbury*. Note that in the third case, the **proper name** consists of common words combined with a *proper noun: Canterbury* (see **nouns**). **Proper names** can consist entirely of common words, as in *Northern Territory*. The uniqueness of the designation makes it a **proper name**, not the words combined in it.

Proper names – personal, geographical and institutional – are normally distinguished by capital letters on every component except the function words. (So words like *the, and, of* are not capitalized.)

However institutional names often shed their capitals when used repeatedly and in abbreviated form in any piece of writing. See further under **capital letters** section 3.

proper nouns

These are single words which serve to identify a unique person or entity, such as *Confucius* or *Hungary*. They contrast with common nouns such as *adult* and *island* which refer to infinite numbers of persons or items of that kind. See further under **nouns**.

Proper nouns are always capitalized, even when their use in the plural suggests they are no longer unique. Thus we write:

We have three Davids on the staff here.

Although reusable **proper nouns** are not listed with the common nouns in dictionaries, they do have some general kinds of meaning which could be specified. For example, the name *Eric* is male and Anglo-Saxon, and *Paola* is female and Italian. Compare *Mitsuhiro* and *Masumi,* whose gender is unclear to those who know no Japanese. Some **proper nouns**, or forms of them, have stylistic meaning built into them, and we recognize *Johnno* if not *Tassie* (= Tasmania) as informal **proper nouns**.

prophecy or prophesy

Up to about 1700 these were interchangeable, but **prophecy** has since been reserved for the noun, and **prophesy** for the verb. This division of labor parallels the one written into pairs such as *advice/advise* (see further under-**ce/-se**). However it is less established in American English than British. *Webster's Third* (1986) allows either word to stand instead of the other, and in data from CCAE more than half the examples of **prophesy** are nouns, as in: *biblical prophesy, a self-fulfilling prophesy.* There are however very few of **prophecy** being used as a verb. *Merriam-Webster* (2000) notes the use of both spellings for the noun, but only **prophesy** for the verb.

proportional or proportionate

These adjectives both mean "being in proportion," and there's little to choose between them – except that **proportionate** normally appears after the noun, as in *profits proportionate to our investment,* but not before it. **Proportional** is more versatile, and could appear either after or before the noun: compare *proportional representation* with *representation proportional to population.* Another small point of difference is that **proportional** seems to express precise numerical ratios, whereas those in **proportionate** are more impressionistic. This second point also emerges when we compare their opposite forms: *disproportional* points out a disparity in numbers, whereas *disproportionate* suggests a more general lack of *proportion.*

propos

See **apropos**.

proposition or proposal

Either of these could be used when it comes to a proposed plan or business offer. Yet the extra syllable and latinate form of **proposition** makes it the more formal choice, and coincides with the fact that **proposal** is definitely the more common of the two, by a ratio of about 3:1 in the BNC. The more formal character of **proposition** has been reinforced by its use in scholarly contexts, especially in mathematics and logic. Yet new idiomatic uses of **proposition** are increasing its popularity, witness *a commercial proposition, an exciting proposition, a different proposition altogether.* In phrases like those, applied to anything from the new motel, to a tempting holiday package, to the freshly signed-up football star, **proposition** becomes a faintly pretentious synonym for "prospect" or "venture." **Proposal** retains its basic link with the verb *propose.*

Another remarkable development is the C20 development of **proposition** as a verb, meaning "seek sexual intercourse with." A similar sense is now also attached to the noun, contrasting dramatically with **proposal** – which is always associated with the proposing of marriage.

proprietary or propriety

These both involve extended senses of the Latin word *proprietas* ("property"). The adjective **proprietary** is rather more concrete and relates to the property of individuals, as in *proprietary rights* or *proprietary company.* A *proprietary product* bears the name of the particular company that profits by it, though it may be made to a generic formula or model. In the southern hemisphere (Australia, New Zealand, South Africa) the *proprietary company* is a private, limited company, indicated by the contraction *Pty,* as in *Computer Systems Pty Ltd.* **Propriety** meanwhile is a noun. It takes "property" in the more abstract sense of the essential character that goes with the social context, hence conventional manners and the "proper code of behavior."

proprietor

This word appears from nowhere in C17, in reference to the *proprietors of the North American colonies.* It looks like a Latin legalism, but the records to prove it are lacking. The *Oxford Dictionary* (1989) is otherwise inclined to explain it as an English concoction out of the Latin adjective *proprietarius* ("proprietary"; see previous entry). **Proprietor** has its own latter-day (C19) English adjective in *proprietorial.*

proscribe or prescribe

See **prescribe**.

prose

The ordinary medium of discourse which we write is **prose**. It contrasts with poetry in having no conventional form to dictate the length of lines or the number of lines which form a unit. It contrasts with scripted dialogue or conversation in being continuous monologue. **Prose** is not in itself a literary form, hence Molière's satire of the "bourgeois gentleman" flattered to be told that he was speaking it.

prospectus

For the plural of this word, see under **-us** section 2.

prostrate or prostate

These two are not to be confused, as in "prostrate troubles." **Prostate** refers to a gland in the male genital organs, whose malfunction in later life may require a *prostate operation.* **Prostrate** is an adjective meaning "lying collapsed on the ground." In that sense it covers both *prone* ("lying face downwards") and *supine* ("lying flat on one's back"). Yet dictionaries all show that the meaning of **prostrate** is closer to *prone* than *supine*, and that it can be a synonym for the former but not the latter.

The difference between **prostrate** and *supine* also comes out in their figurative uses, describing how groups of people behave in the face of powerful forces. **Prostrate** involves total submission and surrender, as in:

> the triumphant dictation of terms to a prostrate enemy

Supine suggests inertness or failure to resist pressure, as in:

> a supine and cowardly press ... intimidated into censoring the truth

Thus **prostrate** implies that the power is not to be resisted, whereas *supine* implies that it should have been.

protagonist and antagonist

These Greek loanwords have been reinterpreted in English so that they complement each other. Modern uses of *pro-* and *anti-* support the notion of **protagonist** as "one who fights for something" and **antagonist** as "one who fights against something" (see further under **ante-/anti-** and **pro-**). But those with a knowledge of Greek, including Fowler and the editors of the original *Oxford Dictionary,* found this very unsatisfactory because the **protagonist** was the leading actor (literally "first actor") in a Greek drama. Fowler therefore claimed that the word could not be made plural (since there was only one **protagonist** in the original context); and he argued that using the adjective "chief" with it (as in *chief protagonist*) was tautologous. They are issues for the cognoscenti. The *Oxford Dictionary* (1989) overruled his first point and allowed **protagonists** in the plural, while insisting that the word be applied to leaders and prominent people only. Yet in BNC data, the **protagonists** are often the unnamed adherents of a cause, as in the *nuclear protagonists' case* or *protagonists of the warm-blooded theory (of dinosaurs).* The *New Oxford* (1998) defines **protagonist** as "leader" as well as "advocate or champion of a cause or idea," noting that this is now widely accepted in standard English. Other dictionaries, both British and American, enter it without any hint of the controversy.

The fact that people nowadays interpret **protagonist** as embodying **pro-** (the Latin prefix meaning "in support of") is not something to lament or condemn. It confirms that common knowledge of Latin word elements in English is much stronger than the knowledge of Greek – and that people like to make sense of the words they use.

protector or protecter

This word might look like an English formation based on *protect* (and therefore to be spelled with *-er*: see **-er/-or**). It was in fact borrowed from French in C14. So the spelling **protector** is long established, and it reigns supreme in both American and British English, by the evidence of CCAE and the BNC.

protest

Everywhere in the English-speaking world, the verb **protest** can be construed transitively as well as intransitively (i.e. with or without a direct object: see

further under **transitive**).

1 *protest one's innocence*
2 *protest that it would spoil the landscape*
3 *protest against the war*
4 *protest at their disregard for the facts*

The third collocation *protest against* usually implies an organized public protest, whereas the fourth (*protest at*) is more likely to be the voice of an individual. *Protest about* and *protest over* are also occasionally found. All four constructions are used in American and British English, yet Americans often use transitive constructions for the third and fourth types as well. For example:

> Civilians on the outskirts of the capital protested French intervention.
> Boris Yeltsin strongly protested the NATO bombing raids.

Transitive constructions like these appear far more often than ones with *against* and *at,* in data from CCAE. They are frequent in news and sports reporting (*protest the game/race*), and support a passive construction: *their arrival was protested by the mayor,* which gets into headlines as *Arrival Protested.* The grammar of **protest** is thus more flexible in American English than British. It includes the intransitive, but emphasizes the transitive side of the verb. In British English the intransitive uses are still to the fore.

Protestant

This term (with a capital *P*) refers to any of the churches which detached themselves from the Catholic Church of Rome at the time of the Reformation. The name was first used of the German princes who spoke out against the counter-Reformation statements of Speyer in 1529. It was then applied to the churches led by Luther and Calvin, and to the Church of England. Further **Protestant** churches were formed in Britain in the next two centuries, detaching themselves from the established Church of England. Dissenting churches, the Methodists, and Presbyterians are therefore also known as *Nonconformist* churches. In the US the largest *nonconformist* churches (upper or lower case) are the Southern Baptist Convention, Uniting Methodists, Lutherans, the Pentecostal Church of God in Christ, and the Mormons.

Note that the term **Protestant** is not used of the Eastern Orthodox churches, which detached themselves from the Church of Rome about AD 1054.

protester or protestor

Given that it's a recent English formation, **protester** is the appropriate spelling – and strongly preferred by American writers represented in CCAE, who have little time for the latinate **protestor**. British writers use both spellings, though still **protester** outnumbers **protestor** by more than 2:1 in data from the BNC.

proto-

This Greek prefix means "first in time" or "original." In English it has developed out of words such as *protoplast* and *prototype,* and provided the initial element for many new scientific terms of C19, especially in zoology, biology and chemistry. These were followed by a spate of words with **proto-** in the humanities and social sciences. Some are generic terms such as *protoculture, protohistory, protosyntax,* while others refer to a specific early culture or language:

proto-Baroque	proto-Renaissance
Proto-Australian	Proto-Indo-European
Proto-Romance	

As the examples show, the prefix is capitalized when it forms part of the name of a hypothetical original language, but in lower case when it refers to an early or primitive form of a given culture. Note also the use of a hyphen with **proto-** before a word with a capital, but not in the generic or scientific terms.

proved or proven

Everywhere in the English-speaking world, **proved** is the dictionaries' primary form for the past participle of the verb *prove,* and **proven** the alternative. Their position is strongly supported by data from the BNC, where the first (as past participle) outnumbers the second by almost 10:1. In American data from CCAE, the ratio is more like 5:2, but still clearly in favor of **proved**. Americans use **proven** in active as well as passive constructions: *has proven impossible, yet to be proven;* and there are examples of both in the BNC, though active constructions are definitely in the minority. All this challenges the claim made in some British style guides that **proven** is *the* American form – as does the fact that British and American writers both use **proven** for the participial adjective, in phrases such as *proven ability,* and legal formulas such as *not proven, proven guilty.*

provenance or provenience

Though **provenience** is sometimes said to be the American equivalent to British **provenance**, there's no evidence of its use in data from CCAE – or the BNC. According to the *Oxford Dictionary* (1989), **provenience** was coined about 1880 by those who objected to the nonclassical (French) form of **provenance**, but the latter has prevailed.

proverb

See under **aphorism**.

provided (that) or providing (that)

Either of these can introduce a condition:

not a problem provided (that) the candidate shows talent and flexibility

... guaranteed permission to go to the West providing (that) they returned to East Germany first

The structures are both equally old, appearing in C15 with a following *that* and, without it, as a quasi-conjunction in C17. Fowler (1926) preferred **provided (that)**, and British writers represented in the BNC endorse it over **providing (that)** by more than 2:1. In American English from CCAE, the ratio is about 3:1. Both constructions are more often used without the following *that* than with it, and when placed at the start of a sentence or after a comma they are unlikely to be misread as parts of the verb *provide.* The second example above would benefit by a comma if the following *that* is to be omitted. Most style commentators agree that these phrases are heavyweight ways of prefacing a condition. If that is the effect you're seeking, they serve the purpose. Otherwise *if* serves for a positive condition, and *unless* for a negative one.

prox.

See under **ult**.

proxime accessit

See under **cum laude**.

proximity agreement

See **agreement** sections 4 and 5.

prudent or prudish

These adjectives recognize very different aspects of human character. **Prudent** implies wisdom and shrewdness, and respect for them in the person or plan credited with them. **Prudish** implies a narrow concern with the conventions of modesty and morality and a tendency to disapprove of others who are more liberal in this regard.

The similarity between the two words suggests a common basis of meaning, but it's deceptive. **Prudent** has a straightforward history going back to an identical Latin adjective meaning "wise." **Prudish** has come to us by a devious route through French. It uses the clipped form (*prude*) of French *prudefemme,* meaning "proud or worthy woman," with the English suffix *-ish* added to make it an adjective. Evidently a certain irony has contributed to its sense development.

pry

There are two different verbs underlying **pry**:
1. "look inquisitively"
2. "prise, lever"

The first is typically followed by *into,* as in:

Far be it from me to pry into a client's financial arrangements

The second collocates with *open,* as in:

... she leaned forward to pry open the packing case

The different particles separate the two usages in North American English (US and Canadian). Neither the British nor Australians make much use of the second.

Pry in the second sense is believed to be a backformation from *prise* – where the third person singular present of the verb – *pries* – suggested a base form *pry.* (Compare *flies/fly.*) The same kind of backformation has contributed several nouns to English (see under **false plurals**). The origin of **pry** ("look inquisitively") is unknown.

The noun for "one who pries" (in either sense of the word) is spelled *prier,* whatever dictionary you consult. But there are no examples in either BNC or CCAE to support the point, and we might otherwise expect it to be the more regular form *pryer.* Compare **drier** and **flyer**.

PS

See under **postscript**.

pseudo-, pseudo, pseud and pseud.

Borrowed from Greek, **pseudo-** meaning "false" first appears in English in medieval religious expressions such as *Pseudo-Christ* and *pseudo-prophet.* But its productive life as an English prefix takes off in C19, in countless new formations. At first they are mostly scholarly, and in biological nomenclature **pseudo-** is used in a relatively neutral way to refer to organs which have a function other than the one you might expect (e.g. *pseudocarp*), or a species which resembles another though it's unrelated to it (*pseudoscorpion*).

In other disciplines **pseudo-** has negative connotations, and points to the falseness of appearances, as in *pseudoclassic* and *pseudoscience*. It is freely used in ad hoc pejorative words and phrases such as *pseudo-charm, pseudo-marble walls*. In examples like the latter, **pseudo** can appear as an independent adjective (*pseudo marble walls*), and is recognized in that role in both *New Oxford* (1998) and *Merriam-Webster* (2000). **Pseudo** is also listed as a noun ("an insincere person"), although the clipped form **pseud**, as in *the ultimate pseud,* is now the more common form in database evidence.

The abbreviation **pseud.** represents *pseudonym* in bibliographies. See further under **nom de plume**.

pseudo-cleft sentence

See under **cleft sentences**.

pseudonym

See **nom de plume**.

psychic or psychical

The first of these adjectives is much more common than the second – except in the phrase *psychical research*. That apart, American and British writers both prefer **psychic**, in academic collocations such as *psychic and social*, and everyday applications such as *psychic breakdown/pain/scars/wasteland*. **Psychic** also serves as a noun for the person considered to have *psychic powers*, as in:

> . . . *only able to communicate with a psychic named Brown*

For other pairs of this kind, see **-ic/-ical**.

publicly or publically

Publicly is an exceptional adverb – because it's formed with *-ly* not *-ally,* as is normal for adjectives ending in *-ic* (see under **-ic/-ical** section on "adverbs"). Dating from C16, **publicly** has remained the standard spelling, and dominates the data from both CCAE and BNC. There are just rare examples of **publically** against hundreds of **publicly**. *Merriam-Webster* (2000) notes **publically** as an alternative to **publicly**, whereas *New Oxford* (1998) has only the latter.

pukka, pukkah, pucka or pucker

This Anglo-Indian word (Hindi for "ripe" or "cooked") gives the nod of social approval wherever it's applied: to the *pukka meal, a pukka racing car,* or the *pukka tones* of a certain accent. *Pukka* is by far the commonest spelling in data from CCAE and the BNC, and prioritized in *Merriam-Webster* (2000) as well as *New Oxford* (1998) – though the latter also lists *pukkah*. *Pucka* was the primary spelling in C19, according to the *Oxford Dictionary* (1989). Any of them serves to distinguish the word from the very different **pucker**, meaning "crease, wrinkle":

> . . . *pucker the top of the bag*
> *The pink lips slide from wide smile to pucker.*

In fact, the grammar of **pucker** as a verb/noun sets it apart from the Anglo-Indian adjective – so it too can be spelled **pucker**, as in the exclusive *Pucker Gallery* in Boston.

pummel or pommel

See **pommel**.

punctuation

The English *punctuation system* has evolved in tandem with the traditions of writing and printing. Some elements of **punctuation** go back to medieval manuscripts, but their shapes and uses varied until well into C17, and were formalized only in C18. The contribution of space to the *punctuation system* (e.g. word space, space between sentences) has only recently been recognized. The *punctuation marks* which appear in modern English are as follows:

* for *sentence punctuation*

brackets/parentheses	colon
comma	ellipsis
em rule / em dash	en rule / en dash
exclamation mark	full stop / period
question mark	quotation marks
semicolon	

* for *word punctuation*

acute	apostrophe	cedilla
circumflex	dieresis	grave
háček	hyphen	solidus/slash
tilde	umlaut	

For more about each, see under individual headings. There are regional differences in the use of *brackets, colon, comma, ellipsis, quotation marks;* as well as the *apostrophe, hyphen, solidus;* and the *stop* in abbreviated words (see **abbreviations**).

Note also the increasing use of sets of bullets, arrows or other devices to mark items in vertical lists. (See **bullets**.)

1 Developments in punctuation. Not all the *punctuation marks* listed above are used regularly, and the use of even the most essential ones has varied since C18. *Punctuation marks* were sprinkled much more liberally through books published a century ago than nowadays. "Lighter" **punctuation** is the taste of our times in continuous prose; and in business letter writing there's a growing preference for "open" rather than "closed" **punctuation** (see Appendix VII for examples of each). Less **punctuation** means fewer keystrokes for the keyboarder, and less time and effort in the production of the day's letters.

2 Punctuation and sentence grammar. Punctuation interacts with the grammar of sentences, marking off separate grammatical units within them (e.g. quotations, parentheses), and always marks the end of the sentence. *Punctuation marks* used to be placed to coincide with almost every phrase of a Victorian novel – and served their purpose, amid the intricate and typically longer sentences of the time. Less complex, shorter sentences can be read comfortably with less internal **punctuation**. It is still vital for presenting itemized material in vertical lists, as in computer manuals designed for print or screen reading. The items can be marked either by conventional **punctuation** or a combination of bullets and space (see **lists**).

The correlation between **punctuation** and sentence elements is otherwise only occasional. An adverbial phrase at the start of a sentence may or may not require a comma after it, depending on its length. Commas may be used with nonrestrictive/ nondefining relative clauses, but are not the only factor that distinguishes them from restrictive/ defining clauses (see further under **relative clauses**).

3 Punctuation, speaking and information delivery. Some people associate **punctuation** with the sound and rhythm of sentences, and see it as a substitute for the stress, rhythm and pausing of living speech. Yet the ordinary patterns of stress and sentence rhythms have to be created by the writer's flow of words. Words needing particular stress are sometimes underlined or italicized – thus going outside the standard *punctuation system*. **Punctuation** mostly correlates with the larger pauses within and between sentences, though not quite as systematically as was thought by C18 writers, who saw the comma, semicolon, colon and full stop as representing increasingly long pauses in sentences. We still regard the comma, (semi)colon and full stop as representing small, medium and large breaks in the structure of sentences (see further under **colon** and **semicolon**). Ideally they are placed at points where readers can safely pause, because of a break or boundary in the structure of information. **Punctuation** serves to pace the *visual* delivery of information, not to control its oral performance. Research by Chafe (1987) showed that readers given *punctuated* texts always added their own prosodic breaks when reading it aloud. The **punctuation** supplied was never quite sufficient to the task.

4 **Meaning in punctuation.** Punctuation is at bottom a device for separating and/or linking items in the continuous line of writing. Many *punctuation marks* do both at once. Commas often separate one phrase from the next, yet they show that the two belong to the same sentence. Hyphens link the two parts of a compound, but also ensure that the boundary between them is obvious to the reader. Research shows that **punctuation** works best in supporting distinctions which are already there for the reader in the words, and cannot really "create" ones which are not already felt.

Punctuation is essentially neutral, and cannot express a writer's attitude unambiguously. Exclamation marks attached to a particular statement could mean that the writer is either shocked or excited by it. The use of "scare quotes" is similarly ambiguous (see **quotation marks** section 1).

For ways of resolving the problem when two different *punctuation marks* coincide in the same place, see **multiple punctuation**.

pundit or pandit

This Hindi loanword, originally *pandita*, means "wise man, scholar," and in the form **pandit** it is still a title of honor, witness *Pandit Nehru*. The pronunciation of the word by Indians makes it sound to English ears like "pundit"; and **pundit** is the spelling attached to the extended use of the word in English, when it refers to ad hoc experts, as in *political pundit, fashion pundit*, or those attached to a particular medium: *TV pundit, Washington Post pundit*. Given this somewhat undiscriminating use of **pundit**, it's preferable to use **pandit** whenever the older meaning of the word is intended.

puns

A **pun** is a play on words, invoking the meaning of two (or more) at once for humorous effect. Though sometimes called the "lowest form of wit," it all depends on the quality of the **pun**. Shakespeare used **puns** to add allusive dimensions to his dialogue, and contemporary news reporters engage their readers with **puns** in headlines. A nice example to head an article on the aristocratic pursuit of gardening was HAUGHTY CULTURE. Advertisers exploit the **pun** in

the naming of products, and help them to linger in the mind, witness ABSCENT for a deodorant, and RAINDEERS for plastic shoe protectors used in the snow belt of North America. As the examples show, a written **pun** commits itself to one meaning by the spelling, and has to rely on the context (verbal/visual/situational) to raise the other.

pupa

The plural of this word is discussed under **-a** section 1.

puritan, puritanical and puritanic

Older dictionaries allow that any of these adjectives can be used to imply moral severity. **Puritanical** is noted as having derogatory overtones, as in *puritanical distrust of pure pleasure*, whereas **puritan** means strict rather than life-denying. It can also be used as a noun: *Don't be such a puritan.* A capital letter is added in historical references to the *Puritan Revolution* (and individual *Puritans*). **Puritanic** is no longer current, by its absence from the BNC and CCAE, and from both *New Oxford* (1998) and *Merriam-Webster* (2000).

purlieu or purlieus

This medieval loanword from French referred to the cleared area on the fringe of the royal forests, where game was still protected under *purlieu law*. In modern English, it has been urbanized to mean the outskirts of a particular place, as in *the photogenic purlieus of Cambridge*. As in that example, **purlieus** is normally pluralized with *-s* not *-x*. See further under **-eau**.

purposely, purposefully or purposively

All three adverbs claim to explain the *purposes* underlying human action, but they take somewhat different perspectives. **Purposely** indicates that what happened was not just a matter of chance, but done intentionally (or *on purpose*). It often relates to small, everyday events: *He purposely kept the memo out of N's hands.* Its opposite is *accidentally*.

Purposefully usually implies movement toward a preconceived goal: *Moran drove purposefully.* Its opposite is *aimlessly*.

Purposively is a more academic word than either of the others, popularized by the theory of "purposivism" a century ago – the idea that the behavior of an individual or organism is always directed toward an end, and is not random:

> The elements of structure have to behave
> purposively, working at and overcoming basic
> human problems.

In **purposively** the perspective is detached, sociological or behavioristic, whereas both **purposely** and **purposefully** are mentalistic. **Purposively** is the rarest of them, though occasionally used for **purposefully** in data from the BNC.

purveyor or purveyer

For centuries this French loanword has referred to those officially designated to provide food and other services to the royal household, or other institutions such as the army. In late C20 English it has been updated to include any kind of capitalism without commercial privilege. One may be **purveyor** of anything from coffee and pizza, to detergents and "insurance-related products." But the newest uses of the word are more figurative: from *purveyor of movies* *galore and unlimited entertainment,* to Hollywood as *purveyor of dreams,* and from *purveyor of gossip* to that of *wild and new paradoxes.* Creative uses like these abound in both American and British English, by the evidence of both CCAE and the BNC – though they may be quite recent, given the lack of comment in either *Oxford Dictionary* (1989) or *Webster's Third* (1986). Figurative use is now acknowledged in *New Oxford* (1998), and embraced by the definition "one who purveys" in *Merriam-Webster* (2000). In fact the verb *purvey* has long been used figuratively, and we may yet see a revival of the English spelling **purveyer** (obsolescent since C17, according to the *Oxford*) to confirm the lively link with the verb.

putrefy or putrify
See under -ify/-efy.

putter or potter
See **potter**.

pygmy or pigmy
The spelling **pygmy** is now strongly preferred in both British and American English, by more than 10:1 in data from the BNC and CCAE. **Pigmy** was used in earlier English up to C16, when its Greek antecedent *pygme* was built back into the spelling by Renaissance spelling reformers (see **spelling, rules and reforms** section 1). However **pigmy** continued to be used, by the numerous citations in the *Oxford Dictionary* (1989), and the two spellings have coexisted, like other *i/y* pairs (see under **i/y**).

Amid C20 concerns over racist language (explicit and implicit) **pigmy** has seemed both unfortunate and linguistically misleading. It suggests animal connections where the word's origins should be found in a Greek unit of length (the *pygme* was a measure from the elbow to the knuckles, rather like a cubit). Both *Oxford* and *Webster's Third* (1986) prefer the spelling **pygmy** for etymological reasons, and usage generally seems to have swung behind it. It affects all uses of the word, whether in reference to one of the Bushman people of Equatorial Africa, or figurative applications such as *an intellectual pygmy;* or adjectival uses for a dwarf species of plant or animal, as in *pygmy pine, pygmy goat, pygmy kingfisher.* When used of the people, the word should bear a capital letter as in *a Congo Pygmy chief* (see **capital letters** section 1). The plural of the noun is **Pygmies.**

pyjamas or pajamas
The first is the standard spelling in Britain and Australia, the second is the one generally used in the US, although *Webster's English Usage* (1989) notes that **pyjamas** occasionally appears in American fashion catalogues, presumably because of its cachet. In Canada both spellings are used, according to *Canadian English Usage* (1997).

The spelling **pajamas** is slightly closer to the word's origins in Hindi *pajama,* based on a Persian word meaning "leg garment." Yet having adapted the word's meaning so that it now refers to a garment for the whole body, we lose part of the argument for keeping the original spelling.

q

In English the letter **q** is almost always accompanied by *u*, a curious convention that goes back through French and Latin to Greek use of *koppa* with back vowels. English words beginning with **q** are typically loans from French (*quality, question*) or Latin (*quip, quota*) which have it before front or back vowels. The *qu* combination was also used by Anglo-Norman scribes before 1300 to respell Old English words beginning with *cw*. Its effects can be seen in *quake, qualm, queen, quell, quick, quoth* and others. Similar respellings have occurred sporadically since then, in *cheque* (around 1700) and *racquet* (C19), though their acceptance has been more variable. See further under **check**, **racket** and, below, **q/k**.

q/k

In words such as *burqa/burka* and names such as *Iraq/Irak,* the **q** represents an Arabic consonant. **Q** used to be replaced by **k** in the process of anglicization, but is now increasingly retained as an element of Arab identity. (See further under **Arabic loanwords**, **burka**, **Iraq** and **Koran**.)

The French digraph *qu* has given us an alternative to **k** in pairs such as *lacquer/lacker, lackey/lacquey, racket/racquet*. In *cheque*, the *qu(e)* substitutes for *ck*. See further under each of these words.

QED

See **quod erat demonstrandum**.

Qoran or Koran

See **Koran**.

qua

This Latin loanword serves in English as shorthand for "in the capacity of" or just "as." It serves to single out one particular viewpoint or angle from any others inherent in the context, as in:

> *He may believe them qua practical man, but not qua scientist.*
> *How far should adult educators, qua educators, engage in activism?*
> *The party qua party was not involved.*

By convention there's never *a(n)* between **qua** and a singular noun following. Fowler (1926) argued that the construction should only be used when **qua** identified a precise element of some larger notion; otherwise *as* was "quite sufficient." Some commentators, extrapolating from this, have argued that **qua** could not be used between repeated nouns, as in the third example. Yet even there, **qua** solicits a different take on the repeated word, and so functions implicitly according to Fowler's prescription. In the second example above, the move is more explicit, with the simple noun following **qua** making only a partial match for the noun phrase before it. Constructions involving repeated nouns are much more common in

BNC data than those without them (like the first example). In North American data reported by *Webster's English Usage* (1989) and *Canadian English Usage* (1997), **qua** was also most commonly found between matching nouns, as in the third construction.

The natural context for **qua** is academic discourse and closely reasoned argument. Though sometimes found in more general kinds of writing, it runs the risk of seeming obscure – irritating to those who don't know it, or pretentious to those who do.

quadr-

This is the Latin prefix for "four," a component of loanwords and neoclassical formations such as:

> *quadrangle   quadrennial   quadrillion*
> *quadrophonic   quadruped*

The examples show that the vowel immediately after **quadr-** is not to be taken for granted. In some words it comes from the stem following, e.g. *-ennial, -illion,* and with stress on that syllable, the spelling is fixed. But those with stress on the first and third syllables (like *quadrophonic*) have at least two possible spellings, because the vowel of the second syllable varies in pronunciation. Is it *quadracycle* or *quadricycle? Quadraplegic, quadriplegic* or *quadruplegic? Quadrasonic, quadrisonic* or *quadrosonic?* The various different spellings are recognized in the *Oxford Dictionary* (1989), and any of them would correspond to the common pronunciation. The point to note is that the spelling with *i* is possible in each case, and indeed the favorite for *quadriplegic,* by the evidence of BNC and CCAE. For *quadraphony* (or is it *quadrophony?*) the spelling depends on whether you stress the first or second syllable.

Note that mathematical words such as *quadrilateral, quadrinomial, quadrivalent* are all standardized with *i,* in *Webster's Third* (1986) and the *Oxford Dictionary*.

quadriceps

For the plural, see under **biceps**.

quadrillion

For the value of this number, see **billion**.

qualifiers

The adverbs whose role is to affect the force of neighboring words, especially adjectives, are **qualifiers**. Some intensify the adjective, as in *very pleased, extremely annoyed*. Others soften its impact, as in *rather excited, somewhat disturbed*.
◊ For more about the first type, see **intensifiers**; for the second, see **hedge words**.

quandary or quandry

The origin of this word meaning "practical dilemma" is itself a puzzle. It appears in Renaissance English, and looks as latinate as its contemporaries *quantum, quorum, quota,* but with no obvious antecedent.

Earlier on, **quandary** was pronounced with stress on the second syllable, but it was moving forward in C18, promoting the two-syllabled pronunciation which is given priority in some dictionaries. Others such as *New Oxford* (1998) and *Merriam-Webster* (2000) make it an equal alternative. The three-syllabled spelling (**quandary**) is still the only one recognized, although *Webster's English Usage* (1989) reports examples of **quandry** from 1950 and 1980. Both BNC and CCAE provide a handful more, suggesting that it may be on the increase, while **quandary** remains the dominant spelling. For Samuel Johnson (1755) **quandary** was "a low word," and still it seems to be at home in everyday interactive writing, not formal prose.

quango or NGO
These latter-day abbreviations may both be defined as "nongovernment organization," but their applications and connotations are quite different. **Quango** originated in the US in the 1960s, as a blend of *quasi nongovernment organization,* and within a decade was being used in the UK. The interplay between the first two elements of the phrase has always been equivocal, since the British **quango** enjoyed government funding and served to further government policy in specialized areas. By 1976 the word **quango** was being explained as *quasi autonomous national government organization* – shifting the emphasis onto its relative independence from the bureaucracy. The word is still rather derogatory, according to *New Oxford* (1998), especially if you feel the **quango** is an unnecessary institution where "failed members of parliament serve on inflated salaries," as one MP put it. Derivatives such as *quangocrat* and *quangocracy* express the same feeling.

Much less contentious is **NGO**, a 1990s abbreviation for the *nongovernment organization* funded by churches or charitable organizations, for example Oxfam, Amnesty International, Community Aid Abroad. It works in foreign countries to assist refugees and other needy people.

While **quango** is an acronym, **NGO** is pronounced as an initialism (see under **acronyms**). For the plural of either word, just add *s:* **quangos**, **NGOs**. See further under **-o**.

quantum leap or jump
The expression **quantum jump** was coined by scientists in the 1920s, as a way of describing the way electrons can abruptly change their state. **Quantum leap** is its common paraphrase, used since 1955 to mean a "sudden large increase or advance" in any sphere of life (*Webster's English Usage*, 1989). In data from CCAE and the BNC, there are *quantum leaps* in *productivity / police powers / our cultural and artistic range / the delivery of government policy,* as well as very specific fields such as *microscopy, video games* and *rug-making.* As the latter examples show, the phrase risks turning itself into a cliché. Popular use of **quantum leap** seems to have impacted back on **quantum jump**, so that it too is used rhetorically on its occasional appearances in nonscientific writing. **Quantum leap** is still commoner by far in American and British data – which may be cold comfort to scientists.

quarreled or quarrelled
On the spelling of this verb, see **-l-/-ll-**.

quarter
This word is differently used in British and American English when it comes to
1 telling the time
2 speaking of fractions
When the time is 15 minutes before or after the hour, standard British English says *quarter to* and *quarter past.* Americans meanwhile may use either *quarter to* or *quarter of* when it's before the hour; and generally prefer *quarter after* to *quarter past.*

When articulating fractions, both the British and Australians speak of *one quarter* and *three quarters.* Americans and Canadians replace the **quarter** in each case, and speak of *one fourth* and *three fourths.* Perhaps this interconnects with the fact that in North America **quarter** refers specifically to the 25 cent coin.

quasi- and quasi
This is a recent prefix (or combining form) meaning "apparently," which gives new life to a Latin conjunction. **Quasi-** suggests that things are not what they seem, and that the rest of the word is not to be taken at face value:

> *quasi-historical   quasi-judicial   quasi-official*
> *quasi-religious*

It freely forms nonce words, both adjectives (as illustrated), and nouns:

> *quasi-career   quasi-expert   quasi-narration*
> *quasi-state*

Recent North American dictionaries allow that **quasi** may also serve as an adjective, i.e. without a hyphen, as in

> *quasi insider   quasi market   quasi privatisation*
> *quasi revenue*

– among examples from CCAE and the BNC. American and British dictionaries both allow that scientific terms formed with **quasi-** may be set solid, as in *quasicrystalline, quasiperiodic.*

quasimodal
This is an alternative term for the *marginal modal* or *semi-modal* verb which shares some of the properties of modals and auxiliaries. See **auxiliary verbs** section 3.

quay
The mismatch between spelling and pronunciation in **quay** results from C17 intervention – intended to distinguish it from two other words: *key* ("locking device"), which goes back to Old English; and *cay,* a Spanish word for "a shoal or reef," sometimes also spelled *key,* as in *Florida Keys* and *Key West.* **Quay** itself was a Celtic loanword, cognate with the word for "fence" in Cornish (*ke*) and Breton (*cai*), and spelled *key* or *kay* in Middle English. The same word in French was/is *quai,* and the anglicized equivalent **quay** makes its debut in Edward Phillips's *New World of English Words* of 1696. The respelling of **quay** is contemporaneous with the adoption of French *qu* in other English words (e.g. *cheque*). See further under **q**.

Quebecer or Quebecker
The inhabitants of *Quebec* may be designated with either spelling. **Quebecer** predominates in Canadian newspapers (*Canadian English Usage*, 1997) and

appears as the primary spelling in *Canadian Oxford* (1998). **Quebecker** is endorsed in *Editing Canadian English* (2000), and more regular in terms of English spelling conventions. See **-c/-ck-**.

question

The various subtypes of **question** are discussed under **questions**. For *beg the question* and *leading question*, see under those headings.

question marks

A **question mark** at the end of a string of words indicates that they form a question, or should be read as one:

> *Did you see the advertisement?*
> *He hasn't come yet?*

The word order of the first sentence (with subject following the auxiliary verb) sets it up as a question. But the second sentence becomes a question only through the mark at the end. If spoken, it would of course be marked as a question through rising intonation.

In the same way, the absence of a **question mark** from an inverted sentence shows that it is not intended as a question, but as a request, invitation or instruction:

> *Could I use your phone.*
> *Won't you come in.*
> *Would you close the door.*

A **question mark** might perhaps be used in the first of those, if the writer wanted to emphasize the politeness of the request, and the fact that the response was not taken for granted. In the second and third cases, the invitation/instruction assumes compliance and is not up for negotiation. Note that **question marks** are used only with *direct questions,* not *indirect questions.* Compare:

> *Where were you last night?*
> *They asked where you were last night.*

Question marks are occasionally used in mid-sentence, beside a date which is uncertain – *Chaucer b. ?1340* – or after a word whose use is questionable. The first is an accepted practice; the second one casts a shadow of doubt on the writer's verbal competence, and should be avoided in a finished MS.

Other punctuation with question marks. The **question mark** takes the place of a period/stop at the end of a sentence. If there are quotation marks or parentheses it stands inside them, unless it belongs strictly to the carrier sentence. Compare:

> *She asked "Who are you?"*
> *Did I hear him say "an old friend"?*
> *Where can I find guitar recordings (classical)?*
> *It's in that tourist pamphlet (What's on in Barcelona?).*

In cases like the last (but not the first) it's usual to close the sentence with a period/stop. (See further under **multiple punctuation**.)

Double **question marks** (??), or combinations of exclamation and **question marks** (!? or ?!), are to be avoided except in informal writing (and in chess). Where they might appear on either side of closing quotation marks (because one belongs to the quote, and the other to the carrier sentence), the sentence should be rearranged to avoid it. Perhaps the *interrobang* will one day solve that problem of needing two punctuation marks at once. See further under **interrobang**.

questions

A **question** is an interactive means of establishing the facts. Through **questions** we elicit information from others, or ask them to affirm or negate a fact which we ourselves supply. The only **questions** which do not work by interaction are *rhetorical questions.* Those who utter them in the course of a monologue mean to provide the answer themselves, and the **question** form is simply a way of securing the audience's attention.

1 Information-seeking questions are also known as *wh-questions* because they're introduced by interrogative words such as *who, when, where, why:*

> *Who were you talking to?*
> *When will the party begin?*
> *Where should we all meet?*
> *Why are you waiting here?*

Note that *how* also counts among the interrogative words, and that it too introduces open-ended *wh-questions.*

2 Questions which seek an affirmative or negative answer are known as *yes/no questions* or *polar questions* (see **polarity**). They are often expressed through inversion of the subject and auxiliary, as in:

> *Have you finished yet?*
> *Were you thinking of lunch?*

Alternatively, a *yes/no question* may take the form of an ordinary statement rounded off with a question mark at the end:

> *The show can go on?*
> *They won't start without us?*

In conversation, **questions** like these would be accompanied by rising intonation.

3 Tag questions serve to underscore the subject and verb of the main **question**, picking up the subject through the appropriate pronoun, and the verb through its auxiliary.

> *The show can go on, can't it?*
> *They won't start without us, will they?*

If there's no auxiliary verb, *do* is recruited for the purpose:

> *You like the program, don't you?*

Note that the *tag question* usually has opposite polarity to that of the main question – negative when it's positive, and vice versa. (See further under **polarity**.)

4 Direct and indirect questions. All the types of **questions** mentioned so far are *direct questions,* i.e. they are expressed as they would be in real interaction with those who supply the answer. At one stage removed are *indirect questions,* ones which report a **question** through the words of another party:

> *They asked where we should all meet.*
> *They queried why we were waiting.*
> *They questioned whether the show would go on.*

Indirect questions differ from *direct* ones in that they use regular subject/verb word order. Note that they may adjust the pronouns (turning the second person *you* into first or third person), and modify the tense of the verb. In the examples above a past tense is used following the past tense of the main verb, even though it would have been present tense in the direct question. (See further under **sequence of tenses**.) No question mark is used with *indirect questions.*

queuing or queueing

The verb *queue* is overendowed with vowels, so dropping the final *e* before adding *-ing* seems eminently sensible, and reflects a general rule of English spelling (see **-e**). **Queuing** is the standard spelling in the US, according to *Merriam-Webster* (2000), and in CCAE it outnumbers **queueing** by about 8:1. In the UK **queuing** and **queueing** are both in common use, appearing in the ratio of 2:1 in data from the BNC. The *New Oxford* (1998) recognizes both (in that order) as does the *Canadian Oxford* (1998) and the Australian *Macquarie Dictionary* (1997).

qui vive

This French tag appears rather curiously in the English phrase *on the qui vive,* meaning "on the alert." In prerevolutionary France, it was the formula by which a sentry accosted anyone approaching, and was intended to elicit the loyal response *Vive le roi* ("long live the king"). So like *goodbye,* it's a remnant of a ritual exchange of greetings. See further under **adieu.**

quick or quickly

Though first and foremost an adjective (as in the *quick brown fox*), **quick** also works as an adverb, especially in conversational idioms such as *Come quick.* (See further under **zero adverbs.**) The regular adverb **quickly** is standard in writing.

In conversation, the comparative form *quicker* also serves as both adjective and adverb, as in *It's quicker by train* or *You'll get there quicker by train.* But in most kinds of writing the comparative adverb would be *more quickly.*

quid pro quo

This Latin phrase means "which in exchange for what." It appears in C16 in reference to substituting one medical remedy for another, though Shakespeare used it figuratively, to mean "tit for tat." Nowadays it still serves to refer to whatever is given in retaliation, or where something is expected in return for a favor. The plural is normally **quid pro quos**, not the Latin *quae pro quo.* (See **plurals** section 2.)

The phrase probably gave rise to the slang word *quid,* a unit of money which varies with the context in which it's used. In C17 it meant a guinea, and after that a pound. In Australia it's now translated into dollars, although it does not pretend to be an exact amount:

Can you lend me a couple of quid?

As that example shows, the plural is often the same as the singular.

quintillion

For the value of this number, see **billion.**

quit or quitted

The past form of **quit** is usually **quit**, for English-speakers everywhere, whether for the past tense or the past participle:

. . . the champion nearly quit the game after an illness

Half of them have quit [smoking] already.

Quitted is still noted as an alternative past form in many dictionaries – *Merriam-Webster* (2000), *New Oxford* (1998), *Canadian Oxford* (1998) and the Australian *Macquarie Dictionary* (1997) – at least for the sense "left," illustrated in the first example above.

But database evidence shows that **quitted** is rare to the point of extinction in most places. In British data from the BNC, **quitted** is outnumbered by past uses of **quit** in the ratio of 1:16, and it's "extremely rare" in Canada (*Canadian English Usage*, 1997). There's no trace of **quitted** in American data from CCAE, or the Australian ACE (Peters, 1995).

While the verb **quit** goes back to C13, **quitted** makes its appearance only in C17. As a regular past form, we might expect it to have increased its grip on the paradigm by now (see **irregular verbs** section 9). Instead it seems to have stalled.

quite

This word is used freely in the US and the UK, but regional differences are there just below the surface. In British English **quite** is the all-purpose qualifier. It can be an intensifier, reinforcing the following word as in *quite right,* or a hedge word that tones it down, as in *quite well.* The first sense ("completely") tends to go with absolute words (see **absolute** section 1), the second ("rather") with those that are gradable and comparable. With verbs the distinction is usually clear cut: compare *I quite forgot* with *I quite enjoyed the meeting.* Yet there are many adjectives in which either sense could apply. If something is *quite original,* is it brilliantly innovative, or just modestly creative? If *quite dangerous,* should you proceed with caution, or take evasive action? In conversation **quite** takes on other roles as well. It draws casual attention to a noun, as in *quite a shock,* and also serves as an emphatic response: *Quite so* or just *Quite!* These contrasting uses mean that **quite** is often ambiguous, though this very ambiguity lends itself to the dynamics of conversation. In data from the BNC, **quite** is disproportionately represented in spoken texts, where it occurs about three times as often as in written texts.

In American English **quite** is much less frequently used in conversation, according to research reported in the *Longman Grammar* (1999). American use of **quite** also differs in that the absolute meaning can be associated even with gradable adjectives, as noted in the *Comprehensive Grammar* (1985). This is the root of some misunderstanding, since Americans who use *quite interesting* to mean "very interesting" are probably heard by the British as saying "rather interesting."

Both British and American writers use **quite** in academic and informative prose to fine-tune their stance, and underscore a view, as in *quite likely/properly/rightly.* Latent ambiguities and regional differences in the use of **quite** tend to be neutralized as the writer develops the discussion.
◊ For other less ambiguous qualifiers, see **intensifiers** and **hedge words.**

quiz and quizzes

See under **-z/-zz.**

quod erat demonstrandum

This weighty Latin phrase means "which was [what had] to be demonstrated." It comes down to us through Euclidean geometry, marking the end of the proof of a theorem. Yet it enjoys wider use as a marker of the conclusion to an argument, when the speaker/writer has pursued the logic of their ideas to the end. *QED* is its abbreviation, where each letter is pronounced as a separate syllable.

quod vide

See **q.v.**

quondam

This Latin adverb is used in English as a lofty synonym for "former," as in *Quondam dissidents joined the establishment.* The writers who use it are now rare, and readers who find it accessible even rarer.

quorum

This enigmatic word is a Latin relative pronoun, a genitive plural meaning "of whom." It seems to come from the wording of commissions that specified how many justices of the peace were needed to constitute a bench. From C17, **quorum** became part of the protocol for nonlegal meetings, indicating the minimum number of people required for business to be conducted. Its use in English makes it an abstract noun, with **quorums** as plural because it's not a regular Latin noun. See further under **-um.**

quotation marks

The common term for the pairs of aerial commas which mark quotations is **quotation marks**, or less formally *quote marks* or just *quotes,* the last being freely used among editors (*Copy-editing,* 1992). In the UK the alternative term *inverted commas* has enjoyed some popularity, but its use is now declining (see **inverted commas**). **Quotation marks** raise a number of punctuation issues, such as the choice between *double* and *single quotes,* and where to locate other punctuation marks in relation to them (see below, sections 2 and 3).

1 Uses of quotation marks. *Quote marks* identify the words actually uttered or written by someone. They appear at the start and finish of the quoted string of words, except when the quotation runs to several paragraphs. Then the *quote marks* appear just at the beginning of each paragraph, until the last one, which has them at both beginning and end. Note that no **quotation marks** at all are needed for block quotations, which are indented and set apart typographically, in a smaller or different typeface.

Quotation marks are often less than essential in separating quoted from nonquoted material. Some famous writers do without them altogether in the articulation of dialogue – including James Joyce, who called them "perverted commas," and preferred to preface segments of dialogue with a dash. (The dash is often used this way in French.) The bible in its "Authorized Version" of 1611 has no *quote marks,* not as a reaction against them but because their use had not then been systematized. Like many aspects of our punctuation system, **quotation marks** were not in regular use until later C18.

Occasional functions of **quotation marks** are to:

* enclose words used to translate others, e.g. *Weltanschauung* "world view"
* draw attention to words which are somehow out of the ordinary. They may be technical, or foreign, or nonce words. The *quote marks* would flank the word on its first appearance, but after that it appears without them. Some writers also use *quotes* as means of emphasis, for expressing irony, or

commenting on a word that they feel is an imperfect choice. *Quote marks* used this way go by various ad hoc names such as "scare quotes," "sneer quotes," "shudder quotes" and "cute quotes." Amid all those effects the *quote marks* do no more than indicate that the word is not one to take for granted.

Using *quote marks* to highlight words for such a range of different purposes is not ideal. Alternative resources for technical and foreign terms are bold and italics, as well as small caps and underlining – depending on the text and type resources. Where *quotes* might be used for personal emphasis, the question to ask is whether they really serve any purpose. The *Chicago Manual* (1993) comments that "mature writers" do not rely on *quote marks* to express irony or other attitudes, but will convey the intended emphasis and meaning through the right choice of words, appropriately arranged. If something is still needed for emphasis, you could resort to bold or italic type. These various strategies help to take the load off **quotation marks** in running text. Most people find they look fussy when used around single words, and their exact significance becomes unclear (see below, end of section 2). *Quote marks* are best reserved purely for quoted material, and for translations or glosses of foreign words, as in many entries in this book.

One other conventional use of **quotation marks** is to identify the titles of shorter compositions which form part of an anthology. So *quote marks* are used to embrace the names of lyric poems which are part of a published collection, and songs which make individual tracks on a record or CD. (On their use for journal articles, see **titles** section 3. On the use of **quotation marks** for the names of radio and TV programs, see **italic(s)** section 5.)

2 Double or single quotation marks. The English-speaking world is rather divided over this. *Double quotes* are the standard practice in the US, and for many Canadian presses and publishing houses. In the UK, *double quotes* are associated with newspapers and some publishers, while *single quotes* are recommended by Oxford University Press and Cambridge University Press in their respective style guides. In Australia the pattern is similar: *single quotes* are recommended for government documents by the *Style Manual* (2002), while daily newspapers and many publishers use *double quotes.*

The argument usually raised for *single quotes* is that they are more elegant than *double quotes* – though this suggests it's a matter of taste. Arguments of space and efficiency are occasionally raised. But the amount of space saved by *single quotes* is negligible; and the fact that *double quotes* involve use of the shift key is of small consequence among all keystrokes used in typing a document. The chief argument in favor of *double quotes* is that they prevent confusion when the typewriter/printer reduces all aerial commas to a straight vertical or backward-leaning stroke. Compare:

"It's John's." with 'It's John's.'

The use of *double quotes* ensures that the apostrophe and quote mark are visually distinct, however limited the type resources.

Whether you choose *double* or *single quotes* as your normal practice, you will need the other when it comes to "quotes within quotes." The alternatives are:

The announcement was that "The council had decided to disallow the cutting of 'significant trees,' even on private property."

or

> *The announcement was that 'The council had decided to disallow the cutting of "significant trees," even on private property.'*

The choice of first level (*double* or *single*) entails the other for the second level.

Beyond this is the question as to which level of **quotation marks** should be used to highlight other words and terms that crop up from time to time in the text. There is no "rule" (Butcher, 1992), and individuals and publishing houses set their own policies. Some use the first level of quote marks for words plucked out of an utterance, and the second level for marking terms – which doesn't necessarily clarify things if the two levels are rarely seen together. Others use the first level of quotes for highlighting both – which leaves readers with the problem of knowing whether a single quoted word was spoken or is being highlighted for some other reason. Similar problems of interpretation arise for quotes within the titles of journal articles that are themselves set in *quote marks* (see **titles** section 3). These various dilemmas show that too much is being asked of **quotation marks**, and the need for alternative highlighting devices such as italics, bold or underlining for key terms.

3 Quotation marks with other punctuation. Which other punctuation marks to use with *quote marks*, and where to locate them, are vexed and variable issues.

a) **Before the quotation begins.** According to older convention, a quotation is preceded by a comma:

> *The old woman declared, "I'll let you in on one condition."*

This is still quite common practice in novels, though a simple space may serve the same purpose:

> *The old woman declared "I'll let you in on one condition."*

In newspapers and magazines there's a strong tendency to use a colon before quoted material:

> *In his summing up, the judge noted: "This was a first offence."*

Note that the quoted material always begins with a capital letter.

b) **Before presentational material.** When a quotation is followed or interrupted by reference to the person who uttered it, any major punctuation mark (exclamation mark, question mark) and the comma which replaces a full stop goes inside the closing *quote marks:*

> *"He's coming up!" they exclaimed.*
> *" Is he coming up?" they asked.*
> *"He's coming," they said.*

That principle is extended to all commas in American editing practice, even those which punctuate the carrier sentence rather than the quotation itself:

> *"Your luggage," they said, "is on the next plane."*

Most Canadian editors do likewise, according to *Editing Canadian English* (2000), and it's commonly implemented in British printing, according to Butcher (1992). The alternative British practice, shown in the *Oxford Guide to Style* (2002), is to place the comma "according to the sense," which means leaving it outside the closing *quote marks* when it's not integral to the quotation:

> *"Your luggage", they said, "is on the next plane."*

The Australian government *Style Manual* also endorses this policy. But its implementation isn't always as obvious as in that example, where grammar can be used to settle the matter. Speech is inherently variable, and the punctuation of scripted speech is always in the hands of the writer, who may well underpunctuate it (see **punctuation** section 3). So the simplicity of the American practice has much to recommend it. British and American editors agree that when a quotation is resumed after the presentational material, the first word is in lower case.

c) **At the end of the sentence.** Where to put the final period / full stop is again a question on which editorial practices divide. In American style (*Chicago Manual*, 2003), it always goes inside the *quotes,* as also for most Canadian editors (*Editing Canadian English*). In British style the conventions are many and varied. According to *Hart's Rules* (1983) the position of the full stop depends on whether what's quoted is complete in itself, and completes the carrier sentence at the same time. If it fulfills those two conditions, the full stop goes inside; if the quotation is only part of a sentence, the full stop goes outside. Compare:

> *The airline clerk said, "It's on the next plane."*
> *The airline clerk said it was "on the next plane."*

The *Oxford Guide to Style* notes the further question as to whether the quotation was a finished sentence in the original (and therefore had its own full stop which would go inside the final quote marks). It concludes that what matters is the grammatical completeness of the quoted form, and placing the final full stop accordingly. A very different policy is indicated in British Standard 5261 (www.bsi.org.uk): that the full stop only goes inside if the quotation stands *by itself* as a full sentence. This would mean putting the full stop outside the closing quote marks in both the last two examples. The Australian government *Style Manual* endorses this latter practice, which has the advantage of making the rules for final punctuation with *quote marks* match up with those for parentheses (see **brackets** section 3).

Whether the reader actually notices the position of the final period / full stop is rather dubious. Editors shed blood, sweat and tears over the issue, wrestling with anomalies not covered by the various rules; and the wastage of editorial time suggests there's a lot to be said for a simple system. The North American practice (put it inside) is still the easiest to apply in texts with a lot of dialogue, because it can be applied to quotations of any length, whether in the middle or at the end of a sentence. But for nonfiction writing, the practice of treating final punctuation for *quote marks* the same way as for parentheses has much to recommend it.

4 Multiple final punctuation with quotation marks. Very occasionally a sentence with an embedded quotation seems to call for punctuation marks on either side of the final *quote marks* – combinations of question marks, exclamation points (exclamation marks) and periods / full stops. American and British style diverge on whether one or two stops are needed: see further under **multiple punctuation**.

quotations

For nonfiction writers, **quotations** are essentially a way of bringing someone else's words into your text. A **quotation** serves to invoke their authority in support of claims or arguments you're making, or as a momentary evocation of their character and style.

Journalists and magazine reporters quite regularly resort to quoting statements made by public figures, in order to relieve the straight reportage and introduce a touch of drama. Yet when it happens in every news article, the switch from indirect narrative to directly quoted speech loses its effect, especially when the words quoted are remarkable for their clichés and low level of significance.

Educational and scholarly writers *quote* the words of other writers to lend weight to their ideas, while avoiding plagiarism. Inexperienced writers sometimes use **quotations** as a kind of academic showmanship ("Look how many authors I've read"), but it's a mistake to *quote* too often on the same page. As in newspaper reporting, **quotations** seem less significant the more a writer resorts to them. Is the writer capable of expressing things independently, the reader begins to wonder.

Introducing quotations. Quotations can only contribute effectively to your prose if they're integrated smoothly into the surrounding text. A little editing may be needed to make them dovetail with the carrier sentence, and avoid a rough transition like the following:

> *Joan Sutherland said that "I'm retiring from now on."*

Either the carrier sentence, or the quotation itself needs a little adapting:

> *Joan Sutherland said "I'm retiring from now on."*
> *Joan Sutherland said that she would be "retiring from now on."*

When the actual wording of the **quotation** is modified by the writer, the word(s) modified or introduced should be marked with square brackets:

> *Joan Sutherland said that "[she would be] retiring from now on."*

For more about the use of *square brackets,* see under **brackets**. The use of ellipsis in **quotations** is discussed under **ellipsis** section 2.

Quran or Koran
See **Koran**.

q.v.
This abbreviates the Latin *quod vide,* which translated literally means "which see," or more freely "have a look at that." **Q.**v. encourages the reader to seek further information under a particular reference, as in *the ideas of pastoral care expressed in Psalm 23 (q.v.).* But its use – like that of many Latin scholarly abbreviations – is in decline. See **Latin abbreviations.**

r or wr

A very few English words may be spelled with either r or wr, over which you may indeed *(w)rack your brains* (see rack or wrack). For most other pairs, only one or other spelling will do. The wr spelling seems in fact to persist as a way of distinguishing the following:

rap/wrap	*reek/wreak*	*rest/wrest*
retch/wretch	*right/wright*	*ring/wring*
rite/write	*rote/wrote*	*rung/wrung*

Note that while *rap* and *wrap* are distinguished for their simple uses, there's some interchange when they are used figuratively. Individual cases are discussed under rap up or wrap up; rapt, wrapt or wrapped, and wrung.

◊ See under reckless for mistaken uses of *wreckless*.

-r-

The letter r is a chameleon sound, changing its color in particular contexts. In English personal names, an "r" sound in the middle has here and there become "l," generating new names such as *Sally* from *Sarah*, *Molly* from *Mary*, and *Hal* from *Harold* and *Henry*. In other names such as *Carolyn* and *Murray*, the medial r is sometimes refashioned as "z," hence *Caz* and *Muzza*, for use among friends. The Australian antihero *Bazza McKenzie* is *Barry Humphries*, using the casual form of his name to ingratiate himself with large audiences.

-r-/-rr-

Verbs ending in -r have it doubled before inflections when the syllable is stressed, as in *deferred*, but not when it is unstressed as in *differed*. For more on this convention, see doubling of final consonant.

rabies

This Latin loanword meaning "madness" is the common English name for "hydrophobia," a dangerous disease transmitted by the bite of infected dogs or other animals. Rabies always takes a singular verb, as in:

> Rabies was eradicated from Britain a century ago.

The singular goes with its Latin past (where it was a singular noun: see -ies) as well as its English present – the fact that it's the name of a disease. See further under agreement section 2b.

raccoon or racoon

This small nocturnal animal of North America is normally spelled raccoon, though US and Canadian dictionaries also allow racoon. In data from CCAE, raccoon is very much more common, by a factor of more than 25:1. In the UK, raccoon is also more common than racoon, by the evidence of a dozen sources in the BNC. The data doesn't support the idea that racoon is *the* British spelling.

racism or racialism

These words are less than a century old, and their application to language usage even younger. Racialism dates from the first decade of C20, whereas racism appears just before World War II. The shorter term has now largely eclipsed the longer one in both American and British English, by the evidence of BNC and CCAE. Preference for the shorter term (based on the noun rather than the adjective) aligns it with others that identify varieties of social prejudice, for example *sexism*, *ageism*. (See further under -ism.)

In the same way *racialist* (from 1917) has given way to *racist* (coined in 1938). *Racist* outnumbers *racialist* by about 25:1 in BNC data, and 150:1 in data from CCAE.

racist language

If racist language was just a means of identifying people as belonging to a particular race or nation, it would be no problem. But terms like those below show built-in prejudice toward ethnic, cultural and national differences. There's a level of contempt in all of them:

Abo	*Balt*	*bohunk*	*boong*
chink	*coon*	*dago*	*darkie*
ding	*frog*	*gook*	*greasy*
Itie	*Jap*	*kike*	*kraut*
nig(ger)	*nip*	*nog*	*polack*
pommy	*raghead*	*slant-eye*	*slope(head)*
spade	*spic*	*towelhead*	*wog*
yid			

At best, such words are offhanded; at worst they are offensive and demeaning. Though it's possible for "insiders" to use them among themselves without prejudice (see for example Jewess), the outsider shouldn't touch them, or try to claim "playful" use of such terms. They put people of different races at an instant disadvantage, and encourage others to stereotype them negatively. Everyone is conscious of ethnic differences, but they are irrelevant in many situations, and drawing attention to them is divisive.

When such differences do need to be acknowledged, it's a matter of choosing the appropriate ethnic or national name: *Aboriginal, American, Chinese, English, French, Greek, Indian, Italian, Korean, Malayan, Nigerian, Pakistani, Polish, Vietnamese* etc. Terms like these offer a description which is both more precise and neutral in its connotations.

◊ See also throwaway terms.

rack or wrack

Several words coincide on these two spellings, and there's no neat division of labor. Historically wrack is a variant of *wreck*, and so associated with shoreline debris, as in *wrack brought in by the tide*. The expression *(w)rack and ruin* preserves the original sense of destruction. (These days *rack and ruin* is the more common spelling in both British and American English, by the evidence of the BNC and CCAE.) Early uses of **wrack** survive also in expressions such as *wrack of seaweed* (cast up or growing on the shore), and the names of tidal plants such as *bladderwrack*. But the *(w)rack of cloud* (= "driven cloud") which appears as **rack** in C14 English is more likely to go back to Old Scandinavian: the noun *rek* ("wreckage," cognate with Old English **wrack**) and verb *reka* ("drive").

Totally independent from all these is **rack** ("framework"), originally Dutch and applied to wooden structures used in medieval crafts and trades, as well as the instrument of torture. These uses of the noun underlie the two major senses of the verb **rack**:

* "store in a rack," as in *life rafts racked ready for the drop*
* "cause pain and/or severe distress": *the persistent cough that racked her*

The second sense, with its deconstructive overtones, is sometimes spelled **wrack**, and finds expression in many personal and political contexts. Nations are *(w)racked by conflict, infighting, rebellion, war* etc., and people *with* or *by doubt, grief, guilt, longing, pressure* etc. The same sense is expressed in *(w)rack one's brains,* and in *nerve-(w)racking* (more often without the *w* than with it, though the ratio between the two is closer in corpus data from the UK than from the US). It spawns compound adjectives as in *violence-wracked townships, the scandal-wracked bank, a recession-wracked economy* – where the *wr* spelling seems to prevail along with the sense of destruction.

Other verbal uses of **rack** resist the alternative spelling. The idiom *rack up* ("notch up"), used in sport and other competitive contexts, is always **rack**:

> *Chiyo racked up a record 1045 wins.*
> *Angus has racked up a hit album.*

The dismissive *rack off!* ("go away") used in Australia and New Zealand probably derives from **rack** meaning a horse's gait (between a trot and a canter).

In wine- and beer-making, **rack** is a technical term: the liquid is *racked* (i.e. drawn off the lees) *into* containers for secondary fermentation or storage. This verb seems to go back to Provençal *arracar* ("separate from the dregs"). Still in the realms of gastronomy, the *rack of lamb* seems to go back to a dialectal word for the "forequarter," i.e. neck and spine of a carcass, probably derived from Old English *hracca,* referring to the back of the skull.

As often, figurative uses of **rack** and **wrack** have enlarged their domains and made the spellings interchangeable wherever the sense of severe stress and destruction apply. **Wrack** seems to be gaining ground there, although still less common than **rack** in collocations such as *nerve-racking* and *racking one's brains.* **Rack** is the regular spelling for the more physical and technical senses of the word, and in collocations such as *rack up/off.*

◊ For other words distinguished by *wr/r* spellings, see **r or wr**.

racket or racquet

Anyone for tennis (or squash, or badminton?)? Whatever the game, you're free to spell the word either way. **Racket** is the original spelling, dating from C16 along with Henry VIII and royal tennis. The French-style spelling *raquet* was also used from C16 on as an alternative for the sporting weapon. Meanwhile **racket** has always been used to spell the informal word for "noise" as in *making a racket,* and

"swindle," as in *running a racket.* The spelling **racquet** was introduced in C19 when French permutations seem to have had special appeal (see **frenchification**); but it too shares the field with **racket**. In fact British writers represented in the BNC are about twice as likely to use **racket** as **racquet** for the sporting implement; and in American data from CCAE, **racket** prevails by about the same ratio in ordinary prose – although **racquet** is common in the names of private sports clubs, the generic "Health and Racquet Club." The *New Oxford* (1998) and *Merriam-Webster* (2000) put **racket** ahead of **racquet** as the headword, whereas the Australian *Macquarie* (1997) does the opposite. The *Canadian Oxford* (1998) also gives priority to **racquet**, and Canadians make more use of it (Fee and McAlpine, 1997) – as elsewhere when both French and English variants are available.

radio-

This prefix has two kinds of use in modern English, to mean:
1 making use of *radio waves,* as in *radioastronomy, radiofrequency, radiotelephone*
2 associated with *radiation,* as in *radioactive, radioisotopes, radiotherapy*

In words like these, the two senses of **radio-** have maintained their distance. But there's now the uncomfortable possibility that the two converge in the hand-held *radio telephone,* otherwise known as *mobile (telephone)* in the UK or *cell phone* in the US. The wireless phone could be a personal source of radiation.

radius

The plural of this word is discussed under **-us** section 1.

radix

For the the plural of this word, see under **-x** section 3.

railway or railroad

Railroad is the standard American word for what in Britain, Canada and Australia is a **railway**, a major transport system which uses heavy rolling stock on a network of parallel rails. Note however that **railway** is occasionally used in the US to refer to a small streetcar system with light vehicles.

As a verb **railroad** is everywhere used to mean "rush something through a legal or legislative process" – with pejorative overtones. Compare the semantically similar verb *fast-track,* which implies that the unusual bureaucratic haste is in the public interest.

raise or rise

Both are essentially verbs, and both by transfer become nouns which can refer to an increase in one's salary. The standard term for this in North America (US and Canada) is a **raise**; and Australians talking about their employment prospects would use it too, although it would seem rather colloquial in a written text. In Britain, a **raise** still sounds American, according to Burchfield (1996), and it hardly appears in data from the BNC. Instead the noun **rise** is used for an increase in one's salary – as for increases on any other more or less quantitative scale: temperature, profits, inflation or corruption.

Curiously, regional usage of **raise/rise** with *flour* works differently. The American term is *self-rising flour*, whereas in Britain and Australia, it's *self-raising*. In Canada both are used.

raison d'être

This useful French phrase means "reason for being." It is typically used to justify the existence of abstract entities, such as institutions or policies (the *raison d'être for computers*), not anything which is itself animate. Its plural is **raisons d'être**, according to *New Oxford* (1998) and *Merriam-Webster* (2000), maintaining the French pattern (see **plurals** section 2). Yet *Merriam-Webster* gives *raison d'etre* as an alternative way of writing the phrase – where loss of the circumflex is a sure sign of its anglicization.

-rance and -erance

A few abstract nouns are spelled **-rance** where you might expect **-erance**. Think of *encumbrance, entrance, hindrance, remembrance,* where the related verb ends in *-er* (*encumber, enter, hinder, remember*). In cases like *entrance,* the **-rance** comes from Old French, but a few like *hindrance* were coined that way in English. In some English adjectives, the *-er* of the related noun is also telescoped (see **-er>-r-**).

The special cases with **-rance** do not change the fact that there are many in which the *-er* of the verb is not telescoped: *deliverance, sufferance, temperance, utterance,* among others. Note also those ending in *-rence,* such as *difference, preference, reference,* which never telescope the *-er* in the spelling, even though they are often pronounced with just two syllables.
◊ For the **-ance/-ence** difference, see under that heading.

rancor or rancour

See **-or/-our**.

rang or rung

See under **ring**.

rangy or rangey

See **-y/-ey**.

ranunculus

The plural of this word is discussed under **-us** section 1.

rap up or wrap up

The word *rap* ("knock") slips easily into colloquial idiom, taking on new expressive meanings as it goes. In C19 British slang and dialect, it could mean "talk" as well as "boast," and these uses have taken off in C20 in different parts of the world. In American English, the first sense has become "talk discursively" (as verb) or *have a rap / rap session* (as noun/atttributive). *Rap music* has no doubt helped to popularize this sense. The second, in Australian and New Zealand idiom, is commuted into meaning "commend"/"commendation": *couldn't rap him up enough, give him a rap (up)*. At this point **rap up** collides with the idiom **wrap up**, used throughout the English-speaking world to mean "bring to a close," whenever the commendation is or could be the peroration. The *Australian National Dictionary* (1988) shows that the spelling with *wr* is common for **rap up** ("commend"), though it may lose the intended sense.

Meanwhile there's some evidence in American English of **wrap up** (when it means "bring to a close") being misspelled **rap up**. The spelling is less crucial for meaning with the curt British idiom *wrap up* = "shut up," because it's normally an imperative (or phrased as *wrap it up!*). Elsewhere, the presence or absence of the *w* may be the defining moment for the reader.

rapt, wrapt or wrapped

These spellings represent two different words whose meanings come close in certain idioms. The adjective **rapt** meaning "totally absorbed" is a Latin loanword, indirectly related to *rapture*. It can be used without hyperbole, as in *rapt in thought, the audience's rapt attention, rapt in my own problems.* The last example shows how *rapt in* converges with informal use of the Anglo-Saxon verb *wrap* in the idiom *wrapped up in* ("be engrossed with"), as in *completely wrapped up in the children*. It amounts to much the same as *rapt in the children*, except that *wrapped up in* seems more colloquial and down-to-earth in style. **Wrapt**, an old past tense of *wrap*, is a rare alternative for **rapt** and for **wrapped** in its physical sense of covering or encasing something.
◊ For other verbs which have / have had a *-t* form for the past, see under **-ed**.

rarefy or rarify

See under **-ify/-efy**.

rather and rather than

The word **rather** has three roles, as:
1 hedge word: *He plays rather well.*
2 comparative adverb:
    a) *The family would rather that she played the flute.*
    b) *I get the news from radio rather than television.*
    c) *He asked for any posting rather than Brazil.*
3 conjunct: *The committee is not against strong views. Rather it's a matter of how they're expressed.*
In its role of comparative adverb, **rather** covers a range of meanings, shown in sentences (a) to (c) above. It may suggest a preference, as in (a); or a very strong determination which allows no alternatives, as in (c). Sentence (b) is somewhere in between and in fact rather ambiguous. Does it express a preference, or a commitment? If the difference is crucial, **rather** needs to be replaced by "in preference to" for the first meaning, and "instead of" for the second.

Ambiguity can also arise between conjunctive use of **rather** and its use as a hedge word. See for example:
    He rather thought that she should pay her own way.
Without more context we cannot tell whether **rather** is there to gently modify the verb, or to make a strong contrast equivalent to "instead."
Grammatical options with rather than. What form of word to use after **rather than** is sometimes an issue with pronouns and with verbs.
• When two pronouns are being compared with **rather than**, standard practice is to give the case of the first one to the second:
    They're coming to talk to him. Rather him than me.
    We rather than they should be doing the course.
However in informal and impromptu speech there's a tendency to use the objective case every time after *than*:

459

We rather than them should be doing the course.
Neither version sounds ideal, and a better result altogether comes with rephrasing the sentence:
We not they should be doing the course.
It's us not them who should be doing the course.
The first version is more formal in style, the second more conversational.

When two verbs are being compared with **rather than**, there are two possible constructions which are stylistically equal but grammatically different: either coordinate the two verbs, or subordinate one to the other. Writers may choose to:

i) repeat the first form of the verb after **rather than** (matching its tense and number):

> *With pulse racing, she trotted rather than walked to the stairs.*
> *It supplements rather than replaces publications of the past.*

In these examples, **rather than** coordinates the two verbs. Note however that if the segment with **rather than** comes first, it effectively subordinates it:

> *Rather than address the problem, politicians look for the quick "fix."*

ii) use the *-ing* form for the second option:

> *Politicians look for the quick "fix" rather than addressing the problem.*

With *-ing,* the **rather than** construction is always subordinate, whether it is effectively a nonfinite clause (with the participle) or a noun phrase (with gerund). It often highlights a preference, as noted in the *Longman Grammar* (1999). In data from the BNC and CCAE, the coordinate construction (i.e. repeating the form of the first verb) is the commoner of the two. The likelihood of the second increases with the distance between the two verbs.

ratio decidendi

See under **obiter dictum.**

ravage or ravish

Both words refer to powerful and usually destructive forces. **Ravage** is used when destruction is spread over a wide area by war or other overwhelming forces: *ravaged by inflation / tribal warfare / acid rain.* **Ravish** typically has a human subject and object, and means "seize, rape" or somewhat paradoxically "transport with delight." The two kinds of meaning have their respective clichés in *ravished virgins* and *ravished audiences,* which are symptomatic of the fact that the word is usually either euphemistic or hyperbolic. The word screens the deed when a man finds his *teenage daughter being ravished by a young police officer.* And when a skilled TV interviewer is said to have *ravished the public,* its praise is somehow laced with irony. The dark forces underlying **ravish** come to the surface in BNC examples such as *the social fabric has been profoundly ravished;* and contamination with **ravage** shows in *Large parts of Africa were ravished by drought.* Compare:

> *Fires have ravaged parts of eastern Australia in recent weeks.*

The rather amorphous and emotive frontiers of **ravish** may well leave readers wondering what is actually meant. It lends itself to parody, as in *I ravished the refrigerator.* Quasi-literary uses of **ravish** in fact seem

to dominate the evidence from the BNC, suggesting that the word is on the brink of self-destruction.

ravel or unravel

These words present a tangle of meanings from their first appearances in late C16 English. Borrowed from Dutch, **ravel** meant "fray out," the way threads or stitches come undone at the edge of a fabric. This image underlies the need [for sleep] to "knit up the raveled sleeve of care," as Lady Macbeth put it. The *Oxford Dictionary* (1989) records other Shakespearean examples in which **ravel** meant "entangle" – as happens with frayed threads. The two senses imply different kinds of negative: disintegration with the first sense, and enmeshed disorder with the second. Add to this the fact that both senses could be transitive or intransitive, and you have ambiguities that would explain the rapid appearance of **unravel** ("disentangle," with positive implications), early in C17. Yet while it was/is an antonym for the second sense of **ravel**, it also serves as a synonym for the first sense. Compare the physical and figurative senses in the following:

* "disentangle"
> *He patiently unravelled the bootlaces*
> *Detectives are trying to unravel the mystery surrounding the death*
* "come apart"
> *Her torn canvas top unravelled in the wind*
> *Then she was stricken with multiple sclerosis and the fairy tale quickly unravelled*

In data from the BNC, figurative use of **unravel** meaning "disentangle" is the most popular of the four just illustrated, and the uses of "come apart" (or "unwind," as in *let the [fishing] line unravel*) are usually physical. Meanwhile **ravel** is rare in both British and American English, with few examples of any of its uses in either BNC or CCAE. **Unravel** has gone some way towards resolving four centuries of ambiguity.

◊ For the choice between *raveled* and *ravelled,* *unraveled* and *unravelled* etc., see -l-/-ll-.

re

This Latin tag is used in official letter writing to identify the subject under discussion. It abbreviates the Latin phrase *in re* ("in the matter of"), and is not therefore a clipped form of "regarding," as is sometimes thought. It prefaces the subject line in a business letter, typically following the salutation, as in:

> *Dear Editor*
> *re: Schedule for production of annual report*
> *Copy for the company's Annual Report will be sent to you…*

In that position it's often set in lower case, and followed by a colon. However **re** can also appear in upper case and without a colon. This is naturally the case when it occurs ahead of the salutation line as in:

> *Re schedule for production of annual report*
> *Dear Editor*
> *Copy for the company's Annual Report will be sent to you…*

This relatively new position for the **re** line makes it more visible, and matches the way in which headers are used to identify the subject of correspondence in both memos and e-mail.

Re is too well established to need italics, and can even be used informally to replace *concerning* or *regarding,* as in *yesterday's discussion re the parents' evening.* But in general contexts like that, **re** still seems a little awkward with its overtones of business and faintly pretentious Latin character. For more about the conventions of commercial letter writing, see under **commercialese,** and Appendix VII for the layout of letters, memos and e-mail.

re-

Drawn originally from Latin, this prefix means "back" or "again." The first meaning is there in words such as *rebound, recall, recover, repress, resound;* the second is in *rebuild, refill, rejoin, reprint, revive.* Yet in many of the French loanwords in which it occurs, **re-** is inseparably bound into the word itself, witness:

> *receive   refuse   remember   repeat   resign*
> *reveal*

In modern English words formed with **re-,** the meaning is always "again," a point which is shown up when we compare the new or ad hoc formations with older ones, for example *re-create/recreate, re-mark/remark, re-serve/reserve.* The hyphen is vital to identify the meanings of the new words and distinguish them from the old. Further examples are:

> *re-act   re-claim   re-collect   re-count*
> *re-cover   re-form   re-fund   re-lay*
> *re-lease   re-petition   re-place   re-present*
> *re-sent   re-sort*

In British, Canadian and Australian English, a hyphen is normally used when **re-** comes up against *e* in forming a new word – whether or not the letters match an old word. See for example:

> *re-echo   re-educate   re-elect   re-emerge*
> *re-emphasize   re-enter   re-equip   re-erect*
> *re-establish   re-evaluate*

They are set solid in American English.

-re/-er

The choice between *centre/center, fibre/fiber* etc. is a matter on which American English and others divide. In the US, spellings with **-er** are standard, whereas in the UK **-re** spellings are strongly preferred. Australians ally themselves with the British on this, as do most Canadians, according to *Canadian English Usage* (1997), though the **-er** alternatives are recognized in the *Canadian Oxford* (1998). The **-re** spellings match the French form of the word, adding to their value in Canada and Britain (see **frenchification**).

The latinate spellings with **-er** were commonly used from C16 to early C18, and appear in editions of Shakespeare and the earliest dictionaries. But *centre* was the headword in Johnson's dictionary (1755), and **-re** spellings became standard in Britain in the decades that followed. Webster however endorsed *center* etc. in his radical dictionary of 1806, and maintained the older spellings in the US.

The words affected by this spelling practice are (in their non-American form):

> *calibre   centre   fibre   goitre*
> *litre   louvre   lustre   manouevre*
> *meagre   mitre   ochre   philtre*
> *reconnoitre   sabre   sceptre   sepulchre*
> *sombre   spectre   theatre   titre*

Some **-re** words nevertheless keep that spelling even in American English, including:

> *acre   cadre   lucre   macabre   mediocre*
> *ogre   timbre*

These words resist **-er** either because it would seem to "soften" the *c* or *g* of the stem (see **-ce/-ge**), or because of other aspects of the word's meaning and identity. (*Timbre* would be otherwise be identical with *timber*.)

Those who use **-re** spellings have the advantage when it comes to forming the derivatives of all those words. The stem of the word remains the same in *centre/central* or *fibre/fibrous,* with just the regular dropping of the final *e* before a suffix beginning with a vowel (see **-e** section 1). Those who use **-er** spellings have to put the stem though a conversion rule before adding suffixes (see **-er>-r-**). The fact that some of the words above are only spelled **-re** makes it the better choice overall.

◊ For the choice of **metre or meter,** see under that heading.

International English selection: The choice of **-re** allows a consistent pattern for all English words of this type, including those which have to be excepted where **-er** is otherwise the norm. The ease of forming derivatives is a further linguistic argument for it. Extensive use of **-re** in Canada adds to its distributional strength, apart from its use in Britain and other Commonwealth countries.

---

reaction signal

See under **interjections**.

reafforestation, reforestation and afforestation

All these words mean "(re)planting with trees" or "converting (back) to forest," though the motives and methods have shifted over the course of time. **Afforestation** is the oldest by far, originating during C15 as the notorious policy of increasing the size of forests to provide hunting grounds for the rich. The pleonastic **reafforestation** was used in the same way in C17. But in the 1880s both **reafforestation** and **reforestation** are recorded as expressing environmental concerns about the loss of the world's natural forests. In current British English **afforestation, reforestation** and **reafforestation** are all used for this, but they stand in the ratio of about 4:2:1 in terms of their popularity with BNC writers. In American English **reforestation** dominates, with scant evidence of either of the others in data from CCAE.

The International Forestry Association in 1971 endorsed both **afforestation** and **reforestation,** using them to distinguish between two kinds of replanting. Thus:

* **afforestation** = planting a species of timber which does not naturally occur in the region, e.g. planting softwood pine trees in Australia
* **reforestation** = reestablishing native trees in areas from which they have been cleared

Outside the circles of silviculturists, this distinction is not regularly observed.

real or really

These words can get overused in impromptu conversation, but both have legitimate roles. **Really** is an adverb with dual functions. It can mean "truly, actually," as in *They were really there*. In addition it's often used as a kind of intensifier, as in *They were really great* (see further under **intensifiers**). The two meanings are not always easy to separate. Both are latent in the second example, and in the ones below where **really** modifies verbs:

> *They really wanted to talk.*
> *What really worries me is their disinclination to act.*

Real has a regular role as an adjective meaning "true, genuine, actual," as in *real friend, real pearls, real life*. *Real estate* and *real property* means assets in the form of land and the buildings on it, i.e. tangible rather than paper assets. From meanings like those, **real** comes to be used in phrases like *real facts* and *a real problem,* in which its role is more the intensifier. Some would object to this as a misuse of **real**, though it has already happened with **really**. The problem with such phrases might rather be that they are clichéd.

The use of **real** most subject to query is its colloquial role as an adverb (once again an *intensifier*): *That's real bad news*. Collocations such as *real good, real quick* are common conversational idioms in North America, and so **real** is much more often an adverb in American conversation than in British. The ratio is about 14:1, according to data examined for the *Longman Grammar* (1999). Americans also make extensive use of **really** in adding emphasis to what's said, using it almost twice as often as the British, according to the *Grammar.* Thus **real** and **really** coexist as adverbs in American speech, sometimes as alternates in the same utterance. This coexistence probably serves as a reminder that **real** is not the fully fledged adverb and therefore nonstandard, like many of the **zero adverbs** (see further under that heading). So despite its relative frequency, American commentators are disinclined to accept **real** in writing, or at least formal writing. *Webster's English Usage* (1989) and *Canadian English Usage* (1997) show that **real** certainly appears in journalistic prose and in fiction, wherever authentic idiom is harnessed for emphasis. But in writing, the adverb **real** quickly becomes conspicuous, and needs to be paraphrased by some other intensifier – that is, if it is needed at all.

realtor, real estate agent, estate agent

These all refer to those whose business is to sell buildings or land, the first two being used in North America, the second in Australia, and the third in Britain. The term **realtor** is claimed by the US National Association of Realtors, and the Canadian Association of Real Estate Boards for their members, as their registered trade mark since 1916. This is why some dictionaries and style guides suggest capitalizing the word (as **Realtor**), and using **real estate agent** for generic purposes. However the proprietary aspect of **realtor** is not widely known, and commentators in the US (Garner, 1998) and Canada (Fee and McAlpine, 1997) both note that the word is widely used without a capital letter.

rebound, redound or resound

Figurative and idiomatic uses bring these close together, though they have quite separate origins. **Rebound** meaning "bounce back" can be used of a ball springing off the ground, or a noise bouncing off the walls or ceiling. In the second case, it begins to overlap with **resound** ("echo"), though the imagery is

a little different. A noise which *rebounds* seems to set up discrete sound waves, whereas one which *resounds* creates an environment of sound. Another extension of **rebound** is to refer to an effect resulting from another kind of action, as in:

> *The reduced flow of fresh water will rebound on fisheries.*

This usage has something in common with that of the now quite rare verb **redound** ("have an effect, contribute to"), as in:

> *The research will redound to the anthropologist's credit.*

As in that example, **redound** now mostly associates with positive entities like *credit, honor, profit,* where **rebound** often entails a negative for those affected. Earlier negative uses of **redound**, as in *May his sin redound on his head,* are now more likely to become *rebound on his head.* Even *redounded to their credit* may these days be paraphrased as *resounded to their credit.* **Redound** has clearly lost out to **rebound** and **resound**.

recalcitrance or recalcitrancy

See under -nce/-ncy.

reciprocal words

Some pairs of words connote actions which complement each other, such as *buy/sell, give/take, teach/learn*. The common cases like these are no problem to adult users of the language, but less frequent ones such as *imply/infer* and *replace/substitute* may be. See **imply**, **replace**, and also **lend**.

recision, recission or rescission

See **rescission**.

reckless or wreckless

The second is occasionally substituted for the first, no doubt because the verb *reck* ("consider") is now archaic, whereas *wreck* (as verb/noun meaning "damage") is current. Amid CCAE's newspaper data, there are mutliple examples of *wreckless driving* – where "wreckful" would put it more aptly. Other curious uses of **wreckless** are the references to *wreckless examiners,* and sportspersons known for their *hustle and wreckless style!* All such examples are paradoxically concerned with the damage caused by **reckless** behavior. But whatever the subliminal explanation, **wreckless** gets no support from any dictionary.

reclaim and reclamation

See under -aim.

reconciliation or reconcilement

Though either could represent the verb *reconcile,* **reconciliation** does it far more often than **reconcilement**. **Reconciliation** has many applications, referring to the coming together of estranged parties, as in the *spirit of reconciliation,* and in the *reconciliation of discrepant evidence,* where courts discuss the consistency and compatibility of the facts. In financial management **reconciliation** is the standard term for *reconciling* one's accounts. **Reconcilement** remains the ad hoc noun, listed in dictionaries as a possibility – and on record since C16 – but little used, or rarely written down. There is no sign of it in the BNC and one solitary example in CCAE.

recourse, resort or resource

See under **resource**.

recto and verso

See **verso**.

recur or reoccur, and recurrence or re-occurrence

Is there any difference between these pairs? **Recur** and **recurrence** are longer established (dating back to C17), and have a wider range of uses. *New Oxford* (1998) glosses **recur** as meaning "occur again, periodically or repeatedly." **Recurrence** has similar scope, and can be used of the pattern of repetition or of a single episode. Compare:

> . . . *minimize the later recurrence of stress and anxiety*
> *The next step is to prevent a recurrence.*

Reoccur and **reoccurrence** focus on the individual episode, as in:

> *Former tennis champion Pat Cash suffered a reoccurrence of a knee injury.*

With **reoccurrence**, the event has happened again but without necessarily being part of a pattern. Its record begins in early C19, according to the *Oxford Dictionary*, but it has little patronage in current British or American English, by the mere handful of examples in BNC and CCAE. Among the few, the hyphenless **reoccurrence** and **reoccur** are preferred to **re-occurrence/re-occur**, even in British English.

redound, resound or rebound

See under **rebound**.

reduced forms

In the flow of conversation we commonly *reduce* the sounds and syllables of words, to ease the process of uttering them, and the amount of decoding for the listener. This results in contractions such as *can't* and *would've,* which embody "weak forms" of *not* and *have* respectively. The weak form of *have* is so common that it's sometimes mistakenly spelled "of," in "could of," "should of," even by adult writers.

Reduced forms of syntax are a common feature of conversation, when we use phrases rather than complete clauses while exchanging ideas:

> [Have you] *Ever tried parachuting?*
> [I wouldn't try it] *Not if you paid me.*

The brackets show roughly what's been left out of the utterance, words which would help to make full sentences but contain repetitive material. The exchange is brisker without them.

Reduced forms of words and contractions are unsuitable for *formal* writing, where they need to be replaced by the fully fledged form. They suggest the informality and the give-and-take of conversation, and may seem to distract from the dignity and authority of the writer's voice. Yet they do reduce the bulk of routine function words and can help to move the underlying rhythm of the prose – which makes them a useful part of any writer's repertoire. They are increasingly seen in expository writing: see **contractions** section 2.

reductio ad absurdum

In Latin this means "reducing [it] to the absurd." It describes an argumentative tactic which makes an extreme deduction from a proposition – one which is obviously contrary to common sense and accepted truth. The technique is used in formal logic to show the falseness of a proposition, but it's also used more informally to discredit someone else's position. For example, those who argue against offering asylum to refugees sometimes suggest that accepting them means the end of the visa system as we know it. The argument thus stretches a proposition (*allow in some displaced persons without visas*) to an extreme (*anyone can enter*). It reduces the social and moral questions embedded in the proposition to bureaucratic procedures.

redundancy

Redundancy is a matter of using more words than are needed to express a point. Sometimes it's matter of sheer repetition as in:

> *They waved a greeting and they went on.*

The second "they" seems *redundant* and clumsy, because English grammar allows us to read the subject of the second clause from the first in a coordinated sentence where the two subjects are the same. (See **ellipsis** section 1.) Very occasionally a writer may wish to repeat something which is normally ellipted for the sake of emphasis, but usually it makes for **redundancy**.

Redundancy often arises through the overlap of meaning between different words which are combined in the same phrase or sentence. Compare "the four members of the quartet" with *all members of the quartet,* where the second version avoids double reference to the actual size of the group. (See further under **pleonasm** and **tautology**.)

Redundant information and strategic repetition. Other kinds of **redundancy** can occur in communicating information, when a detail is reported twice over in a brief stretch of writing, or irrelevant details are included. The document's purpose and its expected readers should settle what needs to be said and what may be beside the point. Avoiding unnecessary repetition is a matter of careful organization, structuring content so that information is presented at the crucial and most productive moment – not too early, so that it has to be repeated. You may nevertheless wish to foreshadow issues in general terms at the start of a longer document, and summarize them at the end. Strategic repetition of that kind helps to underscore document structure; and the more general terms of discussion used in the introduction/conclusion, and the more specific treatment of the issues in the main body of the document, will set them apart and prevent any sense of **redundancy**. See further under **reports** section 1.

reduplicatives

Some English compounds consist of two very similar words, only differing in their first consonants, or their vowels. Examples of the first kind are:

> *fuddy-duddy* *hanky-panky* *mumbo-jumbo*
> *razzle-dazzle* *walkie-talkie*

And of the second:

> *chitchat* *crisscross* *dillydally* *dingdong*
> *mishmash* *riffraff* *tittletattle* *zigzag*

One of the two parts of a **reduplicative** (often the second) may be a meaningful word, and the other then plays on its sound. **Reduplicatives** often have an informal feel to them, and their use can be off-handed or derogatory.

In a small number of cases, English **reduplicatives** involve identical words, as in:

> *fifty-fifty*   *goody-goody*   *hush-hush*   *never-never*
> *pooh-pooh*   *pretty-pretty*   *tut-tut*

As the examples show, they are always the informal word for the concept they refer to.

reek or wreak

See **wreak**.

reference to

Both *in reference to* and *with reference to* are used to highlight a topic or point of interest in a discussion:

> *Not all implications are valid in reference to pedagogy.*

> *. . . a change in my attitude with reference to textiles*

The two complex prepositions often seem interchangeable, and are presented as such in the *Oxford Dictionary* (1998). *In reference to* is the older of the two, dating from late C16, while *with reference to* (from early C18) varies with it, especially in business letters, where it benchmarks the state of correspondence, as in:

> *With reference to your letter of 26 April, I am pleased to report that . . .*

While *in reference to* is fully grammaticalized and fixed in its form, *with reference to* can be varied a little, as in *with frequent/passing/occasional reference to.* Databases show that *in reference to* is much more common than *with reference to,* at least in the UK. The ratio between them is more than 20:1 in BNC data, but about 5:1 in data from CCAE.

In American English *with reference to* also serves as a variant of *by reference to.* Compare:

> *The group justifies the call with reference to the Geneva Convention.*

> *. . . justified by reference to UN resolutions that affirm the right to . . .*

In these cases, the phrase introduced by *with/by reference to* is closely tied to the verb, rather than a detachable adverbial (see **predicate** final note). Comparative data from the BNC and CCAE suggest that *by reference to* is used across a range of writing styles in the UK, whereas in the US it's mostly found in academic writing.

referencing

Writers of reports and scholarly papers often have to refer to other publications to support their own statements and conclusions. There are conventional ways of doing this, so as to provide necessary information for the reader while minimizing the interruption. The five main systems are:

* *short title*
* *footnotes or endnotes*
* *author–date references*, also known as *running references* or (outside North America) as the *Harvard system*
* *author–number system*
* *number system* (*Vancouver style*)

The *short title* system is used in general books, while the others are associated with academic publications. The *footnote/endnote* system is mostly used in the humanities, including history and law. *Author–date* references are used in the sciences and social sciences, and the *number* system in biomedical writing. Some publications use a combination of systems, with *author–date* references for citing other publications, and occasional *footnotes* for a more substantial comment by the writer or editor. *Footnotes* were rather difficult to set or adjust on the earliest wordprocessors, and this probably encouraged wider use of *author–date* references. Other things being equal, *author–date* references are preferable to a *number* system, because they give some immediate information to the reader.

1 Short title references are cut-down variants of full references, with enough distinctive information to remind readers of the identity of the work being invoked (see **short titles**). They have long been used in *footnotes* (see below, section 2), but now increasingly within the text itself. With the abbreviated title and (optionally) its date, they provide more immediate information than either *author-date* references or numbers which take readers away to *footnotes* or the bibliography. They still depend on full references being given in an accumulated *reference list*.

2 Footnotes and endnotes keep reference material out of the ongoing discussion. Only a superscript number intervenes to guide the eye to the bottom of the page, or to the end of the chapter/book when you're ready. The numerals for *footnotes* can recommence with every page, or run through a whole chapter as is usual for endnotes. Occasionally the enumeration runs through the whole book, which makes for increasingly large superscript numbers (often three digits). But their uniqueness is a help to readers searching among accumulated notes at the back of the book.

Some writers use *footnotes/endnotes* to discuss a particular point which might seem to digress from the main argument. These are *substantive footnotes*. But mostly *footnotes/endnotes* serve to identify source publications, and so must include whatever the reader needs to track them down. In the first reference to any source, it's important to name the author, title, date of publication and the relevant page numbers. Unless there are full details in the bibliography, the footnotes should include the place of publication and also the name of the publisher:

> *G. Blainey Tyranny of Distance (Melbourne: Sun Books, 1966) pp. 23–31*

Note that the author's name or initials come in front of the surname (not inverted as in a bibliography). Questions of punctuating the titles and the order of items are discussed under **bibliography**: see final section on "Points to note."

Second and later references to the same work can be cut back, as can endnotes grouped together for the same chapter. The author's name may be sufficient:

> *Blainey, pp. 95–6*

However if another work by the same author is cited in the same group of *footnotes/endnotes*, short titles will be needed for both:

> *Blainey, Spinnifex, p. 66*
> *Blainey, Tyranny, pp. 95–6*

Latin abbreviations used in **referencing** (*ibid., loc.cit., op.cit.*) are discussed at their individual entries.

3 Author–date references explain in passing what source publication is being alluded to, but the reference is kept to the bare essentials: just the author's surname, the date of the publication, and the

relevant pages indicated by numbers only, with no *pp.*
The information is enclosed in brackets, and followed
by a comma, full stop etc. as the sentence requires:
> *Regional usages often stop at state borders in*
> *Australia, as did the earliest railway*
> *developments (Blainey, 1966:95–6).*

The final punctuation is never included inside the
final bracket of a *running reference*, even though it
may be with other kinds of parentheses (see **brackets**
section 2).

If reference is made to two or more authors with the
same surname in the course of an article or book, a
distinguishing initial must be added into the basic
reference. And when referring to more than one
publication by the same author in the same year, the
two need to be distinguished, as 1966a and 1966b, in
the *running references* as well as the bibliography. The
second and subsequent references are identical to the
first, except in the case of publications with joint
authors. The first reference normally gives the
surnames of all authors, unless there are four or more
of them, in which case only the first author is named,
followed by *et al.* This is the regular practice for
second and later references. The *author–date* system
relies very heavily on a full list of references to supply
details of the author(s), titles, and the publishing
information.

4 The author–number system works by enumerating
the works of each author referred to as a set, instead of
using dates of publication. So if four publications by
Blainey are referred to in a particular article, they
will be *Blainey* (1), *Blainey* (2) etc. within the text, and
listed together with those numbers in their
alphabetical place in the bibliography.

5 The number system uses a sequence of superscripts,
or bracketed numbers on the line of text, to refer the
reader to publication details in the reference list. The
use of superscripts is more distinct, but more difficult
to place in relation to other punctuation when the
numbers become large: neither *McBride,*[148] nor
McBride[148], seems ideal. In the *Vancouver* version of
this system, more than one number may be used at the
same point, as in: ... *the evidence discussed by McBride*
[148, 149]. Parentheses may be used instead of square
brackets, though they may then be mistaken for other
kinds of parenthetical material. Some writers,
according to *Webster's Style Manual* (1985), use the
brackets to contain both a reference number and a
page number, the two being separated by a comma,
with the first in italics and the second in roman, e.g.
(*4*, 216). The parenthetical reference is placed after
any punctuation (comma, period / full stop etc.),
which detaches it somewhat from the point it's
intended to detail. Whatever notation is used, the
numbers fix the order of titles in the reference list, so
they are not arranged alphabetically as in other
referencing systems. A further disadvantage is that
the numbering has to be adjusted throughout
whenever a reference is added or taken out. The
Vancouver bibliography style works with minimal
punctuation of authors' names, and abbreviated styles
for titles of journals and publishers' names. See
bibliographies section C, and notes following.

referendum

With its Latin origins, **referendum** has both
referenda and **referendums** as its plurals, though
dictionaries diverge over which to present as the
primary form. *Merriam-Webster* (2000) has **referenda,**
whereas *New Oxford* (1998) makes it **referendums**.
Paradoxically, it was Americans responding to the
Langscape survey (1998–2001) who preferred
referendums, by a majority of 71%, whereas only
43% of British respondents supported it. For the
plurals of other loanwords of this type, see **-um.**

referential

Linguists use this term for one of the three major
functions of language – its ability to *refer* to elements
of the world around us and the way we construct it.
Referential is a synonym for *ideational* in Halliday's
grammar (1994). See further under **textual.**

referred or refereed

Printed side by side, these seem to be anagrams of
each other, but they are more closely related than
most. **Referred** is the past tense of the verb *refer,* with
the final *r* doubled because the syllable it occurs in is
stressed (see further under **doubling of final**
consonant). **Refereed** is the past tense for a verb
made from the noun *referee,* also based on *refer* (see
-ee). The final letter of the verb *referee* is dropped
before the past suffix is added. See **-e** section 1.

reflection or reflexion

Writers overwhelmingly prefer **reflection,** by the
evidence of both British and American databases. See
under **-ction/-xion.**

reflective or reflexive

These adjectives have quite different applications.
Reflective can be applied to any surface that *reflects*
light, heat or sound, as in *reflective glass, heat reflective*
fleece, a reflective barrier. But its most frequent use in
BNC data relates to mental *reflections,* as in *a quiet*
and reflective man or *long, serious, reflective essays.*

Reflexive is much less frequent and largely confined
to academic discourse. It can mean "turned in on
itself," as in *a reflexive, interdependent relationship*
between theory and practice. That apart, it is most used
in grammar, to identify such things as *reflexive*
pronouns and *reflexive verbs* (see next two entries).

reflexive pronouns

The pronouns ending in *-self* or *-selves* are *reflexive,*
and typically refer back to the subject of the sentence.
They include:
> *myself   yourself   him/her/itself oneself*
> *ourselves yourselves   themselves (themself)*

This standard English set of *reflexives* is a mix of
words formed with the possessive pronoun (*my, your,*
our) and the object pronoun (*him, her, it, them*). For
theirselves, see under **themself.**

Reflexive pronouns are selected to correspond in
person and number (and for the third person singular,
in gender) with the subject:
> *I must see for myself.*
> *He shot himself in the foot.*
> *They came by themselves.*

In cases like these, the **reflexive pronoun** serves as
the object of a verb or preposition, and its position in
the sentence is fixed.

Reflexive pronouns can also be used to emphasize
any other noun or name in the sentence, standing
immediately after it:

They talked to the president himself.
You yourselves might go that way.
In shorter sentences where the *reflexive* underscores the subject, it can also appear at the other end of the sentence:

You might go that way yourselves.
Recurrent choices among the **reflexive pronouns** have been found to reflect the genre of writing (*Longman Grammar,* 1999). Fiction writers make most use of the singular personal *reflexives* (*myself, himself, herself*), whereas the impersonal *itself* and *themselves* are most common in nonfiction.

The **reflexive pronouns** are sometimes used without an explicit antecedent, as a bulky substitute for the regular pronoun, as in:

With yourself as project leader, the team is complete.
The idea is for Jan and myself to visit him.
(For the sometimes self-conscious effects of this use of *myself,* see **me.**) In comparative expressions, the **reflexive pronoun** also appears without antecedent, although it may be expressed in the surrounding text.

No-one knew better than ourselves what was meant.
Other comparative prepositions, including *as, but for, except, like* can likewise take **reflexive pronouns** on their own.

reflexive verbs

A **reflexive verb** has the same person as its subject and object. In English it can be formed out of an ordinary verb with a *reflexive* pronoun as object: *The officer cut himself shaving.* But only a handful of verbs must be constructed in that way, like:

She acquitted herself well in the discussion.
Others which require a *reflexive* are:

absent oneself	avail oneself	demean oneself
ingratiate oneself	perjure oneself	pride oneself

All such verbs are in fact French loanwords, where many common verbs are *reflexive* in their construction. The same is true of German and Italian. One example is the verb *remember* which is *reflexive* in all three languages (*se rappeler / sich erinnern / ricordarsi*), but never in English.

reforestation or reafforestation

See **reafforestation.**

refurbish, furbish or refurnish

All these words involve renovation. With **refurnish** you're buying new furniture and perhaps soft furnishings for your home/office, whereas **refurbish** means sprucing up and polishing what you already have. But **refurbish** can be used of other kinds of property from *cruise liners* to *tubular inspection equipment,* and even of more abstract entities, as in *refurbish the economy,* or *a long history to recall and refurbish.* The history of **refurbish** has its own interest. It originated as **furbish** in C14 English, meaning "remove the rust from a weapon," and was then reinvented with the re- prefix in C17, with the more general meaning of "polish up." **Furbish** also took on this meaning, but has lost out to **refurbish** in both British and American English. There are more than 100 instances of **refurbish** to every 1 of **furbish** in data from the BNC and CCAE.

refute

In the standard dictionary definition, **refute** implies the use of a proof to reject a claim or a charge:

Check all the facts and refute them with sound evidence.
Yet the word is often used simply to mean "deny," "reject" without any counterevidence or logical disproof being supplied:

The authors go out of their way to refute the slur in their introduction.
Most ... who work with mentally handicapped people refute the attitude ...
The *Oxford Dictionary* (1989) showed how *refute the allegation(s)* had become the regular idiom, although it called it "erroneous." *Webster's English Usage* (1989) noted that it was common, especially in newspaper reports – and that objections to it are stronger in Britain than America (the two go together). But a decade later the *New Oxford* (1998) comments that the disputed use of **refute** is "now widely accepted in standard English." This is in line with ample evidence of its use in British English, in a variety of texts included in the BNC. *Merriam-Webster* (2000) presents the second definition ("deny the truth of") alongside the first ("prove wrong") without comment. The *Canadian Oxford* (1998) and the Australian *Macquarie Dictionary* (1997) still carry warning labels about using **refute** to mean "deny," though it seems unlikely that the objections can be sustained much longer in the face of usage. It may rankle with those who like to keep words in the state to which they are accustomed, but language moves on.

regalia

The Latin origins of **regalia** associate it with royalty ("emblems of *regal* status"), and make it plural (see **-a** section 2). But in English the word has moved on in both respects. **Regalia** is now democratized, and may be the distinctive uniform (*full regalia*) of almost any group, from *academic regalia* to *cowboy regalia,* not to mention *fish in spawning regalia.* It can be applied to the dress of a particular period, e.g. *1950s regalia, nineteenth century feminist regalia* – and even late C20 *skiers in day-glo regalia,* among the examples from CCAE and the BNC. The phrase *royal regalia* is not felt to be a tautology. With this semantic change, **regalia** has acquired a collective sense that goes with a singular verb, as in:

take great pains to ensure their regalia is authentic.
It entails a singular pronoun:

... her official regalia in all its purple magnificence
Singular agreement occurs more often than plural in BNC data, and *New Oxford* (1998) notes that either may be used. The data in CCAE is grammatically indeterminate, and *Merriam-Webster* (2000) glosses the word only as "noun plural."

regard(s) to

The phrase **regard(s) to** is embedded in complex prepositions such as *in regard(s) to* and *with regard(s) to.* They are wordy conveniences, the stuff of bureaucratic writing and *commercialese* (see under that heading), now used elsewhere in reporting and strategic planning.

The established written forms *in regard to* and *with regard to* are in the singular, though the plural forms *in/with regards to* are also well documented in American and British English. They have probably been affected by yet other idioms: the complex preposition *as regards,* and perhaps the phrase *give my regards to,* popularized in the musical/movie titles *Give my regards to Broadway* (1948) and *Give my regards to Broad Street* (1984). In data from the BNC, the plural forms tend to occur in more interactive discourse (written and spoken), and *Webster's English Usage* (1989) also notes that *in regards to* seems to be in oral rather than written use. This would explain the negative comment which it seems to have attracted, especially from American commentators. But CCAE provides more than occasional examples of *in/with regards to* from newspaper sources, alongside *in/with regard to,* in the ratio of about 1:9. BNC data shows the opposite trend: instances of *in/with regards to* outnumber those of *in/with regard to* by about 4:1. The plural form is thus unremarkable in the UK, but a distraction from the singular form in the US. In both British and American usage, *with regard(s) to* is more popular than *in regard(s) to,* though the difference is much greater in British (by a factor of 5:1 rather than 5:4). The American preference for the singular form (**regard to**) may be aligned with their use of the *s*-less forms of certain adverbs. See **-ward or -wards**.

regime and regimen

Doctors prescribing a course of therapy (diet, exercise etc.) may call it a **regimen**, where the nontechnical term is **regime**. It amounts to the same thing, whether it's a *regimen involving no alcoholic beverages* or a *regime of no booze.* The doctor's avoidance of **regime** probably reflects the fact that it has nonmedical meanings as well, and, like scientists generally, they prefer their words to be unequivocal. The added issue is that when (as often) **regime** refers to a particular system of government, administration or social system, e.g. *a Fascist regime,* its overtones are usually negative. All this is unhelpful for the doctor seeking a patient's compliance with therapy, and so the neutral **regimen** recommends itself. The only snag is its relative unfamiliarity: **regime** outnumbers **regimen** by more than 12:1 in CCAE, and almost 30:1 in the BNC.

Regime does not need an acute accent these days, despite its French background. **Régime** is not suggested by *New Oxford* (1998), *Canadian Oxford* (1998) or *Merriam-Webster* (2000), even as the secondary spelling.

regionalism and regionism

A **regionalism** is, as you might expect, a word or phrase that belongs to a particular *region* and not considered part of the standard variety. **Regionalism** dates from the 1950s, whereas the word **regionism** belongs to the year 2000. It was coined by Wales (2000) to refer to a very old kind of linguistic prejudice, which assumes that the dialect or language variety of your own *region* is superior to that of any other. In the UK, **regionism** mostly works in favor of the southern standard, whereas in the US the more northerly varieties have the advantage. Like any other *-ism,* **regionism** has far-reaching effects on language and social values, and needs watching. See further under **-ism**, and **north, northern and northerly**.

register

The **registers** of music (high . . . low) are the metaphorical starting point for the linguistic notion of **register**. The word was first applied to the range of styles from formal written language to informal spoken language, as if they form a single scale. Nowadays **register** is often used to refer to the distinctive forms of language associated with particular occupations or specializations, e.g. *the register of economics* or *of golf;* and/or the language of particular contexts, such as the **register** of the court, the classroom or the church service.

regrettably and regretfully

Both involve *regret,* but in **regretfully** the feeling is more straightforwardly expressed – *I must regretfully decline* – or else attributed directly to a third party: *He spoke regretfully of his retirement.* In either example the *regret* is expressed openly.

Regrettably is more academic and implies a *regret* that others could or should share:
Regrettably he was not there to speak for himself.
It injects the writer's evaluation of a situation, a view which s/he hopes the reader will endorse.
Regrettably is one of a set of attitudinal adverbs which can be deployed for interpersonal contact in writing. The fact that many of those adverbs end in *-fully* (*delightfully, mercifully, thankfully* etc.) helps to explain why **regretfully** gets mistakenly used for **regrettably**.

regular verbs

The English **regular verbs** are those which simply add *-ed* to make their past forms, as with *departed* and *rolled.* In the same very large group are all those which add the *-ed,* subject to other standard spelling rules, such as:
* dropping the final *e* before the suffix (*arrived, liked*)
* doubling the final consonant before the suffix (*barred, admitted*)
   (See **-e** section 1, and **doubling of final consonant** for more about those rules.)

Regular verbs are very numerous because they include not only all newly formed ones, but also most of those inherited from Old English. The number of *irregular verbs* has been steadily declining over the centuries, and many which were once irregular have acquired regular past forms with *-ed,* at least as an alternative. (See further under **irregular verbs**.)

An alternative term for the **regular verb** is "weak verb," used especially by scholars of Old English and other Germanic languages. The *irregular verbs* are then the "strong" ones.

reindeer

The plural of this word is most often just like the singular, i.e. **reindeer**, in keeping with the word *deer* itself. Many other kinds of wild animals have *zero plurals* like this (see under that heading). However the domesticated **reindeer** associated with Christmas ritual are individualized like horses (*Rudolf, the red-nosed reindeer*), as they take their place in the delivery team. This fosters the regular plural *reindeers,* which is recognized in all major dictionaries.

relaid or relayed

Relaid is the past tense of *relay* meaning "lay again":
> *The railway track was relaid after the earthquake.*

It rarely takes a hyphen, even in British English, by the evidence of the BNC. **Relayed** is the past of *relay* ("communicate by a radio or electronic network"):
> *The performance was relayed by closed circuit TV to viewers in the hall.*

relation or relationship

The choice between these becomes an issue when you want to refer to an abstract connection, because there is some stylistic difference. Data from the BNC shows that **relation(s)** in this sense is mostly associated with academic and official writing, whereas **relationship(s)** is found equally in general and academic writing. **Relationship** is also used in a wide variety of references to personal, social and political connections e.g. *married relationship, loving relationship,* where **relation** could not appear. By the same token, **relation** reigns supreme in the idiom *in relation to.*

relations or relatives

Both can refer to "your sisters and your cousins and your aunts." But in current American and British English, **relatives** is by far the more popular of the two, in data from CCAE and the BNC. **Relative(s)** needs no explanation, whereas **relations** (in the sense of "family") is usually contextualized so as to clarify its use, as in *friends and relations / relations and friends.* Otherwise, **relations** is typically used in more abstract ways, in collocations such as *human/industrial/public/race relations* or *bad/frosty/good/improved relations.* The use of **relatives** for "family" prevents any temporary ambiguity over whether your "political relations" are your cousins in parliament or contacts with people in power.

relative clauses

Sometimes known as *adjectival* clauses, these serve either to define, or to describe and evaluate the noun to which they're attached. They stand right next to it, even if this delays the predicate of the main clause (see **clauses** sections 3 and 4). For example:
> *The radio that we bought at the market has never given any trouble.*

But there are grammatical issues in the connection and relationship between the **relative clause** and the main clause, notably
* the choice of pronoun (and when it can be omitted)
* the status of the **relative clause** in relation to the rest (as a "sentence relative," or as a *restrictive* or *nonrestrictive clause*)

1 **Relative clauses and relative pronouns.** Relative clauses are often introduced by one of the *relative pronouns* such as *that, which, who* etc. (the *wh-pronouns*). The choice is a matter of grammar and style (see below, section 4, and next entry: **relative pronouns**). In certain stylistic and grammatical circumstances there may be no pronoun at all, the so-called "zero relative." Except in the most formal style, the pronoun can be omitted from **relative clauses** of which it's the *object.*
> *The radio we bought at the market has never given any trouble.*

But when the *relative pronoun* is the *subject* of the **relative clause**, it's almost always expressed, whatever the style:
> *The radio that came from the market has never given any trouble.*

Delete "that" from the sentence and it's very likely to be misread, with nothing to signal the fact that "came" belongs to a subordinate clause. In speech it can be signaled through intonation, as in Irish English; but readers need the *relative pronoun* to express the subject of the **relative clause**.

2 **Relative clauses and relative adverbs.** Some **relative clauses** are linked to the main clause by adverbs such as *when, where, why:*
> *I remember the time when we made marshmallow kebabs.*
> *You remember the place where we met.*
> *They remember the reason why we looked so strange.*

The *wh*-adverbs act as relators of the second clause to a noun of time, place or reason in the main clause. ("Time" could be expressed by more particular words such as *year, day, night;* "place" by *house, hotel* etc.) In less formal styles, the *relative adverbs* can be replaced by *that,* as in
> *I remember the time that we made marshmallow kebabs.*

And even omitted altogether:
> *I remember the time we made marshmallow kebabs.*

The *Longman Grammar* (1999) confirms the use of the same alternatives (using *that* or zero relative) for *where* and *why,* with examples from fiction writing as well as conversation. But the omission of *when* is acceptable further up the stylistic ladder. The *Longman* research shows the use of zero relative for *when* across all writing styles from fiction to news reporting and academic prose.

3 **Sentence relatives.** These are **relative clauses** which relate to the whole preceding clause, not to any one noun in it:
> *They wanted to go home by ferry, which I thought was a good idea.*

Sentence relatives are always prefaced by *which.* Some style guides warn against them, and occasionally it's unclear whether the *relative* relates to the whole sentence or the last noun in it. Unless this creates ambiguity, *sentence relatives* are no problem, and they serve to add the writer's comment on the main statement or proposition of a sentence.

4 **Restrictive and nonrestrictive relative clauses.** **Relative clauses** which serve to define or identify something in the main clause are often called "restrictive" – and so others that describe or evaluate or add writers' comments are "nonrestrictive." (Alternative names are *defining* and *nondefining relative clauses.*) Compare the following:
> *People who sign such agreements are crazy.* (restrictive)
> *I met his brothers, who signed the agreement.* (nonrestrictive)

As in these examples, the *restrictive relative clause* helps defines the previous noun, whereas the second simply adds information. Research reported in the *Longman Grammar* (1999) shows that *restrictive relative clauses* are far more common in all kinds of writing. Yet the distinction between restrictive and nonrestrictive is not always clear cut, especially after indefinite antecedents:

> *In the files I found an agreement which was signed under pressure.*

In cases like this, there is no difference in meaning one way or the other. In others it makes a considerable difference, as in:

> *The department shredded all the files from the inquiry which contained embarrassing material.*

Did the department destroy every file (nonrestrictive interpretation), or only those with embarrassing contents (restrictive)? In practice the issue would probably resolve itself in the context of discourse.

Usage commentators have traditionally urged the use of a comma with *unrestrictive relative clauses,* so as to separate them from the antecedent and prevent ambiguity. The principle of a separating comma is widely observed – in 90% of all cases in Meyer's (1987) research – despite the general trend toward lighter punctuation. The complementary prescription is to use *that* rather than *wh-* pronouns with restrictive clauses, but that is far from universally practised (see next entry).

relative pronouns

Words such as *who, which, whom, whose, that,* are the **relative pronouns** that typically introduce *relative clauses:*

> *The doctor who/that came from Sri Lanka spoke well.*
> *The letter which/that I sent you should arrive tomorrow.*
> *The lion which/that escaped from the circus has been found.*
> *A woman whom/that I'd never seen before appeared.*
> *The nurse whose face would cure a thousand ills was frowning.*

As the examples show, *that* can be used for human referents as well as nonhuman and inanimate ones. It serves as an alternative to any of the *wh-*pronouns except *whose* (see further under **who and whose**). The total omission of the **relative pronoun** (= *zero relative*) is discussed under **relative clauses** sections 1 and 2.

The distribution of *that* and the *wh-* alternatives has been a topic of stylistic discussion since C18. *That* is sometimes thought of as informal, and this correlates with it being the most frequent **relative pronoun** in both conversation and fiction, according to *Longman Grammar* (1999) research. By contrast *which* predominates in nonfiction generally, along with *who* in news reporting.

The choice between *that* and a *wh-* pronoun is to some extent affected by whether it prefaces a restrictive or nonrestrictive *relative clause* (see **relative clauses** section 4). The notion that *that* goes with restrictive and *which* etc. with the nonrestrictive is put as an ideal by Fowler (1926), though even he admitted: "It would be idle to pretend it was the practice either of most or of the best writers." Later style commentators note that while *wh-* **relative pronouns** are indeed preferred for nonrestrictive *relative clauses,* both *that* and *which/who* are used with the restrictive type:

> *People who sign such agreements are ill-advised.*
> *People that sign such agreements are ill-advised.*

The *Longman Grammar* shows that *which* (and *who*) are actually used more for restrictive than nonrestrictive clauses in all kinds of writing, from a corpus of British and American English. However the *Chicago Manual* (2003) endorses the Fowlerian ideal as good practice, and American editors and writers more often seem to be exponents of it than their counterparts elsewhere.

In some restrictive contexts, the use of *that* is nevertheless normal worldwide. For example:

* after superlatives: *the best wine that's made in New Zealand . . .*
* after ordinal numbers: *the first hotel that has a vacancy . . .*
* after indefinites (*some, any, every, much, little, all*): *I'll take back any that are unused . . .*
* in a cleft sentence: *It's the label that has a bird on it.*
* when the antecedents are both human and nonhuman:
  > *Neither horse nor rider that fail the water jump find it easy to recover.*

Grammar apart, the choice of **relative pronouns** may be a matter of style and convenience. *That* saves us some decisions about *who* versus *which* (e.g. with babies) – not to mention *who* versus *whom*. With its various restrictive uses, *that* isn't necessarily informal; and it is available as an alternative when *which* with its greater bulk would claim undue attention. *That* makes the linkage with the main clause less conspicuous, and helps the merger in a densely worded sentence. By the same token, *which* is a useful variant for *that* when it is already bespoken in some other role:

> *That is the phrase which appeals most to me.*

Compare the chiming effect of:

> *That is the phrase that appeals most to me.*

Whatever else they do, the **relative pronouns** are a resource for optimizing one's style.

◊ See entry on **that** for its multiple grammatical functions.

relayed or relaid
See **relaid**.

relevance or relevancy
The first is far more common than the second. See **-nce/-ncy**.

remit
The use of **remit** as a verb is centuries old, dating back to C14. Its current use as a noun seems to originate in C18 Scottish law, where it meant the "transfer of a case from one court to another." But only in C20 has the noun **remit** climbed over the wall and taken off in other domains, referring to the "task or area of activity officially assigned to an individual or organization," as *New Oxford* (1998) puts it. In the phrase *beyond their remit,* the word is used to limit the scope and power of others. This use of **remit** is at home in Britain, Australia and New Zealand, but not in North America. *Canadian Oxford* (1998) notes it as "chiefly Brit.," and *Merriam-Webster* (2000) makes no mention of it. In New Zealand, **remit** is also "an item submitted for consideration at a conference," an early C20 meaning that predates its use to mean a "brief" in the UK.

remodeled or remodelled
For the spelling of this verb, see **-l-/-ll-**.

renaissance or renascence

The latinate **renascence** ("rebirth," on record since 1727) is struggling for life with the French **renaissance**, which appeared first in the 1840s and has very largely replaced it. **Renascence** is slightly more evident in American English, with a dozen examples in CCAE, compared with over 2000 of **renaissance**. The one solitary example in BNC data (*Third World renascence*) seems to mark its exit from British English. Writers everywhere are more likely to use **renaissance**, when referring to any kind of rebirth or revival, as in *the artistic renaissance of Birmingham*.

With a capital letter, **Renaissance** is the standard term for referring to the flowering of European culture that began in Italy in C14 and reached Britain in C16. It marked the end of medieval culture with its emphasis on tradition; yet it was at least partly stimulated by the rediscovery of classical scholarship from Greece and Rome. The reading of classical authors brought many Latin and Greek words into English, and occasioned the respelling of many French loanwords acquired during the previous centuries, according to their classical antecedents. (See further under **spelling** section 1.) The relationship between **renaissance** and **renascence** is in fact the opposite – symbolic of the modern era in which classical culture is no longer privileged.

renege or renegue

Four centuries after its first appearance, this word still seems a misfit, with its spelling and pronunciation at odds. Its nearest relative in English is *renegade*, though **reneg(u)e** itself seems to be a clipped form of the medieval Latin verb *renegare* ("deny"). In C16 **renege** had dire overtones of apostasy, and it was only toward the end of C17 that the word became associated with card-playing and with the frenchified spelling **renegue**. The general meaning "go back on a promise or commitment" appears toward the end of C18, though there's scant record of it until C20, and its spelling and pronunciation are still unsettled.

The *Oxford Dictionary* (1989) puts **renegue** ahead of **renege** as the preferred spelling, and it's much more satisfactory in terms of the ordinary rules of English spelling, because *g* followed by an *e* is normally a "soft" sound (see **-ce/-ge**). Yet **renege** is overwhelmingly preferred in both British and American English, by the evidence of the BNC and CCAE. **Renege** is less unsatisfactory as a spelling when you pronounce the word with a long vowel as "rineeg" or "rinayg," as the British do. But most Americans, Canadians and Australians pronounce it with a short vowel. *Merriam-Webster* (2000) lists "rinig" and "rineg" ahead of "rineeg"/"rinayg," as the four possible pronunciations. Garner (1998) notes (without any citations) that contemporary Americans sometimes spell it *renig*, a spelling which goes back to C18, according to the *Oxford*. From its links with *renegade* and *renegare,* we might also expect the spelling *reneg,* but it has only been recorded once or twice.

The general consensus is to use **renege** whatever the pronunciation. It entails the inflected forms *reneged* and *reneging,* registered in all dictionaries –

and we must grin and bear them. On the other hand, we could take affirmative action with the *Oxford Dictionary,* and use **renege**, *renegued* and *reneguing* – in the interests of bringing the renegade into line!

renounce and renunciation

The background to the divergence between these is discussed at **pronounce**.

rent or hire

See **hire**.

re(-)occurrence or recurrence

See under **recur and recurrence**.

repairable and reparable

Both words mean "able to be repaired." But the link with *repair* is stronger as well as more obvious in **repairable**, and it's the one usually applied to material objects which need fixing:

> *If the goods are faulty but repairable, haggle for a discount.*

The latinate **reparable** is more often used of abstract and intangible things needing to be restored or mended, as in:

> *The damage to their self-esteem was reparable.*

Note that the negative of **repairable** is *unrepairable,* and that of **reparable** is *irreparable.*

repellent or repellant

Dictionaries all make **repellent** the primary spelling, for both adjectival and noun uses of this word. *Webster's Third* (1986) and the *Oxford Dictionary* (1989) both allow **repellant** as an alternative for either, but this freedom is exploited more by American writers than their British counterparts. The ratio between the two is about 50:1 in BNC data, and 6:1 in data from CCAE. There's no sign that Americans tend to use **repellant** particularly for the noun. See further under **-ant/-ent**.

repertoire or repertory

At bottom these are the same word, in their French and Latin-derived forms respectively. Both refer primarily to a stock of items which can be performed. The latinate **repertory** is the older of the two by three centuries, borrowed in C16, and since late C19 associated particularly with amateur theatre and the *repertory theatre company,* which offers a set of plays for a short season. **Repertory** has other connections with the stage, referring to the set pieces of other performing groups, in opera, music, dance and other forms of entertainment. Occasionally in the UK and rather more often in the US, it's used of a notional inventory of skills commanded by groups or persons off-stage, as in *an individual's repertory of gestures* or *Florida's culinary repertory.*

Like **repertory**, **repertoire** has both on- and off-stage uses. Borrowed from French in C19, it quickly extended itself outside the theatre and performing hall to include the stock of abilities or skills possessed by a person in almost any field from *tennis strokes* to *coin design,* and on to one's command of ethnic cuisine or scotch whiskies. In scientific use, **repertoire** is applied to biological behavior, as in *the characteristic response repertoire of the species.* These extended uses are more frequent in British English, where **repertoire** is much more widely used than **repertory** (by more than 3:1 among BNC writers). In American English **repertoire** is apparently less popular than **repertory**, by the evidence of CCAE.

repetition

The **repetition** of any word or phrase in a short space of writing draws attention to it. In a narrative the repeated *he* or *she* is the focus of the action; and in nonfiction a set of key words may be repeated throughout the text because they are essential to the subject. If the writing is technical they must be repeated: technical terms cannot be paraphrased without losing the specific point of reference. A certain amount of **repetition** is also important as part of the network of cohesion in any kind of writing (see further under **coherence or cohesion**).

Apart from those functional reasons for repeating words and phrases, there may be stylistic or rhetorical ones. This is what gave and still gives great power to Abraham Lincoln's archetypal statement about American democracy, that it was:

> *government of the people, for the people, by the people . . .*

The repetition of "people" is made all the more conspicuous by being couched in parallel phrasing. (See further under **parallel constructions**.)

Yet **repetition** is sometimes accidental, or not well motivated. Writers get into a verbal groove when they should be seeking fresh ways of expressing an idea. A thesaurus offers a treasury of alternative words, though many of those grouped together are not synonyms and need to be checked for meaning and stylistic consistency. *Fork out* means "pay" everywhere in the world, but it's suitable only for informal contexts.

Repetition can be avoided also by varying the grammar of the sentence. Many verbs, nouns and adjectives have partners which can be pressed into service, with slight rearrangements of other words around them:

> *The demonstrators were protesting about a new road tax.*
> *Truck drivers demonstrated yesterday about a new road tax.*
> *A new road tax was the focus of yesterday's downtown demonstration.*

The choice of an alternative word form (*demonstrator/demonstrate/demonstration*) stimulates a different order and structure for the clause, and creates slots for new information – all of which help to vary your expression. Alternative function words are discussed in various entries in this book: see especially **conjunctions** and **relative pronouns**.

repetitious or repetitive

Both adjectives represent the noun *repetition,* but do they hold the same view of it? Either can appear in negative collocations such as *boring or repetitious work, repetitive and mind-numbing tasks.* Yet in **repetitive** the focus is more often on the repeated pattern itself, as in *repetitive DNA* or *repetitive strain injury* (RSI), and so it's inherently more neutral. That apart, **repetitive** is rather more frequent than **repetitious** in both American and British English. In CCAE data **repetitive** outnumbers **repetitious** by about 3:1, and the ratio in the BNC is 15:1. This accords with the *Oxford Dictionary*'s early C20 view that **repetitious** was "more common in American usage," and the fact that it goes back to C17, whereas **repetitive** is a C19 innovation. But **repetitive** is clearly the more widely used of the two now.

replace, substitute and substituted

The underlying verbs are complementary, in that **replace** means "take the place of" and **substitute** *(for),* "put in place of." So the following statements amount to the same thing:

> *Tom Tough replaced Ray Rough in Saturday's football match.*
> *The manager substituted Tom Tough for Ray Rough.*

In passive constructions, the two can also complement each other:

Ray Rough was replaced by Tom Tough	"had his place taken by"
Tom Tough was substituted for Ray Rough	"took the place of"

But in other passive contructions, **substituted** means "(was) replaced." It may or may not be followed by *with* or *by:*

> *Reserves can be substituted between rounds.*
> *Goddard's anger at being substituted suggests all is not well with the team.*
> *. . . 70% of present fuel consumption could be substituted by use of battery vehicles*

This passive use of **substituted** is particularly common in sports reporting, but not confined to it, as the last example shows. There are others in technical and everyday writing in the BNC. The construction is not new. Its record began in C17, according to the *Oxford Dictionary* (1989), though the *Dictionary*'s note, "now regarded as incorrect," was taken up with a vengeance by Fowler (1926), and the second edition of the *Dictionary* simply labels it "incorrect." The *New Oxford* (1998) restores it to grace with a careful note: "now generally regarded as part of normal standard English." *Merriam-Webster* (2000) simply lists the meaning "replace" for **substitute** without comment, and CCAE contains ample evidence of its use in American English.

If we accept the contrasting meanings of **substitute(d)**, do they ever cause confusion? Not when followed by a preposition, because *for* makes it mean "put in place of," and *by* or *with,* "replace." Without a preposition, the second meaning may not come across to those unfamiliar with the sporting register. So there's still a case for using **replace** or an active form of **substitute** instead:

> *Tom Tough substituted for Ray Rough on Saturday.*

This is the intransitive counterpart of the construction used at the start of this entry (see **transitive and intransitive**). It stands clear of the complications with the passive and the interplay with **replace**. The boundaries between **replace** and **substitute/substituted** are not fixed, and need careful negotiation – as with other reciprocal pairs (see under **reciprocal words**).

reported speech

This is the older name for *indirect speech.* See under **direct speech**.

reports

In their simplest form **reports** give a retrospective view of an enterprise. Written with the advantage of hindsight, they can offer a perspective on what's more and less important – not a "blow by blow" account of events, but one structured to help readers see the implications.

Apart from reviewing the past, **reports** written in the name of industry and government are expected to develop a strategic plan and recommendations for the future. An environmental impact study for example normally begins with an extended description of the existing environment and its physical, biological and social character. This is followed by discussions of the likely impact of any proposed development on all facets of the site, and then by sets of alternative recommendations.

1 Structuring reports. When writing a **report** it's important to identify the purpose of the investigation, so as to focus the document and define its scope. This prevents it from going in all directions, and from being swollen with irrelevant material. A specific brief may have been supplied for the **report** (e.g. to examine the causes of frequent lost-time injuries in the machine shop). If not, it's a good idea to compile your own brief, and to include it at the front of the **report**, to show the conceptual framework within which the work has been done. If recommendations and a management plan are the expected outcome of a **report**, these too need to be presented in summary form at the front (often called an *executive summary*), before you go into the details of the inquiry on which they are based.

Any longer **report** (say more than five pages) needs a table of contents on the first page, to show readers where to go for answers to any particular question. The format for **reports** in government and industry is not standardized (as it is in science), and common sense is your guide in creating a logical structure (e.g. presenting discussion of the status quo before ideas for the future). Within those broad sections, subsections with informative headings need to be devised, ones which can also be used in the table of contents. Tables of statistics are usually housed in an appendix if they occupy full pages, though shorter ones may be included where the discussion refers to them.

2 Science reports are written to a conventional format – the so-called *IMRAD* structure which consists of *Introduction, Method, Results (and) Discussion,* in that order. Two other details to note are that the *Method* may be subdivided into *subjects, apparatus* and *procedures;* and that the *report's* conclusions may be appended to the end of the *Discussion,* or else set apart with their own heading: *Conclusions.* The *IMRAD* format ensures that scientific experiments and investigations are reported in such a way as to be replicable, and allow the reader to separate the facts of the research (the method, results) from their interpretation (discussion/conclusions). The science reporting format is also the basic structure for articles in scholarly journals, and for empirical theses and dissertations.

3 Writing style in reports is necessarily rather formal. Whether written in the name of science or government or industry, they are expected to provide objective and judicious statements on the data examined, and responsible conclusions. They are not a natural vehicle for personal attitudes and values.

Yet the writing style of **reports** need not be dull or overloaded with passives and institutional clichés (see further under **passive verbs** and **impersonal style**). To ensure directness and clarity of style, it always helps to think of the people you're trying to communicate with through the **report**. Imagine them looking for answers to their questions. Readers are interested in clear, positive analysis – not in hedged statements and tentative conclusions. They respond to vitality in style, and to any attempts to supplement the written word with diagrams and visual aids. See further under **Plain English**.

requiescat in pace
See **RIP**.

requisite or requisition
As nouns, these can both mean "item required." But a **requisite** is often just a simple article of food or personal equipment, as in *toilet requisites* for going to hospital. **Requisition** has official overtones. It smacks of supplies for an institution or a national endeavor, as in *army requisitions.* The word **requisition** is often applied to a formal written request or claim for something:

> *Would you put through a requistion for 500 envelopes.*

rescission and recision
The act of *rescinding* finds expression in **rescission**, as in *a rescission motion* or *rescission of the contract.* The word **recision** ("cancelation") is sometimes found instead, at least in American English, witness *recision of the regulatory burden* and the *recision period* associated with such things as door-to-door sales. This is not a spelling mistake, since the word has its own derivation direct from the Latin *recisio(n)-* ("cutting back.") **Recision** and **rescission** appear in equal numbers in data from CCAE, whereas **rescission** stands alone in the BNC. This explains why *Merriam-Webster* (2000) registers both words, whereas *New Oxford* (1998) has only **rescission**. Meanwhile the *Oxford Dictionary* (1989) keeps the record for **recision** up to the end of C19 and a note saying that it was/is "now rare." It seems to have dropped out of British English.

The case for **recision** does not extend to the spellings *recission* or *rescision,* used in earlier centuries, and also reported in the US by Garner (1998), but without actual citations.

resin or rosin
Resin is a broad term, referring to a range of substances obtained from the sap of trees or other plants. It is also applied to similar substances synthesized by chemical processes. **Rosin** refers very specifically to the solid residue of **resin** from the pine tree which remains when the oil of turpentine has been extracted. A lump of **rosin** to rub on the strings of the violin bow is part of a violinist's equipment.

resistor or resister
A **resistor** is a component in an electric circuit, whereas a **resister** is a person who puts up a resistance. The two spellings seem to lend support to the idea that *-er* is used for human agents, and *-or* for an instrument or device. Unfortunately there are more *-or* words which defy that "rule" than ones like

resistor which seem to support it. See further under -er/-or.

resound, redound or rebound

See rebound.

resource, recourse or resort

From independent origins, these three words converge in some idioms. The least common of them nowadays is recourse, a noun which means "someone or something appealed to for help." It appears only in a few phrases such as *no recourse to, without recourse to* and *have recourse to.*

Resort as an abstract noun is also quite uncommon (unlike its more concrete use in *holiday resort*). It survives in the phrase *last resort,* a "course of action adopted under difficult circumstances," and occasionally as a verb meaning "apply to for help." The verb resort is built into phrases such as *resorted to* and *without resorting to,* where its closeness to *without recourse to* may challenge your sense of idiom.

Resource is primarily a noun, used to refer to a means or source of supply in many contexts ranging from *mineral resources* to *resources for teaching*. It comes close to resort when your *last resource* for amusing the children is perhaps also a *last resort.* However the two phrases are essentially different in meaning. The *last resource* for a farmer battling a wildfire might be his water tank, whereas his *last resort* would be to drive away to safety.

respectfully or respectively

Respectfully is a straightforward adverb meaning "full of respect":

They spoke respectfully to the priest.
Respectively has a special role in cuing the reader to match up items in two separate series. They may be in the same sentence, or in adjacent sentences:

Their three sons, Tom, Dick and Harry are respectively the butcher, the baker and the pharmacist of the town.

rest or wrest

See wrest.

restaurateur or restauranteur

The choice between restaurateur and restauranteur (for someone who runs a *restaurant*) highlights the whole process of assimilation. The word was borrowed into C18 English in its French form restaurateur, and this is still the dominant form in print, but the more anglicized form restauranteur has gained ground during C20, probably because it clarifies the link with *restaurant,* its nearest relative in English. Though purists might dub it "folk etymology," the spelling adjustment is helpful rather than distracting in this instance (see further under folk etymology).

Restauranteur is acknowledged as an alternative form in *Merriam-Webster* (2000), and the citations in *Webster's English Usage* (1989) go back to 1926. There it's described as a "standard secondary variant," common in speech; and CCAE contains a sprinkling of examples of it. Both the *Canadian Oxford* (1998) and the Australian *Macquarie Dictionary* (1997) list it as an alternative. But restauranteur struggles for acceptance in the UK. The *New Oxford* (1998) acknowledges its existence as "a common

misspelling," occurring in 20% of cases in the BNC. The *Oxford Dictionary* (1989) documents it with a set of citations from 1949 on, but dubs it "erroneous." Curiously, the *Dictionary* also presents the spelling *restauranter* without comment. In form it's fully English, but it has no currency in either British or American English, by the evidence of BNC and CCAE. Meanwhile restauranteur is widely used and accepted outside Britain as an alternative to restaurateur – whether what the *restaurant*-owner provides is *haute cuisine* or not. It would not be the first loanword to be modified as part of its assimilation into English.

restive or restless

Unsettled or agitated behavior can be indicated by either of these:

The crowd grew restless waiting for the action.
. . . a useful trick when addressing restive or sleepy audiences
Restless is transparently English, meaning "unable to stay still," whereas restive can also imply rebelliousness, whether political or personal:

The parliament ceased to be merely restive, and erupted.
Restive exporters are unlikely to let the government maintain the ban.
The unruly connotations of restive stem from its origins in the French word *restif,* meaning "refractory," used especially of horses balking or chafing at the bit. In English usage the sense of "balking" is rare, and almost all examples of restive in the BNC and CCAE refer to people "impatient for action."

restrictive clause

For the difference between *restrictive* and *nonrestrictive relative clauses,* see relative clauses section 4.

resumé or résumé

This word refers to two kinds of document:
1 a summary overview of events, observations, evidence and such-like, prepared for discussion (see further under summary).
2 a *curriculum vitae,* as when applicants for a job are requested to send a copy of their resumé. This usage originated in North America, but is current and widespread elsewhere – listed without comment in *New Oxford* (1998). For the contents of a resumé, see under curriculum vitae.

Note that résumé often appears with only one accent (on the last syllable). Resumé is in fact the form of the headword in *New Oxford*. The double-accented form appears in examples, and the form with no accents at all is noted as a US alternative. But *Merriam-Webster* (2000) is surprisingly traditional on this, making the double-accented form résumé its headword and the other two its alternatives. It seems unlikely that American writers are more inclined than the British to preserve French accents. Resumé is a useful compromise, sufficient to distinguish it from the verb *resume*. English pronunciation normally gives a short vowel to the first syllable, according to *New Oxford* (1998) and *Merriam-Webster* (2000). This makes the first accent rather artificial, however proper it is in French.

retain and retention

Their divergent spellings are discussed under **-ain**.

retch or wretch

See **wretch**.

reticent and reluctant

These two stand apart in their essential senses:
reticent means "disinclined to speak" while
reluctant means just "disinclined." However the first
is increasingly taking on the sense of the second in the
phrases *reticent to* and *reticent about*:

> I am reticent to ask for help more than once.
> The banks are reticent about admitting fraud is a
> problem.

As these examples show, the newer use of **reticent**
begins where its use involves a slight tautology,
overlapping with a following verb for speaking. This
effectively weasels meaning out of **reticent**, so that it
focuses on a reluctance to speak (or act) rather than
the lack of verbal action. In more developed examples,
there is no act of speaking at all:

> Lots of people are reticent to go into public life.
> He was as reticent about having people to his
> home as ever.

This use of **reticent** to mean "reluctant" is emerging
in both British and American English, though it may
have begun in the US. *Webster's English Usage* (1989)
traces its use in *reticent to* from the 1950s, and
Burchfield (1996) confirms it with British examples of
reticent about from the 1990s. Their respective findings
underscore a small point of regional difference: that
the construction *reticent about* is more common in
British English, and *reticent to* in American. The BNC
provides almost four times as many examples of
reticent about as *reticent to*, whereas *reticent to* is the
regular American construction in data from CCAE.
Examples reported in Canada (Fee and McAlpine,
1997) and Australia (Peters, 2001b), also involve
reticent to. The adapted meaning of **reticent**
associated with these constructions is registered in
Merriam-Webster's (2000), but not in *New Oxford*
(1998). Burchfield nevertheless comments that "it has
the air of inevitability about it." The fact that these
developments for **reticent** also apply to the noun
reticence underscores his point.

retina

The plural of this word is **retinas** rather than
retinae, according to both *New Oxford* (1998) and
Merriam-Webster (2000); and more than 75% of
respondents to the Langscape survey (1998–2001) voted
that way. See further at **-a** section 1.

retro- and retro

This Latin prefix, meaning "backwards" in space or
time, is derived from loanwords such as *retroflex,
retrograde, retrospect*. It appears in some highly
specialized scientific words, as well as some from
aeronautics and astronautics which make their way
into the media, including: *retroengine, retrofire,
retrorocket*. Words formed with **retro-** generally
appear without a hyphen, in British English as well as
American. None of those listed in *New Oxford* (1998)
or *Merriam-Webster* (2000) are hyphened.

Retro has an independent life as an adjective/noun
to refer to recursive changes in taste and fashion. It

originated in French *rétro* in the 1960s, an
abbreviation for *rétrograde* (according to *New Oxford*,
1998) or *rétrospectif* (*Merriam-Webster*, 2000). Either
way, it has quickly spread from dress (*retro chic*) to
music (*retro rock*), to food, furniture and forms of
exercise, at least in the US. Depending on your point
of view, **retro** may mean an inventive revival of past
fashion, or something hopelessly decadent and *déjà
vu*. Applied to a person, as in *he's so retro,* it simply
means "old-fashioned."

Rev. or Revd.

See **Reverend**.

reveled or revelled, reveling or revelling

American and British spelling diverge on this verb,
see **-l-/-ll-**.

revenge, avenge and vengeance

Dictionaries all allow that **revenge** can be a verb or a
noun. Yet databases both American and British show
that it mostly appears as a noun, as in *desire for
revenge* or phrasal verbs such as *get/have/seek/take
revenge*. These phrasal verbs seem in fact to substitute
for its use as a simple verb. The role of verb is also
taken up by **avenge**, used of persons reacting to
injuries and insults, whether suffered by others or by
themselves:

> We must avenge our dead.
> ... a desire to avenge himself in its columns in
> later years

Avenge is gaining figurative uses as in that second
example, and in sports reporting:

> They are out to avenge last season's defeat.

The policy of reserving **avenge** for justifiable
retaliation carried out by a third party is not
"absolutely observed" (as indicated in *Webster's
Third*, 1986, and a usage note carried over from the
Oxford Dictionary's first edition to its second, 1989). It
would depend somewhat on your point of view, as
Fowler (1926) commented.

The nouns **revenge** and **vengeance** are also
sometimes said to be differentiated on the basis that
the first means retaliatory action carried out by the
injured party, and the second the retribution carried
out by a third party. Compare:

> ... an author taking his revenge
> ... claimed as vengeance for the massacre of
> worshippers ...

The ritual connotations of **vengeance** are
underpinned for some by biblical statements such as:

> Vengeance is mine, I will repay, saith the Lord
> (Romans 12:19)

Yet **vengeance** is heavily secularized in database
evidence. It appears in reference to cycles of *violence
and vengeance,* to *bloody crime and popular vengeance,*
and pleas for *justice, not vengeance* – where it clearly
doesn't refer to any "just retribution." There's none in
the *Personal Vengeance* software, which allows you to
act out primitive responses to career frustrations.
Though **vengeance** retains its emotional force in
examples like those, that too is diluted in the single
most common use of the word, in *with a vengeance*. It
accounts for almost half the instances of the word in
BNC data and more than a third in CCAE. For
example:

> Coupés are back with a vengeance.
> I took up dancing again with a vengeance.

Clichéd and casual use of the phrase undermines its point in more purposeful expression:

This was political education with a vengeance.

With a vengeance would be the phrase to avoid, if you want to exploit the full force of **vengeance**.

Reverend, Rev. and Revd

Unless it follows *the*, as in *the Reverend John Bell*, the title **Reverend** is often abbreviated. Fowler (1926) found the abbreviation **Rev.** more usual than the contraction **Revd**, and the trend is underscored at the end of C20 by their relative frequencies in database evidence. In the UK **Rev.** outnumbers **Revd** by about 3:1, by their relative frequencies in the BNC. Elsewhere **Rev.** prevails, appearing in thousands of examples in CCAE, as opposed to just one of **Revd**. Among the Canadian religious titles in Fee and McAlpine (1997), there's no hint of **Revd**, and the Australian *Macquarie Dictionary* (1997) does not register it, because of its lack of currency.

Note that **Rev(.)** may appear with or without a stop, according to editorial policy. (See **abbreviations** section 2.)

◊ For the use of the title **Reverend** in combination with other names, see **names** section 2.

reverent or reverential

The *reverence* involved in these is much the same, except that **reverent** is conventionally associated with religious awe, as in: *a reverent voice, as if speaking in church*. It connects with people and ordinary behavior:

We are hushed, reverent; even the children are subdued.

Reverential recognizes more secular and abstract forms of *reverence*, as in

a reverential rather than a critical approach

...names mentioned in almost reverential tones

This makes **reverential** rather more academic, and the less common of the two.

reversal or reversion

These relate to quite different verbs. **Reversal** is the noun associated with *reverse* ("change to the opposite") as in *role reversal* or a *reversal of fortune/direction/policy*. **Reversion** connects with *revert* ("return to a former state") as in *reversion to polytheism* or to *the home-made and the hand hewn*.

reverse or obverse

See under **obverse**.

review or revue

These are two forms of the same French word, borrowed centuries apart. **Review** came in C16, and its English spelling reflects its full assimilation and its many uses as verb and noun, where the objects under **review** range from a single decision to government policy at large. The spelling **revue** goes with the reborrowing of the word in its pure French form in C20. Its use is mostly confined to theatrical shows offering a mix of amusing or satirical songs and skits, often highlighting topical events and themes. American English also uses **review** for this sense, according to *Merriam-Webster* (2000), but it's not mentioned in other regional dictionaries.

rheme

See **topic** section 1.

rhetoric

This is the ancient and modern art of persuading one's audience. See further under **persuasion**, and **rhythm**.

rhetorical questions

See under **questions**.

rhinoceros and rhino

Dictionaries allow that the plural of **rhinoceros** may be either **rhinoceroses** (the regular English plural) or **rhinoceros** itself (used as a *zero plural;* see under that heading). The British are much more inclined to use the zero plural than the Americans, in data from the BNC and CCAE, and neither use **rhinoceri**, let alone **rhinocerotes**. But the question of the plural for **rhinoceros** becomes rather academic with increasing use of the abbreviation **rhino**. In both British and American databases, **rhino** occurs far more often than the **rhinoceros**, in references to the animal as well as its fabled attributes, in *rhino horn* and the expression *like a rampant rhino*. Its plural **rhinos** takes its place – just like the full form – alongside references to other wild game. Compare:

...3000 gazelle live here, as well as elephants, rhinos, buffalo, lions...

Other species [to see] are elephants, buffalo, rhinoceros, impala, giraffe.

As the examples show, any such list of species may contain both regular and zero plurals, though the preference for zero plurals is more typical of serious environmental writing.

rhotic

English dialects diverge over whether "r" is pronounced when it occurs after a vowel and before another consonant or at the end of words such as *bird, door, ear, perk, tar, thorn*. This makes them either **rhotic** or *nonrhotic*. The **rhotic** dialects that pronounce "r" are located especially in the far north and west of the UK, in Ireland and widespread in North America (including Canada), excluding only New England and the Deep South. The *nonrhotic* group includes southern and eastern British English, South Africa, Australia and New Zealand. **Rhotic** speakers of English outnumber the *nonrhotic* in the world at large, and *rhoticity* is therefore built into the so-called "mid-Atlantic" form of English (see under **mid-Atlantic and mid-Atlantic English**). But for second-language learners, the choice of **rhotic** or *nonrhotic* models would be best decided on the basis of their mother tongues, as suggested by McArthur (2001). *Rhoticity* would come naturally to speakers of Romance and Arabic languages, whereas *nonrhoticity* would be more consistent with Chinese and Japanese. Either way it impinges little on written International English, except in the sets of homophones that depend on the presence or absence of "r," and may subliminally affect one's writing. Thus *fort* and *fought* are homophones for *nonrhotic* speakers, but distinct for **rhotic** speakers.

rhyme or rime

This word for a pattern of sounds was spelled **rime** for centuries, going back to C13. **Rhyme** made its debut in C17 as an alternative spelling, and like many

475

respellings of the time, it linked the word with a putative classical ancestor – in this case the Greek *rhythmos*. This would give **rhyme** and *rhythm* a common source, despite the very different aspects of prosody that they refer to. More recent etymology finds the source for **rhyme** in the Germanic word "rim" meaning "number," which is also associated with accentual verse and its terminal **rhyme**. This sense of the word seems to have been borrowed into Old French (as *rime*), and then into C13 English, to refer to "rhymed verse." These complex origins were obscure to English Renaissance scholars, who could only suggest the connection with *rhythmos*.

The English respelling of **rime** as **rhyme** took some time to catch on, and **rime** was still current in late C18, hence its use in Coleridge's *The Rime of the Ancient Mariner*. **Rime** enjoyed a brief after-life amid the Anglo-Saxon literary revival of later C19, but the spelling **rhyme** was by then too well established in common usage. Etymologically it's inaccurate, yet it serves to distinguish the prosodic word from its homonym **rime** ("hoar frost").

Though *full rhyme* is the hallmark of verse and many kinds of poetry, *half rhyme* is occasionally used by prose writers to create patterned effects (see **assonance**). *Initial rhyme* is another resource for underscoring verbal connections in prose: see **alliteration**.

rhyming slang

Informal expressions for many everyday things have been created by **rhyming slang**, and they lend variety to the all-too-familiar. The *rubbity dub* makes a change from "club" or "pub," and *egg flip* for a gambling "tip." Some **rhyming slang** puts on airs, as does *eau de cologne* for "phone" and *aristotle* for "bottle" – until it's cut down to size as "'Arry." **Rhyming slang** provides ways of skirting round a problem, such as *Farmer Giles* for "piles" and *bang and biff* ("syph[ilis]"). The close ties between **rhyming slang** and a particular community make for different meanings in different places. A *Captain Cook* means a "book" in the UK, but a "look" in both the US and Australia. Local identity is expressed in the different terms coined for the same object: thus *Hampsteads* (from *Hampstead Heath*) serves for "teeth" in the UK, and *Barrier Reef* in Australia.

The examples show how **rhyming slang** selects a phrase of two or three words to highlight the key word, with the rhyming phrase often an amusing distractor rather than a clue to the key word. A few such as *trouble and strife* (for "wife") and *bottle and stopper* (for "copper") are less oblique. Yet the amusement of most **rhyming slang** is its seeming irrelevance to what's being referred to, making it hard for the uninitiated to know what is meant. The habit of abbreviating the rhyming phrase to the first word, and making it an ordinary countable noun, as in *Hampsteads* or *elephants* (*elephant's trunk* for "drunk"), also helps to disguise the reference.

Rhyming slang is certainly for those in the know, and works to exclude outsiders. Once such phrases become well known they lose that value and the major motive for their use. This is why few rhyming slang terms – as far as we know – ever establish themselves in the standard language.

rhythm

Rhythm in prose is certainly no regular **rhythm** as in poetry (see **rhyme**). In good writing **rhythm** is subtly pervasive yet noticeable only here and there. Its effect is wave-like – not the regular pattern of a sound wave, but the infinitely variable movement of waves on the beach, whose shape and size vary with contextual factors. The sentences in a piece of writing can be likened to individual waves in their rise and resolution on the shore. Each wave has a clear crest to mark its place in the continuous pattern. In the same way, every sentence needs a clear focus if it's to contribute to the **rhythm** and momentum of the prose. Shapeless sentences with blurred focus are unsatisfactory in terms of **rhythm** as well as meaning. Very long sentences often impair the **rhythm** unless they are carefully constructed. Yet too many short choppy sentences can also disturb the deeper **rhythms** of prose.

1 Rhythm, variety and balance Continuous variety in sentence length is an important factor in maintaining prose **rhythm**, provided each one is focused and balanced in its internal structure.

> *In Australia alone is to be found the grotesque, the weird, the strange scribblings of nature learning how to write. Some see no beauty in our trees without shade, our flowers without perfume, our birds who cannot fly, and our beasts who have not yet learned to walk on all fours. But the dweller in the wilderness acknowledges the subtle charms of the fantastic land of monstrosities. He becomes familiar with the beauty of loneliness. Whispered to by the myriad tongues of the wilderness, he learns the language of the barren and the uncouth, and can read the hieroglyphs of the haggard gumtrees, blown into odd shapes, distorted with fierce hot winds, and cramped with cold nights, when the Southern Cross freezes in a cloudless sky of icy blue.* (Marcus Clarke, 1876)

The passage shows the skilled writer at work, controlling the shape and balance of sentences. Balance is achieved in the first sentence by inversion of the subject and predicate. The sentence would lose almost everything if it ran:

> *In Australia alone the grotesque, the weird, and the strange scribblings of nature learning how to write are to be found...*

With so much to digest before we reach the verb, it puts a severe strain on short-term memory. The pile-up of phrases has the effect of smothering the latent **rhythm**, until the sentence lets us down with an abrupt jolt at the end. Instead Clarke balances material on either side of the verb. The passage also shows how sentence **rhythm** depends on effective use of the phrase and clause. Note the parallel phrases in the second and fifth sentences which help to create a satisfying **rhythm** and to control the flow of information.

2 Rhythm and the rhetoric of the series. The connection between phrasing and **rhythm** can also be seen in the different effects of combining two, three and four items. When just *two* are coordinated, the effect is neat, tidy and final, as in.

> *We are at once, instrument and end, discoverers and teachers, actors and observers.* (J. Robert Oppenheimer, 1953)

The effect of three coordinated items is more expansive, suggesting both amplitude and adequacy.

Their effect is illustrated in the following sentence

> *I speak of the American in the singular, as if
> there were not millions of them, north and south,
> east and west, of both sexes, of all ages, and of
> various races, professions and religions.* (George
> Santayana, 1920)

The three matched phrases each introduced by "of"
create a breadth of reference points, as of a subject
fully considered. Part of the effect is the careful
grading of the three items, each one a little weightier
than the one before, so that it creates a kind of
cadence. The triplet within the final item shows the
same expansive effect.

Different again is the effect of combining four (or
more) items in a series. A sizable series creates its
own *local rhythm,* and temporarily suspends that of
the host sentence – just as the quartet of information
seems designed to overwhelm the reader, and to
represent a kind of rhetorical pleading:

> *The lion may lie down with the lamb, or at least
> cease eating it; but when will the royalist lie down
> with the republican, the Quaker with the ritualist,
> the Deist with the Atheist, the Roman Catholic
> with the Anglo-Catholic or either of them with the
> Protestant...* (George Bernard Shaw, 1944)

Shaw's use of lists and extended parallelism like this
are a feature of his argumentative prose.

Even from the printed page, the *rhythmic* effects of
well-crafted prose strike the ear and reinforce the
message of the words. The key to writing *rhythmical*
prose is tuning in to the sound of one's own sentences.

rhythmic or rhythmical

The shorter form **rhythmic** is much more frequent in
both British and American English – though
rhythmical is chosen by relatively more British
writers, by the evidence of BNC and CCAE. The
databases show that both words are applied to the
rhythms of music, language and dance, as well as those
of the body and nature. See further under **-ic/-ical.**

ricochet

This C18 French loanword is still usually pronounced
in the French fashion so as to rhyme with "say" and
leave the *t* "silent." With this go the regular spellings
of the verb forms *ricocheted* and *ricocheting,* which are
given priority in all dictionaries. (See further under
-t.) In British English the word can also be pronounced
so as to rhyme with "set," and that pronunciation is
reflected in the spellings *ricochetted* and *ricochetting.*
But the spellings with double *t* make little showing in
BNC data, suggesting a trend away from their use over
C19, when 5 out of the 6 *Oxford Dictionary* citations
had them. There is scant evidence of their use in
current American English, and *Merriam-Webster*
(2000) notes them only as a "British" alternative.

rid or ridded

The verb **rid** may have either **rid** or **ridded** for the
past tense or past participle, according to dictionaries.
Yet database evidence from both the US and the UK
shows that **rid** is the only past form now used, helped
by everyday idioms such as *be rid of* and *get rid of.* The
verb seems to have fended off pressures towards
regularization, though **ridded** has been on record
since C15 for the past participle, and for the past tense
since C17. See **irregular verbs** sections 1 and 9.

right or rightly

Though both words go back to Old English, **right** has
a place in many more idioms and styles than **rightly.**
It carries a range of meanings in its various
grammatical roles as adjective, noun and verb, and as
a multi-faceted adverb in zero form (see **zero
adverbs**). **Rightly** is the regular adverbial form, and
generally keeps its distance, with the meaning
"properly," "justifiably," as in:

> *You rightly suggest that they be included in the
> team.*
> *He was rightly angered at the lack of action.*

However **rightly** and **right** compete in a few idioms
when both mean "correctly":

> *If I remember rightly, the train arrives at 5pm.*
> *If I remember right, the train arrives at 5pm.*

The choice between **right** and **rightly,** meaning
"correct," is a matter of style, **right** being the less
formal of the two (like any zero adverb). Note also how
right when it modifies a verb comes after it, whereas
rightly appears either after or before.

In other adverbial roles not shared with **rightly,**
right always precedes the word or phrase that it
modifies. This is so when it means "exactly," as in:

> *The school is right there.*
> *They should appear right this minute.*

Uses of **right** to modify expressions of time and place
are particularly common in American English,
according to research reported in the *Longman
Grammar* (1999), whereas British speakers are more
inclined to use *just.* For both Americans and the
British, the use of **right** as an adverbial modifier
shades into its use as an intensifier: *The boat was
right out to sea.*

In conversation **right** appears on its own in several
discourse roles. It solicits agreement, as in:

> *You're coming with us. Right?*

It works as an affirmative, indicating understanding
and/or compliance:

> *It's a first step. // Right.*

Right can also signal a new phase of conversation:

> *The visitors will be here tomorrow. Right, let's
> discuss the catering.*

These adverbial uses of **right** in conversation
complement those of **right** as adjective, though
interference between them sometimes causes
problems:

> *At the next intersection you take a left turn. //
> Right! // No, not a right turn...*

Such problems are not so likely in written
communication, because it makes less use of adverbial
right and rather more of the adjectival. In frequencies
from the *Longman Grammar* (1999) corpus, **right**
ranks very high among adjectives for both predicative
and attributive use (see **adjectives** section 1):

> *He was right in believing...* (predicative)
> *... doesn't give the right answer...* (attributive)

The grammatical frame in which **right** occurs as an
adjective usually clarifies its meaning.

Right, right wing and rightist

Being on the **Right** of politics, i.e. on the conservative
side, puts you in what have traditionally been the
government seats in a Westminster-style parliament.
Even in opposition, the conservatives remain *the
Right* and claim a linguistic advantage never enjoyed
by those on the other side of parliament. But

references to them as the **right wing** are not so likely to carry a capital letter. More than 80% of respondents to the Langscape survey (1998–2001) said that they would never capitalize it.

The adjective **rightist** tends to be applied to the more conservative party in foreign governments or social groups, not those at home, for example: *rightist demonstrations in Seoul; Rightist parties such as the Renovación Española.* Though **Rightist** occasionally appears with a capital letter, it is normally without it, in British and American English represented in the BNC and CCAE.
◊ Compare **Left and leftist**.

rigor or rigour
See -or/-our.

rime or rhyme
See **rhyme**.

ring or wring
Ring is in fact the spelling for two different verbs:
1 **ring** ("encircle") with past form *ringed,* as in *ringed with fire*
2 **ring** ("sound") with past forms *rang* and *rung,* as in *ring in the New Year*
The verb **wring** and its past forms are discussed under **wrung**.

The first verb spelled **ring** is regular and quite stable, whereas the second is irregular and somewhat unstable in its past forms. In standard English the past tense is *rang* and the past participle *rung,* distinctions which are generally maintained in writing. But in informal speech, *rung* often serves for the simple past tense, especially when referring to telephone calls (also *rung up*). The form *rung* is recorded in about 40% of cases of the past tense in the transcribed speech of the BNC, yet not acknowledged even in cautionary notes in *New Oxford* (1998). *Webster's Dictionary* (1986) simply presents *rung* as the less common form of the past tense in American English, and *Webster's English Usage* (1989) adds the fact that it's more often heard than seen in print. It nevertheless appears in the past forms of a sprinkling of idioms in CCAE data, including *rung up* (far less common in American than British English), *rung in / rung out, rung hollow* and *rung my/his bell.* The verb **ring** ("sound") is effectively caught between two paradigms, aligning itself with *fling* and *swing* for informal speech among many in the UK, US and elsewhere, but with *sing* for more formal speech, and for writing generally. (See further under **irregular verbs** sections 3 and 6.)

All that apart, *rung* is occasionally found for *wrung* in American sources, on which see **wrung**.

RIP
These initials represent the Latin phrase *requiescat in pace* ("may s/he rest in peace"). The phrase, or the initials, are conventionally written on tombstones and in death notices, as a solemn farewell from the living to those who have recently died.

rise or arise
These verbs have slightly different uses nowadays. **Rise** means "increase, go up" or "get up"; whereas **arise** has only abstract uses: "originate or result

from." In the past **arise** could be used for some of the more physical senses of **rise**, including "get up," but this is now definitely old-fashioned, and begins to sound archaic.
◊ For the use of **rise** as a noun and alternative to *raise,* see under **raise**.

risky or risqué
The French noun *risque* crossed the English Channel in C17, and in its French or English form (*risk*) was quickly applied to hazardous undertakings of all kinds, from climbing sheer cliffs to sinking capital into prospecting for diamonds in the African desert. The English adjective **risky**, dating from the 1820s, took on the same range of ordinary applications.

Risqué is of course the same adjective borrowed freshly from French in the 1870s; and its spelling and accent draw attention to what the English always attribute to the French, namely a ready attention to matters of sexuality. *A risqué joke* has sexual implications and comes close to the limits of what can be shared at a polite dinner party – though what seems **risqué** to some would not raise eyebrows among others. The place that offers a *$100-a-bottle whisky and risqué floor show* may in fact be using **risqué** to cover anything from the *raunchy* to the *pornographic.* The word **risqué** is a "red light" in both senses – a "no-go" signal as well as a lure. The ambivalence of **risqué** lends itself to titillating but not scintillating journalism, as in references to a prince's *string of risqué affairs.* **Risky** was/is occasionally substituted for **risqué**, according to most dictionaries, as in *a risky sense of humor.* But the need to use **risky** as a euphemism for **risqué** has probably passed.

In American English **risqué** frequently appears without an accent (as *risque*) by the evidence of CCAE, and the *Oxford Dictionary* (1989) notes it as an alternative. The contexts of its use help to underscore its meaning, and there's no identical English word to tangle with it.
◊ Compare **resumé**.

rite or ritual
Rite is much more exclusively associated with religion than **ritual**. Typical uses of **rite** are in *last rites* and in *married according to the rites of the Orthodox Church.* **Ritual** concentrates attention on the particular formal procedure, and is often used in nonreligious contexts nowadays, as when we speak of the *Monday ritual of exchanging football news,* or the *greeting rituals* used over the telephone.

rival
On how to spell this word when used as a verb, see -l-/-ll-.

River or river
For the use of capitals in referring to the names of rivers, see **geographical names** section 1.

rivet
On the spelling of this word when it serves as a verb, see -t-.

road or street
The Anglo-Saxon word **road** once served to distinguish the routes connecting towns from accessways within them, known by the Latin word

street. The distinction remains in contrasting idioms: compare being *out on the street* with taking the show *on the road*. The word **street** still predominates in the nomenclature of many capital cities for the same reason. But in Manhattan (New York City), **street** is used systematically for roads going east–west, and *avenue* for those running north–south, as also to a lesser extent in Chicago. The word *avenue* (like *boulevard*) comes from French, and originally referred to a tree-lined street, though the trees tend to be casualties of urban development. These days **streets**, **roads**, *avenues, boulevards* are intermingled in the nomenclature of most English-speaking cities, without discernible patterns. The one regular distinction left is that *lane* designates a minor, narrow way, often adjacent to a major road of the same name. Compare *Collins Street* with *Collins Lane* in Melbourne.

roman
The upright form of type used for all general purposes is known as **roman**. It contrasts with the sloping *italic* type, used to set off such things as titles and foreign words. (See further under **italic[s].**) When referring to type, **roman** never takes a capital letter.
◊ Compare *Roman numerals,* discussed under its own headword.

roman à clef
In French this means literally "novel with a key," but it's used by both French and English to mean a novel in which recent historical events and roles are projected onto fictitious characters. The "key" is the imaginary list which would match the fiction characters with their real-life counterparts. The plural of **roman à clef** is **romans à clef**, according to the French convention (see **plurals** section 2). But in English **roman à clef** is also pluralized as **roman à clefs**, found by Google (2002) in about 1 in 5 English-language documents on the internet. It unfortunately suggests a novel with multiple "keys" rather than several novels.

Roman Catholic
On the use of this expression, see **Catholic or catholic.**

Roman numerals or roman numerals
In general usage, the adjective **Roman** tends to be capitalized, and this is the form listed in dictionaries. But in editorial circles both British and American, references to both *roman* and *arabic* (numerals) are written without capital letters (see *Copy-editing,* 1992; *Chicago Manual,* 2003). In British editorial circles, **Roman numerals** are also called *roman numbers.*

The key symbols in the *roman numbering* system are:

I (1)	*V* (5)	*X* (10)	*L* (50)	*C* (100)
D (500)	*M* (1000)			

All intervening numbers can be created by combinations of those letters. The values are essentially created by subtraction from the left and addition on the right of the key symbols. Thus the lower symbol, e.g., *I*, is subtracted in *IV* (4) but added in *VI* (6). Both principles are worked in numbers such as in *XLIX* (49), and in *MCMXC* (1990).

Because of their variable length, **Roman numerals** raise questions of alignment. When they appear in continuous vertical lists, they are aligned on the left, i.e. the opposite of arabic numerals, according to the *Chicago Manual.* But when used for the purposes of enumeration, they are often aligned to the right, to avoid a ragged right effect next to the start of the regular text. (See further under **numbers and number style** sections 5, 6, 7.)

Roman numerals are frequently used in paginating the preliminary pages of a book, as well as the foreword, preface or introduction. See further under **prelims.** and **preface.**

Romania, Rumania or Roumania
The Romans gave their name to this easternmost province of their empire, hence the spelling **Romania** which is now the official form in English, according to United Nations sources. **Romania** dominates in database evidence from both UK and the US, with thousands of examples, whereas there are only a few score of **Rumania**, and **Roumania** weighs in with less than ten. Dictionaries all now make **Romania** the headword, with **Rumania** as an alternative in some such as *New Oxford* (1998) and *Merriam-Webster* (2000). *Rumania* is the official form in Spanish, and *Roumania* in French.

roofs or rooves
The plural **roofs** is standard in all modern dictionaries, and used overwhelmingly by British and American writers represented in the BNC and CCAE. The data do not support the idea voiced by Burchfield (1996) and Garner (1998) that **rooves** is creeping back in, though it may sometimes be created by analogy with *hoof/hooves.* See further under **-f >-v-.**

root
The **root** of a word is the essential unit of meaning on which various stems and derivative forms may be based. The **root** underlying *course, current* and *cursive* is the Latin *cur-* meaning "run." Two of the Latin stems from it are *curr-* and *curs-*, while *cours-* has developed in French and English.

rosary or rosery
Both involve roses. The **rosary** or set of beads used to tally personal prayers in the Catholic Church is figuratively a "necklace or garland of roses." It comes from the Latin **rosarium** ("rose garden"), which was its first meaning in C15 English. By the end of C16 its now standard meanings of "prayer beads" and "set of prayers" were established. It normally appears without a capital letter in *rosary beads* and in reference to private devotions, but may be capitalized when referring to the formal saying of the **rosary** as at funeral services.

With **rosary** called to higher duty, rose-fanciers were left without a distinctive name for the rose garden – until the C19 coining of **rosery** out of English elements (*rose + -ery,* along the lines of *orangery*). **Rosery** and **rosary** are sometimes mistakenly used for each other, like other *-ery/-ary* words, though their etymologies help to keep them apart. See further under **-ary/-ery/-ory.**

rosin or resin
See **resin.**

rotary or rotatory

Both adjectives mean "turning on or as on an axis," but **rotary** is the everyday word, used in the *rotary dial/excavator/mill/mower* and other mechanical tools. In the US (New England), **rotary** can also refer to a traffic circle; and in the UK, to the *rota* associated with someone's employment, as in *rotary leave*.

Rotatory is the academic and scientic word, applied to things which embody more abstract forms of *rotation*, such as the *rotatory* movement of hurricanes or planets.

Roumania or Romania

See **Romania**.

round or around

See **around**.

rouse and arouse

The idea of "awakening" is in both of these, but only **rouse** means this in the physical sense of "waking up":

She was roused by a scraping sound at the door.

The effect with **arouse** is more internal, raising thoughts and emotions in others:

His smug words aroused their anger.

With such covert behavior you arouse suspicion.

Note also that **arouse** is used of raising sexual excitement, which can be psychological, physiological or both.

route or rout

These words are differently pronounced (with "oo" and "ow" respectively) by the British and by many Americans, and so keep their distance. But they converge in print when used with verb endings. Compare:

All traffic was routed down the main line (**route**)

New Zealand routed Zimbabwe in the second innings (**rout**)

The subject helps to fix the meaning of *routed* in each case: as "set [a] course" in the first case, and "drive [others] into retreat" or "defeat" in the second. Another, technical meaning of **rout** ("cut a groove [in a wood or metal surface]") can also be loaded onto *routed*.

It's been routed from a solid block of wood.

Here too, the context helps to settle the meaning, and is indispensable, given that no alternative spelling is available with the *-ed* inflection.

With the *-ing* inflection, the spelling *routeing* is available to distinguish **route** from **rout**, though it breaks the normal spelling rule for a final *e* (see **-e** section 1). *New Oxford* (1998) makes it the primary choice for **route**, but it's not at all popular with British writers represented in the BNC, who mostly plump for the regular *routing*. Again the context, and collocations such as *routing system* and *routing traffic through...*, generally help to clarify the meaning. In American English, *routing* alone is used according to *Merriam-Webster* (2000), and it's the only spelling found in data from CCAE for all three senses.

Royal or royal

To decapitalize **royal** is not a capital offence. There are good reasons for doing so; and in the Langscape survey (1998–2001), over half the respondents (53%) worldwide said that they would only "sometimes" put a capital letter on the regal word. Add to that the one third

(33%) who said that they would "never" do so, and you may wonder whether republicanism is rampant.

Many generic expressions with **royal** do not require a capital, such as the colors *royal blue/purple*, the writer's *royal we*, or anyone's *royal road to success*. References to a *royal adviser/delegation/family/palace/visit* are similarly left without capitals, whether they are associated with the British or any other sovereign. In context there's usually little doubt which sovereign is meant, and the capital would add nothing to the *Hawaiian royal house*, or to the note that *Queen Elizabeth has visited it, and many of her royal kin*. Only the tabloid-led *Royal-watchers,* looking for a scoop on *the Royals,* seem to insist on capitalizing references to the British *royal family*. The capital is of course required in expressions like *Royal Highness* and *Princess Royal,* because they are official titles.

Royal is most regularly found with a capital in the names of institutions in the UK and overseas which enjoy *royal patronage*. For example: *Royal Navy,* the *Royal Shakespeare Company,* the *Royal Melbourne Hospital,* and the *Royal Canadian Mounted Police.* These high-profile institutions help to explain why a minority of respondents (15%) to the Langscape survey (1998–2001) said that they would "always" capitalize the word. But among the countless **royal** institutions, there are cases which may or may not need to be capitalized. As a generic expression *royal commission* needs no capitals, but as part of the full title it does, as in the *Royal Commission on Environmental Pollution* (1979). Abbreviated references to that particular commission would still be capitalized in British style: *The Royal Commission rejected that solution;* whereas in American style it would probably be decapitalized (see **capital letters** section 3). The term *royal assent,* whereby legislation is signed into law (by the British sovereign or the governor-general or state governors in Commonwealth countries), is regularly found in lower case, and listed that way by dictionaries. Idioms whose connection with royalty is metaphorical are always lower-cased, e.g. the *royal jelly* on which potential queen bees are fed, and the *royal flush* of a lucky poker player, i.e. the winning hand with all the courtly cards, plus the ace and the ten.

The numerous uses of **royal** without a capital are of course neutral in terms of loyalty to royalty, though they still remind us of the further reaches of monarchical management. See further under **capital letters** sections 1a and 1b.

royal we

See under **we**.

RSI

This abbreviation stands for "repetitive strain injury" or "repetition strain injury." The first is the transliteration of *New Oxford* (1998), the *Canadian Oxford* (1998) and the Australian *Macquarie Dictionary* (1997), whereas *Merriam-Webster* (2000) gives priority to the second. In more technical American English it is one of the "cumulative trauma disorders," whereas it becomes "kangaroo paw" in informal Australian English.

RSVP

This French request *répondez s'il vous plaît* (literally "reply if you please") is regularly abbreviated in

English as **RSVP**. The abbreviation conventionally appears at the bottom of formal written invitations, with a date by which to reply, and a contact number or address at which the reply is to be received.

rugby union, rugby league and rugger

Tradition associates the game of *rugby* with *Rugby School*. It supposedly originated in 1823 when a football player picked up the ball and ran with it. By the end of C19 it had developed its own set of rules and a formal governing body, the *Rugby Union*. Until very recently (1995) it was an avowedly amateur sport, whereas the *Rugby League* splintered off from the *Union* in the 1890s, and allowed professionalism. The two games otherwise differ slightly in the number of players per side, and in a few rules and points of scoring. The term **rugger** used to be applied to **rugby union**, but is now generalized to either game, and both suffer from the attentions of *rugger enthusiasts/fans*. The same goes for the *rugger bugger* (a South African term at home in British English since the 1970s). All words are normally written in lower case.

Rumania or Romania

See **Romania**.

rumor or rumour

See **-or/-our**.

run in or run on

American editors use the term **run in** when continuing words on the same line, as opposed to taking them down to the next line. Hence the term *run-in* for entries in an index that provide all information in a solid block (see **indexing** section 2). The question of whether to **run in** or *take down* also arises with longish headings and captions, and in the choice between horizontal and vertical lists (see **lists**). British editors use **run on** rather than **run in**, as do their counterparts in Canada and Australia.

Dictionary-makers everywhere use the term *run-on(s)* to refer to the additional form(s) of a word at the end of an entry, as when the entry for *rustic* (adjective) adds *rustically* (adverb) without defining it at the end. The practice helps to cover more words in abridged dictionaries, but does little to show whether the *run-on* has a life of its own.

rung or wrung

See **ring or wring**, and **wrung**.

running heads

See under **heading, headline, header and head.**

runover lines

See **turnover lines**.

rural or rustic

Both adjectives relate to farming and the countryside, but they diverge in their connotations. **Rural** is neutral and academic, as in *rural incomes* and *rural pastimes*. **Rustic** is value-laden – either positively or negatively – depending on context. The *rustic gate* in a suburban garden is a feature that lends charm to it, whereas *rustic plumbing* on the same property implies crudeness and backwardness.

Russia

It was the largest and most powerful republic in the former *USSR* (Union of Soviet Socialist Republics),

and its name has often been used as a byword for the whole. Such usage was however a double source of dissatisfaction to many within the *Soviet Union*. For one thing, it was properly the title of the Russian imperial regime which was overthrown in 1917. For another, it designated only one of the seventeen republics, and seemed to overlook the others. Within the various republics there were and are more than 100 national groupings, including Armenian, Byelorussian, Estonian, Georgian, Latvian, Lithuanian and Uzbek. To refer to the citizens of such nationalities as "Russian" was to extinguish their identity, and point to centralized control from Moscow.

The dissolution of the *USSR* in 1991 confirms the vigor of nationalist feelings, and it remains to be seen whether any federation will emerge and under what name. The proposed *Union of Soviet Sovereign Republics* has been eclipsed by the *Commonwealth of Independent States,* but what organization will crystallize out of the present situation is still unclear. In the meantime the *Soviet Union's* membership of the United Nations is being continued in the name of the *Russian Federation,* with the support of eleven members of the *Commonwealth of Independent States.* Other former members of the *Soviet Union* are separately represented at the United Nations, including Belarus (formerly *Byelorussia*), Estonia, Latvia, Lithuania and the Ukraine.

rustic or rural

See **rural**.

℞ or Rx

This mysterious symbol appears on doctors' prescriptions prefacing the recipe for a medicament. It represents the Latin word *recipe*, literally "take." As in the scrawled signatures for which doctors are famous, only the first letter of the word is decipherable.

-ry

Strictly speaking this is simply a variant form of the suffix *-ery*. The older spelling of *carpentry* as *carpentery* shows us the process, and it corresponds to the telescoping of *er* to *r* in some other pairs of words (see further under **-er>-r-**). Yet many of the words with **-ry** are centuries old, and we have no record of them with *-ery*.

One noticeable feature of words ending in **-ry** is that they very often have three syllables, and some scholars believe that the **-ry** helped to maintain this pattern, in words which might otherwise have had four syllables:

> artistry   bigotry   devilry   husbandry   pedantry
> punditry   ribaldry   rivalry   wizardry

Compare:

> archery   brewery   butchery   printery
> robbery   smeltery   tannery

where three syllables are maintained through the coincidence of *-er* and *-ery*. And

> eatery   finery   greenery
> popery   shrubbery   thievery

where a single syllable is built up to three with the full *-ery* suffix. Whatever the historical explanation, either **-ry** or *-ery* is now fixed in the spelling of such words. Only in the case of *jewelry* and *jewellery* is there a real choice: see under **jewellery**.

◊ For the choice between **-ery, -ary and -ory**, see under **-ary/-ery/-ory**.

S

s

The letter **s** was the last to acquire a standardized shape in English printing. Well into C18, it had different shapes according to its position in a word. As the first letter or somewhere in the middle, its shape was rather like an *f*. In roman type this type of **s** had only a half cross stroke (just on the left side) as in *fit* and *feat*. In italic it was printed with a descender below the line – the so-called "long *s*"as in *ʃit* and *ʃeat*. At the end of a word, in both roman and italic type, the letter **s** had the serpentine shape we use today: *sits/seats*. The different forms of lower case **s** helped to show when it belonged to the stem of the word, and when it was an inflection (see next two entries). But the capital **s** was always serpentine, and probably helped to fix the shape for the lower case.

-s

This is the most important inflection in English. Paradoxically it marks the singular of the present tense of verbs, and the plural of most nouns. These inflectional uses of **-s**, and others where it is more derivational (see **suffixes** section 2), are discussed below.

1 All verbs except modals have **-s** to mark the third person singular present tense, as in *dances, rocks, rolls, sings* and many more. The variant form *-es* is applied to verbs ending in *o, (s)s, sh, (t)ch, x, y* or *(z)z*, of English or foreign origin:

> echoes hisses finishes clutches lurches
> fixes denies buzzes

2 The **-s** inflection marks the plural of almost all nouns that go back to Old English, and all assimilated loanwords, including *sticks* and *stones, oranges* and *lemons, armadillos* and *aardvarks*. The *-es* variant is applied to nouns ending in *o* or *y* (see **-o** and **-y>-i-**); and in *(s)s, sh, (t)ch, x* or *(z)z:*

> glasses dishes churches patches taxes
> quizzes

Nouns which do not take *-(e)s* are usually very recent loans, such as *kibbutzim,* or else ones which preserve their foreign plurals either for scholarly reasons (*phenomena*) or because of the cachet attached to them (*gateaux*). See further under **plurals**.

Other minor uses of -s, for certain kinds of derivation. These include its use as:

* a marker of *familiarity* (*Comprehensive Grammar,* 1985), in expressions such as *the guilts, up for grabs, got the runs/trots, gone bananas,* and words such as *bonkers, jitters, shakes, starters.* Though some of these can be analyzed as plurals and/or as the names of diseases (Wickens, 1992), they do seem to make a distinct set in terms of their informal tone and the variety of their derivations. These they also share with the "nursery" terms used in talking with infants, e.g. *beddie-byes, cuddles, dindins,* and also the affectionate forms of personal names (*Mabs, Suzykins, Wooz*): see Mühlhäusler (1983).

* a *collective* marker for something composite, whether the elements it consists of are all of one kind, as with *amends, arrears, dregs;* or various, as with *cleaners, headquarters, printers.* The latter have traditionally been analyzed – often awkwardly – as elliptical forms of the genitive (see further under **local genitive**). But clearly they are no ordinary plurals, given that they can be construed in the singular, as in *the cleaners/printers is on the corner.* Rather they seem to embody a collective use of **-s** (see further under **pluralia tantum**).

* *adverbial* marker, as in *Fridays, unawares, westwards* etc., especially in British English (see further under **-ward**). The *-s* ending once marked many more adverbs in English.

-s/-ss-

Several kinds of English words are affected by the issue of whether to write one or two *ss* at the boundary of the stem and affix. Nouns and verbs ending in *-s* raise this question when their *-es* inflections are to be added, though usage generally does not double the *s* (with minor exceptions: see below). When the double is created by a prefix ending in *-s* before a stem beginning with *s*, **-ss-** is usually retained.

1 **Nouns ending in a single -s.** The question of whether to double the *s* before adding the plural *-es* depends on the number of syllables. Those consisting of two or more syllables never double it:

> atlases biases irises proboscises surpluses
> thermoses

This applies also to Latin loanwords ending in *-us,* such as *cactus(es), focus(es)* and *syllabus(es),* whenever they have English plurals (see **-us** section 1). Even with nouns of one syllable, the pattern is normally the same: *buses, gases, pluses.* Spellings with **-ss-** are the secondary ones in each case (see further under **bus, gas, plus**).

2 **Verbs ending in -s** show a little more variability. The regular rules (see under **doubling of final consonant**) apply in cases like:

> biased chorused focused portcullised
> trellised

Though *biassed* and *focussed* are still seen sometimes, their use has steadily declined in the UK as well as the US, according to Sigley's (1999) research on corpora from the 1960s and 1990s. Only in Australia and New Zealand do the double *s* spellings still make around 25% of all usage of the past forms. With **-ss-** spellings, the present tense of those verbs (*biasses, focusses*) jousts with the single *s* used for their plural nouns: *biases, focuses* (see further under **bias** and **focus**). Verbs of one syllable such as *bus* and *gas* normally double the *s* in British English; whereas in American, *bus* gets single *s* and *gas* the double *s* (for reasons discussed at **bus** and **gas**). On the spelling of *canvas* and *nonplus* as verbs, see their respective entries.

3 Complex words formed with *dis-*, *mis-* or *trans-* raise similar word-forming questions about setting one *s* alongside another. In these cases, however, the two *ss* do not result from any conventional doubling but are integral to the prefix and stem. Spellings with -ss- are perfectly regular for words formed with *dis-* and *mis-*, as in:

dissatisfied	*disservice*	*dissimilar*
misshapen	*misspell*	*misstate*

Words formed with *trans-* are less uniform, and some such as *trans(s)hip* and *trans(s)exual* vary between double and single *s*. Hyphened forms are also recorded in the *Oxford Dictionary* (1989), and *New Oxford* (1998) makes *trans-ship* the primary form of the headword, though it's not registered at all in dictionaries elsewhere. Both *Merriam-Webster* (2000) and *Canadian Oxford* (1998) prefer *transship,* and it's the most common form in CCAE. The Australian *Macquarie* (1997) gives preference to the single *s* spelling *tranship,* and this is also registered in *New Oxford* as its second choice. It has a slight edge over both *trans-ship* and *transship* in small amounts of data from the BNC. Usage is more convergent over *transsexual.* The double *s* (unhyphened) form is prioritized by all dictionaries for *transsexual* and its derivatives *transsexualism/transsexuality,* and they are well supported by British and American usage data. Spellings with double *s* outnumber those with single *s* by a factor of 3:1 in BNC data, and by more than 90:1 in CCAE.

Yet single rather than double *s* is the regular spelling for recent scientific terms such as *transonic* (*trans-* + *sonic*) and *transponder* (*trans-* + [re]*sponder*), as well as *transubstantiation,* borrowed from medieval Latin. Thus fully blended spellings with *trans-* occur in both old and recent words, to show that it's not a matter of age. No single pattern holds for this set – thank goodness it's a small one.

's

Compare *Jeremy's work* with *Jeremy's working hard,* and you quickly discover two different uses of the so-called "apostrophe *s*" – as an inflection for nouns and names, and a contraction of certain forms of auxiliary verbs. The inflectional use occurs in all kinds of written English, whereas the second is a feature of scripted speech and more interactive and colloquial writing. Both these are detailed below. A third use of **'s** is as a contraction of *us,* in *let's go,* for which see **let us or let's.**

1 Inflectional 's marks the genitive of English nouns as in *farmer's son* and *the doctor's answer:* see **apostrophes** section 1. Its more variable uses in official and geographical names, as well as personal names ending in *s,* are discussed in **apostrophes** sections 2 and 3.

◊ For the use/nonuse of **'s** in locative phrases such as *at the printers,* see **local genitive.**

◊ The use of **'s** as an embellished form of the plural (on market signs and in unedited prose) is discussed under **apostrophes** section 4.

2 The 's contraction represents one of three auxiliary verbs: *is, has* or (very occasionally) *does,* as in:

That's a good idea.	[is]
Where's he put the coffee?	[has]
What's it matter?	[does]

Despite these coincidences, the grammar of the contracted **'s** is clear enough in context for both readers and listeners. See further under **contractions** section 2.

sabre or saber

See under **-re/-er.**

saccharine or saccharin

See under **-ine/-in.**

sack, sac or sacque

These spellings show what time and fashion can do to a simple word. The progenitor of them all is Old English *sacc,* an early borrowing from Latin of *saccus* ("bag"). The spelling **sack** was and is the standard one for a large woven container for heavy products such as potatoes and wheat. The simpler **sac** was introduced in C17 to refer to a new, loose-fitting style of gown made fashionable by the French. But in the following century *sac* was taken up by biologists in its original sense to refer to a small bag-like structure in the anatomy of a plant or animal, and another spelling had to be found for clothing that went by the same name. Enter **sacque,** a dressed-up form of **sac(k)** with no roots in French, but with that *je ne sais quoi* that is the appeal of other frenchified words (see further under **frenchification**). Its French pretensions were perhaps too obvious. At any rate it never completely displaced **sack** as the spelling for a loose-fitting gown, and later a coat or jacket of the same style. **Sack** remains the standard spelling for most uses of the word.

sacrilegious

Its connections with the noun *sacrilege* help to explain why the adjective **sacrilegious** is spelled as it is. Both noun and adjective embody the Latin stems *sacri-* ("sacred") and *leg-* (here meaning "take/steal"), to create the sense of violating or misusing sacred things. **Sacrilegious** is normally pronounced with a short "i" sound as its third syllable – and this, plus the fact that it's often used in the context of *religion,* helps to explain the confused spelling "sacreligious" which turns up in both American and British databases. It shows a kind of *folk etymology,* though the spelling is not registered in any dictionary. See further at **folk etymology.**

said

The phrase *the said* is a form of cohesion peculiar to legal documents. In expressions such as *the said Gibson* or *the said premises,* it reminds the reader that "Gibson" and particular "premises" have been identified earlier on, and that this reference should be connected with that. In ordinary English the pronouns function this way – though sometimes ambiguously – and so pronouns are studiously avoided in legal writing. We might also note that the sheer length of legal sentences contributes to the danger of ambiguity, and amid the general wordiness of legal prose, even the cohesive devices need to be bulkier. The phrase *the said* helps to highlight a reference more adequately than a simple pronoun or demonstrative. In any other kind of writing, *the said* looks like overkill.

◊ For other kinds of cohesive devices, see under **coherence or cohesion.**

sailboat or sailing boat

The first is used by North American recreational sailors, the second by British and Australian. See further under **inflectional extras.**

Saint, St(.) or S.

The conventions for writing saints' names depend on the context: whether it's a reference to the saint himself or herself, or to an institution or place named after them.

The names of saints are usually prefaced by **Saint** in books which describe their life and works. In the indexes to such books the saint's name is entered alphabetically according to given name, as in

> *Thomas Aquinas, Saint*

However those canonized in modern times are alphabetized according to their family name:

> *More, Sir Thomas, Saint*

When persons canonized are mentioned incidentally in history books and encyclopedias, their title is usually abbreviated: *St. Thomas Aquinas, St. Thomas More.* Liturgical publications such as prayer books use either **St(.)** or the Latin abbreviation **S.**, whose plural is **SS** with no stop (because it thus becomes a contraction rather than an abbreviation: see **contractions** section 1).

When saints' names are written into those of institutions, the shortened form **St(.)** is always used (on the use/non-use of the stop see below). Churches are indicated using the abbreviation, as in *St. John's Church, St. Mary's Cathedral;* as well as other associated organizations: *Brotherhood of St. Lawrence, St. Vincent de Paul Society.* Secularized institutions such as the *St. John Ambulance Association* and *St. Valentine's Day* naturally use the abbreviation. Individuals whose surnames echo a saint's name: *St Clair, St John,* again use the abbreviation – as a glance at the metropolitan phone book will confirm. Geographical names which honor a saint are likewise written with **St(.)**:

> *St Gotthard Pass*
> *St Kilda*
> *St Moritz*
> *St Petersburg*

Abbreviated forms like these are used in the gazetteers of world atlases published by *The Times* and Oxford, among others, and they reflect common usage – *pace Webster's Geographical Dictionary* (1997) which uses *Saint* for all of them.

1 Punctuating saints' names

* **use of full stop / period** The shortened form St is normally left unstopped by British writers and editors, because (a) it's a contraction rather than an abbreviation, and (b) it contains a lower case letter. (For more about these principles, see **abbreviations** section 1.) North Americans using a *saint's name* usually punctuate it as **St.**, as exemplified in the *Chicago Manual* (2003): and this style is carried over into placenames (e.g. *St. Louis*) in encyclopedic dictionaries such as *Random House* (1987) and the *Canadian Oxford Dictionary* (1998).

* **apostrophes** Placenames containing a saint's name normally do without an apostrophe before the final *s* (see **apostrophes** section 2). However institutions with a saint's name may use an apostrophe, especially ones like *St. Vincent's Hospital, St. Joseph's College,* which have a religious affiliation. For other institutions, check the telephone directory.

* **hyphen** In French, both personal and geographical names keep the word **Saint** (or **Sainte** for the feminine equivalent) in full, connecting it with a hyphen to the personal name:

> *Sainte-Beuve*   *Saint-Saëns*
> *Sainte-Agathe-des-Monts*   *Saint-Germain-des-Prés*

Placenames like these are however often abbreviated when they appear in compressed lists, maps and timetables, as:

> *Ste-Agathe-des-Monts*   *St-Germain-des-Prés*

In English-speaking Canada, these abbreviations are normally stopped (**St., Ste.**) whereas in Quebec they are left unstopped, according to *Canadian English Usage* (1997).

2 Indexing names with St(.)

Names prefixed with **St(.)** can be indexed in one of two ways:

* **as if they were spelled out as Saint.** They then appear after *Sah-* in any list, although still abbreviated. Other names involving *Saint-* are integrated with those with **St(.)**, according to their sixth letter. The order is as follows:

> *Sahara Air Conditioning*
> *St Antony's Home*
> *Saint Honoré Cake Shop*
> *St Ignatius College*
> *Saintino Z*
> *St Ives Retirement Village*

* **on a strictly alphabetic basis,** so that names with **St(.)** typically follow *Sp/Sq* in the index (because of the dearth of English words or names beginning with *Sr* or *Ss*).This practice separates them from other words/names which have **Saint** in its full form (which appear after *Sah-*, as just shown).

The second system (strictly alphabetic according to the way they are written) is specified in BS 3700, although Butcher's *Copy-editing* (1992) suggests that the first may be more appropriate and helpful when the names could be written in more than one way and index-users may not be sure of where to look. *Webster's Style Manual* (1985) strongly endorses the first, whereas *Chicago Manual* (2003) indicates its preference for the second. Both the size of the index, and its purpose need to be considered.

◊ Compare the issues in indexing names with *Mac/Mc*, under **Mac or Mc** section 2.

sake

For his sake . . . for my husband's sake . . . for God's sake. These phrases show that **sake** normally involves a genitive; and with nouns and names, this means an apostrophe plus *s*. In the past, the same treatment was accorded to all abstract nouns:

> *for pity's sake   for mercy's sake   for goodness's sake*

However Fowler (1926) noted that the last of those was not regularly written with a final *s* (usually as *goodness' sake*), and that others such as *for conscience sake* were appearing without even the apostrophe. Both these examples involve common nouns ending in a sibilant ("s" sound), and they pose similar questions to names ending in *s*, as a letter or a sound. (See **apostrophes** section 3.) That apart, the phrases are effectively idioms whose meaning is not fully analyzable in terms of individual words, and the genitive construction adds nothing to them. Discarding the apostrophe makes no difference to their meaning, and database evidence shows that most American and many British writers do so. There is no sign of the apostrophe in *goodness sake* in CCAE, and the phrase is punctuated in only a small proportion of the BNC texts (1 in 4).

saleroom or salesroom

British auctions take place in a **saleroom**, whereas the North American and Australian counterpart is the **salesroom**. In this unusual case, the British term does without the inflection used elsewhere. See further under **inflectional extras**.

salination, salinization, salinisation and salinification

During C20 several words were coined for the impact of mineral salts from underground water on agricultural land. The earliest was **salinification**, registered in *Webster's Dictionary* (1911), but now the least used, by the evidence of CCAE and the BNC. **Salinization** or **salinisation** (see -ize/-ise) was first recorded in 1928, according to the *Oxford Dictionary* (1989), while **salination** makes its debut in *Webster's Third* (1961). An internet search (Google, 2003) shows that **salinization/salinisation** is a good deal more popular worldwide than **salination**, by a factor of 4:1; while **salinification** makes very little showing. **Salination** expresses the concept more economically than the others, but is listed only as a run-on to **salinisation** in the *Macquarie Dictionary* (1997), and not at all in *Merriam-Webster* (2000), *New Oxford* (1998) or the *Canadian Oxford* (1998). One other point that might lend support to **salination** is the fact that *desalination* is far more common than *desalinization/desalinisation* on the internet, by more than 7:1 (Google, 2003). The two words come up in rather different contexts however: *desalination* when urban water supplies are under discussion, and **salination** amid agricultural and environmental concerns.

salutary or salutatory

At the root of both these adjectives is the notion of good health, yet both have moved some distance away from it. **Salutary** now serves to describe something as broadly beneficial or helpful in fostering some positive good, as in *salutary experience* or a *salutary effect* on the discussion.

Salutatory has strong links with *salutation* ("greeting": which is ultimately a good health wish). So **salutatory** means "offering a welcome," as in a *salutatory letter from the new landlord*.

same

This word serves as a shorthand device in business and law, as well as in ordinary English. In commercialese **same** stands instead of the details of an order, to save repeating them all:

> *Please deliver three cartons of manila folders 297/211 m, and include invoice for same...*

In law also *the same* saves tedious repetition:

> *the defendant of 31 Low Street, Richmond and his son of the same address...*

These special uses of *(the) same* are well recognized by the style authorities; yet another common use of *the same* gets no mention:

> *We arranged for a taxi, and the visitors did the same.*

There are no overtones of commercialese or legalese in such usage, because it's one of the cohesive devices

of standard English. (See further under **coherence or cohesion**.)

When **same** is used as an adjective in clausal comparisons, the following conjunction may be either *as* or *that*:

> *...at the same time as I was compiling the paper*
> *...at the same time that I was compiling the paper*

Researchers associated with the *Longman Grammar* (1999) found that *at the same time as* and *in the same way as* were both among the most commonly occurring "five-word bundles" in their corpus of conversation. This probably gives them a collocational advantage over constructions with *that,* though their high frequency is helped by the fact that *as* can be complemented by noun phrases as well as finite clauses. But clausal comparisons not involving the words *time* or *way* are more often construed with *that* than *as,* by the evidence of the BNC. Examples such as the following are only tokens of the range in which writers prefer to use *that* following **same**:

> *...subject to the same legislation that governs other foodstuffs*
> *...for the same reason that I did*

The choice of *that* after **same** does not seem to correlate with more or less formal style.

sanatorium, sanitarium and sanitorium

Sanatorium is the standard British spelling for a hospital or residential centre for the chronically ill, and it dominates in data from the BNC. It serves whether the facility is run along medical lines, as in *TB sanatorium,* or something closer to a health resort, as in *take a cure at the local sanatorium*. In American English **sanitarium** is the common spelling for both, by the evidence of CCAE, although **sanatorium** (and to a lesser extent **sanitorium**) are also current. *Webster's English Usage* (1989) notes a slight tendency to prefer **sanatorium** for the treatment of tuberculosis, and **sanitarium** for mental and emotional disorders, perhaps because it lines up with the word *sanity.* These somewhat unsettled boundaries create doubts about the spelling, and *Webster's Third* (1986) records a fourth one: *sanatarium,* though there's no sign of it in CCAE.

Sanatorium and **sanitarium** are about equally used in Canada for the hospital and the health resort, according to *Canadian English Usage* (1997). Neither is much used by Australians, though the analogy with better-known words such as *sanitary, sanitize, sanitation* inclines them towards **sanitarium** (Peters, 1995), as well as the trademark *Sanitarium* attached to health foods.
◊ For the plurals of **sanatorium** and **sanitarium**, see under **-um**.

sanatory or sanitary

See **sanitary**.

sanction

As a verb, **sanction** means putting the official stamp of approval on an action, as in:

> *Agricultural change has to be sanctioned by special committees.*

The noun takes official power one stage further. It can mean "official permission," but its commonest use nowadays is to refer to "coercive action to enforce an official policy," usually in the plural:

> . . . when Washington imposed a package of sanctions on China

Such **sanctions** are typically designed to discourage certain kinds of disapproved action, thus almost the opposite of the facilitatory action expressed by the verb.

sang or sung
See **sing**.

sanguine or sanguinary
Both these go back to the Latin word for "blood," though only **sanguinary** expresses it now, in phrases such as *sanguinary fanatics of the French Revolution,* which refer to bloodshed or to those with a taste for it. Yet the horrific implications of the word are somehow muted in its latinity. If its shocking implications are to be communicated, "bloody" or "bloodthirsty" says it more clearly and strongly.

Sanguine came under the influence of medieval ideas about the four bodily humors which affected a person's temperament: blood, phlegm, yellow bile (choler) and black bile (melancholy). Those in whom "blood" was dominant had a cheerful, energetic character, and so **sanguine** now means "confident" and "optimistic."

sanitarium, sanitorium or sanatorium
See **sanatorium**.

sanitary or sanatory
The first spelling **sanitary** is standard everywhere for this adjective meaning "hygienic" or "concerned with the maintenance of health," as in *sanitary napkin/towel* and *sanitary regulations.* **Sanatory** enjoyed some currency in British English in early C20, alongside *sanatorium,* but has fallen out of use, by its absence from the BNC. It makes no showing in data from CCAE.
◊ For the choice between *unsanitary* and *insanitary,* see **insanitary or unsanitary**.

sank or sunk
See **sink**.

sans serif
See **serif**.

sarcasm
See under **irony**.

sarcophagus
The plural is normally the latinate **sarcophagi** in both American and British English: there's no sign of the anglicized **sarcophaguses** in data from CCAE or the BNC.

sated, satiated or saturated
All three are concerned with the filling of particular needs and capacities, but the first two have much more in common than the third. Both **sated** and **satiated** mean satisfying physical and psychological needs to the hilt, even to the point of overindulgence, as in *sated with TV* and *satiated with chocolate.* Some style commentators suggest that **satiated** connotes excess more often than **sated**, though neither is free of

pejorative connotations. If a neutral word is needed, a paraphrase with *satisfy* (e.g. *satisfy the need for*) would serve.

Saturated in ordinary parlance means "soaked with a liquid, as much as the medium can absorb":

> *The carpets were still saturated after the flood.*

In military jargon it conveys the idea of an area attacked with so many bombs or fighter aircraft as to render it defenseless.

satiric or satirical
Both adjectives connect with *satire,* the literary mode in which writers vent strong criticism of a particular subject (see further under **irony**). The longer form **satirical** is strongly preferred in British English, by a factor of more than 7:1 in data from the BNC. In American English the two are somewhat more evenly matched: the ratio in CCAE data is 3:1, but still in favor of **satirical**.
◊ For other similar pairs, see **-ic/-ical**.

savanna or savannah
The spelling **savanna** stays closer to the original loanword from Caribbean Spanish: *zavana* (in modern Spanish, *sabana,* "plain"). The spelling with two *n*s appeared first in C16, and the variant with *h* in C17. The unetymological *h* suggests that it was thought of as an Indian word, and the spelling **savannah** prevails through the *Oxford Dictionary's* (1989) citations from C19. This explains why it was given preference as headword, and it's still the more frequent of the two in British English, by a factor of about 3:1 in data from the BNC. But in American English **savanna** is given preference by *Merriam-Webster* (2000), and it's the commoner spelling in CCAE by about 10:1 – despite the fact that spellings with *h* are enshrined in placenames such as *Savannah River* and the town of *Savannah* in Georgia.

savings or saving
Both *a savings of* and *a saving of* are used in American English:

> *This is a savings of 40% on the regular price.*
> *This is a saving of 40% on the regular price.*

The two constructions are about equally common in data from CCAE, whereas only the second appears in data from the BNC. British writers thus seem to prefer the strictly singular construction. The plural-with-singular construction makes it a kind of *pluralia tantum,* like *arrears, earnings* etc. See **pluralia tantum**.

savior or saviour
See **-or/-our**.

savoir faire and savoir vivre
The phrase **savoir faire** is French for "knowing what to do" – that almost intuitive knowledge of how to act in any circumstances, which some people possess in larger measure than others. **Savoir vivre** is "knowing how to live." It usually involves experience of good living, and so is more likely to be accessed by those with the means or good fortune to partake of the good life. Yet **savoir vivre** suggests more refined taste than is associated with *la dolce vita:* see under **dolce vita**.

Savoir faire is much better established in English, in spite of being the more recently adopted (first recorded in C19, whereas **savoir vivre** goes back to C18). There is no need for a hyphen in either.

sawed or sawn
The verb *saw* ("cut with a saw") originated as a regular verb in early middle English (C13). But by C15 it had acquired an irregular past participle **sawn**, which has been used as an alternative to **sawed** ever since. British writers clearly prefer **sawn** in both compound verbs (*have/be sawn*) and adjectival uses (*sawn timbers*) by the evidence of the BNC, whereas Americans go the other way, maintaining the regular form for the past participle most of the time, in data from CCAE.

sawn-off or sawed-off
These typically refer to the shortened form of a shotgun used for criminal purposes, or occasionally to clothing (*sawn-off jeans*) and other abbreviated objects. British English writers strongly prefer **sawn-off**, by the evidence of the BNC, and American preferences are equally strongly in favor of **sawed-off**, in data from CCAE. These regional preferences accord with those for the verb *saw* itself (see previous entry).

scalawag
See **scallywag**.

scale and scales
The adjectives *large-scale* and *small-scale* carry rather different meanings according to whether they refer to the **scale** of a map, model, drawing or diagram – or to anything else. In ordinary usage, *large-scale* means "extensive," and *small-scale*, "small in size," as in *a large-scale/small-scale operation*. In references to maps etc., the *small-scale* version covers more ground but offers less detail. The *large-scale* version, by contrast, gives you the fine detail of a relatively small area. It would help walkers but not drivers. So a *large-scale map* might be 1:2000 and the *small-scale map* 1:200 000, though the differences are always relative.

Note that when **scale(s)** means a weighing instrument, usage makes it singular in North America (*stand on the scale*) and plural in Britain and Australia (*stand on the scales*). The singular **scale** seems to refer to the whole instrument, while the plural **scales** conjures up the twin pans of the balance. Either way the word is Germanic in origin and related historically to the word *shell*. But the **scale** of maps is quite unrelated, and goes back to the Latin word *scala* meaning "ladder."

scallop or scollop
The first spelling **scallop** is given preference in all dictionaries, and reflects the word's origins in earlier English *scalop* and Old French *escalope* ("shell"). **Scollop** reflects the common pronunciation of the word, and is a recognized alternative. Its appearance in C18 shows how old our present pronunciation is. Yet **scallop** is the only spelling to be found for the noun or verb in contemporary English databases, British and American.

Should it be *scalloped* or *scallopped*? When used as a verb, **scallop** has no need of double *p*: see **-p/-pp-**.

scallywag or scalawag
The standard British spelling is **scallywag** – the only one to be found in data from the BNC. In American English where the word was first recorded, it's usually **scalawag**, the only spelling in CCAE. Canadians generally use the American spelling, Australians the British. Just where the word came from is unclear, though Barnhart (1987) proposes two alternatives based on Scottish origins. In C19, it referred both to an undersized animal, and to a reprobate or scoundrel, the latter sense being reinforced after the US Civil War, when it was applied to white southerners who collaborated with reconstruction governments for private gain. It remains more derogatory in the US than the UK, where its use is often affectionate: *the old scallywag*.

scant or scanty
Scant is now an old-fashioned adjective, hardly used except in stock phrases such as *scant praise*, and *scant regard* (for their safety/health etc.) In such phrases, it usually combines with abstract nouns. **Scanty** seems to substitute for it in reference to things concrete and practical, as in *scanty clothes* and a *scanty supply of food*.

scarcely
Used on its own, **scarcely** minimizes the effect or likelihood of the verb:
> *They scarcely heard the thunder.*
> *The government will scarcely want an early election after all that.*

Used in tandem with another conjunction, **scarcely** compares the timing of two events:
> *Scarcely had they finished the roof when it began to rain.*
> *Scarcely had they finished the roof than it began to rain.*

The first sentence which uses the temporal *when* is the only correct way of putting it, according to some style commentators. Yet the use of the comparative *than* is quite common, and may indeed sound more idiomatic to some ears. The arguments for it are like those for *hardly than*. (See under **hard or hardly**.)

Following **scarcely** (or other quasi-negative adverbs) at the start of a sentence, subject and verb are usually inverted, as shown above. See further under **negatives**.

scare quotes
See **quotation marks** section 1.

scarfs or scarves
The older plural **scarves** is still the commoner of the two. In British data from the BNC it dominates by about 30:1, whereas in American data from CCAE the ratio is closer to 3:1. See further under **-f > -v-**.

sceptic or skeptic, and scepticism or skepticism
For the choice between these pairs, as well as between *sceptic(al)* and *skeptic(al),* see under **skeptic or sceptic**.

sceptre or scepter
See under **-re/-er**.

schema

This Greek word became English *scheme* in C16. It was then reborrowed in C19 in its classical form, as a technical term for English philosophers of C19 and for psychologists in early C20, referring to a principle of understanding or the cognitive model by which we interpret elements of experience. **Schema** broke out into general usage in mid-C20, as a term for an overview (in the form of a plan, outline or diagram). But in discourse analysis since the 1970s, its use is closer to that of psychologists, as a term for the underlying structure of a piece of prose. The tug-of-war between general and specialized uses helps to explain why both Greek and English plurals are current, in evidence from American and British databases. The Greek **schemata** is mostly found in academic writing (e.g. *experiential schemata*), whereas the anglicized **schemas** is used freely in both technical and more general discourse: *database access schemas, theories that memory is based on schemas.* (See further at **-a** section 1.)

schnorkel or snorkel

See **snorkel**.

schwa

Borrowed from Hebrew by German phoneticians, **schwa** is used internationally to refer to the vowel of unstressed syllables. In English it's the most common vowel of all in terms of frequency, yet it goes largely unrecognized because there's no single letter for it in the alphabet. In fact it can correspond to any of the five vowel letters, as italicized in the following:

*a*bout watch*e*s pol*i*tics phot*o*graph nat*u*ral

Being an unstressed vowel, **schwa** is highly variable in its sound – hence its alternative name "indeterminate vowel." Its indeterminacy means it offers no clues as to the spelling of the syllable it appears in, and many spelling dilemmas, as with *-able/-ible, -ant/-ent* and *-er/-or,* exist because of it.

scientific names

Biological classifications have more levels than we're normally aware of. Both botanists and zoologists work with six levels, as shown below:

botany	zoology
Division	*Phylum*
Class	*Class*
Order	*Order*
Family	*Family*
Genus	*Genus*
Species	*Species*

For ordinary purposes, only the last two levels are used. Most biological names consist of two parts, both of them Latin words, which specify the genus and the species:

Azalea indica   *Azalea kurume*
Python ater   *Python reticulatus*

Occasionally a third word is used to identify a botanic subspecies, typically a cultivar, as in *Azalea indica* var. *balsaminaeflora.* The words designating the species and subspecies may be descriptive, as in the examples above, or may preserve in latinized form the name of the person who identified the species, for example: *Azalea rutherfordiana.*

Biological names are always italicized, but only the first is capitalized, even if others are disguised proper names. Additional proper names are printed in roman after the Latin elements. For cultivated species they appear in a combination of parentheses and quote marks – *Azalea kurume* "Yaya-hiryu" (Scarlet Prince) – when a foreign name or phrase needs translating.

In current zoological nomenclature, the name of the "author" (i.e. identifier of the species) is given in roman after the Latin names – at least once in an article, according to the *CBE Manual* (1994). The name and date are put in parentheses if the classification has changed. The Australian duck-billed platypus was first classified by Shaw as *Platypus anatinus,* until it emerged that the existing *Platypus* genus was used for beetles. A new genus name was found, and it is now *ornithorhincus anatinus* (Shaw, 1799).

Other conventions with scientific names are that when several species of the same genus are mentioned in quick succession, the genus can be abbreviated to an initial (*Azalea indica, A. kurume, A. rutherfordiana*) for the second and subsequent names. Note also that when the Latin word for genus or species is used as the common name for a plant or animal, it's printed with lower case and in roman:

They found azaleas *and* rhododendrons *flowering everywhere.*

The naming principles described above apply throughout the natural world, as well as in medicine. They are used in the naming of body organs, e.g. *Corpus callosum* (the band of tissue which links the two hemispheres of the brain); and in the names of diseases – *Paralysis agitans* (= Parkinson's disease) – and micro-organisms: *Legionella pneumophilia* (the microbe which causes the most familiar form of legionnaire's disease). Note that the initial capital disappears from scientific nomenclature in nonscientific text.

scilicet

This Latin tag meaning "that is to say" is now found only in older scholarly writing. It was used to introduce a detailed list of things which had previously been mentioned in general terms. The standard abbreviation for **scilicet** is *sc.*

Historically speaking, **scilicet** is a blend of Latin *scire licet,* literally "it is permitted to know." The authoritarian overtones of that phrase are a reminder of medieval attitudes to knowledge. The word is first recorded in English in 1387, but its history in medieval Latin is much older. Compare *videlicet* under **vide**.

scissors

Should the verb accompanying **scissors** be singular or plural? See **agreement** section 2.

scollop or scallop

See **scallop**.

Scotch, Scots or Scottish

Conventional uses of **Scotch**, as in *Scotch whisky,* mask the reasons for its replacement by **Scots** and **Scottish** as ways of referring to the people and things associated with *Scotland.* **Scotch** was traditionally used by the **Scots** in referring to themselves, and is enshrined in the writings of Burns and Scott. Yet from mid-C19 on, the English seem to have avoided using

Scotch, on grounds of the "Scotsman's supposed dislike of it" (*Oxford Dictionary*, 1989), making it an early example of (mistaken) political correctness. The retitling of Mendelssohn's "Scotch Symphony" – dedicated to Queen Victoria in 1842 – as his *Scottish Symphony* is symptomatic of the changeover. Perhaps the avoidance of **Scotch** by the English had more to do with the colloquial adjective *scotch* (in lower case) meaning "parsimonious," which was first documented in early C20, but may well have been in use before then. Its negative connotations are no problem for traditional collocations such as *Scotch fir/pine, Scotch mist, Scotch salmon, Scotch thistle;* and *Scotch whisky* is its own trademark. *Scotch Tape* ("adhesive tape") likewise continues as a trademark in North America. But other products were rechristened, so that *Scotch plaid/tartan* is now *Scottish plaid/tartan,* and you wouldn't expect *Scottish beef* or *Scottish beer* to be otherwise. People's *Scotch-Irish* ancestry now tends to be spoken of as *Scots-Irish.*

Broadly speaking, **Scots** is nowadays used in reference to the people, as in *Scotsman* and the *Scots Guards,* while **Scottish** is applied to aspects of the land and its culture, as in *Scottish agriculture* and *Scottish universities.* In some contexts either word is acceptable, as in a *Scots/Scottish accent.* The relative frequencies of **Scots** and **Scottish** in British and American databases suggest that Americans are less inclined to use **Scots** as a general adjective and prefer **Scottish** for that role, whereas the British use both as adjectives. In both the UK and the US, **Scots** serves as a collective noun for the people.

Databases show that the lower case form **scotch** is often used for "whisky," in British and especially American English: *a little drop of scotch.* The lower case form also serves for the quite unrelated verb *scotch* ("quash"), as in *the first argument to scotch* – where whisky is not the secret weapon. Its origins are lost in the mists of C15 English.

sculpt or sculpture
The work of *sculptors* can be indicated by either of these verbs. **Sculpture** dating back to C17 has the longer history; and **sculpt** from C19 is sometimes questioned as a dubious abbreviation of it (see **backformation**). More respectable origins for **sculpt** have however been found in the French verb *sculpter,* and it's now firmly established. In current American English, *sculpted* is a good deal more frequent than *sculptured,* by about 5:2 in CCAE data; and *sculpted* has the edge (8:7) in citations from the BNC. Yet when both occur in the same sentence, some kind of contrast may be intended, as if *sculpturing* involves three-dimensional carving and *sculpting* mostly two dimensions:

> a white marble building surmounted by a series of large sculptured figures with extensive use of decorative sculpted friezes

Dictionaries lend no support to that distinction, and both verbs are freely applied to two- and three-dimensional work, in database evidence from the US and the UK.

seasonal or seasonable
Seasonal reflects the periodic character of the *seasons,* the fact that they come and go in a predictable rotation. So *seasonal employment* is work available each year through a particular season. While

seasonal is a neutral word, **seasonable** affirms that what's happening is right for the time of year, and to be expected then, as for example in the *seasonable heat of the Parisian summer.* **Seasonable** has in fact been recorded with the meaning "timely" since C15.

second cousin or first cousin once removed
See under **cousins.**

second person
See under **person.**

Second World War
See under **World War.**

self
This serves as both prefix and suffix in English, as well as an independent word. As a prefix, it forms new adjective and noun compounds with the greatest ease, using verbs which work reflexively:

> *self-addressed   self-appointed   self-centred self-control*

These examples show that *self-* compounds embody a variety of adverbial relations: for oneself, by oneself, in oneself, of oneself. Note that as a prefix *self-* is always hyphenated, but as a suffix, never. As a suffix *-self/-selves* is the key ingredient in English *reflexive pronouns* (see under that heading).

As an independent word, **self** can be a noun, modified by its own adjective as in *your good self* and *his usual self.* Yet when used on its own and as a substitute for *myself,* as in *a trip for my wife and self,* it sounds a bit offhanded. Using *myself* there (instead of *me*) raises other stylistic issues, though it's natural enough to use *myself* following *my wife.* As Fowler (1926) observed, this is hardly an affectation. See further under **me.**

self-deprecating, self-deprecatory or self-depreciatory
See **deprecate.**

self-raising or self-rising
See under **raise or rise.**

selvage or selvedge
The **selvedge** on each side of a piece of fabric is the "self edge," where threads must be woven back on themselves to prevent fraying. **Selvedge** may thus be the more transparent spelling for some, and British writers clearly prefer it to **selvage,** in data from the BNC. Yet **selvage** (dating from C15) is given priority in the *Oxford Dictionary* (1989) as well as *Webster's Third* (1986), and it's the preferred spelling of American writers represented in CCAE. The *-age* spelling links it with others such as *dosage, linage, shrinkage,* though the internal structure of all such words is more transparent than **selvage.**

semantics or semiotics
These linguistic terms are tossed around in all kinds of contexts these days – so that one hears of the *semantics of police interviews* and of the *semiotics of wearing slippers to a dinner party.* Both words have to do with meaning, but **semantics** is still tied to language, to the meanings of individual words or what

they add up to in discourse. Misunderstandings are sometimes explained in terms of the *conflicting semantics* of what has been said by the parties involved.

Semiotics is concerned with signs and symbols in the widest sense, the significance of material features of a culture and its codes of behavior. The things we surround ourselves with, and the cut and color of what we wear, all say something about individual identity as well as the different value systems within which we operate.

semi- and semi

Derived from scholarly Latin words, the prefix **semi-** means "half" or "partly." In musical words such as *semibreve* and *semiquaver* it means exactly half of a larger unit; whereas the less precise meaning ("partly") is found in *semiconscious* and *semisweet*.

In spite of its Latin origins, **semi-** is now very much at home in English. It combines with everyday English words, as in:

> semi(-)desert   semi(-)final   semi(-)intellectual
> semi(-)official   semi(-)skilled   semi(-)soft
> semi(-)trailer

Words prefixed with **semi-** are usually written with hyphens in British English, as indicated in *New Oxford* (1998). In American English they are equally likely to appear without them, according to *Merriam-Webster* (2000). The dictionaries make no distinction according to whether the word combined with **semi-** begins with a vowel or not (see further under **hyphens** section 1).

Semi also has an independent existence, or rather several. North Americans and Australians use it in speech and everyday writing to refer to *semitrailers*. In Britain, Canada and Australia, **semi** is also used for a *semi-detached house*. In competitive sport the world over, **semi** refers to the *semifinal*. The plural is **semis** for all.
◊ Compare **demi-**.

semi-auxiliary or semi-modal

The term *quasimodal* has been adopted in this book to cover these types of verb: see **auxiliary verbs** section 3.

semicolon

When the average written sentence was much longer, **semicolons** were used much more often as sentence dividers. They are very visible in the narrative of C19 novels such as those by Anthony Trollope and Henry James. Nowadays the **semicolon** is used sparingly, and some writers do without it entirely. Its place in marking items in vertical lists is being superseded by other punctuative devices (see **lists** section 2), and it has a limited role in digital documents (see **digital style**). But **semicolons** still have two very specific functions.

1 The **semicolon** marks the boundary between two independent sentences that are set together as one, usually because the second is strongly related to the first. For example:

> The minister mentioned a possible cut in interest rates; immediately there was a run on the stock exchange.

In cases like that, the two sections could equally well have been set as separate sentences, with a full stop between them:

> The minister mentioned a possible cut in interest rates. Immediately there was a run on the stock exchange.

However the version with the **semicolon** emphasizes the closeness of the two statements, and draws particular attention to the second. Note that the two could also be linked with a comma and a conjunction:

> The minister mentioned a possible cut in interest rates, and immediately there was a run on the stock exchange.

2 **Semicolons** serve as a second level of punctuation, in a series of words or phrases which already have commas to make internal divisions. See for example:

> The minister's announcement resulted in an instant drop in the value of shares; a modest fall in bank rates, at least those offered by the larger ones; and a surprising run on property investments, presumably backed by overseas capital.

In complex horizontal lists such as that, the demarcation of the three subunits would be less clear if commas alone were used. Here again, the greater "weight" of the **semicolon** is put to good use.

semi-modal or semi-auxiliary

See under **auxiliary verbs** section 3.

semiotics or semantics

See **semantics**.

Sen.

In American English this abbreviates the title *Senator*; in British it stands after a name for *Senior*.

seniors and senior citizens

In Latin *senior* means "older" rather than "old," and is relative rather than absolute in sense. This relativity carries over into English, where **seniors** can be applied to persons aged 12 plus, around 18, or 21, or over 65, according to context. At the youthful end of the age spectrum, **seniors** is sometimes used in the UK of students above primary school level (typically 12 years or more), whereas in the US it refers to those either in the high school graduation year (around 18), or else in the final year of college (around 21). None could be called **senior citizens** – the respectful title reserved for those at the grey end of the age spectrum. The phrase originated in American English just before World War II, and has been used in British English since the 1960s. If it began as a euphemism for those over 65 and out of the workforce, the feeling has disappeared in North America, according to *Webster's English Usage* (1989) and *Canadian English Usage* (1997). In Australia it is institutionalized: there and elsewhere it's cheerfully shortened to **seniors** (as in *seniors card, seniors day*), which seems to keep the respect without being cumbersome. It thus seems to avoid the problems associated with other kinds of inclusive language (see further under **political correctness**). Other terms for referring to the elderly are noted at **ageist language**.

sense, sensibility, sensitivity and sensitiveness

The first two of these made a title for Jane Austen, and they focus on the common sense and good judgement of one character, and the tendency to react emotionally in another. Nowadays we're unlikely to use **sensibility** in that way, and would reserve it for responsiveness to the subtleties of experience and of artistic form. The adjective *sensible* has also shifted, from being associated with **sensibility** in its older sense, to being the standard adjective for **sense**.

Both **sensitivity** and **sensitiveness** link up with the adjective *sensitive,* and express the readiness to respond to outside forces. Though both words originated in C19, only **sensitivity** is in common use, outnumbering the other by almost 200:1 in British material from the BNC, and an even larger ratio in American data from CCAE. Stylistically the two are interchangeable, except that in technical fields **sensitivity** is the standard term for the response of a machine or organism to physical and chemical forces, as in:

> ... *the sensitivity and accuracy of its power-assisted steering*
> ... *sensitivity of the pancreas to raised blood glucose*

Compare:

> ... *a thoroughly English writer's sensitiveness/sensitivity to the vagaries of the weather*

where either word could be used.

sensuous or sensual

Both these words mean that the senses are engaged: the question is which senses. Since Puritan times it has been argued that **sensual** implies the gratifying of physical senses including sexual ones, which will probably help to sell a book with the title *Sensual Massage.* **Sensuous** has therefore been reserved by some for that which appeals to the aesthetic senses, as when we refer to a song's *sensuous duet with the flute.* The word **sensuous** seems to have been coined by Milton for just this purpose, to prevent confusion with **sensual.**

Yet the distinction is not so easily applied to what we enjoy eating and drinking, or elsewhere. Should chocolate – or wine – be described as **sensual** because it is a physical pleasure, or **sensuous** to show that it's not a sexual pleasure? The *Random House Dictionary* (1987) suggests that at bottom **sensual** has pejorative connotations which **sensuous** is free of. But **sensual** keeps positive company in American and British English, in examples from CCAE and the BNC:

> *the sensual qualities of light*
> *a sauce so simply sensual*
> *an enticingly sensual opening to this outstanding recital*
> *the furniture's edges, making it more curved, more sensual*

Thus **sensual** can be used to express sensory satisfaction in a variety of contexts that are both physical and aesthetic. *Webster's English Usage* (1989) concludes that the traditional distinction between **sensual** and **sensuous** is honored as much in the breach as the observance. *New Oxford*'s conclusion is similar, that the two are "frequently used interchangeably," and this interchangeability is noted also in *Canadian English Usage* (1997). The interplay

between the two words makes **sensuous** less aesthetic and innocent than Milton intended, in commonplaces such as *sensuous lips* and *a sensuous mouth.* The author who writes of *innocently sensuous lips* reflects the problem – clarifying the meaning for some readers, while creating a tautology for those who read it along Miltonian lines.

The **sensuous/sensual** distinction is blurred for many writers and readers, and artificial because of the complexity of our senses. With two words working much the same semantic territory, one is likely to lose out, and in terms of overall frequency it would be **sensuous**. Already it's outnumbered by **sensual** in both the BNC and CCAE in the ratio of 3:2, and also in Australian data from ACE. In the process, **sensual** loses its more negative implications of sexual excess, and, if they are to be communicated, another adjective or paraphrase has to be found.

Worlds apart is the use of **sensual** in philosophy, where it's neutral in meaning and associated with *sensationalism* (the doctrine that all knowledge is ultimately derived from sensation).

sentence adverbs

This is a term for adverbs that express the writer's attitude to sentence propositions. See further under **adverbs** section 1 ("disjuncts").

sentences

The finite strings of words by which we communicate are **sentences**. A *written sentence* is bounded by a capital letter on its first word, and a full stop after the last. *Spoken sentences* are much more variable in length, marked off by intonation patterns and pauses, though interrupted by internal pauses as well. The two kinds of **sentence** can be analyzed in terms of (a) the particular function that they fulfill; and (b) the common structures they present in strings of words. Both contribute to writing style.

1 The functions of sentences are usually classified as:
a) making statements
b) asking questions
c) uttering commands
d) voicing exclamations

Each of those functions is expressed through a standard clause type: (a) declarative (b) interrogative (c) imperative (d) exclamative. Yet there's no one-for-one correspondence between clause type and sentence function. (For examples, see under **commands**.)

2 The internal structure of a sentence can be analyzed in terms of clause structure: is there one or more of them, and what is the interrelationship between them? The distinctions between *simple, complex* and *compound sentences* turn on this (see under **clauses**).

Our expectations of **sentences** tend to be modeled on the norms of written syntax, where clauses normally have the full subject and predicate, and any subordinate clause has a main clause to support it. Yet many of the utterances in a conversation are not quite like that. Much is understood and left implicit, as in:

> *Where are you going?*
> *To see a movie.*
> *In the city?*
> *No, just the local cinema. Don't have to go further afield.*

Apart from the first question, all the "sentences" in that ordinary piece of dialogue are fragmentary – and would be classed as *sentence fragments* in traditional grammar. The three in the middle have neither subject nor verb, and consist simply of adverbial phrases. The last is more fully expressed, but still lacks a subject. In terms of scripted dialogue they still count as **sentences**, though they differ from those of nonfiction prose.

3 **Sentences and style.** Whether in fiction or nonfiction, **sentences** are the staple of discourse, and their patterning creates the rhythm of prose. (See under **rhythm**.) Variety in length and structure are both important for their effect on intelligibility as well as rhythm. Too many long *complex sentences* will lose the rhythm and the reader. Too many short ones in quick succession create an awkward, repetitive rhythm which distracts the reader from what's being said. Ideally the occasional short **sentence** provides relief from longer ones. In Plain English documents, writers aim to average 20 words per **sentence** (see under **Plain English**). However the average achieved in popular fiction is around 15 words, and this is the target for mass circulation magazines.

Apart from varying in length, **sentences** need variety in their openings, using topicalizing phrases now and then before the grammatical subject, and avoiding anticlimaxes at the end. The **sentence** is after all an infinitely flexible unit, to be rearranged and stretched and compressed in the interests of an elegant style.

sentiment, sentimental and sentimentality

Sentiment has many shades of meaning in reference to thoughts, attitudes and feelings. Its connotations are neutral, and it relies on modifiers to give it particulars and values, as in *a cheerful sentiment* and *a negative sentiment.* **Sentimentality** is somewhat pejorative. It implies an excess of emotion where most people would not indulge it:

> *Their attitude to endangered species showed more sentimentality than scientific sense.*

Sentimental serves as adjective for both **sentiment** and **sentimentality** – for the first in *sentimental value,* and for the second in *sentimental admiration for times past.* However the fact that **sentimental** can be linked with **sentimentality** tends to give it a pejorative flavor generally, and so it's better avoided if you wish to make a link with **sentiment**. Calling someone a *sentimental person* is unlikely to sound like a compliment, as *person of sentiment* once did.

separate and separate out

The verb **separate** ("divide, set apart") has long been used with an object, as in:

> *Two factors separate the German bourgeoisie from its counterparts in Western and Asian nations.*

This simple transitive use is now paralleled by a phrasal form **separate out**, as in:

> *Older people prefer not to be separated out from the adult population.*

The second construction is criticized by some as tautologous – which it would be, if "divide" was the sense intended. But **separate out** otherwise carries the sense of distilling something from a matrix, which could apply to that example, just as it does in:

> *Households are required to separate out recyclable waste.*

This use of **separate out** seems to reflect its C19 origins in physical chemistry, as when a chemical substance is drawn out as crystals from a solution:

> *The silicon will make the aluminium separate out harmlessly.*

Intransitive examples like that pose no grammatical challenge, though passive (i.e. transitive) ones also appear from the start. They emerge also in statistical procedures and social science analyses, as in: *the low-income group were separated out from the rest for averaging purposes.* The first nontechnical examples were recorded in the US in 1962, according to the *Oxford Dictionary* (1989), and have since appeared elsewhere. A hundred-odd examples of *separate(d) out* in BNC data show it to be well established now in British English. It can even be used for fun, as in:

> *I tried to separate out the harmonics in the snoring.*

Despite this, the transitive use of **separate out** is not acknowledged in *New Oxford* (1998). It is registered in both the *Canadian Oxford* (1998) and the Australian *Macquarie Dictionary* (1997).

sept-

This is the Latin prefix for "seven," as in *septet, septuagenarian* and *September* – the seventh month of the Roman year, which has become the ninth month in the modern calendar.

Note that *septic* and *septic(a)emia* embody a different root – the Greek word *septos* ("decayed").

sepulchre or sepulcher

See under **-re/-er**.

sequence of tenses and backshifting

The principle of a **sequence of tenses** originated in Latin grammar, and is sometimes applied in English to the reporting of speech (see further under **direct speech**). By this principle, the tense of the reporting verb in the main clause will influence that of the verb in a subordinate clause. Compare

> *He says they're coming at noon.*
> *He said they were coming at noon.*

In the second sentence, the past verb of the main clause prompts **backshifting** of the tense in the second clause, so that they form a matching sequence. This *backshift* occurs in noun (content) clauses following verbs of speaking as well as verbs of mental process, such as *decide, expect, know.* For narrators, *backshifted tenses* help to coordinate the construction of past events within the "present" shared by writer and reader.

Backshifting also affects sentences that express conditions (see the *Comprehensive Grammar,* 1985). Compare:

> *If he has any money, he will surely invest it.*
> *If he had any money, he would surely invest it.*
> *If he had had any money, he would have invested it.*

In each case the verb in the subordinate clause is one "tense" back from that of the main clause. Expressed in traditional grammar terms, the *sequences* are present v. future, past v. present (conditional), past perfect v. present perfect (conditional). The third sentence shows how **backshifting** into the past perfect creates a remote or impossible condition, instead of an open one (see further under **conditional**).

Though the *sequencing/matching* of tenses occurs often enough in certain kinds of subordinate clause, the convention is varied from time to time because of the nature of the material in the clause. If it contains a statement which is believed to be universally true, it can be expressed in the present tense even when the verb of the main clause is past:

They recognized that all life is sacred.

The present is also used when the writer stands between a reported event in the past and one anticipated in the future:

James told us that Monday is a public holiday.

In both cases, the use of the present tense serves to involve readers in the statement and to lend it vividness, as Fowler (1926) put it. It would also be possible to put the subordinate clauses into the past and observe the regular **sequence of tenses** in them. But this seems to reduce the salience of the statement for the present. The **sequence of tenses** is thus a discoursal resource rather than a grammatical imperative for writers of English.

Serb or Serbian

As adjectives, **Serb** and **Serbian** can both refer to the people of the Yugoslav Republic of *Serbia*, their culture and language. It is then curious that **Serbian** is more than twice as frequent as **Serb** in British sources captured in the BNC, where the opposite holds for American English material in CCAE. The difference may have less to do with regional preferences than the fact that the American data comes largely from newspapers, where American military action is being reported. Research by Kjellmer (2000) on data from CNN showed that **Serb** most typically went with nouns such as *forces, soldiers, target, units,* and **Serbian** with *government, media, orthodox church, television/TV.* The impact of American military sources is evident in both media.

sergeant or serjeant

Sergeant is the standard spelling everywhere for a junior officer in the police and the defense forces, often used in combinations such as *sergeant major* or *police/detective/flight sergeant,* to distinguish ranks and specializations. *Webster's Third* (1986) and the *Oxford Dictionary* (1989) both allow **serjeant** as a variant spelling, though there's no sign of it in American data from CCAE, and very little in BNC sources. It mostly survives in references to the *serjeant-at-arms* attached to the British parliament, whose job is to keep order and to evict unruly members.

serial or series

In both the audiovisual media and in publishing, material may be divided up and offered in several segments. The **serial** and the **series** are two ways of doing it. A television or radio **serial** relates a story through ongoing episodes, as for *Brideshead Revisited.* A **series** presents a set of individually complete stories involving the same set of characters, as in *MASH* or *Dad's Army.* However the two words come together in *miniseries,* which is often a "mini-serial" offering a continuous story in a few larger segments (from two to five).

For the librarian, **serial** is a general word for the magazine or journal which appears regularly, with a different miscellany of short articles each time from the same general field. A published **series** consists of several independent monographs, each of which finds a major subject in the same field.

◊ The plural of **series** is discussed under **Latin plurals**.

serial comma

See **comma** section 3.

serif

Serifs are the feet which mark the ends of letters in many typefaces, including this one. Many people argue that **serif** type is easier to read than its opposite *sans serif* (also written as *sanserif*). However this may have a lot to do with the fact that it has dominated the print medium. On screen, *sans serif* letters give a "cleaner" look because of the lower resolution of the digital medium. They are sometimes used for the text in computer manuals and other technical publications. *Sans serif* fonts are widely used to contrast with **serif** in headlines and headings. Whether they will supersede **serif** fonts as the common medium for the body text – just as roman fonts superseded italic ones – remains to be seen.

The word **serif** is occasionally respelled as *seriph,* either through confusion with the Hebrew word *seraph,* or just through substituting *ph* for *f* in a "foreign" word (see **f/ph**). The *f* is more appropriate seeing that the word is believed to be a variant of the Dutch *schreef* meaning a "stroke." It reminds us that the printing industry developed in England with the help of technology and people from the Low Countries.

serjeant or sergeant

See **sergeant**.

service

This word is increasingly used as a verb, meaning "provide services for", as in *serviced apartments* and *servicing the aircraft* (with consumables such as fuel, food and drink). **Service** often implies a maintenance role, of keeping machinery or other facilities in good running order, as in *servicing the car / gas fire.* Ongoing financial management is the focus of a *serviced debt/loan/investment.* In agriculture, **service** is the standard term for the mating of a male animal with females, as in *a small herd serviced by a pedigree bull.* But if applied to human activity, the implications are obscene, as in the following example from the BNC:

a lady called "Toss-Off Kate," who used to go round the audience and sit beside various isolated gentlemen and ask them if they wanted to be serviced.

This risky side of **service** can be raised unintentionally when the agent of the passive verb is identifiably female, as in *the hostel is serviced by a night nurse.* An abstract or inanimate agent helps to avert the problem, as in:

The hostel is serviced after hours through an external nursing agency.

There and elsewhere with the verb **service**, a nonhuman agent keeps the red light off.

settler or settlor

See under **-er/-or**.

several or a few
See under **few**.

sew
While the past tense of **sew** is always *sewed,* the past participle can be either *sewn* or *sewed,* according to all major dictionaries. The regular form *sewed* reflects the verb's origins in Old English, whereas *sewn* is a latter-day form originating as *sewen* in C17, and consolidated as *sewn* in C19. *Sewn* is now the dominant form in both British and American English, though some Americans make use of *sewed* as the past participle. In data from CCAE, *sewed* is occasionally used in references to domestic or surgical stitching, and especially in the idiom *sew up*:

> *O'Neill has the Republican nomination sewed up.*
British writers represented in the BNC overwhelmingly prefer *sewn up* for this idiom, and only rarely use *sewed* as past participle for the plying of thread.
◊ For other hybrid verbs with both regular and irregular forms, see **irregular verbs** section 9.

sewage or sewerage
Both these words date from mid-C19, when **sewerage** (a system of *sewers*) became part of the infrastructure of cities. The term **sewage** was backformed from *sewer* (and suffixed with *-age*) to refer to the waste material carried by the drainage system. By those definitions, it's taulogous to speak of a *sewerage system,* and *raw sewerage* is inexact. Yet as those examples show, **sewerage** sometimes appears instead of **sewage**, perhaps as a euphemism, or because its derivation is more transparent. The *Oxford Dictionary's* (1989) citations show **sewerage** being used instead of **sewage** from the beginning, and its definitions allow for it. *New Oxford* (1998) labels this "US," although there's a low level of use among British writers – in about 5% of BNC examples – exactly the same rate as in data from CCAE. *Merriam-Webster* (2000) acknowledges it by means of crossreferences.

sex or gender
Sociologists, among others, use these words to distinguish between biological and socially constructed identity, **sex** being used for the first and **gender** for the second. When the distinction is not salient, they are still often used interchangeably, as dictionaries such as *New Oxford* (1998), *Merriam-Webster* (2000), *Canadian Oxford* (1998) and *Macquarie* (1997) all allow. Mostly **gender** replaces **sex**, no doubt because the distractions of the latter word seem to call for avoidance tactics in some quarters. But the standard official form is unlikely to raise either embarrassment or amusement by asking people to declare their identity in the box marked **sex** – despite the broad jokes about what to put in it. See further under **gender**.

sexism in language
English has both natural and conventional ways of expressing human gender, of which the latter raise concerns because of their social implications. There would seem to be a masculine bias in the convention of using *he (his/him)* for generic purposes when the sex/gender is unspecified (see **gender** section 2). The same applies to English compounds and idioms involving *man,* whether or not they apply to both sexes, e.g. *chairman, manpower, man in the street.* Alternatives to various kinds of *sexism* in English are discussed under **nonsexist language**.

shaken or shook
The standard past forms of the verb *shake* are **shook** (past tense) and **shaken** (past participle), as in *shook hands, had shaken hands.* However **shook** is sometimes used as the past participle in conversation, especially in the phrase *all shook up* ("upset"). This was popularized in a songline of Elvis Presley, and is now used in America and elsewhere with a variety of modifiers: *pretty/quite/really shook up* – or with sublime understatement – *a little bit shook up.* Compare the standard form *a little shaken by the experience.*

Shakespearean or Shakespearian
Shakespeare himself varied the spelling of his name, and his ghost is unlikely to be troubled about whether the derivative adjective ends in **-ean** or **-ian**. Usage generally seems to go with **Shakespearean**, which is prioritized in current British and American dictionaries, and overwhelmingly preferred in American data from CCAE. British writers are more evenly divided, and both **Shakespearean** and **Shakespearian** are well represented in BNC data, in the ratio of 7:4.
◊ For other words which vary between *-ian* and *-ean,* see under **-an**.

shaky or shakey
See under **-y/-ey**.

shall or will
Traditional grammar made these complementary forms of the English future tense (see below, section 1). Yet they are not grammatical analogues of the past tense inflections, nor are they the only means of expressing futurity. Periphrastic auxiliary constructions provide a variety of others, such as:
> *am about to (leave)   am going to (leave)*
> *am to (leave)*
In conversational English, contracted forms of the verb phrase are commonly used to project events into the future:
> *I'll leave   I'm going to leave   I'm leaving*
Future events can also be expressed in the simple present tense (see under **present tense** and **future tense**). All these constructions, including **shall** and **will**, provide particular angles on what may come and the speaker/writer's orientation to it – like facets of the proverbial crystal ball. The relationship between **shall, will** and other modal verbs is discussed under **modality**.
1 Not simply the future. Grammarians have known for centuries that **shall** and **will** could express more than predictions of the future, and might indeed express volition or the determination that something should happen. Historically this meaning is associated with **will**, but in current English it's mostly associated with **shall**, as in legal statements to the effect that:
> *The Directors shall file a report on the company's financial posittion twice a year.*
Yet the distinction between intention and futurity can be hazy, and grammarians of C17 and C18 devised an

odd compromise whereby both **shall** and **will** could express one or the other, depending on the grammatical person involved. Their system was as follows:

(express future)

I/we shall   *you shall*   and   *he/she/it/they will*

(express intention)

I/we will   *you will*   and   *he/she/it/they shall*

Research by Fries (1925) into the language of English drama from C17 on showed that this division of labor was artificial even in its own time. The paradigms were however enshrined in textbooks of later centuries and still taught a few decades ago. Their neglect is one of the better consequences of abandoning the teaching of grammar in schools. The reappraisal of **shall/will** as *modal verbs* has provided fresh insight into their roles (see **modality**).

2 Shall and will in statements. Research associated with the *Longman Grammar* (1999) confirms that **will** occurs far more often than **shall** in all registers and modes (spoken and written). **Will** is "extremely common," where **shall** is relatively rare. When it occurs, **shall** more often expresses volition than a prediction of the future. The frequency of **will** is also boosted by use of the contraction *'ll* (as in *we'll*) which occurs so often in conversation. On phonetic grounds *'ll* is unlikely to be a reduced form of **shall**, because the "sh" sound is less likely to merge with surrounding vowels than "w." The decline of **shall** is more marked in the US and elsewhere than in the UK, as shown by Hundt's (1998) studies of comparable corpora of American, British, Australian and New Zealand English. In what follows we focus on the continuing British uses of **shall**, of which there are just residues in other Englishes.

The first question is whether British users of **shall** do prefer it for first person statements of the future. The principle is not backed up by BNC data, where instances of **will** with *I/we* outnumber **shall** in the ratio of 3:2, and the much larger ratio of 5:1 when contractions with *'ll* are factored in. Instead the data on **will/'ll** confirm that **shall** (with the first person) is associated with written rather than spoken style, and has become stylistically marked if not somewhat formal (Siemund, 1993). With second and third person pronouns, the preference for **will** is even stronger, and BNC data finds it in more than 97% of cases. The figure goes down a few percent (to around 92%), if you include third person subjects other than pronouns – those associated with legal or regulatory statements, illustrated above (section 1). But if you add in cases of **will** contracted to *'ll* with third person pronouns, the overall percentage climbs back up. Spoken usage in the UK (as everywhere else) is edging **shall** out.

3 Shall and will in questions. In questions which seek information about the future, **shall** is much more often found with first person pronouns than with second or third. These are the one context in which the old rules for **shall** and **will** (section 1 above) do seem to apply. In data from the BNC, more than 95% of questions using **shall** were in the first person (*I/we*). That is not to say that **will** never appears in first person questions: in fact they make up about 15% of all interrogative uses of **will**. But **will** dominates in second and third person questions. Of those phrased with *you* or *he/she/it/they*, more than 97% used **will**. These strong tendencies apply, whether the questions

asked seek information or advice, offer instructions or pose a request:

> *Shall I bring my lunch?*   *Shall we begin?*
> *Will you put it over there please?*
> *What will it contain?*   *Will he like me, Lily?*

The use of **shall** in first person questions, i.e. "polite" questions which allow others to take the affirmative, is further evidence of its stylistic marking in current British English.

International English selection: **Will** is now the standard choice for expressing future plans and expectations, everywhere in the world. **Shall** is stylistically marked with volitional meaning in legal and regulatory statements, and expresses politeness in first person questions.

---

shammy, chammy or chamois

See **chamois**.

shan't

This contracted negative form of *shall not* is more often used in British conversation and scripted speech than American, in line with the fact that **shall** survives better in the UK than the US (see **shall or will**).

Note that **shan't** usually appears with just one apostrophe nowadays, even though *shall* and *not* are both contracted in it (see **contractions** section 2). The *Oxford Dictionary* (1989) still notes **sha'n't** along with **shan't** as headword, but **shan't** is the only one to appear in *New Oxford* (1998), *Merriam-Webster* (2000), *Canadian Oxford* (1998) and the Australian *Macquarie Dictionary* (1997).

sharif or sherif

See under **sheriff**.

sharp or sharply

Most of the time, **sharp** serves as adjective, and **sharply** as an adverb. However **sharp** appears here and there, in idioms expressing direction, time, and musical pitch:

> *You must turn sharp left at the traffic lights.*
> *He arrived at 8 pm sharp.*
> *The violin was tuned a little sharp.*

In sentences like those, **sharp** is a zero adverb, and the only possible choice whether they are spoken or written. See further under **zero adverbs**.

she

This pronoun has gender built irrevocably into it, which is uncontroversial when you are referring to a female being (see **gender** section 2, on *natural gender*). Other uses of the pronoun **she** are not grounded in nature, but matters of convention. Sailors referring to their ships conventionally use **she**, and pronoun references to the names of countries are sometimes female, as in *Britain and her allies,* especially in rhetorical style. However in plainer contexts of communication this use of **she**/*her* is being steadily replaced by *it/its*.

Yet another use of **she** is neither natural nor conventional but an instrument of affirmative action. This is when writers substitute **she**/*her* for *he/him/his* when referring to an individual of unspecified gender, so as to redress the prevailing imbalance in the use of male and female pronouns for generic purposes. For example:

> Before calling the electrician, make sure you can show her where the fuses are.

Such attempts to create a generic she are distracting when attached to roles not traditionally performed by women, since they violate both cultural norms and linguistic convention. Nor does it help to use male and female pronouns in alternation, as some have suggested, so as to be "evenhanded" and help break down the gender stereotypes:

> The doctor must ensure that his paging device is turned on before she goes into the ward, and be prepared to respond within one minute to calls made to him by hospital staff. In the operating theatre, she should hand his device over to one of the nurses assisting . . .

However systematic the alternation of pronouns, the resulting text is incoherent because we rely on consistent sets of pronouns to provide cohesion in a text. (See further under **coherence or cohesion**.) Gender-free continuity cannot be achieved with either **she** or *he*, but there are other ways round the problem. See next entry, and **he and/or she**.

s/he

This combination pronoun recommends itself as a solution to the problem of how to refer quickly and comprehensively to both sexes. Like the less integrated **she/he**, it foregrounds the feminine pronoun rather than the masculine – and may therefore be a tad too affirmative for some. In fact it was first proposed in the 1970s (Baron, 1986); and *Merriam-Webster* (2000), *Canadian Oxford* (1998) and *New Oxford* (1998) all recognize it. In BNC data there are over 100 examples of **s/he** in various types of nonfiction and institutional prose, and it's more than twice as common as **she/he**.

S/he is effective when the pronoun is the subject, though there's no integrated form for object and possessive pronouns – only *her/him* or *her/his*. A natural solution is to use *them/their* which neutralizes the gender issue (see **they, them, their**).
◊ For other solutions to the pronoun problem, see **he and/or she**.

she-

She- has sometimes served as a simple gender prefix as in *she-goat* and *she-holly*. But in most words formed with it, the gender reference carries derogatory implications of one kind or another, as in *she-devil* and *she-poetry*. In the colonial era, various Australian trees were named with **she-**, including *she-beech, she-oak, she-pine*, where the name implied that the timber was "inferior . . . in respect of texture, colour or other character," according to Morris (1898). The ad hoc names disappeared with the era of heavy logging, to be replaced by latinate ones, e.g *she-oak* by *casuarina*. The disuse of **she-** in its prejudicial sense would seem to be a small victory for nonsexism in language – well before the movement dubbed **political correctness** (see further under that heading).

sheafs or sheaves

The older plural **sheaves** still prevails in American and British English for most uses of the word **sheaf** – whether as the stand of corn in older harvesting methods, or a bundle of cut rice, tobacco leaves or flowers. Only in reference to paper does **sheafs** gain a slice of the action, as in *sheafs of documents / paper orders / proposed legislation*. When **sheaves** is used, there is perhaps a hint of the old-fashioned or out-dated, as in *sheaves of yellowed printout*, but the plural itself often suggests a paper system grown (almost) out of control. See further under **-f/-v-**.

sheared, shore and shorn

This Old English verb has been slowly replacing its irregular past forms **shore** (past tense) and **shorn** (past participle) with the regular **sheared**. As often, the past tense was regularized first, and during C20 **sheared** became the standard form for cutting things off with shears, whether wool off the sheep's back or growth from the hedge: **shore** is now rather archaic. **Sheared** is also used intransitively to refer to metal objects breaking off under external forces, as in *the cable sheared*, or *it sheared the wheel off the wagon*.

As past participle, **sheared** still shares the field with **shorn**, in British and American English. In compound verbs, **sheared** is more likely than **shorn** (by a 2:1 ratio in the BNC as well as CCAE); but **shorn** comes into its own in metaphorical uses, especially coupled with *of*, as in *an economic system shorn of justice*. **Shorn** is also more commonly found as the ordinary attributive adjective, as in *shorn hair, shorn lamb, shorn cornfield*. Only in references to grades of fur, e.g. *sheared beaver*, is **sheared** the regular form of the adjective.

shed or shedded

Written into **shed**, there are two verbs. The older one meaning "drop" or "leave behind" goes back to Old English, and has both physical and figurative uses. Compare *trees shedding their leaves* with *shedding all caution*. It has exactly the same form (**shed**) for past and present (see further under **irregular verbs** section 1). The second verb dating back to C15 means just "put [a vehicle] into a shed." Its past form, usually past participle, is **shedded**, as in *Trams were temporarily shedded at the old depot*.

sheikh, sheik, shaikh or shaykh

The spelling **sheikh** is prioritized in *New Oxford* (1998), and used more frequently than any of the others by writers in the BNC. Yet closer inspection of the British data shows that **sheikh, shaikh** and **shaykh** are most commonly found in titles, such as *Sheikh Mohammed, Shaikh Abdel-Karim Obeid*, while generic uses of the word are quite often **sheik**, as in *an Arab sheik* or *a well-oiled sheik*. The revival of **shaikh** and **shaykh** in the 1990s reflects the revisionary process at work in various Arabic loanwords, bringing it closer to the Arabic source *sayk* ("old man"). Americans meanwhile continue to prefer **sheik/Sheik** in both generic and titular uses of the word, by the evidence of CCAE. This is in line with *Webster's Third* (1986) rather than *Merriam-Webster* (2000).

The choice between **sheikh** and **sheik** impacts also on the noun *sheik(h)dom*. So American data from CCAE shows a strong preference for *sheikdom*, whereas British usage seems mixed, amid very small samples of *sheik(h)dom(s)* in the BNC. The preference of *New Oxford* and *Merriam-Webster* for *sheikhdom* seems to reflect their position on **sheikh**, rather than the facts of usage.

shellac

When used as a verb, **shellac** acquires a *k* before suffixes beginning with a vowel: *shellacked, shellacking.* This is in keeping with the regular spelling practice of doubling the final consonant in inflected forms. See **-c/-ck-**.

sherbet or sherbert

The standard spelling for this sugary food is **sherbet**, reflecting its origins in Turkish *serbet* and relations with the French word *sorbet.* The variant **sherbert** is registered in *Merriam-Webster* (2000) and supported by data from CCAE, where it appears as an alternative to **sherbet** in about 12% of instances. According to *Webster's English Usage* (1989), its currency in the US may have been helped by its use for an ice confection – and in Australia by its slang application to beer: *pumped up by a few sherberts. Webster's English Usage* reports that its most recent evidence is "heavily British," and **sherbert** makes two small appearances in the BNC, though there are ten times as many of **sherbet**. In so far as **sherbert** represents a longish second vowel which has no "r" coloring, it's more likely to turn up in southern British and Australian pronunciation. However both *Webster's Third* (1986) and *Merriam-Webster* (2000) indicate an alternative American pronunciation with "r" in both syllables, matching the use of **sherbert** as an alternative spelling.

sheriff, sherif and sharif

A single letter makes the difference between Anglo-Saxon and American **sheriff** (a law-enforcement officer) and the Arab **sherif** (a Muslim ruler or descendant of Muhammad). But their origins set them far apart: **sheriff** was once a compound ("shire reeve"), while **sherif** is related to the Arabic *sarif* ("noble"). The Arabic source word also explains the trend to replace **sherif** with **sharif**, the standard form in recent dictionaries such as *New Oxford* (1998), *Merriam-Webster* (2000) and the *Canadian Oxford* (1998). **Sharif** is superseding both **sherif** and *shereef,* another older spelling which underscored the long vowel of the second syllable.

shew or show

The use of **shew** for **show** was already an archaism in C19, when the *Oxford Dictionary* found it "obsolete" except in legal use. It enjoys a limited afterlife in historical novels, by the evidence of the BNC, and in CCAE only in historical quotations. See further under **archaisms**.

shibboleth

Ancient and modern uses of this word combine to make it an apt label for linguistic fetishes of C21. The original **shibboleth** was a pronunciation testword used to distinguish those who could pronounce the initial "sh" sound, from others who would make it "s." According to the biblical story (*Judges* 12:4–6) Jephthah used the word **shibboleth** to distinguish his own Gileadite men from Ephraimites fleeing in disguise. In modern English the word **shibboleth** has been extended to the catchcry of a distinct party or sect, or a slogan whose impetus is emotional rather than rational and represents outdated sentiments.

The party **shibboleths** still serve to identify members and to exclude those who don't belong.

Many controversial points of English seem to be **shibboleths** for members of a notional party for the protection of pure English. The insistence on *different from,* the avoidance of split infinitives, and the preservation of the subjunctive are planks in the party platform, endorsed without any critical thought about their basis in contemporary English. More damagingly, they are made the touchstones of "correct" English, to which everyone must adhere or be damned.

This book tries to address issues like those which have tended to become **shibboleths**, to open them up to linguistic analysis, and to query their use by some as all-powerful criteria for judgements about writing. See also **fetish**.

shine

The verb **shine** has traditionally been irregular with *shone* as both past tense and past participle, and *shone* is still standard when referring to light or other kinds of luminescence:

Through the glass shone God's sun.
. . . shone the torch around the shed
His humanity had always shone through.

Other data from the BNC show that British writers occasionally use *shone* for the verb meaning "polish": *I shone a table that she had just aerosolled.* But the regular form *shined* is usual when it's a matter of polishing shoes:

His shoes were shined to perfection.

American writers make more use of *shined,* not only when the verb means "polish," but as an alternative in other senses of **shine**:

The day shined blankly.
. . . shined a flashlight through the hole
Everybody in the team shined.

Such uses of *shined* are regarded as standard by *Webster's English Usage* (1989), though in data from CCAE, *shone* still outnumbers *shined* overall by a factor of 2:1. *Canadian English Usage* (1997) notes it as an acceptable but less common form. The transformation of **shine** into a regular verb is thus ongoing, even in North America. See further under **irregular verbs** section 9.

-ship

Abstract nouns are still being formed with this Old English suffix. They include words associated with particular skills or pursuits, such as:

courtship	friendship	horsemanship
marksmanship	salesmanship	scholarship
showmanship	workmanship	

From these have developed words referring to a distinctive status or position in a given field, as in:

apprenticeship	championship	editorship
headship	internship	leadership
lecturership	tutorship	

Occasionally the suffix refers not to the role of an individual, but to a group or community with a special bond: *kinship, membership, township. Fellowship* is probably the most evolved of the **-ship** words – capable of bearing either the second or third sense, and even functioning as a verb in church communities: *they fellowship(p)ed after the service.* For the spelling, see under **-p/-pp-**.

shishkebab or shishkabob

See under **kebab**.

shit, shat or shitted

The verb **shit** is much rarer than the noun, and its past tense even rarer – hence the uncertainty about its form, and lack of agreement among dictionaries as to what is most likely. *Merriam-Webster* (2000) makes it **shit**, *Canadian Oxford* (1998) **shat**, and both *New Oxford* (1998) and the Australian *Macquarie* (1997) have **shitted**. Database evidence is naturally scarce, though **shat** is more frequent than **shitted** in the BNC, and there's scant evidence of **shit** as a past tense in CCAE (only **shat** and **shitted**). In both the UK and the US, the verb is irregular rather than regular: see **irregular verbs** sections 1 and 3.

shoe-in or shoo-in

See **shoo-in**.

shone or shined

See **shine**.

shoo-in or shoe-in

The dead-certain-to-win candidate is a **shoo-in**, like the horse who wins by fraud, in North American racing slang. The variant spelling **shoe-in** suggests perhaps that a **shoo-in** candidate is *shoe-horned* into a position. Like most spellings based on *folk etymology* (see under that heading), it owes a lot to coincidence.

shook or shaken

See **shaken**.

shoot, shute or chute

See under **chute**.

shore, shorn or sheared

See under **sheared**.

short messaging/message service

See **SMS**.

short titles

The **short title** reduces the full title of a book or article to its key words, in a phrase of from two to four words. So the *Longman Grammar of Spoken and Written English* is referred to as simply *Longman Grammar.* An article with a longish title: *New configurations: the balance of British and American English in Canadian and Australian English* can be short-titled as *New configurations.* **Short titles** can be given more or fewer capitals, according to the context (see **titles** section 1). Titles consisting of less than five words are not usually shortened. **Short titles** are now widely used in referencing, as in this book, and in footnotes instead of Latin abbreviations such as *loc.cit.* and *op.cit.* See further under **referencing** section 1.

should or would

In current English **should** and **would** diverge very markedly in their use, leaving few points at which you might choose between them. They originated as the past forms of **shall** and **will**, and like them used to alternate with each other in first, second and third person constructions (see **shall or will** section 1). But **would** is now almost invariably used for expressing the future-in-past for all three persons, according to *Longman Grammar* (1999) research. For example:

> *I said I would expect to come.*
> *You said you would expect to come.*
> *They said they would expect to come.*

Should serves to express prediction/volition instead of **would** only in deferential style. Compare:

> *I should like to come*   *I would like to come*
> *I should be delighted*   *I would be delighted.*

This rather formal style is much more British than American. Comparative data from the BNC and CCAE show that its use is seven times more frequent in the UK than the US. Even in the UK, **I should** is increasingly formulaic, largely confined to the common verbs of thinking and feeling, e.g. *hope, like, think* – and to the first person singular. The linguistic constraints on it are tighter than for *shall* in its formal and polite uses (see **shall or will** sections 2 and 3).

Other uses of **should** make it a modal verb of obligation and necessity, whereas **would** continues to express volition and/or future possibilities, on which see below. An overview of the relationship between **should**, **would** and other modal verbs is to be found under **modality**.

1 Current uses of should. The major role of **should** nowadays, in English everywhere, is to express obligation or necessity:

> *We should call for submissions from the public.*
> *A teacher should have a sense of humor.*
> *The budget should have been submitted with the proposal.*

Should combines freely with other auxiliaries marking aspect and voice, according to the *Longman Grammar,* and in nonfiction writing especially with the passive (as in the third example). Alternatives to **should** in this sense are the semi-modals *ought (to)* and *need (to):* see under **ought** and **need**.

Should is also frequently found in subordinate clauses (*content clauses*) that express a wish, a plan, a judgement or an obligation:

> *They proposed that we should meet next month.*
> *It's important that we should meet soon.*
> *His insistence that we should meet soon carried the day.*

In British English, **should** constructions like these are the commonest alternative to the *mandative subjunctive,* though not in American and other varieties (see under **subjunctive**).

Meanwhile **should** appears less and less often in conditional statements:

> *If I should never return, you will have proof of their menace.*
> *Should they ask questions, their support is not to be counted on.*

Conditional uses of **should** now sound rather lofty, though the inverted **should** at the start of the clause is still a neat way of prefacing a condition.

2 Current uses of would. Apart from being the usual way to express the hypothetical future, **would** often expresses willingness and preference, as in *I would support that line.* With third person subjects, it expresses a moderate degree of probability:

> *He would have come if he had known.*

The example shows also how **would** readily combines with *have/has* to mark the perfect aspect of the verb, as noted in the *Longman Grammar.*

Less common uses of **would** are to voice a conjecture, and to formulate a habit:

> *That would be the first time they admitted it.*
> *She would walk for half an hour every morning.*

Would is also found in some conventional expressions of politeness:

> *Would the ladies please step this way.*
> *If you would care to look at the screen...*
> *It would be a pleasure.*

The polite use of **would** is often underscored, as in these examples, by its combination with other signals of politeness, e.g. "please," "care to."

The contraction *'d,* commonly found in conversation, is a reduced form of **would** rather than **should**. On phonetic grounds it could hardly be **should**, given that *sh* is a distinctly formed consonant and much less likely to merge with the following vowel than *w*, which is a semi-vowel.

should of or should've

See under **have**.

shoveled or shovelled, shoveling or shovelling

The choice between using single or double *l* is discussed under **-l-/-ll-**.

show or shew

See **shew**.

showed or shown

Dictionaries both British and American allow that the verb *show* may have either **shown** or **showed** for its past participle:

> *Russia has showed its intentions.*
> *The public has shown no great interest in the affair.*
> *Nobody has showed up.*
> *The video has been shown to tourists.*

Yet the two participles are not entirely interchangeable. The *Oxford Dictionary* (1989) notes that **showed** is used as an alternative only in active constructions, whereas **shown** can be either active or passive. The examples above, all from CCAE, confirm that the same governing principles hold in American and British English – although constructions with **showed** as past participle are not very common in either.

shredded or shred

When things are reduced to *shreds,* some dictionaries still allow both **shredded** and **shred** for the past forms (past tense and participle). But there's scant evidence of past uses of **shred** in either American or British databases, and its use as past participle was archaic for Gowers (1965). The form **shredded** is now far more common than any verbal use of **shred**, past or present, by the evidence of CCAE and the BNC. Its uses in culinary products such as *shredded cabbage/coconut/lettuce/wheat* are matched by those freely formed outside the kitchen such as *shredded paper, a shredded tyre, tents shredded by the storm.* **Shredded** is also the form used for simple and compound past tenses:

> *He shredded official documents before vacating his office.*
> *N's confidence was shredded by his rival's desire to win.*

Meanwhile **shred** is much more often used for the noun (*not a shred of evidence*) than as the verb's present or unmarked tense.

shrink

This verb has long had three principal parts: **shrink**/*shrank*/*shrunk*. Yet while *shrank* is the standard past tense, *shrunk* is not uncommonly heard instead of *shrank,* and certainly not an archaism, as Fowler (1926) thought. Mid-C20 regional surveys in eastern and mid-western US found 80% of respondents used *shrunk* rather than *shrank,* and it went round the world in the 1989 movie title *Honey, I shrunk the kids.* Still *shrunk* appears less often than *shrank* in American writing. In data from CCAE, the ratio of *shrunk* to *shrank* is about 1:5, though the examples show a range of constructions, transitive and intransitive:

> *International interest shrunk as the cold war ebbed.*
> *Cold weather shrunk the attendance at the fair.*
> *Their lead shrunk to 31–25 at half time.*
> *...a dry cleaner that shrunk his shirt.*
> *N. shrunk back in the chair.*

All this makes *shrunk* an acceptable alternative past tense in American English, and it's presented as such in *Merriam-Webster* (2000). But there's no recognition of it in *New Oxford* (1998), and less evidence of its use in British writing: just a sprinkling of examples in BNC data.

Note that *shrunken* is strictly an adjective, as in *a shrunken head* or, figuratively, *a shrunken market.*

shute, shoot or chute

See **chute**.

SI units

These form the units of the *Système International* which are the basis of the metric system. See further under **metrication** and in Appendix IV.

Sian

See under **China**.

sic

This Latin word means literally "thus." Scholarly editors use it when they wish to signal that the wording of a quotation is exactly as found in the source, even if the choice of words seems surprising or erroneous in some way. For example:

> "Sydney Harbor Bridge is one of the most elegant suspension [*sic*] bridges in the world"
> "To seperate [*sic*] emotion from pure reason is the ultimate spiritual exercise"

As the examples show, **sic** is placed in brackets immediately after the word in question. It usually appears in italics, and is framed by square brackets rather than parentheses, to show that it's an editorial interpolation. (See further under **brackets**.)

Sic is essentially a neutral device which says "That's how it was." Yet because it questions the wording of another writer, it introduces a critical element. Done too often, it also distracts from the substance of the quotation. One of the less attractive suggestions of Maggio's *Nonsexist Wordfinder* (1988) was to use **sic** to mark sexist usage of *man,* etc. whenever it turned up in quotations. A footnote on the matter could acknowledge the presence of sexist language without intruding on the quotation itself.

sideward or sidewards
See -ward or -wards.

sideways or sidewise
See under -wise or -ways.

signaled or signalled, signaling or signalling
The choice between using single or double *l* is discussed under -l-/-ll-.

signor, signore or signora
These Italian titles and forms of address keep their Italian patterns of inflection, unlike common Italian loanwords (see **Italian plurals**). **Signor** is equivalent to "Mr" and the standard title referring to men, even *Il signor Caruso*. In direct address to men, **Signore** serves as the equivalent of "Sir." **Signora** is used both for "Mrs" in ordinary titles for women, and for "Madam" in direct address. The plural of **signora** is **signore** – just like the masculine singular form of address. But the masculine plural **signori** is distinctive, and keeps the sexes apart.

silent letters
Many English words have **silent letters** in their spelling, i.e. ones which do not correspond to a particular sound in the pronunciation. Quite often they represent sounds which were heard in the word centuries ago, as with *knife, light, write*. Some **silent letters** were added to words in early modern English, either to connect the English spelling with classical antecedents, as with *debt, isle, rhyme;* or to distinguish homophones, as with *grille, racquet, sheriff.* The examples show that most letters of the alphabet can be silent in a few words.

The most common **silent letter** of all in English is *e*. It has developed several roles as a diacritic marker of the sound values of adjacent letters. Following a *c* or *g*, as in *traceable* or *wage,* the *e* serves to "soften" the sound. (See further under -ce/-ge.) In many simple words it serves to show that the vowel before the preceding consonant is long or else a diphthong. Compare:

mate	with	*mat*
mete		*met*
bite		*bit*
rode		*rod*
tube		*tub*

Silent letters have often been the target of spelling reformers, who are inclined to see them as phonetic deadwood. This makes them overlook what **silent letters** do for visual recognition of words, helping us to distinguish homophones at first glance (e.g. *sign/sine*), and forging links between related words whose pronunciation sets them apart (e.g. *sign/signify*). See further under **spelling** sections 1 and 5.

silicon, silicone and silica
The ending makes a crucial difference for chemists and for us all. **Silicon** is a hard, nonmetallic element, commonly found in sand. **Silicone** is a plastic compound that includes **silicon**, carbon and oxygen.

Of the two, **silicon** is better known and more widely used, through the *silicon chip* which is the staple of electronics and the computer industry. **Silicone** is a synthetic rubber, used for such things as artificial limbs and in cosmetic surgery, and also an ingredient of various lubricants and polishes. **Silica** is an alternative name for another **silicon** compound, *silicon oxide* (or *dioxide*), used in the manufacture of glass and ceramics.

silvan or sylvan
See under i/y.

similes
See under **metaphors**.

simple or simplistic
Simple is an uncomplicated word which means "straightforward, easy," as in *a simple solution.* Compare *a simplistic solution*, which is too easy, i.e. it oversimplifies and fails to deal with the complexities of the situation. So **simplistic** is negatively charged, whereas **simple** is neutral or has positive connotations. Because **simplistic** is the longer and more academic-looking word, it's sometimes misguidedly chosen by those who want to make their words more impressive. The result can be disastrous, as in:

> *This software represents the state-of-the-art in information-retrieval systems, and comes with simplistic instructions on how to operate it.*

Heaven help the operator!

simple sentences
See **clauses** section 1.

simulacrum
This Latin loanword meaning "image" is at home among the semioticians. When dropped into everyday prose – in phrases such as *a simulacrum of a dream world / self-management / the eighteenth century, a Disneylandish simulacrum,* or *a danger-free simulacrum [of genuine adventure]* – it seems a hefty way of saying that something presents a likeness (strong or weak) of something else. Perhaps it's the only possible word . . . once you know it! Its academic feel is underscored by the fact that its plural is still almost always the Latin **simulacra**. There's scant evidence of **simulacrums** in the BNC or CCAE, though dictionaries such as *New Oxford* (1998) and *Merriam-Webster* (2000) are prepared for it.

since
As a conjunction **since** is sometimes ambiguous, because it can express a relationship of either time, or cause and effect:

> *They haven't stopped talking since they arrived* (time)
> *The others just smiled since they were too polite to interrupt* (cause)

The first use is more common than the second, and it coincides with temporal use of **since** as an adverb and preposition. Yet the second (causative) use hangs around as an alternative possibility in sentences such as:

> *The children have avoided going out since their father lost his job.*

To settle any ambiguity, it would be better to use a conjunction which is unmistakably temporal or causative. See further under **conjunctions** section 3.

sine

These letters add up to a one-syllabled word used in mathematics (where **sine** contrasts with *cosine*); and a two-syllabled word in several elliptical Latin phrases where it means "without." *Sine die* means "without [setting] a day." It is noted when a formal group disbands without deciding on the date of their next meeting. Sometimes it implies indefinite postponement. *Sine qua non* is literally "without which not." It refers to something indispensable, without which things could not happen or be achieved.
◊ For *sine prole,* see under **decessit sine prole**.

sing, sang and sung

In standard English everywhere, **sang** is used as the past tense, and **sung** as the past participle. But **sung** does replace **sang** in casual conversation from time to time, as in: *the songs that they sung* or *top excutives sung praises for the legislation.* Data from the BNC and CCAE show that past tense use of **sung** very occasionally appears in writing in both the US and the UK, but only *Webster's Third* (1986) and *Merriam-Webster* (2000) allow it as a variant.

Singaporean or Singaporian

The standard spelling for the adjective associated with the island state of *Singapore* is **Singaporean**. The original *Oxford Dictionary* noted the use of **Singaporian**, but there's no sign of it in British or American data from the BNC or CCAE. See further under -**an**.

single for double

The use of *single* or *double consonants* is often crucial to the identity of words, witness *latter* and *later, supper* and *super*. In some verbs this makes the contrast between present (*write*) and past (*written*), and is again a fixed and permanent aspect of the spelling. Yet the use of single and double consonants is also a variable aspect of some words. Like many spelling variables its roots go back to C18. Johnson vacillated over it, and in his dictionary of 1755 we notice pairs such as *distil* and *instill*, and *downhil* versus *uphill*. Discrepancies like those suggest that earlier on in the dictionary he applied a spelling rule which he later abandoned. The practice of reducing two *l*s to one at the end of a word underlies certain distinctive British spellings, such as *appal, enthral, extol* which contrast with American *appall, enthrall, extoll.* It was also applied in the middle of words such as:

> already   altogether   chilblain   dulness   fulfil
> fulness   skilful   wilful

The double *l* has returned to *dullness* and *fullness,* and to the second element of *fulfill* for many people. American English also has it in *skillful* and *willful* (see further under individual headings).

In loanwords, the tendency to replace double with single consonants can also be seen (though more erratically). It creates alternative spellings for some like *cannel(l)oni,* and affects consonants other than *l,* in *cap(p)uc(c)ino, gar(r)ot(t)e, guer(r)illa.* In American spelling it's sometimes seen in *diarrhea* written as *diarhea,* and *hemorrhage* as *hemorhage.* Many loanwords like these are without analogues in

English, so there's no clear rationale for keeping the double consonant.

All this helps to explain why the question of single or double consonants vexes many a writer. Unfortunately it does not change the fact that double consonants are fixed into the spelling of many English words by virtue of their etymology. It is still considered a mistake to write *accomodation* for *accommodation, exagerate* for *exaggerate* etc.

singular

See under **number**.

Sinhalese or Singhalese

See under **Sri Lanka**.

sink, sank and sunk

The standard past tense for **sink** is of course **sank**, and **sunk** the past participle. Yet **sunk** is sometimes heard and seen instead of **sank**, as in:

> ... *the round table approach which sunk the Communist party.*
> *The last European to try it sunk $5 million into the production.*
> ... *inspect the barge for damage incurred when it sunk in November...*
> *It took some time before the lesson sunk in.*
> *That's what sunk me.*

Examples like these – all from writing – show how the typical site for **sunk** as the past tense is a subordinate clause. It is commoner in American than British English, in comparative data from CCAE and the BNC; and **sunk** is allowed as an alternative past form in *Merriam-Webster* (2000) but not in *New Oxford* (1998).

The older past participle *sunken* is rarely found nowadays in the verb phrase, and mostly serves as an adjective, as in *a sunken garden.* However **sunk** too can be an adjective, in technical expressions such as *sunk fence.*

sinus

The English plural **sinuses** was favored by more than 85% of respondents to the Langscape survey (1998–2001), setting aside the zero plural it would have as a Latin fourth conjugation noun. See further under -**us** section 2.

siphon or syphon

See under **i/y**.

Sir

Convention has it that **Sir** cannot be used with a plain surname – unlike most other titles such as *Dr(.), Mr(.), Professor,* which can appear with or without a given name. But with **Sir**, the given name is always mentioned, as for *Sir Henry Wood,* founder of the London Promenade concerts ("the Proms") and never "Sir Wood." The same convention applies to *Dame,* as in *Dame Margot Fonteyn, Dame Judi Dench* etc.
◊ For the use of **Sir** in letter writing, see **forms of address** section 2.

sirup or syrup

See **syrup**.

sissy or cissy

The negative value in this word come from its being an abbreviated form of *sister.* The connection is just visible in **sissy**, but it disappears in **cissy**, suggesting that it's no longer known or thought relevant. **Sissy** remains the only spelling in North America, according to *Merriam-Webster* (2000) and the *Canadian Oxford* (1998). In Britain both spellings are recognized – and occur about equally often in data from the BNC. The personal name *Cissy* (short for *Cecilia*) may be an influence on the spelling.

sister-in-law
See **in-laws**.

situ
See **in situ**.

sizable or sizeable
See under **-eable**.

skeptic or sceptic, skeptical or sceptical, and skepticism or scepticism

Skeptic perpetuates the Greek form of the word and was indeed the earlier form in English, which helps to explain its use in American English. It was also used by Dr. Johnson in his dictionary, and preferred by Fowler (1926) because it works better in terms of English spelling-sound conventions (see **-ce/-ge**). The *Oxford English Dictionary* (1989) gives priority to the French-style spellings with *sc,* and British writers in the BNC overwhelmingly prefer them, despite the occasional confusion of **sceptic** with *septic*, as in: *the Chelsea (football) captain has a sceptic foot and is very doubtful!*

Skeptic/skeptical/skepticism are standard in the US, and preferred by many Canadians, according to *Canadian English Usage* (1997). Australians generally side with the British, despite the **skeptics** among them (see Murray-Smith, 1989).

In choosing between **skeptic/sceptic** and **skeptical/sceptical**, writers of the world unite in preferring the latter for the adjective. Meanwhile **skeptic/sceptic** is used as a noun in about 90% of all occurrences of the word in the BNC, and 99% in CCAE.

> **International English selection:** The classical spellings **skeptic/skeptical/skepticism** recommend themselves in terms of etymology, as well as being more straightforward in terms of pronunciation. This is an advantage for second-language users of English in Europe and elsewhere, apart from their strong base in North America.

skew or skewer

These two sometimes tangle with each other in figurative applications. It happens when **skewer**, used in North American English to mean "criticize" (as in *the research has been both applauded and skewered*) appears instead of **skew** (meaning "distort, bias," as in *results skewed by sampling error*). Examples from CCAE include:

> *The analysis could be skewered by the practice of rehiring.*
> *Spike Lee's skewered gaze at a black college*
> *I have a very skewered version [of the book/movie], because of the people who write to me.*

As in all those cases, **skewer** is used where you would legitimately expect **skew**.

skilful or skillful

The older spelling is **skillful**, and it remains standard in the US, according to *Merriam-Webster* (2000). American data from CCAE shows it's used in about 96% of all instances of the word. In the UK the spelling was modified to **skilful** in C18 and affirmed through Dr. Johnson's dictionary from 1755. **Skilful** has since become the standard spelling in the UK, used in over 95% of all instances in BNC data. Canadians and Australians make use of both spellings, according to the *Canadian Oxford* (1998) and the *Macquarie Dictionary* (1997); but **skilful** is given priority over **skillful**.

skim milk or skimmed milk
See under **inflectional extras**.

slang

Broadly speaking **slang** is language which refuses to conform. It sidesteps the vocabulary of standard English, and creates its own, sometimes offhanded and casual (like *cop*), sometimes direct and coarse (like *rip off* and *in the shit*). **Slang** has frontiers with colloquial language, as well as with the taboo and obscene.

Unlike standard language **slang** is always somewhat limited in its currency. It's often short-lived – witness words such as *cool, neat, unreal. Slang words* of commendation never seem to last long, and even those for tangible things (*the flicks*) lose their currency over time. A few *slang words* work their way into the standard: *bus, cheat, dwindle, mob* are examples from C18. But thousands more live and die in the same century, and even the same decade.

The currency of **slang** is often limited also by being used by a particular group of people, defined by their age, social class, occupation or recreation. The use of *bad (badder, baddest)* to mean "great" has been part of youth slang, just as *googly* is best known among cricketers and their fans. The knowledge of such terms and the natural right to use them goes with belonging to such groups, and the words also serve to exclude those who do not belong. Many *slang words* are limited geographically. Some are confined to the US or the UK, and some only used in a particular state or region, such as the Deep South or Texas. (See further under **dialect**.)

All these limitations on **slang** help to explain why it's usually avoided in formal prose, and in any writing which has to communicate to a wide audience or withstand the test of time. It is more than a matter of style, if you want to be sure that the meaning gets through. Ronald Reagan puzzled the international community as to what deficiencies of character went with the American word *flaky*. **Slang** is a liability if you forget or don't know the limits of its use.

The vigor and vitality of **slang** still makes it a useful resource now and then for making a point. A phrase like *golden handshake* expresses a certain cynicism about the retirement packages offered to company directors, in a way that the standard phrase never could. The Hansard records of parliament nowadays include the **slang** uttered by members in the course of debate, to ensure that the flavor of the debate comes across along with its substance.
◊ See further under **colloquialisms**, **jargon** and **rhyming slang**.

slash (forward or back)

The word **slash** is the general name for the single, forward-leaning oblique stroke (/) used to mark alternatives or to separate segments in an internet address. More specifically it's a *forward slash,* though editors know it by various other names (see further under **solidus**). *Forward slashes* used in pairs are *slash brackets:* see **brackets** section 1d.

The *backslash* (\) is used in computer programming as a metacharacter, to indicate commands and assign special values to regular characters. Mathematicians and logicians use it in set theory to indicate difference.

slated

The verb *slate* is everywhere used to mean "cover with slates," as in *tiled and slated roofs.* But it carries more abstract meanings in both the UK and the US. British speakers and writers use it informally to mean "criticize strongly," as in *the products are slated as boring and overpriced.* North Americans meanwhile use it to mean "propose" or "schedule," especially in the passive, as in the headline *Scottish artworks slated to go west,* or *the trial was slated for November.* This "American" usage is now catching on in Britain, and is actually more common than the British use of **slated** in written data from the BNC.

Slavic, Slavonic or Slavonian

Slavonian is the oldest of the three adjectives (dating from 1598), and now the least used, best known to bird-watchers in the name *Slavonian Grebe.* **Slavonic** (from 1645) is now mostly associated with the languages and culture of the Slavs, as in *Slavonic Studies* and *Slavonic Dances.* **Slavic** is the youngest of the three (from 1813) and the most freely used in reference to recent historical, political and ethnic issues.

slay, slew, slue and slough

The verb **slay** has two almost opposite senses:
1   "kill" in older and literary usage, and
2   "overwhelm with pleasure or amusement," in colloquial usage

For the first sense the past tense is **slew** (*St George slew the dragon*) and the past participle **slain.** For the second it becomes a regular verb with past form *slayed,* as in *she really slayed them.*

Quite independent of **slay** is the nautical verb **slew,** used to mean "swing around," "skid," with *slewed* as past tense/participle: *the plane slewed to the right.* In British English, *slewed* is also an informal word for "intoxicated." In American English **slew** can also be spelled **slue,** as in *the plane slued to the right,* but it's a rarely used alternative in data from CCAE.

Meanwhile **slew** also does service as a noun in the idiom *a slew of* meaning "a lot of." Based on Irish *slua* ("army") it originated in North America, and appears in less formal writing in both the US and the UK, by the evidence of CCAE and the BNC: *a slew of films / papers / endorsements / software packages.* Non-Americans would be surprised to find that this use of **slew** is sometimes mistakenly spelled **slough,** as in "a slough of papers." This has less to do with the despond they create than the fact that the word *slough* ("bog") is commonly pronounced "slew" in American English – everywhere except in New England, according to *Merriam-Webster* (2000). In idiomatic

uses of **slough,** such as *a slough of despair/ignorance/materialism,* the noun following is singular rather than plural. *Merriam-Webster* does not allow **slough** as an alternative spelling for **slew** as a noun.

Slough is nevertheless connected with other variant spellings in *Merriam-Webster.* **Slue** is an accepted alternative for the noun **slough** ("bog"), while *sluff* is listed for the verb **slough** ("cast off"). Both reflect common (local) pronunciation, and find ways out of the *slough of confusion* that goes with words ending in *-ough.* See further under **-gh.**

sled, sledge, sleigh, toboggan or luge

The first three words all go back to a Dutch word for a snow vehicle. **Sled** is the general term used in North America for vehicles on which loads or people are towed, or for the downhill slide enjoyed by children. In Britain both are called a **sledge.** The term **sleigh** distinguishes the larger type of **sled(ge)** used especially for ceremonial purposes (not to mention Father Christmas / Santa Claus). Both **sleigh** and **sled(ge)** have runners for smooth riding, whereas **toboggans** usually do without them – which makes for more exciting travel. **Toboggan** is a loanword from Canadian Indians, but well known internationally through having long been an Olympic sport. Much more recent is the **luge** (borrowed from Swiss French), a light racing **sled** with runners, which is ridden supine (feet first) to enhance the thrills.

slew or slayed

See under **slay.**

sling

Slung now serves for all past forms of the verb **sling,** whether it means "throw" as in *slung the body over the cliff,* or "hook over," as in *a camera slung over his shoulder.* "Slang" was last seen as the past tense in C19, according to the *Oxford Dictionary* (1989).

slink

The verb **slink** lost "slank" as its past tense in C19, leaving *slunk* for both past tense (*they slunk away*) and past participle (*when all the teachers have slunk off home*). There are however signs of a regular past tense on the fringes of both American and British English, witness a handful of examples from CCAE and BNC such as:

He slinked away from a CBS interview.
Onto the stage slinked a tall woman.

Slinked is registered in *Merriam-Webster* (2000) but not *New Oxford* (1998).

Slovak

See under **Czechoslovakia.**

slow and slowly

Formally speaking **slow** is the adjective, and **slowly** the adverb. But **slow** is often used as the adverb in short utterances and commands, such as *go slow,* and in compound adjectives such as *slow-release drugs* and *slow-speaking assistant.*

When it comes to comparatives and superlatives, again the adjective forms *slower* and *slowest* often serve as adverbs too, as in:

My traffic lane moved slower than yours.

Compare:

> *My traffic lane moved more slowly than yours.*

The second sentence would be preferable in more formal styles of writing, but the first is common in conversation. See further under **zero adverbs**.

slue or slew

See under **slay, slew, slue and slough**.

sluff or slough

See under **slay, slew, slue and slough**.

sly

The derivatives of this adjective are usually spelled with *y* rather than *i*: *slyer, slyly, slyness.* See further under **-y>-i-**.

small caps

For editors this is the common abbreviation for *small capital letters,* ones which have the form of CAPITALS but roughly half their height. (In typographic terms, they are close to the x-height of the regular type.) **Small caps** are used in running text to set words off from those on either side, without making them distractingly LARGE. In North American style they are commonly used in time and date abbreviations such as *AM/PM* and *AD/BC*.

small-scale

See under **scale**.

smell

The past tense of this verb can be either *smelled* or *smelt* in British English. In BNC data, *smelt* has the numerical edge over *smelled,* by a factor of roughly 7:5. In American English it's most likely to be *smelled,* by almost 70:1 in data from CCAE. (See further under **-ed** section 1).

Note also that **smell** can be followed by either an adjective or an adverb:

> *It smelled good.*
> *It smelled strongly of coffee.*

In the first sentence, *smelled* acts as a copular verb; in the second it expresses a material event. See further under **verbs**.

smiley or smily

In both the UK and the US, **smiley** is the dominant spelling, whether the word is used as an adjective (*I'm a smiley person*) or as the noun for the "smiley face" icon, popularized on badges and stickers during the 1970s (*a yellow smiley on his lapel*). The regular spelling **smily** (see **-e**) was preferred by the *Oxford Dictionary* (1989); but it has no currency in data from the BNC or CCAE, and neither *New Oxford* (1998) nor *Merriam-Webster* (2000) mentions it. Perhaps Le Carré's spy master *George Smiley,* and *Jane Smiley,* the American prize-winning novelist, have stamped the *-ey* spelling on our consciousness. At any rate, **smiley** has a hold on the future as the spelling for one of the best known *emoticons.* It turns the round-faced icon into one that's more elongated [:>)], but still a token of the happy writer in e-mail or other correspondence. See further under **emoticons**.

smitten

While the verb *smite* slides into archaism, its past participle **smitten** remains perfectly current in the sense of being overcome mentally or emotionally. The only question is whether to construe it with *by* or *with*. The British make about equal use of the two constructions, in BNC examples such as *smitten with remorse* or *by homesickness, smitten with Steve* or *by Sandra's good looks.* Americans are more inclined towards *smitten with* when it's a case of X falling in love with Y: *smitten with a handsome priest / hippie artist.* But they tend to use *smitten by* when referring to other passions and preoccupations: *smitten by ambition / the local wine / Niagara Falls,* in data from CCAE.

smoky or smokey

See under **-y/-ey**.

smoulder or smolder

The first is the standard spelling in Britain and Australia, the second in the US. Both are well used in Canada, according to *Canadian English Usage* (1997). **Smolder** is the older of the two, first recorded as a verb in C15. Its origins are rather obscure, and it seems to have gone underground during C17 and C18 – much like the kind of fire it refers to – before being revived in C19 by Sir Walter Scott.

SMS

This abbreviation is explained as "short messaging service" or "short message system," reflecting the service-provider's point of view, and that of the user. **SMS** represents a large slice of telecommunicated conversation among young people. It provides shortened forms of words and phrases, often omitting the vowels as in *TXT* for "text," and using letters and numbers for their sound values, as in *CUL8R* ("see you later"), or just the first letters of words of a formula, e.g. *BTDT* ("been there done that"). The **SMS** handheld device completes the standardized items for the user after one or two letters have been provided, and so a thumb is all that's needed to set up the message. **SMS** conversations are limited by the resources of the code, yet they have their own kind of appeal even on larger computer screens, and extensions of **SMS** are used among members of certain internet communities. One such is *l33tsp34k,* i.e. "LeetSpeak," where the first element is "elite." The fact that **SMS** engages people so strongly does not mean the end of English or literacy as we know it – just a hi-tech example of the age-old pastime of sharing a code.

sneaked or snuck

After centuries of regular behavior, *sneak* has acquired an irregular past form **snuck** alongside **sneaked**. Whatever its dialect origins, **snuck** was first recorded in the southern US, in later C19. It has since crept into American written usage via fiction and humorous journalism, and is increasingly used as a simple alternative to **sneaked**:

> *. . . an intelligence agent snuck him on board an American submarine*
> *Like it or not, disco has snuck back.*

In CCAE data, **snuck** appears in about 30% of all instances of the past, and is gaining on the 2:7 ratio vis-à-vis **sneaked** which was reported in the *American Heritage Dictionary* (1991). In Canada **snuck** has made rapid strides towards acceptability even in more formal styles, according to *Canadian English Usage* (1997). British writers still keep it at arm's length, where it appears in less than 10% of expressions of the past tense.

The trend towards using **snuck** reverses the usual pattern whereby regular verbs stay regular, and at most acquire irregular past participles over the course of time. See further under **irregular verbs** section 9.

snicker or snigger

The American **snicker** and the British **snigger** both mean a "half-suppressed laugh": each to their own. Canadians live with both words, and so can differentiate between them, giving more malicious intent to **snigger**, according to *Canadian English Usage* (1997). Australians use **snigger** only, for more and less subversive forms of laughter. All parties use **snicker** for the whinnying of a horse, though just what kind of equine emotion it signifies is best left to horse-lovers.

sniveling or snivelling

The choice between these is discussed under -**l**-/-**ll**-.

snorkel or schnorkel

The spelling **schnorkel** harks back to the German *Schnorchel,* originally the name for a submarine's ventilation and exhaust tube (the name is figurative, since it embodies the German verb for "snore"). But in English, this word for a simple underwater breathing apparatus is almost always spelled **snorkel**. When used as a verb, it allows either *snorkeled, snorkeling* or *snorkelled, snorkelling*. The issue of doubling the final *l* is discussed under -**l**-/-**ll**-.

snr(.), sr(.), Sr., Snr and Sr

In lower case, both **snr** and **sr** are abbreviations/ contractions for "senior." The same is true of their counterparts in upper case, although Americans prefer **Sr.** for use in dynastic family names such as *John D. Rockefeller Sr.,* where the British use **Snr**: *Douglas Fairbanks Snr* (or else *Sen.:* see under **Sen.**). The British use of **Snr** for "Senior" may be driven partly by the need to reserve **Sr** for "Sister" in the nursing service or religious orders, for example *Sr Gillian Price, a nun based in Hertfordshire* – though its position before the name makes it different from American **Sr.** anyway. (See further under **names** section 5.) For the American use of stops in shortened forms, see **abbreviations** section 2.

snuck or sneaked

See **sneaked**.

so

A chameleon word, **so** takes its color and meaning from the context – the surrounding words and/or the physical context and particular people involved. This gives it advantages in conversation, where it occurs two or three times more often than in writing, according to the *Longman Grammar* (1999). It frequently appears as an amplifier or intensifier, as in *I was so distressed/excited/pleased/scared,* and in American conversation **so** is more frequent than *very.* When conversing we also use **so** as an affirmative pro-form – *I think so, they hope so* – to pick up a predication made by the previous speaker (see further under **pro-forms**).

Over and above all these roles, **so** very often serves in conversation as a linking adverb (or *conjunct*), as in:
They came on Friday. So did the other speakers.
The program has almost half finished. So let's make the coffee.
Appearing at the start of a supplementary utterance, **so** links it cohesively with what went before (see further under **coherence or cohesion**). At the same time it can serve other discoursal purposes. In the first example it's also a *pro-form,* and in the second it signals a kind of inference or consequence. Inferential **so** often draws on things understood by the people communicating, which are not explicit in the wording (e.g. you wouldn't start watching a program that's half over). Thus **so** supports the interpersonal aspects of discourse rather than the logical or referential (see **interpersonal**).

What makes **so** a useful bond in speaking can be a liability in writing, where ambiguity is to be avoided and logical relations spelled out. This is why older usage commentators preferred to have **so** combined with other conjunctions (forming the subordinator *so that* and the coordinator *and so*). *So that* can still be ambiguous, because of its capacity to express purpose as well as inference/result. See for example:
They left two hours early so that nothing was left to chance.
The sentence is no less ambiguous than when linked with **so** on its own:
They left two hours early so nothing was left to chance.
To clearly express a purpose, the sentence needs to replace *so (that)* with *in order to* or *so as to (leave nothing to chance).* To express result, the sentence has only to replace *so that* with *and so.*

Ambiguity apart, the last example makes **so** a conjunction in its own right – something which traditional grammarians could not contemplate, since for them it was an adverb. Yet the linking adverb/conjunct of conversation is readily turned into a conjunction in the process of transcribing:
The program has already half finished, so let's make the coffee.
Compare this sentence with the previous example. In both, **so** becomes a full conjunction, coordinating the two parts of the sentence (see further under **conjunctions**). The *New Oxford* (1998) presents **so** as a conjunction in its own right, as well as part of a complex conjunction (*so that*). Other dictionaries such as *Merriam-Webster* (2000) acknowledge it as a "sentence connector." The *Comprehensive Grammar* (1985) found the use of **so** as conjunction "rather informal," though *Webster's English Usage* (1989) argued that this stylistic judgement was difficult to prove. Burchfield (1996) finds **so** "unobjectionable" as a conjunction, given mounting evidence of its use in standard fiction and nonfiction.

sobriquet or soubriquet

This French loanword, borrowed in C17, provides a lofty way of referring to a nickname, or (less often) an assumed name. A **so(u)briquet** can be applied to an individual or a group: *"Colonel Screwtop"* for a certain World War II commander, and *"Flying Circus,"* the jokey name among the Allies for a task force of the German Luftwaffe. It can be affectionate or a putdown, in keeping with the original French meaning as "a tap on/under the chin." The standard spelling is **sobriquet**, which dominates in US English and is preferred in the UK. But the C19 alternative **soubriquet** appears in 25% of all instances of the word in BNC data. For other terms for an assumed name, see under **nom de plume**.

social or sociable

Applied to people, these mean much the same. Compare:

> They're very social people.
> They're very sociable people.

The difference – if any – is that **social** embodies the more abstract idea of being inclined to seek the society of others, whereas **sociable** suggests being ready to make friends and be good company.

Beyond that **sociable** has few applications while **social** has very many. It represents the more abstract and impersonal notion of society at large, in phrases such as *social problems, social structure, social welfare*. Other aspects of **social** can be seen in the oppositions it enters into. The *social sciences* contrast with the physical/natural sciences in terms of subject matter (or with the so-called "hard" sciences, in terms of methodology). *Social events* contrast with those at which matters of business are paramount. The *social club* distinguishes itself from ones set up for more specific purposes, such as the tennis club or the wine club.

The antonym of **sociable** is *unsociable*, which simply means "not disposed to be convivial." *Antisocial* is sometimes used that way as well, as in:

> I'm going to be antisocial and watch the TV news.

However *antisocial* can also mean "negatively oriented towards the community at large," as in:

> . . . antisocial, aggressive conduct and delinquent acts

Unsocial is occasionally used this way (*mountain goats are relatively unsocial*), but especially when referring to *unsocial hours* of work that cut into time normally reserved for social activity. Once again, the negative forms of **social** have a wider range of meanings than the negative form of **sociable**.

solecism

Older usage commentators including Fowler (1926) use this word to identify a fault in sentence construction, especially of agreement, as in *you was*. **Solecism** thus contrasted with *barbarism* which was a malformation of a word, for example *brung*. But **solecism** has always had other uses in English, to refer to any error or incongruity, or breach of etiquette, and these are now probably more widely known than its exact linguistic sense.

solemnity or solemnness

Dictionaries allow either as the abstract noun for *solemn*, but **solemnity** is the only one to appear in the reference databases (BNC and CCAE). Perhaps **solemnness** seems too ad hoc for the seriousness of the uses to which it's put.

solidus and slash

Editors worldwide use the term **solidus** for the punctuation mark also known in Britain as the *diagonal, slash* or *oblique*. In North America things have changed rapidly from *virgule* (preferred by *Webster's Style Manual*, 1985), to **solidus** (*Chicago*, 1993), to **slash** (*Chicago*, 2003). Canadian and Australian editors both work with **solidus**, but the

Australian government *Style Manual* (2002) affirms the now wide-spread use of *slash*. Yet another term, used by many when dictating or reading punctuation aloud, is *stroke*. This range of names goes with a variety of uses in different contexts.

1 **The solidus in plain text.** The prime function of the **solidus** is to link words which are alternatives, and invite the reader to consider each in turn:

> They will sponsor road/rail transport for the teams.
> Each applicant must submit his/her birth certificate.

Sometimes the **solidus** offers alternative readings of the same word, as in:

> Everyone can bring their own friend/s.

Style guides such as the *Chicago Manual* (1993) and the *Oxford Guide to Style* (2002) accept also the use of **solidus** to include two successive months or years in a span of time, as in:

> the June/July recess the 2001/2 financial year

But they caution against using the **solidus** more generally to mean "as well as," as in *US/UK support*, on the grounds that it may be misunderstood to mean "or." A reciprocal meaning for **solidus**, as in *an oil/water interface*, is noted in *Copy-editing* (1992), where its role is clarified by the accompanying noun. Others would use an en dash/rule there (see **dashes** section 2).

◊ For the use of *and/or* to coordinate alternatives, see under that heading.

2 **Solidus with numbers.** The **solidus** is conventionally used as a separator in certain kinds of numerical expressions:

* in dates: *21/7/99*
* in fractions: *3/4* when the vertical setting is not available
* as a substitute for *per* in expressions of measurement, when the units of measurement are shown as symbols rather than full words, as in *125 km/hr*.

In the days before decimal currency, a **solidus** was used to separate the shillings from the pence. So *10/6* meant "ten shillings and sixpence."

3 **The solidus for quoting poetry.** When quotations of poetry are integrated with ordinary text, the **solidus** serves to mark the boundary between the lines of the original verse. For example:

> The opening lines of the British national anthem: God save our gracious Queen / Long live our noble Queen *contain two examples of the subjunctive.*

4 **Solidus in writing phonetics.** In phonetic transcription, twin **solidi** (or *slash brackets*) are used to mark the beginning and end of the string of phonemic symbols (see further under **brackets** section 1d).

Historical notes: The word **solidus** is Latin in origin, hence the plural **solidi**. It was the middle denomination of Roman currency, in the series *librae, solidi, denarii*. When abbreviated they were *l.s.d.*, which were then identified with the "pounds, shillings and pence" of British currency. Thus the **solidus** was equated with the shilling. This would explain why the **solidus** is sometimes called the "shilling mark." *Webster's Third* adds that the oblique line which divided the shillings from the pence (in sums like *10/6*) was a straightened form of the "long s" used for shillings. See further under **s**.

soliloquy

See under **monologue**.

soluble or solvable

If the problem has a *solution,* it could be described as **soluble** or **solvable**. **Soluble** is preferred by British writers when the problem is environmental, societal or social. Many American writers use **solvable** for these purposes, where it outnumbers **soluble** in the ratio of 5:1 in data from CCAE. But chemists the world over prefer **soluble** as the adjective to describe a substance that can be *dissolved,* as in *a soluble dye, soluble nutrients.*

sombre or somber

See under **-re/-er**.

some

This word is deliberately nonspecific about how many or how much:

> *Some people resist the trend to metric measurements.*
> *They took some comfort from the results.*

When combined with round numbers, **some** still emphasizes their approximateness, as in *a collection of some two thousand volumes.* But when combined with a more specific number, as in *he drafted some 157 entries for the dictionary,* it simply underscores it, and is strictly redundant. Compare **-odd**.

-some

The string of letters **-some** represents two Old English suffixes, and a latter-day Greek one. The most widely used is an adjectival suffix with roots in Old English *-sum,* found in words such as:

cumbersome	*fearsome*	*irksome*
loathsome	*quarrelsome*	*troublesome*
wearisome	*worrisome*	

Words formed with adjectival **-some** are typically based on verbs, as in these cases. Occasionally the base is itself an adjective, as with *fulsome* and *wholesome.* In *winsome* the base was *wyn,* an obsolete noun for "pleasure." The origins of *handsome* are rather obscure, though it seems to be related to the noun *hand* in rather the same way as the adjective *handy,* but with a shift of meaning from "convenient" to "attractive."

A different suffix spelled **-some** goes back to the Old English pronoun *sum* ("some"), attached to small numbers. It creates informal nouns referring to a small group, as in *twosome, threesome, foursome.*

The Greek combining form **-some** ("body") is distilled out of neoclassical terms such as *chromosome,* and applied in others such as *lysosome, monosome.*

somebody or someone

In database evidence, **someone** is more than twice as common as **somebody**, in both the US and the UK (see **-one or -body**). Otherwise the crucial question is which pronoun or determiner to use in agreement with them. The second element (*-body/-one*) suggests that the following pronoun/determiner should be singular, but this involves choosing between *him/his* and *her,* both of which are regrettably specific in terms of gender. Many people therefore prefer to use

them/their, in spite of their historical association with the plural. See further under **agreement** section 3.

sometimes and sometime

These indefinite words are definitely fluid in their meanings. Though **sometimes** is purely an adverb, **sometime** can be either adverb or adjective. Compare:

> *They sometimes arrive unannounced.*
> *Come up and see me sometime.*
> *They flew in sometime last week.*
> *Meet Mr K., resident and sometime mayor of Richmond.*

The time reference in **sometime(s)** varies with the context, as the examples show. **Sometimes** in the first embraces both past and future in stating a recurrent event. In the next two examples with **sometime** (as adverb), the time reference is framed in the future or past by the tense of the verb. The fourth sentence shows **sometime** as an adjective when its meaning is usually retrospective: "for a period in the past." However it can also mean "occasional" and even "transient" in the phrase *a sometime thing* – popularized by its use in the (1935) Gershwin song *A woman is a sometime thing.* This usage is confirmed by several post-World War II citations in the *Oxford Dictionary* (1989) as well as *Webster's English Usage* (1989), yet it has been rejected by successive usage panels associated with the *American Heritage Dictionary* (1969–2000). It seems to have originated in the South, and worked its way into mainstream American English, according to *Webster's English Usage.*

Both **sometimes** and **sometime** have slightly changed meanings when set as two words:

> *Some times when I visit he doesn't know me.*
> *We've had some times together since then.*
> *Can you find some time to meet me on Friday?*
> *They'll spend some time in Budapest.*

In the first three sentences, *time(s)* means particular times or occasions; in the fourth, it means a period of time.

son-in-law

See **in-laws**.

sophisticated, sophistical or sophistic

Sophisticated is by far the most common, and expresses respect for cultivated taste in whatever field it's applied. **Sophistic(al)** describes a kind of argument which is not really respected: though clever and plausible, it is unilluminating, and does not help to resolve issues. In database evidence, American writers are more inclined to **sophistic** and British to **sophistical** – but the word is too rarely used to suggest that these amount to regional differences. For other **-ic/-ical** pairs, see under that heading.

soprano

In English the plural is usually **sopranos** (not **soprani**). See under **Italian plurals**.

sort of

This is both a considered phrase, as in *this sort of criticism,* and a conversational hedge, as in *he was sort of undermined by it.* Both pose some questions for writers.

Used in the singular, the phrase is normally followed by a singular noun: *this sort of jazz / money / class system.* As in these examples, it's very often an abstract noun. When the phrase is partly or fully pluralized, as *these sort of* or *these sorts of,* it's less clear whether the following noun should be singular or plural. Both constructions are quite well represented in written material from the BNC, where – paradoxically – the phrase *these sort of* behaves more regularly than the other, in that it's always followed by a plural noun: *these sort of fares/features/sentiments.* A plural noun is also often found after the fully pluralized form of the phrase, as in *these sorts of deals / incidents / kick-start measures.* But it's also found with singular nouns in about 15% of examples, such as *these sorts of fibre/character/explanation.* The construction with a singular noun creates an abstraction (e.g. *explanation*) where the plural (*explanations*) would make it countable and more concrete.

Sort of is also a conversational device for hedging a statement, as in:

I think it's sort of employer education.

British speakers make far more use of **sort of** than Americans, according to *Longman Grammar* (1999) research. The American preference is for *kind of.* Frequent use of **sort of** for hedging purposes has generated the merged form *sorta,* as in *It just sorta took over from that.* In BNC data it's mainly used in fiction to signal informality in the narrative voice. American journalists in CCAE also use it when reporting speech, to suggest its naturalness and authenticity: *America's land-based missiles are "sorta like a 1963 jalopy with some new parts."*
◇ Compare **kind of.**

sotto voce

In Italian **sotto voce** is literally "under the voice," i.e. "in an undertone." It refers to something said or sung in a low voice, so that it cannot generally be heard. On stage it's often an aside, used to create dramatic irony.

sound symbolism

The sounds of language create patterns and imagery which can contribute to the meaning. See further under **phonesthemes** and **onomatopoeia.**

south, southern and southerly

For those in the northern hemisphere, **south** and **southern** take you to sunnier places relatively nearer the Equator – whereas in the *southern hemisphere* the overtones are colder and ultimately watery, as you approach the *Southern Ocean.* But everywhere in the world, **southerly** is applied in the same way to winds and ocean currents which stream from the **south.**

When applied to language, **south(ern)** is used for different kinds of discrimination in the UK and the US. See further under **north, northern and northerly.**

South African English

South Africa is one of the most multilingual states in the world, with eleven official languages, one of which is English. Afrikaans is another, a regional variety of the Dutch spoken by the first European settlers of South Africa in C17 and C18, and vigorously maintained through the political contretemps of C19 and C20. The other nine official languages are indigenous African languages of the Bantu family, the mother tongues of up to 80% of the population. Thus in South Africa, English is much more often used as a second language than as a first.

The multilingual context helps to explain why the English used in South Africa from C19 is very diverse. Distinct varieties are associated with the major ethnolinguistic communities, i.e. *Afrikaans English, Black South African English, South African Indian English* as well as the **South African English** associated with the British community there. Collectively these varieties are also called **South African English,** hence some of the difficulty of discussing what is central and peripheral to it.

The pioneering dictionary of **South African English** was Charles Pettman's *Africanderisms* (1913), whose aim was to capture every distinctive aspect of the regional language there, from colloquial words and phrases to placenames. It included various terms not unique to South Africa, yet he was the first to record many loanwords from Afrikaans and Bantu languages which have fed into the South African variety. Later dictionary work led by William Branford and Jean Branford in the 1970s, and culminating in the *Dictionary of South African English* published in 1996, has focused strictly on South Africanisms. Among the 2500 words and expressions listed, about 45% are from Afrikaans and 23% from local African languages. Some of these have moved into international English, notably *apartheid, kopje, trek, veld,* among others from Afrikaans.

Concern with the norms of English usage in South Africa has been vested in prescriptive dictionaries such as the *Dictionary of English Usage in Southern Africa* (1975), which indicated the acceptability of local terms with a cross (×) or a plus sign (+); and the *English Usage Dictionary for South African Schools* (1984) which included only those words which its authors regarded as "good" **South African English.** Normative pressures on the language are institutionalized in the English Academy of Southern Africa, which was set up in 1961 in response to the vagaries of English used in government communication. It has been slow to consider the possibility of **South African English** becoming "a new language" through its contact with so many others, as Ndebele commented in a celebrated speech to the Academy in 1986. *Black South African English* is in fact the language of unity for the majority of the population, and the future of English in South Africa would be strengthened by recognition of its use by indigenous Africans. But for the moment, the standards for written English in South Africa are those codified in British grammars and style guides. The challenge of integrating an "old" native-speaker English with the "new" English of the local non-native speakers lies ahead – as in India, Jamaica, Singapore and elsewhere. See further under **English or Englishes.**

Southeast Asia or South-East Asia

Both forms are used in the UK, whereas US writers overwhelmingly prefer the first. The American use of **Southeast Asia** is in line with their preference for unhyphened forms of *southeast/southwest* etc., where British English prefers *south-east/south-west.* Canadian usage goes with the American on this, according to the *Canadian Oxford* (1998), whereas Australian usage – like the British – is still mixed (Peters, 1995). British writers sometimes leave the capital letters off **southeast Asia / south-east Asia** (in about 15% of BNC examples), presumably feeling it's a descriptive expression rather than an official name. Those bordering the Pacific Ocean do not doubt the significance of **Southeast Asia** as a geopolitical entity, however vast its extent from Indonesia and Malaysia through to Vietnam, and the name is always capitalized.

southern hemisphere
See under **antipodes**.

southward or southwards
See under **-ward**.

Soviet
Until the breakup of the *USSR* in 1991, **Soviet** was a useful adjective for referring to aspects of the union and its citizens. Literally "council," **Soviet** expressed the decentralization of power, and was thus far preferable to "Russian" for most of the diverse peoples in the union. But the word **Soviet** itself is now under a cloud as the byword for Russian communism, and *Russian* is returning as the natural candidate, with the *Russian Federation* representing what remains of the *USSR* at the United Nations. See further under **Russia**.

sow
The past tense of **sow** is always *sowed*. For the past participle dictionaries allow either *sown* or *sowed*, though *sown* is far more common in both British and American English. In BNC data *sowed* appears in less than 2% of all instances of the past participle, and little more than 5% in CCAE. So the historical process of turning this Old English irregular verb into a regular one seems to have stopped with the replacement of the past tense, as with some others. See further under **irregular verbs** section 9.

sox
When *socks* come in pairs, **sox** seems apt, though it defies decoding into the singular for the missing *sock*. It remains an informal spelling, except in the phrase *bobby sox* (= ankle socks as worn by young girls), and the names of American baseball teams, such as the Boston *Red Sox*, the Chicago *White Sox*. For other trimmed spellings, see **spelling** section 5.

soya or soy
Both **soya** and **soy** have been in English since late C17. They represent the oriental compound for "salted beans" + "oil," which was *shi-you* in Chinese and *sho-yu* in Japanese. **Soya** seems to have come via Dutch and colonial activity in the East Indies – hence its popularity with British writers in the BNC, two thirds of whom prefer it. **Soy** corresponds to the abbreviated Japanese form, and it's preferred in American English, by an enormous majority in data from CCAE. Canadians also prefer *soy*, whereas Australians use both words, like the British.

SP, Sp., sp. or s.p.
In full caps with no stops, **SP** abbreviates "starting price" for the racing world, as in *SP bookmaker.* Contrast **Sp.**, which stands for "Spanish." In lower case with a final stop only (**sp.**) it stands for one of several words, including *specimen, species, spelling.*

With two stops (**s.p.**) it represents the Latin *sine prole:* see **decessit sine prole**.

spark plug or sparking plug
See under **inflectional extras**.

spasmodic or spasmodical
The shorter and earlier form **spasmodic** seems to have won out over the longer **spasmodical**, last seen in mid-C19. There's no trace of it in either the British or American reference databases.

-speak
George Orwell bequeathed us **-speak** via the term *newspeak,* coined in the novel *Nineteen Eighty-Four* (1949) for a repressive type of public language that entails *Doublethink.* The two concepts merge in the term *doublespeak,* coined in 1957 for language that is deliberately ambiguous or deceptive. Newer uses of **-speak** make it the language of a particular medium or specialist group, as in *adspeak, computer-speak, education-speak.* Such compounds can be faintly pejorative, mostly because the jargon they refer to tends to be extravagant and somewhat exclusive. "LeetSpeak" or rather "*l33tsp34k*" on the internet is strictly for its own members (see under **SMS**). Other forms of **-speak** such as *Californiaspeak* and *Thatcherspeak* are simply an ad hoc way of referring to idiosyncrasies of speech associated with a place or person.
◊ Compare **-ese**.

speaking (of)
The combination of **speaking** and an adverb, as in *practically speaking / speaking frankly,* often serves to adjust the topic under discussion or highlight a particular perspective on it. *Strictly speaking* they are *dangling participles* (see under that heading). But their conventional discourse role is what readers respond to, in
> Generally speaking the Church has tended to support the hegemony.

The grammar/semantics of the word **speaking** is superseded in all but a perverse reading of the sentence. (It's not about what the Church might say about itself.) The same holds for the idiom **speaking of**, used in spoken discourse to adjust the conversational focus: *Speaking of which . . .*

special, specially and especially
Though **special** has supplanted *especial* in contemporary English, **especially** is much more common now than **specially**, according to the evidence of English databases. **Especially** dominates by more than 8:1 in the BNC, and by 20:1 in data from CCAE. This large difference in frequency is because **especially** works as a general-purpose subjunct and modifier of adjectives and whole phrases, as in:
> There was nothing especially difficult in the plan.
> She wanted it especially for the children.

The meaning of **especially** ranges from "very" (an intensifier) in the first example, to "above all" (a particularizer) in the second. In conversation **specially** could be used in such sentences, but in writing it would look somewhat informal.

Specially does however have an adverbial use of its own, meaning "for a specific purpose," as in:

> *. . . specially commissioned music*
> *. . . a chair specially designed for people with short legs*

As in those examples, **specially** typically modifies the past participle of a verb, and is technically an adjunct rather than a subjunct. (See further under **adverbs**.) **Especially** could not be used in such sentences without blurring the meaning.

special pleading

This phrase originated in the courts where it refers to a lawyer's statement of the particular issues affecting the case about to be heard. It also points out new matter which will be presented to refute the arguments of the opposing counsel. From these strictly legal applications, the phrase **special pleading** has been reinterpreted to mean an unprofessional style of argumentation found in many ordinary contexts – a one-sided style of argument, which concentrates on what is favorable to the case being argued, and avoids counter issues.

specialty or speciality

These words can apply either to a special product (*special(i)ty of the house*), or to a special pursuit (*election coverage a special(i)ty*); and dictionaries confirm that they are interchangeable. But database evidence shows that for both meanings Americans overwhelmingly prefer **specialty**, while the British are inclined to prefer **speciality** over **specialty**, by more than 3:1. Australians also use both (Peters, 1995), whereas **specialty** is the choice of most Canadians, according to *Canadian English Usage* (Fee and McAlpine, 1997).

species and specie

The Latin word **species**, used to mean "[a] kind [of]," is both singular and plural: *this species / these species of birds*. (See further under **Latin plurals**.) Against this, **specie** is very occasionally heard and seen for the singular, as in "a dying specie." Technically it's a backformation, and not recognized in any of the major dictionaries (see **backformation**).

But the dictionaries do note the term **specie** used by financiers to refer to money in the form of coins:

> *. . . desperate attempts to obtain silver specie from Colorado in 1862*

This usage is based on the legal Latin phrase *in specie*, meaning "in visible form." **Specie** is in fact the ablative form of **species**: see further under **ablative**.

spectre or specter

See under **-re/-er**.

spectrum

This Latin loanword has both scientific and general uses in English, and so dictionaries note two plurals for it: **spectra** and **spectrums**. Scientific uses account for most instances of the word in American and British databases, as in the *atomic spectra of sunlight*, and so the latinate plural prevails in raw numerical terms. The English plural **spectrums** is nevertheless confirmed by cases like *all spectrums of music,* and *representatives of all spectrums of Philippine society*.

speed

Dictionaries all show that the past forms of **speed** can be either *sped* or *speeded*, but they diverge on their applications. *New Oxford* (1998) associates them with different senses of the word, *sped* with the rapid motion of a train, tram, bus, automobile or even skis or skateboard:

> *The jeep sped on towards the crossroads.*

and *speeded* with driving at excessive speed:

> *The truck had speeded all the way to Richmond.*

as well as the more abstract sense of accelerating an activity or procedure:

> *The appeals process should be speeded up.*

These distinctions seem to hold in British English, by the evidence of the BNC, but not so systematically in American English. In CCAE *sped* is used for physical and for the more abstract uses of **speed**. *Merriam-Webster* (2000) simply allows both forms for any of the three meanings.

spelled or spelt

When *spell* means "give the letters of a word" or "explain fully" (*spell out*), the past form may be either **spelled** or **spelt**. British English uses both, though more of **spelt** by a factor of about 2:1 in BNC data. In American English **spelled** is almost unchallenged, by the evidence of CCAE (see further under **-ed** section 1). When *spell* means "give a spell (or rest) to," the only possible past is **spelled**.

spelling, rules and reforms

English **spelling** is the product of a long period of evolution. It embodies the changing culture of centuries of history. It preserves mutants and fossils along with the mainstream of more or less regularly spelled words. Some claim that about 85% of English words conform to *spelling rules,* though the irregular ones are the focus of most comment and criticism. See for example sets such as:

> *cough dough plough rough through thorough*
> (words with the same spelling but different sounds)
> *eat   meet key quay   chief   receive*
> *people police ski amoeba faeces*
> (multiple spellings for the same sound)

There are thus two dimensions of irregularity in English, where other languages such as French and German have only the second. Cutting across both is the extent to which the spelling of individual words or groups reflects their origins. These several factors explain why English *spelling rules* rarely work in 100% of cases, and why attempts at regularizing English **spelling** have always been piecemeal.

1 Spelling adjustments of the past. Attempts to reconnect the **spelling** of English words with their sounds are to be found in almost every century. Anglo-Norman scribes revised the spelling of various consonants and vowels in the wake of the Norman Conquest, bequeathing us digraphs such as *gh* and *th*, and respelling sequences such as *-es/-se* with *-ce* (as in *once, bodice, dice*). The introduction of printing to England in C15 created *multiple spellings* for many words as printers grappled with new technology. They reduced the blank spaces in a line by adding an extra *e* to words here and there, or swapping an *i* for a *y*. These erratic uses of **spelling** (as well as shifting pronunciations which changed the relationship between sounds and letters) left C16 scholars skeptical about linking a word's spelling to its sound, and more inclined to base it on its historical form. Renaissance scholarship brought to light the classical antecedents of many English words, showing how the spelling had diverged over the centuries, and confirming some of the respellings which had already begun to filter through from French sources. Though the *classical respelling* movement petered out in France, it continued in England, adapting loanwords which had been left untouched in French. This accounts for the bracketed letters in all of the following, which were spelled without them in Middle English:

a(d)venture dou(b)t fau(l)t recei(p)t t(h)rone

Some medieval and Renaissance respellings were misguided. Words with no classical ancestry were touched up according to classical **spelling** analogies:

a(d)miral – from Arabic (made like *admire*)
i(s)land – from Old English (made like *isle*)
s(c)ythe – from Old English (made like *scissors*)

Debate continued as to whether it was more useful to base **spelling** on the etymology or the sounds of a word. But the **spelling** of most common words was standardized during C17, and only fine-tuning took place in C18, such as removing "superfluous letters" (as in *logic[k]* and *music[k]*), and the respelling of *k* with the French *qu*, as in *quay* and *cheque*.

2 Standardization in English spelling. In comparison with pronunciation, **spelling** is very highly standardized, yet not all English words have the same spelling everywhere. The biggest divide in spelling is between British *standard spelling* and the American standard, both of which are known in Canada, Australia and elsewhere. American **spelling** sometimes differs from British when it preserves the older forms (as with *check* ("money order"), and *skeptic*), which were taken across the Atlantic in C17 and C18, and untouched by the francophile tastes of Victorian England. Later British **spelling** often differentiates words (such as *ensure/insure* and *kerb/curb*) which have the same **spelling** in American English. In general British **spellings** follow those of Dr. Johnson's dictionary of 1755, while American **spellings** are mostly in line with those of Webster's dictionaries of 1806 and 1828. American **spelling** applies the rules to more of the susceptible words in any set, and is less inclined to create exceptions on grounds of etymology. In Britain the reverse is true. So American English uses *-ize* everywhere possible, allowing it in words like *advertize* and *realize* where etymology argues for *-ise*. It extends the rule to words with *-yze*, preferring *analyze* to *analyse*. The main points on which American and British spelling differ systematically are detailed in entries such as:

ae/e   i/y   -ize/-ise-   -l/-ll   -l-/-ll-   oe/e
-or/-our   -re/-er   -yze/-yse

Overall American **spelling** is more *standardized* than British, though not without its own anomalies.

3 Spelling rules. All varieties of English make use of certain conventional practices in **spelling**, which are presented with examples at the following entries:

-c/-ck-   -ce/-ge   **doubling of final consonant**
-e   -ed   -f >-v-   ie > y   i before e   -o   -y > -i-

The extent to which these rules are applied is nevertheless somewhat variable. In cases such as **doubling of final consonant, -e** and **-ed,** this contributes to British–American divergence.

4 Spelling reform. Most *spelling reformers* recognize that it is an enormous challenge to overhaul the present system and iron out its inconsistencies – even in one English-speaking country like Australia, let alone through the whole English-speaking world. There is no constitutional authority to enforce **spelling** changes, and even if there were, it seems

doubtful whether people would be willing to follow it to the letter. Dr. Johnson doubted whether British citizens of C18 would have been willing to obey the dictates of a language academy, and his arguments still ring true today:

> *The edicts of an English academy would probably be read by many only that they might be sure to disobey them ... The present manners of our nation deride authority ...*

Yet we could perhaps achieve something by way of streamlining, preferring more *regular spellings* wherever they are already used by a group of significant size, or familiar even as minority variants. In Britain and Australia, **spellings** such as *archeology, color, defense, fulfill, spelled, traveler* (and others in each set) would be prioritized. In North America it would involve words currently spelled *-er* rather than *-re* (preferring *centre* to *center*). None of these *spelling adjustments* would be revolutionary. They simply represent further extensions of rules which are already applied in the region to the **spelling** of other words.

A more proactive step, though still not revolutionary, would be to extend a *standardized spelling* to all words in large sets such as the following:

-able/-ible   -ant/-ent   -er/-or

In each case the vowel is indeterminate, whatever variety of English you speak (see **schwa**). The rationale for spelling the suffix this way rather than that is buried in individual word history, and makes no difference to the meaning. Some pairs in each set are already interchangeable, for example: *collapsable/collapsible, dependant/dependent, convener/convenor.* Because neither the sound or meaning of the suffixes is affected, it seems perverse that differences in **spelling** should be maintained for so many of them – differences which may get the better of otherwise excellent writers. It would be a kindness to all to allow alternatives, or else to suggest that the most common suffix in each set (*-able, -ent, -er*) be used for all words included in it. Those who wished could of course continue to use the traditional **spelling** for each word in the set. Others could use a *standardized spelling* for the suffix, without fear of being ridiculed for *bad spelling*. It seems unfortunate when adults with a full secondary education still have to reach for the dictionary. The arbitrariness of the *spelling system* may be the problem, rather than the adequacy of the education system! A strategic policy of *reform*, that embraces traditional **spellings** while targeting *standardized* ones for the future could facilitate transitions that otherwise seem unthinkable. This would lighten the load for both first- and second-language learners, consolidating the rules that are already there, and progressively streamlining the *spelling system*.

5 Trimmed spellings. The redundancies of English **spelling** have been noted by language scholars since C17, though relatively few words have had their *silent letters* removed. In some cases, there may be good reasons for retaining them (see further under **silent letters**). Other words could lose a letter or two from their conventional **spelling** with no loss of identity. Webster listed many in his much published C18 **spelling** book, such as *bilt, bred, frend, giv, hed, relm,* all of which speak their meaning perfectly well in the reduced form. Others like *altho, prolog, tho, thoro, thru* were among the 300 recommended by the

Simplified Spelling Board in 1906, which President T. Roosevelt endorsed as US government style – but he was quickly overruled. Since then advertisers and others have launched trimmed spellings such as *donut, lite, nite, sox, thru* with some success, in that they are known worldwide. Yet only *lite* seems to appear in standard prose (see individual headings). English-users generally are strongly constrained by pressures to use conventional **spellings**, and to avoid the trimmed versions which would be more straightforward and efficient.

Communicators on the internet and via SMS have nevertheless taken things into their own hands with a repertoire of curtailed **spellings**, such as *U* ("you"), *F2F* ("face to face"): see further under **SMS**. As in these examples, they tend to reduce whole syllables to a single letter. Some are more transparent than others, but they circulate widely on the internet, and could be established through it. By the same token they are mostly used for social communication, as a colloquial style to counter the impersonality of the digital medium. There's little incentive to use them in less personal forms of communication, so their passage into standard English style should never be taken for granted. We need not fear a future of monosyllabic, acronymic prose.

spick or spic

These spellings cover two kinds of concepts:
1 "neat/clean," as in *spic(k) and span,* and only found there. British English prefers *spick and span,* and American *spic and span,* by the evidence of the BNC and CCAE, although in each case the database shows minority use of the other spelling. The phrase is quite often hyphened in attributive use, as in *a spic-and-span Dutch ship,* but sometimes also when used predicatively: *the room is impossibly spick-and-span* (see **hyphens** section 2c). Whichever way, it abbreviates the Middle English phrase *spick and span-new* ("absolutely new"), which embellished the Old Norse *span-nyr* ("a new chip") with the English *spick* ("spike, nail") – when fresh carpentry was a general sign of newness.
2 a racist term for a "Hispanic." In American English this is spelled both **spic** and **spick**. See further under **Hispanic** and **racist language**.

spiky or spikey

See **-y/-ey**.

spill

The past forms of **spill** can be either *spilled* or *spilt*. British writers are more inclined to use *spilled* for the past tense, and *spilt* for the past participle or adjective, though the overall trend in BNC data is towards *spilled*. American writers overwhelmingly use *spilled* for all past uses, except in the phrase *spilt milk,* in data from CCAE. See further under **-ed** section 1.

spin and span

The verb **spin** once had three principal parts **spin**/*span*/*spun*, but is now reduced to two, with *spun* used for both past tense and participle. In *Oxford Dictionary* (1989) citations from C19, *span* and *spun* appear in equal numbers. But *spun* has since prevailed in both literal and more figurative uses of the word: *the vehicle spun out of control; he spun out the agony.* The disuse of *span* as the past of **spin**

probably coincides with more frequent use of the quite independent verb **span** meaning "extend across" (derived from the noun *span*). Although spatial uses of the verb **span** have been on record since C17, it is now very often used in relation to time and other numerical scales, as in the headline: *Council rents span wider band.*

spiraled or spiralled, spiraling or spiralling

For the choice of spelling in each pair, see under **-l-/-ll-**.

spiritual or spirituous

Spiritual has everything to do with the *spirit* and the human soul, and strong religious overtones. **Spirituous** is totally secular. It relates only to *spirits* in the sense of distilled alcoholic beverages. The word is little used in print, though often seen above the doorway of the public bar, identifying the publican as a *licensed vendor of fermented and spirituous liquors.*

spirt or spurt

See **spurt**.

spit

As the verb meaning "expectorate," **spit** has alternative past forms in *spat* or *spit*. British English prefers *spat,* according to *New Oxford* (1998) and it's overwhelmingly preferred in data from the BNC. American English makes equal use of both; compare *spat on and beaten,* with *chewed it up and spit it out,* among examples from CCAE. Either way the verb is irregular (see **irregular verbs** sections 1 and 3).

When **spit** means "put on a spit," its past forms are quite regular, as in *chickens were spitted over makeshift fires.*

splendor or splendour

See under **-or/-our**.

splice

For a discussion of the so-called *comma splice,* see under that heading.

split infinitive

The "problem" of the **split infinitive** stems from misconceptions about English infinitives: the assumption they consist of two parts (*to* + the verb itself, as in *to read*), and that the two parts can never be split. In fact English infinitives do not necessarily come with the preceding *to* (see **infinitives**); and **split infinitives** were used for centuries before they became the *bête noire* of C18 and C19 grammarians. Their censure cast long shadows into C20, extended by computer style checkers which can so easily be programmed to pick them up.

Reactions to the **split infinitive** still beg the question as to what is wrong with it. The answers to that question vary from "It's ungrammatical" to "It's inelegant." The first comment has no basis, as we've seen. The second is often subjective, though individual cases do need to be examined in their own terms. Having an adverbial phrase between the *to* and the verb can make awkward reading, as in:
I wanted to above all be near her.
It reads more smoothly as:
I wanted above all to be near her.

Yet there's no alternative place for the adverbial phrase in:

He wanted to more than match that offer.

A single-word adverb runs in smoothly enough, especially an intensifier:

He wanted to really talk to her.

If we made a point of not splitting the infinitive in that case, the result is less elegant and more ambiguous:

He wanted really to talk to her.

In some cases, the effort to avoid splitting the infinitive alters the meaning of the sentence. Compare:

He failed completely to follow the instructions.

with

He failed to completely follow the instructions.

There's little virtue in a sentence which avoids the **split infinitive** so clumsily as to make obvious what the writer was trying not to do:

The failure adequately to brief the pictorial editor was inexcusable.

Most usage guides including Fowler (1926) recommend a judicious approach to *splitting infinitives,* and do not endorse the knee-jerk reaction of C19 pedagogues or the latter-day computer style checker. The consensus is:

* Don't split an infinitive if the result is an inelegant sentence.
* Do **split infinitives** to avoid awkward wording, to preserve a natural rhythm, and especially to achieve the intended emphasis and meaning.

spoil

The past form of this can be either *spoiled* or *spoilt.* In British English they are both freely used for the past tense and the past participle – though the *spoilt child* appears rather more often than the *spoiled child* in BNC data. In American English, *spoiled* is preferred for all uses, and *spoilt* is very rare, by the evidence of CCAE. See further under **-ed** section 1.

sponging or spongeing

The verb *sponge* tests the general rule by which the final *e* of the word is dropped before adding a suffix (see **-e**). But the preferred spelling in both American and British English is **sponging,** by the evidence of their respective databases, with one solitary example of **spongeing** in the BNC. There is of course no verb "spong," so no risk of misinterpretation; and the other relevant spelling rule allows that "g" followed by "i" makes a "soft" sound, as in *changing.* See **-ce/-ge.**

spoonfuls or spoonsful

See under **-ful.**

spouse and spouse equivalent

The term **spouse** has traditionally been used for one's married partner (man or wife). This understanding is built into the bureaucratic expression **spouse equivalent,** used to refer to the person involved in a long-term domestic arrangement other than that of man and wife, and to the other partner in a homosexual or heterosexual relationship. It is however a tad cumbersome, and usage has found an easier way out by stretching the meaning of **spouse,** to include both non-married partners, and ones of the same or different sex. These extensions to the meaning of **spouse** are noted in *Webster's English Usage* (1989) with an example from 1975, and

recognized in *Canadian English Usage* (1997), but not yet hinted at in the definitions of *Merriam-Webster* (2000) or *New Oxford* (1998). In the meantime, **spouse** itself has to be qualified, e.g. by **spouse equivalent** or *same-sex spouse,* as appropriate. *Married spouse* is then not a tautology.

English presents a range of other terms for the "significant other," though their connotations often rule them out. *Lover/mistress* are too direct, *paramour* and *inamorata/o* too exotic, while *fiancé(e)* invokes the very marital conventions that are being circumvented. Journalists create makeshift expressions such as *apartmate* and *live-in friend,* but neither they nor the sex therapists' term *spousal unit* seem very usable. *De facto,* though widely used in Australia and New Zealand, sounds legalistic when applied to one's own closest friend. *Significant other* itself is rather intellectual, and no more transparent when acronymized to *SIGO.* The term *partner* is probably the most serviceable of all, though subject to its own ambiguities (see **partner**).

The lack of a standard term obliges people to invent their own, which is no bad thing, given the infinite variety of human relationships.

spring

The past tense of the verb **spring** may be either *sprang* or *sprung* in American English, as indicated by *Merriam-Webster* (2000), and amply illustrated in data from CCAE. There's some evidence of *sprung* in British English too, in BNC examples such as *asylums which sprung up after the Lunacy Act of 1847,* which occur in both spoken and written data (especially in subordinate clauses). The *New Oxford* (1998) notes it as "chiefly American," but it is evidently found closer to home. In Canada it's the less common past tense, but not incorrect, according to *Canadian English Usage* (1997).

spry

When the adjective **spry** has to be compared, you may wonder how to spell the comparative and superlative forms. British English prefers *spryer, spryest* according to the *New Oxford* (1998), whereas *Merriam-Webster* (2000) indicates the American preference for *sprier, spriest.*

spurt or spirt

The older spelling **spirt** seems to be extinct in both British and American English, despite Fowler's (1926) attempt to find a role for it. **Spurt** is the only one of the pair to appear in data from the BNC and CCAE.

square brackets

For the uses of **square brackets,** see **brackets** section 1b.

square metres or metres square

The order of the words makes a big difference to the size of the area being described. A room whose area is *6 square metres* may be 2 metres long and 3 metres wide (the two dimensions multiplied together make the square metrage). But if the room is *6 metres square,* its walls are all 6 metres long (its dimensions 6 m × 6 m), and the room is definitely square in shape. The first would be about the size of a ship's cabin: the second large enough for table tennis.

squirreling or squirrelling

For the choice between these, see under **-l-/-ll-**.

Sr(.) and sr(.)

See **snr(.), sr(.), Sr., Snr and Sr** for a discussion of all these shortened forms.

Sri Lanka, Sinhala and Sinhalese

Since 1972 **Sri Lanka** has been the official name of the large Indian Ocean island which was formerly *Ceylon*. The largest single group within the *Sri Lankan* community (75%) are the **Sinhalese**, who originated from Northern India. The Tamils from South India are the next largest group (20%). Since 1956, **Sinhala** has been the official language, though Tamil serves some official purposes in some areas. **Sinhalese** has also become the adjective for referring to the culture and main language of **Sri Lanka**, replacing the older spelling *Singhalese* – and the now archaic *Cinghalese*.

St. or Saint

See **Saint**.

-st

This ending is fixed in *against*, but decreasingly used in *amidst, amongst, whilst* where it survives only as the minor alternative (see under **amid, amidst, among or amongst** and **while or whilst**). In all of them the final *t* is something acquired over the centuries, like verdigris on a copper roof. The suffix was originally just *-(e)s* as with some other adverbs (see further under **-s**). But from C16 on, the *t* seems to have been added by analogy with the superlative ending.

stadium

For the plural of this word, see under **-um**.

staff, stave and staffer

Some uses of the word **staff** ("stick, rod") are very old, hence the plural **staves** in which its *ff* is replaced by *v* (see further under **-f > -v-**). It still appears when the sticks referred to serve some special purpose, as ceremonial instruments or as primitive weapons, as in:

> *Royal serjeants-at-arms, staves in their hands, moved into the hall.*
> *. . . militants armed with iron bars and bamboo staves.*

British writers occasionally use the plural **staffs** in reference to historical and ritual events, as in *twisted snakes on ceremonial staffs,* but in BNC data it's usually **staves**. Likewise *tipstaves* is used as the plural of *tipstaff,* the term used of the judge's assistant who precedes him into court, bearing a metal-tipped **staff**.

The singular **stave** is a C14 backformation from **staves**, used to refer to a strip of wood used in making vessels (*barrel stave*) or in the construction of buildings and fences: *. . . splitting timber into staves for the stockade.* Because its plural is also *staves*, the line between it and the plural of **staff** ("stick") when used as a weapon is sometimes fuzzy.

Stave also varies with **staff** in the scoring of music. It originated as a single line (=**staff/stave**), against which the notes were set, and was gradually extended to the set of five lines conventionally used today. In the strict sense of the word, it was a bundle of **staves**, but

staff/stave remained the term for it, acquiring a collective meaning in the process. For musicologists, **staff** is the primary term, according to the *New Grove Dictionary of Music and Musicians* (2001), and it remains in *staff notation*. But general dictionaries vary: *New Oxford* (1998) and the Australian *Macquarie* (1997) give priority to **stave**, whereas *Canadian Oxford* (1998) and *Merriam-Webster* (2000) make it **staff**.

By far the most common use of **staff** these days is to refer to the body of people who work in a particular institution. Its plural is always **staffs**, as in *their respective embassy staffs*. **Staff** in this sense is again a collective noun, raising the question as to whether it takes a singular or plural verb in agreement. In British English both are equally common:

> *They told me that the staff was/were on strike.*

American English prefers singular agreement for such collective words (see further under **agreement** section 1).

Collective use of **staff** creates the need for a word to refer to the individual member, which can be met by **staffer**. The word originated in American English of the 1940s, and has since been taken up in Britain and elsewhere. Its plural is of course **staffers**.

stained glass or stain glass

Stained glass is the standard expression for the colored glass of church windows and Tiffany lamps. **Stain glass** is sometimes heard but rarely seen in print. In British and American database evidence it appears only in transcribed speech, suggesting that most writers find the *-ed* a necessary *inflectional extra:* see further under that heading.

stalactite or stalagmite

Most people need a mnemonic to remind them which of these grows downwards and which grows upwards – as well as which has *c* and which has *g* in it. Both points are covered if you remember that the **stalactite** descends from the ceiling or top of the cave (which gives you the *c* and *t* of the spelling); whereas the **stalagmite** grows from the ground or mud on the cave floor (the *g* and *m* are there).

Both words are neoclassical, dating from C17 but formed with Greek stems. The first embodies a verbal adjective meaning "dripping or trickling," and the second a noun meaning a "drop."

stamen and stamina

The plural of **stamen**, the pollen-bearing organ of a flower is usually **stamens**. Very rarely it appears as **stamina**, which is its correct Latin plural. This is one and the same word as **stamina** meaning "physical resilience." In Latin *stamen/stamina* meant "thread(s)," and as Roman myth had it, the threads of life were spun by the Fates until a person's dying day. So the idea that **stamina** related to longevity is very old, though our use of it to refer to someone's staying power on the tennis court (and elsewhere) is relatively new.

stamp or stomp

The verb **stamp** has multiple meanings in British and American English, from *stamp one's foot* to *stamp a passport* or having an idea *stamped on* or *stamped out*. These uses are standard everywhere, except that **stomp** shares the field when it comes to heavy use of the feet. In American English **stomp** is more frequent than **stamp** in this sense, in data from CCAE, whether it's people (*students clapping and stomping in their seats*) or animals (*herds of buffalo stomping through clouds of dust*). The verb can also connote bad temper, as in *stomped off in a huff* / *stomped out of the room,* or brutality, as in *stomping on his face while he lay unconscious.* **Stomp** has dialectal origins, before making its mark in written American English in the 1910s. It has now established itself in British English, and is found in 100 or so BNC examples describing the *stomping horse* and the *stomping noise from the kids,* as well as adults who *stomp away/off/out.* There are a few examples of *stomping ground* in the BNC, though the British still prefer *stamping ground* – for the moment. Americans are comfortable with both versions of the phrase, by the evidence of CCAE.

stanch or staunch
See **staunch.**

stand in line or stand on line
See **in line or on line.**

standard English
People sometimes speak of **standard English** as if it were a simple reference norm, like a standard gauge on the railway. But what "standard" can we refer to in choosing between expressions like *eccentric, off-beat, way-out, flaky?* There is no easy answer, because words are not physical objects with linear dimensions. A standard in language is more abstract and more value-laden. The notion of **standard English** is often invoked by those who want to claim that a certain expression is correct and that another is effectively *substandard.*

A less value-laden approach to **standard English** is to relate it to the many expressions that have a particular stylistic, regional or social character, which limits their usefulness in other contexts. Words with strong colloquial associations (such as *way-out*) are unsuitable for formal prose. *Eccentric* meanwhile is on the more formal side of the style range. This suggests that we could well define **standard English** as the kind of language which has no strong stylistic connotations, or – put the other way round – language which is neutral in style. An enormous body of words can in fact be used in any kind of context, forming a broad band between colloquial and slang on the one hand, and formal and technical language on the other.

FORMAL	TECHNICAL
STANDARD ENGLISH	
COLLOQUIAL	SLANG

Apart from being stylistically neutral, **standard English** is neutral as to region. It avoids words with a strong local flavor, or ones which might not be understood outside the region of the world in which they are current idiom. An American colloquialism such as *flaky* is unsuitable for international communication. The words used in **standard English** could have originated anywhere in the English-speaking world. In this sense it's close to the notion of *international English* (see further under that heading).

The most contentious aspect of **standard English** is how far it is or can be neutral in social terms. Many would associate it with "educated English," and this seems to make it the prerogative of those who have enjoyed access to a full formal education. Yet **standard English** should not be equated with written English or bookish modes of expression. Again we would assert its neutrality in the social–educational spectrum of usage, so that **standard English** occupies the middle ground between illiterate expression and pedantic usage. It prefers *you* to *youse,* but would not go out of its way to use *whom.* (See further under **whom** and **yous.**)

Standard English is not the exclusive property of any social or regional group, but a resource to which English-speakers at large have access.

standard units
See **SI units, metrication** and Appendix IV.

stank or stunk
See under **stink.**

start (to)
The verb **start** ("begin") can be complemented by either a *to-infinitive* or a verbal noun in *-ing:*

　　　started to laugh　started laughing

The two constructions are equally frequent in British English (Mair, 1998), whereas the *-ing* construction is more common in American.
◊ Compare **begin (to).**

state or State
In both the US and Australia, the federated **states** often come up for discussion, raising the question as to whether the word **state** needs a capital letter. The answer from the *Chicago Manual* (2003) is only when it's "an accepted part of the proper name": compare *Washington State* with *the state of Washington.* Any references to state facilities, as in *state government,* need no capitalizing. The same is broadly true in Australia, where the word would be capitalized in the official title *State of Victoria,* but not in writing about its *state schools.* It thus obeys the general practices associated with institutional names (see **capital letters** sections 1a and 3). However official government documents are inclined to retain the capital letter on **State** in paraphrases and abbreviations of the official name (Peters, 1995).
◊ Compare **federal.**

statements
In terms of sentence functions, **statements** contrast with questions and exclamations. A **statement** simply offers a piece of information and is not primarily intended to stimulate a reaction from the reader or listener. Contrast the ways in which questions, commands and exclamations work: they are indeed designed to elicit a response, either linguistic, behavioral or emotional, from the other party.

Sentences which are **statements** are phrased with the verb in the indicative, and always end with a full stop. See further under **indicative** and **mood.**

stationery or stationary
The choice of spelling is in line with the grammar of the two words: the spelling **-ery** is only applied to nouns, whereas **-ary** can be for either nouns or adjectives (see further under **-ary/-ery/-ory**). **Stationery** is therefore the only possible spelling for the noun referring to paper goods, which leaves

stationary for the adjective meaning "not moving." Yet the mistaken use of the latter in an advertisement for a "stationary cabinet" suggests the need to look for furniture which doesn't get up and walk away.

statistics

The choice between a singular or plural verb with statistics is discussed under -ic/-ics, and agreement section 2b.
◊ For the treatment of numbers in written documents, see numbers and number style.

status

In English usage status has both an anglicized plural statuses and the (zero) plural status. The second results from its being a Latin fourth declension noun (see further under -us section 2); but it also correlates with English use of the word as a mass noun, as in *considering their relative status*. The second issue seems the more likely explanation as to why 50% of respondents to the Langscape survey (1998–2001) endorsed status for the plural form.

status quo

This elliptical Latin phrase means the "state in which." It refers to an existing state of affairs, in contrast with proposed changes and alternatives. Status quo sometimes seems to imply a state which has been discontinued, as in *things have returned to the status quo*. Strictly speaking the phrase should then be *status quo ante*, the "state in which [things were] before" – though that phrase is hardly well known.

staunch or stanch

Staunch is the standard spelling for the adjective meaning "loyal," "steadfast," as in a *staunch supporter of civil rights* or a *staunch gun-control opponent*. In British and American databases, it dominates the evidence, although dictionaries allow stanch as an alternative.

When the word is a verb meaning "stop the flow of or from," usage divides along regional lines. Stanch is very strongly preferred in American English, by the evidence of CCAE, and Canadians are the same way inclined, according to *Canadian English Usage* (1997). Meanwhile BNC data shows a strong British preference for staunch which is shared by Australians (see Peters, 1995).

staves or staffs

See staff, stave and staffer.

stem

This is the part of a word to which affixes are attached, the common element in sets of words like:
escalate escalator escalating de-escalated
The stem can appear in more than one form in different words. In the case of *escalat(e)* it appears with and without a final *e*. For others like *refer(r)*, the final consonant may be doubled in some words but not others, witness:
refers reference referred referring
In other languages such as French and Italian, individual stems vary a good deal more than in these English examples. See for example the set of stems for the French verb *venir* ("come"):
viens venons viennent viendrai
◊ Compare root.

stencil

When used as a verb, should stencil become *stenciled* or *stencilled?* See under -l-/-ll-.

step or steppe

Step is the Russian word for "lowland," as it was borrowed into English in C17, and indistinguishable from the Germanic word for a leg movement or a stair. The use of steppe for the vast treeless plain of Russia was introduced into English from French, and became the dominant spelling in C19. It might otherwise owe something to the "olde Englysshe" mode of archaizing familiar words.

-ster

There's life in this very old suffix, judging by C20 coinings such as *bopster, jivester, popster* to refer to the devotees of various types of popular music. Better known are the words for writers and composers of other kinds: *pulpster, punster, rhymester, songster;* as well as those for "con-artists" in other fields: *gangster, huckster, shyster, tipster, trickster*. Almost all recent formations are deprecating in some way, except *youngster,* and words such as *dragster, roadster, speedster, teamster*, which refer to a means of transport or those who use them.

According to the *Oxford Dictionary* (1989), -ster has an intricate history. It was originally a female agentive which paralleled -er for males. Yet scattered evidence in the following centuries suggests that it gradually became associated with the professional conduct of a trade by either men or women, whereas the -er suffix was used for the occasional practitioner. Thus the *brewer, spinner* and *weaver* turned their hand to the trade from time to time, while those whose livelihood depended on it were named *brewster, spinster* and *webster* respectively. (*Pollster* is a modern example.) But the use of -ster varied in different parts of Britain, and it continued to be applied to women in the south until 1500, while carrying the professional meaning in the north from as early as 1300. The gender and professional/part-time distinctions were further complicated by the pejorative overtones of the suffix, which begin to be registered about 1400. The word *spinster* seems to suffer from all these complications.

stereotypical or stereotypic

The longer form stereotypical is very much preferred by both British and American writers, in data from the BNC and CCAE. See further under -ic/-ical.

stigma

This Greek loanword has both Greek and English plurals: stigmata and stigmas. Stigmata is very strongly associated with religious tradition in the Catholic Church (the mystical marks which symbolize the piercing of nails on the crucified body of Christ). Stigmas is the usual plural in secular use (when it means a mark of disgrace), and in its various scientific uses.

stimulus and stimulant

Both these are used to refer to a physiological mechanism that stimulates the function of a body organ. The stimulus is normally that which initiates a process, while the stimulant increases it. Elsewhere their roles are quite different. Stimulant means a food (such as chocolate) or drink (such as coffee) or medication (such as pep pills) that stimulates the body. **Stimulus** is a more abstract word for anything which motivates and mobilizes us to action.

The plural of **stimulus** is usually **stimuli**, in keeping with its Latin origin, though **stimuluses** is common enough in informal contexts. See **-us** section 1.

sting

The past tense and past participle are both now *stung:*
> *His words (had) stung them.*

The use of *stang* seems to have died out in C19, by the *Oxford Dictionary* (1989) record.

stink

The past tense of this is either *stank* or *stunk,* with both *New Oxford* (1998) and *Merriam-Webster* (2000) giving preference to *stank.* Data from the BNC shows that *stunk* as past tense is mostly found in speech, whereas *stank* prevails in writing. But in American written data from CCAE *stunk* is three times more frequent than *stank* for the past tense. This usage of *stunk* has in fact been on record since C16.

stoa

This Greek architectural term for a colonnade comes to us via Latin, so either **stoai** or **stoae** could be used as its plural in English. The *Oxford Dictionary* (1989) actually gives priority to **stoas** (see further under **-a** section 1). The Athenian **stoa** was the birthplace of Stoic philosophy. See under **stoic.**

stoic or stoical

References to the Greek philosophy of the **Stoics** (as adjective or noun) are always written as **Stoic.** But the adjective meaning "steadfast and forbearing" is also typically written as **stoic** in both British and American English. It outnumbers **stoical** by about 5:3 in BNC data, and by 8:1 in data from CCAE. Neither database lends support to Fowler's (1926) notion of a division of labor, whereby **stoic** was preferred for attributive use, as in *stoic resignation,* and **stoical** for the predicative role: *be stoical.* Rather both forms occur in both roles.
◊ For other *-ic/-ical* pairs, see under that heading.

stomp or stamp

See under **stamp.**

stony or stoney

See **-y/-ey.**

stops

The word **stop** is sometimes used as:
1 a term for any punctuation mark
2 a shortened form of *full stop* (i.e. *period*), especially in reference to punctuating abbreviations.
◊ For further information about *punctuation marks,* see **punctuation.**

storey or story

In British English, as well as Canadian and Australian, these spellings differentiate the word for the floor or level of a building, from the word for a tale or account of something. This distinction is however less than a century old. The original *Oxford Dictionary* (1884–1928) had both spelled **story,** and this

is current American usage. The plural for the first spelling is **storeys,** while for the second it's **stories.**

Whether the two words come from one and the same source is a matter of scholarly debate. Some trace both words back to the Latin *storia,* with the picturesque notion that the levels of older buildings were differentiated by the different tales told in their windows. Others suggest that **storey** ("level of a building") developed, like the noun *store,* from an Old French verb *estorer* ("build").

The British use of **storey** entails *multistorey* where Americans use *multistory.* Other derivatives involve even more variants: *two-storey* or *two-storeyed* for the British, and *two-story* or *two-storied* for Americans. (See further under **inflectional extras.**)
◊ For the question as to whether the second **stor(e)y** is the first or second floor, see **floor and storey.**

straight, strait and strai(gh)tened

Straight is that very common adjective describing a line or edge with no curves or kinks in it. It can also be an adverb meaning "directly" or "immediately":
> *Head straight for the river.*
> *Go straight to bed.*

Strait is an archaic adjective/adverb meaning "narrow" or "restricted," which survives in compounds such as *straitjacket* and *strait(-)laced.* Both words are occasionally spelled with **straight.** *Straightjacket* has been recorded continuously since C16, according to the *Oxford Dictionary* (1989), and is recognized as an alternative in *New Oxford* (1998) and *Merriam-Webster* (2000). No doubt people think of the garment as one which keeps your arms and legs **straight** – not just one which restricts your movements. Likewise it's tempting to reinterpret *strait-laced* as *straight-laced,* i.e. "keeping to the straight and narrow," especially when it goes with *straight-faced.* Almost half of all instances of the word in CCAE were *straight-laced* (mostly hyphened), and more than half in the BNC (all hyphened), and it's recognized by the reference dictionaries. *Merriam-Webster* (2000) lists both *straightlaced* and *straitlaced* without hyphens, whereas *New Oxford* (1998) has them with.

The phrase *straitened circumstances* (ones in which you feel the financial pinch) is also sometimes written as *straightened circumstances.* It appears in both British and American databases, but is not sanctioned by either of the reference dictionaries.

stranded preposition

See **prepositions** section 2.

strata

This plural of the Latin **stratum** meaning "level," "layer," has taken on a singular life of its own in English. See further under **stratum.**

strategy or stratagem

A **strategy** is an overall plan or method for tackling a problem or managing a campaign. A **stratagem** is a specific trick or ruse, used to deceive. They differ thus in scale, as well as their implications: a **stratagem** involves deviousness, whereas a **strategy** means legitimate planning.

Both words go back ultimately to Greek *strategos* ("a general"). **Stratagem** entered English in C15 with a French modification to the spelling of the second syllable. **Strategy** arrived in C17, amid the English Renaissance when the classical forms of words were better known.

stratose or stratous

Both adjectives are related to the Latin stem *strat-* meaning "laid down," but they belong in different fields. **Stratose** is a botanical term meaning "arranged in layers," first recorded in 1881. **Stratous** is older, used since 1816 in meteorology to refer to a layered cloud formation. It corresponds to the noun *stratus*. See further under **-ous**.

stratum and strata

The Latin **stratum** meaning "layer" was borrowed into English in C16, along with its Latin plural **strata** (see **-um**). Its technical uses in medicine and geology are now paralleled in the social sciences, with references to social and institutional levels as in *a stratum of farmers* or *upper class stratum of entrepreneurs*. Expressions like these have made it into everyday parlance, but the plural remains **strata**, rather than the anglicized **stratums**. The latter doesn't appear in either the British or American databases, though it is occasionally heard in conversation.

Like other Latin loanwords with plurals ending in *-a*, **strata** has been used as a singular word since C18, like *candelabra* and *data* (Peters, 2001). Collective and indeterminate uses pave the way, in examples such as *the same social strata, the bottom strata of the well*. Singular agreement and singular use of **strata** are still rare in current British English, with just a sprinkling of examples in the BNC: *a strata, a particular strata, this strata*. In American English it's more freely used, judging by the more elaborate examples in CCAE, such *a whole strata of music (going unrecognized), a different economic strata, the absence of that middle strata*.

The next evolutionary step is for **strata** to acquire its own English plural **stratas**. This is more often heard than seen, but the single example in CCAE adds to those recorded earlier by *Webster's English Usage* (1989). *Merriam-Webster* (2000) notes it as "persistent" though not particularly frequent. As usage it's no stranger than turning *agenda* into a singular, countable word: see **agenda**.

street

While British speakers typically say *I live in Market Street*, American idiom has it as *I live on Market Street*, or just *on Market* (see further under **on/in**).
◊ For the differences between **street**, *road* and other terms in the same set, see **road**.

streptococcus

The plural of this word is discussed under **-us** section 1.

strew

Dictionaries allow either *strewn* or *strewed* for the past participle. American writers use *strewed* very occasionally, in about 3% of all instances of the past participle in CCAE. British writers don't do so at all, by the evidence of the BNC.

stride

The past tense of this verb is definitely *strode*, but some doubt hangs over its past participle. Though

stridden is the dictionaries' first choice (in line with the verb *ride*), *strode* is also a possibility. The option is rarely used in British English, and *stridden* prevails in BNC data. Canadians endorse it too, according to the *Canadian Oxford* (1998). Americans meanwhile use *strode* all the time for past participle in data from CCAE, and there's no evidence of *stridden*. Australians find themselves torn between them. In an Australian survey (Peters, 1995), 47% endorsed *stridden* and 38% *strode* for the past participle, though many expressed discomfort about the choice.

strike

Struck now serves for both past tense and past participle of this verb:

> *At one o'clock the clock struck six.*
> *The phantom raspberry-blower had struck again.*

The old past participle *stricken* lives on as an adjective in metaphorical uses of the word, as in *stricken with age* and *poverty-stricken*.

string, stringed and strung

In *stringed instrument*, the word **string** is essentially a noun. The phrase refers to instruments such as the violin and cello, which produce sound through the vibrations of their strings – just as the phrase "wind instruments" identifies the sound-producing medium of the flute, oboe etc. **Stringed** can thus be analyzed as an inflected noun (see **-ed** section 2). Alternatively, it might be derived from the verb **string**, meaning "fit with strings" or "suspend." But its past tense and past participle are **strung**, whether it's a guitar *strung with fresh gut* or a clothes line *strung between apartment buildings*. Though originally regular, the verb has used irregular parts (especially **strung**) since C16, according to the *Oxford Dictionary* (1989). **Strung** prevails also in more abstract and compound uses:

> *He was strung up about something*
> *Knowing how highly strung she was...*
> *They strung the discussion out for the whole morning.*
> *We were hamstrung by the lack of funds.*

strive

The past tense of **strive** can be *strove* or *strived*, and the past participle either *striven* or *strived*. Both *New Oxford* (1998) and *Merriam-Webster* (2000) give priority to the irregular forms, and there's little use of the regular *strived* in BNC data. The examples (mostly of the past participle) are almost entirely from spoken sources. But in American data from CCAE, *strived* serves as both past tense and participle, in about 25% of instances of the first, and more than 40% of the second. So in the US the regularization of the verb is still underway, whereas in the UK it seems to be becalmed.

strong and weak

These terms have been used by Germanic philologists to distinguish

* irregular and regular verbs: see further under **irregular verbs**.
* major and minor classes of nouns: see further under **declension**.

structure in writing

See under **headings** and **subheadings**.

stub

See under **tables**.

stucco

For the plural see **-o**.

stunk or stank

See **stink**.

stupefy

See under **-ify/-efy**.

sty or stye

Many dictionaries give these as alternative spellings for (a) pigs' accommodation (and by analogy, that of humans), and (b) the small swelling which comes up like a boil on an eyelid. In fact **sty** prevails for both words in data from CCAE and the BNC, and there's little sign of **stye**. When used in the singular, **stye** always refers to a *pig stye,* although some of the BNC examples of **styes** refer to the eye problem. The other plural form **sties** is applied only to accommodation fit for pigs (animal or metaphorical).

style

Some do it with **style** – and others presumably without it. But writing always has a **style** or **styles** built into it, generated by the very language used. Whether the **style** is formal, informal or something in between depends on the words (see **formal words** and **colloquialisms**), and the grammatical choices. A lively **style** makes use of active verbs and concrete imagery, and avoids too many abstractions and nominalizations. (See further under **abstract nouns** and **nominal**.) A clear **style** is helped by effective use of sentences, so that their length and structure correspond with the units of meaning being expressed.

Certain writing **styles** have strong links with particular institutions. Documents written in the name of government often embody officialese, just as those associated with business often contain commercialese. Legal writing and scientific writing have recurrent features, such as long sentences, and passive and impersonal constructions. Many academic writers have a **style** which is abstract and impersonal, in keeping with the theoretical emphasis of university work. Thus the writing **style** of many people employed by those institutions is at least somewhat institutionalized. It may indeed be seen as part of their professional competence. Yet no-one would deny the negative aspects of *institutional styles,* and the need to consciously combat them with *Plain English* (see further under that heading).

Institutional and professional writing often involves **style** in that other sense of *house style,* the conventions of spelling, word form, punctuation and usage to be used by everyone who works for that company or department or publisher. The *style guide* which describes the *house style* is intended to standardize the documents or publications produced, and so is normative or prescriptive.

Individual writers are free to cultivate their own **style** in both senses of the word: to create their own flexible "house" **style** according to the various contexts in which they write; and to create their own distinctive writing **style**, making it clear and lively, and attractive and readable.

stylus

New Oxford (1998) and *Merriam-Webster* (2000) both give priority to the Latin plural **styli** rather than the English **styluses.** Yet a majority of respondents (72%) to the Langscape survey (1998-2001) preferred **styluses.** This makes it one of the better assimilated Latin loanwords of its type: see further under **-us** section 1.

stymie or stymy

Golfers coined this word for the frustrating situation when an opponent's ball lies directly between yours and the hole. For them the uncertainty of the spelling is of no consequence, but it becomes a question for others when the word is used in the general sense of "thwart." In British and American English **stymie** is preferred, according to *New Oxford* (1998) and *Merriam-Webster* (2000) respectively; and it has the numbers (in *stymieing* as well) in data from the BNC and CCAE. **Stymy** might seem to be supported by the very occasional use of *stymying* in the BNC – except that it embodies the spelling rule that changes *-ie* to *−y* before *-ing,* as for verbs such as *die, lie, tie* (see further under **ie > -y-**). There's no sign of the C19 spelling *stimy.*

◊ For other words in which *y* has replaced *i,* see **i/y**.

sub-

This Latin prefix meaning "below," is found in all kinds of verbs, adjectives and nouns of which the following are just a token:

> *submarine submerge submit subordinate subterranean*

Sub- often means "below" in physical terms, as in *subcutaneous, subsoil, subway.* From this it has developed metaphorical meanings, such as "inferior to," in *subhuman, subnormal, substandard.* It can also mean "below" in terms of structure or organization:

> *subcommittee subcontract subdivide sublet subplot subroutine subsection subtitle*

In a handful of words, this meaning is further extended to designate a rank or position by reference to the one immediately above it, as in:

> *subdean subeditor sublieutenant*

sub poena

See under **habeas corpus**.

sub rosa

This Latin phrase means "under the rose," but in English (and other languages such as Dutch and German) it's used to mean "confidentially" or "privately." The phrase has a long history. Some trace it back to the ancient Egyptian god Horus, whose symbol was the rose. Horus was identified by the Greeks with Harpocrates, their god of silence, who was represented as a naked boy sucking his finger. In Roman myth, Harpocrates was given a rose by Cupid, to bribe him not to disclose the amorous affairs of Venus. Thus the rose became the symbol of silence in western civilization. In more recent times it was sculptured on the ceilings of banquet rooms, as a reminder to the diners that what was said in their cups was not to be repeated outside. A rose was also set above the door of some C16 confessionals. At this point the secular symbolism of the rose begins to overlap with its symbolism in the Christian tradition, where it was associated with the Virgin Mary and other female saints. See also **rosary or rosery.**

subconscious or unconscious

The prefixes make some difference to the meaning of these words. **Subconscious** as an adjective means "just below the level of consciousness," as in:
> *Her smile revealed subconscious relief at the decision.*

Unconscious as an ordinary adjective means "having lost consciousness":
> *The victim lay unconscious on the footpath.*

In psychology **unconscious** is used both as noun and adjective in *the unconscious (mind)* to refer to mental processes and psychic material which a person cannot bring into consciousness. The word **subconscious** is sometimes used nontechnically in the same way:
> *My subconscious is telling me I need a drink.*

subcontinental

In British English this adjective is used to refer to the *subcontinent of India,* as in the provocative suggestion that *Cricket is a subcontinental game.* More seriously it's used alongside *Asian* to refer to distinct ethnic Indians and Pakistanis in the UK.

Elsewhere **subcontinental** is mostly used by geologists, to mean "below the continent" as in *the composition of the subcontinental, lithospheric mantle,* or to a subsection of a continent, as in *a continental or subcontinental scale.*

subject

The grammatical **subject** of a clause is the person or thing which operates the verb:
> *On Saturday I go to the markets at 6 am.*
> *Wholesale business begins much earlier.*
> *The stalls are closed in the afternoon.*

The **subject** also decides whether the verb is singular or plural, though with some variability (see further under **agreement**). The easiest way to locate the **subject** of each of those clauses is to identify the verb and make it the focus of a question:
> *Who or what goes?* ("I")
> *Who or what begins?* ("wholesale business")
> *Who or what are closed?* ("the stalls")

In statements, a **subject** almost always comes before the verb, though in questions it's usually delayed until after the auxiliary part of the verb phrase. (See under **inversion**.)

The **subject** is often the first item in a sentence, hence the standard pattern of *SVO (subject verb object)* etc. (see further under **predicate**). However the **subject** can be preceded by a conjunction, and adverb or adverbial phrase, as in the first example in this entry above. Any kind of phrase which precedes the **subject** draws attention to itself, and can be used to alter the focus of discussion. (See further under **topic**.)
◊ For what grammarians call a *dummy subject,* see under that heading.

subject−verb agreement

See **agreement**.

subjective case

This is a name used by some English grammarians for the case of the *subject* of a clause. Traditionally it has been called the *nominative case.* See further under that heading.

subjunctive

The **subjunctive** is a pale shadow of what it used to be. In older English grammar, the *subjunctive forms* of verbs diverged from those in the indicative, and were used for special purposes such as expressing a wish or a hypothesis. Compare:
> *God bless America* (**subjunctive**, for a wish)
> *God blesses America with . . .* (indicative, for a plain statement)

What's left of the **subjunctive** manifests itself by default, the absence of an *-s* on verbs in the third person singular present tense (*bless* rather than *blesses*).

English once had both present and past forms of the **subjunctive** for all verbs. But for most the only residue is the third person singular *present subjunctive.* As shown in the example above, it differs from the indicative in having no *-s* suffix. Only for the verb *be* is there a set of alternative forms for the *present subjunctive,* all of which are different from the indicative. Compare:

	I am	*you are*	*he/she/it is*	*we are*	*they are*
(if)	*I be*	*you be*	*he/she/it be*	*we be*	*they be*

The verb *be* also retains some distinct forms for its *past subjunctive,* at least in the singular. Compare:

I was	*you were*
he/she/it was	*we were*
they were (indicative)	
I were	*you were*
he/she/it were	*we were*
they were (**subjunctive**)	

The most visible differences are in the first and especially the third person singular, and these provide us with evidence of the surviving uses of the **subjunctive**, detailed below.

1 The mandative subjunctive. This is the kind of construction that calls for a particular action, as in:
> *They recommended that he present hard evidence for the claim.*

Mandative constructions use the present forms of the **subjunctive**, and so are often only detectable in the third person singular, although the switch of tenses (present following the past of the main clause) is another sign of their presence. Compare:
> *They proposed that he come the next day.*
> *They proposed that we come the next day.*

Mandatives can be prefaced by any one of a number of verbs including:

advise	ask	beg	demand
desire	direct	insist	move
order	propose	recommend	request
require	stipulate	suggest	urge

Adjectives such as *essential, important, necessary, vital,* and conjunctions such as *in order that* and *on condition that,* also introduce mandative clauses which typically take the **subjunctive**. The *mandative subjunctive* is used regularly in North American English, as well as Australian and New Zealand English (Hundt, 1998; Peters, 1998a; and *Canadian English Usage,* 1997). It appears in positive and negative constructions:
> *The doctor insisted that she (not) be allowed out.*

In British English, the *mandative subjunctive* declined during C20, perhaps because of Fowler's (1926) general onslaught on the **subjunctive**, on the basis that it was either misused or pretentious. Gowers left it unchanged in his revised version of Fowler (1965), and British grammarians since then have tended to say that it's primarily associated with formal style, as do

the authors of the *Comprehensive Grammar* (1985).
Instead, British writers have expressed the mandative
by means of the modal verb *should,* as in
> *The doctor insisted that she should (not) be*
> *allowed out*

Signs of a late C20 revival of the *mandative
subjunctive* in British English have been detected by
Overgaard (1995), so this regional difference may
disappear in C21.

**2 The subjunctive in "unreal" or impossible
conditions.** The only surviving past form of the
subjunctive, i.e. *were,* is the one most associated with
expressing conditions that could never apply, after *as
though, as if,* and especially *if.*
> *The room had a strange effect on her, as if she were*
> *floating in space.*
> *If he were a good manager, I wouldn't mind.*

But after plain *if* there's a growing tendency to replace
the **subjunctive** with indicative, whether the
condition is strictly real or unreal:
> *If he was a good manager I wouldn't mind.*

The *Oxford Grammar* (1996) notes that the
were-subjunctive is also associated with formal style,
and growing use of the indicative. From the
Australians surveyed (Peters, 1993a) came the
comment that the use of *if* was all that it took to
express the hypothetical condition, and so there was
no need for the **subjunctive**. The motivation for using
the *were-subjunctive* is stylistic rather than
grammatical.

3 Formulaic uses of the subjunctive. In C21 English,
we still use the **subjunctive** in conventionalized
wishes and other formulaic phrases. For example:

Be that as it may	*Come what may.*
Far be it from me.	*If I were you...*
If need be.	*As it were.*
God bless you.	*Heaven forbid.*

Fixed expressions like these would not arrest the
general decline of the **subjunctive**, nor decreasing use
of the *were-subjunctive*. Yet the *mandative subjunctive*
is still in regular use outside Britain, which could
facilitate its return. Widespread and productive use
makes the *mandative subjunctive* stylistically neutral,
which enhances its chances of persisting for some
time. There's life in the old paradigm yet.

subjuncts

See under **adverbs**.

subordination and the subordinate clause

The grammatical aspects of **subordination** are
discussed under **clauses** sections 3 and 4.
◊ For the role of **subordinate clauses** in controlling
the delivery of information, see **information focus**.

subpoena or subpena

See under **habeas corpus**.

substantial or substantive

Both words are related to the noun *substance,* and
though both could appear in the same context, they
differ in focus. **Substantial** is the commoner of the
two by far, with the physical and general meaning of
"large in size or proportion," as in a *substantial
distance* or a *substantial contribution*. The meaning of
substantive is more abstract, and implies that there
are real issues in whatever's being described that way,
such as *substantive decisions* or *no substantive*
evidence. The same discussion paper could be both
substantial and **substantive** – if it was long and
large as well as significant in terms of the issues it
raised. However a weary reader would no doubt prefer
it to be **substantive** rather than **substantial**.

substitute or replace

See under **replace**.

substitute verb

See **pro-forms**.

subtitles

For the use of capital letters in **subtitles**, see **titles**
section 1.

such and such as

The grammar of **such** has not been well understood
until recently, making it the target of anxiety and
censure on several fronts. For many dictionaries it's
just a pronoun and adjective, as in the following:
> *Such is the fate of many of us* (pronoun)
> *Such people are hard to convince* (adjective)

But these two complementary uses of **such** are now
recognized as those of pronoun and *determiner*. **Such**
is also a determiner in extended noun phrases:
> *Such conscientious people are hard to convince.*

though some dictionaries would explain its use there
as that of *adverb*. Yet another grammatical puzzle was
the construction *such a,* as in *such a fate*. The
Comprehensive Grammar (1985) explains this use of
such as making it a *predeterminer* (see further under
determiners). All these are "classifying" uses of
such, and important as cohesive devices in spoken
and especially written discourse (see **coherence or
cohesion**).

In conversation, the determiner **such** also plays a
slightly different part, that of *intensifier,* as in
They're such clever people. This is the usage dubbed
"informal" by some usage writers, though it appears
often enough in print for *Webster's English Usage*
(1989) to dismiss the criticism. Research associated
with the *Longman Grammar* (1999) showed that
intensifying use of **such** was twice as common in
fiction and conversational data as in news reporting
and academic prose. Issues of style intersect with the
grammar and meaning of **such** in all the
constructions discussed below.

1 Clausal links with such. **Such** is sometimes
questioned when used in combination with relative
pronouns, most notably *that:*
> *The document was phrased in such a way that*
> *made it thoroughly incomprehensible.*

The *Oxford Dictionary* (volume issued in 1917) said
that constructions with the relative were "rare" and
"now regarded as incorrect." Perhaps this was true
for the pronouns *which* and *who;* but with *that* the
issues are rather different. It creates a hybrid
(relative–adverbial) construction, whose ambivalence
presumably had to be resolved to satisfy older usage
commentators. Their solution was to replace *that* with
as, although this could not be done in all cases, as
Fowler (1926) noted. Modern English grammars like
the *Comprehensive Grammar* recognize the
combination of *such ... that* as a kind of correlative,
and as a complex coordinator expressing result –
which also lends something to the interpretation of
the sentence above. Like *so ... that,* the two

521

components (*such, that*) can be used together or apart, but with different stylistic implications. Their use together goes with a style on the formal side of standard, as in:

> *Ignorance was such that they became afraid of normal social contact.*

Such that mostly occurred in the academic texts of the *Longman Grammar* corpus. Meanwhile uses of *such . . . that* spread across other kinds of writing from news reporting to fiction; and the longer string *in such a way that* was one of the relatively common "lexical bundles" of conversation – more common in fact than *in such a way as*. Burchfield (1996) found constructions with *such that* and *such . . . that* perfectly idiomatic.

2 Such as to introduce examples. Such as has traditionally been preferred to *like* as a way of introducing examples. Compare:

> *He preferred tropical fruits such as pineapple and mango.*
>
> *He preferred tropical fruits like pineapple and mango.*

The argument for **such as** was that it prevented the ambiguity that might sometimes beset *like* (though the case seems to have been exaggerated: see **like** section 1). Yet this concern probably explains why **such as** is more than a thousand times commoner in academic writing than in speech. **Such as** is also found in fiction and news writing, but much less often. These facts of usage make **such as** more formal and academic in style, whereas *like* is straightforward and direct.

Pronouns following **such as** are normally in the accusative (objective) case:

> *. . . Stephen King. They would only consider well-known writers such as him.*

It was once argued that the nominative form (*he*) ought to be used in such cases, on the basis that **such as** introduces the remnant of an elliptical clause (*such as he was*). Modern grammarians are less inclined to argue from what is not there, and to allow that **such as** is a *complex preposition* rather than conjunction – which means that the accusative *him* is the case to use. (See further under **case**.)

3 Such as a cohesive device. Such as a pronoun/determiner is a useful aid to cohesion, which is no doubt why it often appears at the start of a sentence, in written as well as spoken discourse:

> *Such is the way of the world.*
>
> *Such indifference I can't understand.*

In each case, **such** forges a strong link with something said in the previous sentence or sentences, and is prominent as the first word. The second example shows how this can impact on word order, with the object of the clause moved to the front (see further under **inversion**). Upfront use of **such** is part of the fiction writer's repertoire, by the various examples presented in the *Longman Grammar*. But the use of the pronoun **such** in mid-sentence is associated much more exclusively with legal writing. For example:

> *Any person found borrowing test instruments for use at home, or using such for private purposes while on government premises will be prosecuted under Section 522 of the Government Property Act.*

The intricate language of law makes it necessary perhaps to have **such** rather than the regular, unobtrusive pronouns *them/it*. Whatever the

necessity there, using **such** in the same way elsewhere creates an official and rather pompous style.

suffixes

These are the add-on units at the ends of words which modify their grammar and/or meaning, witness:

> *hyphen* hyphen*s* hyphen*ate* hyphen*ated* hyphen*ation*

In that set of words there are two essential types of **suffixes**:

* inflectional
* derivational (or lexical)

1 Inflectional suffixes are ones like the plural *-s* and the past tense *-ed*, which simply adapt the basic word within its own grammatical class (noun or verb in those cases). A plural noun is still a noun, just as a past tense verb is still a verb. The range of *inflectional suffixes* in English is quite small when compared with those of other European languages. See further under **inflections**.

2 Derivational suffixes have a much more radical effect on the word they're attached to, often moving it from one grammatical class to another. In the set above, *-ate* converts the noun *hyphen* into a verb, while *-ion* turns the verb into an abstract noun. Note that **suffixes** which convert concrete nouns to abstract ones (*cork > corkage*), or to agentive nouns (*farm > farmer*) and vice versa, are also considered to be *derivational*. The range of *derivational suffixes* in English is very large, comprising those maintained from Old English (e.g. *-dom, -ship*), as well as many acquired via French and Latin loanwords (e.g. *-ery, -ment*), and even some from Greek (e.g. *-archy, -logy*). Others are the fruit of internal development in English itself, over the course of centuries (e.g. *-ful, -man*).

Derivational suffixes can be grouped in terms of their effect on the grammar of words, those which convert:

* verbs into nouns, either agentive (*-er, -ant, -or* etc.) or abstract (*-al, -ation, -ment* etc.)
* adjectives/nouns into verbs (*-en, -ify, -ize*)
* adjectives into adverbs (*-ly*)
* nouns/adjectives into adjectives/nouns (*-an, -ese, -ite* etc.)
* concrete nouns into other types of noun (*-eer, -hood, -ie, -y*)

English words often carry more than one **suffix**, though four derivational ones seem to be the limit. The verbal noun *editorializing* (*edit/or/ial/iz/ing*) is a useful mnemonic for this. All *derivational suffixes* precede inflectional ones. The last *derivational suffix* decides the grammatical role of the word. Note that words with three or four *derivational suffixes*, each of which in turn modifies the word's role, put some strain on the reader. Writing which relies on multi-suffixed words is heavy-going (see further under **nominal**). The uses of many common **suffixes** are discussed in this book under their individual headings.

sui generis

In Latin this means literally "of its own kind." It is used of something which (or someone who) stands apart as the only one of their kind. Strictly speaking it's an adverbial phrase – not a noun, a usage which the *Oxford Dictionary* (1989) dubbed "illiterate." The reason for such heavy censure is not however obvious to those without Latin, and the grammar of the phrase is ambiguous in English sentences such as *This publication is sui generis.*

sulfur or sulphur

In American English, **sulfur** is the standard spelling, where British English uses **sulphur**. But **sulfur** is also the professional choice for chemists everywhere in the world, recommended by the International Union of Pure and Applied Chemistry. The *f* spelling is also used in the names of **sulfur** compounds such as *sulfuric acid, copper sulfate, hydrogen sulfide*, and *sulfurous* when used in technical contexts. It applies also to *sulfa drugs* or *sulfas* (sometimes *sulpha drugs* in the UK). British writers – including scientists other than chemists – still prefer **sulphur**, by the almost overwhelming use of it in BNC data. Journalism that focuses on *sulphur dioxide* as a cause of "acid rain" uses the nonspecialist's spelling; and it persists in the names of animals such as the *sulphur-bottom* (= blue whale) and the *sulphur-crested cockatoo*.

Sulfur is usually traced back to Latin, where it was variously spelled *sulpur, sulphur* as well as *sulfur*. Beyond that its origins are obscure, though cognates in Germanic languages (including the Anglo-Saxon *swefl*, "sulfur, brimstone") suggest that it goes back to Indo-European rather than Arabic sources (see **Indo-European**). *Webster's Third* (1986) notes a precedent in the Oscan language, an early Italic language that was replaced by Latin. In medieval French it was *sulfre*, and *soufre* at first in Middle English. From C14 on there were more than a dozen variants with *ph* or *f*, but Johnson's dictionary (1755) lists only *sulphur*, and most of the *Oxford Dictionary*'s (1989) citations from C18 support it. However the *Dictionary* acknowledges the use of **sulfur** in American English, and it's clearly in line with the rational spellings endorsed by Webster. See further under **spelling** section 5.

sumac or sumach

The tree that lends its rich color to the North American fall can be spelled either way, but **sumac** is given priority in *Merriam-Webster* (2000) and *New Oxford* (1998). This is in line with American usage, by the relative frequencies of the two spellings in CCAE. The British however seem to prefer **sumach**, which gets twice as much use as **sumac** in the BNC.

summa cum laude

See under **cum laude**.

summary

How different are the following:

> *abridgement abstract précis resumé summary synopsis*

All refer to a shortened version of a text, and are sometimes used loosely as substitutes for each other. Yet they differ in the way they summarize the original text.

* An *abridgement* gives you a shortened version of the text of a book. The less important parts are cut out, and the rest remains in the author's own words.
* An *abstract* is a very brief statement (usually one or two paragraphs) about the work reported at large in a document. The *abstract* pinpoints the issues addressed and the results of the inquiry, as well as the conclusions drawn from it. *Abstracts* are

much used in reporting the essence of research endeavors in academic journals.

* A *précis* restates the contents of a piece of writing in a much more limited number of words (usually specified). Compression is achieved by repackaging the ideas in alternative wording.
* A *resumé* is an overview of action so far taken or of something proposed. (For other uses of the word, see the individual entry for **resumé**.)
* A *synopsis* give you a bird's eye view of the various topics discussed in a work, without detailing what is said about each.
* The word *summary* may be reserved for a brief recapitulation of the points argued in a piece of writing. However it's often used to cover reporting of the main substance of a document, and thus in much the same way as *synopsis*. For *executive summary*, see **reports** section 1.

summation plurals

See **pluralia tantum**.

summons

This legal noun is always construed as a singular in English, as in *expecting a summons at any moment*. The grammar reflects its origins as an abstract noun in Old French (*sumunse*), which became *som(o)unce* in Middle English. In C15 English it was refashioned along classical lines and with a final *s*, but the singular sense has survived – hence the need for the plural **summonses**. The noun also provides the base for the verb which is regularly inflected as *summonsed, summonsing*. The verb **summons** spells out the legal imperative for someone to appear in court, though in practice it's the same when one is *summoned*.

super- and super

This is a Latin prefix meaning "above," derived from words such as:

> *superficial superlative superordinate supersede supervisor*

In modern English formations, it often means "above and beyond," as in:

> *superhuman supernatural superpower supersonic superstructure*

This meaning has been extended in popular formations to mean "outstanding, very special," as in *superman* and *supermarket,* and this extension has proved useful to advertisers, with their generic *superproduct,* as well as *superwash, supercleaner* etc.

Super served for decades of C20 as an adjective meaning "great." It was used very freely in conversation to express approval: *a super holiday, it was just super!* Fowler (1926) railed at overuse of the word, and it has since fallen out of fashion like many heavily indulged words. Its chief uses nowadays as an independent word are semitechnical: in reference to the highest grade of petrol, and as an abbreviation for *superannuation* (allowance).

◊ For the older chemical use of **super-**, as in *superphosphate*, see under **per-**.

supercede or supersede

See **supersede**.

supercilious and superciliary

Both these words focus on the eyelid, in Latin *supercilium*. The literal meaning is there in

superciliary, a recent scientific word used in anatomy and zoology to refer to a ridge or mark above the eye. **Supercilious** is the common adjective for "haughty," an attitude which even the Romans associated with raising one's eyebrows.

superior

In Latin **superior** is a comparative adjective meaning "higher" – which has consequences for its use in English. One is that **superior** should not be further compared with "more" (which would make it a *double comparative:* see under that heading). Another is that when **superior** expresses comparisons, the prepositional link should be *to* rather than *than,* according to usage commentators as well as grammarians. For example:

> *The wealthy enjoy schooling far superior to that of poor people.*

In fact most British and American writers prefer to do this, by the evidence of the BNC and CCAE. Yet the objections voiced to using *than* with **superior** suggest that it is sometimes used, and not so surprisingly when it creates comparative constructions, as in:

> *Education for the wealthy is far superior than that of poor people.*

Written evidence of *superior than* is however elusive in both British and American databases, and it remains spoken rather than written idiom.

superlative

In common usage this word means "excellent" and it lends itself to hyperbole, as on a menu card which describes a dish as:

> *A superlative combination of fresh seafood, lightly cooked in batter and served with a garnish of roasted pinenuts*

This usage probably makes it an *absolute adjective* (see **absolute** section 1).

Grammarians use **superlative** for the highest degree of comparison for an adjective, as *freshest* is for *fresh* (see **adjectives** section 2). Some **superlatives** nevertheless seem to exist without regular comparison, e.g. *darndest* (see "absolute superlatives" under **absolute**).

◊ For the use of *double superlatives,* see individual entry.

superordinate

In logic and language this refers to a concept or word which is at a higher level of generality or abstraction, as *residence* is in relation to *house, home unit, hut, mansion* and *weekender.* The **superordinate** stands as a cover term for a whole class of more specific words, and includes them within its ambit. Between the **superordinate** and the specific terms (*hyponyms*), there's a strong bond of meaning which can be exploited to provide cohesion. (See further under **coherence or cohesion,** and **hyponyms.**)

supersede or supercede

The spelling **supersede** is the standard one, reflecting the etymology of the word. Its second element is the Latin root *sed-* ("sit"), but it's the only word in English which uses the root that way – hence the temptation to spell it like the larger set of those with the root *ced-* meaning "yield." **Supercede** appears often enough in American English for *Webster's Third* (1986) to register it as a variant, and *Webster's English Usage*

has several recent citations from later C20 prose. Data from CCAE confirms its position as the minority variant, outnumbered by **supersede** in the ratio of almost 1:10. In British English, **supercede** has been marginalized by the *Oxford Dictionary's*(1989) comment on it as a "variant, now erroneous" of **supersede.** This is echoed by *New Oxford* (1998), though it does not prevent the occasional appearances of **supercede** in BNC data, in the ratio of about 1:50 to **supersede.** The forces of analogy are still with it.

◊ For other words ending in *-cede,* see **-cede/-ceed.**

supine or prostrate

See **prostrate.**

supper or dinner

See under **dinner.**

suppletive verbs

See under **irregular verbs** section 8.

suppose or supposing

Either of these can be used to preface a suggestion or a speculative idea ("what if"):

> *Suppose/supposing you put the question to them.*

Some stylists prefer **suppose** for a more formal effect, and it's easier to justify in terms of grammar. There may however be regional preferences, judging by database evidence. **Suppose** is the only one used in BNC citations when the word is followed by *that,* whereas it's **supposing** in American data from CCAE. Compare:

> *Suppose that the Chancellor has decided in favour of the petitioner*
> *Supposing that I was allowed to set up my own business*

Supposing is the only possibility when the word is used as a subordinator in sentences presenting an open condition:

> *We'll go to the gallery today, always supposing it's open.*

In such sentences **supposing** means "assuming." The condition that it prefaces makes the utterance more tentative, often as a token of politeness.

sur-

This prefix comes to us in French loanwords such as:

> *surface surpass surplus surprise survey survive*

As the French form of *super,* it essentially means "above," although that meaning is submerged in most of the words just listed. The pronunciation of some of them (especially *surprise*) seems to erode the prefix away, hence the spelling "suprise" found in children's writing. However **sur-** appears in full force in a few English formations such as:

> *surcharge surclip surprint surtax surtitle*

And of course *surname.*

surname

This is the traditional English way of referring to one's *family name* or "second name." See further under **names** section 1, and **first name, forename or given name.**

surprised by or surprised at

The preposition following *surprised* holds the key to two different meanings. When the phrase means "caught unawares," it's **surprised by**, whereas **surprised at** means "struck with amazement." Compare:

> The intruders were surprised by the security guard.
> She was surprised at how quickly it had grown.

In some contexts either meaning might apply, and so **surprised by** could possibly be used in the second sentence. But **surprised at** could not be used in the first without changing its meaning.

Surrey or Surry

In Britain **Surrey** is the only form of this geographical name associated with a county south of London. In North America and Australia, spellings with and without the *e* are used, so that it's **Surrey** for the Melbourne suburb and the Canadian municipality in British Columbia, but **Surry** for the county in Virginia, and the Sydney suburb of *Surry Hills*.

surveil or surveille

This verb, backformed from *surveillance*, is better known in the US than the UK, judging by its absence from the BNC and (modest) presence in CCAE. The shorter spelling **surveil** is the only one to appear in the American data, for both military and civilian uses, as in:

> a satellite able to surveil more than 80% of Soviet territory
> ... ordering him not to threaten, surveil, follow or telephone her

The *Oxford Dictionary* (1989) also lists **surveille**, which would explain the inflected forms *surveilled* and *surveilling* used even in American English (*Merriam-Webster,* 2000). With **surveil** as the base form, the double *l*s are irregular, because the preceding vowel (*ei*) is a digraph (see **doubling of final consonant**). The only problem is the lack of evidence for **surveille** in *Oxford* citations or CCAE. It seems that **surveil** itself operates under *surveillance*.

sus or suss

See under **suspect**.

susceptible

In common use **susceptible** is followed by *to:*

> The plant was susceptible to frost and to many kinds of bug.
> Were they ever susceptible to doorstep persuasion?

In such cases it means "easily affected or influenced by." In its more abstract use, where it means "capable of," **susceptible** is followed by *of:*

> The paper was susceptible of several interpretations.

These days the collocation with *of* sounds rather formal.

suspect or suspicious, suspicion and sus(s)

These adjectives differ in that **suspect** applies to the object of *suspicion,* while **suspicious** describes the attitude of the person holding the **suspicion**. Compare:

> Their commitment to the project was very suspect.
> I was suspicious of their motives for joining the group.

Suspicious is however also used to mean "giving rise to suspicion," especially in police reporting on *suspicious circumstances*. The adverb *suspiciously* has to do service for both adjectives, as in:

> The children were suspiciously quiet.

(their behavior was suspect)

> The teacher looked suspiciously round the room.

(he had reason to be suspicious)

Both **suspicious** and **suspect** are reduced to **sus(s)** in colloquial Australian usage, as in *That seems pretty suss to me.*

Meanwhile in British English **sus** abbreviates **suspicion**, hence the notorious *sus laws,* whereby a person could be arrested *on suspicion* of illegal behavior. This also explains the verb *suss (out),* occasionally *sus out:*

> The counsellor came to suss me out.

This verb meaning "investigate," "check out" is the most frequent use of the word in BNC data. Canadians and Australians also know it, according to their respective dictionaries, but it's not so familiar in the US, by the label "chiefly British" attached to it in *Merriam-Webster* (2000). Yet other British uses of **suss** are its role as a noun meaning "shrewdness," as in *extra degrees of vim, suss and humour,* and for the related adjective meaning "shrewd."

suspense or suspension

Both have you *suspended,* but they work in different worlds. **Suspense** hangs you up emotionally, as in:

> I'm still in suspense over the scholarship application.
> The play kept us in suspense until the last act.

Suspension is usually a physical state of being *suspended.* It may be in the air as on a *suspension bridge,* or close to the ground when it's the shock-absorbing system of a vehicle. In chemistry the word refers to being *suspended* in a liquid, as when particles of chalk *form a suspension* in water. One other use of **suspension** is more an administrative matter: the *suspension of a driver's licence* (or anything else) means that certain rights have been temporarily withdrawn, or that a regular system of some kind has been discontinued.

◇ For editors in North America **suspension** is the technical term for one kind of contraction: see **contractions** section 1.

suspicious or suspect

See **suspect**.

suss or sus

See under **suspect**.

swam or swum

See **swim**.

swap or swop

All major dictionaries have **swap** as the primary spelling. It expresses the presumed etymology of the word in an old onomatopoeic verb *swappen,* meaning "strike or slap hands [in a bargain]." In modern English **swap** also serves as a noun, as in *Is this a fair swap?* Though colloquial in flavor, it is a standard term in financial reporting when referring to a *share swap* and other kinds of *swap deals*. The alternative spelling **swop** expresses the word's pronunciation, and is the commoner of the two, according to Gowers (1965). Yet **swap** outnumbers **swop** by about 9:1 in BNC data. **Swop** is not used in the US, according to

Merriam-Webster (2000), and there's no sign of it in data from CCAE.

swat or swot

In both British and American English, **swat** is the preferred spelling for "strike [a fly]" or "instrument for striking flies," according to *New Oxford* (1998) and *Merriam-Webster* (2000). In BNC data the spelling **swot** is sometimes found instead, but only a minority of writers use it for this purpose. Mostly **swot** is reserved for a different set of colloquialisms associated with studying: the verb "stuff oneself with information for exams," and the related nouns meaning "hard study" or "person who studies (too) hard." None of these is used in American English.

swathe or swath

These two antique words were once distinct, **swathe** being a verb meaning "wrap" and **swath** a noun referring to the strip of land cleared by a stroke of the scythe. But in British English **swathe** is taking over the uses of **swath**, and can now refer to a physical area or a notional domain:

> . . . a new road cutting a swathe through the countryside
> . . . cuts a swathe through NZ rugby
> . . . withdraw from a swathe of constituencies

As the third example shows, **swathe** becomes a collective word for any significant number. In BNC data **swathe** is far more popular than **swath** for these applications, outnumbering it by more than 5:1. In American English the opposite holds, by the evidence of CCAE. **Swath** dominates in hundreds of examples like *a wide swath of public opinion,* and **swathe** is rare.

swear words

This phrase covers the wide variety of coarse, blasphemous and obscene language used in swearing, and in angry or excited exclamations. Their effect is to shock or offend, though the degree of offense depends on how inured those listening are to them. Intensifiers such as *bloody* and *fucking* are used so often in some quarters (such as a football crowd or building site) that they cease to be shocking or to offend those around. However **swear words** which are deliberately used to insult are likely to create shock waves even when the person targeted is thoroughly used to them. This is the reason why people can be charged with "swearing and offensive language" under Australian law – not that the police are unaccustomed to such words.

◊ See further under **four-letter words** and **taboo words**.

sweat

The past forms of this verb can be either *sweated* or *sweat,* according to *New Oxford* (1998), which puts them in that order; and *Merriam-Webster* (2000) which reverses it. Database evidence shows that *sweated* is strongly preferred by both British and American writers, and there's scant evidence of *sweat* for the past in either the BNC or CCAE. Thus in the US and the UK, **sweat** is now a regular verb. See further under **irregular verbs** section 9.

swelled or swollen

Both **swelled** and **swollen** serve as past participles for the verb *swell,* but they tend to be used in different domains. **Swollen** is usually used when the swelling is physical and visible, as in:

> His ankle became badly swollen.
> The river had swollen to three times its usual size.

Swelled is used especially for increasing numbers, and increased extent:

> By noon the crowds had swelled to 120,000.
> . . . their French possessions were swelled by grants of English land

Note that **swollen** tends to suggest that something has gone wrong, or is developing in an undesirable way. The negative associations carry over to its use as an adjective, as in *eyes swollen with crying,* and the more idiomatic *swollen head,* a metonym for "conceited" in British English. However this is usually *swelled head* in North American and Australian English.

swim

In North American English, as well as British and Australian, the standard past tense of **swim** is *swam* and the past participle *swum.* However the past tense is not entirely stable, and *swum* is sometimes heard in casual conversation. There are a very few examples in CCAE, and *Webster's Third* (1986) acknowledges it simply as an alternative. Its absence from the BNC is in line with the *Oxford Dictionary* (1989) indication that it disappeared in C19.

swing

The past form of **swing** (for both past tense and past participle) is now *swung.* "Swang" was still around a century ago, but the *Oxford Dictionary* (1884–1928) noted it then as "rare." With only one past form, **swing** now lines up with *sling* rather than *sing.*

swiveled or swivelled, swiveling or swivelling

For the choice between these, see under **-l-/-ll-**.

swollen or swelled

See **swelled**.

swop or swap

See **swap**.

swot or swat

See **swat**.

swum or swam

See under **swim**.

syllabify, syllabicate or syllabize

These were coined in C19, C18 and C17 respectively. Modern dictionaries show by their crossreferencing that **syllabify** has largely eclipsed the other two, though they diverge on second preferences. *New Oxford* (1998) makes it **syllabize**, whereas *Merriam-Webster* (2000) has **syllabicate**. The reference databases provide too little evidence to discriminate any further.

syllables and syllabification

The boundaries of **syllables** in both speech and writing are far from clear cut. Linguists debate them, and typesetters and others who divide words at the end of a line often vary in where they make the break, for practical reasons. Dictionaries differ over them partly because of the question as to whether to go by the sounds or the structure of the word. The principles are discussed under **wordbreaks**.

syllabus

This Latin loanword began life as a misreading of the Greek *sittyba*, meaning "title slip." Borrowed into English in C17, it has a Latin plural **syllabi** as well as the English **syllabuses**. A majority (just over 60%) of respondents to the Langscape survey (1998–2001) endorsed *syllabuses:* see further **-us** section 1.

syllogism

A **syllogism** is one of the classical forms of deductive argument. See further under **deduction**.

sylvan or silvan

See under **i/y**.

symbols and symbolism

A **symbol** stands for something beyond itself. In specialized fields such as chemistry, mathematics and logic, there are conventional **symbols**; in others, writers create their own. The first group are often like abbreviations, witness the chemical **symbols** *C* for carbon and *N* for nitrogen. They also serve as **symbols** for SI units, C for the coulomb, and N for the newton. These conventional **symbols** are never given stops like other abbreviations. For the **symbols** used in the SI set, see Appendix IV.

The **symbols** created by writers are different altogether. They are focal images which carry significance beyond themselves by being developed steadily through the language and substance of a literary work. **Symbols** often begin unobtrusively in a poem or the narrative of a novel, grounded in its physical world. But they reappear in successively different contexts, and take on a complexity of values which help to give the original physical image its greater power. The albatross of Coleridge's *Ancient Mariner* begins as part of the oceanic ambience, yet becomes a symbol of an evil system of values. In Carey's *Oscar and Lucinda,* the symbolism of glass is developed slowly but surely from its first introduction as the mysterious object in Lucinda's hand. It is both the plain object of manufacture, and the metaphysical medium of the church which is the apex of aspirations in the novel. Through the work the **symbol** becomes an element much more important than it originally seemed, and a unifying element in a long and complex narrative.

Symbols differ from metaphors in being much less closely tied to the specifics of language for their effect. For the difference between **symbolism** and *allegory,* see **allegory**.

sympathy with or sympathy for

The preposition after it makes a difference to the meaning of *sympathy*. **Sympathy with** is an intellectual identification with someone's values and point of view – endorsing their ideas. **Sympathy for** is an emotional identification with the problems of others – feeling compassion for them.

symposium

For the plural of this word, see under **-um**.

synagogue or synagog

See under **-gue/-g**.

sync or synch

Both these are clipped forms of *synchronize,* used in discussing the operation of computers and film-making. But the word appears increasingly in general usage, especially in the phrase *out of sync(h),* and so it raises spelling questions that impinge on us all.

Sync is the primary spelling in both *New Oxford* (1998) and *Merriam-Webster* (2000), and generally preferred by British and American writers. In data from the BNC **sync** outnumbers **synch** by 2:1, and in CCAE it's closer to 4:1. The spelling of **synch** might seem to rhyme with "winch" or to be a mistake for "cinch." At any rate **sync** works fine until you want it as a verb with the standard verb suffixes attached. Then the regular forms *synced* and *syncing* don't seem ideal in terms of the spelling rule by which a *c* is normally softened to "s" by a following *e* or *i*. The conventional way to avoid this is to add a *k*, as in *trafficking* (see further under **-c/-ck-**), though there's no sign of *syncked/syncking* in the databases. Instead *synched/synching* appear in both British and American data, and in the BNC they are the only spelling. In CCAE there's some use of *synced* alongside *synched* (in the ratio 1:3); and *syncing* is on a par with *synching,* especially in *lip-syncing* – where the first element helps to identify the compound. But as a simple verb, **synch** has its place in supporting the inflected forms.

synchronic and diachronic

Linguists contrast these two perspectives on language. The **synchronic** looks at language structure and variation at a particular point in time. The **diachronic** takes a historical perspective on both, and so traces changes in the language system and in its elements over the course of time.

synecdoche

This is the classical name for a figure of speech in which either:
* a part of a familiar object is used to refer to the whole, or
* the name of the whole stands for the part.

An example of the first is *tied to the kitchen sink* (where the proverbial "kitchen sink" represents a range of household duties). The second can be illustrated by the use of *Washington* to refer to the American federal government which has its headquarters there. Either way **synecdoche** works allusively, inviting the reader to translate the expression offered into something broader, or more specific. The first type of **synecdoche** is also known as *meronymy:* see under **metonymy**.

synonyms

"Words with the same meaning" is a common definition of **synonyms**. But when you ask whether *chair* and *seat,* or *tap* and *faucet,* or *buy* and *purchase* are **synonyms**, clearly there's more to be said. Words embody many kinds of meaning: denotative, connotative and stylistic; and relatively few words match up on all those dimensions. The denotation of *chair* is more specific than *seat*. (A chair has legs and can be moved around independently, whereas a seat at the opera is different on both counts.) The connotations of *faucet* make it North American, whereas *tap* is at home in Britain and Australia. The stylistic overtones of *purchase* are much more formal than those of *buy*. Few pairs of words like those are perfect **synonyms**.

Yet words which diverge more than any of those can function as **synonyms** for each other. So *high* can stand for *secondary* when referring to schooling, even though it could never do so in *secondary symptom*. The fact that you can interchange them in one particular phrase without changing the meaning makes them **synonyms** there, for the purposes of the argument. Words may be **synonyms** within a particular text without being so in the abstract.

synopsis

See under **summary**.

syntax

This term is often used in alternation with *grammar* when talking about the structure of English. The two are however distinct when one gets down to details. *Grammar* is the broader term, embracing:

1 **syntax** (i.e. the grammatical relations between words as they're strung together in phrases, clauses and sentences)
2 **morphology** (i.e. the grammar of words as shown by their suffixes and inflections)

Because there are relatively few inflections in modern English, **syntax** is much more important in our *grammar*, in the broader sense.

Syntax embodies the principles that underlie the *syntagmatic* axis of any language. This is the so-called "horizontal" dimension of meaning, vested in the order of words, and the way that adjacent words set up expectations about each other's roles. We become most conscious of this axis of meaning when it's unclear, as in the following headline:

CLEANER TRAINS IN TEN YEARS

If we take the first word as a noun, it becomes the subject of the verb we anticipate in "trains" – and we get a vision of the most thoroughly trained cleaner in the universe. Yet if we read the first word as a comparative adjective, we anticipate that the second word is the noun it describes – and it paints a gloomy picture of rail car maintenance.

◊ Compare the *paradigmatic axis*, under **paradigm**.

synthetic

Apart from its everyday uses, this word has two technical meanings in relation to the use of language. A *synthetic language* is one which has many kinds of inflections to express the grammatical relations between words. So *synthetic languages* like Latin contrast with those like English or Chinese, in which grammatical meaning is vested much more in the syntactic arrangements of words. (See further under **syntax**.)

A *synthetic statement* is one whose validity can be tested by empirical evidence. See further under **induction**.

syphon or siphon

See under **i/y**.

syringing or syringeing

The regular spelling **syringing** is endorsed for American and British English by the reference dictionaries, and **syringeing** makes no showing at all in data from CCAE or the BNC. There is of course no need for the *e*, given that the *-ing* suffix serves to "soften" the preceding *g*. See **-ce/-ge**.

syrup or sirup

The first spelling is given preference in all dictionaries, British, American, Canadian and Australian. Even in the US, **syrup** is strongly preferred, and the only CCAE evidence of **sirup** goes with quotations of how things used to be. The word seems thus to have affirmed its *y* instead of replacing it with *i*. See further under **i/y**.

systematic or systemic

The first of these has many more uses, to describe something that works methodically, e.g. a *systematic approach to recycling,* or a person who is well organized: *a systematic secretary.* The latter has positive overtones.

Systemic is a more academic word, used to refer to things organic to the whole body – whether it's the human body or the body politic. In medicine *systemic diseases* or *drugs* are those that affect the whole body; whereas in political and social science, problems such as *systemic discrimination* are built into the system itself. *Systemic grammar* shows how sentences and parts of them work in the language *system* and support the larger functions of language.

-t

Several sets of words with **t** as their final letter raise questions of spelling:

1 Two-syllable English words ending in -t: should it be doubled before inflections such as *-ed* and *-ing?* The question comes up with words like *budget* and many others, including:

ballot	*banquet*	*billet*	*blanket*
bracket	*buffet*	*bullet*	*cosset*
debit	*docket*	*ferret*	*fidget*
fillet	*jacket*	*junket*	*limit*
market	*orbit*	*picket*	*plummet*
profit	*rivet*	*rocket*	*target*
ticket	*trumpet*		

In all of them the syllable ending in -t is unstressed, and so the -t remains single before inflections, as in *debited, marketing, profited, targeting* etc. (see further under **doubling of final consonant**). These uncluttered spellings help to preserve the identity of the underlying noun, while their *transfers* into the role of verb or adjective are marked by inflections, as in *budgeting for a surplus / a budgeted surplus* (see **transfers**). The same principle of *not* doubling the -t applies to three-syllabled words such as *benefit* and *deposit,* when they become verbs. (See individual entry on **benefit.**)

Yet there are exceptions among compound nouns used as verbs, e.g. *input/output,* and others, e.g. *format,* whose second element (*mat*) seems to be separable. It then dictates the spelling, and so the -t is doubled (*formatting, inputted/outputted*), according to the rule for doubling the final consonant of a monosyllable.

◊ For the spelling of *bayonet* and *combat* when inflected, see **bayonet** and **combated or combatted.**

2 French loanwords ending in a silent -t: what happens when they serve as verbs? Words to which this question applies include:

ballet	*beret*	*bouquet*	*buffet*
cabaret	*chalet*	*crochet*	*debut*
depot	*parquet*	*sachet*	*valet*

The final -t remains silent even when the standard English verb suffixes are added, as in *bouqueted, debuting, valeted.* Their spelling is thus very straightforward, though the relationship between spelling and sound is quite unconventional for English. The verb *ricochet* is a special case, with two pronunciations and two sets of spellings (see **ricochet**).

3 Monosyllabic English verbs whose past ends in -t: when is it standard? The -t suffix is the standard past form for English verbs like the following:

build (built)	*buy (bought)*	*creep (crept)*
deal (dealt)	*keep (kept)*	*leave (left)*
mean (meant)	*send (sent)*	*sleep (slept)*
teach (taught)		

For other verbs the -t is an alternative to *-ed,* as with:

burn	*dream*	*kneel*	*lean*	*leap*
learn	*smell*	*spell*	*spill*	*spoil*

Regional differences provide a backdrop for the choice of -t or *-ed.* See further under **irregular verbs** sections 2, 4 and 5.

tabbouleh, tabouleh or tabouli

These spellings, and other permutations and combinations like them, are used to refer to a Lebanese salad made of cracked wheat, parsley and tomato. The word is a recent borrowing (1955) from Arabic, where it appears as *tabbula,* apparently a derivative of *tabil* ("spice"). The *Oxford Dictionary* (1989) registers the word as **tabbouleh** but notes the alternative spellings *tabbouli* and *tabbuuli,* while **tabouleh** is the one spelling to be found in the BNC. Clearly there are several points of variability, although **tabbouleh** is the only spelling indicated in *New Oxford* (1998) and the *Canadian Oxford* (1998). *Merriam-Webster* (2000) also makes **tabbouleh** the standard spelling, but registers both **tabouleh** and **tabouli** in crossreferences. All three appear in CCAE data, though **tabbouleh** and **tabouleh,** in the ratio of 2:1, are much better represented than **tabouli.** In the Australian *Macquarie Dictionary* (1997) **tabouli** is prioritized as the preferred spelling. Like other loans more or less directly from Arabic, **tab(b)ouleh** has come into English in dialect forms which are in tension with classical rendering of the word. See further under **Arabic loanwords.**

table d'hôte

See **à la carte.**

tableau

The French plural **tableaux** is still strongly preferred over **tableaus** in both British and American English, in data from the BNC and CCAE. See further under **-eau.**

tables

A **table** is an effective and efficient way of communicating a lot of numerical information in a small space. **Tables** allow the reader to make instant comparisons horizontally and vertically, and to see overall trends. They are (or should be) designed to be read independently of the surrounding text, and must contain all the information necessary for that reading.

Every **table** needs an explanatory title, highlighting its topic or the general trends which it shows. The wording must be specific enough to allow browsing readers to make sense of the figures, and may therefore run to two or three lines. Beneath the title comes the box containing the column headings for the **table,** showing what kind of entries are entered in the field or body of the **table,** and what unit of measurement they're calibrated in. Abbreviations can be freely used in column headings.

Numerical issues in designing tables: the unit of measurement should be chosen so as to minimize excess zeros, or zeros that are nonsignificant in the figures cited. (So *59 kg* is preferable to *59 000 gm*.) The whole set of figures must be expressed in terms of the same unit for easy comparison. If percentages are used, readers also need to know the actual size of the population analyzed, and the raw number (*n* = whatever) should be given in the footnotes to the **table**.

Table: The relationship between age of respondents and their support for a set of spelling changes (data from Australian Style Council Surveys 1986–7)

Spelling changes	Age groups		
	10–25	*26–45*	*46+*
	% support	*% support*	*% support*
1 Change *-our* words to *-or* (*colour>color*)	38	41	55
2 Use *-er* for all agent words (*investor>invester*)	22	32	42
3 Use *-able* for all words with-*ible* (*digestible>digestable*)	61	56	63
4 Use *-l-* for *-ll-* before suffixes (*traveller>traveler*)	50	56	59
5 Drop final *e* from root before *-able* (*likeable>likable*)	61	63	68
6 Reduce *ae* to *e* (*paediatrics>pediatrics*)	38	73	75
7 Reduce *oe* to *e* (*homoeopath> homeopath*)	38	67	73
	n = 18	*n* = 158	*n* = 232

Tables these days work with a minimum of horizontal rules drawn in, and no vertical rules, to allow the eye to move freely across and down.

The side headings in a **table**, known collectively as the *stub*, are set flush with the margin, as is the numbering in the illustrative **table**. Turnover lines may be indented if there's sufficient space, or else set flush left with a line space between each heading. The headings begin with a capital letter, but have no final full stops. The wording of all headings needs to be made consistent. In the example, all headings begin with an imperative form of the verb. See further under **lists**.

tablespoonful

For the plural of this word, see **-ful**.

taboo words

Words which many people avoid because of the offense they may give are **taboo words**. In current English they typically involve private subjects such as defecation (*shit*), urination (*piss*) and copulation (*fuck*): see further under **four-letter words**.

Earlier on in English, **taboo words** linked up with religion, as they still do in other languages. Religion is often a focus of taboos, because religious words uttered without reverence are naturally an offense to those who take religion seriously. Some of our common expletives are disguised religious references: *by Crikey* is a veiled form of "by Christ"; and *bloody* is believed to be a disguised form of "by our Lady." In

those forms they are less directly blasphemous, and do not seem to violate religious taboos – though *bloody* can still be offensive to some as a *swear word* (see further under that heading).

The force of **taboo words** is that they evoke the taboo subject in a blatant or blasphemous way. Disguised expletives serve to reduce the problem in speech, and latinate words like those mentioned above help writers to deal with taboo subjects when necessary.

The word *taboo* is an English respelling of the Tongan word *tabu* ("forbidden"), though *tabu* itself is occasionally used as the spelling. In New Zealand the same word is *tapu*, a Maori loanword.

tabouli, tabouleh or tabbouleh

See under **tabbouleh**.

tabula rasa

In Latin this means "a tablet scraped clean" – a clean slate. But in English this phrase is used where someone knows nothing about a subject and is ready to receive any information about it. Psychologists use it to refer to the human mind at birth.

tag questions

See under **questions**.

talc

This word for an everyday cosmetic is ultimately Arabic *talq* ("mica"), but *talcum (powder)* marks its passage through Latin, and **talc** was its spelling in French. In English **talc** raises questions only as a verb, when used to describe the process of *talc(k)ing* or being *talc(k)ed*. *New Oxford* (1998) endorses the forms without the *k*, going for simple regularity rather than the general rule for words ending in a "hard" *c* (see **-c/-ck-**). There's no evidence either way in the BNC. *Merriam-Webster* (2000) does not suggest that **talc** can be used as a verb, though American English is at least as tolerant of such *transfers* as British. See further under **transfers**.

tant pis

See under **faute de mieux**.

target

The metaphor of the firing range has faded in new uses of **target**, as a noun and verb. The *target market* still provides a focus, but it's more diffuse than a bullseye, and the product may have to be *tightly targeted* to find its niche. A *sales target of 70 houses by the end of the year* adds further relativity to the goal. The idiom of *achieving a target* makes it clear that **target** often means "objective," and this broader sense is now registered in both *New Oxford* (1998) and *Merriam-Webster* (2000). It coexists with the sense of a **target** as something you hit, still there for the missile *targeted against enemy submarines*.
◊ For the spelling of this word when it's used as a verb, see **-t**.

tarmac

This word for the hard surface of a road or runway blends the medium *tar* with the first syllable of *Macadam*, the name immortalized also in *macadamize*. It belonged to John Macadam, the originator and advocate of the road-making technique,

who was made surveyor-general of British
(metropolitan) roads in 1827. The unabbreviated noun
tarmacadam is now much less common than **tarmac**
in BNC data, and the verb *tarmac(ked)* seems to have
ushered out the older verb *macadamize(d)* since the
1960s. Inflected forms of the verb are usually spelled
with the additional *k*, as recommended by *New Oxford*
(1998), and in keeping with the usual rule for words
ending in *c*. (See further under **-c/-ck-.**)

New Oxford (1998) makes no suggestion that **tarmac**
should be capitalized, whereas the *Canadian Oxford*
(1998) lists it as **Tarmac**, and its proprietary origins
are noted in *Merriam-Webster* (2000). The capital is
sometimes seen in American newspaper data in
CCAE, as in *on the Tarmac*, no doubt in fear of legal
retribution from the trademark owners. But many
American reporters/editors take the risk with the
lower-case form **tarmac**. There's no evidence of any
anxiety among British sources in the BNC, where
tarmac is the only form.

tasseled or tasselled
See under **-l-/-ll-.**

tautology
This is a matter of saying the same thing twice over, as
in: *A capacity crowd completely filled the stadium.* A
tautology involves redundancy, though there are
times when it serves a purpose (see **pleonasm**
section 2).

Philosophers use **tautology** to refer to an *analytic
statement,* i.e. one which is self-defining or
self-validating. See further under **induction**.

taxi
As a verb, **taxi** raises questions when it takes on the
-ing inflection. Should it then be *taxiing* or *taxying?*
Dictionaries are unanimous in preferring *taxiing*
(without any hyphen), and do not suggest that the *i*
should be converted to *y* (see **-ie>-y-**). British writers
in the BNC nevertheless make use of both spellings,
where their American counterparts in CCAE have
only *taxiing*.

tea or dinner
See **dinner**.

teaming or teeming
See **teeming**.

teaspoonful
For the plural of this word, see under **-ful**.

technical or technological
The first is a good deal older than the second.
Technical has since C17 been applied to *techniques* of
all kinds, in fields ranging from art to arithmetic and
from angling to leatherwork. **Technological** is a C20
word, associated with the *technology* of science and
industry. Both *technology* and **technological** have a
learned ring to them, and *institutes of technology* can
offer university-style degrees, while *technical colleges*
do not.

Differences like those are matched in the words
technologist and *technician*. As a job title, *technologist*
presupposes professional knowledge and skills
developed through a four-year degree, and often some

postgraduate study. The skills of a *technician* are
typically underpinned by two-year training courses.

technologese
This word takes its place alongside *commercialese,
journalese* and *legalese,* to designate the writing style
of a particular institution or profession. The suffix *-ese*
has negative overtones, and **technologese** is loaded
with technical terms and abbreviations, which are
hurdles for nontechnical readers and bound to
alienate the technophobe. For them **technologese**
becomes *technospeak* or *technobabble*.

That said, technical writing in science, medicine,
engineering, economics or any other specialized field
does depend on the use of technical jargon (see
terminology). It allows specialists to communicate
precisely and efficiently with each other, and, in
documents for a limited readership, the use of
technical terms is perfectly legitimate. Technical
writers do however need to be able to adjust their
style, if they have any ambitions to communicate with
the public, let alone win them over. Apart from
limiting the technical terminology, they need to avoid
the typically impersonal style of technical and
scientific writing, and replace it with lively and direct
expression. See further under **impersonal style** and
passive verbs.

technological or technical
See **technical**.

teeming or teaming
Ultimately these two go back to the same Germanic
stem meaning "offspring" or "those in tow." But they
have led separate lives under different spellings, with
teem strictly a verb, and *team* mostly a noun – until
recently. American English now makes frequent use of
team as verb, especially when describing sports or
business partnerships, and this has made *teaming
with* a familiar construction. In British English it's
there, but usually *team up with*. This explains why
teaming with occasionally appears for *teeming with* in
American sources, in references to a fishing ground
teaming with life or the streets *teaming with bicyclists*.
Examples like those from CCAE were not to be found
in data from the BNC, where **teeming** and **teaming**
keep their distance.

teetotalism
The practice of avoiding alcoholic drink is
teetotalism in both British and American English.
But when it comes down to the individual, s/he is a
teetotaller in the UK and a *teetotaler* in the US. No
prizes for seeing which is more consistent. See further
under **-l-/-ll-**.

tele-
These letters represent two Greek prefixes, one in
common usage, the other mostly confined to
philosophy.
1 The very familiar prefix tele- means "distant" or
"over a distance." It derives from *telescope*, first
recorded in English in C17 along with new
developments in optics. Other **tele-** words are
monuments to technological developments, including
telegraph (1794), *telephone* (1835), *telemeter* (1860) and
television (1909). In both *television* and
telecommunication, the Greek prefix forms a linguistic

hybrid with a Latin word; and it now combines with ordinary English words in *teleprinter, teletext, teletype.*

Some other simple formations with **tele-** are really blends of *television* and other words:

    telecast   telemovie   teleplay
    teleprompter   televiewer

(see further under **portmanteau words**).

2 **The much less common prefix tele- or teleo-** means "end or goal." Best known in the philosophical term *teleology*, it refers to the theoretical approach which looks for evidence of design in nature, and for the ultimate purpose in any phenomenon.

temblor, tremblor or trembler

See under **tremor**.

tempera or tempura

These similar words are very different in origin, though by coincidence eggs are involved in both. **Tempera** is an Italian word for a method of mixing paint, combining the pigments with egg yolk. It was once known as *distemper,* but that word has been annexed by home decorators to refer to paints which are made with sizing materials less expensive than eggs. A new word had to be found for the original egg-based technique of fine art, and **tempera** has been used in English for this since 1832.

    Tempura is a Japanese word meaning "fried food." It refers to a dish in which seafood or vegetables are deep-fried in a very light batter, again making good use of egg yolk.

template or templet

Templet is the original spelling of this word for a pattern or mould used to reproduce a design on another surface or in another medium. The word comes from Latin *templum* ("timber, beam") via French (where a diminutive ending *-et(te)* was added on), and so **templet** meant "small timber." This background was obscure to English users, and the C19 spelling **template** injects some sense into the second syllable, helping it to displace **templet** entirely. It is however a *folk etmology:* see further under that heading.

temporary or temporal

The time in **temporary** is always limited, and sometimes very brief: *a temporary appointment, a temporary shelter from the storm.* The pressure of time seems to be felt in the word itself, at least in British English, so that it's commonly pronounced with only three syllables (and sometimes only two – which occasionally registers as the spelling "tempory" in unedited writing). American pronunciation preserves the four syllables with a secondary stress, and helps writers to produce the standard spelling.

    Temporal relates to time at large. In academic fields such as linguistics it means "expressing a time factor," as in *temporal conjunction.* In religion it expresses finite human time, in contrast with eternal, spiritual time. So the *Lords Temporal* (in the English House of Lords) have a lesser brief than the *Lords Spiritual.*

    The adverb *temporarily* (like **temporary**) suffers from an overdose of weak syllables in British pronunciation and is sometimes short-circuited so that it sounds like "temporally," exactly like the regular adverb associated with **temporal**, as in *culturally and temporally specific.* It sometimes shows

in transcriptions of speech, as in: *He went temporally insane.* But edited writing has no reason to reflect pronunciation – and every reason to maintain the distinction between *temporarily* and *temporally.*

tempura or tempera

See **tempera**.

tend or attend

See **attend**.

tendinitis or tendonitis

The inflammation of a *tendon* is spelled **tendinitis** (rather than **tendonitis**), according to *New Oxford* (1998) and *Merriam-Webster* (2000), and it preserves the Latin stem *tendin-* at the heart of the word. But actual usage is less uniform. While the vast majority of American writers in the CCAE use **tendinitis**, those in the BNC are more inclined to use **tendonitis**. This alternative spelling which builds the *tendon* into **tendonitis** makes some sense, and is recommended for Australians by the *Macquarie Dictionary* (1997). The *Canadian Oxford* (1998) prioritizes **tendinitis**.

tensed verb

See under **finite verbs**.

tenses

Any language has its ways of indicating whether an event is in the past, present or future; and many do it through the forms of their verbs and especially through different inflections. These sets of inflections which represent time differences are the **tenses** of a language. English has only two **tenses** in this sense: *present* and *past.* They are the time differences represented in the forms *rest/rested* and *write/wrote.* (See further under **present tense** and **past tense**.) The future is expressed in English through compound verbs, i.e. ones involving auxiliaries:

    will rest/write
    shall rest/write
    am/is/are going to rest/write
    am/is/are going to rest/write

(See further under **future tense**.) The English future has much in common with compound verbs which express such things as inclination and possibility, such as *might rest/write* or *could rest/write.* (See further under **modality**.)

◊ See also **sequence of tenses**.

terminology

Technical terms go with any specialized activity, whether it is the craft of knitting (*one purl one plain*) or computing (*booting the DOS*) or any other. Nonspecialists are effectively excluded by such **terminology**, and the word *jargon* is often used to express their sense of frustration and alienation. When writing for a general reader, it's important to use words in common use wherever possible, and to provide an explanation beside any technical terms which cannot be avoided (or else a glossary at the back of the document).

    Technical **terminology** should not be applied in fields other than the one it belongs to. It may be tempting to say of someone who's just got up and is acting like a zombie that "he hasn't yet booted the DOS." But neither the point nor the joke would get through to those who know nothing of computers. See further under **jargon**.

terminus or terminal

As nouns, these are both associated with *public transport,* and both can mean a "station at the end." **Terminus** is the older word for the final station on a train, tram or local bus line, where the passengers get on and off. **Terminal** has always been the point of arrival and departure for aircraft, including helicopters, for shipping, and more recently for long-distance buses. In computing, a **terminal** (never a **terminus**) is the word for the workstation which accesses a computer network.

Like other Latin words ending in *-us,* **terminus** has two plurals: **termini** and **terminuses**. In spoken English **terminuses** is common enough, and respondents to the Langscape survey (1998–2001) endorsed it by a small majority (53%). But **termini** is overwhelmingly preferred in written material in the BNC and CCAE. See further under **-us** section 1.

terminus ante quem and terminus ad quem

Historians use these Latin phrases to refer to the final point of a period in which something must be dated. The first means literally "endpoint before which [something happened]," and makes a firm reference point. The second, "endpoint towards which [something was heading or tending]," implies less certainty about the continuity of events up to the terminal date. The contrasting phrase for the beginning of the dating period is *terminus a quo,* the "point from which [a certain period began]."

terra

In both Latin and Italian, this is the word for "earth" or "land." English has it in several borrowed phrases:
* *terra cotta* from Italian is literally "cooked earth." This is the clay out of which reddish, unglazed pottery is made, and a name for the pottery itself.
* *terra firma* from Latin is "solid land," nowadays used to distinguish solid, dry land from sea. Originally it seems to have been used in reference to the mainland, as contrasted with offshore islands, though this use became obsolete in C18.
* *terra incognita* from Latin is "unknown [or unexplored] land." It frequently appears on early maps of the world, and is still used metaphorically.
* *terra nullius* from Latin means "land of no-one." It embodies the now discredited legal notion held by European colonialists that lands which seemed uninhabited or used only for nomadic lifestyles were subject to no particular title-holders.

terrible or terrific

Colloquial use has reduced the element of *terror* in both of these. The essential meaning of **terrible** is still there in phrases such as *terrible destruction* and names such as *Ivan the Terrible.* But in everyday use **terrible** has become an all-purpose negative, as in *a terrible performance* – unpleasing to musicians although not life-threatening. The associated adverb *terribly* is often just an intensifier, as in *It's terribly kind of you,* with no negative value at all.

Terrific has become a word of commendation, as in *a terrific performance* – even if it sounds rather exaggerated. The adverb *terrifically* also serves as an intensifier: *It's terrifically exciting.*

◊ Compare **horrible, horrid, horrendous, horrific or horrifying**.

tertium quid

This is the Latin equivalent of a Greek phrase which means the "third something." English uses it in several ways. In scholarly argument it refers to a notional elusive something which is related to but distinct from two other known entities. A more specific use of **tertium quid** is to refer to something which is a medium between two others, or an intermediate between opposites. Another, less academic use of the phrase is to refer to the third party in an "eternal triangle," a use which is immortalized in the Kipling story which begins: "Once upon a time there was a man and his wife and a tertium quid."

tête-à-tête

This French phrase means literally "head to head." In English it's most often used of a private conversation between two people, though it has also been applied to an S-shaped piece of furniture for seating two people face to face. As a noun meaning "private conversation," **tête-à-tête** usually bears hyphens, though they seem rather superfluous when it's printed in italics with a full quota of accents. As a compound adjective the same applies (see **hyphens** section 2c). Dictionaries vary on whether the accents may be omitted. Both *Merriam-Webster* (2000) and the Australian *Macquarie* (1997) allow for the possibility, but not *New Oxford* (1998) or the *Canadian Oxford* (1998).

◊ Compare the Italian phrase *a quattr'occhi,* discussed under **au pair**.

textual

Connected discourse depends on the integration of ideas, and on cohesion between the statements that express them (see **coherence or cohesion** section 2). The cohesive elements realize the *textual function* of language, its ability to support and develop discourse. The *textual function* is complemented by (a) the *referential function,* the power of language to articulate ideas and refer to the world around us; and (b) the *interpersonal function,* i.e. the role of language in establishing a relationship between the sender and receiver of a text. See further under **interpersonal** and **referential**.

-th

This Old English suffix is found on numerical adjectives (*fourth, fifth* etc.), and in a number of common abstract nouns, such as:

breadth	depth	filth	growth
health	length	stealth	strength
truth	warmth	wealth	width

Since C17 there have been no lasting coinages with **-th**. The most notable example since then was *illth* (1860), coined by Ruskin as an opposite to *wealth* (in its older sense of "well-being"), but which never caught on.

Note that *drought* and *height* were once "drought" and "heighth." The spellings with plain *-t* began to be used in C13, and have long since taken over except in dialectal use.

than

Questions about the grammar of **than** were energetically debated in C18, and still today are sometimes asked. By origin it is a subordinating conjunction, used to introduce comparative clauses, as in:

> He knows more than I do about the family history.

The use of the subject pronoun *I* anticipates the verb (*do*), and confirms that a clause is to follow. This is proof that **than** is indeed a conjunction – in that sentence. But older commentators were inclined to think, "once a conjunction, always a conjunction," and to disregard common constructions like the following:

> He knows more than me about the family history.

In that alternative version of the sentence, the object pronoun *me* shows **than** operating as a preposition, which normally takes an object. Prepositional use of **than** with an object pronoun has been recorded since C16, yet prescriptive grammarians still argue that the subject pronoun is the proper one to use after it; and they would "correct" the second sentence to:

> He knows more than I about the family history.

To many people this sounds less natural, but its proponents argue that it is an elliptical version of the first sentence above, i.e. that a whole clause is to be understood after **than**, and so *I* is the correct pronoun. Yet there's no need for this elaborate argument if we allow that **than** is both a preposition and a subordinator. Research associated with the *Longman Grammar* (1999) showed that speakers mostly use **than** (and *as*) as prepositions (i.e. with a following object pronoun) and only rarely with a following subject pronoun. Fiction writers make about equal use of the two constructions, while academic writers use neither. Academic comparisons more often turn on correlative phrases with comparative adjectives:

> He possessed a greater sense of history than others of his time.

You could therefore say that the problem is academic! It rarely comes up in academic prose, and in fiction and conversation where **than** is much more often used with simple pronouns, the use of object forms is quite idiomatic. In practice the issue only arises with first or third person pronouns that have distinct forms for the subject and object (*I, we, he, she, they*). For the second person pronoun *you*, the third person *it*, it makes no difference – or for nouns and proper names: *He knows more than John (does) about the family history.*

A different issue with **than** is its potential ambiguity when used elliptically, as in:

> She's kinder to her dog than the children.

To settle the ambiguity in sentences like that, the point needs to be spelled out more fully. (See further under **ellipsis**.)

Combinations with than:

1 **Than** and what. The most extended use of **than** as a preposition is to be seen in nonstandard usage such as: *He wanted it more than what I did.*

Such constructions provide an empty object for **than** but ensure the use of the subject pronoun in the following clause. It could thus be seen as a kind of hypercorrective response to the grammatical "problem" (see **hypercorrection**). The *what* is unnecessary because the sentence could perfectly well be: *He wanted it more than I did* (or *more than me*). The construction *than what* is associated with impromptu talk – one of the various redundancies that occur

when we construct sentences on the run, which need to be edited out of written documents.

2 Following **than** it's possible to use either an infinitive or an *-ing* form of the verb. Compare:

> She rushed on rather than let us catch up.
> She was rushing on rather than letting us catch up.

But as these examples show, the choice can effectively be made by matching the forms before and after **than**: the *-ing* follows a continuous/progressive form of the main verb, while the infinitive goes with other aspects and tenses.

3 **Than** with quasi-comparatives. A number of adjectives and adverbs imply comparisons without having the standard comparative suffixes such as *-er* or *more*. They include collocations like *different/differently than* (and *superior than*) which are used especially in speech as alternatives to constructions with *from* or *to*. Other constructions which sometimes use **than** are sequences such as *hardly . . . than, scarcely . . . than,* where the alternative is to use *when* as the subordinator. Purists are inclined to argue that **than** has no place in such phrases, because the comparison remains implicit rather than explicit in the form of words. Yet common idiom endorses such combinations. See further under **different from, hardly** and **scarcely**.

thank you and thanks

These expressions differ a little in style. **Thank you** is the standard and neutral way of expressing one's gratitude:

> Thank you for your attention.

Thanks is more informal, and works either as a friendly acknowledgement or a brisk refusal:

> Thanks for being with us.
> No thanks. I've had enough.

The expression *many thanks* gets the best of both worlds. It embodies warmer feeling than **thank you**, while avoiding the informality of **thanks**.

Note that when **thank you** becomes a compound noun or adjective, it is either set solid or hyphenated, as in *said their thankyous* and *wrote a thank(-)you note*.

thankfully

This adverb now serves as both adjunct and disjunct, in other words as an adverb of manner, as well as an attitudinal (or sentence) adverb (see **adverbs** section 1). Compare:

> They spoke thankfully of their rescue.
> Thankfully the damage was minimal.

The second type of usage has gained ground since the 1960s, according to *New Oxford* (1998), and is now its dominant use in BNC data (found in approximately 80% of all instances of the word). The role of **thankfully** as a "sentence adverb" is thus established in British English, and recognized also in American by *Merriam-Webster* (2000). Objections to disjunctive use of **thankfully** – like those against *hopefully* – are difficult to justify on grounds of grammar or usage.
◊ Compare **hopefully**.

that

The workhorse of the English language, **that** has uses as a demonstrative pronoun and determiner, as a relative pronoun, two kinds of conjunction, and occasionally as an adverb.

1 As a demonstrative, that complements this. That represents something further away than whatever we might apply *this* to: *This goes with that* as they say in a certain fashion store. **That** draws attention to something at a remove from the reader and writer, whereas *this* draws them together over it. Yet in conversation **that** often refers to something in the physical context, and is very much more common than *this* – by a factor of more than 7:1 in the *Longman Grammar* (1999) corpus. In writing **that** must have an antecedent (phrase or clause) to refer to in the text itself:

> *To go to Japan – that was her number one ambition.*

The examples so far have shown **that** as a pronoun, whereas in *that trip* and *that exciting trip* it serves as a determiner (not "adjective," as in traditional grammar and older dictionaries). As determiner or pronoun, **that** is a useful cohesive device, like the personal pronouns. (See further under **coherence or cohesion**.)

2 That as a clause-connector. That serves to link embedded, complementary and subordinate clauses to the main clause in one of three ways:

* as a relative pronoun (like *which, who*)
* introducing a noun (complement) clause
* introducing an adverbial clause

These three uses of **that** are detailed in sections (a), (b) and (c) below. **That** also appears in several compound subordinating conjunctions:

> *in order that   provided that   so that*

a) When **that** introduces a relative clause it can be omitted – and often is, depending on both grammatical and stylistic factors. It often disappears when it's the object of the relative clause, as in:

> *The TV program (that) we saw last night had a powerful impact on us.*

Compare the obligatory use of **that** in:

> *A TV program that had a powerful impact on us was shown last night.*

In the second sentence **that** is the subject of the relative clause and must be expressed in current written English. Yet the deletion of **that** as object pronoun is normal in conversation, and these days common in writing (see **relative clauses** section 1). ◊ For the choice between **that** and *which,* and their use in *restrictive relative clauses,* see **relative pronouns**.

b) When **that** prefaces a noun (complement) clause (also called a *content clause*), it's often omitted after verbs expressing a mental or verbal process:

> *We knew (that) the idea was yours.*
> *He thought (that) he said it.*

Constructions like these, with **that** omitted, abound in everyday discourse. They serve to express the speaker's stance or that of others, and are equally useful and common in fiction writing, according to *Longman Grammar* (1999) research. The omission of **that** very often happens when a personal pronoun is the subject of the following clause, and especially when it refers back to the subject of the main clause, as in the second example above. But in academic style, when the clause complements an abstract noun for a mental or verbal construct, e.g. *assumption, belief, doubt, suggestion,* **that** is normally expressed. For example:

> *Doubts that the government would fund the project . . . quickly surfaced*
> *The suggestion that younger people were included was quickly . . .*

The divergent patterns of speech / fictional writing and more formal written English would explain why the omission of **that** from complement clauses is often thought of as "informal," though it's really a matter of different constructions.

c) In various kinds of adverbial clauses, **that** is also omitted, depending on the formality of style. This is expecially true when it functions as part of a compound conjunction, for example:

> *We were so exhausted (that) we didn't care.*
> *They would be there provided (that) we did all the catering.*

The constructions without **that** present the briskness of speech, rather than the decorum of formal writing.

3 That as an adverb. Some adverbial uses of **that** are more or less standard English, as when it serves as an intensifier of other adverbs, in nonassertive contexts (*Comprehensive Grammar*, 1985).

> *Is it that far to Moscow?*
> *The course isn't that easy.*

Apart from its use in negative and interrogative constructions, **that** serves occasionally as a modifier of *much*:

> *It should be that much easier to do.*

But the use of **that** as an intensifier of adjectives is still quite colloquial:

> *They were that excited about the trip to Russia.*

The standard intensifying word for modifying adjectives is *so*. See further under **intensifiers**.

the

This common and humble word is surprisingly significant in conveying ideas. In traditional grammar it was the *definite article* in a class of its own, though contemporary grammars now class it as one of the *determiners*. Its major roles are outlined below, as well as issues of its use in journalism and when citing proper names.

1 Cohesive the. In the grammar of English, **the** has the very important role of signaling that a noun is to follow. It very often implies that the noun is one with which readers are already acquainted, as in:

> *The result was not declared immediately.*

Effectively **the** says, "You know which one I mean," and reminds us of an earlier reference to the same thing in the text. Thus it's an important cohesive device (see further under **coherence or cohesion**). **The** often links up with a phrase introduced by an indefinite article (*a* or *an*). Yet **the** makes connections with all kinds of noun phrases, and can forge a link with a whole clause or sentence, as in:

> *He asked if we would cover the costs. The answer from my boss was predictable . . .*

2 Universal and generic uses of the. The use of **the** sometimes appeals to common knowledge outside the text, rather than working cohesively with other words and phrases within it. Examples like *the government, the radio* call on our social and cultural experience, and *the sun, the world* on what we know of the universe. Common knowledge is also invoked in the so-called "generic" use of **the** with a singular noun:

> *A conservation program for the white rhino is now in place.*

In the one-teacher school, older students act as
mentors to younger ones.

We assume that these sentences are about rhinos and
one-teacher schools in the plural, despite the singular
construction with **the.**

3 Journalistic omission of the. In everyday news
reporting journalists often delete **the** when providing
readers with a thumbnail identity of the person just
mentioned in the report:

Peter Carey, (the) author of Oscar and Lucinda
and ex-advertising man has a gift for graphic
description.

As an appositional structure, this is grammatically
straightforward. But the practice is sometimes
applied before mentioning the person's
name:

Novelist and ex-advertising man Peter Carey has
a gift for ...

This gives the person a "pseudo-title" (Meyer, 2002), a
style which is well established in American news
reporting but resisted in other quarters of the
English-speaking world. It is strongly associated with
journalese (see further under **journalism**).

There is of course no problem in omitting **the** when
it refers to a unique office:

As coach, he was a tireless motivator.

He was voted co-president for a second year.

Omission of **the** under these circumstances is
acceptable in any writing style.

4 Issues involving the within proper names.
*The in geographical names. The English form of
certain placenames has included the word **the,** which
may or may not still be capitalized. The Dutch city of
The Hague is one case where the official name
includes the definite article, with a capital letter even
in mid-sentence. Data from the BNC has it written
that way in a large majority of instances (about 75%).
The Dutch kingdom was once *The Netherlands,*
though the official English form of the name is now
just *Netherlands,* as shown in the United Nations
members list (www.un.org). Yet most BNC texts (about
70%) have it as *the Netherlands*, as in *Queen of the*
Netherlands, suggesting that the word **the** remains
idiomatic, for the moment. With *Lebanon,* things have
moved further, and only a minority of BNC writers
make it *the Lebanon* (translating the French *Le Liban*).
Most simply call it *Lebanon.* Informal designations
such as *the Trossachs* and *the Grand Tetons* always
have the written in lower-case (in mid-sentence).
*The in titles of books, newspapers and magazines.
The titles of many publications include **the,** witness
Michael Ondaatje's novel *The English Patient* and
reference books such as *The Gentle Art of Flavoring.*
In such cases, **The** needs a capital, as an intrinsic part
of the title, even when cited in mid-sentence:

Ondaatje's novel The English Patient *became an*
Oscar-winning movie.

However style guides agree that if retaining the **The**
makes an awkward sentence, it can be dropped:

Have you read his Gentle Art of Flavoring?

Likewise it's accepted that when referring to titles
prefaced by *A* or *An* (e.g. *A New English Dictionary*),
the indefinite article may be replaced by **the.** It would
not be capitalized as part of the title:

Information on many a cultural question can be
found among the words listed in the New English
Dictionary.

In the mastheads of newspapers and magazines, **The**
no longer needs to be cited. Earlier style guides used
to recommend it, perhaps because *The Times* and *The*
Economist were known to insist on it. But the
preferences of less well-known publications could be
hard to ascertain, and so the simple practice of
leaving **The** out makes a reliable rule for all. Some
publications such as *New Scientist* have deliberately
shed **The** from their mastheads, lest there be any
doubt about it. The practice also simplifies adjectival
use of such titles, as in:

They have a collection of 100 Times *editorials.*

The use of italics for newspaper titles is discussed at
italic(s) section 5.

theatre or theater

See under **-re/-er.**

theirself and theirselves

See under **themself.**

theme

For the **theme** and *rheme* of a sentence, see under
topic.

themself and themselves

Themself is still more often heard than seen, and
noted with reservations ("colloquial," "not widely
accepted") by those dictionaries that do register it.
Themself was in fact standard English until mid-C16,
when it was replaced by **themselves.** The *Oxford*
Dictionary (1989) still treats it as obsolete, yet there are
fresh British citations for it in a score of BNC sources,
as well as American ones in CCAE. For example:

How can someone hang themself?

... the person involved may justify themself

somebody starts talking to themself

a candidate who just talks about themself

The singular reference in **themself** obviously serves a
purpose, especially after an indefinite noun or
pronoun. If we allow the use of *they/them/their* for
referring to the singular (see **they**), **themself** seems
more consistent than **themselves.** We make use of
yourself alongside *yourselves* in just the same way.
Themself has the additional advantage of being
gender-free, and thus preferable to both *himself* and
himself/herself. It's time to reinstate it to the set of
reflexive pronouns!

The alternatives *theirselves* and *theirself* are
registered in both *Oxford Dictionary* (1989) and
Webster's Third (1986), as nonstandard items. They are
of course consistent in their makeup with *myself,*
ourselves, yourself, yourselves in using a possessive
adjective for the first element – whereas **themself** and
themselves match up with *himself* and *itself* in using
the object pronoun. The two sets provide conflicting
analogies, but with the second set at least the third
person reflexives are all consistent with each other.

thence

See under **hence.**

theoretical or theoretic

The longer form **theoretical** is very strongly
preferred everywhere, by the evidence of both British
and American databases.

◊ For other similar pairs, see **-ic/-ical.**

there

In the same sentence **there** can play two different grammatical parts:

There were more people there than you'd expect.

Without any particular thought we decode the first **there** in its "existential" role of indicating a topic, and the second as demonstrative adverb. Both are multi-faceted.

1 As a demonstrative adverb, there means "in/on/at/towards that place." In speech as well as writing, it's used to refer to a place already mentioned, whether geographical or abstract:

We went there on foot.

Turn to the diagram on p.10 and look at the details there.

The lecture moved to government policy on the environment, and there he became very strident.

There sometimes occurs at the start of a sentence, as in:

There we found the start of the waterfall.

Whatever its position in the sentence, **there** is cohesive with something said in a previous sentence. It binds conversational utterances together, and occurs much more often in speech than any kind of writing, according to the *Longman Grammar* (1999).

Adverbial **there** combines with other adverbs/prepositions to form complex adverbs of place:

down there   over there   up there

Note that *from there* is now used instead of *thence* (see further under **hence**); and that **there** itself has taken over from *thither*.

◊ Compare the legal adverbs compounded with **there** in first place, discussed at **thereafter**.

2 Existential there is the grammarians' name for the **there** which introduces a topic, as in:

There is no place like home.

There are no winners in this situation.

This use of **there** is very conspicuous, often at the start of a sentence, yet semantically empty – just a grammatical slot-filler to provide the subject for a significant complement (see **predicate** section 1c). Some grammarians therefore call it a "dummy subject," like the "ambient *it*" in *It was raining.* This similarity explains why some older dictionaries label *existential there* as a "pronoun." But unlike normal pronouns, it's not a substitute for a previously mentioned word, and not at all cohesive like adverbial **there**. It is freely used in writing of all kinds as well as speech, according to the *Longman Grammar,* though frequently contracted to *there's* in speech: see further in section 3 below.

Existential there is almost always coupled with the verb *be* in the *Longman Grammar* corpus: in 99% of cases in spoken data, and 95% in fiction and academic prose. Just occasionally it combines with *exist* (in academic writing), and with longer paraphrases of *be,* such as *seem/appear/used to.* In fiction a sprinkling of other verbs combine with *existential there* to set the scene:

On the bed there lay a small figure.

There remained the small matter of money.

There comes lends itself to various idioms such as:

There comes a time when even a politician prefers early bed.

There comes a point where one begins to suspect . . .

Inversion of the normal subject–verb word order underscores the significance of the moment being described. (See further under **inversion**.)

3 There's. Existential *there* can be contracted with *is,* as often happens in everyday discourse. It appears in writing, but much more often in fiction than other kinds of prose (Kjellmer, 1998): in almost 45% of all possible instances. *There's* is however increasingly seen on the pages of the newspaper. Westergren-Axelsson (1998) found it in 15% of possible instances in journalism of the 1990s, though *there's* is still much less common than other contractions such as *it's* and *that's.*

Existential there couples with either singular or plural verbs (*there is / there are,* according to the following noun phrase), as shown at the beginning of section 2. This formal agreement is strictly maintained in academic writing. But in narrative and everyday writing, *there is* and especially *there's* is found even with plural nouns.

There's tears in her eyes.

There's certain ways of getting round it.

There's lots of new plays being written.

In conversation the combination of *there's* with a plural noun is in fact more common than *there are,* according to the *Longman Grammar.* It goes especially with quantitative statements, indefinite and definite:

There's lots of questions to be answered.

There's enough people to tackle the problem.

. . . the lectures. There's six of them.

There's four bedrooms.

Negative statements also seem to attract *there's,* as in:

There's no telephones with outside lines.

There's precedes collective phrases using *a set/handful/crowd* etc. with a following plural noun:

There's a whole crowd of protesters on the steps.

When a compound subject follows, *there's* rather than *there are* is selected:

There's a post office and a small church on the corner.

In such cases both *formal* and *proximity agreement* help to select the singular verb (see further under **agreement** sections 3, 4 and 5).

These various uses of *there's* with plural (or notionally plural) noun phrases show how the structure is working its way into the standard. It seems to be evolving into a fixed phrase, rather like the French *C'est . . . ,* serving the needs of the ongoing discourse rather than the grammar of the sentence.

thereafter, thereby, therefor, therein, thereon, thereunder etc.

All these, and others like them, are at home in legal documents where they appear instead of using the standard pronouns. **Thereafter** only means "after it/that," but it's more conspicuous than the plain phrase in a long sentence and may perhaps reduce ambiguity. (Compare *the said.*)

In other kinds of writing, these words sound very formal and slightly archaic. The only one which enjoys some general use is **thereby**:

She was known to lace claret with malt whisky, thereby ruining both drinks.

In modern English **therefor** has become archaic as a way of saying "for that purpose" (except in law). Meanwhile the variant form *therefore* meaning "consequently" is taking on new roles. See next entry.

therefore

No-one doubts that **therefore** is an adverb meaning "consequently" or "for that reason." The question is whether it can sometimes be a conjunction. It typically forges a logical link between the two parts of a sentence, as in:

> *The weather deteriorated, and therefore they thought the trip was off.*

In sentences like that, **therefore** is a *conjunct*, not a full conjunction because the grammatical connection depends on *and*. But in everyday speech, the sentence might equally have been:

> *The weather deteriorated, therefore they thought the trip was off.*

In speech there is of course no punctuation, but the comma there equates with a brief (mid-sentence) pause, and suggests that speakers do use **therefore** like an ordinary conjunction – an emphatic alternative to *so*. There's no lack of examples in the more argumentative spoken texts of the BNC, as speakers draw out their reasoning. The famous *I think therefore I am* shows that this usage is not simply colloquial. But traditional grammarians and dictionary-makers are disinclined to recognize **therefore** as a conjunction, and editors working on the same principle would probably repunctuate the travel example with a semicolon:

> *The weather deteriorated; therefore they thought the trip was off.*

It is a nice distinction – a single dot making the difference between formal and informal style, and maintaining the boundaries between grammatical classes. Yet it doesn't do to make too much turn on a semicolon, as more and more documents are read via computer screens (see under **digital style**). One way or another, **therefore** is on the threshold of becoming a sentence connector, as noted by the *Collins Dictionary* (1998). It is recognized as a conjunction by the Australian *Macquarie Dictionary* (1997). See further under **conjunctions**, and compare **however** section 3.

therein, thereon, thereunder

See under **thereafter**.

there's

Can this ever take a plural noun in agreement? See **there** section 3.

thesaurus

The Latin plural **thesauri** is given priority over **thesauruses** in both *New Oxford* (1998) and *Merriam-Webster* (2000). British writers in the BNC do indeed seem to prefer **thesauri**, whereas their American counterparts in CCAE clearly prefer the English **thesauruses**. See further under **-us** section 4.

they, them, their

When we need to refer back to something in the third person plural, the pronoun **they/them/their** serves the purpose. It also serves generic purposes, in statements which claim universal validity: *They also serve who only stand and wait.* "Universal" use of the third person plural pronoun is also the one found in statements like:

> *Everyone has to consider their future.*

This of course is more contentious. Purists might say that it's ungrammatical to use **their** after *everyone*,

because *one* requires a singular pronoun. Many others would say that generic/universal **their** provides us with a gender-free pronoun, avoiding the exclusive *his* and the clumsy *his/her.* It avoids gratuitous sexism and gives the statement broadest reference. With determiners such as *each,* the same things apply:

> *Each member of the group must be prepared to bring in samples of their work to discuss.*

Again the use of **their** following an indefinite noun phrase allows it to remain gender-free and inclusive.

They/them/their are now freely used in agreement with singular indefinite pronouns and determiners, those with universal implications such as *any(one), every(one), no(one),* as well as *each* and *some(one),* whose reference is often more individual. For those listening or reading, it has become unremarkable – an element of common usage. In fact the *Oxford Dictionary* (1989) has it on record since C16, but its acceptance was preempted by C18 grammarians, whose anxieties about formal agreement were reiterated in C20 by Fowler (1926) and Gowers (1965). The singular use of **they/them/their** after *everyone* and other indefinites can now be explained as a kind of "notional agreement" (see under **agreement**).

Current dictionaries register the singular use of **they, them** and **their** among its definitions, often with an explanatory usage note. *New Oxford* (1998) treats their acceptability after indefinite pronouns as given, and is willing to embrace the next stage (use with indefinite nouns) in dictionary definitions. *Merriam-Webster* (2000) takes both for granted. The *Canadian Oxford* (1998) plays down the objections against its spreading use, and underscores its usefulness in avoiding sexist language. *Webster's English Usage* (1989) illustrates current uses of singular **they/them/their** following indefinite nouns and pronouns in various kinds of publication from the mass-circulating to the academic. Australian research by Eagleson (1995) finds singular use of **they/them/their** in a range of writing from advertising to professional publications and legislation. The Australian government *Style Manual* (2002) endorses it as "standard idiom in most contexts." All this evidence from different quarters of the English-speaking world shows that singular use of **they/them/their** after indefinites is now well established in writing.

Language historians would note that the trend towards using **they** for both plural and singular is exactly what happened with *you* some centuries ago (see **you and ye**). The trend is probably "irreversible" (Burchfield, 1996). Those who find it uncomfortable can take advantage of the various avoidance strategies mentioned under **he and/or she**, to be used when grammatical liberties with **they/them/their** are unthinkable. Yet that kind of response to singular **they/them/their** is no longer shared by the English-speaking population at large. Writers who use singular **they/them/their** are not at fault.

International English selection: The appearance of singular **they/them/their** in many kinds of prose shows its acceptance by English writers generally. It recommends itself as a gender-free solution to the problem of agreement with indefinite pronouns and noun phrases.

---

think of or think to

Mental plans whether formulated or not can be expressed with **think of**. For example:
> *We might think of going for a walk.*
> *We didn't think of going for a walk.*

But **think to** seems to be used only when things are not thought of:
> *I didn't think to ask her address.*
> *The desk clerk will never think to stop us.*

See further under **complementation**.

third person

The **third person** is a grammarian's term for the person(s) or thing(s) being talked about in a sentence. The different perspectives of the three *persons* show up in the differing sensitivities of *I, you* and *s/he,* in humorous paradigms such as:
> I am firm (*first*)
> You are stubborn (*second*)
> S/he is pig-headed (*third*)

In conversation we use all three *persons,* whereas most writing depends heavily on the **third person** to convey information. Some formal and institutional styles oblige writers to keep to the **third person** and avoid the *first* and *second persons* entirely, which makes for detached and impersonal prose. See further under **person** ("first- or third-person style").

Third World

Coined in French (as *tiers monde*), this term was used after World War II to refer to the least developed countries of Asia, Africa, Latin America and the Pacific. It had both political and cultural implications: that the countries concerned were not politically linked with western alliances such as NATO or with the Soviet bloc; and that they had neither an industrial infrastructure nor a high standard of living.

The term can be explained either by assuming that the **Third World** is the newest international frontier after the "Old World" (Europe) and the "New World" (North America) – or by the idea that the "First World" and the "Second World" are, respectively, the West and the former Soviet bloc, and then the **Third World** includes all those not aligned to the first two. In the Chinese view, however, they are the **Third World**. This then requires a further expression "Fourth World," for referring to the poorest and most dependent nations of the world.

thirty-second note

See under **demi-**.

this

Like *that,* **this** is a demonstrative pronoun and determiner: see **that** section 1.
◊ For the choice between **this** and *next,* as in *this Saturday* and *next Saturday,* see **next**.

tho

See **though**.

-thon

Formations with this ending are discussed under **-athon**.

thorax

The plural of this word – should you need it – is discussed at **-x** section 2.

thou and thee

These were once the ordinary English pronouns by which English-speakers addressed each other. **Thou/thee** was for the individual, while *ye* and *you* were for more than one person. This division of labor was maintained in the King James bible (1611), and it underlies the difference between two otherwise similar comments:
> *O thou of little faith.*
> *O ye of little faith.*

The first was said by Jesus to Peter, when the disciple seemed to be thinking twice about his ability to walk on water. The second was addressed to the crowd assembled to hear the sermon on the mount. In fact this biblical grammar was somewhat old-fashioned in its own day.

Shakespeare's plays suggest that by about 1600, the singular/plural distinction between **thou** and *ye* had already been replaced by a style distinction in which **thou/thee** was used for friendly and intimate address to an individual, while *ye/you* was for neutral, public and more distant address, to either an individual or a group. This is comparable to the distinction still made in French, German and other modern European languages. But for some reason the distinction was short-lived in English, and by the end of C17 **thou/thee** had been replaced by *you* for almost all second person uses, both singular and plural. **Thou/thee** survive in everyday use in some British rural dialects, and among Quakers. Otherwise, they are now the hallmark of religious language, as a special form of address to the divinity:
> *Praise be to thee, O God.*

And of literary rhetoric:
> *O wild west wind, thou breath of autumn's being...*

The lofty overtones of **thou/thee** contrast now with its humble origins.

though or although

In spite of appearances, **though** is not to be thought of as simply a cut-down version of **although**. In fact **though** predates **although** by some five centuries. Dictionaries treat them as equals, sometimes crossreferencing **although** to **though**, and they are interchangeable in sentences like the following, where either one could be used to mean "despite the fact that":
> *Though the door is still intact, the lock needs repairing.*
> *Although the door is still intact, the lock needs repairing.*

Although is of course the bulkier of the two, and it gives greater emphasis to the subordinate clause. If it seems more formal than **though**, that goes with it being the commoner of the two in academic prose by a factor of 3:1, according to *Longman Grammar* (1999) research. In fiction the reverse is true: instances of **though** outnumber those of **although** by 3:1.

Though has other roles than that of concessive subordinator which it shares with **although**. It also serves as a contrastive subordinator (like "but"), as in:
> *He was reserving judgement, though he considered it a hopeful sign.*

It works as a contrastive adverb, meaning "however," at any point in a sentence including the end:
> *I wouldn't stake my life on it, though.*

As in that example, **though** often serves to link an utterance with one that preceded it. This is indeed its major role in conversation, for both British and American speakers, according to the *Longman Grammar.* It would explain why the *Canadian Oxford* (1998) deems adverbial use of **though** to be "informal." Nevertheless it's registered without any stylistic judgement in *New Oxford* (1998), *Merriam-Webster* (2000) and the Australian *Macquarie Dictionary* (1997). Adverbial uses of **though** are also found in the *Longman* corpus of fiction and British/American news reporting, though they are rare in academic prose.

Other conjunctive roles of **though** (but not **although**) are to combine with *as* and *even* in compound conjunctions:

> *As though it had been commissioned, the sun began to shine.*
>
> *Even though we were indoors, the mosquitos found us out.*

Even though is more emphatic than **although** or **though**, and draws extra attention to a concessive statement when it's needed.

Both **though** and **although** have alternative spellings in *tho'/tho* and *altho'/altho*. Unlike many abbreviations, they have no effect on the pronunciation of the word, and they do tidy up the surplus letters. Despite this, neither abbreviation has caught on generally. Most of those in BNC data were in transcribed speech rather than published texts, and those in CCAE appeared in direct reporting of newsworthy statements. *Webster's English Usage* (1989) finds *tho* only in advertising and certain technical journals. The forms with the apostrophe declare their informality, and those without it are perhaps too different from the regular spelling. Eminently sensible as they are, *tho'/tho* and *altho'/altho* remain beyond the pale of standard English.

◊ For other examples of trimmed spelling, see **spelling** section 5.

thrash and thresh

Both **thrash** and **thresh** come from the same source word "thresshe," the variant spelling with an *a* making its appearance first in C16. The different spellings have since linked up with different strands of meaning: **thrash** with the verb "beat" and **thresh** with "separate the grains of wheat from the stalks." The divorce is not total, in that there are occasional examples of **thresh** in both British and American databases which do not relate to harvesting, as in *the thresh of his emotions* and *a threshing mass of children*. By the same token, there are no examples of **thrash**/*thrashing* that refer to harvesting. That apart, it's **thrash** that's gaining ground as the one used for newer figurative meanings, in the *thrash metal band, thrashed his opponent, thrashing out an agreement.*

thrive

Database evidence shows unmistakably that the past tense/participle of **thrive** is now *thrived*. The use of *throve* has declined almost to the point of extinction in both the UK and the US, with very few examples in either the BNC or CCAE. There's no evidence at all of *thriven*.

throes or throws

The idiom *in the throes of* ("struggling with") probably preserves a lost English word *throwe* meaning "threat." Its standard modern form **throes** may owe something to "woes." Given its isolation in current English, it's no surprise that writers occasionally spell it as *in the throws of* – but no doubt **throws** is written under the influence of sport, rather than an echo of the origins of the word.

through and thru

With the meaning "from one end to another," this word can be used in the dimensions of either space or time. Compare:

> *They walked through the park.*
>
> *They walked through the night.*

In such cases, **through** governs a noun which is a unit of space or time.

A slightly different temporal use of **through** has developed in American English, by which it links two words specifying the beginning and the end of a time period:

> *The gallery will be open Monday through Thursday.*

Here **through** means "from Monday up to and including Thursday" – though it's a neater way of saying it, and it has the advantage of making it clear that the period runs until the end of Thursday. The alternative expression *Monday to Thursday* leaves it not entirely clear whether the period includes the whole of Thursday. The use of **through** to define a period or time is now widely recognized and understood outside North America. Yet there's scant evidence of its actual use in BNC texts, hence the restrictive label "North American" in *New Oxford* (1998) and "US" in the Australian *Macquarie Dictionary* (1997).

The abbreviated spelling **thru** is not generally used in documentary writing, even though it appears on street signs (*NO THRU ROAD*), and in catalogues and advertising. In American English it also appears in newspaper headlines: *BROADWAY THRU A KEYHOLE,* in data from CCAE, and in entertainment schedules, as in *showing Tuesday thru Friday.* Canadians too use it this way (*Canadian English Usage,* 1997). **Thru** renders the word simply and directly, and has everything to recommend it. Major American institutions such as the National Education Association and the *Chicago Tribune* tried to establish it, among others, during nearly a century of spelling reform. (See further under **gh**.) Compounds such as *thruway* and *drive-thru* are isolated monuments to the endeavor, but **thru** still lacks broad acceptance in its own right. In BNC data it appears only in computing notes and a few transcriptions of speech.

◊ For other trimmed spellings, see **spelling** section 5.

throwaway terms

Because languages reflect the culture of the people who use them, they also show something of their values and attitudes to others – those they admire and those for whom they have no respect. Every language has expressions like the English *Chinese copy, Dutch courage, French leave,* which enshrine stereotyped criticism of the peoples concerned.

Throwaway expressions have no factual basis, though they sometimes emerge in a century when relations with another country are particularly vexed. The *Oxford Dictionary* (1989) notes that rivalry between the English and the Dutch in C17 seems to have generated various phrases critical of the Dutch, including *Dutch bargain, Dutch gold, Dutch treat, Dutch uncle*. The phrases imply stereotypes of the Dutch as stingy and moralizing. **Throwaway terms** for the French tend to project them as licentious, witness *French kiss, French letter, doing french*. Speakers of languages other than English return the compliment. To express what the English call *French leave,* there are expressions in Italian, French and Norwegian which translate as "leave like an Englishman."

The prejudices and stereotypes embodied in **throwaway terms** are very persistent, and it would be better for neighborly relations if they passed into oblivion. Dictionaries too can do their bit by removing the capital letter from **throwaway terms**, so that there's no subconscious stimulus to read them as national or geographical terms. The fact that *French Guiana* comes just before *French leave* in the headword list is no reason to insist on keeping the capital letter on the second.

thru or through
See **through**.

thrust
The present and past tenses of this verb are spelled **thrust**, as is the past participle. A regular past form *thrusted* was used between C17 and C19 according to the *Oxford Dictionary* (1989), but it makes no showing in current British or American databases.

thus
This has two roles, as:
1 a demonstrative adverb meaning "in this way"
2 a conjunct meaning "consequently"
Both uses of **thus** contribute to the cohesion of a piece of writing (see **coherence or cohesion**). The second is particularly useful in argument, suggesting logical connections between one statement and another. This is why **thus** sometimes comes to be used as a *conjunction* in argumentative speech:
>... the government's agenda is to abolish state pension, thus more and more people will rely on private and company pension.

In that example from transcribed speech in the BNC, **thus** introduces a finite clause like an ordinary conjunction. Much more often it's followed by a nonfinite clause, and remains a conjunct as in:
>... reduce the cost of subscriptions thus encouraging trade union membership.

The role of conjunction is less far advanced for **thus** than for other conjuncts such as *therefore* and *however.* See further under those headings, and **conjunctions** section 3.

thusly
This is a C19 American invention, often used for amusement or to make an ironic point. In data from CCAE it usually prefaces a portentous or otherwise extraordinary quotation, as in:
>The novella begins thusly: "In our family there was no clear line of division between religion and fly-fishing."

>... described his goals thusly: "Just survivin' this gig"

There's little sign of it in British English, judging from its rarity in the BNC. It is nevertheless registered by *New Oxford* (1998) as an informal variant of **thus** (as demonstrative adverb). See previous entry.

tick or tic
These spellings are associated with quite different words. **Tic** is reserved for a convulsive motion by the muscles of the face (*a nervous tic*), while **tick** covers all of the following:
• the small sound made by a clock
• the small mark (✓) used to check items off
• the small bloodsucking insect
• the cover of a mattress or pillow (also *ticking*)
Those four meanings come from three different sources. Only the first two stem from the same source, which they share with the verb **tick**. Apart from its standard uses, **tick** is used in informal idioms such as *just a tick* ("just a moment") and *on tick* ("on credit"), used in many English-speaking countries, though not in the US.

As a set, the words spelled **tick** are remarkable in that most refer to something small. This suggests that there's sound symbolism at work: see further under **phonesthemes**.

ticketed
For the spelling of this verb, see **-t**.

tidbit or titbit
See **titbit**.

tieing or tying
See **-ie>-y-**.

tight or tightly
Tight can be either an adjective as in a *tight fist*, or an adverb, especially in informal idioms such as *hold tight* and *sit tight*. It usually follows the verb it modifies. **Tightly** is the regular adverb which expresses the firmness of a grip, as in *clamped tightly between the teeth,* or the closeness of an arrangement, as in *tightly packed congregation*. It can appear either before or after the verb, as in those examples. See further under **zero adverbs**.

tike or tyke
See **tyke**.

tilde
This accent is most familiar in Spanish and Portuguese, though it has different functions in each. In Spanish it only occurs with *n*, as in *señor,* to show that it's pronounced to rhyme with "tenure" rather than "tenor." In Portuguese it appears with *a* and *o* to show that they are nasal vowels, whether as single sounds or as the first vowel in a diphthong as in *curação*.

till, until or 'til
In most contexts **till** and **until** are equally good, witness:
>The formalities can be delayed till they arrive.
>The formalities can be delayed until they arrive.

The extra syllable seems to make **until** a little more formal, though **till** is not an abbreviated form of it, but an independent older word. **Until** is however very much more common in current English, outnumbering **till** by about 8:1 in BNC data and more than 30:1 in data from CCAE. Both words can be used as prepositions and conjunctions, in the dimensions of time and space. Note that neither **till** nor **until** needs to be combined with *up*. "Up till" and "up until" are both tautologies, though sometimes used for special emphasis.

The form **'til** explains itself as an abbreviation of **until**, but is strictly redundant when **till** stands in its own right, as we have seen. In data from the BNC and CCAE, **'til** is used in quotations to suggest direct speech, as in "the game ain't over 'til it's over," and in titles and slogans: *shop-'til-you-drop.* But in both databases, **'til** with or without apostrophe is the least used of the three forms.

timbre or timber

These are not alternative spellings like *centre/center,* but totally independent words. **Timbre** is the quality of sound made by a musical instrument, or the singing or speaking voice. It comes from the French word for a small bell. A rare alternative spelling is *tamber,* which was coined by British linguists in the 1920s to render the sound of the French word. **Timber** is never used, even in American English.

Timber is of course the collective word for wood which has been harvested and sawn up for use in buildings etc. It originated in Old English as the word for "wood" or "wooden construction."

time

In the Anglo-Saxon tradition, *time of day* is reckoned in terms of two equal parts, with twelve hours before noon (*a.m.*) and twelve before midnight (*p.m.*). Questions about which of the threshold hours belong to which are discussed at the entry for **p.m.** With the twenty-four-hour clock, neither *a.m.* nor *p.m.* are needed, and the problem disappears altogether.

◊ For regional divergences in the use of fractions of an hour, see **half past or half after**, and **quarter**.
◊ For matters of historical time, see **dating systems**.
◊ For geological time, see **geological eras** and Appendix II.
◊ For the use of the apostrophe in expressions such as *six months time,* see **apostrophes** section 2.

time zones

The world is divided into 24 unequal **time zones**, roughly longitudinal but bent around certain cities and geographical forms for strategic reasons. The *zones* stretch westward from the International Dateline in the mid-Pacific, so that a new day dawns first in Fiji and New Zealand, and last in Hawaii. But the universal time reference is set in Greenwich, London; and so for practical purposes, *GMT* (Greenwich Mean Time) plus or minus so many hours is the common way of indicating relative time. In non-English-speaking countries and internationally, it's referred to as *UTC* (see individual entry).

• New Zealand time is GMT + 12.
• Australia is divided into three **time zones**. The eastern states (Queensland, New South Wales, Victoria and Tasmania) work by Australian Eastern Standard Time (GMT + 10); South Australia and Northern Territory by Central Standard Time (GMT + 9.5); and Western Australia by Western Standard Time (GMT + 8).

• Major South Asian countries are as follows: Japan and Korea (GMT + 9); China, Taiwan, Hong Kong and Singapore (GMT + 8); Thailand (GMT + 7); India and Sri Lanka (GMT + 5.5).
• Middle East: Iran (GMT + 3.5); Baghdad (GMT + 3); Israel (GMT + 2).
• Europe: from Spain to Hungary (GMT + 1); Greece and Turkey (GMT + 2); Russia (GMT + 3); Britain and Portugal (GMT + 0).
• Africa: Egypt and South Africa (GMT + 2).
• North America: the US has four major **time zones**: Eastern, including New York, Washington, Atlanta, Miami (GMT − 5); Central, including Chicago, Dallas and New Orleans (GMT − 6); Mountain, including Denver (GMT − 7); Pacific, including Los Angeles and San Francisco (GMT − 8). Anchorage is (GMT − 9), and Honolulu (GMT − 10). Canada uses the US **time zones**, so that Montreal, Ottawa and Toronto use Eastern time, while Winnipeg is on Central time, and Vancouver on Pacific time.
• Central and South America: Mexico (GMT − 6); Brazil and Argentina (GMT − 3); Chile (GMT − 4)

Daylight saving adjustments are applied independently by nations and states to their standard time. Their sovereign right to decide when summertime begins and ends can result, temporarily, in further **time zones**: an additional hour's difference, or the negation of it.

timpani or tympani

See under **tympanum**.

tingeing or tinging

The verb *tinge* ("give a faint color") needs the *e* in **tingeing** to distinguish it from **tinging**, which goes first and foremost with the verb *ting* ("make a ringing sound"). See further under -e section 1e.

-tion

Many abstract nouns in English end this way, though strictly speaking the *-t* belongs to the stem, and the suffix is **-ion**. See further under the headings **-ation** and **-ion**.

tipstaff

The plural of this word is **tipstaves.** See under **staff.**

tire or tyre

See under **tyre.**

tiro or tyro

See **tyro.**

titbit or tidbit

While **titbit** is standard in British and Australian English, in American and Canadian it's **tidbit**. The word is something of a mystery, but both Bailey (1721) and Johnson (1755) record that *tid* could mean such things as "nice, delicate, tender, soft," which seem to come closer to the meaning than *tit,* a "small animal or object." This suggests that the North American **tidbit** is closer to the origins of the word – though the British spelling **titbit** also dates from C18.

titer or titre

See -re/-er.

542

titles

The **titles** of publications and creative works demand special treatment to set them apart from ordinary strings of words. This entry deals in turn with books, journal articles, newspapers and magazines and audiovisual media. (For the **titles** used by people, see under **forms of address**.)

1 Book titles are distinguished in print by italics, and in handwriting or typing by underlining. On the question of which words in the **title** to capitalize, all agree that the first word must carry a capital letter, but after that there's considerable divergence from one journal or publishing house to the next. Opinions range from minimal use of capitals to something like maximal:

a) capitalize nothing apart from any proper names:
      For the term of his natural life
b) capitalize all nouns:
      For the Term of his natural Life
c) capitalize all nouns and adjectives:
      For the Term of his Natural Life
d) capitalize all nouns, adjectives, pronouns, verbs and adverbs (i.e. everything except function words):
      For the Term of His Natural Life

Librarians and bibliographers work with minimal capitals, i.e. option (a), yet options (b) to (d) are well established in literary tradition. For many people there's virtue in using option (a) in lists and bibliographies (see further under **bibliographies**), but using one of the other options for **titles** quoted in the course of a written discussion. Option (b) is quite sufficient whenever an italic typeface or underlining is used to set the **title** apart from the text in which it's embedded.

These options also allow us to contrast the **title** and *subtitle* of a book with heavier and lighter capitalization. Thus any of the options (b) to (d) can be used for the main **title**, and option (a) for the *subtitle*, as in:

The Life and Times of the English Language: the marvelous history of the English tongue.

The use of option (a) for the *subtitle* also settles a minor bone of contention over whether to capitalize its first word. There is no need. The principle of minimal capitals means lower case for everything (except proper names) in the *subtitle*, as shown above.

2 The use of short titles (an abbreviated form of the book's **title**) is on the increase. They replace the Latin *ibid.* etc. in footnotes, and also appear in the main text in second and subsequent allusions to a publication. Within the text, it's helpful to have more than minimal capitalization. (See further under **short titles**.)

3 Titles of journal articles. The setting of the **titles** of scholarly articles varies from journal to journal, reflecting the decisions and preferences of individual editors. A traditional style is to enclose the **title** of the article in quotation marks, and to use italics (or underlining) for the name of the journal itself. More recent style does away with quotation marks, and simply uses typography to contrast the **title** of the article (in roman) with the name of the journal (in italics). It avoids the problem of "quotes within quotes," whose status is unclear – apart from their rather fussy appearance within quote-marked **titles**. Abbreviations for the stock items in journal

references, such as *J* for *Journal,* are increasingly used, especially in the Vancouver style. (See **bibliographies** section C.)

4 Titles of newspapers and magazines. The mastheads of newspapers and magazines are set in italics, normally without *The* (see **the** section 4). The date of issue and the edition, where necessary, are given as well as the section number or name, if the paper is produced in separate units. Page references are optional according to both the *Chicago Manual* (1993) and *Copy-editing* (1992).

5 Titles of radio and TV programs, feature films, sound recordings etc. The **titles** of these are capitalized, as for books. Again it's desirable to have more than minimal capitalization when the **titles** are cited in running text, using any of the options (b), (c) or (d) noted in section 1 above. Quotation marks are sometimes used to distinguish the subunits of a TV or radio series (as with individual poems in an anthology). Otherwise the **titles** of audiovisual items are distinguished chiefly by the use of italics (see further under **italic[s]**). For more details about citing audiovisual and digital media, see **audiovisual media**.

titre or titer

See **-re/-er**.

to

This small word is the focus of several usage questions about how it relates to verbs and to particular adjectives.

1 To with verbs. To is commonly thought of as an essential part of the infinitive of English verbs, but it's not necessarily so. (For a discussion of the so-called "split infinitive," as in *to really understand,* see **split infinitive**.)

To often serves as the link between semi-auxiliaries or catenatives and the main verb, for example:

be going to	*dare to*	*had to*	*need to*
ought to	*begin to*	*like to*	*mean to*
try to	*want to*		

Note that the **to** is sometimes omitted with *dare, need, ought,* especially in negative statements (see individual headings).

◊ For the choice between **to** (plus infinitive) and *of* (plus *-ing*) after verbs like *begin, like, try,* see under **complementation**.

2 To after certain adjectives. To has always been used after adjectives (and adverbs), especially those which suggest likeness or closeness, for example:

  adjacent to close to similar to near to

It also works with many kinds of words to suggest a particular orientation or relative position, as with:

amenable to	*averse to*	*comparable to*
conducive to	*different to*	*oblivious to*
susceptible to		

For some of these, the collocation with **to** is an alternative, but for others it's the only one used. Adjectives with a related verb (e.g. *compare, differ*) often have alternatives. See further under **compared**, **different** and **oblivious**.

tobacco

The plural of this is **tobaccos**, by the consensus of dictionaries and writers represented in the BNC and CCAE. There's no support for *tobaccoes*.

toboggan or sled

See **sled**.

toilet or toilette

When first borrowed into English in C17 (as **toilette**), this French loanword referred to a cloth associated with dressing and grooming. Within the context of getting dressed it developed a number of other meanings, almost all of which have been disabled since about 1900 – because as **toilet** it then became the standard word for a lavatory.

The older and wider associations with dressing and grooming live on in derivatives such as *toilet kit/bag, toilet set, toiletries,* and in the occasional use of **toilette** (with French pronunciation) to refer to personal ablutions. In writing, the French spelling helps to distance the word from the WC. No longer is it possible to say: *She appeared in a blue toilet,* as in C19; and the possibility of a **toilet** being a "reception held while dressing" (a C18 usage) is unthinkable. The word's history is a living example of the operation of language taboos. See further under **taboo words**.

tolerance or toleration

These abstract nouns both embody the verb *tolerate,* but **tolerance** is the broader and more sympathetic word. It implies a characteristic willingness to give place to attitudes and practices other than one's own. **Tolerance** also has certain technical meanings:

* in medicine and pharmaceutics, "capacity to endure," as in *low tolerance for alcohol*
* in engineering, "acceptable deviation from the specified dimensions," as in *the measurements have tolerances of only 1 mm.*

Toleration is mostly used of a specific instance of **tolerance**, as in:

> *Don't count on their toleration of swear words.*

It implies more strongly than **tolerance** that there are limits to what people put up with. This is still so when it comes to *religious toleration,* which often suggests the need to accept other religions because of their presence in the community, rather than any desire to endorse them. These differences are neutralized in *intolerance,* which serves as the negative form for both **tolerance** and **toleration**.

tomato

For the plural, see **-o** section 1.

ton, tonne and tonnage

The word **ton** belongs to the imperial system of weights and measures (equivalent to 2240 lb). Extended terms such as *gross ton* or *long ton* help to distinguish it from the *short ton* of 2000 lb, which is used in the US. (The latter is therefore sometimes called the "American ton" by outsiders.) The **tonne** is a metric unit of mass equal to 1000 kg. See further under **imperial weights and measures** and Appendix V.

Ton derives from *tun,* a word for a large cask of wine or beer, which has also served as a unit of measurement for liquids. The spelling **ton** was simply a variant of *tun* that became the word for a standard of weight during C17. **Tonne** was borrowed from French in C19, though it too is ultimately the same word.

The word **tonnage** ("volume of freight") originated with the imperial system, and dictionaries still tend to refer to the **ton** in defining it. But the word is quietly embracing the metric **tonne**. In current British usage **tonnage** is expressed as often in **tonnes** as **tons,** in BNC examples such as as:

> *...great ship with a gross tonnage of 80 000 tons*
> *Net tonnage of goods broke the four million tonne mark.*

When **tonnages** are specified like this there's no doubt about what they amount to. Much of the time, **tonnage** is used abstractly as in *the tonnage of raw potatoes processed* or of *bombs dropped,* and it makes no difference whether readers think in terms of **tons** or **tonnes.**

tonite

This compact version of *tonight* has little currency in standard prose, but a life apart in advertising: *Tonite, atop the Empire State Building.*

◊ For other trimmed spellings, see **spelling** section 5.

tonsillitis or tonsilitis

Though **tonsillitis** is standard for both *New Oxford* (1998) and *Merriam-Webster* (2000), it shares the field with **tonsilitis** in both British and American English. The spelling with single *l* appears in 20% of all BNC examples of the word, and in about 25% of those in CCAE. **Tonsilitis** accords better with the core spelling conventions: see **-l-/-ll-**.

too

This diminutive adverb has two distinct roles, as an intensifier and as an additive marker, both linked to particular styles:

* as *intensifier,* **too** modifies adjectives or adverbs, as in *It was too hot to hold* or *That's going too far.* In conversation **too** is commonly heard from both British and American speakers – whereas academic writers make little use of it, according to *Longman Grammar* (1999) research.
* as an *additive adverb,* **too** appears immediately after the item (word, phrase, clause) which is to be added to one mentioned before: *My brother came, and his wife too.* In this role it complements *also,* but where **too** is most common in speech and speech-like writing, *also* prevails very strongly in expository and academic writing, according to the *Longman Grammar.* In "private speech" it's most likely to be positioned at the end of the sentence (Taglicht, 1984), whereas almost 60% of written examples followed the first sentence element, putting the spotlight on it: *Russell too used that metaphor.* On rare occasions **too** is the very first word. The original *Oxford Dictionary* (1884–1928) noted that this could no longer happen, but revoked the comment in its second edition (1989), with a fresh set of examples. *Webster's English Usage* (1989) presents several American examples since World War II, while noting that it's far from common.

topic

The beginning of a sentence is its most important "slot." Whatever is there gets foregrounded for the reader as the ongoing focus of interest, whether it's something talked about in the preceding sentence(s), or a new focus of attention. Compare:

> A) *James Rand had always wanted to go to Africa. He had met Moroccans in Spain who seemed to exude the mystery of the dark continent. He also knew there was business to be cultivated*

in Nigeria, and he could amuse himself with a
little big game hunting as recreation...
B) James Rand had always wanted to go to Africa.
But until things settled down in Nigeria, you
wouldn't look for business there. The big game
hunting grounds of Africa were still an
attraction...

Notice how version (A) seems to focus on JR the man
himself, whereas version (B) is concerned with
locations. These different perspectives develop from
the different openings to the second and third
sentences. Both versions begin with a statement about
the man and the place, but (A) turns the spotlight on
"he" and (B) on "Nigeria" and other African places.
Thus the focus of the passage, and what it foregrounds
as a whole, is controlled by what appears at the
beginnings of successive sentences.

1 Sentence positions. The all-important first slot in
the sentence is often referred to as the *topic*. The rest
of the sentence is then known as the *comment*. In these
terms the first sentence above is structured thus:

TOPIC	COMMENT
James Rand	*had always wanted to go to Africa.*

The *topic position* can of course be occupied by
different grammatical items. It's often a name,
pronoun or noun phrase which is the grammatical
subject of the sentence. But it can also be an opening
adverbial phrase or clause, as in sentence 2 of version
(B):

But until things settled down in Nigeria...

The **topic** may be preceded by a conjunction/conjunct
(in that case *but*), which helps to show that the focus is
changing. In closely argued writing the **topic** is quite
often preceded by a conjunct and/or an interpersonal
cue such as *perhaps, regrettably,* which again helps to
frame the *topic item* for the reader.

What happens in the *comment* slot (the latter part of
the sentence) is less important for information focus.
It does however serve to introduce information which
can be developed in the following sentence. The
reference to "Africa" in the *comment* of the first
sentence gives the writer a basis from which to
develop the subject and to refer to "Moroccans" in the
second sentence (version A) and "Nigeria" (version B).

Note that some linguists replace the terms **topic**
and *comment* with *theme* and *rheme* respectively.

2 Topicalizing phrases. Because the *topic position* is so
important, what goes there should not be dictated by
the routine grammar of the clause. Ordinarily a
clause begins with its subject, as noted above; yet
something else can be put ahead of it to highlight the
point at issue. The phrase or clause which does that is
known as a *topicalizing phrase/clause.* In
documentary writing there are stock *topicalizing
phrases* which serve to alter the focus:

*In a similar/later/larger study, researchers found
that...*
*From a historical/theoretical point of view, it
seems that...*

For other examples, see under **dangling participles.**
3 Topicalizing with the passive. Another resource for
getting something into *topic position* is using the
passive – which puts the spotlight on the object of the
verb instead of the subject. Compare:

*The Moroccans embodied all the mystery of the
dark continent.*
*All the mystery of the dark continent was
embodied in the Moroccans.*

The first version sets the **topic** up as people, the
second as an intriguing place.
4 Using a cleft sentence to establish the topic. Cleft
sentences provide a more pointed way of indicating a
topic. For example:

*It was the Moroccans who embodied all the
mystery of the dark continent...*
*It was the mystery of the dark continent that the
Moroccans embodied...*

The cleft sentence can extract either the subject or
object of an ordinary sentence as the focal **topic.** (See
further under **cleft sentences.**)

With these various strategies, writers can manage
their focus of discussion within paragraphs and
extended texts, purposefully maintaining or changing
it. Other details of information management are
discussed under **information focus.**

topic sentences

These are the sentences that signal what a paragraph
is to be about. See under **paragraphs.**

tormentor or tormenter

Dictionaries always give first preference to
tormentor, and unabridged ones list **tormenter** as a
legitimate alternative. Very few writers in fact use the
alternative, in data from either the BNC or CCAE. But
it's there for those who would connect the noun
directly with the verb *torment.* See under **-er/or**
section 1.

tornado

Both **tornados** and **tornadoes** serve as plurals, and
are much of a muchness where British respondents to
the Langscape survey (1998–2001) are concerned.
However American respondents and those based in
Continental Europe were strongly in favor of
tornados, by a majority of 80%. See further under **-o.**
◊ For the difference between **tornado,** *hurricane and
cyclone,* see under **cyclone.**

torpedo

The plurals **torpedos** or **torpedoes** seem to have
adherents in different regions of the English-speaking
world. A large majority of American and Continental
respondents to the Langscape survey (1998–2001) –
more than 80% – favored **torpedos,** whereas
torpedoes was preferred by about 70% of British
respondents. See further under **-o.**

torpor or torpour

See **-or/-our.**

torso

Borrowed in C18, **torso** came with its Italian plural
torsi, which is listed as an alternative to **torsos** in
both *New Oxford* (1998) and *Merriam-Webster* (2000).
Torsos is the only plural used now in British and
American English, by the evidence of both BNC and
CCAE. Everyday uses of **torso** far outnumber those in
artistic and literary scholarship, where the Italian
plural might have survived. See further under **Italian
plurals.**

torturous or tortuous

Though there's *torture* in it, **torturous** is usually used
metaphorically, as in sports training conducted at *a
torturous pace* or music with *torturous violin and*

vocals. The pain caused may be physical, but not usually life-threatening. **Tortuous** means "twisting, winding," and so lends itself to the description of rough mountainous tracks: *a tortuous climb across the cliff.* By the same token, a walk across the glacier could be both **tortuous** and **torturous**, i.e. a difficult and grueling passage.

Tortuous has figurative uses too, in describing verbal processes and negotiations, as in *tortuous legal battles* or the *tortuous takeover of a motel chain.* It sometimes describes language itself, as in a *tortuous explanation* or *tortuous metaphors,* with the sense of "convoluted." Here *torturous metaphors* is also possible – if they were particularly excruciating!

At any rate, figurative uses of **torturous** and **tortuous** converge in more than one place, when indicating physical stress for the athlete/performer, and mental stress for the observer. If negative stress is all that matters, either **torturous** or **tortuous** might do. Overall **tortuous** is the commoner of the two by far in database evidence, and may itself seem to connote some kind of *torture,* for many writers and readers. But if the cause of the stress is to be pinpointed, it's probably better to use a synonym like one of those mentioned above.

total of
Should the verb following be singular or plural?
A total of 34 students was/were arrested.
Both constructions are possible. It depends on whether you wish to focus on the collective set, or the individuals of which it consists. See further under **agreement** section 5.

totaled or totalled, totaling or totalling
Whether or not to double the *l* is discussed at **-l-/-ll-**.

toto
See in **toto**.

tour de force
This French phrase means literally "feat of strength." In English it usually refers to a feat of technical skill, as in:
The soprano's high trills were a tour de force.
The phrase can be used admiringly, but it often implies that what was done was spectacular rather than having particular artistic or intellectual value.

toute de suite
In English this is usually taken to mean "at once, immediately," while in French it means "following straight on." Thus it's open to the same kind of ambiguity as *momentarily,* as to how soon the intended action will actually take place. See under **momentary** or **momentous**.

toward or towards
The choice between these prepositions is mostly a matter of where you live. In the UK, most people plump for **towards**, whereas in the US it's **toward**. In each case the regional preference is strongly marked, so that it appears in about 95% of all instances of the word, in their respective databases. Australians fall in with British usage on this (Peters, 1995), and Canadians with American usage, according to the *Canadian Oxford* (1998).

◊ For the variation between *-ward* and *-wards* with adjectives and adverbs, see under **-ward**.

toweling or towelling
For the choice between these, see **-l-/-ll-**.

town names
Towns and cities named after the same person or place sometimes diverge in spelling: see for example **Columbia** and **Surrey**. The variables in personal names such as *Phil(l)ip* and *Stewart/Stuart* are reflected in variable geographical names, as are the alternative spellings of *Mc.* See under **Mac or Mc**.

toxemia or toxaemia
See under **ae/e**.

trachea
The plural is discussed under **-a** section 1.

tract, track or tack
Track is by far the commonest of the three, which would explain why it sometimes turns up instead of **tract** or **tack**, in particular idioms. The convergence has been noted by American and Canadian commentators, but there's some evidence of it in British sources as well.

Track converges with **tract** very occasionally in reference to a largish extent of something, often land, as in the following from the BNC and CCAE:
The Trust owns several tracks of land in the area.
. . . vivid vertical tracks of color in symmetrical composition
In each case **tracts** might be expected, but the idea of "long strips" (of land/color) would explain the substitution of **tracks.**

The convergence of **track** and **tack** can be seen in examples such as:
This season's results could take a different track.
He set us on a new track with human rights violations.
Tack in the nautical sense of the "course" set at sea is a good deal less familiar than the land-based idiom of finding a **track**. Land-lubbers take note!

trademarks
When first created, **trademarks** and tradenames are jealously guarded commercial property, to be used only by the company that owns them. The shareholder may nevertheless rejoice to hear the product name becoming a household word. If your fortunes depend on HOOVER, it's reassuring when people use *hoover* as a noun or verb to refer to any vacuum cleaner or to vacuum cleaning – as if it's the only product of its kind on the market. It suggests that the word is becoming generic, and would merit a place in the dictionary.

The point at which a word moves from being a *tradename* to being a generic word is in one sense a matter of law. Unpleasant lawsuits are fought over what is considered by one party to be a protected *tradename*, and by the other to be common lexical property. Dictionaries are sometimes invoked to show whether a word is generic, and can find themselves in the gun for including words which began life as *tradenames*. Their defense is to say that such words would not be in the list if they were not already generic, while noting that the word originated as a

trademark. A surprising number of ordinary words began life as **trademarks**, including:

aqualung	biro	cellophane	crimplene
dictaphone	escalator	jeep	kleenex
laundromat	levis	linotype	masonite
nylon	plasticine	polaroid	primus
pyrex	rollerblade	technicolor	thermos
vaseline	velcro	walkman	xerox
zipper			

There are many more. Unfortunately, dictionaries do not indicate the currency of any **trademark** mentioned, and a good many are out-of-date.

Newspapers and mass-circulating magazines are more often challenged over the use of a *tradename* than dictionaries. They are vulnerable because they also contain advertising, and editorial use of *tradenames* may be seen as promoting one product at the expense of others. Most newspapers take no risks therefore, and urge their journalists to avoid **trademarks** altogether by means of a paraphrase. Thus "sticking plaster" is used instead of *band-aid* in the UK, and "adhesive strip" in the US. Their other strategy when the word cannot be avoided (as in verbatim quotes) is to capitalize it, to show that it's not being used carelessly. Yet the effect can be quite unfortunate: . . . *according to the minister: "It was just a Band-aid solution to the agricultural problem."* The use of the capital letter invites a literal rather than figurative interpretation of *band-aid.* A way out in this case would be to put quote marks round "band-aid solution."

The currency of **trademarks** varies from place to place. *Aspirin,* for example, is still protected in Canada, but no longer in Britain, the US, South Africa, Australia and New Zealand. The status of **trademarks** can be ascertained in:

* the UK, through the website at www.patent.gov.uk/tm/
* the US, through the *Trademark Checklist* (USTA 1990), updated by the International Trademark Association (formerly the US Trademark Association)
* Canada, through the *Canadian Trade Index,* published by the Canadian Manufacturers' Association
* Australia, through the website at www.ipaustralia.gov.au
* New Zealand, through the website at www.nztrademark.com.

traffic

For the spelling of this word when it serves as a verb, see **-c/-ck-**.

tranquilizer, tranquillizer or tranquilliser

In American English **tranquilizer** is dominant, and the only one of the three to appear in data from CCAE. The second and third spellings are used in British English, **tranquilliser** somewhat more than **tranquillizer**, by their relative frequencies in the BNC. These preferences are in line with US/UK practices on *-ize/-ise,* and their treatment of derivatives of words ending in *l* (in this case *tranquil*). See **-ize/-ise** and **-l-/-ll-**.

trans-

The Latin prefix meaning "across, through" comes to us in a large number of loanwords, especially verbs, but also adjectives and related nouns:

transcribe	transfer	transfigure
transform	translate	translucent
transmigrate	transmit	transparent
transpose		

In modern English the prefix has mostly helped to create geographical adjectives. Following *trans-Atlantic* (1779) came:

transalpine	trans-Andean	trans-Canadian
transcontinental	trans-Pacific	transpolar
trans-Siberian		

An exceptional example where **trans-** is used more figuratively is *transsexual.*

◊ For the spelling of *trans(s)exual* and *trans(s)hip,* see **-s/-ss-**.

transatlantic or trans-Atlantic

Both spellings are current in British and American English, though the merged form **transatlantic** is the more common of the two, by a factor of about 4:1 in data from the BNC and 2:1 in CCAE.

◊ For the notion of *trans-Atlantic English,* see **mid-Atlantic English**.

transcendent and transcendental

In common usage either of these may be used to mean "surpassing ordinary standards or limits," though they have few applications in everyday life. **Transcendental** is most familiar in the phrase *transcendental meditation,* a profound yet fully conscious state of relaxation deeper than sleep, which is reached by a technique derived from Hinduism. In western philosophy **transcendental** is used in reference to a particular style of argumentation, whereas **transcendent** refers to that which is beyond experience. In Christian theology **transcendent** is the term used to express the idea of a divinity existing beyond the created world. Still in the realms of the abstract, **transcendental** is used in mathematics to describe a number which cannot be produced or expressed by algebraic operations.

transexual or transsexual

See under **-s/-ss-**.

transferable, transferrable or transferrible

The spelling with one *r* (**transferable**) is overwhelmingly preferred by British and American writers. Some dictionaries such as *Merriam-Webster* (2000) also list **transferrable**, which reflects the fact that the stress is usually on the second syllable (see **doubling of final consonant**). Yet **transferrable** occurs in only about 10% of examples of the word in CCAE, and is very rare in the BNC. The rather latinate spelling **transferrible** is listed in the *Oxford Dictionary* (1989) and *Webster's Third* (1986) – but makes no showing in either BNC or CCAE.

◊ Compare **inferable**.

transferor, transferrer or transferer

With options like these, you would expect **transferor** to be associated with legal writing (see **-er/-or**), and the other spellings with general usage. Both *New Oxford* (1998) and *Merriam-Webster* (2000) propose **transferrer** as the nonlegal spelling, which accords better than **transferer** with common pronunciation (i.e. having stress on the second syllable: see **doubling**

of **final consonant**). However neither of the *-er*
spellings appears in the BNC or CCAE. Instead,
transferor seems to be there for all uses of the word.

transfers

Words often acquire new roles and meanings by being
transferred from one grammatical class to another.
Shakespeare made it happen in much-quoted
examples like *spaniell'd me at heels*. A C21 example
would be *We scubaed down to the sunken wreck*. The
same grammatical process can be applied to
compounds, as in:
> They were short-changed at the restaurant.
> He button-holed me in the corridor.

The conversion of nouns and noun compounds to
verbs has fostered innumerable new usages since the
Middle English period, when the number of
inflections used for different classes of words was
reduced to the few we use for verbs and nouns today.
Many of the **transfers** produced by Shakespeare are
now unremarkable elements of the English language.
Even recent examples are quickly assimilated, such as
the following verbs, all from the first half of C20:
> audition   contact   date   debate   feature
> package   page   pressure   process   service

The reverse process, by which verbs are converted
into nouns, is also common enough. The following are
all very old **transfers** of this kind:
> aim   contest   fall   hunt   laugh
> lift   look   move   push   reject
> ride   scan   shudder   sneeze   split

Adjectives also lend themselves to grammatical
conversion, and have generated new verbs all through
the history of English. Examples from C13, C14 and
C15 include:
> black   blind   brown   calm   crisp   dim
> dirty   empty   equal   humble   secure   treble

Even comparative adjectives can become verbs,
witness *better* and *lower*.

All those examples show that English permits and
even encourages such **transfers**. Some **transfers** are
nevertheless resisted when new, especially nouns
pressed into service as verbs, such as *action, impact,
interface, profile*. The usage panel of the *American
Heritage Dictionary* (2000) still votes solidly (74%)
against the use of *author* as a synonym for "write,"
and only 53% of its members accept the use of *host* as a
verb, when it means welcoming guests at a show or
public reception. The panel rejects the use of *buy* and
quote as nouns (61% and 85% respectively). **Transfers**
launched in one variety of English may take a while to
reach others, and find resistance when they do.
Dictionaries, including dictionaries of neologisms,
vary in their readiness to list them (Ayto, 1998), and
their absence may or may not correlate with local
usage. *Merriam-Webster* (2000) lists verbs such as
voucher ("provide a voucher for") which are not
countenanced in *New Oxford* (1998). By the same
token *New Oxford* records the use of *trial* as a verb,
but *Merriam-Webster* does not.

Other linguistic terms for **transfers** or the
conversion of words from one grammatical class are
functional shift, and *zero derivation*, because the word
changes class without any derivational suffix. See
further under **suffixes**.

tranship or transship

See under **-s/-ss-**.

transient or transitory

Both these are about impermanence. But they differ
slightly in connotation, since **transitory** can have a
certain elegiac melancholy about it, as in *the
transitory freshness of youth*. **Transient** is quite
matter of fact about the brevity of things, and
transient workers are simply "short-term."

transitive and intransitive

In traditional grammar these words provide a
two-way classification of verbs. A *transitive verb* is
one with a direct object as the focus of the action it
expresses, as with *pick* (a team) or *send* (a letter).
Intransitive verbs are ones without an object, such as
appear and *vanish*. But many verbs can be used either
transitively or intransitively, witness:

transitive	intransitive
They flew me to Singapore	The birds flew away.
She boiled the kettle.	The kettle boiled.

Note that verbs in the passive are automatically
regarded as **transitive**, because they involve using
the object of a verb as the subject. Compare: *I was
flown to Singapore* with the first example above.
Reflexive verbs are also regarded as **transitive**,
because of the reflexive pronouns which function as
their objects: *She drove herself to the airport*.

The *transitivity* of verbs is not set in concrete, and
intransitive verbs can acquire new **transitive** uses
(and vice versa) through particular idioms.
Transitive use of *progress*, as in *progress the changes*
is relatively new, as is the **intransitive** use of *enjoy*, in
the friendly imperative *Enjoy!* when you say you're off
to a show. Increasing use of **intransitives** has been
noted in both American and British English, in
examples like *the word derives from Spanish*, or *the
word is spreading*. While **intransitive** use of *derive* is
commoner in American sources, and *spread* in British
(McMillion, 1998), the overall rate of innovation is
much the same. (See further under **ergative**.)

The fluid boundary between **transitive** and
intransitive can also be seen in the way certain verbs
are differently construed in American and British
English. In the US *cater* can be used transitively,
whereas in the UK it's always followed by a
preposition (see **cater for or to**), making it
intransitive, according to the traditional
terminology. This, and other issues of *transitivity* are
discussed below.

1 Complex transitivity. In all the **transitive** examples
so far, the verb has had one object (V+O) and is
therefore *monotransitive*. There are also *ditransitive*
verbs, which have both indirect and direct objects in
that order (V+O+O), as in *They wrote me a letter*.
Different again are the *complex transitives* themselves,
which have both a direct object and another kind of
obligatory *complement* or *adverbial* (V+O+C,
V+O+A). (See further under **predicate** section 3.)

2 Transitivity extended. Certain kinds of verbs are
transitive by virtue of the noun (or content) clause
which is their normal object. Typically they are verbs
which express a mental or verbal process, such as *say,
think*:
> I know (that) he'll do well.

The concept of *transitivity* is also extended by some
grammarians to verbs which take an infinitive,
treating the infinitive as a noun and as the object of
the verb. (See further under **verbal nouns**.) This

makes *want* a *transitive verb* in constructions such as: *They want to swim after work*. The alternative analysis is to regard *want to* as a catenative verb, and *swim* as its complement – by which *want* is then **intransitive**. See further at **complementation**.
3 **Phrasal and prepositional verbs** present another kind of challenge to the concept of *transitivity*. Compare:
> *He lives down the road.*
> *He can't live down his past.*

In the first example, *down* creates a prepositional phrase, making *lives* **intransitive** (V + A). But in the second, *down* is closely associated with *lives* as a *phrasal verb*, and together they form a **transitive** construction (V + O), according to the *Comprehensive Grammar* (1985) and the *Longman Grammar* (1999). These grammars extend the concept to *prepositional verbs* such as *rely on*, as in *I'm relying on you*, and call its object (*you*) a "prepositional object." Both the name and the concept may be debated, but there's no doubt that there are many such verbs in English, using particles such as *for* (*ask/call/pay/wait/wish for*), *in* (*believe/give/hand/take in*) and *up* (*bring/fix/put/turn up*), on which to base such analysis. Allowing that *prepositional* and *phrasal verbs* are **transitive** also helps with the complexities of *phrasal–prepositional verbs* such as *come up with*, so that *come up* can be analyzed as the verbal unit, and *with* as the head of a prepositional phrase. (See further under **phrasal and prepositional verbs**.)
4 **Copular verbs** also challenge the **transitive/intransitive** distinction, as in *I feel uneasy*. They are usually felt to have more in common with **intransitive** verbs, because the item after the verb is not its object but a complement for the subject. (See further under **copular verbs**.)

Despite these grammatical advances, the traditional notion of *transitivity*, as a two-way division of verbs into **transitive** and **intransitive**, persists in some dictionaries. Others embrace *copular verbs,* and *auxiliaries/modals,* to classify verbs better in terms of how they work in English syntax. A theoretical reanalysis of *transitivity* is presented in the *Introduction to Functional Grammar* (1985).

transitory or transient[1]
See **transient**.

translucent, transparent or opaque
A **transparent** material lets the light through, as well as the detail of images on the other side. **Translucent** lets the light through, but only very fuzzy shapes or colors. The adjective **opaque** is usually understood to mean "not letting light through" (see **opacity**). However the "opaque glass" used in buildings is normally **translucent**.

transmission or transmittal
Though the verb *transmit* has two abstract nouns, **transmission** bears most of its technical and general applications, from *electricity transmission* to the *transmission of disease*. **Transmittal** is used primarily for the processes of law, as in *transmittal letter* or *memo,* and also in official and financial contexts, for the formal reporting of strategic information, as in *transmittal of wartime secrets to Moscow*. But increasingly **transmittal** is used to refer to things other than verbal information that are

transmitted, as in the *cash transmittal industry,* and computer software that organizes data for *transmittal to the printer.* Contrast the *signal transmission* that is part of the hardware.

transparency or transparence
When referring to a photographic image, only **transparency** will do. Dictionaries allow either word for the abstract noun that describes the quality of being *transparent,* but database evidence shows that **transparence** is hardly used, and **transparency** is overwhelmingly preferred.
◊ For the difference between **transparent** and **translucent**, see **translucent**.

transpire
This word has been shifting its ground for the last three centuries, against stout resistance from Dr. Johnson and other commentators. Its first role in English was to refer to the biological process of *transpiration,* as it still does. But during C18 it began to be used of news filtering through, and during C19 to refer to events themselves, as in *much has transpired in Poland.* These shifts are unsurprising, given that a written comment on what *transpired* might refer to something happening and/or to reports about it. The ambiguity can be seen in current examples of **transpire** in BNC data:
> *It transpired that somehow the clips had twisted and become detached ...*

This very frequent construction with *it* as "dummy subject" draws its meaning from the subordinate content clause; thus the grammar itself distances us from the facts. With other subjects than *it,* **transpire** clearly means "happen," as in:
> *There are conflicting accounts of what actually transpired ...*
> *Nothing so romantic ever transpired there.*

This use of **transpire** to mean "happen" is now common in both British and American English – occurring in about 25% of examples, according to *New Oxford* (1998), and "standard" according to *Webster's English Usage* (1989). If **transpire** still seems a tad pretentious, it is perfectly idiomatic.

transsexual or transexual
See under **-s-/-ss-**.

transship or tranship
See under **-s-/-ss-**.

traveled or travelled, traveler or traveller, traveling or travelling
The choice represented in these pairs is discussed under **-l-/-ll-**.

travelogue or travelog
See under **-gue/-g**.

tread, trod and treaded
The regular past forms of **tread** are **trod** (past tense) and *trodden* (past participle), although **trod** is quite freely used as an alternative to *trodden,* as in:
> *Like all bathroom scales, ours are trod with hope and trepidation.*

In BNC data *trod* is used for *trodden* in about 1 in 4 cases, whereas in CCAE it's 1 in 2. Americans actually prefer **trod** over *trodden* in compound forms such as *well-trod* and *little trod,* in data from CCAE. *Untrod* is their preferred form of the negative adjective, and it's listed ahead of *untrodden* in *Merriam-Webster* (2000), though not at all in *New Oxford* (1998). British usage is firmly with *untrodden.*

Trod is also used in the US as a verb in its own right, meaning "walk [in pursuit of something]," as in *trod(ding) the boards* – an idiom associated with the acting profession. (In the UK it's *tread(ing) the boards.*) The American use of **trod** has a long history in dialect, and seems to have come via Scottish to more general currency in C20. In CCAE data it turns up in various transitive collocations, such as *trodding the road/path/sidewalks,* and can be used intransitively, as in: *apt to trod over party lines. Canadian English Usage* (1997) reports recent examples from the western provinces.

The form **treaded** is occasionally found for **trod** as the past form, in idiomatic uses, especially in American English. It occurs when it's a matter of "treading water":

> *Most of us would have treaded water or sunk.*
> *The new party treaded gently.*

Treaded is also found in both British and American English in reference to the *tread* of tyres or shoes – for example: *deep-treaded sneakers* and *changing from slick to treaded tires.*

treasonable or treasonous

These are equivalent, though **treasonable** is the one for most purposes. It serves in law, as in *treasonable offence,* as well as in ordinary usage, as a general synonym for "traitorous." **Treasonous** is sometimes used instead, as in *treasonous mismanagement of the economy,* but it's outnumbered by a factor of more than 5:1 in database evidence. For Fowler in 1926 it was "comparatively rare," so little has changed through C20.

treble or triple

See **triple**.

trellis

When used as a verb or verbal noun, as in *trellised, trellising,* there's no reason to double the *s*. See **-s/-ss-**.

tremor, trembler, tremblor or temblor

All these are used to refer to earthquakes, but some are more local than others. **Tremor** is the general as well as technical term, used by vulcanologists as they measure its magnitude on the Richter or other scales. (There is no parallel spelling "tremour" to set British and American usage apart here.)

The Spanish loanword **temblor** (literally "a trembling") is also applied to earthquakes on the west side of the North American continent, and standard since the Californian earthquake of 1906. But writers unfamiliar with it sometimes turn **temblor** into **tremblor** or **trembler**, both listed in *Webster's* (1986). This respelling with *tremble* is apt, yet strictly *folk etymology* (see under that heading). Both are therefore felt to be nonstandard, or at best colloquial, according to *Webster's English Usage* (1989) and *Canadian English Usage* (1997).

tri-

This Latin prefix for "three" is found in common words such as:

> *triangle tricycle trident triple tripod*

It also plays a vital part in scientific words, in chemistry:

> *trichloride trinitrotoluene (=* TNT*) trioxide tritium*

and in medicine:

> *triceps tricuspid trinodal trivalve*

Tri- appears in expressing time periods. In *trimonthly* and *triweekly* it means "happening every three months/weeks," and *triennial* "every three years." *Tricentennial* is "every three centuries," but much less common than *tercentenary* for "three hundredth anniversary." Compare **bicentennial or bicentenary**.

The prefix **tri-** appears with a shortened vowel in words such as *trilogy, trinity, trivial.* The last word is probably connected with *trivium,* the three-part curriculum that was the foundation level of medieval schooling: see **trivia**.

trialed or trialled, trialing or trialling

The choice of spellings for this relatively new verb are discussed under **-l-/-ll-**.

triceps

For the plural see under **biceps**.

trillion

For the value of this number, see under **billion**.

triple or treble

Both these are modern forms of the Latin *triplus,* which comes to us direct in **triple**, and as **treble** via Old French and Middle English. Both words can work as adjectives, nouns or verbs, though database evidence shows up some differences in their use. Americans strongly prefer **triple** for all uses, in data from CCAE; whereas British and Australian writers make substantial use of both. **Treble** is however more frequent as a verb, and **triple** as noun and adjective, in data from the BNC and ACE (Peters, 1995). Writers who use both words sometimes maintain a distinction made by Fowler (1926), that **treble** means something has become three times as large in size, e.g. *Aid trebled to US$649 million;* whereas **triple** means "consisting of three parts," as in *triple alliance* or *triple jump.* Yet *New Oxford* (1998) lists the verb **triple** as meaning "become three times as much or many," and the BNC provides plenty of examples like *Its turnover has tripled in the past decade.*

For musicians, the two words still stand far apart. **Treble** refers to the highest voice part in a musical score, and to instruments whose range corresponds to it, such as the *treble recorder.* **Triple** refers to musical rhythm in which there are three beats to a bar (as in a waltz), and contrasts with duple and quadruple time signatures (as in a march).

triumphant or triumphal

The first of these expresses a personal feeling of *triumph,* as in *She was triumphant after winning the contract.* **Triumphal** has ceremonial overtones, as in a *triumphal arch* or *triumphal march.*

trivia

This Latin loanword is the plural of **trivium**, a word used in medieval schooling for the lower or elementary curriculum. In modern English **trivia** means "petty details," though it may be construed as either plural or singular, according to *Webster's Third* (1986) and the *Oxford Dictionary* (1989). Both constructions can be found in BNC data. Compare:

> the endless trivia that surround most criminal prosecutions
>
> the apparent trivia is also serious

Yet the fact that the BNC contains examples of *these trivia* but not *this trivia* suggests a continuing preference for the plural, and it's glossed that way in *New Oxford* (1998). By contrast *Merriam-Webster* (2000) affirms that **trivia** can be singular or plural in construction. Data from CCAE provides a few examples of *this trivia* but not *these trivia,* and otherwise almost always singular constructions (*trivia that matters, trivia is king!*). Its most frequent use is as a modifier in *trivia question/answer* where the singular/plural distinction is neutralized. On the evidence then, British usage inclines more to the plural and American to the singular, but there's also acceptance of the other construction. **Trivia** has not been a focus of concern like *data* or *media* (see under those headings). *Canadian English Usage* (1997) comments that few object to the singular construction.

-trix

This is sometimes thought of as a feminine suffix, because it identifies the feminine gender in pairs like *aviatrix/aviator,* coined from Latin. Strictly speaking, the operative ending is *-ix,* since the *t* and *r* belong to the stem. It appears in very few other words in English, only *executrix* and *testatrix,* which are confined to law; and *dominatrix* (the "Madam Lash" of sado-masochism). Given their specialized character, the **-trix** words would seem unlikely to impact on the status of women generally – unlike those formed with *-ess,* a more frequently used feminine ending. (See **-ess.**)

When used in the plural, words with **-trix** can maintain their latinity with *-trices* or become more English with *-trixes* – according to context. See **-x** sections 2 and 3.

trod or trodden

See **tread.**

trolley or trolly

These spellings once served to distinguish a type of lace (**trolly**) from a four-wheeled vehicle (**trolley**). The former is now hardly known, and **trolly** is beginning to be reused as a simple variant for **trolley** in database evidence. But **trolley** is still overwhelmingly preferred in data from both CCAE and the BNC. See further **-y/-ey.**

trompe l'oeil

This French phrase means literally "deceive the eye." It refers to a type of painting which creates the illusion of three-dimensional space as hyperreal art does; or to interior decor which suggests spatial features which are not there, such as painted panels which make a passage seem longer or a room look larger.

-tron

This C20 suffix finds its source in references to the subatomic particle, e.g. *neutron,* and to electronic devices such as the *cyclotron* in which particles can be accelerated. Its use at the frontiers of technology has prompted fictional coinings in *Star Trek* and other kinds of science fiction – all of which makes it less attractive in everyday coinings such as *waitron.* See **waiter, waitress or waitron.**

troop or troupe, trooper or trouper

All these go back to the French *troupe(au)* meaning "organized group of people," but the spellings with "oo" and "ou" are associated with different activities. The older English (C16) spelling **troop** (used in the singular) refers to certain kinds of military unit, in artillery, armored formation and cavalry. In the scouting movement, a **troop** is a group of three or more patrols. The plural **troops** is military usage for the whole body of soldiers, rather than units within it. The French spelling **troupe** was reborrowed in C19 to refer to a group of actors or entertainers, and is readily modified as in *dance troupe, Moscow circus troupe, troupe of traveling players.*

The distinctions between **troupe** and **troop** carry over to **trouper** and **trooper**. **Trouper** refers to a member of an entertainment group, and **trooper** (in the UK) to a soldier associated with an armored unit or cavalry, and, in the US, a member of a state police force. The first is proverbially a committed and experienced performer, the second the archetypal champion at swearing. Compare:

> He carried on like a trouper.
>
> He swore like a trooper.

While **trouper** is often embellished with adjectives like "real" and "old," **trooper** is a plain job title. However the *Oxford Dictionary* (1989) noted that **trooper** was sometimes substituted for **trouper,** and the BNC provides examples such as *the good trooper that she is.* It happens in more than 1 in 4 instances of the word, though the accompanying adjective leaves no doubt about the meaning.

tropical or tropic

For the most part, **tropical** and **tropic** complement each other as adjective and noun respectively. Just occasionally **tropic** is used as adjective in reference to the delights of the warm zones (*tropic island/ skies/sun/breezes*) as well as their downside (*tropic heat/rot*). But in both British and American English, **tropical** is much more usual, by database evidence.

Tropic (but not **tropical**) is sometimes used instead of *trophic* when describing the action of hormones, as in *the tropic effect of CCK on pancreatic growth* – nothing to do with the climate!

truculence or truculency

The older spelling **truculency** (from C16) seems to have been ousted by the C18 spelling **truculence** – the only one to make its mark in the reference databases.

truism

This is a word to be wary of. In logic, a **truism** is a tautology, i.e. a self-validating statement such as *A triangle has three sides.* But the word is also commonly used to refer to a self-evident truth, one which requires no proof. As such it may be an axiom, or, worse, a platitude so obvious that it does not bear uttering. This last possibility makes **truism** an unreliable word, and one to avoid if you want to stress the fundamental truth or factuality of something, as in:

> *It's a truism that violence breeds violence.*

With **truism** embedded in it, the statement runs the risk of either being thought pretentious, or to mean that you think the observation is superfluous. Either way you need to express the thought in other words.

trumpet

For the spelling of this word when used as a verb, see under -t.

try and

Try and is a paraphrase of *try to,* typically used in informal promises and instructions, as in:

> *I'll try and keep in touch with her.*
> *Try and come soon.*

It expresses a supportive attitude, as Fowler (1926) noticed, and has a particular interpersonal role to play, hence its relatively high frequency in conversation. Even there it's outnumbered by *try to* in the ratio of about 2:5, in the *Longman Grammar* (1999) corpus. The data show that **try and** is a stranger in nonfiction writing (both newspaper journalism and academic prose), altough it does occur sometimes after *to,* in the structure *to try and,* where it helps to avoid the echoic *to try to.* **Try and** is more common in British than American English, judging from fictional data in the *Longman* corpus.

The conversational tones of **try and** have tended to raise eyebrows about its use, but it's grammatically straightforward. The expression is curiously fixed since no other part of the verb (*tries, tried, trying*) can go with *and.* Fowler queried whether it could be used in the negative, but with 60 instances of *Don't try and* . . . in a variety of BNC sources, there's no doubt about it.

Try and isn't the only construction of its kind in English. Analogues can be found with other common verbs such as *come/go/stop,* as in:

> *come and see   go and ask   stop and think*

These are in fact more flexible than **try and**, since they can also be construed in the past: *came and saw, went and asked, stopped and thought.*

tsar or czar

See under **czar.**

tubercular or tuberculous

With TB largely scotched, we may think twice about which of these to use. Dictionaries allow either for the adjective, and both are there in the BNC. Yet **tubercular** is clearly preferred to **tuberculous** by the ratio of texts (5:2) in which each appears. In CCAE **tubercular** dominates the evidence. There's no sign of **tubercular** being used as a noun in either British or American data.

tumor or tumour

See under -or/-our.

tunneled or tunnelled, tunneling or tunnelling

See -l-/-ll-.

tuppenny or twopenny

See **twopenny.**

turbid or turgid

Writing which fails to communicate may be **turbid** (muddy, unclear, confused) or **turgid** (inflated, pompous) – or both. When trying to identify the problem, you need to know which, although generalized criticism of a style often conflates the two. Our ability to separate them is hampered by the fact that neither is much used now in its essential physical sense: **turbid** in reference to a liquid with particles stirred up in it, and **turgid** as "swollen." Either way, plain English is needed as an antidote to **turbid** and **turgid** writing.

turfs or turves

The choice of plurals for **turf** is discussed under -f>-v-.

turnover or runover lines

Turnover lines is the editorial term used in the UK for lines which run on to the next one. In the US they are known as **runover lines.**

After a paragraph indent, *turnovers/runovers* are of course set flush left. But in an index or the stub of a table, they go the other way and are normally indented 1 em from the left alignment in an index, or the left margin in a table (see **indexing** and **tables**). In captions to pictures, the *turnovers/runovers* may be aligned on the left, indented, or even centred.
◊ For questions of word division at the end of a line, see **wordbreaks.**
◊ For how to divide strings of numbers, see **numbers and number style** section 1.
◊ For how to handle longish internet addresses, see under **URL.**

turret

When inflected, this becomes *turreted* with no extra *t.* See further under -t.

twingeing or twinging

The choice between these is discussed under -e section 1e.

twopenny or tuppenny

Currencies change but this word remains, reminding us of things that once cost "two pence," and as a byword for something considered of little value. Dictionaries put **twopenny** first as the etymological spelling, and it's the only one to be found in American data from CCAE. British writers rather prefer the phonetic spelling **tuppenny,** by the evidence of the BNC. Yet both *New Oxford* (1998) and *Merriam-Webster* (2000) show the pronunciation as having the first syllable rhyme with "up." The mismatch between it and the standard spelling seems odd.

-ty

This masquerades as an English suffix in abstract nouns such as:

> *casualty   certainty   cruelty   frailty   loyalty*
> *safety*

All of these have closely related adjectives from which they might seem to be derived. In fact the nouns were borrowed ready-made from French, and none have been formed independently in English.
◊ Compare -ity.

tyke or tike

As an informal word for a child or young person, **tyke** takes on a variety of tones. In American English it can be quite neutral, as in *went fishing as a tyke with his father.* But in British English it's often applied to those whose behavior is unruly or unsociable, and its overtones vary from indulgent as in *plucky little tyke,* to deprecating: *greedy little tyke.* According to both *New Oxford* (1998) and *Merriam-Webster* (2000), **tyke** can also be used in reference to a mongrel dog, but there's no sign of this in either the BNC or CCAE – or of the alternative spelling **tike**.

Note also the strictly local use of **tyke** in Britain to refer to someone from Yorkshire; and in Australia and New Zealand to mean "a Roman Catholic."

tympanum, tympani and timpani

In the medical profession **tympanum** refers to the ear drum. Like other scientific words borrowed straight from Latin, it becomes **tympana** in the plural. See further under -**um**.

Timpani is the standard spelling for a "set of kettle drums," as in: *heavy strings and timpani rolls.* Ultimately it's the same Latin word borrowed through Italian, with its Italian meaning and plural ending. In American English it's sometimes spelled **tympani**, but rarely in British English, by the evidence of CCAE and the BNC.

type of

When it's *this type of,* the word following is normally singular, as in *this type of accident/game/garden/ sausage.* The corresponding plural phrase: *these types of* is much less common in both American and British English, by a factor of 1:7 in CCAE and 1:10 in the BNC. *These types of* takes both plural and singular nouns following, as in *these types of drama* and *these types of plays.* The compromise form *these type of* is rare in both databases, and mostly found in speech. Some uses such as *these type of things* show it as a routine pause filler, but others are deliberate: *these type of games / links / specials / victim-based surveys.*
◊ Compare **kind of** and **sort of**.

typhoid or typhus

Typhoid means "typhus-like" and is a reminder that these two different diseases have similar symptoms. **Typhus** was identified first by de Sauvages in 1759, as a severe and often fatal infection, characterized by great lassitude and the eruption of reddish spots. It was associated with crowded human habitations, such as camps, hospitals, jails and ships, hence some of the earlier names for it: *camp fever, jail fever.* Somewhat later its cause was found in the micro-organisms transmitted by fleas and lice in crowded places.

Typhoid fever has similar febrile symptoms, and was not distinguished from **typhus** until mid-C19. Its source is a dangerous bacillus in contaminated food or drink, which causes severe intestinal inflammation and ulceration – again often fatal.

typhoon, tornado or cyclone

See **cyclone**.

typographical or typographic

The longer form is preferred in both the US and the UK. But while the American preference for **typographical** over **typographic** runs at more than 15:1, it's more like 2:1 for the British, in data from CCAE and the BNC.
◊ For other pairs of this kind, see -**ic/-cal**.

tyre or tire

In British and Australian English, these two spellings are used to distinguish the rubber shock-absorber round the rim of a wheel (**tyre**) from the verb meaning "exhaust" (**tire**). In American and Canadian English, **tire** serves for both meanings.

The words are quite separate in origin. **Tire** meaning "exhaust" goes back to Old English, whereas **tyre** is a contracted form of *attire,* a loanword from French. At first it could refer to any kind of wheel covering, such as the metal rim on a cart wheel, later made of wood or cork. The use of rubber was a byproduct of C19 colonialism, and the first inflatable rubber **tyre** was patented in 1890. All through this time, the word could be spelled either **tire** or **tyre**, and **tire** was endorsed by the *Oxford Dictionary* (1884–1928), and by Fowler (1926). However the spelling **tyre** was the one used in the patent, and subsequently taken up in Britain as C20 progressed. It has no etymological justification, but appeals to those who prefer that homophones should not be homographs as well. In fact the grammar of the two words keeps them apart, and North Americans do without **tyre**, at no obvious cost to communication.

tyro or tiro

In classical Latin the novice was a **tiro**, and this spelling was preferred by the original *Oxford Dictionary* (1884–1928). But medieval Latin had it as **tyro**, and this is now the preferred spelling in British and American English, by the evidence of the BNC and CCAE. **Tiro** makes no showing at all. For the plural, both *New Oxford* (1998) and *Merriam-Webster* (2000) recommend **tyros**. The Latin plural **tyrones** was last seen in 1824.

U

U and non-U

No other letter of the alphabet has the touch of class that goes with **U**. In the late 1950s it acquired unforgettable social and linguistic significance as the letter/symbol for "upper class," and especially for the speech habits of the British aristocracy. Class differences in speech had certainly been recognized before in Shaw's *Pygmalion* (1913), which dramatized the contrast between the languages of the upper crust and the working class. **U** and **non-U** are different in that they focus on the differences between upper and middle class, seen as upwardly mobile.

The terms **U** and **non-U** were coined by Alan Ross in an academic article published in 1954. They might never have caught on but for the reduced version of the article that appeared two years later in a small anthology of essays, *Noblesse Oblige,* edited by Nancy Mitford. Ross identifies differences in pronunciation, in greetings and modes of address, and especially in the choice of words, for example:

U	non-U
drawing room	*lounge*
jam	*preserve*
lavatory	*toilet*
napkin	*serviette*
rich	*wealthy*
scent	*perfume*
vegetables	*greens*
writing paper	*note paper*

For the traditional **U**-person, the alternative terms in the **non-U** list point to the pretensions of the *nouveau riche* or the would-be *riche.* Many are borrowings from French, to which the English have always turned for verbal sophistication (see further under **frenchification**).

The language has of course moved on since the 1950s, and some of Ross's **non-U** words have eclipsed their **U** equivalents in terms of general currency (not that this would enhance their value for the **U**-person). The terms **U** and **non-U** have enlarged their scope and can now refer to social etiquette as well as language behavior. Outside Britain it's less clear who are the defining group to whom **U** and **non-U** refer, and there are no American examples of their use in data from CCAE.

UK

These days **UK** stands for the *United Kingdom of Great Britain and Northern Ireland.* The "United Kingdom" wasn't built in a day, but over centuries by strategic treaties. England and Wales were united by treaty in 1536, and Scotland joined in 1707 to form *Great Britain.* The so-called "Act of Union" brought the whole of Ireland into the "United Kingdom" in 1801, but in 1921 the south of Ireland (Eire) regained its independence, and now only Northern Ireland remains.

The abbreviation **UK** is useful shorthand – not just in addresses, tables and lists where space is at a premium. In everyday writing it provides a brisk identification whether the discussion focuses on *UK lagers* or *UK hospitals.* The phrase *UK government* is arguably more accurate than "British government," though the latter is preferred in official documents. **UK** forms a useful contrast with *US* where British/American differences are being discussed, as often in this book. The abbreviation needs no stops because it's in upper case: see **abbreviations** section 2.

Ukraine and Ukrainian

The standard adjective for the **Ukraine** is **Ukrainian**, which leaves the stem unchanged. The spelling *Ukranian* (used on the analogy of *Iranian* perhaps) also appears in some edited texts in British and American databases. Most writers prefer **Ukrainian** (more than 90% in the BNC, and more than 95% in data from CCAE), and it remains the only spelling presented in dictionaries.

ukulele or ukelele

This musical instrument combines two Hawaiian words in its name: *uku* ("flea") and *lele* ("jumping"). So **ukulele** renders them exactly, and is the preferred spelling in all dictionaries. But common pronunciation turns the second vowel into a *schwa* (see under that heading), and **ukelele** is also recognized in both *Webster's Third* (1986) and the *Oxford Dictionary* (1989). It appears in some well-respected musical references, e.g. Scholes (1977). The two spellings are more or less equally represented in British texts in the BNC, whereas in American data from CCAE, **ukulele** outnumbers **ukelele** by about 7:1.

ulna

This Latin word for the thinner of the two bones of the forearm can be pluralized as **ulnae** or **ulnas**. See **-a** section 1.

Ulster

See under **Ireland and Irish**.

ult.

The Latin abbreviation **ult.** was once used regularly in business letters:

> *Thank you for your letter of 23 ult.*

It stood for *ultimo mense* ("last month"), and contrasted with *inst.* (*instante mense,* "this month") and *prox.* (*proximo mense,* "next month"). All three smack of older styles of correspondence. Current business style is to give the name of the month, as in:

> *Thank you for your letter of 23 August.*

See further under **commercialese**.

ultimatum

Most respondents to the Langscape survey 1998–2001 (almost 90% worldwide), endorsed **ultimatums** for the plural of this word. See further under **-um**.

ultra- and ultra

Latin **ultra** was an adverb and preposition meaning "beyond." In modern English it works as a prefix for various adjectives, with the meaning "beyond the range of," as in *ultrasonic* and *ultraviolet*. Some scientific formations of this kind have become household words, in abbreviations such as *UHT milk* ("ultra-heat-treated") and the *UHF wave band*, meaning "ultra-high frequency." But in common words **ultra-** often means "extremely or very," as in *ultrafashionable* and *ultramodern*.

Ultra can also be used as an independent adjective, as in:

They were voting with the ultra conservatives.

Its use as a noun for "one who goes to extremes" can be seen in:

Punks are the ultras of counterfashion.

In both these uses, and some of the compound adjectives, **ultra** carries the value judgement "excessive." This meaning seems to have originated in the French loan *ultrarevolutionary*, first recorded in 1793, and latent in many nonscientific words which have been coined with **ultra-** since then.

ultra vires

This Latin phrase means "beyond the powers [of]." It represents the judgement that a particular issue is beyond the legal power and authority of a person, committee or institution to deal with. Compare it with *intra vires* meaning "within the powers [of]," which affirms that the issue in hand is within the jurisdiction of the authority concerned.

-um

Words of two or more syllables that end in **-um** usually have Latin connections. Many are classical loanwords; others are neoclassical formations from C16 on. They serve in many different fields:

aquarium	*atrium*	*colloquium*
compendium	*condominium*	*consortium*
continuum	*cranium*	*curriculum*
emporium	*encomium*	*equilibrium*
euphonium	*forum*	*fulcrum*
gymnasium	*harmonium*	*honorarium*
mausoleum	*maximum*	*medium*
memorandum	*millennium*	*minimum*
moratorium	*ovum*	*pendulum*
planetarium	*podium*	*referendum*
rostrum	*sanatorium*	*sanctum*
serum	*solarium*	*spectrum*
stadium	*stratum*	*symposium*
tympanum	*ultimatum*	*vacuum*
velum		

The key question is whether their plurals should still be Latin ones with *-a*, or English ones with *-ums* – or perhaps either. Overall, the more the word appears in everyday use, the more likely it is to take the English plural, as with *aquariums, compendiums, condominiums, emporiums, forums, gymnasiums, pendulums, planetariums, ultimatums, vacuums.* Those which most often appear in scholarly or institutional contexts maintain their Latin plurals,

e.g. *colloquia, curricula, memoranda, millennia*. Words that lead a double life with both everyday and scientific uses, e.g. *equilibrium, spectrum, stratum,* appear with the **-ums** plural in writing for a general audience and the **-a** plural in writing for the specialist. These stylistic tendencies emerged through the Langscape survey (1989–2001), as well as regional divergences. British respondents were always more inclined than either Americans or Australians to use the **-a** plurals, making a majority for *consortia, moratoria, referenda* though elsewhere it would be *consortiums, moratoriums, referendums*. A few scholarly words ending in **-um** are found with Latin plurals everywhere in the world, namely *addenda, corrigenda, desiderata, errata, ova*.

Some words ending in **-um** always have English *-s* plurals, notably plants and flowers such as:

capsicum	*chrysanthemum*	*delphinium*
geranium	*nasturtium*	

A miscellany of everyday words also have English *-s* plurals:

album	*asylum*	*conundrum*
euphonium	*harmonium*	*momentum*
museum	*nostrum*	*premium*
quorum	*vademecum*	

The reasons why these have English plurals only are intertwined with their individual histories. None of them have straightforward connections with Classical Latin nouns.

Note finally that the Latin and English plurals express different meanings for some words:

* *mediums* – the means or material for doing something; or spiritualist links with the supernatural
* *media* – channels of communication, especially mass communication: particular materials or techniques of art
* *stadiums* – sports grounds
* *stadia* – stages of a disease.

umlaut

This accent consists of two strokes, which in German and Swedish are placed above a back vowel to show that it is pronounced further forward in the mouth than the same vowel without **umlaut**. So the first syllable of the German Hütte ("hut") and Hut ("hat") sound a little different, rather like the difference between "Hugh" and "who."

Umlauts also appear in some other languages such as Hungarian, but loanwords from there are so few that their use of the **umlaut** is unfamiliar. German loanwords such as Fraülein and Führer are however seen occasionally in English with their **umlauts**. When the **umlaut** is unavailable in English wordprocessing or printing fonts, an *e* is sometimes inserted after the umlauted vowel as a substitute. The English spelling of *muesli* embodies this practice, whereas in (Swiss) German it's *müsli*.

◊ Compare **dieresis**.

un-

Negative words are created very freely in English with the prefix **-un**. Most simply it means "not," as in adjectives such as:

unable	*uncertain*	*uncommon*	*unfit*
unjust	*untidy*	*unusual*	*unwilling*

When attached to certain verbs, **un-** reverses the action expressed in it, as in:

uncover   undo   undress unfasten
unleash   unload   unlock   unplug
untie   unwind

With verbs like these, there is some attachment or cover that can be affected by the prefix. Many other verbs cannot be reversed in this way: e.g. *break, expect, seek, smile.* **Un-** has no semantic value in verbs such as *unloosen* (= "loosen") and *unravel* (= "ravel"), discussed under **loosen** and **ravel**.

In longer adjectives, especially those ending in *-able*, **un-** is tending to replace the Latin negative prefix *in-*. So *unarguable* is more widely used than *inarguable* etc.: see further under **in-/un-**.

unaccusative
See **ergative**.

unarguable
See **inarguable**.

unattached participles or phrases
See under **dangling participles**.

unaware or unawares
Unawares is the relatively rare adverbial form, used as in:

> *Some have entertained angels unawares.*
> *FBI surveillance tapes that caught him unawares*

The latter idiom with *caught* (or *taken*) is occasionally constructed with **unaware**, at least in American English. It appears in about 1 in 3 cases of the idiom in CCAE data. Most of the time **unaware** serves as a predicative adjective, complemented by an *of*-phrase or clause, as in:

> *Gill was unaware of the local ordinance banning political signs.*

◊ For the use of *-s* as an adverbial suffix, see **-s** ("minor uses").

unbeknown or unbeknownst
Both forms are current in British and American English. But where British writers in the BNC prefer **unbeknown**, their American counterparts in CCAE go for **unbeknownst**. The ratio is about 4:1 in each case. Canadian usage reflects the American preference, and Australian usage the British, by their respective dictionaries.

uncharted or unchartered
See under **charted or chartered**.

unconscious or subconscious
See **subconscious**.

uncountable
For *uncountable nouns,* see **count and mass nouns**.

under-
This English prefix has both physical and figurative functions. It means:

* "below or underneath," as in *undercarriage, underground, undermine, underpants*
* "less than normal," as in *underestimate, undernourished, underprivileged, underweight*
* "lower in status or rank," as in *underdog, undergraduate, undersecretary, understudy*

Under- combines freely with both English and Latin/French words, and with nouns, verbs and adjectives.

underhand or underhanded
Tricky things lie below the surface with both these words, as well as regional differences in their use. In British English **underhand** usually means "sly" or "deceptive," as in *underhand profiteering,* and **underhanded** is very occasionally used for the same purpose. For Americans, this is the normal use of **underhanded**, in *underhanded sales tactics* and numerous other examples from CCAE.

Meanwhile the primary American use of **underhand** is more literal. It refers to a throw or shot of the ball where the momentum comes from below the shoulder, as in an *underhand toss* in baseball, or an *underhand serve* in tennis. Though British sports writers occasionally use **underhand** this way (in BNC examples such as *his underhand bowling was formidable*), the usual term is *underarm*. To add to the complexity, **underhanded** is occasionally found instead as an alternative to **underhand** in American sports reporting, in about 1 in 14 instances in data from CCAE. The overlap with the primary sense is acknowledged and played on in a comment that *softball and politicians are both underhanded*. There the literal and more figurative meanings, the neutral and the negative are all vested in **underhanded**.

Note also that **underhanded** can – in the US and Canada – refer to a team or working group that's short of the full complement of players/workers, as in *the home side was underhanded*. It thus becomes a synonym for *shorthanded* (or *short-handed* in British and Canadian English).

underlay or underlie
Like *lay* and *lie*, these verbs tend to tangle with each other. The additional problem is that both can be used transitively, as in:

> *Before putting the carpet down, we underlay it with rubber.*
> *. . . skills and technology that underlie arms production*

In practice, **underlay** mostly serves as a noun meaning "something laid underneath," and the verb when used refers to a practical process of laying something down. **Underlie** meanwhile refers to a foundation which is already there, not through (conscious) human intervention.

Still there's slight discomfort in the fact that the past tense of **underlie** coincides with **underlay** (present), as in:

> *patterns of investment control that underlay the whole operation. . .*

Without any explicit time reference, we might wonder which of the two verbs was intended there. A preceding past verb (e.g. "disturbed"), or a following past time phrase (e.g. "in the 1990s") would confirm it as the past tense of **underlie** – rather than a mistaken use of **underlay** in the present.

While the past participle of **underlay** is *underlaid,* that of **underlie** is *underlain:*

> *The pools are underlaid by another concrete floor* (= **underlay**)
> *The route is underlain by sedimentary rocks* (= **underlie**)

Occasionally *underlaid* is found where *underlain* might be expected, as in *Much of Iowa is underlaid with limestone*. But data from CCAE and the BNC confirm that *underlain* is surviving relatively better than *lain* itself, in both physical and metaphoric uses of **underlie**. See further under **lie or lay**.

understatements

Provided your readers know what you're referring to, **understatement** can be as effective as *overstatement* in drawing attention to it. For example, if you have been severely reprimanded by someone, you could say that X had "come down like a ton of bricks on you." But if others know X's style, it may be just as effective – and more amusing – to say that "X told you how to improve yourself." **Understatement** suggests restrained judgement, whereas overstatement implies a willingness to dramatize or exaggerate things. See further under **figures of speech**.

undertone or overtone

See **overtone**.

underway or under way

With the fading of its nautical origins, this phrase is increasingly written as a single word. The *Shorter Oxford* (1992) gives priority to **underway**, and its popularity with British writers is strongly confirmed in data from the BNC. But **under way** is still well used in American English, and outnumbers **underway** by about 3:1 in data from CCAE.

undiscriminating

See under **discrimination**.

undistributed middle

Using the *undistributed middle term* in a syllogism is a logical fallacy. See **fallacies** section 2.

undoubtedly, indubitably, doubtless and doubtlessly

All these aim to banish the reader's doubts, and therefore have an interpersonal role to play in writing (see **interpersonal**). Of the four, **undoubtedly** is the most forceful and widely used, whereas **indubitably** has little use except in very formal style. **Doubtless** comes between them in terms of frequency, but is relatively less popular with American than British writers. The ratio between **doubtless** and **undoubtedly** is about 1:3 in BNC data and 1:4 in CCAE.

Though **doubtless** is itself an adverb, the more obviously adverbial form **doubtlessly** is also recognized by dictionaries. It makes little showing by comparison with the other doubt-negating adverbs in the British and American databases, though Americans are relatively more inclined to use it. The ratio of **doubtlessly** to **doubtless** is about 1:12 in CCAE and more like 1:80 in the BNC. The existence of **doubtlessly** suggests the discomfort people feel with *zero adverbs:* see further under that heading.

unexceptional or unexceptionable

See under **exceptional**.

unfurl or furl

When the historical novel has ships "furling their sails," can you confidently imagine what is happening? By its origins (from the French compound *fer[me]*, "firm" + *lier*, "tie"), the verb **furl** means "tie up." But unless you are a sailor, you may still doubt the meaning of **furl** when hearing how luxury yachts have *their sails furled and set by computer*. *Furled umbrellas* are part of the stereotypical uniform of bureaucrats on the streets of London or Washington, yet that use of **furl** has also been obscure to at least some English users since C18, as the *Oxford Dictionary* (1989) notes. The writer describing how *the smoke furled dreamily from its nostrils* is not alone in confusing **furl** with **unfurl**.

These days **unfurl** is gaining ground over **furl**, with a variety of uses that make its position more secure. It is regularly used for the displaying of banners and flags:

> *Demonstrators unfurled a banner on the White House lawns.*

It serves to describe the emergence of new growth or life (*maple trees unfurling their leaves; butterflies emerging with unfurled wings*). In American English **unfurl** is now also being used figuratively to mean "reveal," as in *unfurled a strategy*. In data from CCAE it also appears as a variant of "unfold," as in *As the story / the nineteenth century unfurled*, a further non-physical use which is registered in *Merriam-Webster* (2000). There are small signs of this in BNC data, though it has yet to be recognized in *New Oxford* (1998).

uni-

The Latin prefix **uni-** ("one") is found in everyday English words such as *uniform, unilateral, unisex*. It appears in scientific words such as *unidirectional, unipolar, univalve*. In shortened form (*un-*) the same prefix appears in *unanimous* and *unanimity*, and it's integrated into loanwords such as: *unify, union, unit, unity* whose meanings focus on "oneness."
◊ Compare **mono-**.

uninterested

See under **disinterest**.

unique

This word has received an extraordinary amount of critical attention, with various rights and wrongs made to hang on its use. In its primary and historical sense, the word singles something out as the only one of its kind:

> *Sydney's Opera House is a unique building.*

In this absolute sense, the word cannot be qualified by words such as *more* or *very*. By implication, there are no degrees of *uniqueness*. Yet Fowler (1926) argued that some modifiers such as *almost, really, truly, absolutely* could be used with it, because they focus on whether the state of *uniqueness* is actually achieved. Fowler also allowed that *quite unique* was possible, provided you were using *quite* as an intensifier rather than as a hedge word (see further under **quite**). Since British English is more inclined than American to use *quite* as a hedge word, uses of **unique** that are unobjectionable in the US may be queried in the UK.

That apart, the dispute over **unique** turns on the idea that it has a single, absolute meaning, which is itself an oversimplification. Dictionaries such as *New Oxford* (1998) and *Merriam-Webster* (2000) recognize that in many of its applications, **unique** means "outstanding," "remarkable," "unusual." Some would call it a "loose" application, but it can equally be thought of as an extension of the word's range – something that happens to many words over the course of time. With its extended meaning, **unique** can legitimately be qualified by words such as *more, very* etc., and they in fact show that it's not being used in an absolute sense. Without such qualifiers, it still means "the only one of its kind" – other things being equal. Those who doubt whether **unique** continues to express an absolute meaning can take advantage of other words such as *sole*.

United Church or Uniting Church

These are respectively the Canadian and Australian names for a composite Protestant church, formed in Canada in the 1920s and in Australia in the 1970s out of the Methodist, Congregationalist and Presbyterian denominations. In both cases some Presbyterians have remained independent of the amalgamation.

units of measurement

The SI system is discussed at **metrication**, and set out in full in Appendix IV. For **imperial weights and measures**, see under that heading. Note that the symbols representing units of measurement in either system do not take stops: see further under **abbreviations**.

unless

This subordinator helps to introduce clauses that express a negative condition, equivalent to *if . . . not*, as in:

> *Unless it snows, we'll move the furniture tomorrow.*

Unless identifies a very specific, often exceptional condition. In older usage it was followed by a subjunctive form of the verb, as in:

> *Unless the Lord build the house, they labour in vain that build it.*

In modern English **unless** is rarely used with the subjunctive, in either the US or the UK (Johansson and Norheim, 1988). Instead the verb is indicative or formed with the modal *can*. **Unless** can also be followed by a nonfinite clause, as in *Unless otherwise instructed, you should proceed . . .*

◊ For positive equivalents to **unless**, see **in case** and **provided (that)**.

unlike

For the problems posed by this word in negative sentences, see under **like**.

unloose or unloosen

See under **loose**.

unpractical or impractical

See under **practical**.

unravel or ravel

See **ravel**.

unsanitary or insanitary

See **insanitary**.

unsatisfied or dissatisfied

See **dissatisfied**.

unshakable or unshakeable

See under **-eable**.

until or til

See under **till**.

unwieldy or unwieldly

Unwieldy is the standard spelling and the only one recognized in current dictionaries. Yet there's a sprinkling of **unwieldly** in British, American and Canadian databases, and the *Oxford Dictionary* (1989) identifies it as a legitimate variant from C16 on. Its rarity in current English does mean that it's liable to be thought a mistake.

upper case

For the origins of the name, see under **lower case**. For the use of upper case / capital letters, see **capital letters**.

upward or upwards

See under **-ward**.

urban or urbane

In C16 English, these two were simply spelling variants, expressing the same meaning ("associated with the city"). This is now attached exclusively to **urban**, as in *urban transport* or *urban development*. The extended sense of "sophisticated" developed in C17, and the spelling **urbane** has since been attached to it. Though it originates in the social stereotypes of town and country life, it allows us to note that *urban dwellers* are not necessarily **urbane**.

urethra

The plural is discussed under **-a** section 1.

URL

Whether you regard this as an acronym or an initialism (pronouncing it with one syllable or three), it's the *uniform resource locator* – or *universal resource locator* – by which you track down sources of information on the internet. Both explanations are credited in *New Oxford* (1998) and *Merriam-Webster* (2000), but they give preference to *uniform*.

When quoting a(n) **URL** or e-mail address, some writers enclose it in a pair of chevrons, while others set it on a fresh line, and use the space as terminator (instead of a stop/period):

> *information available at <www.m-w.com>*
> *information available at*
> *www.m-w.com*

Both methods ensure that there's no confusion with the punctuation associated with the carrier text.

Longish **URLs** that take the visitor deep inside a website can be handled in either of those ways. When run on straight after the carrier sentence, the **URL** may need to be divided at the end of the line, in which case the break is made after the forward slashes or any other punctuation mark within the address:

> *Information can be downloaded free of charge from <http://www.askasia.org/image/maps/india4.htm>*

Hyphens should never be used to mark the break in the address.

-us

This ending is very often found on Latin loanwords, and often means that their plurals need special attention. They come from several Latin declensions, and their Latin plurals are still used extensively in writing, though often replaced by English plurals in speech.

1 Many **-us** words are from the Latin second declension or modeled after it. Examples include:

abacus	bacillus	cactus
crocus	focus	fungus
gladiolus	hibiscus	incubus
narcissus	nucleus	phallus
radius	stimulus	streptococcus
stylus	syllabus	terminus
uterus		

In Latin the regular pattern was for the **-us** ending to become **-i** in the plural (*stimulus > stimuli*), which often happens in English too. The Latin plural is occasionally replaced by the regular English one (*stimuluses*), especially for the names of flowers and plants e.g. *crocuses*. The fact that the English plural involves a concentration of sibilants at the end of the word does not seem to prohibit their use in speech, as is sometimes thought. Among the various words tested in the Langscape survey (1998–2001), a majority of respondents preferred English plurals for *focuses, papyruses, phalluses, styluses, syllabuses, terminuses*. (British respondents were however much more inclined to *termini,* and Americans to *syllabi* than the others.) There was clear agreement worldwide on using the Latin plural for **-us** words which belong to specialized discourse, such as *nuclei, radii,* and generic botanical names such as *cacti* and *fungi.*

The *-es* plural is the only one for **-us** words whose English use has no antecedent in classical Latin, such as *bonus, campus, circus, virus.* For *genius,* the choice of plural depends on the intended meaning (see **genius**).

2 A small number of **-us** words come from the fourth Latin declension, where the plural was spelled the same way as the singular (i.e. a *zero plural*). English loanwords from this group include:

apparatus	census	excursus
f(o)etus	hiatus	impetus
nexus	prospectus	sinus
status		

When plurals are needed in English, these words are usually given the regular **-es**, since the Latin zero plural is ambiguous. They should never be given plurals in *-i,* as if they were members of the second declension.

3 An even smaller group of **-us** words are from the Latin third declension. Their plurals have a characteristic inflection with **-ra**, and a preceding change of vowel. The commonest loanwords are *corpus, genus, onus, opus* which have Latin plurals in *corpora, genera, onera, opera,* which tend to be used by academics in the relevant field. Yet a majority of respondents to the Langscape survey (1998–2001) preferred English plurals for *corpuses, genuses, onuses,* especially those from outside Britain.

4 Some **-us** words are not Latin nouns at all, and so are not heirs to any Latin plural suffix. They include *ignoramus, minus, omnibus, rebus,* which can only be given English plurals: *ignoramuses, minuses,*

omnibuses, rebuses. Most scholars prefer to give English plurals also to words whose source material is Greek rather than Latin, as with *chiasmus, chorus, hippopotamus, octopus, platypus, thesaurus,* though plurals ending in *-i* are around for some of them: see **hippopotamus, octopus, thesaurus**.

USA and US

Both are standard abbreviations for the *United States of America.* **USA** is often seen in writing – especially outside North America – in followup references after the full name has been given, and as the primary form in addresses, lists etc. Meanwhile **US** is common in both spoken and written discourse, and favored by Americans themselves. The *Chicago Manual* (1993) notes its use "in serious writing," but not "the most formal." *The US* is some 15 times more frequent than *the USA* in data from CCAE, and more than twice as common in BNC data. It occurs freely as the adjectival modifier in phrases such as *US government* and *US president.* In those and similar examples, the abbreviation **US** is strictly speaking more accurate than using "American" – which refers rather loosely to the whole continent, not the *United States* in particular (see further under **America**).

No stops are needed in either **USA** or **US** in British style, because they are in upper case (see **abbreviations** option c). In American style, they are now optional, though the *Chicago Manual* (2003) notes the traditional preference for periods in *U.S.*

usable or useable

With these two there's no question that **usable** is to be preferred. It appears as the first spelling in current dictionaries (*New Oxford*, 1998, *Merriam-Webster*, 2000); and it was the *Oxford Dictionary*'s (1989) choice on grounds of sheer usage as well as the fact that it embodies one of the most general spelling rules of English, the dropping of *e* before a suffix beginning with a vowel (see **-e** section 1). In data from the BNC and CCAE, **usable** far outnumbers **useable**. The analogy with *usage* also makes **usable** preferable. In *usability testing* (of website structure and design), the use of **usable** is again to be applauded.

usage or use

In some contexts, **usage** is no more than an inflated substitute for **use**, witness:

> The usage of public transport has declined in the last two decades.

Since the sentence is about actual **use**, the simple noun would work better than the abstract **usage**. Yet **usage** comes into its own as a reference to a prevailing linguistic or social habit. Compare the roles of the two words in:

> Common usage now sanctions the use of different than.

As that example shows, **use** needs postmodification, to specify what is being used, whereas **usage** has enough intrinsic meaning to stand on its own.

Though **usage** has always referred to actual use (of language or anything else), it acquired the additional meaning of "approved use," through appeals to Fowler's *Modern English Usage* (1926). So *usage guides* are expected to embody "correct" **usage**, and to prescribe how language should be, rather than

describe how it actually is. See further under
descriptive or prescriptive.

useable or usable

See **usable**.

used to

This quasi-auxiliary verb is a curious remnant of an
older idiom. It refers to a custom or habit, as in:

> *We used to sleep in every morning.*

Used to is fixed in the past tense, and as with other
fringe auxiliaries there's some uncertainty as to how
its negative works. Should it be:

* *We used not to get up early.*
  (This makes it an auxiliary, which takes the
  negative itself.)
* *We didn't use to get up early.*
  (This makes it a lexical verb, which needs an
  auxiliary to precede the negative.)
* *We didn't used to get up up early.*
  (Here it's still a lexical verb, which relies on the
  auxiliary to take the negative but duplicates the
  tense marking.)

The second construction (*did not use to*) seems
rather strange since there's no longer an infinitive
"use" pronounced to rhyme with "loose." This
helps to account for the third version, despite the
oddness of having the past tense marked in two places.
In conversation, it's impossible to know whether
the "d" is there or not, because of the following "t."
So the choice between *use to* and *used to* is an
artefact of the transcriber's ear or writer's eye for
what should appear on the page. In BNC data
didn't used to is in fact the commonest of the three
constructions, outnumbering *didn't use to* by more
than 3:2 – though almost all citations for both come
from transcriptions of speech. *Used not to* is the
least well represented, but scattered over various
kinds of writing as well as speech. The relativities are
much the same in data from CCAE, except for the
dearth of examples of *used not to*. The data challenge
the comments of both the *Comprehensive Grammar*
(1985) and *Webster's English Usage* (1989), that *didn't
use to* is preferred/usual in British and American
English.

When it comes to phrasing questions with **used to**,
there are the same alternatives, treating **used to** as
auxiliary and as a lexical verb:

> *Used you to get up early?*
> *Did you use(d) to get up early?*

The construction: *did you use(d) to* is overwhelmingly
preferred in British and American English, and in
Australian English as well. Yet Collins's research
(1979) also showed Australians' discomfort in using
the dubious *use(d) to*, and an inclination to avoid it by
means of paraphrase. The following are some of the
alternatives for construing the question:

> *Did you get up early when you were younger?*
> *Did you make a habit of getting up early?*
> *Were you used to getting up early?*

All this shows the erosion of auxiliary use of **used to**,
now more or less confined to affirmative statements.

USSR

See under **Russia**.

UTC

This initialism translates the French *Temps Universel
Coordonné* into "Universal Time Coordinate(d)," but
usually becomes "Coordinate(d) Universal Time" in
English. It refers to the system by which the world's
time is reckoned at standardized intervals around the
globe. Anglophone countries generally prefer to refer
to it as "Greenwich Mean Time" (GMT). See further
under **time zones**.

utilize/utilise or use

Most of the time **utilize/utilise** seems to be a
heavyweight substitute for **use**, as in:

> *If the fax machine fails, would you utilize the
> telephone.*

There's little justification for **utilize** when it only
serves to make the statement sound more important.

Yet for some writers **utilize** still connotes
something more than **use**, i.e. the implication that a
resource has been turned to good account, and used in
a profitable, effective or ingenious way:

> *They utilized water from a nearby stream to cool
> the engine.*

This subtle extra dimension of **utilize** is
unfortunately jeopardized by pretentious use of it
elsewhere.

utmost or uttermost

See under **-most**.

U-turn, about-turn, about-face or volte-face

All these can refer to an abrupt reversal of policy. The
most recent (**U-turn**) is already the most frequent in
British English by the evidence of the BNC; and it has
the force of its other very familiar use in describing
the 180° change of direction of a vehicle. Both
about-turn and **about-face** come from the military
parade ground, though their imperatives are muted.
In British English **about-turn** is somewhat more
common than **about-face**, though both are current. In
American English **about-face** is by far the commoner
of the two, and almost as popular as **U-turn**. Neither
British nor American writers make much use of
volte-face, a French calque of the Italian *voltafaccia*
("[a] turn [of the] face)."

-v-/-f-

The letters *v* and *f* are alternatives in some verbs and participles which derive from older English nouns ending in *-f* or *-fe*, e.g. *hoofed/hooved, knifed/knived*. The words are all ones which as nouns have *v* in their plural forms (see further under **-f/-v-**). The use of *v* or *f* sometimes affects the meaning, as shown in the table below.

Noun	verb	Inflected verb
calf	*calve* "give birth to a calf"	*calved*
dwarf	*dwarf* "cause to look small"	*dwarfed (dwarved)*
half	*halve* "divide in two"	*halved*
hoof	*hoof* "have hoofs"	*hoofed/hooved*
hoof	*hoof* "kick," "go on foot," "dance"	*hoofed*
knife	*knife* "stab"	*knifed (knived)*
leaf	*leaf* "have leaves"	*leafed/leaved*
leaf	*leaf* "turn pages"	*leafed*
loaf	*loaf* "be idle"	*loafed*
roof	*roof* "put roof on"	*roofed*
sheaf	*sheaf/sheave* "make sheaves"	*sheaved/sheafing*
shelf	*shelve* "put on the shelf"	*shelved*
thief	*thieve* "be a thief"	*thieved*
turf	*turf* "cover with turf," "throw out"	*turfed*
wolf	*wolf* "eat ravenously"	*wolfed*

The -f- spelling prevails for the majority, except *calve, halve, sheaf, shelve, thieve*, where the verbs with -v- are centuries old. For *dwarf* and *knife*, -v- spellings are only a rare alternative, in data from the BNC and CCAE. But the -v- spellings provide a significant variant for the compounded forms of *hoof* (compare *cloven-hoofed* and *large hooved animals*), and *leaf* (compare *flat-leafed parsley* with *glossy-leaved orange trees*). The alternatives may correlate with the fact that they may be regarded as deverbal (with -f-) or denominal (with -v-), since the latter aligns them with the inflected noun (*hooves/leaves*) in each case. (See further under **-ed** section 2.)

The -v-/-f- option normally used for the verb is applied in adjectives such as *dwarfish, thievish;* and in other derivatives (*dwarfism, thievery*) before a suffix beginning with a vowel.

◊ For the choice between *elvish/elfish* and *wolfish/wolvish*, see under those headings.

vaccinate

See under **inoculate**.

vacuity or vacuousness

Both these provide an abstract noun for *vacuous* ("empty"). **Vacuity** is the more latinate of the two, but well established (from C16) with a range of meanings from physical emptiness to absence of mind or

purpose. **Vacuousness** is a C17 English formation, but used only sporadically, and rarely seen in print, by the evidence of both BNC and CCAE. When it is, its bulk helps to underscore the critical point, as in *the prince of privileged vacuousness*.

vacuum

For the plural of this word, see under **-um**.

vademecum

This Latin phrase means literally "go with me." Since C17 it has been used to refer to portable reference manuals on subjects as diverse as theology and theatre, opera and archeology etc. etc. The pocket computer, replete with information on everything from the local tides to astronomical configurations, is its C21 counterpart. For the plural of **vademecum**, see under **-um**.

vagary, vagaries and vague

Vagary derives from the Latin verb *vagari* ("wander"). But in English it has long been used more figuratively to refer to a digression in discourse ("rambling"), and to capricious conduct. This last meaning is regularly enshrined in plural uses of the word, such as the *vagaries of fashion* or *of the money market*. From this it's used to describe anything unpredictable, as in the *vagaries of the weather/friendship/life*. The word is only rarely used in the singular now, by the evidence of British and American databases.

When **vagaries** refers to erratic patterns of thought or speech, it may seem to involve *vagueness* as well, as in:

> ...*upbeat vagaries at the end of the documentary*
> ...*subject to the vagaries of the interviewer's memory*

That some find *vague* in **vagaries** is clear in its occasional misspelling as "vagueries," found in both BNC and CCAE, e.g. "the vagueries of stylistic relationships." Though strictly *folk etymology* (see under that heading), "vagueries" is underscored by common pronunciation in both the UK and the US, which puts stress on the first syllable. In older English the second syllable took the stress, as shown in the second pronunciation of the *Oxford Dictionary* (1989).

vague words

Communication isn't always about precision, and so **vague words** have a role to play in spoken and (sometimes) written discourse. People's *vagueness* may be deliberate – not because of any desire to hide information, but because the situation is informal, where you wouldn't put too fine a point on the facts being communicated. The most obvious **vague words** are fill-ins such as *thingy, thingamajig, whatsit, whatchamacallem*, whose key elements (*thing, what*) draw attention to their own lack of content. They are also rather amorphous, with shorter and longer forms

561

used according to whim, and substitutable bits: compare *thingamajig* with *thingamabob* and *whatchamacallem* with *whatchmacallit*. The spellings vary especially in unstressed syllables (compare *thingamajig/thingamyjig*), and there are a few regional differences which may reflect local pronunciations. *Thigamajig* and *thingamabop* seem to be US variants (Kaye, 1990) of the two main forms of the word. *Doohickey, deelebob* and their variants are American rather than British, whereas **vague words** based on *thing* and *what* are common to both (Channell, 1994).

Vague language can also be found in the use of hedges to soften the impact of precise numbers: *We had about 40 visitors*. With round numbers, the hedge may reflect some unknowns. But when someone says *We had about 43 visitors*, the chances are that it's intended to mitigate the cold precision of the count, and to promote some give and take in the conversation. As an interpersonal strategy it has less value in writing, except to underscore the informality of the style. See further under **interpersonal**.

valence, valency and valance

Valence is the standard American spelling for the term used by chemists to describe the combining power of an element. It is also applied by sociologists to social and political forces (*the political valence of popular music*), and by grammarians to the power of verbs to combine with other clause constituents (see further under **cases**). In British English, **valence** and **valency** are both used for these applications, by the evidence of the BNC, though **valency** has a slight edge over **valence**. This kind of spelling alternation occurs in various nontechnical words (see further under **-nce/-ncy**). Both spellings modernize the Late Latin *valentia* ("power," "competence").

Worlds apart in terms of seriousness is **valance**, a quite independent word now mostly known in the contexts of motoring and soft furnishings. In early motorcars it was the name for a cover over the wheel. Its analogue on the home front is that hanging piece of drapery which covers the upper part of a window, or the lower part of a piece of furniture. It seems to derive from an Old French verb *avaler* ("descend").

valet

For the spelling of **valet** when it's used as a verb, see under **-t**.

valiant, valorous, valorise or valorize

The Latin *valor* ("bravery," "courage") underpins both **valiant** and **valorous**, but the adjectives differ stylistically. **Valorous** is the formal word, used especially in official recognitions of bravery, as in military and police awards for *valorous conduct*. **Valiant** is the everyday word used in appreciating all kinds of *valor*, from moral and political courage to the heroics of ordinary life:

> He was a valiant campaigner on environmental issues.
>
> ...valiant attempts to reduce the phone bill

As the examples show, **valiant** has plenty of warmth, where **valorous** is rather cool in its formality.

The verb **valorize/valorise** is derived from the French *valorisation*, which is based on *valeur* ("value"). It was first used in C20 English in reference to official price-fixing, but now more generally to mean "give value to," "affirm the validity of," as in *the valorization of women's voice*.

◊ For the choice between **valorize** and **valorise**, and *valorization/valorisation*, see **-ize/-ise**.

valor or valour

For the choice between these, see **-or/-our**.

valorize or valorise

See under **-ize/-ise**.

valuable and invaluable

Both **valuable** and **invaluable** put a positive spin on something, though they look like opposites. Put another way, that which is **invaluable** is in fact very **valuable**: compare *a valuable contribution to science* with *an invaluable contribution to science*. The negative prefix on **invaluable** says that the *value* cannot be calculated (because it's so great) – not that it has no value. The *Oxford Dictionary* (1989) record shows that **invaluable** was formerly used to mean "worthless" as well, but citations for it stop in C19. In C21, **invaluable** gives unqualified praise, where **valuable** is somewhat measured.

van/Van and von/Von

These are unremarkable prepositions meaning "from," in Dutch/Flemish/Afrikaans and German respectively. In their home languages the words **van/von** would not bear a capital letter, yet the Dutch have long been inclined to capitalize **van** in surnames which stood alone (Ritter, 2002): compare *Vincent van Gogh* with plain *Van Gogh*. The German practice with **von** is to leave the particle out, so *Baron von Trapp* would become *Trapp*. In English the general trend is to capitalize the particle (see **capital letters** section 1), though it seems to happen faster with the Dutch **van** than the German **von**, by the evidence of the BNC. The style for famous persons can of course be settled by reference to a dictionary of biography, and for a correspondent by checking against previous letters or the telephone directory.

The process of capitalization is moved along by two editorial practices:

* **van/von** are always capitalized at the start of a sentence, whether or not the name is conventionally written with lower case:

    > ...postwar immigrants such as Wernher von Braun. Von Braun's impact on the American space program ...

* **van/von** are usually capitalized when the surname appears directly after a title, or without the first name. Thus *Dries van Heerden* becomes *Mr. Van Heerden*, and *Federica von Stade* just *Von Stade*.

Surnames with **van/Van** and **von/Von** raise further questions when it comes to indexing. In principle, their place depends on whether the particle is capitalized or not, so that *von Eisenblatt* would be alphabetized with the *E*s and *Von Eisenblatt* with the *V*s. This makes it rather unpredictable for the index-user, however. So dictionaries and directories often enter the **van/von** surnames in their alphabetic places under *V*, and indicate there the preferred upper- or lower-case style (i.e. the usual practice for names beginning with **Mac** or **Mc**). Helpful indexes also provide a crossreference at the other point where the **van/von** names might be looked for.

Vancouver style

In Britain, Australia and New Zealand, **Vancouver style** is the name for a type of number referencing system developed in the late 1970s and used especially in biomedical journals. Other names for it are

* *author–number system* (*Oxford Guide to Style*, 2002)
* *number system* (*Webster's Style Manual*, 1985)
* *citation-sequence system* (*CBE Manual*, 1994).

It works by assigning a reference number to every work cited in the text, and this decides their order of appearance in the list of references at the end. See **referencing** section 5.

vapor or vapour

For the choice between these, see under **-or/-our**.

variant and variety

The term **variant** is used in linguistics to describe alternative spellings, words and constructions without leaping to judgement on their status (as being "correct"/"wrong," "acceptable"/"unacceptable"). The term **variety** is similarly used to refer to dialects and styles of any kind, so that they can be discussed in relation to their contexts of use, rather than some normative notion of "standard English." See further under **descriptive or prescriptive**.

variety in writing

To keep the reader with you, *variety* is vital. Even a shortish piece of writing is a relatively long monologue for readers; and if the style is pedestrian and repetitious, they're likely to switch off. Writers need therefore to consciously *vary* their style, by such things as:

* *varying* the shapes of sentences, both in length and structure (see **sentences**)
* extending the choice of words with suitable synonyms (see **synonyms**)
* *varying* the word forms used (see under **-ation** and **nominal**). This incidentally helps to *vary* both the vocabulary and the shape of sentences.

variety of

This phrase can be construed in either singular or plural. Compare:

> a variety of US businesses have pulled out
> a variety of influences has altered the art's course

As the examples show, the use of singular agreement suggests a collective meaning for **variety**, whereas the plural gives it multiplicity. In data from CCAE the plural construction was better represented than the singular, in the ratio of 8:5, showing that *notional* or *proximity* agreement governs its use, more often than not. See **agreement** sections 1 and 5.

vegetarian or vegan

The **vegetarian** and the **vegan** both maintain a meat-and fish-free diet. But the **vegan** takes *vegetarian principles* much further and avoids eating any animal produce, including eggs, milk, butter and cheese. *Vegetarian diets* have of course been obligatory at various times and seasons in earlier centuries, and in other cultures. But the idea of voluntary *vegetarianism* contrasting with the omnivorous eating habits of others seems to arise with the first record of **vegetarian** in 1839. **Vegan** first appears in 1944.

veld or veldt

Modern dictionaries all make **veld** the primary spelling, in line with usage in South Africa itself. But **veldt** continues elsewhere, and is in fact more common than **veld** in American data from CCAE, by a factor of 3:1. In BNC data, **veld** outnumbers **veldt** in the same ratio. Common pronunciation of the word still involves a "t" at the end, according to both *New Oxford* (1998) and *Merriam-Webster* (2000).

vellum or velum

Despite its latinate appearance, **vellum** (the parchment of medieval manuscripts) comes from Old French *velin,* a word for veal and calfskin. **Velum** is genuine Latin where it meant a "veil" or "covering." Among its anatomical uses, it refers to the soft palate used in articulating nasal vowels.
◊ For the plurals of these words, see under **-um**.

venal or venial

See **venial**.

vendor or vender

These spellings both date from the last decade of C16. **Vendor** originated in law and represents the role of anyone who disposes of property by sale. **Vender** also exists for the person or machine that "vends" things, often in the street. But there's no sign of **vender** in British data from the BNC, and only a very small sprinkling in CCAE, despite its being recognized by *Merriam-Webster* (2000) as an alternative spelling. The legal spelling **vendor** has effectively become the general spelling.

vengeance or revenge

See **revenge**.

venial or venal

The spelling marks the crucial difference between that which is pardonable (**venial**) and that which involves bribery (**venal**). Compare:

> She had the disarming but venial habit of plying him with questions.
> A venal police force is the first symptom of the breakdown of law.

Both adjectives have their own abstract nouns: *veniality* and *venality*, where once again the *i* in the second syllable makes a big difference in meaning.

Note that because a *venial sin* is forgivable, it can be atoned by prayer and other good works. In theological terms it's the opposite of a "mortal sin," i.e. one which means spiritual death and condemns the soul to hell.

venturous or venturesome, adventurous or adventuresome

All these are recognized in modern dictionaries as words meaning "daring, or ready to take risks." **Venturous** was put to good use in past classics of English literature, but it's become the least used of the four in current British and American English. **Adventurous** is now far and away the most popular in the UK, in data from the BNC. In American English it also outnumbers the others, but American writers also make considerable use of *adventuresome* and *venturesome,* by the evidence of CCAE.

veranda or verandah

The spelling **veranda** was preferred by the *Oxford Dictionary* (1989), probably because it was closer to its origins in the Portuguese and Hindi word *varanda*. But its citations show that **verandah** was popular in C19, and it's supported by many British writers in the BNC, who prefer **verandah** to **veranda** in the ratio of about 3:2. Americans meanwhile prefer **veranda**, which outnumbers **verandah** by almost 2:1 in data from CCAE. A regional divide has thus opened up, despite the fact that both *New Oxford* (1998) and *Merriam-Webster* (2000) give priority to **veranda**.

verb phrase

This term means different things in different grammars.

1 In traditional grammar verb phrase meant the finite verb of a clause when it consisted of more than one word:

> *was playing*
> *was being played*
> *will have been played*
> *would have been being played*

The **verb phrase** has a main verb (*playing/played*) as its head, and the first of the accompanying auxiliaries (the *operator*) marks the verb's tense (see **auxiliary verbs**).

2 In modern English grammars the term **verb phrase** is given extended applications. It can refer to *nonfinite verb phrases*, as well as the finite ones illustrated in section 1, though they differ in having no *operator*, and usually no subject. They can be simple or complex, and consist of infinitives or participles (*be/being/been, have/having/had*), as illustrated in the following:

> Having *your arm* twisted *is no fun.*
> It *was* supposed to be played *on the glass harmonica.*

(The *nonfinite verb phrases* are shown in roman. They can be discontinous, as in *having ... twisted.*) *Nonfinite verb phrases* may support *nonfinite clauses* as in the first example, or work as an extension of a *finite verb phrase*, as in the second. Grammarians would debate whether the second example consists of one or two **verb phrases** – whether to regard *be played* as part of a complex **verb phrase** operated by the catenative *was supposed to* or to explain the sentence as a sequence of two verb phrases, one *finite* and the other *nonfinite*. (See further under **catenatives**.) The syntactic and theoretical implications of nonfinite verbs/clauses are still being weighed up: see the *Comprehensive Grammar* (1985).

3 In transformational-generative grammars the term **verb phrase** comes close to meaning the "predicate" of a clause. A sentence is said to consist of an NP + VP, i.e. a *noun phrase* which is the subject, and a (finite) *verb phrase* which includes not only the verb but also its object and/or any adverbial elements attached:

NP	VP		
The assistant	*put*	*the clock*	*on the counter.*
(S)	(V)	(O)	(A)
subject	verb	object	adverbial

This notion of the **verb phrase** is the most comprehensive of the three, and ties in with more abstract analyses of verb complementation and verb valency. It is however rather cumbersome when the verb's complement consists of several adverbials, with their own internal structures.

These divergent uses of the term **verb phrase**, and their connections with particular theoretical frameworks show what has to be put on the table before any discussion of **verb phrases** takes place. The term "verb group," used in the *Introduction to Functional Grammar* (1985) for the **verb phrase** of sections 1 and 2 above, helps to distinguish it from the other applications.

verbal and verbalize

The more you deal with language, the more ambiguous **verbal** seems. It can mean:

1 "spoken" (as opposed to "written") as in *verbal agreement*
2 "in words" (as opposed to images) as in *verbal and visual warning signs*
3 "using verbs" (rather than nouns) as in *verbal style* (see further under **nominal**)

The first of these uses of **verbal** is the commonest of the three, judging by their relative appearance in the BNC.

Verbal is also used as a verb in British and Australian English. It refers to a police procedure whereby the remarks of a defendant noted in a police interview are presented in court as evidence against him. The inflected forms of the verb often appear with double *l* (*verballed, verballing*), though there's strictly no need. (See under **-l/-ll-**.)

Compare **verbalize**/*verbalise*, the verb used in English worldwide for the process of putting words to ideas, whether in speech or on paper – involving verbs, nouns and all classes of words. The choice between *-ize* and *-ise* spellings is discussed under that heading.

verbal nouns

Various kinds of noun embody the action or process of a verb. The most familiar are those with the *-ing* suffix, as in *skiing* (see further under **-ing**). Yet abstract suffixes such as *-al, -ation, -ence, -ment* also create **verbal nouns**, as in *disposal, alienation, preference, abridgement*. Some **verbal nouns** have no derivational suffix at all, e.g. *rise* as in *sunrise* (see further under **transfers**).

In traditional grammar, infinitives were regarded as **verbal nouns**, because they seemed to function in the same way as *-ing* forms: compare *liked to go / liked going*. Alternatively the infinitive may be analyzed as part of the verb phrase or clause complement (see **verb phrase** section 2).

Verbal nouns, especially those formed with abstract suffixes, tend to create a *nominal style*, which is heavy-going in many communicative contexts. See further under **nominal**.

verbiage and verbosity

Both mean an excess of words, but while **verbiage** applies to the text itself and the expression used in it, **verbosity** can also be applied to the writer or speaker. As in:

> Amid the *verbiage and jargon of these investigations* ...
> ... the *verbosity of official pronouncements*
> Don't indulge the *verbosity of the amateur.*

The adjective *verbose* ("wordy") can likewise be applied to the discourse or the communicator.

verbs

The **verb** is the prime mover of the clause, and the item that makes something happen. **Verbs** may be classified in three ways, in terms of their meaning, their grammatical roles and their grammatical form.

Many **verbs** are dynamic and express events. They may be physical events such as *push, pull, rise, fall,* which can be observed by anyone; or the verbal (speech) events referred to in **verbs** of communicating such as *call, exclaim, speak, shout*. Other **verbs** express internal, mental events, such as *decide, hope, remember, think*. Another group, sometimes called "stative" **verbs**, expresses states of being, for example, *involve, mean, seem*. With these semantic differences go different grammatical constructions. Event-oriented **verbs** may be *transitive* or *intransitive,* whereas stative **verbs** are typically *copular* (see under **transitive** and **copular verbs**).

The **verbs** discussed so far are ones which would be the *main verb* within a *verb phrase* (in the strictest sense of the term: see **verb phrase** section 1). Other names for the *main verb* are *lexical verb* or *full verb*. The *main verb* may be prefaced by *auxiliary* or *modal verbs* such as *be, have, do* or *can, must, should,* as in *am calling / can call* (see further under **auxiliary verbs** and **modality**). When coupled with *auxiliaries/modals* they are *nonfinite* rather than *finite* (see **finite verbs**). They may be *active* or *passive,* according to whether their subject carries out the activity of the *verb phrase* or not (see further under **voice**). Some **verbs** have strong links with a following particle (see further under **phrasal verbs**).

Most **verbs** vary in form according to tense and/or aspect, adding particular inflections (*called, calling*), or changing their appearance in other ways (*felt/feeling, stood/standing*). **Verbs** which mark their past tense and past participle with *-ed* are historically *regular verbs,* though the distinction between *regular* and *irregular* is not straightforward in modern English. See under **irregular verbs** and **principal parts**.

vermin

This derogatory word is mostly used collectively, of a set of animals – or occasionally of people:

> *The vermin were inside the pillow*
> *There are racist vermin out there . . .*

Vermin can also be applied to an individual (animal or person), as in:

> *He is regarded here as vermin with a malicious streak.*

Singular applications of **vermin** to a human being are recognized among *Merriam-Webster* (2000) definitions of the word, whereas *New Oxford* (1998) defines it by reference to the plural only. There are few examples in either CCAE or the BNC, though their sheer offensiveness tends to keep them out of print.

vernacular

In older views of language, the **vernacular** was one's native language, as opposed to Latin, once the lingua franca of Europe. This meaning survives in liturgical contexts, e.g. *celebration of the Mass in the vernacular*. With the recognition of modern languages such as French, Italian, English etc. after the Renaissance, the term **vernacular** was reapplied to the "low" forms of those languages, as spoken by the working class, and

others in informal situations. The phrase *in the vernacular* often means "slang," as when computerspeak is said to *innovate in the vernacular* with terms such as "hack attack" for a storm of computer hackers. In the US it's freely applied to any distinctive idiom: *showbiz vernacular, the confrontational vernacular of the 70s, the vernacular of a college jock*. **Vernacular** is built into the abbreviations *AAVE* and *BEV* for Afro-American English: see **Black English**.

verso

This word is short for the Latin phrase *verso folio,* which is used in book production to refer to the left-hand page of an open book. The right-hand page is *recto* i.e. *recto folio*.

versus

This Latin word, meaning "against," is at home in everyday English, witness its use in sporting contests: *Tonight's cricket: England versus Australia*. In law it's conventionally used to refer to the opposing parties in a law suit: *Kramer versus Kramer*.

In the titles of law suits, **versus** is regularly abbreviated to *v*. British style has it in roman, according to *Copy-editing* (1992), whereas the *Chicago Manual* (2003) prefers italics – in keeping with the names on either side. In both British and American style, *v*. normally appears with a stop.

Beyond the contexts of law, both *v*. and *vs*. (with stops) are used as abbreviations for **versus**. In sports reporting and elsewhere, the abbreviations are left in roman, like others from Latin which have become commonplace.

vertebrae

This is the regular Latin plural of **vertebra**, the word for an individual bone of the spinal column. Compare:

> *She has cracked a vertebra.*
> *Three vertebrae need to be fused to protect the spinal cord.*

Though **vertebrae** is the standard plural in English, it is sometimes replaced by *vertebras* in informal discourse – at least in American English. *Vertebras* is a recognized alternative plural in *Merriam-Webster* (2000), but not in *New Oxford* (1998).

vertex or vortex

The first word **vertex** means "apex." It mostly appears in mathematical and scientific writing, in reference to the apex of a cone or triangle, or to the crown of the head (in anatomy and zoology). **Vortex** means a "whirlpool [of water, air or fire] around an axis." It can also be used figuratively, of whirling forces which threaten to engulf people.

Vertex and **vortex** have Latin plurals **vertices/vortices** as well as English ones **vertexes/vortexes**, for use in specialized and everyday contexts respectively. *New Oxford* (1998) and *Merriam-Webster* (2000) recognize both types, in that order. See further under **-x** section 2.

very or most

In some contexts these seem interchangeable as intensifiers:

> *That's most/very kind of you.*
> *They were very/most determined about it.*

Grammarians find a small difference between them in that **very** works as a "booster" of the adjective on a notional scale, whereas **most** is a "maximizer" (see under **intensifiers**). **Most** forms a kind of *absolute superlative* (see **absolute** section 1). As an intensifier, **most** can only be used with qualities that are subjectively assessed, like those in the examples above – not ones like "brief," "sudden" etc. There are no such restrictions for **very**, which is in fact the commonest intensifier in both formal and informal kinds of discourse, according to the *Longman Grammar* (1999).

veterinary or veterinarian

The first of these is usually an adjective as in *veterinary surgeon,* though it could stand alone as a noun in older British usage. The equivalent American term for the animal professional is **veterinarian** – always a noun.

veto

The standard plural (or third person singular verb) is **vetoes,** in both British and American English. The form **vetos** is nevertheless found occasionally for both noun and verb in data from CCAE, and it's acknowledged as an alternative in *Merriam-Webster* (2000). Other variable plurals of this kind are discussed under **-o** section 1.

via

This Latin loanword means "by way of." Its essential use is to spotlight the route by which you go from A to B, as in flying to London via Kuala Lumpur. The C20 saw its use extended to refer to the channel by which something is transferred, as in:

> *The signal is broadcast via satellite.*
> *You can get that information via dozens of reports.*
> *The policy is mediated via senior management.*

Some would allow the first two applications of **via,** but not the third, so as to restrict it to an impersonal channel. This is implicit in the examples of *New Oxford* (1998). Other dictionaries including the *Oxford Dictionary* (1989) and *Merriam-Webster* (2000) embrace all three uses of **via** with the definition "by means of," and a wider range of examples. The traditional prepositions *through* or *by* could of course be used in the third example.

vice or vise

In British and Australian English **vice** is the spelling for all three of the following:

1 the Latin loanword/prefix: *Vice Chancellor* (see next entry)
2 the word meaning "bad habit," as in *vices and virtues*
3 the term for a mechanical gripping device, as in *held in a vice*

In American English, the first two are spelled **vice** while the third is **vise.** Both **vice** and **vise** were used this way in medieval times, and **vise** continues to be used in the US and Canada to distinguish the mechanical device from the bad habit (**vice**). **Vise** occurs also in derivatives (*a vise-like grip*) and as a verb *vise(d).*

◊ For the use of **vice** as a prefix, see next entry.

vice, vice- and vice versa

In Latin **vice** had two syllables, and meant "in place of." This particular usage survives only in rather academic discourse, as in:

> *The bursar attended the meeting vice the financial manager.*

Much more often, **vice-** is used as a single-syllabled prefix, as in *vice-captain, vice-chancellor, vice-president* to indicate that the incumbent deputizes regularly for the more senior person (*captain, president* etc.). In the same way the *viceroy* exercised royal authority over a colony, and *viceregal* affairs are those associated with the governors of the Crown.

Vice versa embodies the same word, literally "with the place turned around" or more approximately "with things the other way round." It can be used when people's roles or the order of items are being reversed. Compare:

> *You should support his request and vice versa.*
> *We'll visit the gallery and then have lunch,*
> *or vice versa.*

The expression has been thoroughly assimilated into English since C17, and is sometimes abbreviated to *v.v.*
◊ For other uses of **vice,** see previous entry.

vide, videlicet and viz.

These instructions are all based on the Latin verb *videre* ("see"). **Vide** is the imperative, sometimes found on its own but more often in the crossreferencing instruction *quod vide.* It is usually abbreviated to *q.v.* (see under that heading).

Videlicet is a telescoping of *videre licet,* literally "it is permitted to see." It introduces a more precise explanation of something already stated in general terms. (Compare *scilicet,* used to introduce examples.) **Videlicet** is rarely seen in full nowadays, and is much better known in the abbreviated form **viz.** The *z* is the printer's equivalent of the scribal mark ȝ, which was the standard abbreviation for *-et.* Thus **viz.** is strictly speaking a *contraction* (see further under that heading).

vie

When used to describe competition between people, **vie** usually collocates with the particle *with,* as in

> *Banks vie with each other to finance mergers.*

In British English this is the only pattern, whereas in American English it sometime combines with *against:*

> *... vying against one another to get the most with the least*

In both the US and the UK, *vying* (not "vieing") is used for the participle. See further under **-ie > -y-.**

Vietnam or Viet Nam

For most of three decades following World War II, **Vietnam** was divided into a northern communist zone with Hanoi as its capital, and a southern zone whose capital was Saigon. The country was reunified in 1976, as the *Socialist Republic of Vietnam,* and Saigon renamed as Ho Chi Minh City.

In English the name is normally written as a single word (**Vietnam**) – in almost 99% of BNC examples, and closer to 99.5% in American data from CCAE. However it's written as two words (**Viet Nam**) for United Nations and other official purposes.

vigor or vigour

For the choice between these, see under **-or/-our**.

vilify

This verb embodies the Latin stem *vili-* ("of low value"), hence the accepted spelling **vilify**. Think of *vile*, which is its only relative in English. But because there are rather more English words with two *l*s, it sometimes appears as "villify." An internet search (Google, 2003) found *villify* in more than 10% of all instances of the word. Its users may see a meaningful connection with *villain*, though it's strictly *folk etymology*. See further under that heading.

villain or villein

Historically speaking, these are simply alternative spellings for the medieval word for a farm laborer. The word was however used with derogatory connotations as early as C14, and they are strong enough to do disservice to honest farmhands. Yet only since C19 have the two spellings been regularly used to differentiate the scoundrel **villain** from the medieval farm worker **villein**. Modern dictionaries still allow that **villain** may be used for **villein**, but not vice versa.

virgule

See **solidus**.

virtuoso

The choice between **virtuosi** and **virtuosos** for the plural is discussed under **Italian plurals**.

virus

For the plural of this word, see **-us** section 1.

vis-à-vis

In French this means literally "face to face." From this it comes to mean "opposite," and in earlier times it could mean a carriage or piece of furniture which one shared with another person sitting opposite. Nowadays it's most commonly used as a preposition meaning "in relation to" or "with regard to," as in:

We discussed the arrangements vis-à-vis their costs.

In English the phrase is sometimes written without a grave accent, especially when printed in roman, but always with hyphens.

viscous or viscose

From C15 on, these were interchangeable as adjectives meaning "sticky, glutinous." **Viscose** disappeared from the record in C18, but was signed up for service again in late C19 as the name of an artificial fibre or sheet made from cellulose. For similar pairs, see under **-ose**.

vise or vice

See under **vice or vise**.

visible or visual

The essential difference between these is that **visible** emphasizes the fact of being seen, as in *visible signs of emotion.* **Visual** points to the fact that sight rather than any other form of perception/communication is involved, as in: *a day-long visual and alimentary orgy,* or *wordplay and visual imagery.*

Yet **visual** is used in some scientific contexts where we might expect **visible**, as in *visual symptoms* (of a disease), and *visual rays of the sun.* Note also that **visible** is developing along more metaphorical lines with the meaning "in the public eye." See for example:

Ministers of Education are more visible than they used to be.

visitation, visit, and visit to/with

Anyone can pay a **visit**, but **visitation** implies extra formality, and often has official connotations. In the UK it refers to the formal visits of government inspectors, or of clergymen to those in hospital or jail. In the US, it's also applied to the legal access of a noncustodial parent to his/her children (*visitation rights*), as well as viewing the deceased prior to a funeral. The numbers of visitors to a tourist attraction such as a national park can be described in terms of *visitation rates.* **Visitation** also serves for supernatural appearances such as those of ghosts, aliens or angels; as well as devastating natural events, e.g. *visitations of the plague,* though such phrases sound rather archaic now. The biblical *visitation of the Virgin Mary* to her cousin Elizabeth (Luke 1: 39–56) is commemorated in the names of churches and convents.

The ordinary noun **visit** is followed by *to* if what follows is a place, as in *a visit to Alaska.* This applies in both American and British English, but when it comes to people, usage diverges somewhat. In the US it's usually **visit with**, as in *his visit with the doctor,* or *a weekend visit with relatives.* In examples like those the British normally use **visit to**, by the evidence of the BNC, though there are a few cases of **visit with**, as in the question: *Visit with old Fanshawe go alright?* The social aspect of *visiting* goes further in American and Canadian English, so that *a visit with* can also be used to mean "a chat with [someone]," face to face or on the telephone. However *cybervisits* are expressed in terms of *a visit to our website* (rather than *with our website*), suggesting the metaphor of travel rather than social encounter.

Visit with is commonly used for the verb construction in North American English when people are mentioned, as in *a request from London that you go visit with them.* In British and Australian English this would be just *visit them,* using **visit** as a transitive verb. **Visit** is used transitively everywhere when it comes to *visiting* places real or virtual: *visit our website at www . . .*

visual or visible

See **visible**.

vita

This Latin word for "life" is used in American English as an alternative to *curriculum vitae (CV).* **Vita** originated as a term for a brief biographical sketch, but the new application makes it a kind of autobiography. See further under **curriculum vitae**.

viva voce

This Latin phrase meaning literally "with living voice" is occasionally used to mean "by word of mouth." In British and Australian universities it refers to an oral examination at which students are quizzed by one or more examiners. Colloquially such an exam is a **viva**.

viz.
See under **vide** and **Latin abbreviations**.

vocal chords or vocal cords
See under **chord**.

vocative
This is one of the six grammatical cases recognized in Latin and some other languages. It is associated with direct address, as in *Et tu Brute?* from Shakespeare's *Julius Caesar,* where "Brute" is the **vocative** form of *Brutus.*

English has no special inflection for the **vocative** case, though it's sometimes ascribed to names used in direct address:

> *John, would you bring the sugar?*

Apart from such everyday uses, the English **vocative** is associated with liturgical and literary language, as in *O Land of our Fathers,* and often prefaced by *O.* See **O or Oh**.

vogue words
Fowler created this term in 1926 for trendy expressions used by people to show they are swimming with the cultural tide. The **vogue words** of earlier C20 included *modern* and *progressive,* which were replaced at the end of the century by ones like *alternative* and *sustainable.* As those examples show, **vogue words** embody contemporary values, and reflect changes in them.

Some **vogue words** are drawn from the technology of the times. Expressions like the *global village* and the *intelligent building* embrace the revolution in communications, with that element of hyperbole that often goes with the use of **vogue words** and expressions.

Many **vogue words** are less obviously connected with cultural developments – simply expressions which have somehow become very popular, such as:

> crisis   dialogue   facelift
> front runner   grass roots   marathon

Such words are grist for reports on almost anything in the mass media, and quickly become clichés. Today's **vogue words** are likely to be old hat within the decade, just because they're worked so hard. Those used as intensifiers, such as *cosmic, fantastic, mega, unreal* wear out even faster.

Apart from the **vogue words** in general usage, there are those which seem to be the hallmarks of academic, bureaucratic or corporate discourse. They include words like:

> factor   framework   image   interface
> parameter   profile   situation   syndrome
> target

Whatever their stylistic weight, the effect is undermined by overuse, and their being often redundant, as in *the classroom situation.*

voice
In traditional grammar **voice** is the term used to cover the *active* and *passive* forms of the verb phrase, which show different relationships between the verb and its subject. In languages such as Latin there were separate sets of inflections for *active* and *passive* verbs. In modern European languages, including English, the *passive* is expressed through a complex verb phrase. See further under **active verbs** and **passive verbs**.

vol-au-vent
For the plural in English, see **plurals** section 2.

volcano
The choice between **volcanoes** and **volcanos** for the plural seems to vary round the world. American respondents to the Langscape survey (1998–2001) were much in favor of **volcanos**, as were those from Continental Europe. British and Australian respondents, and those resident in Asia, voted the opposite way, preferring **volcanoes**. See further under **-o**.

volte-face or about-face
See under **U-turn**.

Von
The alphabetization of names beginning with **Von** is discussed under **van and von**.

vortex or vertex
See **vertex**.

vouch or voucher
In American English, **voucher** is both a noun and a verb. As a verb it can be used to mean "provide a voucher for" as in *We were vouchered for hotel accommodation.* In the combination *voucher for,* it means "establish the validity of," as in *he had M to voucher for his whereabouts.* This way it overlaps with the verb **vouch** as in *vouch for,* which is the only possible construction in British English.

vowels
A **vowel** is at the heart of any syllable we pronounce. Consonants are the sounds that accompany the **vowel**, coming before and/or after it. In English there are about twenty different **vowels** (including diphthongs) by the standard analysis based on the International Phonetic Alphabet. A complete inventory of English **vowels** and consonants is to be found in Appendix I.

The Roman alphabet has only five **vowel** letters (*a, e, i, o, u*) which naturally means that they correspond to more than one sound in English. Even *vowel digraphs* generally represent more than one **vowel**, witness the different sounds for *ea* in *beat, great, hear, heart,* or for *oo* in *flood, good, goose, poor.* One consequence is that readers make more use of consonants than **vowels** in identifying written words. If every **vowel** in a sentence is blanked out we still have a fair chance of reconstructing the words from the consonants and the inherent grammar. So while **vowels** are indispensable to spoken language, the consonants are more fundamental to the written word, at least in English. Classified advertisements, and text-messages (*TXT*) compress words by omitting **vowels** rather than consonants: see further under **SMS**.

vox populi
This Latin phrase is an abbreviated version of *vox populi vox Dei* ("the voice of the people is the voice of God"). From C15 on it was often cited to affirm the importance of common opinion. In C20 the phrase was further curtailed to *vox pop,* but given new life in radio and TV programs where brief statements

extracted from street interviews are broadcast to give a spectrum of opinion on a current issue.

vs. or v.
See under **versus**.

vulgar
These days **vulgar** means "rude," "coarse" or "obscene." But when used by the *Oxford Dictionary* (1884–1928) of some expression, it meant that it belonged to popular usage, reflecting the Latin noun *vulgus* ("the common people"). **Vulgar** expressions were therefore colloquialisms, to be avoided if you were aiming at literary style. For Fowler (1926) and other usage commentators, the word served to discredit more informal styles of writing. Its negative value underlies some of the current shibboleths of usage, which still make formal English the only correct form. See further under **shibboleth** and **barbarism**.

vying or vieing
See **vie**.

wagon or waggon

The spelling **wagon** is preferred in all modern dictionaries, including *Merriam-Webster* (2000) and *New Oxford* (1998). In C18 and C19 England there was strong support for **waggon**, indicated by the *Oxford Dictionary* (1884–1928), though it preferred **wagon** on grounds of etymology (the word being derived from Dutch *wagen*). Current database evidence shows the decline and fall of **waggon**, which is outnumbered by **wagon** in the ratio of of 1:10 in BNC data, and makes no showing at all in CCAE.

wainscot

The origin of this word for the wood paneling low down on walls is quite obscure – though we can rule out any connection with the Scots, and live with the uncertainty. Decisions do have to be made about its spelling when used as a verb: should it be *wainscoting* or *wainscotting, wainscoted or wainscotted?* The spellings with one *t* are given priority in both *New Oxford* (1998) and *Merriam-Webster* (2000); and database evidence backs this up. The double *t* forms get a little use in both BNC and CCAE, but the single *t* forms are clearly in the majority.

wait or await

Both **wait** and **await** can be used as transitive verbs. Compare:
> *We're awaiting their arrival.*
> *You'll have to wait your turn.*
The first sentence shows **await** with its typical object – an abstract noun. The use of a human or tangible object now sounds rather formal: *We await her (plane).* The second sentence shows one of the relatively few idioms in which *wait* by itself takes an object. Much more often it finds its object through phrasal verb constructions, especially with *for.* See next entry.

wait for, wait on and wait up

In English everywhere, the expression **wait for** is standard for being in expectation of something or someone:
> *They waited for the President's cavalcade.*
Wait on also has some widely accepted uses, such as the rather formal sense of "serve" (as in *waited on the Queen*) and the religious idiom *wait on the Lord (God).* Its use in *waiting on tables* is also standard everywhere. But the use of **wait on** as an alternative to **wait for** has been questioned, especially since it was declared "obsolete" by the *Oxford Dictionary* (1884–1928). In fact it is alive and well in the US, Canada, Australia and New Zealand, with both personal and impersonal objects: *wait on the President / the results of the elections.* Dictionaries in North America and the antipodes register it as standard usage, and *Merriam-Webster* (2000) makes a point of saying that it is current and not confined to the American South. *New Oxford* (1998) meanwhile notes

only intransitive use of **wait on** in the sense of "be patient" (*Wait on, Marie*), and describes it as "informal," and associated with "Northern English." But in BNC data there are ample examples of **wait on** being used in the same way, at least before impersonal objects, in various kinds of prose:
> *...did not wait on a Home Office ruling*
> *Aries will wait on market response before planning any [expansion]*
> *Manchester United wait on BR's decision on his fitness*
> *Important matters had to wait on his attention.*
Perhaps **wait on** is enjoying a revival in British English. At any rate it's being used without inhibition by UK writers, and seems to be standard (if minority) usage there, as elsewhere.

Wait up means "stay up late for someone to return home" wherever you are. But in North America, especially Canada, **wait up** can also mean "slow down so that others can catch up." There are some small examples of it in CCAE, although it's not mentioned in *Merriam-Webster* (2000).

wait in line or on line

See **in line or on line**.

waiter, waitress or waitron

The push towards nonsexist language means that **waiter** is preferred by many, whether the person providing table service is male or female. When *calling the waiter,* it's unnecessary to draw attention to the sex of the person concerned, except when their dress (or lack of it) makes it something you cannot overlook. The trend is reflected in gender-free definitions in most dictionaries (*a person / one who provides table service*) in North America, Australia and New Zealand. *Editing Canadian English* (2002) comments that **waiter** has become "understood as gender-neutral," and it recommends against using unnecessary female forms derived with *-ess* (see further under that heading). The *Oxford Guide to Style* (2002) likewise speaks of referring to occupations in "asexual" terms. In Australia and New Zealand, government style manuals have made recommendations along these lines since 1988 and 1997 respectively.

Waitron was concocted in the US in the 1980s, though it has never caught on, by the dearth of evidence in CCAE. The ending was supposed to represent "one" (i.e. "person"), but it probably smacked of the robotic *automaton,* the last thing you want in restaurant service. With **waiter** redefined to cover both sexes, **waitron** has already passed its use-by date. See further under **-tron**.

waive or wave, waiver or waver

Anglo-French law gave us **waive** and **waiver**, as ways of referring to official concessions. Even in nonlegal use they keep their official overtones:

The committee must agree to waive the prerequisite.

A visa waiver can be obtained at the border.

Wave meaning "signal with the hand" comes from Old English, with roles as noun and verb that are quite distinct from **waive**, most of the time. They only come close in idioms such as *wave aside* meaning "dismiss." For example:

He waved aside my offer of payment.

Wave aside still differs from **waive** in being a personal dispensation rather than an institutional one.

Note also the verb **waver** ("hesitate"), borrowed from Old Norse. Its only chance of being confused with **waiver** is on the rare occasions when it's used as a noun:

There wasn't a waver in the line of protesters.

The two words still contrast, in that **waver** suggests indecision whereas **waiver** always connotes some form of decision-making.

wake, waken, awake or awaken

These verbs present a confusion of choice to refer to emerging from sleep or rousing someone from it. In practice **wake** is the most popular by far in both American and British English (often in the phrasal form *wake up*). In both the US and the UK, its past forms are *woke/woken*, with scant evidence of *waked* in data from the BNC or CCAE. **Waken** (*wakened*) is the least popular of the four verbs in both databases, though surviving better in British English, in a wider variety of discourse than in American English.

Awake now most often appears as an adjective or adverb, in combinations such as *be/keep/lie/stay awake*. Curiously, the verb **awake** in the present tense is rare in both BNC and CCAE, yet quite well represented by the irregular past *awoke,* providing an alternative to *woke up.* The irregular past participle *awoken* complements it in British English, but is rare in American, in comparative evidence from the databases. Neither the Americans nor the British seem to use the regular past form *awaked,* for either past tense or past participle.

Awaken provides another alternative to the verb **wake**, though database evidence shows that it's more popular in American than British English. In particular, the relatively high frequency of *awakened* as past participle in CCAE suggests that it may also do service for *awoken*. **Awaken** is used in both varieties to refer to waking from sleep, but it's also the most likely of the four to be used figuratively, as in:

. . . to awaken memories of summers past

. . . awaken the stock market to its present peril

Not to mention *awakening* the proverbial *sleeping giant.*

English seems always to have had multiple expressions for "wake." There were two simple verbs in Old English, one strong, one weak, which gave us *woke* and *waked.* Another was **waken**, with *n* added into the present stem to make it *inchoative,* i.e. carry the sense of just beginning to **wake** (see under **inchoate**). **Waken** was reinforced by its Old Norse counterpart *vakna,* and preserved in more northerly medieval writing. **Awake** and **awaken** once provided intransitive alternatives to the others, but can now be used either transitively or intransitively – as can they all. No-one has felt the need to standardize their roles.

wallop

For the spelling of this word when it serves as a verb, see **-p/-pp-**.

wangle or wrangle

In British English these two keep their distance: **wrangle** means "quarrel" (*they always wrangled over details*), and **wangle** "extract [something] with difficulty":

He had wangled a meeting with Mr Bush.

Americans use **wrangle** to refer to quarreling, as well as to achieving something not to be taken for granted, as in:

. . . wrangled a refund from the company

She wrangled herself a job with the basketball team.

The councilman had wrangled the use of an empty building to house his collection.

These and other examples from CCAE should not be seen as mistakes where "wangled" was intended. In fact this use of **wrangle** probably owes something to the American frontier where the *horse wrangler* (in Spanish *caballerango*) was the legendary master of things. In movie credits the *animal wrangler* is noted, though the movie casting is not yet attributed to the "people wrangler." The verb **wrangle** has nevertheless gone ahead, and, in all the examples listed above, it involves manipulating people. *Merriam-Webster* (2000) registers this meaning by crossreference to **wangle**, but its background makes it independent of both **wangle** and **wrangle** ("quarrel.") The origins of **wrangle** are usually found in Low German *wrangeln* ("struggle") – which also accounts for the Cambridge University **wrangler**, i.e. a first-class graduate of the mathematics tripos.
◊ Compare **cum laude**.

-ward or -wards

These endings on adjectives and adverbs imply movement in a particular direction: *downward(s), upward(s)* etc. In British English the choice between them is governed by grammatical principles, which are largely neutralized in American.

The general practice in the UK is to use **-ward** for the adjective, and **-wards** for the adverb, as in *downward pressure/spiral/trend* and *climb/move/slope downwards.* The **-wards** form makes productive use of the adverbial *-s* ending, which is otherwise only residual in English (see further under **-s**). But in American English, **-ward** serves for both adverb and adjective most of the time. Compare:

an immediate downward spiral

. . . spiraling downward into criminal activity

American writers occasionally use *downwards* when the word's use is more adverb than adjective (e.g. *hold it face downwards*), by the evidence of CCAE. But they don't make systematic use of the **-wards** form. These regional divergences apply to others in the set, including:

eastward(s)	heavenward(s)	homeward(s)
inward(s)	landward(s)	northward(s)
onward(s)	outward(s)	seaward(s)
sideward(s)	upward(s)	westward(s)

They apply also to ad hoc words such as *skyward(s).*

The regional/grammatical differences just described for British and American English work less than perfectly for the most common cases such as

backward(s) and forward(s). In BNC data backward is
found for the adjective in about 85% of instances (e.g.
backward thinking, a backward society), the rest being
clearly adverbial. And though backwards is an adverb
in about 95% of instances in the BNC, as in
face/go/lean backwards, there are two notable kinds
of exception. One is when referring to a physical
direction, which is normal for backwards, whereas
backward is often figurative, meaning "not
progressive," as in the examples above. The need to
avoid the negative implications of backward explains
the use of backwards as adjective in contexts such as
sports reporting: a backwards pass would be strategic,
but a backward pass might not. Adjectival use of
backwards is also common when it follows the noun,
as in a step backwards. (See further under
postpositive.) Backwards also makes its mark in
American data from CCAE, as the less common form
but clearly current. It appears in sports reporting for
reasons explained above, and more generally in
well-established idioms such as bend over backwards,
go(ing) backwards, spelled backwards – not to mention
the compound adjective of software designers:
backwards-compatible.

With forward(s), the grammatical distinction
between adverb and adjective hardly seems to apply,
even in British English. Forward is very commonly
used as an adverb, as in bring/carry/lean/look
forward, and there are thousands of examples like
those in BNC data, as opposed to a few hundred of
forwards. In combinations like backwards and
forwards, it still tends to match the other in its
adverbial form. But forward seems to be taking over
generally in the UK, with forwards often a plural noun
(sports reporting again!), as almost always in
American data from CCAE.

In Canadian English, the grammatical distinction
between -ward and -wards is not regularly observed
(Fee and McAlpine, 1997), and it seems to be waning in
Australia (Peters, 1995). We may lament its passing as
the last bastion of adverbial -s – or embrace the
process of streamlining.
◊ For the choice between **toward or towards**, see
under that heading.

International English selection: With the
increasing use worldwide of -**ward** for both
adjective and adverb, and the loss of adverbial -s,
it makes sense to prefer it, except in idioms where
the -**wards** form is fixed.

---

warden or warder

In British English, **warden** is the name for officials of
several kinds ranging from church and traffic wardens
to the Warden of Winchester College. **Warder** is an
older term for the rank-and-file prison officer, as in the
headline: Warder taken hostage by prisoners. As a job
title, it's now replaced by prison officer, in both the UK
and Australia.

In North American English, the **warden** is the
superintendent of a prison, and jailer is used for the
regular prison guard: see **jailer**.

warranter or warrantor

See under -**er/-or**.

warranty or warrantee

This word originated as **warranty** in C14 feudal law,
but two centuries later began to be used in its
commercial sense of a "pledge as to the reliability of
goods sold." The second spelling **warrantee** is labeled
as erroneous by the Oxford Dictionary (1989), though
its citations from C17 on are complemented by some
in speech transcriptions in both the BNC and CCAE.
In law **warrantee** is reserved for the person to whom
a **warranty** is given. But outside the law the roles of
warrantee/warrantor and the **warranty** are of much
less interest than the pledge itself, and the context
makes the focus plain whichever spelling is used. The
same issues arise with guarantee/guaranty, and the
spelling **warrantee** may well be prompted by the high
frequency of guarantee (see further under that
heading). In fact all these go back to the same French
source, which was warantie in the northern dialect
and garantie further south.

In common usage, the functional domains of the
warranty and the guarantee overlap. Some
distinguish them in terms of the guarantee's
commitment to repair or replace, and **warranty**'s
pledge that the goods have been fully tested and
checked before being marketed. Caveat emptor!

wash up

Americans use **wash up** for the washing of face and
hands as a refresher:

Okay guys, wash up for dinner ... and use soap.
For the British the verb **wash up** implies the
dish-washing chore at the end of a meal. Canadians
know both uses of the phrasal verb, but Australians
would expect it to happen in the kitchen rather than
the bathroom. Other informal uses of **wash up** are
also regionalized. In the UK and Australia, the noun
wash-up can be used to refer to the debriefing process
after an event, but it's not known in North America.
In American slang washed-up is used of has-been
sportsmen and performers of many kinds. It levels the
washed-up boxer / hockey star with the washed-up
comic / rodeo cowboy, not to mention washed-up
veterans and investment advisers. There are small
signs of this in BNC data, but not yet the range of
applications found for it by American writers in
CCAE. The adjective probably picks up the sense of
things washed up by the tide on the shoreline.

WASP or Wasp

This rather derogatory American acronym stands for
white Anglo-Saxon Protestant, all aspects of the
established power-wielding set in American society.
Like other well-established acronyms, **WASP** can be
written with just an initial capital letter, and **Wasp** is
given as an alternative form in Merriam-Webster
(2000) and as the primary one in New Oxford (1998).
Database evidence from the BNC and CCAE shows
that **WASP** is commoner by far in both British and
American English. But either way the capital letter –
and the context – distinguish it from the disagreeable
insect. The adjective Waspish ("characteristic of the
WASP") depends entirely on the capital to distinguish
it from waspish ("easily angered, snappy").

waste or wastage

British style guides following Gowers (1965) are
inclined to distinguish these two, using **waste** for

careless use of resources, and reserving **wastage** for loss by wear and tear, decay and other natural processes. Compare:

> *The lecture was a waste of time.*
> *We hope to reduce the work force by natural wastage.*

By this distinction **waste** has negative connotations and **wastage** is neutral.

Yet both the *Oxford Dictionary* (1989) and ones more recent show that the distinction just illustrated is not watertight: **wastage** is also applied to human *wastefulness,* and used as a synonym for **waste**. This may reflect the seductive power of the longer word, as Fowler (1926) thought, and/or the fact that **wastage** has acquired some of the negative coloring of **waste**. So if you need a neutral way of referring to the natural attrition of a resource, it's best to spell it out as *natural wastage* – or else seek an alternative expression.

wave or waive, waver or waiver
See **waive or wave**.

wax
The verb **wax** meaning "grow" is somewhat archaic – except in reference to the moon's *waxing and waning,* and to expansiveness in people:

> *He waxed lyrical about the glories of England in the spring.*

This construction makes **wax** a *copular verb,* and so its complement "lyrical" is properly an adjective, not an adverb. See further under **copular verbs**.

way and the way
Apart from being a very common noun, **way** has additional roles as an adverb and conjunction, especially in conversation and in everyday writing.
*****way is an adverb in:**

> *AR finished way ahead.*
> *The speech was way off the mark.*
> *. . . the danger of inflating the person way out of proportion to the job*

There **way** means "far" or "a long distance," a usage which is well established, on record since 1849. *New Oxford* (1998) still bills it as "informal," though expressions such as *way ahead/off/out* appear in a variety of written texts in the BNC. There's some evidence too of **way** serving as a general intensifier, in examples such as: *way too polite,* and *B. takes way too long to resolve the plot.* The use of **way** as an intensifier is certainly very common in American English, and registered without stylistic restrictions in *Merriam-Webster* (2000).
*****the way serves as a conjunction in sentences such as:**

> *The birds don't sing the way they used to.*

In traditional grammar, this use of **the way** was regarded as elliptical for *in the way that,* and some writers still spell it out in academic and formal contexts. Yet research associated with the *Longman Grammar* (1999) showed that **the way** (in its elliptical form) was used almost as much in academic writing as in fiction and conversational data, and that it actually appeared less in news reporting than the other genres. This suggests that British sensitivity to the use of **the way** as a complex conjunction has diminished since Mittins *et al.* (1970) found strong reactions to its appearing in formal speech and writing. In the US it has long been accepted, as demonstrated by research

before and after World War II, and *Webster's English Usage* (1989) finds it unexceptionable.

waylay
The past form of this is *waylaid,* not *waylayed.*

-ways or -wise
See **-wise**.

we
Questions of grammar and style are raised by this pronoun. Its use often embodies a particular sense of identity, as in *we blind people,* which resists grammatical change when it might be expected, as in:

> *This is a familiar experience for we blind people.*

As object of the preposition *for,* "us blind people" would be the regular grammatical form. In speech **we** can pass unnoticed, masked by the appositional structure (see **apposition**). *Webster's English Usage* (1989) notes examples from print as well, always in apposition – as are some of those in the *Oxford Dictionary* (1989). Despite the apposition, *us* would be expected in formal writing, in both American and British English.

The plural **we** is conventionally used by a single person in several kinds of context. "Royal *we*" is of course a linguistic privilege of the British monarch, though sometimes assumed by other heads of state: the "presidential or premier *we*" (Wales, 1996). Doctors, psychiatrists and other health carers use the "doctor *we*" to involve the patient in his/her own treatment (e.g. *We need strategies to cope with stress*). Teachers too use an *inclusive we* when trying to engage children in productive activities: *Now we mustn't poke the person next to us, Stevie.*

In some institutional genres of writing, **we** is the conventional persona for projecting an argument. Newspaper editors use it, speaking on behalf of the nation or the newspaper; as do scientists and academic writers when seeking to involve the whole academic community in their point of view. This use of **we**/*us* is unlikely to raise eyebrows, except when the opinion attributed to the pronoun is contrary to that of the reader. Therein lies the rub. But persuaders and narrators of all kinds use **we** to establish solidarity with their audience, and create a feeling of common identity. It thus serves a rhetorical purpose in many a context. See further under **person**, "first- or third-person style."

weak and strong
◊ For the **weak** forms of words, see **reduced forms**.
◊ For **weak** and **strong** classes of verbs and nouns, see **strong and weak**.

wean
The verb **wean** has traditionally been used to refer to the process of detaching an infant or baby animal from breast-feeding. In figurative use, other kinds of detachment are expressed with the prepositions *off* and *(away)from,* as in: *weaned off drugs / from Puritanism.* Applications like those go back to C16, whereas it's only recently that **wean** (plus *on*) could be used to put the spotlight on formative psychological influences, as in: *weaned on baseball, faith in learning, a diet of Hollywood fantasy,* or *patronage and coercion. Webster's English Usage* (1989) finds the earliest evidence of *weaned on* in the 1930s,

but it seems not to have taken off until the 1970s. In both American and British English, this is now the commonest phrasal construction, by the evidence of CCAE and the BNC. Meanwhile the construction of **wean** with *onto (on to)* is typically gastronomic:

> *Patients were gradually weaned onto a normal, unrestricted diet.*
> *Lionfish can be weaned onto non-living foods.*

weasel

For the spelling of this word when used as a verb, see under -l-/-ll-.

weasel word(s)

Theodore Roosevelt popularized this term for individual words which suck the meaning out of their neighbors. A "meaningful discussion" implies that there might be meaningless ones. Something that's "virtually unheard of" could well happen. So *meaningful* and *virtually* are **weasel words**, robbing those next to them of their force.

Weasel words is however often used more loosely, to refer to a misleading statement or empty promise:

> ... *a few weasel words in a newspaper do not constitute a policy of nuclear deterrence.*

Shorter dictionaries are inclined to note the second application of **weasel words** without the first.

weave

The verb **weave** has two kind of past tense (*wove* and *weaved*), which go with different senses of the word. When it refers to the *weaving* of a fabric, or of verbal texture of some kind, *wove* is usually the past tense (and *woven* the past participle):

> wove nets of hemp   densely woven fibres
> wove fancies from fact   subplots rooted in
>   family are deftly woven

Weaved is used especially for the past forms when describing the winding movement of a person or a vehicle, in phrases such as *weaved from side to side* and *she had weaved her way across the garden.* Yet *wove* is occasionally used by both British and American writers when describing patterns of movement: *the car wove through the traffic* (it occurs in about 15% of instances of the word in the BNC and CCAE). *Weaved* is very occasionally used in describing verbal webs, as in *weaved his/her/their magic.* Those are minority variations on the specialization of *wove(n)* and *weaved,* which gives complementary roles to the regular and irregular forms. See further under **irregular verbs** sections 7 and 9.

webpage, web page or Web page

At the turn of the millennium, users of this new compound still tend to space it out. A search of the internet (Google, 2003), found **web page(s)** twice as often as the solid form **webpage(s)**. Dictionaries that list it vary: *New Oxford* (1998) and *Canadian Oxford* (1998) have **web page**, whereas the Australian *Macquarie* (1997) has **webpage** as its primary form. The solid setting seems likely to increase worldwide, because it's (i) the common trend for compound nouns consisting of monosyllables (**hyphens** section 2d); and (ii) already established in *homepage* and *website*. On this, and the use of a capital letter in **Web page**, see next entry.

website, web site or Web site, and the World Wide Web

Internet users unite in preferring **website** for a location on the **World Wide Web**, according to a Google search (2003). Dictionaries still tend to show it spaced as **web site**; and for *Canadian Oxford* (1998) it's **Web site** with a capital letter (*Web page* as well), as if both terms are subject to proprietorial constraints. But writers everywhere leave them uncapitalized, suggesting that **web** is seen as a generic element (see further under **trademarks**).

The **World Wide Web** declares itself with three capitals, and is usually spaced, though with the use of *intercaps*, it occasionally appears set solid as *WorldWideWeb* (see **capital letters** section 4). The ultimate compact form is *W3,* enshrined in the *W3 Consortium,* which provides advice on such things as the coding of internet documents. **World Wide Web** is otherwise abbreviated in lower case as the *www* prefixed to many URLs: see **URL**.

wed and wedded

As a verb meaning "marry," **wed** is faintly old-fashioned, except as a conveniently short word to use in newspaper headlines. When it appears in ordinary text, **wed** is used for the past tense/participle as well as the present in reference to being married:

> *The couple officially wed two years ago*
> ... *was to be wed in the cathedral*

The regular past form **wedded** is rarely found in the sense "marry," except in clichés such as *wedded and bedded,* and as adjective in *wedded bliss.* Most of the time *wedded* is coupled with *to* to express figurative bonding (*wedded to the bank / big government / the gesellschaft model*) in myriads of examples from the BNC and CCAE.

welch or welsh

See **welsh**.

well and good

See **good**.

well and well-

The adverb **well** is used to modify parts of verbs, as in:

> *The parents were well dressed.*
> *Their children were well behaved.*

In sentences like these, **well** and the word following are independent parts of the verb phrase and not to be hyphenated. But when the same combinations form compound adjectives and become part of a noun phrase, then they need hyphens, as in:

> *We met well-dressed adults and well-behaved children.*

The use of hyphened **well-** depends thus on the grammar of the phrase or sentence – not whether it's part of an established compound adjective, listed in a dictionary.

Compound adjectives with **well-** may be made comparative and superlative in one of two ways:
* with *better/best*
* with *more/most*
Compare:

> *They wanted a better known architect for the job.*
> *They wanted a more well-known architect for the job.*

and

He was the best loved author of his generation.
He was the most well-loved author of his generation.

(For the absence of hyphen in compound adjectives using *better* and *best,* see **hyphens** section 2.)

Some authorities such as the *Oxford Guide to the English Language* (1984) indicate their preference for the forms with *better* and *best*, and they are certainly neater. Yet they lose a shade of meaning which is there in *well-known* and *well-loved* – an indication of celebrity. The forms with *better/best* are certainly unsuitable for various adjectives compounded with **well-**, where only *more–most* seem to work. See for example:

He took the most well-done steak on the barbecue.
A more well-rounded person you couldn't imagine.

In such cases the idiomatic meaning of the compound is lost if **well-** is converted into *better/best.* The problem is deepened by the fact that *better/best* are related to *good* as well as **well**, which also lends ambiguity to many **well-** compounds.

welsh or welch

All dictionaries make **welsh** the primary spelling for this colloquial word meaning "duck one's responsibilities" (financial or otherwise). **Welch** is indicated as the minor variant, though it appears almost as often as **welsh** in admittedly small numbers of examples in the BNC and CCAE. **Welch** is the one to prefer if you wish to play down any possible disparagement of the people of Wales. The word may well have originated as a "throwaway term," expressing English prejudice against the Welsh, though dictionaries such as *New Oxford* (1998) say its origins are obscure. See further under **throwaway terms**.

were

The usual role of **were** is as the plural past tense of the verb *be.* For its use to express wishes, suppositions and conditions, see under **subjunctive**.

west, western or westerly

These all appear in lower case when used to refer to a geographical point, area or direction which is 90° left of the north/south axis for a given place. The meaning is always relative: compare *west of the Appalachians* with the *western suburbs of London.* Note that both **west** and **western** normally mean "toward(s) or in the west." But when **west** or **westerly** are applied to winds or ocean currents, they mean "from the west."

Both **West** and **Western** also appear with capital letters as the first element in official geographical names, such as *West Indies, West Pakistan, Western Australia, Western Samoa.* **West** appears in lower case as the second element in *Midwest* (the central and northern farming lands of the US), but is upper-cased in *Far West* (the states west of the Rocky Mountains). The "Wild West" was never strictly a geographical term, but rather a notional frontier region where stable government and law and order had yet to be established. Tales from the *Wild West* are of course the stuff of *westerns*, always in lower case.

For the world at large, *the West* has become a political designation for the capitalist countries of Europe and North America, as opposed to the communist or socialist states of eastern Europe and the former Soviet Union. The adjective **Western**

contrasts with *Eastern* in broad cultural terms, as in *Western governments* and *Western-style democracy*. But in *western medicine* the implied contrast is between Euro-American culture and traditions, and those of Asia. These uses of **western** are often capitalized, according to *New Oxford* (1998) and *Merriam-Webster* (2000), and **Western** appears in about 90% of political/cultural uses of the word, in both BNC and CCAE.

The verb *westernize/westernise* ("adapt to the culture and customs of the West") is usually written without a capital letter. A large majority of respondents to the Langscape survey (1998–2001) preferred the lower case form for *westernization,* and only 18% said that they always wrote it as *Westernization.*

westward or westwards

See under **-ward**.

wet and wetted

The past forms of the verb **wet** are often just the same as the present:

The footprints disappeared when rain wet the dust on the road.
The cat has wet the armchair.

Wetted is used for the past tense when some deliberate action is involved, as in:

He wetted his lips in a theatrical way.

The choice between **wetted** and **wet** for past participle again helps to show whether it's the product of human intervention, or a more or less natural result:

. . . his straight brown hair, freshly wetted and parted in the middle
The wall had been wet by a broken pipe for years.

In BNC data, **wetted** is sometimes mistakenly used for *whetted,* as in "wetted our appetite." See under **whet**.

wh- words

See **interrogative words**.

wharfs or wharves

The traditional plural **wharves** is still more common than **wharfs**. See further under **-f > -v-**.

what

The use of **what** as interrogative pronoun is straightforward in questions both direct and indirect. Compare *What's the matter?* and *You asked what I thought.* There it's the only possible choice. But for the interrogative determiner, it could be **what** or *which:*

What train did you catch?
Which train did you catch?

In questions like that, either word would do, though **what** is indefinite, implying no prior knowledge about the times of the trains, whereas *which* suggests that the questioner knows something about them.

What also has a special use introducing indefinite noun clauses, where it's equivalent to *that which* or *those which:*

I did what I thought was right.
They looked for batteries and bought what there were.

As these examples show, the verb following **what** may be singular or plural, depending on the grammatical number of the noun it has to agree with (singular or plural). Note also how this use of **what** differs from its use as a relative pronoun in nonstandard speech: "The man what came to the door looked upset." The *Longman Grammar* (1999) notes that this is more common in the UK than the US. The standard form for both speech and writing would be *who* or *that came to* ...

A final issue with **what** is its sometimes unnecessary appearance in comparative clauses:

> She remembered the meeting in more detail than (what) I did.
> I'd like to have the same dish as (what) I had before.

In such sentences the conjunctions *than* and *as* are quite enough to join the two clauses.

◊ For the use of **what** in topicalizing clauses such as *What the world needs now ...* , see under **cleft sentences** and **information focus**.

whatever or what ever

See under -**ever**.

whence

Like *hence* and *thence,* this word now draws attention to itself as being either formal or slightly old-fashioned. See further under **hence**.

where-

In earlier English there was a large set of conjunctions compounded with **where**-:

whereat	*wherefore*	*wherein*
whereof	*whereon*	*wheresoever*
whereto	*whereunder*	*wherewith*

None of these is current in ordinary usage, and if used they bring a slightly stuffy or old-fashioned flavor to the style. They are easily paraphrased with *which,* so that *whereat* becomes "at which," and so on.

The only **where-** conjunctions remaining in general use are *wherever* and *whereas* (see **whereas**). *Whereby* is restricted to some formal constructions such as *a means whereby ...* ; and *whereupon* survives in certain traditional styles of narrative. Other remnants of the set are used as nouns: *whereabouts, wherewithal, wherefores* (as in *whys and wherefores*).

whereabouts

Should it be:

> The president's whereabouts remain a secret.

or

> The president's whereabouts remains a secret.

In both British and American English, the plural verb is much more likely than the singular, by the evidence of the BNC and CCAE – though both are established, according to *Webster's English Usage* (1989). Singular agreement seems to happen more often when **whereabouts** is separated from the verb, as in: *the whereabouts of the Chinese traveling companion is unknown.* In examples like that, *proximity agreement* seems to take over from *formal agreement.* See further under **agreement** section 5.

whereas

This has two quite distinct uses. As a comparative or contrastive conjunction, **whereas** enjoys widespread use in various styles of writing:

> She went on to become an architect, whereas I did history.

In legal usage only, **whereas** means "given the fact that," and introduces a formal recital of background material to an agreement:

> Whereas this document witnesseth the determination of the two parties ...

As in that example, the archaic nature of such "recitals" is signaled by this use of **whereas** and the -*eth* verb form that follows. Plain language lawyers (Asprey, 1996) argue that they often create ambiguity, and that if anything operational is introduced by the **whereas**, it should be in the body of the agreement.

whet and whetted

The days of **whet** ("sharpen") seem to be numbered, judging by its uses in British and American databases. In BNC data, its appearances are largely restricted to *whetting the appetite*. Americans use a wider range of objects, e.g. *whet my interest / your curiosity / their fantasies,* in data from CCAE. But these variations on the theme are heavily outnumbered by examples using *appetite*. Examples of its literal use, as in *a whetted knife,* can be counted on the fingers of one hand. A further sign of its decline is the way its past form **whetted** is sometimes replaced by *wetted* (see **wet**). Apart from their very similar – if not identical – pronunciations, the two verbs seem to be juxtaposed in English idiom. Compare:

> The walk had whetted their appetite.
> They had already wetted their whistle.

The phrase *wet one's whistle* goes back to C14, to Chaucer and "The Reeve's Tale."

whether

In indirect questions **whether** is equivalent to *if,* though it's slightly more formal in style:

> The student asked whether/if she could record the lecture.

In some cases **whether** is preferable to *if* to prevent ambiguity (see under **if**). **Whether** is the only possible conjunction in some contexts:

* when there's a preposition: *His appointment depends on whether we can make savings elsewhere.*
* when there are alternatives to introduce: *You must make a decision whether to go or not.*
* when the meaning is "regardless of X or Y": *Whether they want him or not, he'll volunteer.*

When *whether or not* sets up the alternatives, they do not need to be underscored by antonyms, as in "Whether or not we succeed or fail ..." The point comes through more clearly as either:

> Whether or not we succeed ...
> Whether we succeed or fail ...

whetted or wetted

See under **whet** and **wet**.

which

This word has several roles, in introducing direct and indirect questions, as well as relative clauses, which raise different questions of grammar, meaning and style.

1 In direct (and indirect) questions, which can be an interrogative pronoun or determiner:

> Which is your house?
> Which train do we take to the city?

In either case **which** implies a set of known alternatives. Compare the use of *what* as an interrogative (see **what**).

2 In relative clauses, which often provides an alternative to *that* in reference to things:

*I bought tickets at the kiosk which/that was
opposite my hotel.*
The choice between **which** and *that* may be influenced
by the nature of the clause it introduces – whether it is
"restrictive" or "nonrestrictive." (See further under
relative pronouns.) That apart, the choice is purely
stylistic, a matter of their relative weight, and the
need to vary one's pronouns. With other uses of *that*
(as demonstrative or conjunction) in the vicinity,
which is a useful alternative.
3 Which as a sentence relative. Sometimes **which**
introduces a relative clause that refers back to a whole
preceding clause, not just something within it. The
difference can be seen in:
James is buying a house, which is great news.
James is buying a house which he will be proud of.
In the first of these sentences, **which** effectively
summarizes the whole of the preceding statement
and is a "sentential relative." The construction
used to be frowned on, but the *Comprehensive
Grammar* (1985) treats it as a regular part of English
syntax.

while or whilst

With its several meanings, **while** is overworked and
potentially ambiguous. Its essential and oldest use is
as a temporal conjunction:
While the Titanic was sinking, the band played on.
This temporal use of **while** overlaps with a concessive
sense, which is more distinct in:
*While the recovery may be sluggish, there is reason
to be optimistic.*
The concessive use shades into one which is more
clearly contrastive. For example:
*While the other states have been losing jobs,
Connecticut's labor market is improving.*
The sense of contrast may be affected by the position
of **while** in the sentence. When used in mid-sentence,
it seems a good deal weaker:
*The adults wanted to talk while the children
pressed for a video.*
Neither contrast nor time could account for the use of
while in everyday examples such as:
*The barbecue is planned for Friday, while
Saturday is games night.*
In such sentences **while** is not much more than an
additive conjunction, and some would deprecate this
"modern colourless use," as the *Oxford Dictionary*
(1989) calls it. The larger problem in writing is just
which sense of **while** is intended, at which point it's
often best to seek alternatives. For the temporal sense,
there is *when;* *(al)though* (for the concessive); *whereas*
(for the contrastive); and even *and* (for additive use). If
of course you want a conjunction that combines two
or more of those senses, **while** could be handy –
provided your readers can decide which!
The choice between **while** and **whilst** is a matter of
regional dialect and style. **Whilst** is rare in American
English (outnumbered by almost 1500:1 in CCAE). In
British English they come much closer: the ratio of
while to **whilst** is 10:1 in data from the BNC. Like
while, it can bear temporal, concessive and
contrastive meanings. **Whilst** appears in British
prose ranging from formal to standard, though rarely
in the daily press (Peters, 1995), or in conversational
data.
◊ Compare **amid(st) and among(st)**.

while away or wile away

The use of *while* as a verb meaning "take time" goes
back centuries, and **while away** has been on record
since 1635. It implied leisurely activity rather than
anything particularly purposeful or subversive:
*… while away the rest of the evening in expensive
surroundings*
Wile away might suggest that the time is being used
proactively, and it's recognized in *Merriam-Webster*
(2000). But examples in the BNC and CCAE do not lend
support to this hypothesis: people **wile away** *their
time / idle hours / Saturday afternoons* in the sauna,
on the golf course, or meandering on the waterways of
Chesapeake Bay. **Wile away** is not a frequent
alternative in either database, and its
meaninglessness leaves it without any real basis of
support.

whimperative

This whimsical word, coined by grammarians in the
1970s, is a blend of *whimper* and *imperative*. The
whimperative is the verbal strategy that requests
action of someone without using a direct command. A
typical **whimperative** is the polite question: *Could
you please open the window.* See further under
commands and **imperative**.

whingeing or whinging

This informal British verb meaning "complain" is
usually spelled **whingeing**, at least in edited writing.
Almost all examples of **whinging** come from
transcriptions of speech in the BNC. However
whinging is presented as the primary spelling in both
Merriam-Webster (2000) and the *Canadian Oxford*
(1998). It is of course the more regular spelling: see
further under **-e** section 2e.

whisky or whiskey

Within the trade, these two spellings distinguish the
grain-based spirit of Scotland, Canada, Australia and
Japan (= **whisky**) from those of Ireland and the US
(**whiskey**). However British writers use **whisky** as
the generic spelling for the spirit, whatever its source.
The fact that **whisky** outnumbers **whiskey** by more
than 10:1 in BNC reflects their spelling preference not
their drinking habits. The same applies in American
English, where **whiskey** is generic, and outnumbers
whisky by 6:1 in data from CCAE.
The two terms keep their difference in the plural.
For **whisky** it's **whiskies**, and for **whiskey**,
whiskeys.

whiz, whizz and wiz

These spellings are spread unevenly over two main
areas of meaning:
* rapid movement (as verb or noun), probably
onomatopoeic
* an expert (or something remarkable), an
abbreviation of *wizard*
In North America and Australia, **whiz** is the
preferred spelling for both senses, for *trains whiz by*
and *a former Wall Street whiz*. In data from CCAE
there were hundreds of instances of **whiz**, and only
handfuls of the others – slightly more of **wiz** used in
the second sense, as in *the computer wiz* or *a wiz at
video games*. Yet **whiz** was the dominant spelling for
whizkid and the exclamation *gee whiz*.

The *Oxford Dictionary* (1989) preferred **whizz** for both words, and it's the most common form for both senses in British data from the BNC:

> *The particles whizz around at a great rate*
> *... not such a whizz at car, boiler or electrical*
> *appliance repairs*

Examples of **whiz** turn up only in "gee whiz," and occasionally as the verb of quick motion: *should be able to whiz through that*. This use of the single consonant is in line with British convention for the base form of verbs such as *fulfil,* where the double consonant is reserved for the inflected forms (*whizzed, whizzing*): see further under **-z/-zz**. At that point it makes no difference whether you regard the base form as **whiz** or **whizz**.

The choice between *whiz-bang* and *whizz-bang* goes with your preference for **whiz** or **whizz**. The first spelling is preferred by *Merriam-Webster* (2000) and the *Canadian Oxford* (1998), the second by *New Oxford* (1998). Note also the distinction between the American *whizkid* ("exceptional person"), and the British slang *whizz-boy* ("pickpocket"). Other divergences are the North American slang use of **whiz** to mean "urinate," and British use of **whizz** as a byword for amphetamines.

who and whose

Who works as a pronoun both interrogative and relative for referring to people:

> *Who is calling?*   (interrogative)
> *A caller who gave his name as Steve just hung up.*
> (relative)

The examples show **who** in its typical *nominative* role, i.e. as subject of the clause (see further under **cases**). But in conversation **who** can take on the role of object pronoun: see further under **whom.**

In the examples above, **who** is singular, but it also covers the plural as in *Who were the first men on the moon?* It's the more likely relative pronoun when referring to an organized group of people: *committee, team,* etc. – although *which* is also possible:

> *It was the committee who agreed to those terms.*
> *... not on that committee, which operated quite*
> *democratically.*

The use of *which* projects the *committee* as a single administrative unit, whereas **who** makes them individual people.

Whose is the possessive form for both **who** and *which* (for both people and things) in relative clauses:

> *The soldier whose arm was raised in salute had*
> *disappeared.*
> *We were sideswiped by a truck whose brakes had*
> *failed.*

Yet the idea that **whose** can only be applied to people dies hard, and many a sentence has been made awkward by the use of *of which* rather than **whose**. Compare this version of the second sentence above:

> *We were sideswiped by a truck the brakes of which*
> *had failed.*

Fowler (1926) argued strenuously for the use of relative **whose** in reference to inanimates, and the controversy even then was 150 years old. Note however that when **whose** appears in questions at the start of a sentence, it is effectively limited to people. The question *Whose computer lost its mouse?* could never mean "Which of the computers has lost its mouse?" Interrogative use of **whose** concentrates

attention on the computer's owner, and cannot relate to the computer itself.

wholistic or holistic
See **holistic**.

wholly or wholely
English usage is now entirely with **wholly**. The more transparent form **wholely** was used up to C19, but is now so rare it would be thought a mistake.

whom
Whom is the object form of *who,* and a remnant of the once much more extensive case system in English (see further under **cases**). Its use overall has declined, and while it survives in writing, it's becoming rare in speech. Its decline is more marked in the US than the UK, and this adds some regional and stylistic coloring to its use. For both interrogative and relative **whom** there are alternative constructions, which help to account for its disuse.

1 Whom as an interrogative pronoun appears as the object of a verb or preposition, and so it does in *Whom did she marry?* But this rather formal construction was already being questioned at the end of C18, when Noah Webster argued that it should rather be:

> *Who did she marry?*

Whom was not what people actually said, he noted; and he deplored the efforts of those who rewrote passages of Shakespeare and other classical authors, to ensure that **whom** appeared according to grammatical rule. Then as now, *who* is preferred to **whom** when the *wh-* word comes up first in a question. In the *Longman Grammar* (1999) corpus, this preference held for all genres of writing from fiction to academic, but was of course most pronounced in conversational data, where 1000 instances of *who* were not matched by a single instance of **whom**.

Interrogative **whom** is still used after a preposition in written genres, as in:

> *To whom were you speaking?*

But when the preposition moves to the other end of the sentence, **whom** once again gives way to *who:*

> *Who were you speaking to?*

These two constructions show the contrast between formal and standard/informal styles, with the second now commonly used in writing as well as speech. In both direct and indirect questions, **whom** makes for a high style:

> *They asked to whom I was speaking.*

Compare:

> *They asked who I was speaking to.*

The construction that delays the preposition (in this case *to*) is termed *preposition stranding*. (See **prepositions** section 2.)

2 Whom as a relative pronoun serves as direct object, but again is often replaced by *that* or a zero relative. Compare:

> *He is the person whom I wanted to see.*
> *He's the person that I wanted to see*
> *He's the person I wanted to see.*

There is an obvious scale of formality here, although the use of **whom** probably seems more formal to Americans and Australians than to the British. In the US, **whom** as object pronoun is associated with academic and expository prose rather than fiction (Peters, 1992), whereas British writers use it across the generic range. The same regional differences hold for using **whom** after a preposition. **Whom** is required in some prepositional constructions, e.g. partitives such as *none/both/some/all of whom,* and they occur across all genres. But in other constructions, e.g. with *in,* **whom** can be paraphrased with the help of *that* or a zero relative. Compare:

> *She needs someone in whom she can confide.*
> *She needs someone that she can confide in.*
> *She needs someone she can confide in.*

Prepositional **whom** is less frequent and stylistically marked for Americans and Australians, occurring much more often in expository and academic prose than the daily press or fiction (Collins and Peters, 2003).

3 **Debatable use of whom.** The propriety of using **whom** in parenthetic constructions has challenged grammarians, because of conspicuous examples in Shakespeare and the King James bible, e.g. *Whom do ye say that I am?* which becomes *Who do you say that I am?* in the Revised Standard version (1952). Fowler's (1926) strong arguments against this use of **whom** are reproduced by Gowers (1965), but without Jespersen's equally energetic defense of it in the third volume of his grammar (1909–49). Both note that the problem is a kind of *hypercorrection* on the part of those who worry about not using **whom** in the right place (see **hypercorrection**). In some examples, the *wh-* *word* seems in fact to be both object and subject, as in:

> *They asked me whom I thought was best suited to the task.*

The fact that the quasi-object role comes up first would explain why **whom** is used. It is a dilemma, and the *New Yorker* once found enough examples to run a column titled "The Omnipotent Whom." It was discontinued when the editor found that "almost nobody knew what was wrong with them." The construction is ambivalent.

If **whom** gets a little extra airing in parenthetic constructions, this doesn't change the fact that its use overall is shrinking. In most styles, writers paraphrase it by means of one or other alternative, and so it has become stylistically marked and associated with formal style for many readers. Only the wise old owls are continuing to say: *To whit, to whom!*

Whorfian principle

One of the tantalizing questions of language is whether it influences the society and culture we live in, or whether they determine it. Are we predestined to see the world as we do because we speak English or any other language, or does our language simply reflect what happens in our culture?

The relationship between language and culture was one of the profound questions raised by Benjamin Lee Whorf, an American linguist of the 1930s. Whorf was an engineer by profession, but he spent any leave he had investigating the unwritten languages of American Indians, and eventually became a full-time field worker.

While working with the Hopi Indians, Whorf ascertained that they made no use of tense with their verbs, and it occurred to him that this went hand in hand with their stable, very traditional lifestyle, which recognized no landmarks of history and anticipated no change of state in the future. It seemed to Whorf that the absence of tenses in language worked against any possible perception of historical

change, and that language could perhaps condition the outlook of a people. This kind of linguistic determinism is now generally referred to as the **Whorfian principle.**

Yet linguistic evidence often allows either a *Whorfian* or *counter-Whorfian* interpretation. Many Australian Aboriginal languages have highly developed case systems and demonstratives to express the location and direction of objects. You could argue that these linguistic resources have supported a nomadic way of life, or that they have developed in response to the necessities of that lifestyle. Many people would prefer a compromise interpretation: that such language resources develop hand in hand with a nomadic lifestyle, and are not simply a cause or effect of it. Language has a dynamic relationship with culture.

This dynamic reinterpretation of the **Whorfian principle** lends strength to attempts to rid English of sexist and racist elements. While they are there, they may sustain and foster sexist and racist attitudes in the community. By consciously replacing them with nonsexist and nonracist words, we have some hope of consolidating equal opportunity attitudes and practices.

whose

See under **who**.

wh-words

See **interrogative words**.

widow or widower

The *-er* ending on **widower** now marks it as the male counterpart of **widow**, and gives us a clear sex distinction between the two words. For centuries the word **widow** could refer to the bereaved of either sex, but the last dialectal traces of this are well in the past. The distinction which we now make between **widow** and **widower** confers no obvious advantage on the latter except perhaps in retirement villages, and has not attracted attention in the debate about sexist language. See further under **nonsexist language**.

widows and orphans

In editing and text design, these terms refer to words or single lines that are separated by page breaks from the rest of a paragraph. A **widow** is a line or part-line that finishes off a paragraph at the top of the next page. Its counterpart is the **orphan**, which is the first line of a paragraph at the bottom line of the previous page. Editors and typesetters often intervene to prevent the discontinuity, adding a line or forcing an early page break as the case may be. **Widows** are regarded by some as a bigger problem than **orphans** (Ritter, 2002), and while **widows** are discussed in American style books, there's no mention of **orphans**. Note that the **orphan** is also known as a *club line* in British editorial circles.

wilful or willful

The spelling **wilful** dates from C14, and is standard in the UK. **Willful** makes its first appearance in C17, early enough to cross the Atlantic with the first American settlers, and become firmly established in their English. Current English from British and American databases confirm the difference, and so BNC data is polarized towards **wilful**, and CCAE data towards **willful**. Canadians know both spellings but prefer **wilful** (*Canadian Oxford*, 1998); for Australians it's the only possibility, according to the *Macquarie Dictionary* (1997).

will

For the choice between **will** and *shall*, see **shall or will**.

winey or winy

This adjective meaning "like wine," as in *a win(e)y taste,* is relatively uncommon in print, despite being on record since C14. The spelling **winey** takes no chances, and continues to be used as much as **winy**, in small amounts of data from the BNC and CCAE. See further under **-y/-ey**.

wiry or wirey

Wiry was preferred by the majority (more than 70%) of respondents to the Langscape survey (1998–2001). Its uses in the last two centuries have become increasingly figurative, so the connection with *wire* does not need to be underscored through the spelling **wirey**. **Wiry** is of course the more regular spelling of the two: see further under **-e**.

-wise or -ways

In some words, **-wise** and **-ways** are alternatives, as in:

crosswise/crossways	edgewise/edgeways
lengthwise/lengthways	sidewise/sideways

Both suffixes have ancient pedigrees, **-wise** meaning "in a particular manner" and **-ways** "in a particular direction," though this is no longer straightforward in common examples such as *always* and *clockwise*. The original *Oxford Dictionary* (1884–1928) emphasized the need to distinguish **-wise** and **-ways**, and not to substitute one for the other. But often now they express regional divergence between the US and the UK: Americans use the **-wise** form where the British prefer **-ways**. For example *crosswise, edgewise, lengthwise* are overwhelmingly preferred in American English, by the evidence of CCAE, whereas *crossways, edgeways, lengthways* are the majority preference in data from the BNC. British usage is in fact more mixed than the American on most of the examples above. The one remarkable exception is *sideways,* which reigns supreme in British English, and is very strongly preferred (over *sidewise*) even in American English. That apart, there's a clear trans-Atlantic divide, with Canadians sharing the American preference for **-wise** in examples like *crosswise* etc. Australians share the British inclination to use **-ways** when both are available.

The spelling **-wise** is quite stable in several other uses, and there's no variation anywhere in the world for the following:

1 **-wise** in long-established adverbs such as *clockwise, likewise, otherwise*
2 **-wise** in newer adverbs of manner, e.g. *crabwise*
3 **-wise** meaning "clever, smart" in compound adjectives such as *streetwise*. Ad hoc words can be formed in this way without raising eyebrows:
   She's as computerwise as anyone in this office.
Being adjectives, these **-wise** words are built into the core of the sentence either *predicatively* (as in the example) or *attributively,* as in *a computerwise person.* (See further under **adjectives**.)

Grammar is the issue with one final group of words formed with **-wise**, where it's at its most productive in current English. They are the ad hoc adverbs in which **-wise** means "where X is concerned," as in:
   Computerwise it's the only solution.
These **-wise** words are *disjunctive adverbs* (see **adverbs** section 1). This makes them grammatically mobile (unlike group 3 above), and they're often used to begin a sentence. Given that they announce a new focus of attention, it's their natural place. They are in fact a *topicalizing* device (see further under **topic** and **information focus**). But being improvised and conspicuous at the start of a sentence, they're a ready target for those who react negatively to innovations in language. *New Oxford* (1998) dubs this use of **-wise** "informal," whereas *Merriam-Webster* (2000) takes it in its stride. Words formed this way are convenient shorthand for a longer phrase, and more often spoken than written, though that's no reason to ban them from writing. The grammar of the sentence distinguishes them from any matching adjective, as shown above.

wisteria or wistaria

The glorious climbing plant with pendant clusters of blue flowers is usually said to be named after Caspar Wistar 1761–1818, an American anatomist, scientist or doctor, depending on which dictionary you consult. The spelling **wistaria** renders the surname more closely, and is preferred by the *Oxford Dictionary* (1989). **Wisteria** was the spelling used by Thomas Nuttall, curator of the Harvard botanical gardens 1822–34, who gave the flower its name. Horticultural references variously use **Wistaria** or **Wisteria** for the genus name, but common usage is strongly in favor of **wisteria**, judging by its dominance in database evidence from the US and the UK. **Wisteria** is the primary spelling in *New Oxford* (1998) and *Merriam-Webster* (2000), as well as the *Canadian Oxford* (1998) and the Australian *Macquarie Dictionary* (1997).

Apart from the spelling issue, we may wonder whether the plant was actually named after Caspar Wistar the anatomist/scientist, or whether it might not reflect appreciation of the work of another Caspar Wistar, actually the grandfather of the anatomist, who founded the American glass industry in New Jersey. The products of Wistar the elder's foundry (known as *Wistarberg glass*) were beautiful green vessels decorated with swirls and threads of applied glass – rather reminiscent of the tendrils of the climbing **wisteria**.

without

This was once the opposite of *within*, and a synonym for "outside." So in Shakespeare's *Macbeth*, a servant could say of visitors: *They are, my lord, without the palace gate*. This meaning of **without** goes back to Old English. The modern meaning "lacking" began to appear in Middle English, and has completely taken over. The old meaning can only be revived in a contrived way by combining it with *within*, as in *a house clean within and without*.

Without is a preposition in English everywhere, used to preface a phrase or nonfinite clause as in:
   You don't mean to climb all day without a rest stop.
and
   You don't mean to climb all day without stopping to rest.

In older English, and some current dialects in the UK and the US, **without** also serves as a conjunction to introduce a finite clause:

> You don't mean to climb all day without we stop for a rest.

The *Comprehensive Grammar* (1985) thought that conjunctive use of **without** was increasing in informal discourse, and most examples in the BNC are from transcriptions of speech.

wiz, whiz or whizz
See under **whiz**.

wog
This word makes a pariah of anyone it's applied to. **Wog** seems to have begun as British army slang for an Arab, explained ironically as an an acronym for "western oriental gentleman." It quickly became a derogatory word for any non-white person (see *New Oxford*, 1998); and *Merriam-Webster* (2000) defines it as meaning "dark-skinned, especially from the Middle or Far East." But chauvinism being what it is, **wog** is also a pejorative term for "foreigner" in general, as noted in the *Oxford Dictionary* (1989), *Canadian Oxford* (1998) and the Australian *Macquarie Dictionary* (1997). It becomes anglo-centric in comments such as "incomprehensible wogs," and phrases such as *wog languages,* indifferently associated with immigrants and tourists. Though **wog** can be used affirmatively by immigrants themselves (as in the Australian drama *Wogs out of work*), it's an inflammatory word on the lips of anyone else. Part of its offensiveness is that it lumps all immigrants and foreigners together, with no attention to their individual backgrounds or identity. See further under **racist language**.

wolfish or wolvish
Though **wolvish** is still listed in *Webster's Third* (1986) and the *Oxford Dictionary* (1989), it makes no showing against **wolfish** in data from either the BNC or CCAE. The American *wolverine* has not evidently helped to preserve the adjective with *-v-,* even in the US. This preference for **wolfish** is in line with other words of this type: see further under **-v-/-f-**.

woman or lady
See under **lady**.

woolen, woollen, woolly or wooly
The spelling **woolen** observes the convention that consonants are not normally doubled after a vowel which is a digraph (see **doubling of final consonant**). Compare *leaden, wooden* etc. In American English **woolen** is the standard spelling and dominant in data from CCAE. But **woollen** is equally strongly preferred in BNC data, and it matches the British use of double *l* in other derived words such as *traveller,* though they normally have more than two syllables (see **-l-/-ll-**). Regional consistency slips with **woolly**, which is preferred in both the US and the UK. Americans do make use of **wooly** as well, but it's clearly the minor variant, outnumbered in CCAE by almost 6:1.

Wool(l)en is the older adjective of the two, dating from C11, and still used strictly to refer to things made of *wool* for a commercial market. **Woolly** was coined in C16, and has several semantic domains of its own:

* referring to garments made of *wool,* but not as commodities of commerce: e.g. *wearing a red woolly hat.* In British English, **woolly** also serves as an informal noun for a pullover: *in a baggy woolly and corduroys.*
* describing animals other than sheep with *wool-like* coats, from *woolly monkeys* to the *woolly mammoth.*
* passing judgement on language which is imprecise (*woolly platitudes*) or muddled thinking (*woolly-headed*).

Note that *wild and woolly* means "rough," "unkempt" when applied to people, but "unrestrained," "lawless" when applied to a place or an era. Compare *the outlaw's wild and woolly look* with *Colorado's wild and woolly past.*

word classes
See **parts of speech**.

word order
In English, **word order** is a significant factor in grammar (syntax). The normal **word order** for statements has the subject preceding the verb, and the verb before its object or complement. This basic order is modified for questions and occasionally for other grammatical reasons. (See under **inversion**.)

Beyond the essential grammar of **word order**, we can and do vary the position of elements of the sentence for reasons of style and emphasis. Knowing that the beginning of a sentence is its most conspicuous part, we may well want to move a significant phrase into that position (see further under **topic**). Adverbs and adverbial phrases can often be moved around; and a sentence with a lot of them reads better when they are not all clustered together at the end. Compare:

> The speaker drew attention again at the end of his speech to the number of members absent from the meeting.
> At the end of his speech, the speaker again drew attention to the number of members absent from the meeting.

The second version is clearer and more effective.

wordbreaks
In printed texts, especially those with narrow columns, it's necessary from time to time to divide the last word in the line, and put some of it on the line below. Readers are notified that the word has been divided by the hyphen placed after the first part. Longer words can often be divided in more than one place, as with *re + spect + ive + ly*. Thus the **wordbreak** can be made so as to optimize the use of space at the end of the line.

Some dictionaries indicate the points at which the headwords can be divided, yet they are far from unanimous about it. Some go by the pronunciation of the word and how the sounds combine in the syllables; others go by the word's structure. Compare:

> *tran + scend* with *trans + cend*
> *des + pite* *de + spite*

American dictionaries are often said to go by the pronunciation, and British ones by the structure; yet both compromise between the two principles on particular words. Because English words are so diverse in structure and spelling, the best general practice is to ask what the reader would make of the string of letters on the upper line. Will they provide a helpful lead on to the rest of the word – or prove distracting? Clearly it's not ideal to break *mother* into *moth + er*, nor *therapist* into *the + rapist*.

Apart from that basic principle, the following points are worth noting:

1 Words of less than six letters should not be divided; less than seven letters is better.
2 Words of one syllable should never be divided, e.g. *straight*.
3 Other things being equal, there should be at least three letters of the word on each line. Exceptions would be words beginning with a two-letter prefix e.g. *indebted, recaptured*.
4 Letters which together form a digraph or grapheme should stay together, thus *budg + et, beaut + iful* and *feath + er* or *fea + ther*.
5 Ideally a consonant is carried over to begin the second part of the word. Thus *pano + rama*, except where word structure overrules this as with *draw + ing, system + atic* etc.
6 *Wordbreaks* between two or more consonants (so long as they don't form a digraph/grapheme) are usually acceptable, as in *democ + racy, dif + ferent* and *ser + vice*.
7 Breaking a compound at the junction of its two parts is always acceptable, as in *Anglo + Saxon, awe + inspiring, heavy + duty*.
8 Proper names of any length should not be broken. The computer's automatic *wordbreaking* system can be set to execute some of these principles, but the output still needs an editorial eye to check for infelicities.

words

We take them for granted, yet it's quite difficult to define what they are. Loosely speaking they are the strings of letters which are separated by space from their neighbors in the line of print. So *foot, foothold* and *UFO* all qualify, as would *foot-and-mouth,* in *foot-and-mouth disease*.

Compounds test our definition of **word**, because the hyphens in *foot-and-mouth* seem to make it a **word**, even though they would be three separate **words** in other contexts. Compare: *The disease affects both foot and mouth*. In that sentence the same **words** make up a freely formed phrase, whereas in *foot-and-mouth* they form a conventional compound adjective. (See further under **hyphens** section 2c.) Yet many recognized compounds such as *cash register* do not have hyphens and are set with space between their components. Does that disqualify them as **words**? The answer depends on whether you want to include all compounds in the definition, or only those which are visually unified by means of hyphens or being set solid.

Other issues affecting the definition of **word** come up when we ask whether *armor* and *armour* are different **words**, or *adaption* and *adaptation*, or *orange* and *oranges, child* and *children*. Linguists handle these differences with special terminology, saying that in each pair we have the same *lexeme* but variant spelling or morphology. The reverse problem also arises – the need to recognize that *bear* ("large furry animal") and *bear* ("carry") are different lexemes/**words**.

In the examples of the previous paragraph we used word meanings to help decide on their status as individuals or members of the same lexeme. The grammar inherent in **words** is also part of their identity and, for some, their most important contribution to the sentence. *Function words* such as *a, and, to, the, that* mostly serve to string other **words** together to form phrases and clauses. Meanwhile the grammar of *content words* e.g: *cloud, float, rise, crowd* is more malleable (all those could be nouns or verbs). Either way they invest phrases and clauses with their distinctive semantic content. *Function words* can be just one or two letters, whereas the *content words* are mostly a minimum of three. *Go, ox* and *ax* (in American English) are among the few exceptions, apart from abbreviated **words** such as *ad, ex, ma, pa*. The fact that *content words* normally consist of at least three letters would explain the reluctance of some to use spellings where the word's stem is reduced to two, as in *aging* (cf. *ageing*).

In fact we seem to need several definitions of **word** for different purposes, depending on whether we're thinking of them as printed items on the page, or in terms of their linguistic form, function and meaning.

World War

The two **world wars** of C20 may be written as either:

> World War I or First World War
> World War II Second World War

All dictionaries and style guides agree that the words should be capitalized. But they diverge in that style guides such as the *Chicago Manual* (2003) and the *Oxford Dictionary for Writers and Editors* seem to prefer *World War I/II*, whereas general dictionaries such as *New Oxford* (1998) and *Canadian Oxford* (1998) indicate a preference for *First/Second World War* by their crossreferencing.

World Wide Web or WorldWideWeb

See under **website**.

worrisome or worrying

In North American English **worrisome** is a well-established adjective for something that causes serious concern, as in *a worrisome Education department report* or *white backlash is substantial and worrisome*. In British and Australian **worrisome** is rare, and instead **worrying** is used as adjective, both attributively (*a worrying report*) and predicatively (*the backlash is worrying*).

worse or worst

The most awful possibilities we can imagine are when *worse comes to worse . . .* Or when *worse comes to worst . . .* Or when *the worst comes to the worst*. In American English the forms with *worse* are more common, by the evidence of CCAE, where *worse comes to worse* outnumbers *worse comes to worst* by 10:6. In British data from the BNC, the phrase almost always takes its most emphatic form: *if the worst comes to the worst,* where superlatives underscore the agony, as well as the repeated *the*. Who said the British tended to understate? But then American English provides the phrase *worst case scenario* – to simulate the ultimate disaster.

worshipped or worshiped

British and American English diverge over how to spell the inflected forms of *worship*. In the US both **worshiped** and **worshipped** are used, in the ratio of about 2:1, by the evidence of CCAE. In the UK worshipped is strongly preferred. The pattern is the same for *worship(p)er:* the spelling with two *p*s is standard in the UK, whereas both spellings are used in the US, *worshiper* more often than *worshipper.* See further under **-p/-pp-**.

worthwhile, worth-while or worth while

This expression has been steadily compacted since C19. Then it was *worth the while* meaning "worth the time that it took." This became **worth while** (*the excursion was worth while*), and from this predicative use has evolved the attributive: *a worthwhile excursion.* The unhyphenated form **worthwhile** is now by far the most common form in British and American English, for predicative as well as attributive use, in data from the BNC and CCAE. **Worth-while** was favored for the attributive use by those who wanted to distinguish it from the predicative **worth while**, and punctuate it like other compound adjectives (see **hyphens** section 2c). Yet the hyphenated form is the least common of the three in the BNC as well as CCAE. British writers have probably been resistant to **worthwhile** because Fowler (1926) found no place for it (only **worth while** and **worth-while**); and Gowers (1965) too kept it at arm's length. In the same vein, Burchfield (1996) found **worthwhile** "regrettably common" for the predicative. He thereby affirms what the databases show, that **worthwhile** is now standard for all uses of the word.

would or should
See **should**.

would of or would've
See under **have**.

wove or weaved
See under **weave**.

wr or r
For most words there's no choice between these. See further under **r or wr**, and individual entries.

wrang or wrung
See **wrung**.

wrangle or wangle
See **wangle**.

wrap up or rap up
See **rap up**.

wrapped or wrapt
See under **rapt**.

wrath, wroth and wrathful
Despite its literary flavor, the noun **wrath** is current in both British and American English. When something stronger than "anger" or "fury" is needed, **wrath** serves the purpose, in hundreds of contemporary examples from the BNC and CCAE. The *wrath of the business community* is thus equal and opposite to the *wrath of the unions,* and the **wrath** of secular leaders from General Noriega to Mrs Thatcher becomes an analogue of the *wrath of God.* Both seem to be embodied in *The Grapes of Wrath,* Steinbeck's powerful novel from the 1930s.

Meanwhile the adjective **wroth** has disappeared. Its demise was signaled by Fowler (1926) through cases where **wrath** was being used instead. In data from BNC and CCAE there's no sign of **wroth** or of any adjectival use of **wrath**; and when an adjective is needed, **wrathful** serves the purpose. Requiescat in pace.

wreak or reek
These two have something in common – their pronunciation and negative connotations – but other things set them apart. While **wreak** is contracting to a few savage idioms such as *wreak havoc/vengeance/ mayhem/destruction,* **reek** is expanding its domain. As a verb it means "smell" in the physical sense as well as figuratively (being suffused with some negative quality). Compare its use in:
> *The house reeked of popcorn.*
> *His comments reek of other ambitions.*
As in these examples, **reek** is construed with *of,* whereas **wreak** takes *havoc* etc. as a direct object. Thus grammar as well as idiom set them apart, though Garner (1998) reports the occasional substitution of one for the other in American sources. Both **reek** and **wreak** have regular past tenses (*reeked, wreaked*), although *wrought* is sometimes substituted for *wreaked.* See **wrought**.

wreckless or reckless
See **reckless**.

wrest or rest
These two are almost opposite in meaning. **Rest** as a verb means "take it easy," whereas **wrest** means "take by force or struggle" (often figuratively), as in:
> *The home team wrested victory from their opponents in the last two minutes.*
Note that *wrestle,* where the emphasis is often on physical struggle, is a derivative of **wrest**: see **-le**.

wretch or retch
Neither word has pleasant associations. **Retch** as verb or abstract noun refers to an involuntary spasm which precedes vomiting. **Wretch** is an emotionally charged noun used to describe someone pitiable or despicable, and occasionally as a term of abuse.

wright or write
In words like *shipwright, wheelwright,* **wright** survives as a noun and was once the ordinary word for "worker," Only in *playwright* do we sometimes pause, with the thought that it could perhaps be "playwrite" – though it would be very awkward use of the verb **write**. When it comes to *playwriting,* the same issue arises: see further under **playwright, playwrighting and playwriting**.

write me
The verb *write* can be construed in several different ways:
* intransitively, as in *Do write when you've settled in.*
* monotransitively, as in *Do write me, when you've settled in.*
* ditransitively, as in *Do write me a letter, when you've settled in.*
American English has all three constructions, whereas British usage allows the first and third only.

◊ For other regional differences in transitivity, see under **transitive.**

wring or ring
See under **wrung.**

wrong or wrongly
Wrong can be an adjective or noun, as well as an adverb:

>   *It was the wrong answer.*
>   *A grave wrong was committed there.*
>   *The plan went wrong after a few weeks.*

In the last sentence **wrong** is a zero adverb (see further under that heading).

Wrongly only works as an adverb, though it cannot be freely interchanged with **wrong** in that role. It could not replace **wrong** in the third example, or in the many ordinary idioms with *do, get, go, have,* such as *Don't get me wrong.* On the other hand, only **wrongly** can be used with more formal expressions such as *wrongly accused/attributed/decided/judged* etc.

Note that although **wrongly** comes before the past participle in those examples, it can also come after the verb:

>   *He had applied the concept quite wrongly.*

◊ Compare **right or rightly**.

wrought or wreaked
Wrought is a well-disguised past form of the verb *work* (which gained its regular past *worked* only in C15). It survives mostly as a past participle in idioms such as *wrought iron,* and *overwrought / wrought up*

meaning "stressed." Yet it also serves instead of *worked* for past tense and past participle, in combinations such as *wrought change/miracles/transformation,* as well as *wrought havoc/damage/destruction.* **Wreaked** (from **wreak,** "cause/inflict") is used as an alternative to **wrought** in the second set (i.e. those expressing negative events). Database evidence from CCAE and the BNC show that **wrought** is slightly more common than **wreaked** in such constructions, but both are established idioms.

wrung, wrang or wringed
What is the past form for the verb *wring?* The *Oxford Dictionary* (1989) confirms that **wrang** and **wringed** were current in earlier centuries, but that modern usage has settled on **wrung** for both past tense and past participle:

>   *The lawyer wrung his hands nervously.*
>   *She had wrung his heart.*

With **wrung** as its only past form, *wring* is like *fling* and *sling* rather than *ring,* which still has two past forms: *rang/rung.* (See **irregular verbs** sections 3 and 6.)

Wrung and *rung* sometimes collide, at least in American English. Examples such as *all rung out,* and *the party that rung the neck of apartheid* can be found in CCAE, to add to those of Garner (1998). Despite the lapses of spelling, the idioms speak through.

www
See under **website.**

X

-x

The letter *x* often marks a spot needing special attention – especially at the ends of English nouns. Because of their diverse origins, nouns ending in -**x** may or may not take regular English plurals. The patterns are as follows:

1 **Regular English plurals** (with -*es*) are used with:
a) everyday nouns of one syllable such as *box, fax, flax, flux, fox, hex, jinx, lynx, tax, wax*
b) commercial names such as *durex, kleenex, pyrex, telex, wettex*
c) loanwords from Old French or Late Latin such as: *affix, annex, circumflex, crucifix, equinox, paradox, prefix, reflex, suffix, syntax*

2 **English as well as Latin plurals** (where -*ces* replaces the **x**) are found with various loanwords from Classical Latin. They include *apex, appendix, calyx, helix, ibex, index, latex, matrix, phalanx, thorax, vertex, vortex*. In everyday writing for the general public, these can take English plurals (with -*es*); whereas the Latin plurals are conventional in scholarly, scientific and legal writing. More details are given at individual entries on **apex**, **appendix**, **index**, **matrix**, **phalanx** and **vertex or vortex**. (See also -**trix**.)

3 **Latin plurals only.** Specialized terms of science, medicine, mathematics, paleography and theology which come from Classical Latin or Greek are always pluralized as they were in Latin, i.e. with either:
*-**ces**: as for *anthrax, calix, caudex, cicatrix, codex, cortex, fornix, pollex, radix*
or
*-**ges**: as for *coccyx, larynx, pharynx*
Note finally that the letter *x* is itself a plural suffix for two kinds of words:
* French loanwords, such as *adieux, fabliaux, gateaux* etc. Such words also have -*s* plurals. (See further under -**eau**.)
* a small number of English words ending in *k* or *ck*, such as *sox, thanx*. These are mostly used to suggest informality, and not yet standard spellings. See **spelling, rules and reforms** section 5.

Xian
See under **China**.

-xic or -ctic
See under -**ctic/-xic**.

-xion or -ction
See under -**ction/-xion**.

Xmas
This abbreviation for *Christmas* is over a thousand years old. The *X* represents the Greek letter *chi*, which is the first letter in the Greek form of the name *Christ*. In the first centuries of Christianity the letter *chi* was often used as a symbol of the faith, and there are citations for its use in abbreviations for *Christian* in C15 and C16. In modern English **Xmas** rarely appears in edited prose, in either the UK or the US. Data from both the BNC and CCAE have it mostly in transcriptions of speech – apart from signs, headlines and greeting cards, where space has to be conserved.

X-ray or x-ray
To capitalize or not to capitalize: that is the question. The upper-case form **X-ray** is strongly preferred in both American and British databases. Less than 5% of instances in CCAE and only 10% of instances in the BNC are **x-ray**. Even as a verb, *X-rayed* is much more common than *x-rayed*. The capital letter is in line with the usual practice for writing letters as words, especially within compounds. See **letters as words**.

y/i

For words with variant spellings in **y** and **i** (e.g. *gypsy/gipsy*), see **i/y**.

-y

Both nouns and adjectives in English have this ending:

1 Adjectives formed with -y typically have it added to a single-syllabled noun, as in *cloudy, dirty, risky, woody, wordy* and countless others. A minority such as *crazy, edgy, icy, shady* and others, delete the final *-e* of the noun (*craze, edge* etc.) before adding the **-y**, thus conforming with the standard rule (see **-e** section 1, as well as **-y/-ey**). Note that when the basic word itself ends in **-y**, the adjective ending is *-ey*, as with *clayey* and *flyey*. Plural nouns can also provide the base for such adjectives, as in *newsy* and *rootsy*. Many adjectives of this kind are formed ad hoc and do not appear in dictionaries.

2 Nouns ending in -y fall into two major groups:

a) abstract and often rather formal words like *capacity, novelty, revelry, tracery*, many of them borrowed ready-made from French or Latin. (See further under **-ity** and **-ry**.)

b) informal words which are always English formations. Some are associated with talking to children, such as *doggy, nanny, piggy;* but many are used freely by adults: *brolly, footy, hippy, telly*. Many words of this kind can also be spelled with *-ie*, as with *footie, hippie*. See further under **-ie/-y**.

-y/-ey

Some well-established English words ending in **-y** have variant spellings in **-ey**. They include nouns such as:

> bog(e)y   curts(e)y   doil(e)y   fog(e)y
> stor(e)y   troll(e)y   whisk(e)y

In some cases different meanings are attached to the different spellings (see under individual headings for each).

Adjectives whose spelling can be either **-y** or **-ey** are typically informal words, whose recorded history is relatively short and recent. The nouns on which they are based are much more familiar in print, and some writers and editors prefer to preserve the whole noun within the spelling of the adjective. Others allow them to lose the final *-e*, in keeping with the general rules of English spelling (see **-e** section 1, and **-y** section 1). For example:

> bon(e)y   cag(e)y   chanc(e)y   choos(e)y   cliqu(e)y
> dic(e)y   dop(e)y   gam(e)y   hom(e)y   hors(e)y
> jok(e)y   lim(e)y   lin(e)y   loon(e)y   mop(e)y
> mous(e)y   nos(e)y   phon(e)y   ponc(e)y   pric(e)y
> rang(e)y   scar(e)y   shak(e)y   smil(e)y   smok(e)y
> spik(e)y   ston(e)y   win(e)y   wir(e)y

(The non-italicized words are further discussed at their individual entries.) The sample presented in the Langscape survey (1998–2001), drew mixed responses, though the majority gave regular **-y** spellings to the oldest (C16) examples (*bony, stony, wiry*) and *-ey* to

those coined in C19 and C20 (*cagey, dicey, gamey, nosey, pricey*). Age and other factors correlated with the mix of responses. Young respondents (under 25) preferred **-ey** spellings, either because they seem to be "safe" spellings, or because of their unfamiliarity with the rule that trims the *-e*. In contrast, the second-language users of English were more inclined to use the rule-governed spellings that trim the *-e*. Among first-language users, the British are more inclined than Americans to **-ey** spellings (Sigley, 1999), by the increased numbers in late C20 databases, often in new coinings. Apart from their newness, it may be that their nonconforming spellings help to emphasize their informality. But both these effects wear off over time, and it does the language no favor to increase the number of irregular spellings.

If there is any problem in recognizing the regular spellings, it could be with examples like *cagy* and *dicy*, where dropping the *-e* leaves only three letters to indicate the root word. Yet *icy* is well established with only two. In these and others like *chancy, poncy, pricy, rangy*, the **-y** takes over the role of "softening" the preceding *c* or *g* – again in accordance with English spelling rules (see **-ce/-ge**). Overall there's no reason to delay spelling these words in the regular way. For *phoney*, it only helps to perpetuate a spurious etymology (see **phony**).

> **International English selection:** Given the general rules for *-e* dropping in words formed with **-y**, it makes good sense to endorse such spellings for all established words of this type, not the **-ey** variants.

-y > -i-

When **-y** occurs at the end of a word after a consonant, it often changes to *i* before inflections beginning with *-e*. It happens with:

* verbs ending in **-y**. These change to **-i-** before *-ed*, as in *apply>applied, copy>copied, fry>fried*. The same change is seen before *-er,* in agent words such as *copier*.

* nouns ending in **-y**. These change before the plural suffix *-es*, as with *city>cities, estuary>estuaries, spy>spies*. Note however that proper nouns ending in **-y** do not change for the plural: *three Hail Marys, four Gregorys*. Compounds also resist the change, witness *laybys, standbys*.

* adjectives with two syllables change **-y** to **-i-** before *-er/-est: gloomier/gloomiest*. Note however that this is not necessarily done with one-syllabled words, as seen in common examples such as *drier/dryer* (see further under that heading).

The change of a final *y* to *i* also affects many other words formed with suffixes. The following are just a token:

> alliance   beautify   bounciness   denial
> gloomily   marriage   merriment   pitiless
> plentiful   reliable

586

Only when the suffix begins with -*i* does the final *y* remain, for example in *allying* and *copyist*.

The major exceptions to *y/i* change are words in which a vowel precedes the final **-y** before the suffix. Note the unchanged *y* before regular inflexions in:

* verbs, e.g. *delayed, employed, surveyed*
* nouns, e.g. *alloys, days, donkeys, guys*
* adjectives, e.g. *coyer/coyest, grayer/grayest*

The change to *i* does however take place in three very common verbs, where the suffix is fused with the root:

lay>laid   pay>paid   say>said

and in two rather uncommon nouns:

obsequy>obsequies   soliloquy>soliloquies

But otherwise the presence of a vowel before the final **-y** seems to inhibit the change, in numerous formations such as:

betray   conveyance   employment
joyless   playful   repayable

yack or yak

This slang word meaning "nonstop talk" or "talk nonstop" is found worldwide spelled as **yak** and **yack**, and they're about equally represented in data from the BNC and CCAE. The dictionaries all make **yak** their primary spelling, often reduplicated (as **yak yak**), or embellished (as **yakety yak**), so there's little risk of confusion with the Tibetan bovine.

ya'll or y'all

See **you-all**.

Yankee

Outside the US this term is used rather casually and sometimes disparagingly to refer to Americans and things American (see further under **racist language**). To Americans themselves it has historical overtones: it originally referred to the inhabitants of New England, and subsequently to northerners at large, especially those who fought for the Union in the Civil War. The abbreviated form *Yank* was applied in World War II to American soldiers overseas, and since then to any American.

The origin of **Yankee** is debated. Most dictionaries trace it back to *Jan Kees,* a derisive nickname meaning "John Cheese," which was supposedly applied by early Dutch settlers in New York to the English colonists in Connecticut. It was then interpreted as a plural by English-speakers, and the singular **Yankee** derived from it. (For other words derived this way, see **false plurals**.) Other scholars believe the word comes from an Amerindian word *Yengees,* used in reference to the English-speaking settlers.

ye and you

See **you**.

yes

This word needs no comment, except to say that when used as a noun its plural could be **yeses** or **yesses**. Database evidence shows that the two are about equally current in both British and American English. But the dictionaries lean towards **yeses**. This is explicit in *New Oxford* (1998) and implicit in the lack of indication in *Merriam-Webster* (2000), by which a regular plural (**yeses**) can be assumed.
◊ Compare **bus** and **gas**.

yet

This can serve as a conjunction, conjunct or adverb, as shown in the following sentences:

He offered no help, yet assumed his right to sell our project.
(conjunction)
They stayed home. Yet they must have thought about coming.
(conjunct)
It hasn't come yet.
(adverb)

In the first sentence, **yet** serves as a synonym for "but," and in the second for "however," though it seems to make the contrast more gently than either of them (see further under **conjunctions** sections 1 and 3). In the third sentence **yet** is a gentle alternative to "still." Compare *It still hasn't come.* The choice of **yet** rather than one of its synonyms is a matter of style and emphasis, and it provides a useful alternative for discursive writing. In the *Longman Grammar* (1999) corpus, **yet** was more than twice as common in academic prose as in conversation.

Adverbial **yet** combines with *to* in signaling processes that have still to take place, or thresholds still to be crossed:

The conductor has yet to confirm the terms of his Berlin contract.
Their skills are yet to be tested in a tougher economic climate.

The examples show that *yet to* may be construed with the auxiliary *have* or *be,* though constructions with *have* are very much more common, in British and American databases. Those formed with parts of the verb *be* make up less than 5% of examples in the BNC and CCAE. Idioms such as *the best is yet to be,* and formulas such as: *This film is yet to be classified by . . .* do not seem to exercise much influence on common usage.

yodel

The question of whether to double the *l* when verb suffixes are added is discussed under **-l/-ll-**.

yogurt, yoghurt, yoghourt and yogourt

For the ubiquitous cultured custard, the first two spellings are much more common than the third or fourth. In the US **yogurt** is standard, and it dominates the data from CCAE. In the UK both **yogurt** and **yoghurt** are current, but British writers clearly prefer **yoghurt**, by the evidence of the BNC where it outnumbers **yogurt** by almost 3:1. **Yoghourt** is also listed in American and British dictionaries, but not popular in either place, by its absence from CCAE and the mere handful of examples in the BNC. The more French-looking **yogourt** is given priority over **yogurt** in the *Canadian Oxford* (1998), although *Canadian English Usage* (1997) notes that **yogourt**, **yoghurt** and **yoghourt** are all relatively rare, and that **yogurt** is by far the most common – as it is across the border. Australian usage is like the British, with **yoghurt** and **yogurt** both current but **yoghurt** ahead on database evidence (Peters, 1995).

Yog(h)urt was in fact borrowed into English in C17, since when no fewer than eleven different spellings have been recorded. The original *Oxford* (1884–1928) made **yogurt** the headword, which is surprising given its absence from the citations, and the fact that it renders the original Turkish less closely than **yoghurt**. Closer inspection finds **yogurt** listed as a variant spelling (as well as headword), while **yoghurt** is not mentioned, and we might suspect that **yoghurt** was intended to be the headword. Be that as it may, **yogurt** remains the primary spelling in the second edition of the *Oxford Dictionary* (1989), with **yoghurt** as the secondary alternative. This still seems curious in light of the fact that each occurs only once in the five citations from C20, while **yoghourt** is in three of them. *New Oxford* (1998) also makes **yogurt** its first choice – on the basis of product labels perhaps?

Yogyakarta
See under **Jakarta**.

you and ye
Until the later C16, **ye** and **you** shared the role of the second person plural pronoun, with **ye** used when the word was the subject of a clause, and **you** when it was the object. (See further under **cases**.) The King James bible still observes this in:

Ye have not chosen me; I have chosen you.

But this case distinction was already breaking down in Shakespeare's and Ben Jonson's plays, and early C17 grammarians made the two words interchangeable. **You** was in fact taking over, and by C18 **ye** had been ousted from the standard language and survived only in literary and lofty use. The takeover went still further, for **you** also subsumed the singular roles of *thou/thee* (see further under **thou**).

The lack of *case* distinction between **you** and **ye** was no great loss, since English syntax helps to show subject and object. But the merging of plural and singular second persons leaves English without a simple way of showing whether someone's remarks are meant solely for the person addressed, or for others whom s/he represents as well. Many an invitation has been complicated by this fact. Expressions such as *you both* and *you all* help to clarify the situation, and in informal contexts *you guys* and *you lot*, as well as *youse/yous* (see further under **you-all** and **yous**). Still there's no regular way of expressing the singular/plural distinction in the English second person.

Special uses of you and ye
1 Apart from its regular use in second person address, **you** can be used *indefinitely,* so that it reaches beyond the second person, as in:

After all that you'd think he would compromise.

In such sentences, **you** is an informal substitute for *one*, a pronoun which is somewhere between second and first person (see further under **one**). *Indefinite you* invokes something that **you** and I might agree on, and proposes a kind of solidarity without insisting on it. As in the example, it's normally done in passing, in the flow of conversation.

All this explains why *indefinite you* hardly lends itself to the cause of Plain English paraphrase – though it's sometimes suggested as a cure for the impersonal or authoritarian style which besets government documents. The idea is that statements such as:

All tax returns must be filed by March 31.

might be translated into

You must file your tax return by March 31.

But **you** is then very far from *indefinite*. From the printed page it speaks with the directness of the ordinary second person pronoun, especially when reinforced by *your,* and underscored with *must,* a modal verb of obligation. As a device for pressuring people into paying their taxes, it succeeds. But it fails if a friendly and tactful form of address is intended. To work *indefinitely* **you** needs to be used sparingly and out of the topical spotlight at the start of a sentence (see **topic**).

2 *Pseudo-*ye. The most familiar use of **ye** nowadays is perhaps its appearance in old-fashioned shop signs: *Ye Olde Tea Shoppe.* This use of *Ye* is not related to the second person pronoun, but uses the *Y* to match the Old English character "thorn" (borrowed from the runic alphabet) which represented "th." So *Ye* is simply *The.* In Tudor handwriting and printing, *y* was used instead of *th* in *the* and a number of other words: *that, this, they* (and sometimes *them, their*) to save space. It ceased to be common practice by C18, but it lingers in the *Ye* of pub and shop signs, wherever the whiff of antiquity seems to be a commercial asset.

you-all and you all
This complex pronoun is associated particularly with the southern and southwestern parts of the US. It provides an explicitly plural form of the second person pronoun, which English has lacked since C17 (see **you and ye**). *Merriam-Webster* (2000) and others note that **you-all** is occasionally used in addressing a single person, though even then it may be explained as a way of referring to the notional group represented by that person. It has suffered from stereotyping by outsiders, but **you-all** is part of the speech repertoire of educated Americans from the South (Garner, 1998). Database evidence from CCAE shows its use in both public and private contexts:

I remember years ago I told you-all about TM...

"You-all on your way out?" the waitress asked.

You-all is normally hyphenated, so as to distinguish it from other juxtapositions of *you* and *all*. The *Oxford Dictionary* (1989) notes the setting **you all** as an alternative, but on the printed page it runs the risk of not being seen as the complex pronoun – at least with non-American readers. The standard contracted form is *y'all*, although Garner notes the occasional use of *ya'll*. It presumably owes something to the use of *ya* to represent informal pronunciation of *you;* and perhaps also the influence of other contractions such as *I'll, we'll, you'll*. In those *'ll* represent "will," of course, so it's best not to make the contraction of **you-all** match up with them.

◊ Compare **yous**.

Yours faithfully, Yours sincerely, and Yours etc.
The use of **Yours faithfully** at the close of a formal letter is declining. It was once used widely in official and commercial correspondence in which the relationship was strictly one of business. **Yours sincerely** was then reserved for letters to friends. Nowadays, businesses seek friendly relationships with their customers; and within corporations and bureaucracies, the tone of communication is generally collaborative rather than distant and authoritarian. Either way **Yours sincerely** is more in keeping with the prevailing style, whether or not the correspondents are acquainted. **Yours faithfully** is increasingly reserved for correspondence addressed

to the unknown reader (*Dear Sir/Madam*) at a government institution, and in legal correspondence.

In personal letters, closure can take whatever form seems right for the relationship between the correspondents. With **Yours sincerely** used increasingly in business letters, the shortened form **Yours** becomes the more informal closure for veteran letter writers. But many prefer alternatives such as *Best wishes* or just *Best* (in American English); *Regards* or *Kind regards* (in British English); and others such as *With thanks (Thanks), Cheers, Good luck, Much love (Love), Bye*. All these and more are used in personal e-mails (Li, 2000), although about 20% of messages have just the sender's name by way of closing.
◊ For the opening salutation in letters and e-mail, see under **Dear**.
◊ For older and newer styles in business letters, see **commercialese** and **letter writing**.
◊ For the layout of letters and e-mail, see Appendix VII.

yous or youse

These colloquial or slang forms of **you** are found in many varieties of English: northern British and American, Irish, Australian. They no doubt exist as responses to the lack of distinct singular and plural pronouns for the second person (Wales, 1996). The spelling **yous** suggests plurality, on the analogy of regular nouns – a rather weak analogy, since the word is a pronoun. **Yous** is nevertheless a good deal more popular than **youse** in data from the BNC, and was given priority by the *Oxford Dictionary* (1989). But *New Oxford* (1998) prefers **youse**, as does the *Canadian Oxford* (1997) and the Australian *Macquarie Dictionary* (1997). *Merriam-Webster* (2000) also prefers **youse**, but in CCAE data it hardly occurs except in *youse guys*, rendering rough speech. **Yous** meanwhile is associated with the plural forms of conventional phrases such as *thank yous, I love yous, how are yous, what have yous*.

Yous(e) is not invariably used in plural reference, despite the fact that it seems to fill a gap in the English pronoun system (see further under **you and ye**). Singular reference is clear in BNC examples such as *Yous will be left on your own*, and others suggest singular address even if the person addressed is seen as representing "another or others," as *Merriam-Webster* notes.

Whatever its number value, **yous(e)** is unmistakably informal in style – so much so that it can be a liability. Dictionaries always enter it with restrictive labels or cautionary notes. *New Oxford* dubs it "dialectal," while the *Random House Dictionary* (1987) associates it with "urban speech" in the northern US, notably New York, Boston and Chicago. The *Canadian Oxford* notes it as "unacceptable in writing or cultivated speech." In Australia it's heard in casual exchanges in both metropolitan and country speech, but still associated with a shortage of education. The *Macquarie Dictionary* labels it "nonstandard."
◊ Compare **you-all**.

youth and youths

In the singular, **youth** is most often found as an abstract or collective noun, in reference to one's early years (*in my youth*) and referring to young people

generally (*the youth of today*). These uses are gender-neutral, and can involve either or both sexes. But when **youth** is individualized or pluralized, it is strictly masculine, as in

> *a pin-striped youth in his early twenties*
> *Though youths were predominant, there was no shortage of older men . . .*

-yse/-yze

See under -yze/-yse.

yuck or yuk, yucky or yukky

Slang words are under less pressure than most to conform, and both **yuck** and **yuk** appear for this relatively recent (1960s) exclamation of distaste. Database evidence shows that Americans are more inclined to **yuck**, and the British to **yuk**, though both are current everywhere. When it comes to the adjective there's more convergence in the data, and **yucky** is clearly preferred to **yukky**, by the evidence of CCAE and the BNC. Dictionaries everywhere prefer **yucky** as the spelling for the adjective, while allowing **yukky** as an alternative. The use of **yuck(y)** helps to normalize the word(s) according to standard English spelling conventions (see further under **k/c**). In American English the spelling **yuck** helps to distinguish the word from older slang use of **yuk** (*yuk yuk*), used to represent a sardonic laugh.

Yugoslavia

This name means a state for "Southern Slavs," though it covered a diverse group of people inhabiting the western side of the Balkan peninsula, amalgamated in 1918 out of Serbia, Montenegro and parts of the Austro-Hungarian Empire. Until 1990 **Yugoslavia** consisted of six socialist republics: Bosnia-Herzegovina, Croatia, Macedonia, Montenegro, Serbia and Slovenia. There were three official languages: Serbo-Croatian, Slovenian and Macedonian, with Serbs and Macedonians using the Cyrillic alphabet, and Croats and Slovenians the Roman. In religion too the population of **Yugoslavia** was divided, with a majority adhering to the Eastern Orthodox Church, and others to Roman Catholicism and to Islam. Such diversity became the basis of division and civil war, and by May 1992 three states (Bosnia-Herzegovina, Croatia, and Slovenia) had declared their independence and been recognized as separate members of the United Nations. Macedonia's attempt to assert its independence has been complicated by controversy with Greece over the use of the name "Macedonia," and it remains "The former Yugoslav Republic of Macedonia" on the UN members' list (2003). Until February 2003, the states of Serbia and Montenegro retained the name **Yugoslavia**, but this has been changed in favor of "Serbia and Montenegro."

Dictionaries still note *Jugoslavia* as an alternative spelling for **Yugoslavia**, but it's rare in British data from the BNC, and not used at all by American writers represented in CCAE.

yuk and yukky

See under **yuck**.

yuppie or yuppy

This 1980s word for the upwardly mobile person is usually spelled **yuppie**, according to both dictionaries and database evidence. There's little sign of **yuppy** being more popular with British writers, as some dictionaries suggest. The *-ie* ending probably makes the word look more informal (see further under -ie/-y), though the capital letter sometimes given to it (*Yuppie*) reminds us of its origins as an acronym. In fact it's an amalgam of two acronyms: *young urban professional*, and *young upwardly mobile person*. As originally coined, **yuppie** and *yumpie* identified two social types both preoccupied with acquiring status symbols, the first distinguishable by superior education, and the second by social pretensions (cf. **U and non-U**). By now the word **yuppie** has outperformed *yumpie*, incorporated its image as part of its own, and "professional" is part of the definition of current dictionaries, whether British, American, Canadian or Australian. A third variation on this theme – not yet registered in dictionaries – is the "yummie," the *young upwardly mobile Marxist*, identified by Australian writer Murray-Smith with the repopulation of older suburbs of Melbourne and Sydney.

-yze/-yse

These are alternative spellings for the following verbs:

analyze	*catalyze*	*dialyze*
electrolyze	*hydrolyze*	*paralyze*

American English makes the **-yze** spellings its standard, while British English prefers **-yse**, as indicated in *Merriam-Webster* (2000) and *New Oxford* (1998). However the BNC provides some evidence of British use of **-yze** spellings for *analyze,* and a little for *paralyze* (see **analyze** and **paralyze**). Australian usage is like the British, and Canadian like the American, according to the *Macquarie Dictionary* (1997) and *Canadian Oxford* (1998).

American use of **-yze** aligns these words with the much larger set in which *-ize* is used (see **-ize/-ise**). British English puts more weight on etymological issues, and the spellings with **-yse** express the fact that they came via French or Latin, as well as their connections with nouns such as *analysis* and *paralysis*. The fact that many British writers use *-ise* spellings predisposes them towards **-yse**; and the same holds for Australian English.

International English selection: Though there are arguments for both spellings, **-yze** aligns these few words with a much larger set, and makes it eminently teachable and learnable. The fact that Canadians and a few British writers use **-yze**, as well as Americans, gives it a broad basis of distribution.

Z

-z/-zz

Very few words allow you to choose between one or two *z*s at the end, only *friz(z)* and *whiz(z)*: see further under those headings. Beyond those there are a few which always have a single z, and a lot which always have double z.

Those with single z are mostly colloquial words, such as *biz, squiz* and *swiz*. They're often abbreviations, as *biz* is for "business" and *swiz* for "swizzle." The word *quiz* may likewise have originated as a clipped form of "inquisitive" or "inquisition," though it's now a standard English word. Note that all such words double the z before suffixes are added to them. So the plural of *quiz* is *quizzes*, and *quizzed* is its past tense. Derivatives such as *quizzical* also show the tendency to double.

The majority of words ending in z have two, and double z is the regular spelling with:

> buzz   chizz   fizz   fuzz   jazz
> mozz   razz   tizz   zizz

Such words need no special treatment, whatever inflections are added.

zed or zee

The letter *Z* goes by the name **zee** in the US, and **zed** in the UK and Australia. Canada uses both names, according to the *Canadian Oxford* (1998). So the North American expression *catch/bag some zees,* and the Australian *push up / stack zeds* both mean "get some sleep" (from the use of *ZZZZZ* in cartoon speech bubbles, to represent a person sleeping). Z is ultimately the Greek *zeta,* which came into English via French, where it was *zède.* **Zed** is the earlier of the two English forms, dating from C15, whereas **zee** is a late C17 variant.

zero

The plural of **zero** can be either **zeros** or **zeroes**, and both are current in English everywhere. In the US the two are about equally current, in data from CCAE, whereas the UK preference is for **zeros**, which outnumbers **zeroes** by about 6:1 in BNC texts.

◊ For the uses of *naught/nought* and *zero*, see under **naught**.

zero adverbs

The fact that many English adverbs are formed with suffix *-ly* leads some people to assume that all adverbs have it. Thus the adverb for *slow* is expected to be *slowly,* and the adverb *doubtless* gets touched up as *doubtlessly.* A moment's thought shows that many kinds of adverbs never end in *-ly:*

* adverbs that double as prepositions: *above, after, before*
* negative adverbs: *not, never, no*
* adverbs of time: *often, soon, then*
* focusing adverbs: *also, even, only*
* modifying adverbs: *rather, quite, very*

Other adverbs can appear both with and without *-ly,* according to context and idiom. They include:

> bad   cheap   clean   clear   close
> deep   direct easy   fair   flat
> high   loud   quick   right   sharp
> short   slow   tight   wide   wrong

The form without *-ly* is actually more common for some, including *cheap, close, flat, high, right, wrong.* All are caught up in idioms which require the zero form:

> come close   going cheap   fall flat   fly high

Where there's a choice, the zero form is usually more colloquial: compare *come quick* with *come quickly.* Research associated with the *Longman Grammar* (1999) found that **zero adverbs** (of all kinds) predominate in spoken discourse, whereas in academic writing, it's the *-ly* adverbs. But in some cases the **zero** and *-ly* forms differ in meaning (see **direct, just** and **low**).

The distribution of **zero adverbs** and *-ly* forms also has a regional dimension. In parallel corpora of British and American writing, Opdahl (1991) found **zero adverbs** more often than *-ly* ones (where there was a choice) in the British data. Her findings were confirmed by elicitation tests in which American and British speakers chose between *low/lowly* and *direct/directly* in a set of sentences, and the American preference for the *-ly* forms was very clear. It reflects the more general American tendency to prefer rule-governed forms where they are available. Compare the alternatives discussed at **-ed, spelling** section 2, and **apostrophes** section 3, for example.

zero conjunction

Not all subordinate clauses are introduced by a subordinating conjunction. English allows the conjunction *that* to be omitted before a noun (content) or adverbial clause, as in:

> I thought (that) you were in the office.
> It was so difficult (that) they gave up.

This omission of *that* (i.e. **zero conjunction**) is associated particularly with speech and more informal writing. See further under **that** section 2b and c.

zero derivation

This is a linguist's term for words that appear in new grammatical roles without any derivational suffix to mark the change. See further under **transfers**.

zero past tense

A number of common English verbs of one syllable ending in *t* or *d* have no special form for the past tense (or the past participle). Compare:

> You just cut out the order form and send it off
> (present)
> I cut my finger while doing the vegetables
> (past tense)
> They have cut off my telephone (past participle)

Other verbs which operate with **zero past tense** are:

> bid   burst   hit   hurt   let   put   set
> shut   slit   split   spread   sweat   thrust

See further under **irregular verbs** section 1.

zero plurals

Several kinds of English nouns are the same whether they're singular or plural. They include:

* collective words for animals, e.g. *deer, fish, giraffe, pheasant, sheep*, especially when they're the quarry for hunting, or the focus of environmental analysis. The **zero plural** is also associated with animal husbandry, as in *raising alpaca/crocodile/emu.*
* a few Latin loanwords whose plurals were the same as the singular in Latin, including *series, species, status* (see further under **Latin plurals** and **-us** section 2)
* a few French loanwords, such as *chassis, chamois*

For all such words, the plural is shown by the use of a plural verb.

Other English words that do not distinguish singular from plural are those which already end in a plural *s*, such as:

> binoculars   clothes   dregs   earnings   gallows
> means   news   scissors   trousers

For them there's no singular noun with the same sense, nor can they be further pluralized. Grammarians treat them as "summation plurals" or *pluralia tantum* (see under that heading). They mostly take plural verbs, but not always: see **agreement** section 2.

zero relatives

See under **relative clauses** sections 1 and 2.

zincic or zincky

See under **-c/-ck-**.

Zionist

See under **Israel**.

zombie or zombi

When you reach this end of the alphabet you may not care how **zombi(e)** is spelled! Since the 1930s it has been applied to a detached mental state and/or clumsy physical behavior (*acting/feeling/staring/walking like a zombie*), hence *zombie-like*. The word was popularized through *zombie movies* after World War II, as well as *zombie rock (music),* which probably helped to make **zombie** the standard spelling. At any rate, it's stamped on other extended uses, such as *zombie-cold scrambled eggs.*

The alternative spelling **zombi** is as close as anyone can get to the original African word, now current only in the Kongo word *nzambi*. It referred to the python god worshipped in voodoo ceremonies, who was believed to have the power to bring a dead person back to life. The word then became associated with the corpse thus revived – and so to the person who behaves like the living dead. Anthropologists who study surviving cults of this kind, in Haiti and elsewhere, sometimes use **zombi** to distinguish the word from its popularized counterpart, but it's otherwise very rare, in both American and British databases.

Appendix I

International Phonetic Alphabet symbols for English sounds

Vowels

/iː/	as in	"seat," "sweet"
/ɪ/	as in	"sit"
/e/	as in	"set"
/eɪ/	as in	"sate," "say," sleigh
/æ/	as in	"sat"
/aɪ/	as in	"sight," "site"
/ʌ/	as in	"shut"
/ɪə*/	as in	"shear," "seer"
/eə*/	as in	"share"
/ə/	as in	"aside"
/ɚ/	as in	"cider"
/ɜː/	as in	"serve"
/aː/	as in	"shard"
/aʊ/	as in	"shout"
/ɒ/	as in	"shot"
/ɔɪ/	as in	"soil"
/ɔː/	as in	"short," "sought," "saw," "sore"
/oʊ/	as in	"show"
/ʊ/	as in	"sugar"
/uː/	as in	"shoot," "shoe," "souvenir"
/ʊə/*	as in	"sewer"

Consonants

/b/	as in	"bet"
/d/	as in	"debt"
/f/	as in	"fed," "photo"
/g/	as in	"get"
/dʒ/	as in	"jet," "edge"
/h/	as in	"head"
/tʃ/	as in	"cheddar," "hatch"
/k/	as in	"kettle," "cat," "quit," "excite"
/l/	as in	"let"
/m/	as in	"met"
/n/	as in	"net"
/ŋ/	as in	"sing," "anchor"
/p/	as in	"pet"
/r/	as in	"red"
/s/	as in	"said," "cedar"
/ʃ/	as in	"shed," "chevron"
/t/	as in	"tetanus"
/ð/	as in	"then"
/θ/	as in	"thread"
/v/	as in	"vet"
/w/	as in	"wet," "suede"
/j/	as in	"yet"
/z/	as in	"zip," "xerox"
/ʒ/	as in	"genre," "beige"

> Not all these vowel sounds occur in every variety of English. Those marked with an asterisk * are found only in non-rhotic varieties, e.g. Southern British, Australian and New Zealand. The vowel /ɚ/ occurs in rhotic varieties, e.g. General American and Canadian.

Appendix II

Geological Eras

Era	Years BP	Period	Epoch	Evolutionary events
Precambrian	4550 m.	Archean		hardening of earth's crust
	2500 m.	Early Proterozoic		spores; bacteria; marine algae
	1600 m.	Riphean		
	650 m.	Vendian		
Paleozoic	570 m.	Cambrian		marine invertebrates
	500 m.	Ordovician		primitive fish
	430 m.	Silurian		shellfish; fungi
	395 m.	Devonian		age of fishes; first amphibians
	345 m.	Carboniferous		age of amphibians; first insects
	280 m.	Permian		development of reptiles
Mesozoic	225 m.	Triassic		first dinosaurs
	190 m.	Jurassic		age of dinosaurs; flying reptiles
	136 m.	Cretaceous		last dinosaurs; modern insects
Cenozoic	65 m.	Tertiary	Paleocene	development of mammals
	53 m.		Eocene	modern mammals; modern birds
	37 m.		Oligocene	browsing mammals
	26 m.		Miocene	grazing mammals
	5 m.		Pliocene	formation of Alps, Andes, Himalayas
	1.8 m.	Quaternary	Pleistocene	widespread glacial ice; early man
	.1m		Holocene (Recent)	modern man

Adapted from the *Cambridge Encyclopedia of Earth Sciences* (1981)

Appendix III

Perpetual Calendar 1901–2008

Years				J	F	M	A	M	J	J	A	S	O	N	D
	25	53	81	4	0	0	3	5	1	3	6	2	4	0	2
	26	54	82	5	1	1	4	6	2	4	0	3	5	1	3
	27	55	83	6	2	2	5	0	3	5	1	4	6	2	4
	28	56	84	0	3	4	0	2	5	0	3	6	1	4	6
01	29	57	85	2	5	5	1	3	6	1	4	0	2	5	0
02	30	58	86	3	6	6	2	4	0	2	5	1	3	6	1
03	31	59	87	4	0	0	3	5	1	3	6	2	4	0	2
04	32	60	88	5	1	2	5	0	3	5	1	4	6	2	4
05	33	61	89	0	3	3	6	1	4	6	2	5	0	3	5
06	34	62	90	1	4	4	0	2	5	0	3	6	1	4	6
07	35	63	91	2	5	5	1	3	6	1	4	0	2	5	0
08	36	64	92	3	6	0	3	5	1	3	6	2	4	0	2
09	37	65	93	5	1	1	4	6	2	4	0	3	5	1	3
10	38	66	94	6	2	2	5	0	3	5	1	4	6	2	4
11	39	67	95	0	3	3	6	1	4	6	2	5	0	3	5
12	40	68	96	1	4	5	1	3	6	1	4	0	2	5	0
13	41	69	97	3	6	6	2	4	0	2	5	1	3	6	1
14	42	70	98	4	0	0	3	5	1	3	6	2	4	0	2
15	43	71	99	5	1	1	4	6	2	4	0	3	5	1	3
16	44	72	00	6	2	3	6	1	4	6	2	5	0	3	5
17	45	73	01	1	4	4	0	2	5	0	3	6	1	4	6
18	46	74	02	2	5	5	1	3	6	1	4	0	2	5	0
19	47	75	03	3	6	6	2	4	0	2	5	1	3	6	1
20	48	76	04	4	0	1	4	6	2	4	0	3	5	1	3
21	49	77	05	6	2	2	5	0	3	5	1	4	6	2	4
22	50	78	06	0	3	3	6	1	4	6	2	5	0	3	5
23	51	79	07	1	4	4	0	2	5	0	3	6	1	4	6
24	52	80	08	2	5	6	2	4	0	2	5	1	3	6	1

Days of the week

S	1	8	15	22	29	36
M	2	9	16	23	30	37
T	3	10	17	24	31	
W	4	11	18	25	32	
T	5	12	19	26	33	
F	6	13	20	27	34	
S	7	14	21	28	35	

The three tables allow you to discover what day of the week any date fell or would fall on, e.g. Christmas Day (25 December) in 1988 and 2008.

- Read across from the relevant year (*1988, 2008*) to the **Months** table and extract the number for December (in these cases 4 and 1).
- Add the number to the actual day of the month (25) = 29 and 26.
- Check that composite number on the **Days of the week** table above to find the actual day . . . *Sunday* (1988) and Thursday (2008).

Appendix IV

International System of Units (SI Units)
Physical quantity

Base SI units	SI unit	Symbol
length	metre	m
mass	kilogram	kg
time	second	s
electric current	ampere	A
thermodynamic temperature	kelvin	K
amount of substance	mole	mol
luminous intensity	candela	cd

Supplementary units		
plane angle	radian	rad
solid angle	steradian	sr

Derived SI units		
energy	joule	J
force	newton	N
pressure	pascal	Pa
frequency	hertz	Hz
power	watt	W
electric charge	coulomb	C
potential difference	volt	V
resistance	ohm	Ω
capacitance	farad	F
conductance	siemens	S
inductance	henry	H
magnetic flux	weber	Wb
magnetic flux density	tesla	T
luminous flux	lumen	lm
illumination	lux	lx

Prefixes for SI units					
exa-	E	10^{18}	deci-	d	10^{-1}
peta-	P	10^{15}	centi-	c	10^{-2}
tera-	T	10^{12}	milli-	m	10^{-3}
giga-	G	10^{9}	micro-	μ	10^{-6}
mega-	M	10^{6}	nano-	n	10^{-9}
kilo-	k	10^{3}	pico-	p	10^{-12}
hecto-	h	10^{2}	femto-	f	10^{-15}
deka- (deca-)	da	10^{1}	atto-	a	10^{-18}

Appendix V

Interconversion Tables for Metric and Imperial Measures

Metric unit		Symbol	Conversion factor to imperial unit	
Length	centimetre	cm	1 cm	= 0.394 inches
	metre	m	1 m	= 3.28 feet or 1.09 yards
	kilometre	km	1 km	= 0.621 mile
area	square centimetre	cm²	1 cm²	= 0.155 sq. inches
	square metre	m²	1 m²	= 10.8 sq. feet or 1.20 sq. yds
	hectare	ha	1 ha	= 2.47 acres
	square kilometre	km²	1 km²	= 0.386 sq. mile
volume	cubic centimetre	cm³	1 cm³	= 0.0610 cubic inches
	cubic metre	m³	1 m³	= 35.3 cubic feet or 1.31 cubic yards or 27.5 bushels
volume (*fluid*)	millilitre	mL	1 mL	= 0.0352 fluid ounces
	litre	L	1 L	= 1.76 pints
	cubic metre	m³	1 m³	= 220 gallons
mass	gram	g	1 g	= 0.0353 ounces
	kilogram	kg	1 kg	= 2.20 pounds
	tonne	t	1 t	= 0.984 ton
velocity	kilometre per hour	km/h	1 km/h	= 0.621 miles per hour
angular velocity	radians per second	rad/s	1 rad/s	= 9.55 revolutions per minute
energy	kilojoule	kJ	1 kJ	= 0.948 British thermal units
	megajoule	mJ	1 mJ	= 9.48×10^{-3} therms
force	newton	N	1 N	= 0.225 pound-force
pressure	kilopascal	kPa	1 kPa	= 0.145 pounds per square inch
(meteorology)	millibar	mb	1 mb	= 0.0295 inch of mercury
power	kilowatt	kW	1 kW	= 1.34 horsepower
temperature	degree Celsius	°C	$(°C \times \frac{9}{5}) + 32 = °F$	

Imperial unit		Symbol	Conversion factor to metric unit	
length	inch	in	1 in	= 25.4 millimetres
	foot	ft	1 ft	= 30.5 centimetres
	yard	yd	1 yd	= 0.914 metres
	mile		1 mile	= 1.61 kilometres
area	square inch	in²	1 in²	= 6.45 sq. centimetres
	square foot	ft²	1 ft²	= 929 sq. centimetres
	square yard	yd²	1 yd²	= 0.836 sq. metres
	acre	ac	1 ac	= 0.405 hectares
	square mile	sq.mile	1 sq.mile	= 2.59 sq. kilometres
volume	cubic inch	in³	1 in³	= 16.4 cubic centimetres
	cubic foot	ft³	1 ft³	= 28.3 cubic decimetres
	cubic yard	yd³	1 yd³	= 0.765 cubic metres
	bushel	bus	1 bus	= 0.0364 cubic metres
volume (*fluid*)	fluid ounce	fl oz	1 fl oz	= 28.4 millilitres
	pint	pt	1 pt	= 568 millilitres
	gallon	gal	1 gal	= 4.55 litres
mass	ounce	oz	1 oz	= 28.3 grams
	pound	lb	1 lb	= 454 grams
	ton		1 ton	= 1.02 tonnes
velocity	mile per hour	mph	1 mph	= 1.61 kilometres per hour
angular velocity	revolution per minute	rpm	1 rpm	= 0.105 radians per second
energy	British thermal unit	Btu	1 Btu	= 1.06 kilojoules
			1 therm	= 106 megajoules
force	pound-force	lbf	1 lbf	= 4.45 newtons
pressure	pound per square inch	psi	1 psi	= 6.89 kilopascals
(meteorology)	square inch of mercury	inHg	1 inHg	= 33.9 millibars
power	horse power	hp	1 hp	= 0.746 kilowatts
temperature	degree Fahrenheit	°F	$(°F - 32) \times \frac{5}{9} = °C$	

Appendix VI

Selected proofreading marks: British and American

Action	Marking on text of MS	Marginal indicators
Leave as printed	~~words to be retained~~	(stet)
Delete character	words$ to be retained	𝖺 or ⤶
Delete and close up	w𝟇ords to be retained	𝖺 or ⤶
Delete string of characters	words not to be retained	𝖺 or ⤶
Insert in text	words / be retained	to ⋏
	words / be retained	[each new item to be followed by a /]
Substitute in text	words to be re/gained	t/
Insert as superior or superscript	"words / to be retained	⤳ or ⤳
		[for quote marks, apostrophes and superscript letters or figures]
Insert hyphen	words to be re/marked	| - | or =
Insert or substitute	words retained/remarked	, or ५| [for comma]
Insert or substitute	words retained/and	;| [for semicolon]
		?| [for question mark]
		!| [for exclamation mark/point]
Insert or substitute	words retained/Remarking	⊙/ [for full stop/period, colon]
		⊙/
Insert or substitute	words retained/remarked	⦸/ [for solidus]
Change to capital letter	words to be retained	(caps) or ≡
Change to lower case	w(ORDS)to be retained	(l.c.) or ⧣
Change to italic	words to be retained	(ital) or ⊔⊔
Change to roman	words(to)be retained	(rom) or ⊔⊔
Change to bold	words to be retained	(bold) or (bf)
Reduce space between words	words to ⌣ be	⊤ or less #
Reduce space between lines	words to (be retained	⟵ and ⟶
		or
	words to > be retained	less #

598

Insert space between characters	words to be	⅄ or #
Insert space between lines	words to be retained	⌐—and —⌐ or # [amount of space can be indicated]
	words to be retained	
Transpose characters	words to be retained	(trs) or (tr)
Transpose matter	words be to retained	(trs) or (tr)
Correct vertical alignment	‖ words to be kept ‖ in alignment	(align) [place lines at right or left of lines to be adjusted]
Move matter to left	words to be retained	⌐ or]
Move matter to right	words to be retained	⌐ or [
Move to next line or page	words to be checked and retained	(take over) or ⌐_⌐
Move to previous line or page	words to be retained	(take back) or ⌐⌐
No fresh line or paragraph	words to be retained	(run on) or (run in)
Begin new paragraph	...out. Words to be retained ...out. Words to be retained	(NP) or ⌐⌐

Notes

- Words used as marginal indicators are ringed to show that they are instructions and not to be set as part of the text.
- If there are several corrections for the same line, divide them between the left and right margins, and present in left-to-right order on each side.
- Editorial corrections to the MS are conventionally made on the text itself between the lines, assuming that the MS is double-spaced. Marginal marks are designed for easy reference by the proofreader/typesetter.
- Where there are alternatives, the first is the usual British mark, the second the American. For a comprehensive listing of proofreading marks, consult the *Oxford Guide to Style* (2002), *Chicago Manual of Style* (2003).

Appendix VII

Formats and styles for Letters, Memos and E-mail

1 An official letter, with fully blocked format and open punctuation

Date at left hand side

Addressee's details, no punctuation

Subject line

All paragraphs begin at left margin

Complimentary close at left margin

Writer's position stated

TAXAID

Specialists in personal income tax
Acme House Kingston 2604
(PO Box 997 Kingston 2604)

3 March 2004

Mr. John Evans
99 Cheltenham Road
CHELTENHAM 2119

Dear Mr. Evans

ADVICE ON CLAIMING EDUCATION EXPENSES

Self education expenses are allowable deductions if the education received is directly relevant to the activities by which the tax payer derives his/her assessable income, and if the study leads to an increase in income earning activities in future.

It is not deductible where the study is designed to enable a tax payer to get employment or to open up a new income earning activity.

According to the information supplied in your letter, the study trip was strongly supported by your employer with study leave and a financial contribution. The study workshop and the conference you attended is directly connected with your current job. They help you to keep up to date and to improve your ability to perform existing duties or to earn your current income. The expenses incurred in your overseas study trip are therefore an allowable deduction and qualify under sec 51(1), having the necessary connection with your current rather than future employment.

The claim for education expenses of $4,279 should therefore be allowed in full.

Contact the undersigned for further information on the matter.

Yours faithfully

L.S. Deer
Chartered Accountant

Letter style
- formal explanation
- language is neutral, logical

2 A more personal letter, with semiblocked format and closed punctuation

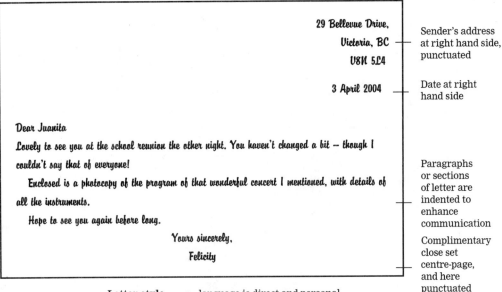

29 Bellevue Drive,

Victoria, BC ——|— Sender's address at right hand side, punctuated

V8N 5L4

3 April 2004 ——|— Date at right hand side

Dear Juanita

Lovely to see you at the school reunion the other night. You haven't changed a bit -- though I couldn't say that of everyone!

   Enclosed is a photocopy of the program of that wonderful concert I mentioned, with details of all the instruments. ——|— Paragraphs or sections of letter are indented to enhance communication

   Hope to see you again before long.

Yours sincerely,

Felicity ——|— Complimentary close set centre-page, and here punctuated

      Letter style
- language is direct and personal
- has emotive and evaluative elements

3 Format of memo

MEMO TO: PROFESSOR K. WONG Chair of English — Addressee before sender

Header indicates titles and status of correspondents —

FROM: DR. G.G. KING
SUBJECT: CONFERENCE PLANS
DATE: 20 February 2002

Style generally formal, distanced but courteous —

The Executive of the Global English Association will consider offers to host the 2004 conference at the forthcoming meeting in Hawaii. Would you like me to indicate the willingness of the department to host it here next December?

4 Format of e-mail message (as received)

Header makes it person to person —

DATE: Thursday 21 February 2002
FROM: Kathleen Wong <kwong@eng.hkbu.hk>
TO: Gregory King <gking@langc.hkbu.hk>
SUBJECT: Conference

— Sender before addressee. Position of date and subject vary with the e-mail system.

Style can be personal and/or business-like —

I will send you in hard copy a formal letter of welcome to present to the GEA Executive hosting the 2004 conference. Thanks for moving things forward. K

Appendix VIII

Layout for Envelopes: 1) US, UK, Canada, Australia 2) Continental Europe, Asia

1

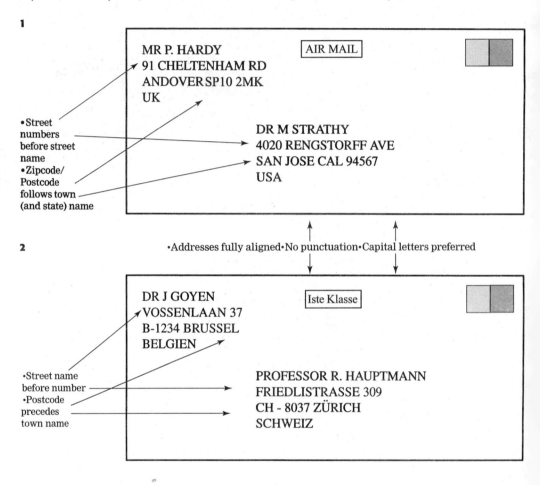

MR P. HARDY
91 CHELTENHAM RD
ANDOVER SP10 2MK
UK

AIR MAIL

DR M STRATHY
4020 RENGSTORFF AVE
SAN JOSE CAL 94567
USA

•Street numbers before street name
•Zipcode/Postcode follows town (and state) name

•Addresses fully aligned•No punctuation•Capital letters preferred

2

DR J GOYEN
VOSSENLAAN 37
B-1234 BRUSSEL
BELGIEN

Iste Klasse

PROFESSOR R. HAUPTMANN
FRIEDLISTRASSE 309
CH - 8037 ZÜRICH
SCHWEIZ

•Street name before number
•Postcode precedes town name

Appendix IX

Currencies of the World

	unit	symbol
Argentina	peso	PS
Australia	dollar	A$
Austria	schilling (Euro)	Sch/€
Bangladesh	taka	Tk
Belgium	franc (Euro)	Bfr/€
Brazil	real	R$
Canada	dollar	C$
Chile	peso	peso
China	yuan	Y
Cuba	peso	peso
Czech Republic	koruna	Kcs
Denmark	krone (Euro)	DKr/€
Egypt	pound	£E
Fiji	dollar	F$
France	franc (Euro)	Fr/€
Germany	Deutschmark (Euro)	DM/€
Greece	drachma (Euro)	Dr/€
HongKong	dollar	HK$
India	rupee	Rs
Indonesia	rupiah	Rp
Iran	rial	IR
Iraq	dinar	ID
Ireland	pound/punt (Euro)	I£/€
Israel	shekel	NIS
Italy	lira (Euro)	L/€
Japan	yen	¥
Jordan	dinar	JD
Korea (North and South)	won	Won (N), W (S)
Malaysia	dollar/ringgit	M$
Mexico	peso	peso
Netherlands	guilder (Euro)	G/€
New Zealand	dollar	NZ$
Norway	krone	NKr
Pakistan	rupee	PRs
Philippines	peso	P
Portugal	escudo (Euro)	Esc/€
Russia	ro(u)ble	Rbl
Singapore	dollar	S$
South Africa	rand	R
Spain	peseta (Euro)	Pta/€
Sweden	krona	SKr
Switzerland	franc	SFr
Taiwan	dollar	NT$
Thailand	baht	Bt
Turkey	lira	TL
United Kingdom	pound	£
United States	dollar	$
Vietnam	dong	D

Bibliography

—Aarts, B and Meyer, C (1995) *The Verb in Contemporary English*. Cambridge University Press
—Aarts, J, de Haan, P, and Oostdijk, N (1992) *English Language Corpora: design, analysis and exploitation*. Rodopi, Amsterdam
—Aijmer, K (2001) *A Wealth of English: studies in honour of Göran Kjellmer*. Gothenburg University Press
—Alford, H (1863) *Good Words* (March issue)
—Algeo, J (1988) British and American grammatical differences. *International Journal of Lexicography* 1:1
—Algeo, J (1991) *Fifty Years among the New Words*. Cambridge University Press
—Algeo, J (1995) Having a look at the expanded predicate. In *The Verb in Contemporary English* → Aarts, B and Meyer
—*American Heritage Dictionary of the English Language* (1969) Houghton Mifflin
—*APA Style Manual* → *Publication Manual*
—Asprey, M (1996, 2nd ed.) *Plain English for Lawyers*. Federation Press, Sydney
—*Australian Government Style Manual* (1994, 5th ed.) Australian Government Publishing Service, Canberra
—*Australian Government Style Manual* (2002, 6th ed.) → *Style Manual*
—*Australian National Dictionary* (1990) Oxford University Press
—*Authors' and Printers' Dictionary* (1938, 9th ed.) Oxford University Press
—Ayto, J (1992) A minuscule question: orthography and authority in dictionaries. *Euralex 92 Proceedings*
—Ayto, J (1998) Lexical life expectancy – a prognostic guide. In *Words* → Svartvik, J
—Baker, R (1770) *Reflections on the English Language*. London
—Baker, SJ (1945, 1st ed.; 1966, 2nd ed.; repr. 1978) *The Australian Language*. Currawong Press, Sydney
—Barnhart, RK (1987) *The Barnhart Dictionary of Etymology*. HW Wilson
—Baron, D (1986) *Grammar and Gender*. Yale University Press
—Bauer, L (1994) *Watching English Change*. Longman
—Benson, M, Benson, E and Ilson, R (1986) *Lexicographic Description of English*. John Benjamins, Amsterdam
—Bernstein, T (1958) *Watch your Language*. Channel, Great Neck NY
—Bernstein, T (1965) *The Careful Writer*. Atheneum
—Bernstein, T (1971) *Miss Thistlebottom's Hobgoblins*. Farrar, Strauss and Giroux, New York
—Biber, D *et al.* (1999) *Longman Grammar of Spoken and Written English*. Longman
—Bliss, AJ (1966) *A Dictionary of Foreign Words and Phrases in English*. Routledge and Kegan Paul
—Bolinger, DW (1941) Among the new words. *American Speech* 16:4
—*Brewer's Dictionary of Phrase and Fable* (1981, 2nd ed.) Cassells

—Bryant, P (1989) SouthEast Lexical Usage Region of Australian English. *Australian Journal of Linguistics* 9
—Burchfield, RJ (1986, 1st ed.; 1997, 2nd ed.) *New Zealand Pocket Oxford Dictionary*. Oxford University Press, Auckland
—Burchfield, RJ (1996) *New Fowler's Modern English Usage*. Oxford University Press
—Butcher, J (1975, 1st ed.; 1992, 3rd ed.) *Copy-editing*. Cambridge University Press
—*Cambridge Encyclopedia of Earth Sciences* → Smith
—*Cambridge Encyclopedia of Language* (1987) → Crystal (1987)
—*Cambridge Grammar of English* (2002) → Huddleston, R and Pullum, G
—*Cambridge International Dictionary of English* (1995) Cambridge University Press
—*Cambridge World Gazetteer* (1990) → Chambers/Cambridge World Gazetteer
—*Canadian English Usage* (1997) → Fee and McAlpine
—*Canadian Oxford Dictionary* (1998) Oxford University Press
—Carver, M (1987) *American Regional Dialects: a word geography*. University of Michigan Press
—*CBE Manual: Scientific style and format* (1994, 6th ed.) Cambridge University Press
—Chafe, W (1987) *Punctuation and the prosody of Written Language*. Center for the Study of Writing, University of California (Berkeley), and Carnegie-Mellon
—*Chambers/Cambridge World Gazetteer* (1988; 1990)
—*Chambers English Dictionary* (1988) W and R Chambers, Edinburgh
—Channell, J (1994) *Vague Language*. Oxford University Press
—*Chicago Manual of Style* (1993, 14th ed.; 2003, 15th ed.) University of Chicago Press
—Collins, PC (1978) "Dare" and "need" in Australian English. *English Studies* 59
—Collins, PC (1979) *Elicitation experiments on acceptability in Australian English*. Working Papers of the Speech, Hearing and Language Research Centre, Macquarie University
—Collins, PC (1988) Semantics of some modals in Australian English. *Australian Journal of Linguistics* 8
—Collins, PC and Peters, PH (2003) Australian English morphology and syntax. In *Handbook of Varieties of English* → Kortmann
—*Collins English Dictionary* (1991) Harper Collins, Glasgow
—*Comprehensive Grammar of the English Language* (1985) → Quirk *et al.*
—Copperud, R (1980) *American Usage and Style: the consensus*. Van Nostrand, Reinhold, New York
—*Copy-editing* → Butcher
—Couture, B (1986) *Functional Approaches to Writing Research*. Frances Pinter Bibliography

—Creswell, TH (1975) *Usage in Dictionaries and Dictionaries of Usage*. University of Alabama Press

—Crystal, D (1984) *Who Cares about English Usage?* Penguin

—Crystal, D (1987) *Cambridge Encyclopedia of Language*. Cambridge University Press

—Crystal, D (1997) *Cambridge Encyclopedia of the English Language*. Cambridge University Press

—Crystal, D (2001) *Language and the Internet*. Cambridge University Press

—DARE (1985 on) → *Dictionary of American Regional English*

—de Bono, E (1990) *Atlas of Management Thinking*. Penguin

—*Debrett's Correct Form: standard styles of address for everyone* (1992) Headline Book Press

—*Dictionary of American English* (1938–44) Chicago University Press

—*Dictionary of American Regional English* 5 vols. (1985 on) Harvard University Press

—*Dictionary of Americanisms* (1951) University of Chicago Press

—*Dictionary of English Usage in Southern Africa* (1975) Oxford University Press, Cape Town

—*Dictionary of New Zealand English* (1997) → Orsman (1997)

—*Dictionary of Newfoundland English* (1984) University of Toronto Press

—*Dictionary of Prince Edward Island English* (1988) University of Toronto Press

—*Dictionary of South African English* (1996) Oxford University Press

—Eagleson, R (1995) Singular use of "they." (Corporations Law Simplification Program.) Attorney General's Department, Australian Government

—*Editing Canadian English* (1987, 1st ed.) Douglas and McIntyre

—*Editing Canadian English* (2000, 2nd ed.) McFarlane, Walter and Ross

—Empson, W (1961, 3rd ed.) *Seven Types of Ambiguity*. Penguin

—Engel, D and Ritz, M-E (2000) Present perfect in Australian English. *Australian Journal of Linguistics* 20:2

—*English Usage Dictionary for South African Schools* (1984) Perskor, Johannesburg

—Estling, M (1997) Going out (of) the window. *English Today* 15:3

—Evans, B and Evans, C (1957) *Dictionary of Contemporary American Usage*. Random House

—Fee, M and McAlpine, J (1997) *Oxford Guide to Canadian English Usage*. Oxford University Press

—Fennell, B and Butters, RR (1996) History and contemporary distribution of double modals in English. In *Focus on the USA* → Schneider

—Fischer, A, Tottie, G and Lehmann, HM (2002) *Text Types and Corpora: studies in honour of Udo Fries*. Bunter Narr Verlag

—Follett, W (1966) *Modern American Usage*. Hill and Wang, New York

—Fowler, FG and Fowler, HW (1906; 1931, 3rd ed.) *The King's English*. Oxford University Press

—Fowler, HW (1926) *A Dictionary of Modern English Usage*. Oxford University Press

—*Fowler's Modern English Usage* (1965, 2nd ed.) → Gowers (1965)

—Francis, WN and Kucera, H (1982) *Frequency Analysis of English: usage and lexicon*. Houghton Mifflin

—Fries, CC (1925) The periphrastic future with "shall" and "will" in modern English. *Publications of the Modern Language Association of America* 40

—Fries, CC (1940) *American English Grammar*. Appleton, Century Crofts, New York

—Fries, U, Tottie, G and Schneider, P (1993) *Creating and Using English Language Corpora*. Rodopi, Amsterdam

—*Gage Canadian Dictionary* (1983) Gage Publishing Ltd

—Gains, J (1998) Electronic mail – a new style of communicating or just a new medium? *English for Specific Purposes* 18:1

—Garner, BA (1998) *A Dictionary of Modern American Usage*. Oxford University Press, New York

—Gowers, E (1954; repr. 1962) *Complete Plain Words*. HM Stationary Office

—Gowers, E (1965) *Fowler's Modern English Usage*. Oxford University Press

—Graddol, D (1997) *The Future of English?* British Council

—*Grammar and Gender* (1986) → Baron

—*Grande Dizionario della Lingua Italiana* (1962–95) UTET, Turin

—Grove, G (1879–89) *Dictionary of Music and Musicians* London

—Hale, C (1996) *Wired Style*. Hardwired

—Hall, RJ (1962, 2nd ed.) *Leave Your Language Alone*. Doubleday

—Halliday, MAK (1985, 1st ed.; 1994, 2nd ed.) *Introduction to Functional Grammar*. Edward Arnold, London

—Halliday, MAK (1988) On the language of physical science. In *Registers of Written English*, ed. M Ghadessy. Pinter, London and New York

—*Handbook of Nonsexist Writing* → Miller and Swift

—*Handbook of Varieties of English* → Kortmann

—*Hart's Rules for Compositors and Readers* (1983, 39th ed.) Oxford University Press

—Hector, LC (1966, 2nd ed.) *The Handwriting of English Documents*. Edward Arnold

—Hofland, K and Johansson, S (1982) *Word Frequencies in British and American English*. Norwegian Computing Centre for the Humanities

—Holmes, J and Sigley, R (2002) What's a word like "girl" doing in a place like this? In *New Frontiers of Corpus Linguistics* → Peters, P et al. (2002)

—Huddleston, R (1984) *Introduction to the Grammar of English*. Cambridge University Press

—Huddleston, R (1988) *English Grammar: an Outline*. Cambridge University Press

—Huddleston, R and Pullum, G (2002) *Cambridge Grammar of the English Language*. Cambridge University Press

—Hundt, M (1998) *New Zealand English Grammar: fact or fiction*. John Benjamins

—*Indexing, the Art of* → Knight

—*Introduction to Functional Grammar* → Halliday (1985/1994)

—*Introduction to the Grammar of English* → Huddleston (1984)

—Ireland, RJ (1979) Canadian spelling. Unpublished Ph.D. cited in *In Search of the Standard in Canadian English* → Lougheed

—Jespersen, O (1909–49) *A Modern English Grammar*. George Allen and Unwin

—Jespersen, O (1948, 9th ed.) *Growth and Structure of the English Language*. Macmillan

—Johansson, S and Norheim, E (1988) The subjunctive in British and American English. *ICAME Journal* 12

—Johnson, S (1755; facsimile 1989) *A Dictionary of the English Language*. Longman

—Kaye, A (1990) Whatchamacallem. *English Today* 6:1

—Kirkman, J (1980) *Good Style for Scientific and Engineering Writing*. Pitman

—Kjellmer, G (1986) On the spelling of English "millennium." *Studia Neophilologica* 58

—Kjellmer, G (1998) On contraction in modern English. *Studia Neophilologica* 69

—Kjellmer, G (2000) On Serb and Serbian. *English Today* 16:2

—Knight, GN (1979) *Indexing, the Art of*. Allen and Unwin

—Kortmann, B (2003) *Handbook of Varieties of English*. Mouton De Gruyter

—Krug, M (1994) Contractions in present-day English. Unpublished MA thesis, University of Exeter

—Krug, M (1998) Gotta: the tenth modal in English. In *Major Varieties of English* → Lindquist *et al.*

—Labov, W (1972) *Language in the Inner City*. University of Pennsylvania Press

—Labov, W (1991) Three dialects of English. In *New Ways of Analyzing Sound Change*, ed. P Eckert. Academic Press, New York

—Landau, S (2001, 2nd ed.) *The Art and Craft of Lexicography*. Cambridge University Press

—Langenscheidts *Grosswörterbuch* (1997) Langenscheidt KG, Berlin

—Lanham, R (1974) *Style: an Anti-textbook*. Yale University Press

—*Larousse gastronomique* (1984) Mandarin, London

—Leech, G and Culpeper, J (1997) The comparison of adjectives in modern English. In *To Explain the Present: studies in honour of Matti Rissanen*, ed. T Nevalainen, L Kahlas-Tarkka. Société Néophilologique, Helsinki

—Lehrer, A (1983) *Wine and Conversation*. Indiana University Press

—Levey, S (2003) He's like "Do it now" and I'm like "No." *English Today* 19:1

—Levin, B (1986) *In these Times*. Sceptre

—Levin, M (1998a) On concord with collective nouns in English. In *Explorations in Corpus Linguistics* → Renouf

—Levin, M (1998b) On concord with collective nouns in British and American English. In *Major Varieties of English* → Lindquist *et al.*

—Li Lan (2000) Email: a challenge to standard English. *English Today* 16:4

—Lindquist, H. (1998) Comparison of adjectives in -y and -ly in present-day British and American English. In *Major Varieties of English* → Lindquist *et al.*

—Lindquist, H, Klintborg, S, Levin, M, Estling, M (1998) *The Major Varieties of English*. Växsjö University

—*Longman Grammar of Spoken and Written English* → Biber *et al.*

—Lougheed, W (1985) *In Search of the Standard in Canadian English*. Occasional Paper 1, Strathy Language Unit, Queen's University, Ontario

—*Macquarie Dictionary* (1997, 3rd ed.) Macquarie Library, Sydney

—Maggio, R. (1988) *The Nonsexist Wordfinder*. Beacon Press, Boston

—Mair, C (1998) Corpora and the study of the major varieties of English. In *Major Varieties of English* → Lindquist *et al.*

—Mair, C and Hundt, M (2000) *Corpus Linguistics and Linguistic Theory*. Rodopi, Amsterdam

—McArthur, T (1992) *Oxford Companion to the English Language*. Oxford University Press

—McArthur, T (1998) *The English Languages*. Cambridge University Press

—McArthur, T (2000) Netcronyms and emoticons. *English Today* 16:4

—McArthur, T (2001) World English and world Englishes. *Language Teaching* 34:1

—McMillion, A (1998) Ergative verb variation in British and American English. In *Major Varieties of English* → Lindquist *et al.*

—Mencken, HL (1919) *The American Language*. Knopf, New York

—Mencken, HL (1945) *The American Language, Supplement I*. Knopf, New York

—*Merriam-Webster's Collegiate Dictionary* (2000, 10th ed.) Merriam-Webster

—*Merriam-Webster's Geographical Dictionary* (1997, 3rd ed.) Merriam-Webster

—Meyer, C (1987) *A Linguistic Study of American Punctuation*. Peter Lang

—Meyer, C (2002) *English Corpus Linguistics* Cambridge University Press

—*Microsoft Manual of Style for Technical Publications* (1998, 2nd ed.) Microsoft Press, Washington

—Miller, C, and Swift, K (1988) *Handbook of Nonsexist Writing*. Harper and Row

—Milroy, J and Milroy, L (1985) *Authority in Language*. Routledge and Kegan Paul

—Mitford, N (1956) *Noblesse Oblige*. Hamish Hamilton, London

—Mittins, W, Salu, M, Edminson, M, Coyne, S (1970) *Attitudes to English Usage*. Oxford University Press

—*MLA Style Manual* (1985, 1st ed.) Modern Language Association of America

—Modiano, M (1998) The emergence of Mid-Atlantic English in the European Union. In *Major Varieties of English* → Lindquist *et al.*

—Moore, B (2001) *Who's Centric Now?* Oxford University Press, Melbourne

—Morris, EE (1898; repr. 1972) *A Dictionary of Austral English*. University of Sydney Press

—Mühlhäusler, P (1983) Stinkipoos, cuddlepies and related matters. *Australian Journal of Linguistics* 3:1

—Murray-Smith, S (1989, 2nd ed.) *Right Words*. Viking, Ringwood, Australia

—*Naming Systems of Ethnic Groups* (1990) Department of Social Security, Australian Government

—*New Grove Dictionary of Music and Musicians* (2001, 2nd ed.) Macmillan, London

—*New Oxford Dictionary of English* (1998) Oxford University Press

—*New Westminster Dictionary of Liturgy and Worship* (1986) Westminster Press, Philadelphia

—Opdahl, L (1991) -ly as adverbial suffix: corpus and elicited material compared. *ICAME Journal* 15

—Orsman, H (1989) *Heinemann New Zealand Dictionary*. Heinemann

—Orsman, H (1997) *Dictionary of New Zealand English*. Oxford University Press

—Övergaard, G (1995) *The Mandative Subjunctive in American and British English in the 20th Century*. Uppsala University Press

—*Oxford Dictionary for Writers and Editors* (1981) Oxford University Press

—*Oxford Dictionary of New Words* (1998) Oxford University Press

—*Oxford English Dictionary* 13 vols. (1884–1928) Oxford University Press

—*Oxford English Dictionary* 20 vols. (1989) Oxford University Press

—*Oxford Guide to English Language Usage* (1984) → Weiner

—*Oxford Guide to Style* (2002) → Ritter

—Partridge, E (1942) *Usage and Abusage*. Harper, New York

—Peters, P and Young, W (1997) English grammar and the lexicography of usage. *Journal of English Linguistics* 25:4

—Peters, P, Collins, P and Smith, A (2002) *New Frontiers of Corpus Research*. Rodopi, Amsterdam

—Peters, PH (1992) Corpus evidence on some points of usage. In *English Language Corpora* → Aarts, J *et al.*

—Peters, PH (1993a) Feedback report (on the subjunctive). *Australian Style* 2:1

—Peters, PH (1993b) American and British influence on Australian verb morphology. In *Creating and Using English Language Corpora* → Fries, U *et al.*

—Peters, PH (1993c) *Style on the Move*. Dictionary Research Centre, Macquarie University

—Peters, PH (1995) *Cambridge Australian English Style Guide*. Cambridge University Press

—Peters, PH (1998a) The survival of the subjunctive. *English World-Wide* 19:1

—Peters, PH (1998b) In quest of international English. In *Explorations in Corpus Linguistics* → Renouf

—Peters, PH (1999a) Feedback report: dating the new millennium. *Australian Style* 7:2

—Peters, PH (1999b) Research findings on variable points of style and usage (plus supplement). Report to AusInfo, Style Council Centre, Macquarie University

—Peters, PH (2000) Paradigm split. In *Corpus Linguistics and Linguistic Theory* → Mair and Hundt

—Peters, PH (2001a) The Latin legacy. In *A Wealth of English* → Aijmer

—Peters, PH (2001b) On being reticent. *Australian Language Matters* 9:4

—Peters, PH (2003) Me or my. *Australian Language Matters* 11:2

—Peters, PH and Delbridge, A (1997) Fowler's legacy. In *Englishes around the World: studies in honour of Manfred Görlach*, ed. EW Schneider. 2 vols. John Benjamins

—Preston, D (1996) Perceptual dialectology. In *Focus on the USA* → Schneider

—Pride, J (1982) *New Englishes*. Newbury House Publishers, Rowley (MA), London

—*Publication Manual of the American Psychological Association* (2001, 5th ed.) American Psychological Association, Washington DC

—Quinion, M (2003) *Ologies and Isms*. Oxford University Press

—Quirk, R (1978) On the grammar of nuclear English. Paper for conference on English as an International Auxiliary Language. EastWest Center Hawaii

—Quirk, R, Greenbaum, G, Leech, G and Svartvik, J (1985) *Comprehensive Grammar of the English Language*. Longman

—*Random House Dictionary of the English Language* (1966, 1st ed.; 1987, 2nd ed.) Random House

—Reaney, P (1967) *The Origin of English Surnames*. Routledge, Kegan, Paul

—Reid, W (1991) *Verb and Noun Number in English*. Longman

—Renouf, A (1998) *Explorations in Corpus Linguistics*. Rodopi, Amsterdam

—*The Right Word at the Right Time* (1985) Reader's Digest Association, Pleasantville

—Ritter, R (2002) *Oxford Guide to Style*. Oxford University Press

—*SBS World Guide* (1999) Text Publications

—Schneider, EW (1996) *Focus on the USA*. John Benjamins, Amsterdam

—Scholes, P (1975, 10th ed.) *Oxford Companion to Music*. Oxford University Press

—*Scientific Style and Format for Authors, Editors and Printers – CBE Manual* (1994, 6th ed.) Cambridge University Press

—Siemund, R (1993) Aspects of language change in Progress. Unpublished MA thesis, University of Freiburg im Breisgau

—Sigley, R (1999) Are we still under England's spell? *Te Reo* 42

—Simon, J (1980) *Paradigms Lost*. Clarkson N Potter, New York

—Simpson, J (2001) The Queen's English and people's English. In *Who's Centric Now?* → Moore

—Smith, DG (1981) *Cambridge Encyclopedia of Earth Sciences*. Cambridge University Press

—Strang, B (1962) *Modern English Structure*. Edward Arnold, London

—Strang, B (1970) *A History of English*. Methuen

—Strunk, W and White, EB (1972, 2nd ed.) *The Elements of Style*. Macmillan, New York

—*Style Manual* (2002, 6th ed.) John Wiley, for the Australian Government

—*Style Manual for Aotearoa New Zealand* (1997) → *Write, Edit, Print*

—*Peters 1993c*

—Svartvik, J (1996) *Words: an International Symposium*. Kungl. Vitterhets Historie ok Antikvitets Akademien

—Taglicht, J (1984) *Message and Emphasis: on focus and scope in English*. Longman

—*Terminology Bulletin no. 342: Country Names (1990–2)*. United Nations Secretariat

—Todd, L (1995) *Guide to Punctuation*. Cassell

—Tottie, G (1991) *Negation in English Speech and Writing*. Academic Press London

—Tottie, G (2002) *An Introduction to American English*. Blackwells

—Ungerer, F (2002) When news stories are no longer just stories. In *Text Types and Corpora* → Fischer *et al.*

—Wales, K (1996) *Personal Pronouns in Present-Day English*. Cambridge University Press

—Wales, K (2000) North and south: an English linguistic divide. *English Today* 16:1

—Webster, N (1806) *A Compendious Dictionary of the English Language*. Hartford

—Webster, N (1828) *An American Dictionary of the English Language*. New York

—*Webster's Dictionary of English Usage* (1989) Merriam-Webster

—*Webster's Geographical Dictionary* (1997, 3rd ed.)
Merriam-Webster
—*Webster's New International Dictionary* (1934, 2nd
ed.) G and C Merriam, Springfield, MA
—*Webster's Standard American Style Manual* (1985)
Merriam-Webster
—*Webster's Third New International Dictionary* (1961;
repr. 1986) Merriam-Webster Inc.
—Weiner, E (1984) *Oxford Guide to English Language
Usage*. Oxford University Press
—Westergren-Axelsson, M (1998) *Contractions in
British Newpapers in the Late 20th Century*. Uppsala
University

—Whitbread, D (2001) *The Design Manual*. UNSW Press
—Wickens, M (1992) *Grammatical Number in English
Nouns*. John Benjamins, Amsterdam
—*Wired Style* (1996) → Hale
—Wolfram, W and Schilling-Estes, N (1998) *American
English*. Blackwell
—Wong, I (1982) Native speaker English for the third
world today. → Pride
—Worcester, J (1860) *Dictionary of the English
Language*. Boston
—*Write, Edit, Print: Style Manual for Aotearoa New
Zealand* (1997) Australian Government Publishing
Service and Lincoln University Press